REAGAN'S 1968 DRESS REHEARSAL: IKE, RFK, AND REAGAN'S EMERGENCE AS A WORLD STATESMAN

Gene Kopelson

REAGAN'S 1968 DRESS REHEARSAL
by Gene Kopelson

Published by
FIGUEROA PRESS
840 Childs Way, 3rd Floor
Los Angeles, CA 90089
Phone: (213) 743-4800
Fax: (213) 743-4804
www.figueroapress.com

Figueroa Press is a division of the USC Bookstores
Produced by Crestec, Los Angeles, Inc.
Printed in the United States of America

If unwittingly, the author has infringed on the copyright of any institutions or persons, the author hopes they will accept his sincerest apologies and tell him of this oversight.

Library of Congress Cataloguing-in-Publication Data
Gene Kopelson
REAGAN'S 1968 DRESS REHEARSAL
ISBN-13: 978-0-18-219884-9
ISBN-10: 0-18-219884-7
Library of Congress Number: 2016935886

This work is dedicated to my parents, Jules and Isabelle Kopelson. They instilled in me my love for America by having me first join the Cub Scouts, and continue on as a Boy Scout attaining the rank of Eagle Scout. I hope through my children, Barry, Charles and Michelle, that my grand-children, Eli, Max, Samuel and others yet unborn, will continue our shared love of America and its freedom and liberty.

Table of Contents

AUTHOR'S NOTE

Look, then, into thine heart, and write!
Yes, into Life's deep stream.
All forms of sorrow and delight,
All solemn Voices of the Night,
That can soothe thee, or affright,—
Be these henceforth thy theme.
Henry Wadsworth Longfellow, Prelude to *Voices of the Night*

I ran for president of the United States in 1968. Sort of. Growing up in Oceanside, an affluent Long Island suburb of New York City, my top academic interests always were in science. But history ran a close second. I had gained local on-stage fame in sixth grade when I starred as The King in our school's two and-a-half hour musical production of *The King and I*. Three years later, I won second place in our junior high school's speech contest. By senior year, a mock presidential mini-campaign and debate was planned. Knowing that I still was active in the Boy Scouts, now a Junior Assistant Scoutmaster and active member of the Order of the Arrow, the high school administration asked me if I would play the part of Richard Nixon.

I had not followed much of the election up to that point. My main concerns were college applications and my advanced placement courses. The prior June, the day after Robert F. Kennedy's assassination, my main priority was learning the result of my SATs. Later I learned that Rep. Allard Lowenstein was our Congressman, the Democrat who pushed Edward Kennedy to become the candidate of the liberals right after RFK had been assassinated. My upbringing was conservative, but not in any active way. Politics was only discussed around election time. Discussing the debate offer with my parents, we decided it would be a good experience—doing something far removed from science and college worries.

So I became "Richard Nixon" for a week. I went to local Republican Party headquarters and gathered campaign materials. I read as much as I could about Nixon's plans for the nation. So I dressed in a suit and wore a large "I'm Dick Nixon" campaign button that had been created for me. I had a small table, and during free periods, I greeted students and handed out Nixon materials. Believe it or not, I was not given a hard time by my classmates. I debated "Hubert Humphrey," a friend whom I have known since kindergarten. He had bested me at the junior high speech contest and now bested me at the 1968 mock debate---the students voted overwhelmingly for Humphrey. But afterwards, a number of students came up to me congratulating me on a job well done. Many said they were for Nixon, but because their friends were for Humphrey, they conformed to peer-pressure and had raised their hands for Humphrey.

I recall zero about Ronald Reagan running for president at the time, and I thought that my week as Nixon and the final debate was the end of my brief career in politics and history and government.

Flash forward five decades. I view the presidency of Ronald Reagan as a golden age for America and for the world. Reagan had defeated communism and brought freedom to millions in Eastern Europe without firing a single shot. He revived America's economy and created more than 20 million jobs. I decided to learn why and how he first decided to run for the presidency. While I was reading the beginning of Craig Shirley's history of Reagan's 1976 campaign, Shirley made the point that because nobody had written about this 1976 "first" Reagan run for the presidency, he would. Shirley then proceeded briefly to mention that Reagan did in fact run in 1968 but Shirley's work focused on 1976.

I thought, how odd. If indeed Reagan did run in 1968, and I had no idea that he had, why had nobody written about 1968 as his first campaign? And if Shirley wanted to write about Reagan's first presidential campaign, why had he skipped 1968? But Shirley was not the only one to skip 1968.

So did Reagan, who left virtually no written record of the campaign. Unlike when he was president,[1] Governor Reagan kept no diary, and basically he ignored the subject altogether in his second, post-presidential, autobiography. As we will see, after 1968 both Nancy and he would deny the campaign's very existence. So my preliminary research initially concentrated on Steven Hayward and then Reagan historian Lou Cannon's two classic works on Reagan's gubernatorial years. In *Ronnie and Jesse* and in *Governor Reagan*, Cannon described the divisions between Reagan's advisors who wanted him to be president versus those who did not. For instance, Cannon's second analysis gives the reader a fourteen-page brief summary of the campaign, yet I felt that there possibly were many gaps in the story. Historian Glen More wrote a brief academic summary of the campaign as well. A group of British authors who attended the convention soon thereafter had chronicled the events as well. The above works concentrated on the late spring of 1968.

Yet a work by historian Kiron Skinner et. al., one of whose team was Condoleeza Rice, wrote, "In one way or another, the California governor had been campaigning for the GOP nomination since late 1966."[2] I wanted to learn more, as I saw that the spring of 1968 was but the endpoint of an important missing link in the Reagan saga. I wanted to help fill that missing piece. I realized that there were untold stories of those grass roots activists across the country who wanted to see Reagan elected in 1968. Perhaps some were still alive and would be willing to relive that period?

Filling that void took almost three years of hard work. I made personal visits to presidential libraries and historical archives. After much digging and searching, I found and met a cadre of wonderful Reagan activists who granted me in-person and telephone interviews or written communications. Most of the stories of these grass roots Reagan workers have never been told before. I knew I had begun to fill the void.

But who needs another book about Ronald Reagan? As remains true with historical giants such as Washington, Lincoln, Theodore Roosevelt, Winston Churchill and Ronald Reagan, new books appear several times a year. Other than supplying missing new history about the 1968 presidential campaign, could I contribute something even more important?

The answer—completely unexpected and what turned out to be my most important findings, the hidden mentor-protégé relationship of Eisenhower and Reagan—began from a cryptic sentence by authors Skinner, Anderson and Anderson in *Reagan: A Life in Letters*. Their research indicated there was a bit more information on Eisenhower, Reagan, and a mutual golfing friend, in the Eisenhower Presidential Library in Abilene. Historians Gibbs and Duffy in *The Presidents Club* found some additional communications.

But my visit to the Dwight D. Eisenhower Presidential Library revealed much, much more about the relationship of Ike and Dutch. Then I learned of Ike's post-presidential diary and have become one of the very few historians who have examined it. I then sent away for Reagan's gubernatorial audiotapes from the Ronald Reagan Presidential Library, whose archivist said in the twenty-some years he had been working there, nobody previously had ever asked for them. Listening to scores of hours of Reagan speeches and press conferences, delivered on the campaign trail in 1967 and 1968, I was amazed. What a thrill it was for me to hear Reagan's voice again. And to me they were brand new—not the classic Reagan speeches I had known so well. And to history, these Reagan speeches and press conferences never have been heard or analyzed before

The speeches often were his standard campaign and fund raising speech during this period, updated with new statistics on his success in down-sizing California state government. Many of his inspiring words remain timeless and quite relevant to early 21st century America. I kept nodding my head in agreement as I heard Reagan's stirring words on domestic policies, wishing he were here as president, because many of his solutions are needed once again in our time. I mention many specifics in this work, but the reader is urged to order a few selections from Simi Valley to hear Reagan anew. They will not be disappointed.

But whereas most of his campaign speeches concentrated on his domestic accomplishments and how he was running for president to bring those solutions to the nation as a whole, to me the most amazing segments were about world affairs. A good deal of Reagan's growing stature as a world statesman, the major theme of my work, initially took place in his press conferences, where the press constantly asked him about Vietnam, and culminated in Reagan delivering five White Paper speeches about foreign affairs.

And the press had no idea that Reagan's policies on Vietnam— actually wanting to win the war—stemmed in large measure from the man who had been mentoring Reagan behind-the-scenes: former President Dwight D. Eisenhower. Reagan and Eisenhower's interactions began in depth in the early and mid 1960s, a time period just prior to the main events in the present story. Via personal meetings, phone conversations, and via specific advice delivered from Eisenhower to Reagan via intermediaries, Eisenhower became Reagan's political mentor. The present work for the first time documents in detail Eisenhower's mentoring of Reagan from 1965 through 1968. By 1966, Eisenhower had certified Reagan as presidential timbre and then encouraged Reagan to run for the nation's highest office. Their relationship blossomed into the arena of foreign affairs. My Epilogue continues that analysis through the end of Reagan's presidency. I feel this is the most important contribution to history that I can make.

During the course of his first presidential campaign, Reagan spoke out on issues way beyond that of an average governor. And there were many examples in 1967-1968 which foreshadowed events to come later. For instance, Reagan bemoaned President Johnson's use of "despair," just as Reagan would against President Carter's "malaise" a decade later.

Most of Reagan's growth into a world statesman is seen in the area of world affairs. Reagan saw a nation adrift, without leadership. With apologies to Senator Edward Kennedy's memorable words at his brother's funeral in June, 1968, Reagan saw crime and wanted to fight it. He saw bloated federal government and wanted to cut it. And Reagan saw war and wanted to win it.

Specifically, Reagan saw America in a war led by an administration that seemingly did not want to fight to win. So for Vietnam, Reagan, lone among the candidates running for president—Democratic or Republican—pushed to win the war. He wanted to use specific military tactics and threats against North Vietnam, just as Eisenhower successfully had done against North Korea. Those details will be reviewed here.

But there was more, much more, to Reagan in 1968 than being a lone hawk on Vietnam. During his 1968 campaign, Reagan actually for the first time in public called—indeed a number of times— for the Soviets to tear down the Berlin Wall. He for the first time publicly pushed for an anti-missile defense shield. Reagan even found ways to call for freedom for Croatia and Latvia in Eastern Europe. He told the press how he would deal with hostages. He was unafraid to upset the cart of political correctness. He knew right from wrong. Reagan told the public that America should not stay neutral in the Middle East: he wanted us to side clearly and forcefully with Israel. He foresaw that communism could not survive both a growing American economy and a growing American military. He would negotiate with the communists, but only from positions of strength and not from weakness. This is vintage President Reagan, but seen for the true first time in 1967-1968, as emerging world statesman.

Press reports and historical works of the era hardly mention Reagan's growing expertise in foreign affairs. It was only via listening to his frequent press conferences and his five White Paper and numerous other speeches, by watching relevant old film clips of the era, and by studying the Eisenhower-Reagan correspondence, that I heard and understood how Reagan, as student of his mentor Eisenhower, was transforming from a domestic governor into a true national contender for the presidency.

But isn't it preposterous to claim a direct link between moderate Eisenhower and conservative Reagan? I hope my work will serve to open the door for future scholars to assess the true and continuing influence of Eisenhower throughout the years of the Reagan presidency and beyond. For indeed Eisenhower saw conservative Reagan as well within the wide tent of mainstream Republicanism.

The general realized that Reagan's solutions to problems were the same common sense solutions as he had recommended. Ike never saw Reagan as an extreme right winger. Eventually, Reagan would fulfill Eisenhower's vision and, likely as a shock to many readers, be one of Eisenhower's protégés and political heirs. Indeed future analysis may conclude that Reagan became Ike's major protégé and heir. And that, as will be seen, is how Reagan saw himself as well.

Likely also surprising to many readers, Reagan's main antagonist during this era was Robert F. Kennedy. The story of how Robert F. Kennedy became Reagan's nemesis during the 1960s is detailed here, culminating in how, once Kennedy announced his candidacy, Reagan transformed his campaign anew.

Some aspects of the final portion of Reagan's campaign, starting just prior to and at the convention, have been told before in works by Chester et.al., Cannon's two works discussed above, Skinner et.al., Moore, and in a brief Eureka College course by Craig Shirley. Tom Reed was Reagan's national campaign director for 1968. Via personal meetings, many chats and written communications, his willingness to share his written notes and personal reflections was priceless. Reed gave me access to the chapter on 1968 and his list of campaign meetings, which were to become part of his book on the Cold War. I have cited Reed extensively here. But recently, Reed changed direction and published his own memoirs, which concentrate on his own personal role and recollections of his observations of Reagan in the 1960s.

Reed acknowledges that it was my research on Eisenhower and on Kennedy, which I shared with him, that he then used in his book. Only after I reviewed my findings with Reed, did he understand that what Reagan had said and had done in 1968 became crystal clear. For at the time, Reed had no idea how Eisenhower had been mentoring Reagan and had almost no idea of the many years-long antagonism between Reagan and Kennedy. In a portion of his memoir, Reed details the Reagan campaign from his point of view but gets into almost no detail of what was happening across the country as people wanted to see Reagan elected in 1968.

This work details the earliest stirrings of grass roots Reagan-for-President groups across the country. The stories of these activists and the behind-the-scene Reagan campaign history, is the second theme of this work. From 1964, when a group in Owosso, Michigan, formed the first Reagan for President group, to the histories of grassroots activists in the three critical 1968 primary states of Wisconsin, Nebraska, and

Oregon, through the political antics at the Miami Beach convention, are all detailed here for the first time.

Reagan's transformation into a world statesman and presidential contender was not a straight line. Reagan's first presidential campaign hit many bumps, not the least of which was Reagan's reticence openly to declare his official candidacy until the convention and the decision not to visit any of the three critical primary states in 1968. Reagan's campaign was almost derailed several times. But each time, Reagan arose anew, like a political phoenix, and transformed his campaign, culminating in the final drive at Miami Beach.

For me, this has been a quite fun adventure—a chance to have others share in learning many new things about Reagan before he was president. Reagan would use the term "silent majority" more than a full year before Nixon and would use the military term "surge" a full four decades before the American public would hear it again during the Iraq War. Plus there are lessons that now need to be "un-learned." For instance, Reagan did not first utter his "pale pastels" speech in 1975. He did not first publicly call in the mid 1980s for the Soviets to tear down the Berlin Wall. Reagan did not first call for America to have an anti-ballistic missile defense shield after he became president. He did not first call for freedom in Eastern Europe as president. He did not first call for a strong and quick response to hostage situations in the late 1970s during the Iran Hostage Crisis when he was running against Jimmy Carter. For in fact, all of these "firsts" happened while Reagan was running in his first presidential campaign. I invite the reader to see the first time Ronald Reagan offered America his new, bold leadership—to right the veering ship of state—and in the process became a world statesman and true contender for the presidency, when he first ran for the highest office in the land.

Endnotes

1.   Reagan and Brinkley
2.   Skinner et. al. pp. 78-79

ACKNOWLEDGMENTS

The final stage of writing a book is when you "kill the monster and fling him about to the public."

Winston Churchill, quoted by Richard Langworth (*Finest Hour* 61: 165, 2015)

I want to thank the following individuals for their help with research: Kevin Bailey, Kathy Struss, and Christopher Abraham (Dwight D. Eisenhower Presidential Library, Abilene, KS), Steve Branch and Jennifer Mandel (AudioVisual Department, Ronald Reagan Presidential Library, Simi Valley, CA), Charles Wascher (Shiawassee County Historical Society Archives, Owosso, MI), Kathy Lafferty and Jenna Roberts (Henry A. Bubb Archives, University of Kansas Spenser Research Library, Lawrence, KS), David Vail (Morse Department of Special Collections, Kansas State University), Monica Blankley (Graham Molitor Papers, Nelson A. Rockefeller Archives, Sleepy Hollow, NY), Marion Watkins, Erin Wolfe, Audrey Coleman and Bill Lacy (Dole Institute of Politics, Lawrence, KS), Heather Furnas (Clifton White Archives, Cornell University, Ithaca, NY), Frank Mackaman (The Dirksen Congressional Center, Pekin, IL), Jenny Fichtman (Kathryn R. Davis papers, Hoover Archives, Stanford University, Palo Alto, CA), Joanne Drake (Reagan Foundation), David Kessler (Bancroft Oral History Program, University of California at Berkeley, Berkeley, CA), Bill Landis (Yale University Library Archives, New Haven, CT), Anthony Glass (Melick Library, Eureka College, Dixon, IL), Lori Sotelo (King County Republican Party), Omaha Nebraska Public Library (1968 Presidential Election Collection, Omaha, NE), Tom Putnam and Aubrey Butts (Robert F. Kennedy Collection, John F. Kennedy Presidential Library, Boston, MA), Liz Nepreis (Ivy Baker Priest Papers, J. Willard Marriott Library, University of Utah, Salt Lake City, UT), Nancy Dehlinger (Republican National Committee), John D. Morris (Ronald W. Reagan Society, Eureka College, Eureka, IL), Dee Dee Hamilton and Ron Robinson (Young Americans Foundation, Washington, D.C.), Michael Zupan (Croatian-American Cultural Center, Los Angeles,

CA), Tara Setmayer and Ken Grubb (Office of Congressman Dana Rohrabacher), Jacob Pomrenke (Society for American Baseball Research), Claire Falkner and Beth Montgomery (Office of Bill Bradley, AllenCo, New York, NY), Susan Wigler (Chubb Fellowship, Timothy Dwight College, Yale University, New Haven, CT), David Kessler (William F. Knowland Papers, Bancroft Library, University of California at Berkeley, Berkeley, CA), Professor Jim Johnson (University of Arizona, Tucson, AZ), Drew Vattiat (*The Oregonian*, Portland, OR), Michael Florer (Eisenhower Gettysburg Home, National Park Service), Chris Peterson (Oregon State University Archives), Addie Maguire (Albany Regional Museum), Ned Seaton (*The Manhattan Mercury*), Bill Kelly (Nebraska Public Television), Frank Donatelli, Mike Lennon, Ariel Gross.

Special mention must be made of the generous insight and help provided by Thomas C. Reed. Reed sent me his own unpublished book chapter on 1968, his logs of campaign meetings, and took the time to read and critique the early chapters of this work.

The author thanks nationally-syndicated radio host and commentator Michael Medved for his encouragement and for suggesting part of the title.

The author is indebted to the following academicians who discussed and/or read sections of this work and/or provided invaluable advice, insight, and constructive criticism in improving it: Historians Lou Cannon, Jed Donahue, Chip Bishop, Ambassador Gil Robinson, John Morris (Ronald Reagan Society at Eureka College), Bruce Chapman (Discovery Institute) and W. Bruce Weinrod (Potomac Foundation). Professors and historians Paul Kengor (Grove City College), Evan Thomas (Princeton University), Fred Greenstein (Princeton University), Andrew Polsky (City University of New York), Bill Tilchin (Boston University), Douglas Brinkley (Rice University), Annelise Anderson (Stanford University), Carlos Gil (University of Washington), Henry Nau (George Washington University) and Kevin Ashley (University of Pittsburgh).

Participants in events of those times also advised the author and/ or critiqued sections of the work include: Dick Derham, Ned Lange, Don Hodel, Kathryn Forte, Peter Murphy, Judges James C. Goode and Paul Haerle, Randy Teague, Fred Van Natta, John and Sally Gram, Don Taylor, Shawn Steel, Pat Nolan, Ron Docksai, the Honorable Diarmuid O'Scannlain, Austin Hoyt, and Tanya Melich. The author is eternally grateful to all of the above.

The author wants to thank his cover designer, Smutesh Mishra, and his publisher, Tiffany Quon of the Figueroa Press at the University of Southern California, whose decisions and help were invaluable. I also give special thanks to my early reviewers. Your feedback is greatly appreciated: The Honorable George Shultz, senior staff economist on President Eisenhower's Council of Economic Advisors and secretary of state under President Reagan; the Honorable Edwin Meese III, attorney general under President Reagan; Thomas C. Reed, special assistant to President Reagan for national security policy and Governor Reagan's presidential campaign director 1966-1968; Paul Kengor, Ph.D., professor of political science at Grove City College; Fred I. Greenstein, professor emeritus of politics at Princeton University; Craig Shirley, renowned Reagan historian; and Fred Barnes, executive editor of *The Weekly Standard*.

My three children, Barry, Charles and Michelle, provided encouragement, critiqued sections of the work, and helped with computers and photography. Last but certainly not least, I thank my wife, Mindy, who patiently gave up many afternoons and evenings while I did my research and writing but took the time to bring added color and language to enliven my story and added her expertise in audiovisual computer technology.

INTRODUCTION

After "The Speech"

Ronald Reagan turned over in bed the evening of October 27, 1964 to kiss his wife Nancy good night, but he was worrying about the speech, *A Time for Choosing*, he just had given on behalf of Republican candidate for president, Barry Goldwater. "I hope I haven't let Barry down," he fretted.[1] The Reagan's had returned home after watching his nationwide speech at the home of some friends who would become his future political supporters.[2]

A scant two hours after going to sleep, shortly after midnight, Reagan was awakened by the shrill ring of their telephone. It was the operator from Citizens for Goldwater headquarters office in Washington, D.C., who barely could contain herself, yelling, "The switchboard has been lit up ever since you signed off. It's three A.M. and there's been no let up!"[3] Political operative F. Clifton "Clif" White, running the office, was amazed by the initial nationwide response to Reagan's speech.

Some politicians had not watched Reagan. George Romney was on a speaking tour in Michigan. Robert F. Kennedy, running for the Senate as a New Yorker, was busy campaigning in Long Island and had been conversing with President Johnson. But former vice-president and losing nominee for the presidency in 1960, Richard Nixon, did watch. Nixon had been grateful to Reagan for campaigning on his behalf two years earlier, when Nixon had run for governor of California and had lost. Nixon's keen political insight knew a winner when he saw one. He also could see a potential political competitor and threat as well. Immediately after watching The Speech, Nixon clearly noted that the one Republican winner emerging from the Goldwater debacle was not even on the presidential ballot: Ronald Reagan. Nixon likely started to mull the ramifications of Reagan's speech. He may have started to sense that Reagan's clear call for individual freedom, coupled with his brand new emergence into the national political limelight could threaten, from the conservative political right, Nixon's musings possibly to seek the Republican nomination once again.

Besides these political luminaries, a number of other ordinary citizens watched Reagan also. In California, a high school freshman named Pat Nolan huddled with his family, watching on their tiny black-and-white television set. Nolan, who had heard Reagan speak once before, kept nodding vigorously throughout the speech because of the truths that Reagan was espousing. Reagan's speech changed 12-year-old Doug Boyd's life forever; his half-century of involvement with conservative Republican politics in California began that day.[4] Another young conservative also was watching on his black-and-white set; Don Hodel, the secretary of the Clackamas County, Oregon, Republican Central Committee, felt that Reagan's speech resonated tremendously within him. In Pennsylvania helping with nationwide delegate work at the time, another young Republican Party worker from Oregon, Fred Van Natta, thought that Reagan's speech was the best in the entire 1964 campaign. Van Natta decided from that point on, Ronald Reagan was the man to watch. A third Oregonian, Diana Evans, who had worked for her congressman in the nation's capital and later had created a group of young Goldwater activists in Portland, had watched Reagan and became an instant believer. In his Queens, New York basement, student Ron Docksai was captivated by Reagan for his common sense, patriotism and fairness.

Not everyone in 1964 could afford the luxury of a television to watch Reagan—not even a bank executive. A young Wisconsin Republican activist named Don Taylor—a rising bank executive— and his wife had to listen to Reagan on their radio, but nevertheless came away extremely impressed. Near the nation's capital, a young student named Bruce Weinrod thought the man he was watching on television should be president *now*! In Pittsburgh, a political operative working his first campaign, Tom Reed, saw in Reagan an articulate spokesman for individual freedom who delivered a highly polished and professional speech. Reed felt he had been hit by a bolt of lightning sent directly from Ronald Reagan. Immediately he also envisioned that Ronald Reagan should be president of the United States—forget Goldwater!

The lives touched that evening by Reagan's speech, and the history of the United States and of the world, would never be the same. These political operatives would become the nucleus of Ronald Reagan's first campaign for the presidency in 1968. And each of their lives had been transformed by the inspiring words they heard that October evening from Ronald Reagan.

Across the nation, especially in the three major primary states where most of the 1968 action would be, these and many other hard working grassroots Reagan activists would lay the groundwork for what was to come later. They would come close, ever so close, to seeing Ronald Reagan chosen as the Republican nominee to be president in 1968.

But one other person watched Reagan's speech too. Former President Dwight D. Eisenhower carefully studied Reagan and his speech that evening. Only two years earlier, Eisenhower and Reagan jointly had made a Republican Party publicity record, not mentioned in any known Reagan or Eisenhower biography, entitled, *Mr. Lincoln's Party Today*. Reagan had used some of the same phrases about individual liberty in their joint 1962 recording as he just had spoken in his speech. The general, as he preferred to be called after he had left the White House in 1961, had watched and heard Reagan praise the courage of American soldiers during World War II and challenge the free world not to leave Eastern Europe in perpetual occupation by the Soviet Union. Just before Reagan had spoken the immortal words, "rendezvous with destiny," Reagan had quoted Eisenhower's World War II colleague, Winston Churchill. Eisenhower—the leader of D-Day as Supreme Allied Commander and then president of the United States—was an astute judge of character, of politics, and of nations. Looking and listening to Reagan, a new Republican star in the making, Eisenhower liked what he saw and heard.

Eisenhower then enthusiastically picked up the phone and called his former attorney general to say what a fine speech Reagan just delivered. Eisenhower was not done yet praising Ronald Reagan. After further reflection, then he phoned his former special assistant to say what an excellent speech he had heard from Reagan. Eisenhower had not been a fan of the Goldwater candidacy, and as he had been following the race closely, the former president began to plan how to rebuild the Republican Party after the likely huge Goldwater loss. Eisenhower long had felt that his party had failed in marketing and communicating their ideals.

Right in front of him, Eisenhower was seeing an articulate Republican who clearly was a great communicator. Perhaps Eisenhower, who knew that Reagan had campaigned for Nixon in 1962, had become a Republican at the same time, and had been California co-chairman of the Goldwater campaign, wondered if Ronald Reagan nursed any future political ambitions of his own and thus might become an important part of Eisenhower's plans for the future of the Republican Party.

Over the next few years, after winning the governorship of California, Reagan would begin his first campaign for the presidency.

In the process of his cross-country campaigning and in his speeches and press conferences, Reagan's expertise on world affairs would grow exponentially. Mentored by Dwight Eisenhower and fighting Robert Kennedy, Reagan initially only would briefly mention Vietnam. But during his campaign, Reagan would expand his vision: decrying the loss of America's military prowess which was squandered during the Kennedy-Johnson years from its prior height during the Eisenhower administration, giving specific strategies and tactics to win in Vietnam, pushing multiple times to tear down the Berlin Wall, calling for an American missile defense shield, pushing for freedom in Eastern Europe, wanting America to stand firmly with Israel, and teaching how to deal with hostage taking.

This is the inspiring yet untold story of how Ronald Reagan created a positive image for America during his first presidential campaign. Reagan's ultimate goal was to restore America to the road of greatness during Eisenhower's stewardship of the nation. Reagan first became Eisenhower's political student and later an Eisenhower protégé. Little did Reagan realize that under the mentorship of Eisenhower, Reagan first would be transformed into a world statesman, national candidate, and contender for the highest office in the land. Eisenhower was not left without a political legacy. Ultimately as president, Ronald Reagan would succeed in fulfilling Dwight Eisenhower's lofty goals. Ronald Reagan truly was one of Dwight Eisenhower's political heirs.

Endnotes

1. Evans, *The Education of Ronald Reagan*, p.169
2. Colacello, Bob "Ronnie and Nancy" *Vanity Fair*, 7/98 p.134
3. Evans, op. cit.
4. Doug Boyd, personal communication 2/27/2016

PART ONE

BEFORE THE CAMPAIGN

PROLOGUE: BEFORE "THE SPEECH": RFK, RN, AND IKE

> When it comes to the presidency its not candidates who
> make the decision whether to run, its public opinion—the
> people make the decision.
>
> ~ Ronald Reagan[1]

"Reagan 'the movie star?'" Nixon replied, "Yes."[2]

Presidents take inspiration from their predecessors. They hang
portraits and place busts of, and cite and quote in speeches and press
conferences, those who previously occupied the Oval Office. Ronald
Reagan was no exception. Upon taking office, Reagan placed a small
statue of Theodore Roosevelt (TR) in his private study.[3] Reagan
then took down Harry Truman's portrait and replaced it with that of
another of his heroes, Calvin Coolidge.

Reagan admired Coolidge's conservative principles and knew
that as governor of Massachusetts, Coolidge had fired striking public
employees: police officers. In the White House, Coolidge had lowered
taxes, which then had led to a booming economy. Reagan's actions
would mirror those of Coolidge.

Coolidge, after entering office when Harding had died and then in
1924 won election in his own right, had stunned the political world by
announcing that he would not seek reelection in 1928: "I do not choose
to run." Some, including Coolidge's vice-president, speculated that in
fact Coolidge was hoping for a draft from the people and from his
party.[4] Besides honoring TR and Coolidge, Reagan placed a portrait
of Taft on one wall of the Cabinet Room. But Reagan admired another
former president most of all, and to honor his favorite, Reagan did not
stop with hanging just one small portrait.

For Reagan placed a photograph of Dwight D. Eisenhower on
a small table behind his own Oval Office desk, placed a bust of
Eisenhower in his small study adjacent to the Oval Office, and then
hung a huge, towering portrait of General Eisenhower over the mantel
in the Cabinet Room.

Reagan knew that Eisenhower was another president whose
election was tied intimately with being drafted for office. In his

second autobiography, Reagan was recalling his initial support for Eisenhower in the early 1950s, at a time when Eisenhower may have been reluctant to seek the presidency. Reagan had seen that during 1952, Eisenhower had won an unexpected victory in the New Hampshire primary followed by a massive write-in drive in the Minnesota primary, which had delivered more than 100,000 votes for Eisenhower. This public draft, aided by grass roots activists, rather than the opinions of professional politicians, is what had swayed Eisenhower to reconsider his original position and then to enter the Republican primary race.[5]

So Reagan wrote this crucial comment: "When it comes to the presidency, it's not candidates who make the decision whether to run, it's public opinion—**the people make the decision**."[6] (author's emphasis)

Reagan's hero Coolidge had waited for a draft from the people to seek reelection. Eisenhower in 1952 had accepted the mantle only when the people had spoken. And this became Reagan's political mantra in 1968: he would not overtly seek the office. But if the people and the delegates wanted him as their presidential nominee, and once the people had spoken, he would not argue.

But why did President Reagan so personally honor President Eisenhower? Was it just placing mementos of the last Republican— other than disgraced Richard Nixon and Reagan's 1976 party opponent Gerald Ford—to have been elected? Or was there something more specific as to Reagan's choice of a photograph, a bust, and a large portrait?

The reader cannot be faulted for wondering how could Eisenhower and Reagan possibly have had anything directly to do with each other? After all, Reagan was elected in 1980, and prior to Eisenhower's death in the spring of 1969, did not Ike just play golf during the 1960s? This work for the first time will demonstrate the profound and direct link, in fact a mentor-student relationship between the two, such that Ronald Reagan was in fact one of Dwight Eisenhower's major protégés and may be considered his political heir. Preposterous, wonders the reader. Profound and true, answers your author.

But three busts or portraits or photographs Reagan had no intention of placing in his Oval Office, or elsewhere in the White House, were those of Presidents Kennedy or Nixon or of Attorney General Robert F. Kennedy.

RN

Richard Nixon liked to sign his memos with his initials, RN. Ronald Reagan and Richard Nixon had a relationship that spanned five decades, from when they first met in 1947 until Nixon would suffer a stroke and pass away in April of 1994. Two major reviews of their decades-long interactions are by historians Nancy Gibbs and Michael Duffy[7] and another by historians Kiron Skinner and Annelise and Martin Anderson.[8] The two "California Boys" now rest for eternity near each other in the part of the United States where they had begun their political lives.

In 1947, young Congressman Nixon heard that the new president of the Screen Actors Guild (SAG) had been worrying about the communist leanings of some union members. So Nixon had thought he might have found a good witness for his House Un-American Activities Committee. Reagan testified as a friendly witness, answering in a "clear, concise way."[9] Yet Reagan "upheld the rights of others to free speech and their participation in the electoral process."[10]

But three years later, Nixon and Reagan were on opposing sides back home in California. Reagan supported Nixon's opponent for the Senate and campaigned against Nixon, because Helen Gahagan Douglas was the wife of Reagan's friend, actor Melvyn Douglas.[11] Both John and Robert F. Kennedy supported the staunchly anti-communist Nixon and indeed Democrat JFK even quietly donated money to Republican Nixon's campaign.[12] Reagan's early, staunchly conservative views were noted by RFK and other Kennedys.

Reagan admitted that after the 1950 campaign he had "still carried around some bitter feelings" against Nixon. Some historians have even cited a letter Reagan wrote to a friend questioning Nixon's honesty.[13] Eventually, Reagan's friend and patron at General Electric, Ralph Cordiner, urged Reagan to take another look at Nixon.[14] And in 1952 and 1956 Reagan would vote Nixon as vice-president under Dwight D. Eisenhower.[15]

Reagan for Ike

During World War II, Ronald Reagan was assigned to the First Motion Picture of the Army Air Force, under the command of General "Hap" Arnold. Historian Kiron Skinner unearthed a little noted January, 1944 radio show to sell war bonds, entitled *Let's All Back the Attack*, in which Capt. Ronald Reagan of the Army Air Force's Public Relations Unit had played a soldier in battle. Another voice heard on that same show was that of the military leader of the Allies, who in five months would launch the D-Day Invasion, General Dwight D. Eisenhower.[16] This was Reagan's and Eisenhower's first interaction. Of course they did not meet. Between January and November, 1944, Reagan temporarily was assigned to New York City as part of the opening of the sixth war bonds appeal and Eisenhower of course was in Great Britain; their separate voice parts were united in the studio.[17][18]

Reagan was proud of America's multi-ethnic society. After Pearl Harbor, a Los Angeles market owner had fired five Japanese-American workers as a "patriotic" act. Reagan was incensed and gathered market customers and convinced them and the owner that the five Japanese-Americans were loyal citizens who were deserving of fair play. The owner rehired the workers. In December, 1945, General Joseph Stillwell had pinned the Distinguished Service Cross on a Japanese-American woman to honor her deceased brother; both were former internees at internment camps earlier in the war. Earlier in the year, Reagan had narrated a film (*The Stilwell Road*) about Stillwell's bravery in Burma. Reagan was at the ceremony and spoke later: "America stands unique in the world—the only country not founded on race but on a way, an ideal. Not in spite of but because of our polyglot background, we have had all the strength in the world. That is the American way."[19] Decades later, President Reagan would sign a bill authorizing restitution for the internment of Japanese-American civilians during World War II; during his remarks, he would reference his 1945 speech.[20] In Santa Ana, California, a plaque honors Reagan's 1945 speech. Thus early on his career, Reagan already was demonstrating his concern for minorities within American society.

As World War II had ended, Eisenhower had seen first hand the horrors of the holocaust and was in charge of de-Nazification and displaced persons camps. After returning to the United States, he became the president of Columbia University and not long after was puzzled by the Truman administration's slow military response in Korea.[21] However Eisenhower fully had supported Truman's decision to oppose the communists with military action.[22] Furthermore, unpopular Truman needed the help of highly popular Eisenhower, as Truman asked Eisenhower temporarily to leave Columbia University to become the head of NATO.[23] Eisenhower and Reagan both would find themselves supporting another Democratic president's mismanaged war in Southeast Asia a decade later.

Reagan had supported President Truman in 1948.[24] But by 1951, General Douglas MacArthur, fired by Truman, warned Congress and the American people, stating, "There is no substitute for victory." Reagan heard the speech, and seeing how the Korean War was being mismanaged, this was an early trigger for him to change parties.[25] Reagan recalled in his second autobiography that he, as had MacArthur, felt a strong "moral responsibility to do everything we can to win the war we put them in." Reagan then cited a prophetic remark by MacArthur, "If we don't win this war in Korea, we'll have to fight another war—this time in a place called Vietnam."[26] Reagan had become a disaffected Democrat. As Truman's popularity plummeted, the eyes of the nation, and of Ronald Reagan, turned to Ike.

Reagan wrote that in the early 1950s he had "greatly admired" Eisenhower,[27] and the Reagan's had sent the announcement of their March 4, 1952 wedding to the Eisenhower's.[28]   In 1952, Reagan still officially was a Democrat, and he sent a telegram to Eisenhower "urging him to run for president as a Democrat." But when Eisenhower instead ran as a Republican, Reagan recalled that he reasoned if he had considered Ike to be the best man for the job as a Democrat, he still should be Reagan's choice. So Reagan "campaigned and voted for Ike—my first for a Republican."[29] In fact Reagan was officially a Democrat for Dwight D. Eisenhower in 1952 and Reagan would vote for the Eisenhower-Nixon ticket again in 1956.[30] It would not be the last time that Reagan would think it a good idea for a Democrat to vote for a Republican.

Because the political pros controlled the delegates, and Eisenhower needed to win the nomination as an outsider, a group of supporters had helped push Eisenhower toward the candidacy by creating "Citizens for Eisenhower."[31] The co-founders of that national effort eventually would create over 800 "Eisenhower Clubs" across the country and would enlist over a million grassroots volunteers.[32] Eisenhower had been further persuaded to run by a February, 1952 rally at Madison Square Garden in Manhattan and the results of primaries in New Hampshire and Minnesota.[33] In addition, just as Eisenhower's biography, *Man From Abilene*, appeared, Eisenhower thought it important to publish his political philosophy, which he did via a paperback and series of newspaper articles.[34]

The first days of June, 1952 should go down in presidential history as quite consequential. On June 2, conservative actor Ronald Reagan delivered a commencement address at William Woods College (now University) in Fulton, Missouri. It was only a few years after Fulton had made world-wide headlines as the location of Winston Churchill's famed "Iron Curtain" speech. Reagan entitled his address, "America the Beautiful." He spoke about individual freedom and how it had been challenged, most recently, by "Hitlerism" and before that, by "Kaiserism." In words from Lincoln that foreshadowed what Reagan and Eisenhower together would use a decade later, Reagan warned the students, "No group can decide for the people what is good for the people so well as they can decide for themselves." Reagan closed by again using Lincoln's words: that America was "the last best hope" of mankind.[35]   Reagan would use those same phrases again many times in the future. And little did Reagan realize that he would return to Fulton decades later, after his presidency, to praise Churchill's warning about the Iron Curtain, as Reagan himself would bring the Berlin Wall, the most glaring symbol of the Iron Curtain, crashing down upon the ash heap of communism.

Reagan, who hated to fly, had written his address during an eastbound train trip from California. After speaking in Fulton on June 2, he headed back west the next day past Abilene, Kansas, where an important announcement was about to be made by Abilene's hometown hero.

On June 4 in Abilene, Dwight Eisenhower made his official announcement that he was launching his campaign for the race for the presidency. And only two days later came the eighth anniversary of D-Day: June 6, 1952. As reviewed by historian Michael Beschloss, new candidate Eisenhower's still-evident painful memories of having sent soldiers to die caused Eisenhower, speaking to a veteran's group that day, and being so overcome, to cover his face with a handkerchief so as not to show his tears.[36] The photograph was seen in newspapers of the day and it is not inconceivable that Reagan, officially a Democrat-for-Ike and almost back home in California, had seen it during his train ride west.

Reagan may have learned that fellow actor and the president of SAG immediately prior to Reagan, Republican Robert Montgomery, had advised the general on television speech techniques. Later in July, Reagan may have read that at the Republican Party convention, and after much credentials committee infighting, Eisenhower eventually had prevailed over Taft.   During the fall general election, among various voting blocs that nominee Eisenhower's campaign had targeted successfully, to be discussed in more detail later, were those of Southerners and Hispanic Americans.[37]

Atoms for Peace

On Election Day 1952, Eisenhower had won in a massive election victory. Several critical aspects of Eisenhower himself and the

Eisenhower administration would impact Ronald Reagan, both during his 1968 presidential campaign, and beyond. As shown recently by historian Evan Thomas, Eisenhower, who hated war itself, had had no compunction about bombing Berlin and other German cities during World War II; Ike had wanted the full fury of the entire Allied military unleashed on Germany so that the war could be won and won quickly. Later, as the Eisenhower administration began, Eisenhower felt that nuclear weapons should be viewed as part of the continuum of America's weaponry arsenal. He not only *threatened* to use nuclear weapons on North Korea and even China, he gave orders that the *military should act as if it intended to use them.* For Eisenhower, the threat of their possible use is what he wanted the North Koreans and Chinese to feel, even if he kept hidden only to himself whether he actually truly would use them. It was the Eisenhower threat, plus the additional factors of Stalin's death and China's fear of an American amphibious landing, that ended the Korean War.[38] Reagan would learn these lessons well during his first presidential campaign, and it would be Eisenhower who would mentor Reagan on these specific tactics.

Indeed Reagan likely paid particular attention to the new president, for whom he had just voted, and his new Republican policies. Indeed many of Eisenhower's policies and methods of governance would be carried forth later by Reagan.

In office for a few months, on June 14, 1953, President Eisenhower had the pleasure of signing a proclamation making the following week, "Theodore Roosevelt Week." It was the official public opening of TR's old home, Sagamore Hill. Eisenhower, a military student of the Civil War, held Lincoln with highest respect as a role model. But Ike admired TR as well and urged the nation to review his great achievements. Reflecting on the multi-faceted life of his Republican predecessor, including TR's career as leader of the Rough Riders and hero of the Spanish-American War, Eisenhower reminded the nation that TR "was a man who understood his fellow human beings. He understood those things for which they yearned and which they deserved under the principles in which he believed...Nothing was too difficult for him to tackle."[39] No truer words could describe future President Reagan as well.

On October 1, 1953, the United States-Republic of Korea Mutual Defense Treaty was signed, to deter future attacks by North Korea and to provide continental bases for U.S. military forces in Asia. Eisenhower then tried to help the countries of the Mideast, who never reached a final peace agreement (due to Arab intransigence, still wanting to destroy Israel) after 1948. During that same autumn of 1953, Eisenhower sent a special ambassador to the Middle East to establish a comprehensive water plan for the regional development of the Jordan River. Only Israel and Jordan complied with the final hydrological logistics. But throughout Eisenhower's two terms, the major problems were not in the Middle East but were with communism.

Eisenhower, like Reagan, felt that the Soviet system could not compete with democratic free market capitalism. In 1948, as talks to lift the Soviet blockade of Berlin had failed and the Soviets had denounced America's plan to control nuclear weapons, Eisenhower had seen that the Soviets clearly had shown their intentions never to seek compromises with the West.[40]

As reviewed by historian Peter Gilbert, Eisenhower felt strongly that many of the actions of the communists against the West were to force western nations to spend their treasuries in all the various hot spots in which the communists had created trouble. Eisenhower did not want to over react to communist threats and thus was able to fund major new technological triumphs for America's military while simultaneously holding the line on military over-spending. Eisenhower felt that the best way to defeat communism was for them to educate their citizens. Once the citizens behind the Iron Curtain could learn about freedom, democracy, and free-market capitalism, at most communism would last another four decades—i.e. into the 1990s. Eisenhower certainly got that prediction exactly correct.[41] In the decade after his presidency, Eisenhower would communicate these ideas to Ronald Reagan.

In early December, 1953, President Eisenhower had met with Prime Minister Winston Churchill to discuss a possible new summit meeting with the Soviet Union. Eisenhower lashed into the Soviet leadership and communist system, calling them the same old "whore" as always.[42] The next day, Eisenhower had threatened that if the truce in Korea broke down, he wanted to "unleash atomic weapons on Chinese bases."[43] But after issuing the threat, and after the Churchill meeting, Eisenhower flew to New York City to propose peace.

The next day on December 8, 1953, Eisenhower delivered his "Atoms for Peace" speech before the United Nations, wherein he proposed an initial reduction followed by a complete reduction of nuclear arms and handing all weapons over to an international atomic energy agency under the aegis of the United Nation. The hooker was that the Soviet Union had to agree; they rejected Eisenhower's proposal.[44] As will be seen, future President Reagan, who wished for the complete elimination of nuclear arms as well, not only would cite Eisenhower's speech repeatedly when negotiating with Gorbachev and other Soviet leaders about arms control, Reagan specifically would tell reporters that as official Reagan policy, he wished to bring to completion those very same policy proposals which Eisenhower had started.

Eisenhower also had proposed an "Open Skies" initiative, in which the airspace over America and the Soviet Union would be open for visual inspections. The Soviets had rejected that too. It was the forerunner of what future President Reagan would call "trust but verify."

On April 7, 1954, Eisenhower made his famous "domino theory" speech, at a point when, if strong measures were not taken, the looming French defeat in Vietnam seemed a precursor of other future Southeast Asian disasters for the West. Immediately thereafter, Eisenhower called Churchill and invited Britain to join the United States in again threatening the Chinese, who now were supporting the Vietminh rebels.[45]

After pressure from the Mexican government, which wanted to retain its workers to aid in the nation's plans to industrialize, that May the United States initiated Operation Wetback. When Eisenhower learned of the illegal immigrants staying in the country, he appointed a West Point classmate to lead the Immigration and Naturalization Service. Obeying the law always was paramount to Ike. Border agents rounded up illegal immigrants and transported them back to Mexico. A parallel-program, however, Bracero, issued temporary work permits to Mexicans to work the agricultural fields in America's Southwest.

On July 10, President Eisenhower tied together domestic agriculture with world peace by establishing the Food for Peace program, Public Law 480, in which America started shipping excess food supplies to needy countries.

Later that year, Eisenhower used threats once again. Communist China shelled the two small islands off Formosa (Taiwan): Quemoy and Matsu. America had pledged to defend the islands, and President Eisenhower once again made the clear use of threats. On December 2, the Mutual Defense Treaty between the Republic of China and the United States was signed, and the next month, Congress passed the "Formosa Resolution," which granted President Eisenhower the authority to defend Taiwan militarily. As reviewed by historian David McCullough in a film history, Ike staged maneuvers off the coast of China and tested battle-field atomic weapons in the Nevada desert. Eisenhower wanted the tests and maneuvers made public and then even staged a mock evacuation of the White House. Red China, convinced America would stay firm on its commitments to Formosa and use atomic weapons, backed down.[46] As reviewed by historian Shannon Tiezzi, "the Republic of Taiwan probably owes its continued existence to U.S. foreign policy and security decisions made under Eisenhower."[47]

Eisenhower's thoughts on military and political strategies and tactics and the use of threats, in Taiwan, Korea in the 1950s and Vietnam in the 1960s, would all be critical precedents to Reagan in the next decade. In 1967 and 1968, Reagan repeatedly would cite Eisenhower's forceful dealings with the communists in 1953 and 1954 and how the general wanted to see Vietnam handled in 1968.

In 1955, President Eisenhower helped renegotiate America's rights and obligations in the Canal Zone, and this new treaty with Panama, the first since the days of Theodore Roosevelt, was called the Remon-Eisenhower Treaty. Three years later, shortly after Vice President Nixon had a difficult trip to Latin America due to anti-American feelings, Eisenhower sent his brother Milton to Panama for additional discussions.

On September 11, 1956, Eisenhower established the Sister Cities International Program, a People-to-People program, to help foster global ties. That same year when Eisenhower had threatened Britain, France and Israel to force an end to the 1956 Suez Crisis, if Ronald Reagan knew the details of these events at the time, it is not known. But as will be seen, that event would make a lasting impression on him. For in 1968 Reagan would invoke Egypt's Nasser and his 1956 nationalization of the canal, the true origin of the crisis, as an example of how in the future to deal—swiftly but differently—with such political crises.

In his 1957 State of the Union Address, President Eisenhower welcomed efforts to form a European Union, and on October 25 he and British Prime Minister Harold MacMillan established a Technical Cooperation Program to share defense technologies between the two nations. In 1958, President Eisenhower sent troops to Lebanon but when asked if the troops should be based on land, his military training arose instantly. President Eisenhower ordered that the troops be stationed on American ships for added security. It would be a critical lesson not used by Reagan three decades later.

But there were domestic lessons about the Eisenhower administration, too, that Reagan observed. On June 29, 1956, President Eisenhower established the Interstate Highway system.

Politically, for much of the Eisenhower administration, the president had to deal with a Congress controlled by the opposition. Thus any major plans of Eisenhower to halt or stem the rise of big government over the prior decades faced intense congressional opposition. But Eisenhower did not hesitate to use his veto pen. Reagan would face similar difficulties during his governorship and during his 1968 presidential campaign would discuss those similarities with the press. Plus the "style" of the Reagan administration in Sacramento would be compared to the Eisenhower administration in the nation's capital via a quite disdainful elite eastern press at the end of 1967; to Reagan, such a comparison to Eisenhower probably was the highest political compliment that he could receive. Indeed historian Lee Edwards has noted that the eventual styles of governance of President Reagan— decision-making via consensus of the cabinet—would be compared favorably with those same processes of Eisenhower.

POW in Korea

After his service in World War II came to an end, Ronald Reagan's activities in the 1950s—actor, president of the Screen Actors Guild (SAG), public speaker—are well documented by others. But of major importance is a little-remembered Reagan film from 1954. In *Prisoner of War*, Reagan starred as an American army officer who volunteers to go underground to investigate terrible living conditions in North Korean POW camps. He finds things worse than anticipated: brainwashing, psychological torture, violence and starvation. He keeps the other prisoners alive while planning his escape.

To form the basis of the story, the screenwriter personally had visited the first ship of returning American POWs from the Korean War. Actor Reagan likely learned firsthand of the story, because future Governor Reagan would make certain he would be there first to greet the captain of an American ship captured by North Korea in 1968: the *U.S.S. Pueblo*. An advisor to the film, who worked closely with Reagan, was Capt. Robert H. Wise, who in World War II had spent one year in a Nazi prison camp and in Korea had spent three years in a North Korean POW camp.

One of Reagan's co-stars, portraying the American army officer who assigns Reagan's character the job to go to Korea, was actor Harry Morgan. Decades later, Morgan would gain his greatest fame— again in Korea—portraying fictional surgeon Col. Potter in *M*A*S*H*. In retirement, Morgan would revisit his co-star in the White House, and besides reminiscing about *M*A*S*H*, the two would recall their Korean War film.

During the filming, the peace talks in Panmunjom dragged on and on. Every newspaper headlined accounts of returning POWs. Reagan recalled, "Every torture scene and incident was based on actual happenings documented in official Army records."[48]

Thus Reagan—the tough negotiator as president of SAG—had almost-first-hand experience of what prolonged peace negotiations meant, what the Korean War had meant to those who had fought it, and what life in Nazi and North Korean POW camps had meant.

One of Eisenhower's last trips abroad as president was to Taiwan, in June, 1960. This visit marked the first time an American president had visited the island-nation. Over 500,000 Taiwanese came in person to hear and see the American leader, who in 1953-1954 had saved their nation from the possible military takeover by Red China preceded by Quemoy and Matsu. Eisenhower's "bold crusade," and his 1960 visit, "cemented his legacy in Taiwan's historical memory." He remains as the American president held in highest regard in Taiwan.[49]

As Eisenhower's second term was coming to an end and Vice-President Richard Nixon was heading the 1960 Republican ticket, the Democratic candidate was the young senator from Massachusetts, John F. Kennedy. Eisenhower called him "Little Blue Boy."[50] Eisenhower later would have harsher words about Kennedy's younger brother.

1960: Reagan Versus Joe Kennedy

In 1959 as the Eisenhower years were waning, Reagan still was spokesman for General Electric. Reagan sent Vice-President Nixon an analysis of the present tax situation, which generated a congratulatory response from Nixon.[51] Reagan answered via letter on June 27, 1959, telling Nixon that during his travels he had seen a "groundswell of economic conservatism."[52] Nixon continued via letter noting, "You have the ability of putting complicated technical ideas into words everyone can understand." Nixon was "helping to launch Reagan's political career whether he intended it or not."[53]

After Nixon's famous "kitchen debate" with Khrushchev in Moscow that summer, Reagan had congratulated Nixon on standing up to communism. Reagan wrote that he could only believe in coexistence when Russia "abandoned the Marxian precept that Communism must be imposed on the whole world."[54] Reagan, anchoring the Rose Bowl for ABC on New Year's Day 1960 and hoping to meet Nixon in person, even invited Nixon, who would be Grand Marshal, to meet; Nixon declined.[55]

After watching the Democratic Party nominate Kennedy, Reagan wrote a letter to Nixon on July 15, 1960. Reagan noted that Kennedy's ideas were for a bigger federal government with more federal spending. Reagan added that if some "short-sighted" Republicans tried to "out-liberal" Kennedy, "this would be fatal." Reagan had a strong feeling that the "20 million non voters in this country just might be conservatives." Reagan had one last thought for Nixon— that someone should tag Kennedy's program with its "proper age…it is still old Karl Marx." [56]

After sending the letter to Nixon, Reagan planned to support him publicly.[57] Historian Marc Eliot has cited several reasons for Reagan's intense support for Nixon, including Reagan's "intense dislike and distrust of both Kennedy brothers…He believed they were too rich, too young, and too opportunist to properly serve the country."[58] But most of all, Reagan felt that even though RFK had served briefly on Senator McCarthy's staff, which earned at least some positive feeling from Reagan, "JFK was too soft on communism."[59] There "was no one more anti-communist than Richard Nixon."[60] But there was one more reason. Walter Annenberg was a man whose opinion Reagan had respected. Annenberg had told the executives at General Electric what a fine job Reagan had been doing plus he had put Reagan on the cover of his popular magazine *TV Guide*. Despite Reagan's 1952 apparent concern about Nixon's honesty as mentioned earlier, when Annenberg told Reagan he had been supporting Nixon, that sealed it for Reagan.[61]

Reagan, the movie star?

During the summer of 1960, Nixon was deciding on whom to choose as his vice-presidential running mate. Two initial possibilities were conservative Barry Goldwater or liberal Nelson Rockefeller. A new organization, Youth for Goldwater, had tried to get Nixon to choose their favorite.[62] Reagan agreed and sent an urgent telegram to Nixon, advocating that he choose Goldwater because "cannot support ticket if it includes Rockefeller." An unnamed Nixon aide was incredulous when he saw that the telegram had been signed, "Mr. and Mrs. Ronald Reagan" and wrote a quick note in effect asking, "Reagan, the Movie Star?" Nixon answered, "Yes!"[63][64]

Nixon's staff wanted to use Reagan in the campaign, thinking that Reagan could attract others from Hollywood to endorse Nixon.

Reagan even offered to change parties. Nixon said his support would mean more if he did so as a Democrat, so Reagan, the former Democrat for Ike, now became vice chairman of Southern California Democrats for Nixon.[65] Reagan learned a valuable political lesson; for in 1966, when a prominent Mexican-American supporter would ask Reagan if he should become a Republican, Reagan would tell him it would be better to stay as a Democrat for Reagan.[66]

Reagan then made a public statement against the Democrats. This enraged Joseph Kennedy.[67] Kennedy, patriarch of the Kennedy's and financial backer of his son's campaign, called Reagan[68] and insisted on visiting Reagan in the hopes of dissuading Reagan from supporting Nixon and instead to support JFK. Reagan recalled, "I turned him down."[69] Whether the elder Kennedy definitely discussed this Reagan visit with JFK or RFK is pure conjecture, but one may presume he did. Reagan would not switch parties officially for another two years until Nixon ran for governor of California. This episode is not mentioned by Joe Kennedy's biographer.[70]

Reagan made note of one major part of John F. Kennedy's campaign theme—that President Eisenhower supposedly had permitted a "missile gap" with the Soviets to develop. Reagan would return to Kennedy's charge, later disproven as completely false, during the 1968 campaign.

After the narrow Nixon loss that fall, conservative leaders William Rusher and William F. Buckley, Jr. wanted to change the Republican Party and they turned to a rising star of conservatism, Barry Goldwater.[71] That conservatism might be on the upswing, especially in the South, was evidenced by the election of John Tower, the first Republican senator from Texas since Reconstruction. Tower had been elected to fill the vacancy when Lyndon Johnson became vice-president.[72]

Ruthless RFK Launches Ronald Reagan's Political career

Ronald Reagan had been the spokesman of *General Electric Theater* since 1954. During that time as part of GE's marketing plan, he "visited one hundred twenty-five plants, met 250,000 GE employees and spent hours in serious conversation with the conservative businessmen who ran the company."[73] When the Kennedy administration's National Labor Relations Board filed charges against GE in 1961 alleging unfair labor practices, the company management "complained of government harassment and expansion."[74] Although Reagan was not named in any part of the lawsuit, the case "would continue through the beginning of Reagan's California governorship and his first attempt to capture the Republican Presidential nomination."[75] The case would not be settled until 1969 and because Reagan worked for GE, it served as the first example of the Kennedy administration's potentially involving Reagan. RFK was not involved yet against Reagan, but that was about to change.

Historian Evan Thomas has noted that RFK had remained cognizant of the abuses of the McCarthy Committee, on which RFK had served as an attorney.[76] In 1961 shortly after taking office as attorney general, Kennedy, who previously also had been chief counsel of the Senate Rackets Committee,[77] announced on television that he was seeking anti-trust convictions against GE for alleged price fixing. Although the case had begun just prior to his taking office, Kennedy pursued it. The chief judge imposed fines on GE of millions of dollars and sentenced several GE executives, including a vice-president, to jail. GE's stock lost a third of its value. Then over 4,000 civil suits against GE began.

Once again, Reagan was untouched by this second Kennedy administration legal quest against GE. But this was the first time RFK had entered the fray directly. For Reagan, "the charges, that had been directed at the company and some of its key executives, were never used in any meaningful way against him."[78]

But the third brush that Reagan had with the Kennedy administration, and his second with RFK, would lead directly to the major change in Ronald Reagan's career. Historian Marc Eliot has reviewed how Reagan was subpoenaed to testify before a grand jury on February 5, 1962 about his role with MCA and the Screen Actors Guild (SAG). How Reagan had felt after Nixon had lost to the Kennedys "was nothing compared to how he felt when Robert Kennedy....ordered the Department of Justice to open an extensive investigation into MCA."[79] Kennedy was pursuing what he considered to be anti-trust violations again, but rather than within the electric industry and GE as he had earlier, this time he dealt with the entertainment industry. MCA had obtained a waiver and became the only company that had a talent agency and a television film production company. Kennedy attempted to prove "that the grant of this 'blanket' waiver was effectuated by a conspiracy between MCA and SAG."[80] Although historian Thomas has felt that RFK "was careful not to fling around baseless charges," he does admit that RFK had a "scattershot method," which produced "many more headlines than indictments."[81] Kennedy's theory was that there was a "possible payoff by MCA to Reagan for his aid in securing the SAG grant" for the waiver.[82]   Kennedy now was after conservative Reagan directly.

Kennedy's direct involvement with the SAG/MCA case began in March 1961 when the head of the Antitrust Division in Washington had told Kennedy that MCA was being investigated.[83]   The investigation continued, and on August 25, 1961, "Attorney General Robert F. Kennedy authorized a federal grand jury to be convened in the Southern District of New York to investigate the numerous charges against MCA."[84]   That October, the Grand Jury was moved from New York to Los Angeles after Kennedy had approved the change in venue.[85]

Robert Kennedy not only pursued the case, but his "reinvigorated investigation into MCA dragged on for months with stars, executives, and department heads regularly subpoenaed to testify."[86]   Although the national media did not cover the hearings very much, "the local Hollywood trades seemed interested."[87]

Living in Hollywood, Reagan "knew it was only a matter of time before the Committee would get around to him."[88]   Reagan "feared the investigation was really a retaliatory action on the part of the Kennedys against him personally for his enthusiastic support of Nixon during the presidential campaign."[89]   Reagan was warned by GE to lessen his verbal attacks on federal governmental policies. But Reagan not only did not relent, he "kept ramping it up…and continued his thinly disguised attacks against the Kennedy administration, accusing the country of turning soft on communism and hard on the working man."[90]

Eventually, Reagan indeed was called before the grand jury and testified on February 5, 1962. Reagan had spent the morning on the set of GE Theater and then testified "for nearly two hours without a break and acquitted himself well."[91]   The first time the previously-sealed 1962 Reagan testimony was printed in its entirety was by historian Dan Moldea. How Reagan was grilled by Kennedy's team for many hours is evidenced by the fact that his complete testimony occupies a full thirty-four pages of single-space type at 41 lines of testimony per page.[92]

After the unexpected death of Kennedy's chief prosecutor, and due to lack of evidence against Reagan, the case was settled and Kennedy had to announce the details. Reagan was "excused from all further testimony including the much-anticipated public trial, which many in the Kennedy administration had wanted to be broadcast in the same uninterrupted manner as the McCarthy…hearings."[93]   What Kennedy felt when his plans—to rake Reagan over the coals in a public trial—failed is unknown. But Kennedy was not yet done with Reagan.

Although Reagan survived the initial ordeal of Kennedy's Justice Department and was exonerated completely, he and Nancy Reagan were not off the hook yet. Indeed Kennedy's Justice Department ordered an IRS audit of both of their tax returns for the prior ten years.[94] In his memoirs, Thomas Reed felt that RFK's audit of the Reagan tax returns was related to RFK's continuing search for evidence of the SAG-MCA payoff.[95] But despite Kennedy's harassment of the Reagan's in the grand jury room and in arranging for the IRS audit, "no charges were filed against anyone."[96] Did Reagan feel he was the only conservative being targeted by a Kennedy vendetta? As will be seen shortly, the details of the secret Kennedy-IRS plan to audit conservatives would not become known until years later.

After his dual ordeals by the hands of Robert F. Kennedy, Ronald Reagan did not back down on his opinions on governmental interference in the lives of individuals. His experience with Kennedy served only to intensify his feelings for individual freedom and knowledge that government had gotten too big and had reached too far. Indeed shortly thereafter, Reagan "resumed his vocal attacks on the Kennedy administration, accusing Robert Kennedy of having conducted a meat-ax operation against MCA."[97] But Reagan did not feel only that he himself was the victim of Robert Kennedy's ruthlessness. Reagan "publicly bemoaned the fact that thanks to Robert Kennedy's insistence that MCA divest itself of its talent agency, hundreds of actors were now without adequate representation."[98]

Reagan did not bow to RFK's tactics of intimidation. But Kennedy had another trick up his sleeves to discredit Reagan.

One month after his testimony and the signing of the consent decree, Reagan still was the host of *General Electric Theater* on Sunday evenings at 9PM on CBS for its eighth, and ultimately last, season. The ratings of the show usually had been in the top ten and it was described as an "extremely successful show."[99] But in March 1962, the show was cancelled abruptly, and thus Reagan's weekly appearances in the homes of American viewers were over.

For many years, several theories as to why Reagan's show was cancelled were put forth in numerous books. However, the true reason, which involved RFK directly, was revealed only recently by the Reagan family. One theory was that CBS could not "cope with a program that had an outspoken conservative as a front man."[100] Another was that the decision was not politically-motivated but reflected the show's loss of audience ratings due to NBC's highly-rated *Bonanza*,[101] especially because Reagan's show was a half-hour "anthology melodrama"[102] program in black-and-white and "was no match for the appeal of the hour-long color western."[103] [104]   Another theory advanced by the same author was that Reagan's testimony amidst the MCA-SAG scandal had tainted him and "it was shortly thereafter that GE cancelled" his show.[105] A fourth theory was that after the GE anti-trust charges and jailing of some of its employees, a new management team at GE "decided that Reagan's road tour should be confined to pitching the company's products. When Reagan balked at this suggestion, he left GE, and the television program was terminated."[106]

However two eye-witness accounts from members of Reagan's immediate family confirm the true origin of the decision as indeed political—but the origin of the decision lay not with CBS but with Robert F. Kennedy pressuring the show's sponsor, GE. In a 2011 op-ed in *Investors Business Daily*,[107] Reagan's son Michael relates the true story, which his dad had related to him. His dad had been criticizing the Kennedy administration in several speeches. At the same time, GE was negotiating several contracts with the federal government. Attorney General Robert F. Kennedy dictated new terms to GE: that "if the company wished to do business with the U.S. government, it would (have to) get rid of 'General Electric Theater' and fire the host."[108]   Maureen Reagan corroborated Michael's recollections, adding that Ronald Reagan spoke to his boss, Ralph Cordiner, who confirmed the intimidation by Kennedy but told Reagan, "Don't worry. We won't be blackmailed."[109]

But within two days of the call from RFK to GE, Ronald Reagan came home to tell Michael, Maureen, and the rest of the family that CBS "hadn't cancelled the highly rated show. Instead GE pulled the plug."[110]   It would prove to be not the last time that CBS would be involved with the orders of Robert F. Kennedy against Ronald Reagan.[111] Historian and author Lee Edwards had contacted CBS to look at their files on Reagan, but Edwards was told that the files no longer existed.[112] Historian Lou Cannon interviewed a CBS executive who had been present at the meeting where the decision was made to cancel Reagan's show. Cannon was told it was because of ratings.[113] Regardless of the true reason for the cancellation, whether the actual decision lay with GE or CBS, as related by his children above, the important point is that Ronald Reagan blamed Robert Kennedy.

One can only imagine how Ronald Reagan felt about Robert Kennedy at that time. First, Kennedy's father had attempted to muscle Reagan into supporting JFK in 1960. Then Reagan was threatened indirectly by two Kennedy administration lawsuits, one run by RFK, against GE. Third, Reagan was forced to testify for RFK's grand jury in the SAG-MCA matter and was found innocent. Fourth, RFK had arranged to audit Reagan's tax returns. And now came the final straw: Reagan believed that RFK arranged for Reagan's show to be cancelled, which thus threatened his family's source of income. Would Reagan ever get the chance to meet RFK? Could he somehow turn the tables on RFK?

Now Ronald Reagan was unemployed. As historian Marc Eliot has summarized, Ronald Reagan was "angered by this decision"[114] knowing "the Kennedys were behind it all."[115]   And Reagan was not angry at Kennedy solely for Kennedy having had the show cancelled; Reagan began having difficulties finding any other work in Hollywood. Reagan "would never forget or forgive Robert Kennedy for leading the charge against MCA that left him, Reagan, almost completely shut out of the entertainment mainstream." Indeed Reagan "felt blacklisted as a result of his testimony... There was nobody beating down his door to give him a job, and for that there was no one else to blame, he believed, than the Kennedy brothers."[116]

The Ideological Organizations Project

Why the Kennedys fought American conservative institutions and individuals, and the secret methods they employed to harass and discredit them, only came to light in the mid 1970s. Historian John A. Andrew III has detailed the congressional findings, which will be summarized only briefly here. Shortly after taking office, Attorney General Kennedy "assailed the Right as a 'tremendous danger' to the United States."[117]   The administration then began to "monitor the activities of right-wing organizations."[118]   At the behest of the administration, a United Auto Workers official sent the Kennedy brothers a memorandum outlining steps that were both "secret and illegal," which became the "first step in what became a covert effort to discredit the right wing and undercut its sources of financial support."[119]   Anyone on the Right who challenged "mainstream thinking" was lumped together as a threat to the liberal Kennedy administration and the Democrat Party.

Amongst the recommendations of the memorandum were to choke off money flowing to right wing organizations,[120] and to use the Internal Revenue Service along with sending undercover FBI and Treasury department agents.

But the most "far-reaching effort" taken by the Kennedy brothers was a secret plan called the Ideological Organizations Project, which was launched in 1961 to audit some 22 right-wing groups.[121] In order to cover their tracks somewhat, the administration added "a couple of left-wing groups for balance."[122] The plan was to audit 10,000 tax-exempt organizations and non-exempt right-wing groups such as Young Americans for Freedom (YAF) for which, as we will see later, Reagan was on the National Board and was a cherished speaker.[123]

The entire covert auditing project was made official when the IRS Office of Chief Counsel, under pressure from either the President or his brother the Attorney General, granted the Kennedy family's accountant—special consultant to the president—access to tax returns in early 1961.[124]

The first phase of the Ideological Organizations Project ran from the fall of 1961 until 1963,[125] and it was during this time period that RFK had arranged for the IRS audit of the Reagan taxes after Reagan had been exonerated after the SAG-MCA testimony.

As reviewed by historian Andrew, the entire secret project of the Kennedys to discredit their opposition was only made public during the mid 1970s Senate Select Committee on Intelligence Activities, the Church Committee. Thus only now in retrospect can one see that RFK's harassment of Reagan fit in quite naturally with his and his brother's larger goals of destroying as much of their opposition from the right wing as possible. First RFK attacked the institutions, and then he went after the individuals such as the prime, outspoken, national celebrity and defiant spokesman for conservatism in the 1950s and 1960s—Ronald Reagan. Neither the IRS nor the Kennedys ever apologized to the Reagan's for the harassment. It would be another four decades until similar IRS harassment of conservative groups and individuals would come to light during the Obama administration as a major scandal in 2013. It would not be until 2014, more than fifty years after the Kennedy's had gotten the IRS to audit Reagan for political revenge, that the IRS would apologize to conservatives.[126] One can only guess as to how long the Kennedy's had planned to continue their IRS harassment in regard to the 1964 election.

As a direct result of his livelihood being threatened at the hands of Robert F. Kennedy, Ronald Reagan refocused his efforts away from television and Hollywood and into a political direction. Michael Reagan's op-ed piece related this one bright spot in the story of Reagan having been fired. It was a "classic case of the liberals outsmarting themselves. If Bobby Kennedy had let Ronald Reagan continue hosting his successful TV show, would my father have run for governor? Doubtful. And if he had not been elected governor, he certainly would not have run for President of the United States."[127] So in a "backhanded way, Bobby Kennedy launched Ronald Reagan's political career."[128]

Reagan Again Helps Nixon

So after cancellation of Reagan's show in March, 1962, Reagan started to focus on the world of politics. Reagan at the time was on the National Advisory Board of one of the targets of Kennedy harassment: YAF, the organization of young conservatives founded in 1960 at the Sharon, Connecticut estate of *National Review* editor William F. Buckley, Jr. On June 18, 1962, Reagan enclosed the following note with his financial contribution to YAF:

> I know of no other group in the nation which is going to be more effective in preserving and extending our cherished goals. There is no need to emphasize that these young people are the future leaders of the nation. As they grow and develop, so will our country.[129]

Reagan may not have known that YAF also was in cross-hairs of the Kennedy's, for the 1975 investigation would reveal that the Kennedys' Ideological Organizations project also had arranged for the IRS to audit and harass the YAF, as had been done to Reagan. But besides thinking about the growth of conservatism in the future with YAF, Reagan turned to how he might be of help with more-pressing political goals and decided to help Kennedy's old 1960 opponent, now running for governor of California, Richard Nixon.

Nixon had moved to New York City, but when he had returned to California to run for governor in 1962, he was viewed by many California conservative Republicans as too liberal. Nixon turned to Reagan for advice on how to gain their support. Reagan tried to help but was still officially a Democrat. But while speaking in Los Angeles at a Nixon Republican fundraiser, a woman asked Reagan "Have you registered as a Republican yet?" When Reagan said he intended to, the woman, a local registration official, handed him the correct form. As the audience cheered, Ronald Reagan became a Republican Party member that day.[130]

After this pivotal political change in 1962, Reagan would be asked to narrate a Republican Party publicity record which would involve the four major Republican political figures of the era and with whom

Reagan would interact in 1968: Nixon, New York Governor Nelson A. Rockefeller, former candidate Barry Goldwater, and the man who would become his political mentor and coach, former President Dwight D. Eisenhower.

Ike

As discussed by historian Jim Newton, Eisenhower had grown up in a family with five other brothers and had to find common ground with them to survive. Eisenhower's capacity to find similar "common ground" with difficult wartime personalities such as Roosevelt, Churchill, De Gaulle, Montgomery, Truman, and Brooke had made him an ideal commander during World War II.[131] Ike was the ultimate team player. Eisenhower was an astute judge of character and had seen upfront the worlds of politics in the army and between nations. He sought the same finding of common ground with various Republicans after his presidency, and a prime example of his philosophy of bringing together all Republicans, which Reagan would continue in 1968 by never criticizing in public any of his Republican competitors while at the same time trying to reach out to Democrats and Independents, is an LP recording that has been unknown to historians.

Mr. Lincoln's Party Today

Deep in the Eisenhower Library archives lies a script of a recording made in 1962. The script and the resultant record brought together six Republicans whose careers spanned virtually the entire nineteenth and twentieth centuries: Abraham Lincoln, Dwight D. Eisenhower, Richard M. Nixon, Nelson A. Rockefeller, Barry M. Goldwater, and Ronald W. Reagan. Very few copies of the record still exist. The title was *Mr. Lincoln's Party Today*. It was a "declaration of Republican belief" and was based on a 1962 report of the Joint Committee on Republican Principles.[132]

Historian George Kabservice recently reviewed Republican intra-party squabbles during that time. The GOP was responding to a March, 1962, public critique that had been made by discontented liberals. Eisenhower had stayed informed of the views of the malcontents. At a late June, 1962 gathering—held at Eisenhower's Gettysburg farm—called the All-Republican Conference, Eisenhower urged attendees to study the criticisms. Also at the gathering, the formation of a new party outreach organization called the National Republican Citizens Committee was announced. Its purpose was to bring onboard

Independents and discontented Democrats. Eisenhower had been unhappy with what he saw as his party's major weakness compared to the opposition: poor salesmanship. As a result of these efforts, Wisconsin Congressman Melvin Laird had created a "declaration of principles" upon which Republicans of 1962 could agree. Kabaservice concluded that Eisenhower and Laird's lofty goals ended in failure by a combination of inertia and conservative opposition from Goldwater.[133]

But the existence of *Mr. Lincoln's Party Today* proves that conservative Goldwater not only did not oppose Eisenhower's plans to enlarge the GOP tent, he would be at the forefront of the national effort. And the first step in Eisenhower's (and Laird's) plans was to create the script and hire a narrator.

Why and how Ronald Reagan was chosen to be the narrator of the 1962 record is not known. After all, Reagan, while campaigning in California for Nixon, just had registered to become a Republican. But ever since his 1952 speech in Fulton, Missouri, Reagan had been espousing conservative, essentially Republican ideas for more than a decade as a speaker for General Electric as well. Indeed Reagan was so popular a conservative spokesman that one GE executive told Reagan that he was, "more in demand as a public speaker than anyone in the country except President Dwight D. Eisenhower."[134] To be compared favorably with Eisenhower, as noted above, may very well have been in Reagan's mind the highest political accolade that Reagan ever could receive. It would not be the last time the comparison would be made.

It is inconceivable that the chosen narrator for such an important new party publicity project would not have passed Eisenhower's muster. Did Eisenhower recall their joint war bond radio program in January, 1944? Most likely Eisenhower and the other decision makers within the Republican Party decided this was a good way for Reagan—the brand-new Republican—to be introduced to party members by using his well-known radio and television voice and personality. The record jacket wording listed that the record company was indebted to the Republican National Committee, and specific thanks were given to twelve individuals one of whom was Laird. The back of the jacket had photographs of the speakers with short biographies; Reagan was listed as a film and television star without any political wording.

Reagan was to narrate the record, whose specific theme was that the founding principle of the Republican Party in Lincoln's time, individual freedom, still applied in the early 1960s. The main idea was that the Republican Party of today—1962—indeed still did hold to the principles espoused by Lincoln when he had delivered the Gettysburg Address. But that because times, ideas, and issues had changed, Republicans needed to be reminded, and all Americans needed to be educated, on what it meant to be a Republican in the space age.

The original script in the Eisenhower Presidential Library indicated that Reagan would speak to two ordinary citizens about a given topic and then each of the four main Republican leaders would answer with detailed explanations accompanied by specific sound effects. The record would end with General Eisenhower speaking from his farm at Gettysburg, which of course tied the ending back to Lincoln's Gettysburg Address, the last words of which Reagan recited as he had at the beginning of the record.

A fascinating aspect to the script of the record is the hand-written revision that Eisenhower added. As noted, the individual who had chosen the speakers was not stated. After hosting the party gathering on his farm, this was another example of Eisenhower's involvement in his party after 1960. More would follow.

Eisenhower wrote onto the original script, "Good Republicans can, and do, have divergent individual beliefs...There are good so-called conservative Republicans; good middle-of-the-roaders; good so-called liberal Republicans. But on this fundamental document, Republicans of many differing views on individual issues are agreed." During his 1968 presidential campaign, Reagan would say repeatedly that he did not like the terms of "conservative-" or "liberal-" Republican—telling the reporters that he did not like labels or hyphens; Reagan would preach the unity of the party. Eisenhower's insertion of his own beliefs into the script that Reagan read may have been one major source for Reagan's thinking on the issue of divisiveness versus unity even prior to the future scars that would be generated from the 1964 Republican convention.

What is also significant is that Eisenhower must have been very comfortable that brand-new Republican, conservative Ronald Reagan, had agreed to be the narrator of such an important new party outreach program. Eisenhower had modified the script as noted; he never wrote that the producers should get someone else to narrate. Conservative Reagan fit quite well within Ike's broad tent Republican Party. Although in this script, Reagan would read some of the words that Eisenhower had written, in the years ahead Eisenhower himself directly would suggest that Reagan should use these very same themes as Reagan was beginning his political career.[135]

The final version of the record as sold to the public did not follow the initial script exactly. Reagan did speak at the beginning by framing the entire recording with Lincoln's thoughts that government ought not to interfere with what individual citizens could do for themselves. Reagan then introduced the four speakers, asking each to reply whether those principles still applied today—in 1962. Little did Reagan realize how crucial these four individuals would become to him in 1968.

Nixon and Goldwater spoke about small government and individual freedom, and Rockefeller espoused individual initiative and private enterprise. Eisenhower reviewed that Lincoln's party, believing in the preeminence of the individual, indeed could meet new challenges in the twentieth century. He said that the function of government is to "let us take risks." He used the analogy of his Interstate Highway System saying that only those drivers who were having major difficulties on the road of life needed to exit and go into the lane of the federal government to help guide them.

Eisenhower summarized his deepest-held political philosophy: that whatever could be done by private effort should be done by private effort first; if a problem must be done by government, then people should decide first if it can be done at the state level; and whatever could only be done by the federal government should be done as a last resort at that federal level. Eisenhower eloquently had espoused the cherished themes of small government and individual freedom.

"World Divided" Speech

Reagan then spoke again to conclude the recording. Having spoken about Lincoln at the beginning of the recording, Reagan revisited his hero again. Reagan referenced Lincoln's famous "House Divided" speech of 1858, when Lincoln had proclaimed that because of the vastly different philosophies and economies of the North and South, "I do not believe this government can long endure, half slave and half free."

Ronald Reagan then updated and universalized Lincoln's well-known words for the world of 1962, where communism and liberal, democratic capitalism were competing for the minds of mankind. Reagan warned the world about the loss of political and religious freedoms in the Soviet Union and occupied Eastern Europe: "The world cannot exist half slave and half free." Historians might look back and call this recording Ronald Reagan's "World Divided" speech.

Reagan ended the recording by using phrases he had made in Fulton a decade earlier and that would echo later in his famed 1964 speech and beyond. Reagan cautioned his listeners that America's problems should not be sent to "an intellectual elite in a far away capital," who thought they could plan better than we can for ourselves. Reagan ended by warning that if citizens gave up their rights of solving problems for themselves, they would give up "the last, best hope for man on earth."[136]

How the record was used by the Republican Party is not known nor what the sales were. The record is not mentioned in any other Reagan or Eisenhower or Nixon or Rockefeller or Goldwater biography to your author's knowledge.[137]   It does demonstrate clearly however, that Reagan, thought highly enough by Ike and in party circles to be chosen to be its narrator, indeed had been an ideal choice.

The message of the record, that Republicans of divergent views shared a common core set of principles would reverberate for both Eisenhower and Reagan in the years ahead. Eisenhower would use these same themes repeatedly in his political advice he would give to Reagan, and during the 1968 campaign, Reagan not infrequently would tell the press that he and his Republican competitors for the nomination shared this common set of Republican principles and that is why he felt he could support for president whichever Republican candidate won the nomination.

The main message of Reagan was but a prelude to his famed October, 1964 *A Time for Choosing* speech. His 1962 Lincolnesque warning to the world, that enslaved societies in the Soviet Union and its Eastern European satellite countries soon would face their reckoning, would be undertaken by candidate Reagan during his 1968 campaign and reach its conclusion with President Reagan's ultimate peaceful defeat of communism two decades later.

By the manner in which the 1962 recording was produced, those four Republican speakers did not meet together in the same studio to record their ten minute answers to Reagan's initial question. Eisenhower's only "interaction" with Reagan was having thanked Reagan on the recording just prior to starting his own answer. Thus, as with their earlier joint war bonds radio program two decades earlier, there was no actual direct contact between the two men in 1962.

Nixon Loses Again

Despite the campaign help from Reagan, Nixon lost his 1962 gubernatorial campaign to Democrat Edmund "Pat" Brown, father of Jerry Brown. One prominent Mexican American leader who had campaigned for Brown was a physician and banker named Dr. Francisco Bravo. Bravo hoped Brown would appoint many minorities to office.[138]

Nixon ended his final press conference with the famous, "You won't have Dick Nixon to kick around anymore." The actual tape of the 1962 Nixon press conference would play a role six years later. All five Republicans who were part of *Mr. Lincoln's Party Today* were about to play critical roles in the upcoming 1964 and 1968 elections. Richard Nixon was now a double political loser: in 1960 and 1962. It looked like Nixon's political career, let alone any future second quest for the presidency, was finished. But Ronald Reagan's was about to begin.

Endnotes

1. Ronald Reagan, *An American Life*, p. 133
2. Gibbs, p. 197
3. See Illustrations
4. Gilbert, p. 229. Gilbert reviews various other theories behind Coolidge's decision.
5. Jacobs, p. 276- 278
6. Reagan, op. cit., p. 133
7. Gibbs
8. Skinner, et. al.
9. Boyarsky, p. 86
10. Moldea, p. 72
11. Reagan, op. cit., p. 132
12. Ambrose, *Nixon*, p. 210-211
13. Spitz, Bob, personal communication, 8/31/2015
14. Reagan, op. cit., p. 133
15. Mann, p. 8
16. Cited in Skinner, *Reagan: A Life in Letters*, p. 132
17. Eisenhower later made a second radio appeal after D-Day, which was broadcast that November as Reagan was returning to California
18. *Evening Independent*, "Eisenhower Says His Forces Need Additional Arms," 11/24/1944, p. 1
19. http://www.discovernikkei.org/en/journal/2012/12/21/masuda-family-5/. Columnist Carl Cannon in 2015 discussed Reagan's 1945 speech in relation to Islamic immigration. (www. realclearpolitics.com, 12/13/2015)
20. Reagan, Ronald "Remarks on Signing the Bill Providing Restitution for the Wartime Internment of Japanese-American Civilians," 8/10/1988
21. Jacobs, p. 249
22. Jacobs, p. 274
23. Jacobs, p. 252
24. Reagan, *An American Life*, p. 132
25. Reed, p. 35
26. Reagan, op. cit., p 133
27. Reagan, op. cit., p.133
28. Eisenhower, Mamie: Papers, SHAPE Series, Box 2, America-Personal Friends, Dwight D. Eisenhower Presidential Library
29. Reagan, op.cit. p. 133

30. "The Winning 'Loser,'" *NYT,* 1/3/67, p. 24
31. Jacobs, p. 270
32. https://www.youtube.com/watch?v=NMW-d3t676c
33. Another perspective is offered by historian William Pickett, who felt that Ike had in fact orchestrated his run behind the scenes, even as early as 1948. Pickett's is the minority view, as most historians feel that Ike reached his decision to run for president after he had seen the grass roots support in Madison Square Garden and in the New Hampshire and Minnesota primaries, as noted. But if Pickett's thesis is correct, it is conceivable that Reagan may have modeled his 1968 stealth presidential campaign mode after what Ike did behind-the-scenes twenty years earlier. (Pickett, William R. *Eisenhower Decides to Run.* Chicago: Ivan R. Dee, 2000.)
34. Jacobs, p. 276
35. Reagan. Ronald, Commencement Address, William Woods College, 6/2/1952
36. Beschloss, Michael "Why Ike Wouldn't Celebrate the D-Day Anniversary," *NYT,* 5/19/2014
37. Trende, Sean, "Eisenhower's Coalition," *Sabato's Crystal Ball,* 11/20/2014
38. Thomas, *Ike's Bluff*
39. Eisenhower, Dwight D. "Remarks at the Dedication of the Theodore Roosevelt Home at Sagamore Hill, Oyster Bay, New York, as a National Shrine." 6/14/1953
40. Jacobs, p. 113
41. Gilbert, Peter, "Eisenhower and Reagan," Vermont Public Broadcasting radio talk, 9/16/2004
42. Leaming, p. 243
43. Leaming, p. 244
44. Thomas, Ikes Bluff, p. 111
45. Leaming, p. 252
46. *The American Experience: Eisenhower,* PBS
47. Tiezzi, Shannon "How Eisenhower Saved Taiwan," *The Diploma*t, 7/29/2015
48. "Prisoner of War," *International Movie Data Base*
49. Tiezzi, Shannon, op.cit.
50. Buchanan, p. 158
51. Gibbs, p. 195
52. Skinner, Anderson, et. al., p. 702
53. Gibbs, p. 196
54. Skinner, Anderson, op. cit., p. 703
55. Gibbs and Duffy, pp. 196-197; Skinner, Anderson, op. cit., p. 704
56. Skinner, Anderson, op. cit., p. 705
57. Eliot, p. 304
58. ibid
59. ibid
60. ibid
61. Eliot, Marc, p. 304-305
62. Andrew, p. 27-28
63. This reminds one of the line in *Back to the Future* when Professor Emmett Brown in 1955 is shocked when Marty McFly tells him who the president—former actor Ronald Reagan—is in 1985. President Ronald Reagan loved *Back to the Future* and so enjoyed the part where Professor Brown is incredulous that Reagan is president in 1985 that he made the White House projectionist stop the film so the scene could be shown several times while Reagan laughed. Reagan then referenced the ending of the film in his 1986 State of the Union Message when he said, "As they said in the film *Back to the Future,* where we're going, we don't need roads.'" Reportedly director Robert Zemeckis offered former President Reagan the part of the 1885 mayor of Hill Valley so Reagan could dedicate the film's clock tower, but Reagan declined. Reagan was a part of other scenes in the movie trilogy, including: the 1955 movie marquee showing his film *Cattle Queen of Montana* (made while Eisenhower was president), his likeness was portrayed on the television in the 2015 Café 80s, the headline that Reagan would seek a second term appeared in the newspaper when the timeline was restored in 1985, and the headline that Reagan would have surgery appeared in the newspaper Mr. Strickland received in the alternate 1985!
64. Gibbs and Duffy, p. 197
65. Cannon, p. 112
66. Kopelson, Gene. 2014C
67. Gibbs and Duffy, p. 198
68. Evans, p. 159
69. Reagan, *An American Life,* p. 134
70. Nasaw
71. Frisk, p. 143
72. Frisk, p. 152
73. Boyarsky, p. 99

74. Boyarsky, p. 100
75. Evans, p. 160
76. Thomas, Evan, p. 85
77. Moldea, p. 119
78. Evans, p. 163
79. Eliot, p. 305
80. Edwards, p. 478
81. Thomas, op. cit.
82. Edwards, p. 478
83. Moldea, p. 155-156
84. Moldea, p. 161
85. Moldea, p. 164
86. Eliot, p. 305
87. ibid
88. Eliot, p. 306
89. ibid
90. ibid
91. Edwards, p. 478
92. Moldea, p. 167-201
93. Eliot, p. 319
94. Edwards, p. 478
95. Reed, *Reagan Engima*, p. 87
96. Moldea, p. 203
97. Eliot, p. 319
98. ibid
99. Boyarsky, p. 102
100. Gibbs and Duffy, p. 199
101. Edwards, Anne, p. 476
102. Eliot, p. 320
103. Boyarsky, p. 102
104. This would not be the first time *Bonanza* entered the Reagan-RFK saga as will be seen later
105. Edwards, p. 478
106. Evans, p. 163
107. Reagan, Michael, "Ronald Reagan's Son Remembers the Day When GE Fired His Dad," *Investors Business Daily*, 2/4/2011
108. ibid
109. Reagan, Maureen, p. 110
110. ibid
111. Reed, *The Reagan Enigma* p. 88-89. Reed, who interviewed both Michael and Maureen, also reviews other theories from historians.
112. Edwards, personal communication, 4/17/2015
113. Cannon, personal communication ,4/25/2015
114. Eliot, p. 319-320
115. Eliot, p. 320
116. Eliot, p. 326
117. Andrew, p. 152
118. Andrew, p. 156
119. Andrew, p. 153
120. Andrew, p. 155
121. Andrew, p. 157
122. Andrew, p. 158
123. Andrew, p. 158-159
124. Andrew, p. 159
125. Andrew, p. 160-161
126. "New IRS chief apologizes to targeted conservative groups after House hearing," www.foxnews.com, 2/5/2014
127. Reagan Michael, op.cit.
128. ibid
129. Thorburn, p. 79
130. Reagan, *An American Life*, p. 136; Gibbs, p. 199
131. Newton, Jim, *Eisenhower: The White House Years*. Eisenhower's finding common ground is the theme of the book.
132. See Illustrations
133. Kabaservice, George. *Rule and Ruin*. New York: Oxford University Press, 2012, p. 55-60
134. Cannon p. 112

135. Recording Script, Eisenhower, Dwight D.: Post-Presidential Papers, 1961-1969, 1962 Principle File, Box 38, Lincoln, Dwight D. Eisenhower Presidential Library

136. Reagan, Ronald, narrator "Mr. Lincoln's Party Today," recording, Schwalbe, Stuart A. producer, Heritage Records, Saratoga CA, 1962.

137. An unattributed photograph appears in Reed's book *The Reagan Enigma*, which this author gave to Reed

138. "Francisco Bravo, 80: pioneer in Development of East L.A." *Los Angeles Times*, 5/11/90

CHAPTER 1: 1964-1966: OWOSSO, IKE, COMMON SENSE, AND THE CITIZEN-POLITICIAN

"I <u>could</u> be President."
~ Ronald Reagan[1]

"I do remember being struck by the intensity with which Reagan studied Eisenhower."
~ Gore Vidal[2]

"It's very premature to talk about 1968."
~ Ronald Reagan[3]

"You can bet he will become a Presidential possibility."
~ Dwight Eisenhower[4]

After Reagan's October, 1964 speech was seen on television, political operative F. Clifton "Clif" White, at the Citizens for Goldwater headquarters in the nation's capital, watched in amazement as the office was "snowed under" with calls and, over the next few days, with visits of newly energized conservatives.[5]   White encouraged repeat showings of the Reagan speech to maximize the impact of what Reagan had accomplished. Reagan had "found a way to marry the medium that loved him to the message he loved."[6]

What some other politicians who would play important roles in 1968 were doing when Reagan had delivered his 1964 speech varied, and what they had thought about what Reagan had said was left unspoken except for Nixon, whose comment on The Speech was noted earlier. Michigan Governor George Romney, a Republican liberal, was in Kingston, Michigan at the time on a speaking tour.[7] Nelson A. Rockefeller, of the same political persuasion as Romney and who had lost to Goldwater, had stayed out of the campaign. Neither man had endorsed Goldwater; both would be castigated by Reagan after the election for having created the party fracture. On the Democratic side, Robert F. Kennedy—now former attorney general and no longer able to try to destroy Reagan in any official capacity—was running for the Senate and was in New York. He just had appeared in the cover story of *Time*'s October 30, 1964 issue, which had analyzed his campaign against Republican Senator Kenneth Keating. Kennedy was planning a campaign swing to Long Island and was on the phone asking President Johnson to visit those New York City suburbs with him to shore up support.[8]

Back in California, after the telephone operator in White's Goldwater campaign office had awakened Reagan with the good news of how successful his speech had been, Reagan may have smiled with satisfaction and then reflected for awhile, before trying to go back to sleep, on the events of 1964 which had culminated in his *A Time for Choosing speech*—which afterwards forever would be known simply as "The Speech."

Early 1964

In early 1964, feeling that his *General Electric Theatre* had been cancelled by the coercion of Kennedy and having survived the ordeal of having his taxes audited due to Kennedy, Reagan had made his last movie, *The Killers*. Based on an Ernest Hemingway short story, an earlier version had had a young Burt Lancaster make his screen debut. Reagan had fifth billing,[9] and for him it was a "bold, innovative move."[10] Reagan's agent had come up with the idea to cast Reagan as the sadistic, unrepentant villain who slapped Dickinson hard in her face. In that scene, the vision of Reagan hitting Dickinson left audiences "gasping."[11] But the film bombed. As historian Thomas Evans reflected, "The public simply refused to accept Ronald Reagan in such an unfavorable role."[12]

Reagan remained on the Advisory Board of YAF. He was "financially well off" and, free for the first time in a decade, spent part of 1964 at his Malibu ranch, Yearling Row, attending to ranch chores.[13] But then his brother Neil Reagan, vice-president of the advertising firm that handled the account of the United States Borax Company, contacted him saying that a new host was needed for its weekly dramatic television program, *Death Valley Days*. Reagan was hired.[14]

When not at the studio, in spite of the harassment he had received from the Kennedys, Reagan continued to deliver the same conservative-themed speeches he previously had been delivering for General Electric. As a new member of the Republican Party since the losing Nixon gubernatorial run in 1962 and then having been selected as narrator of *Mr. Lincoln's Party Today*, he had been following politics even more closely ever since.

Volunteer for Goldwater

Earlier in 1964 well before The Speech, Reagan likely observed the progress of conservative Goldwater. Goldwater had won a number of primaries but had been stymied in Oregon when Rockefeller had taken the time to campaign personally. Nixon's name had been placed on the Oregon primary ballot too and Rockefeller ended up winning an upset. Then in California, a grass roots army of some 8,000 YAFers and Young Republicans had gone to some 600,000 homes seeking primary votes for Goldwater to counter the Rockefeller campaign, which had a $2 million budget and was being run by a political company run by Stuart Spencer. Goldwater won in California—but narrowly.[15]

Reagan was ready to take his next step into politics to help the conservative cause. Reagan was in San Francisco on business and stopped at a Goldwater campaign office. Reagan walked up to a young woman at the desk and introduced himself, saying he wanted to offer his services to the Goldwater campaign and asked the woman what could he do to help?

The woman, Kay Valory, knew immediately who the handsome celebrity was. Quickly she called Goldwater campaign headquarters, explaining that this was a golden opportunity too good to pass up— that of actor Ronald Reagan helping Goldwater. Valory and her colleague Jim Ince, who we will meet again in New Hampshire, decades later recalled that Valory arranged for Reagan to speak on behalf of Goldwater "all over California" in the late spring, early summer and later during the fall of 1964.[16] Valory, the future head of Consumer Affairs during the Reagan administration in Sacramento, was assigned by the Goldwater campaign to be Reagan's chauffeur and assistant.

The San Francisco Republican Convention

After weeks of hard campaigning for Goldwater, Reagan prepared to go to the Republican national convention in San Francisco. During this time, Nixon, who had presumed the opposition to Goldwater would be so extensive as to force a deadlocked convention, sought to create the deadlock singlehandedly "by launching an eleventh hour effort to stop Goldwater," which columnist Robert Novak characterized as "the worst political performance" of Nixon's career.[17] Reagan's reaction to Nixon's last-minute campaign is not known. By the end of the proceedings, Nixon introduced nominee Goldwater before his acceptance speech.[18] Nixon friend and advisor Robert Finch realized that Nixon's subsequent decision to campaign for the party and for Goldwater, even though Nixon knew Goldwater would be trounced, was a strong indication that Nixon had decided to seek the presidency once again in 1968.[19] Meanwhile another supporter praising Goldwater was Ronald Reagan.

At the convention, Reagan initially was introduced at a pro-Goldwater speech "to an audience of several hundred."[20] By the second night of the convention, Reagan became the master of ceremonies at a youth rally for Goldwater. Buckley recalled it was "one of the highlights of the entire week."[21] The auditorium was jammed with young Goldwater supporters anxious to see both Goldwater and Reagan; more than 5,000 were turned away. The next day, Reagan was recruited once again to speak at another Goldwater youth rally. He said to the crowd, "You were at this long before many, and God bless you for it."[22]

This was Ronald Reagan's first national political convention as a Republican; he had attended the 1960 convention as a Democrat for Nixon. It was only two years since he had switched parties while campaigning for Nixon and then had narrated *Mr. Lincoln's Party Today*. He likely recalled the excitement he first had felt when he had spoken on a political stage decades earlier at Eureka College. His more recent speeches on behalf of GE may have confined him somewhat, as he still was company spokesman. But at the convention he could speak more freely about what he truly felt politically. Now that he had given speeches at three political rallies at the 1964 national convention, he could see first-hand the reaction from his audiences: thunderous applause.

One convention attendee who was attending his first national convention and who marveled at the enthusiasm for conservative Goldwater was a young savings and loan executive and treasurer of the Nebraska Republican Party, Dale Young. Young recalled he had not seen Reagan's convention speeches at the youth rallies but had hoped for a turn in the nation's direction by a Goldwater victory in the fall.[23] Little did Young know at the time how critically important he would become in 1968 to the future success of the party's next conservative leader, Ronald Reagan.

Reagan Watches Eisenhower

But one keen observer who did watch Reagan at the Cow Palace was CBS reporter Walter Cronkite. Both Cronkite and Reagan had gotten their professional starts as Midwestern sports announcers. Cronkite was impressed. Cronkite's biographer, Douglas Brinkley, recalled that while watching Reagan and analyzing the implications of Reagan's speech, Cronkite presciently thought, "Reagan could be president someday."[24]   While clearly wide awake in 1964 at the Republican convention, in 1968 Cronkite, as we will see, would be so bored that he would doze off on the air! Just as Cronkite watched Reagan, another liberal observer was watching Reagan as well.

Liberal writer Gore Vidal was in attendance and happened to be standing and leaning on a metal railing that enclosed the space where Ron and Nancy Reagan were watching Eisenhower deliver his convention speech. Vidal, whose analysis of the 1968 convention in conjunction with William F. Buckley, Jr. will be discussed later, revealed his 1964 initial observations of Reagan while reflecting on President Reagan's inauguration in 1980.[25]   Vidal observed that someone at the 1964 convention created a diversion while Eisenhower was speaking. Nancy was furious. "She turned, lip curled with Bacchantish rage, huge unblinking eyes afire with a passion to kill the enemy so palpably at hand." Vidal observed her husband, the actor and conservative speaker and soon-to-be Goldwater California co-chairman. Reagan was "slumped in a folding chair, one hand holding up his chins; he was totally concentrated on Eisenhower." In his later reminiscence of 1964, Vidal reflected, "I do remember being struck by the intensity with which Reagan studied Eisenhower...The understudy examines the star's performance, and tries to figure out how it is done. An actor prepares, I said to myself: Mr. Reagan is planning to go into politics."[26]

Vidal had gotten it half right, but neither he nor anyone else picked up the thread. Reagan was indeed studying Eisenhower. But it was not in the abstract. Reagan was not studying just any politician. Vidal had no idea of the history of the two men. But for Reagan, it was a direct and personal link to the former president. Reagan had first made the 1944 war bonds radio appeal with Eisenhower. Then Reagan had turned toward being a Republican by sending the telegram to Eisenhower, by becoming a Democrat for Ike, and by voting for Eisenhower in 1952 and 1956. A decade later, and only two years ago, both men had made *Mr. Lincoln's Party Today*. Now Reagan was moving toward entering politics himself. But who would teach him and show him the ropes? Reagan was entering politics later in life. So had Eisenhower. Could he ask the general for advice? Would Eisenhower be willing to share his political wisdom? That Reagan in private was seeing Eisenhower as a political role model to emulate, possibly as early as 1952, was evident in public clearly in 1964.

As Reagan watched intently and heard Eisenhower speak at the convention, the general repeated, in some sections almost verbatim, the message of their joint 1962 record. Eisenhower began his convention address by reviewing Lincoln and the party's founding. Eisenhower then noted, "In all those things that the citizen can better do for himself than can his government, the government ought not to interfere...Our party's programs have reflected concern for the individual...All public responsibilities (should) be carried out wherever possible by local and state governments (and) by the federal government only when necessary."[27] It was his and Reagan's exact 1962 message repackaged for 1964.

Just as Cronkite and Vidal watched Reagan, once Eisenhower was done, Reagan continued observing everything at the convention. As Reagan saw the specific 1964 campaign and convention tactics unfolding in front of him, likely he filed them away in his memory—just in case he might need to use them in the future should he himself definitely decide to run for office. Reagan's ability to observe and file away information for future use was outstanding.[28] As a Board member of YAF, he likely saw first-hand what these young Republicans had been doing for Goldwater.

Role Models for 1968

Youth for Goldwater, which would serve as a model for Students for Reagan in 1968, was "basically a YAF-run organization."[29] YAF had sent cheering members to almost every Goldwater campaign appearance. For instance, in Grand Rapids, Michigan, YAF had organized a 40-car Goldwater motorcade. In Wisconsin in 1967, Don L. Taylor would orchestrate a similar motorcade for candidate Reagan. The Greater Boston YAF chapter had arranged that Goldwater was greeted by "twenty young ladies in white cowboy hats, red Goldwater sashes and blue shirts"[30] As Hillary Rodham Clinton would tell NPR in January 1996, in 1964 she (as Hillary Rodham) had been a proud "Goldwater Girl." In 1968 there would be *The Reaganettes* in Miami Beach. YAF had sent its members to numerous college mock conventions and had convinced college Republican clubs to endorse Goldwater.[31] Four years later, Students for Reagan would do the same for their hero.

YAF had arranged for a group of conservative folk singers, "The Goldwaters," to tour college campuses and the group actually had an album, *Folk Songs to Bug the Liberals*.[32] At the convention, YAF had sponsored a two-hour cruise of San Francisco Bay on the *S.S. Young Conservative* at which "The Goldwaters" sang. Their lead singer, Ken Crook, noted, "Our songs are funny but they have a serious message."[33] Hundreds of YAF demonstrators had greeted candidate Barry Goldwater when he had landed at the airport. Students for Reagan would do the same four years later. YAF had arranged for a flat-bed truck outside the Cow Palace and it was here where the YAF national director had introduced Reagan as discussed earlier. YAF had a Dixieland band on the back of the truck, which later was driven into the middle of a televised Rockefeller rally. There was even a Goldwater cable car. Every convention delegate was sent copies of *The New Guard* plus a personal letter from Texas Senator John Tower.[34]

Besides Reagan learning specific tactics for the future and thriving amidst the enthusiastic young conservatives, another observer was watching too. William Rusher, publisher of *National Review*, also was fascinated by the tactics of the Goldwater college students and in particular by a parked trailer just outside convention hall in which Clif White, a delegate hunter, was using remote audio to direct Goldwater delegates on the convention floor.[35]

White and his conservative political friends, sometimes termed the *Syndicate*, together had launched the National Draft Goldwater Committee. Goldwater let White run his successful primary campaign. White then innovated at the San Francisco convention. Besides his central communications trailer with remote hookups, White had roving messengers on the convention floor with walkie-talkies. The trailer itself also was equipped with multiple televisions to watch convention coverage by all the networks. His team had the electronic capability to listen in on their opposition's communications and believed they themselves had taken precautions to prevent the reverse.[36] These innovations from 1964 would be used and updated by Reagan and his team in Miami Beach in 1968.

The convention ended with Goldwater's loyalists booing Rockefeller. For Rockefeller, as well as for Reagan, this would have major impact four years later when Rockefeller would be debating whether he should enter various 1968 primaries. Historian Geoffrey Kabaservice observed that the 1964 convention had marked the point of the vast demographic changes within the country leading to power shifting within the party to the South and the West.[37]

Reagan is California Goldwater Co-Chairman

After the convention, on August 21 Reagan appeared before the California Citizens for Goldwater-Miller meeting to run as state chairman. But Reagan had come under a "blistering attack" by a southern California businessman, who had led Goldwater's victory over Rockefeller in the California primary that spring; the businessman told the audience that they didn't want their Goldwater national headquarters on the east coast forcing them to accept a "Johnny-come-lately" as state chairman.[38]

Clif White, who had run Goldwater's successful primary campaign but after the convention had been disappointed by Goldwater making him national head of the Citizens group instead of being appointed head of the Republican Party, was sitting next to Reagan and rose to defend him. But quietly Reagan told White, who would become Reagan's main delegate hunter in 1968, "No, Clif. This is my fight. Let me handle it."[39] Reagan hit the issue straight on, telling them that he knew he was inexperienced but that the California Citizens for Goldwater-Miller should not be fighting each other but rather should be seeking unity. After "resounding applause," Reagan and Davis were elected co-chairmen.[40] Reagan was already demonstrating his abilities as a party uniter and not a divider.

White likely noted Reagan's political acumen and speaking skills at that meeting, which would be greatly enhanced when White's office started getting all those donations from The Speech soon thereafter. After being elected co-chairman, Reagan continued being driven around by Kay Valory for many additional appearances on behalf of Goldwater that summer and fall.

Autumn Campaign

Not all Republicans were enthralled by the Goldwater candidacy. As historian Kabaservice has reviewed, Dan Evans, running for the governorship of Washington State, agreed to be seen with Goldwater but managed to have someone else wiggle his way between the two so that no photographs showed Evans next to Goldwater. Evans made sure his Democratic opposition did not have that ammunition to use against him.[41]

As noted, Romney and Rockefeller refused to endorse Goldwater. Eisenhower's support in public initially was luke-warm, but he was the good party soldier and had made the convention speech, which Reagan had studied so well. But later after Goldwater had praised

Germany's military, Eisenhower was infuriated and told Nixon, "Before we had this meeting I thought that Goldwater was just stubborn. Now I am convinced that he is just plain dumb."[42] Nixon campaigned for Goldwater but wrote privately that Goldwater was "inept."[43]   But Reagan campaigned enthusiastically. Soon both Eisenhower and Reagan would be called in to help Goldwater directly.

Looking past the looming Goldwater defeat, Buckley spoke at the YAF convention and sought to explain what lay ahead. "The 1964 campaign was merely the first step in a long crusade for conservative principles, not the final chapter. The purpose of Goldwater's candidacy," he observed, was "to recruit legions to the conservative cause."[44]   Goldwater wanted YAF members to look ahead to the "well-planted seeds of hope" that would lead to victories not in 1964 but in "Novembers to come."[45]

Indeed YAF staff did heed Buckley's advice and "planned for future crusades" by starting to "develop plans to perpetuate the conservative cause" in case Goldwater might lose.[46]   Conservatives had started to plan for a new leader to take over the mantle of conservatism from Goldwater.

The Speech

For the upcoming general election campaign for 1964, White came up with the idea of a campaign film, which was to highlight Goldwater's stance against street violence. The film, *Choice*, never made it onto national television, because Johnson devotee, columnist Drew Pearson, saw an advance copy and branded it "racist" as did Goldwater, who cancelled the film project for the same reason.[47] Rusher saw the film debacle as a "substantial opportunity lost."[48] But in 1968 the idea of using a campaign biographical film would be resurrected by Reagan and expanded by Reagan and his team into one of the Reagan campaign's most successful tactics. Rusher's keen interest in, and personal involvement in, the tactics employed in 1964 would lead him to advise their use again four years later to aid Reagan's 1968 candidacy in Miami Beach.

As discussed by historian Kasey Pipes, Eisenhower had met with Goldwater on August 6 and then the two men made a new attempt at a Goldwater campaign film. It was filmed in Gettysburg and then was shown to some party leaders. But before the plans to show it nationally were finalized, the broadcast time had been purchased by Reagan's financial backers, in order to show Reagan's *A Time for Choosing*. According to historian Pipes, the Eisenhower-Goldwater campaign film was never broadcast nationally.[49] However Goldwater biographer Lee Edwards noted that it was, in fact, seen later.[50] Thus there were two last-ditch television efforts to aid the floundering Goldwater campaign: the Reagan speech that was broadcast and made history and an Eisenhower-Goldwater film that was not seen at the time. It is not known if in October Eisenhower had been surprised to learn that Ronald Reagan's speech, *A Time for Choosing*, would replace his own planned Goldwater film broadcast. Goldwater was not pleased that his nationwide film with Eisenhower had been replaced by one featuring a conservative upstart actor.[51] In some versions of the events, Goldwater and Reagan then chatted about the non-enthusiastic reaction of party leaders to the Gettysburg film and went with Reagan's film. Thus there were several versions of the origin of how Reagan was asked to deliver *A Time for Choosing* as well as Goldwater's involvement with the decision and the broadcast itself.

Briefly, "The Speech" was in essence the same speech, honed and polished over eight years, which Reagan had been delivering to workers at General Electric and to small, local public audiences.[52] But *A Time for Choosing* was Reagan's first political speech to a national audience. Many readers are quite familiar with it, but a few points should be emphasized.

Reagan praised Eisenhower's troops who had fought in World War II. Then Reagan castigated the West: "(We) never open up our mouths about the millions of people enslaved in Soviet colonies in the satellite nations." Reagan later quoted Winston Churchill, who had said men had the duty to stand up for freedom. In a lead up to the final section, Reagan again called for freedom in Eastern Europe: "A billion now in slavery behind the Iron Curtain" should not be told to give up their dreams for freedom because the West was too selfish and would buy their own security by bargaining with the Soviet Union.[53] Reagan's calls for freedom in Eastern Europe, begun in the 1962 recording, thus continued in the autumn of 1964.

After the speech was broadcast, he had fretted that night in late October until he had been awakened by the phone call from Goldwater headquarters. Reagan had the satisfaction of having been told by Clif White's telephone operator, "Thousands of people have called pledging support and saying they're sending in checks....The staff of the Republican Finance Committee say they've never seen anything like it. I'm sorry to call so late, but I thought you'd like to know."[54] The broadcast of "The Speech" netted some $8 million, not including what later local rebroadcasts—arranged at the behest of White—had netted, and the windfall from Reagan's broadcast "exceeded any previous campaign-fund-raising event."[55]

Ike is Impressed by "The Speech"

One person who did watch Ronald Reagan deliver "The Speech" on national television was Dwight Eisenhower. Regardless of whether Eisenhower was relieved or annoyed at not having his own joint film with Goldwater broadcast, Eisenhower watched Reagan praise Eisenhower's troops during World War II, then quote Eisenhower's friend, Churchill, and twice call for freedom in Eastern Europe. Eisenhower, the supreme Allied commander, judge of character, of men and of nations, liked what he saw and heard from Reagan's speech.

Immediately thereafter, on Friday October 30, 1964 at 10:15 AM, he called his former Attorney General and political advisor Herbert Brownell and told him it was a "fine speech by Ronald Reagan."[56] Busy with other activities, but the span of several hours affording him the time for further reflection, the same afternoon at 3:00 PM Eisenhower talked with his former special assistant Bryce Harlow and was even more enthusiastic than in the morning: "Reagan's speech was excellent."[57]

Almost in the same breath as praising Reagan, Eisenhower ended his talk with Harlow by discussing rebuilding the party after the likely loss by Goldwater the following week, and Eisenhower then sent such a message to Republican leaders. Clearly Eisenhower had continued to feel that he had a new responsibility in the world of politics again after his despair after his vice-president's loss in November 1960 to JFK.

Eisenhower had been consulted by Kennedy a few times, especially after the Bay of Pigs fiasco, but after all, Kennedy represented the Opposition.[58] After the Gettysburg meetings in 1962 about Republican marketing, the resultant *Mr. Lincoln's Party Today* record with Reagan as narrator, and now seeing Reagan as a clear future national party leader, Eisenhower likely felt that his "hidden-hand" techniques, so successfully utilized during his presidency as analyzed by historian Fred Greenstein, were being used successfully to guide the party into the mid 1960s and beyond.[59] If Reagan and his speech were parts of Eisenhower's thoughts on how to rebuild the party, his appointment summary did not disclose.[60]

And whether Eisenhower had recognized some of the phraseology of *A Time for Choosing* being repeated directly from their joint

1962 *Mr. Lincoln's Party Today* recording is not known. Certainly the general had used his own 1962 phraseology when speaking at the San Francisco convention. Of his own personal hero, Lincoln, Eisenhower had said at the 1963 centennial celebration of the battle of Gettysburg, "We have not paid to his message its just tribute until we—ourselves—live it. For well he knew that to live for country is a duty, as demanding as is the readiness to die for it."[61] But Eisenhower and Reagan soon would begin their own coach-player relationship that would culminate in Eisenhower's endorsing Reagan as presidential timbre. Meanwhile, under the looming likelihood of a Johnson landslide, Eisenhower, Reagan, and Goldwater went to vote, as did a small group of conservative activists in Michigan.

The First Reagan-for-President Club in History: Owosso, Michigan

Despite the enthusiastic reception and financial windfall that Reagan's national speech had netted, Goldwater was soundly thrashed by a huge Johnson victory. Amongst the few bright spots for the Republicans, Dan Evans was elected governor of Washington, the Oregon House of Representatives had gone Republican, and Reagan's friend, fellow actor George Murphy, defeated former Kennedy administration spokesman Pierre Salinger to become California's newest senator.

Despite Goldwater's crushing loss, Nixon observed astutely, "One Republican winner was not on the ballot." Nixon saw that the one winner—Reagan—had what Goldwater had lacked: "the ability to present his views in a reasonable and eloquent manner." What Nixon had noted privately about Reagan in June of 1959 now received nationwide acclaim five years later.[62] Nixon, continuing to plan his own political renaissance for a run in 1968, may have then realized that his most formidable future opponent might in fact be the charismatic, conservative, and telegenic Reagan. Clearly, "The Speech" had proven that Reagan had all the qualities of electability that he, Nixon, lacked. But at this point, who knew what political plans, if any, the washed-out actor Reagan might harbor? And it was not only Nixon who saw a new Republican winner emerge from the election debacle. As Buckley had foreseen and in the words of historian Joseph Lewis, "The American public got a preview of post-Goldwater conservatism: Reagan combined Taftian beliefs with Ike's charm."[63]

On November 3, 1964, as the ink dried on newspaper headlines across the country, which proclaimed the victory of Lyndon Johnson and the landslide defeat of conservative Republican Barry Goldwater, not all conservatives sat in stunned silence. For I. Walter Jorgensen, the president of Mark Manufacturing Company and Robert Smith, the head of Smith Research Products,[64] the Goldwater defeat was a call to action. On Election Day 1964, the two men met in Owosso, Michigan to forge a new path with a brand new presidential candidate for America: Ronald Reagan.

Up to that point, the small town of Owosso had become somewhat famous because of whom had been born there: 1948 Republican Party nominee Thomas Dewey.

As Jorgensen and Smith told the press shortly afterwards, the purpose of their small grass roots group was to push Reagan first to be governor but then aim for "the 1968 Republican presidential nomination."[65] The group felt that Reagan's "The Speech" had been "just a sneak preview of what the man can do."[66] No one knew it at the time, but that small group in Owosso, Michigan just had started the long process which would take three campaigns—1968, 1976, and 1980—over sixteen years finally to culminate in Ronald Reagan being elected president of the United States.

This very first Reagan-for-President club in history had fifteen local campaign workers in Owosso and had "received letters and contributions from several thousand persons across the country."[67] Besides Jorgensen and Smith, the principals included three other grass roots activists: a local reviewer of books, a widow, and a local attorney.[68] Jorgensen told the press that although most of the Reagan supporters had been former backers of Goldwater, because Goldwater had campaigned "negatively for President, while Reagan is obviously able to approach the campaign positively," the allegiance of the group had switched clearly from Goldwater to Reagan.[69] The group in Owosso had been very impressed by "The Speech." Jorgensen reflected, "He demonstrated the ability not only to sell himself but to sell Republicanism."[70] Smith claimed that there was much interest in Reagan "on college campuses across the country" and the group planned a national newspaper and hoped to attract "ten million members" within a year-and-a-half.[71]

Reagan's "The Speech" was described by the *New York Times* as "the most cogent exposition of the conservative political philosophy during the campaign of 1964."[72] Shortly thereafter, the national media was quick to note the beginning of the movement for Reagan for president in 1968. Within a month of its formation, the Reagan for

President in 1968 club in Owosso was mentioned in *Life* magazine. The article noted that Smith had been a county chairman for Citizens for Goldwater in Michigan and that the Owosso group had been created shortly after Reagan had delivered "The Speech." The *Life* reporter characterized the purpose of the group as "a Republican group to back Ronald Reagan for President in 1968."[73] Even Owosso's famous son Thomas Dewey was interviewed and asked what he thought of the Owosso club that had formed to promote Reagan's candidacy for president in 1968. The town's famed son answered that he had been "surprised to learn there was an organized group called Republicans for Ronald Reagan" and that he was even "more surprised" that the headquarters was in Owosso.[74] Dewey did not mention what he thought of the nascent Reagan campaign for president.

Reagan himself was informed of the formation of the Reagan for President Club in Owosso. His reaction was muted but realistic: "It's very flattering to think that anyone would even harbor such thoughts, but it's very premature to talk about 1968, and I personally have never thought of myself in that regard."[75] Yet Reagan may have forgotten that at one point the idea of him someday being president already had occurred to him. A pair of letters exchanged between Reagan and his daughter, Maureen, in 1962 was shown decades later to historian Lou Cannon.[76] She had written to her father urging him to run for governor and that he "could" be governor; Reagan replied using her family nickname and underlined one word: "Well, if we're talking about what I could do, Mermie, I could be president."[77] Reagan's statement to the press about the Owosso group likely was Ronald Reagan's first *public* statement about seeking the presidency.

The Owosso group, as we will see, would make its presence known again as it would work quietly to see Reagan become president in 1968. But despite Reagan's wonder that anyone would be thinking of him as president, others besides those in Owosso in fact did.

Friends of Ronald Reagan

The story has been told often, and will not be detailed here, of how a group of wealthy southern California conservative businessmen saw *A Time for Choosing* and decided that Ronald Reagan should enter politics.[78] Besides the Owosso group, these businessmen also foresaw that Reagan could become president.[79] Compared to Goldwater, Reagan was seen as someone who had the same philosophy but could "express his thoughts" and thus "get through to people."[80] This was identical to Nixon's observation. But upon further reflection, the group agreed that he needed more experience and thus tried to convince him first to run for senator of California, but there were no openings, as Reagan's friend George Murphy just had been elected senator, plus California's incumbent senator, liberal Republican Thomas Kuchel, was not up for re-election in 1966.[81] Eventually the group decided instead to push Reagan to run for governor. Within six weeks of Goldwater's defeat, the group had raised anywhere from $36,000[82] to $135,000[83] for Reagan's gubernatorial campaign and founded Friends of Ronald Reagan. But according to one historian, "From that moment, Reagan had his eye on the Presidency."[84]

Whether he did indeed have his eye on the presidency in those years will be examined throughout this book via Reagan's comments and actions. As we will see, he would constantly deny in public that he was running and he would voice a fatalistic willingness to accept the nomination if it were God's will. Reagan felt it was his duty to accept the 1968 nomination only if the people and his party cast their collective eyes on him. The origin for Reagan's thoughts, seen clearly in his autobiography as discussed earlier, was his observation of Eisenhower's acceptance of his call to duty after the Madison Square Garden rally and the huge write-in votes of the 1952 New Hampshire and Minnesota primaries.

But support for Goldwater amongst conservatives did not fade gently on election night. Many moderate and liberal Republicans, including Governors George Romney and Nelson A. Rockefeller, and Congressman John Lindsay, had refused to support the conservative Goldwater, and Reagan was livid. Shortly after the Goldwater debacle, Reagan spoke to the Los Angeles County Young Republicans noting bitterly, "We don't intend to turn the Republican Party over to the traitors in the battle just ended. The conservative philosophy was not repudiated."[85] Then Reagan wrote in the December, 1964 issue of *National Review* that those who had voted for Goldwater, some 26 million Americans, were "committed to freedom." Those who voted for Johnson "did not vote against the conservative philosophy" but had voted against a "false image" of conservatism that had been created by the Democrats.[86]

The pitting of Goldwater against Rockefeller, and the resultant refusal of Rockefeller and Romney to endorse the Republican ticket that year, would have major ramifications during Reagan's 1968 campaign for the presidency. During 1967-1968, Reagan frequently would say at speeches and press conferences that he wanted Republican unity and that he himself would back whomever the party would choose as its nominee. Reagan was not angry at the Republican liberals for their views but for their refusal to support the party's nominee. Reagan wanted a large political tent and Rockefeller, Romney, Lindsay and others had refused to enter Goldwater's tent. Historian Geoffrey Kabaservice observed that it would be Reagan who was about to "modulate conservatism and make it a more inclusive, realistic, and successful political force."[87]

But Reagan privately did think that Goldwater's campaign had been "inept" and, looking toward a future career in politics himself, Reagan "was certain he could have done better."[88] Historian Lou Cannon felt that in his *National Review* article, Reagan "had sounded like a prospective candidate."[89] Indeed historian Anne Edwards felt that shortly after Goldwater's crushing defeat, Reagan was "thinking of announcing himself as a 1968 Presidential candidate."[90] But historian Steven Hayward felt such an announcement seemed "out of character with Reagan's persistent modesty and realism."[91]

But pragmatism took over the ultimate goals of his backers, for before running for the presidency in 1968—"before going for the 'big one,'"[92] —Ronald Reagan needed to prove his mettle by winning both a primary and a general election campaign, and then establishing a track-record of governing before his own eyes might turn toward the White House in 1968. And almost immediately a stumbling block appeared across the road to a Reagan White House in January, 1969, and it came from the very conservative nominee on whose behalf Reagan had campaigned and made The Speech.

On January 22, 1965, seemingly out of the clear blue and years too premature for such a commitment, conservative Goldwater announced publicly that he would support moderate Nixon for the 1968 nomination.[93] Historian Patrick Buchanan details why Goldwater came out so early for Nixon.[94] The main point of the endorsement, as it impacted Reagan's future 1968 chances, was clear: if Nixon was conservative enough for Goldwater, then was he not acceptable to most conservatives too?[95]

Early 1965: Death of Churchill

A week later was the major international news story of the month: the final illness, death, funeral and burial of the man of the century, the man many considered the greatest Briton of all time, Winston Churchill. The newspapers and magazines were filled with coverage, as kings, queens and presidents came to London for the funeral. Likely Reagan followed all the details, as Reagan just had quoted Churchill in his *A Time for Choosing*. First, Reagan would have seen that President Johnson did not attend. Johnson felt that Churchill had slighted the memory of President Franklin Roosevelt twenty years earlier by not attending Roosevelt's funeral in April 1945, even though at the time Churchill was managing the final end of the war in Europe; he had wanted to attend but had been convinced that it was more important to stay in Britain.[96]

Reagan had been, and would to continue to be, an ardent admirer of Churchill, as explored recently by historian Steven F. Hayward in *Greatness*.[97] After having quoted Churchill in "The Speech," Reagan often would quote Churchill during his 1968 presidential campaign. Indeed Reagan would get the chance directly to honor the memory of Churchill when on November 19, 1990, Reagan would receive an honorary degree and would dedicate a sculpture created out of the remnants of the Berlin Wall at Westminster College in Fulton, Missouri, where Churchill had delivered his famous "Iron Curtain" speech in 1946, and where (across town at William Woods College), Reagan had delivered his 1952 address, "America the Beautiful."[98] In 1990, Reagan would tie together three critical events: the warning against communism that Churchill first had uttered; Reagan's own call to tear down the Berlin Wall—to be uttered first in 1967 and several times thereafter during his first presidential campaign; and the final fall of communism in 1989.

In early 1965, Reagan likely observed that the man who did deliver America's eulogy for Churchill was Churchill's comrade and friend from those years, and the man who was the centerpiece of their joint 1944 and 1962 publicity records and whose recent 1964 convention speech had been so intensely scrutinized by Reagan: Dwight Eisenhower. The importance of individual freedom to Eisenhower (and to Churchill and Reagan) cannot be overstated. In his Inaugural Address as the president of Columbia University, Eisenhower had stated that Americans placed one thing above all others: "That priceless thing is individual liberty."[99] Only six months before Churchill's death, at the 1964 Republican convention—while the Reagan's had sat, transfixed—the general had repeated the same theme of individual freedom.

While planning his eulogy address, did Eisenhower reflect on Reagan's recent two calls for freedom for Eastern Europe in *A Time for Choosing*, which Eisenhower so recently had praised to his associates, or recall Reagan's updating of Lincoln's "House Divided" speech in their joint recording?

Eisenhower's 1965 funeral oration for Churchill received major press coverage in the United States and is reviewed in The Churchill

Centre's 2015 commemorative issue of *Finest Hour*. Eisenhower spoke on January 30 and ended his eulogy stating that throughout all time, one phrase would always stand out in describing Churchill, "Here was a champion of freedom." Eisenhower then looked ahead, "May we carry on his work until no nation lies in captivity."[100] No truer words would describe both Eisenhower and Reagan as well.[101]

Perhaps as Reagan watched and read more about Churchill and Eisenhower's eulogy speech and then reflected on their leadership and the importance of individual freedom—of course the major theme of his 1952 address, the 1962 publicity record and such a major component of The Speech and his own speeches to GE workers— he might have wondered if he himself could take over the mantle of conservatism and enter the world of politics now that he had delivered "The Speech" and Goldwater had been defeated. Perhaps Reagan asked himself if specifically he somehow could carry forth the lofty goal of freeing captive nations that Churchill, Eisenhower, and he himself had championed.

Vietnam

At this time, Vietnam began creeping into the headlines in America. Historian Andrew Johns has reviewed the entire saga of Vietnam and the war's effects on the Republican Party in the 1960s, on Eisenhower, and on the 1968 party candidates for the nomination.[102] As noted earlier, JFK had consulted with Eisenhower after the Bay of Pigs fiasco and the Cuban Missile crisis. But as Johns reviews, Eisenhower nevertheless had become increasingly upset about Kennedy's foreign policy blunders.[103] But things had worsened once Johnson became president. And now Ike became involved directly.

Immediately after returning to America from Churchill's funeral, Eisenhower intimately was involved in what Johns described as the "most important week of the entire American involvement" in Vietnam: Eisenhower met at the White House with Johnson and his advisors on February 17, 1965.[104] Eisenhower's own philosophy was never to get American troops involved directly in a land war in Asia. For two hours, Eisenhower gave ideas on avoiding putting America's boots on the ground, other than as advisors. Eisenhower told the group to get more support from America's allies, to boost morale, to decentralize the military effort, to start an effective propaganda campaign, and to get South Vietnamese troops to improve and carry the burden. Eisenhower advised that Johnson begin a massive air campaign against North Vietnam and, via secret channels, to threaten

Beijing and Moscow not to intervene. Eisenhower told Johnson to let the communists know that the use of nuclear weapons was not off the table. America never should negotiate from a position of weakness.[105] Afterwards, the general started getting briefed biweekly on Johnson's Vietnam situation by General Andrew Goodpaster, Eisenhower's former defense liaison.[106]

As spring began, Nixon, returning the favor of Goldwater's endorsement, was the main speaker in Phoenix at a testimonial dinner for Goldwater. Reagan was at the dinner too and had been invited to introduce Nixon. Afterwards, Nixon wrote a thank you letter to Reagan, admitting that although he did not know "what your political plans eventually will turn out to be," he cautioned Reagan, "Resist the temptation of 'striking back' at any of the other potential candidates." Nixon feared that in California in 1966, Brown would win again if there were Republican infighting, as had been seen a few months earlier when Rockefeller and Romney had failed to support Goldwater. Reagan wrote back that he would "speak no evil." These were the early stirrings of the Eleventh Commandment, which Dr. Gaylord Parkinson would formalize for California in 1966.[107] Former President Eisenhower would expand it for the national convention in 1968.

Reagan Fills the Void

Although Nixon remained in the political limelight, Reagan did indeed begin to fill the void in conservatism left by the defeated Goldwater. Paradoxically at first, Goldwater's defeat seemingly had strengthened conservatism. Conservatives were busy. To create a conservative organization for those too old for YAF, Bill Rusher and William F. Buckley, Jr. helped found the American Conservative Union in mid December, 1964. By this time, YAF itself had "eighteen full-time employees at a 'posh' headquarters in Washington, D.C."[108] YAF had   "hundreds of new applicants," which culminated in a full 5,400 new members joining in the second half of 1964. The circulation of *National Review* increased from 61,000 to 94,000.[109] The strengthening conservative forces began looking ahead towards a new candidate after Goldwater, and Reagan was emerging as Goldwater's heir and replacement. So YAF decided to give Reagan a big nudge forward.

Not using the behind-the-scenes route of Reagan's businessmen backers, YAF members openly prodded Reagan to agree to run for governor by featuring him on the cover of the June, 1965 issue of *The*

New Guard. Reagan relished the chance to offer hope to more young conservatives and proceeded to speak to 1,200 Santa Ana Young Republicans, calling on them to "rise from defeat" and begin "the second round to defend the Republic."[110]

That same month, watching in the audience as Reagan delivered a Republican fund-raising speech in Cincinnati, reporter and columnist Robert Novak observed Reagan's speech-making style. In his next column, Novak compared Reagan to the charismatic President Kennedy. The column was assailed by liberal reporters: how dare their assassinated but beloved JFK be compared to a "washed-up B movie actor."[111] By 1968 Novak would make additional insightful observations of Reagan's growing support and would play a critical role during the 1968 convention.

Meanwhile, Reagan had appreciated Nixon's recent brief bit of written political advice, but how was Reagan to prepare to change careers from actor to candidate and then governor? Reagan had a core set of conservative principles. He favored individual freedom and smaller government. He favored a strong America and hated communism. He was not making politics a life-long career; he had been a successful radio announcer, actor, and rancher. He had had excellent preparatory personal experience as president of the Screen Actors Guild, a Democrat for Ike in 1952 and 1956, speaker for General Electric, a campaigner for Nixon in 1960 and 1962, and co-chairman of the California Goldwater campaign in 1964. Initially, he had been thinking of entering politics to help bring conservative solutions to the nation.

But now he himself actually was contemplating running for political office and was being urged by his backers to seek the top executive job and top political and party job in the nation's biggest state. Ronald Reagan needed mentoring on how to enter politics and how to become an effective Republican Party candidate and leader. To whom could Reagan turn for guidance? He needed a wise, elder, experienced statesman who would be discrete.

Reagan turned to the most experienced leader in the nation and the man who still was held in highest esteem by the American public: former president Dwight D. Eisenhower. After all, Reagan had made the 1944 war bonds radio appeal with General Eisenhower, had sent the Eisenhower's the 1952 Reagan wedding announcement, had sent Ike the telegram urging him to run for president, and had been a Democrat for Ike. More recently in 1962, Reagan had been the new Republican narrator of Eisenhower's and the party's *Mr. Lincoln's Party Today*, with Eisenhower's and his own emphasis on smaller government and individual freedom. The Reagan's had watched Eisenhower intently at the 1964 convention as Eisenhower had delivered his address. Clearly Reagan had observed how the man at the top—Ike—was master of politics. After The Speech, his financial backers were pushing him to run for office. Now in mid 1965, Reagan likely earlier had seen Churchill's funeral and Eisenhower's eulogy. The aims of Eisenhower and Churchill clearly matched Reagan's own: individual freedom and freedom for those under the yoke of communism. In the early summer, YAF was pushing him to seek office. Reagan reached a critical decision. The die was cast. After Reagan made the decision to enter politics, he knew exactly how to obtain political advice from the master, Eisenhower.

Reagan contacted Eisenhower through a mutual friend in July, 1965, and this would lead to a multi-year long friendship, which would have critical effects upon Reagan's political future in 1968 and which would extend throughout future President Reagan's years in office. The relationship between Reagan and Eisenhower is critical and has been unknown to his closest advisors as well as virtually most historians up to now.[112]

Eisenhower's Coaching Begins

Dwight Eisenhower, former junior varsity football coach at West Point, laid out in the 1960s a comprehensive political game plan for his prize student, "the Gipper"—Ronald Reagan—to follow. Both Dwight Eisenhower and Ronald Reagan had loved football. At West Point, Eisenhower had been starting running back and linebacker. In 1912 he had tackled the legendary Jim Thorpe before a knee injury, sustained after trying a second time to tackle Thorpe, later forced Eisenhower into coaching.[113] Eisenhower observed that football tended to "instill in men the feeling that victory comes through hard—almost slavish—work, team play, self-confidence, and an enthusiasm that amounts to dedication."[114]

Reagan had played football in high school, and at Eureka College by sophomore year he was promoted to first string guard.[115] Both men must have been quite comfortable in their respective roles as political coach and student, for the historical records documenting Eisenhower's teaching of Reagan, and of Reagan's words and actions from 1962 through the end of his presidency, all show quite clearly the profound direct influence Dwight Eisenhower had upon Ronald Reagan.

Dwight Eisenhower had loved to read westerns in the evening, as long as there was no romance in the plot. As president, he loved to watch westerns in the White House theater. Had Eisenhower watched actor Reagan at the movies? During Eisenhower's presidency, Reagan had appeared in several westerns including *The Last Outpost* (1951), the remake (unrelated to the television series) of *Law and Order* (1953), *Cattle Queen of Montana* (1954)[116] and *Tennessee's Partner* (1955). Eisenhower's favorite movie was *High Noon*.[117] But it is not known if Eisenhower had seen any specific Reagan films—westerns or others—before, during, or after his presidency.[118] As we will see, Eisenhower would make one reference to having watched Reagan on television, but whether Eisenhower specifically had watched episodes of *General Electric Theatre* or *Death Valley Days* or had enjoyed television reruns of old Reagan westerns similarly is not known.

Historian Evan Thomas has noted that Eisenhower had told his wife Mamie only on two occasions that life was no longer worth living: that day when he had been told he could no longer play football because of the injury and the day when Nixon lost the presidency in 1960 to John F. Kennedy[119] According to Thomas, Eisenhower had started to contemplate his legacy in 1959,[120] and Ike thought a summit with Khrushchev—to begin a test ban treaty—would be his lasting presidential legacy to the nation. But the shooting down of the U-2 spy plane and capture of its pilot, the initial denials and subsequent changes in official explanations, and then the Soviets' walking out of the summit all helped to scuttle the idea. Eisenhower had made some notable blunders during Nixon's campaign and due to illness he could not campaign much for his vice-president. Eisenhower and Nixon had never been close, and the general left office feeling as if his entire eight year term had been wasted; to make matters much worse, Kennedy was the new president.[121]

Eisenhower had for the most part stayed out of politics during the early years of his retirement and although he had met President Kennedy several times as noted, Eisenhower did not choose sides during the Rockefeller versus Goldwater primary campaigns in 1964. As we have seen, privately the general did not think highly of Goldwater but had tried to help with the Eisenhower-Goldwater campaign film, which was replaced by *A Time for Choosing*. Plus Ike had delivered his address at the convention. But the notion that Eisenhower spent the 1960s only golfing in Gettysburg or Palm Springs is not true. Historian Fred Greenstein's seminal work on Eisenhower's "hidden-hand" approach to power analyzed Eisenhower during his presidential years.[122] But likely other Eisenhower historians did not know to what extent Eisenhower had continued his hidden-hand techniques into the 1960s. For as we will see, the former president would start planning for a post-Goldwater Republican Party and slowly would start to see in Ronald Reagan someone who not only showed the same common sense political solutions to domestic problems as he had, but was also someone who could win elections unlike his former vice-president. And the relationship between Eisenhower and Reagan was not unidirectional. For although Eisenhower's advising of Reagan would be crucial to the novice politician's political career as we will see, for Eisenhower, Reagan may have begun to fill the void as heir of Eisenhower's political legacy that Eisenhower had felt so keenly in November, 1960.

Through a series of personal letters of political advice and via private meetings and conversations between the two men, old football coach Eisenhower would map out specific instructions to Reagan on how to begin his career in politics. Then Eisenhower would advise and guide Reagan throughout his 1966 gubernatorial primary and general election campaigns. Finally Eisenhower would mentor him about foreign affairs during Reagan's 1968 campaign for the presidency. As will be seen, Ronald Reagan would emerge in 1968 as a world statesman due directly to Dwight Eisenhower.

Freeman Gosden

Eisenhower loved to play golf. One of his "Golf Gang" was Freeman Gosden. Gosden, known as the father of the situation comedy for having co-created the original *Amos and Andy* radio show, also had starred as Amos.[123] After Eisenhower left office, Eisenhower's "Golf Gang" as he called them, played together at Augusta National, Gettysburg Country Club as well as at courses in Palm Springs, California where the Eisenhower's spent their winters.

David Eisenhower recalled that the Gosden's were Ike and Mamie's "most treasured friends in the years after the White House."[124] Gosden also would be Eisenhower's golf partner in February 1968 when Eisenhower would shoot the only hole-in-one of his career at an executive course in Palm Springs shortly before Eisenhower's third heart attack—the heart attack that would confine him to Walter Reed Army Hospital for the final eleven months of his life; it would be from that hospital room where he would address the 1968 Republican Convention.[125] The friendship of Ike and Gosden "blossomed into an intimate partnership based on affection and trust."[126]

In late June, 1965, as the war deteriorated, Johnson made his critical decision and authorized sending 95,000 American troops to Vietnam. On July 2, 1965, Eisenhower spoke to President Johnson, urging him to "to go all out" in Vietnam.[127] Eisenhower felt that once America made the decision to send in troops, it had to win and win quickly. A few days later, Eisenhower met with Goodpaster to relay to Johnson that Eisenhower wanted the president to "swamp the enemy with overwhelming force."[128] This critical advice from the general would not be heeded by Johnson and would remain unlearned well into the second decade of the 21st century, with similar disastrous results.

Ike's Critical First Advice to Dutch

A few days after meeting with Goodpaster, while Eisenhower was thinking about Vietnam and what Johnson would do, suddenly Eisenhower heard from Gosden about Ronald Reagan. It was a little more than eight months after Eisenhower had phoned his aides to tell them what a fine speech Reagan had delivered on behalf of Goldwater. On July 14, 1965, Gosden, who lived in Beverly Hills at the time, phoned Eisenhower asking what Eisenhower had thought of various speeches and statements that actor Ronald Reagan had been making and asked Eisenhower for advice on how Reagan could enhance his image as a relatively new Republican Party member. Most likely Gosden, also a friend of Reagan, had chatted with the actor at some point in early July as Reagan was contemplating changing careers into politics. Whether Gosden offered to ask for Eisenhower's advice or whether Reagan asked Gosden to contact Eisenhower is not known. Clearly Gosden had become the conduit to reach Eisenhower.

Eisenhower's initial thoughts about this news that Ronald Reagan might be entering politics, and that he had asked for help and advice from the former president, are not known. Indeed the Eisenhower Library in Abilene has no post-presidential diaries of Eisenhower from those years.

The next day, Eisenhower answered by writing a long, thoughtful letter to Gosden, which of course was to be transmitted by Gosden to Reagan. Eisenhower for the first time gave detailed, thoughtful, multi-step advice on how specifically Ronald Reagan should enter the political arena. Eisenhower recommended first that Reagan should declare he was a loyal and faithful Republican; second that Reagan should state clearly that in 1964 he had done his utmost to help his party and its candidates, but that in 1964 he was a party worker thus not responsible for policy or platform. Third, Eisenhower urged Reagan to point out that the Republican Party, could, in seeking "**common sense** solutions to problems, accommodate men of quite different views concerning details." (author's emphasis)

Here was the theme of the 1962 record carried forward by Eisenhower to Reagan. Being loyal to the party and to support the party's nominee, be it 1964 or 1968, would be used by Reagan: Reagan would use these exact words when announcing his formal candidacy for the governorship and use them again throughout the 1968 campaign whenever he was asked whom he would support. Reagan's answer would always the same at every speech and press conference where the subject arose: that the Republican Party had a fine field of candidates in 1968 and he would support whomever was the party's nominee. When the subject would arise about the lack of support for Goldwater from Rockefeller and Romney and Lindsay, Reagan would not hesitate to criticize their lack of support for the 1964 ticket, although Reagan virtually never would criticize them by name. When Reagan would be asked about liberal-Republican versus conservative-Republican, Reagan always would echo Eisenhower's advice: that labels were not helpful and the party could accommodate members of differing views within one set of great principles. The origin of Ronald Reagan's emphasis on Republican Party unity, of course which could have arisen within himself, on the other hand clearly can be seen here to have arisen in both Eisenhower's words on the 1962 record which Reagan read as narrator as well as from Eisenhower directly when in 1965 he had begun advising Reagan on how to enter politics.

Eisenhower's use of "common sense" deserves a brief discussion. In the 1950s Eisenhower had used the phrases, "modern" Republicanism, and "forward-looking," but after he left the White House, he began to use the new term, possibly borrowed from Thomas Paine's publication of the same name during revolutionary times, "common sense." Eisenhower had used the term when campaigning in Maryland in 1962, when campaigning for Everett Dirksen that same year, and when he had encouraged Henry Cabot Lodge to run for the presidency for 1964.[129] Thus Eisenhower was not using a new term when he wrote to Reagan.

But Reagan did pay marked attention to what Eisenhower had recommended. Reagan took special notice of Eisenhower's theme of common sense solutions to problems, for as we will see it would become Reagan's exact campaign slogan for 1966 and would continue to President Reagan's Farewell Address in 1989. The pattern of

Reagan learning from his mentor and incorporating what Eisenhower had suggested to Reagan was just beginning, but this is the exact point where Eisenhower's direct influence upon novice politician Ronald Reagan began. And as we will see, one far distant effect would be the winning of the Cold War.

But Eisenhower gave additional crucial political advice to Reagan in his answer: how to attract what history would know as Reagan Democrats. Fourth, he advised that Reagan should always present himself as a Republican who is seeking the support of all citizens—Republicans, Independents, and disillusioned Democrats—by offering strong leadership in combating crime and in bringing **"common sense"** and integrity to government. (author's emphasis) As mentioned briefly earlier, analyst Sean Trende recently has reviewed the historical importance of Eisenhower's 1952 and 1956 victories in building lasting coalitions resulting in Republican victories.[130]   By following Eisenhower's advice, Reagan would carry the political coalition-building ball forward for another four-plus decades.

For his 1966 gubernatorial run, Reagan directly would incorporate Eisenhower's suggestions. Reagan would make "common sense" his campaign theme, and he would ask disenchanted Democrats and Independents to find common ground and to join him under a new Republican banner. These were the very early Reagan Democrats long before 1980. Reagan's seeking Republican unity along with Democrats and Independents may indeed be traced back to these very words of tutelage from Dwight Eisenhower to Reagan in 1965. And Reagan not only would follow Eisenhower's advice during his gubernatorial campaign, he also would use Eisenhower's very words to announce his 1966 candidacy and later in his standard 1968 presidential campaign speech given throughout the nation.

As noted earlier, Eisenhower had started his own political career with the publication of a paperback and various newspaper articles.[131] So the general suggested, his fifth detailed recommendation, the next thing Reagan, if he wanted to seek public office, do was to define his own political convictions and present these to the public "at every possible opportunity." Eisenhower ended his letter by his sixth point of advice to Reagan: urging Reagan to meet often with the media."[132]

Being a Mentor, Being a Student

Coach Eisenhower had given student Reagan a clear, precise and direct multi-step game-plan on how to run for political office. What would Eisenhower receive personally by mentoring Reagan? In the

Philippines, Eisenhower had learned under Douglas MacArthur. But earlier in Panama, as a young army officer, Eisenhower had been mentored by the man he always would idolize as the "ablest man I ever knew," General Fox Conner.

Historian Edward Cox has analyzed Conner's mentorship of Eisenhower. Conner was Eisenhower's superior officer as they served together in the Canal Zone, and this is where Conner had instructed his protégé on military history. Afterwards, for more than two decades, the men kept up a private correspondence. Even in the midst of World War II, Ike, in July, 1942, sought the counsel of his old mentor.[133]

Perhaps as the Reagan-Eisenhower relationship flourished, it grew from mentor-student, as Eisenhower had experienced with Conner, into Reagan being viewed by Eisenhower as one of his own political protégés. It may have been Eisenhower's strong feelings that a dedicated team is what led to victories, and he saw himself as the elderly coach and Reagan as the new political player and both were needed vital elements in Republican victories. Eventually, the general likely saw in Reagan someone to carry on the Eisenhower legacy, which he thought had been lost with the election of Kennedy in 1960.

In addition, Eisenhower, as political teacher, had the personal satisfaction of seeing the mentoring of his new political student pay off handsomely. Eisenhower thought very highly of the profession of being a teacher—someone who, Eisenhower reflected, "through the ripened viewpoint from which he sees youth's questions, and the high average of wisdom he uses in helping them solve their problems," had mentored others.[134] Eisenhower, in his private letters to Reagan, was gratified by the political progress Reagan was demonstrating. But the general never commented in public about his specific advising Reagan on entering and succeeding in Republican Party politics.

How did Reagan feel about Eisenhower's advice? As we will see, Reagan would end up following Eisenhower's recommendations and advice almost to the letter. And how did Reagan feel about being in the position of novice player to coach Eisenhower? Tom Reed in his recent memoir discusses the psychology of having an absent, alcoholic parent, as Reagan had experienced. Historians have recounted how a young Reagan saw in Sid Altschuler, a Kansas city businessman married to a woman from Dixon, IL, and for whom Reagan had done swimming coaching, an early mentor. Later, Reagan confirmed how Altschuler had guided him into his first career choice. Similarly, historian Lou Cannon addressed the analogous subject of Reagan as a young football player, being mentored by his college football coach during sophomore year. At the time, "Reagan played his heart out for the coach and the team."[135]   Indeed Cannon cites a revealing Reagan comment, "I'm a sucker for hero worship." But the greatest hero and mentor to Ronald Reagan was in fact Dwight Eisenhower.[136]

Before, during, and long after his 1968 campaign, Reagan would play his heart out for coach Eisenhower and the team of the American people. Via the Reagan-Eisenhower correspondence, Reagan thanked his mentor many times. And as we will see, as Eisenhower would lie in a hospital bed just weeks before the Miami Beach convention, Reagan finally would get the opportunity to express in public what a true inspiration coach Eisenhower had become to his new political player and student.

Historian Douglas Brinkley has felt that Reagan embraced Franklin D. Roosevelt as his "high-water benchmark" for a commander-in-chief. However as will be seen below, when Reagan would announce his candidacy for 1966, he would castigate FDR's domestic policies. Brinkley felt that future President Reagan often justified decisions by following FDR's "leadership standard."[137]   Brinkley mentions Reagan's frequent quoting of FDR and radio addresses as additional justification for seeing FDR as Reagan's hero.[138] Yet your author believes that the present work, including its analysis—to be discussed—of citations from President Reagan's speeches, in fact will demonstrate clearly that it was Dwight Eisenhower who was Reagan's true role model, hero, and mentor.

While Reagan thought about what Eisenhower had recommended, the summer of 1965 saw the Watts riots in Los Angeles. Eisenhower, champion of having citizens obey the law, sternly warned that America was permitting a "policy of lawlessness," and proposed "greater respect for the law." Astonishingly Robert F. Kennedy—the former attorney general and chief law enforcement officer in the land—quickly lashed back, "There is no point in telling Negroes to obey the law."[139] The theme of whether citizens should obey the law, argued in public between Reagan's mentor and his nemesis, would have major repercussions in the spring of 1968. This exact same issue—who is exempt from the law—unfortunately still remains in the headlines of the second decade of the twenty-first century.

While Watts burned, trouble continued in Vietnam. Eisenhower told a wavering Johnson, "We are not going to be run out of a free country that we helped establish." On August 3, Eisenhower proposed to mine Haiphong Harbor.[140]   On August 27, Johnson spoke to Eisenhower and said flatteringly that the general's use of psychological warfare in the North Africa campaign in World War II had been Johnson's model to conduct secret radio broadcasts, dropping leaflets and instigating a strategic "black letter campaign" designed to implicate North Vietnamese leaders in treason.[141] Meanwhile with the 1966 election a little more than a year away, Eisenhower studied more about the man he had begun advising, Ronald Reagan.

Ike Studies Dutch

Within days, Eisenhower found himself defending Reagan against charges that Reagan was a right-wing extremist. Eisenhower wrote a friend, "For quite awhile I have been reading all I can find about Mr. Reagan." Also watching Reagan on television, Eisenhower noted that Reagan had a pleasant and appealing personality. Eisenhower wrote that Reagan had earnestly supported the Republican ticket in 1964, but whether this represented, as reported, political convictions of a "rightist" complexion or merely Republican loyalty was "something I do not know." The general added that he had been "disturbed" when he had received another note, which had "referred to Mr. Reagan as the 'darling' of the far-out right."[142]

Clearly for Eisenhower, one criteria to obtain his support was having been a loyal Republican by supporting and endorsing prior party candidates. And Reagan as a new Republican politician must have not only piqued the general's interest, Eisenhower had been reading all he could about Reagan for "quite a while" in the midst of Eisenhower's planning the future of his party.

Reagan had taken Eisenhower's tutelage and specific recommendations into account, and after many discussions with his financial supporters and his wife Nancy, Reagan reached a momentous decision. He announced on September 9, 1965 that he was going to travel throughout the state to see if there was grass roots support for him to seek the gubernatorial nomination of the California Republican Party. Just as Eisenhower had not declared his candidacy in 1952 until the people had shown their support in Manhattan, Minnesota and New Hampshire, Reagan needed to see proof that Californians wanted him to be their governor. After criss-crossing the state and receiving enthusiastic reaction, Reagan's formal, televised announcement would occur in January.

Kuchel Versus Owosso

Eisenhower began to reflect more fully on the upcoming California gubernatorial race. At this point, another potential Republican candidate was liberal Senator Thomas Kuchel. What was most important to Eisenhower, and always would be, was electability. Eisenhower's worries about electability would last to the summer of 1968. After all, his former vice-president had lost in 1960 and then the governorship in 1962. Eisenhower reviewed two recent polls with Gosden, one showing Reagan favored by Republicans over Kuchel but another showing that in a general election, Kuchel would beat Brown by a wider margin than would Reagan. Eisenhower mused that Reagan's five point margin in the general election poll was "too narrow a margin for comfort…The present political image of Reagan in the minds of all Californians is not nearly as appealing as that of Kuchel."[143] Gosden quite likely transmitted Ike's thoughts directly to Reagan.

Liberal Republican Kuchel did not agree with Eisenhower's feelings on party loyalty or Reagan's prior comments about liberals Rockefeller and Romney and Lindsay after their lack of support for Goldwater the year before. When Kuchel told the press that he himself was not going to run for governor but added an icy warning to the California Republican Party that it had better repudiate candidate Reagan, Reagan's grass roots group from Owosso sprung to action once again. Robert Smith, "national chairman of Republicans for Ronald Reagan," sent a telegram to Kuchel telling him of their resentment at his remarks.[144] Of course the Jorgensen and Smith group in Owosso, as seen earlier, had backed Reagan for governor but also was pushing for his presidential candidacy in 1968.

On October 26, CBS broadcast for the first time an international television debate show via satellite. Called *Town Meeting of the World*, the subject was Vietnam, and Harvard professor Henry Kissinger led a group of academicians who supported the war effort. As revealed in his post-presidential files, Eisenhower, deeply involved in thinking about the war and advising Johnson, sent for a copy.[145] The initial townhall program in 1965 would have a successor program in 1967 that would become a critical Reagan triumph and have major implications for the 1968 presidential race.

A few months after the brief Kuchel controversy, *Life* magazine would run a story on Reagan in January, 1966 and cite the Owosso "fan club" as having "launched a Reagan-for-President-in-1968 movement."[146] But Smith would take exception to how his Owosso group had been characterized and wrote a letter to the editor, which appeared in print the next month. Smith wrote: "Ours is a Republican organization with supporters in every state of the union, not a fan club."[147] After their initial splash on Election Day 1964—as the first group in the country to form a Reagan for President in 1968 club—there are only a few further references to the grass roots group from Owosso. How many members joined the Owosso group is not known, but as we will see, they would make their presence known three more times. On Election Day 1966 when Reagan would become governor of California, they would make a big splash. Jorgensen and Smith would continue their Reagan grass roots campaign into 1967 when Smith would appear on ABC's *Summer Focus,* shown on Detroit's WJRT, as he would advocate Reagan's 1968 candidacy.[148] And in the summer of 1968, they would urge Senator Everett Dirksen to support Reagan for president.

Reagan's Campaign Tactics in 1966

Reagan's 1966 primary and general election campaigns and subsequent victories are detailed in Lou Cannon's *Governor Reagan,* historian Matthew Dallek's *The Right Moment,* and an unpublished thesis by Kevin McKenna entitled *The "Total Campaign."* Reed has detailed his own role as northern California chairman too.[149] Two schools of thought have emerged over why Reagan won his two elections in 1966. Dallek has argued that it was the convergence of then-current issues such as student unrest in Berkeley, the riots in Watts, civil rights and Vietnam, which enabled Reagan to emphasize his theme of law and order.[150] But McKenna has argued that it was the successful strategies and tactics of Reagan's campaign management team which enabled Reagan's victories that year.[151] Both of those specific strategies and tactics would be modified but used again when he would run for president in 1968. But some aspects of Reagan's 1966 campaign, not mentioned by other historians, are chronicled here because those specific parts of the 1966 Reagan campaign would continue straight into his 1968 presidential campaign.

At Goldwater's recommendation, Spencer-Roberts became Reagan's political management firm for the 1966 primary and general election campaigns.[152] Reagan had seen them in action in California in 1964 when they had used several innovative tactics including: sending direct mail to registered Republicans, organizing a grass roots activist volunteer base, and succeeding in newly registering some 50,000 blacks so they could vote for Rockefeller.[153]

At first Spencer and Roberts were skeptical about taking on the 1966 campaign of Reagan, but they were convinced when Reagan demonstrated his sense of humor. The men had been discussing communism and Reagan then sat down for drinks in the living room and was wearing red socks. Not known to be fan of the Boston Red Sox, Reagan clearly was showing his self-deprecating humor on the "red" issue.[154] Reagan would do a better job than Christopher in unifying the party and Reagan had a better chance of beating Brown in the fall election.[155] Decades later, Spencer would admit that Reagan was the best candidate for whom he ever had worked because Reagan had a core set of principles.[156]

Spencer-Roberts suggested that Reagan begin to make speeches away from heavily Democratic big cities in California and concentrate on smaller population centers such as Modesto. Reagan's format was a speech, audience questions, and then press conferences where Reagan demonstrated his being "more comfortable with reporters than most conservative Republicans."[157]

Unbeknownst to any of his advisors, Reagan already had asked for, and received, detailed political advice from Eisenhower. Also, Reagan used public opinion to pinpoint issues important to voters to aid in his conservative solutions to problems.[158] This approach fit in naturally with Reagan's theme that the people were the ones who should choose their candidates.

1966 Primary Campaign

Reagan's ease with media and audiences, and his years of giving those speeches to GE audiences, led historian Cannon to describe Reagan in 1965 and 1966 as, "a president in waiting almost as soon as he began campaigning."[159] When reporter Lyn Nofziger was deciding whether to accept the offer to become Reagan's press secretary, he predicted that Reagan "might one day become president."[160] Nofziger observed a special "connect between Reagan and the people,"[161] and later reflected, "I wanted Ronald Reagan to be President in 1968, and that's what I was working toward."[162] Nofziger would try to help Reagan accomplish just that goal.[163]

On January 4, 1966 via a televised statewide address, Ronald Reagan formally declared his candidacy for the governorship of California. In his speech, one not only can hear the clear echoes of Eisenhower, one can hear his earlier, exact words to Reagan. In addition, some of the words used likely indicated the two men had had discussions of the issue of Americans being subdivided by Democrats into ethnic categories to find grievances and thus attract votes:

"Its high time we stopped hyphenating ourselves, Irish-Americans, Negro-Americans, Italian-Americans....These blocks were set up for political expediency so cynical men could make cynical promises in the hunt for votes."

As will be discussed, Reagan and Eisenhower formally would discuss the subject (first enunciated by Reagan's hero, Theodore Roosevelt) via letter six months later. But Reagan's use of the theme in his campaign announcement likely indicates he and Eisenhower had discussed the issue already.

After citing Winston Churchill's change in party for principle, and then asking Democrats to read Franklin Roosevelt's First Inaugural Address and its call for smaller government and asking which party today followed those principles, Reagan, very likely modeling his campaign persona after Eisenhower's 1952 "Citizen-Soldier," told his audience, "I think I can lay claim to being called a Citizen-Politician." Reagan then explained that since he became a Republican, he had worked as "actively as I could" for candidates in 1960, 1962, and 1964. In those campaigns, "I supported all the party's nominees, men with basic and widely differing philosophies."[164] Reagan had followed through on Eisenhower's initial letter of six months earlier, and indeed used the exact same wording. Then, after his formal announcement of his quest for the governorship, candidate Reagan got down to campaign business.

Reagan's advertising firm targeted television, radio, newspapers and billboards.[165] Such state-wide efforts then were brought to the local level as county and regional chairmen reached out to local media as well. A direct-mail campaign was supplemented by informal coffee hours for voters with both Nancy and Ronald as well as town-hall gatherings especially at colleges.[166] Polls were commissioned to further target certain voting precincts.[167] Reagan again was featured in YAF's *The New Guard*. The February 1966 article, "The Republican More Like JFK Than Any Other," by Lee Edwards, echoed the earlier commentary by Robert Novak, and praised Reagan's communication skills, good looks, and mastery of television.

On a practical level, sometimes Reagan campaigned by a chartered DC-3, dubbed "The Turkey Bird" by the press, as well as mainly by bus. As noted earlier, Reagan did not like to fly, so in 1966 he stayed on land whenever he could. Reagan endured a grueling schedule of multiple stops for multiple events each day across a vast state.[168] It would be good practice for the hectic pace he was to maintain during his first presidential campaign. As will be discussed, Reagan's fear of flying and his relentless campaigning—all via jet in 1967 and 1968—will be reviewed as proof of his commitment to winning.

Goldwater activists quickly switched onto the Reagan bandwagon in 1966 and a "Register for Reagan" drive asked each of them to add six new members for Reagan; all were kept informed by a Reagan campaign newsletter.[169] Grassroots Reagan groups were set up in each county, and local Young Republican and Republican Women clubs hosted small Reagan gatherings. College Republicans and Youth for Reagan distributed campaign materials, walked precincts, helped register voters and volunteered their time and energy.[170]

County chairmen recruited precinct captains who canvassed their districts door to door searching for likely Reagan voters; then after using phone banks to reach other Republicans, the campaign team had Reagan "Victory Squads" help bring voters to the polls.[171] Finally, a massive Reagan rally on the last day attracted some 4,000 people coupled with Reagan then flying to eight cities each with its own rally culminating in a final rally at a Los Angeles area airport.[172]

Republican State Chairman and obstetrician Dr. Gaylord Parkinson, in order to unify the State Republican Party after divisions brought on by the Goldwater-Rockefeller infighting in 1964, instituted the fabled Eleventh Commandment ("Thou Shalt Not Speak Ill of a Fellow Republican"), which kept Christopher's primary fight against Reagan on a short leash.[173] Reagan continued this theme of unity by disavowing the use of the terms "liberal-Republican" or "conservative-Republican," just as Eisenhower had suggested.

Prior to his January, 1966 announcement, Reagan had made only two out-of-state campaign trips while he had been assessing support for his possible run for the governorship. Reagan had spoken at the New Haven Arena on September 28, 1965 as guest of honor for a rally by the Connecticut Republican Citizens Committee, which had not been recognized officially by the GOP State Central Committee. Reagan witnessed first-hand the difficulties in fighting the political establishment as an outsider. Fearing the rise of Reagan, "Both the state and local leadership of the Republican party boycotted the rally." After a rousing performance by the Westport Young Republican Band, Reagan was introduced by his friend, Ralph Cordiner, former chairman of the board of General Electric. In addition to helping Reagan's career as GE spokesman, three years earlier Reagan had been told by Cordiner of Robert Kennedy's pressure to get Reagan fired.

The crowd of 3,500 had interrupted Reagan's 50-minute speech with "applause more than twenty times."[174] Despite the boycott by Republican state leaders, he closed on a plea for party unity amongst Republicans. Reagan received a standing ovation when he had made a very brief remark, calling for the soldiers in Vietnam to "be allowed to win."[175] Thus even before declaring his candidacy, let alone winning the nomination or general election, Reagan thus had spoken up about an area not normally in the purview of gubernatorial candidates: foreign policy. It was the first small step in his long road towards becoming a world statesman.

Later in Boston, Reagan had spoken first at a Republican finance luncheon. Then in front of the National Federation of Republican Women, he "brought down the house."[176] Reagan had made a special visit to meet the black attorney general of Massachusetts, Edward Brooke.

Reagan, after January 4 an official candidate, traveled outside of California once again, albeit quite briefly, as of course he needed to concentrate on California. But Reagan was becoming a sought-after speaker for the GOP. On March 28, 1966, Reagan gave a short, domestic-themed talk at the Republican Party Founders Day celebration in Lincoln, Nebraska.[177] Little did Reagan know how critical one active GOP member from Lincoln, Dale L. Young, would become to Reagan's presidential aspirations exactly two years hence. Reagan then flew east to the Detroit Economic Club. The speech, on economic policy, was not open to the public. He said that Michigan Governor Romney was a "fine governor" but when asked, Reagan thought that Nixon was more likely to win the 1968 Republican nomination for president. When Reagan then was questioned about his never having held political office before, he countered that Governor Romney similarly had not held political office prior to his election as governor of Michigan.[178]

Reagan was an old hand at deflecting anyone questioning his lack of working in government. That fall, he would cite the memory of California Governor Hiram Johnson as a man who had had no prior governmental experience but had been elected governor with subsequent great success in office. Reagan would state, "Experience in office was, and remains the problem, not the solution."[179] These out-of-state visits to New England and to the Midwest had begun the process of establishing political outsider Reagan as a future candidate for national office. In 1967 and 1968, his out-of-state presidential campaign travels would dwarf those of his gubernatorial campaign.

Rockefeller and Lindsay Against Reagan

Meanwhile during the California primary campaign, two prominent New York liberal Republicans, Governor Nelson Rockefeller and

New York City Mayor John Lindsay, each got involved in attempting to thwart conservative Reagan. Each of course had refused to endorse Goldwater in 1964. At this point Rockefeller made a "sizeable grant" to the Christopher campaign.[180] Lindsay sent a key aide to California for research to collect "incriminating statements from Reagan."[181]

Rockefeller advisor George Hinman said of Reagan's primary opponent, San Francisco Mayor George Christopher, "We hope he can prevail." After Reagan won the primary, Rockefeller "cringed at the news." Hinman said Rockefeller was "greatly disappointed," and Reagan's campaign as the official party nominee was "moving to the right out there in a most depressing way." Hinman, as Rockefeller's spokesman, did adhere somewhat to the fabled Eleventh Commandment and wrote to other conservative California Republicans praising Reagan's 'smashing victory.'"[182]

Columnist Drew Pearson soon tried to destroy Reagan's chances. Pearson was a known Johnson supporter, and historian Arthur Schlesinger, Jr. described him as a close friend of Johnson. Indeed Johnson would relax with Pearson and discuss politics.[183] It never hurt to have friends in the media who would write articles supporting you and destroying your enemies! Pearson, whose articles would become very popular in 1968, got involved directly with the race in California. Pearson was fed a story by Governor Brown and his aides. Pearson proceeded to publicize a 1940 arrest of Christopher—when he had been in the dairy business—in the hopes that by getting rid of Brown's opponent Christopher, Reagan would be left: as the "weaker 'fringe' candidate."[184] It would not be the last time Pearson would have it in for Reagan.

In March, *Esquire* ran a story theorizing about the 1968 Republican nominee. A survey of 162 GOP heavyweights showed that only one would vote for Reagan.[185] Meanwhile Nixon, defeated in 1960 and in 1962, was shoring up his support amongst party conservatives in preparation for another shot at the presidency.

More Eisenhower Advice

Eisenhower had been keeping a close eye on the Republican gubernatorial primary race, especially because he wintered in California and wanted intra-party unity. But Eisenhower had a personal stake in the outcome: Reagan was becoming his political student. Gosden wrote to Eisenhower on May 29, 1966 asking for Eisenhower's advice once again to help Reagan. Gosden had enclosed some polling information from Reagan headquarters; Gosden thought

Eisenhower should see it. Gosden asked the general for suggestions on how Reagan, should he win the primary on June 7, could get Christopher backers behind Reagan.

Eisenhower answered via letter on June 2, 1966, and this letter revealed that Reagan and Eisenhower had conversed personally. Eisenhower first thanked Gosden for sending him the Reagan poll and then mentioned at least one prior conversation he had had with Reagan ("Once when I was talking to Ronald Reagan") about a Reagan critic. Eisenhower then continued his political mentoring: "It is obvious that Reagan has made great gains in the primary campaign...Mr. Reagan should give more attention to his 'image' in the northern part of the State...On top of this he must be successful in getting a lot of Independents and Democrats to vote for him."[186] Eisenhower did not specify that his conversation had been the only one he had had with Reagan; thus one may surmise that the conversation mentioned was but one of several.

In 1952, Republican nominee Eisenhower had generated controversy on the liberal campus of Columbia University when he had met with his opponent in the primary, the defeated Senator Robert Taft, a conservative.[187] But Eisenhower had known the critical importance of healing wounds to restore intra-party unity prior to a general election. Eisenhower did not want Reagan to repeat the mistakes of 1964. After Reagan's triumph in the primary, getting the support of former Christopher supporters would be key. Eisenhower already was looking ahead to Reagan seeking Independents and Democrats in the general election.

Once again as he had done in 1965, Eisenhower's specific advice to Reagan was to seek party unity, and the idea that history would know as the Reagan Democrats again may be traced to Eisenhower's very words of advice he continued to give Reagan.

After Gosden told Reagan of Eisenhower's detailed advice, Reagan followed through exactly by concentrating on the north and seeking out Christopher supporters. Prior to the primary election day, Reagan sent out a mass mailing to known Christopher supporters, telling them that if Christopher won, Reagan would support him. Reagan said of his liberal Republican Party members, "We don't win elections by destroying them."[188]

In his announcement on January 4, he had offered an outstretched hand to Democrats when he had asked them to read FDR's Inaugural Address and to realize that it was only the Republican Party which was calling for limited government. Reagan's team also sent a message to supporters of conservative Los Angeles Mayor Sam Yorty (who was running against Brown in the Democratic primary) by inviting them to "come aboard."[189] Would all of Eisenhower's mentoring work?

Primary Victory and Unity

Reagan won the Republican primary by an astounding 77 percent.[190] Immediately speculation arose again about Reagan's aiming for the White House. His primary win had "splashed new colors" onto the 1968 Republican field. Although Reagan likely would head the California delegation and throw its weight towards Nixon with a likely Romney counter-offensive, one reporter felt that in fact the "most extreme possibility" was that Reagan might "capture the 1968 Republican Presidential nomination" for himself.[191]

The *New York Times* speculated that if Reagan won the general election, "He will, in the judgment of many Republicans, automatically become a factor in the 1968 Presidential race" and added that Reagan might "emerge as a Presidential prospect himself."[192] But a few days later, one of their elitist, liberal reporters derided the thought of Reagan as president writing, "If Ronald Reagan of California is suddenly put on the list of Republican presidential possibilities," then why not the president of Yale? The reporter added, "Mr. Reagan is an actor, which is really in his favor, for all politicians are actors. But if Goldwater, the authentic conservative article, could not make it, why (would) a Hollywood type playing the role of Goldwater?"[193] That reporter would not be the last to underestimate Ronald Reagan.

After winning the primary, Reagan followed through on Eisenhower's advice and sought party unity by immediately asking Christopher for his support and by hiring a number of Christopher supporters to work in the general election campaign.[194] Christopher campaign director Casper Weinberger was made chairman of the Reagan campaign's Executive Committee.[195] Not only did the former campaign team for Christopher start to work for Reagan immediately, it was an Eisenhower administration appointee who made the announcement that they were all "completely united" in supporting Reagan for governor in the general election. The appointee told the press that Reagan "comes very close" to Eisenhower's philosophy of "conservative in all things fiscal, liberal regarding problems where government help is needed." Regardless of whether the assessment on the latter point was correct, one Reagan backer was pleased: "The GOP, seldom united in recent years, has finally come through in one piece."[196]

Once Reagan won the primary, the September, 1966 issue of *The New Guard* arrived early with a recorded copy of a Reagan speech.[197] In California, Reagan activist Shawn Steel converted his YAF chapter into Youth for Reagan and he became high school state chairman.[198] By the time of the 1966 summer YAF conference, after having followed and contributed towards conservative Reagan's victory in his primary campaign and the start of his general election campaign for governor, the YAF leaders were polled about whom they wanted for president in 1968. Their order of preference was: Reagan (53 percent), Goldwater (30 percent) and Nixon in last place (15 percent.)[199] It was a harbinger that America's conservative youth might be the ones to lead the party and the nation into Reagan country.

One unique Youth for Reagan sub-group was the *Reagan Girls*, organized by former Goldwater Girl, Cherie Adams. Besides helping with the same volunteer work as other Youth for Reagan, their purpose was the "addition of beauty, personality, and energy to political campaigning."[200] Nancy Reagan personally selected the group's clothing as "the most attractive campaign outfit ever designed."[201] They wore red berets and brightly-colored white and red clothing.[202] The *Reagan Girls* attended campaign meetings, rode in campaign cars, served as receptionists, and baby sat on Election Day so mothers could vote.[203] They also answered phones for surveys on behalf of Reagan.[204] The *Reagan Girls*, along with the Boston YAF cowgirls mentioned earlier, by the summer of 1968 would morph into *The Reaganettes*.

The head of Students for Christopher was brought into the fold of Youth for Reagan.[205] Reagan even mended fences with Kuchel, after the Owosso controversy, for the future.[206] But like Lindsay and Romney would do in 1968, Kuchel refused to support Reagan in 1966.[207] Coach Eisenhower, though, just saw his political student get his first victory. But Eisenhower did not know that his involvement as political mentor and coach to Reagan was about to intensify.

Reagan had not asked Nixon to participate in the primary campaign. Reagan knew that his populist conservatism campaign might not be helped by those who viewed Nixon as too moderate.[208] When Reagan won, Nixon had trouble getting through via telephone to congratulate Reagan and had to write a letter instead. Nixon complimented Reagan writing, "your primary race was conducted with great ability, dignity and effectiveness."[209] On June 25, 1966 in Los Angeles, Nixon congratulated Reagan in public saying, "Ronald Reagan, by his track record as a candidate, has demonstrated he is a politician of the first rank and has great potential for leadership."[210]

Despite the earlier endorsement by Goldwater for 1968, Nixon, continuing to think about a possible Reagan threat to his nomination in 1968, started to court other conservative leaders directly.[211] Nixon eventually would come to understand how presciently true his acclaim for Reagan was.

1966 General Election Campaign: Common Sense, the Citizen-Politician, and Ike's Endorsement

As Reagan unified the party, the fall election came into sharp focus. Just as Eisenhower had been the nation's "citizen soldier," Reagan, as he had proclaimed on January 4, continued to call himself the "citizen-politician" and espoused such a populist theme frequently during the campaign. But now the campaign had to expand in full force to attract voters besides Republicans.[212]

A few days after winning the Republican primary nomination, Reagan wrote on June 10, 1966 to Eisenhower to thank him for his advice. As best as can be determined, this was the first letter Reagan had sent the general since his first 1952 telegram in which Reagan had urged Eisenhower to run for president. Specifically Reagan wrote, "I want to thank you for your invaluable advice and suggestions…My TV appearances profited by a reduction in verbiage and the resultant slower pace drew some appreciative comments."

Clearly at some prior point the old general had advised the famous actor on speechwriting and on television speechmaking skills! And Reagan had followed Eisenhower's specific suggestions with success. This Reagan-Eisenhower interaction is reminiscent of the television advisory role that Reagan's friend and SAG president predecessor, actor Robert Montgomery, had given Eisenhower both before and during Ike's presidency. Besides Freeman Gosden, had Montgomery also been an intermediary between Reagan and Eisenhower? Your author has been unable to find any direct link.

Of course, Reagan—the decades-long actor—may in fact not have needed Eisenhower's advice at all. But Reagan did allude to what Eisenhower likely had advised over the phone: to speak more slowly and to shorten the text. More importantly, Reagan added, "Most of all, I'm deeply grateful for your willingness to share your time, thoughts, and philosophy with me. I know you'll be happy to learn that party unity in California is becoming a reality. Pledges of support are coming in from campaign workers and chairmen in the Christopher camp."[213] Eisenhower and Reagan clearly had spent time discussing politics and issues of importance facing California even before their first meeting.

At what exact point Reagan started to view Eisenhower as a political father figure and mentor is not certain, but clearly Reagan turned to Eisenhower many times for advice, initially via friends such as Gosden, and now directly. Eisenhower advised, or perhaps tutored, Reagan on how to present his political philosophy to the public, how to seek a united Republican Party, how to start seeking Democrat and Independent voters, and even how to change his speech-writing and television speechmaking. Perhaps Eisenhower began to think that it might be Ronald Reagan who could continue his own "common sense" Republican solutions to California's, and the nation's, problems into the 1970s and beyond.

Eisenhower wrote back to Reagan on June 13, 1966, noting how glad he was that his political advice to Reagan had not been worthless. Eisenhower added, "There is no need for me to tell you how much I hope for your success this fall....You should go through to a splendid victory."[214] In fact, Eisenhower was about to express his good wishes in person. This would be the first of four crucial face-to-face meetings that would change world history.

June 1966 Meeting with Eisenhower

Within a few days of Ronald Reagan's first victory in any political election, Reagan became a new star within the Republican Party. The national media announced on June 14 that Reagan had been invited to Washington D.C. to meet with Republican Party leaders and the California delegation. But with whom did Reagan choose to meet as soon as he had won? First he would meet with his mentor and political coach, Dwight Eisenhower.[215]

Behind the scenes, Eisenhower had continued getting his biweekly updates on Vietnam and sending his advice to Johnson via General Goodpaster. The prior October, when informed that the U.S. was sending in major ground reinforcements, Eisenhower wanted to see "overwhelming strength" used.[216] Eisenhower then got impatient with Johnson's slow build-up of American forces.[217] It seemed to be a repeat of the tragedy of the Korean War, when Truman's gradualism had led to Eisenhower being called in to the rescue. Eisenhower had felt that he was forced to rescue Truman's "chestnuts from the fire."[218] This expression may have been a favorite of the general's. For as will be seen, it would be used in 1968 by candidate Reagan in a very similar situation, and its origin most likely came to Reagan directly from Eisenhower.

In Vietnam, Ike did not want to see another long drawn-out conflict. Eisenhower wanted to see Vietnam get massive American military force so the war would be won and thus "brought to an end as soon as possible."[219] At the time of the Reagan visit, Eisenhower just had told Goodpaster that he supported "hitting the enemy where it hurts."[220] Reagan would use Eisenhower's exact phrase many times. Vietnam is what was in the front of Eisenhower's mind as he greeted his new guest: his party's nominee for governor of California, which happened to be the location of his own winter home.

During the summer months, the Eisenhower's were at their Gettysburg farm. After the drive from the nation's capital, Reagan and Reed first arrived at Eisenhower's Gettysburg College office. Then Reagan and Eisenhower met privately for a full 55 minutes.[221] [222] Then it was time for lunch.

As one learns today on tour when visiting the Eisenhower home, Mrs. Eisenhower insisted that all guests, including her husband—the former president—as well as their grand-children, had to sign in every single time they entered; thus multiple visits the same day required multiple signatures. So on June 15, after his private meeting with the general, Reagan arrived at the Eisenhower home, signed the guest book, and sat with the general for lunch.[223]

Facing reporters after the luncheon, Eisenhower and Reagan were asked, what had the two men discussed? Reagan had told Eisenhower more details about the new Republican unity in California and Eisenhower told reporters he was very gratified by Reagan's report. When asked about Reagan's candidacy, Eisenhower officially endorsed him for governor of California: "Mr. Reagan is a man of great integrity and **common sense** and I know he's a Republican and I'm for Republicans." (author's emphasis) And when asked about segments of the party, Eisenhower interjected, "If the Republican Party has any label at all it ought to call itself the **common sense** party." (author's emphasis) Because of his heart attack, Eisenhower added, he could do no active campaigning for Reagan.

Reagan told the press that he knew the plan of his Democratic opponent was to paint him, Reagan, as a right wing extremist. Eisenhower continued the detailing of their private conversations, stating that the Republican Party had members of varying political specifics and that the party could accommodate such a wide group of men. Eisenhower was confirming in public what he had, and would, write in private: that he in no way saw Reagan as a right-wing extremist.[224] Eisenhower saw Reagan and Reagan's political philosophy as well within the wide tent of mainstream Republicanism. Eisenhower then decided personally to help launch Reagan well beyond the governorship in Sacramento and potentially right into 1600 Pennsylvania Avenue.

When Eisenhower then was asked if a Reagan victory in the fall would propel Reagan into the 1968 Republican presidential race, Eisenhower answered, "You can bet he will become a presidential possibility." Reagan winced, as he did not want the idea of his presidential plans interfering with his gubernatorial election.[225]

Eisenhower's words made front-page national news.[226] The accompanying photograph of smiling Reagan and Eisenhower was entitled, "Eisenhower Endorses Reagan."[227] Eisenhower had thrown Reagan's hat into the ring for 1968 and had done so forcefully. Nobody there, other than Reagan and Eisenhower, knew about their political relationship, which had grown and blossomed since Ike's first letter of advice.

Neither Eisenhower nor Reagan ever commented again in public about their Gettysburg meeting. Eisenhower made no mention of their meeting other than what he told the press. His post-presidential diary did not yet exist, as it would not begin until August. But afterwards Reagan told Reed about the specifics of the long talk with Eisenhower. Eisenhower had advised Reagan about campaign tactics but then brought up Vietnam. Eisenhower proceeded to critique Johnson's handling of the war. Eisenhower favored massive force, instructing Reagan, "Gradual escalation will not work."[228] This may be somewhat surprising as Reagan just had become nominee and had not yet won the general election.

But with Vietnam occupying so much of Eisenhower's thoughts at the time, perhaps he could unburden his feelings about Johnson's mismanagement of the war to this young, rising Republican. Eisenhower had heard Reagan, in The Speech, twice call for freedom for Eastern Europe. Clearly Eisenhower had loved Reagan's The Speech and been mentoring Reagan for a full year on domestic politics and campaign strategy and tactics. Eisenhower must have seen sufficient potential for the national political stage in his protégé that discussing world affairs was prudent.[229] And then a few minutes later at the press conference, he had certified Reagan as presidential timbre.

Eisenhower and Reagan also discussed Robert F. Kennedy. As will be reviewed in more detail later, the former president, shortly after the Kennedy assassination and concerned about RFK's abuses of power, had cautioned President Johnson about RFK in late 1963. Now in 1966, Eisenhower cautioned Reagan about RFK.[230] Reagan, on the receiving end of harassment from RFK, needed little mentoring about the dangers to individual freedom of Robert Kennedy.

Had Eisenhower and Reagan also discussed executive branch organization for a president versus a governor? Or dealing with a hostile legislature in Washington, D.C. versus Sacramento? Did Eisenhower again use the phrase "common sense" (which he used again with the press) when recommending to Reagan what policies he might recommend? As we will see, future governor and presidential candidate Reagan would be compared to President Eisenhower on those very same issues soon thereafter as well as many decades later.

After that initial mentoring from the general, Reagan reflected more on Vietnam. In his encyclopedic mind,[231] Reagan was filing away the new military analysis from the man who had led the European Allies in World War II and who had ended the fighting in the Korean War. Reagan was about to speak in Seattle three days later, and for the first time to a national audience as a candidate for governor of the most populous state in the nation and a possible future candidate for the presidency, Reagan would discuss the Vietnam War.

The *New York Times* was quick to follow their positive front-page story with a more negative commentary about Reagan's presidential chances a few days later. Arthur Krock, Washington bureau chief for the newspaper, admitted that Reagan just had received "his certification as potential Presidential timbre by General Eisenhower" but added, "In the two years before the Presidential election of 1968, Reagan could only have made a start" in solving California's massive problems. But if Reagan "can show sufficient progress with the task in two years to justify to the voters of California and the nation his leaving of it in a quest for the Presidency," then Reagan "will have performed a miracle of administration and leadership." Reagan would perform his miracle in six months.[232]

Campaign Preview: Seattle, 1966

Reagan's first speech on the national political stage occurred in Seattle a few days after the Eisenhower meeting. This was Reagan's only out-of-state major public campaign speech during the general election campaign, as his prior speeches in New Haven, Boston, and the Midwest were delivered during the primary race. Now he was the full-fledged nominee of his party to become the governor of the nation's most populous state. Thus what gubernatorial candidate

Reagan would say, and how he would be received, portended a preview of how presidential candidate Reagan would be received on the national campaign trail starting early in 1967.

Reagan was invited to come north by a Boeing engineer, Ken Rogstad, the conservative Republican leader in the Seattle area. Rogstad had fought for several years with the party's liberal elements under the control of Governor Dan Evans. As noted earlier, Evans had been one of the few Republican victors in 1964.[233] Rogstad, seeking a nationally-known conservative speaker for the 1966 Republican King County convention to be held in Seattle, announced that candidate Reagan would arrive to address the expected 4,000 delegates.[234] Hoping to attract a wide audience, which might not know that famous actor Reagan was running for office, newspaper advertisements spread throughout the *Seattle Times* showed that the admission was only $1![235]

And what did the public think about an actor-turned-politician? A *Seattle Times* poll asked, are "show-business personalities are fully justified in running for public office?" An astounding 80% answered: Yes.[236]

Most Republicans at the King County convention were elated to have Reagan there in person as their main speaker, although Evans was not.[237] Reagan's speech was the first he ever gave on the national scene as an official Republican Party candidate with national presence and national appeal. In front of 1,297 delegates, alternates, and the public, he did not speak against incumbent Brown in Sacramento. Rather, Reagan already was running against incumbent Johnson in Washington, D.C. As will be seen, decades later President Reagan would reflect that one major domestic thrust of his presidency was not to undo FDR's New Deal but rather to undo LBJ's Great Society.

In front of the eyes of that Seattle audience, Reagan began transforming himself into a national candidate. His talk was national in scope about problems facing the country as a whole. He "lambasted the Johnson administration, its economic policies, poverty program, social planning, and Vietnam policy." Reagan was "interrupted numerous times by applause and laughter" as he attacked the Democratic administration in Washington, D.C. The attendees gave a "roaring, standing ovation to the actor-politician."[238] The Seattle speech and the preceding poll proved that former actor Ronald Reagan could be accepted outside of California as a serious politician discussing serious issues and policies. And Reagan spoke about problems of serious national concern.

Reagan had visited with Eisenhower at Gettysburg just three days earlier. By addressing Vietnam ever so briefly for the first time, as he had done briefly in New Haven when running in the primary, Reagan again was demonstrating that he could speak intelligently—albeit quite briefly—about foreign affairs. Over the next two years, his public forays into foreign policy would expand exponentially both in scope and detail. But New Haven and Seattle were the first steps, where Reagan initially put his toe into the vast ocean of thorny international issues. This was way beyond what gubernatorial candidates normally addressed. Seattle was an inflection point when Reagan was seen, away from the political comfort of his home base in California, for the first time as a national candidate.

The influence of Eisenhower upon Reagan is quite clear. Reagan was using in public a number of Eisenhower's ideas. Coach Eisenhower had gone from mentoring Reagan about politics and domestic policies into the realm of foreign affairs. From this humble beginning in 1966, Reagan would take the lessons he would learn from Eisenhower—about military policies and strategy in World War II and how he had fought against communist aggression in Korea—and Reagan would apply them to detailed strategy and tactical recommendations about Vietnam during 1967 and 1968. The world eventually would see the final stage of Eisenhower's mentoring of Reagan about foreign policy culminate in the collapse of communism and the great decline in nuclear arsenals of the superpowers two decades in the future under President Reagan.

One person not happy that Eisenhower had thrown Reagan's hat into the 1968 presidential ring was Eisenhower's former vice-president. When at the Gettysburg press conference Reagan had winced after Eisenhower's public certification, it was for concern as to whom those words would mean the most. Indeed Nixon was offended.[239] Yet still Reagan was running for governor in California, so on June 23, Nixon helped launch Reagan's official gubernatorial campaign as the Republican nominee at a Republican victory dinner at the Sports Arena in Los Angeles. Senator George Murphy was there too, and newspaper photographs showed the three engaged in a three-way handshake.[240] At a press conference, Nixon predicted RFK would run for president in 1968, and at an NBC interview, Nixon confirmed he planned to campaign for Reagan for governor in 1966.[241]

After the Eisenhower endorsement and certification of presidential timbre, Reagan wrote a thank you letter to Eisenhower, "Your generous comments, and the fact of our meeting have done more than you could ever know to unify the Party here in California."[242] Eisenhower was delighted that former Christopher supporters declared for party unity and cheerfully were giving their support to Mr. Reagan.[243]

Eisenhower Defends Reagan Against Charges of Anti-Semitism

The issue of anti-Semitism arose the following month. On July 7 Gosden wrote to Eisenhower telling him that a false accusation of Reagan being anti-Semitic was spreading. Gosden told Eisenhower that a Jewish man had told Gosden about it. Gosden affirmed to Eisenhower that Reagan absolutely was not anti-Semitic. Gosden also told Eisenhower of campaign difficulties in the northern part of the state. Gosden asked Eisenhower for advice on how to help Reagan now in the general election.[244]

It is well beyond the subject of this work to delve into Eisenhower's feeling towards Jews in general or the Jewish vote in the 1950s or similarly for Reagan. But Eisenhower had made a special trip to witness first hand what the world later would call the holocaust, when in May, 1945 he and Generals George Patton and Omar Bradley had visited Ohrdruf, a sub-camp of Buchenwald, which was the first camp liberated by American soldiers. Seeing and smelling the decaying dead bodies heaped up in piles by the depraved Nazis, fearless Patton vomited. Seeing ahead to a day when the holocaust might be denied, Eisenhower had a film crew document the entire grisly and horrific circumstances before he made the local German populace tour the camp as well and to bury the bodies. Eisenhower then proceeded to arrange for members of Congress and the press to be flown in to see anti-Semitism at its worst extreme in all of human history.

After liberation, some Allied authorities wanted Jews placed in separate displaced persons camps, but Eisenhower would not permit it, for "this reminded him of how the Nazis had discriminated against them."[245] In order to learn more about the problems the Jewish survivors were experiencing, Eisenhower appointed a new adviser on Jewish affairs and then had met with future Israeli Prime Minister David Ben Gurion, who at the time was the head of the Jewish Agency. On Yom Kippur 1945, Eisenhower had made a surprise visit to the displaced person camp Feldafing, where he said in part, "I know how much you have suffered and I believe a sunny day will still come for you."[246] The Jews in the camp, still suffering the physical and mental effects of the holocaust, gave Eisenhower a standing ovation.[247]

At the future commemoration service at Arlington National Cemetery honoring the Warsaw Ghetto uprising, as the Holocaust Museum in Washington, D.C. was being planned, Eisenhower's son

John would read a letter from his father honoring the memories of the six million Jewish victims of the Nazis. The Eisenhower Presidential Library website has the details of Eisenhower and the holocaust.

So Eisenhower likely was particularly incensed when anyone would be called an anti-Semite via vague rumors; nobody needed to tell Dwight Eisenhower what anti-Semitism was. And although Eisenhower probably was unaware of Ronald Reagan's own personal experiences with anti-Semitism, Reagan was no anti-Semite. Reagan as a youngster had observed first hand how his father had refused to stay at a hotel that had refused to admit Jews, and the two had slept in their car. During World War II, Reagan was stateside in the Army's Motion Picture Unit and made *For God and Country*, which "aimed at promoting unity among Catholics, Protestants and Jews"[248] along with other anti-Nazi propaganda films. A post-war FBI dossier on Reagan portrayed him as "an emotional foe of anti-Semitism who denounced persecution of the Jews in radio broadcasts and nearly came to blows at a party with a guest who said that the Jews had profiteered from the war."[249] Later when married to Jane Wyman, Reagan had quit a local country club when he learned that it did not admit Jews.[250]

Finally, in the future when he would talk to Israeli Prime Minister Yitzhak Shamir and Nazi-hunter Simon Wiesenthal, President Reagan would become "so carried away in denouncing the horrors of the Holocaust that he talked about photographing Nazi death camps during World War II."[251] We will see how Reagan would visit Bergen-Belsen concentration camp in 1985. And just as his two terms would end, while speaking at the dedication of the site of America's Holocaust Memorial Museum, President Reagan would urge the world not to view the holocaust as incomprehensible. Rather, Reagan would say that study of the holocaust was critical—that "the future depends upon it."[252]

So in the summer of 1966, Eisenhower continued his mentoring of Reagan and offered Reagan an elegant solution to clearly negate the false charges of anti-Semitism by sending a detailed reply letter to Gosden on July 11. Ike wrote:

"I suggest that Mr. Reagan make arrangements to see that, at the first major press conference he holds, some individual question him about as follows: 'Mr. Reagan, I hear that you have disavowed any connection with the John Birch Society but, at the same time, I've heard reports that you are anti-Semitic. Do you have anything to say on this point?'"

Eisenhower suggested Reagan's answer to be "emphatic and short" and gave an example—"I've heard of this malicious accusation. It is not true. Anyone who repeats this rumor is guilty of a deliberate falsehood."

Eisenhower then continued, as Theodore Roosevelt first had pronounced decades earlier,[253] and echoing the words Reagan already had used in his January 4 declaration of candidacy, that Reagan should add elsewhere in his first press conference, "I do not exclude any citizen from my concern and I make no distinctions among them on such invalid bases as color or creed...There are no 'minority' groups so far as I'm concerned. We are all Americans." Eisenhower also advised Reagan, "Get some fine women on the staff and in every group set up" and closed giving his warmest personal regards to Nancy.[254]

Gosden then wrote back on July 15, telling Eisenhower that he had read the entire letter personally to Reagan, who was extremely grateful. Gosden wanted Eisenhower to know that most of Eisenhower's suggestions already were being implemented by Reagan, and the rest of Eisenhower's advice to Reagan would quickly be added.[255] Reagan, as he had begun on his January 4 address, would emphasize in 1966, and more so during his 1968 campaign, that he did not want people broken into subgroups. Be it Republicans classified as liberal or conservative or some Americans being called Irish-Americans: they were Americans plain and simple. As Reagan had surmised, both Eisenhower and Reagan knew that their Democratic opponents usually placed individuals into groups, which then could be characterized as having been discriminated against in some manner.

The very first official written historical appearance of documented Reagan Democrats was a newspaper clipping, which Gosden had enclosed with his July 15 letter to Eisenhower: in the primary, Republican gubernatorial nominee Reagan had received 27,422 Democrat cross-over write-in votes.[256] Undoubtedly Gosden had discussed it with Reagan, and now Eisenhower saw that Reagan, whom he had been advising for more than a year to attempt to attract Democrats and Independents, was not only following his advice— Reagan was succeeding brilliantly.

An analysis from the *New York Times* thought that Reagan, if he would win the governorship in the fall, might play a "decisive role in the 1968 Republican Presidential maneuvering." One idea was that Reagan would then become the darling of California's conservative Republican wing, which "would destroy the chances of Richard M. Nixon for the Republican Presidential nomination in 1968." A second thought was that Reagan could sway the nomination to either Romney or Nixon. The third idea, attributed to Nixon supporters, was that a Reagan win for governor in the fall would "almost guarantee" a Nixon nomination in 1968 because California's huge delegation would prefer Nixon over Romney. Nixon was reported to believe that Reagan "would not be in a position to seek the nomination for himself," but would help Nixon with conservatives in western states.[257]

Romney-Reagan or Romney vs. Reagan

Fortuitously, new nominee Reagan was the host for the next governors conference and George Romney was to be there. In the summer of 1966, Romney and Nixon were viewed as the two major probable Republican candidates for 1968. Yet as soon as Reagan had won his gubernatorial primary, his swift rise "from political obscurity" into possibly winning the governorship of California was thought to let Reagan "play the decisive role in the 1968 Republican Presidential maneuvering." Reagan was thought to be in a position to swing the nomination to either Nixon or Romney. If such a maneuver by Reagan for Romney were made, "the Vice Presidential nomination could be his reward and there already was talk of a Romney-Reagan alliance." Another view was that if Reagan became governor, he would be California's favorite son and this would be "fatal" to Nixon's chances. In that case, in 1968 "Mr. Reagan then would become the conservative champion in a showdown with Mr. Romney."[258]

The day after that analysis appeared, the National Governors Conference met in the posh Century Plaza Hotel in Los Angeles. The politics and policy discussions were described as "tentative and half-hearted," attributed to the luxurious setting next to 20th Century Fox's movie studio, or the weather and the lure of golf and swimming, or a "decreasing degree of control over their own destinies." The sixteen Republican governors who attended "caucused frequently and came out issuing manifestos," but "in the end their only decision was to meet again in December." Although most had favored Romney in 1968, "They trooped off as a group to have breakfast with, and say kind things about, Ronald Reagan, the Republican candidate for Governor of California."[259] But this seemingly benign, happy breakfast was to become the first instance of an obvious rift between Reagan and Romney.

Reagan hosted all the Republican governors at the Los Angeles Country Club. Suddenly, Romney set himself as the group's leader and asked out loud what they all thought of Republican nominee Reagan's views on civil rights?   Reagan answered that he hated bigotry but had indeed opposed the 1964 Civil Rights Act; Reagan had said many times that he had opposed it because it took away the rights of business and property owners. Romney, the guest of Reagan, was "the one governor who broke the veneer of formal cordiality." Romney was simply quite rude to his host. Romney then proceeded to attempt to oust Idaho Governor Robert Smylie, a future Reagan supporter in 1967-1978, from chairmanship of the group. As the meeting ended, the Republican governors were described as wanting in 1968 a choice other than Nixon or Romney.[260]

As his post-primary victory vacation on the beach was coming to its end, Reagan wrote directly to Eisenhower on July 22. He wrote to Eisenhower, "Freeman called and read your letter to me with the very sound advice and suggestions—some of which are already being put into action," just as Gosden himself had written as noted above. But then Reagan detailed how he again was following Eisenhower's political mentoring and reflected in private to Eisenhower the exact words he himself had spoken when he had announced his candidacy six months earlier and for which the general had just written and Reagan was replying: "I am in complete agreement about dropping the hyphens that presently divide us into minority groups. I'm convinced this 'hyphenating' was done by our opponents to create voting blocks for political expediency…Once again I'm indebted to you for giving me the benefit of your thinking and experience."[261]

The original hand-written two-page letter from Reagan to Eisenhower on July 22, 1966 lies now in a special vault for preservation at the Dwight D. Eisenhower Presidential Library in Abilene. Throughout his future 1968 campaign, anytime Reagan would be asked about liberal versus conservative Republicans, he would echo Eisenhower's advice that hyphenating was a divisive tactic and instead Reagan wanted everyone called Republicans. Plus Reagan would follow Eisenhower's lead, as noted first enunciated by President Theodore Roosevelt many decades earlier, by applying the same idea to Americans as a whole when Reagan, echoing his own January 4 broadcast, ended his letter: "One is not an Irish-American for example but is instead an American of Irish descent."   Reagan did not refer to Roosevelt at the time, but Reagan in 1968 would demonstrate his detailed knowledge of his predecessor Roosevelt's handling of a major foreign crisis involving hostages.

Common Sense

Eisenhower corresponded with another friend, and on August 19, 1966, Eisenhower answered the friend's prior letter, which had predicted a Reagan victory that fall. Eisenhower in part wrote:

"Over the past year I have had two or three **satisfying** conversations with Ronald Reagan and on top of that have had some correspondence with him… He is *not* the 'darling of the far right.' He seems to me to represent a **common sense** and progressive philosophy of government and an individual's relationship to his government."[262]   (author's emphasis)

Thus by the summer of 1966 Eisenhower was quite comfortable in endorsing and continuing to advise Reagan, via multiple phone conversations and letter writing. What Eisenhower and Reagan had discussed during their multiple conversations beyond those at Gettysburg, which Eisenhower found satisfying, is not known. But clearly further political advice, specific discussions on domestic policies and Vietnam or other discussions of foreign affairs, perhaps Eastern Europe and dealing with the Soviet Union, are most likely.

Eisenhower's use of "satisfying" is significant as well, for it indicated that in Eisenhower's mind, Reagan had passed muster. Indeed this may be the point where Reagan passed from Eisenhower's political student to one of his political protégés.

But there is much more to Eisenhower's direct influence on Reagan in 1966 than endorsement and advising. In fact, Ronald Reagan's entire gubernatorial campaign themes, "citizen-soldier" and "common sense," came from Eisenhower. As we will see, Reagan would make his gratitude and indebtedness to Eisenhower known at a press conference in July, 1968. Reagan clearly had seen Eisenhower's letters to him and those written to go-betweens like Gosden and Jones.

Besides "common sense," the other major Reagan 1966 campaign theme, announced in his January 4 speech, was Reagan as "citizen-politician." Eisenhower had viewed himself as the "citizen-soldier," a latter-day Cincinnatus.[263] It is highly likely that Reagan, who modeled so much of his campaign after Eisenhower and the general's direct advice, modeled his own "citizen-politician" campaign slogan directly after Eisenhower's "citizen-soldier." Reagan's 1966 motto would morph into his 1968 campaign film, *Ronald Reagan, Citizen Governor*.

But the 1966 Reagan campaign theme of "common sense" was used by him often as well, and clearly the source for this term was none other than Eisenhower. As author Lou Cannon quotes of

Reagan's numerous speeches at the time, "I am an ordinary citizen... and it's high time that more ordinary citizens brought the fresh air of **common sense** thinking to bear on these problems."[264] (author's emphasis) What better way to pay homage to his mentor than by continuing to follow coach Eisenhower's instructions exactly and to model himself after his coach?

Eisenhower began to keep a diary in August, 1966, which was the first diary he had kept since he had left office in 1961. The hand-written comments mainly reflected his medical status: symptoms of any chest pain, his use of nitroglycerine, and his general health. But at this time as the fall elections loomed, his diary notes indicate that he was becoming more involved with Republican Party politics once again.

Over the next six weeks, Eisenhower had lunch at the White House, visited the Army War College, attended a Republican dinner in Chicago, spent a full day at a Republican advisory committee, and went to the Defense College.[265]

On October 6, Eisenhower told the press that as America had decided to use force to help an ally remain free from communism, it should use "whatever way is necessary to do it." That meant the full force of the American arsenal.[266] Eisenhower made no specific diary entries about Reagan at this point, but likely his ongoing political coaching of Reagan contributed to his feeling of reinvolvement with his party.

Hollywood

Reagan appeared on the cover of *Time* in early October, and in the cover story, Reagan's media campaign was noted. No one could know that exactly a year later, Reagan's appearance on a future *Time* cover would stir even more political speculation. Meanwhile, Reagan's gubernatorial campaign team created simple, spot announcements for television to lessen the number of personal appearances Reagan had to make.[267] Reagan's team needed Hollywood's expertise, but suddenly it was in Hollywood where an old campaign problem resurfaced.

On October 26, Gosden wrote to Eisenhower telling of a fund-raising dinner that had just been held at the home of Hollywood mogul Jack Warner. At the dinner, fellow mogul Samuel Goldwyn, who had been born into a Chasidic Jewish family and who previously had written a letter praising Reagan and America, had a pro-Reagan letter he had written read aloud by actor Jimmy Stewart. Goldwyn, by endorsing Reagan this way, clearly put to final rest any lingering concerns that Reagan harbored any anti-Semitism. Reagan agent Taft Schreiber was at the dinner, and he commented that Goldwyn's letter about Reagan was very heart warming, and Stewart's reading of it had had great effect upon everyone at the dinner. Gosden wanted Eisenhower to read the Goldwyn letter and asked Eisenhower to follow-up himself to Goldwyn.[268]

Eisenhower helped Reagan again on October 31. He first wrote to Gosden that Goldwyn's letter about Reagan was a "masterpiece." The same day, Eisenhower wrote the letter to Samuel Goldwyn, commenting on Goldwyn's letter supporting Reagan for governor, "I was deeply touched by your eloquent statement expressing pride in your American citizenship and the love you bear for your country."[269] Gosden wrote back to Eisenhower that Goldwyn was deeply touched by Eisenhower's letter. Indeed, Mrs. Goldwyn cried when she listened to the general's thoughts.[270]

One of the points Eisenhower had made to Reagan in that first 1965 letter was to seek out the press. Nofziger, always suspicious of the liberal, biased media, helped to maintain Reagan's good relations with the press.[271] As Reagan's run for the 1968 nomination began, he would meet with the press before and after almost every campaign stop or speech and in airplanes and busses. And Reagan would make numerous television news and interview appearances coupled with major articles in national magazines and newspapers during his first presidential campaign.

Reagan continued to use his Eisenhower-inspired term "citizen politician." As seen earlier, Reagan pushed the idea that he was an outsider; he wanted to bring fresh "common sense" solutions to Sacramento. This forced Brown to defend himself against being called a "professional politician."[272] Reagan's travels and televised talks showcased "his strongest political asset—his speaking ability— as a means of building support."[273] Reagan would modify "citizen politician" into "citizen governor" for 1968.

Reagan appealed to, and was helped by, politicians across the political spectrum in 1966; in 1968 he would emulate those tactics. As noted, Nixon did campaign for Reagan for governor. But Nixon was busy shoring up support with conservatives and cementing his relationship with Goldwater.[274] Nixon campaigned across the country, but in one instance he did more harm than good. On October 24 while in Oregon, he forgot the name of the Republican gubernatorial candidate. He blurted out "Bob McCall," until the audience shouted out, "It's Tom! It's Tom!" McCall was miffed.[275] Payback would follow in 1968.

Meanwhile Yorty, the conservative Democrat who had lost to Brown in the Democrat primary, had met Reagan to discuss how he could help Reagan.[276] Back in 1952, Congressman Yorty had helped actor Edward G. Robinson fend off accusations of being a communist. Reagan's testimony for the congressional HUAC committee, of which Nixon was a member, was discussed earlier. By 1960, conservative Democrat Yorty had so despised the Kennedys that he had penned an anti-Kennedy book.

In 1966, Yorty helped Reagan establish closer ties to the Mexican American community, and Reagan's appeal to conservative Hispanics led to the formation of Mexican American Democrats for Reagan. As a model to emulate, Eisenhower had targeted minority groups in 1952 and in 1956 with the slogans "Me Gusta Ike" and "Yo Quiero Ike" (I Like Ike; I Want Ike) run by Latinos con Eisenhower and a Los Angeles businessman.[277] In 1966, Mexican American Democrats for Reagan, headed by businessman Dr. Francisco Bravo, created the slogan "Ya Basta?!" (Had Enough?) for Reagan.[278] Reagan's huge 1966 success in attracting a large plurality of Mexican American voters is reviewed by your author elsewhere.[279] Bravo would return to help Reagan in 1968.

Reagan again followed Eisenhower's advice, and besides going after the Mexican American vote, Reagan targeted other groups typically thought of as in the Democrat fold. As a result, there were "Labor For Reagan," "Farmers For Reagan," "Union Workers For Reagan," "Youth for Reagan" and "Senior Citizens For Reagan" groups.[280] Reagan, eyeing the more than a million Democrat votes cast against Brown in the Democrat primary, went out of his way to continue inviting disaffected Democrats to join him.[281] And what of Reagan and Eisenhower's multiple comments not to break Americans into subgroups? Historian Curtis Patrick reviews that Reagan objected to the names of the various pro-Reagan support groups. But there is no indication Reagan made any attempt to stop them. For example, Reagan joined in and enjoyed riding horseback in Mexican American communities.[282]

Eisenhower's public endorsement of Reagan defused any accusations that Reagan was an extreme far right-wing candidate. Reagan knew from Eisenhower that he had difficulties in more liberal northern California, and thus Reagan followed Ike's advice to target Northern California. Reagan's northern California director, Tom Reed, arranged for Reagan to campaign specifically in smaller cities, towns and rural areas instead of liberal San Francisco and Oakland.

Individual Reagan campaign booklets addressed a different campaign topic, such as "crime" or "academic freedom."[283] Television ads featured actors John Wayne, Jimmy Stewart and Irene Dunne all endorsing Reagan.[284] Some 50,000 copies of the Reagan autobiography *Where's the Rest of Me?* were distributed.[285] In 1968, Students for Reagan would send out more Reagan political biographies and Reagan speeches to campuses across the country.

As the campaign neared its end, Reagan issued the first of several "Issue of the Week" speeches, which would serve as the template for Reagan's 1968 series of White Paper speeches. Then Reagan participated in telethons and answered voter questions. The first modern campaign house party, "Reagan Team Barbecue," reached thousands of voters via simultaneous broadcasts across California.[286] The Reagan television final blitz reached its zenith just before Election Day, with over 400 television spots and a five-minute pitch every night on each of thirteen key California television stations.[287] In 1968 such last minute Reagan television blitzes in Wisconsin, Nebraska and Oregon, and a special newspaper tabloid insert in Portland, all would have their origins in what Reagan had pioneered in 1966.

Meanwhile Democrat Brown's own foray into Hollywood became a nightmare. When Brown attacked Reagan because he was an actor, the actor Jack Palance walked out of a Democratic telethon in disgust.[288] Liberal actor Robert Vaughn, television's *Man from U.N.C.L.E.*, sent a telegram to Reagan saying, "You have covered yourself with dignity."[289][290] Frank Sinatra, also a known Democrat, was so upset that he called the Reagan campaign and offered, "What can I do?"[291]

Rockefeller Helps Reagan's Opponent

As seen earlier, New Yorkers Rockefeller and Lindsay had attempted to defeat Reagan in the primary. Historian Todd Holmes has unearthed documentation that Rockefeller was an active opponent of Reagan's run for the governorship in the general election too. Rockefeller had broken from the party and had not supported Goldwater in 1964, yet there is no evidence that he supported Johnson publicly. Yet in 1966 Rockefeller decided actively to help the Democrat incumbent against fellow Republican Reagan. Governor Brown wrote a letter to Rockefeller in which Brown thanked Rockefeller for "his fine campaign advice." What this advice was not clear in the historical record.[292] After Reagan would win the race for governor, Hinman would write that Rockefeller had "very mixed feelings about the result out there."[293] But another liberal New Yorker was about to take a much more active role against Reagan in the fall campaign: Reagan's old nemesis, Robert F. Kennedy

RFK Campaigns Against Reagan

Whether Kennedy asked Brown if he could come to campaign against his enemy Reagan, or whether Brown asked Kennedy, is not clear. But the memories of his multiple attempts to thwart and discredit Reagan certainly must have been fresh in Kennedy's mind, and likely Kennedy relished the chance to aid directly in Reagan's defeat for his first run for political office.

As reviewed by historian Joseph Lewis, Brown aired a campaign commercial showing him accosting a group of black children, saying, "I'm running against an actor, and you know who shot Lincoln, don'tcha?" Invoking the assassinated Lincoln would perhaps foreshadow events to occur in the near future to both RFK and Reagan. The ad, attempting to link actor Reagan with actor John Wilkes Booth, was created in extremely poor taste. But despite Republican outrage and demands that it be withdrawn, the Democrats "showed it around the clock in the last week."[294]

What is not so well known is that the campaign film segment that had attempted to associate Reagan with Booth was just one segment of a longer thirty minute film documentary about Brown which had been created by a documentary expert, Charles Guggenheim. The biographical film, *Man vs. Actor*, was scheduled to be shown one-hundred times before the election.[295] Guggenheim had sifted through thousands of film clips to create the film. Prior to being flown to California for the film project by local California Democrats, Guggenheim had worked for Robert Kennedy in New York. Whether RFK had spoken to Guggenheim about Reagan before Guggenheim left RFK to work for the Brown campaign is not known. But to attempt to link Reagan with Booth to a group of black youngsters and the film viewers demonstrated an intense hatred for candidate Ronald Reagan.

Historian Craig Shirley noted that not only were California voters "appalled" by the Brown campaign ad, but actor Dan Blocker, who played Hoss Cartwright on the television western *Bonanza*, the success of which as we have seen may have been one factor in the cancellation of Reagan's *General Electric Theater*, was so upset by the Brown ad attacking Reagan that actor Blocker "renounced his endorsement of Brown."[296]

But as historian Bill Boyarsky has related, RFK also came himself to California to campaign directly against Ronald Reagan. During the final pre-election months that fall of 1966, Brown's campaign had not been doing well against Reagan. First, Vice-President Humphrey came to help by campaigning against Reagan in late September, which temporarily gave the Brown campaign "a lift."[297] President Johnson was to visit but the trip was cancelled due to surgery. Brown's main outside help against Ronald Reagan turned out to be from Reagan's nemesis, Robert F. Kennedy.

Kennedy landed in California late on October 21, 1966. Although he was greeted by some three hundred people at the Los Angeles airport, "Roughly half the placards they carried were hostile, carrying such inscriptions as... 'Beware this is Yorty country.'"[298] Earlier in the year, "Kennedy had become involved in an argument with Los Angeles Mayor Samuel Yorty...over Yorty's handling of Negro slums." [299]As noted, Yorty had run against Brown in the Democrat gubernatorial primary and had lost. Afterwards, Yorty had become a "leader-and a symbol-of the Democrats who had left their party and gone over to Reagan,"[300] and as we have seen, Reagan and Yorty had met resulting in Yorty's suggestion to go after Hispanic voters. At the future Reagan victory party the night Reagan would win the governorship, one of the first people "hurrying over to congratulate Reagan was Mayor Sam Yorty".[301] Yorty's further deteriorating relationship with the Kennedys will be discussed below.

That evening, "The Senator made a single veiled reference to Governor Brown's Republican opponent, Ronald Reagan," wondering in part "whether California will retreat to the answers of another day, searching for a certainty that is gone, shrinking from the burden of leadership and decision in this last third of the twentieth century." [302] One can only speculate what RFK, had he lived, would have thought of those words of pessimism about Reagan which he had uttered in 1966 after future President Reagan's triumphs of masterminding the peaceful fall of communism, of creating a booming economy, and of reinstilling pride of nation in the spirit of the American people. As we will see, at a future White House ceremony, RFK's brother Ted would feel differently about Reagan than his brother had in the 1960s.

The next day was October 22 and "in the interest of defeating Ronald Reagan, Senator Robert F Kennedy tried today to make up with Los Angeles." RFK held television interviews, news conferences, and spoke at rallies all day on behalf of Brown. He mentioned Yorty, who had just three days before accused Kennedy of "having come to California to run for President"; Yorty had predicted that Kennedy's visit "would hurt rather than help the Brown cause."[303] As discussed, Yorty had supported Nixon over Robert's brother John in the 1960 presidential election and had even written a book *Why I Can't Take Kennedy* at that time. One can surmise that Yorty's support for Reagan must have intensified RFK's dislike for each.

But the reporter did note, "Senator Kennedy went to some lengths to avoid specific criticism of Mr. Reagan." Kennedy was asked two specific questions about Reagan: Did RFK think the former motion picture actor "was qualified to be Governor?" Kennedy did not answer the question directly but just praised Brown. When he was next asked if he had an opinion about Reagan's qualifications, RFK again did not answer directly but just said that Reagan was "not as good as Pat Brown."[304]

Then RFK made a "high-speed tour"[305] campaigning alongside Brown "in the southern and northern parts of the state. With Kennedy at his side, Brown drew his biggest crowds; he (Brown) later said that if he won, the credit would have to go to the senator."[306] But in fact the crowds were there mainly to see Kennedy himself and were described as "young people more interested in joining a Kennedy crusade."[307]

But as occurred when he had landed in California a few days before, Robert Kennedy once again would encounter hostility when he campaigned against Ronald Reagan towards the end of that short October campaign trip.

Norwalk, California lies south of Los Angeles and in 1966 was a community of skilled and semi-skilled workers especially in the local aerospace industry and government mental health hospital in town. Although a clear majority of voters had been traditionally Democrat, concerns about taxes, burgeoning welfare programs and open-housing laws were mounting. Reagan had campaigned here in April 1966 and "the reception was enthusiastic".[308] Specifically at Lakewood Shopping Center, even though he visited midweek, "Reagan was surrounded by more than five hundred people yelling 'Good luck" and 'Give 'em hell about the unions.'"[309] A later photograph in the *Los Angeles Times* shows Reagan at the shopping center being greeted by banners proclaiming not domestic themes but rather "H-Bomb Hanoi," and "Support Our Troops in Vietnam."[310]

Unmentioned in any of the classic or recent RFK biographies, historian Bill Boyarsky related that Kennedy, in mid October, went to the same shopping center as Reagan had months earlier. But when RFK appeared, teenagers held signs "telling Kennedy to go home. Obscene slogans were scrawled on many of the signs, and the senator had difficulty speaking as the mob milled about him. Bobby Kennedy was no hero to the youngsters at the Lakewood Shopping Center."[311] Perhaps RFK, used to adulation from the young, may have started to sense for the first time that Ronald Reagan was no ordinary political opponent and also was someone who could attract young voters by offering hope. Kennedy and the Democrats had a seeming lock on minority voters. But a new challenger had arisen who was attractive to minority voters too: Ronald Reagan. And Dr. Bravo continued his campaigning for Reagan to make inroads with this normally Democrat constituency.

Incumbent Brown, in his "political death throes" as the campaign was winding down, started telling his crowds that Reagan's ultimate goal was not in Sacramento but in Washington, D.C.[312] Nofziger flew twice to the nation's capital to warn conservative media columnists that if they wanted "to sink Ron, the best way in the world is to keep mentioning him as a possible Presidential candidate."[313] The columns, which speculated about Reagan's 1968 campaign stopped, at least temporarily, until he had won.

Eisenhower's Letter

Historian Maria Petrini showed, via analysis of White House audiologs, that on September 30 in Chicago, Eisenhower's comments on the war were interpreted by the press as calling for the "use of all necessary force" in Vietnam.[314] On October 3, Eisenhower told Johnson that if he still were president, he would want to be "winning as quick as I could…I think that winning the war should be the number one priority."[315] Johnson appreciated Republican Eisenhower's advice but also shrewdly, Johnson had included the general in his outer group of advisors in case anything went wrong.[316] But it was the height of election season and partisan Johnson continued attacking Republicans.

During mid October, Eisenhower wrote in his diary that Johnson's political attacks during the election campaign were "far from inspiring." Johnson had called the Republicans a "party of fear," and Eisenhower—upset enough at Johnson's mishandling of Vietnam—then described Johnson's political actions as "weak and cowardly." Eisenhower wrote that his hero, Lincoln, "could laugh" at his opponents—in contrast to Johnson's comments, which were "all so false."[317]

One tangible, though admittedly small, direct help that Eisenhower made was a financial contribution to the Reagan for governor campaign.[318] Then Eisenhower thought about how else he could help his new protege, as he could not campaign directly for Reagan—or any other Republican—due to his own heart condition. The *Los Angeles Times* just had endorsed Reagan for governor, and Eisenhower himself had done the same previously as seen earlier. So in the Sunday edition of the newspaper, Eisenhower wrote a letter to the newspaper commending it "for its endorsement of Reagan." Then Eisenhower, after explaining to California voters that although he did winter in Palm Desert he was still a legal voter in Pennsylvania, he added,

"As one who has deep affection for California, if I were a citizen of your state, I would enthusiastically vote for the entire Republican ticket and would urge my California friends to do the same,"[319]

The headline became "Eisenhower Backs Reagan and GOP California Slate."

The Media's Nightmare

Some news reporters indeed did wonder in 1966 if Reagan was thinking of running for president in 1968. After his Seattle speech, at an early summer news conference when a reporter had asked him whether if he were elected governor whether he would serve all four years, Reagan answered in the affirmative. The same reporter quickly then followed up asking if Reagan could make a "flat statement about his intentions," to which Reagan replied, "I have. What more flat statement could I make?"[320] Reagan soon would learn that he would be asked continuously about his desires to enter the 1968 presidential race for another two years.

Once the general election campaign had begun, it did begin to dawn—even on some at the *New York Times*—that Reagan might indeed win the governorship and have his eyes on the White House. In one mid-summer review about potential Republican presidential candidates for 1968, three names were listed: "George Romney, Richard Nixon, Ronald Reagan."[321]

As the fall general election approached, as noted earlier, *Time* did a cover story on Reagan and discussed his campaign techniques. The magazine noted, "A victory for Reagan will inevitably catapult him onto the national scene…His name is certain to crop up in connection with the party's vice presidential and even presidential nominations in 1968."[322]

Governor-Elect

Ronald Reagan was elected governor of California by almost a million vote margin over incumbent Brown. Reagan's massive victory was made possible in no small measure by votes of former Christopher supporters, votes of labor union members (some 40 percent of union members and half the votes of union members' wives)[323] , votes of young Republicans, votes in heavily Democratic districts, and by somewhere between 20 to 50 percent of the votes of Mexican Americans.[324]   With these Mexican American voters, Reagan "ran more strongly in this community than any Republican had ever done."[325]   But behind the scenes had been Reagan's hidden mentor, Ike.

Dwight Eisenhower first had advised Reagan to enunciate clearly and precisely what his political principles were, to repeatedly state them forcefully to the public and also to meet the press so that his policies would receive wide coverage. Eisenhower never advised Reagan to change his political philosophy with the political winds and fickle public opinion.

Reagan did not win in 1966 by compromising, or by changing his conservative views, to appeal to Independents and Democrats. He stayed a consistent conservative and made those Democrats and Independents realize that his views were their views. He never attempted to be a Democrat-lite. The Democrats and Independents came to Reagan's conservative philosophy and not vice-versa.

Kennedy's fight against Reagan on behalf of Brown did not work. The fall of 1966 marked the initial and only time when RFK campaigned directly against Reagan prior to 1968. Even though RFK was a surrogate for Brown, in the election results with Reagan's landslide victory, Kennedy did not seem to be able to make any significant impact with voters when he fought against Reagan.

When one imagines what a 1968 Reagan-RFK national election might have been like, one must realize that in 1966 Reagan was able to attract not insignificant numbers of supporters from the youth, from unions, as we have seen from minority groups such as Mexican-Americans, and thus Kennedy—besides the drubbing he would receive by debating Reagan the following spring—may have had a very difficult time if he would have faced Reagan in the fall of 1968. How well Reagan had fared, despite Kennedy's personal campaigning on behalf of Brown, coupled with how well Reagan would debate Kennedy six months later, all would have major impact on the thinking of Republicans as to who would be their best nominee for 1968.

Eisenhower was elated with the election results, and these Republican victories impacted his health—for the better. Prior to Election Day, he wrote in his diary that his angina was due to either over-eating or "tension." On the morning of November 9 after the results were known, he wrote, "The world looks better... the Republicans made significant gains...No pains." On November 9 he again wrote, "No pains," and by November 29 he wrote proudly, "I've had no serious chest pains—in the past ten days."[326] Eisenhower did not write the names of any specific Republican winners in his diary, but as we will see he certainly was proud that he had been the hidden political coach, and public endorser and advocate, of the new governor-elect of California.

Other prominent Republicans, of course, watched the national election results too. When Rockefeller was re-elected, he declared that he was finished seeking the presidency and endorsed Romney for the 1968 nomination.[327] Nixon took a suite at New York's Drake Hotel to watch the returns. After Reagan won, Nixon did not have to worry about not being able to phone Reagan this time, as Reagan called him first to offer congratulations for all the hard work Nixon had done helping Republicans including himself. Nixon took the call and came out saying, "He's all right, Ron is—it's a sweep in California too."[328]

For Richard Nixon, who had lost to Brown four years earlier, now to have to congratulate Reagan who had defeated Brown, it must have been awkward at best. Nixon does not mention how he felt in his autobiography. But his new advisor Patrick Buchanan knew that Nixon's main threat for 1968 was not Rockefeller. Nixon's main threat was Mr. Conservative; for Reagan "could pull the conservatives away from Nixon."[329] And in the spirit of the children's game rock-scissors-paper, the theme of "Brown beats Nixon, Reagan beats Brown" would end up as a major part of the most effective tactic the Reagan campaign would use against Nixon in 1968.

Even the *New York Times* saw where Reagan was headed: "Without a day in public office, he became the favorite presidential candidate of Republican conservatives."[330] In particular, young conservatives were thrilled. New conservative political star Reagan "represented the political future for those in Young Americans for Freedom."[331]

Eisenhower's teaching to enlarge the party's tent had helped Reagan achieve victory with the aid of labor and Mexican-Americans. In Massachusetts, Republican Ed Brooke had made history by being the first black senator elected by a white majority and Reagan immediately wrote to him congratulating him on a victory over bigotry, for showing Americans that a man could rise as far as his abilities and talents could take him, and that the Republican Party was a party of "all the people."[332] Previously when Reagan had traveled to New England in late September 1965, Reagan had met Brooke who was the attorney general of Massachusetts. Reagan cared not that Brooke was black, for Reagan was described as the "most inclusive" politician anyone had met.[333] Reagan, when asked in November, 1966 if the party's victories were due to white racism, answered, "I find it very difficult to assess the Republican victory on the basis of white backlash when it's the Republican Party that elected the first Negro to the United States Senate in almost a hundred years."[334]

But Reagan was not given time to enjoy the fruits of his victory, for his winning of the governorship in front of his staunch, eager, and enthusiastic grass roots supporters and his campaign team eyed him onwards to the presidency in 1968. During his first run for the presidency, he would need all the wisdom he was learning from Eisenhower coupled with all the strategies, skills, and tactics he had witnessed in 1964 and had used triumphantly himself in 1966.

Endnotes

1. Cannon, p. 133
2. Vidal, Gore "The Best Years of Our Lives" *New York Review of Books*, 9/29/1983
3. Alexander, Shana "My Technicolor Senator," *Life*, 12/4/64, p. 30
4. "Eisenhower Meets Reagan and Backs Him for Governor," *NYT*, 6/16/66, p. 1
5. White and Gill, p. 24
6. Eliot, p. 334
7. Kingston Enterprise 5040, 10/30/64
8. Highlights of LBJ's Telephone Conversations, Citation 5968, Robert F. Kennedy, Tape WH6410.15, Program No. 1, 10/26/64, Lyndon Baines Johnson Presidential Library
9. the newer 1964 version featured John Cassavetes, Lee Marvin, Angie Dickinson, and Reagan.
10. Evans, p. 164
11. Evans, p. 164-165
12. Evans, p. 165
13. ibid
14. Boyarsky, *The Rise of Ronald Reagan*, p. 103-104
15. Frisk, p. 185
16. Valory, pers int 1/20/13; Ince, pers int 1/18/13; Curtis Patrick vol II., p. 294
17. Novak, p. 153
18. Buchanan, p. 15-16
19. White, p. 48
20. Frisk, p. 189
21. Thorburn, p. 123
22. ibid
23. Young, pers. Int., 6/15/2015
24. Brinkley, D. personal communication, 5/6/2015
25. Vidal, Gore
26. Vidal, ibid
27. Eisenhower, Dwight D "Speech to the 1964 GOP Convention," *NYT*, 7/15/1964
28. Reed, The Reagan Enigma, p.54
29. Andrew, p. 192
30. Thorburn, p. 108

31. Thorburn, p. 121
32. Andrew, p. 192
33. Thorburn, p. 119
34. Thorburn, p. 122
35. Frisk, p. 189-190
36. White, p. 159-161
37. Kabaservice, p. 114
38. Evans, p. 165
39. ibid
40. Evans, p. 166
41. Kabaservice, pp. 119-120
42. Nixon, p. 262
43. ibid
44. Andrews, p. 203
45. ibid
46. Andrew, p. 206
47. Edwards, Lee, personal communication, 4/30/2015
48. Frisk, p. 193-194
49. Pipes, p. 290-291
50. Edwards, Lee, pers. communication, 4/30/2015
51. Reed, *Reagan Enigma*, p. 65
52. Lewis, Joseph, p. 51
53. Ronald Reagan, "A Time for Choosing"
54. Evans, p. 169
55. Evans, p. 169
56. Memorandum of Conversation: Dwight D. Eisenhower and Herbert Brownell, 10/30/64, Eisenhower, Dwight D.: Post-Presidential Papers, 1961-1969, DDE Appointment Books Series, Box 1, Calls and Appts 1964, Dwight D. Eisenhower Presidential Library
57. Memorandum of Conversation: Dwight D. Eisenhower and Bryce Harlow, 10/30/64, Eisenhower, Dwight D.: Post-Presidential Papers, 1961-1969, DDE Appointment Books Series, Box 1, Calls and Appts 1964, Dwight D. Eisenhower Presidential Library
58. Reed, Reagan Enigma pp 44-45
59. Greenstein, Fred
60. Memorandum of Conversation: Dwight D. Eisenhower and Herbert Brownell, 10/30/64, Eisenhower, Dwight D.: Post-Presidential Papers, 1961-1969, DDE Appointment Books Series, Box 1, Calls and Appts 1964, Dwight D. Eisenhower Presidential Library.
61. Eisenhower, Dwight D., Address Commemorating the Centennial of the Battle of Gettysburg Nov. 19, 1963
62. Nixon, p. 263
63. Lewis, Joseph, p. 7
64. Charlie Wascher, Shiawassee County Historical Society, personal communication. 2/9/13
65. Sandner, Al "Owosso Group Backs Reagan's Candidacy" Owosso Argus-Press 2/20/65 p. 13
66. ibid
67. ibid
68. Wascher op.cit.
69. Sandner, op.cit.
70. ibid
71. Sandner, op.cit.
72. Krock, Arthuer, "In the Nation," *NYT*,11/19/64
73. Alexander, Shana "My Technicolor Senator," *Life*, 12/4/64, p. 30
74. Owosso Argus-Press, 5/7/66, p. 1
75. Alexander, ibid
76. Cannon, *Governor Reagan*, p. 133
77. ibid
78. Cannon, *Governor Reagan,* p. 131-136; Edwards, Anne p. 487-489; Boyarsky, The Rise of Ronald Reagan p. 105-110; Deaver, A Different Drummer p. 20; Colacello, Bob "Ronnie and Nancy," *Vanity Fair*, 7/98 p. 135-136
79. Lewis, Joseph p. 11-12
80. Chester et. al., p. 194
81. Cannon, p. 131
82. Edwards, p. 488
83. Colacello, Bob
84. Edwards, Anne, p. 488
85. Boyarsky , *The Rise of Ronald Reagan*, p. 104
86. Cannon, *Governor Reagan*, p. 131-132

87.   Kabaservice, p. 122
88.   Cannon, p. 132
89.   Cannon, p.133
90.   Edwards, Anne, *Early Reagan*, p. 488
91.   Hayward, Steven "Here We Are on the Late Show Again," *Claremont Review of Books*, 8/31/2001
92.   Edwards, Anne, *Early Reagan*, p. 488
93.   Rusher, p. 195
94.   Buchanan, p. 14-19
95.   Buchanan, Chapter 2
96.   for a recent review of Johnson's decision not to attend Churchill's funeral see   http://townhall.com/columnists/davidstokes/2013/12/10/the-world-leader-who-didnt-attend-churchills-funeral-n1760692; reviews of Churchill and the FDR funeral are available at www.winstonchurchill.org
97.   Hayward
98.   Reagan, Ronald "The Triumph of Churchill's Principles", November 19, 1990
99.   Jacobs, p. 120
100.   Eisenhower, Dwight D. "Here was a Champion of Freedom" Finest Hour 166: 15, 2015
101.   Plumpton, John "The Funeral of Sir Winston S. Churchill" Finest Hour 66: 1990
102.   Johns
103.   Johns, p. 28
104.   Johns, p. 86-89
105.   Johns, p. 87
106.   Ambrose, p. 559
107.   Gibbs, p. 200, Skinner p. 706
108.   Frisk, p. 200-201
109.   Andrew, p. 211
110.   Thorburn, p. 145
111.   Novak, p. 165
112.   Reed's chapter 5 of *The Reagan Enigma*, Eisenhower the Mentor, was in fact the research this author gave Reed. Reed acknowledges this in his Acknowledgements but not in his text.
113.   In later years, Eisenhower would praise Thorpe
114.   Mills, Nicholas, "How His West Point Football Experience Inspired Eisenhower," *The Daily Beast*, 11/11/2014
115.   Boyarsky, p. 49-53.
116.   As discussed earlier, this film is seen on the 1955 movie marquee of Reagan's favorite movie, *Back to the Future*
117.   Its Always 'High Noon' at the White House," *NYT*, 4/25/2004
118.   Eliot, Mark, pers comm. 8/18/2013
119.   Thomas, Ikes, *Bluff*, p. 393
120.   Thomas, p. 363
121.   Thomas, p. 393
122.   Greenstein
123.   "President Resurrects Andrew Hogg Brown," *NYT*, 5/5/66, p. 11
124.   Eisenhower D., p. 281
125.   Eisenhower, David, p. 243
126.   Eisenhower, p. 59
127.   Ambrose, p. 559; Johns, p. 93
128.   Johns, p. 97
129.   *New York Times* ,10/7/1962; *Chicago Tribune,* 10/28/1962; *New York Times,* 12/8/1962; thus candidate Donald Trump's claim in early 2016 that he had coined the term "common sense conservative" in reality is not correct
130.   Trende, Sean, "The Underrated Eisenhower Coalition," Sabato's Crystal Ball, 11/20/2014
131.   Jacobs p. 276
132.   Dwight D. Eisenhower to Freeman Gosden, 7/15/65 letter, Eisenhower, Dwight D.: Post-Presidential Papers 1961-1969, Files of the Secretary of Dwight D. Eisenhower 1962-1966, Box 2 Politics PL-California, Dwight D. Eisenhower Presidential Library
133.   Cox, p. 16-17
134.   Jacobs, p. 44
135.   Cannon, p. 30
136.   Cannon, p. 17
137.   Brinkley, p. 114
138.   Brinkley, p. 115
139.   Schlesinger, Blumenfeld, Ralph "Bobby and Ike Clash over Riots," *NY Post,* 8/18/1965, p. 840

140. Ambrose, p. 559-560
141. Petrini
142. Dwight D. Eisenhower to Jim Murphy, 9/8/65 letter, Eisenhower, Dwight D.: Post-Presidential Papers 1961-1969, Files of the Secretary of Dwight D. Eisenhower 1962-1966, Box 2 Politics PL-California, Dwight D. Eisenhower Presidential Library
143. Dwight D. Eisenhower to Freeman Gosden, 9/22/65 letter, Eisenhower Post-Presidential Papers 1961-1969, Files of the Secretary of Dwight D. Eisenhower 1962-1966, Box 2 Politics PL-California, Dwight D. Eisenhower Presidential Library
144. "Local Group Raps Kuchel" Owosso Argus-Press 9/22/65, p. 16
145. IN-7 "Town Meeting of the World" 10/26/1965 CBS broadcast, Box 7, Dwight D Eisenhower Post-Presidential Papers 1961-1969, 1965 Principal File, Dwight D Eisenhower Presidential Library
146. Oulahan, Richard, and Lambert, William, "The Real Ronald Reagan Stands Up," *Life,* 1/21/66, p. 70-71
147. Smith, Robert letter, *Life*, 2/11/67, p. 17
148. Owosso Argus-Press 8/17/67, p. 7
149. Reed, *The Reagan Enigma*
150. Dallek
151. McKenna, K
152. Cannon, p. 134-135
153. McKenna, K, p. 28-29
154. Evans, Thomas, *The Education of Ronald Reagan*, p. 172
155. Kabaservice, p. 170
156. Curtis Patrick, vol 1, p. 225
157. Cannon, p. 137
158. Cannon, p. 138; Boyarsky, *The Rise of Ronald Ragan* p. 143; McKenna, K, p. 30-31
159. Cannon, p. 140
160. Cannon, p. 141
161. Curtis Patrick, vol. 1, p. 168
162. Kelley, p. 165
163. Gizzi, John, "The First Reaganaut," *Human Events*, 3/28/2006
164. youtube 0VNUOO7POXs
165. McKenna, K, p. 33
166. McKenna, K, p. 34
167. McKenna, K p. 35
168. Cannon, p. 144
169. McKenna, K, p. 41
170. McKenna, K, p. 43
171. McKenna, K, p. 50
172. McKenna, K, p. 51
173. McKenna, K, p. 46
174. Barclay, Tony "Reagan Hailed by Arena Crowd, Warns of 'Government Tyranny,'" *Yale Daily News*, 9/29/65, p. 1. At the time, GE was still in CT
175. ibid p 3
176. Reed, *Reagan Enigma*, p. 25-26
177. Lincoln Star, 3/28/1966, p. 15
178. "Nixon Seen More Likely Candidate," *Reading Eagle*, 3/28/66, p.4
179. Reed, *Reagan Enigma*, p. 53-54
180. Kabaservice, p. 171
181. ibid
182. Holmes, p. 7-8
183. Schlesinger, p. 934
184. Kabaservice, p. 172
185. Buchanan, p. 41
186. Dwight D. Eisenhower to Freeman Gosden, 6/2/66 letter, Eisenhower Post-Presidential Papers 1961-1969, Files of the Secretary of Dwight D. Eisenhower 1962-1966, Box 2 Politics PL-California, Dwight D. Eisenhower Presidential Library
187. Jacobs, p. 283-284
188. Kabaservie, p. 173
189. Dallek, p. 210
190. Kabaservice, p. 172
191. Donovan, Robert J. "Reagan's Victory: Nixon's Gain?," *Milwaukee Sentinel*, 6/12/1966 part 5, p. 3
192. "The Star Is Reagan," *NYT*, 6/12/66, p. 208
193. Reston, James "Washington: The Tragedy of the Republicans," *NYT*, 6/12/66, p. 218

194.   Dallek, p. 213
195.   Dallek, ibid
196.   Hill, Gladwin, "Reagan receives Pledge of Unity," *NYT*, 6/14/66, p. 28
197.   Thorburn, p. 146
198.   Thorburn, p. 146
199.   Frisk, p. 215
200.   McKenna, p. 43
201.   McKenna, p. 43-44
202.   Curtis Patrick. vol. 1, p. 138
203.   McKenna, p. 44
204.   Curtis Patrick, vol. 1, p. 138
205.   Nolan, pers int, 5/18/13
206.   Dallek, p. 214
207.   Kabaservice, p. 238
208.   Gibbs, p. 200
209.   Gibbs, p. 193
210.   Chester, p. 433
211.   Rusher, p. 201; Buchanan, p. 36-39
212.   Cannon, p. 139
213.   Skinner, Kiron, *Reagan: A Life In Letters*, p. 699-700
214.   Dwight D. Eisenhower to Ronald Reagan, 6/13/66 letter, Eisenhower, Dwight D.: Post-Presidential Papers 1961-1969, 1966 Principal File Box 44, Dwight D. Eisenhower Presidential Library
215.   "GOP Plans to Hail Reagan In Capital," *NYT*, 6/15/66, p. 22
216.   Ambrose, p. 560
217.   Ambrose, p. 561
218.   see Jacobs for Eisenhower's annoyance at being called away from the presidency of Columbia University to help Truman
219.   Ambrose, p. 561
220.   Johns, p. 112
221.   Broder, David "Eisenhower Meets Reagan and Backs Him for Governor," *NYT*, 6/16/1966, p. 1
222.   See Illustrations
223.   See Illustrations
224.   press conference at www.reagan68.com
225.   Reed, *The Reagan Enigma*, p, 47
226.   press conference available at www.reagan68.com
227.   "Eisenhower Meets Reagan and Backs Him for Governor," *NYT*, 6/16/66, p. 1
228.   Reed, *The Reagan Enigma*, p. 48
229.   Reed, Tom, personal communication, 9/18/2014
230.   Reed, *The Reagan Enigma*, p. 48
231.   described fully by Reed
232.   Krock, Arthur "In the Nation," *NYT*, 6/19/66, p. 175
233.   Kopelson, Gene, 2015A
234.   Burt, Lyle, "Reagan to Address GOP Here Saturday," *Seattle Times*, 6/13/66, p. 1
235.   *Seattle Times*, 6/17/66, p. 7,14,26,29
236.   Skreen CJ, "Actors in Politics Get 'Green Light', *Seattle Times*, 6/19/66, p. 97
237.   Kopelson, Gene, 2015A
238.   Lyle, Burt, "Conservative-Minded GOP Convention Cheers Reagan," *Seattle Times*, 6/19/66, p. 1
239.   Reed, *The Reagan Enigma*, p. 47
240.   "GOP Candidates Reagan, Nixon and Murphy," *Chicago Tribune*, 6/24/1968
241.   NBC News clip 5118369328_s01
242.   Ronald Reagan to Dwight D. Eisenhower, 7/6/66 letter, Eisenhower, Dwight D.: Post-Presidential Papers 1961-1969, 1966 Principal File, Box 44, Dwight D. Eisenhower Presidential Library
243.   Dwight D. Eisenhower to Leigh Battson, 6/24/66 letter, Eisenhower, Dwight D.: Post-Presidential Papers 1961-1969, Special Names Series, Box 5, Gosden, Freeman, Dwight D. Eisenhower Presidential Library
244.   Gosden to Dwight D. Eisenhower, 7/7/66 letter, Eisenhower, Dwight D.: Post-Presidential Papers 1961-1969, Special Names Series, Box 5, Gosden, Freeman, Dwight D. Eisenhower Presidential Library
245.   Hoffman, p. 28
246.   Hoffman, p. 36
247.   ibid

248. Cannon, p. 68
249. Cannon, *President Reagan*, p. 140
250. Cannon, p. 15
251. Cannon, *President Reagan*, p. 69, 518
252. Reagan, Ronald, "Remarks at the Site of the Future Holocaust Memorial Museum" 10/5/1988
253. TR was incensed that Americans were using hyphenated nationalities, initially fearing eventually it could lead to the break-up of the country. Historian Clay Jenkinson reviews Roosevelt's earliest call to avoid naming hyphenated Americans, while TR still was in the Dakota Territory, on July 4, 1886 in Dickinson. Later, TR saw the threat from German-Americans and from other similar immigrant groups during World War I. For a full discussion, see Thompson, J. Lee. Never Call Retreat. New York: Palgrave MacMillan, 2013
254. Dwight D. Eisenhower to Freeman Gosden, 7/11/66 letter, Eisenhower, Dwight D.: Post-Presidential Papers 1961-1969, Special Names Series, Box 5, Gosden, Freeman, Dwight D. Eisenhower Presidential Library
255. Freeman Gosden to Dwight D. Eisenhower, 7/15/66 letter, Eisenhower, Dwight D.: Post-Presidential Papers 1961-1969, Special Names Series, Box 5, Gosden, Freeman, Dwight D. Eisenhower Presidential Library
256. "Democrats Give Reagan 27,422 Votes," *Los Angeles Times*, 7/15/66, p. 36
257. Wicker, Tom, "Reagan's Role in '68," *NYT*, 7/8/66, p. 13
258. ibid
259. Broder, David, "The Governors Seem Out of the Mainstream," *NYT*, 7/10/66, p. 146
260. Evans and Novak, "Romney for First Time, Makes Leadership Move," *The Free Lance-Star*, Fredericksburg VA, 7/12/66, p. 4
261. Skinner, Kiron, p. 700-701
262. Dwight D. Eisenhower to Charles S. Jones, 8/19/66 letter, Eisenhower, Dwight D.: Post-Presidential Papers 1961-1969, Special Names Series, Box 11, Jones, Charles S. 1966, Dwight D. Eisenhower Presidential Library
263. Thomas, Ikes Bluff, p. 26
264. Cannon, p. 137
265. Eisenhower, Dwight. Diary Aug. 11, 1966-Dec. 8, 1966. Dwight D. Eisenhower Presidential Library, entries 8/26,66; 9/1/66; 9/29,66; 10/4/66; 10/11/66.
266. http://efootage.com/stock-footage/86873/Eisenhower_On_Vietnam_War_Stratagey_-_HD/
267. Boyarsky, *The Rise of Ronald Reagan*, p.138; Reed, *The Reagan Enigma*, p. 38
268. Freeman Gosden to Dwight D. Eisenhower, 10/26/66 letter, Eisenhower, Dwight D.: Post-Presidential Papers 1961-1969, Special Name Series, Box 5, Gosden, Freeman 1963-1966, Dwight D. Eisenhower Presidential Library
269. Dwight D. Eisenhower to Samuel Goldwyn, 10/31/66 letter, Eisenhower, Dwight D.: Post-Presidential Papers 1961-1969, Special Names Series, Box 5, Gosden, Freeman, Dwight D. Eisenhower Presidential Library
270. Freeman Gosden to Dwight D. Eisenhower, 11/2/66 letter, Eisenhower, Dwight D.: Post-Presidential Papers 1961-1969, Special Names Series, Box 5, Gosden, Freeman, Dwight D. Eisenhower Presidential Library
271. Boyarsky, p. 141
272. Boyarsky, *The Rise of Ronald Reagan*, p. 137
273. Hayward, Steven, "Here We Are On The Late Show Again," *Claremont review of Books*, 8/30/2001
274. Buchanan, p. 42-47
275. Buchanan, p. 83
276. Hill, Gladwin, "Rivals on Coast Chart Campaigns," *NYT*, 6/26/66 p. 43
277. Burt
278. See Illustrations
279. Kopelson, Gene, 2014C
280. McKenna, p. 64-66
281. Hill, Gladwin "Brown and Reagan Both Seek Votes From the Other's Party," *NYT*, 7/3/66, p. 16
282. Kopelson, 2014C
283. McKenna, p. 57-58
284. McKenna, p. 60
285. Langguth, Jack,"Political Fun and Games in California," *NYT*, 10/16/66, p. 248
286. McKenna p69
287. Hill, Gladwin "Indications are That California Voters Will Choose on Emotion and Instinct," *NYT*, 10/23/66, p. 80
288. Cannon, p. 151
289. Lewis, J, p. 136
290. Your author's attempt to interview Vaughn in the summer of 2015 went unanswered

291. "Interview with Stuart Spencer," Ronald Reagan Oral History Project, Miller Center of Public Affairs, University of Virginia, 11/15/2001, Tape 3, p. 29
292. Holmes, *The Ever-Shrinking Middle Ground*, p. 7-8
293. Holmes, p. 9
294. Lewis, J, p. 137
295. Hill, Gladwin, "Indications Are That California Voters Will Choose on Emotion and Instinct," *NYT*, 10/23/66, p. 80
296. Shirley, *Rendezvous with Destiny*, p. 10
297. Boyarsky, p. 127
298. Weaver Warren Jr, "Kennedy Praises California Gains," *NYT*, 10/22/66, p. 14
299. Boyarsky, p. 135
300. Boyarsky, p. 155
301. ibid
302. Weaver, op.cit., *NYT*, 10/22/66, p. 14
303. Weaver, Warren Jr, " Kennedy Courts Voters for Brown in Los Angeles," *NYT*, 10/23/66. p. 81
304. Weaver, ibid
305. Hill, Gladwin "Indications Are That California Voters Will Choose on Emotion and Instinct," *NYT*, 10/23/66, p. 80
306. Boyarsky, p. 127
307. ibid
308. Boyarsky, p. 134
309. ibid
310. *Los Angeles Times*, 11/5/1966
311. Boyarsky, p. 135
312. Lewis, J, p. 154-155
313. ibid
314. Petrini
315. Petrini
316. ibid
317. Eisenhower, Dwight. Diary Aug. 11, 1966-Dec. 8, 1966, 10/12/66
318. PL-3 Political Affairs, Box 11, Dwight D Eisenhower Post-Presidential Papers 1961-1969, 1966 Principal File, Dwight D. Eisenhower Presidential Library
319. "Eisenhower backs Reagan And GOP California Slate," *NYT*, 10/27/66, p. 52
320. Spartanburg Herald-Journal, 7/6/66, p. 1
321. Weaver, Warren Jr. "Republicans and '68: Platform takes Shape," *NYT*, 7/24/66, p. 133
322. "Ronald For Real," *Time*, 10/7/66, p. 31
323. Kabaservice, p. 190
324. Kopelson, 2014C
325. Cannon, p. 152
326. Eisenhower, Dwight. Diary Aug. 11, 1968-Dec. 8, 1968. 11/9/66; 11/10/66; 11/29/66
327. Rusher, *The Rise of the Right*, p. 192
328. Safire, p. 41
329. Buchanan, p. 40
330. Weaver, Warren Jr. "GOP Finds '68 Outlook Brighter as It Counts Election Successes," *NYT*, 11/10/1966, p. 1
331. Thorburn, p. 147
332. Kabaservice, p. 188
333. Reed, *The Reagan Enigma*, p. 27
334. http://www.upi.com/Archives/Audio/Events-of-1966/1966-Midterm-Election

CHAPTER 2: THE GOVERNOR-CANDIDATE

"He's going to be President someday."
~ Theodore H. White[1]

"Reagan controls 250 convention votes just by being elected."
~ Reagan staffer[2]

From Governor-elect to Presidential Candidate

Presidential historian Theodore H. White sat transfixed in front of the television on Election Day 1966. As the on-screen reporters turned to California's results, behind an elated Ronald and Nancy Reagan, a large "Reagan for President" banner was unfurled. White started taking notes on the new figure about to enter the national political scene: Ronald Reagan. When one of his friends asked White why he was bothering to watch a "broken-down actor" run for governor, White disagreed. White quickly did the political calculus and came to a momentous prediction, answering, "No. He's going to be President someday."[3][4]

Reagan's landslide win of almost a million votes made front-page news across the nation. The *New York Times* confirmed that "an enormous 'Reagan for President' banner was promptly unfurled,"[5] and the victory instantaneously had "magnified the 55-year old actor's state and national political stature."[6] At a press conference a few minutes after he had won the governorship, Reagan admitted that he "might play a significant part in the 1968 national election" but "conspicuously stopped short of any of the historic renunciations of Presidential interest."[7] Student activist Pat Nolan was at the Biltmore Hotel that evening and recalled seeing that Reagan-for-president banner unfurled. Nolan thought to himself that it was "too soon," as Reagan needed to prove himself first as governor.[8] Nolan also recalled that the banner itself did not stay unfurled for very long, because Reagan campaign aides quietly were saying, "No," and hastily took down the banner.[9] Although the banner was gone, the actual plans for Reagan to run for president in 1968—having been launched in 1964—would ascend further almost immediately.

Nancy Reagan later would recall that the very next morning, "The press was already asking whether he was planning to run for president as a favorite-son candidate in 1968. I guess that's the first time I remember thinking that the White House might be a possibility."[10] Her comments are somewhat disingenuous as she just had excluded his 1968 run in her list of his campaigns and counted only 1976 as "the only one he lost."[11] Also, she seems to have qualified her recollections saying that the press had asked about his plans to run as California favorite-son, but the press actually had no such qualification and wanted to know if he was running for the presidency directly in 1968.

The following day, although the *New York Times* front-page looked ahead to 1968 and concluded that Reagan had become, "without a day in public office, the favorite Presidential candidate of Republican conservatives,"[12] the editorial page felt that for Reagan, "talk of the presidency is distinctly premature in his case; he has yet to demonstrate any talents as Governor."[13] They would not be so critical of a political newcomer in 2008.

It took only one more day for other politicians to start to think of Ronald Reagan as a candidate for the 1968 presidency. Barry Goldwater told a news conference on November 10 that there were five possible Republican presidential candidates for 1968, one of whom was "Gov.-elect Ronald Reagan of California."[14]

On November 20, Reagan appeared on ABC's *Issues and Answers*. Despite his election as a domestic governor, immediately the press shifted the focus to foreign affairs. Governor-elect Reagan showed no hesitation in answering and invoked the name of his mentor by stating, "I agree with former President Eisenhower on Vietnam... The nation has a moral obligation to impose its full response to end it as soon as possible."[15]

Eisenhower Looks Ahead

As the California gubernatorial campaign had been nearing its end, Eisenhower friend and newspaper publisher Walter Thayer had sent Eisenhower a letter of his analysis of where things stood at that point for the 1968 Republican possibilities. Thayer did not seem enthusiastic about Rockefeller, Nixon, Romney, nor Percy. Then Thayer brought up Reagan, wondering to Eisenhower, if Reagan wins in California, Reagan would carry importance for 1968. Thayer was looking for a brand, new candidate for the presidency and asked Eisenhower if the general had any better suggestions?[16]

Eisenhower's answer on October 24, 1966 is most illuminating. Eisenhower devoted only one sentence to Nixon, writing that Nixon had "matured a great deal." He dismissed Percy in a few words. But Eisenhower devoted the largest paragraph to Reagan and went out of his way to tell Thayer that he had devoted time and energy to Reagan's campaign and that Eisenhower's analysis of Reagan indeed was quite positive—especially in Reagan again using common sense, or in this case, horse sense:

"I have had a number of talks with Ronald Reagan. By no means do I consider him the 'darling of the right wing.' In our discussions of specific issues, he has exhibited **good horse sense and considerable imagination**...He also is showing some maturity and **I for one have contributed my time to his campaign**."[17]   (author's emphasis) Eisenhower did not mention that he had made a financial contribution as well.

Here Eisenhower again mentions his multiple private conversations with Reagan and discussions of issues followed by Eisenhower's positive analysis of Reagan. So one may surmise that the two men chatted many times over the telephone, even though there are no such post-presidential phone logs at the Eisenhower Library. Or there may have been other personal meetings, besides that one noted earlier, the two men had which did not appear in the press. Likely they continued the topics Reagan and Eisenhower had discussed in person the prior June: domestic politics, Republican unity, and the war in Vietnam. It is also not unreasonable to assume that Eisenhower discussed how he had ended the Korean War by threatening to use nuclear weapons, the similarities and differences between the Korean and Vietnam Wars, and with both men having called for freedom, how to combat communism.

But as Eisenhower clearly was devoting his time to help coach Reagan, he was becoming more and more impressed with Reagan as one of his political protégés. And perhaps in his mind he confirmed his prior initial thinking that Ronald Reagan was fitting in quite well with his plans for the future of the party nationally. And perhaps he was starting to see that for the future of the Republican Party, winner Ronald Reagan might be replacing loser Richard Nixon. After all, Eisenhower had given Reagan much specific campaign advice and Reagan had followed Eisenhower's recommendations to the letter. As soon as Reagan had passed his first political test by winning the California primary, Eisenhower had endorsed Reagan for governor, had certified Reagan as presidential timbre, and had continued mentoring him with further advice. Now coach Eisenhower must have been quite pleased that his protégé had passed his second political test—being elected governor of the country's most populous state— with flying colors!

Just prior to Election Day, Reagan wrote a final letter of thank you as Republican Party gubernatorial nominee. Dated November 1, 1966, Reagan wrote to Eisenhower, not only to thank him, but to acknowledge Ike's original recommendation of stating Reagan's political beliefs and to seek his mentor's approval: "I'm deeply grateful to you. As I told you I'm working on a speech designed to make plain what are my political beliefs. If you wouldn't think it presumptuous I'd like to submit it to you once it takes shape and **have the benefit of your judgment**."[18] (author's emphasis)

After Reagan won the governorship, Eisenhower sent Reagan a congratulatory telegram on November 9, 1966: "Needless to say I am delighted that the voters of California have given you this great opportunity to all its citizens…A lot of hard work lies ahead and I am confident that your accomplishments as governor will command admiration and respect."[19]

Ike and Dutch: Foreign Affairs

Eisenhower was looking ahead, both to Reagan's inauguration and further into the future. In June, Eisenhower had critiqued Vietnam for Reagan. Now world affairs would become the next area that Eisenhower would mentor his protégé—just as Reagan would make his first run for the presidency.

On December 22, 1966, from Walter Reed Army Hospital in Washington, D.C., Eisenhower sent Reagan a letter of apology that due to his illness, he would be unable to attend Reagan's forthcoming inauguration as governor. But Eisenhower added, "**I do hope that sometime during the winter I can get a chance to talk with you— more about world affairs**."[20] (author's emphasis)

Here is the crux of Eisenhower's mentoring of Reagan as the future of the party. Previously Eisenhower had coached Reagan on entering Republican politics, and had some discussions of Vietnam at their first meeting and had continued coaching him repeatedly for the 1966 election. Reagan had followed Eisenhower's advice virtually to the letter and had succeeded as a major winner and new force within the national party. Why expand coaching Reagan—just a new governor-elect—further on world affairs? The answer is obvious: Eisenhower now wanted to expand his mentoring and start coaching Reagan, just elected with a huge margin of victory in the country's largest state, for the national stage as a future candidate for the presidency.

Owosso (again)

Exactly two years had passed since Owosso, Michigan had made national news when the Ronald Reagan for President in 1968 club announced its existence. But although the group had settled on a slightly different title, Republicans for Ronald Reagan (RRR), they made their presence known again as soon as Reagan won the governorship. At a news conference, Chairman Robert Smith reminded reporters of the original goal of his group and predicted, "The next President of the United States will be Ronald Reagan."[21] Smith revealed that over the past two years, RRR had been enrolling members in "nearly every state" accompanied by an "outpouring of bumper stickers, membership cards, and bulletins."[22] By the time Reagan had been elected governor, RRR had approximately 1,000 members and received their funding directly from members with no financial hidden "angel."[23]

The four RRR officers, mentioned earlier, revealed that had met privately with Reagan. They stressed that they could not "speak for Reagan," and said that their group had "not been discouraged by him" but neither had they "been encouraged by him."[24] When the RRR officers were asked by the press if they were part of a "Draft Reagan" movement, they answered emphatically that "more than that, Republicans for Reagan considers itself the spearhead of such a movement."[25] Finally when they were asked if it were not premature for a "Reagan for President in 1968" movement, Jorgensen and Smith did acknowledge that their original goal two years ago, the day Goldwater had lost to Johnson, of wanting Reagan to run for president in 1968, indeed had been premature. But now that Reagan was the new governor of California, such a grass roots effort to send Reagan to the presidency in 1968 was hitting its stride.[26]

Romney

In early November, a Louis-Harris poll had been released showing that Romney would beat President Johnson in 1968 by 54 percent to 46 percent and the pollster commented, "Mr. Romney stands a better chance of winning the White House than any Republican since Dwight D. Eisenhower." So on November 20, on ABC's *Issues and Answers*,

Reagan was asked if someone who had not supported Goldwater in 1964, i.e. Romney, should be nominated by the Republican Party. Reagan likely thought back to how Romney, his guest, had treated him in Los Angeles.

Reagan had strong personal opinions on the question, as evidenced by those angry comments directed at Republican "traitors" he had made after the Goldwater loss. The touchy subject had been reinforced by the advice and comments he had received in 1965 and thereafter by Eisenhower. Reagan showed, though, that he could forgive such a traitorous political act if the perpetrator saw the error of his ways. Reagan had not spoken ill of any fellow liberal Republican. He was giving Rockefeller, Romney, Lindsay and others a chance to say they had been wrong in 1964. Reagan answered the reporter, "Well a lot of that would deal with whether the individual repented or not. I don't think that a convention would probably support someone, let's say, who stayed aloof or who actually opposed the will of the party and then was completely unregenerate about this and said 'I was right, and the party was wrong.'"[27] But at the same time, Reagan was issuing a warning to his liberal Republican comrades that the party would not forgive a second time of failing to endorse the party's nominee. As we will see, despite Reagan offering a helping hand to Republican liberals, Reagan's warning to Romney would go unheeded.

Indeed he then tried to extend an olive branch to Kuchel. Reagan had not campaigned against Kuchel. Despite earlier Eisenhower pleas for unity from Kuchel, Kuchel had refused to endorse candidate Reagan. It was Reagan who now demonstrated "his inclusive spirit and magnanimous leadership" to Republican liberals and moderates.[28]

Eisenhower, Reagan, and the Eleventh Commandment

In his autobiography *An American Life*, Reagan explained that the origin of the famed Eleventh Commandment (Thou Shalt Not Speak Ill of Any Fellow Republican) had been during the California primary when Dr. Gaylord Parkinson first had suggested it.[29] Historian Craig Shirley recently reviewed how some politicians have misinterpreted the Eleventh Commandment by not wanting ever to criticize another Republican but having forgotten that Reagan cited the Eleventh Commandment solely to have Republicans avoid personal attacks on one another.[30]

Yet only a short time after Parkinson had proposed it for the California gubernatorial primary, Dwight Eisenhower proposed a corollary: that his own version of the Eleventh Commandment be applied on the national level for the 1968 campaign, and Eisenhower's decision-making involved Reagan too. A few weeks after Reagan's gubernatorial victory, as well as after the many Republican victories, Eisenhower wrote a letter to Republican Party National Chairman Ray Bliss. In it Eisenhower said he wanted to do something "to persuade Republican leaders to avoid any divisive efforts."

Eisenhower proposed hosting a luncheon with Bliss and all potential 1968 presidential candidates. Eisenhower listed, in this non-alphabetical order: Nixon, Romney, Percy, Reagan, Rockefeller and Hatfield. The general must have taken great pride to add to the list his newest protégé: Reagan. The purpose of the meeting would be to urge these "prospective aspirants the need for speaking of all the others only in favorable terms." Of course if this were impossible, Eisenhower suggested, "The next best thing would be to keep silent."[31] Thus one might argue that equal credit for the fabled Eleventh Commandment should be given not only to Parkinson but also to former President Eisenhower. However as a keen observer of the recently-completed California primary and general election campaigns, Eisenhower may have known of Reagan's and Parkinson's thoughts of party unity at the state level and only had sought to formalize it at the national party level.

Clearly in Eisenhower's astute mind, Reagan already had made the jump from political novice to governor-elect to presidential possibility. And surely Eisenhower realized that it was he who had guided Reagan on the trajectory to the top. In effect, Dwight Eisenhower had mentored novice politician Ronald Reagan and helped guide him to winning the governorship and now a potential president of the United States.

Johnson 67, Reagan 33

Newsweek ran its election analysis by reviewing Spencer-Roberts' hugely successful Reagan campaign techniques. Of course the subject of Reagan running for the 1968 presidency arose. One Reagan staffer told the magazine, "If he does a reasonably good job as governor, you're going to see the goddamndest draft movement for Reagan you've ever witnessed."[32] And others speculated about expanding Reagan's campaign style to "nationwide potential" for a 1968 run.[33] But other Reagan anonymous Reagan staffers disagreed saying, "Reagan just doesn't have the all-consuming desire to be President that Nixon has," and "to plunge immediately into a national thing—well it wouldn't come together."[34] However one thing was for sure. If Reagan did decide to run for the presidency in 1968: "Reagan could claim the delegate-rich Goldwater apparatus for the asking," as one staffer calculated that "Reagan controls 250 convention votes just by being elected."[35]

It took the Harris national polling organization just a few days to start asking voters whom they preferred for president in 1968. Now Reagan started to be included amongst those choices in trial heats. On November 20, it was reported that President Johnson handily would beat Reagan by 67 to 33 percent. But for Reagan, seen now as a 1968 presidential candidate, who just had won his first general election and who had not even taken office yet, to become the choice of one-third of American voters, simply was astounding.[36]

Then the *New York Times* took notice of Reagan as a full-fledged 1968 presidential candidate. On Thanksgiving weekend, the newspaper's *Sunday Magazine* ran a major analysis of all 1968 GOP candidates and included Reagan as an official contender. The multi-page spread was accompanied by a drawing of the Republican contenders on the "Good Ship G.O.P."[37] Reagan was drawn as a mid-shipman with a huge smile while holding two American flags. Ironically, a year later most of those Republican presidential contenders would be together on a real ship for a governors cruise to the Virgin Islands which would engender even more political speculations about 1968.

The magazine finally admitted they had to "stop making dull jokes" about the old Reagan Hollywood movies and from then on would "judge Reagan as a public servant and politician."[38] Reagan was described as having a "fast mind," but the eastern, elitist magazine made certain to add disdainfully that Reagan had a "somewhat primitive philosophy." The reporter conveniently forgot to add that the same philosophy had attracted a decisive majority of voters in the country's most populous state a few weeks before. Reagan used the same themes as had Goldwater but Reagan was seen as more plausible and reasonable.

The reporter then asked the main question: "Will Reagan become a real live candidate for President?"[39] Reagan could wait for 1972. Or Reagan could turn his conservative voters towards Nixon and possibly become Nixon's running mate. Or Reagan could become a running mate of Romney. But it also was noted that Reagan might "have difficulty avoiding being carried to the convention on the shoulders of the undaunted Goldwater forces."[40]

One national media celebrity who threw cold water on the speculation that Reagan, who still had not been inaugurated governor, might be seeking the presidency was conservative icon William F. Buckley, Jr. In his syndicated column on December 1, 1966, "Reagan for Prez?" Buckley thought any such move to be way too premature until Reagan had established some track record in Sacramento.[41] Buckley at this time was becoming close to Nixon.[42]

Nixon and the Reagan Threat

Richard Nixon long had foreseen that Ronald Reagan would be the major threat to his plans to capture the 1968 nomination. In late December, Buckley, along with Rusher and others attended a meeting at Nixon's Fifth Avenue apartment. Nixon was asked who he thought would be eligible to run in 1968. Nixon gave the expected names but then "added Ronald Reagan's." Buckley said he thought Reagan as a presidential candidate was inconceivable. Nixon responded, "Why? Suppose he makes a very good record as Governor of California?" [43] Buckley's biographer John Judis recorded Nixon as saying, "It isn't preposterous. Anyone who is the governor of California is *ex officio* a candidate for President."[44]

Reagan's Inauguration and Vietnam

In deference to the huge vote from Americans of Mexican descent which he had received, Ronald Reagan's inauguration and the related festivities had a distinctly California and Mexican American theme, with Reagan being sworn in using one of the oldest bibles in the state and mariachi bands playing at the parties.[45] In his formal address, delivered on January 5 even though he actually was sworn at midnight as January 1 began, he spoke about individual freedom and how once freedom was lost or squandered, how difficult it was to replace. Reagan called his domestic programs his "Creative Society," as a counterpoint to President Johnson's "Great Society." But Reagan's political creativity in regards to world affairs was evident at the inaugural ceremony itself.

Likely mindful of Eisenhower's request to meet him again to delve further into the vexing problems in world affairs, as well as his own concern for the administration's increasing mishandling of the war, Reagan arranged to bring foreign affairs, specifically the Vietnam War, right into the ceremonies. At that moment, Reagan initiated a tradition—which he would carry through his presidency—of citing specific citizens and their individual actions. At the end of his speech and pointing up to the ceiling where a small California flag was flying, Governor Reagan—who had arranged that the special small flag be raised that evening—wondered with his audience, "If, in glancing aloft, some of you were puzzled by the small size of our State Flag … there is an explanation. That flag was carried into battle in Vietnam by young men of California. Many will not be coming home. One did—Sergeant Robert Howell, grievously wounded. He brought that flag back…It might remind us of the need to give our sons and daughters a cause to believe in and banners to follow."[46]

It would not be the last time Reagan, as a sitting domestic governor in Sacramento or on the campaign trail for the presidency, would find ways to insert world affairs, into the minds of his listeners. And this early call by Reagan, to reinstill pride in America, which he would do throughout his first run for the presidency, would see fruition in the 1980s.

By the time Reagan was inaugurated, the reality of his being governor started to sink in to the national media and speculation about Reagan's running for the presidency seemed to quiet down. A January 3, 1967 *New York Times* biographical analysis did not mention his running for president at all,[47] but shortly thereafter a *Los Angeles Times* reporter asked the new governor if he would run in 1968 as favorite-son. Major media outlets "were soon buzzing with rumors" and "the idea took hold."[48] Clearly those same outlets had missed the facts that grass roots efforts for a 1968 Reagan run had started more than two years earlier.

But now that Ronald Reagan was governor, he had to govern and lead his state. Though "in the minds of some of Reagan's advisers, Sacramento appeared to be merely on-the-job training for the Presidency,"[49] what he accomplished as governor in 1967-1968 provided a necessary template for what he could accomplish as president.

Governor Reagan

Who Reagan chose as his advisors, staff, and Cabinet will be reviewed later when some of those same people became part of, or in some cases opposed, the 1968 Reagan presidential campaign.

Even before taking the oath of office, in mid-December, 1966, Reagan, Nofziger, Reed—who as we will see by then had become Reagan's Appointments Secretary—and Chief of Staff Phil Battaglia all flew to a meeting of Republican governors in Colorado Springs.[50] Reagan later would tell William F. Buckley Jr. on the show *Firing Line*, that at the meeting, he had proposed a mechanism for the federal government to return a small percentage of each state's federal tax revenues to the state instead of all the monies going to the federal government. The Colorado Springs meeting was the first of numerous such meetings of governors, Republican governors, and western governors that Reagan would attend in 1967-1968. Reagan not only would learn and interact with his fellows, but the venues would establish Reagan as a national political figure who was an equal—if not a leader—of the other governors and to gain for Reagan precious exposure to the national press, national audiences, and potential supporters for 1968.

During his 1966 primary and general election campaigns, his speeches had cited all the problems with big government. Reagan's inauguration day speech emphasized cutting budgets from all California state departments, described as a "financial blueprint for the biggest retrenchment of California government since the depression." During his presidential campaign, his speeches would continue his earlier campaign themes. But no longer would Reagan only criticize big government; Reagan started to document exactly how he had begun successfully to solve those problems by down-sizing California's bloated state bureaucracy and then telling his audiences that Washington D.C. needed the same shrinkage.

What Reagan would accomplish as governor, highlighted by historian Lou Cannon, will only be touched upon in this work briefly—when he would cite his achievements as models to apply to the federal government during his campaign speeches. During his first year in office, Reagan cut costs and decreased governmental waste and inefficiencies. He brought in private industry experts, who worked at low state salaries for six months, to apply regular business practices to state government. Reagan would tell future audiences proudly how he had saved the state the entire cost of a new office building, which was no longer needed. Reagan created the stricter use of state automobiles and restricted out-of-state travel for state employees unless there was proven need. He had saved the state the cost of hiring seasonal workers by staggering the renewal dates of licenses. Then he had saved millions in state telephone bills by taking advantage of a free program to improve phone efficiencies. Reagan had cut the growth in government employees by not hiring replacements for retiring or disabled workers. Reagan even sold former Governor Pat Brown's state airplane. Then he had his office staff save even more money by, instead of throwing out Brown's stationery and buying new Reagan stationery, just crossing-out Brown's name and writing in Reagan's name by hand.[52] Reagan really enjoyed telling his audiences of that savings.

One particular program, started by private businessman H.C. McClellan[53] before Reagan was elected, sent employment recruiters to Watts after the riots there for the purpose of finding jobs for the unemployed.[54] Reagan expanded the program statewide. Reagan also proposed a new method of selecting judicial appointments, which moved the process away from patronage and into a new system, which rated potential judge appointees on a point system.

But not all of Reagan's innovative cost-cutting policies were greeted positively by all the segments of California, which the prior general positive statewide poll approval numbers in 1967 had indicated. Reagan proposed that students at the previously tuition-free state colleges and universities start to pay 10 percent of their tuition costs; massive student and faculty protests ensued. Because the student and faculty protests "failed to ruffle Reagan…more and more people looked upon the California governor as a leading possibility for the Republican presidential nomination in 1968."[55]

Reagan started a program to treat mentally-ill patients away from costly, inpatient hospitals via outpatient and home programs. Once the numbers of mentally-ill inpatients declined and inpatient staffs thus were lowered, he was accused by the liberal media and Democrats of not caring for the mentally ill. Once Reagan explained how his innovative and cost-cutting program worked, the accusations lessened. Reagan's innovative programs were a forerunner of the shift to outpatient medical care in the 1980s and 1990s.

For all of these innovations, which Reagan had set in motion shortly after becoming governor, he would keep up-to-date follow-up statistics for each program, which he would give to audiences in 1967-1968. Governor Ronald Reagan had accomplished a great deal that first year, and the media started to notice and speculate how his significant accomplishments as governor would impact his running for president in 1968.

Reagan would appear on the cover of the May 22, 1967 edition of *Newsweek* and the cover-story article would address his accomplishments as governor as well his work style, and home and family life since inauguration.[56] By the fall and early winter months of late 1967, Reagan would be nearing the end of his first year in office and more analyses of his governorship would appear. But Reagan had his turn first. Reagan would give a pre-holiday *Report to the People* television address on December 17, 1967. He would tell his fellow Californians that much had been accomplished, but much work needed to be done. He would cite as one example his highway department, for whom Reagan had appointed the first Asian American as a commissioner as we will see, which was doing thirty percent more miles of paving with eleven percent fewer employees. He would emphasize his goals of "putting our fiscal house in order" and ended saying a line he had emphasized in campaign speeches throughout 1967 and would again in 1968, "we cannot afford anything and everything simply because we think of it."[57] At the same time the *New York Times* would run a feature article assessing Reagan as governor and listed his accomplishments of streamlining government, working with a hostile legislature and being a forceful decision maker, but much of the article, as we will see later, would be about his presidential aspirations and how Reagan governed being compared to how Eisenhower had governed.[58] Not all conservatives were pleased by the new governor's accomplishments for 1967. A major critique of Reagan's first year from the right appeared as a book whose title, *Here's the Rest of Him*, was chosen as an answer to Reagan's autobiography *Where's the Rest of Me?*[59] Reagan "took the attack with stride," pleased that he had a "growing reputation as a responsible executive who refused to let ideology interfere with effective governance."[60]

Ronald Reagan could take great pride in what he had done in 1967 as governor. But while he was working hard as governor and achieving major accomplishments, his first campaign for the presidency had begun as well.

Endnotes

1. Kelly, p. 143
2. *Newsweek,* 11/21/66, p. 36
3. Kelley, p. 143
4. For more on White, see http://www.politico.com/magazine/story/2015/04/teddy-white-political-journalism-117090_Page3.html#.VTmrniFViko
5. Davies, Lawrence, "Reagan Elected by a Wide margin," *NYT,* 11/9/66, p. 1
6. Hill, Gladwin, "Reagan Emerging in 1968 Spotlight," *NYT,* 11/10/66, p. 1
7. Hill, ibid
8. Nolan, pers int, 5/18/13
9. Nolan, ibid
10. Reagan, Nancy, *My Turn,* p. 178
11. ibid
12. Weaver, Warren Jr "GOP Finds '68 Outlook Brighter," *NYT,* 11/10/66, p. 1
13. "…and New Republicans Win," *NYT,* 11/10/66, p. 46
14. "Goldwater Lists 5 in GOP For '68 Presidential race," *NYT,* 11/11/66, p. 32
15. "Reagan for President? Not in 1968, He Says," *Milwaukee Sentinel,* 11/21/1966, part 1, p. 2
16. Walter Thayer to Dwight D. Eisenhower, 10/20/66 letter, Eisenhower, Dwight D.: Post-Presidential Papers 1961-1969, Special Names Series, Box 19, Thayer, Walter 1963-1966, Dwight D. Eisenhower Presidential Library
17. Dwight D. Eisenhower to Walter Thayer, 10/24/66 letter, Eisenhower, Dwight D.: Post-Presidential Papers 1961-1969, Special Names Series, Box 19, Thayer, Walter 1963-1966, Dwight D. Eisenhower Presidential Library
18. Skinner , Kiron, p. 701
19. Dwight D. Eisenhower to Ronald Reagan, 11/9/66 telegram, Eisenhower, Dwight D.: Post-Presidential Papers 1961-1966, 1966 Principal File, Box 44, Dwight D. Eisenhower Presidential Library

20. Dwight Eisenhower to Governor-Elect Ronald Reagan, letter 12/22/1966, Post-Presidential Papers, 1966 Principal Files, Box 6, folder IV-2 "Invitations-Declined", Dwight Eisenhower Presidential Library
21. "Owosso Group Spearheads Drive to Put Reagan in the White House," *Owosso Argus-Press*, 11/12/66
22. ibid
23. ibid
24. ibid
25. ibid
26. ibid
27. Turner, Wallace "Reagan Cautions Romney On 1968," *NYT*, 11/21/66, p. 24
28. Kabaservice, p. 189
29. Reagan, *An American Life*, p. 150
30. Shirley, Craig "Exploring Reagan's 'Eleventh Commandment'" Politico, 6/16/2011
31. Dwight D. Eisenhower to Raymond Bliss, 11/25/66 letter, Eisenhower, Dwight D.: Post-Presidential Papers 1961-1966, 1966 Principal file, Box 11, Dwight D. Eisenhower Presidential Library
32. *Newsweek*, 11/21/66, p. 36
33. ibid
34. ibid
35. ibid
36. "President Trails Romney, 46% to 54, in Harris Poll," *NYT*, 11/21/66, p. 22
37. Weaver, Warren Jr "Four Hearties of the Good Ship GOP," *NYT*, 11/27/66, p. SM26
38. ibid
39. ibid
40. ibid
41. Frisk, p. 219
42. Buchanan, p. 36-39
43. Buckley, William F "Reagan: A Relaxing View," *National Review*, 11/28/67
44. Judis, p.280
45. Kopelson, 2014C
46. Reagan, Ronald, Inaugural Address, January 5, 1967
47. "The Winning 'Loser,'" *NYT*, 1/3/67, p. 24
48. Morrell, p. 192
49. Boyarsky, *The Rise of Ronald Reagan*, p. 158,
50. Boyarsky, ibid, p. 169
51. Boyarsky, ibid, p. 7
52. Lewis, J, p. 174
53. Chad
54. Boyarsky, *The Rise of Ronald Reagan*, p. 207-208
55. White and Gill, p. 71
56. See Illustrations
57. Reagan, Ronald "A Year of Achievement and the Challenge Ahead," 12/17/67, courtesy Kathryn Forte
58. Duscha, Julius, "Reagan Gives a Surprising Performance: Not Great, Not Brilliant, But...," *NYT*, 12/10/67, p. 296
59. Author Kent Steffgen attacked Reagan's first term agenda because Reagan had been forced to raise taxes. But Reagan had inherited a huge undisclosed budget deficit due to last-minute and hidden spending under Governor Brown. Steffgen had a laundry list of perceived Reagan sleights to conservative backers who had voted him into office.
60. Cannon, p. 200

Chapter 3: Assembling the Campaign Team

"In 1967-68, Ronald Reagan actively sought the Republican nomination for President of the United States. He did so consciously and deliberately."
~ Thomas C. Reed[1]

"Elementary, my dear Watson. They were elsewhere."
~ William Rusher[2]

Tom Reed

In the second decade of the twenty-first century, Tom Reed has returned to his roots of nuclear physics and remains a consultant to the National Laboratory at Lawrence-Livermore CA. His hair now is all white, and he walks with a slow gait. Reed also requires the help of a personal assistant to drive and accompany him. But his gregarious conversation, bright smile, cheerful personality and keen sense of humor all convey warmth and intense interest in talking about the events of some forty-five years earlier. Reed reminded the author of a best professor, who took a genuine interest in his students, listened attentively, and also imparted critically important wisdom. Reed's two memoirs review how Reagan recruited him, and the reader is referred there, and to works by Cannon and Skinner et. al., for background details on Reed's military and political careers and on the initial formation of Reagan's team.

After "The Speech," Reed saw Reagan as the conservative leader to whom he could pledge his allegiance and for whom he could work—and work hard. "Reagan believed that honesty was not negotiable, that truth was absolute, and that leaders were to lead—not to poll their constituents....You knew what his beliefs and policies were. You could do your job secure in the knowledge that they would not change on the morrow."[3] Reagan was a man of "utmost integrity. He did not run for office for the perks and power."[4] What Reed saw in Reagan that set him apart from others was his "overarching sense of vision and a mental clock speed that far outran everyone else. He had a depth and clarity of vision that gave him the confidence to ignore criticism, media abuse and the countervailing advice from advisors, cabinet members and staff."[5] Reed's sole purpose was to "help make Ronald Reagan President of the United States…and Tom Reed would expend his last breath of air on this earth to achieve it."[6]

Was Reagan's candidacy in 1968 the half-hearted, wishy-washy, last-minute attempt in Miami Beach that so many historians have characterized? Absolutely not. Reed, at the epicenter of action, states emphatically, "In 1967-68 Ronald Reagan actively sought the Republican nomination for President of the United States. He did so consciously and deliberately, driven by a concern for his country, not by ambition run wild."[7]

As Reed has related, Reagan's first meeting to plan his first presidential campaign was nine days after he won the election, i.e., November 17, 1966. Both Reed and Nancy attended. Neither of the Reagan's had initiated the meeting or asked that a presidential campaign be started. But each was involved in the planning, with Reagan at the end authorizing the efforts to start the hunt for delegates.[8] The man needed for that job was famed delegate hunter Clif White.

F. Clifton "Clif" White

Clif White was described in the mid-1960s as a "tall, somber-looking man with a penchant for bright bow ties that go oddly with his saturnine appearance."[9] He was in his early 50s and his main occupation was as a public affairs consultant advising corporations on how to relate to the political structure. But also he accepted jobs as a campaign consultant and had become "the best-regarded delegate-hunter in the business."[10] White's extensive political background prior to 1968 is reviewed in two biographies.[11] White's personal documents of his many years of political activity are at Cornell University, but unfortunately this author could find no files or documents related to the 1968 Reagan campaign. Only a brief summary of White's background ensues.

As Reagan had been urging Eisenhower to run for president in 1952 and likely had followed the Republican convention, it had been White who was credited for the "convention floor tactics that shot down Taft," which enabled Eisenhower to become the Republican nominee.[12] Amongst the mechanics of politics that White had mastered included the critical importance of controlling the credentials committee. We will see later in Washington State, which in 1968 might have sent a Reagan-majority delegation to Miami Beach, those lessons had not been learned. White felt that the most important lesson he had learned from his many years in politics was that elected officials had no knowledge of the "fundamentals of practical politics."[13] But Reagan would soon start expanding his political knowledge by following White's trailblazing path.

In 1964 after helping Goldwater win the nomination at the convention Reagan had attended, White was given chairmanship of Citizens for Goldwater-Miller as a consolation prize from Goldwater. It was in this role that he had been sitting next to Reagan, when Reagan was elected California State co-chairman for Goldwater. In 1965, several members of White's conservative friends, the *Syndicate*, would form Public Affairs, Inc, a nationwide consulting service. The head of their Topeka, Kansas office had a close friend and colleague, John Kerwitz.[14] Kerwitz would in a short time become Executive Director of the Citizens for Reagan National Information Center, the main national clearing-house for 1968 Reagan presidential campaign materials, and he would work closely with Reed and White. White was not involved with either of Reagan's 1966 campaigns, as he was expanding the conservative base, but he did stay in phone contact with Nofziger.[15]

Intricate Minuet

White knew columnist Robert Novak, and Novak later reflected, "White saw Reagan as the candidate he had hoped Goldwater would become but never did."[16] White signed on to the Reagan campaign initially as an advisor in 1967 to survey the political landscape and as delegate-hunter in 1968. While Reagan was busy in Sacramento, White would plan all Reagan activities outside of California.[17] Novak saw that White was ready to "reassemble his nationwide team that had won the nomination for Goldwater."[18]

The projected budget for Reagan's campaign for 1967 was $100,000[19] and for 1968 was $440,000.[20] Of the latter, the actual spending in 1968 would be $366,000 of which $163,000 was to be spent at the convention.[21]

Reed has related that on November 21 at the Reagan residence, the Reagan's had a second meeting where they both confirmed the campaign plan to hunt for delegates. The Reagan's then had to leave for the first and only transition meeting with defeated Governor Brown, so they did not have time to discuss details, but clearly "they approved."[22] Reagan again approved the hunt for delegates and the overall presidential campaign on November 30 at the St. Francis Hotel in San Francisco for his third confirmatory meeting.[23] The much longer fourth meeting occurred the next day, December 1, again at the Reagan residence. Ron and Nancy Reagan again were there and Reed recalled, "Both were fully involved."[24] Other than the Reagan's, it was just Reed and White. By the end of that fourth planning meeting, Reagan and White came to a "meeting of the minds."[25] Both Nancy and Ronald Reagan "were unequivocally involved in structuring the deal."[26] But as the Reagan's were focused on their move to Sacramento and the governorship, they did not get involved in the details for White, which Reed had arranged. Reed and White agreed on a system of compensation and expense reimbursement.

As will be discussed later, Reed, who would hold some one hundred campaign meetings with Reagan, remains perturbed and upset by subsequent claims by the Reagan's that they had no idea what Reed had been doing,[27] although some of those denials to the press were a deliberate part of Reed and White's tactics. As far as Reed was concerned, as of December 1, 1966, "the campaign for the nomination in 1968 was underway."[28]

White told Reagan that because he was governor of the largest state in the union and thus a leader of the party, "He was bound to be considered for the Presidential nomination."[29] He regarded Reagan as Goldwater's heir apparent, and that if Reagan wanted to run for the 1968 Republican nomination, "I would be happy to support him in any way I could."[30]

Reporter Novak later recalled that White had told him that the campaign plan was in fact an "intricate minuet."[31] The initial plan was for White and "a few emissaries" to cross the country in secret and "try prying delegates from Nixon," while Reagan would vow in public he was only California's favorite son.[32] Meanwhile Reagan would begin a rigorous series of trips across the country, doing party fundraising, swearing he was not a candidate, but at the same time searching in earnest for delegates.[33]

Nixon Spills his coffee and his scotch

White not only met with the Reagan presidential campaign team, he also was being courted by almost every other Republican candidate too. Governor Romney had invited White to Michigan "several times" asking him to work on the Romney campaign, but White did not feel that he and Romney were close enough philosophically for him to accept the offer.[34] Rockefeller also "tried to bring me into his campaign," White reflected.[35]

But the most determined effort to hire White was made by Richard Nixon. White had been director for Volunteers for Nixon-Lodge in 1960 and tried to convince Nixon to contest the presidential election results, which had shown a tiny Kennedy victory amidst charges against more than 600 election workers of Democratic voter fraud in Illinois, Missouri, South Carolina, and Texas.[36] Early in 1967, Nixon and White met at Nixon's law office in Manhattan. After his secretary brought coffee to the two men, Nixon asked White if he would run his 1968 campaign. White recalled telling Nixon that he couldn't make any such decision unless he discussed it first with his 1964 Goldwater group—the *Syndicate*. Nixon proceeded to spill his coffee.

Nixon tried again to convince White, with this second attempt taking place at Nixon's Fifth Avenue apartment. Nixon poured scotch whiskey for both men. This time, trying to appeal to White's hurt over Goldwater's slight from 1964, Nixon offered, "I want you to be Republican National Chairman after I'm elected." But White answered, "No thank you. I don't want to be National Chairman." Nixon then proceeded to spill his scotch.[37] White wanted the Republican Party directed from the White House, which is what eventually Nixon would do. White wrote, "Ronald Reagan, of all the potential Republican candidates for 1968, was the only one I really wanted to see nominated."[38]

Spencer-Roberts: "The Office Seeks the Man"

Stuart Spencer and Bill Roberts successfully had managed many political campaigns before they agreed to work for Reagan.[39] But Spencer began to have some misgivings, which he then expressed privately to Reagan. In his 2001 oral history, Spencer recalled one particular meeting in which the presence of White meant that Reagan indeed was seriously going to run for president. Spencer thought a Reagan run would be quite difficult.[40]

Spencer stayed with the Reagan's after the meeting had adjourned. He asked Reagan what he was doing? Reagan gave a short answer about his planned campaign but Spencer answered that neither Reagan nor White at this point had enough qualified staff to run the kind of campaign needed to win the presidency.[41]

After advising Reagan on whom to get if he indeed seriously wanted to run, such as Ray Bliss—the Republican National Chairman, Spencer recalled that Reagan proceeded to give him the greatest quote he had ever heard. Reagan would tell many of his advisors, including Spencer, "The office seeks the man." Reagan did not elaborate on how his mentor Eisenhower's vote tallies in New Hampshire and Minnesota had been the model for Reagan of how the people had told the politicians whom they preferred for the highest office in the land.

But Spencer was not amused by what he had perceived as Reagan's naivete and retorted that Reagan had to fight and fight hard to win. Spencer indeed had found the fatal flaw in Ronald Reagan's drive to the presidency in 1968. Reagan would use the phrase—"the office seeks the man"—during his 1968 campaign and again when writing his autobiography decades later.

The Growing Conservative Base

But White would feel that Reagan did give his utmost in 1968. In his 1981 book *Why Reagan Won*, Clif White traced the rise of Reagan within the context of the modern conservative movement in America. White reflected, "Over a period of a dozen years—from 1968 to 1980—he waged three campaigns for the Republican Presidential nomination. In every one of those campaigns he went all out."[43] And in the first of those, Reagan believed America could turn the defeat of conservative Barry Goldwater into the victory of conservatives. Previously we have seen how individuals coalesced around Reagan starting on the evening Reagan had delivered "The Speech." But institutions existed within a broader conservative political milieu as well. The institutions, and the individuals who controlled them, would have major impacts on Reagan's 1968 campaign.

At this time, William F. Buckley, Jr. was editor of *National Review* along with its publisher, William Rusher. Buckley had both a weekly column and television program, *Firing Line*, and Reagan soon would appear as Buckley's guest. Buckley had founded the conservative college organization Young Americans for Freedom, which soon would spawn an off-shoot organization called Students For Reagan.

The magazine *Conservative Digest* had been published by direct mail expert Richard Viguerie, who would help Reagan in 1968, and had as its original editor Lee Edwards, who would become editor of the Young Americans for Freedom magazine, *The New Guard*. All the above of course are in addition to the Republican Party or the Young Republicans or College Republicans. But there was one particular Clif White group from which a number of Reagan's campaign staff would originate.

The *Hard Core*

On January 31, 1965 in Chicago, Clif White had organized a meeting of members of his original Draft Goldwater group along with some other conservative individuals to form a new political club called the *Hard Core*. In White's *Why Reagan Won* are listed all the founding charter members, but of future importance to Reagan's 1968 campaign were: Rusher, Anderson Carter of New Mexico who would become Reagan's first 1968 Western Campaign Director until he would become ill and would be replaced by Fred Van Natta, Montana newspaper publisher Frank Whetstone who in 1968 would be in charge of Montana, attorney Don Pearlman of Oregon who would become an important part of the Reagan team in this most critical of the 1968 primaries, and Reed.[44] White recalled, "the conservative cadre was now complete for its first big test—the effort to win the Republican Presidential nomination for Ronald Reagan in 1968."[45]

The Strategy Takes Shape

In *The Making of the President 1968*, author Theodore H. White describes how Reed and White "drew up a meticulous master plan for seizure of the nomination, timed in five phases and date-deadlined from December, 1966 to nomination in August, 1968." Reed shared his plan with your author too. Reed's first phase, November 17 to December 1, 1966, was described above.[47]

As noted earlier by Novak, one of the key initial ground rules was that "the entire operation at that point was conducted in utmost secrecy."[48] Reed was to be the director of operations for Reagan, raising money and serving as liaison between Reagan and White and the others.

To keep his Reagan activities clandestine, White retained his Manhattan-based political consultancy business.[49] For White, "maintaining secrecy entailed me flying out to California frequently to meet with Reagan and his people under an assumed name since the media would have been able to figure out what was going on if they knew about my visits."[50] White's official title for public consumption was "consultant to the California delegation"—as he did actually work for the delegation and did need to be seen at some delegation meetings in that time period.[51]

Meanwhile Reed, after staying in office as Reagan's Appointments Secretary for 100 days, would go underground and run the Reagan campaign from Reed's office, north of San Francisco.[52] Rusher recalled that many political reporters had "ransacked" Sacramento looking for Reagan's presidential campaign office. Because they could not find it, the reporters assumed there was no such campaign. Rusher chuckled, "Elementary my dear Watson. They were elsewhere."[53]

Developing the Plan

During the two-month period of December, 1966, and January, 1967, Reagan met Reed, White, and Spencer-Roberts dozens of times to review details.[54]

At first, Reagan's team still was in the heady excitement of the election results from the month before. Besides Reagan's massive victory, there were many other triumphs for conservatives and Republicans. Fully twenty-seven of the forty-eight Democrat freshmen Congressmen lost, as Republicans "more than recouped their losses in 1964."[55] Also "Republicans won their first gains in party identification in twenty years."[56] The most spectacular gains in 1966 were at the gubernatorial level. Of the fifteen Republican governors up for re-election, fully thirteen won.[57] Of the ten new governors, nine were Republican. At the state level, of thirteen Western State legislatures, fully twelve were Republican. "Republicans now controlled statehouses representing 293 out of the 535 electoral votes."[58] And even in New York, the new Conservative Party garnered more votes than the Liberal Party.[59]

Certainly much of the credit, deservedly so, had gone to Richard Nixon, who had campaigned vigorously for Republicans all across the country.[60] Those Republicans who won because of Nixon clearly had an IOU in their back pocket awaiting a 1968 Nixon call to cash it in. But despite owing their initial political careers to Nixon, did those same Republicans think Nixon could win?

One other aspect of the 1966 Republican triumph might have portents affecting 1968. Because 1966 was not a presidential election year, Republican candidates had run their campaigns "more or less as they pleased."[61] Thus Reagan won in the West as a conservative while Romney in the Midwest and Rockefeller in the East had won as liberal Republicans. For 1968, these same new potential candidates for the presidency would have to unite behind one eventual winner in Miami Beach or face a repeat of the 1964 disaster of the Goldwater fiasco where Republican liberals had refused to endorse their Republican standard-bearer.

In 1968, as was true in most presidential elections in mid twentieth-century America, few actual delegates were elected directly in primaries. In 1968, less than twenty states had them, and most delegates were elected at state conventions. As we will see in Washington State as a perfect example later, state conventions were in turn based on prior county conventions or local office holders. As the conventions approached, "party bosses worked in those smoke-filled rooms to develop a consensus on who would be their most electable candidate."[62] By 1964, Clif White and others on his Draft Goldwater Committee had wrested control of the Republican Party from Northeastern, establishment party members by getting control of the party apparatus at the precinct and county level from the ground up. "No county meeting was too small or too remote to escape the attention" of White and his committee.[63] And White himself was there with Reed and Spencer-Roberts to use his and all their combined areas of expertise to forge a battle plan for Ronald Reagan to win in 1968.

Meanwhile Reagan had to govern, and as planned, Reed first did become Appointments Secretary. Reed had a deputy, a young attorney named Paul Haerle, who later would become active in the campaign. Reed would be important in fostering Reagan's appointments of minorities to positions within the new administration.[64] For example, Reagan appointed Dr. Francisco Bravo, his critical 1966 liaison to the Mexican American community, and Croatian American Jack Pandol, to the state Board of Food and Agriculture. In 1968, Mexican Americans and Croatian Americans were to play important parts in Reagan's campaign. Reed would remain Reagan's official Appointments Secretary and Traveling Secretary for one hundred days until his planned leave to embark on the next phase of the Reagan campaign, as planned.

Reagan's team chose the 1964 White model of building a bottom-up organization. White had stayed in contact with many of his Syndicate members from 1964 and friends in the *Hard Core*: Anderson Carter in New Mexico, Frank Whetstone in Montana and Don Pearlman in Oregon. Then "others began to show up in Sacramento, San Francisco, or Los Angeles waiting to enlist in a Draft Reagan movement."[65] In his memoirs, Reed admits that a crucial error he made was not including Reagan's financial backers in the presidential campaign plans. More would follow.

The Republican Leaders

Reagan needed to court the major leaders of the party: Senate Minority Leader Everett Dirksen of Illinois, former nominee Barry Goldwater, and Senators John Tower of Texas and Strom Thurmond of South Carolina.[66] These leaders would control the delegate votes that mattered most.

When planning Reagan's campaign, Reed never considered contacting Eisenhower, seen now in retrospect to have been an obvious major omission. But at the time, Reed was not aware of any of the behind-the-scenes mentoring efforts of coach Eisenhower.[67] Although Reed had been present at the Gettysburg meeting the prior June, Reed never asked Reagan about Eisenhower and thus never understood the critical importance that the general had been playing behind the scenes in mentoring Reagan.

Everett Dirksen

Illinois was not only a delegate-rich state, it was Ronald Reagan's birthplace and where he grew up and went to college at Eureka College. Dirksen was not an activist and thus would not solicit delegates on behalf of Reagan. Dirksen was needed to "look favorably on the upstart from California. We wanted him to spread the word that Reagan was a winner."[68]

Barry Goldwater

Goldwater, the loser of the 1964 election, posed several problems for Reagan for 1968. Goldwater had recommended Reagan hire Spencer-Roberts for 1966. And despite Reagan having worked hard for Goldwater, including having had to fight to be elected State Co-Chairman, Reagan and Goldwater did not have a warm relationship. Plus Goldwater had come out for Nixon in early 1965. William Rusher called Goldwater's refusal to endorse fellow conservative Reagan in 1968, and later in 1976, as one of the "most baffling mysteries" of modern American conservatism.[69]

Goldwater initially may have objected that Reagan's *A Time for Choosing* speech had replaced the one he had filmed with Eisenhower. Perhaps it may have been "Goldwater's jealousy of Reagan's success as the Goldwater campaign collapsed."[70]   Or perhaps Reagan objected to Goldwater's abrasive style of speech, which turned off many voters. Because Goldwater had lost so badly in 1964, his name was "poison to many middle-of-the-road Republicans."[71] Some had viewed Goldwater in 1964 as a lost opportunity because "Reagan was wasted as cheerleader while Goldwater was out there fumbling passes."[72] Whereas people had laughed at Goldwater, they laughed with Reagan, making Reagan a "dream candidate" who might have won in 1964.[73]   Reagan, realizing likely he would never garner Goldwater's blessing, needed Goldwater at least to remain neutral.[74]

Goldwater had not made things easy for potential Reagan supporters. At one point Goldwater wrote to Nixon, worrying that if Reagan ran in 1968, the conservative vote would be split, thus allowing Romney or Rockefeller to win the nomination. Goldwater then urged Nixon to have Reagan as his vice president. Goldwater concluded one letter to Nixon, "let us not allow Reagan to get into this unless he knows full well what he is taking on and full well what it might do to his chances and the Party's chances."[75]

Strom Thurmond

The third leader was the Senator from South Carolina, "Ol' Strom." He had begun his political life as a Democrat and had run as a States' Rights candidate for president in 1948. In 1964 he had become a Republican. Even though Goldwater lost nationally, he did carry five southern states in large part due to the help of Thurmond. Afterwards, Ol' Strom became the "de facto trustee of Republican fortunes in the South."[76] Reagan needed Thurmond's support, as well as that of Thurmond's campaign operative Harry Dent, and this critical thrust would become the heart of Reagan's Southern Strategy.

John Tower

A second critical part of Reagan's Southern Strategy was to garner the support of Texas' new and first Republican Senator, John Tower, and the State Republican Chairman, Peter O'Donnell.[77]

Reagan felt that if these four key Senators supported him for 1968, then he might win; but if they opposed him, there was no chance of success. But there were other leaders as well who played important roles: the thought leaders of conservatism. Reagan's team held the keys to practical campaign strategy and tactics. But the two major leaders who ran the political and philosophical framework behind conservatism in the 1960's—and beyond—were William A. Rusher and William F. Buckley, Jr. They would fight between themselves on whom to support in 1968.

William A. Rusher

Rusher's biographer details how Rusher became a conservative at Princeton and later at Harvard.[78] In 1948 he met Clif White[79] and they became close friends. Rusher became increasingly anti-communist and at a Young Republican meeting in 1955, he had first heard Barry Goldwater speak. Once Rusher had decided that he himself would not enter a political career and would work behind the scenes, he decided to join forces with the editor of the new conservative magazine, *National Review*: William F. Buckley, Jr.[80]

The Two Bills

While Buckley worked on the daily management of the magazine, Rusher was described as the "ambassador between National Review and the YAF leaders."[81] Buckley's Young Americans for Freedom provided a training ground for young conservatives wanting to enter politics. Lee Edwards, the founding editor of YAF's magazine *The New Guard*, described Buckley and Rusher as "the two Bill's."[82] Young conservatives looked to Buckley for intellectual and personal inspiration and to Rusher for practical political nuts-and-bolts guidance.[83]

After the narrow Nixon loss in 1960, it was Rusher and Buckley who had nudged the party toward conservative Goldwater.[84] Rusher had thought that the best man to lead the drive for Goldwater in 1964 was Clif White, and the effort to move the party to the right was managed from a small office at 42nd Street and Lexington Avenue, which they called Suite 3505.[85] But both White and Rusher were stunned shortly thereafter when Goldwater had told them that he was not a candidate and would not permit a draft.[86] Goldwater would change his mind, but for Clif White, his dealings in 1963 with a reluctant Goldwater was just a precursor to how he would have to deal with another reluctant candidate—at least in public—in 1968, Ronald Reagan.

Rusher had written a February 12, 1963 *National Review* essay, "Crossroads for the GOP," predicting that the 1964 nomination of a conservative Republican would "lay the foundations for a truly national Republican Party, ready to fight and win in 1968."[87]

After Goldwater's crushing defeat, it was White's Draft Goldwater group—the Syndicate—along with cheerleading from Buckley and Rusher, Buckley's new American Conservative Union, and groups of Young Republicans and members of Young Americans for Freedom who yearned for another shot at the presidency in 1968—but with someone more telegenic and charismatic than Goldwater.

A year after Goldwater's defeat, Buckley himself had entered the New York City mayoralty race against Republican and Liberal Party nominee Congressman John Lindsay. Lindsay, who as noted had not endorsed Goldwater in 1964, continued to base his campaign on maximally distancing himself from conservatism. Rusher advised Buckley to ask Lindsay publicly if he would support Ronald Reagan or Richard Nixon if either were to be the 1968 Republican nominee, but Buckley never did.[88]   After losing the mayoralty race, Buckley began hosting a new television debate show, *Firing Line*, and started writing a new syndicated column, *On the Right*.

Bill Vs. Bill in 1968

But as attuned and as in sync to the needs of conservatism and the Republican Party that Bill Buckley and Bill Rusher were, they did not see eye-to-eye on whom should be the party nominee in 1968.

Of the two Bill's, Rusher was for Reagan from the beginning. In 1966 as conservative Young Americans for Freedom were polling their highest votes for Reagan as we will see, Rusher wrote to a friend asking help in arranging a visit to London. Rusher wrote that he would be grateful and would reciprocate the favor "when Ronald Reagan is President."[89]   Nixon seemed too familiar and too tired.[90]   If a new, fresh, younger liberal Republican entered the fray as a replacement for Nixon, Rusher wanted there to be a conservative new face too: Ronald Reagan.[91]   Rusher wrote to a friend that the performance of the new governor of California had been impressive and that "if it continues to be impressive I see no reason why he should not be the Republican candidate in 1968."[92]   Plus Reagan did not owe a lot of political favors; he was "not sullied by the political process."[93]

By November, 1966, Rusher had "no doubt" that Reagan should be the choice of conservatives for 1968.[94]   Rusher felt that Reagan's approval of Clif White, his old friend, was sound. Rusher suggested that White's job be Reagan's "national prospector."[95]   Reagan's choice of White would "signal to the world that Reagan intended to run for the nomination in 1968."[96]   Over the remainder of Reagan's 1968 campaign, Reed would keep Rusher up-to-date.

But the other Bill, Buckley, did not agree. Patrick Buchanan has related how he had patched things up between Nixon and Buckley so that Buckley had remained a loyal Nixon supporter.[97]   Buckley had addressed the possibility of a 1968 Reagan candidacy when he wrote that December 1, 1966, "Ronald Reagan for Prez?" article, in which Buckley had felt the odds of such a Reagan candidacy for the 1968 presidency were "unlikely, to say the least."[98]   Buckley presumed that Reagan would not have enough time to establish a good track-record as a new governor in just eighteen months before the convention, plus Reagan did not have the requisite "obsessive personal ambition"[99]   to become president.

Buckley would not become involved directly with the 1968 Reagan campaign except twice: he would interview Reagan and later would meet the Reagan's at Buckley's alma mater, Yale University, when Reagan would stay as an honored Chubb Fellow in early December 1967. Buckley's support for Nixon continued, but despite this, Reagan would have kind words for his old friend. In a speech in New Orleans in May 1968, Reagan would declare, "Bill's a good friend of mine. He's my pride and joy. He's the one fellow we got on our side who makes some of those intellectual liberals have to run."[100] Buckley also became friends with celebrity novelist Norman Mailer; both would be called to Miami Beach and would write about Reagan.[101]

The two Bill's would remain at loggerheads over whom to support as the Reagan campaign got off the ground and then again eighteen months later as the Miami Beach convention would approach.

A Spy and a Demotion

Sometime early on in the campaign planning, Reed had detected a leak and was determined to find out from whom the leak had originated. In both Reed's and White's memoirs and Spencer's oral history, all indicate that Reed traced the presumed leak to Spencer—a trusted member of the Reagan 1968 presidential campaign inner circle. Reed initially had viewed Spencer-Roberts and their third partner Haffner as the "manager-strategists" of his campaign team, those who would recommend to Reed who to hire.[102]

But as seen earlier, Spencer had had misgivings about the campaign, which he personally had expressed to Reagan. Spencer felt that Reagan did have the possibility of being president of the United States, but it was too soon. When discussing Reagan's oft-repeated phrase that "the office seeks the man," Spencer told Reagan to find someone else.[103] How far Spencer took these misgivings is not clear.[104]

Spencer's phone records were checked because he was being accused of still being in Rockefeller's camp, having run the Rockefeller primary campaign against Goldwater in 1964.[105] Spencer recalled that he indeed had spoken to Rockefeller but only occasionally.[106] But Spencer had spoken to Nixon. Nixon had called Spencer asking him to run Nixon's campaign but Spencer explained that as the owner of a political consulting business in California, he had to stay on the good side of the state's new governor, Ronald Reagan. But the words used by Spencer seemingly indicated he did confirm to Nixon that

Reagan had his eyes set on higher office.[107] Nixon very likely knew immediately that Reagan indeed was going to run for the presidency in 1968.

Spencer recalled in his oral history that after these accusations, his role within the Reagan campaign changed and from then on he was placed in charge solely of putting the California delegation together.[108]

But White recalled things differently. White noted that Spencer had been calling Rockefeller's national political consultant, George Hinman and "feeding him information about what we were up to, what Reagan's plans were, what his schedule looked like." Although White knew that campaign inside information often was exchanged amongst different campaigns, what was being revealed was "the most guarded information of all—Reagan's interest in the Presidency."[109] White then was present at a meeting, which included Reed, Reagan, and Bill Clark. It was this meeting which decided that from then on, Spencer was to be "disinvited" from all future key campaign meetings but would be left to round up delegates from California as noted above.[110] White recalled that he felt that Spencer had gotten "a bit too greedy" thinking that Rockefeller may have more to offer him.[111]

Lyn Nofziger

In his 1992 autobiography *Nofziger*, Reagan's press secretary reflected back that just after Reagan had been elected governor, "nobody had locked up" the 1968 convention and at the time "a few of us around Reagan believed" in his chances to become president in 1968.[112] Placing himself equally with Reed at the time, Nofziger recalled that the meetings with the Reagan's, which had confirmed the plans for him to run, had been made and that he had been one of the "perpetrators of this affair."[113] After the four meetings with Reagan, Nofziger was part of a "low-key, unofficial, and easily deniable 'Reagan for President' organization (which) was hatched that functioned all the way to the 1968 Republican National Convention in Miami Beach."[114] Nofziger reflected that he saw only one problem: that Reagan would not cooperate and become an active candidate.

Looking back in 1992 from the vantage point of almost three decades later, as Bill Clinton just was elected and thinking of Presidents Nixon, Ford and Carter, Nofziger thought that the Reagan supporters had been "right:" that the Reagan of 1966-1968, "despite his innocence," fared quite well compared with those men, besides Reagan in 1980 and 1984, who became President from 1960-1992.[115]

Nofziger felt in 1966 that Reagan had to "strike while the iron was hot," because he was a "hot political figure, the natural successor to the aging and irascible and forever defeated Barry Goldwater."[116] If Reagan would wait until 1972 it would be too late. If another Republican would win in 1968, Reagan would have to wait until 1976 at which point he would be "a little old" to seek the presidency; by then as a two-term governor he would be wearing "ten years worth of political scars."[117] During the next eighteen months, Nofziger would manage to keep his eye "on the goal I had set for my leader—the Presidency."[118]

Paul Haerle

Pauel Haerle is a life-long Republican. The earliest childhood memories that he has are at age four wearing a sunflower campaign button from the 1936 campaign of Alfred M. Landon and crying himself to sleep when Thomas E. Dewey lost.[119]   Haerle's ties to his alma mater, Yale, would play a prominent role during the 1968 Reagan campaign when he would help arrange for Reagan's 1967 Chubb Fellowship.

A long-time Reagan devotee north of San Francisco, once Reagan won the governorship in the fall, it was only a short time before he was asked to take over Reed's job as Appointments Secretary once Reed was to leave to begin the stealth phase of the Reagan campaign.[120] By early 1967, Haerle agreed.[121]   Haerle recalled that besides helping with the Yale visit by Reagan in late 1967, he would accompany Reed on Reagan's two campaign visits to Oregon in 1967, would ask fellow Oregonian Don Hodel to chair the Oregon Reagan campaign, would help to choose the California delegation, and would be sent by Reed to be advance man for the Miami Beach convention effort.[122]

Norman "Skip" Watts and Frank Woods

Watts was brought into the campaign as political advance man, due to his prior national experience working for Nixon and his grand-father's conservative credentials. Watt's wife would become Reed's secretary when Reed would go into stealth mode and run the Reagan campaign from Reed's own northern California business office.[123] Woods had gone to college with Reed and was brought on-board also as an advance-man.[124]   Although Nofziger, Haerle, Watts, and of course Reed were all quite committed to seeing Reagan be elected president in 1968, not everyone on Governor Reagan's staff was excited for Reagan to be running for president.

Edwin Meese III

Another Yale graduate from the west coast is Edwin Meese III. An attorney, debater, and conservative, Meese met with Reagan and became Reagan's Legal Affairs Secretary, a position he would hold through the end of 1968.[125]

Meese reflected that he shared the same view as William Clark, who we will meet shortly, that neither felt that Reagan should run for the 1968 presidency and indeed Meese felt that Reagan "did not intend to run for President"[126] in 1968. During 1967-1968, Meese noted, "I didn't feel that he was running."[127] Meese did know that Reagan would run as California's favorite son but Meese felt that Reagan "had plenty to do in California"[128] and hence a true run for the presidency was out of the question.

Meese took no part in planning any of Reagan's out-of-state campaign and fundraising trips with the exception of planning the Reagan's participation in a trip to Hawaii. But in June 1967 when Reagan would prepare to debate Robert F. Kennedy—which would become a critical part of the Reagan campaign—Meese would be Reagan's debate coach.[129] In Miami Beach, Meese would help establish Reagan's security, but ironically Meese would not be at the convention because he would be called away for military duty because he still was in the reserves at the time.[130]

William P. Clark

Little did a young "Billy Boy" Clark know that the Hollywood star he had just met would meet him again five decades later in the State Department. Four-year old William Clark had the thrill of pinning a badge on Hollywood starlet Shirley Temple because Ventura County's sheriff, Billy's uncle, had arranged that Billy would officially "deputize" her. Decades later under President Reagan, when Clark would be second in command at the State Department, Shirley Temple Black would be a foreign affairs officer.[131]

As Goldwater supporters in 1964, Clark and his wife saw Ronald Reagan speak at the Los Angeles Sports Coliseum; he and his wife told themselves that if Reagan ever would run for office, they would volunteer to help. A year later, Clark accepted Reagan's offer to become Ventura County Chairman for Reagan.[132]

As Reagan's gubernatorial term began, Clark served on a governmental reorganization task force but as he was about to return to private practice, Reagan asked him to stay on in a cabinet position as Secretary. Thinking about the offer, Clark decided to stay on, not so much because of Reagan's domestic priorities and plans, but because Reagan wanted to solve international problems that were of major importance to Clark: the Vietnam War and relations with the Soviets.[133] Clearly, Clark had entertained thoughts that Reagan at some future time would not be in Sacramento but would be in Washington, D.C.

Yet as Meese had recalled earlier, it was Clark and Meese who did not want Reagan to run for president in 1968 because he just had been elected governor. And Reagan biographer Lou Cannon confirmed that Clark "was not anxious for him to become a quixotic presidential candidate."[134] Yet Clark would not remain completely aloof from Reagan's first presidential campaign and would voice his concern about Reagan's declarations of non-candidacy as the convention would approach. Unfortunately, Clark's biographers do not mention Clark's recollections of the 1968 campaign in their biography except the episode of the resignation of Phil Battaglia.[135]

Phil Battaglia

Clark would become Governor Reagan's Chief of Staff in late August, 1967, when Phil Battaglia would resign. Battaglia became the center of a homosexual scandal whose details are detailed by historian Lou Cannon[136] and Reed.[137]

Reagan, who had thought Battaglia might be ill or under strain, made the final decision and let him go.[138] Reagan's backers "worried that the Battaglia affair would harm Reagan's chances for the Presidency," because what would the public think if his top staff person left office after only eight months? And any negative publicity could "undermine Reagan's credibility."[139]

After the announcement of the Battaglia resignation, reporters Rowland Evans and Robert Novak felt that the staff shake-up was a "turning point" in the Reagan administration. Feeling that it had indicated major problems in the Reagan organization with moderate Battaglia infighting with favored staff conservatives, Evans and Novak felt that Reagan could not afford to let such conflicts simmer and thus "if Reagan is ever to run for president, it will have to be now—in 1968—or never."[140]

From the vantage point of the 21st century, the actions in the firing of Battaglia seem extremely harsh and would be illegal today, but 1968 was a different time with different cultural norms in regards to homosexuality. Some historians have felt that the Battaglia affair ruined whatever chances Reagan may have had for 1968. Yet Reed reflected decades later that the Battaglia affair was "not major to '68."[141]   Rusher and White both agreed: the Battaglia affair had minimal impact on Reagan's 1968 campaign.[142]   But effects from the Battaglia affair would resurface during a gubernatorial cruise and would ensnare Nofziger himself.

Reagan's team was assembled. Now it was time to plan specific strategies and tactics to get Reagan the 1968 Republican nomination.

Endnotes

1.   Reed, p.1
2.   Rusher, p. 206
3.   Patrick, p. 271
4.   Patrick, ibid
5.   Patrick, p. 273
6.   Patrick, p. 275
7.   Reed, p. 1
8.   Reed, Tom. *The Reagan Enigma,* p. 57-60
9.   Chester, p. 201
10.   Chester, p. 200
11.   White; Gill and White
12.   Steffgen, p. 164
13.   Frisk, p. 42
14.   Steffgen, p. 171
15.   White and Gill, p. 66
16.   Novak, p. 166
17.   Reed, pers int 10/17/12
18.   Novak, p. 166
19.   Reed, p. 8
20.   Cannon, Gov Reagan, p. 265
21.   Cannon, ibid
22.   Reed, p. 8
23.   Reed, p. 8
24.   Reed, p. 8
25.   Reed, p. 9
26.   ibid
27.   Reed, p. 8
28.   Reed, p. 9
29.   White and Gill, p. 88
30.   White and Tuccille, p. 173
31.   Novak, p. 166
32.   ibid
33.   Novak, p. 166
34.   White and Gill, p. 85
35.   ibid
36.   ibid
37.   White and Gill, p. 86
38.   White and Gill, p. 87
39.   This author left several voicemail messages for Spencer in the hopes of obtaining an interview, but they never were returned.
40.   "Interview with Stuart Spencer," Ronald Reagan Oral History Project, Miller Center of Public Affairs, University of Virginia, 11/15/2001, tape 3, p. 34
41.   ibid
42.   ibid
43.   White and Gill, p. 15
44.   White and Gill, p. 69
45.   White and Gill, p. 80
46.   White, p. 35
47.   Reed, p. 5-9
48.   White, p. 174
49.   Rusher, p. 205

50. White, p. 174
51. ibid
52. Rusher, p. 206
53. Rusher, p. 206
54. Reed, p. 9; Reed, pers int 10/17/12
55. Chester, p. 185
56. Perlstein, p. 163
57. Chester et. al., p. 185
58. ibid
59. Perlstein, p. 164
60. Chester et. al., p. 253-254; Weaver, Warren "Nixon 'bats' .686 for 1966 Season," *NYT,* 11/13/66
61. Chester et. al., p. 186
62. Reed, p. 4
63. Reed, ibid
64. Kopelson, Gene. 2014C
65. Reed, p. 9
66. Reed, *Reagan Enigma,* p. 64-66
67. Reed, pers int 10/20/2013
68. Reed, p. 10
69. Rusher, p. 197
70. Reed, p. 10
71. Reed, p. 10
72. Chester et. al., p. 194
73. Chester et. al., p. 190
74. Reed, p. 10
75. Buchanan, p. 45-46
76. Reed, p. 11
77. Reed, p. 11
78. Frisk, p. 19-35
79. Frisk, p. 41
80. Frisk, p. 70-73
81. Frisk, p. 123
82. Frisk, p. 124
83. ibid
84. Frisk, p. 143
85. Frisk, p. 157
86. Frisk, p. 164
87. Frisk, p. 162
88. Frisk, p. 204
89. Frisk, p. 215-216
90. Frisk, p. 218
91. ibid
92. Frisk, p. 218
93. Frisk, ibid
94. Rusher, p. 203
95. Frisk, p. 220
96. Rusher, p. 204
97. Buchanan, p. 36-39
98. Frisk, p. 219
99. ibid
100.   RRL tape 342
101.   Frisk, p. 205-206
102.   Reed, pers int 10/17/12
103.   "Interview with Stuart Spencer," Ronald Reagan Oral History Project, Miller Center for Public Affairs, University of Virginia, 11/15/2001, tape 4, p. 34
104.   voicemail messages left by this author asking to interview Spencer in Palm Desert in 2013 again were not returned.
105.   Reed, pers comm., 10/2/2013
106.   "Interview with Stuart Spencer," Ronald Reagan Oral History Project, Miller Center for Public Affairs, University of Virginia, 11/15/2001, tape 4, p. 35
107.   ibid
108.   ibid
109.   White, p. 174
110.   White, p. 175
111.   ibid

112.   Nofziger, p. 65
113.   Nofziger, ibid
114.   Nofziger, p. 66
115.   Nofziger, ibid
116.   Nofziger, ibid
117.   Nofziger, ibid
118.   Nofziger, p. 68
119.   Haerle, Paul, "Paul R. Haerle, Ronald Reagan, and Republican Party Politics in California 1965-1968," an oral history conducted by Sarah Sharp, in "Appointments, Cabinet Management, and Policy Research for Governor Ronald Reagan, 1967-1974," Regional Oral History Office, The Bancroft Library, University of California, Berkeley, 1983, p. 2
120.   Reed, pers comm. 10/17/12
121.   Patrick, p. 50
122.   Haerle, pers int 11/22/12
123.   Watts, oral history, p. 12
124.   Watts, p. 16
125.   Meese, p. 30
126.   Meese, pers int 1/3/2013
127.   ibid
128.   ibid
129.   ibid
130.   ibid
131.   Kengor and Doerner, p. 9
132.   Kengor and Doerner, p. 60-61
133.   Kengor and Doerner, p. 62
134.   Cannon, p. 259
135.   Your author attempted to interview Clark, but he was too ill and died in August, 2013.
136.   Cannon, p. 242-245
137.   Reed, *The Reagan Enigma*, ch 11
138.   Cannon, p. 245
139.   Kengor and Doerner, p. 67-68
140.   Evans, R and Novak R, "Moderate Leaves Reagan, Division in Camp is Blamed," *Milwaukee Sentinel,* 9/12/1967 part 1, p. 16
141.   Reed, pers comm. 6/2/2014
142.   Rusher, p. 206

PART TWO

1967

CHAPTER 4: THE CAMPAIGN BEGINS

Reagan, as California's favorite son, was a "godsend."
~ Chester et. al.[1]

"Reagan was building himself a limited, but emotional, national constituency."
~ Chester et. al.[2]

"Oregonians had never heard a presentation as he had made...It was an amazing amount of enthusiasm...People were star-struck....like a rock star."
~ Fred Van Natta[3]

"The crowd looked ready to march under Reagan's banner: they whooped and cheered for nearly a full minute before letting him go."
~ *Newsweek*[4]

"The next Republican candidate for President is likely to be Ronald Reagan."
~ A group of Republicans[5]

As Reagan had prepared for his inauguration during the two-month transition period, Reagan's team had added more personnel. Two prominent members of the *Hard Core* were brought on-board. Frank Whetstone of Cutbank, Montana, became a second-in-command to White, and Anderson Carter of Lovington, New Mexico, was put in charge of Western states. Nofziger described each as "a bear of a man, well over six feet and burly" with Whetstone being called "Uncle Frank."[6] Each was a wealthy businessman with many business and political contacts in the West. As each went politicking, they "would drop the word that Reagan was running for President."[7] When excited reporters then called Nofziger asking if it were true, Nofziger would deny it. The next day, the local reporters would write that Reagan indeed was running. So Nofziger would call Carter and Whetsone, tell them what a great job they were doing, and encourage them to continue. When Carter became ill, Fred Van Natta of Oregon replaced him. The reason a great deal of effort was made in the West was because this was Reagan's home region, Republicans had won major victories in the West in 1966, and two critical primary elections would be held there in 1968: Oregon and California. For the critical South, Reed and White would bring onboard Robert Walker, as will be seen.

Favorite Son

The rationale of a state having a favorite son candidate, such as their governor or senator, was that such a leader could unify discordant elements within the state's delegates. Plus at the convention, delegates vote as the leader thinks best in order to "preserve their leverage" with all the candidates who are seeking the nomination.[8]

Reagan's prior 1966 campaign had been "littered with pledges to serve out his term as Governor."[9] Having promised not to use Sacramento as a mere stepping stone to Washington, D.C., Reagan knew that he overtly could not seek the nomination. Rather, Reagan would need a ground-swell of support—from seasoned politicians and the public—for his candidacy. Reagan had "made it clear he wanted to be the favorite son candidate and that he did not want to see a 'divisive' presidential primary conducted within the state" according to one historical analysis.[10] For Reagan, being the favorite son from California "was a god-send: in one stroke it eliminated his most immediate problem—namely, how to ensure that his name would be placed in nomination without his being an open candidate for the Presidency. It also gave him a healthy eighty-six vote base to build on."[11]

Not only was California in need of a strong unifying leader given prior intraparty infighting, having Reagan as favorite son provided a perfect mechanism for him to be an acknowledged candidate—even if only as California's favorite son. Reagan now was assured that his name would be placed in nomination "without his being an open candidate for the Presidency."[12]

The Three Targeted Opt-Out Primaries

In 1968, only some 34 percent of the delegate votes cast in the primaries would be binding at the convention and only 17 states held primaries.[13] In most states it would be the usual state conventions and the selection or election of delegates, which would determine for which candidate they would vote for in Miami Beach. As historian Kiron Skinner and her co-historians put it, "The institutional makeup of the electoral system in 1968 reinforced the power of party leaders."[14]

Reagan could not be seen as "running around seeking the nomination" early-on in the campaign, but at some point "some tangible evidence of Reagan's firepower at the ballot box would be necessary."[15] But there was a new way for Reagan to be on the ballot without announcing his formal candidacy.

The problem with those states holding primaries was that in most of them either serious candidates, such as Nixon, would be filing, or they would have their own favorite sons. Reagan not only would not file papers in any of those states—because that would be public proof that he was running for president having just been elected governor— as we will see Reagan's team would actively succeed in withdrawing Reagan filing papers in New Hampshire which a Reagan grass-roots campaign organization previously had filed.

But there were three states in 1968 whose citizens and public officials had felt that they had been ignored by candidates in prior primary elections: Wisconsin, Nebraska, and Oregon. So their legislatures came up with the ingenious idea of an "opt-out" state primary. A state official or a panel would look over the field of potential national candidates—usually by reading newspapers—and select those names which had been mentioned frequently as potential 1968 candidates for the presidency for listing on their 1968 primary ballot. If such a named individual did not want to be listed on the primary ballot, he or she had to execute a signed affidavit to confirm that they were not a candidate for president and wished to withdraw.

For Reagan, the opt-out primaries in Wisconsin on April 2, Nebraska on May 14, and Oregon on May 28 afforded a chance for Reagan to not need an open declaration of candidacy to get onto those three primary ballots. Thus the key campaign strategy for Reagan to win the Republican nomination in 1968 emerged. Increasing campaign efforts would be made: initially minimal in Wisconsin, then more in Nebraska and finally the major effort in Oregon, so that Reagan would win sequential increasing vote tallies in each of those three primaries. Coupled with the 86 delegates he would garner at the June 4 California primary, he would sail into Miami Beach with unstoppable momentum towards the nomination. Yet behind this winning strategy lay the realization that the odds still favored Romney or Nixon. Thus the main goal was to stop any candidate from a first ballot victory. Then Reagan's conservative stalwarts would vote on a second or third ballot to see Reagan become the 1968 nominee.

What would happen if Reagan were asked about signing a withdrawal affidavit? Reagan had the perfect answer: because he would be California's favorite son, he could not sign any withdrawal affidavit because that statement would state that he was not a candidate for the presidency. As he was in fact California's favorite son for the presidency, he could not sign any such withdrawal affidavit. During the forthcoming campaign, Reagan would be asked that very question many times and would give that same answer each and every time up to the point his name would be placed in nomination in Miami Beach.

So Reagan's team decided to place incremental campaign efforts into those three states. Wisconsin would not provide a major vote percentage—perhaps ten percent. Reed actually felt that "no campaign" was his objective there.[16] But Reagan would meet with the very first state chairman in history for a campaign for Ronald Reagan for President: Don L. Taylor, who would run the entire Wisconsin Reagan campaign in 1968.

In Nebraska, Reagan hoped that "only local support" would achieve a "better-than-expected result."[17] Several Reagan for President grass roots campaign groups would form in Nebraska. Yet the creation of a Reagan campaign film, *Ronald Reagan, Citizen Governor*, would lead to primary results few had anticipated.

The all-out push was to be made in Oregon, where as envisioned initially by Reed, Reagan was to achieve victory. In Oregon, a full Reagan team would be created. Its foundation and framework in early 1967 would pave the way for a May, 1968 primary win.

In early 1967, White's preliminary delegate count showed that of the 667 needed to win, Michigan Governor George Romney was the leading contender with some 320 delegates, Nixon had around 310, and Reagan (with his 86 from California assumed) was in the 200-300 range.[18]

Reagan had the perfect excuse as to why he needed to travel so frequently during 1967 and 1968: he was in high demand. Ever since his *A Time for Choosing* speech in the fall of 1964, Reagan had been besieged by requests to speak all over the country. His 1965-1966 out-of-state campaign trips to New Haven, Boston, Detroit and Seattle were evidence of the beginning of his initial national appeal.

For public consumption, Governor Reagan had been invited to speak across the country and he was giving speeches to raise monies for fellow Republicans because he was seen as the new star of the party. His Hollywood and political appeal could attract donors. But although this indeed was true, Reagan had the luxury of so many invitations, this permitted him the luxury to sift out and select to where he should go to benefit his presidential campaign.

Reagan was expected to remain in California during each week, and during the time period of 1966-1968, he continued to give many speeches within California on state issues. But weekends often were free for the governor, except when the Legislature was in session and for which Reagan had to stay in-state. Reagan would plan visits, mainly during those free weekends, which would all fit in with the stealth presidential campaign: the three opt-out primary states, meetings of governors, and speeches to major public policy organizations and media interviews, all of which would enhance his being seen as a major national political figure and thus natural contender for the 1968 presidency.

By traveling to various Republican fundraising events, and then being the main speaker, he could broaden his appeal and be brought into direct contact "with the kind of men who would be delegates at the convention."[19] Reagan's gubernatorial responsibilities could not be interfered with, nor did Reagan need to go to every "fifty-dollar-a-head steak-and-eggs breakfast to thousand-dollar-a-head cocktail parties and dinners."[20] Rather Reagan had very specific campaign targets in mind.

Reagan would visit the opt-out primary states of Wisconsin, Nebraska and Oregon, but would not visit states that did not fit into campaign plans. New Hampshire or Massachusetts, which although they were to have primary elections, Reagan would not enter. For if he did, he would run the risk of being perceived as truly running for president. Reagan would need to visit with Dirksen, Goldwater, Thurmond and Tower and would visit with Eisenhower several times for private mentoring on foreign affairs. Reagan also would receive two prestigious academic honors, which would enhance his national stature: giving the Landon Lecture at Kansas State University and becoming a Chubb Fellow at Yale University. Reagan would speak at a number of national press meetings as well as speak before economic institutions. Plus there were many upcoming conferences for governors. All these were planned to enhance Reagan's stature by being seen as a serious national figure by the public and the press.

Yet the campaign visits did in fact have the secondary goal, but the primary goal to be seen by the public, of fundraising for the Republican Party and local Republicans. An agreement was reached that for the monies Reagan would raise, Reagan's team would keep five percent to cover their travel expenses as well as to fund future visits of those out-of-state Republicans whom Reagan had met on his travels and who wanted to return the favor and campaign for Reagan in California in the future.[21] One historian noted that by January, 1968 after one year of out-of-state campaigning and fundraising, Reagan had raised "the impressive sum of $1.5 million for the Republican Party."[22] The *New York Times* felt that Reagan had raised even more: $2-million.[23] One result of Reagan's efforts was that party officials throughout the country had met Reagan, heard what he had to say, had raised a ton of money for the party, and were put "politically in his debt."[24]

Although the Reagan presidential campaign truly began at that first meeting, shortly after the November, 1966 election, Reagan had delivered his first speech as a national political figure—beyond just California—in Seattle in June, 1966, while he had been campaigning for governor. As noted earlier, Reagan's speech had won standing ovations from the crowd and attracted attention in the press. Indeed his Seattle speech can be seen as the first public one in his 1968 bid for the presidency.[25]

One group of British historians attacked Reagan and his campaign, feeling that Reagan was a robotic political force, "totally devoid of any concept of objective morality," and "more dangerous" because he could be pointed at whatever direction was wanted by whoever "is at the controls."[26] Of course this was pure nonsense.

Reed got many chances directly to observe Reagan, besides as candidate, also as speechwriter during the campaign. Reagan wrote his own speeches, but he did get added help to obtain "new information, easily digestible facts to nail his case shut, along with well-written phrases that captured the spirit of what he is trying to say."[27] Michael Deaver recalled that Reagan was constantly reading, especially books on economics, which Deaver saw was Reagan's "relaxation." Deaver observed that Reagan was extremely competitive and wanted to be knowledgeable.[28]

As Deaver recalled and as your author can attest from listening to tens of hours of them, Reagan's typical campaign speech during 1967 and early 1968 often was a modified version of *A Time for Choosing*, always updated with current statistics and timely welcoming jokes about his Democratic opposition. For instance, his attacks on RFK started out early in the campaign as humorous jokes when incumbent President Johnson seemingly again would be the Democratic nominee. As a gubernatorial candidate, Reagan had attacked big government. But once he started to run for the presidency, he not only continued to attack big government in general, but Reagan then started to cite example after example of how his successful policies in Sacramento had begun to tame the beast of big state government, which set the stage for him to apply those same solutions on the federal level as president. Sometimes he would speak out on cherished topics, which will be explored, such as when he would speak about the dangers of student indoctrination by elite professors when he would speak at several colleges and universities along the campaign trail. But it would not be in the area of domestic affairs that would transform Reagan into a national contender.

Foreign policy, specifically the Vietnam War and relations with the communists, had not been addressed by Reagan during his gubernatorial campaign—with the exception of his very brief remark during his talks in New Haven and Seattle—but once he started to run for the presidency, they began to appear as small sections of his campaign speeches. But at most of his press conferences, which Reagan typically held before and after every campaign visit and speech, the reporters repeatedly asked more questions about Reagan's foreign policies than about domestic matters. Former President Eisenhower, characterized by Princeton historian Fred Greenstein as the "hidden-hand" president because of the behind-the-scenes control he exerted during his administration,[29] continued as the hidden-hand mentor and advisor to Reagan. Once Reagan was elected governor, Eisenhower's role changed from advising his political student on domestic politics to mentoring on foreign affairs.

Reagan would cite Eisenhower's experiences and policies in the Korean War as models to follow on how he wanted to see the Vietnam War won. And the fact that as a new domestic governor, Reagan spoke out about foreign affairs in almost every presidential campaign speech, and that foreign affairs comprised a great portion of reporters' questions at every press conference, all indicate that Reagan was being transformed from a local California political figure into a national figure and potential president. By the time the summer of 1968 would arrive, Reagan would be giving specific military tactical suggestions on how to win in Vietnam and would address issues of national security including how to deal with hostage situations such as the *U.S.S. Pueblo*, his advocacy of an anti-ballistic missile shield, and he would begin to push openly for freedom in Eastern Europe.

Reagan was able to excite his audiences, and many press reports described standing ovations and spontaneous cheers for Reagan. The previously-mentioned contrasting reactions in Norwalk, California to the enthusiastic Reagan visit versus the "Bobby Go Home!" RFK campaign stop is but one example. Individuals who one day would join the Reagan team as grass roots activists in 1968 will recount their excitement when they first heard Reagan speak. To the Students for Reagan who we will meet, their passions for political involvement were kindled by hearing Ronald Reagan speaking on the presidential campaign trail at the time. One historian concluded, "Reagan was building himself a limited, but emotional, national constituency."[30] But this view—that Reagan's loyalists were limited in number—will be seen not to be true when Nixon's slender margin of victory would be counted.

Unexpected Invitations

Many critical Reagan campaign appearances were not arranged by Reed. One Reagan supporter would arrange for a series of crucial Veteran's Day appearances in Oregon in the fall of 1967. But some trips would fall into the lap of Reagan and he would take full advantage of the opportunities. Reagan's invitations to be Chubb Fellow at Yale and to deliver the Landon Lecture at Kansas State University would come from others but would become major triumphs for Reagan during the campaign. But amongst the most important successes would be Reagan's May, 1967, triumph over his nemesis Kennedy at an international debate, and what would escape notice at the time was that for the first time in public that spring of 1967, Ronald Reagan publicly would call for the Berlin Wall to be torn down—almost a full two decades before exhorting Gorbachev to do so. Candidate Reagan would expand his foreign policy expertise and pronouncements well beyond his initial campaign comments on Vietnam.

The Governor Conferences

Unless there were overriding concerns back in Sacramento or other major schedule conflicts, Reagan would attend every governors conference from Inauguration Day in 1966 until the Miami Beach convention in August, 1968. Indeed even before Reagan had been sworn in, as seen, Reagan had attended one such meeting in Colorado Springs. Nofziger recalled that Reagan "showed up at every governors' conference—national, regional, Republican—much to the dismay of the other governors because Reagan clearly dominated the meetings, not so much with his knowledge of government as with his personality and celebrity status."[31] The press virtually would ignore the other governors by concentrating their questions on Reagan's presidential candidacy. Thus the public, and Republican activists, would read articles on the growing Reagan candidacy, no matter what denials Reagan would tell the press. Reagan's national stature would ascend on its trajectory with each passing conference.

The First Weeks

Within weeks of Reagan's inauguration, one member of the national press began an anti-Reagan campaign via his nationally syndicated newspaper column, which would continue through the convention a year-and-a-half later. Columnist Drew Pearson along with his investigative reporter, Jack Anderson, wrote *Washington Merry-Go-Round*. Pearson was described as "LBJ's hatchetman."[32] As mentioned, in 1966 it had been Governor Brown who had fed Pearson controversial information about Reagan's primary opponent in the hopes that once Christopher was defeated, candidate Reagan would be an easy target for Brown to defeat.

Pearson surprisingly had made no comments in his column attacking Reagan's "The Speech" on behalf of Johnson's opponent Goldwater in late October, 1964. Yet likely Pearson had been shocked by Reagan's victory over his confidant, Brown. Pearson must have seen Reagan as a huge 1968 presidential threat to Johnson, because he began attacking Reagan immediately in late January, 1967. Pearson attacked Reagan for cutting the budget of the University of California while at the same time he praised how New York's Rockefeller was increasing spending massively. Pearson decried Reagan's plan to ask students at state colleges and universities to pay a small fraction of their tuition.[33] A few weeks later, Pearson seemed to salivate when he proclaimed, "there will be a statewide recall vote to remove Governor Reagan from office."[34]

Reagan's potential candidacy was discounted by the *New York Times* editorial page, which felt that Nixon was the likely candidate and that the new governor of California "was hip deep in state problems and was unlikely to interfere with the emerging strategy of Mr. Nixon."[35] This incorrect analysis suited Reagan just fine, as his campaign was to remain under-the-radar. As Nixon had surmised with Buckley and Rusher days earlier, unlike the leading newspaper, Nixon saw the Reagan threat quite clearly.

So Nixon then planned a new, more secret second meeting to get advice on the Reagan threat. On January 7, 1967, Nixon held a meeting for his top advisors, including historian William Safire, newly-elected California Lieutenant Governor Bob Finch, who Safire characterized as "close to RN (Richard Nixon) as a son," and Fred La Rue, the State

Chairman of the Mississippi Republicans.[36] Buchanan recalled that first they searched the room for electronic eavesdropping devices.[37]

Nixon told the group, "I think we can assume that the Vietnam War will have ended by the 1968 election." Nixon admitted that his biggest problem was the perception that "Nixon can't win," having lost the 1960 presidential and 1962 California gubernatorial elections. Nixon then laid down the odds. Nixon predicted, "Reagan is four to one."

Nixon debated whether he should do anything at all, when LaRue commented, "Reagan could shoot us down in two minutes." Nixon agreed adding, "It's the reverse of '64 when the liberals could never get it together." Nixon was worried that Reagan and he would split the conservative vote if Reagan attempted to run himself for president in 1968. Finch, of course Reagan's lieutenant governor, offered to "get George Murphy and others to lean on Reagan" so as not to run.

Then Finch offered a different idea. What if Reagan became Nixon's stalking horse, just as Rockefeller was using Romney? Safire saw a flaw in that approach saying, "What if Romney offers Reagan the Vice Presidency? Then you have the stalking horses running away with the wagon." Finch admitted it was a danger but said Nixon then could "offer Reagan the top spot on a silver platter in 1972 if we lost." Nixon smiled and disagreed saying it might work if Reagan would go for it, but added that Reagan wouldn't. One person asked if they should float out a "hint that Reagan will be our VP?" The idea was shelved quickly with a, "Hell, no—talk left," as more liberal Republicans were thought best to pair with Nixon rather than a more conservative Reagan.

Nixon decided to take no overt action for the nomination at that point, letting Romney take "all the savaging that the press corps reserves for the front runner." Nixon assessed his delegate strength that January 1967 at 603 of the 667 needed to win on the first ballot in Miami Beach.[38]

Meanwhile, Reagan planned his first campaign-fundraising speeches to two of the three critical opt-out states for 1968: Oregon, where he would speak in Eugene on February 11, and Nebraska, where he would speak in Omaha and Scottsbluff in late June. The first, described afterwards as "enormously successful," was to Eugene.[39]

Reagan's First Presidential Campaign Trip: Lincoln Day in Eugene, Oregon

The very first trip the new governor of California made outside the state was to Oregon on February 11-12, 1967. Reagan's team arranged that newly inaugurated Oregon Governor Tom McCall, a liberal Republican, officially had invited him.[40] McCall was no particular friend of Nixon's, as it had been McCall whose first name Nixon had forgotten during a 1966 campaign rally as seen earlier.[41] McCall in fact made no secret that he was for Rockefeller.[42] Reagan hired Travis Cross, a political staffer also working for Romney, to make local arrangements.[43]

Reagan flew from Sacramento to Salem and had a luncheon with Governor McCall and his Welfare Department.[44] A public relations colleague of Cross, Fred Van Natta, future Reagan Western states campaign director, was present. Van Natta had heard Reagan's The Speech in October, 1964 and had marked Reagan as "the man to watch."[45] Van Natta was not yet working for the Reagan presidential campaign but he would always remember the first time he had ever met Reagan and shook hands with him.[46] That meeting would be mentioned by Reagan when he would return to Oregon that November.

In the afternoon Reagan was driven to Eugene for the main event, the Lincoln Day dinner. Reagan spoke to somewhere between 700[47] and 900 people.[48] Republican stalwarts paid $10 per plate to hear and see Reagan, which would have been close to $75 per plate in 2015 dollars.[49] The banquet, held at the Lane County Fairgrounds, officially was sponsored by the Lane County Republican Central Committee.[50] McCall was in attendance, as were members of the state legislature, Reed, Haerle, and a conservative Oregon Republican activist, Don Hodel.[51] Hodel remembered receiving Reagan's firm handshake in the receiving line. Hodel and Van Natta would become major participants in Reagan's Oregon campaign team.[52]

Both Reed and Haerle were scouting out Oregon conservative Republicans and laying the initial groundwork for the future Reagan Oregon campaign. Reagan needed a competent conservative to head the Reagan staff in Oregon. As Oregon was to be the final of the three opt-out state primaries, here is where Reagan wanted to achieve a final primary win over likely opponent Nixon and sail into Miami Beach with unstoppable campaign winds behind him.

Reagan's speech was typical for what he would say at each campaign stop over the next seventeen months. Only a few of his initial campaign speeches will be quoted here. Although his domestic themes would predominate in his early speeches, it would be his increasing discussion of world affairs during press conferences and in his later speeches that would mark his growth as a presidential contender. For although most presidential elections are decided chiefly on the domestic concerns of the electorate, the time period of the late 1960s had the equally important worries of Americans in the realm of foreign policy.

Reagan warmed up his audience with some jokes and anecdotes. He cited Abraham Lincoln and Daniel Webster. A natural and gifted communicator, Reagan had honed his speaking skills for fifteen years as the national spokesman for General Electric.[53] Plus of course he had campaigned in California for Nixon in 1962, Goldwater in 1964, and himself in 1966.

Reagan did acknowledge his relatively recent switch to the Republican Party by admitting that he was "still getting used to being a Republican." There were many laughs. He felt that after a period of years when the Democratic Party controlled all phases of government, the recent 1966 fall elections had restored the nation's two-party system. The Republican Party, now an effective opposition party, would oppose the growth of government. He analyzed that voters had voted against the War on Poverty. Reagan explained that Republicans had no quarrel with the humanitarian goal of the Great Society, but he warned the audience, "if it cannot remain a free society, the price is too high." There was thunderous applause.

Reagan said he was disturbed when he had been asked if newly elected representatives were identified with the liberal or conservative wings of the party; he wanted one united Republican Party. This theme—of not wanting people broken into named interest groups— had come to Reagan from Eisenhower as seen. Reagan decried the growth of the federal government since 1900, citing that although the Gross National Product had increased some 33-fold, that the cost and size of the federal government had increased 234-fold. Reagan attacked the "unprecedented federalization of American life," a comment which also drew great applause. Reagan then warned fellow Republicans, "Read the signs correctly; we were not elected to perpetuate that which the people voted against."

The new California governor explained that the Watts riots had left that area of Los Angeles devastated. Businesses had shut down or fled the area with resultant massive unemployment. He then cited recent progress there by private industry, via Chad McClellan as noted earlier, which had created more than 2000 new businesses and had halved the unemployment rate. Reagan approved of this solution but then contrasted it to the advice of the local Democratic congressman who had said that only massive *federal spending* could solve the problem.[54]

Although Richard Nixon's fall 1968 presidential campaign later would be remembered for the term "Silent Majority," Ronald Reagan uttered those exact same sentiments for the first time to a national audience that evening in Eugene:

"There is a bloc out there that you and I should be talking to, and that bloc is made up of many unsung heroes. They're of every race and religion, they're in every economic bracket, and they certainly have every ethnic background. I'm talking about that great unsung body of Americans who've been carrying the load and paying the bills. They go to work, they send their kids to school, they contribute to their church and charity, and they make the wheels of the local community go 'round by their contributions, civic and otherwise."[55]

The *New York Times* described his audience as being "enthusiastic," and his speech was "well received" with frequent applause.[56]

But Reagan got a standing ovation when he discussed foreign affairs. This was Reagan's first major pronouncement on foreign affairs after his brief comment in Seattle. He made it forcefully. He said that if Republicans were in charge of Vietnam policy, "If this country continues to ask its sons to die, we'll let them win."[57] Here in Oregon, Reagan uttered just a few words and treaded lightly on Vietnam at this very early point in his 1968 campaign. Orders of magnitude of more intensity would follow.

Van Natta's personal recollections were vivid. "Oregonians had never heard a presentation as he had made...It was an amazing amount of enthusiasm...People were star-struck....like a rock star."[58] *Newsweek* agreed and reported that when Reagan had finished, "The crowd looked ready to march under Reagan's banner: they whooped and cheered for nearly a full minute before letting him go."[59]

Perhaps this very moment in Oregon, those in the audience and the national press who were there may have begun to realize that not only was Reagan of presidential timbre as Eisenhower had proclaimed, but perhaps as early as 1968 they might envision a President Ronald Reagan in the near future. Reagan had delivered his 1964 "The Speech" but he had done that on behalf of Goldwater. His 1966 speeches were delivered when he ran as a domestic gubernatorial candidate. Although his Seattle speech that year was in fact his first appearance as a gubernatorial nominee to an audience beyond California, it received sparse press coverage and he had not yet won the general election.

But now he was Governor Reagan, the chief executive of the nation's most populous state, speaking about foreign affairs, in neighboring Oregon. Reagan's campaign for the presidency, begun and planned behind closed doors, became public in Eugene, Oregon in February 1967. It would take two additional campaigns and some fourteen years to culminate in his inauguration in 1981.

After spending the night at the Eugene Hotel, Reagan held a "closed breakfast meeting with eighty persons."[60] At this meeting, which "included some of the most important Republican Party managers and financial contributors in this key state,[61] Reagan and his team obtained their "first organizing leads."[62] Hodel and Van Natta were being targeted as prime future campaign managers for the Reagan's Oregon campaign.

A few minutes after the private breakfast, Reagan met the press. He reiterated that he had "no intention of campaigning for the Republican nomination."[63] Reagan, for not the only time as will be seen, was asked if he would issue a response as had General William Tecumseh Sherman, who famously had said in the late 1800s that he would decline the nomination and if elected he would not serve. As will be discussed later, Eisenhower had thought Sherman's comment foolish because individuals called to continue to serve their country should do so without hesitation. In a future press conference, Reagan even would mention that at one point Ike had told him this personally on the golf course. But at this time in February, 1967, Reagan countered only that making such a statement would be "presumptuous and ridiculous."[64] As we have seen, Reagan was waiting for the people to proclaim their support for him. Reagan wanted it known that if the public wanted him to be their president, he would serve enthusiastically.

Reagan's first out-of-state trip, his first as an unannounced presidential candidate for 1968, was "enormously successful."[65] The eastern press editors also took note that presidential ambitions for 1968 might have sent Reagan there to begin his campaign. "Before the Lincoln Day audiences in the crucial state of Oregon, he was enthusiastically received at public meetings and at closed-door sessions for wealthy and influential kingmakers."[66]

March, 1967 Trips to the East Coast

In March, Reagan was busy flying back and forth on trips to the east-coast. He would joust with three of his major 1968 opponents: his old nemesis: Democratic Senator Robert Kennedy of New York and for the Republican nomination, liberal Republican Governors Nelson Rockefeller of New York and George Romney of Michigan.

Romney

Governors and presidential candidates Romney and Reagan had met previously in Los Angeles at the July, 1966 governor's meeting, when Romney had been so rude to Reagan, the new nominee and his host. But when Reagan and Romney met in early March 1967 at a Republican fundraising dinner at the Washington Hilton, it would be viewed as a major turning point in their respective campaigns. New Republican senators and governors attended, as did more than two thousand Republican contributors who paid $500 apiece to hear Reagan and Romney. Reagan was the new governor and rising conservative star and Romney was the established liberal Republican who was the major contender for the 1968 nomination besides Nixon.

Romney bombed. His speech consisted "almost entirely of jokes that did not produce much laughter."[67] Romney had an "uninspiring speaking style, particularly when he appeared with a scene-stealer like Reagan."[68]

But Reagan delivered "a rousing summons to Republican conservatives to base the 1968 campaign on what he said were the lessons of 1966." The diners were not solely composed entirely of wealthy Republican conservatives. In fact more than a quarter was composed of Congressional staffers who were given tickets by other contributors. Reagan was described as a "resounding success, rousing a previously indifferent audience to round after round of applause. Most significantly, Governor Reagan managed in the process to overshadow unmistakably the only other Presidential possibility on the speaking list, Gov. George Romney." One of Romney's staunchest supporters admitted, "It was not a good night for Romney. He didn't seem to belong in the same ballroom with Reagan. It was only one night, but I don't know how many more of those we can take." The dinner pointed up one of Romney's difficulties in the presidential race: he seemed impressive when alone but suffered immensely by comparison next to "fast-thinking, facile speakers like Governor Reagan." Those in attendance left, predicting, "The next Republican candidate for President is likely to be Ronald Reagan."[69]

Washingtonians were so impressed by Reagan, who had drawn so much more applause and laughter than Romney, that many spoke of the event as a "turning point in their comparative fortunes."[70] Reagan "again stole the show. He was 'on,' his lines properly mixed substance and humor. His timing was flawless."[71] Afterwards, Reagan met with Reed, White and Nofziger to discuss the encouraging reception in the nation's capital and to plan their return visit in a week to face RFK.[72]

At his press conference, Reagan was asked about mining Haiphong Harbor. His answer clearly showed Eisenhower's earlier advice. Reagan answered emphatically, "Yes," adding that once America had asked its young men to fight and possibly die, the country owed its military that it would use the nation's "full resources" to win the war as "quickly as possible."[73]

Back in California, Reagan sought to downplay any speculation about the presidency by telling the press that his role would be limited to being California's favorite son.[74] In Sacramento, when the press was told of an upcoming second D.C. trip for the Gridiron Dinner to be followed by a third trip to D.C. the following Saturday to attend the Governor's Conference called by President Johnson, Battaglia grinned and added, "When you read about these frequent Washington trips, please don't read anything into it."[75] Meanwhile Reagan returned east and his first stop was to meet a second presidential opponent: Nelson Rockefeller.

Rockefeller

According to historian Craig Shirley, Rockefeller and Reagan "were actually good friends."[76] Your author however has found that conservative Reagan was no fan of liberal Rockefeller and the feeling was mutual. As discussed, in 1960 Reagan had sent a telegram to Nixon, who had been deciding on his choice for vice-president, saying, "Cannot support ticket if it includes Rockefeller."[77] Rockefeller had returned the favor by becoming an active opponent of Reagan's run for the governorship in 1966, as we have seen, first by having supported Christopher financially in the primary and then by having aided Democrat Brown in the general election.[78] Thus the 1968 presidential campaigns of these two governors began with definite political and likely personal animosity too. How ironic that in 1967 and 1968 both men would be asked constantly by the press about being running mates.

Of course Reagan had known of Rockefeller's public refusal to support Goldwater in 1964 and had described such actions as traitorous. Then Reagan had been tutored by Eisenhower about the importance of such party loyalty. But could either Eisenhower or Reagan conceive that Rockefeller might actually work for the Democratic opponent of a Republican? Whether Reagan knew of Rockefeller's behind-the-scenes support of Christopher in the 1966 California Republican primary, or of Rockefeller's secret advice to his Democratic opponent Brown in the general election, is not known. But once Reagan was inaugurated, a meeting of the Republican governors of the country's two most populous states, and likely candidates for the presidency in 1968, was in order.

Reagan and Rockefeller met privately for the first time, along with their wives, on March 9, 1967 at Rockefeller's fifteenth-floor apartment overlooking Central Park in Manhattan. Speaking to reporters before the get-together, Rockefeller said, "We're just going to discuss mutual state problems. This is a social event and we're not going to discuss politics."[79] Reagan told the press that "there were no differences" between himself and Governor Rockefeller. Then the two men adjourned for a private one-hour meeting accompanied only by a Rockefeller servant.

Rockefeller's New York City apartment at 812 Fifth Avenue was on the eleventh floor of the same building as Richard Nixon's on the fifth floor. Author Theodore White described Rockefeller's Manhattan home as "light and airy; its mood changed from room to room— by turn stark modern, elegant soft, traditional solid, each setting a background for painting and sculpture. The art, lovingly collected and placed, ranged from primitive to latest modern, reflecting a curiosity refined by boldest taste and sustained by infinite resources."[80]

Afterwards Rockefeller told the press they had met "just for cocktails" and to discuss mutual state problems. They each "ruled themselves out as possible Republican candidates for the Presidency."[81] Neither Reagan nor Rockefeller revealed the details of their hour long conversation, and thus whether there was an airing of political differences and/or discussions of the hidden support of Reagan's two opponents by Rockefeller remains unknown. Reagan and Rockefeller would meet again at several governors conferences, including a cruise later in 1967, and by coincidence in New Orleans in May, 1968. After leaving Rockefeller, Reagan met with Reed, Nofziger, White for a two-hour campaign review session chaired by White.[82]

Then Reagan flew to the nation's capital and spoke on Capitol Hill. After a breakfast with 143 Republican members of the House, Reagan held a luncheon for all congressmen from California. Even columnist Pearson surprisingly characterized the visits as "Reagan's Goodwill" and admitted that Reagan was "gracious."[83]

Reagan then held his usual press conference. The *New York Times* commented that Reagan "moved into the Washington scene with ease and agility, discussing every issue from Vietnam to reclamation of California's Imperial Valley."[84] The reporter noted that Reagan "was treated more like a rising Presidential candidate."[85] Reagan then confirmed that he would become California's favorite son candidate at the convention—for intrastate party unity purposes—but also hoped that no Republican "would be able to tie up the Republican nomination before the convention."[86]

As was starting to become commonplace, the press asked Reagan mainly about foreign affairs. Reagan minced no words when he was asked about using nuclear weapons in Vietnam saying, "The last person in the world that should be told we won't use them is the enemy in Vietnam."[87] Reagan, mentored by Eisenhower on foreign affairs—and about to meet Eisenhower again—had begun to apply the policies by which Eisenhower had brought the North Koreans to the negotiating table—the threat to use nuclear weapons—to Vietnam. Now Reagan was discussing specific military tactics and the use of threats.

But the meetings and dueling with his Republican rivals Romney and Rockefeller were only preparatory for the next encounter, for Reagan now was to face his nemesis: Democrat Kennedy.

Fighting RFK at the Gridiron Dinner

In pure irony, it may not only have been true that Kennedy had launched Reagan's political career by coercing General Electric and CBS to cancel *General Electric Theatre* in 1962, as Michael Reagan has recalled that his father had believed, but it would turn out that a few years later Reagan would become RFK's most formidable opponent in the 1968 presidential campaign.

Reagan and Kennedy first met in person at the prestigious Gridiron Dinner on March 11, 1967 in Washington, D.C. Walter Trohan of the *Chicago Tribune* was club president and invited Reagan as speaker for the Republicans and RFK for the Democrats. Reagan, in such a prominent Washington D.C. spotlight position, certainly fit into his plans to be viewed as a national figure and potential 1968 presidential candidate.

During March of 1967, Kennedy was seen as true heir to the legacy of his slain brother and thus was viewed as a potential challenger to the incumbent Lyndon Johnson, as the latter's unexpected announcement that he would not seek re-election would be exactly one year in the future. Having both possible 1968 presidential nominees together— Reagan and RFK—might provide insight as to how they would tangle the following year.

The dinner, closed to reporters, usually was (and is) a semi-comedic series of political spoof-skits aimed at politicians. But having such a comic event during the spring of 1967 was lamented by columnist James Reston, who felt the "present melancholy air" in the capital was due to the twin problems of war and poverty and neither of which were funny.[88] But Republicans in California had seemed elated during the same time period because of their new governor and his successful new programs. Reagan had already made one trip to the nation's capital the week before to attend the Republican fundraising dinner, and California Republican National Committeeman Gardiner Johnson called attention to the "tremendous reception" that Reagan had received.[89]

But not everyone in the political arena was pleased by the invitation extended to Reagan to be the Republican speaker in the national limelight at the Gridiron Dinner. Richard Nixon wrote to Reagan on February 24, 1967, "Through my private intelligence, I have learned that you will be the speaker at the Gridiron dinner. The purpose of this note is to wish you well." Nixon explained that he could not attend due to his own upcoming world tour but continued telling Reagan, "The Gridiron speech, as you know, is quite a test for the average political figure. My guess is, however, that this white tie audience will present no significant problem for you." The psychodynamics of this letter for the Nixon-Reagan relationship is discussed at length by historians Gibbs and Duffy. [90] Nixon, already having begun years earlier to view Reagan as a potential threat from the right wing of the Republican Party for 1968, now was seeing his worst nightmare becoming reality: Reagan was supplanting Nixon on the main political stage in the nation's capital.

The March 11, 1967 Gridiron Dinner turned out to be a bipartisan series of parodies, skits, songs, and self-deprecating humor. One skit featured the voice of Senator Everett Dirksen, as the Oracle of Delphi, trying to discern who would be the Republican nominee in 1968. President Johnson was hailed in song as "King of the Road." RFK was shown in a parody of "Winchester Cathedral," and other impersonators of George Romney, Hubert Humphrey, and Richard Nixon brought on laughter. A second RFK impersonator was a long-haired newsman dressed in a leather jacket who was preceded by motorcycle roars and accompanied by a gang of disciples. There even was a duet sung by impersonators of Soviet Premiere Kosygin and Chairman Mao Tse-tung of communist China[91]

The comments at the Gridiron Dinner traditionally were off-the-record, but some observers did make subsequent comments. Kennedy introduced Reagan as, "the 'acting' governor of California."[92] Reed commented that Kennedy "was masterful; his jokes were self-deprecating one-liners about himself, his family, and his problems with President Johnson. His timing was great and his humor was perfectly attuned to that Washington in-crowd."[93] Reagan's performance was "light and his jokes good, but they were too California-oriented. They did not make much sense to the Washington insiders. Reagan tried to wind up with a short, serious pitch, but it failed."[94] Newspaper reporter Bill Boyarsky said that Reagan had "bombed out."[95]

What Reagan thought of RFK during the dinner is not known. During the remainder of the evening, if Reagan and Kennedy between them discussed Reagan's termination from his CBS program five years earlier due to the direct intervention of RFK, or discussed any of their other interactions discussed earlier, it has not come to light.

For Reagan and RFK in their first in-person head-to-head encounter, Reed reflected, "Bobby won. Reagan departed as a country bumpkin not yet ready for prime time. As a pro, however, he had learned some lessons."[96] But in just two months, the tables would be turned.

Despite Battaglia's earlier announcement of a third trip to the nation's capital in the short span of three weeks, Reagan could not make this third visit due to state duties in Sacramento. But Reagan's presence and his presidential aspirations were felt. The Republican governors were deciding if they should support any of Johnson's domestic or foreign policies. The national press noted that any such help to Johnson would be "politically embarrassing" for the governors who were viewed as potential presidential candidates: Romney and "Ronald Reagan of California."[97]

Being Taken Seriously

The same day, another *New York Times* writer commented, "Some of Ronald Reagan's closest aides are talking seriously about 1968 and Reagan himself has shown no reluctance to become a 'favorite son.'"[98] The writer wondered if their 1968 nominee could unify the party after the divisions of 1964? Could "Reagan...furnish that kind of unity?"[99] But at this point the newspaper columnist felt that Johnson was "unlikely to retire and is going to be hard to beat."[100]

The young, liberal Republican research and policy organization headquartered in Cambridge, Massachusetts, the Ripon Society, issued a warning in its March issue of *The Forum*, writing that signs of Reagan's presidential candidacy were "growing rapidly."[101] It noted that besides California, Reagan might go to the Republican convention in 1968 as the favorite son of "several Western States" plus it had received word that Reagan would enter primaries in New Hampshire, Oregon, Nebraska, and Wisconsin. The liberal think tank worried that a Reagan nomination in Miami Beach would make "1968 another year of disaster and disunity for the Republican Party."[102] Obviously the Ripon Society felt that Republicans should unify only if the party's choice was liberal.[103] [104]

Another liberal media bastion, the *New York Times*, decided that the Ripon Society's warning and attack on Reagan was so good, they decided to reprint the entire article from *The Forum* as an opinion piece a few days later. Entitled "Another Opinion: A Republican Attack on Reagan," the newspaper itself made no editorial comment per se but certainly left the reader with the distinct impression that the newspaper was in full agreement with the attacks on a potential Reagan presidential bid for 1968.[105]

A Harris Poll at the time showed that Reagan already was in third place of GOP voters for the 1968 nomination, behind Nixon and Romney but ahead of Rockefeller or Percy. The growing Reagan bandwagon was joined by Governors Tim Babcock of Montana, Stanley Hathaway of Idaho, and Don Samuelson of Idaho. Speculation was that Southern Nixon delegates "would join the Western Reagan bloc at the earliest opportunity."[106] Ronald Reagan's "Presidential ambitions must be taken seriously."[107]

While the media debated the Reagan candidacy, the citizen-governor was about to revisit the citizen-soldier.

Endnotes

1. Chester et. al., p. 197
2. Chester et. al., p. 200
3. Van Natta pers int 7/30/12
4. Newsweek 5/22/67, p. 36
5. Weaver, Warren "Reagan Outpoints Romney at Dinner," *NYT*, 3/3/67, p. 23
6. Nofziger, p. 68
7. Nofziger, ibid
8. Reed, p. 11
9. Chester et. al., p. 197
10. Jonas, Frank H. and Harmer, John L., p. 469
11. Chester et. al., p. 197
12. Chester ibid
13. Skinner et. al., p. 34
14. Skinner et. al., p. 34
15. Reed, p. 11
16. Reed, p. 12
17. Reed, p. 12
18. Reed, p. 12
19. Chester et. al., p. 199
20. Chester et. al., p. 199
21. Reed, pers int 10/17/12
22. Chester et. al., p. 199
23. Hill, Gladwin, "Reagan Finishing National Swings," *NYT,* 1/21/68, p. 41

24. Chester et. al., p. 199
25. Kopelson, G 2015A
26. Chester et. al., p. 197
27. Reed, *Reagan Enigma*, p. 130
28. Deaver, oral history, p. 9
29. Greenstein
30. Chester et. al., p. 200
31. Nofziger, p. 69
32. Thomas, Evan, p. 378
33. Pearson, Drew, Washington Merry-Go-Round, 1/23/67
34. Pearson, Drew, Washington Merry-Go-Round, 2/13/67
35. "GOP Hopefuls Warm Up for '68," *NYT*, 1/29/67, p. 162
36. Safire, p. 42
37. Buchanan, p. 109
38. Safire, p. 42-26
39. Reed, p. 13; Reagan-Reed planning meeting 2/3/1967 at San Francisco hotel
40. Walth, p. 202
41. Buchanan, p. 83
42. Kopelson, Gene. 2014D
43. Turner, Wallace "Reagan Attracts Backing In West," *NYT*, 2/13/67, p. 26
44. Hoover papers, Governor's schedule 7-11-67 to 7-12-67
45. Van Natta, pers int 7/30/12
46. Van Natta, pers int 7/30/12
47. "Reagan Warns Against Feuding in GOP," *Seattle Times*, 2/12/67, p. 2
48. Turner op.cit.
49. *Newsweek*, 5/22/67, p. 36
50. Hoover archives
51. Hodel, pers comm. 8/25/12
52. Van Natta, pers int 7/30/68
53. Evans, Thomas
54. RR 269
55. RR 269; *Newsweek*, 2/22/67, p. 36
56. Turner op.cit.
57. Turner op.cit.
58. Van Natta pers int 7/30/12
59. *Newsweek*, 2/22/67, p. 36
60. Turner op.cit.
61. Turner op.cit.
62. Reed, p. 13
63. Turner op.cit.
64. Turner op.cit.
65. Reed, p. 13
66. "Another Opinion," *NYT,* 3/26/67, p. 155
67. Weaver, Warren "Reagan Outpoints Romney at Dinner," *NYT*, 3/3/67, p. 23
68. Kabaservice, p. 210
69. Weaver, et. al.
70. "Another Opinion," *NYT,* 3/26/67, p. 155
71. Reed, p. 13
72. Reagan-Reed, 3/2/1967
73. www.efootage.com/tape 78307
74. Cannon, p. 231
75. ibid.
76. Shirley, *Reagan's Revolution*, p. 12
77. Gibbs, p. 197
78. Holmes, p. 7-9
79. "Rockefeller Talks With Reagan in City," *NYT*, 3/10/67, p. 35
80. White, Theodore, p. 43
81. "Rockefeller talks…" *NYT*, op.cit.
82. Reagan-Reed, 3/9/1967
83. Pearson, Drew, Washington Merry-Go-Round 3/11/67
84. Herbers, John, "Reagan Greeted on Capitol Hill," *NYT*, 3/11/67, p. 13
85. ibid
86. ibid
87. ibid
88. Reston, James, "Washington: Why Not Try Laughter?," *NYT*, 3/12/67, p. 205

89.   Davies, Lawrence E, "California GOP Praises Reagan", *NYT,* 3/5/67, p. 40
90.   Gibbs and Duffy, p. 208
91.   "Capital Newsmen Spoof Politicians," *NYT*, 3/12/67, p. 36
92.   Adler, Bill, "The Quotable Kennedys," *Harper Collins*, NY 1997.
93.   Reed, p. 14
94.   Reed, p. 13
95.   Humphrey, Hall, "Book Rates TV Image of Politicians," *The Oregonian,* 5/31/68 sec 2, p. 13
96.   Reed, p. 14
97.   "25 GOP Governors to Chart Strategy," *NYT*, 3/16/67, p. 93
98.   Wicker, Tom, "In the Nation: Counting Votes Before They Hatch," *NYT*, 3/16/67, p. 46
99.   Wicker, ibid
100. Wicker, ibid
101. "Ripon Society Fears Reagan Candidacy," *NYT*, 3/22/67, p. 26
102. ibid
103. The entire history of the liberal Ripon Society's attacks upon conservative Republicans was chronicled recently by historian Geoffrey Kabaservice
104. Kabaservice
105. "Another Opinion: A Republican Attack on Reagan," *NYT*, 3/26/67, p. 155
106. ibid
107. ibid

CHAPTER 5: COACH EISENHOWER, PART ONE

"Governor Reagan is one of the men I admire most in this world... I will support Governor Reagan for president if he is the party's nominee."

~ Dwight Eisenhower[1]

"I did get some sound advice."

~ Ronald Reagan[2]

"There was "no doubt in Reagan's mind that a serious campaign was underway. He certainly acted that way."

~ Thomas C. Reed[3]

Eisenhower Advises Reagan on the 1968 Presidential Campaign

Traveling west after the Gridiron Club fiasco with Kennedy, Reagan paid a second visit to Eisenhower, who was wintering near Palm Springs. Eisenhower had seen himself as a latter day Cincinnatus, the citizen-soldier "reluctantly but dutifully" returning to "lead his nation."[4] This was what Reagan first had observed about Eisenhower. As mentioned, it was early 1952 when the combination of "Citizens for Eisenhower," the huge rally at Madison Square Garden, coupled with his unexpected New Hampshire primary victory plus the spontaneous write-in campaign for Eisenhower in the Minnesota primary—of more than 100,000 write-in votes "forced Eisenhower" to reconsider his prior position and to enter the Republican race.[5] The public had forced Eisenhower to accept the mantle of leadership in 1952 and Reagan was awaiting the same mantle in 1968.

When Reagan would be asked about his own presidential ambitions and plans for 1968, he often would tell the press that he initially had been reluctant to enter political office, just as he would remind the nation when delivering his Farewell Address in 1989. For 1968, if the delegates and party wanted him as their nominee, he would not refuse, as it was his duty to serve. As Reagan recently had discussed with the press, he thought that General Sherman's famous refusal to serve was ill-conceived. As will be seen, Reagan would confirm to the press that his own thoughts on the subject had come from Eisenhower. Both viewed their duty as caring very much about "being seen as a man of principle, the kind who never cuts corners or resort(s) to expediency."[6]

Reagan had taken Eisenhower's 1952 citizen-soldier persona and had become the "Citizen-Politician" for 1966, which in 1968 would morph into the "Citizen-Governor." Reagan's 1966 "common sense" campaign slogan had originated with coach Eisenhower's first letter. Lastly, Reagan in 1966 had followed Parkinson's Eleventh Commandment for California and "never attacked an opponent by name."[7] In 1968 Reagan would follow Eisenhower's expanded, national version of the commandment and never would attack, indeed hardly ever would speak, the names of Republicans Nixon or Romney or Rockefeller. Instead Reagan's campaign speeches would focus entirely on attacking the Democratic Kennedy-Johnson administration; even then Reagan almost never would refer to his presumed general election opponents by name.

After Reagan won the 1966 primary and general elections by following Eisenhower's detailed advice, Eisenhower's friend, publisher William E. Robinson, had sent Eisenhower updates on Reagan during the winter of 1966-1967. In late December, Robinson discussed the political situation and suggested that Romney was his present choice for president but that Reagan should be vice-president. Days after Reagan's inauguration as governor, Robinson sent Eisenhower a new letter stating that Reagan represented Ike's brand of Republicanism better than any prominent Republican on the scene today. Reagan was described as bold as well as unique, in being one of the first political executives who said he intended to cut expenses. Robinson theorized to Eisenhower that should Reagan and Romney could get together on the general's kind of Republican doctrine, they would be unbeatable in 1968.[8]

Eisenhower's answer showed he was up-to-date on issues facing the new governor: "So far he has made some very splendid appointments and some solid moves. However he has all the intelligentsia against him because he wants to have a tuition of reasonable amount for all students at state-supported colleges." Eisenhower was in favor of Reagan's proposal, discussed earlier, to have students pay ten percent of their tuition costs. Eisenhower added however that with all of California's budget mess and high property taxes, "Reagan starts off, I think, with a problem that almost defies solution."[9]

Had Eisenhower considered in detail Robinson's first observation—that Reagan best represented Eisenhower's brand of

Republicanism—and its implications? Or indeed was this just the growing confirmation of what Eisenhower already had been thinking about Reagan as his political heir? Could Ronald Reagan indeed be a better political heir of Eisenhower than the 1968 front-runner Nixon?

The relationship of Eisenhower and Nixon has been analyzed by many historians. For whatever good or bad, political or personal, qualities Eisenhower had found in Nixon, Eisenhower also knew that Nixon had lost in 1960 and in 1962. But Reagan just had won in the nation's most populous state with an impressive margin of almost a million votes. Plus by following coach Eisenhower's recommendations, Reagan had attracted disaffected Democrats and Independents including having attracted substantial union and Mexican American voters. As seen earlier, for Eisenhower, electability had always been uppermost in his mind, and Reagan already had proven his electability when he had won the California primary and governorship versus the string of election losses with Nixon.

March 1967 Meeting

It was in late December when, as noted, Eisenhower had written to Reagan asking to meet with Reagan to discuss foreign affairs in more depth. Their first in-person meeting had been at Gettysburg the prior June when Eisenhower had discussed Vietnam, had endorsed Reagan and had certified him as presidential timbre. Just before their upcoming March meeting, Eisenhower was becoming more and more distressed at Johnson's mishandling of the war. Eisenhower could not "believe America would cut and run."[10]

This time Eisenhower and Reagan met at Rancho Mirage, where Eisenhower had a home and which would become the Eisenhower Medical Center. Although their meeting was described to the press as "primarily a social gathering," they did admit to the press they had discussed problems in California and Vietnam. Reagan said, "I did get some sound advice." A photograph of the two men that day talking to reporters showed them smiling happily together.

The facts that Eisenhower had asked to meet Reagan to discuss world affairs, that Governor Reagan and General Eisenhower followed through and indeed did again discuss Vietnam and perhaps other world hotspots, that Eisenhower advised Reagan about it, and the men revealed this to the press are all critically significant. Via Eisenhower's mentoring, Reagan was continuing broadening his areas of strength beyond domestic affairs. And who better to coach Reagan than the man who had carried the world to victory in World War II and who had ended the Korean War fighting upon his assumption of the presidency—Eisenhower!

At the meeting, Eisenhower gave Reagan specific and detailed military strategic and tactical lessons. Their lunch meeting lasted a full two and-a-half hours. A lot of significant ground was covered. Eisenhower mentored Reagan to use the tactics that had worked so well for the general in winning World War II and in ending the Korean War by threats.

Eisenhower told Reagan what had worked in Korea and what he had been urging Johnson privately for eighteen months. He said, "I'd mine Haiphong Harbor." Ike mentored Reagan that his own recommendation was to bomb "hard." Eisenhower then recommended a policy from which many would recoil in horror when Reagan or Eisenhower would broach the subject later. North Vietnam was in the war already, offering sanctuary and killing American soldiers. The general told Reagan that he wanted no safe sanctuaries in adjoining countries, urging "hot pursuit of troops or aircraft into havens."

Eisenhower then changed from giving Reagan specific critiques of current administration policies to what might seem to be tactics that a future Commander-in-Chief Reagan might order come January, 1969: "Plan for amphibious landings on northern turf. Head for their capital; bomb the dams; flood the place."[11] Here was Eisenhower not just prepping a new politician, but mentoring a protege who might in fact become his political heir at the White House.

Reed recalled that Reagan's "vast internal hard drive" absorbed everything his mentor had advised. Eisenhower's principle of overwhelming force would become a new theme for Reagan. Thus Eisenhower had helped Reagan's expertise in foreign affairs grow exponentially.

Subsequent Reagan comments indicate that he learned a great deal from the general that day. At the press conference, a smiling Eisenhower is evidence that his wish to continue to mentor Reagan beyond domestic policy issues—specifically on world affairs, the original purpose of the meeting—had been a huge success.

What follows is pure speculation on additional aspects of their conversations. Based upon Reagan's subsequent speeches and press conferences during the 1968 campaign, the thread of ideas and policy recommendations directly from Eisenhower to Reagan is clear. During his presidential campaign in 1967-1968, Reagan would not ask staff members to research policies or statements of Eisenhower for use in Reagan speeches or press conferences. Indeed other than what will be cited here, there are no known notes or diaries from Reagan or his staff, which cite anything related to Eisenhower (or Robert Kennedy) at all. As will be seen, Reagan's citing of Eisenhower would stem from his own observations (likely starting as early as 1953 as discussed earlier), readings and internal analyses, and then the private meetings (there would be four) and multiple phone conversations and letters exchanged with the general.

Eisenhower had taken office after Korean peace talks with the Truman administration had stalled; during this period, thousands of American soldiers had died. As new president, he had campaigned on going to Korea to reassess the military situation. Eisenhower had sent out warnings in early May 1953 that "American patience had worn out and the United States was making its final offer at the negotiating table."[12] Many times during the 1968 campaign, Reagan—who had seen first-hand the dragged out real peace negotiation headlines during the filming of *Prisoner of War*—would make similar warnings that America should set a firm deadline for Vietnamese negotiations and would emphasize that they would not drag out as had happened in Korea during Truman's watch. In addition, he would say that a new president in 1969 presumably a new President Reagan—should reassess the military options for Vietnam just as Eisenhower had done in Korea.

In Korea, Eisenhower had threatened to use nuclear weapons. He had told the military to come up with a "massive order of attack, including nuclear weapons if necessary, to end the war."[13] Specifically, historian Stephen Ambrose noted that in May 1953, Ike had put pressure on Red China by threatening that if a truce could not be arranged, America would use atomic weapons. Then Eisenhower had backed up his threat by transferring atomic warheads to American bases in Okinawa. The Chinese accepted the truce.[14] The next year on April 7, 1954 was when Eisenhower had pronounced his domino theory.[15]

The mainstay of Reagan's Vietnam policy, asserted tentatively at first in New Haven in 1965 and Seattle in 1966, and which was repeated vigorously and often by Reagan throughout the campaign in 1967 and 1968, similarly would be that the Americans should fight to win. And part of that policy should include the threat to use nuclear weapons, as Reagan had first told the press earlier. Indeed was Eisenhower's use of threats in the early 1950s, transmitted to Reagan in the mid-to-late 1960s, a direct precursor of future President Reagan's sending nuclear-tipped cruise missiles and Pershing missile launchers to Europe in the early 1980s as a way to send a similar message to threaten the Soviet Union and thus force them into losing an arms race?

For Eisenhower, like Reagan, it was the *threat* that was critical. Historian Evan Thomas explains that the military foundation of Eisenhower's entire presidency was to threaten that atomic weapons might be used, be it in Korea or against Red China or the Soviet Union. And of most importance, "the threat had to be real."[16] That is why Eisenhower had changed the command structure for atomic weapons and had turned them over to the military, with him as Commander-in-Chief, from the civilian administrative control that had existed before. And of more importance, to make his enemies feel that the threat from Eisenhower was real, he had ordered that the military place the atomic weapons near planes "ready to fly"[17] and to American bases on Okinawa as noted. Similarly during the 1968 campaign, Reagan had once already, and would repeatedly, tell the press that America should threaten North Vietnam with atomic weapons, and often Reagan would suffer tremendously negative liberal press analysis claiming how awful Reagan's policies were. But the liberal press missed the point. As Reagan likely learned from Eisenhower at their meetings or conversations, they each wanted the enemy to feel threatened regardless of whether either man might ever have ordered their use. As Johnson had failed to learn from Eisenhower, and in the second decade of the 21st century when President Obama would fail to learn from Eisenhower and would tell America's enemies exactly when he would withdraw all troops from Iraq and Afghanistan, Reagan knew to never reveal your hand to the enemy, to in fact threaten to do worse, and to leave them "quaking in their beds" until coming to the peace table in earnest.

Indeed historian Thomas' thesis is that Eisenhower never told any single person, possibly not even his son John or his brother Milton, whether or not he ever would use those weapons. Reagan would be in a different situation, as Vietnam became his first area for foreign policy starting in 1966. Several times at press conferences he would tell the reporters that he did not intend to use them but was quick to add that those Americans in charge of the conflict, i.e. President Johnson, should nevertheless issue the threat. The policy of both Eisenhower and Reagan was that "the essence of effective deterrence is to never let on that you are not willing to use your ultimate weapon."[18]

Conventional forces were not to be ignored however. In World War II when American military planners initially did not want to join Britain in a planned air raid against the city of Berlin, Eisenhower had overruled them saying, "I am always prepared to take part in anything that gives real promise to ending the war quickly."[19] In Korea, in addition to the threats of atomic bombs, Eisenhower had sent U.S. planes to bomb "hydroelectric plants, dams, and irrigation canals. Much of North Korea was blacked out and flooded, and with the rice crop ruined, the country faced famine."[20] And in Korea, as discussed by historian Evan Thomas, the end of the active conflict was due to a combination of the threat of atomic weapons, the actual conventional attacks on both military and non-military targets, the death of Stalin (who was the North Korean patron), and the fear the Chinese had of an American amphibious landing.[21]

During the 1968 campaign, Reagan once again followed his mentor's advice almost to the letter, just as he had done in 1965-1966. Reagan would want Haiphong Harbor mined regardless of how it might impact the civilian population. Reagan would recommend that enemy Vietcong or North Vietnamese troops who fled into sanctuary sites in adjacent countries be chased and attacked from the air. As will be seen, in July 1968 Reagan would follow through on Eisenhower's March, 1967 advice and advocate that American jets should bomb the dams that supplied water for North Vietnam's crops. Just as Eisenhower had told his air force to threaten to use the atomic bomb by placing the equipment next to military aircraft and that the Chinese were fearful about an amphibious landing, Reagan would recommend that the American navy should practice amphibious invasion drills off the North Vietnamese coast so that both the civilian and military populations would worry about an imminent invasion from the sea. Clearly Ronald Reagan saw himself carrying on Eisenhower's successful military policies from World War II and the Korean War into the new conflict in Vietnam. Reagan was seeing himself as Eisenhower's heir; the general was quite comfortable mentoring Reagan, likely sensing and/or hoping that some day in the future, Reagan would succeed in carrying forth those same goals and methods.

Indeed during the 1968 campaign, Reagan would become the only Republican candidate to recommend those exact same policies as Eisenhower. As detailed by historian Andrew Johns, Romney and Rockefeller were decidedly on the dove side, while Nixon's policies for Vietnam never became very specific, even through the general election. When Eisenhower and Reagan would recommend attacking sanctuary sites, Nixon would say he never would, even though as president his invasion into Cambodia in the spring of 1970 would generate massive student protests.

Did Reagan and Eisenhower also discuss communism and how to achieve its downfall by means other than war—such as military spending while at the same time free market capitalism could outshine planned statist economies? Did they discuss the elimination of nuclear weapons, which Eisenhower had proposed at the United Nations in 1953? Eisenhower's "Atoms for Peace" speech, as will be seen, made such a lasting impression on Ronald Reagan that it was to become official policy of his future presidential administration and to become the basis of his agreements with Gorbachev. Is it not likely that Reagan and Eisenhower discussed the subject at some point during this time period?

Future President Reagan would pursue Eisenhower's goal of the elimination of nuclear weapons if a defensive shield—"Star Wars" or the Strategic Defense Initiative—were in place to protect America from incoming missiles. As we will see later, Reagan would get involved in discussions about an anti-ballistic missile system in the fall of 1967, which would continue into the summer of 1968. Reagan's initial advocacy for such an anti-ballistic missile shield would be initiated during the 1968 campaign, more than a decade before the idea of the Strategic Defense Initiative would be reborn during his future first presidential term. Might he and Eisenhower have discussed such ideas in 1967?

Eisenhower had faced the specter of rising military costs, over-estimates of their true military needs, and associated inflated costs during his entire military and presidential careers, which then had culminated in his famous Farewell Address warning about the Military-Industrial complex. As an example, on April 4, 1949, Eisenhower had told an audience, "We pay for a new destroyer with new homes that could have housed more than 8,000 people."[22] Likely Eisenhower had discussed such military spending with his protégé, for in the summer of 1968 as we will see, Reagan would warn his countrymen about military over-spending with similar warnings equating the cost of one fighter jet versus the number of schools that could have been built instead.

It was Eisenhower, "more than other top commanders in World War II" who had been "comfortable with scientific advancement in the art of war."[23] Eisenhower, who previously had advanced the idea of tanks along with Patton (as had Churchill in Britain), "pushed for high tech advances in weaponry and radar."[24] During the Eisenhower presidential years, technology had flourished. Major achievements had included the creation of America's intercontinental ballistic missile system, the U2 spy plane, the launching of reconnaissance satellites, and America's nuclear weapons arsenal. It would be Reagan at Cleveland and at Amarillo in the summer of 1968 who would cite those Eisenhower years—of technology flourishing—in comparison to how much of a military technological decline there had been under Kennedy-Johnson.

Did Reagan and Eisenhower, who had discussed RFK briefly a year earlier at their first meeting at Gettysburg, again discuss Kennedy, who would be the heir-apparent if Johnson decided not to run in 1968, and whom Reagan was about to debate? Eisenhower had "regarded Robert Kennedy as a dangerous force in American politics."[25] In fact within a day of the assassination of President Kennedy in 1963, Eisenhower and new President Johnson had conferred next to the Oval Office and Eisenhower "fervently pressed Johnson to curb Robert Kennedy's rumored abuses of the Justice Department and his use of intimidation tactics to silence critics of the Kennedy administration."[26] Indeed David and Julie Eisenhower in their recent book honoring his grandfather's last ten years, although the authors do not mention the meetings Eisenhower had with Reagan nor their growing relationship, they do cite a memo of the conversation with Johnson saying that business leaders who were having their finances audited were asked "political party" types of questions. Plus there had been threats by Kennedy's Justice Department that if a corporation or university gave Congress any testimony unfavorable to the Kennedy administration, all future government contracts with that corporation or university would be cancelled.[27] Eisenhower then had let known his feelings about Kennedy's election as New York Senator in 1964 via a letter he had written to Rockefeller in 1966. He had disdained the New York electorate when they had elected in 1964 "a stranger from another state to be their senator and reject a good citizen of their own."[28]

As we have seen, Ronald Reagan had felt he had been one of the prime recipients of Kennedy's harassment: as noted, Michael Reagan confirmed that Reagan's *General Electric Theatre* television show had been cancelled because Kennedy had threatened to cancel future General Electric contracts unless GE got rid of Reagan, and then Reagan felt that Kennedy directly had the IRS audit the Reagan tax returns. If Eisenhower and Reagan ever discussed Robert Kennedy this second time, Reagan could have gone on for hours providing Eisenhower with exact specific examples to prove that the rumors about Kennedy's abuses were in fact true.

And Kennedy's present policies in Vietnam, to give up and quit, were anathema to both Eisenhower and Reagan. After all, Reagan just had met Kennedy at the Gridiron Club. As will be seen, Reagan's expansive knowledge about Vietnam, to be showcased at an upcoming debate with RFK, may in fact have had, in major part, its origin with his mentor, Ike. It is not unreasonable to assume that Eisenhower not only gave Reagan a pep talk about the Gridiron Club encounter, but may indeed also have advised Reagan with important preparatory background information about Vietnam for Reagan to use during the upcoming debate. After all, the debate with RFK would be on exactly the topic of highest importance to mentor Eisenhower and his political student, Reagan: how to win in Vietnam.

Dieting

One topic that might indeed have come up was the Democrats' targeting of poverty. Historian Evan Thomas cited an April, 1959 speech of John Kennedy declaring, "Seventeen million Americans went to bed hungry every night."[29] Told of the speech at a meeting of Republican leaders, Eisenhower callously replied, "They must all be dieting."[30]

Eight years later, Ronald Reagan's standard campaign speech during his 1968 campaign often cited Robert Kennedy's exact same claim about hunger. Reagan's answer was, "They all must be on diets." Regardless of the merits of the claims about hunger, and we later will review President Eisenhower's generous program to help feed the world's hungry, the point is that Reagan used Eisenhower's exact words. Did Reagan know of what Eisenhower had said in 1959? Most likely Eisenhower had told Reagan of his 1959 comment during one of their numerous conversations or meetings and then Reagan incorporated Eisenhower's exact words into his standard 1968 presidential campaign speech.

At Rancho Mirage, Reagan and Eisenhower told the press that they had discussed problems within California, and certainly the prior Watts riots may have been part of their discussions. As historian Kasey Pipes has noted, Eisenhower felt that one direct reason for the riots was the "heightened expectation levels produced by the New Frontier and Great Society."[31] When those unrealistic expectations were not met quickly, the riots had ensued. Throughout the campaign speeches Reagan would make in 1967-1968, he often would cite those false expectations as a reason why minorities should vote for the policies of Republicans, which clearly he felt were more realistic.[32] Eisenhower and RFK had had the verbal spat about the Watts riots, when former attorney general RFK had said that blacks did not have to obey the law. As will be seen, Reagan would deliver a white paper speech on that exact subject a year hence.

Admiration for Reagan and Ike's Tentative Endorsement for President

The luncheon was only part of the almost 4 hours they spent together on March 13. As reported by the *Desert Sun* on its cover story that day, both men heartily endorsed the fact that the Eisenhower Medical Center was being built without any federal funds. Then Eisenhower said he would support Reagan for president "if he is the party's nominee." Ike added that if Reagan were drafted at the 1968 convention, "he'll respond if duty calls." Unlike what Governor Romney would declare in 1968 prior to the convention, that he would refuse to support Reagan as nominee, and what would occur in 2016 when various Republicans would announce in advance they would refuse to support Donald Trump if he were the nominee, Ike knew quite well in 1967 that Reagan was well within the wide political tent of Republicanism.

But what happened next to Eisenhower and Reagan at their March, 1967 impromptu joint press conference generated misunderstandings, an apology from newsman Walter Cronkite, became the subject of sections of several Eisenhower biographies, yet may have obscured the true importance of the meeting to the press and the public.

Reagan recently had announced officially that he was going to be California's favorite son at the convention. At the joint press conference, Reagan was asked about his presidential aspirations, as had been asked of him many times by that point. He gave his standard answer that he would "make his own decision" about seeking the Republican nomination. Then the reporters turned to Eisenhower.

The *New York Times* headline would run, "Eisenhower Says He Admires Reagan," and the story would state that Eisenhower had told reporters, "There are a number of men who would make fine presidents in our party. Governor Reagan is one of the men I admire most in this world."[33]

Eisenhower biographers Stephen Ambrose and Arthur Larson each described what actually happened. Larson explained that Eisenhower had told him the true details personally afterwards. Eisenhower was besieged by all the reporters at the press conference. Simultaneously, one reporter on Eisenhower's right side asked his opinion of Nixon while a second reporter on his left side asked his opinion of Reagan. Eisenhower turned to the reporter who had asked about Nixon saying, "he is one of the ablest men I know and a man I admire deeply and for whom I have great affection." But most of the other reporters had only heard the question about Reagan and assumed that Eisenhower's answer was about the governor. So the next day's headlines, exemplified by The *New York Times* above proclaimed, "Governor Reagan is one of the men I admire most in the world."

What could Eisenhower do? He told Larson that if he went out of his way to issue a clarification saying that Reagan was *not* one of the men he had most admired, that would have made things much worse. In fact, he told Larson he did like Reagan. So Eisenhower let the matter rest.[34]

Walter Cronkite reported the story on his CBS evening news program using the *New York Times* headline as his source. When Eisenhower called Cronkite to tell him what really had happened, Cronkite was "chagrined to admit his information came from a newspaper and he hoped some day to change it."[35] Cronkite never corrected the error, and the episode is not mentioned by Cronkite biographer, historian Douglas Brinkley.[36] The press mix-up obscured the true historical importance of the Eisenhower-Reagan meeting that day: the mentoring of Ronald Reagan on world affairs which was the natural continuation of all the advice Eisenhower had been giving to Reagan all along. Then Reagan returned to California.

Had Reagan and Reed been able to see into the future, they might have altered Reagan's California travel plans slightly. On that same day, a rising young member of Great Britain's Conservative Party named Margaret Thatcher was in Los Angeles as part of the State Department's International Visitor Program. [37] Perhaps Reagan might have met her for the first time then. In fact, Thatcher would not meet Reagan in person until 1975.[38]

Press Speculation

Reagan returned to Sacramento while Reed stopped off in Milwaukee to begin planning Reagan's first primary campaign. Reed had campaign meetings with Reagan either in Sacramento or via telephone on April 19, 23 and May 2.[39] Meanwhile the national press began to contemplate that Reagan had a serious presidential campaign ongoing. Indeed some in the media thought that Reagan could indeed become the nominee.

The *New York Times* reported that neither Nixon nor Romney had clear paths to victory. They might end up dividing up wins in several 1968 primary states. So Reagan's support initially was interpreted as "vital to a Nixon bid." But on the other hand, Reagan's own growing strength then was seen as a direct threat to a Nixon victory:

"If Mr. Reagan holds the votes of California and some of the more conservative Western states for himself, probably not even primary victories could win for Mr. Nixon."[40]

The newspaper analyzed the Republican race with a photograph that was symbolic of where the three major contenders were both physically in the photo and philosophically. Romney was at the left, Nixon was in the center, and Reagan was to their right, and indeed both Nixon and Romney were looking to Reagan with smiles. It was true that Nixon was seen as the only Republican with foreign policy experience "needed to lead the nation in these troubled times." But the "key to the whole puzzle, however, may possibly be found in California where Governor Reagan controls the second largest convention delegation." As a result Reagan "will acquire a significant bargaining position" in Miami Beach. Indeed Nixon's team regarded Reagan as "an independent force" with "the power to split the conservatives and make the nomination of a moderate candidate measurably easier."[41]

Unnamed conservative Republicans then turned upside-down the entire earlier analysis of Reagan in a secondary role. They wondered if Reagan "would hold out votes needed to nominate Richard Nixon. Others think Mr. Nixon should throw his support to a fresher face and a more certifiable conservative in the person of the California governor."[42] Clearly the national media viewed Reagan as the governor controlling the California delegation and conservatives nationally. The unnamed Republicans, but not the newspaper, got it right. After all, Reagan was already months into the campaign.

Reed Goes Underground

At the end of Reagan's first one-hundred days, Reed as had been planned, left Sacramento to pursue the Reagan campaign without the duties of being Appointments Secretary. Haerle took his place. Reagan was given weekly progress reports on the campaign and once a month was given a delegate total.[43] There was "no doubt in Reagan's mind that a serious campaign was underway. He certainly acted that way."[44]

And as if to emphasize the seriousness of the campaign, Ronald Reagan was about to face the most important campaign event up to that point in the late spring: confronting again his nemesis, Robert F. Kennedy. But rather than at a private, humor-filled political event like the Gridiron Club, this time the confrontation would be a serious international debate to be viewed by millions and would cover an area in which Reagan clearly was becoming an expert thanks to his continuing discussions with Eisenhower: foreign affairs.

Endnotes

1. "Eisenhower Says He Admires Reagan," *NYT*, 3/14/67, p. 26; Kramer, Chuck, "Reagan, Ike Praise Private Fund Concept," *Desert Sun*, 3/13/1967, p. 1
2. ibid
3. Reed, p. 14
4. Thomas, Ikes Bluff, p. 26
5. Jacobs, p. 276- 278
6. Thomas, p. 46
7. Thomas, p. 47
8. William E. Robinson to Dwight D. Eisenhower, 1/7/67 letter, Eisenhower, Dwight D.: Post-Presidential Papers 1961-1969, Special Names Series, Box 17, Robinson, William 1967, Dwight D. Eisenhower Presidential Library
9. Dwight D. Eisenhower to William E. Robinson, 1/14/67 letter, Eisenhower, Dwight D.: Post-Presidential Papers 1961-1969, Special Names Series, Box 17, Robinson, William 1967, Dwight D. Eisenhower Presidential Library
10. Ambrose, p. 561
11. Reed, *The Reagan Enigma*, p. 48
12. Thomas, p. 75
13. Evans, p. 74
14. Ambrose, Stephen "The Age of Ike," *New Republic*, 5/9/1981
15. Ambrose, p. 357-364
16. Thomas, p. 72
17. Thomas, p. 72
18. Thomas, p. 80
19. Thomas, p. 76-77
20. Thomas, p. 76
21. Thomas, p. 81
22. Thomas, p. 64
23. Thomas, p. 146
24. Thomas ibid
25. Eisenhower, David, p. 204
26. Eisenhower, David, p. 204-205
27. Eisenhower, David, p. 205
28. Dwight Eisenhower to Governor Nelson Rockefeller, letter 11/7/ 1966, Post-Presidential Principle Papers, 1966 Principle File, Box 11, folder "PL-4: Political Affairs, Funds" Dwight Eisenhower Presidential Library
29. Thomas Ikes Bluff, p. 362
30. ibid
31. Pipes, p. 296
32. RRL Tape 348 Part I
33. "Eisenhower says He Admires Reagan," *NYT*, 3/14/67, p. 26
34. Larson, Arthur, Eisenhower, p. 191-192
35. Ambrose, Eisenhower, p. 565.
36. Brinkley, Cronkite
37. Scott-Smith, p. 18
38. Hannaford, Peter, "Thatcher Passes," American Spectator, 4/8/2013
39. Reagan-Reed, 4/19/1967-5/2/1967
40. Wicker, Tom, "In the Nation," NYT, 4/16/67, p. E13
41. Weaver, Warren Jr, "GOP Hopeful on 1968 if It Can Avoid Party Strife," NYT, 4/24/67, p. 24
42. ibid
43. Reed, p. 14
44. Reed, p. 14

CHAPTER 6: DEBATE, DRAFT, AND DÉTENTE

"The first eyeball-to-eyeball test of the two men who may very well meet on the road to the White House;" the debate might be a "dry run for some future set of Great Debates" between them.

~ *Newsweek*[1]

"If Ronald Reagan decides he wants to run, he will be the Republican nominee in 1968."

~ Barry Goldwater[2]

"Do something Bobby! He's killing you, he's killing you!"

~ Ethel Kennedy[3]

"I've never seen anything like it, and I've been covering them since Truman. There isn't anybody who can touch Reagan."

~ Warren Weaver[4]

"How long has it been since an American has spoken as did Dwight David Eisenhower when the Red Chinese threatened the invasion of Formosa and he bluntly replied, 'They'll have to crawl over the 7th Fleet to do it.'"

~ Ronald Reagan[5]

As May began, Reagan's campaign received some national attention via a surprising press comment from Nixon supporter Barry Goldwater in Saint Louis: "If Ronald Reagan decides he wants to run, he will be the Republican nominee in 1968. But I don't think he wants it."[6] But at the time, Reagan in fact was prepping to debate the very person whom he expected to face in the general election in the fall of 1968.

On Monday, May 15, 1967, Reagan sat silently as he prepared to enter a television studio in Sacramento. He seemed tense and did not hear the "chatter of his assistants."[7] As an accomplished actor and then governor, most likely he was not nervous. Yet he was about to debate his arch nemesis, Robert F. Kennedy, before an audience of millions. And the debate was to be live and would be broadcast across the globe.

Two months before at the Gridiron Dinner, Reagan had been seen only by those members of the national press who were there to watch him live in-person. While running for governor and since his election, most of his audiences were comprised of Californians, local press, and the occasional national reporter. In his Seattle speech in 1966 he had been seen as a politician on the national stage for the first time, but by few reporters. Similarly in Eugene in February for his first out-of-state and campaign speech, few reporters were there.

But now he would be seen for the first time by a nation-wide television audience as a national Republican political leader on an international stage who also was representing his country. America had known Ronald Reagan as a movie star and then television star of *General Electric Theatre* and *Death Valley Days*; some Americans may even had known he had campaigned the year before and won election as governor of California. But now he was to be watched and analyzed by nationwide press via an international satellite broadcast —as a potential 1968 Republican opponent to either Democratic President Lyndon Johnson or Robert F. Kennedy.

Reagan approached such political appearances "as a business that required dedication and hard work."[8] Reagan had studied well. He knew that Kennedy had bested him three months earlier, although admittedly no subjects of weighty political importance had been discussed. This time Reagan had "prepared for the telecast by studying a twelve-page memorandum".[9] Assistant Press Secretary Clyde Beane had prepared the fact-based paper and recalled decades later that Reagan "carried it around in his suit pocket—took it out and studied it in the limo or whenever he wanted to."[10] Beane reflected that Reagan was a "marvelous reader—a marvelous study. He picks things up so fast."[11] Afterwards Republicans across the country wanted copies of Reagan's Vietnam policies from the debate. On the final preparatory day, Ed Meese had helped with a rehearsal dry-run.[12] But probably Reagan's greatest hidden asset was the mentoring on Vietnam and global affairs he had received from Eisenhower, most recently at their March meeting.

If Reagan had in fact been nervous in any way, once the program began, "Reagan was calm and quick-witted."[13]

Don Hewitt of CBS had invited Reagan. As mentioned earlier, Hewitt's program, *Town Meeting of the World*, was not brand new. The concept, that of a satellite-beamed program between Great Britain and America featuring a debate on important international topics, had featured a previous debate on Vietnam. In the fall of 1965, Hewitt had gone to the Harvard campus and recruited two young students and Professor Henry Kissinger to debate some Oxford students. One of the pro-war American students was a young Bob Shrum, future Democratic strategist.[14] At the same time as Kissinger and Shrum had debated the anti-war Oxford students, Kissinger and 190 Harvard colleagues had signed a pro-Johnson petition.[15] As mentioned earlier, Eisenhower had sent for a copy of the October, 1965 broadcast, indicating he had watched the new format—televised discussions of Vietnam—with interest.[16]

Did either Kennedy or Reagan want to accept the invitation to debate? Frank Mankiewicz, press secretary for the newly-elected New York senator, thought it was a great opportunity for RFK. Mankiewicz recalled in 2006 that at the time, he "saw no downside" and thought that "RFK would virtually destroy this 'B-movie actor,' who had somehow stumbled into the governorship of California."[17]

However Reagan initially was less enthusiastic. In fact he "did not want to appear at first, but when he heard the Senator from New York was the guest, he jumped at the chance."[18] Reporter Bill Boyarsky, who earlier had noted that Reagan had "bombed out" at the Gridiron Club, felt Reagan "had to prove himself" against Kennedy this time.[19] Reagan press secretary Nofziger agreed that Reagan should go for it.

For Reagan, here was a chance to redeem himself from his relatively poor performance at the Gridiron Club. But Reagan's acceptance ran much deeper than this reason alone. Reagan may have sensed that he might never get the chance to confront Kennedy again. Such a debate opportunity might be the only chance he would ever have at least to question RFK's changing policies on Vietnam, whose new dovish tones Reagan so detested.

But for Reagan, it also was personal. Reagan knew how Ike felt about RFK. Plus the old hurts were there. Reagan had felt threatened when Kennedy had pursued GE with two lawsuits in the early 1960's, followed by Kennedy forcing Reagan to testify for hours at the SAG-MCA trial. Even when Reagan was exonerated, Kennedy arranged for Reagan's taxes to be audited. Then Reagan believed that Kennedy's coercion led directly to the cancellation of Reagan's show. Kennedy was indirectly behind the spiteful Brown campaign ad, which had attempted to link Reagan with Lincoln's assassin. Then Kennedy came to California to campaign personally against Reagan. Kennedy had bested him at the Gridiron Club, but here was a chance to best Kennedy in front of millions.

Once again Reed and his 1968 Reagan presidential team had not been behind the invitation, recalled Norman "Skip" Watts.[20] Reed later thought that the idea was invented by Reagan's television press secretary.[21] But clearly Hewitt's 1965 show predated this by two years.

For 1967, Hewitt and CBS did not want the well-known Republicans, such as Nixon or Rockefeller, to oppose Kennedy. Rather "the network people just saw Reagan as somebody that was articulate and formidable...so they asked him."[22] On the other hand, some may surmise that the liberal network may have thought they had arranged the perfect ambush, expecting Kennedy easily to triumph over Reagan. They forgot that in 1966, liberals Pearson and Governor Brown had wanted Reagan to beat Christopher in the primary because Reagan, so they had thought, would be an easy pushover in the general election.

The potential importance of the program was previewed by *Newsweek* as "the first eyeball-to-eyeball test of the two men who may very well meet on the road to the White House."[23] The Reagan-Kennedy debate might be a "dry run for some future set of Great Debates" between them.[24]

The *New York Times* commented, "The CBS selection of Governor Reagan to appear as a Republican spokesman on international television in itself has some political significance. His willingness to participate as a specialist in international affairs is not likely to diminish talk over his political ambitions."[25] Reagan had prepared well as noted above. But Reagan's comfort in discussing foreign affairs, and his growing expertise in areas not normally the purview of a domestic governor, can in large measure be attributed to the coaching of Eisenhower.

The program was broadcast to some fifteen million viewers on Monday evening May 15, 1967 at 10:00-11:00 PM EDT and also was simulcast over the CBS radio network. The program was not actually called a formal debate but rather had the official title of *Town Meeting of the World*. The specific topic addressed "The Image of America and The Youth of the World."

At first, CBS planned that Reagan would be in a studio in Sacramento and Kennedy at a studio in Syracuse, New York, with the student audience being taped in the afternoon local time in Great Britain.[26] Later the plans for RFK were changed to Washington, D.C., although decades later Reagan aide Michael Deaver thought that Kennedy had been in Paris for the taping.[27] Host Charles Collingwood was on the London set with the eighteen students. It was the latest in Telstar, also called Early Bird, satellite television transmission technology at the time, although Telstar was a generic name.[28]

The students, attending universities in Great Britain, were from Europe, Asia, and Africa. Why they specifically were chosen and who chose them was never made clear. Given the anti-war and anti-American feeling prevalent in Great Britain at the time, it would have been difficult to find students who were sympathetic to the U.S. Yet to have all non-American students so completely hostile to America makes one think that perhaps whoever chose the students had a definite political agenda.

The one American student was named Bill Bradley. Later as Senator (D-N.J.), he would lose to Al Gore for the Democratic nomination in 2000. Bradley reflected that he had never been asked about his recollections of the debate before agreeing to be interviewed by your author. In the mid-1960s, Bradley's name was a household word to an American television audience. He had been a Princeton University basketball star, held many Ivy League and Princeton basketball records and had won an Olympic gold medal in basketball. He had interned for Congressman Richard Schweiker (R-PA); in 1976 Senator Schweiker would be named by Reagan as his choice for vice-president.

At the time of the debate, Bradley was a second year Rhodes Scholar at Oxford but also worked for CBS radio's London office. His being familiar to the CBS London office staff is what prompted his invitation as the one American student participant.[29] Prior to the debate, the only other debate student Bradley had met was the Indian Rhodes Scholar, Montek Singh.

Reagan and Kennedy were shown in color but Collingwood and the students were shown in black-and-white; indeed the images of the latter had a grainy appearance. The students were sitting in two rows with name placards of their country of origin. Bradley recalled that the television and satellite formats were indeed novel to him but he remembered he could see clearly both Kennedy and Reagan on large television screens in front of the students.[30] The viewer would sometimes see Reagan watching Kennedy and vice-versa, and at the beginning they were shown together on a split-screen. Yet RFK may not have been familiar with the camera techniques, as it was noted by one observer, "the senator often was found looking into the wrong lens while Reagan kept his gaze riveted on the right camera."[31] Indeed *Newsweek* noted that although Reagan missed his monitor's picture of Kennedy and that of the students because he looked at his camera, to the American audience at home it appeared as if "he was carefully following every nuance."[32] Reagan's decades of experience as an actor—being quite used to cameras—clearly had paid off in the political arena.

At first, both Reagan and Kennedy did seem to be relaxed, often smiled, and their relative cheerful manner and demeanor contrasted sharply with the always hostile non-American students. If the true topic was to be a discussion of the image of the United States as viewed by the students of the world, almost all of the non-American students seemed completely hostile to America. The topics mainly covered Vietnam (for example the role of the U.S., draft-dodging, participation of the National Liberation Front in peace negotiations), but also there were questions on race relations in the U.S. and aid to Greece.

Once the questions began, however, and the students hammered away about Vietnam, Kennedy's demeanor became noticeably sullen and he looked quite uncomfortable as the representative of the United States and having to defend the Johnson policies. Reagan on the other hand seemed quite at ease in defending his country.

The first student question set the tone of the entire hour-long town meeting: "I believe the war in Vietnam is illegal, immoral, politically unjustifiable and economically motivated. Could either of you agree with this?"[33]

A few minutes later a second accused and convicted America by proclaiming, "In 1954 you refused to sign the Geneva Convention, you refused to allow independent elections in Vietnam, you forced the Diem regime on the Vietnamese people….it put six million in forced prison camps. This was your puppet regime….You've refused to come to the negotiations with the Vietcong…Every time you ask for a peace talk, all you do is escalate the war."

Then a third student poured on more gasoline to the debate flames by charging that the United States "breached the U.N. Charter, the U.S. Constitution, and the Geneva Agreements. What can you say about that?" He seemed like a spoiled child who had prepared his remarks well in advance and couldn't wait to let out his multiple anti-American invective. These were no calm discussions of the image of America by the youth of the world; it was a series of anti-American rants that went on and on.

Kennedy the Apologizer

Robert Kennedy was in a difficult position, as many of America's Vietnam policies had been promulgated by himself and his now-slain brother, President John F Kennedy, and then had been continued by

President Johnson. RFK slowly was transitioning his views away from what he and his brother had initiated, but RFK was not yet at the point of breaking completely with the Kennedy-Johnson policies.

On screen, Kennedy appeared friendly. He was "all smiles" as he sympathized with the anti-American students.[34] Although his initial answers reminded the students that the goals of the U.S. had been to bring self-determination to the people of South Vietnam, his subsequent answers almost always were apologetic in nature. Clearly he felt he had to apologize to these students, and possibly the world, for America and his own role in creating those exact policies that the students, and now he, decried. Indeed as *Newsweek* observed, "More often than not, Kennedy essentially agreed with the students' sharply worded critiques...He seemed essentially sympathetic to the students' complaints about U.S. involvement in Viet Nam."[35]

Kennedy never seemed to dispute the premises nor supposed facts of the student questioners. Rather he seemed to join them in turning the meeting into one long critique of America and its policies. *Newsweek* observed that when one student grossly erred by exaggerating that "a million civilians" had been killed in Vietnam, Kennedy "didn't quibble," adding himself, "I would regard it as a mistake."[36]

His initial answer to the first student was, "I have some reservations...about some aspects of the war." When the second student asked a follow-up question about holding elections in South Vietnam, RFK seemed to ask for the students' forgiveness: "there were mistakes that were made over the period of the last ten years. There were mistakes in which I was involved—excuse me." He added, "I don't go on this program...saying that we never made a mistake and that we never erred, because I think we have.....I don't say that we are without fault. I don't say that even the administration that I was involved with—President Kennedy—was without fault."

Then apparently attempting to side with the students against American policy, when the second student cited that the U.S. was "spending 20 billion dollars a year destroying the country," Kennedy corrected him to the upside: "It's about 25 billion" and smirked. Then Kennedy continued his apologies: "I said in the beginning that there were mistakes and things done that I would disagree with in South Vietnam."

As the debate was about to end, Kennedy asked moderator Collingwood if he could say a final word. All that he did though was to continue to apologize: "We make major mistakes within the United States" and advised the students that in the future "where you see that we make mistakes, that you continue to criticize." Robert F. Kennedy felt clearly that the image of America with the youth of the world was poor. Clearly Kennedy felt that poor image was deservedly so; Kennedy's own comments throughout the debate added and reinforced that negative perception.

After World War II and throughout the 1950s, Americans were proud of their country. The Vietnam War became a clear inflection point where many Americans saw their war efforts as wrong. But this debate was in 1967. Most Americans, including Bill Bradley, still wanted to help South Vietnam maintain its freedom and to fight off communist Vietcong insurrection and military infiltration from North Vietnam. One may not unreasonably point to RFK's apologies as the beginning of the attitude of the "blame America first" crowd mentioned by future President Reagan's United Nations ambassador Jeanne Kirkpatrick. Apologizing for American actions, apologizing to foreign leaders, refusing to see American exceptionalism, continue well into the Obama administration.

But not everyone in that 1967 debate was anti-American. Both Ronald Reagan and Bill Bradley stood up for their country, did not apologize for the United States, and indeed voiced the only clearly positive and inspiring words about America that were uttered all evening. Historian Paul Kengor noted that those Americans watching who were looking for a defense of the United States from the hostile charges were chagrined by Kennedy's "lame responses," whereas they were "buoyed by Reagan's strong retorts."[37] Ronald Reagan remained fiercely pro-American. He saw the war being mismanaged and wanted to win. He knew that not only were America's goals in Vietnam laudatory, the original policies had been established while RFK was his brother's closest advisor. Given the debate structure—answering the charges from the students—Reagan was not free to discuss all of his thoughts on Vietnam. RFK had not yet broken completely with Johnson administration policies. Presidential candidate Reagan's time publicly to attack RFK directly for the first time would come exactly one year in the future in Hawaii.

Reagan to the Rescue

In the third studio thousands of miles away in California, and on-screen to millions of American viewers and potential voters, Governor and presidential candidate Ronald Reagan showed himself a steely debater. Reagan's knowledge of Vietnam was "encyclopedic."[38] He not only knew his facts and history about Southeast Asia, but was about to propose an idea for the first time in public which would forever be associated with him and the course of world history some twenty years later: tearing down the Berlin Wall.

Some of the initial student questions centered on dissent and draft-dodging, in which RFK had made blanket answers and statements that dissent was in fact patriotic. But Reagan countered, "When dissent takes the form of actions that actually aid the enemy...such as avoiding the draft, refusing service, blocking troop trains and shipments of munitions...this is going beyond the dissent that is provided by our present governmental system."

Also, Kennedy and Reagan had opposite opinions on whether the Vietcong's political arm, the National Liberation Front, should be part of the peace negotiations. Whereas Kennedy stated, "I'm in favor of the National Liberation Front being represented at the conference table," Reagan answered, "Here we're in disagreement" and explained he wanted the South Vietnamese to negotiate directly with the Vietcong alone. Kennedy wanted a four-part negotiation officially including the North and South Vietnamese, the U.S and the Vietcong. Reagan considered the Vietcong a rebel force. Indeed one student tried to compare the fight of the Vietcong to the American Revolution. Reagan countered by saying he didn't think the Vietcong's war of liberation was a "legitimate uprising of a people" like America in 1776 but rather felt they were a "tiny minority instigated by an outside force, namely North Vietnam."

When one student was in the midst of his many hostile anti-American statements and questions, unlike Kennedy who never challenged the premises of the questioners, Reagan immediately spoke up stating firmly, "I challenge your history." Two minutes later when the student accused the South Vietnamese of putting six million citizens into "forced prison camps", Reagan immediately countered, "I challenge your history again. There is absolutely no record that six million people were put in concentration camps. They only have sixteen million to begin with." Reagan then cited a specific United Nations report that had cleared the Diem regime of all charges made against it. Reagan's clear use of facts seemed to stop the barrage of criticism.

Later Reagan gave the students a history lesson on the Geneva Agreement, the 17th parallel, and the fact that a million people had fled the north towards freedom in the south. Reagan was able to use facts and figures to show the American audience that much of what America was being accused of, and that Kennedy was apologizing for, was not true.

Bill Bradley's Turn

Young Bill Bradley finally got his chance to ask his one allotted question about mid-way through the debate. In 2012, Senator Bradley recalled his growing discomfort at the debate—with all the hostile anti-American questions—even though he himself knew of the growing concerns about the war in America and shared them. It "awakened in me the need to defend my country."[39] Bradley recalled that his own comments and follow-up questions were spontaneous. Bradley began by emphasizing, "The United States is not out to achieve a position of power in land or economic force in the world." It was the one pro-American sentence that any of the students uttered during the entire town meeting.

Indeed later on, Reagan continued Bradley's theme: "At the end of World War II, one nation in the world had unprecedented power, had not suffered any damage in its industrial complex, had the greatest military force the world had ever seen put together, the United States…We had the atomic bomb…But the United States disarmed. The United States made no effort to impose its will on the rest of the nations. Can you honestly say in your heart that had the Soviet Union been in a comparable position with that bomb, or today's Red Chinese…with that great military force, that the world would not today have been conquered by that force? But this country did not."

It was a shining defense of America's beneficence that was sorely needed to stand solidly against all the student anti-American charges and contrasted sharply with Kennedy's apologies. Clearly with Ronald Reagan and Bill Bradley, and perhaps the fifteen million Americans watching the attacks against their country unfold before them on television, the image of America as a force for good had two proud champions that evening. Reagan had remained "firm in his support of the U.S. and its quest for freedom."[40]

Bill Bradley had another part to his allotted time and continued his initial theme by turning the debate away from Vietnam into a broader perspective on America's role and commitment to Asia. He asked in general terms what negotiations for Asia would mean. He asked if America should shrink from its responsibilities in Asia: "Does it mean that the United States should be absent, and let revolutionary forces take their course?" After thus answering his own question to remind the other students and the American audience of the consequences of an American withdrawal from the region, he then turned to his friend Mr. Singh from India asking, "If the Chinese happened to attack India, to whom would he first go for help? Would he go to the Soviet

Union, or would he go to the United States?" Bill Bradley's prescient warning, that America should not abdicate its responsibilities in Asia, unfortunately is not being recalled in the middle years of the second decade of the twenty-first century.

Unfortunately the moderator changed the direction to another student before Mr. Singh from India could answer, but the clear intent of Bradley's was to point out that when international crises arose, America was the first country to help. Bradley's statement and rhetorical questions remained the only pro-American student comments in the entire hour-long debate. Shri Montek Singh Ahluwalia, future Deputy Chairman of the Planning Commission of the Republic of India in 2012, recalled that had he not been cut off by Collingwood, he would have answered Bill Bradley's question by discussing China's attack on India in 1962 and Nehru's asking President Kennedy for help.[41]

Bradley had begun his comments by saying that after discussions on Vietnam somehow seemed to degenerate into "polemical accusations and disputations of facts," and later Reagan picked up on Bradley's comments. Reagan commented, "This ties in with something that Bill Bradley said, and it's very significant—among people of good will in the world today, there is too much of a tendency to argue, challenging or suspecting the other fellow's motive, when perhaps what we're challenging is only the method that has been suggested." Clearly both Bradley and Reagan were attempting to tone down both the student rhetoric aimed against the United States as well as not to impugn the motives of any of the nations nor individuals attempting to achieve peaceful solutions.

Some forty-five years later, former Senator Bradley reflected in 2012 that these last Reagan comments above, and Reagan's praise of Bradley, were a "very astute political move" because the Reagan comments were seen and heard by the American audience, which identified with both Bradley and Reagan.[42]

Reagan closed on an uplifting note to the students and the American audience by stating the ideals he had shared with Eisenhower and Churchill and the Republican Party: "The highest aspiration of man should be individual freedom and the development of the individual," and Reagan ended speaking about man reaching for the stars. Robert Kennedy "gulped in restrained agony"[43] and "had little to say."[44]

Reagan's First Public Call to Tear Down the Berlin Wall

Looking back on the debate/town meeting from the vantage point of the 21st century, it is clear that communism in general, as opposed to the Vietnam War specifically, seemed to be a small part of what was discussed that spring of 1967. However a Soviet student did manage to go on a tirade saying that eventually "the Communists will be all over the world because it is a very good system."

Historian Paul Kengor felt that in 1967, Reagan "lacked the ability to shape national policy toward the Soviets."[45] It is true Reagan held no power to effect new policies until he hopefully was to win the 1968 nomination and then the general election. But Reagan's May 1967 speech marked an inflection point where he began to call publicly for specific steps to shift America's foreign policy in the direction he wanted. And one giant step was about to be promulgated by candidate Reagan.

In hindsight, the far most important part of the evening turned out to be Reagan's answer to being asked about normalizing relations with Red China. His answer began when he discussed the best way to build bridges with the communist nations and his feeling that "we haven't been hard-nosed enough in getting…concessions."

Then he reflected on the recent signing of a Consular Treaty with the Soviet Union:

"I think that there were things we could have asked in return. **I think it would be very admirable, if the Berlin Wall, which was built in direct contravention to a treaty, if the Berlin Wall should disappear.** (author's emphasis) I think that this would be a step toward peace, and towards self-determination for all the peoples if it were."

Reagan did not stop with just one mention of his idea of getting rid of the Berlin Wall.

A minute later he added:

"We don't want the Berlin Wall knocked down so that it's easier to get at the throats of the East Germans. We just think that a wall that is put up to confine people, and keep them within their own country instead of allowing them the freedom of world travel, has to be something wrong." (author's emphasis)

Here was not-yet vintage Ronald Reagan telling a 1967 audience almost exactly what, in twenty years, he would shout again as, "Mr. Gorbachev, Tear Down This Wall!" Did anyone in the 1967 audience think about Reagan's Berlin Wall proposal? Could anyone other than Ronald Reagan have the imagination even to propose such an idea in 1967 and share that hope with a huge American television audience?

Historian Douglas Brinkley has reviewed the apparent near-term background of Reagan's future 1987 Berlin Wall speech, yet no analysis of what Reagan had first said in 1967 was discussed.[46] But no matter what President Reagan's advisors and speechwriters recall about the origins of Reagan's call to Gorbachev and their own speechwriting musings in 1987, the true origin clearly was from candidate Reagan himself in 1967. And it would not be the last time that Reagan would call for the Soviets to tear down the Berlin wall during his first presidential campaign.

What did the students themselves on the panel in London say at the time to Reagan's idea to tear down the Berlin Wall? Stunned by Reagan's audacious plan to bring potential freedom to East Berlin, the French student only managed to stammer, "I don't think you are really answering my question." One wonders if that particular French student, or anyone else in the room or in the living rooms of those Americans who had watched the debate, remembered Reagan's 1967 words when he would give his famous Berlin speech and win the Cold War, without firing a shot, twenty years later.

History can now re-emphasize that the first time Ronald Reagan called publicly for the dismantling of the Berlin Wall was on May 15, 1967 as he had begun his first quest for the presidency.

Moderator Collingwood ended the program abruptly without any summary. Apparently afterwards the film editors of the debate found that the debate's general "tone was so insulting that CBS edited out thirty minutes of the taped program."[47] Clearly the image of America with the youth of the world, at least university students in England, was quite poor from before the show began and most likely did not change afterwards. No opinion polls were taken in Europe about the impact of the town meeting.

But in the United States, the impact of the debate was profound and would become of critical importance to the Reagan campaign when RFK would enter the presidential race some ten months later.

Reactions to Kennedy's performance uniformly were poor whereas Reagan's were excellent. Reagan biographer Lou Cannon simply noted, "Reagan...bested Kennedy,"[48] but elsewhere Cannon said that Reagan's performance was "stellar."[49] Norman "Skip" Watts watched the debate live and commented that he had been "impressed with Reagan and his ability to stand in there with Bobby Kennedy. In fact he really did Bobby in on that show."[50] One observer noted, "Kennedy anguished through questions about the war"[51] and that by the end of the show, "Kennedy looked as if he stumbled into a minefield."[52]

The tables indeed had been turned from the earlier Gridiron Club meeting of Reagan and Kennedy. Reporter Bill Boyarsky felt that Reagan did prove himself and although he was "tense right beforehand...when he got on camera, he made Kennedy look ill at ease."[53] Clif White felt, "If I myself had any doubts about Reagan's prospects, they were dispelled...Reagan ...slaughtered Bobby Kennedy."[54] David Halberstam wrote, the "general consensus was that Reagan...destroyed him."[55] *Newsweek* added, "Reagan effortlessly reeled off more facts and quasi-facts about the Vietnam conflict than anyone suspected he ever knew....The ease with which (Reagan) fielded questions about Vietnam may come as a revelation... it was political rookie Reagan who left old campaigner Kennedy blinking when the session ended."[56] One Kennedy aide commented, "Reagan was talking to an American tv audience; that's why Reagan was the big gainer."[57] Tom Reed said of Reagan, "It was a brilliant performance, a nice recovery from the dismal Gridiron Club face-off with RFK just two months before, and it was done before an audience of millions."[58] Reagan biographer Stephen Hayward felt that the debate was "Reagan's most significant showing in 1967."[59] William F. Buckley Jr. commented with his usual tongue-in-cheek sarcastic wit, "I mean, it is more than flesh and blood can bear: Reagan, the moderately successful actor, the man ignorant of foreign affairs, outwitting *Bobby Kennedy* in a political contest. It's the kind of thing that brings on...nightmares."[60] Historian Paul Kengor emphasized that the debate served as a "wakeup call to those who underestimated Ronald Reagan."[61]

It should be noted that much of the above analyses of Kennedy's performance were from the Reagan side. Yet Frank Mankiewicz recalled, "The debate...was a disaster for our side." Mankiewicz sensed that the RFK team was "in trouble" as soon as the first question had been asked because RFK had given "a lengthy explanation" and never "did he make eye contact with the camera."[62] In the studio in Washington D.C. near Kennedy, Mankiewicz recalled, "as the questions continued from students in India and elsewhere in Asia, it only got worse." But perhaps the person closest to Kennedy summed up everyone's reaction: Kennedy's wife Ethel not only was displeased, to put it mildly, she kept shouting at the television set, "Do something Bobby! He's killing you, he's killing you!"[63]

In fact, "The press verdict that Reagan won the debate was virtually unanimous."[64] At the time there was little analysis from the liberal perspective other than the few comments above, and indeed afterwards the debate was not mentioned in either Arthur Schlesinger

Jr.'s classic biography of RFK,[65] nor in a more recent biography,[66] nor in a recent work, which focused on RFK's presidential campaign[67]. The slain Senator's brother Ted would give a touching reflection on the debate some fourteen years later with President Reagan. The reviewer from the *New York Times* gave scant appraisal of either Reagan's nor RFK's debate performance but instead chose to note that an obvious weakness in the debate format was the lack of a true representative from the Johnson administration.

After the debate, Reagan's office was "deluged with thousands of letters of his support for his 'standing up for America.'"[68] Those letters were used by Reed and his team to "begin determining who might be for Reagan throughout the nation."[69] Reagan's 1968 presidential campaign continued. If the Gridiron Dinner had created any pause for reflection or reassessment of Reagan's viability as a national candidate for the nation's highest office, any such doubts were dispelled by Reagan's masterful performance in the town debate with one of his two most likely opponents at the time, Robert F Kennedy.

What did the candidates themselves think of the debate and their performances? Reagan himself credited his own careful preparation saying, "that was one time when woodshedding really paid off."[70]

But Robert F. Kennedy was "furious"[71] immediately afterwards shouting, "Who the fuck got me into this?"[72] and telling his aides never again to put him on the same stage with "that son-of-a-bitch;"[73] Reagan aide Michael Deaver confirmed hearing this story years later.

A short time later when RFK saw his press secretary who had arranged his participation in debating Reagan, Frank Mankiewicz, Kennedy castigated him saying, "You're the guy who got me into that Reagan thing." But RFK's debate loss to Reagan clearly irked Kennedy to such a point that RFK would bring it up frequently from then on. Indeed Mankiewicz recalled that for the remaining year of RFK's life, whenever RFK and his 1968 campaign team would debate the pros and cons of a certain campaign activity, RFK would turned to Mankiewicz and ask ruefully, "Aren't you the fellow who urged me to debate Ronald Reagan?" Mankiewicz reflected, "It was the most one-sided, awful debate I have ever seen. Reagan was a polished performer and Robert Kennedy…looked disinterested and his answers were too long. It was chaos."[74] Kennedy's bitterness about the debate would last almost to the end of his life.

Reagan spoke publicly about the debate for the first time a few days later at Chico State College. Reagan said it had been "shocking" to hear the diatribes against America uttered by the students. Reagan told his listeners that first he had thought the Oxford students might have been brainwashed. Then he had thought that America had failed to sell its image. But Reagan told his audience that instead he had concluded that America had been trying to "buy love in the world when we should have been earning respect." America should stand tall and proud that it was helping the Vietnamese remain free.[75]

Reagan's May 20 speech at Chico College became more than just an obligatory gubernatorial duty. After discussing the Kennedy debate as noted, and after addressing higher education by discussing his tuition proposal as well as permissiveness on campus, he warned his audience of faculty and students that his administration would remove any educational policies which had "allowed a political foot in the door."[76] Reagan later would expand his concerns that professors should teach all points of view and not just promote liberalism when he would speak in Nebraska, Kansas, and Connecticut.

Reagan emphasized his belief that America should "keep forever" it's tradition of "building a floor beneath which no human being should live in degradation." But Reagan wanted to pass on to the students the heritage that instead of having pre-determined and equally set outcomes in life, each individual had a "sacred right to fly as high and as far" as each individual's strength and abilities could take them.[77]

Reagan reminded his listeners that America was an exceptional country. He quoted Churchill again in the spirit of freedom that Eisenhower had spoken at the January, 1965 funeral, saying, "When great forces are on the move in the world we learn we are spirits, not animals." Duty called Americans. America's love of freedom meant we should lend a helping hand to those, like in Vietnam, who yearned to be free.[78]

Reagan was educating modern Americans that they should be proud to carry forth the goals of freedom that had been inherited from Churchill and Eisenhower. Reagan would carry forward the theme that Vietnam was a just war, which was a definite part of America's national interest and should be won, not only throughout the campaign but as will be seen, well into the ending days of his presidency.

The RFK debate would resurface briefly during the May 1968 Oregon primary, when Reagan's Oregon supporters would ask CBS for a copy of the town debate so they could show it on local Oregon television. Kennedy "refused permission"[79] and "CBS, naturally, acceded to his request."[80] CBS would relent as will be seen. Clif White thought the debate to have been so positive for Reagan that he obtained a copy and "played it at Republican gatherings so people could see for themselves just how effective Reagan was. It was an education for everyone who saw it."[81]

It is not known with certainty if coach Eisenhower watched Reagan debate Kennedy. Based upon the copy of the 1965 CBS townhall program in the files at the Eisenhower Library, discussed earlier, it is highly likely he did watch Reagan and RFK in May of 1967. As a keen observor of the political scene, Eisenhower likely watched to see how his protege, Reagan, would do against a man they both despised. After all, Eisenhower also had no love for any of the Kennedys, especially after John Kennedy's false charges of a missile gap during the 1960 campaign as well as Eisenhower's disdain for communist hunter Joseph McCarthy, on whose committee Robert Kennedy had served during the Eisenhower years. To say nothing of how Kennedy had to come crawling to Eisenhower for advice *after* the failed Bay of Pigs invasion.[82] What Eisenhower thought of Robert Kennedy has been discussed.

Certainly Reagan had prepared well ahead of time for his debate with Kennedy by studying the history of the Vietnam War, which his aide had prepared, and by sparring with Meese as preparatory debate foe. But even more important in Reagan's preparation had been Eisenhower and the numerous talks Eisenhower and Reagan had had.

After the debate, Reagan's presence as a viable candidate for the presidency soared. Although the May 22, 1967 cover-story of *Newsweek* analyzed Reagan's many gubernatorial accomplishments, Reagan's presidential candidacy was highlighted as well. Behind Nixon and Romney, Reagan was "strengthening his hold on third place among GOP Presidential contenders" noted the magazine and indeed with support for Romney sliding somewhat recently, "Republicans and independents are giving increasing support to Reagan."[83] The magazine reported that Reagan faced the same barrage of questions almost at every one of his frequent press conferences held either in Sacramento or wherever he traveled. He "denied he was a Presidential candidate," but did not hesitate to speak out on foreign affairs about his disagreements with the Johnson administration over Vietnam and his support of policies advocated by his secret coach, Eisenhower.

The magazine reported that besides sending out conventional reports to the people on varying subjects, Reagan's team had created two-minute commercial news spots which had aired on local and national television news programs as well as having the audio sections available for radio. Reagan's media aide, Nancy Reynolds, who had come up with the idea, beamed after learning that her idea had been used on Walter Cronkite's CBS evening news program saying, "That's 19 million viewers;" *Newsweek* noted that most of those Cronkite viewers "cast their votes outside California—a fact that delights the eager Reagan forces as they dream of '68."[84]

Reagan of course already had proclaimed himself the favorite son from California in order to have a united California Republican Party and to heal the wounds left from 1964. Yet *Newsweek* noted that while Reagan only "modestly disavows any interest in running for the White House," Reagan's "staffers talk Presidential strategy quite openly."[85] Those same staffers tended unemotionally to make delegate calculations whereas Reagan himself had "an almost mystical fatalism about the Presidency," as one unnamed high state official noted that Reagan "tends to think 'if this is God's will, so be it.'"[86] Reagan's early comments to Stu Spencer were now being said to other Reagan supporters nation-wide.

But there is another interpretation of Reagan's supposed fatalism that has not been discussed previously. Reagan did not believe God would perform a miracle to make him president. Rather, Reagan always had believed that it was the people who called upon a candidate to become their leader. It was Reagan's observation of how Eisenhower had accepted his duty to enter the race after the 1952 New Hampshire primary and the write-in vote in Minnesota both had shown Eisenhower that the people had wanted him. As Reagan would write in his later second autobiography, Reagan in 1968 would await the calling of the people's delegates to select him to be their nominee. And unlike Sherman, Reagan would serve—just as had Eisenhower.

But if Reagan announced publicly, could he win in 1968? One Reagan enthusiast answered, "If Reagan does decide to go, he can win. He'll be the guy in the white hat again. There are no scars on him."[87] *Newsweek* theorized that Reagan's main hope was a deadlocked convention. At that point, with Reagan having his own 86 delegates from California, in the back rooms it would not be "inconceivable that he could wield a bloc of up to 400 Western and Southern delegates."[88] And then at such a deadlocked convention, if Reagan stood up and made a speech for party unity, one Reagan backer lit up proclaiming, "I guarantee you that convention'll say: 'You're the guy, Ronnie! You're it!'"[89]

Reagan's real appeal "would be as the telegenic leader of a new American crusade to restore the old American virtues—morality, thrift, industry, honesty—to their hallowed place on the national mantelpiece."[90] The article ended by citing the comments Reagan had received quite recently from a former Pennsylvanian who had just moved to California: "Everyone back home wants you to be our next President."[91]

The magazine also ran a side-bar story about new potential GOP candidates which included Reagan. It noted, "If Ronald Reagan shows interest in the Presidency, some of the state organizations now strongly for Nixon—Georgia, Indiana and Mississippi—might dump him and switch to Reagan."[92] Indeed if Reagan made himself "slightly available," he could "pick up as many as 300 delegates, almost entirely at Nixon's expense."[93] That total did not even include the 86 delegates from California.

With all the massive positive reaction to the debate triumph, Reagan met in Santa Barbara with Reed, Nofziger, White and Spencer and Roberts to discuss the campaign status and future travels.[94]

The hugely positive pro-Reagan publicity from the debate showed Nixon that indeed his perception was correct: that his major threat was Reagan. Nixon had been busy that spring lining up delegates, following the plan he had formalized in January.[95] And a major portion of Nixon's original plan was that the major threat to his campaign would come from Reagan, as mentioned earlier via Buchanan.

A new analysis of the Reagan-Nixon political competition appeared a week after the initial analyses of the debates from the *New York Times*. Reagan's advisors reportedly saw their candidate as "a natural successor rather than a rival" to Nixon. One unnamed California Republican leader commented that he did "not see these two men on a collision course." Rather, if Nixon were failing by the time of the California primary in early June 1968, "Reagan stands to be the residual beneficiary of most of his strength." Reagan supporters were reported as astonished that Nixon had "not made even the most casual approach to the Governor" because "Governor Reagan's support could be the key to a Nixon nomination." The California Republican leaders acknowledged Reagan's public statements that he was not a candidate other than the formality of his being California's favorite son, but the leaders were all convinced that Reagan "could be drawn into the situation as it develops." It was thought that Reagan could not declare openly his candidacy for the nomination because "if he did he would offend Nixon conservatives, unify the liberals against him, and cause himself more trouble in the state Legislature than he already has." One leader's comments ended the analysis by saying that his television communication skills were those of a "genius" and he came across as a "rational, sincere individual." The leader concluded, "He's got to be a formidable politician."[96]

Nixon thus read that some party leaders thought he was to supplanted by Reagan. Nixon prided himself on his expertise in foreign policy. Yet it was Reagan who had been chosen to represent the Republican Party and its foreign policy in the Kennedy debate. So Reagan already was supplanting Nixon. And the Reagan triumph was seen internationally and by millions of Americans. So who needed Nixon now that Reagan was here—Reagan the conservative, Reagan the proven winner of elections, Reagan the genial communicator who handled the media so well—and now Reagan the winner of the Reagan-Kennedy debate?

It must have been Nixon's worst nightmare. It must have been too much for Nixon to bear. Something needed to be done to hold off the growing Reagan threat. So Nixon began with a letter of *rapprochement* with Reagan some two weeks after the Kennedy debate and just four days after the newspaper assessment. Nixon wrote to Reagan on May 31, 1967: "I was still in Latin America when the program was carried but from all sides I have heard nothing but the highest praise for your handling of the joint television appearance with Bobby Kennedy. When *Newsweek* gives you rave notices, it must have been tops!"[97]

For Richard Nixon, loser of the famous 1960 televised debate to John F. Kennedy (although radio listeners thought Nixon had won), and then loser to Pat Brown in 1962 for California governor only to see Reagan beat Brown just the year before in 1966, writing such a letter of congratulations to competitor Reagan—who had just bested Robert Kennedy—must have been impossibly difficult indeed.

A few days later in early June, Israel stunned the world when it defeated multiple Arab armies in the Six Day War. General Eisenhower, who had directed Operation Torch in World War II let alone D-Day, must have followed the tank battles and the entire Middle East situation with keen interest. As president, he had put a stop to the joint Israeli, British and French forces in 1956 when they initially had triumphed against Egypt after the nationalization of the Suez Canal. One wonders if he might have discussed the Middle East with Reagan, as surely Reagan would be asked about the Six Day War soon.

In the midst of the war, on June 11, Reagan spoke at a Hollywood Bowl pro-Israel rally.[98] Reagan would get a chance to speak about Israel's victory at his upcoming next out-of-state campaign speech, in Nebraska.

Meanwhile, campaign seeds that Reagan's speeches and visits had planted were starting to germinate elsewhere in the nation. As we will see, Don L. Taylor was filing with the Wisconsin secretary of state the first organizational papers in history for Ronald Reagan to become president of the United States. But Reagan would not yet visit the first opt-out primary state of Wisconsin until the fall, as he was about to visit instead the second opt-out state, Nebraska. But before leaving, in preparation for seeking support from the South, Reagan was introduced in San Francisco to Mississippi state Republican chairman Clarke Reed.[99] As will be seen, Clarke Reed was recalling how an earlier call to Reagan for political help had gone unanswered. Clarke Reed's perceived affront would last to the convention in Miami Beach.

Campaign Visit to Nebraska, June, 1967: Sickly Pastels

Of the three opt-out primary states of Wisconsin, Nebraska and Oregon, Reagan had visited crucial Oregon in February. Reagan was achieving growing national media attention as a serious candidate because of his proven experience solving domestic problems in California. And now Reagan had achieved a tremendous breakthrough as an expert in foreign affairs when he had trounced Kennedy.

Basking in the glow of that triumph, Reagan visited Nebraska. It was a trip that targeted both professional Republican Party stalwarts as well as the young. Reagan received a "tremendous response from the national Young Republican convention," spoke at Hiram Scott College, and met with "200 Party leaders in eastern Nebraska."[100] Reagan's Nebraska grass roots team started to be assembled then, including White's friend Charles Thone, who was assistant to Nebraska Governor Hruska at that time.[101] The three major Nebraska grass roots Reagan campaign offices—those by Dale L. Young in Lincoln, and by Dr. William H. Thompson and William H. Sherwood in Omaha—would not be formed until 1968.

The Young Republican National Federation previously had met in San Francisco in 1963 and had given their enthusiastic support for Barry Goldwater. But by 1967, the group's allegiance had switched to Reagan so markedly that the national press commented that the convention's pro-Goldwater forces only consisted of "two delegates raising a lone nostalgic banner" for Goldwater.[102] In contrast, overhead was a "rising cluster of balloons (and) a big picture of Ronald Reagan;" indeed Reagan's presence dominated with "demonstrable superiority over all opponents in posters, straw hats, balloons, (and) buttons."[103] There was almost no detected enthusiasm for Nixon: "There was not a single Nixon sign or button on view," "None of the usual Nixon traveling representatives showed their faces in Omaha," and "There was no Nixon hospitality suite."[104] This lack of any presence for Nixon was a deliberate strategy, as "Nixon did not want to be placed in the position of competing with the avid young Reagan enthusiasts."

There was no effort for Romney as his advisors felt he had a "slim chance for success" with the conservative group; but Romney did send his wife to speak on his behalf.

Why did Nixon make a deliberate decision to make no effort for the Young Republicans? Perhaps he sensed that it was a losing battle to challenge Reagan for the hearts and minds of the young conservatives, yet these committed Young Republicans were the future of the party. An informal straw poll of 333 convention voters was done by the United Republicans of America, a group described as a "post-1964 offshoot of the Goldwater movement." Of the major contenders, the tally had Reagan winning with 152 votes (46%) followed by Nixon at 100, Rockefeller at 36, and Romney at 21.[105] It should be noted that the group Students for Reagan had not yet formed officially but some members of Young Americans for Freedom who were at the Omaha meeting may have begun to plan the formation of this specific Reagan-for-President student organization at that time.

The convention in Omaha ended with Reagan's speech on June 23, 1967 as the highlight. For those listening at the time, who would hear what Reagan years later would say in 1975, they might recall that Reagan uttered the words "sickly pastels" in 1967 some nine years before his famous 1975 "pale pastels" speech. Reagan entitled his speech "Read the Meaning of 1966."

It took the shouts of "We Want Reagan" almost a full minute to quiet down before he could begin.[106] Reagan began by recalling earlier visits he had made to Nebraska, in Grand Island in 1961 and Lincoln in 1966. He decried those who became angry when anyone attempted to lessen governmental power. He blasted federal government relative growth, in dollars and personnel, versus population during the Kennedy-Johnson years. He then explored a new public topic for him by pointing out that over the past seven years, despite the costs of the war in Vietnam, the growth of non-military spending had outpaced military spending.[107] He was delving further into foreign affairs and now into defense spending. And again Eisenhower had been the inspiration to expand his expertise in these areas.

After going through all the specific domestic initiatives he had made during his first few months in office, points he would make at virtually every speech during his 1968 campaign, Reagan got to the main theme suggesting his audience study what the results of the November Republican triumph had meant. Reagan used a theme he would reiterate time and time again over the next decade—that Republicans should "raise a banner" for those of all parties to rally towards. But Reagan then warned those listening to choose those colors well. Reagan said that those citizens who had voted for Republicans the prior November were **"not in the mood to follow the <u>sickly pastels</u> of political expediency**." (author's emphasis)

These were not the exact words he would utter in March 1975—a date that almost all readers may think was the first time Reagan had used those words which would become one of his immortal phrases. But it was here in 1967—during the early phase of his first run for the 1968 presidency and almost a full ten years before his famous 1975 speech, that he first would use the "pastels" exhortation.

Reagan then proceeded to devote the majority of his talk to world affairs. He began by noting the hand wringing about Vietnam and the worries of a communist invasion. Virtually confirming that he and Eisenhower had conferred recently, Reagan gave a short history lesson about the South China Sea by reminding his listeners of a time in the 1950s, when Red China had threatened the offshore islands of Taiwan. Reagan continued, "a firm voice in a tone we haven't heard in our land for a long time," Dwight D. Eisenhower, had told the communists, "they'll have to climb over the Seventh Fleet to do it." There was no invasion, Reagan reminded the audience, and the audience cheered.[108] Coach Eisenhower's protégé, Reagan, was doing very well.

Then for the first time publicly, Reagan moved elsewhere in the world and made a pronouncement on the Middle East. And he did not proclaim America should remain neutral with both sides. Indeed Reagan wanted his audience to understand that America should not stay neutral. He received loud applause when he proclaimed, "this nation has a need for statesmanship."[109] Obviously Reagan again was referring to Eisenhower, whose presence in the White House Reagan and countless others sorely missed. The Six Day War just had occurred as had Reagan's appearance at the pro-Israel rally at the Hollywood Bowl. Reagan was concerned about the seeming non-definitive decision made by the Johnson administration as to who was in the right. Reagan knew who was in the right and made no hesitation to say it loudly and with distinct moral clarity where he wanted America to stand: **"Our national interest is inextricably woven into the fabric" of Israel.**[110] (author's emphasis)

Was Reagan's solution, as would occur via other administrations over the next many decades, to go to the United Nations? No. Reagan understood the inherent problems of the UN and proceeded to caution that finding any specific peaceful long-term solution could not be found via the United Nations "as presently constituted."[111] Reagan had objected to the undue voting influence of new and small nations in the General Assembly. Had he discussed the UN with his mentor?

Reagan then told his Nebraska audience that the presence of America's Sixth Fleet demonstrated the Mediterranean and Middle East region's importance to America. On July 15, 1958, President Eisenhower had launched Operation Blue Bat, to bolster the pro-Western government of Lebanon, by sending the Sixth Fleet to the Mediterranean Sea. It was Ike's first use of his new Eisenhower Doctrine, in which America would protect countries threatened by international communism. One can almost hear coach Eisenhower discussing these same topics with Reagan either in March in person or over the phone shortly after the Six Day War.

Reagan then showed his audience that his growing expertise in foreign affairs extended beyond Vietnam, Taiwan and Israel. He turned his attention to communism versus the West and negotiations over Vietnam and other world hotspots. He decried the appeasing attitudes that Americans and the Johnson administration sometimes felt toward the Soviet Union and Communist China, and he used the example that Russia was free to mine waters off South Vietnam but we refused to mine Haiphong Harbor for fear we would be accused of escalating the war.

Reagan ended by returning to domestic issues again. Invoking Eisenhower's 1965 advice, Reagan told his audience that Republicans should "broaden the party" and reminded his listeners about the Eleventh Commandment—that no Democrat should be able to use any Republican's words which had been spoken against a fellow Republican. Last, he decried the use of Democrats' advocating programs, which gave money to the poor for "political nest building."[112]

The press observed that Reagan's "half-hour speech was repeatedly interrupted by applause," and there were six standing ovations. His themes were for "greater American militancy against Communism abroad" and he had asked his audience to pledge that once the primaries were over to be united. The analysis by the national media was that if Nixon did not do well in New Hampshire and Wisconsin, then "Nebraska may see a strong conservative swing to Mr. Reagan."[113]

Even Nixon supporter Barry Goldwater may have started to change his mind somewhat. Goldwater commented that if Reagan became a "real, live candidate," Goldwater might "re-examine" his "allegiance" to Nixon.[114] One may presume that former nominee Goldwater, the darling of Republican youth only three years before, in Omaha was a forgotten figure who was seeing the new conservative stalwart, Ronald Reagan, receiving the cheers of the convention. Jealousy alone may have reinforced Goldwater's support for Nixon despite his comments. As we will see, later Goldwater would attempt to push Reagan out of the race altogether.

Even the liberal Ripon Society had to admit that the Young Republicans in Omaha were the "advance guard of the Reagan Presidential candidacy."[115]

Historian Kiron Skinner and her group felt that Reagan's speech did not broaden his political base.[116] But Reagan was in fact widening his tent. He was asking for liberal Republicans as well as disaffected Democrats to join him in his new crusade for the presidency, just as they had the year before for Sacramento.

The next day, June 24, 1967, Reagan attended two more campaign events in Nebraska. He had a campaign breakfast with 400 Douglas County Republicans. Reagan got right into foreign affairs, wanting America to threaten North Vietnam. Harkening back again to his mentor's detailed advice, Reagan told his audience, "I think we should win that war as quickly as possible…Ho Chih Minh should be sitting on an apple crate asking for help!"[117] The delighted supporters gave Reagan "round after round of applause" and left "singing his praises."[118] The breakfast was the "second impressive Nebraska welcome for Mr. Reagan in 12 hours." The national media summarized the two events as, "Ronald Reagan is going to be a formidable candidate in the next Presidential primary here next May."[119] At each locale Reagan "denied again, as he does almost daily, that he is a Presidential candidate."[120]

Warren Weaver, the *New York Times* reporter who was covering Reagan in Nebraska and had filed the above stories, was amazed at Reagan's charisma and the enthusiastic support he was observing. Weaver then blurted out "impulsively" to a fellow reporter, "I've never seen anything like it, and I've been covering them since Truman. There isn't anybody who can touch Reagan."[121]

After leaving the breakfast, Reagan flew to Scottsbluff, where he was greeted by the president of Hiram Scott College and a large crowd at the airport and then spoke at the college's Midwest Theater.[122] He wove together themes of world affairs with American ideals at home. Speaking to the students' aspirations for a better world, he reminded them that his generation had known World Wars I and II as well as the Korean and Vietnam wars. He warned the students to be aware of the philosophy of "the omnipotence of government" to solve all problems.[123] Echoing what he had narrated and Eisenhower and the other Republican leaders had said for *Mr. Lincoln's Party Today* in 1962, Reagan emphasized that the government indeed had the legitimate role of providing maximal individual freedom and liberty short of law and order. He contrasted the freedom of America versus the lack freedom in communist countries. Harkening back also to Eisenhower's funeral oration for Churchill, Reagan reminded the students that "Freedom is never more than one generation from extinction," which would be a phrase Reagan would use many times in the future.[124]

Spontaneously he opened his speech to questions from students. The first question was whether was running for president. Reagan answered, "I am not a candidate" but said that he wanted to help improve government in California just as the students should help improve government in Scottsbluff.[125] He was asked if any Great Society programs had worked, and he said the Head Start program was a good idea, but he did emphasize that his main objection of most Great Society programs was that he felt local problems could be solved best at the local level and the added that governmental bureaucracy wasted too much money. Reagan quoted the medieval Jewish sage Maimonides, saying the best way to help the poor was to teach them to help themselves. Reagan ended by emphasizing again the Republican creed that America was founded on the idea of individual freedom.[126]

West Yellowstone Governor's Conference

After Reagan left Nebraska still basking in the limelight of the numerous tumultuous ovations he had received, Reagan's destination was the Western Governor's Conference in West Yellowstone, Montana. But first Reagan made a campaign stop in Great Falls, Montana.

Montana Governor Tim Babcock and Wyoming Governor Stanley Hathaway were Reagan supporters. As early as March, they were described as "new passengers on the Reagan bandwagon."[127] Of course Whetstone had been in charge of these two states for Reagan, and Whetstone arranged for Reagan's stop just prior to the conference.

Reagan flew into the Great Falls, Montana airport on June 24 where he was greeted by "a crowd of about 300." Later that evening, Reagan spoke at C. M. Russell High School where more than 1,500 people paid $3 per person to hear him. There was also a private reception just before the speech. Those attending both, several hundred people, paid $15. Although those numbers did not approach the numbers Reagan had received in Eugene, Oregon earlier in the year, considering the sparse population of far north central Montana, these size crowds were considered to be "respectable."

Reagan expanded the scope of his speech beyond the Vietnam War, where he said we should fight to win. Reagan again entered the world of Mideast politics and policy again but now gave more nuanced details. He again praised Israel's recent victory in the Six-Day War but now drew a moral lesson for his audience by tying Israel's triumph to freedom at home. Reagan noted, "A small nation faced with the denial of its sovereignty, indeed of its very existence, has reminded us that the price of freedom is high but is never so costly as the loss of freedom."[128]

The next day, Governor Babcock, official host to the conference, gave Reagan a pair of western riding pants, cowboy boots, and a jacket. Reagan wore them proudly to an initial news conference. But the presence of Reed did not escape the notice of the press. Reagan was asked about Reed's true function and whether Reed was there seeking support for a Reagan run for the presidency for 1968. Reagan denied the charge claiming that Reed was there to keep him "out of trouble" by keeping him from "stumbling into some political booby trap" and that Reed was only his advance man and "adviser on out-of-state appearances."[129] Then Reagan elaborated by adding a new nuance to the role Reed had in arranging his out-of-state appearances: that Reed was attempting to get speakers who would return Reagan's favor—of speaking across the country—by having them come to California to speak at local GOP fundraisers there. This was exactly what Reagan had planned to say if ever he was asked about his fundraising trips. The reporter noted at the conclusion of the conference that Governor Babcock appeared "ready to follow any Reagan move for the Republican Presidential nomination" and that Governor Hathaway felt "warmly" toward Reagan as well.[130]

Indeed the next day Governor Babcock described Reagan as "a strong contender if he decides to be a contender." Whetstone attended the meeting with Clif White along with other Reagan supporters, including fund-raiser Charles Barr, the vice-president of Standard Oil of Indiana.[131]

Finally, Reagan mysteriously told reporters that he had "taken steps" to stop the formation of a group supporting him in the New Hampshire primary.[132] Later we will examine Reagan's comments in the context of the apparent theft and retrieval of Reagan filing papers in the New Hampshire capital.[133]

The reporter noted the growing support for Reagan amongst Western governors. Many of the governors spent "much of their time answering questions about Mr. Reagan."[134] They would have to get used to it, because those same questions about the 1968 Reagan candidacy would be asked of them up to the convention. But as we will see later, other Western Republican governors in attendance, such as Dan Evans of Washington and Tom McCall of Oregon, were not Reagan fans. McCall, likely jealous of all the attention Reagan was receiving and who we will meet later, made a number of comments about Reagan at the conference, as well as made a proposal for moderate Republican governors to agree to a unity candidate.

Reagan Open for a Presidential Draft

McCall was not the only governor thinking of party unity. Reagan was asked what he thought of a Rockefeller candidacy and answered that he thought it would be too divisive based on Rockefeller's refusal to endorse Goldwater in 1964. Indeed Reagan spoke of Republican unity, which would be a constant theme in virtually all of his speeches and press conferences in 1967 and 1968.

In the midst of an interview with an Idaho newspaper, suddenly Reagan announced that he would be open for a draft stating, "If the Republican Party comes beating at my door, I wouldn't say 'get lost fellows.'"[135] Quickly he added, "That isn't going to happen."[136] But Reagan's admission that he was open to be drafted for president of the United States did make the national press. Reagan had gone from being only California favorite son to a true potential nominee.

The *New York Times* noted that Reagan now was the "rising star" of the Republican Party and indeed had "stolen the show" in West Yellowstone.[137] Reagan demonstrated "decreasing reluctance to look like a candidate." But any such Reagan candidacy might be a "blessing in disguise for Romney," because Reagan and Nixon would split the party's conservative vote. Looking further into the future, a strengthened Romney might beat Nixon in New Hampshire. But later in Oregon, Romney "surely will have the opportunity to meet Reagan head-on, no holds barred."[138] As it would turn out, Nixon would win in New Hampshire and have to face Reagan head-on in Oregon.

Then the venue switched to Jackson Lake Lodge for the Republican Governor's Conference on June 28.[139] Reagan could not attend due to budget problems back home. At the meeting, the press reported that besides Romney, Reagan was one of two governors "regarded as major Presidential candidates."[140] Clif White did attend in Reagan's absence. The press picked up on the significance of White's presence. White, the press reviewed, had been the main organizational driver behind Goldwater's successful primary campaign against Rockefeller in 1964. Now White "flew in with several of the men who helped him pull off that coup. All are believed to lean toward Reagan."[141]

Eisenhower sent a telegram to the governors asking them to "exert their unified influence" as a way to restore the Republican Party "to the national leadership which it deserves and the country needs." Eisenhower was continuing the same theme of party unity for which he had been advising Reagan for several years. And likely his continued mentoring of, and friendship with, Reagan was an important part of Eisenhower's growing re-involvement with national politics.

As the conferences ended, one reporter noted that Reagan was truly a major presidential candidate. [142] This led to rising speculation about a formal Reagan candidacy announcement. The presence of Reagan campaign team members and the noted growing support of fellow Western governors fueled such speculation. *Time* considered a possible Rockefeller-Reagan ticket because of recent favorable comments Rockefeller had spoken about Reagan. Such speculation would crest a few months later when that theoretical ticket would be featured on the magazine's cover. Also the magazine observed, "Reagan's ascendancy poses a threat of a conservative split. Reagan in fact said of Nixon to one Republican governor: 'this guy's a loser. Any guy who can lose to Pat Brown can't win the Presidency.'"[143] The major media blitz of the 1968 campaign, the film *Ronald Reagan, Citizen Governor*, would be based on that exact premise.

In fact, after Reagan's comment about Nixon appeared in the magazine, both men were aghast. The "whole rationale for Reagan's supposedly secret candidacy suddenly was out in the open. And if *Time* was right, Reagan himself had put it there."[144] So Reagan, "to cover his tracks,"[145] fired off an angry letter to *Time* demanding to know to whom he allegedly had said such a thing about Nixon and then sent a copy of the magazine article and his letter to Nixon. *Time* refused to reveal its source and Nixon wrote back a short, polite note suggesting that Reagan had been the victim of press malfeasance, as had Nixon himself so many times in the past.[146] But most likely Reagan's off-the-cuff comments only served to confirm, as seen earlier, what Nixon had learned before: that Reagan indeed had his sights set on the presidency.

But of most importance was the change in the nature of his candidacy as reported by the national press to the public: Reagan had grown beyond being only the favorite son from California into a candidate willing to accept a draft to become the party's nominee in

1968. And in a careless slip of the tongue, he had revealed his own major strategy to win in 1968. A meeting between Reagan and Nixon was needed to iron out their plans and perhaps heal their political wounds and differences.

Of course Republican Reagan was not invited to the annual Western States Democratic Party Conference held in Los Angeles that summer, but his presence was felt nevertheless. One top California Democratic Party official considered Reagan a "definite possibility" for the GOP nomination after acknowledging how successful Reagan's gubernatorial campaign had been the year before.[147]

Reagan-Nixon Summit at Bohemian Grove: Détente with Nixon?

Fifty miles north of San Francisco sits the Bohemian Grove, a group of ancient redwood trees occupying some 2,700 acres where for decades the nation's politicians and giants of industry and finance had met to discuss politics, business, and to laugh at a musical theatrical production called the Grove Play. The Bohemian Club was a private, male-only organization begun in the 1800s. A famous meeting of members of the Manhattan Project had occurred there in 1942 to plan the atomic bomb. The club's symbol was an owl, for knowledge, and at its yearly special ceremony in front of a specially constructed Owl Shrine, the voice of the Owl in 1967 was that of member Walter Cronkite.

There were some 130 individual camps, each organized by the fields of members' expertise, and they were all maintained by camp valets. Nixon was a member of the Cave Man's Camp of which the late President Hoover had been a member. It was at the Grove in 1950 where Hoover first had introduced Nixon to Eisenhower. In 1967 Nixon had been invited to be the keynote speaker and would dedicate his talk to Hoover.[148] Years later Nixon would be heard complaining of the Bohemian Grove on a Watergate tape, yet he would call this talk the one "that gave me the most pleasure and satisfaction in my political career…it marked the first milestone on my road to the Presidency."[149]

Governor Reagan had been invited by Preston Hotchkis, a Los Angeles ranch manager, and both stayed at his Lost Angels Camp. According to a Reagan associate, the governor had been invited to attend the meeting a month earlier but then "last week Nixon called him and suggested they get together for a talk." Undoubtedly it was time to clear the air from the *Time* affair and learn what Reagan's true presidential intentions were. It was time for détente. Before arriving,

Reagan told the press, "I have a strange hunch that 1968 won't even come up in our discussions."[150]

Before arriving, Nixon had told the press that he would respect the favorite son status of Reagan. Nixon added, "Any potential candidate should respect the right of any favorite son to have his delegation and should not interfere with the makeup of that delegation." Nixon's feelings in this regard would change by the following June. At one breakfast held at Owl's Nest camp, Reagan and Nixon sat somewhat formally dressed for the rustic redwoods.[151]

Then "Nixon cornered Reagan to pin him down about his plans for 1968."[152] With Senator George Murphy sitting with them on a bench in Lost Angels Camp, Nixon told Reagan he would seek the presidency but would run against Johnson and not against any other Republican. Reagan said he was "surprised, flattered and somewhat concerned about all the presidential speculation surrounding him."[153] He told Nixon that he did not want to be California's favorite son but would permit his name to be used so that California would have a unified delegation. Reagan told Nixon he would not enter the primaries. Whether Nixon had interpreted this to mean that Reagan would not enter any primary, or whether Nixon knew that Reagan would not withdraw from the Wisconsin, Nebraska and Oregon primaries due to the wording on their withdrawal affadavits, was not clear. Reagan would reiterate his position on the primaries at numerous press conferences.

Did Nixon believe Reagan's avowed goal of only being California's favorite son? About this time, Spencer had told Nixon that Reagan had had the stars in his eyes.[154] Nixon now knew that Reagan was serious about seeking the presidency in 1968. So whether Nixon thought Reagan was lying or had changed his mind is not clear. But seemingly there was now a Reagan-Nixon détente.

Was there a true, secret agreement between Reagan and Nixon? As will be discussed later, Patrick Buchanan felt that based on a Nixon memo, Nixon's reaction, and some of Reagan's future actions in 1968, Reagan and Nixon did in fact reach a secret deal.

Did Goldwater act as intermediary? Rusher recalled that at Bohemian Grove, Reagan also met with Goldwater, and that the secret agreement for Reagan to openly seek the nomination only if Nixon had stumbled had been mediated via Goldwater.[155] Author Kitty Kelley noted that a few weeks after Bohemian Grove, Goldwater told Vice-President Humphrey about the Goldwater-Reagan conversation. Humphrey then sent a memo to President Johnson. Reportedly Goldwater had told Reagan to not kid himself thinking he could beat President Johnson and to not be fooled by the enthusiastic loud, hard-core conservatives. Goldwater also told Humphrey that Reagan refused to run in the second spot to Rockefeller.[156]

But at Bohemian Grove, within a day, the Reagan-Nixon truce fell apart. It set a record for the shortest détente in world and political history. Columnists Roland Evans and Robert Novak reported that the Nixon camp was attempting to isolate Reagan by unloading right wing extremists onto Reagan. Nixon had reportedly declared, "Let Ronnie have the kooks."[157] As veteran columnist Robert Novak noted, "The last thing Nixon wanted was a quarrel with Ronald Reagan."[158]

A new apology, this time from Nixon to Reagan, was needed. Historian Buchanan revealed his own role at this critical point. Buchanan felt that whoever leaked this information had committed an "act of paralyzing stupidity." For they had insulted Reagan, and Reagan was a "far more serious rival than Rockefeller."[159]

On July 31, Reagan had prostate surgery for benign disease in Los Angeles. By August 8 he was feeling well enough to host a campaign update meeting at his Los Angeles home with Reed. The two reviewed travel plans and campaign organization.[160]

Meanwhile Buchanan drafted Nixon's August 4, 1967 letter of apology to Reagan, and in it Nixon referenced the earlier *Time* incident where Reagan had had to apologize to Nixon. Reagan then wrote back on August 16, 1967 writing, "We shouldn't believe any quotes unless we hear them ourselves."[161] Novak revealed years later that the Nixon insider who had revealed the "kook" phrase to Evans and Novak was professional politician Bob Walker, who later would join the Reagan campaign in 1968.[162]

Time had gotten hold of a memo about Nixon from Reagan's public relations firm. In the memo, Reagan's advisors felt "the one thing that could rejuvenate Nixon would be color TV. In black and white he looks sinister with his black beard." They were referring to Nixon's late-in-the-day beard shadow.[163] Nixon then chatted with a young television executive producer named Roger Ailes. Ailes, future Chairman of Fox News Channel decades later, would in 1984 help coach President Reagan toward a winning performance in his second debate against Walter Mondale. While Ailes and Nixon chatted about politics, Nixon—the loser of the television debate to Kennedy in 1960—admitted that he thought TV was a gimmick. Ailes disagreed telling Nixon he knew it was "the most powerful means of communications ever devised."

Unlike Nixon at the time, Reagan—the great communicator—not only had long known the power of television and its durability, he was using it successfully during his campaign. Nixon must have changed his mind, for shortly thereafter he hired Ailes.[164]

During the summer, the *New York Times* ran a front-page story which analyzed where the 1968 Republican race stood with roughly a year to go until the Miami Beach convention. After the New Hampshire primary on March 12, 1968, the "major contested primaries" would be Wisconsin on April 2, Nebraska on May 14, and Oregon on May 21. Besides Romney and Nixon, those three states "will almost certainly include a third prospect, Gov. Ronald Reagan of California."[165] The analysis continued, "Mr. Reagan is in a strong position to take advantage of any Nixon slippage. The Governor has said he will not withdraw his name from the Nebraska or Oregon ballots because this would require a seeping renunciation of Presidential ambition that would be inconsistent with his planned role as California's favorite son....Such a rationale would apply with equal validity to the Wisconsin primary."[166]

So there it was: a front page story from the nation's newspaper of record outlining clearly that Ronald Reagan would enter three key primaries in 1968 and that should Nixon slip, Reagan was waiting to take his place as Republican standard-bearer a year hence. Plus the rationale for Reagan's refusals to sign withdrawal affidavits was made crystal clear and unassailable. Reed and White were thrilled at what Reagan had achieved. His campaign continued accelerating on its upward trajectory.

Endnotes

1. *Newsweek*, 5/29/1967, p. 26
2. Lewis, Joseph, p. 185
3. White, p. 168.
4. Buckley, William F, "Reagan and California" www.NationalReviewOnline.com/1967200511170828.asp
5. Ronald Reagan, Young Republican National convention, Omaha, Nebraska, June 23, 1967
6. Lewis, Joseph, p. 185
7. ibid
8. Boyarsky, p. 23
9. Lewis, Jos, p. 196.
10. Curtis, p. 19-21
11. Curtis, p. 118
12. Meese, pers int 1/3/2013
13. Boyarsky, op.cit., p. 23
14. Shrum, p. 15
15. Isaacson, p. 119
16. IN-7 "Town Meeting of the World, 10/26/1965 CBS broadcast, Box 7, Dwight D. Eisenhower Post-Presidential Papers 1961-1969, 1965 Principal File, Dwight D Eisenhower Presidential Library
17. Mankiewicz, Frank, "Nofziger: A Friend With Whom It Was a Pleasure to Disagree" Washington Post, 3/29/2006
18. Lewis, Jos, p. 197
19. Humphrey, Hall op.cit., *The Oregonain*, 5/31/68

20. Watts, oral hist
21. Reed, *The Reagan Enigma*, p. 87-88
22. ibid.
23. *Newsweek*, 5/29/67, p. 26
24. ibid
25. Gould, Jack, "TV: Dialogue With London Students," *NYT*, 5/16/67, p. 91
26. "Reagan and Kennedy Will Share TV Spot," *NYT*, 4/26/67, p. 94
27. Miller Center of Public Affairs, Presidential Oral History Program, University of Virginia, Interview with Michael Deaver, 9/12/2002, tape 2, p. 12
28. Reed, *The Reagan Enigma*, p. 89
29. Bradley, int 9/14/12.
30. Bradley, int 9/14/12
31. Lewis, Jos, p. 197
32. *Newsweek*, 5/29/67, p. 27
33. the debate transcript in full is available on-line at www.reagan2020.us and a video is available from the Ronald Reagan Presidential Library
34. Reed, *The Reagan Enigma*, p. 90
35. *Newsweek*, 5/29/67, p. 26-27
36. *Newsweek*, 5/29/67, p. 27
37. Kengor, p. 34
38. Reed, *The Reagan Enigma*, p. 90
39. Bradley, int 9/14/12
40. Reed, p. 15
41. Ahluwalia, pers comm. 9/24/2012
42. Bradley int 9/14/12
43. Lewis Jos, p. 197
44. Reed, p. 15
45. Kengor, p. 33
46. Brinkley, p. 209-212
47. Hayward, p. 168
48. Cannon, Governor Reagan, p. 260
49. Cannon, Ronnie and Jesse, p. 264.
50. Watts, oral hist, p. 10
51. Lewis, Jos, p. 196
52. Lewis, Jos, p. 197
53. Humphrey, Hal op.cit., *Oregonian*, 5/31/68
54. White , Politics, p. 168
55. Beran, p. 150; Halberstam, p. 110
56. *Newsweek*, 5/29/67, p. 26-27
57. ibid
58. Reed, p. 15
59. Hayward, *Age of Reagan*, p. 168
60. Buckley, "Reagan and California," *National Review*, 11/28/67
61. Kengor, p. 33
62. Mankiewicz, Frank "Nofziger", op.cit., *Washington Post*, 3/29/2006
63. White op.cit., p. 168
64. Cannon, *Governor Reagan*, p. 260
65. Schlesinger, Arthur Jr., RFK
66. Thomas, Evan Rfk His Life…
67. Clarke, Thurston
68. Hayward, p. 170
69. Watts Oral History, p. 10
70. Cannon Ronnie and Jesse, p. 264
71. Hayward, p. 170
72. ibid
73. Kengor 2007, p. 3
74. Rothstein, Betsy, "20 Questions with Frank Mankiewicz," *The Hill*, 12/9/2008
75. Reagan, Ronald Address at Chico State College, May 20, 1967
76. ibid
77. ibid
78. ibid
79. Hayward, p. 170
80. Kengor 2007, p. 3
81. White and Tuccille, p. 168
82. On the way to meet Kennedy, Eisenhower told his son John, "I don't do failed invasions."

83. *Newsweek*, 5/22/67, p. 27
84. *Newsweek*, 5/22/67, p. 30
85. *Newsweek*, 5/22/67, p. 36
86. *Newsweek*, ibid
87. ibid
88. ibid
89. ibid
90. ibid
91. ibid
92. *Newsweek*, 5/22/67, p. 28
93. *Newsweek*, 5/22/67, p. 29
94. Reagan and Reed, 5/26/1967
95. Pearson, Drew, "Washington Merry-Go Round," 5/8/67
96. Weaver Warren, "Role For Reagan After Nixon Seen," *NYT*, 5/27/67, p. 14
97. Gibbs and Duffy, p. 209
98. See Illustrations
99. Reagan-Reed, 6/15/1967, San Francisco hotel
100. Reed, p. 15
101. Reed pers int, 10/17/12
102. Weaver, Warren, "Young Republicans," *NYT*, 6/25/67, p. E3
103. ibid
104. ibid
105. ibid
106. RRL, Tape 275
107. RRL, Tape 275
108. Reagan's recorded words are slightly different than his prepared speech
109. RRL, Tape 275
110. RRL, Tape 275
111. ibid
112. RRL, tape 275
113. Weaver op.cit.
114. Weaver, ibid
115. Kabaservice, p. 208
116. Skinner et. al., p. 52
117. Lewis, Joseph, p. 196
118. Weaver, Warren, "Young GOP Unity Urged by Reagan," *NYT*, 6/24/67, p. 12
119. Weaver, ibid
120. Weaver, ibid
121. Buckley, William F, "Reagan and California" www.NationalReviewOnline.com/1967200511170828.asp
122. "Reagan to Speak Here on June 24" Hiram Scott College Scrapbook, 6/15/67
123. RRL, Tape 275
124. RRL, Tape 275
125. RRL, Tape 275
126. "Arrives in Scottsbluff," *Scottsbluff Star-Herald*, 6/25/67
127. "Another Opinion," *NYT*, 3/26/67, p. 155
128. Turner, Wallace, "Reagan Denies Advance Man Seeks Support for race in '68," *NYT*, 6/26/67, p. 20
129. ibid
130. Turner, Wallace, ibid
131. Turner, Wallace, "Reagan Doubts He'll Be Drafted," *NYT*, 6/27/67, p. 24
132. Turner, ibid
133. Turner, Wallace, "Reagan Denies Advance Man Seeks Support for Race in '68," *NYT*, 6/26/67, p. 20
134. Turner, Wallace, "Reagan Doubts He'll Be Drafted," *NYT*, 6/27/67, p. 24
135. ibid
136. ibid
137. Wicker, Tom, "In the Nation: Down but Not Out in Wyoming," *NYT*, 6/29/67, p. 42
138. ibid
139. ibid
140. Weaver, Warren Jr., "Eisenhower Asks Republican Unity," *NYT*, 6/29/67, p. 9
141. "Waiting Game," *Time*, 7/7/67, p. 14
142. Weaver, Warren Jr, "Eisenhower Asks Republican Unity," *NYT*, 6/29/67, p. 9
143. Time, ibid
144. Gibbs and Duffy, p. 210

145. ibid
146. Gibbs and Duffy, p. 211
147. Hill, Gladwin, "Democrats Open Parley in West," *NYT*, 8/25/67, p. 16
148. Gibbs and Duffy, p. 211
149. Nixon, RN, p. 284
150. Lewis, Joseph, p. 192
151. Davies, Lawrence "Nixon and Reagan in Informal Talks," *NYT*, 7/24/67, p. 14
152. Gibbs and Duffy, p. 211
153. ibid
154. Spencer oral history, p. 35
155. Rusher, p. 207
156. Kelley, p. 165
157. Novak, p.154
158. Novak, p. 154
159. Buchanan, p. 122
160. Reagan-Reed, 8/8/1967, Reagan residence
161. Gibbs and Duffy, p. 212-213; Skinner, Anderson, p. 706-707
162. Novak, p. 155
163. Safire, p. 46-47
164. Diamond, p. 155-157; Nixon RN, p. 304
165. Weaver, Warren, "Republicans Face 4 Key Primaries for President," *NYT*, 7/9/67, p. 1
166. Weaver, ibid

CHAPTER 7: IKE WANTS REAGAN TO RUN FOR PRESIDENT

"DE also encouraged RR to run for favorite son."
~ Memorandum of Conversation: Dwight D. Eisenhower
and Bob Kennan[1]

As Reagan was conferring with Nixon at Bohemian Grove and recovering from surgery, coach Eisenhower was about to encourage his protégé to follow his own footsteps and seek the highest office in the land. At the time, Eisenhower remained emphatically opposed to a 'war of gradualism" in Vietnam.[2] Domestic politics also remained key, and on July 26, 1967 at 4:40 PM, Eisenhower spoke at length to former Louisiana Governor Bob Kennon, who thought that one key to winning in 1968 was the South but he was concerned about the appeal of George Wallace. Kennon had just spoken to Reagan about 1968. Kennon called to tell Eisenhower that Reagan had said, "he had a job to do in California." Eisenhower's secretary's notes for the call stated that:

"DE agreed to contact Reagan...DE encouraged him to stick with the job there, not far away from entertainment world yet. He agreed and said he had no intention of doing it (Presidency). **DE also encouraged RR to run for favorite son.**"[3] (author's emphasis)

Thus Dwight Eisenhower indeed did encourage Ronald Reagan to run for president in 1968, albeit as a favorite from California. Surely an astute a politician as Eisenhower, not aware of Reagan's stealth campaign (still hunting for delegates with the specific campaign plans for the opt-out primary states) realized that there was some chance that Reagan might be nominated by the Republican Party in 1968. Eisenhower had had the same thought once Reagan had been elected governor as we have seen, and that at some point if Reagan were the nominee he might need to point out that Eisenhower had encouraged his entrance into the race for the presidency.

Around this time, Battaglia resigned, entangled in the homosexuality scandal discussed earlier. After the announcement, which did not reveal the reason behind the departure, reporters Rowland Evans and Robert Novak felt that the staff shake-up was a "turning point" in the Reagan administration as noted earlier. Feeling that it had indicated major problems in the Reagan organization with moderate Battaglia fighting with favored staff conservatives, rather than the true reason of Battaglia's sexuality, Evans and Novak felt that Reagan could not afford to let such conflicts simmer: "If Reagan is ever to run for president, it will have to be now—in 1968—or never."[4] White felt that after this event, Reagan's campaign never recovered.[5] But as discussed, Reed felt at most this was a minor bump in the road for a campaign that had started in November, 1966 and lasted until the last day of the convention some 22 months later.

A second shakeup then ensued. Reed in his memoir discusses the details of how he was terminated as campaign director because he had failed to inform Reagan's financial backers about the campaign. A series of meetings was held, culminating in a summit held at the Reagan residence. The status of the presidential campaign to-date was reviewed, as were the details for all of the planned fall campaign trips. After successful earlier trips to Oregon and Nebraska coupled with the Governors' Conference in Montana, Reagan had a full slate of fall campaign trips scheduled. Who was in charge of his 1968 presidential campaign: Reed and White and Spencer? Nofziger? Reagan's backers? The Reagan's were confused and told Reed to cancel most of October's travel schedule.[6]

As new chief of staff, Clark—as we have seen—was not in favor of the Reagan presidential campaign; he hoped the "whole Presidential quest would go away."[7] The Los Angeles backers complained of Reed's inexperience. Reagan began to have doubts about Reed and the team Reed had created.

The final confrontation came on September 19, 1967 when Reagan and Reed met in San Francisco. Reagan's golden parachute for Reed was to secure for Reed the position of the next Republican National Committeeman from California. But Reed did not exit the 1968 campaign altogether. He took over the job that had been assigned originally to Spencer, who had left by then, and Reed started to run Reagan's out-of-state travels. Clif White was the one left "in limbo."[8] Reagan told Reed that he wanted a new person to be the chairman of the presidential campaign: William French Smith. Smith was one of Reagan's original financial backers. Reed felt that Smith did not have the ability to lead, plus Smith had "neither the time nor inclination" to travel on Reagan's fall campaign trips.[9]

With the crisis of campaign leadership seemingly settled, Reagan turned his thoughts back to his young supporters. Reagan never had young people far from his mind. As we have seen, Reagan—on the National Advisory Board of YAF—had received a tremendous reception at the 1964 Republican convention and in 1966 had his own cadre of enthusiastic young supporters. In June, 1967, he had traveled to Nebraska to the Young Republican national convention where he had received the tremendous reception and the national media had begun to see how conservative youth were switching loyalty from Goldwater to Reagan.

YAF held its convention in Pittsburgh, and on Sept. 1, 1967, a brand new grass roots Reagan for President group announced its official formation: Students for Reagan (SFR). The announcement was made by Mike Thompson, and "Representatives were out in force at the convention, signing up members from a hospitality suite at the Pittsburgh Hilton."[10] It would not be until 1968 that SFR would become organized and functional.

As had happened in Omaha in June, the national media took notice once again at the transformation that was occurring within conservative youth. Reagan bumper stickers and buttons were as popular as those for Goldwater had been four years earlier.[11] Reagan posters and pins "dominated" the YAF convention as SFR said its goal was to "drum up campus support for the Governor's expected bid for the Republican nomination in 1968."[12] Clearly despite Goldwater's endorsement of Nixon, the allegiance of YAF members had shifted completely from Goldwater to Reagan.

Several of the founders of SFR, who we will meet shortly— David R. Jones, Randal C. Teague, and Kathryn Forte—attended that Pittsburgh convention. Reagan took time out from his busy fall campaign schedule to send greetings:

"You are America's future and you have the responsibility to weigh everything in the line of government, law and economic theory that is proposed to you. And you should weigh it on this scale: does it offer some kind of security in exchange for your right to go as far and as high as your own ability will take you? We can maintain a floor under which no one should have to live in degradation, but we must never put a ceiling on the individual."[13]

Reagan wanted equality at the starting line of life's endeavors but clearly did not want members of American society to be guaranteed equal results. Those same choices would echo still in the 21st century when liberals would propose to cap how much an individual could contribute to his/her retirement plans as they would feel they should cap how much an individual should be permitted to live off of per year.[14]

Vietnam remained ever present. As was almost a custom among reporters at the time, in mid September at a Sacramento news conference (just prior to flying east to Milwaukee), again Reagan was asked if he advocated the use of nuclear weapons in the war. As will be discussed in more detail later, Reagan answered, "I still repeat what President Eisenhower said some time ago, that perhaps one of our great mistakes was in assuring the enemy in advance of our intention not to use them—that the enemy should still be frightened that we might."[15] A few days later, Eisenhower's original recommendations to Johnson shown through again when Reagan added, "If the escalation that the United States had undertaken during the last two or three years had occurred suddenly, the war might have ended, because doing it all at once might have brought the enemy to the bargaining table."[16]

On September 18, Reagan was featured in the political section of *U.S News and World Report* under the banner, "Ronald Reagan in the Limelight As '68 Maneuvering Starts." The magazine noted that Reagan "has become the fastest-rising prospect in public opinion polls for the 1968 Republican Presidential nomination." According to unnamed White House sources, even President Johnson was "becoming concerned about the rising public appeal of Ronald Reagan." Reagan had risen to third in Republican polls behind Romney and Nixon, and Reagan's stock was "rising nationwide with 'independents' and among Democrats." The magazine speculated on a potential Reagan-Lindsay ticket for 1968, pairing Reagan— the governor of the nation's most populous state—with the liberal Republican mayor of New York City—the nation's biggest city to offer "geographic balance."[17]

The magazine took note that Reagan was "setting out on a cross-country speaking schedule which will take him into key States."[18] The three opt-out primaries of Wisconsin, Nebraska and Oregon would be crucial as would the first primary in New Hampshire. If Nixon did not win, he admitted he would be "washed up." Romney supporters echoed those sentiments. If neither emerged with a commanding lead, then Nixon added, "It would be best to have a new man."[19]

Reagan as governor had battled with a legislature controlled by Democrats and had emerged "with the reputation of being a cool, experienced, and skilled political operator." When he appeared on television, he was "particularly effective at explaining his position on issues in plain language that people can understand."[20] Clearly the magazine was stating that Reagan, recognized even then as The Great Communicator, could transfer his skills in dealing with California's legislature to Congress in the nation's capital.

As Reagan's star was rising as presidential candidate, Nixon was busy behind the scenes. Columnist Pearson reported of a major September meeting, in follow-up to the late December-early January strategy session held at Nixon's apartment and of course after the failed peace at Bohemia Grove. The new Nixon meeting consisted of forty advisors, clearly many more than the first meeting in January. Dr. Gaylord Parkinson, who along with Reagan and Eisenhower had come up with the fabled Eleventh Commandment, had been Nixon's first campaign director. Parkinson returned, though, to California to attend to his ill wife and was replaced. Others felt that the reason Parkinson had been replaced was that "he was sharing" Nixon's secrets with Governor Reagan.[21]

Pearson wrote that a radio network official plus two members of the executive staffs of *Time* and *Newsweek* were there. Nixon's secret opinion of his major GOP rival was disclosed next. The "biggest danger to Nixon, it was decided, is that in the early primaries, especially New Hampshire, supporters of Ronald Reagan would write his name in…This could take conservative votes away from Nixon (and) help Romney." A poll from New Hampshire was discussed which showed Nixon far ahead of his other rivals and indeed Reagan came in fourth behind Romney and Rockefeller as well. In homage to his main rival, or more likely in spite of Reagan, Nixon's meeting ended not with "win one for the Gipper" but "win big with our boy Dick."[22] Patrick Buchanan recalled he had created a "Counter Reagan" strategy trying to make sure Reagan never found an issue in which Nixon was to the left of Reagan and for which Reagan could drive a wedge with those conservatives favoring Nixon.[23]

Nixon was preventing Reagan from gaining ground to his political right, so Reagan decided to shift left, albeit within the party. Before leaving California for his fall campaign swings, Reagan decided to mend some political fences with one of his liberal rivals for the 1968 nomination, George Romney. Romney and Reagan had spoken in the nation's capital the prior spring with Reagan clearly triumphing. Over the summer Romney had made his infamous "brainwashing" comment and his poll numbers declined rapidly yet he still campaigned.

The national media thought that Romney's brainwashing comment could, however, turn out to be a bonanza for Reagan. The *New York Times* editorialized that as a result of Romney's mistake, "If Gov. Ronald Reagan of California persists in his present intention of leaving his name on the ballot in Wisconsin, Nebraska, and Oregon, (and) if Messrs. Nixon and Romney kill one another off in the primaries, the less active candidates will move into contention, notably Governor Reagan."[24]

Governor and Mrs. Romney were invited for lunch on September 24, 1967 at the Reagan's Pacific Palisades home. Amidst tropical greenery and bougainevilla, the Romney's limousine drove up the steep driveway. The Reagan's and Romney's spoke together in the driveway amidst some forty reporters and photographers before going inside. The film is available online.[25] After a luncheon of cold salmon and mixed vegetables, the two governors met formally with reporters.

Whether Reagan and Romney reached an informal truce, just exchanged banal pleasantries, debated the weather, or had heated arguments was not revealed. Indeed they men told the reporters that they had "purposely skirted political issues." Reporters asked Romney about a new Gallup poll, which had shown his poll numbers drop ten points in three weeks. Romney had dropped to fourth place amongst Republicans at fourteen percent and now trailed Reagan's sixteen percent. Romney said the results were "interesting." Reagan was asked about a Romney-Reagan ticket in 1968 and answered that he was not going to discuss politics. But no reporter asked about a Reagan-Romney ticket. Reagan's upcoming trip to Wisconsin, Illinois, and South Carolina was being viewed as "an early tentative move toward seeking the party's 1968 nomination."[26]

Reagan also told reporters that he had not invited Romney to enter the California primary where Reagan was set up to be favorite son. The California delegates, as we will see, were only committed to Reagan on the first ballot. For Romney, this "did not rule out a careful, but intensive, effort to win the support of the delegates and the party leadership in California for the second ballot." At this point, there were some California Republican activists "who were willing to make that effort" on behalf of Romney but "almost nothing was done." Perhaps this was another item discussed at the Reagan luncheon.[27] But Romney would drop out long before he would have to worry about whether to challenge Reagan in California in 1968.

Reagan would be asked about Romney's brainwashing comment several times that fall, and Reagan would use it as an opportunity to not speak ill of a fellow Republican. Reagan would honor Eisenhower's extension of Parkinson's Eleventh Commandment. Reagan could have used it as an opportunity to attack Romney as Romney had attacked him on civil rights earlier, but Reagan used it as an opportunity not only to defend Romney but used it to attack the Johnson administration. "I think he (Gov. Romney) has made an explanation of the context in which he used the term brainwashing.

Perhaps he expressed at the same time the concern a lot of Americans should have as to whether they are getting all of the facts that they are entitled to have about foreign and domestic policy."[28]

Another example of Reagan helping Romney that fall would be during a Chicago press conference on October 27, 1967. Reagan would be asked about a comment Romney had made earlier in the day calling President Johnson a "phony" and if Reagan thought this comment had destroyed whatever remaining chances Romney had for the nomination. Reagan quickly would come to Romney's defense.[29]

Perhaps ruffled feathers were smoothed over at their luncheon after all.

A month after the Pittsburgh YAF convention, Lee Edwards, by this time the former editor of *The New Guard*, released *Reagan: A Political Biography*, and Edwards' chief researcher was Bruce Weinrod. As will be seen, Edwards also had been editing an autobiography of Senator Strom Thurmond. Meanwhile in California, "thousands of Californians" tried to convince Reagan to run not merely as favorite son but to become a full-fledged candidate.[30] At the forefront of this effort were California YAF members including Dana Rohrabacher, who recalled his activities as being Reagan's "advance guard."[31]

U.S. News and World Report then previewed Reagan's upcoming cross-country trip.[32] Reagan was going on quite a whirlwind campaign swing. Reagan jetted east to campaign in two of the three opt-out primary states and would begin his own Southern Strategy in South Carolina. But Reagan's first stop was to the critical state where for the first time outside California, Reagan would appear on the ballot: Wisconsin.

Endnotes

1. Memorandum of Conversation: Dwight D. Eisenhower and Bob Kennan, 7/26/67, Eisenhower, Dwight D.: Post-Presidential Papers 1961-1969, DDE Appointment Books Series, Box 3, Calls and Appts 1967 4, Dwight D. Eisenhower Presidential Library
2. Ambrose, p. 562
3. Memorandum of Conversation: Dwight D. Eisenhower and Bob Kennan, 7/26/67, Eisenhower, Dwight D.: Post-Presidential Papers 1961-1969, DDE Appointment Books Series, Box 3, Calls and Appts 1967 4, Dwight D. Eisenhower Presidential Library
4. Evans, R and Novak R, "Moderate Leaves Reagan, Division in Camp is Blamed," *Milwaukee Sentinel*, 9/12/1967, part 1, p. 16
5. White, p. 36
6. Reagan-Reed, 8/8/1967 through 9/23/1967; Reed, *The Reagan Enigma*
7. Reed, p. 16
8. Reed, ibid
9. Reed, p. 19; Reagan-Reed, 9/19/1967-9/23/1967
10. Thornburn, p. 164
11. Thornburn, p. 164
12. Bigart, Homer, "Youth Unit Shifts Fealty to Reagan," *NYT*, 9/2/67, p. 10
13. YAF National Convention program, 8/31/67-9/3/67, Pittsburgh PA, courtesy Kathryn Forte

14. Marotta, David John, "Is a $3 Million IRA Sufficient For Retirement?," *Forbes On-Line*, 4/21/2013
15. Boyarsky, Bill, "Reagan Prepares for 'Hawk' Tour," *Gettysburg Times*, 9/13/1967
16. "Reagan Urges Escalation to Win War Quickly," *NYT*, 9/13/1967, p. 5
17. *U.S. News and World Report*, 9/18/67, p. 52
18. ibid
19. ibid, p. 53
20. ibid
21. White, p. 135
22. Pearson, Drew, "Washington Merry-Go-Round," 9/21/67
23. Buchanan, p. 140-141
24. "Romney vs. Nixon," *NYT*, 9/10/67, p. 218
25. http://www.efootage.com/clip_list.php?query=September%2025,%201967
26. Weaver, Warren, "Romney Is Guest At Reagan Home," *NYT*, 9/25/67, p. 38
27. Hart, David K, "Pilgrim's Progress", op.cit., p. 106
28. "Reagan Urges Escalation to Win the War 'Quickly,'" *NYT*, 9/13/67, p. 5
29. RRL, Tape 301
30. Thorburn, p. 165
31. ibid
32. *U.S. News and World Report*, 9/18/67, p. 52

CHAPTER 8: WISCONSIN REAGAN FOR PRESIDENT CLUB

"I was giddy with excitement."
> ~ Don L. Taylor[1]

"It's good to meet the man in Wisconsin that I've heard so much about."
> ~ Ronald Reagan[2]

Ronald Reagan's first test as a national candidate was not his 1976 primary run against President Gerald Ford. It was not his 1980 campaign as Republican nominee against President Jimmy Carter. Also it was not his run in the 1968 New Hampshire primary because as we will seen, his campaign papers were withdrawn; his name was not on the New Hampshire ballot and he received only a few hundred write-in votes. Rather, Ronald Reagan's very first test on any ballot as a national candidate was in 1968 in the Republican Wisconsin primary.

Because of the new campaign laws that had been passed in Wisconsin, Nebraska and Oregon, Wisconsin was in fact the first step in Reagan's master campaign plan from the very beginning. Wisconsin would hopefully start the ball rolling for Reagan. With sequential increasing vote tallies afterwards, including his winning in California, he would sail into Miami Beach with the combined momentum of these three primaries at his back.

When the state's new election law was passed in the summer of 1967 and signed by Governor Warren P. Knowles, Wisconsin had emerged as the first "full-scale testing ground" for the 1968 presidential election. A bipartisan committee would meet on February 6, 1968 and list "all potential candidates" on each party's ballot. To be listed as a candidate, someone had to be "generally advocated or recognized in the national news media throughout the United States." If a named person did not want to remain on the ballot, he or she could withdraw by filing an affidavit "stating without qualification that he is not and does not intend to become a candidate." The thirty delegates so elected on April 2, 1968 were to be pledged to support the winner of the primary at the national convention, "until he releases them or falls below a third of the votes cast at the convention."[3] Besides the method of being chosen by the committee, there was also a second path to appearing on the ballot via filing petitions with 35,000 signatures.[4]

Wisconsin's new law was almost identical to those passed in Nebraska and Oregon. It was the unique primary structure of these three states that had been used to plan Reagan's campaign strategy and tactics. Reagan's name would automatically appear and he certainly would not withdraw. The Wisconsin primary, because of the new law, was seen as being completely different than the primary to be held in New Hampshire on March 12, 1968, which was to be the only other primary prior to that in Wisconsin. The *New York Times* said that with Wisconsin's new law, "the Wisconsin primary is expected to be the first test of strength for Governor Reagan."[5]

Taylor is Chosen to Chair 1968 Reagan Wisconsin Campaign

The story of Reagan's Wisconsin campaign is the story of one man who still is active in Republican Party politics: Don L. Taylor. Taylor self-published a monograph entitled *A Devotion to Liberty, The Political Life of Don L. Taylor* and its third part, entitled *Early Efforts for Reagan* chronicled Taylor's activities during 1966-1968 on Reagan's first presidential campaign. Taylor kindly shared the monograph with your author during his interview.

Taylor was, and still is, a bank executive in Waukesha County, Wisconsin, which is west of Milwaukee. A life-long Republican, by 1963 he was a member of the Republican Party of Wisconsin Executive Committee and was Wisconsin Federation of Young Republicans State Chairman from 1963-1965. He and his wife heard Ronald Reagan deliver his *A Time for Choosing* speech on the radio, as they did not yet own a television set. They were totally impressed.

Taylor got interested in flying during World War II when he had watched yellow Cub trainers, flown by future Army Air Force pilots, fly over his family farm while he looked up from farm fieldwork. During the same memorable weekend that he received his Bachelor degree, he passed his flight test and became a commissioned Reserve Officer in the U.S. Army. Taylor would put his flying skills to good use on behalf of Ronald Reagan's first campaign for the presidency.

In 1967, Taylor was solicited to join the Nixon effort in Wisconsin, but Taylor declined. Not only did Taylor not like Nixon personally, his "heart belonged to someone else."[6] Taylor and his wife hoped that Reagan, whom they had followed in the news ever since they had heard "The Speech," might be president some day. Taylor wrote to Reagan and urged him to run for president. In the letter, Taylor volunteered to work for Reagan in Wisconsin, listed his credentials, and offered personal references of Governor Knowles and GOP Wisconsin Chairman Ody Fish.

Within days of mailing the letter to Governor Reagan, to his "pleasant surprise,"[7] Taylor received word that Reagan wanted him to meet Reed. While Reagan had left Eisenhower and had returned to California, Reed had arrived in Milwaukee and met Taylor. Taylor then learned the entire Reagan 1968 presidential campaign strategy. Reagan would not declare his candidacy initially, but Reagan would give full support behind the scenes. Reagan's plan was to get ten percent of the vote in New Hampshire on March 12, fifteen percent in Wisconsin on April 2, thirty percent in Nebraska on May 14, and then win the Oregon primary on May 28. That would be enough to convince the nation, especially the South, that Reagan should be the Republican nominee. The specific percentages as goals would change slightly in the future, New Hampshire would be eliminated as the first step and the Oregon expectations would be lowered from outright win to a hoped-for tally higher than Nebraska's—as we will see—but Reagan's plan essentially would stay intact up to the convention.

Taylor felt "giddy with excitement not only to be informed of Reagan's grand design, but to be included in it!" Taylor was being appointed Wisconsin State Chairman for Reagan; the appointment however was to be "unofficial and confidential." Thus Don L. Taylor became the very first state chairman for the candidacy of Ronald Reagan for the presidency of the United States.

Wisconsin Reagan for President Club

Taylor got to work for Reagan's 1968 presidential campaign at once. On April 28, 1967, Taylor announced the formation of the Wisconsin Reagan for President Club with himself as chairman. Organizational papers were filed with the secretary of state's office in Madison the same day. The document listed as the club's nature to promote "the candidacy of Gov. Ronald Reagan of California for President of the United States in 1968." As your author has been unable to locate any papers filed by the Owosso group in Michigan, Taylor's statement is the first official legal form ever filed on behalf of the candidacy of Ronald Reagan for president of the United States.

Governor Reagan then wrote to Taylor personally on May 1. Reagan wrote, "Thanks for your good letter and the honor you do me in wishing to support me for the Presidency. I feel now however that my role must be to do the best job possible here in California." [8] Taylor read Reagan's denial, smiled secretly for Taylor was now an insider who knew better, and felt he was part of Reagan's unheralded team. On May 20, Taylor flew his Piper Comanche to Eau Claire, which would become one of many flights on behalf of Reagan, to attend the GOP state convention in order to promote the Reagan candidacy. Taylor already had reached out to Reagan youth in Wisconsin.

Over the next few months as news about Taylor's Reagan presidential club spread, Taylor received phone calls and letters from many enthusiastic Wisconsin voters, who offered to help the nascent Reagan grass roots campaign. Taylor was so inundated by eager Reagan enthusiasts that he soon had more invitations and opportunities than he could handle himself. So Taylor then found and delegated additional campaign responsibilities to new Reagan campaign leaders and organizers to such a point that eventually he had more than four hundred card-carrying Reagan volunteers working all over Wisconsin.

The national press did not report directly on the activities of Taylor on behalf of Reagan. Indeed early that summer the only national media comment about Reagan's Wisconsin campaign was at the same time the new Nixon campaign team had been announced to the press on July 29. It was felt at the time that Nixon did not yet have the Wisconsin Republican primary sewn up because Nixon "will have to head off a drive among members of the Young Republican Clubs for Mr. Reagan," as Reagan's young supporters were "his staunchest supporters in the state."[9]

In August 1967, black violence came to Milwaukee and Gov. Knowles sent in National Guard tanks to restore order. Taylor noted that people in Wisconsin were "nervous," and his own efforts for the Reagan candidacy "were intensified."[10]

That same month, Republican State Chairman Ody Fish convened a meeting of the leaders of all three Wisconsin Republican presidential teams at his home. At the meeting, the Reagan campaign in Wisconsin was given full and equal status with the others. Fish suggested that each campaign limit their out-of-state donations to $75,000 so as to leave other donations for other party candidates and activities in 1968. Out-of-state contributions could continue without limit. The Romney budget for Wisconsin was $350,000 and Nixon would spend $500,000. Taylor recalled, "I kept quiet for we would spend less than $10,000 and we had no expectation of receiving outside funds."[11]

Later that summer when discussing the implications of Wisconsin's new primary law and the withdrawal affidavit process, the national media finally began to focus somewhat on the presidential campaign of Ronald Reagan in Wisconsin. The *New York Times* felt, "the Wisconsin primary is expected to be the first test of strength for Governor Reagan."[12] Whether Reagan would withdraw from the Wisconsin ballot was discussed at a late September news conference where Reagan and Governor Knowles appeared as part of Reagan's Wisconsin campaign and fundraising trip to be discussed shortly. Reagan told the press that he just had learned the details of the new Wisconsin primary law but he had not yet made any final decision about signing the withdrawal affidavit. If Reagan did withdraw, the press noted this would be "a substantial help to Mr. Nixon who has indicated that he considered Mr. Reagan's possible candidacy a major threat to his own aspirations."[13]

Reagan's comments about the withdrawal affidavit were made at the end of a three-day campaign and fundraising trip to Wisconsin in late September 1967. The Wisconsin State Republican Party officially had invited Reagan to be their main speaker. The visit, like virtually all visits Reagan made away from California, were offered officially by local Republicans who wanted to see Reagan in person and as fundraising vehicles. But behind the scenes of course it was Reagan's team who had made all the arrangements and had decided to accept that specific invitation. Milwaukee was a prime targeted campaign stop in the opt-out states, of which Wisconsin was the first to hold its primary on April 2, 1968. For Reagan, he would gain national stature and continue growing his grass roots teams, headed in Wisconsin by Taylor, in this first critical opt-out primary state.[14]

Throughout the entire Wisconsin primary campaign in 1967 and 1968, Fish continued to be "more than fair in giving" the Reagan campaign team "equal treatment," but Fish himself, as state party chairman, had to remain neutral.[15] Taylor's Reagan campaign, his Wisconsin Reagan for President Club officers, and its hundreds of volunteers campaigning for Reagan were never made to feel a second-class or less-important part to the Wisconsin Republican Party.

Reagan Visits Wisconsin

Taylor saw Reagan's visit as a great opportunity to promote his presidential candidacy. That Reagan was to appear at a "$100-a-plate state Republican dinner" on Sept. 30 had been mentioned twice in The *New York Times* over the summer.[16] But the true story, of what sounded like a simple campaign and fundraising dinner featuring Ronald Reagan, would in fact turn into a nightmare for Taylor and would demonstrate the active involvement of the campaign team Reed had assembled far away in California into the details of Reagan's drive to the presidency in 1968.

As noted by the *New York Times* above, the tickets were sold for $100, but Fish arranged for the Milwaukee Arena's upper gallery to have seats sold to the public for just $5. The State GOP Finance Committee had approved the plan even though some Wisconsin Republican leaders were opposed. On September 5, Taylor's Wisconsin Reagan for President Club received two thousand of the $5 tickets on consignment, and Taylor that very evening met with Young Republican leaders from Racine, Waukesha and Milwaukee in order to start the process of selling tickets to students. As an enticement, Taylor's club offered a one-year membership in the Young Republicans, a subscription to their newsletter, plus the Reagan speech ticket all for the same $5. Taylor planned to publicize the Reagan speech and the club's offer via campus posters, articles and ads in the newsletter, and Taylor also planned to write personal letters to seventy leaders of the Young Republicans in Wisconsin.[17] In addition, Taylor planned to coordinate publicity with the Wisconsin State Republican Party, to include a mailing to more than 20,000 Wisconsin Republicans plus radio and newspaper articles and advertisements.

Taylor planned this major effort because he knew this would be Reagan's only visit to Wisconsin before the primary. Taylor knew that this planned Reagan visit was not just a Republican fundraising visit to help local Wisconsin Republicans. Reagan's prior out-of-state speeches and talks at governors conferences were raising his national stature. Reagan's Milwaukee visit, and the Wisconsin primary to follow in 1968, was to be the first step in getting to the nomination in Miami Beach. It would be Ronald Reagan's crucial first test with voters outside of California.

But suddenly on September 12, Taylor received a phone call from Reed's team in California, who told him to cancel the entire $5 ticket program. Reed's representative instructed Taylor, "Governor Reagan is not a candidate for anything and therefore the events should avoid any appearance of campaigning." In addition, there was fear of being accused of the loss of money if the upper gallery seats were sold for just the planned $5 rather than having been sold for the full $100. Reed reflected decades later that he did not recall this occurrence and thought it possible that the orders had originated from Clif White at the time.[18]

Taylor recalled he was "shocked" but then summoned his courage and "fired off a letter" to California. Taylor outlined that the Young

Republicans were in fact the selling agents, that they had relied on Taylor's Reagan club, that the plan had been approved by the party's finance committee, and it had been widely publicized already.[19] Taylor explained that now in fact Fish and the party regulars were counting on Taylor's $5 ticket sales to be their profit and if Taylor backed out now, the party would be angry at the Reagan group. Plus if the upper gallery were seen as being empty, observers would say that Reagan could not draw a crowd. Taylor added that they would have to throw out the 23,000 printed letters, and then the Reagan campaign committee would appear to be indecisive and confused.[20] But Reed's team remained unmoved, forcing Taylor to cancel the $5 ticket program, "to the dismay of Ody Fish and the state GOP." [21] Taylor had already sold 355 tickets and remitted that amount to the state party. Taylor and his volunteers were not pleased. Despite the micromanaging from California, Taylor continued by using the Young Republican network and writing letters to local Republicans themselves.

But besides canceling the $5 ticket plan, Reed's representative vetoed Taylor's original plan to have a caravan of cars escort Reagan from the airport to his downtown hotel. Taylor recalled that he did not have the heart to tell the national campaign team that he had printed hundreds of 28-inch signs that the Young Republicans would wave: REAGAN in '68.

Despite all the obstacles placed in Taylor's way, the crowd that greeted Reagan at the airport was "excellent." However a new battery-powered bullhorn, which Taylor had bought for Reagan to use for the occasion, ultimately was not used because now Taylor "avoided any possible appearance of a Presidential campaign."[22]

That afternoon at the hotel, Taylor met Reagan personally for the first time. Taylor recalled that as he entered Reagan's suite at the Pfister Hotel, his "heart was thumping madly." Reagan rose to greet Taylor with a warm smile and said, "It's good to meet the man in Wisconsin that I've heard so much about." Reagan and Taylor chatted in private for more than an hour. Taylor admitted that he had been "in a daze" but that he recalled Reagan and he discussed the country, the recent race riots in Milwaukee, and family, but they did not discuss any details of Reagan's 1968 presidential campaign.

After meeting with Taylor, Reagan held a thirty-eight minute press conference before the dinner speech. Reagan, as usual at any press conference, was asked about the Vietnam War. For the first time, he said in public one of the new tactical military ideas promulgated to him by Eisenhower earlier. Reagan said that if invading North

Vietnam would bring the North Vietnamese to the negotiating table, he was in favor of it. Here was Reagan advocating what Eisenhower had mentored to him privately and what MacArthur—fifteen years earlier related to Korea—had been fired by Truman for advocating in public. No sanctuary sites would be allowed.

Reagan was asked about the draft and said he advocated a volunteer army when the country was not in the midst of a war as it was at the time. Reagan was asked about civil disobedience and the recent riots. Reflecting on RFK's earlier answer—after the Watts riots—to Eisenhower's call for citizens to obey the law (when RFK had said that blacks did not have to obey the law), Reagan said that if citizens did not obey the law, "our civilization could come apart like a wet cigar."[23] He pointed out that the militants represented only a tiny fraction of the law-abiding majority of the black community.

When asked about whether he was a candidate, he said he had tried in every way to say he was not a candidate. He was asked about his favorite son candidacy and the upcoming primaries in 1968 and explained that Wisconsin was like Nebraska and Oregon where his name would be on the ballot. Reagan's presidential ambitions were asked again in terms of the withdrawal affidavit. He reiterated that he could not sign the affidavit because then he would be lying, as he was going to be a favorite son presidential candidate from California. When asked if he would campaign in Wisconsin, he said "No. No. I have no intention of campaigning." Reagan explained that although he did not like the favorite son status in California, because of prior intra-party discord, he had been asked to be California's favorite son in 1968. Reagan told the reporters that the plans for him to be in Milwaukee for the Republican fundraiser had been set up prior to the passage of the new Wisconsin primary law. Reagan pointed out that the Wisconsin law was different than that in Nebraska or Oregon because it was a commission in Wisconsin that was to decide who would be on the ballot versus the secretaries of state in Nebraska and Oregon.

That evening, Reagan's Milwaukee speech began when from the podium he recognized the enthusiastic students in the gallery who cheered him. Warming up the audience, he poked fun at inflation and the $100 per person cost of the fundraising dinner by saying if the Democrats stayed in office, "What you paid tonight will soon be the regular price for dinner." He told his Make Love, Not War joke. ("I was picketed in California by youngsters with signs saying, 'Make Love, Not War' and from the look of them, they didn't have the capability of doing either.")[24]

Reagan then made his appeal to disaffected Democrats who had become Republicans by addressing the question if they had felt any feeling of betrayal when reregistering their party affiliation. Reagan explained:

"There was a betrayal but the guilt was not yours. When the leadership of the Democratic Party repudiated the constitutional concepts of individual freedom, local autonomy and states' rights, when it embraced the nineteenth century philosophy of rule of the many by the few, that one man, even if he's in the White House, is omnipotent and that a little intellectual elite in the nation's capital in social tinkering even to the extent of telling the working men and women of this country how and with whom they must share the fruit of their labor, then I say the leadership of that party betrayed and left you."

Reagan's moving message of hope and his opening of his hand of goodwill towards any wavering Democrats was the continuing phase, begun after receiving the cogent advice from Eisenhower via Freeman Gosden prior to and during his gubernatorial campaign and now continued during his first campaign for the presidency, of what would be known as Reagan Democrats.

Reagan spoke of the results of the past November 1966 election, which had seen the major Republican gains and the implications of these results:

"Ours was not a narrow partisan victory…Millions of Americans, Democrats and Independents and Republicans, are joining hands voting against what's been going on. They voted last year against going deeper and deeper into debt as a nation…They voted against the idea that as a nation we can afford anything and everything simply because we think of it. The voting men and women of this country voted against taxing themselves to provide medical care and a standard of living for others that often is more than they are able to afford for their own families."

This drew sustained applause.

Reagan reflected that Republicans were historically accused of favoring money over human concerns but wanted Republicans to tell their critics that it was not the spending of money on social ills that was the problem—*if* the governmental programs had worked. Reagan said that indeed Republicans would spend *more* if they worked. The issue was that the ill-conceived Democrat programs were "failures."

Towards the end of his Milwaukee speech, Ronald Reagan spoke once again, as he had done first in Omaha a few months before, the 1967 version of what would become a landmark speech he would give in its final version in the future. Indeed those readers who think that Ronald Reagan's "Pale Pastels" speech was delivered first in 1975 might again take note of what he did say first in 1967:

"It is our destiny—the destiny of our party—to raise a banner for the people of all parties to follow. But choose the colors well, for the people are not in a mood to follow the *sickly pastels* (author's emphasis) of political expediency—the cynical shades of those who buy the people's votes with the people's money."[25]

As noted earlier, "sickly pastels" would get transformed into "pale pastels" by the end of his 1968 campaign. But Reagan spoke those words publicly for the first time in 1967—in Omaha and now in Milwaukee.

Taylor's reaction to Reagan's speech was quoted in the *Waukesha Freeman* when he said, "It was one of the greatest speeches I ever heard." [26] The *New York Times* reported that 2,000 diners had attended plus 1,000 in the gallery and that in his speech Reagan had decried the "arrogant misuse of poverty funds for political nest-building."[27] *Time* however was less than enthusiastic and characterized Reagan's speech in Milwaukee just as a "rerun" of his 1964 "The Speech."[28] What *Time* failed to realize was that Reagan's "The Speech" and its various variants delivered by Reagan both before and after 1964, such as the version he used in Milwaukee, would be destined for the ages.

The attendance numbers for the Milwaukee speech from the local Republicans in Wisconsin was somewhat different. Fish reported that exactly 2,823 hundred-dollar tickets had been sold as well as 3,000 five-dollar balcony seats. Taylor felt the "entire evening was a spectacular success for Reagan" and he had "raised a huge sum for the Republican Party of Wisconsin."[29] Even Reed's team changed its tune after its earlier micromanaging. Taylor received a letter that was half-apology and half-appreciation: "After all the confusion that we caused you, the people that turned out at the airport rally and for Governor Reagan's speech were outstanding." Taylor had been vindicated.

But Reed's later personal assessment was more muted. Although Wisconsin Governor Knowles had accompanied the Reagan team, "there was no closure with anyone."[30] As had occurred in Eureka, whether it was Reagan's reticence or lack of preparation on how to ask Knowles for support, the Milwaukee visit, in Reed's opinion, was another partially-lost opportunity.

But Taylor was ecstatic. Immediately after Reagan left Milwaukee, Taylor was so enthused by the campaign stop and meeting Reagan that he drafted a detailed paper, which set forth the "assumptions, aims and means"[31] of his Wisconsin Reagan for President Club. Taylor knew that Reagan probably would not return in person, but may have hoped otherwise. Taylor also knew that Reagan would not withdraw his name from the ballot. Plus Taylor knew that Reagan would not announce his candidacy officially until the convention. The immediate aim of Taylor was to promote Reagan and his ideas and obtain as many primary votes and delegates for Reagan as possible. If Nixon faltered during the Wisconsin primary season or before, Taylor's Reagan campaign staff could "seize the initiative and promote Reagan as the new front-runner"[32] in Wisconsin. Then hopefully the Reagan steamroller would pick up speed in the Nebraska primary, win the Oregon primary, and then onwards to win the nomination.

And indeed not all those Republicans who had heard Reagan in Milwaukee had been pleased with the momentum that the Reagan campaign was achieving. Wisconsin GOP officials had "good reason to fear that Reagan would cut into Nixon's conservative strength" and this might possibly aid Romney.[33] Nixon clearly saw the Reagan threat. The *New York Times* said that Reagan was coming under "strong pressure" from the Nixon camp to withdraw in Wisconsin, because in their view "Reagan would only be a spoiler in Wisconsin."

Reagan still invoked the same reasoning he would use not only in Wisconsin but eventually in Nebraska and in Oregon—that if he signed the withdrawal affidavit stating he was not a candidate for president, he would be lying because in fact he was going to be one as California's favorite son candidate at the convention. The analysis concluded, "If Mr. Nixon should be forced to drop out of Presidential competition, a good deal of his support among Republicans who are Southern, conservative, or both, would almost certainly shift to Governor Reagan, whatever his primary record, making him a major convention contender."[34] It would not be the last time Nixon would feel threatened by Reagan's growing strength.

Then on October 26, Taylor sent his detailed letter to Reagan's team outlining the specifics of his forthcoming Reagan campaign in Wisconsin. Taylor planned a vigorous grassroots effort, which would include having speakers and materials throughout Wisconsin and by sponsoring newspaper ads and television spots in order to educate Wisconsin Republicans about Reagan.

For the remainder of 1967, Taylor and his Wisconsin Reagan for President Club remained busy speaking, signing up new members, and preparing to follow through on the tactical plans he had sent, all in preparation for the all-important first opt-out primary the following April.

But while Taylor was focusing like a laser on Wisconsin, Reagan was continuing his hectic autumn campaign travel schedule. As a small preview, on the trip back West after Milwaukee, Reagan stopped again in opt-out Nebraska—a planned refueling stop and visit to Grand Island—where Reagan would be greeted by Clif White and local Reagan grass roots campaign teams. But many more campaign visits would follow, including the next, a visit home.

Endnotes

1.   Taylor, Don L. A Devotion to Liberty, Part III Early Efforts for Reagan, published privately, p. 3
2.   ibid, p. 10
3.   Janson, Donald ,"Wisconsin's New Primary Law Signed by Governor," *NYT*, 7/26/67, p. 16
4.   Weaver Warren, "Republicans Face 4 Key Primaries," *NYT*, 7/9/67, p. 29
5.   Janson, op.cit.
6.   Taylor, p. 2
7.   Taylor, p. 3
8.   Taylor, p. 4
9.   "Wisconsin Group is Pushing Nixon," *NYT*, 7/30/67, p. 39
10.   Taylor, p. 5-6
11.   Taylor, p. 12
12.   Janson, Donald, "Wisconsin's new Primary Law Signed by Governor," *NYT*, 7/26/67, p. 16
13.   Hill, Gladwin, "Reagan Weighing Wisconsin Stand," *NYT*, 10/1/67, p. 32
14.   Reed, pers int, 10/16/12
15.   Taylor, p. 7
16.   Janson, op.cit., 7/26/67; "Wisconsin group," op.cit., 7/30/67
17.   Taylor, p. 7
18.   Reed, pers comm, 3/10/13
19.   Taylor, p. 8
20.   Taylor, p. 8-9
21.   Taylor, p. 9
22.   Taylor, p. 10
23.   RRL, Tape 284
24.   RRL, Tape 285
25.   RRL, Tape 285
26.   Taylor, p. 11
27.   Hill, Gladwyn, "Reagan Weighing Wisconsin Stand," *NYT*, 10/1/67, p. 32
28.   "Reagan's Road Show," *Time*, 10/13/67, p. 28
29.   Taylor, p. 12
30.   Reed, p. 20
31.   Taylor, p. 13
32.   Taylor, p. 14
33.   "Reagan's Road Show," *Time*, 10/13/67, p. 28
34.   Weaver, Warren Jr, "GOP Sees Reagan Playing Key Role in Two Primaries," *NYT*, 10/15/67, p. 32

Chapter 9: Return to Eureka

"Then why are all those stickers saying, 'Reagan in '68'?"
~ Young Girl in Eureka[1]

Ronald Reagan, D.H.L.

Reagan relished another chance to come home to Illinois, especially to return again to his beloved alma mater. But Reagan knew the main reason for the trip, besides the library dedication, was to meet privately with Senator Everett Dirksen. Dirksen was the first of the Republican Party leaders who had been targeted as part of the master strategy for Reagan's 1968 campaign. Reed recalled that the minority leader was not an activist and was not expected "to solicit delegates."[2] Rather he was the nominal head of the party and was viewed as the "pre-eminent party boss in the finest sense of that word."[3] Reagan needed Dirksen, the delegate-rich state of Illinois, and the U.S. Senate to "look favorably on the upstart from California."[4] Dirksen hopefully would "spread the word that Reagan was a winner."[5]

Of course Illinois was Reagan's home state where he had been born in Tampico, had lived for a short time in the Hyde Park section of Chicago, and had grown up in Dixon. Eureka College was where Reagan had gone to college starting in 1928 and from where he had graduated four years later. He earned his degree in economics and sociology; lettered in track, swimming and football; was in theater and a member of the drama fraternity; served three years as president of the Booster Club and was cheerleader for the basketball team; was feature editor of the yearbook; and became president of the Student Senate for one year and class president during his senior year.

But it also was at Eureka where he had started his career as a public speaker. The school's president at the time, Bert Wilson, was unpopular with the students because he had banned drinking, had banned dance music on campus, and had proposed budget cuts due to the declining economy of the Midwest.[6]

Historian Anne Edwards and reporter Bill Boyarsky described that a group of students had started a movement to force Wilson out, and as soon as Wilson's proposed cuts had been approved by the college trustees, one-hundred and forty-three students, including Reagan, had signed a petition advocating Wilson's dismissal. Tuesday November 27 was the big football game against Illinois and students were to leave for Thanksgiving break after the game. Reagan was on the bench, his usual spot on the team that freshman year. Suddenly in the second half, newsboys had started shouting that the trustees had refused to act on the student petition. "The students were in a fury."[7] At 11:45 PM, the students had prepared to strike and they had rung the college bell to announce a meeting in the chapel. An over-flowing crowd of students, faculty, and even college graduates living in town all had crammed into the chapel, which held just two hundred people.[8]

Eureka freshman traditionally had remained silent, but student leaders had decided that freshman Reagan should stand up and read the charges. Reagan was, "they all agreed, the best and most enthusiastic speaker they had, and they needed someone whose impassioned words could stir up the student body into demanding Wilson's resignation."[9] Reagan, about to speak publicly for the first time in his life, had been coached by the student leaders. He had reviewed the history of the negotiations, assailed the administration and trustees, and called for a strike.

Reagan had found that night that he loved public speaking. He had sensed he was able to carry the crowd with him. Reagan recalled, "Giving that speech—my first—was as exciting as any I ever gave. For the first time in my life, I felt my words reach out and grab an audience, and it was exhilarating."[10] At the end they all had cheered him with a standing ovation and one co-ed had fainted.[11] After President Bert Wilson's subsequent resignation, the student and faculty unrest had ended.

The story of the strike had been reported in the national press, but the name of Ronald Reagan was not mentioned. Thus the honor to have written the first national press story in 1928 about Ronald Reagan had been lost.[12]

Reagan had returned to Eureka College in 1947 as "grand marshal of the Pumpkin Parade;" in 1955 he had received a special citation in honor of the college's centennial celebration.[13] Ten years later he had returned, this time with Nancy, to receive an honorary degree of Doctor of Humane Letters (D.H.L.), given for having exposed the influence of communists when he had been president of the Screen Actors Guild.[14]

In a speech there on June 7, 1957 he had wondered what government should provide to the people, saying that there were well-meaning people who: "work at placing an economic floor beneath all of us so no one shall exist below a certain level or standard of living, and certainly we don't quarrel with this. But look more closely and you may find that all too often these well-meaning people are building a ceiling above which no one shall be permitted to climb"[15]

During his 1968 campaign, Reagan would repeat these thoughts, which, as mentioned earlier, would turn out to be so prescient in the second decade of the 21st century under President Obama.

In 1958, Reagan had donated twenty acres of land from his Los Angeles landholdings to the college.[16] Reagan also had spoken at Eureka College in 1961 during a speaking tour. But his most famous visit to his alma mater was about to occur during his first campaign for the presidency.

1967 Visit to Eureka College

The biggest event to hit Eureka College and the city of Eureka, Illinois was Governor Ronald Reagan's return visit to his alma mater in late September, 1967 to dedicate the college's new Melick Library. Eureka Mayor Thomas P. Tracy made an official proclamation of spiritual unity between the town and college in honor of the event and "his presence and continued support of the college."[17] Detailed plans for the event were announced to the public well ahead of time. Merchants painted storefronts and placed signs of welcome in their windows.

Students were photographed carrying books from the old library at Burgess Hall to the new library. The campus was closed to traffic and many streets in town became one-way for the day. Over 15,000 people were expected to "swarm into the town of 2,500."[18] Guests included three former Eureka College presidents (but not former Eureka College President Wilson who had resigned after the Reagan-led strike decades before), the presidents from other regional colleges, the Melick family, Eureka College graduates who had obtained M.D. or PhD. Degrees, and political invitees who will be discussed later. Nancy Reagan did not fly in with her husband, but her parents did attend and a photograph showed Reagan greeting and kissing his in-laws as he arrived.[19]

Reagan landed at 3:30 PM in Peoria for his whirlwind seventeen hour visit.[20] Reagan was greeted by county and college officials. A photograph of the scene mentioned that Reagan used both hands to greet well-wishers "in a manner reminiscent of presidential candidates."[21]

First Reagan held the customary press conference. He was asked about the rights of public employees to strike and he said, "I do not believe you can extend that right to those entrusted with education or protection against fire and lawlessness."[22]

Knowing the history of his hero President Coolidge's career as governor of Massachusetts and his firing of striking state workers, a future President Reagan would apply that exact principle when faced with a strike of airport control tower workers in 1981; that issue would resonate still in the second decade of the 21st century in several states, most notably Wisconsin, where Governor Scott Walker would survive a recall attempt and win re-election because of his strong stand against public employee unions.

When asked what he thought of a Rockefeller-Reagan ticket, Reagan smiled and answered, as he had and would so many times during his 1968 campaign, "I'm not interested." When asked if he would permit his name to be entered on presidential primary ballots in several states he said, as he would so often, "I'm doing nothing to encourage this and everything to discourage it."[23]

When asked what he thought about recent polls, he said that politicians should not run their political lives by polls. Reagan then quoted Winston Churchill again, saying, "Keeping your ear to the ground is a rather undignified position." When asked point blank if he was running for president he answered directly, "I am not running for President." Reagan was asked if there any differences between the student unrest of the 1960s versus his student strike at Eureka decades before. Reagan said that after all their negotiations, in his day, "we simply stayed home from class…we kept up with our studies." There were no violent protests at Eureka College in Reagan's time. Reagan was asked about the funding for his trip and he said that arrangements were made via the Republican National and Illinois State Committees and that no California state employee had made any arrangements.[24] As noted, Reed long since had departed the Reagan administration in Sacramento and was working privately from near San Francisco as Reagan's stealth out-of-state travel agent.

After the press conference, Reagan was driven into Eureka where he switched to a convertible automobile. County sheriffs and state police guarded all intersections along I-74 and state highways. After his convertible was led to the courthouse square by the Eureka High School band, at 5:10 PM Reagan received a key to the city from Mayor Tracy.

The mayor first had met Reagan in 1947; the mayor was on the college's football team then and Reagan was visiting for the pumpkin parade. The mayor recalled that Reagan had given his team a pep-talk and Tracy told the crowd, "He was our Gipper."[25] The key that Tracy gave Reagan was made of walnut and brass by one of Reagan's old classmates.[26] Inscriptions on the key recalled events in Reagan's numerous prior associations with the college: his graduation in 1932, his 1947 visit when he had crowned the queen of the Pumpkin Parade, the 1955 centennial citation, his 1957 honorary doctorate, and his 1961 visit.[27]

Reagan was photographed seen smiling and was described as a "HAPPY MAN surrounded by admirers, young and old." Promptly at 5:30 PM he was at a small reception at the home of the Eureka College president and then had dinner on campus with the students. The academic processional began at 7:15 PM.[28]

The library dedication was held outdoors and some elderly women were photographed having sat down hours earlier for front row seats and being dressed in hats, coats and many added blankets.[29] Despite the earlier predictions of 15,000, "seats for more than 4,000 were filled and hundreds stood." Temperatures were described as seventeen degrees colder than normal for the end of September but few people left the event.

It was "the largest press delegation ever to assemble in Eureka."[30] As many as seventy-five reporters and photographers were there including those from the *New York Times*, the *Los Angeles Times*, and Long Island's *Newsday*.[31] Indeed as soon as he had landed at Peoria, Reagan had been "literally mobbed by cameramen." Those who had gathered downtown in Eureka to get a glimpse of Reagan were "cheated of their view; the Reagan convertible was surrounded six-deep by cameramen."[32]

The *Peoria Journal Star* announced, "Ronald Reagan, Governor of California and possible Republican candidate for President of the United states makes his triumphal return tonight."[33]

Yet the political ramifications of Reagan's visit began well before his arrival in Eureka. In the files of Senator Dirksen at the Dirksen Congressional Center in Peoria is a folder of letters from many Illinois Republicans who wrote to Dirksen asking for his help in getting Reagan to speak to their groups during the planned Eureka trip. Dirksen wrote to Reagan and forwarded requests from the Coles County Republican Central Committee, the Republican Workshops of Illinois, the Tazewell County Republican Central Committee, and the Peoria County Republican Central Committee. Reagan had no time to visit with any.[34]

Reagan's press secretary told the press, "The Governor's trip to Illinois is not for political purposes," but did admit Reagan in fact was going to meet several Republicans, since he 'hadn't much time for his Party duties up to now."[35] Prior to his visit, Reagan had been proclaimed the "number one choice for President among Illinois Republicans by the Cook County Republican chairman."[36]

Dirksen, who was scheduled to introduce Reagan at the dedication, had generated great political speculation prior to Reagan's visit when he had told the *Washington Post* that he planned to give Reagan "a humdinger of an introduction that...will look like a nominating speech."[37] One local editorialist noted that Dirksen and Reagan had much in common, with both coming out of "a homespun Midwest background and they make homespun virtues their political stock in trade...The Dirksen-Reagan partnership is natural, two hometown boys who have made good and yet have never lost the hometown touch."[38]

But there was more to the commonality of Illinois that made Dirksen a potential supporter of Reagan and someone who might endorse Reagan early and work hard for his nomination and election. Dirksen had worked tirelessly for conservative Goldwater in 1964 and was a fellow hawk with Reagan on Vietnam.[39] Historian Andrew Johns has reviewed Dirksen's views on Johnson and Vietnam during this period. With Dirksen likely to formally endorse Reagan, Reagan's visit was thought to be "his first national appearance with the 1968 presidential campaign in the not-too-distant future."[40]

Illinois Senator Charles Percy, another potential Republican contender in 1968, initially was not planning on attending the dedication.[41] But when he heard what Dirksen had said about his forthcoming introductory speech on behalf of Reagan and thus the forthcoming Dirksen-Reagan appearance "assuming such political importance," Percy changed his plans and decided to attend. He wanted to see his conservative opponent up close.[42]

Also attending was Congressman Robert Michel, who was from Peoria. In the future Michel would become Minority Leader for the 97th-103rd Congresses. President Reagan would campaign for him in 1982 and confer upon Michel the Presidential Citizens medal in 1989. Other attendees at Eureka to see Reagan included Illinois Republican national committeeman and committeewoman, the chairman of the party's statewide county chairmen's association, and the chairmen of the central committee of Cook and Woodford Counties. One reporter described the event as having "been blown up into one of major political proportions."[43]

Dirksen's introduction of Reagan touched on humor about show business, and he noted that Reagan's birth month of February was the same as Washington and Lincoln. He then praised Reagan for having stayed "loyal to the precepts and principles instilled here at Eureka College" and for having kept the covenant with the people of California. Dirksen quipped that had Reagan been born a few miles south of Tampico, he would have been a constituent of Dirksen's when he was in the House of Representatives; but that since he represented now all of Illinois, he was claiming Reagan as a constituent anyway. Dirksen closed by echoing Reagan's 1966 campaign theme, which Reagan had borrowed directly from Eisenhower, saying that Reagan had a gift and "that gift is common sense."[44] But there was no ringing endorsement of Reagan. In fact Dirksen had said almost nothing of consequence at all.

Listeners who had hoped for Dirksen to continue his analogy between Reagan and Washington and Lincoln were disappointed. High expectations had been dashed. Dirksen in effect had "tantalized, then darted away from any reference to Reagan as presidential timbre in 1968."[45] An editorial in a local newspaper noted, "The national press, perhaps over-anticipating a bit, was prepared for a presidential launching," but added, "Those who expected Sen. Everett Dirksen to give Reagan his blessing for bigger things were disappointed."[46]

After Dirksen finished, it was Reagan's turn. Reagan spoke about the communication gap between old and young, saying that his generation did not need to be ashamed of its accomplishments, for "No people in the history of the world have shared so widely its material resources." He urged the students to use their new library, and he pleaded for morality and high principles. Reagan defined the purpose of America as "unleashing the full talent and genius of the individual" and not that of creating "mass movements with the citizenry subjecting themselves to the whims of the state."[47] Reagan quoted Jesus and again the medieval Jewish rabbinical sage and physician, Maimonides.[48]

Reagan saw how the increasingly liberal faculties in America's universities had turned the sons and daughters of the generation who had fought World War II away from traditional American values. In a theme he would use more fully at Yale a few months later but which he had used in Nebraska at Hiram Scott College in June, he told the faculty and students that the purpose of a university was not to teach just facts but to "teach wisdom." In Eureka, he did not give the added warning not to indoctrinate as he would at Yale. [49]

Reagan did not deliver his standard 1968 campaign speech but rather had delivered a more heart-felt philosophical speech about the purpose of the country and the educational system. The purpose was not to get the Republican base standing and cheering. He did not bring up world affairs. Reagan was home to relax amongst friends.

Afterwards, Reagan was described as having addressed the audience "with polished ease and fluency."[50] Yet another local paper felt the opposite noting, "Mr. Reagan said nothing to further his political future" and adding, "If anything, one could wonder if his chances were not chilled by his remarks." They felt Reagan's speech "was not a humdinger, even as non-political speeches go. He drew no applause during the course of the address."[51] Unmentioned was that Reagan had not planned to deliver a campaign speech despite whatever expectations the press had had. Rather he had come home to Illinois, to his alma mater, and wanted to speak personally from the heart to this next generation of students. Plus the weather was freezing as everyone in the photographs was seen wearing gloves. Conveniently unmentioned in the editorial was that students thought the talk was just fine. Afterwards, Reagan was mobbed by friendly students.

Another negative editorial appeared from liberal columnist Mary McGrory a few days later. She complained that Reagan "desperately needs a new script writer" and besides the weather being frosty, Reagan "was, unaccountably, a frost too." She complained that Reagan spoke "in a rambling, incoherent, sentimental manner for 25 minutes and was heard in chilled silence." McGrory added, "This is hardly the kind of thing that sets the prairies on fire." In case anyone had any doubts about her elitist attitudes towards Reagan, she concluded, "He also found himself in the uncongenial position of praising books and learning."[52]

But at least one local reader took exception to what he had read. Sherman Stetson of Neponset wrote a letter denouncing McGrory. "I feel anyone who had heard Ronald Reagan at Eureka would dismiss her opinion as very unfair." Stetson warned Reagan to be on the lookout for the same biased, liberal media "that succeeded in scuttling Goldwater." Stetson noted how people had been given the chance to meet the person "who may well become our next chief executive." Stetson's view of Reagan's speech was the exact opposite of McGrory, observing that Reagan's "national image was elevated to new heights by his straight-forward message about our problems and their solutions." He continued, "Her distorted view of Reagan's speech and his views of learning were anything but fair reporting....

she admitted that one student said he was 'really impressed.' She forgot the many more who felt the same way." Stetson ended by saying that he knew the good citizens of Illinois "are smart enough not to fall for the ultra-liberal line that Mary tried so hard to give the readers."[53]

The dedication exercises concluded at 8:45 PM. Afterwards hundreds attended a reception at Dickinson Commons.[54]

The last planned event for the day was a private reception for Republicans and friends at the home of Eureka attorney Sam Harrod. Harrod had been a close friend of Governor Reagan, and at college Harrod's father had been a professor and dean. Earlier in the day, Harrod had met Reagan at the Peoria airport. Harrod had told the press that Reagan was coming to Eureka "as a gesture to the old school…he doesn't want to make this any political clambake."[55]

Finally came the crucial meeting of Reagan and Dirksen. But when Reagan huddled with Dirksen, "the talk was of football. Reagan gave vague answers to Dirksen's questions, and they both moved on to cookies and punch. That was it."[56] When rumors circulated in the press about the evening gathering being filled with "political maneuvering between Reagan, Sen. Everett Dirksen, Sen. Charles Percy and other powerful Illinois Republicans," Dirksen denied it all. Dirksen confirmed that they only "ate cookies and cheese sandwiches and swapped a few lies."[57]

After the meeting, Reagan was mobbed by that group of well-wishing students. The governor, referencing his problems in California with hostility to his program to have students pay ten percent of tuition, quipped, "You'll never know how thrilled I am to see so many who are paying tuition."[58]

Reagan's last morning featured a return visit to his Tau Kappa Epsilon fraternity for breakfast. He was met by a group of fraternity brothers and a "huge poster of himself as a motion picture cowboy."[59] Reagan made a surprise donation of thirteen historic newspaper editions to the new library and they were photographed for the public to view. Reagan personally donated $50,000 towards the library construction.[60] At the airport as he was leaving, Reagan was asked what he thought of the political air in Illinois, and he answered, "It's the same air that started stirring across the country in 1966. I think people want a change."[61]

As Reagan was leaving, one reporter wondered, "How far down or away from the road toward running for President he will be is anybody's guess. For all its non-political intent, however, the political engineers of the Eureka dedication may have won another one for the Gipper."[62] Another editorialist, when summarizing the Reagan-Dirksen trip to Eureka, commented, "If Reagan should move up in the Presidential sweepstakes, with the mark of success clearly evident, their rendezvous could be a forecast of the Republican future."[63] One national commentator noted that the "pros concede Reagan is a potential candidate for President", and that for conservatives frustrated by the futile Goldwater campaign, "Reagan represents a hope for the future. They see him as a conservative with enough mass appeal to win a national election."[64] Even nationally-syndicated columnist and Johnson hack Pearson took note of the Reagan trip. Undoubtedly having reported it all to Johnson, Pearson characterized Reagan as a "potential candidate for President." After referencing Reagan's autobiography *Where's the Rest of Me?* for his readers, Pearson forecast that Reagan's "prose will make interesting reading if he ever really runs for President."[65]

In the end, Dirksen had not given the anticipated rousing endorsement speech for Reagan. In private Reagan had not asked Dirksen for his support. It was true that Reagan had met local Republicans in Illinois and had strengthened his friendship with the Senate Minority Leader. Even the *New York Times* noticed, remarking that Reagan's visit had "helped dim the image of anti-intellectualism acquired in his jousting with the University of California. And it brought him into constructive elbow-rubbing contact with the wheels in Illinois' Republican establishment."[66]

But Reagan might have gotten much more out of this meeting with one of the four leaders of the GOP. Reagan had no preparatory discussions with his campaign staff prior to arriving in Eureka. The reason for the private meeting was "obvious."[67] The presence of liberal Percy at the Harrod home, however, was an unnoticed major factor. As Buchanan had detailed above, Percy was in the midst of forging his own candidacy. Thus liberal Percy's presence was a major impediment to Reagan asking Dirksen for his support. Plus Reagan's campaign just had undergone its major shake-up. Finally, as we will see throughout his campaign up to the following spring, Reagan also felt that the party needed to come to him and ask him to be its nominee.

Reagan's October 4, 1967 formal letter to Dirksen, thanking him for participating at Eureka, had a hand-written personal note appended at the bottom, which read, "You'll never know what your presence meant to that little college. You gave it a position in the Sun and they'll be forever grateful."[68]

After Reagan had left, some local Eureka youngsters were interviewed and were asked if they thought Reagan would be the next president. The first student said, "No. I heard him say on television that he wasn't running." But her friend then chimed in, "Then why are all those stickers saying 'Reagan In '68'?"[69]

Chicago

But Reagan was not done visiting Illinois and staying in close contact with Senator Dirksen. Reagan and Dirksen exchanged letters related to federal and California governmental business and on October 31, 1967 Reagan requested that Dirksen veto an amendment which would have eliminated the federal government's purchase of the northern unit of what would become Redwood National Park.[70]

Reagan's trip to Eureka and meeting Republican leaders was bearing fruit, despite the failure to obtain the Dirksen endorsement. Illinois Republican State Party Chairman Victor Smith arranged for Reagan to visit Chicago on October 27, 1967 to speak to the Chicago Chamber of Commerce. On October 23, Reagan invited Dirksen to join him. Dirksen wrote back about the huge throng of grass roots supporters who would attend Reagan's address: "Your luncheon was not only a sell-out, but there were demands for literally thousands of tickets over and above the capacity of the ballroom at the Palmer House." Dirksen suggested a closed-circuit television hook-up so that the overflow guests could be seated in another ballroom and still watch and hear Reagan.[71]

In Chicago, Reagan explained to his audience that his Republican goals of helping defeat poverty and unemployment were the same as the Democrats but that his methods were different. Reagan observed, "The great society is growing greater every day. It is greater in size, greater in cost and greater in wasteful inefficiency." Reagan then warned, "Government talks political equality and ends up trying for income equality."[72]

Reagan attacked governmental interference with private business by complaining of the IRS's recent decisions to lessen business deductions for gifting and business entertainment expenses. Reagan, having been the personal recipient of the political abuse of the IRS from Kennedy, was especially annoyed that supplicant business leaders had gone to the federal government bureaucrats with the only purpose of negotiating the terms of how they would bend to the federal government's whim. Reagan got large and sustained applause when he said, "What business should have said is 'so long as we're legitimately spending the money in the belief that it helps to produce a profit, it isn't any of government's business how much we spend.'"[73]

At his press conference, most questions, as usual, centered about Vietnam.[74]

Senator Dirksen had never made it to Chicago in time to hear Reagan, but during the remainder of 1967 would keep in touch both professionally and personally. Unlike his earlier unsuccessful attempt to get Nixon to lead the Parade of Roses, Reagan this time would arrange for Dirksen to lead the parade and then would invite the Dirksen's for dinner at his and Nancy's Pacific Palisades home for dinner on December 27, 1967.

Dirksen would continue to forward to Reagan many requests for Reagan to return to speak in Illinois. On November 28, Dirksen would ask Reagan if he would speak in Chicago the next February to the United Republican Fund of Illinois. Dirksen would entice Reagan by writing, "Republicans are getting themselves in top shape in the state and your appearance at this dinner would be a real shot in the arm."[75] As we will see later, the Champaign County Young Republicans would invite Reagan to be their Lincoln Day speaker and Dirksen's office would add to the chorus of speaking requests for Reagan in Illinois. Reagan would fulfill that request the following May. In 1968, Reagan's and Dirksen's private correspondence would continue.

Thus Reagan had two somewhat successful trips to his home state of Illinois in the fall of 1967. Unfortunately, although the friendship of Reagan and Dirksen would continue into the Miami Beach convention, Reagan was unable or unwilling to ask for Dirksen's support in his quest for the presidential nomination.

In the interim, the national news media reported more encouraging signs for Reagan for president in Illinois after his visits. Perhaps Dirksen knew that in fact he was open to a Reagan candidacy when he told the national press that he wanted the "Illinois delegation to go 'unpledged' to the Republican nominating convention. At the same time the national press took note that "Reagan is 'making fast progress' in public-opinion polls at county fairs" in Illinois.[76] But ultimately the hopes for Dirksen to change his support away from Nixon would be dashed.

Reagan had faced his largest barrage of national exposure thus far on the campaign trail. He had handled the myriad of questions about his candidacy well. Despite whatever difficulties he had had asking Dirksen for direct support, there was obvious increasing momentum for Reagan for president. Reagan had visited two of the three critical opt-out states—Wisconsin, Nebraska—and then his home state of Illinois within a short amount of time. Flying to his next campaign visit, to South Carolina, Reagan—as was his custom to keep current by reading voraciously as discussed—based on comments he soon would make in Seattle, picked up the current issue of the nation's most popular national magazine, whose cover story was about a proposed missile shield for the United States.

Endnotes

1. "Eureka Swells to Greet 'Favorite Son,'" *The Pantagraph,* 9/29/67, p. 3
2. Reed, p. 10
3. ibid
4. ibid
5. ibid
6. Boyarsky, p. 43-44
7. Edwards, Anne, p. 90
8. Boyarsky, p. 45
9. Edwards, p. 90
10. Reagan, *An American Life*, p. 48
11. Edwards, p. 91
12. "Students Strike at Eureka College," *NYT*, 11/29/28, p. 23
13. Boyarsky, p. 53
14. Boyarsky, p. 53
15. Reagan, Ronald, Commencement Address at Eureka College, 6/7/1957
16. Streckfuss, Dick, "Eureka College Set for Reagan's Visit," *The Pantagraph*, 9/22/67, p. 3
17. "College Preparing For 15,000 People At Library Dedication," *Woodford County Journal*, 9/21/67, p. 1
18. Klein, Jerry, "Eureka Set to Welcome Gov. 'Dutch,'" *Peoria Journal Star*, 9/24/67, p. C-1
19. *Peoria Journal Star*, 9/29/67, p. D9
20. Reed, p. 19
21. *Peoria Journal Star*, 9/29/67 p. D-9
22. https://www.youtube.com/watch?v=-i4pg7_p41g
23. Childs, Marquis, "Eureka May Be Historic Jumping Off for Reagan," *The Pantagraph*, 9/29/67, p. 10
24. RRL, tape 280
25. "Eureka Swells To Greet 'favorite Son,'" *The Pantagraph*, 9/29/67, p. 3
26. "Reagan in Eureka Today; He'll Receive Key to City," *The Pantagraph*, 9/28/67, p. 3
27. "Reagan To Receive Key To City Of Eureka," *Woodford County Journal*, 9/28/67, p. 1
28. "Reagan Gives 17 Busy Hours To Eureka," *Woodford County Journal*, 10/5/67, p. 1
29. *Peoria Journal Star*, 9/29/67, p. D9
30. "Reagan Tells Students They Are Needed," *Woodford County Journal*, 10/5/67, p. 1
31. Klein, Jerry, "Eureka Set To Welcome Gov. 'Dutch,'" *Peoria Journal Star*, 9/24/67, p. C-1
32. "Eureka swells To Greet 'Favorite Son,'" *The Pantagraph*, 9/29/67, p. 3
33. "Reagan Returns," *Peoria Journal Star*, 9/28/67, p. B-12
34. Dirksen Congressional Center, EMD Papers, Alpha 1967, Reagan
35. "Reagan to Meet GOP Leaders At Eureka," *The Pantagraph*, 9/26/67
36. Streckfuss, Dick, "Eureka College set For Reagan's Visit," *The Pantagraph*, 9/22/67, p. 3
37. Childs, Marquis, "Eureka May Be Historic Jumping Off for Reagan," *The Pantagraph*, 9/29/67, p. 10
38. ibid
39. Skinner et. al., p. 39
40. Childs, op. cit.
41. At this time, Percy was being thought of as a back-up if Romney failed. Rockefeller's campaign sent a message to Percy that if he dared enter, Rockefeller would crush him. A Percy candidacy would split the liberal Republicans. It signaled that Rockefeller indeed was serious about running.
42. Klein, Jerry, "Eureka Set to Welcome Gov. 'Dutch,'" *Peoria Journal Star*, 9/24/67, p. C-1
43. ibid
44. "Remarks of Senator Everett Dirksen, Minority Leader, United States senate, in introducing Governor Ronald Reagan at the Dedication of the Melick Library at Eureka College, Eureka Illinois" Dirksen Congressional Center, EMD Papers, Remarks: Releases. 9/28/67
45. "Eureka Swells To Greet Favorite Son," *The Pantagraph*, 9/29/67, p. 3
46. "Reagan Star Winks Cold," *The Pantagraph*, 10/1/67

47.   Streckfuss, Dick, "Plug generation Gap, Reagan Tells Youth," *The Pantagraph*, 9/29/67, p. 3
48.   Rabbi Moshe Ben Maimon
49.   RRL, tape 279
50.   "Reagan Tells Students they Are Needed," *Woodford County Journal*, 10/5/67, p. 1
51.   "Reagan Star Winks Cold," *The Pantagraph*, 10/1/67
52.   McGrory, Mary, "Reagan Met Frost In Eureka," *Peoria Journal Star*, 10/3/67
53.   Stetson, Sherman, "McGrory Distorted Reagan," *Peoria Journal Star*, 10/7 67, p. A-4
54.   "Reagan Gives 17 Busy Hours To Eureka," *Woodford County Journal*, 10/5/67, p. 1
55.   Klein, Jerry, "Eureka Set to Welcome Gov. 'Dutch,'" *Peoria Journal Star*, 9/24/67, p. C-1
56.   Reed, p. 19
57.   "Eureka Returns To Normal," *The Pantagraph*, 9/30/67, p. 13
58.   "Eureka Swells To Greet 'Favorite Son,'" *The Pantagraph*, 9/29/67, p. 3
59.   "Visits Fraternity House," *The Pantagraph*, 9/30/67, p. 13
60.   "Eureka Swells To Greet 'Favorite Son,'" *The Pantagraph*, 9/29/67, p. 3
61.   "Eureka Returns to Normal," *The Pantagraph*, 9/30/67, p. 13
62.   Klein, Jerry, "Eureka Readies All-Out Welcome for 'Dutch,'" *Peoria Journal Star*, 9/24/67, p. C-2
63.   Childs, Marquis, "Eureka May Be Jumping Off for Reagan," *The Pantagraph*, 9/29/67, p. 10
64.   Boyarsky, Bill, "There's No Business Like Politics," *Peoria Journal Star*, 9/28/67, p. B-12
65.   Pearson, Drew, "Washington Merry-Go-Round," 9/28/67
66.   Hill, Gladwin, "As A Non-Candidate, Reagan Is a Non-Slouch," *NYT*, 10/8/67, p. E3
67.   Reed pers comm. 8/23/13
68.   Reagan Letter to Dirksen, 10/4/67, Dirksen Congressional Center, EMD Papers, Alpha 1967, Reagan
69.   "Eureka Swells to Greet 'Favorite Son,'" *The Pantagraph*, 9/29/67, p. 3
70.   "Telegram LLH299 47 LA349, 1967 Oct 31", Dirksen Congressional Center, EMD Papers, Alpha 1967, Reagan
71.   Reagan Letter to Dirksen, 10/23/67 and Dirksen Letter to Reagan, 10/26/67, Dirksen Congressional Center, EMD Papers, Alpha 1967, Reagan
72.   RRL, tape 300
73.   RRL, tape 300
74.   RRL, tape 301
75.   Dirksen to Reagan letter, 11/28/67, Dirksen Congressional Center, EMD Papers, Alpha 1967, Reagan
76.   *U.S. News and World Report*, 9/18/67, p. 52

CHAPTER 10: SOUTHERN STRATEGY

"In 1968 the South was to be one of the most important regions in terms of winning both the nomination and the election.....It was Ronald Reagan who set the hearts of many Southern Republicans aflutter. He spoke their conservative language articulately and with great passion, and there was always a possibility that Southern delegates could be lured at the last minute by his ideological siren song. Until I had the nomination, therefore, I had to pay careful attention to the dangers of a sudden resurgence on the right."

~ Richard Nixon[1]

Reagan is "one of the leading figures of the world today."
~ Strom Thurmond[2]

"Reagan was No. 1 in Republican hearts."
~ Harry Dent[3]

The term "Southern Strategy" is accepted in virtually all historical circles to mean Richard Nixon's 1968 decision to seek out delegates and voters from the part of the country that had voted Democratic—often segregationist Democratic—ever since post-Civil War Reconstruction: the South. As we will see, Ronald Reagan had exactly the same strategy in 1968 as Nixon.

But neither Nixon nor Reagan originated the idea that a Republican renaissance could start in the South. In actuality, as several historians have reviewed, the growth of the Republican Party in the South had preceded both Nixon and Reagan. The realignment had received a major boost from Eisenhower's campaign strategies in 1952 and 1956. Historian Sean Trende observed that Eisenhower had won three Southern states in 1952 and five in 1956, had won a majority of the South's popular vote, and had achieved at least "one-third of the vote in every state in the Old Confederacy."[4]

In February, 1963, Rusher had written an essay in *National Review* entitled "Crossroads for the GOP" which summarized the basis of the Southern Strategy: that if Republicans nominated a conservative for the presidency, that nominee would attract many Southern voters. But were Republicans just trying to attract racist whites? Rusher felt the opposite was true: that southern Republicans were far less racist than their southern Democratic counterparts and lived in the growing suburbs and cities of the South as opposed to rural areas where racism was more entrenched.[5] By the spring of 1967, columnist Tom Wicker of the *New York Times* wondered the same thing: if unhappiness with Johnson's domestic programs might give Republicans "rosy prospects" in a Southern state like Virginia, yet would hawkish stands by Republicans on Vietnam be as attractive to voters in the more liberal states? Wicker wondered if this question "could be asked about Ronald Reagan."[6]

By 1968 the Southern Strategy would become targeted to the near-term goal of winning Southern delegates in the Republican nomination race, with leaving the later Southern Strategy tactics for the fall election to be used by whoever the party nominee was in the general election. In the run-up to the convention, "astute Dixie Republican leaders" wanted to stay "loose and uncommitted: they would have to be courted, and they knew they would be."[7] For the Miami Beach convention, the South would control some 356 convention votes, more than 50 percent of the total needed. And those Republican votes from the South were "going to be used shrewdly."[8]

Nixon in his autobiography felt, "In 1968 the South was to be one of the most important regions in terms of winning both the nomination and the election…. it was Ronald Reagan who set the hearts of many Southern Republicans aflutter. He spoke their conservative language articulately and with great passion, and there was always a possibility that Southern delegates could be lured at the last minute by his ideological siren song. Until I had the nomination, therefore, I had to pay careful attention to the dangers of a sudden resurgence on the right."[9]

Another figure lurking in the background of the South was segregationist Democrat George Wallace. Of course Wallace's support only would impact Reagan if Reagan would win the Republican nomination and then would face the possibility of having to split conservative Southern votes between Wallace and himself. Reagan would be asked questions about Wallace throughout 1967 and 1968. How Reagan, instead of Wallace, was able to become the "spiritual godfather" of Southern conservatives in 1968, and beyond, was the subject of a recent historical analysis, in which the answer was that Reagan's rhetoric and personality appeared less harsh than Wallace and that Reagan's populist appeal was more consistent and more broad.[10] But in a good portion of the 1960's, the only politician in the South looked upon with more reverence than Wallace was Strom Thurmond.

Ol' Strom

South Carolina Senator Strom Thurmond's biographers, in *Ol' Strom*, tell the story of a segregationist, anti-communist, States Rights candidate for president in 1948, and conservative governor and then senator who became more and more dissatisfied with his Democratic Party.[11] In September, 1964, as Thurmond had addressed his constituents in a speech stressing that the Democratic Party no longer represented their views, at the bottom of the screen, Thurmond's party affiliation dramatically was seen to change from D-S.C. to R-S.C.[12] Due in no small measure to Thurmond's efforts, Goldwater had won South Carolina, Georgia, Louisiana, Mississippi and Alabama besides his native Arizona. Thurmond's support in 1968 would be crucial for Reagan or any potential nominee.

By 1966, Harry S. Dent, Sr. was State Republican Chairman for South Carolina and had been recommended to Thurmond by James B. Edwards, who later would become governor and Reagan's Secretary of Energy.[13] A critically important meeting of the minds was about to take place by accident during the 1966 campaign. But first a bit of political lore must precede the telling of the meeting.

The Dent's family dog had been run over by a car and shrewd Nixon sent the Dent's children a new pet. As thanks, Dent told Nixon how to win Thurmond over: by praising the Senator in public.[14] Shortly thereafter, Nixon arrived in Columbia. Dent had invited Nixon, who still was practicing law but had been criss-crossing the country to help fellow Republicans and at the same time establishing IOU's for 1968. Nixon followed through on Dent's advice and told a reporter that Thurmond was not a racist and in fact was a man of integrity and courage. As Dent recalled, "Thurmond never forgot those unapologetic, gracious comments by Nixon—nor did any member of the South Carolina GOP."[15] Thurmond's gratitude would impact Reagan's chances for the 1968 nomination profoundly.

Nixon's return jet was late, so Nixon and Dent chatted in Dent's car. Dent presented the case to Nixon that the South was ripe for the GOP. Nixon "made clear his intention to seek the top job again in 1968"[16] but expressed some reluctance to run because he feared that Wallace would siphon off white voters thereby preventing his victory. Dent told him that the answer to Nixon's dilemma was Strom Thurmond, for Thurmond would "take Wallace head-on for Nixon and 'stiff him.'"[17] Six months later, Nixon sent a representative to see Dent to check if he still had Thurmond's support, and Dent again reaffirmed with Thurmond, and then back to Nixon, that the Senator indeed would support Nixon.[18] As Dent recalled later, a "twist of fate—a plane running late—launched the 1968 Southern Strategy."[19]

Corn Pone and Hog Jowls

A year later, Reagan arrived in Columbia on September 29. The national media observed that in South Carolina, Nixon, "until a few months ago" appeared to "dominate Republican thoughts here about 1968" until that is, Reagan arrived and "pre-empted the spotlight."[20]

Dent had finalized arrangements for the Reagan visit when Dent had visited Sacramento earlier that summer. A deal seemed almost set for a Reagan endorsement by Thurmond. In fact, Dent recalled that there had been much press speculation in South Carolina about Dent's prior visits to Reagan, "making it appear that the Nixon-Reagan battle in the South Carolina GOP was underway."[21] Then "talk swept the state about how Thurmond and Dent were committed to Reagan" and were busy stealing delegates from one prominent pro-Nixon State Republican.[22] Dent though felt that at the time both he and Thurmond were not committed to either Nixon or Reagan, despite the assurances Dent had given to Nixon previously. Later, Dent admitted that the major reason he was so anxious to get Reagan to Columbia was because the state party had been $40,000 in debt and he had signed the note; he needed Reagan to come to South Carolina "to get that note paid off."[23]

At the airport, Reagan received a "big and enthusiastic greeting."[24] Reagan was greeted by a crowd of 500.[25] At the main event, the Republican finance dinner held for 3,000 supporters at the Columbia Township Auditorium, "the auditorium rocked with the jubilation of a triumphal political rally when Governor Reagan was escorted in."[26] Thurmond introduced Reagan to cheers, calling Reagan, "one of the leading figures of the world today."[27] He welcomed Reagan for his integrity, vision, his love for American and his true patriotism. Reagan received a standing ovation.[28]

Reagan thanked Thurmond as the man in the arena—echoing Reagan's hero Theodore Roosevelt's phrase from decades before—and gave his standard campaign speech to an audience that had never heard Reagan give a political speech previously. The applause was thunderous, and Reagan's appearance was described as "boffo box office."[29] Dent recalled that Reagan had "set Republican hearts afire."[30] The $100-a-plate dinner had netted $150,000 and was described as "the largest political fund-raising event in state history."[31] The *New York Times* reported that Dent was "enthusiastically supporting Mr. Reagan for the Presidential nomination."[32] One newspaper reported that Reagan was "the greatest thing to come along since corn pone and hog jowls."[33]

Private Meeting with Thurmond and Dent

Then Dent and Thurmond met privately with Reagan, Reed, and Nofziger for the critical true purpose of the trip. But as in Eureka with Dirksen, again the conversation went nowhere. Thurmond asked specifically and repeatedly as to Reagan's presidential plans. The governor's response was vague, and neither Nofziger nor Reed wanted to clarify to Thurmond or Dent as to what Reagan had meant to say.[34] Dent wondered if Reagan could win. Reed thought Reagan was "entranced by the idea" of being president but seemed to be basically not ambitious for the job at this point in his life.[35] This observation seemed to confirm Spencer's concerns nine months earlier. Reagan would accept the nomination if the people and his party offered it to him. Yet Reagan's national base of support, critical in the fall if Reagan were the nominee, still had to grow: the campaign had to continue.

Star Wars?

That very day, the cover story of *Life* was an interview with Defense Secretary Robert McNamara about the administration's new anti-ballistic missile (ABM) program, whose purpose was to shield America from a nuclear attack from Communist China. McNamara revealed that the Soviets were building a missile shield system to protect Moscow from an American attack, but when asked why the United States was not similarly building such a shield to protect the nation from a Soviet attack, McNamara answered that the country could not defend itself; the Soviets had too many offensive missiles. Plus, thought McNamara, if America built such a defensive capability, the Soviets would respond by building more offensive weapons. But since Communist China did not have as many intercontinental ballistic missiles (ICBM's) as the Soviets, the United States could build such an ABM system to shield the nation from a Chinese attack.[36] Someone who most assuredly immersed himself in that article on the day of Reagan's visit was Thurmond.

Thurmond at this point was completing work on an autobiographical book that had been edited by Reagan's earlier biographer, Lee Edwards,[37] and would be published the next year, the subject matter of which was Thurmond's political philosophy. Entitled *The Faith We Have Not Kept*, in it Thurmond reviewed his strong convictions about national defense. A prominent component of the programs he advocated was the possibility of an anti-ballistic missile defense.[38]

Whether Thurmond and Reagan discussed the *Life* cover story on the ABM program or Thurmond's opinions on the subject from his forthcoming book is lost to history. It is difficult to imagine they did not, given the subject's importance to Thurmond and the fact that the magazine cover story had hit the newsstands a few days earlier. For as we will see, the next spring the ABM would become a prime factor in Thurmond's mind to endorsing a presidential candidate. Plus the issue would increase in importance nationally by the summer.

Very likely, Reagan found time to read both the *Life* article and Thurmond's book. For in November while in Seattle, Reagan would be asked about orbital weapons and his answer would indicate his deep knowledge on the subject. As will be seen, Reagan would tell the press he had been reading magazine articles, and more, on the subject. And later he would take the time to make an extended, personal visit to Lawrence-Livermore National Laboratories to see first-hand what was being done to build an antimissile defense system. A few other historians have noted Reagan's November visit as a contributing factor to future President Reagan's vision for SDI. But to your author's knowledge, none have explained the origin of *why* Reagan decided to visit the laboratory to learn about missile defense. Very likely it was the *Life* article combined with the Thurmond meeting and biography. As Reagan would reveal in Seattle, his encyclopedic mind was busy expanding his expertise in world affairs—way beyond the complex lessons Eisenhower first had initiated—into the realm of missiles and a defense shield. But somewhat closer to the ground, Reagan had to fly—virtually every weekend with multiple flights—to campaign. And Ronald Reagan hated to fly.

Ambition and Aviophobia

Reagan would deny to the press repeatedly that he was a candidate; he would make those denials almost up to the day he would fly off to Miami Beach. The press would report the mystic fatalism which Reagan would express by telling others that he would be a candidate if it were God's will; he would tell the press that if the people and the party offered him the nomination, that it would be his duty to accept. As Reed and Spencer had thought, and as historian Cannon has reviewed, none of these sounded like Reagan had drive necessary to win the White House.[39]

Cannon cites an October 2 memo from Reagan advisor Jack B. Lindsay, sent to Reed and Nofziger, emphasizing that Reagan's constant denials of his candidacy were not believed and that although his denials seemed a good idea during the fall of 1967, Republican Reagan supporters wanted to see a true announced candidacy soon.[40]

But the same denials had been true for him when running for governor. It was only after a fair amount of arm twisting from his backers that he consented to run. But when he did run, he gave it all he had.

Yet in 1966 and for the 1968 campaign, there is one aspect to Reagan's personality that few have discussed yet demonstrated that indeed not only he did have the ambition to be president for 1968, but he actively sought it. And it comes from Cannon's second book about Governor Reagan. Cannon outlines how Reagan was terrified of flying ever since he had experienced a turbulent plane ride 30 years earlier.

Cannon then would witness first-hand how frightened of flying Reagan would remain in 1968. During one flight that would have mechanical problems, Reagan briefly would discuss his fear of flying, and Cannon would ask to interview Reagan so the governor's mind was taken away from the flight. While flying and campaigning all over the country, covering tens of thousands of miles from February 1967 through early August 1968, sometimes in a small plane, really impressed historian Cannon.[41] Reagan then had another harrowing mishap when his jet landed on the wrong runway in Redding, California that fall. After emerging to a group of startled, disbelieving locals, who never had seen a jet land there, Reagan smiled, saying humorously "I'm your governor. You probably wonder why I called you here."[42]

Spencer told Cannon, "Reagan's acceptance of the necessity of flying had made him aware that Reagan was more ambitious than he seemed."[43] For an individual with aviophobia, to have to endure multiple flights every weekend for eighteen months in order to campaign for the presidency and to raise party funds, shows steely courage. Reagan's actions in overcoming his fear of flying at least partially disproves Reed and Spencer's theory that Reagan had no real ambition to go out and seek the nomination in 1968.

Nevertheless, a critical opportunity with Thurmond was lost. With the newspaper account indicating that Dent was for Reagan, coupled with the assertion that Dent was arranging a deal between Reagan and Thurmond, would not Thurmond be willing to endorse Reagan if Reagan had indicated he truly was running? Or were Dent and/or Thurmond purposely misleading the media? Or were Dent and Thurmond in fact playing Reagan because they were for Nixon all along? Regardless of what Thurmond and Dent had thought, had Reagan affirmatively told them that he was running for president in 1968, the entire course of history might have been different.

But likely an even more critical event had occurred: with Reagan and Thurmond likely discussing both the *Life* article and Thurmond's forthcoming autobiography, the idea and implications of America having an antimissile shield had been kindled and stored in Reagan's encyclopedic mind. Reagan began reading all he could in the press and in magazine articles about a possible shield.

Meanwhile, Dent and Thurmond would return to prominence again later in the spring of 1968. But Thurmond was not the only GOP leader from the South that Reagan needed to court.

Texas

Peter O'Donnell, the Texas Republican state chairman, along with Clif White, had broken the stranglehold that Northeastern state politicians had held over the Republican Party.[44] O'Donnell was an early target for Reagan's team.[45] The new and first Republican senator from Texas, John Tower, was the key. O'Donnell and Tower were a formidable pair of political strength plus they had access to "oceans of conservative political money" in Texas.[46]

O'Donnell once had been a Nixon supporter but by the spring of 1967 had dropped out. On March 27, O'Donnell equivocated on the matter of a presidential candidate.[47] O'Donnell and Tower would not be ready to meet with Reagan until autumn.

On September 1, at the Reagan Los Angeles residence, Reed and Reagan met with the finance committee of a new grassroots Reagan for President group from Texas.[48] A few days later, Reagan received a call from Senator Tower. They wanted to meet.[49] A "Texas Summit" took place at the Reagan residence in Sacramento on September 17, and Nancy Reagan was present along with Nofziger and William Clark. Texas National Committeewoman Anne Armstrong and her rancher husband "arrived ready to support Reagan for the Presidency."[50] Senator Tower, who previously had decided not to seek the nomination himself, was "ready to deal" and O'Donnell was listening.[51] All of the Texas visitors wanted to know if Reagan was going to run. If they committed themselves, would Reagan "become an active (and winning) candidate?"

But Reagan "never answered the question" and the Texans left "perplexed if not unconvinced."[52] Two weeks later, after Reed had been demoted to handling Reagan's out-of-state travels, Tower called again and asked to see Reed for any new answers.[53] Reed had none.[54] Reagan had left Tower with the impression that his campaign was a "vague and headless monster and that he was going to wing it;" men such as Tower and O'Donnell "did not want to get caught on the losing side of a struggle for the nomination."[55] Within a week, Tower joined the Nixon team.

Louisville, Houston and Dallas

Tower's decision to go to the Nixon camp had occurred just three days after Strom Thurmond had introduced Reagan in Columbia to a rousing reception and fundraiser. Thus there was still hope for the South. During that busy autumn, shortly after appearing on Buckley's *Firing Line* show, to be discussed shortly, Reagan was off to Louisville, Kentucky just prior to a governors cruise.

One part of the Kentucky visit was to help gubernatorial candidate Louis Nunn. At the time, young, conservative activist Morton Blackwell, on leave from his job as national executive director of College Republicans, had been serving as Nunn's youth coordinator. In preparation for Reagan's visit, Blackwell and his group organized putting some 5,000 bumper stickers, with the permission of the cars' owners, onto several thousand cars. Blackwell observed that Nunn became an enthusiastic Reagan supporter at the time of the visit.[56] After Reagan arrived at Freedom Hall, and with a $10 per person ticket price, Reagan raised over $200,000 for Nunn and the state party.[57] But his visit clearly was for a national audience.

In his press conference, once again world affairs dominated. Reagan attacked the Johnson administration policies in Vietnam, but now by accusing the president of only telling the American people the truth about the war when it was "politically advantageous."[58] At the main speech, he called for Democrats to join Republicans to "repudiate" Johnson.[59] Reagan had growing political viability for his "had enough?" appeal to "normally Democratic middle class voters."[60] Reagan had used the Spanish version of "Had enough?!", "Ya Basta?!" as his 1966 campaign theme to attract normally Democratic Mexican Americans, and the phrase would be used again in 1968.[61]

During the Louisville visit, on October 14 Reagan's team met privately with Alfred Goldthwaite, the Alabama state Republican chairman.[62] A conservative not afraid to buck Thurmond, Goldthwaite gave his unequivocal support, and that of much of his delegation, to Reagan.[63]

After the cruise (to be discussed), Reagan would be back on the campaign trail in Texas for visits to Houston and Dallas on October 26. Historian Sean Cunningham has commented upon Reagan's appeal to Texans—Republican and Democratic—in 1967 and 1968, plus how with Wallace receiving the brunt of criticism that he was a racist, Reagan easily was able to deflect such charges.[64] Reagan told the press he was "crusading" for party unity, victory in 1968, and helping to add to party coffers.

Cunningham notes that Reagan "set the standard for LBJ-bashing" in Johnson's home state.[65] In Dallas at the Marriott Hotel, 750 turned out for Reagan at a luncheon and another 1,200 attended to see him at dinner. After quipping initially about Johnson and Robert Kennedy, Reagan got serious and attacked the liberal programs of the Great Society, whose programs had been failing. Reagan then attacked the re-election candidacy of Senator Edward Kennedy of Massachusetts. Reagan said that Kennedy had never held any public office prior to becoming senator four years earlier, and "come to think of it, he never held a job before."[66] Many years later at a White House ceremony honoring the slain Robert Kennedy, as we will see, Reagan and Edward Kennedy would be effusive in their recollections of the 1968 campaign.

O'Donnell later introduced Reagan as 'a man who may become President of the United States."[67] O'Donnell then enunciated all of "Reagan's potentialities for the Presidency."[68] Reagan closed the final news conference by restating that he was California's favorite son. When asked about what O'Donnell had said for the introduction, Reagan told the press, "It scared me. Obviously I'm honored. But I'm not a candidate."[69]

Cunningham noted that Reagan appealed to Texas businessmen and yet maintained a populist image with the party's rank-and-file.[70]

One new Reagan grassroots group was forming in Texas. In the files of Senator Everett Dirksen of Illinois is a letter he received from the chairman of Citizens for Ronald Reagan, Bob Dent (no known relation of Harry Dent). The letterhead was from Fort Worth, Texas and had been mailed to Dirksen as an invitation to join. Dent wrote that his group had opened, and was maintaining, "a Ronald Reagan Headquarters in Tarrant County, distributing bumper stickers, buttons and literature." Dirksen wrote on the letter, "Texas Favorite Son."[71] One may presume that Bob Dent had been in contact with the Reagan national information office that was forming in Topeka, but there is no other information available about this Reagan grassroots group in Texas, although it may indeed have been the group that had flown to Sacramento on September 1.

Ever since meeting with Reagan in Columbia, when Reagan had not given the forceful affirmative voice to Thurmond and Harry Dent that he was going to run for the presidency, Dent stayed in close contact with Reagan's team. But Dent kept wondering, "Can Reagan win?"[72] So Dent decided to seek the answer himself by traveling across South Carolina. He found out that "although Reagan was No. 1 in Republican hearts, Nixon was the choice for President, with Reagan as his running mate…He could arouse the GOP stalwarts, but he would be rejected in a national election because of his inexperience in national and international affairs."[73] Nobody was realizing how well Reagan was burnishing his skills in America's defense and space policy.

Reagan would visit Tulsa, Oklahoma, as part of the Southern strategy on January 16. The Oklahoma delegation, the first in the nation, was to be formed on February 24. As Reagan would end his Tulsa visit, Reagan supporters "predicted 12 to 15 Reagan supporters will be included on the 22-man Oklahoma GOP delegation when it finally is selected."[74] The Reagan movement in Oklahoma was spearheaded by Oklahoma Republicans for Reagan, which would announce it was mailing out 14,000 Reagan postcards. National attention would start focusing on the Oklahoma delegation's formation, because as the first in the nation, the movement toward Reagan "might trigger similar action in other conservative states where Richard Nixon is the expedient candidate, but Reagan is the preferred one."[75]

Thurmond may have been reconsidering his private confirmation via Dent that he would support Nixon, as well as despite the reservations Dent was starting to have himself about Reagan's electability. For on February 15 at the national meeting of the Eagle Conference of Republican Women held in St. Louis, Thurmond would tell the 270 attendees from 30 states to " go back home and work diligently to bring about the nomination of a candidate for President who comes nearest" to standing for conservative principles. The only candidate Thurmond mentioned was "that great conservative Republican in California—Gov. Ronald Reagan."[76]

Thus Reagan's Southern strategy, begun in the fall of 1967 would still be alive and kicking in early 1968. In the two most important Southern states with two of the four GOP leaders, in Texas although Tower had gone over to Nixon, O'Donnell was still in the Reagan camp. Alabama and its chairman Goldthwaite were for Reagan. And in South Carolina, although Dent had pretty well made up his mind for Nixon, Thurmond was telling his national party to vote for the candidate who came closest to standing for conservative principles— Ronald Reagan. But it would not last.

Endnotes

1.   Nixon, Richard, RN, p. 304
2.   RRL, Tape 283
3.   Dent, p. 78-79
4.   Chester et. al., p. 187; Thomas, Ikes Bluff , p. 220, 233; Trende, Sean,"Southern Whites' Shift to the GOP Predates the '60s,'" RealclearPolitics.com, 4/30/13
5.   Frisk, p. 160-162
6.   Wicker, Tom "In the Nation: The Candidate Nobody Knows," NYT, 3/23/67, p. 34
7.   Chester et. al., p. 189
8.   Chester et. al., p. 189
9.   Nixon, Richard, RN, p. 304
10. Ritter
11. Bass and Thompson
12. Bass and Thompson, p. 205
13. Bass and Thompson, p. 222
14. Perlstein, Rick, "The Southern Strategist," NYT Magazine, 12/30/2007
15. Dent, p. 77
16. Dent, p. 77
17. Bass and Thompson, p. 223
18. Bass and Thompson, p. 224
19. Dent, p. 77
20. Hill, Gladwin, "Reagan Aids GOP in South Carolina," NYT, 9/30/67
21. Dent, p. 78
22. Dent, ibid
23. Dent, p. 78
24. Reed, p. 19
25. Hill op.cit.
26. Hill op.cit.
27. RRL, Tape 283
28. RRL, Tape 283
29. Reed, p. 19
30. Dent, p. 78
31. Hill op.cit.
32. Hill op.cit.
33. Cannon, Ronnie and Jesse, p. 264
34. Reed, p. 19
35. Reed, pers comm. 8/23/13
36. "The Chilling Facts Behind the Decision to Build the Anti-Ballistic Missile," Life, 9/29/67, p. 28A-28C
37. Edwards, Lee, "The Last Dixiecrat" Wall Street Journal Bookshelf, 8/31/2012

38. Thurmond, p. 69-72
39. Cannon, Ronnie and Jesse, p. 266
40. Cannon, Ronnie and Jesse, p. 265
41. Cannon, Governor Reagan, p. 323-324
42. Reed, *The Reagan Enigma*, p. 133
43. Cannon, p. 324
44. Reed, p. 4
45. Reed, p. 9
46. Reed, p. 11
47. Reed, p. 17
48. Reagan-Reed, 9/1/1967
49. Reed, p. 16
50. Reed, p. 17
51. ibid
52. Reed, p. 18
53. Reagan-Reed, 10/4/1967, Sacramento
54. Reed, p.20
55. Reed, p. 20
56. Blackwell, Morton, personal communication, 11/19/2015
57. Franklin, Ben, "GOP in Kentucky Hoping for Upset," *NYT*, 10/16/67, p. 28
58. ibid
59. Franklin, Ben, "Reagan Assails Welfare Costs," *NYT*, 10/14/67, p. 41
60. Franklin, 10/16/67 op.cit.
61. Kopelson, Gene, 2014C
62. Reagan-Reed, 10/14/1967
63. Reed, *The Reagan Enigma*, p. 146
64. Cunningham, p. 88-91
65. Cunningham, p. 91
66. Hill, Gladwin, "Reagan Tour Aids GOP War Chest," *NYT*, 10/27/67, p. 34
67. ibid
68. ibid
69. ibid
70. Cunningham, p. 90
71. Dirksen Congressional Center, EMD Papers, alpha 1967, Reagan
72. Dent, p. 78
73. Dent, p. 78-79
74. "The Moving Finger Writes 'Reagan,'" *The State Journal*, Topeka, 1/30/68
75. ibid
76. Janson, Donald, "Strategy Shaped by Conservatives," *NYT*, 2/16/68, p. 19

CHAPTER 11: THE GIPPER MEETS THE JUICE, AND STAR WARS

"I am one who has followed with interest the discussion in the press and in magazine articles...statements and interviews by various people associated with both the military and space."

~Ronald Reagan[1]

"Perhaps we are under-spending in the military areas of space."

~ Ronald Reagan[2]

"He listened carefully and interrupted maybe a dozen times. Every one of his questions was to the point. He clearly comprehended the technology."

~ Dr. Edward Teller[3]

Reagan "rides his horse right into the front lawn of the White House...and proceeds to the throne."

~ William F. Buckley Jr.[4]

"That's not a dream ticket, it's a nightmare."

~ Ronald Reagan[5]

If Reagan thought he had been busy campaigning during the early autumn, visiting Illinois, South Carolina, Wisconsin, Nebraska, Kentucky, and Texas and planning for his January visit to Oklahoma, Reagan was in for a rude but pleasant shock: the next four weeks would be even more hectic. The national media was starting to take notice of Reagan's burgeoning presidential campaign.

Dutch Defends Ike

On October 12, Reagan was interviewed by William F. Buckley, Jr. on *Firing Line*. Buckley made a point at the start of the program that he would avoid asking anything about Reagan's presidential ambitions. Indeed one historian felt that Buckley originally had not wanted to "subject Reagan to the intellectual rigors of *Firing Line*," as Buckley supposedly had not felt that Reagan was truly ready for "prime-time" political debate.[6]

But Reagan was ready. While discussing the relationship between the federal government and the states, Reagan recalled that at the late 1966 Governors Conference in Colorado Springs, he had taken the initiative and proposed that two percent of all federal income taxes be returned to each state in which it had been collected. He explained that the present system was not only redistributing individual incomes by federal taxation and spending with wealthy individuals subsidizing poor individuals, but that the federal government was also redistributing the income of each state: wealthy states were subsidizing poorer states. Reagan wanted the system modified to permit each state to keep its share of monies taken by the IRS. Then Reagan took a forceful stand on the issue of federal protection of minority rights when he said the federal government should come in "with bayonets if necessary" to protect the constitutional rights of minorities.[7]

Suddenly Buckley attacked former President Eisenhower because Eisenhower, according to Buckley, had not dismantled Franklin Roosevelt's New Deal by shrinking the bloated federal bureaucracy. Buckley may have thought that conservative Reagan would agree about Eisenhower, but Buckley was in for a rude awakening from his fellow conservative.

Previously Reagan had been asked by the press why certain of his policies had not been implemented in Sacramento. He had reminding the reporters that he, like Eisenhower, had had to deal with hostile legislatures.

So when Buckley criticized his coach in front of a national audience, Reagan quickly delivered a sterling defense of President Eisenhower:

"What has been overlooked a great deal is one of his most notable achievements. He vetoed 165 spending measures in his term in office... I'd add something else in there. In only one term of his entire eight years did he have a Congress of his own philosophy and of his own party. He was a president isolated by a Democrat congress that was carrying on literally the philosophy that had been in existence since 1932. The greatest thing that he could do was in those numerous vetoes."[8]

Many times during the 1968 campaign, Reagan would bring up this similarity between his own hostile legislature in Sacramento and his planned use of the veto and President Eisenhower's similar predicament and forceful solution. Reagan was continuing to model himself after his mentor.

Ike Again Advises Reagan:
Disclosure of Previously Undocumented Prior Meeting

Meanwhile, Clif White convened his Hard Core for a critical three-day meeting in Miami. White straddled the line as both Reagan campaign spokesman and as leader of his old group. The Hard Core became official members of the Reagan campaign.[9] Three days later in Manhattan, a day before the cruise departed, Reagan was interviewed by ABC political editor Bill Lawrence on *Issues and Answers*.

The first question was whether Reagan would be willing to give a firm declaration that he did not want any supporters to involve him the race for the presidency. Reagan said he had been doing that "over and over." He cited that he had sent a letter to "every paper" in New Hampshire "disavowing the efforts being made on my behalf." Lawrence revealed that his own recent travels across the country showed "there is a lot of rising Reagan for President sentiment," and asked Reagan if he had noted it too.

Reagan was careful in his response, noting that he had not made "an effort to find out how deep is it." Reagan felt honored that any citizen would consider him for president. After Reagan declared that he was not a candidate, he was asked why he continued to make so many out-of-state visits. Reagan answered by saying that he did think some reporters thought that this issue was his "Achilles heel," but he was doing it all to help the party and other Republicans. Reagan then said that the locations of his visits were determined by the chairmen of the Senate and Congressional Campaign Committees in Washington, and by George Murphy and Bob Wilson, respectively. Reagan was needed where the party stood the "best chance" and needed to make "the most effort."

Reagan cited his upcoming visit to Kentucky and brought to the attention of the ABC reporters that four other governors and senators also would campaign there. Reagan said he had refused most invitations from January through August in 1967 because the California Legislature had been in session, so now he was cramming many visits into the autumn. Reagan was asked if he had any favorite candidates now that he himself was not one? Reagan explained that because he would be the favorite son for California, he had to stay neutral. When asked what he thought of a Reagan-Rockefeller ticket, Reagan laughed, saying, "I'm not a candidate for that either." It was virtually the only time a reporter ever asked about pairing Reagan with Rockefeller with Reagan at the top of such a ticket.

When asked if he would accept a draft, first he reflected that he had discussed this at the Western Governors Conference a few months before. Reagan then started to discuss the Sherman statement. Reagan first had been asked about the Sherman statement while in Eugene the previous February and at that time, Reagan had told the press that Sherman's response had been ridiculous. Reagan continued on *Issues and Answers* by adding new information. He revealed that when chatting with Eisenhower on the golf course, the former president had been the one who told Reagan that even Sherman should not have made the remark. Reagan continued that if the party called on him, he had no right to refuse to serve his party and his country.[10]

Reagan's innocent and humorous answer, however, disclosed information quite important to history. Clearly, mentor Eisenhower once again directly had advised his political student. What is not clear is to which golf outing with Ike was Reagan referring when the two had discussed the vice-presidency? As discussed in detail earlier, neither their June, 1966 meetings at Gettysburg (first at the college and then at the Eisenhower home) nor their March, 1967 meeting in Palm Desert (a multi-hour discussion session) were a golf outing. As will be seen, their last known documented meeting, truly a golf outing, would not occur until March, 1968. Thus there is a strong likelihood, from Reagan's comments to the press, that the two men had at least one other, previously undocumented, meeting. Given that Reagan only became governor in late 1966, most likely this previously unknown meeting had taken place earlier in 1967. And this other meeting also had included playing golf. Thus there seemingly were at least four meetings between Reagan and Eisenhower and at this 1967 meeting, the vice-presidency, and not unreasonably to assume, the presidency, were discussed.

Time Cover

Time magazine's cover on October 20, 1967 showed two faces: for President: Rockefeller of New York and for Vice-President: Reagan of California. It may have been the first introduction of the American public to the idea that such a team indeed could be sent to the White

House. But it also may have kindled the idea with the public, asked of Reagan earlier, that perhaps the roles might be reversed.

The cover story gave an in-depth review of where the Republican 1968 campaign stood that fall. A Gallup poll showed that Rockefeller-Reagan easily would defeat Johnson-Humphrey by 57 percent to 43 percent. The magazine speculated that Reagan would attract votes in the West and South while Rockefeller would get the votes of urban blacks and intellectuals But there major issues to surmount. First, Rockefeller had not supported party nominee Goldwater in 1964. Independents outnumbered Republicans, thus and any Republican nominee would need to attract Democrats and Independents in order to win. And both Rockefeller and Reagan had been divorced which was thought to be a possible handicap for 1968.

If Rockefeller wanted to gain the top spot, first he would have to derail the "bandwagons for Reagan" and second he would have to "strike a deal with the conservatives in advance by guaranteeing the second spot to Reagan."[11] But would Republicans forgive Rockefeller for 1964? If Reagan were on the ticket, they might. In fact according to the report, "signs of grudging support for an R. & R. ticket are beginning to sprout even in the South's stony soil."[12]

But how could liberal Nelson Rockefeller share a ticket with conservative Ronald Reagan? Many Republicans doubted they could or feared the public would view the ticket as too expedient politically. Indeed as discussed, Eisenhower had berated the idea. But New York Republican Senator Jacob Javits cautioned that Rockefeller indeed could accept Reagan ideologically.[13] After Reagan's impressive gubernatorial victory the prior fall by almost a million votes, Rockefeller had told friends to take Reagan seriously. Rockefeller predicted that once Reagan had to govern, rather than campaign, "you'll find he is no extremist."[14]

And what about reversing the *Time* cover with a ticket of Reagan-Rockefeller? Reagan for president "becomes more of a possibility when it is realized that the South and West will have more votes than the Midwest and Northeast at Miami Beach."[15] Based on Reagan's very successful trip to South Carolina two weeks before, followed by talk that they would "jilt faithful old Dick Nixon if the charismatic Californian will only whistle," some Republicans started to contemplate seriously such a ticket headed by Reagan. In fact although a recent poll of GOP county chairmen had shown Nixon in the lead, Reagan beat Rockefeller 233 to 67.[16]

Governors Cruise to the Virgin Islands

Forty-two governors, half Republican and half Democrat, boarded the *S.S. Independence* on October 16 for an eight-day working cruise conference sailing from Manhattan to the Virgin Islands. Press photographs showed the Reagan's and the Romney's on deck as they passed by the Statue of Liberty.

As each governor opened their cabin, there lay a copy of the Rockefeller-Reagan "dream ticket" issue of *Time* which had been placed under every cabin door.[17] This most elegant of the gubernatorial conferences Reagan attended—or would attend—during his first campaign for the presidency was described as a place where "pols let their hair down in exotic locales, gossiped, jockeyed, sized up who was who, put on a show for reporters, flaunted their privileges as men who ran the world."[18]

Politics just oozed out of the ship's rafters. Besides Romney and Rockefeller being aboard, it was noted that on the small ship "Reagan might be the third full-fledged Republican Presidential aspirant."[19] With Governors Volpe of Massachusetts, Chafee of Rhode Island, Rhodes of Ohio, Knowles of Wisconsin, Love of Colorado, Cargo of New Mexico, and Evans of Washington all there, so many potential vice presidential candidates created "a traffic jam on the promenade deck."[20]

Aboard the ship, there were many social events. At a tropical-themed costume ball, Nancy and Ronald Reagan were noted to be at the edge of the dance floor. Rockefeller was seasick and had told reporters that he was not interested in being president. At the ball, all eyes were on the seemingly constant meetings of Rockefeller and Romney. At other times Romney made three visits to Rockefeller's cabin on the sun deck, all of which fueled speculation that Romney would become Rockefeller's stalking horse even though Romney had begged Rockefeller to "let him off the hook."[21]

Reed accompanied the Reagan's[22] as did Nofziger and Clarke; all told there were some 700 aides and journalists onboard. Besides the partying, there was actual gubernatorial work to be done. Reagan and Romney got into a disagreement over a resolution, which endorsed an increase in federal taxes. Reagan objected to the wording and offered an amendment to the resolution with the wording "we support those members of Congress who are insisting on a prompt and meaningful cut in non-defense spending."[23] Governor Romney objected to Reagan's amendment because his main concern was inflation.[24]

Reagan, in office less than a year compared to most of his colleagues, did not hesitate to get involved beyond domestic matters. He was becoming a statesman and dove right into his new area of expertise, world affairs. Reagan objected to adopting a resolution on Vietnam because he did not want to introduce "partisan politics into the Governors' Conference."[25]

The partying and the gubernatorial work all took second place to politicking. Romney's candidacy clearly was diminishing because of his brainwashing comment, yet with all of the meetings with him and Rockefeller, coupled with Rockefeller telling reporters that he did not want to be president, it was assumed that Romney still was going to be Rockefeller's stalking horse.

At a first morning breakfast meeting, Reagan met with Reed to plan shipboard networking for his presidential campaign. Later Reagan met with Reed, Nofziger, and Clark to review the new structure of the campaign and to delineate responsibilities.[26]

Reagan held a news conference during the cruise as Rockefeller and other governors sat in the audience. Reagan was asked if he wanted to be president. Reagan answered that it was up to the people and to the convention to decide. When asked about a Reagan-Rockefeller ticket, so soon after the same question only days earlier in Manhattan, Reagan answered that he could not conceive of it.[27]

There were two somewhat bizarre episodes on the cruise, which made national news and had implications for Reagan's candidacy. During the cruise, Lyn Nofziger was accosted persistently by reporters, who were asking about the prior Battaglia resignation. Historian Lou Cannon's review of the Battaglia affair, mentioned earlier, included analyses of columns written by Johnson-operative Drew Pearson.[28] Pearson of course did whatever he could to attack opponents of Johnson, and one of his columns attacked Reagan's supposed slow reaction to the scandal, speculating that "it will be very interesting to note the effect the incident has on the governor's zooming chances to be President."[29]

Reagan, trying to protect the reputations and family of his advisors, called Pearson's charges untrue but later would issue a retraction. Because there had been no explanation to the press when Battaglia had left office previously, but then on the cruise Nofziger had told reporters the true reason why Battaglia had resigned, eventually the embarrassment thus created ensnared Nofziger, who left office as well.

The false charges that Reagan had covered up the affair would reappear intermittently as far into the future as 1980. Indeed historian

Cannon would think he was in the Bill Murray movie *Groundhog Day* because to Cannon, and likely to Reagan, the same day and the same false charges which had to be denied would appear again and again.[30]

Some historians have felt that the initial Battaglia affair and the subsequent reappearance of it during the cruise ruined whatever chances Reagan may have had for 1968. As noted earlier, Reed to this day insists that the Battaglia affair was "not major to '68."[31]

The second incident involved Johnson and Reagan directly, and historian Andrew Johns called this the "biggest news" of the voyage.[32] David Brinkley of NBC news reported that President Johnson sent a telegram on the cruise to one former governor—on the cruise as liaison between the White House and the governors—asking him to drum up support for Johnson's Vietnam policies while on the cruise. But the telegram was sent to Reagan's cabin by mistake and Reagan told the press of the telegram's contents.

Reporter Brinkley's team was on the ship and asked some of the governors what they thought of the mis-delivered telegram. Reagan said it was "a sealed envelope delivered to me" and was amongst many similar envelopes he had received and he had opened them all. There was a debate between those governors who felt Reagan was morally in the wrong by revealing the telegram's contents versus those who thought that what Reagan had done was the correct moral course by exposing how Johnson was attempting to influence opinions and the news.[33] President Johnson ended the entire misdirected telegram matter humorously when he proclaimed that he wanted Ronald Reagan "to be elected the president of Western Union."[34]

As the Reagan's debarked from the cruise back on the United States mainland, Reagan then visited Iowa and the two stops in Texas discussed earlier. In Des Moines, after delivering a short speech to a rally, Reagan and Reed met with local Republican politicians to garner more delegates.[35] After leaving Dallas, an important honor for Reagan awaited in Kansas.

Landon Lecture

Ronald Reagan's first trip to Kansas during his 1968 presidential campaign was to deliver the prestigious Alfred M. Landon Lecture on Public Issues at Kansas State University on October 26, 1967. Governor Landon of Kansas had been the 1936 Republican Party nominee for president. Governor Landon, who would meet Reagan in Topeka the following spring, had inaugurated the speaker series in 1966, and the third speaker chosen was Governor Reagan. Reagan would be invited to deliver the lecture a second time, this time as president, on September 9, 1982—the only person to have been asked twice to deliver the prestigious talk. Landon would pass away at age 100 in 1987.

Reagan's topic in 1967 was "Higher Education: Its Role in Contemporary America," and a photograph of Reagan at the lectern[36] shows a distinguished gentleman named Henry A. Bubb seated at a floor-level dais a few feet from Reagan.

Bubb was the initiator of Reagan's visit via Reed as the intermediary. Bubb would become the founder of Reagan's national campaign office a few months later and would work closely with Reed and other grass roots Reagan offices. Indeed letters from Reagan to Bubb in 1968, to be discussed later, would reveal a friendship between Bubb and Reagan which had started at a talk Reagan had given ten years earlier.

Reagan began his speech by telling the audience that he was neither a politician nor an academician. Reagan used again his citizen-candidate term from 1966, which had originated with Eisenhower. For one of the few times during his campaign, Reagan did not discuss world affairs. Also he did not discuss his policy triumphs as governor or raise any banner for conservatives to follow. He focused like a laser on education, just as he had done at Hiram Scott College, Eureka College, and soon would do again at Yale.

Reagan provided details of his recently announced plan in California to ask state college and university students to start to pay ten percent of the costs of their education. Reagan's idea had generated student protests and opposition from the Democrats in the state legislature, which he characterized as "cataclysmic." Reagan explained that he had to do this because "the cost of education is increasing faster than the increase in public funds." But he proceeded to tell his audience that the resultant monies received from the tuition increase would be targeted to provide educational assistance. Reagan explained, "half of the funds from the proposed tuition increase would go for a combination of loans and grants-in-aid to needy students." Reagan had targeted disadvantaged Mexican American students to receive the aid, as will be discussed later. Then a quarter would "provide for 250 new teaching chairs at the University and the remaining fourth could be applied for capital construction of needed facilities." Redistribution was fine for the Democrats as long as monies came from someone else, but when Reagan wanted students to pay ten percent of tuition in order to provide aid to minorities and new teaching jobs, they were in opposition.

Reagan then spoke of the duties of universities. Reagan urged professors not to abandon the notions of right and wrong. An "educator is wrong who denies there are any absolutes—who sees no black and white, right or wrong, but just shades of gray." Reagan said that educators "cannot escape a responsibility to aid in students' development of character and maturity." Reagan cautioned professors that they had "no right to indoctrinate students with his view of things" and ended those comments stating it "is the university's obligation to teach, not indoctrinate."

His next theme was how society viewed equal opportunities versus equal results, a problem echoed well into the second decade of the 21st century. Reagan explained that each American was "equal before God and the law." But Reagan saw clearly that society could not guarantee equal results or achievements for all. He stressed the importance of the individual by saying every man had a right "to achieve above the capacity of his fellows." Neither government nor society should attempt to create equal outcomes as he used an analogy from baseball. "Certainly major league baseball would not be improved by letting every citizen who wanted to have a turn at playing Willie Mays' position." America, well into the 21st century, still is grappling with the concerns Reagan expressed.

Finally Reagan spoke about a favorite theme of his, the increasing encroachment of the federal government into the individual states and federal versus state rights and obligations. Echoing a divisive issue facing his fellow governors some five decades later, whether or not to implement federal mandates of Obamacare, Reagan cautioned his listeners, "Let us think very carefully before switching to a system in which these states become administrative districts enforcing uniform laws and regulations."[37]

A short time after the Landon Lecture, due to state business, Reagan could not attend the Western States Republican Conference in Denver. But Reagan's candidacy was the subject of much speculation. Reagan support was noted to be "high" in the West, and continuing discussions about a potential Rockefeller-Reagan ticket "fascinated many" at the meeting.[38] The *New York Times* reported that in the three days of late October, Reagan "drew audiences totaling about 50,000," and that was on just one of his four planned swings in the fall.[39]

Those on the left were starting to get nervous with the growing support for Reagan for president. Columnist Pearson, who had gotten his knives out for Reagan in his October 30 column on the Battaglia affair, tried to stir up further anti-Reagan sentiment in the same column. He wanted his readers to know that Nancy Clark, in charge of Reagan's television appearances "expected to be the first woman press secretary ever to serve in the White House."[40] Just imagine: a pro-Democratic columnist complaining that a conservative Republican was for women's rights in the workplace! Reagan was following Eisenhower's long-ago advice to bring women onto his staff, and here another prominent Democrat with a byline[41] was attacking him for it.

October ended with Reagan's follow-up Chicago visit (discussed earlier) and another campaign assessment from the *New York Times*. The editorialist felt that on the cruise, Reagan had made "some progress in closing his own credibility gap," and despite having made public the mis-routed Johnson telegram, Reagan "did succeed in convincing many correspondents and fellow governors that he would make a believable candidate for President." But the editorialist could not resist his liberal biases and had to add, "Reagan has little experience and his shallow opinions on some questions have terrifying implications, but he is urbane, self-possessed and a smooth performer on camera and at news conferences. His political potential has—most unfortunately—to be judged a serious matter."[42] That Reagan spoke quite well off the cuff without the need for a teleprompter at many press conferences was not noted, and one wonders where that editorialist was in 2008.

In early November, a new polling organization called Trend Line Analysis released their findings. The people behind the six-state poll, of California, New York, Pennsylvania, Ohio, Illinois, and Michigan, were the AFL-CIO union, the Brotherhood of Airline and Railway Clerks. The union admitted they did not like the results because of their usual Democratic leanings, but the poll's conclusions were that Reagan was the Republicans' "most powerful vote getter, strongest maintainer of the GOP's strength, and leads all others in the presidential race in turning out the electorate." Specifically, Reagan ran "plus 23 percent" above Nixon or Rockefeller or Romney or Percy. Clearly, the candidate to win the most disaffected Democrats remained Reagan.[43]

On November 2 in Sacramento, Reagan met with Reed to discuss future campaign travels and speechwriting.[44] A week later at a governor's residence breakfast meeting and with Nancy Reagan, Reed and Clif White all present, Reagan again reviewed his campaign.[45]

Reagan then set his sights on making his second campaign swing to the Pacific Northwest. Before visiting the critical opt-out primary state of Oregon, first he would visit Seattle, where he had made his first out-of-state speech as nominee of the Republican Party for governor a year-and-a-half earlier and first had been seen as a national candidate.

Return to Seattle

In the interval between his Seattle visits, Reagan had become a true contender for the presidency, and his political stock had soared. King County conservative Republican leader Ken Rogstad had charged just $1 to entice the public to see and hear the new nominee for governor of California back then. Now in mid November, 1967, Reagan's political stock had soared 100-fold to become a $100 per plate luncheon at the Olympic Hotel. More than 1100 people jammed the hotel's Grand Ballroom and an overflow crowd was placed in an adjoining hall to watch and hear Reagan via closed-circuit television. The event was described as "the biggest political fund-raising luncheon in terms of income ever held" there and the crowd in both ballrooms cheered Reagan's comments. [46]

Governor Dan Evans was on the dais. Evans was a Rockefeller supporter and had done his best to rid his party of conservative Republicans like Rogstad.[47] Reagan began his speech explaining that when he had first been elected governor of California, one of the first people he had called for advice was Evans.

Reagan paraphrased Winston Churchill twice. When he attacked the Johnson administration for spending $425 million to promote publicity, Reagan quipped: "never have so few spent so much to tell us so little," which was greeted with great applause. Following the large tent philosophy he had learned from Eisenhower and he had so successfully used in 1966, Reagan urged Democrats to think about switching officially to join the Republicans when he again cited Churchill: "Some men change principle for party and some men change party for principle."

Unlike at his press conferences, foreign affairs still took a back seat to domestic matters in his speeches at this point, but his brief comment on Vietnam generated huge applause. Using similar wording to what he had declared in Seattle a year-and-a-half earlier, Reagan said that if the government asks families to send their sons to war and that they might die for freedom, "their sons should be allowed to win it."[48]

After the speech, as usual it was at his press conference where the reporters honed in on Reagan's positions on foreign policy and Reagan shined again. Asked immediately about Vietnam, Reagan said he wanted America to "turn the full resources of this nation to ending this conflict as soon as possible." Come January, 1969, proclaimed Reagan, Republicans would achieve honor and freedom for the peoples of Vietnam "using whatever steps are necessary." Reagan's comments on Vietnam were becoming more specific. Reagan had learned well Eisenhower's dictum that it was the threat that counted. He did not elaborate yet on which specific steps a Republican president would use to win in Vietnam, but that soon would change.

Inevitably, the press asked about Reagan's role in the upcoming 1968 presidential election. He affirmed, "I am not a candidate" and when asked the same question 15 minutes later he reiterated, "I am not a candidate!" He elaborated that "Republicans cannot afford disunity" and that "we have a responsibility to win" but also affirmed that he would remain loyal to the party and would "support whoever is the nominee." A reporter asked Reagan what he thought of coverage by the media and he answered that with the exception of a few columnists, likely meaning Pearson, so far it had been "very fair and objective." The media was about to launch a question whose implications would reverberate well into the 21st century.

Star Wars

Suddenly out of the clear blue, Reagan was asked about America's expenditures for weapons in space. Reagan was asked if America should match the development of "orbiting nuclear bombs" that the Soviet Union was working upon. Immediately what had simultaneously occurred in September came to mind: the ABM magazine article in *Life*, Thurmond's new autobiography and his strong feelings in favor of America's needing anti-ballistic missiles, and his own meeting with Thurmond. The reporters had not understood that the previous political and press discussions had been about a defensive shield against incoming missiles. But Reagan revealed much more to the press: Reagan explained for the very first time in public that indeed for months he had been educating himself about the idea of a missile shield for America.

He answered,

"I am one who has followed with interest the discussion in the press, and in magazine articles, and so forth, statements and interviews by various people associated with both the military and space and am one who leans toward the belief that perhaps we are understating and underspending in the space program with regard to the military possibilities of space."[49](author's emphasis)

The one newspaper account only mentioned a small subsegment of what Reagan had disclosed: "Perhaps we are under-spending in the military areas of space."[50]

Reagan had been processing the idea of a missile defense shield for two months. Reagan had read everything he could on the subject: articles, interviews, and statements. Now he had made his very first public proclamation on what would, a decade and a half later, be called "Star Wars," the Strategic Defense Initiative. Historians have made a number of analyses of the origins of SDI but none have mentioned this critical Reagan press conference. Your author believes that this Seattle press conference was in fact its exact origin—Reagan's first public comment on offensive or defensive systems in space—based on the earlier September *Life* article, Thurmond's forthcoming autobiography, and what the two men had discussed in September. More public pronouncements about America's antimissile defense by Reagan would occur the following summer.

Meanwhile, Reagan needed to learn more about a possible antimissile defense for America and see the technology first-hand for himself. After all, he was running for president and in a year might become commander-in-chief, but now was only a domestic governor and Washington outsider. Where could he learn more for himself? Just as Reagan had sought the advice of Eisenhower when first Reagan had contemplated entering politics, Reagan needed to meet the scientist who was at the forefront of the nation's missile defense planning. Reagan soon would find the answer and the person back at home in California.

Both governors ended their joint press conference agreeing that the West would have greater say in Republican politics due to the population shift westward. Governor Evans may have begun to realize that Reagan not only was a serious and well-spoken contender for the presidency, but that there was some possibility he could become party nominee at the convention in nine months. Evans would wind up telling ABC News that he could in fact work hard to support a Reagan candidacy if Reagan were the nominee. But as will be seen, Evans would try his best to prevent Reagan having many delegates from Washington State.[51]

That day, Reagan spoke of Republican Party unity and attempted to bring together the 1964 conservative-Goldwater members with the liberal-Rockefeller members. He continued to want to win the Vietnam War. Following Eisenhower's dictum of maximum force, now Reagan had the confidence to start urging to the public and national press the use of whatever was necessary to achieve that victory.

But now Reagan had been thrust briefly publicly into the realm of defensive and offensive weapons in space. When asked by the Seattle reporters, Reagan did not demure, saying he was not an expert in the field. On the contrary, Reagan forcefully had told reporters his very first public utterance on what history later would call "Star Wars," or Reagan's Strategic Defense Initiative.[52] Reagan was far afield from the usual gubernatorial areas of domestic policies. Reagan's growing expertise and confidence in world affairs and military technology soon might launch him to the White House. Reagan's mind quickly got back to earth as he left for Oregon. He was looking forward to tomorrow's big Veteran's Day football game and the new star on the playing field: O.J. Simpson.

The Oregon Invitation

Ronald Reagan's second, and last, visit to Oregon during his first presidential campaign took place in November 1967 and would create the nucleus of his Oregon supporters who would all play major roles in his 1968 primary campaign. The momentum that had started in February in Eugene grew tremendously in November, and once the team was assembled, would snowball during the spring of 1968 into a group of very hard-working loyal Reaganites. Today the members of the Reagan Oregon 1968 presidential campaign recall those events as if they happened yesterday.

Reagan received his invitation from James C. Goode. Judge Goode, who would be appointed Oregon Circuit Judge in 1981 and is still active in 2014, comes from a long-standing family loyal to the Republican Party. Goode had been the Linn County campaign chairman for Tom McCall for governor, and they became friends. Once a week McCall called Goode for political discussions and advice; the two also had family vacation homes on the Oregon coast. Then in 1967, Goode was appointed to obtain dignitaries for the well-known Albany Veteran's Day Parade, the largest Veteran's Day parade west of the Mississippi.

Goode's parents, recently moved back from California, were loyal fans of Governor Reagan. Every week "their side of the conversation always included raves of things Reagan was doing."[53] So Goode, a conservative Republican, decided to learn for himself all about Reagan. Once Goode read about Reagan, Goode knew he had found his speaker. Reagan as a rising conservative star in the Republican

Party in next-door California seemed a perfect fit for the parade. But Goode recalled that it was the possibility of Reagan running for president that sealed the deal. Goode recalled "Word of Reagan as a possible presidential hopeful made it an ideal time for me to try."[54]

Goode knew that Governor McCall had been to the Albany event many times before, so Goode called his friend with the idea. McCall initially declared, "Its worth a try," and a week later reported to Goode, "I'm optimistic." McCall and Reagan each loved and rode horses, and Goode recalled that the governor mused, "So we'll both ride horses." And within two weeks the final decision was made—Yes to the Reagan invitation.

What is not clear is why it took two weeks for McCall to decide to extend an invitation to Reagan for an event that fall when previously he had invited him to attend the Eugene event that spring. Why had McCall agreed with Goode's suggestion to invite Reagan in spite of McCall's earlier skepticism about Reagan's candidacy for president? Don Hodel speculated that had McCall opposed Reagan's run fervently, "He would not have given Reagan the visibility in Oregon nor extend his welcome to him."[55] Indeed Hodel recalled, "McCall didn't have a mean bone in his body." The true reason was that Reagan's presence "would heighten the publicity and that McCall would be co-equal in the spotlight as host governor."[56] That McCall had added the comment above about the both of them riding horses seems to confirm Hodel's answer.

Besides the parade and political events, Reagan's visit would include attending what would become a famous football game. And Goode would spend considerable personal time with Reagan. But first Goode had to make many arrangements as advance man for Reagan under the Linn County Veteran's Council.

Reagan in Portland

At the end of his Friday November 10, 1967 press conference in Seattle, after his comments on orbiting nuclear weapons, Reagan was asked if he was going to Oregon to campaign for the presidency? He answered that he had been invited by the Oregon governor, had been asked to ride in a parade, had wanted to see a football game with USC, and was asked to attend two fundraisers. When asked if the fundraiser was related to the upcoming presidential primary in Oregon the next spring, he answered that indeed he had been advised to go to the fundraiser well in advance of the Oregon primary.[57]

Reagan then flew to Portland the same afternoon and was met by Governor McCall. Had McCall truly been against a Reagan candidacy in 1968, or had been extremely jealous of Reagan, he could have found an excuse not to greet Governor Reagan. On the way downtown, they stopped to meet the Oregon Dairy Princess and both governors toasted her with large glasses of milk. The photograph of Reagan, McCall and the princess made the front page of *The Oregonian.*[58]

At their press conference, Reagan was asked about a possible run of McCall's in the future for the Senate. Reagan turned to McCall and said, "Anytime your Governor McCall finds himself running against a Democrat, I'll be happy to support him."[59] Reagan's 1968 bid for the presidency came up quickly. Reagan was asked about his California favorite son candidacy and the Oregon affidavit process, which stated that he was not a presidential candidate, and why he would not sign it. He said that as in Wisconsin and Nebraska, he could not sign the Oregon affidavit because he would have to affirm he was not a presidential candidate. "I can't fulfill the terms of your affidavit because I'd either be a liar in the affidavit or been a liar when I became a favorite son."[60] He said that in states where he could withdraw, as in New Hampshire, he already had. He was asked about the qualities of the Republican 1968 nominee and he answered that the party had a "wealth of manpower" but that he did not want to name anyone specific. He told the press, as he had learned from Eisenhower, that he did not like the labels of liberal-Republican nor conservative-Republican and wanted to reiterate his repeated callings of "the necessity to drop the hyphen."[61] When asked about his national speeches, he answered, "I am one of many" who was traveling on behalf of the party and cited that just the prior week he and Richard Nixon were in Chicago at the same time.[62]

Then of course came world affairs. He was asked about the war in Vietnam and addressed the importance of the war for America: Reagan said firmly that it was in the national interest of the U.S. to be there. Echoing his mentor, Reagan declared that America, once it was at war and its young men were fighting, had a moral responsibility to put "its full resources" into winning the war and winning it "as quickly as possible."[63] He said he stood against the appeasement of aggression by North Vietnam. Reagan then got into specific military tactics. He said he was pleased by the recent expansion of military targets of the U.S against North Vietnam.

Reagan was honing his message to the public. He wanted America as a united country and not a disparate group of citizen groups, balkanized into public interest groups using hyphenated name groupings. He defined one of America's clear national interests: Vietnam. He had said so much at the Kennedy debate and was repeating it now. He got down to specific military tactics by approving of the expansion of targets in North Vietnam. He didn't say it, but "full resources" included nuclear weapons. As he had learned from Eisenhower, he wanted the North Vietnamese quaking in their beds, wondering if a President Reagan would leave their country a smoldering cinder in one year.

Governors Reagan and McCall and their teams then proceeded to the Coliseum where Reagan was the featured speaker at a $50 per plate fundraiser dinner for the Multnomah County Central Committee of the Oregon Republican Party. Some 1,200 persons attended, "joined by an estimated 400 high school students" as well.[64]

McCall introduced Reagan and did not shy away from mentioning the 1968 Reagan for President campaign. McCall predicted, "Reagan would play a key role in the 1968 campaign."[65] Hodel reflected later that this remark was "classic McCall who wanted to be liked and thus aligned himself with the predominant pro-Reagan sentiment of the audience."[66] Don Hodel and his wife were at the dinner. The venue, in the exhibit hall of the Coliseum, had a very high ceiling and tables that were spread somewhat far apart. The arrangement created acoustical difficulties for Reagan to deliver his speech properly.

Hodel recalled, "I never saw Reagan work so hard to warm up an audience." At first Reagan's usual humor seemed flat. But it was not because the audience did not like what he said. Rather one could barely hear the people at one's own table laughing, let alone hear the laughing from the rest of the audience. Hodel recalled that Reagan was extremely patient and non-plussed, probably spending "three times as long as normal with anecdotes and humor until he finally got the audience laughing and responding loudly enough to hear each other." At that point Reagan went on with his speech to a very responsive audience. Although the later press reports made no comment about the acoustics and initial difficulties Reagan had, Hodel felt he himself had "learned a huge lesson from observing him in action at that event."[67] Reagan had kept his cool.

Reagan had begun his speech by addressing the Oregon affidavit issue head on: "if I am in your primary it will not be my doing," and he told the audience, as he had at the press conference earlier, that he could not be a California favorite son and sign the Oregon withdrawal affidavit which would declare he was not a presidential candidate. He reminded his audience that this was his second visit to Oregon since the 1966 elections. Reagan told the audience that at the

February 1967 Eugene visit, "Very graciously your governor made it possible for me to bring some of our personnel from our own welfare program up here to do a little brain-picking to find out what was going on." Not only did Reagan thank McCall for having arranged for those earlier joint February discussions to discuss mutual problems, he told the audience that the two governors had also just discussed the tax burdens in Oregon and California. Reagan continued, "Now, however, we're aligned on something else, I'm happy to say, and that is the necessity…to find an answer…to attack the property tax that must be made more reasonable." The audience applauded loudly. Hodel recalled that McCall had seemed delighted at these favorable references from Reagan. By doing this, Reagan had made it harder for McCall to remain openly hostile to Reagan's 1968 candidacy.[68]

Reagan's difficult dealings with the Democratic-controlled California legislature were discussed humorously when he said he had often wondered "what the Ten Commandments would have looked like if Moses had to run them through the legislature first." Reagan added four standard jibes about his nemesis, Robert Kennedy, which will be detailed later. After his standard speech, as he had done in Nebraska, he ended that the Republican Party must "raise a banner that the people of all parties can follow. But choose the colors well. They're not in the mood to follow the sickly pastels of expediency and the cynical shades of those who would buy the people's votes with the people's money… Now we have it within our power to broaden the base of our party. There must be many former Democrats and some who are still Democrats, perhaps some still here tonight, who look to us for leadership because they just plain can no longer follow the tortuous trail, the leadership their own party has taken."[69] "Sickly" pastels still had not morphed into "pale" pastels.

Reagan's mid November speech would turn out to be midway between his debate triumph over RFK and a future first White Paper speech (in May, 1968) attacking RFK. In each, the major subject was Vietnam. Now in Portland, Reagan extended his expertise on Vietnam into neighboring Laos. The headline ran "Reagan Blames Viet War on Laos Failure" and detailed Reagan's attacks on the Kennedy years.

In a preview of what he would say in Albany the next day, Reagan assailed President Kennedy's failure to "stand up against the Communists in 1961" as the direct cause of the war in Vietnam. Reagan stated it was in the "national interest" of America to stay in Vietnam until the war was won. Reagan told his audience that communist aggression "must be resisted." Reagan pushed to win the war. Reagan did not think the North Vietnamese were being "hit hard enough." Reagan added that the communists would come to the negotiating table only when "it hurts too much not to come."[70] Reagan's fundraiser dinner in Portland "raised more money than any other affair in recent history."[71] Plus he had expanded his foreign policy expertise once again.

Reagan's Oregon Chair

Immediately after the speech that evening, Don Hodel met in a hotel conference room with Tom Reed and Paul Haerle. Reed told him that Reagan would be on the Oregon presidential primary ballot for 1968. Reed also affirmed that Reagan would not sign the "I am not and never will be a candidate for President" Oregon affidavit.[72]

Reed and Haerle also explained to Hodel that some of the Oregon Reagan supporters were somewhat "inexperienced,…outspoken… and hard-core conservatives. They would make perfect targets for the liberals to brand Reagan as marginal if they were prominent in his campaign."[73] Reed and Haerle told Hodel that one important job for him was to make certain that anyone not well versed in dealing with the press was not to play too prominent a role in the forthcoming Reagan Oregon presidential campaign. So who should lead the Reagan effort in crucial Oregon?

They then asked if he, Hodel, would officially chair the campaign. Hodel demurred, telling them that he was too young, did not have enough stature in the eyes of high-level state Republicans, had recently turned down Bob Packwood's request to chair his upcoming campaign for the U.S. Senate—explaining to Packwood that he intended to get out of politics—and was "severely limited" in what he could do for the 1968 Reagan campaign because he was a full-time attorney with Georgia-Pacific and simply lacked the time necessary to do the job that was needed.

Reed then countered offering that Governor Reagan could call the CEO of Georgia-Pacific to ask if they could cut Hodel "some slack."[74] Hodel's boss, the company general counsel, said Reagan's call would not be necessary: Hodel could be Oregon Reagan campaign chairman during 1968 as long as he got his work done.

Hodel, as we shall see later, worked long and hard on the campaign, yet he recalls ruefully, "I was unable to do my work as well as I should have and it cost me a raise at the next performance review period following the campaign….That…still stings a bit."[75] But Hodel, thinking back to the conversation he had had with McCall the prior summer, told Reed and Haerle that he thought he could recruit someone who did have the proper credentials.[76]

Veteran's Day Parade

As advance man, Goode arranged that all of Reagan's meals were planned campaign events: breakfasts at the Albany American Legion Hall and all lunches and dinners at the Albany Elks Lodge. Reagan's time was completely filled in. Reagan stayed at a local hotel. Reagan's room had a large sitting room, and several times Goode had a chance to spend a few minutes with Reagan between all the planned events. Goode recalls that Reagan was "quiet" but was "amicable and easy going." Reagan and Goode chatted but no major political discussions ensued.[77]

Goode recalled that Reagan "put his feet up on a coffee table and was very relaxed. We didn't talk about anything political—just the parade, the football game…The governor smiled and laughed a lot. He made jokes and laughed at other people's jokes….The whole time he was here, it was very easy and very positive. He never projected his ego or star image."[78]

For Reagan to relax was his style. Reagan, the former actor, needed to decompress after a speech. His adrenalin needed to leave his system. This post-speech time was when he could relax and open up with friends and colleagues when the public was not present.[79]

Veteran's Day, November 11, 1967, began with Reagan attending the Albany Oregon Veteran's Day Parade. Goode had planned in advance that both Governors Reagan and McCall would ride horses in the parade and each would be Grand Marshal. Both governors were known as avid horsemen and each looked forward to the parade. The weather report looked like rain, so Goode arranged that Reagan's horse had wet-rubber parade horseshoes. Goode fondly recalls that Reagan's saddle was made of leather but "shined like silver." Reagan's horse, a three-year old filly named Sassy, was large at seventeen hands and was on loan from the sheriff's mounted posse.[80]

Goode arranged that his own group, the Albany Woodpeckers, wore their formal red coats and yellow hats, and Reagan approved. The three-hour parade, as noted earlier the largest west of the Mississippi, had approximately 200 floats, twelve military groups, twelve bands, and an Oregon National Guard jet fly-over. The rain held off during the parade.

As Reagan and McCall rode their horses, Reagan then took off his hat and Goode saw that "the people went nuts;" Reagan received a "tremendous positive response."[81] Onlooker Paul Pritchard recalled in 2015 that in 1967 he had newly arrived in Oregon from Indiana only two months earlier and enjoyed attending his first Albany Veterans Day Parade. Pritchard took a photograph of both governors on horseback.[82]

Another onlooker was forest products manager Peter Murphy, who as a Notre Dame freshman had been hooked by Reagan when he had watched the movie *Knute Rockne*. Murphy had been slightly active in Republican politics in the southern end of the Willamette Valley in middle-western Oregon, but when he learned that his hero Reagan would be in the parade, he had to see Reagan in person. Murphy recalled that it was "impressive" seeing Reagan "all fixed up" in his riding clothes and saddle.[83]

Reagan's horse bore a sign that Reagan was the Grand Marshal of the parade. Some of the only known film footage of Reagan in the parade would appear the next month in a CBS documentary. After he dismounted, Reagan smiled, telling Goode, "We dazzled the people."[84]

Not everything Reagan did received media attention. Goode accompanied Reagan during a private meeting with at least twenty wounded veterans on Veterans Day.[85] Reagan, powerless to direct any aspects of foreign policy from Sacramento or on the campaign other than by swaying public opinion via speeches and media attention, did what he could. He helped the troops by visiting and giving moral support. As historian Douglas Brinkley has reviewed, Reagan, who by the end of World War II had become a captain in the Army Air Corps, always was in awe of the brave American soldiers of World War II. In the 1960s too many Americans ignored the bravery of the troops in Vietnam because all the public had seen were America's few missteps. Future President Reagan would try to rectify that misperception. President Reagan would emphasize Vietnam veterans at his 1982 State of the Union Address.[86] Perhaps Veteran's Day, 1967, just as at his inaugural address ten months earlier when he had arranged to fly the military base flag and greet the wounded veteran, is where he began to think of more ways he, as a domestic governor, could take direct action in world affairs. Reagan would make additional visits to wounded troops.

Reagan then got a hair raising, high speed ride. Time was running short between the end of Reagan's activities in Albany and his need to be in Corvallis for the kickoff. It was normally a twelve minute drive from Albany to Corvallis, but Veteran's Day had "horrendous" traffic due to the two big events and the roads were clogged. Indeed the towns were "bursting" as Goode remembered. Goode drove Reagan's car, a 1965 Lincoln-Continental, which followed Governor McCall's car, which was driven by a state trooper lieutenant who was a friend of Goode. Goode wondered out loud to the lieutenant how could they possibly get there in time with all the traffic? The lieutenant bet Goode $5 "that everyone would be at the game on time." Goode took the bet as there was "no way" he could lose.

"The lieutenant told me just to get on his tail and follow. We drove so fast that we made it, partly because all of the traffic had been pulled over."[87] The ride was "hair raising. I thought I was gonna die," Goode recalled.[88] Reagan kept any comments to himself but seemed to enjoy the ride. Perhaps he had had more fun in the parade riding Sassy.

The Juice

Orenthal James Simpson, O.J.—"The Juice," had received good medical news from his doctors just prior to his hoped-for 1967 Veteran's Day football game. Simpson had been out of action the prior week, yet his University of Southern California Trojans had still beaten California. But the upcoming Oregon State game would be "another matter completely."[89] O.J. would be needed to face the Oregon State Beavers on November 11 in a game described as "the giants meet the giant killer."[90] Indeed the 1967 Oregon State team had earned the name "Giant Killers" when they would become the only team to go undefeated against three top-two teams in one season.

The 1967 USC Trojans had been ranked the number 9 team of the 20th century as of that date, and they already had defeated number 1 ranked Notre Dame at Notre Dame by a 17-point margin, which became the largest home loss at Notre Dame between 1963 and 1976.

The Trojans came to Corvallis to face the Beavers for the very first time (prior Beaver home games versus the Trojans having been played in Tacoma and Portland) and arrived having averaged winning every game by more than 20 points while playing a very difficult schedule. Half-back O.J. Simpson led the country with 1,050 rushing yards. At kick-off the #1 ranked Trojans were a 13-point favorite over the #13-ranked Beavers.

Reagan arrived in grand style at Parker (now Reser) Stadium in Goode's car. Then Reagan was joined by McCall, and both were transferred to a convertible car on a track so the crowd could see them. Then the rain arrived. Both governors wore ponchos, waving to the crowd, which gave return applause.[91]

Lt. General Jimmy Doolittle, who had come to many prior Veterans Day events in the Albany-Corvallis region to do some hunting, came over to shake the hands of both governors.[92] Shortly after the end of World War II, Reagan had narrated a documentary about Doolittle's victory parade in California, *Target Tokyo*. Likely Reagan did not know that his mentor President Eisenhower had thought highly of Doolittle and had him create a secret report on the CIA in the 1950s.[93]

Even for Reagan, who twice had met Eisenhower personally, a chance to shake the hand of another of America's military heroes must have been thrilling. It is not known if Doolittle spoke to Reagan at any length. But the brief Reagan-Doolittle interaction that day did have lasting effects. In the future, President Reagan would give Doolittle his fourth star in 1985, and Reagan would mention Doolittle in his Farewell Address in January, 1989.

Reagan could not wait for kickoff for one of the most highly anticipated games of the college football season. Of course as discussed in his relationship with fellow football player Ike, Reagan loved football. As a youngster Reagan had seen in stores the new football high school uniforms, and his "heroes were the high school stars." By the time he was in high school, his "goal and aim in life" was to make the team because "everything is a game except football." He had made the team in junior year but due to poor eyesight had been assigned a guard.[94]

At Eureka College, for Reagan "most important was the football field," where as a freshman he had "sulked on the bench" every week in the local small college conference called the "Little 19." But by second year his "bruising practices" had caught the attention of his coach who had promoted him to first string guard. He was thought of as a college football hero.[95]

Reporter Bill Boyarsky reflected, Reagan "retained the love of football as an adult. No role was more enjoyable to him than that of George Gipp in the Knute Rockne movie."[96] As governor, Reagan would soon give a job to Buffalo Bills quarterback Jack Kemp, and as governor and then later as president, Reagan would often couch "problems in the context of a football game."[97]

Indeed Reagan may have been torn for which team to root, as the USC Trojans had just defeated his beloved Notre Dame yet they were still the home team from California that day. But Reagan, confident in his state's team and in Simpson, bet McCall that he would hand-pick a box of oranges for McCall if Oregon State won, and McCall said he would give a fresh silver salmon to Reagan if USC won.

Besides General Doolittle and the two governors, other dignitaries at the Veteran's Day game included ten generals and admirals, the Air Force Academy Drum and Bugle Corps, and three Congressional Medal of Honor winners. There was an overflow crowd of 41,494 fans filling the 40,750-seat stadium and it was the most-attended single sporting event in Oregon history as of then. The Beavers had moved up to 13th in national polls. The thousands of good-luck telegrams took more than five hours to clear the local telegram office. OSU radio announcer Bob Blackburn broadcast the game in his tuxedo; Blackburn also was the announcer for the brand-new Seattle SuperSonics basketball team. Yet USC was still an 11-point favorite. All the pre-game excitement was reviewed not long ago on the OSU official website.[98]

Reagan and McCall sat in a press box area under an overhang so they would not get wet from the rain. Murphy was a friend of Hobie Wilson, the founder, owner, and radio personality of the conservative radio station in Eugene, KPMW. Wilson had arranged that Murphy could say hello to his hero, and to this day Murphy recalls his excitement when he and Reagan shook hands.

By now it was raining hard. Murphy recalled his annoyance at the playing conditions in those days before artificial turf. Murphy called it a "mud bowl."[99] Knowing about O.J.'s prior injuries, Reagan agreed with Murphy, and with a twinkle in his eye, turned to Goode, predicting, "O.J. will perk up, but this mud-bog is a poor excuse for a football field."[100]

On the Trojan's opening drive, Simpson rushed for forty yards but the team settled for a 36-yard field goal attempt which went wide right. The Trojans would never get closer than that for the rest of the game. Even though "Simpson threatened to run away with the game in the first half, racking up 131 yards on 18 carries," Simpson's efforts were to no avail.[101] One play that would become lore at OSU was when OJ was mowed down from behind during the second quarter. The Beavers scored a field goal that same quarter and the half ended 3-0. In the second half, there were a number of fumbles and penalties including a Simpson fumble on his last carry. The Juice scored no touchdowns despite his total 183 rushing yards. The game ended in a 3-0 Beaver triumph. That 1967 Oregon State Beaver team, having defeated Purdue and USC and tied UCLA, remains the only college football team in history to remain undefeated against three top two teams in one season. Your author was unable to interview Simpson, who in 2016 remains in prison.

As the game progressed, Reagan was "more silent" recalled Goode. A somber Reagan, no longer with his twinkle, commented to Goode afterwards, "I think the weather and the field conditions beat us rather than the players."[102] Reagan told the press he would contribute to a fund to purchase a new tarp and his office in Sacramento told OSU that Reagan's $1 check would be sent out shortly.[103] With the historic game over, Reagan reflected on the important political speech on world affairs he was about to deliver and the ongoing search to complete his Oregon campaign team.

The Price We Must Not Pay

Reagan stood in front of an Albany Elks Lodge audience of 1,000, each of whom had paid $5 to see him.[104] Reagan delivered a much more detailed and nuanced speech than he had earlier in Portland. His critical address was entitled, "The Price We Must Not Pay for Freedom."[105]

For his Veteran's Day topic, for the first time in his career, Reagan ignored any domestic theme and concentrated on foreign affairs head on for the full speech. During his May townhall debate with Kennedy, Reagan had addressed negotiating with communist countries and had proposed tearing down the Berlin Wall. But since then his comments on world affairs had been short pronouncements: a few sentences in speeches or in press conferences—give our soldiers the tools to win, or we should use our full resources.

But now Reagan would expand his previous focused comments about Vietnam and Laos into a sweeping, broad historic critique of both communism and how his Democratic opponents had mishandled foreign policy for the past six years. This address would clearly place candidate Reagan for the first time squarely in the center of America's role in world affairs—a topic both worthy and critically important for those seeking national office.

Reagan began his speech noting the theme of freedom from Eisenhower and Churchill, "We hear the cry for peace everywhere, but another word seems absent—no voices seem to be crying 'freedom.'"[106] The United States had an obligation to "not stop fighting until the security of our allies has been assured in freedom and independence."[107] With an eye towards both President Johnson and potential challenger former Kennedy administration advisor, Attorney-General, and now Senator Robert F. Kennedy, Reagan noted that the "fundamental error was made just six years ago" on Kennedy's watch, when the Soviet Union and Ho Chi Minh "decided to test, at places of their choosing, the nerve and stamina of a new administration."[108] Reiterating his earlier comments in Portland, Reagan assailed Kennedy for having failed the test when he had "decided not to stand in Laos."

Reagan then traced the military history of America in Vietnam during the prior six years. Unlike what would occur in the second decade of the 21st century when President Obama would tell America's enemies in Iraq and Afghanistan exactly when American troops would withdraw, Reagan in 1967 particularly was critical of the Johnson administration tactics of "being too late with too little, while tipping our hand to the enemy so he always knew in advance what we proposed."[109] He chastised Johnson asking, "Isn't it time that we either win this war or tell the American people why we can't? Isn't it time to recognize the great immorality of sending our neighbors' sons to die with the hope we can do so without angering the enemy too much?"[110]

Reagan expanded the scope of his remarks to well beyond Vietnam. He did not use the exact words "evil empire" to characterize the Soviet Union, but he did basically the same when he accused it of seeking world domination. The United States needed to find the courage to "fight" such an enemy. For Reagan, America could not lie passive. The solution could not lie with the United Nations but had to rest with the United States.[111]

At the time, the media did note that Reagan had determined that the Vietnam War "must be fought through to victory....We have been patient long enough and our patience wears thin. Stop the bombing (of North Vietnam), and we will only encourage the enemy to do his worst." His address on Vietnam and the Soviet Union was Reagan's "first major venture into the field of foreign policy."[112] Reagan had transformed completely from a domestic governor into a national candidate for the nation's highest office and had made his first full speech on foreign policy.

Subsequently, the only historian to discuss Reagan's 1967 Albany speech was Paul Kengor in 2006. Kengor cited Reagan's words as "revealing of his Cold War intentions" and felt his speech was one of a number of speeches showing Reagan's decades-long commitment to defeat communism.[113] Kengor also pointed out that Reagan did not use the word "fight" to mean a military attack upon the Soviet Union.[114] As discussed here earlier, Reagan had learned from Eisenhower the value of threats. Might Reagan have processed Thurmond's book and the *Life* article into realizing that he was becoming an advocate of an anti-ballistic missile shield? A decade and a half later, it would be

Reagan's threat to build his missile defense system coupled with his actual buildup of America's military and the American economy that would in large measure cause the collapse of the Soviet Union.

Reagan was not finished speaking about the handling of the Vietnam War. Indeed his critiques would become more frequent and detailed from then on. And from Albany onwards, he would continue speaking forthrightly about all aspects of American foreign policy. And his growing expertise in world affairs no longer would be confined to a few words, if reporters asked, at press conferences.

After the Veterans Day speech, Reagan, Reed and Nofziger met with Reagan's Oregon financial backers twice: a late-evening meeting in Albany on November 11 and a breakfast meeting in Salem on November 12.[115]

After Reagan returned to California, he sent Goode a letter to thank him for being his host and chauffeur. Reagan also helped Goode arrange for comedian Bob Hope to be the Grand Marshal and speaker for the 1968 Albany Veteran's Day Parade the following year. Perhaps by then Reagan could return as president-elect and join Hope and Goode. Meanwhile, Murphy decided to take action and see that vision—of a President-Elect Ronald Reagan—become a reality.

Reagan-Lindsay: The Nightmare Ticket

The following week back in Los Angeles, Reagan met New York City Mayor John Lindsay for the first time at Reagan's suite at the Biltmore Hotel. Lindsay had been another of the 1964 Republicans who had refused to endorse Goldwater and in 1966 had gone to California to dig up political dirt on Reagan as seen earlier. Historian Richard Reeves was present that day at the Reagan-Lindsay meeting and noted that Lindsay had been sent by Rockefeller to "size up" Reagan, especially after the *Time* cover the prior month and the speculation of a Rockefeller-Reagan ticket.[116] Reeves accompanied Lindsay to Reagan's room where the two men exchanged pleasantries before Reeves was dismissed.

It was a half-hour courtesy meeting of two major Republicans with eyes on the White House. Reagan and Lindsay discussed the pressures each had experienced when governing.

Earlier that day, Lindsay had seen his first "Lindsay for President" signs and was "euphoric." When Reagan later was asked what he thought of Lindsay as a possible Republican contender in 1968, Reagan told the press that "the Republican Party is rich in talent, and traditionally the Mayor of the largest city should be considered." It was just what others had said of Reagan as soon as he had taken office as governor some eleven months earlier. Reagan was to return the visit to meet with Lindsay in Manhattan in January.[117] Reagan did add that Lindsay should be considered "a possible nominee for President or Vice-President in 1968" adding that he did think Lindsay was "qualified and capable" to be president.

When Reagan was asked about a potential Reagan-Lindsay ticket, Reagan laughed saying "That's not a dream ticket, it's a nightmare."[118] Lindsay's biographer does not mention any of these Lindsay-Reagan interactions in the mid-to-late 1960's.[119]

Neither Reagan nor Lindsay knew that in a few months, Lindsay would return to Oregon to campaign actively for the presidency against Reagan.[120] Meanwhile a more dangerous political foe of Reagan's was busy.

Nixon Bats First and Reagan Second?

At this time, Nixon was worried because of "Reagan storming into the primaries."[121] After Bohemia Grove during the fall, Nixon had visited many Republican governors and party leaders in preparation for his formal announcement of the start of the campaign. A short article appeared in *Human Events* by Ralph de Toledano, which claimed that Reagan and Nixon had an agreement that Nixon would run in the New Hampshire and Wisconsin primaries unchallenged by Reagan. But if Nixon faltered, Reagan would run openly. Nixon staffer Patrick Buchanan showed the article to Nixon, who checked it off without any comment. To Buchanan, it was true: Reagan had agreed at some prior point that "Nixon bats first."[122]

Besides having hired Buchanan and Roger Ailes, Nixon hired former advertising executive Harry Treleaven Jr. to create campaign spot advertisements. Treleaven just had run the successful 1966 campaign for Congressman George Bush and later in 1968 would create the slogan, "Nixon's The One!"[123]

But besides being Nixon's new media consultant, Treleaven did another thing very well: he kept personal files filled with all Nixon campaign memoranda that had been used and discussed during all the secret Nixon campaign staff meetings. Treleaven later would give access to the files to author Joe McGinnis in preparation for the author's 1969 book *The Selling of the President 1968*.

One of the memos was a November 1967 analysis by Nixon staffer William Gavin, which attempted to review for Nixon the media aspects of Nixon's competitors. Gavin wrote about how to appeal to both younger and older generations of voters, and then disparagingly wrote of Reagan, "Reagan manages to appeal to both at the same time; he's the tv candidate, who instinctively reaches the aural-tactile; he speaks with a linear logic, and his quick simplicisms appeal to children old and young."

Nixon advisor Ray Price wrote a November 28, 1967 memo under the title, "Recommendations for General Strategy from Now through Wisconsin." He wrote that Reagan continued to exercise his attractions from the sidelines. "Reagan's strength derives from personal charisma, glamor (sic), but primarily the ideological fervor of the Right and the emotional distress of those who fear or resent the Negro, and who expect Reagan somehow to keep him 'in his place'— or at least to echo their own anger and frustration."[124]

Meanwhile Reagan was not staying in place. It was time for Reagan to reenter the world of missiles, space and the defense of the nation he loved. As he had revealed to the press in Seattle, he kept reading all he could about a missile defense shield. He found the place to learn in person more about orbiting weapons. The place was just around the corner from his home in Sacramento. And the individual personally to mentor Reagan was a world-renowned physicist.

Lawrence-Livermore

Less than two months after the *Life* cover story on America's ABM system and his meeting with Thurmond and likely discussion of Thurmond's forthcoming book with its chapter on missile defense, and less than two weeks after discussing missiles while in Seattle and then delivering his stirring first speech dedicated completely to world affairs, Reagan made an extended tour of the Lawrence-Livermore National Laboratory. Reagan became the first governor of California to take the time to visit the facilities. One of the laboratory's major projects was America's first anti-ballistic missile defense system.

Now Reagan could see first hand all the cutting-edge details of America's missile defense shield. This would not be a brief visit. There would *not* be a big press contingent for a publicity stunt. Reagan wanted to spend significant, thoughtful time to see first-hand what was being developed at the forefront of America's defense. He had spent two months reading all he could on the subject. Now he wanted to learn in-person all he could. He would ask probing questions.

Director Dr. Edwin Teller and his staff showed Reagan "all the complex projects. He listened carefully and interrupted maybe a dozen times. Every one of his questions was to the point. He clearly comprehended the technology. And there was no skimping on time. He came in the morning and stayed over lunch."[125]

Historian Peter Schweizer felt, "Reagan was an instant convert," and that Reagan "had caught the ABM bug."[126] Historian Lou Cannon commented, "It is certainly conceivable that this briefing planted in his mind the seeds of an alternative to mutually assured destruction."[127]

Yet these two eminent historians were off by two months. Reagan had told the Seattle press that he had been studying the subject in detail well before November's visit to Teller. It was Reagan's campaign discussions with Thurmond, the *Life* story, and Thurmond's autobiography with its section on an ABM defense, that all had converged to become the true trigger for Reagan's initial interest in the subject. Reagan's voracious pursuit for knowledge on the technology and its implications, which he first had revealed in public to the press in Seattle, culminated with his extended, personal visit with Teller. Clearly, presidential candidate Reagan had wanted, and received, up-to-date details on this most cutting edge part of America's defense, which of course the world would know the next generation version some fifteen years later as SDI—Reagan's Strategic Defense Initiative, or "Star Wars."

Plus Reagan was running for the presidency. His expertise on military strategy and tactics had expanded rapidly under Eisenhower's tutelage. In one year, should he be the nominee and then win the general election, Reagan would be commander-in-chief. Reagan was preparing to fill those shoes using whatever means he could on the campaign trail and out in California.

Taking this keen interest in the nation's defense, well beyond what might be considered typical for a governor, unless that governor were seeking higher office in the nation's capital, Reagan's late 1967 conversion to being an advocate for an anti-ballistic missile system would not be his last foray into this area during his 1968 campaign. History has shown clearly that his plan for America to be able successfully to defend itself from incoming missiles—envisioned by Reagan first during his 1968 campaign and of course to be expanded later as SDI during his presidency—would become a reality. Indeed by the second decade of the twenty-first century, missile defense would become "one of the biggest items in the Pentagon's annual budget."[128] Indeed in 2014, the Pentagon would announce that it had begun planning east coast missile defense bases to complement those on the west coast,[129] just as laser-based systems—the original SDI—were becoming a reality.[130]

As November ended, Reagan could look back on a busy month. With his return visit to Seattle, he had strengthened conservatives like Ken Rogstad. Don Hodel was working on finding someone he thought was even better than himself for the critical Oregon primary campaign leadership job. Peter Murphy wanted to help in mid Oregon. In Albany he had delivered his first major speech on world affairs. And to top it all off, Reagan vastly had expanded his initial knowledge of defense strategy and tactics by visiting Lawrence-Livermore and quickly had expanded his knowledge and understanding of the details and overall importance of the technological leadership America was developing for an anti-missile defense. Reagan was now a bona fide national candidate for the White House.

But in fact, all was not well with the campaign. Reed's demotion and the ascension of Clarke as a campaign director, who had no plans to "light the prairie fire" for Reagan, meant that in fact Reagan's campaign was leader-less. The disintegration of the campaign was discussed at a November 27 meeting, attended by Reagan, Reed, Clarke, White, Spencer, Smith and Nofziger.[131]

Reagan made one more major appearance in the press that November. The Thanksgiving 1967 issue of *National Review* featured an article of political reflection by editor William F. Buckley, Jr. Entitled *Reagan: A Relaxing View*, Buckley—who had just interviewed Reagan on *Firing Line* as we have seen—gave a tongue-in-cheek assessment of Reagan as governor. But he did begin the article telling his readers of his supposed nightmare: that in 1968 neither Nixon nor Romney do well and Reagan "rides his horse right into the front lawn of the White House…and proceeds to the throne."[132][133] After discussing how the Left feared Reagan, Buckley surmised that Reagan indeed "may become a part of American history."[134]

December and the holidays were approaching, as was the end of Reagan's first year in office. But before he could relax and ride into the White House, Reagan the conservative was to reenter the heart of enemy country: an elite, liberal Ivy League institution in New Haven, Connecticut.

Endnotes

1.   RRL, Tape 307
2.   Burt, Lyle, "Reagan Blasts Welfare Programs," *Seattle Times*, 11/11/1967, p. 15
3.   Broad, William J., "Reagan's Star Wars Bid: Many Ideas converging," *NYT*, 3/4/1985
4.   Buckley, William F. Jr., "Reagan: A Relaxing View," *National Review*, 11/28/67
5.   Reeves, Richard, "Lindsay Confers with Reagan As He Begins Los Angeles Visit," *NYT*, 11/17/67, p. 1
6.   Judis, p. 281
7.   RRL, Tape 289

8. RRL, Tape 289
9. Rusher, p. 204-205
10. RRL, Tape 289
11. *Time*, 10/20/67 p. 19
12. ibid
13. ibid
14. ibid
15. *Time*, 10/20/67, p. 20
16. *Time*, 10/20/67, p. 20
17. Perlstein, p. 217; White, p. 60
18. Perlstein, p. 216
19. *Time*, 10/20/67, p. 17
20. ibid
21. White, p. 60
22. See Illustrations
23. "Proceedings of the National Governors' Conference," Fifty-ninth Annual Meeting, National Governors' Conference, Chicago IL, 1967, p. 105
24. ibid, p. 107
25. ibid, p. 111
26. Reagan-Reed, 10/17/1967
27. http://www.youtube.com/watch?v=5Txhvm4rCGo
28. Cannon, p. 248-251
29. Pearson, Drew, Washington Merry-Go-Round, 10/30/67
30. Cannon, p. 252
31. Reed, pers comm, 6/2/2014
32. Johns, p. 181
33. RRL, Tape 292
34. Pearson, Drew, Washington Merry-Go Round, 11/18/67
35. Reagan-Reed, 10/25/1967
36. See Illustrations
37. Landon Lecture by Ronald Reagan, Oct 26, 1967 http://ome.ksu.edu/lectures/landon/trans/Reagan67.html
38. Kneeland, Douglas, "Confidence Noted at Parley of GOP," *NYT*, 10/30/67, p. 16
39. Hill, Gladwin, "Reagan's Speeches at Dinners Crafted for Cheers and Laughs," *NYT*, 10/29/67, p. 54
40. Pearson, Drew, Washington Merry-Go-Round, 10/30/67
41. Term from Glenn Reynolds of Instapundit.com
42. "The Republican Outlook," *NYT*, 10/30/67, p. 44
43. Riesel, Victor, "Reagan is Strongest" November, 1967 unidentified newspaper article, Henry A. Bubb Collection, University of Kansas
44. Reagan-Reed, 11/2/1967, Sacramento
45. Reagan-Reed, 11/9/1967, Sacramento residence
46. "Burt, Lyle, "Reagan Blasts Welfare Programs," *Seattle Times*, 11/11/67, p. 15
47. Kopelson, Gene 2015A
48. RRL, Tape 307
49. RRL, Tape 307
50. Burt, Lyle, "Reagan Blasts Welfare Programs," *Seattle Times*, 11/11/1967, p. 15
51. Kopelson, Gene, 2016
52. RRL, Tape 307
53. Goode, pers comm, 11/12/12
54. Goode, ibid
55. Hodel, pers comm. 10/7/12
56. ibid
57. RRL, Tape 307
58. Hughes, Harold, "GOP Governor Visits Portland," *The Oregonian*, 11/11/67, p. 1
59. RRL, Tape 305
60. RRL, Tape 305
61. RRL, Tape 305
62. RRL, Tape 305
63. RRL, Tape 305
64. Hughes op.cit.
65. Hughes, ibid
66. Hodel, pers comm. 10/7/12
67. Hodel, pers comm. 10/7/12
68. Hodel, pers comm. 10/7/12

69. RRL, Tape 306
70. Hughes, Harold, "Reagan Blames Viet War on Laos Failure," *The Oregonian*, 11/11/1967, p. 1
71. ibid
72. Hodel, pers comm. 8/25/12
73. Hodel, op.cit.
74. Hodel pers comm. 8/24/12
75. Hodel ibid
76. Hodel, op.cit.
77. Goode, int 8/16/12
78. Ingalls, Cathy, "Remembering Reagan's Visit," *Corvallis Gazette-Times*, 6/12/2004
79. Reed, *The Reagan Enigma*, p. 33-34
80. Ingalls, Cathy, "Remembering Reagan's Visit," *Corvallis Gazette-Times*, 6/12/2004
81. Goode, int op. cit.
82. See Illustrations; Paul Pritchard, pers int 7/14/2015
83. Peter Murphy, pers int 8/16/2012
84. Goode, op. cit.
85. Goode, int op. cit.
86. Brinkley, p. 162
87. Ingalls, op.cit.
88. Goode, pers int op.cit.
89. "Beavers After Another Giant," *Seattle Times*, 11/10/67, p. 66
90. ibid
91. See Illustrations
92. Goode, op.cit. int
93. Thomas, Ike's Bluff, p. 143-149
94. Boyarsky, p. 34-35
95. Boyarsky, p. 49
96. Boyarsky, p. 35
97. ibid
98. http://www.osubeavers.com/ViewArticle.dbml?DB_OEM_ID=30800&ATCLID=207868052
99. Murphy, pers int 8/16/2012
100. Goode, int 8/16/12
101. "Beaver Field Goal Tips Trojans, 3-0," *The Seattle Times*, 11/12/67, p. 77
102. Ingalls, op.cit.
103. http://www.osubeavers.com/ViewArticle.dbml?DB_OEM_ID=30800&ATCLID=207868052
104. "Bomb Halt Opposed by Reagan," *Spokesman-Review*, 11/12/1967, p. 6
105. Reagan, Ronald. "The PriceWe Must Not Pay for Freedom," 11/11/1967, courtesy Students for Reagan
106. ibid
107. ibid
108. ibid
109. ibid
110. ibid
111. Kengor, p. 36
112. "Bomb Halt Opposed by Reagan," *Spokesman-Review*, 11/12/1967, p. 6
113. Kengor, p. 35
114. Kengor, p. 35-36
115. Reagan-Reed, 11/11/1967-11/12/1967
116. Reeves, Richard, "My Years with Ronald Reagan" American Heritage magazine 571: 2006.
117. Blumenfield, Ralph, "Reagan Plans to return Lindsay's Visit," *LA Times*, 12/12/67
118. Reeves, Richard, "Lindsay Confers with Reagan As He Begins Los Angeles Visit" *NYT*, 11/17/67, p. 1
119. Cannato
120. Kopelson, Gene. 2014D
121. Buchanan, p. 149
122. Buchanan, p. 234-235
123. Diamond, p. 156
124. McGinnis, p. 187-190
125. Broad, William J, "Reagan's Star Wars Bid: Many Ideas Converging," *NYT*, 3/4/85
126. Schweizer, p. 74-89
127. Cannon, Pres Reagan, p. 276
128. Shala-Esa, "Exclusive: Pentagon to boost missile defense spending by over $4 billion" Reuters.com, 2/7/2014

129. Shalai-Esa, Andrea, "Pentagon to further study 4 possible East Coast missile defense sites," Reuters.com, 1/31/2014

130. Kirsch, Joshua, "Israel Wants to Use Lasers to Shoot Down Missiles," www.popularmechanicsonline.com, 2/18/2014

131. Reagan-Reed, 11/27/1967, Sacramento residence

132. Buckley, William F. Jr "Reagan: A Relaxing View," *National Review*, 11/28/67

133. one candidate for the presidency, an American cowboy named Americus Liberator, did have a platform to have his horse, Pard, graze on the White House lawn. Liberator is the only candidate to have run against Reagan three times and lost each time. Kopelson, Gene 2014B

134. ibid

CHAPTER 12: PROFESSOR REAGAN GOES TO YALE

"(when) it hurts them more by continuing to fight than they want to be hurt."

~ Ronald Reagan[1]

"But you have erected a wall through Berlin which is illegal," and we could deliver the wheat to you faster if "we didn't have to go through that wall."

~ Ronald Reagan[2]

"If the Republicans nominate Reagan, they'll hang The Bomb around his neck the way they hung it on Goldwater. What they don't know this time is that The Bomb is hanging around Johnson's neck."

~ California Democrat[3]

"There is a very real possibility ...that Governor Reagan will be the next Republican nominee for president."

~ Harry Reasoner[4]

Ronald Reagan was looking forward to his December, 1967 visit to the east coast for two main reasons. Up to that point, he had traveled on his campaign trips almost always on weekends while Nancy had stayed home with the family. This time things would be different: Nancy would be accompanying him. Secondly, for one week he would become a professor at Yale.

In July, Yale University had invited Reagan to New Haven to be a Chubb Fellow.[5] The unexpected invitation looked like a sure-fire bonanza. Little did Reagan foresee the controversies the visit would create or that Reagan's visit would remain legendary at Yale well into the 21st century.

William F. Buckley, Jr., a Yale graduate, first had explained the Chubb Fellowship to his readers in 1958 in a short article entitled, "What Hath Chubb Wrought?"[6] Buckley explained, "Chubbs are used to bring to Yale, specifically to Timothy Dwight College, men of practical experience in world affairs. The Chubb Fellows take up residence in Timothy Dwight for one week, during which period they are accessible to students and faculty who quiz them about practical affairs in the practical world." Buckley then proceeded to decry half-heartedly Yale's 1958 choice of Harry Truman.

Perhaps the last time Yale had experienced such publicity about a man who might occupy the Oval Office was when ex-Presidents Taft and Roosevelt came to the university to attend the funeral of a mutual friend, an expert on Chaucer, in April of 1915. At the time, speculation was rising that Roosevelt, returning to the fold of the Republican Party, likely once again would be their next presidential candidate.[7] Fifty-two years later for Reagan's visit, the speculation was ascending as well, but this time it would involve an expert on Dante

Reagan was no stranger to talking politics in New Haven. As we have seen, it was in New Haven where, a few weeks after declaring that he was embarking on a tour to assess if the people wanted him to run for governor, he had spoken as a Republican outsider to 3,500 cheering onlookers.[8] It was here where, for the first time to an audience outside of California, he had called for soldiers to be allowed to win in Vietnam and had received a standing ovation.[9]

By March, 1967, Paul Haerle had replaced Reed as appointments secretary as planned. Haerle as an undergraduate had been a member of Timothy Dwight College. At Yale, one of Haerle's friends was Charles Lichenstein who had helped found the Chubb Fellowship program. Haerle recalled working with Lichenstein in helping with the arrangements for Reagan's trip to New Haven.[10] Lichenstein, Research Director for the Republican National Committee in 1964-1965, would be appointed by President Reagan as an alternate delegate to the United Nations and would stir a controversy that would make headlines world-wide. After the fateful shooting down of Korean Airlines flight 007 by the Soviet Union and retaliatory landing rights issues would surface for Soviet officials to land in America, the Soviet delegate would wonder if the United Nations still should be in the United States. Lichenstein, furious, would answer famously that any member who felt that way could leave and that the US mission "will be down at the dockside waving you a fond farewell."

That Reagan was running for president was quite clear to Yale, its students, faculty and guests in 1967. Two months before Reagan's visit, the editor-in-chief of *The New Republic* had spoken on campus. Decrying the Vietnam War, his prediction for which candidate would become president in 1968 made the front page: "I personally have bet on Reagan."[11] The editor made a follow-up comment that if Reagan planned to end the war quickly, "The New Republic might have no choice but to support him...Even Reagan's conservatism could be tolerated." The editor ended by hoping such a Reagan's conservatism would moderate in the White House: "just as every President before him became a moderate, so would Reagan."[12]

A few days later, Buckley was interviewed by the *Yale Daily News* and was asked his personal choice for the 1968 Republican Party nominee. The distinguished alumnus gave his answer, the first sentence of which by then had become classic in conservative circles, "I'm for the guy who is the most conservative and who stands the best chance to win. Which means I'm for Nixon if he wins the primaries." And if Nixon doesn't win the primaries? Buckley had added "And if he doesn't win the primaries then of course it will necessarily be Reagan." Buckley proceeded to analyze the Miami Beach convention if the Vietnam War had worsened by then, predicting, "There is going to be a tremendous and thundering fight within the Republican Party with Nixon and Reagan leading one side and Dirksen leading the other."[13]

A more humorous element was introduced next when Hollywood entertainer and comedian Art Linkletter arrived in New Haven four days later to be guest-of-honor at a "house party" (the name of his television program) sponsored by the Conservative Party of the Yale Political Union. Linkletter had been active in California Republican politics and was asked about Reagan's candidacy. Linkletter told the Yale audience, "Ronnie has all the attributes needed for success: good looks and a good personality. But he lacks experience." Questions then revolved around Reagan and his Hollywood background. Linkletter reflected that actors still faced "a built-in prejudice against entertainers entering into the sober and astute field of politics."[14] Reagan had conquered that obstacle via the poll done in Seattle in June, 1966.

Next, Yale's Divinty School entered the fray. Yale Chaplain William S. Coffin Jr. had been urging resistance to the draft.[15] Three Yale Divinty School students had formed an anti-war group whose goal was to elect a dove to the presidency. But what would the group do if the 1968 election were between Johnson, viewed as a hawk, versus Reagan, even more of a hawk? It would put the Yale seminarians "in a real bind."[16]

So the Yale community and New Haven keenly were aware that not only Reagan was running for president but already had contemplated a Reagan versus Johnson general election. Some at

Yale then attempted to rescind Reagan's invitation. Professor Thomas G. Bergin was Sterling Professor of Romance Languages. Two years earlier he had published a popular handbook to commemorate the 700th anniversary of the birth of Dante. Bergin, lauded as a "witty raconteur," had been master at Timothy Dwight College for fifteen years.[17] Bergin now would be forced to defend his Reagan invitation to the entire Yale community.

Reagan Right, Parry Left

By late October, word filtered out that Reagan had been invited and the first formal protest was from a colleague at Timothy Dwight College. Adam Parry, Associate Professor of Classics and a fellow of Timothy Dwight College, wrote a letter to the *Yale Daily News* that was published on Halloween. In it he said he was "surprised that there has been so little protest over this invitation." Parry cited Reagan's views as a hawk on the Vietnam War claiming Reagan was "one of the most savage proponents of American belligerence." Parry asked "why should we invite him to Yale?" Parry invoked the 1968 presidential campaign of Reagan when he added, "We are aiding him (for the Chubb Fellowship will be a minor feather in his cap) in his current campaign for the presidency." Parry wondered, "What need has Yale University to be watering his burgeoning political career?" Parry complained of Reagan's advocacy for a "sharp escalation" which in Parry's view would "make more possible such crimes against humanity." He concluded by recommending, "Let's get rid of Reagan."[18] It was classic liberal intolerance.

Bergin began the defense of his having invited Reagan by noting several previous controversial political Chubb Fellows: Harry Truman and Lord Attlee. Bergin fought back explaining that the fellowship was not an honorary degree nor did it imply anyone nor the university shared the opinions of Governor Reagan. But because Reagan was a "very prominent public figure," it was very proper to have invited him. Bergin there were many at Yale looking forward to Reagan's visit: "Judging by the requests we have had for Governor Reagan's time I would say a very eager audience awaits him."[19]

An op-ed writer took a different tact noting, "A retraction would be a worse mistake than the invitation ever was." There would be a boomerang: headlines might run across the country that Yale had slighted Governor Reagan. Then Reagan might say "nuts to you" to "considerable popular applause." Reagan might come to speak any way in which case the applause for Reagan would be "thunderous."

Yale's claim to intellectual freedom would be destroyed. Indeed Yale would appear as a "crude censor and an impolite bully." The op-ed writer then thought it would be good for Reagan to come so that ivy-league Yale could help educate this "misguided southwestern politician." Emphasizing the 1968 Reagan campaign of which the Yale visit was clearly to be a part, "Perhaps the education of this hot presidential property could begin right here in New Haven."[20]

Parry fought back by attacking Reagan's campaign for the presidency, saying that Yale should not "award money and honor to anyone actively engaged in a campaign for high political office." Parry then made it personal. If he would be forced to "drink and dine and engage in friendly conversation" with Reagan, then his "conscience revolts at the possibility." He concluded his rebuttal by stating "I am not alone in considering him a man capable of doing enormous harm to our country and to the human race."[21]

Some rose to Reagan's defense and questioned the supposed intellectual freedom that Yale was supposed to enshrine. An incensed freshman wrote a letter in which the possibility of Reagan becoming president was addressed and how such reaction to him at Yale might then be perceived in 1968. The writer bemoaned Parry's "lack of tolerance and honesty." Reagan not only was governor of America's most populous state, but Reagan was "presently more popular than the President, and possibly (will be) our next President."[22]

William F. Buckley, Jr., who had not written about the Chubb Fellowship since 1958, had followed the controversy from afar but then entered the fray. Buckley nationalized the whole affair by writing a somewhat tongue-in-cheek column on November 16, 1967, which appeared for his nationally syndicated column "On the Right" in over 200 newspapers. Buckley revealed that Reagan would receive $500 for his fellowship. Buckley criticized those "who think of themselves as liberals but would sooner die than extend to conservatives such rights as conventional courtesy." Buckley then pictured Professor Bergin using Dante's words to lament the furor over his decision to invite Governor Reagan. Buckley ended by imagining a future when "a decade hence, ex-President Reagan, retired, might be able to say that he owed his office to the marginal nudge of Adam Parry of Yale University, who might then be persuaded to leave off his studies of the Golden Age of Greece, in order to report, at first hand, on the Golden Age of America, and his own glorious role in it."[23] [24]

Dressed for Political Success

Despite the months' long controversy that occupied most of the fall, at long last the visit of Governor Reagan approached. But one famous enterprising local New Haven business decided to capitalize on the arrival of presidential candidate Ronald Reagan. The Yale Co-op placed an advertisement for sport coats in the *Yale Daily News*, which addressed the Republican contest directly. "Neither Romney, Reagan, Nixon nor Rockefeller wear Deansgate Sport Coats...No wonder 3 of them are going to lose" ran the advertisement. The name order was not alphabetical yet Reagan was listed second.[25]

Just prior to Reagan's arrival, an anti-Reagan student-faculty petition was circulated in undergraduate and graduate dining halls. One student leader, who planned to present it personally to Reagan, was asked what he thought would be Reagan's reaction. He answered: "I hope it shocks the hell out of him!"[26] The actual protest petition was printed in its entirety as a letter to the editor. The student leader explained that the importance of Reagan's visit was "the fact that he is often mentioned as a national Republican candidate for 1968."[27] The student leader claimed his petition would garner 800 signatures, but his efforts spawned a second student group to counter with a more pro-Reagan petition, which asked students "to withhold judgment until Gov. Reagan has had a chance to convey his views personally to the student body."[28]

Arrival

The Reagan's arrived late Sunday evening December 3, 1967.[29] They went "directly to their suite at Timothy Dwight College" according to the Yale press release.[30] In actuality, they were guests of Professor and Mrs. Bergin in their home at Timothy Dwight College.

Nancy Reagan's unauthorized biographer Kitty Kelly related that one of Nancy's friends, a resident of New Haven, described the trip to Yale as, "really tough for the Reagan's."[31] Nancy had attended Smith College, some two hours north of New Haven, and used her time that December week to visit Northampton one day to see her old campus and room.[32]

Professor Bergin may have admonished Professor Parry to show civility towards Governor Reagan, but Mrs. Bergin did anything but that to Mrs. Reagan and the governor. Nancy's friend related that as soon as Nancy had arrived, she had invited Nancy to have lunch. Nancy declined because she was to be with Mrs. Bergin. Soon thereafter Nancy called back saying Mrs. Bergin "was so horrid to her," that she would have lunch after all. What had happened was that when Governor Reagan was picked up, Mrs. Bergin turned to Nancy saying, "Well Mrs. Movie Star, I'm sure you have a lot of plans on your own so I will see you later," and then proceeded to leave Nancy to fend for herself.

At a small gathering at the Bergin's, before other guests had arrived, Reagan asked for a vodka martini. Professor Bergin refused, saying with disdain, "At Yale we make our martinis with gin." Reagan claimed an allergy to gin and asked if in fact he could have what he had asked for. When Bergin refused again, the husband of Nancy's friend got so exasperated that he made the governor his preferred drink himself.[33]

But besides these examples of social rudeness given by the Bergin's to the Reagan's, there was also a political facet to how the Bergin's treated the Reagan's. When the Reagan's were first shown to their rooms, the professor's wife "had stacked all this filthy, virulent anti-Reagan reading material on their bed stands."[34]

Monday: Teacher

On his first full day at Yale, his morning consisted of a press conference and him teaching History 40A, "Education and Society in the U.S.," for which only students were permitted. A get-acquainted lunch was held with the Mott Wooley Council, a group of 20 Timothy Dwight undergraduate students, plus California students who were at Timothy Dwight. In the afternoon, Reagan was interviewed separately by the *Yale Daily News*, by WYBC radio, and by students from Hartford High School. The Reagan's had cocktails and dinner with 50 fellows of Timothy Dwight and their wives at the Bergin's home. Yale President Kingman Brewster attended as well.

At the morning's press conference, when Reagan was asked about his reaction to the petition that had been circulated, Reagan quipped, "I believe in civil rights, even for Governors."[35] Reagan questioned the methods and motives of the many intolerant Yale liberals who had attempted to block his visit. He said that a "liberal is the one most guilty...of charging that anyone who opposes the method is opposed to the goal." Reagan explained that liberals falsely accused conservatives of wanting "the poor to die in the street; you want the ill not to have a doctor." Reagan sought unity. He told the reporters that as Americans, he didn't want people to be labeled but wanted those on the left and those on the right to sit down together to find solutions to common problems.

Then the focus switched to his presidential campaign. When asked about George Wallace and racial discrimination, Reagan said he had been opposed to discrimination and bigotry his whole life and cited the example of his having editorialized against formal whites-only rules in the official baseball handbook while he was a sports announcer in Iowa.

The recent *Time* magazine cover of Rockefeller and Reagan was brought up and he was asked how he felt about being vice-president. He said to him it "seems strange" to think of a Rockefeller-Reagan ticket but he did not elaborate or mention Eisenhower's disdain for the pairing. He said emphatically that he wanted to be governor of California rather than vice-president. When asked if the Miami Beach convention were deadlocked and he was then asked to be the Republican nominee in 1968 what he would do, he answered by saying, "I'm not a candidate."[36]

Reagan's first day as a Yale Chubb Fellow made national news. The *New York Times* ran an article that showed a five-column wide photograph of Governor and Mrs. Reagan answering student questions at Timothy Dwight. The reporter quoted an undergraduate who had been in Reagan's morning class and said, "He handled himself beautifully. He's got much more depth than I thought." The reporter noted that besides secretaries leaning out windows to glimpse the former movie star, there "were students rushing up to shake his hand." Reagan's fee of $500, mentioned initially in Buckley's column, was being handed over to charity.

Nancy Reagan was asked how she liked Yale. Wisely not complaining about how she and Governor Reagan had been mistreated by the Bergin's, she told the reporter that when she had been a student at Smith she had visited Yale and added, "I never thought I would be spending the night in one of the buildings."[37]

Of course the first full day of the Reagan visit also made the front page of the *Yale Daily News*, which concentrated on Reagan's thoughts on foreign affairs. When Reagan was asked about negotiating with North Vietnam, his answer showed Eisenhower's mentoring in action, reflecting what Eisenhower had said to Goodpaster in June, 1966 just before the first Eisenhower-Reagan meeting. Reagan answered first that American had been too slow in upping its troop strength in Vietnam. Reagan then reminded his listeners that when America had negotiated in Korea during the Truman administration, the communists had used negotiations as a stalling tactic.[38] Reagan continued that the only way to negotiate now in Vietnam is for the U.S. to threaten escalated force until "it hurts them more by continuing to fight than they want to be hurt."[39]

Tuesday: *Ronald Reagan At Yale*

Just when Reagan was fitting into his role as visiting professor, suddenly he was called on to star in a movie. Film and television producer Austin Hoyt arrived on campus to film a documentary on Reagan's visit. *Ronald Reagan at Yale* is still legendary at Yale in the 21st century.

In the mid 1960s, public television was in its infancy. The Ford Foundation funded a small organization, the Public Broadcast Laboratory (PBL), which was based in Manhattan. PBL had four bureaus nationwide, including WGBH in Boston, and ran a two-hour Sunday evening broadcast seen nationwide by National Educational television affiliate stations.

Austin Hoyt, a Yale graduate, had won a UPI Tom Phillip's award for a documentary about LSD advocate Timothy Leary. By 1967 he was producer for WGBH and also was on-air personality for the Sunday evening PBL program. The Board of Directors of WGBH, officially the Lowell Institute Cooperative Broadcasting Institute, included Yale. Thus when Ronald Reagan was invited to be the Chubb Fellow, Yale contacted WGBH and invited the station to come to New Haven for two hours of private access to Reagan.

The planned film was described by Hoyt not as a documentary but rather as "Ronald Reagan Goes to School". Yale's supervisor for the film, David Walker, told the press that he did not think that the filming of Reagan would interfere with Reagan as a Chubb Fellow.[40]

Hoyt arrived in New Haven with a mobile unit and personally taped Reagan appearing before an economics class. Then with his full film crew, Hoyt filmed Reagan's public appearances starting on Tuesday December 5, 1967, when the Reagan's had breakfast with the Bergin and coffee with undergraduates.

For the remainder of Tuesday, Reagan taught an informal political science seminar and lunched with members of the Aurelian Society, an honor society. At the graduate school, Reagan met a group of political science graduate students. Reagan had dinner with students in the Timothy Dwight dining hall followed by an informal conversation with undergraduates.[41]

Wednesday: George Who?

Wednesday December 6, 1967, was the busiest day for Reagan. In the morning, he taught both Economics 42A "Fiscal Policy" and Political Science 15A, an introductory course. But while Reagan spoke, the young assistant professor, who was behind Reagan on stage, "chuckled sarcastically" and "shook his head meaningfully at his students." It was too much even for Bergin. That professor's rudeness, along with the hostility of some student questions, prompted Bergin to post a special notice to students and faculty reminding them to "comport themselves accordingly. Let us leave in his memory a healthy impression of Yale."[42]

Later Reagan was handed the final student protest petition which by then had garnered 928 signatures. Reagan was described as having "retained a cool composure, often flashing a broad smile." However Reagan was noted to have "showed some bitterness" when he told one group that he had known that some of the hostile student questions were read from a mimeographed list of 18 hostile questions that had been circulating on the Yale campus. The list was called "Questions for Governor Reagan."[43]

Yet Reagan did not duck from the students' hostilities. Indeed he answered student questions, hostile or not, for the entire week. As one independent journalist noted when radical students tried to make it difficult for him, Reagan "gave them better than he got." Reagan's skillful handling of an opponent was noted: "if there is anyone better in the United States at mollifying an opponent than Ronald Reagan, I'd like to know his name."[44] Reagan, who years before had negotiated so successfully as SAG president and then had skillfully won the debate with RFK seven months earlier, was honing the skills he would use to his utmost some nineteen years hence.

Reagan lunched at Mory's, then a private club, with members of the Political Science Department. In the afternoon he toured New Haven urban renewal projects with the mayor of New Haven.

That evening the Bergin's threw a cocktail party for eighty people and then had twenty-five couples for dinner. Governor Reagan's advance schedule did mention that Mr. and Mrs. William F. Buckley, Jr. would be attending,[45] but no other important political attendees had been brought to Reagan's attention beforehand.

As recalled later by Buckley, Reagan had shaken many, many hands at the cocktail party reception line. Reagan recognized the Buckley's immediately and gave them a warm greeting. But then a tall, thin gentleman approached Reagan, gave Reagan a big handshake, and then seemed quite disappointed that Reagan did not recognize him immediately. George H.W. Bush, Yale graduate and Reagan's future vice-president, had not been listed as a guest and indeed it took Reagan an extra second to recognize him.[46]

Thursday: On Camera

Reagan's last teaching duties at Yale consisted of him teaching a graduate seminar on "Political Parties and Interest Groups." Then the Reagan's prepared for Hoyt and some students. Having filmed various public appearances of Reagan on Tuesday as per the direction of Yale, Hoyt then was given his choice of the second venue. He chose a familiar setting: the intimate setting of the pool room of Hoyt's old Yale fraternity, Saint Anthony Hall. Hoyt invited six students: two liberals, two conservatives, and two drama students.

Reagan stood between two pool tables, and Nancy Reagan stood by the cue rack. The camera crew was positioned there too, which made for some elongated shots of Reagan, from under looking up. Hoyt recalled that although the drama students and conservative students were fairly quiet, the two liberal students "went after Reagan."[47] After one lively exchange about Vietnam that went on for several minutes without any breaks or re-takes, Nancy Reagan complained off-camera of filming such a long segment. One of the two liberal students was young Daniel Yergin, who would win the 1992 Pulitzer Prize for his analysis of global energy markets. [48]

Hoyt's film began with Reagan being asked about the presidency, and he answered anyone who wanted to be president was "out of his skull." Quickly the subject switched to Reagan's foreign policies. He was asked who had advised him about Vietnam, and Reagan answered that he had turned to leaders in industry such as aerospace manufacturers in California. When Reagan was challenged that such companies were war profiteers, he mirrored President Eisenhower's Farewell Address (when Ike had used the term "military-industrial complex") by answering that the "American-Industrial complex" did "far better in a peacetime economy than wartime." Reagan was challenged as to which scholars he had spoken about Vietnam. Possibly expecting Reagan to say he had never discussed the situation with any eastern elite Ivy League universities, the student was quieted when Reagan said he had spoken to scholars at Cal Tech, Stanford and also several state universities in California. Reagan then turned the tables on the badgering students by telling them that university professors had the obligation to present them with all points of view and not to indoctrinate their students. Reagan then suggested that the students should read some Republican literature to broaden their own perspectives.

Reagan's ideas of attempting to broaden the minds of university students in this manner, and warning professors not to indoctrinate, and students not to be passively indoctrinated, had been used by him in Nebraska the prior spring and at the Landon Lecture two months previously.

Nancy Reagan was seen at this point standing up against the cue rack with her arms folded seeming less than amused by the whole exchange. The film ended with Associate Chubb Fellow Professor Leonard Barkin commenting that Reagan "was a bigger hit than Goldwater."[49] Segments of the Reagan visit are available at youtube.[50]

Following the filming, Reagan attended another lunch at Mory's with officers of the Yale Political Union.

Reagan's finale was his speech at the Yale Law School auditorium to a capacity crowd of members of the Yale Political Union. It was planned as a fifteen minute opening address followed by questions from groups of three students who were chosen by the union's president.

Reagan began his speech by acknowledging the controversy his visit had elicited via the letters to the Yale newspaper. His tone, as Reagan always did to warm up an audience, was humorous when he remarked sarcastically "the *Yale Daily News* doesn't appear to be subsidized by the CIA" which drew laughs.

He admitted that he did not think he could convert anyone at Yale to his conservative approach to problems. He then addressed higher education by discussing information flow between government and universities. Reagan called his visit "the politician and the intellectual."

As the questions began, Reagan got to the major point. As he had delivered at Hiram Scott College and at the University of Kansas and during the earlier Hoyt filming, Reagan cautioned the Yale faculty and administrators that schools of higher learning had an obligation "to teach, not indoctrinate" by giving their students every point of view and letting the students make their own decision. Reagan's remark was greeted with warm applause.

This was not a press conference, but rather was a question-and-answer session with students. Nevertheless, foreign affairs quickly became the major focus. But this time Reagan was asked not about Vietnam but rather he was asked about a more general theme: coexistence with the communists. He answered by saying "we will coexist with the Soviet Union." But when it came time for more concessions, Reagan felt the West had done all the giving without receiving anything meaningful in return.

Reagan then returned to the same example he had used in his *Town Meeting of the World* debate with Kennedy six months earlier. He said that when the Soviet Union asked for wheat, we should say Yes. But then the United States should add, "But you have erected a wall through Berlin which is illegal," and we could deliver the wheat to you faster if **"we didn't have to go through that wall."** (author's emphasis)

As during the RFK debate, here was Reagan once again out his idea—for anyone listening carefully enough to discern—of ending the Cold War some twenty years before he would say "Mr. Gorbachev, tear down this wall!"

Reagan got his loudest applause twice: when he accused the Johnson administration of hiding facts about Vietnam from the American people, and again when saying any Republican candidate who was elected would plan to use whatever methods were necessary to end the war as quickly as possible.

At the end of the speech and questions, Reagan thanked Yale and the students telling them he would never forget his visit.[51] The audience "responded with a standing ovation."[52]

Reagan finished his Chubb Fellowship at Yale with a meeting with some fifteen law and graduate students who were members of the Young Republicans. Governor and Mrs. Reagan then departed to address the Republican State Central Committee in Hartford.

The final assessments of the Reagan visit to Yale appeared in the press shortly thereafter. One student who had been turned into a Reagan presidential supporter wrote, "Maybe I'm being snowed; it will be interesting to find out in about five years."[53] One alumnus, shocked at how the assistant professor had mocked Reagan and how hostile the students had been to their guest, suggested, "Yale University should hang its collective head in shame."[54] One smug op-ed writer ended with a sarcastic, elitist comment: "Now Reagan's acting career is ostensibly in the past."[55] Another called Reagan "frighteningly naïve" and his ideas "banal and occasionally inane."[56]

The *New York Times* managed to take a broader view noting that Reagan had sounded "to observers very much like a candidate running against Mr. Johnson." Clearly Reagan was "considered by many a leading contender for the Republican Presidential nomination," especially when he made an appeal to Democrats who might be "deeply disturbed...as we have moved from the New Frontier to the Great Society."[57]

A month later, Yale's alumni magazine, never mentioning all the domestic and foreign policy issues Reagan had discussed in classes, speeches, interviews, press conferences, and social gatherings for the week, assessed Reagan as a performer-candidate who had dazzled many of the students into passivity. Sheepishly the writers did admit, "A great many of the Governor's opinions are not extreme by Yale's or any other standards." Reagan's conservative views were now characterized as a "slice of moderation" which "did not go unnoticed."

The writers turned last to Reagan as presidential candidate in 1968, when they felt "a strong hunch that Reagan harbors a private urge to be President." If Nixon faltered in the spring primaries, Reagan would "do better with Nixon's disappointed backers than George Romney or Nelson Rockefeller. He would do better with the mass electorate than Barry Goldwater did." They proclaimed, "We are more convinced than ever of Ronald Reagan's capacity to become a big-time, perhaps even presidential performer." They could not help themselves from referring to Reagan as a mere actor.[58]

Ronald Reagan's trip to Yale as a Chubb Fellow had generated much controversy in New Haven during the months prior to his arrival and while he was there. Reagan faced some hostile students, perhaps more hostile but definitely rude faculty members, inconsiderate hosts, a petition, and mainly negative press reaction. Yet Reagan handled the students with grace, spent many hours patiently answering their questions and participated in radio interviews plus took part in the WGBH film being created while he and Nancy were there. He was a western governor running for president in the midst of an Ivy League elitist, liberal university. Reagan not only held his own, he triumphed.

Ronald Reagan Goes to Yale

Meanwhile film producer Austin Hoyt sent the take and film rushes to the New York City office of PBL. He and his editor went to work in the early hours of Friday morning, and early Sunday morning Hoyt himself recorded narration for the film. Hoyt's film *Ronald Reagan Goes to Yale* was thus completed in approximately forty-eight hours —record time. With almost no advance publicity, PBL aired the film to a nationwide television audience via the NET affiliate stations that Sunday evening.

Prior to seeing the Reagan film, the viewers of PBL on Sunday evening December 10, 1967 initially saw a joint concert of world-renowned violinist Yehudi Menuhin and sitar master Ravi Shankar. Then Beatle George Harrison was interviewed.[59]

PBL ended the evening with Hoyt's film. After watching Reagan interact with the students in the pool hall, one reviewer felt that "Reagan fielded their questions ably and engagingly." He concluded saying "the moral seems to be: if you are a conservative Republican, keep Reagan."[60] The *New York Post* noted that Reagan "kept his temper, answered in earnest and at the end complimented the students on their interest in world affairs."[61] A Seattle entertainment critic observed that as the students had attempted to trip Reagan, "one was reminded of Cool Hand Luke's comment: 'there's a failure of communication here.'"[62]

But out of the blue, suddenly Hoyt had competition from a major network. CBS was to show its own brand-new documentary on Reagan just two days later.

What About Ronald Reagan?

CBS showed a one-hour documentary tracing the life and political career of Governor Reagan on December 12, 1967. Host Harry Reasoner began in Reagan's birthplace of Tampico, IL and set the stage for the viewers when his narration began: "There is a very real possibility ...that Governor Reagan will be the next Republican nominee for president. This frightens some people but delights others," and added "a lot of people who didn't like Goldwater like Reagan." Reasoner added that Reagan "might go all the way," and he cited a CBS poll showing that Reagan's support for the nomination was stronger with delegates than with Republican rank and file members however. He said Reagan's strongest support was with Protestants, well-educated but low-income people and those in the South.[63]

Reasoner explained that Reagan had run for political office because he had accumulated a great concern about the direction America was going. Nancy Reagan, his closest advisor, explained that her husband did a lot of his thinking about issues out loud to get her opinions and insights. Of those who had known Reagan best over the years, Reagan was characterized as an "honest, decent fellow" and an "all American square." Reagan's brother thought that the one word to show his appeal as a candidate was his "credibility." One backer noted Reagan's "capacity to move people." One of the most perceptive and prescient comments was uttered as far back as 1941. Press agent Bob Michaels was interviewed by Reasoner, and he recalled being told by actor Alan Hale Sr. that in 1941 on a movie set when he was near Reagan, Hale became so exasperated at Reagan's continued mini-speeches on politics that Hale bellowed, "This guy and his speeches may bring him to the White House some day!"[64]

Reasoner noted that the phenomena of "Reagan has gone beyond state boundaries."[65] Reagan was seen campaigning earlier in 1967 in Omaha, Louisville, Houston, Milwaukee, Cincinnati, Concord, and Albany, Oregon. The latter film clip showed Reagan on horseback with Oregon Governor Tom McCall for the Veteran's Day Parade, which had occurred exactly one month earlier. Reagan was seen expounding on domestic and foreign affairs. Reasoner observed that Reagan was greeted "with the enthusiasm that goes with a winning candidate."[66] Reasoner presciently added, "Much of what he said has paved the way for him to run against LBJ," but if for some reason Johnson were not the candidate, Reagan was prepared to battle RFK.[67] Reagan then was seen attacking Kennedy. Reagan was "treated everywhere like a candidate," and clips of Reagan grass roots activists opening a Reagan campaign office in Concord N.H—accompanied by two young girls singing Reagan's praises on a guitar—were seen next.[68]

Finally, Reasoner did discuss the just-completed visit of Reagan to Yale. Reagan had created a favorable opinion for middle-of-the-road voters and showed everyone at Yale that he was a "serious and capable public figure."[69]

Reasoner ended by interviewing Reagan, praising his speech-making abilities and his abilities to handle the press. After explaining Reagan's continued denials of running for the Republican nomination but Reagan never denying that he would accept a draft at the convention, Reasoner ended the documentary on a more poignant note saying that for Ronald Reagan, 1968 was "probably his last chance for the White House."[70]

Reagan got the additional nationwide publicity with no input from his campaign staff in California and also at no cost to his campaign. Despite the television critics preferring the Hoyt documentary over the CBS special,[71] the clips of Reagan making campaign stops, especially riding on horseback for Veteran's Day in Albany Oregon with Governor McCall, are priceless as they likely are some of the only film clips of his presidential campaign for calendar year 1967. CBS had shown that indeed support for Reagan as president was growing nationally.

Reverberations

Ronald Reagan's visit had repercussions for Yale students and the conservative movement the following spring. "Irked by the exclusively liberal preachings of other campus publications," four Yale students published a brand-new conservative magazine in February, 1968. Entitled *Alternatives*, its first issue was sixteen pages and received "great moral support" from William F. Buckley, Jr. The new magazine was distributed to all Yale undergraduates. One of the editors was Anthony R. Dolan who would achieve fame under the Reagan administration. The first issue had an interview with Reagan.[72]

Long after the Reagan presidency, the memory of Reagan's Chubb Fellowship visit in December 1967 and the documentary *Ronald Reagan at Yale* live on well into the 21st century. Members of the class of 1968 watched the film at subsequent reunions including one in 2008. Film excerpts also have appeared on youtube and in short video clips. One historian, who had written one of the op-eds discussed earlier, reflected in 1997 upon the Reagan visit saying that when he and his fellow students had become "increasingly frustrated," Reagan "merely by maintaining his cool, easily got the better of us."[73] In 2011, an op-ed in the *Yale Daily News* recalled the hostility which Reagan had faced and how Reagan had overcome the obstacles presented to him by the rude Yale students and faculty. Reagan "created common ground out of which grew more serious discussion." The writer contrasted the civility with which Reagan taught the left "don't demean conservatives; they too have hearts." Yale had given Reagan a standing ovation "not because they agreed with his views, but because of how he expressed them. He injected intellectual diversity into the university, presenting himself not as an ideologue, but as a thinker. He transcended political difference to reach his audience with openness and good will."[74]

Reagan finished his Yale visit as the critical first year of Reagan's governorship was coming to an end. It also was the end of the first year of Reagan's first campaign for the presidency. The *New York Times* surprisingly complimented Reagan in an editorial entitled, "Reagan and the Press." The newspaper commented that "Reagan's knack for dealing with complex issues in a simplified, free-flowing manner is best shown at his press conferences."[75] No teleprompter was needed.

Meanwhile, presidential politics remained at the forefront. Rockefeller announced he was open for a draft. Romney still seemed to be Rockefeller's stalking horse. Plus Rockefeller did not want to face the ire of conservative Republicans due to his failure to have supported Goldwater in 1964. Some Republicans felt that a Rockefeller run actually would benefit the Reagan drive toward the presidency. It was felt that any effort by party moderates or liberals to stop Nixon "would simply help Gov. Ronald Reagan in supplanting Mr. Nixon."[76]

After leaving Yale, The Reagan's and Reed flew south to join the Republican governors meeting in Palm Beach.[77] Governor Rockefeller had financed a 250-page analysis of domestic programs for use in drafting a party platform for the convention. Rockefeller's wheeling and dealing "would make it more difficult for the Party to nominate Gov. Ronald Reagan of California."[78]

A Look Back at Year One

The *New York Times* ran its major analysis on Reagan's first year on December 10, 1967. Surprisingly, there were a few positive comments. The article's title was *Reagan Gives a Surprising Performance: Not Great, Not Brilliant, But...* Reagan "turned out to be a man of some strength who likes to make decisions, and makes them easily. In less than a year, he has become one of the three or four leading candidates for the Republican Presidential nomination in 1968...Reagan is not a politician like Nixon or Johnson. He's much more like Eisenhower and he has a good deal of the Kennedy glamour."[79] If Reagan and Eisenhower read this section, likely each smiled.

Even California Speaker of the House Democrat Jesse Unruh, Reagan's likely opponent should Reagan run for reelection in 1970, when reflecting upon Reagan's success at lessening the size and scope of government, had told reporters that Reagan "would be the ideal Republican candidate next year."[80] The reporter then explained that it was Reagan's success at working with a legislature controlled by the opposition, especially on the issue of taxation, which explained why "he remains so popular in California as well as why he could win the Republican nomination next November."[81]

After reviewing a number of Reagan's first-year accomplishments, especially those in the area of streamlining government, cutting out governmental inefficiencies and lessening its size, the reporter— referencing Spencer's earlier comment to Nixon—felt, "All of these state efforts may be overshadowed by a campaign for the Republican nomination. 'He has stars in his eyes,' said a friend with whom Reagan has talked about the Presidential possibilities."[82] A group of close friends told Reagan to concentrate on doing a good job as governor and "not to campaign actively for the Presidential nomination but leave the door open. And he has followed just that advice."[83]

It did not escape the reporter's notice that, as we have seen, Reagan during 1967, despite telling reporters that he was not a candidate, "made speeches in such Presidential primary states as Wisconsin and Oregon and in such dependably conservative states as Texas and South Carolina."[84] Despite having missed Reagan's speeches in the primary state of Nebraska, the reporter from the nation's newspaper of record did end up describing the first part of the basic strategy of Reagan's 1968 drive towards the White House.

Reagan had never stated that he would never accept the nomination. If front-runner Nixon faltered, "no one doubts that his supporters would take Reagan as a second choice, and there are already indications that Reagan may be the first choice of some nominal Nixon backers."[85] And here was the second part of the strategy.

But could a Republican nominee named Reagan defeat incumbent President Lyndon Johnson? Prior successful Republican newcomers who attained the presidency were Ulysses S. Grant and Dwight D. Eisenhower. And Eisenhower was mentoring Reagan all along. In 1966, Reagan successfully had turned Pat Brown's charges of Reagan's inexperience into a battle of the citizen-politician versus the professional politician, and Brown had been clobbered. If Reagan were to face Johnson, "a man whose name is synonymous with the word 'politician,' once again Reagan may find himself to be the right man in the right position at the right time."[86] Reagan's continuing ideas to lessen the size of government, first in California and then applied to the country as a whole, were seen as "a philosophy to which millions of Americans subscribe and for which a majority might vote in 1968."[87]

The same issue of the newspaper had another review of the Republican race. Reporter Tom Wicker warned Democrats not to fall in 1968 into the "Pat Brown Syndrome" in which Brown had thought Reagan would be "the easiest opponent to defeat" in 1966 but instead ending up losing to Reagan in a landslide.[88] President Johnson and "most of his political advisers" still suffered from the Pat Brown Syndrome, thought Wicker, as one of the latter said, "Reagan would be the weakest candidate they would put up against Johnson."[89] Wicker reported that shortly after the Reagan visit to Yale was over, a professional organizer had been hired to "work up a Reagan-for-President campaign."[90] Little did Wicker know that Reagan's campaign had been underway for a year.

Wicker warned the Democrats that Reagan was different than other candidates. Reagan had "a nearly irresistible parlay going for him" and he could not be judged "by the old standards. He makes them obsolete."[91] He was seen as "the ultimate political product of the television tube."[92] But just as Reagan had explained this crucial point many times to reporters over the course of his 1968 campaign, his use of television made his impressions onto the electorate that much more personal. Television had wiped out any phoniness because as Reagan explained, "people can see for themselves and make up their own minds now" instead of listening to Party ward captains or Party officials.[93] Reagan's greatest asset was that he was "not trying to fool anybody; he is simply saying what he thinks, which is what a lot of other Americans think."[94] Reagan was seen as "an ordinary fellow- not a politician," which suited Reagan just fine.

Wicker ended with another warning to Johnson by alluding to Reagan's hawkish policies on Vietnam and his threats to use nuclear weapons. Wicker quoted a California Democrat who said that Johnson's advisers told him, "If the Republicans nominate Reagan, they'll hang The Bomb around his neck the way they hung it on Goldwater. What they don't know this time is that The Bomb is hanging around Johnson's neck."[95]

At his year-end press conference, Reagan looked ahead to the 1968 race and thought an important issue would be the "slackening of moral standards" as evidenced by the rise in crime across the country. Reagan gave thanks to those advocating for him as a presidential candidate but reiterated that he was not a candidate.[96]

Seabee Reagan

Reagan continued to show how important Vietnam and foreign and defense policies were to his heart. As governor, of course domestic issues remained number one. But as candidate for the presidency, he had visited the Lawrence-Livermore National Laboratory a few weeks before the Yale visit, and as we have seen he had become an advocate of an anti-missile defense shield.

Vietnam remained much in the news. As we will see, former President Eisenhower took the private advice he had given Reagan and now publicly was advocating specific military tactics to help win the war. All the while Reagan continued to discuss Vietnam almost every day at press conferences.

After returning to California from Yale and Palm Beach, Reagan participated in a special ceremony in front of the State Capitol in Sacramento. On December 13 he received the state flag, which had flown over the Navy Seabee Camp Barnes in Dong Ha, Vietnam. Governor Reagan beamed with pride as he was made an honorary Seabee by the unit's Commanding Officer.[97] [98]

Reagan had found something new that let him in some small way act in the area of world affairs. A month earlier in Albany, Oregon, quietly and without press coverage, Governor and Mrs. Reagan spent many hours "comforting wounded Vietnam war veterans." Afterwards Nancy wrote letters, made telephone calls and spent time with individual soldiers. They did these deeds "without fanfare or a desire for recognition" and never permitted the press to cover the events.[99]

The Seabee ceremony was a new way for Reagan to insert himself into the arena of world affairs, albeit far away from the nation's capital. Reagan's foreign policy *bona fides* would ascend even further in the new year.

On December 20, Reagan met with Reed and Clarke to coordinate campaign travel for early 1968.[100] But as 1967 ended, although Reagan still spoke to audiences as what seemed to be a candidate for the presidency, his campaign had developed a split personality. The actual campaign, theoretically run now by William French Smith, was in fact leaderless and sailing without a rudder. Reagan's abilities giving speeches and at press conferences during campaign stops were almost flawless. But nobody from Reagan's original campaign team was out in the country "fanning the prairie fire." But across the country, grass roots activists, especially in the three opt-out states, were continuing their hard work or were just starting to get into high gear. Reagan was continuing his attacks on the Johnson administration, and Eisenhower was continuing to coach Reagan behind the scenes. But Reagan's nemesis, Robert F. Kennedy, soon would send shock waves into the Reagan campaign, which would change everything.

Endnotes

1. Gray, Joe, "Reagan Hits Dissent, Welfare," *Yale Daily News*, 12/5/67, p. 14
2. RRL, Tape 313
3. Wicker, Tom, "In the Nation," *NYT*, 12/10/67, p. 257
4. *What About Ronald Reagan?*, CBS 12/12/1967, courtesy Ronald Reagan Presidential Library
5. "Gov. Reagan to Visit With Yale Students," *NYT*, 7/23/67, p. 46
6. National Review, 3/8/58, p. 223
7. After many years of bitter political wrestling, including being opponents in the 1912 election resulting in the election of Woodrow Wilson, at Yale TR and Taft saw each other for the first time and began their reconciliation. See Thompson, J. Lee. *Never Call Retreat*. New York: Palgrave Macmillan, 2013, p. 78
8. Barclay, Tony, "Reagan Hailed by Arena Crowd, Warns of 'Government Tyranny,'" *Yale Daily News*, 9/29/65, p. 1
9. ibid, p. 3
10. Haerle, pers int 11/22/12
11. Moore, Paul, "Editor Mocks LBJ," *Yale Daily News*, 10/18/67, p. 1
12. Leslie, Jacques, ""Normalcy or Apocalypse?," *Yale Daily News*, 10/19/67, p. 2
13. *Yale Daily News*, 10/20/67, p. 3
14. Newman, Scott, "Linkletter Details "Darndest Things,'" *Yale Daily News*, 10/24/67, p. 3

15. Hundt, Reed, "Brewster Raps, Defends Coffin," *Yale Daily News*, 10/30/67, p. 1
16. Kannar, George, "Seminarians Form New Peace Group," *Yale Daily News*, 10/30/67, p. 1
17. NYT obituary, 11/3/87
18. Parry, Adam, "Reagan's Visit," *Yale Daily News*, 10/31/67
19. Bergin, Timothy, "Bergin vs. Parry." *Yale Daily News*, 11/7/67, p. 2
20. Macgillis, Donald, "Is Ronald Reagan Welcome at Yale?," *Yale Daily News*, 11/7/67, p. 2
21. Parry, Adam, "Parry Replies," *Yale Daily News*, 11/7/67, p. 2-3
22. Koford, Kenneth, "Intolerance," *Yale Daily News*, 11/13/67, p. 2
23. "Buckley Column Lampoons T.D.-Reagan Controversy," *Yale Daily News*, 11/15/67, p. 3
24. Buckley, William F Jr., "The Troubled Conscience of Adam Parry," *On The Right*, 11/16/67
25. Yale Daily News, 11/9/67, p. 7
26. "Reagan faces Protest Letter," *Yale Daily News*, 12/1/67, p. 1
27. Hanson, Robert, "Reagan Statement," *Yale Daily News*, 12/1/67, p. 2
28. Gray, Joe, "Reagan Visit Starts Amidst Controversy," *Yale Daily News*, 12/4/67, p.1
29. Gray ibid.
30. *Yale News Bureau*, #160, 11/22/67
31. Kelly, p. 168
32. ibid, p. 167
33. ibid, p. 169
34. ibid, p. 168-169
35. Borders, William, "Reagan in New Role: Yale Lecturer in History," *New York Times*, 12/5/67, p. 49
36. RRL, Tape 313
37. Borders, William, "Reagan in New Role: Yale Lecturer in History," *New York Times*, 12/5/67, p. 49
38. RRL, Tape 313
39. Gray, Joe, "Reagan Hits Dissent, Welfare," *Yale Daily News*, 12/5/67, p. 14
40. Gray, Joe, "Television's PBL to Film Reagan," *Yale Daily News*, 11/30/67, p. 1
41. Office of the Governor, 11/29/67 Revision #3, Hoover archives
42. Borders, William, "Reagan Keeps Smiling at Yale Despite Sneers and Hostile Air," *NYT*, 12/7/67, p. 30
43. Borders, William, "Reagan Keeps Smiling at Yale Despite Sneers and Hostile Air," *NYT*, 12/7/67, p. 30
44. Chamberlain, John, "Reagan in the Ivy League," *Evening Independent*, 12/14/67, p. 11
45. Office of the Governor, op.cit.
46. Buckley, William F, "The Reagan I Knew," p. 222-223
47. Hoyt, pers int. 11/9/2012
48. Through his agent, Yergin declined to be interviewed by this author. Marn, Jeff, pers comm. 11/20/12
49. Austin Hoyt, dvd of film, pers comm.
50. https://youtube/cyMt_X6vQGU
51. RRL, Tape 313
52. Gray, Joe, "Reagan Decries Lack of Political Dialogue," *Yale Daily News*, 12/8/67, p. 1
53. Gray, Joe, "Reagan Scored by Students," *Yale Daily News*, 12/7/67, p. 1
54. Harvey S. Bennett '40 letter to President Kingman Brewster, 12/20/67, Brewster files, Yale University Archives
55. Lander, Ed, "Of Acting," *Yale Daily News*, 12/7/67, p. 2
56. Roe, David, "Ronald Reagan: The Politics," *Yale Daily News*, 12/7/67, p. 2
57. "The Great Society Assailed by Reagan," *NYT*, 12/8/67, p. 34
58. Rae, Douglas W., and Lupsha, Peter A., "Politics As Theater: Ronald Reagan at Yale," *Yale Alumni Magazine*, January 1968, p. 41-43
59. Newton, Dwight, "It's What's Happening," *San Francisco Examiner*, 12/11/67
60. Newton, ibid
61. *New York Post*, 12/11/67
62. Voorhees, John, "Travels with Charlie," *Seattle Post-Intelligencer*, 12/12/67, p. 26
63. *What About Ronald Reagan?*, CBS 12/12/67, courtesy Ronald Reagan Presidential Library
64. ibid
65. ibid
66. ibid
67. ibid
68. ibid
69. ibid
70. ibid
71. Lee, Mary Ann, "TV News and Views," *Memphis Press Scimitar*, 12/13/67, p. 3

72. Raymont, Henry, "A Magazine for Conservatives Appears at Yale," *NYT*, 3/6/68 p.41L; "Magazine Formed," *Yale Daily News*, 2/20/68, p. 1
73. Leslie, Jacques, "The Yale of My Day: Viet Nam on Our Mind," *Yale Alumni Magazine*, 3/97
74. Zelinsky, Nathaniel, ""Remember the Great Communicator," *Yale Daily News*, 2/7/11, p. 2
75. "Reagan and the Press," *NYT*, 12/10/67, p. 348
76. Weaver, Warren, "Rockefeller refuses to Rule Out His Acceptance of a Draft in '68," *NYT*, 12/9/67, p. 1
77. Reagan-Reed, 12/7/1967-12/8/1967
78. Weaver, Warren Jr. "GOP Governors, Balked on Nominee, Push Liberal Issues," NYT, 12/10/67, p. 1
79. Duscha, Julius, "Reagan Gives a Surprising Performance: Not Great, Not Brilliant, But…" *NYT*, 12/10/67, p. 296
80. ibid
81. ibid
82. ibid
83. ibid
84. ibid
85. ibid
86. ibid
87. ibid
88. Wicker, Tom, "In the Nation," *NYT*, 12/10/67, p. 257
89. ibid
90. ibid
91. ibid
92. ibid
93. ibid
94. ibid
95. ibid
96. "Morality is Big Issue in 1968, Reagan Says," *Milwaukee Sentinel*, 12/28/1967 part 1, p. 5
97. See Illustrations
98. www.mcb11.com
99. Curtis Patrick, vol 1, p. 303
100. Reagan-Reed, 12/20/1967, Sacramento office

PART THREE

1968

CHAPTER 13: COACH EISENHOWER, PART TWO

"The best known Republican hawk."
                                    ~ John Chamberlain[1]

"Never maltreat the enemy by halves. Once the battle is joined, let 'em have it."
                                    ~ Winston Churchill[2]

"I would not necessarily select the man I thought best qualified to be president...I would like to see the convention pick a man who can win over Johnson in November."
                                    ~ Dwight Eisenhower[3]

The President and the Governor

New York Times reporter Duscha's 1967 year-end review of Reagan's first term had made a number of comparisons between the Reagan and his administration in Sacramento in the mid 1960s and Eisenhower and his in the nation's capital in the 1950s. Not surprisingly from the liberal newspaper, the tone of the comparisons was that, of course, both Republican administrations' policies were bad. Yet from Reagan's and Eisenhower's points of view, the analysis may indeed have further confirmed in both the minds of Reagan and Eisenhower that the old coach was succeeding in his mentoring of his protégé. The first year of the Reagan administration not only was a success, but in large measure it had been a success because Reagan had modeled his administration on that of Eisenhower.

Duscha commented[4] that like General Eisenhower, Reagan had a "view of government which holds that the best government is the least government." When choosing members of the Cabinet and other high governmental appointments, "Reagan also has the same faith Eisenhower had in the judgment of businessmen." Of course both Eisenhower and Reagan chose to appoint those businessmen because of their expertise in their own field of specialty. When commenting upon Reagan's use of mini-memos to summarize and simplify complex topics, the reporter felt, "Again, the Eisenhower

Administration comes to mind." Of course the elite, liberal reporter clearly was disdainful of both Eisenhower and Reagan, but many commentators over time would note quite clearly how adept Reagan was in simplifying complex topics to explain them easily to the public. Finally, it was noted that amongst top-level Reagan appointees for his administration in Sacramento were two prominent Eisenhower appointees: Agriculture Department Director Earl Coke, who had been an Assistant Secretary of Agriculture for Eisenhower; and State Director of Industrial Relations Albert C. Beeson, who had been on Eisenhower's National Labor Relations Board. And U.S. Treasurer Ivy Baker Priest, who had performed her job in the Eisenhower administration, recently had moved to California, where she did the same job at the state level. Later as Ivy Baker Priest Stevens, she would place the name of Ronald Reagan for nomination for president of the United States in Miami Beach. Reagan's appointing to office previous members of the Eisenhower administration, begun when he was governor, would continue when he would become president. After all, if his mentor Ike thought highly enough of an individual to appoint him or her to office in the 1950s, should not Reagan follow through in the 1960s and 1970s and then do the same later in the 1980s?

Eisenhower Continues Advising Reagan On Foreign Affairs

The war in Vietnam had occupied increasing attention from Eisenhower in late 1967, and Reagan's campaign speeches and press conferences during that same period clearly had demonstrated the continued direct influence of Eisenhower. In 1968, foreign affairs would continue as an increasing portion of Reagan's campaign speeches and would culminate in a series of detailed attacks on all aspects of Kennedy-Johnson foreign policies by the early summer of 1968 in Cleveland and Amarillo. Indeed historian Andrew Johns feels that not only for Eisenhower and Reagan, but for all Republicans running in 1968, "The candidates' positions on the Vietnam War proved to be pivotal."[5]

It had been at Hiram Scott College the prior June when Reagan had expanded his view of how to deal with world trouble spots by reminding his audience to recall President Eisenhower's stern warning to Communist China, that America's commitment to freedom was strong and ever watchful. Reagan reviewed that when Communist China had threatened Taiwan's offshore islands, Eisenhower's words, "They'll have to climb over the Seventh Fleet!" had kept the communists at bay.[6] Presidential candidate Reagan would want the nation to understand that as president, Reagan would continue the same firm and assured stances against communist expansionism as had Ike.

For Vietnam, the main foreign policy issue before the public in the mid and late 1960s, Reagan consistently since 1965 had called for the United States, since it was sending young men possibly to die in battle, to give them the full abilities to win the war. As discussed, President Eisenhower had ended the Korean War fighting when he had said he would reassess all military options, one of which was the threat to use nuclear weapons. During his presidential campaign, Reagan said the same threat should have been used against the North Vietnamese and he had been attacked constantly by the press and his critics for those comments. At the same time, Eisenhower had been one of the few Republicans who had voiced agreement with the Johnson Administration over the war but like Reagan, Eisenhower's criticism of the Johnson policies was that the war was not being fought to win.

Eisenhower had reiterated his threat to use atomic weapons, when he told the press, "I would not automatically preclude anything."[7] As discussed, it had been at a mid September Sacramento news conference when Reagan, having been asked about the use of limited nuclear weapons, had answered, "I still repeat what President Eisenhower said some time ago, that perhaps one of our great mistakes, however, was in assuring the enemy in advance of our intention not to use them—that the enemy should still be frightened that we might."[8]

Historian Nina Tannenwald has reviewed in detail Eisenhower's thoughts and policy recommendations on using nuclear weapons in Vietnam and why he did not believe the Soviets or Chinese would retaliate.[9] Eisenhower soon would tell the public the same thing.

Reagan continued what he had learned from his mentor's sagacity when in public Reagan also had favored a "surge" in American troop escalation, rather than the gradual escalation that the Johnson administration had done. The term surge would not come into common parlance for this type of escalation until the Iraq War in the early 21st century. But in September, 1967, Reagan had stated, "If the escalation that the United States had undertaken during the last two or three years had occurred suddenly…the war might have ended, because doing it all at once might have brought the enemy to the bargaining table."[10] Clearly, Reagan was adding to his foreign policy credentials after his June, 1966 and March, 1967 meetings with Eisenhower. As we will see, Reagan was about to use the actual term "surge" in early 1968. As discussed, Reagan and Eisenhower previously had reviewed those specific military tactics—the sudden escalation or surge—which President Johnson had failed to follow.

During the early fall of 1967, Eisenhower had reached the conclusion that neither China nor the Soviet Union would pressure North Vietnam to settle the war at the negotiating table because the conflict already "was causing the United States so much distress."[11] He then urged his contacts with the American military to strike enemy sanctuaries: "hot pursuit," in Laos and Cambodia.[12] Whenever there was discussion of a halt in the bombing, Eisenhower bristled, asking, "Who wants to stop the bombing? The communists do because it is hurting them."[13]

The only Republican presidential candidate who agreed with Eisenhower's positions was Ronald Reagan, who in November in Oregon and Washington State again had pushed for a sudden troop escalation and warned of the communists' use of negotiations as a stalling tactic. As we have seen, it was during this time that Reagan had visited the Lawrence-Livermore National Laboratory to learn more about technological advances for America's defense including the anti-ballistic missile system, he had visited veterans in Oregon and he had been made an honorary Seabee by naval officers returning from Vietnam.

Ike's Republican Hawk

The issue of electability, as we have seen earlier, was of paramount importance to Eisenhower; and Reagan had won a year earlier with almost a million votes whereas Nixon's most recent track record was his lost elections in 1960 and 1962. Historian Andrew Johns has reviewed the discussions Eisenhower and Nixon had about Vietnam during this time.

Eisenhower had stayed neutral during the 1964 primary and he acknowledged in December that "his 1964 neutrality pledge may have been a mistake." Looking ahead to the race for the presidency and the 1968 Miami Beach convention, it was reported that Eisenhower did not expect to endorse any one candidate prior to the Republican convention but hoped to attend if his health permitted. Who was Ike favoring? An analysis of where Eisenhower's preference for president appeared, in which Eisenhower supposedly had sent a "golf buddy" to represent him to chat with a reporter. In reality, it might have been just Eisenhower himself wanting to convey his controversial opinion without attaching his name.

The Eisenhower Engima

When discussing Nixon, Eisenhower had said, "Even if I had the power to name the next Republican Presidential nominee, I would not necessarily select the man I thought best qualified to be president...I would like to see the convention pick a man who can win over Johnson in November." By his comments, Eisenhower had "knocked Nixon down." Eisenhower was saying that he thought Nixon was the best man for the job but could not win.

Of Romney, a dove on Vietnam and whose post-brainwashing poll numbers were plummeting, Eisenhower had said that he had sounded like a "man in a panic." Of Rockefeller, also a dove, Eisenhower had said he retained an open mind, yet Rockefeller's refusal to endorse nominee Goldwater in 1964 had remained a sore point. For Eisenhower, staying loyal to the party was critically important as he himself, no fan of Goldwater, had endorsed his party's 1964 standard-bearer. Plus Ike had made the film with Goldwater, which had been replaced by Reagan's *A Time for Choosing*.[14]

And what of rumors of a Rockefeller-Reagan ticket? Eisenhower then added that it "would be a mistake for the Republican Party to put Gov. Ronald Reagan of California on a Republican Presidential ticket headed by Governor Rockefeller," because "such a ticket would have to be regarded as a marriage of convenience."[15]

The reporter next asked Eisenhower's "golf buddy" about Reagan as nominee. There was no direct answer. But indirectly, "by inference or implication," Eisenhower warned, "If a Republican or Democrat suggests that we pull out of Vietnam, and turn our backs on the more than 13,000 Americans who died there in the cause of freedom, they will have to contend with me."

The reporter questioned if Reagan was "in" with these comments. The "golf buddy" did not answer, but the reporter answered his own query with, "You might say 'Yes.'" In the face of what the reporter felt was growing dovish leanings in America, Eisenhower's preferences still were that the nominee "must be....hawkish enough to stick to Saigon even if it means a Republican defeat." And of all the Republican candidates at that time—Nixon, Romney, Percy,

Rockefeller—Reagan was described clearly as "the best known Republican hawk."[16]

Patrick Buchanan acknowledges that Eisenhower clearly had thought of Nixon as a loser but did not know why Nixon had been slighted.[17] One answer from the above is that for Eisenhower, Reagan fit the bill as Nixon never could.

The reporter never pushed the "golf buddy" further asking him to be clear and specific as to whether candidate Reagan was or was not "in" as the choice for the nomination. But it is not unreasonable to assume that Eisenhower was using the same "hidden hand" techniques of obfuscation, which the general had used so well in the 1950s as described by historian Fred Greenstein, to keep his true feelings purposefully said but unsaid—plausible deniability.

It is reasonable to assume, and your author believes, that Dwight Eisenhower, through the use of the fiction of a "golf buddy," was telling the world that his true preference for 1968 was to see a Republican winner, Ronald Reagan, become the nominee rather than the man most qualified, Nixon, and risk another loss as in 1960. Could Eisenhower have declared this preference in public at the time, with his former vice-president still the avowed favorite and with Ike's grand-son dating Nixon's daughter? Of course not.

Ike's Vietnam Committee

Eisenhower had kept current on Vietnam as the war was deteriorating. In late October, 1967, Eisenhower, former President Truman, and General of the Army Omar Bradley had formed a non-partisan working group called the Citizens Committee for Peace with Freedom in Vietnam. The committee issued an initial report, which Eisenhower had edited "in longhand," that supported the Johnson policy goals. The committee viewed itself as representing the "great silent center, the understanding, independent and responsible men and women who have consistently opposed rewarding international aggression from Adolf Hitler to Mao Tse-Tung."[18] Reagan would use similar words as "great silent center" throughout many of his 1968 campaign speeches, and as discussed, one may credit Reagan with the idea for the campaign term "silent majority" before Nixon would use it in the fall.

A few weeks later after Thanksgiving, CBS television newsman Harry Reasoner while doing background work on *What About Ronald Reagan?* had served as moderator for an interview of Eisenhower and Bradley at Eisenhower's Gettysburg farm. The question of pursuing

Vietcong troops into neighboring countries arose. Eisenhower clearly had said, "I would be for what we call 'hot pursuit,' even from the air...or on the ground." He added, "If you're chasing some people and they step over into Cambodia or Laos—it wouldn't bother me. I'd go at 'em as long as they'd come in there in the first place. And in the same way, the air, if an airplane attacked me, and we wanted to chase him, I'd go in wherever his base was." When asked if that included China, Eisenhower answered, "Yes, wherever his base comes."[19] Eisenhower did stress that he was not calling for an invasion of North Vietnam, but a limited attack: "just removing an annoyance and a menace." Bradley had concurred adding, "You're suggesting an end run around the DMZ and knock their artillery out." Both retired generals had agreed that such an end-run could be made by sea or land and that "American forces should have limited access to Cambodia and Laos."[20] As we will see, Reagan would follow-up on what the Eisenhower had recommended and would call for threatening to land an amphibious force in North Vietnam just as the Red Chinese had feared Eisenhower would do in North Korea as discussed earlier. Eisenhower made quite clear that he did not see either the Soviet Union or Red China becoming directly involved.[21]

Eisenhower's comments were interpreted as a warning both to Romney, who had taken an "independent" position on the war and to Rockefeller, who was thought to be wavering on the war. Nixon said he respected Eisenhower's military judgment but "from a political point of view" could not invade Laos or Cambodia.[22] [23] Of course in the future President Nixon would invade Cambodia in 1970. Reagan however was the only Republican candidate who had agreed entirely with Eisenhower's analysis and recommendations. In regard to Romney and Rockefeller and others, Eisenhower warned, "If any Republican or Democrat suggests that we pull out of Vietnam and turn our backs on the more than 13,000 Americans who died in the cause of freedom there, they will have me to contend with."[24] And in a subsequent *Readers Digest* article to be discussed later, he would promise to "stump against any candidate...who ran on a 'peace at any price' platform."[25]

Eisenhower's citizens committee issued its final report in early January, 1968. Eisenhower "had taken a very active part in drawing up the statement," which said that if North Vietnam stopped sending men and material to the south, then the United States would prepare to de-escalate in the hopes of mutual continuing de-escalation.[26]

In an interview with *Look*, to be discussed shortly, when asked about his prior comments on wanting to win the war, Reagan would answer, "I am in agreement with what former President Eisenhower said on the air." Reagan would say he advocated closing the harbor in Haiphong and keeping ever-present the threat of invasion. Reagan would say he favored "hot pursuit." Reagan favored using ships to make maneuvers threatening North Vietnam because it would tie up "half a million men." Reagan said he did not fear the consequences of hot pursuit into Laos or Cambodia.[27] Reagan was following Eisenhower's and his own ideas for winning the war. Reagan summarized his position on Vietnam saying, "I believe that the United States and the American people would feel a lot better about this... if the government of the United States would put this country on a war footing and ask the people of the country to sacrifice in some measure...and say we're going to win this as quickly as possible."[28]

In a March, 1968 *New York Times* interview with James Reston, Reagan actually would use the term "surge." When commenting on whether America could win the war, Reagan would say that if the Johnson administration had followed the prior recommendations of the military, an escalation "as a sudden **surge** and thrust of power, the war could well be over by now."[29] (author's emphasis) America would learn more of the importance of a military surge some 45 years later in Iraq.

In May on NBC's *Meet the Press*, Reagan would be asked about a possible confrontation with Red China during a time when negotiations had begun in Paris and American deaths had increased. He would answer by saying that in the Korean War, while negotiations between the Truman administration and North Korea were going on, more than 20,000 American troops had been killed. Reagan would continue by reminding the press and the nation that when Eisenhower had come in as a new president, he "brought an end to the negotiations and end to the conflict by simply releasing the word that the United States was going to review its options with regards to weapons, theaters of operation, manner of fighting." Reagan would say he advocated those exact same Eisenhower policies as applied now to Vietnam and explained that if the North Vietnamese were using the negotiations to gain battlefield advantage, that we should threaten them with force: "And I think that the same conditions that President Eisenhower submitted would be the same conditions here: a review of our strategy, a review of targets, a review of theaters of operation."[30] Clearly, 1968 presidential candidate Reagan was using Eisenhower's successful strategy in the early 1950s, which had ended the Korean fighting, as the basis for his own ideas on Vietnam. And as an added bonus, once the commission made its report, Eisenhower had reiterated those same views to the American public. As *Meet the Press* would end, Reagan would discuss John F. Kennedy's false charge of a missile gap in the 1960 election and brought the Kennedy's into his discussions of Eisenhower. Shortly thereafter in Cleveland, as will be seen, Reagan would expand upon his defense of Eisenhower and would turn Kennedy's charge on its head.[31]

Meanwhile in early 1968, there still were other candidates seeking, or thinking about seeking, the Republican nomination.

Endnotes

1. Chamberlain, John, "Who is Ike's Man for 1968? You Figure it Out," *Milwaukee Sentinel*, part 1, 1/2/1968, p. 10
2. Churchill quoted in *Finest Hour*, 170: 35, 2016
3. ibid
4. Duscha, Julius, "Reagan Gives a Surprising Performance: Not Great, Not Brilliant, But…" *NYT*, 12/10/67, p. 296
5. Johns, p. 133
6. RRL, Tape 275
7. Ambrose, p. 562
8. Boyarsky, Bill, "Reagan Prepares for 'Hawk' Tour," *Gettysburg Times*, 9/13/1967
9. Tannenwald
10. "Reagan Urges Escalation to Win War 'Quickly,'" *NYT*, 9/13/67, p. 5
11. Eisenhower, David, p. 216
12. Eisenhower, David, p. 217
13. Eisenhower, David, p. 220
14. Chamberlain, John, "Who is Ike's Man for 1968? You Figure it Out," *Milwaukee Sentinel*, 1/2/1968, part 1, p. 10
15. Belair, Felix Jr, "Eisenhower bars Major Role in '68; Cool to Romney," *NYT*, 12/25/67, p. 1
16. Chamberlain, op.cit.
17. Buchanan, p. 157-158
18. Kenworthy, E.W., "Eisenhower Joins Truman In Group Backing War," *NYT*, 10/26/67, p. 1
19. "Eisenhower-Bradley Interview Excerpts," *NYT*, 11/29/67, p. 14; Ambrose, p. 562
20. "Eisenhower backs U.S. Land Forays In North Vietnam," *NYT*, 11/29/67, p. 1
21. https://www.youtube.com/watch?v=yCahzYUDadE
22. Eisenhower, David, p. 229
23. Johns, p. 183
24. Wicker, Tom, "In the Nation: Eisenhower Rides Again," *NYT*, 12/28/67, p. 30
25. Eisenhower, David, p. 219
26. Sheehan, Neil, "Citizens' Panel Backs Johnson on Bombing Pause," *NYT*, 1/16/68, p. 3
27. RRL, Tape 326
28. ibid
29. Reston, James, "Reagan View: Fresh Leader Wanted," *NYT*, 3/4/68, p. 1
30. RRL, Tape 343
31. Naughton, James, "JFK's 'Missile Gap' Now Exists—Reagan," *Cleveland Plain Dealer*, 5/23/68, p. 1

CHAPTER 14: ROMNEY, ROCKEFELLER, AND NIXON

The possible Reagan candidacy was "hampering their efforts to raise campaign funds. Nixon supporters say that potential California contributors are waiting to see if Reagan enters the race before they open their purse strings."
~ Nixon supporters[1]

Romney

As we have seen, Romney had attacked candidate Reagan in 1966 in Los Angeles and later had suffered in comparison to Reagan at their joint appearance in the nation's capital in early 1967. Romney and Reagan had their fence-mending luncheon that fall. After Romney had made his infamous "brainwashing" comment and his poll numbers plummeted, the *New York Times* analyzed Romney's error in relation to Reagan: "If Gov. Ronald Reagan of California persists in his present intention of leaving his name on the ballot in Wisconsin, Nebraska, and Oregon, and if Messrs. Nixon and Romney kill one another off in the primaries, the less active candidates will move into contention, notably Governor Reagan."[2]

As noted earlier, Reagan had used the repeated questioning by the press about Romney's ill-fated comment as an opportunity not to speak ill of a fellow Republican. Reagan could have used it as an opportunity to attack Romney, as Romney had attacked him on civil rights. Instead Reagan not only had defended Romney but had used it to attack the Johnson administration on Vietnam: "I think he Gov. Romney has made an explanation of the context in which he used the term brainwashing. Perhaps he expressed at the same time the concern a lot of Americans should have as to whether they are getting all of the facts that they are entitled to have about foreign and domestic policy."[3] In October, Reagan had been asked to comment after Romney had called President Johnson a "phony." Reagan was asked if Romney had destroyed whatever remaining chances Romney had for the nomination. Reagan quickly came to Romney's defense.[4]

By 1968, despite comments from liberal commentators that his race was a lost cause,[5] Romney's campaigns continued in the three opt-out states of Wisconsin, Nebraska,[6] and Oregon.[7] Romney and Rockefeller poked fun at Reagan at this time.[8] But the handwriting was on the wall for Romney. Thus as 1968 began, political eyes turned away from Romney as Rockefeller's stalking-horse and turned directly towards Rockefeller.

Rockefeller

Despite historian Craig Shirley's earlier-noted assertion that the two governors were close friends, your author has found that Rockefeller and Reagan's relationship—pun intended—was quite "rocky". As seen earlier, Reagan had telegrammed Nixon he could not support a ticket in 1960 if liberal Rockefeller was to be Nixon's running mate. It was here where Nixon's aide had asked incredulously, "Reagan, the movie star?"[9]

Having lost in 1964 to conservative Goldwater, liberal Rockefeller had disdained the rise of the newest Republican conservative: Reagan. In 1966 Rockefeller had supported Reagan's opponent for the Republican nomination and actively had helped Reagan's Democratic opponent. Thus twice Rockefeller did not remain neutral; rather twice he had wanted Reagan defeated. Yes, they had met privately at Rockefeller's home and had appeared on the *Time* cover just prior to the governors cruise. Both had had to face the press many times to discuss a possible joint ticket. It was this possible ticket that Eisenhower had disdained. Rockefeller's work in late 1967 on the Republican platform was an attempt to cut off the influence of conservative Reagan.

Rockefeller's biographer observed that Rockefeller was one of many who had underestimated Reagan. Rockefeller "resented that Reagan's political successes seemed to be based wholly on the former actor's speaking skill." Rockefeller had called Reagan a "lightweight" and felt that Reagan "doesn't deal with tough issues."[10] But Rockefeller was taking no chances. He had seen Reagan as a true threat to his own chances to be the 1968 nominee. And Rockefeller had hired the perfect operative to keep track of Reagan.

Graham T.T. Molitar could probably attest the veracity of the value of being a wealthy politician. For Molitar owed his career to such a mover and shaker. Molitar, a former legislative counsel for the U.S. House of Representatives, had been hired by wealthy Rockefeller to be Director of Candidate Research for Rockefeller's ill-fated 1964 campaign for the presidency. Molitar had stayed on to fulfill the same role for 1968. Molitar's extensive files at the Rockefeller Archive Center show that he had considered the nominating period, rather than the general election, to be most crucial. Molitar wanted future historians to understand that "the nominating period is a time in the overall presidential campaign process when ideological appeals are strongest." It is the period when "the substantive and ideological delineation between parties is greatest."[11]

Molitar's files for Rockefeller on Reagan are extensive, consisting of separate thick folders occupying many separate boxes. Each folder is arranged by subject such as Reagan's views on: crime, the arts, defense, conservation, civil rights, aerospace, civil defense, welfare, youth, Supreme Court, Vietnam, South-east Asia non-Vietnam to name a few. In each were hundreds of newspaper clippings of press releases and articles from national and regional newspapers. For example, Reagan's positions on aerospace were in Box 27, Folder 654 of the Molitar papers.

Then Molitar had summarized and analyzed where Reagan stood on each subject so as to make it easy for Rockefeller to refer to, or agree or disagree with, Reagan's various opinions and positions. As 1968 began and Romney's polling declined, Rockefeller had to decide if he would enter the presidential race and face Nixon and Reagan. If so, Rockefeller had plenty of armamentarium to aid in his quest. During this time, New York City was suffering through a sanitation workers strike. New York City Mayor John Lindsay agreed to some of the demands, but the city became a mess. Unlike how Reagan's hero, Calvin Coolidge, had handled the Boston police strike—when Coolidge had said emphatically that no union had the right to strike against public health or safety, Governor Rockefeller solved the problem by caving in to the demands of the strikers. New Yorkers favored Lindsay overwhelmingly.[12] Likely Reagan was taking notes on comparing how his hero had handled a strike of public employees versus how his own modern political opponents were handling the same problem. How President Reagan, shortly after taking office, would deal with striking governmental workers airport controllers in this case would reverberate well into the 21st century to Wisconsin Governor Scott Walker.

Molitar would show his usefulness to Rockefeller in regards to Reagan again later in the campaign. On May 26, Reagan would be interviewed on *Meet the Press* as will be seen later, and afterwards Molitar would analyze Reagan's answers. When asked if a divorced man could run successfully for president, Reagan would answer that

Adlai Stevenson—divorced—had run twice in 1952 and 1956. Reagan had been prepared for that question for years, as he had been divorced as well. But Rockefeller was divorced also, and Molitar's careful watching of the Reagan interview might be of help to Rockefeller, as no one in his staff had realized what Reagan had mentioned.[13]

RN: Richard Nixon

Richard Nixon remained the frontrunner for the Republican nomination. Yet as seen earlier it was at Nixon's private January, 1967 strategy meeting for 1968 where he had told his supporters that his major competition would be from Reagan.[14] Confirmatory comments from his speech-writer Patrick Buchanan and reporters Evans and Novak show that Nixon always had foreseen Reagan to be his major threat.

To Nixon, Reagan initially had been the rising conservative governor whose electability and proven success in solving California's domestic problems had made him a formidable opponent. But ever since Reagan had been chosen to represent the Republican Party at the Gridiron Club and then on the *Town Meeting of the World* debate and then had trounced Kennedy in front of millions, Reagan clearly was also a formidable expert in foreign affairs. Plus Reagan had continued speaking out, mainly about Vietnam, in press conferences after the debate. There was no way Nixon could match Reagan's affability, ability to communicate with the common man, and ease with television and the media. To his advisors and with the press, Nixon had spoken with deference about Reagan as a candidate and competitor.

To make matters worse, Eisenhower had certified Reagan as presidential timbre in the summer of 1966 and clearly based upon the recent Eisenhower interview, Eisenhower may have revealed that because of Reagan's hawkish position on Vietnam and proven electability in the country's most populous state, Reagan might in fact be Eisenhower's personal choice for president, even if the general would never say such a thing in public.

Front runner Nixon was worried. Rather than being concerned about Rockefeller, in fact for Nixon, "More formidable was the new Republican governor of California, Ronald Reagan." If Reagan officially and openly entered the race, he could give "the Nixon campaign some anxious weeks."[15]

As was discussed, Patrick Buchanan felt that Reagan and Nixon had reached a secret agreement in which only if Nixon would falter in the first two primaries would then Reagan officially enter the race. Rusher thought that Reagan had reached such the agreement through Goldwater. But nonetheless, Reagan never stopped his campaigning, almost every weekend still criss-crossing the nation, holding frequent campaign meetings with his campaign staff, and having his grass roots activists start gearing up their campaigns, especially in the three opt-out states.

By early 1968, indeed *Newsweek* reported that Nixon workers were complaining that the possible Reagan candidacy was "hampering their efforts to raise campaign funds. Nixon supporters say that potential California contributors are waiting to see if Reagan enters the race before the open their purse strings."[16] Rusher and Buckley, Jr. had their quarterly *National Review* editorial meeting the same month. As discussed by Buckley's biographer, Rusher was unable to convince Buckley to support Reagan, and the magazine decided to remain neutral between Reagan and Nixon. But in public, Buckley voiced strong support for Nixon, as did Rusher for Reagan.[17]

It would only be years later that Nixon's candid opinions of Reagan would come to light. Nixon's secret tape recordings, under transcription and analysis at the Miller Center for Public Affairs at the University of Virginia, reveal these comments which would be made by President Nixon about Reagan on November 17, 1971: Nixon was speaking to Kissinger and said that Reagan was "pretty shallow," and that of Reagan and foreign affairs, "It shows you how a man of limited mental capacity simply doesn't know what the Christ is going on in the foreign area."[18]

While at Camp David in August, 1972, Nixon would tell Haldeman that on a personal basis, Reagan was "terrible. He just isn't pleasant to be around...strange."[19] And in 1973 when thinking about his possible future successors, one of whom might be a future President Reagan, Nixon would be aghast saying "Good God. Can you imagine— can you really imagine—him sitting here?"[20] As we will see in the Afterword, Nixon would see his worried imaginings come to fruition when he himself would become the supplicant.

Nixon had tried to sound out Reagan on his true intentions at Bohemian Grove. After the short-lived détente there, Reagan's star had continued to rise. During the spring of 1968, Reagan's campaigns in Wisconsin, Nebraska and Oregon would prove that Nixon's prescience—about the threat Reagan posed—to have been correct. And at the Miami Beach convention, the Reagan threat would test Nixon's political skills to the utmost.

Endnotes

1.   *Newsweek*, 1/15/68, p. 9
2.   "Romney vs. Nixon," *NYT*, 9/10/67, p. 218
3.   "Reagan Urges Escalation to Win the War 'Quickly,'" *NYT*, 9/13/67, p. 5
4.   RRL, Tape 301
5.   Pearson, Drew, "Washington Merry Go-Round," 1/1/68. p. 3
6.   Kopelson, Gene. 2014A
7.   Kopelson, Gene. 2014D
8.   https://www.youtube.com/watch?v=K-aCwD83Csk
9.   Gibbs, p. 197
10.   Persico, p. 271
11.   Molitar, Graham T., letter to Dr. Darwin Stapleton, Rockefeller Archive Center, 12/28/94
12.   Buchanan, p. 208
13.   "Favorable-unfavorable Rockefeller Comments," Rockefeller archive Center, Graham Molitar papers, IV 3A 18, series NAR RWR Ticket, Box 29, Folder 711, 5/26/68
14.   Judis, p. 280
15.   Gould, p. 29
16.   *Newsweek*, 1/15/68, p. 9
17.   Judis, p. 282
18.   http://tapes.millercenter.virginia.edu/transcripts/index.php/Nixon/620-008
19.   *NYT*, 12/11/03
20.   Gibbs, p. 353

CHAPTER 15: EARLY 1968—GUNS FIRST

"Reagan stands as more of a threat to front-runner Dick Nixon than either Romney or Rockefeller."

~ *Newsweek[1]*

"I've no evidence that anyone has a grab on the convention. I still believe …that it's going to be a wide-open convention."

~ Ronald Reagan[2]

The tumultuous year of 1968 had dawned. Children would see a new Disney-animated version of the beloved book character "Tigger" and the brand new *Mr. Rogers' Neighborhood*. The news program *60 Minutes* premiered. America seemingly was obsessed with space—real or science fiction. In real space, Apollo 8 would orbit the moon at Christmas. In fictional space, *Star Trek* was in its second season but there were indications of poor ratings and likely it would end and never be seen again. There were premieres of the movies *Planet of the Apes*—starring Reagan's old friend Charlton Heston—and *2001: A Space Odyssey*. Not yet a terminator, an immigrant from Austria would arrive in America who would become an admirer of Reagan; Arnold Schwarzenegger, who lifted weights and hoped someday to become an actor, immediately became fascinated with the 1968 American political scene and with Republicans.[3] In what would become known as Silicon Valley, a startup called Intel would be founded. The first successful heart transplant, 911 phone system, bank ATM, computer mouse, and McDonald's Big Mac all would debut. Abroad, a little known figure, Saddam Hussein, would help stage a coup d'etat in Iraq. Meanwhile as the Vietnam War intensified, anti-war protests in America grew.

In politics, 1968 was to be the year of the R's. On the Republican side, George *R*omney was running against *R*ichard Nixon, who signed all his memos as *RN*. Nelson *R*ockefeller—*R*ocky—and *R*onald *R*eagan were the next contenders. The Democratic side started out with President Johnson as presumed candidate for reelection, but the brother of slain President JFK, *R*obert F. Kennedy—*RFK*—was looming in the background. It would take almost fifty years for another set of R names to appear in the presidential race: Mitt *R*omney and Paul *R*yan in 2012. With the dawn of the new presidential election year of 1968, the nation's media cast its collective eye anew upon the candidacy of Ronald Reagan.

The Media in Early 1968

On January 1, 1968 columnist Drew Pearson, the Johnson supporter based inside the Beltway, stated, "Gov. Ronald Reagan of California is too far to the right for the GOP and for a public which includes so many underprivileged voters."[4] A Gallup poll showed his support amongst Republicans dropped fully five points, to 8 percent, from two months earlier. But any weakness for candidate Reagan is not what other national commentators saw in the political trenches.

Good Housekeeping ran an article on what eighteen "smart" women thought of Reagan, but the year's truly first comprehensive review of the Republican candidates was by columnists Rowland Evans and Robert Novak in the January issue of *Harper's* magazine entitled, "The Road to Miami Beach."[5] They began their analysis examining the state of Wisconsin, where Nixon had sewn up the support of party leaders "long ago" and that Nixon's organization there was "virtually a roster of the state's regular party organization."[6] In theory then, the Wisconsin primary should have been ceded immediately to Nixon. But it could not because "the perfervid volunteers who marched for Barry Goldwater in 1964—ferociously conservative Young Republicans, svelte society matrons from the North Shore suburbs above Milwaukee, small-town businessmen—are far more attracted to Governor Ronald Reagan of California than to Nixon."[7] Clearly the hard work of Wisconsin State Chairman for Reagan, Don L. Taylor, who was following the detailed plan he had sent after meeting Reagan during the Milwaukee visit in the fall, was starting to take root.

Evans and Novak felt that the divided loyalties seen in Wisconsin were a "microcosm of the national Republican party," as it was sensing victory against the unpopular President Johnson.[8] The columnists divided the party into four groups. At the state and county levels, "the second choice of the Regulars, by a wide margin, is Reagan."[9] Amongst the 26 Republican governors, fully one-third preferred Reagan. Amongst Republicans in Congress, Nixon was the favorite but with "not with much enthusiasm."[10] However, although Reagan was viewed as a political newcomer, "the kind words of Senator Everett McKinley Dirksen of Illinois are lessening this handicap."[11] Reagan's visits to Illinois and his continuing private correspondence with the Senate Minority leader were starting to bear fruit. Dirksen seemingly was moving toward Reagan and was speaking to members of Congress pushing the Reagan candidacy. Perhaps Reed's initial pessimistic assessment of the failure of Reagan's meeting with Dirksen, after the library dedication at Eureka College, had been incorrect.

But there was a fourth major group within the Republican Party: the grass roots conservatives. Evans and Novak characterized them as the "volunteers…those doughty foot soldiers of the Goldwater movement" who did not "fade away" as had been expected but rather had continued their conservative political activities by raising money, addressing envelopes, and making "their wishes known vocally."[12] The conservative volunteers had been "unenthusiastically for Nixon," but "they switched dramatically to Reagan and continue to back him in full force."[13] The grass roots activists were "mesmerized by Reagan's charisma and neo-Goldwater rhetoric."[14]

The growing national grass roots movement for Reagan for President, at that point spearheaded by Don Taylor in Wisconsin and the group in Owosso, was noted by Evans and Novak and soon would form the tactical basis of a renewed Reagan campaign. Indeed as Taylor was recruiting other grass roots campaign volunteers in Wisconsin, other similar groups were forming in Nebraska, Oregon, and elsewhere with a national information center coalescing in Topeka.

Evans and Novak noted that all four blocs within the Republican Party shared one common goal: "not to make a premature commitment."[15] Nixon had been viewed in the fall of 1967 as having an "open road to Miami" but this was "before the phenomenal rise of Reagan, that is."[16]

In upcoming New Hampshire, a likely write-in campaign for Reagan would give Reagan "at least 10 to 15 per cent of the vote;" such Reagan strength, taking votes away from Nixon, could throw New Hampshire to Romney.[17] Wisconsin was being transformed by a "mounting Reagan boom" from a "sure Nixon situation to a serious Nixon hazard" especially because Democrats could cross-over and create whatever "mischief" they wished.[18] It might be Rush Limbaugh's 2008 Operation Chaos—in reverse—some four decades early. And if Nixon somehow managed to survive, he had to go next to Nebraska, "where Reagan is strong" and then to Oregon whose streak for independent thinking was well known.[19]

Evans and Novak still viewed Reagan as the 'absentee candidate." But the authors felt that Reagan's growing appeal came from groups that favored his foreign policy theme of "unleashing the military on Ho Chi Minh," as well as from discontented middle class constituents, who were "anti-government, anti-politician, anti-intellectual, and anti-international."[20] Reagan was felt to have "enormous political appeal" and was viewed as hurting Nixon "dearly" in Nebraska and Oregon, possibly to such an extent that with Reagan and Nixon splitting those conservative votes, Romney could win some of the forthcoming spring 1968 primaries.[21]

The authors brought up that in the South, Reagan was seen as "the Republican most likely to stave off the third-party threat of George Wallace."[22] And if Nixon faltered in the primaries, party regulars in Illinois would "try to deliver the state's 58 delegate votes to Reagan, particularly if the flirtation between Reagan and Dirksen ripens as it promises to."[23] Behind the scenes, Reagan was building support amongst Republican governors and he had "worked hard and effectively to carve out a leadership niche" on the recent governors cruise.[24] His first year as California governor was seen as "turbulent but highly successful," while Reagan's rising presidential campaign was described as a "public relations spectacular."[25]

Rockefeller's only hope was that "fifteen or more governors will hold their delegations under tight control while the Reagan boom dies down."[26] When Evans and Novak wondered what would happen if Nixon did not win on the first ballot and Reagan and Rockefeller were left as the second and third ballot choices? Clif White answered, saying if by the third ballot Reagan might have 550 delegates and Rockefeller had 250, "I'd like to see the guy that goes up to Reagan and says 'Ron, Rocky will take you as Vice President if you give him your delegates.' I just don't think it can be put together."[27]

Evans and Novak continued the scenario of a Nixon nomination loss, by speculating that for Reagan to become the Republican nominee, Nixon's blessing "might still be decisive," even though if Nixon would fall in the primaries, "much of the blame can justifiably be put on Reagan."[28] But very likely Nixon the consummate politician would not "hesitate to give" Reagan "a push over the top at Miami Beach."[29]

Evans and Novak concluded their analysis by noting that the forthcoming Republican Party convention promised to be "the most exciting Republican contest perhaps since 1912, when Colonel Theodore Roosevelt" ran as a third party candidate. The authors gave Nixon the booking odds of 5 to 1 and Reagan in second place at 10 to 1; Rockefeller was 15 to 1.[30]

The *New York Times* did not hide its opinion when it declared in the opening sentence of the first page story for 1968 that amongst Republicans, it was for Rockefeller.[31] Their survey showed that in a hypothetical matchup, Johnson would defeat Reagan "decisively."[32]

Reagan would win only 13 states against Johnson: Maine, Vermont, North Carolina, Kansas, Ohio, South Dakota, Iowa, Wisconsin, Nebraska, New Mexico, Idaho, Wyoming and Montana. If Wallace were included as a third party candidate, he would beat both Reagan and Johnson in Louisiana, Alabama, and Mississippi. On an Electoral College basis, Johnson would get 413 electoral votes to Reagan's 98 and Wallace's 27.[33]

The most detailed analysis after *Harper's* was in *Newsweek*, whose cover featured caricatures of the major Republican candidates sliding down the trunk of an elephant and which devoted six full pages to it's review, entitled, "Politics 1968: The Big Show."[34] The "only Republican to spark any real fervor among the GOP faithful" was Reagan.[35] Reagan supporters were "noisily trying to ignite boomlets in his behalf from New Hampshire to the mountain states."[36] The magazine commented, "Reagan, indeed, stands as more of a threat to front-runner Dick Nixon than either Romney or Rockefeller" and cited that if Reagan achieved a substantial vote in the Oregon primary, it "could jeopardize Nixon's Presidential hopes."[37] Indeed if Nixon faltered, "Many of those who have tentatively signed on with Nixon would delightedly defect to a Reagan bandwagon."[38]

Reagan was observed "doing little to discourage his sympathizers," and his denials of interest at press conferences were noted to have been buffed by Reagan into a "tantalizing sheen."[39] He was doing not overt campaigning but his name remained on the ballots in the three opt-out states. And what had Reagan thought of the "evident support for him around the country?"[40] Reagan found it gratifying. And did Nixon have the nomination sewn up? "No" said Reagan who added, "I've no evidence that anyone has a grab on the convention. I still believe …that it's going to be a wide-open convention."[41]

As of early January, *Newsweek*, which would publish updates of its delegate tally up to Miami Beach, had Reagan in third place with 201 delegates. Specific state-by-state analyses included: Alabama if Nixon did not sweep the primaries, it would go for Reagan, Georgia if Nixon falters, "bring on Reagan", Idaho if Nixon slips, state leaders could move to Reagan, Louisiana unless Nixon loses his loser image, "they'll go Reagan, Mississippi if Reagan wants the nomination, Republicans here "would go nuts for him", Nebraska for Nixon but Reagan was gaining, Oregon Reagan could win with a "rousing campaign", Texas GOPers here wanted Nixon or Reagan, and Wisconsin Reagan will cut Nixon's lead over Romney[42]

Pressure was building upon the national media to find out directly from Reagan as to where all the speculation about his candidacy was heading. At a Sacramento press conference on January 10, Reagan "firmly dashed...the hopes of his backers." When he was asked, "Can you conceive of any set of circumstances that would lead you to campaign in your own behalf before Presidential primaries in Oregon and any other states?" Reagan replied, "No. I can't. I have no such intention."[43] But Reagan cleverly had not answered the real, underlying question. His answer, that he would not campaign personally in any of the three opt-out states in 1968, did not mean he had stopped his first quest for the presidency. Indeed the campaign was about to intensify dramatically.

Reagan's grass roots teams had sprung into action. Don Taylor was hard at work gaining new Wisconsin supporters for Reagan. In Oregon, Don Hodel was planning the official state and Portland Reagan campaign staffs. In Kansas, a Reagan national information center was opening headed by Henry Bubb, who then would arrange the Reagan offices in Nebraska.

And even if visits to the three opt-out states were off the table, Reagan did not sit at home in California and ignore his campaign. By not angering his home-state constituency not being seen as actively campaigning in those three states where his name was on the ballot, he still could continue his campaign and fundraising trips elsewhere.

Once the new year began, candidate Reagan immediately got back to work on his presidential quest. On January 2, Reagan met with Reed, Clarke and Nofziger to finalize the upcoming campaign travel logistics for Tulsa and a return trip east. The next day Peter O'Donnell arrived from Texas, followed by a January 10 meeting with Texas financial fundraisers for Reagan.[44] After campaigning in Tulsa on January 16 as discussed, where the Oklahoma Republicans for Reagan tried to blunt any momentum for Nixon by sending out a massive postcard mailing, Reagan flew to New York City.

Reagan's January Travels

Two major addresses occurred on January 17. For candidate Reagan, the most important speech as the new year began was Reagan's January 17, 1968, speech before the Economic Club of New York.[45] Reagan had demonstrated his expertise in economics when he had spoken in Detroit during the gubernatorial campaign. After all, economics had been Reagan's area of expertise in college. In an era when few Americans went to college, Reagan had graduated Eureka College with a B.A. in economics and social science. Reed had envisioned this speech as the kickoff of Reagan's true campaign.[46]

In New York City, Reagan spoke about his policies in California—Reagan's answer to Johnson's "Great Society" as Reagan's "Creative Society." But in words that readers in the second decade of the 21st century will find all too familiar, Reagan warned about the "relentless inch by inch encroachment on, or usurpation of, rights traditionally held to be the proper possession of the people...I do not remember a time when so many Americans regardless of their economic or social standing have been so suspicious and apprehensive of the aims, the credibility and the competence of the federal establishment."[47] Reagan decried the proposed Johnson administration calls for Americans to sharply reduce investment abroad and to stop foreign travel. Reagan's main theme was to cut governmental spending and the role of free markets. The chairman of the Chase Manhattan Bank was extremely impressed, writing Reagan that he had done a "superlative job" and had handled all the tough questions "well."[48]

Reagan flew to the nation's capital and after a brief press conference, he met with Republican leaders late on January 17.[49] The second, and of course more important speech for the nation that day, was President Johnson's State of the Union Address. The next morning, in response to what Johnson had said to the nation, to be discussed, Reagan and Reed began working on new speech ideas for the campaign.[50]

Although the current issue of *Time* had focused on Rockefeller, with scant attention paid to Reagan,[51] one of those Democrats who had noted the growing public excitement with Reagan was in fact President Lyndon Johnson. Virtually very single presidential campaign speech candidate Reagan had delivered since Seattle in 1966 had as its primary political target Johnson's Great Society programs. Johnson needed political help to deflect the Reagan threat. He knew it and he started arranging to shore up his political defenses.

Meanwhile, Johnson delivered his State of the Union Address on January 17. Johnson observed that in America there was a "certain restlessness—a questioning." Johnson added, "I spoke of despair."[52] Whether Jimmy Carter was watching and taking notes—that perhaps a better phrase for future use might be "malaise"—is not known!

But one person observing Johnson's words and tone was Ronald Reagan. In the spring, once Reagan's new speech ideas were finalized, Reagan would use Johnson's words against him, just as he would against Carter some twelve years later.

After departing the nation's capital, Reagan spoke at Convention Hall in Philadelphia. Then while at the University of Pittsburgh, Reagan "drew loud cheers from a largely student audience."[53] Reagan told about a recent scandal of favoritism for providing aid in Alaska to a small motel owned by a state Democratic Party leader versus much smaller aid given to a much larger motel, which was owned by the Republican governor. Reagan was incensed by not only the favoritism as an abuse of public funds, but told the audience of a media correspondent who did not seem to care. Reagan cited this as an example of the country's moral decay and stressed that citizens should demand that "no place in the nation shall have higher standards of integrity and honor than in the halls of government—the very temple of freedom, and we'll settle for nothing less." When Reagan charged that there was a morality gap in government, both "young and old applauded," reported the political editor of the *Pittsburgh Press*.[54]

At his first press conference, when asked about his planned role at the August convention, he stressed his role as favorite son.[55] At his second press conference, he was asked if he had any organized campaign workers in western Pennsylvania; Reagan answered emphatically, "Well I don't. I'm not unaware of what some people are saying or doing. While it's flattering, it is not done with any cooperation with me or any approval from me…I am not a candidate."[56] But Reagan did add, "I think the nomination is still open and will be decided at the convention."[57] The columnist from the *Pittsburgh-Gazette* caught the "essential reaction of people everywhere to Ronald Reagan and wrote that 'even determined Democrats would admit that Reagan, at 56, generates excitement.'"[58]

A few days later it was reported that Johnson, still assessing reaction to his State of the Union Address, had solved his Reagan problem. Johnson brought into his cabinet Clark Clifford as Secretary of Defense to help bolster support for the Vietnam War. Congressman George H. W. Bush just had returned from a two-week fact-finding trip to the region and gave a positive assessment by urging America to have the will and patience to win.[59] But public opinion was heading downhill. Johnson had an ulterior motive for bringing onboard the former Truman administration official. Clifford had helped Truman change his image and go on the offensive and win against a ticket of two Republican governors in 1948: Dewey of New York and Warren of California. To Johnson in 1968, the prospect of facing another pair of Republican governors, this time Reagan of California and Rockefeller of New York, was the ticket "the Democrats fear the most."[60] Clifford was hired to once again work another miracle for Johnson as he had for Truman. But within days, Clifford would have a whole slew of new problems, not the least of which would be Reagan's attacks on Johnson foreign policies. Indeed Johnson's restlessness and his own despair were about to get markedly worse.

Foreign Affairs Intrude: Ike, the Pueblo and Tet

Eisenhower may have had some foreboding about the year 1968. Historian Evan Thomas relates that Eisenhower had a theory that "the eighth year of every decade was somehow especially arduous and climactic for him."[61] Eisenhower would find that this would be especially true this time. For the former president, sadly it would be his last year ending with an 8. But first there was some good news for Ike. As alluded to earlier, while golfing with Gosden in Palm Springs at the par 3 executive golf course at Seven Lakes Country Club, Eisenhower shot the only hole-in-one of his life.[62] But in mid-summer his feared bad luck for years ending in "8" would reappear, when he would suffer the worst cardiac event of his life.

At the January 17 press conference in the nation's capital, Reagan had brought up the Eisenhower committee on Vietnam. Reagan said the conclusion of Generals Eisenhower and Bradley, to let troops and air power go after fleeing North Vietnamese and Vietcong—who were fleeing into neighboring countries "hot pursuit"—had made "a great deal of sense." The two generals had made a clear distinction between hot pursuit versus invasion, and Reagan said he would "abide by their judgment."[63] When asked about negotiations with the North Vietnamese, Reagan brought up the failed negotiations with North Korea during the Truman administration, reminding the press that America had suffered more military losses during the negotiating period than before.[64]

On January 20, Reagan campaigned in St. Louis. Reed arranged to film a Reagan rally and speech for future campaign use.[65] Reagan then got a call from his mentor.

Eisenhower wrote in his diary on January 20, "I got ahold of Governor Reagan."[66] The diary notation was that the two men had discussions about the makeup of the California delegation to Miami Beach, but given the ongoing events at home and abroad, likely the mentor and his protege discussed much more.

Johnson's phrases about "restlessness" and "despair" likely were discussed, because shortly thereafter Reagan specifically would begin attacking Johnson's speech and its wording and phrases. Vietnam, Eisenhower's Vietnam Committee, Reagan's public support for his mentor's military recommendations, Reagan's reminders to the press of the parallels between the Korean and Vietnam wars, and the hard lessons of the perils of negotiating with the enemy learned in Korea that Reagan urged be applied in Vietnam, likely were all at the forefront of Eisenhower's thoughts at the time of his conversation with Reagan.

Their last understanding about the 1968 presidency was that Reagan was going to run for president in the role that Eisenhower had urged—that of California favorite son. It seems highly unlikely that Reagan shared his confidential campaign plan to seek delegates to prepare to win the Republican nomination in 1968. And in just a few days after Eisenhower and Reagan had spoken, two major foreign policy crises were about to hit America and the Johnson administration. The first came from a country last dealt with successfully some fifteen years earlier by Eisenhower himself: North Korea.

Only one week after Johnson delivered his State of the Union address, headlines blared that the *U.S.S. Pueblo* was captured by North Korea. The United States maintained that the naval surveillance vessel was in international waters, but North Korea claimed it had strayed into their territory. Then North Korea launched a commando raid against the presidential mansion in South Korea, the Blue House, termed thereafter, "The Blue House Raid." The Johnson administration seemed paralyzed with indecision as to whether a strong military response or threat was needed and decided to do neither. Two recent analyses show that behind-the-scenes, the situation was more complex.[67] But Reagan saw, as did the nation and the world, an American president who seemingly was powerless to decide, powerless to act and powerless to save the crew.

The ship's crew became hostages. They were made prisoners, beaten repeatedly, tortured, and starved. Then an eleven-month drama unfolded with daily newspaper stories and television stories about the fate of the crew and Johnson's decision to watch and wait. As will be discussed, the crew would be released at year's end and Governor Reagan would be the first to greet the crew. Decades later the ship still was moored as a museum ship in North Korea. It remains as the only commissioned ship being held by a foreign nation, although the North Koreans did give it a fresh coat of paint in 2013.[68]

A week after the massive media reports on the *U.S.S. Pueblo* capture and lack of any American response, the headlines suddenly returned to Vietnam. The American public suffered a second major shock when the Tet offensive in Vietnam began. American television audiences—just days after reeling with the news of the *U.S.S. Pueblo*—listened to television commentators, especially Walter Cronkite of CBS, bemoan the war and Tet, even though the military result was in fact an American and South Vietnamese triumph.[69]

Americans' restlessness and despair worsened dramatically. Reagan had commented on Vietnam repeatedly during the campaign thus far; he discussed it at each campaign speech, and was asked about Vietnam at almost every press conference as we have seen.

Reagan would continue pushing for his Eisenhower-inspired Vietnam policies—i.e., to win—for the remainder of his 1968 campaign.

Harold MacMillan

As soon as Eisenhower learned of the Pueblo incident, he spoke to General Goodpaster. Then two days later Eisenhower had a visit from former British Prime Minister Harold MacMillan, who was stopping off prior to a visit to an ancestral family home in Indiana.[70]

On January 11, Macmillan had received an honorary degree from Columbia University, where of course in the late 1940s, Eisenhower had been its president. Macmillan urged a new peace initiative from the United States to the Soviet Union. Macmillan told the press that he knew that America and the Soviets were in discussions "on a treaty to prevent the spread of nuclear weapons."[71] Later in Chicago, Macmillan regretted that Britain, unlike Australia and New Zealand, "was not sharing with the United States the burden of the war in Vietnam," adding, "Those who don't share in the burdens and dangers have no right to criticism."[72] On January 15, Macmillan met President Johnson at the White House and proceeded on to Gettysburg to see Eisenhower followed by visiting Indiana.[73]

Eisenhower's diary discloses nothing about their conversations. Yet besides the news about Columbia, and the antimissile shield, most certainly Tet, the *U.S.S. Pueblo*, and Reagan were discussed, for as will be seen, later Reagan would reveal that MacMillan had approved of how Reagan believed the Pueblo hostage crisis, and any future hostage crisis, should have been handled.

After Macmillan departed, Eisenhower kept up his political appointments and kept up-to-date on both of the new Asian crises with former CIA Director John McCone and then with General Goodpaster, who also gave Eisenhower a "fine briefing, not only on Viet Nam, but on the comparative strengths of Russia and the United States in missiles, bombs and so on."[74] [75]

To Eisenhower, the Tet offensive was eerily reminiscent of World War II. When Nazi Germany had surprised the Allies in December, 1944 with the Battle of the Bulge, Eisenhower quickly had asked for reinforcements to destroy the Germans and got them and won. But in 1968, Eisenhower had observed that when General Westmoreland, the American commander, had asked for reinforcements to complete the destruction of the North Vietnamese Army and their Viet Cong allies, the Johnson administration answered not with more military help but rather placed a ceiling on manpower. Likely Eisenhower was livid.[76]

On February 19, President Johnson unexpectedly would pay a quick visit to Eisenhower in Palm Desert, and Johnson and his advisors "briefed me on the latest news of the Viet Nam war" as well as on "the moves made by the government in the Pueblo case." Eisenhower would add in his diary that Johnson seemed "to be worried more about the political opposition within his own Party— Kennedy, Mr. Fulbright, and Mr. McCarthy, than about some of his obvious problems."[77]

Clearly Eisenhower disdained Johnson's concerns, more worried for his own political survival rather than the good of the country. But Eisenhower's writing also confirmed his own strong dislike of Kennedy by the lack of dignifying his name in the diary entry by not adding a "Mr." before Kennedy.

After their January 20 telephone call, did Eisenhower and Reagan speak again during this time? It is not known. Eisenhower's personal post-presidential diary certainly is not a minute-by-minute secretarial log. But it is quite likely. As Eisenhower was Reagan's coach, the two men indeed likely spoke again after Tet, the Pueblo incident, the Vietnam briefings, the MacMillan visit, the Johnson visit and concern about Kennedy, and the briefing on Soviet missiles. Perhaps such discussions had broadened beyond America's problems in Asia to discussions of the anti-ballistic missile shield, which had so impressed Reagan at Lawrence-Livermore only weeks earlier, for which Macmillan had discussed with the press days earlier, and for which Eisenhower had just been updated.

From then on, Reagan was not hesitant in attacking Johnson's handling of these problems. Indeed Reagan would mention the *U.S.S. Pueblo* almost as often as Vietnam for the remainder of the spring. Reagan always would be quick to caution reporters that only the president had all the facts. But as we will see, in July Reagan would have his clearest enunciation of his policy about how to handle a hostage crisis—and would reveal MacMillan's approval of it—which eerily would foreshadow similar hostage-taking events to come in 1979-1980, when he would run for president for the third time, as well as a future hijacking at sea in 1985. But at this point in early 1968, this first major travel phase of the Reagan campaign was winding down.

Reagan Curtails His Campaign and Fund-raising Travels

As January was ending, the *New York Times* collated Reagan's travels over the past 14 months. Reagan had visited 14 states and had spoken to some 60,000 persons. As a fund-raiser, Reagan had been outstanding. He had raised $2-million for Republican coffers.

But the newspaper felt that if his cross-country travels had "bolstered his prospects" for the presidential nomination, they remained "enigmatic."[78] Reagan for President movements had "sprung up in many states;"[79] his strategy was one of "gently advertising his availability and palatability, while waiting to exploit a nomination deadlock."[80] Reagan told the press that he was going to curtail his out-of-state travels in order to concentrate on his Creative Society programs and his budget in Sacramento.

In Oklahoma, the draft-Reagan movement had backers of twelve to fifteen of the state's 22 delegates.[81] Northeastern Republican governors met in Manhattan on January 27 and "there were indications of support for Governor Ronald Reagan if he became an active candidate."[82] But those in New York City who kept up-to-date on presidential politics got more than just a tid-bit of news about Ronald Reagan during that time period.

In the *New York Post* magazine section, a detailed analysis on Reagan's presidential candidacy appeared by columnist Murray Kempton. Entitled "Ronald Reagan," Kempton's article had an unflattering photo of Reagan from his 1942 film, *King's Row*. Kempton saw Reagan as a man following orders, who could not think for himself or make independent decisions. Reagan was a "contract player. He accepts the part for which the company casts him."[83] Kempton thought that this was the reason "to doubt that he will drive himself to the ordeal of moral and physical exhaustion demanded for a Presidential nominee."[84] Spencer and Roberts were interviewed for the article. Of Reagan's travels, Spencer said that Reagan was a "team player" who "never makes an appearance unless he has a fund-raising reason for being there."[85] However Roberts countered that Reagan had formidable qualities as a candidate, with a "hell of an ability" to connect with the common man, and had "the ability to be a great leader."[86]

Kempton ended by discussing the role of Mrs. Reagan. Kempton felt that Nancy was "plainly more ambitious for him than he is for himself" yet at the same time, her calling him "Ronnie" to reporters was viewed as an "unlikely" name used by a "woman who is thinking very seriously about her husband as President."[87]

Spencer and Roberts were not the only Reagan campaign team members who caught the eyes of the press. At this time, Clif White had been assigned to put together the California delegation. The press asked Reagan about White. Reagan confirmed White's role. The press felt that White's hiring made it "more difficult" for Reagan to continue to deny that he was a candidate for president.[88] When asked if White's planned "nationwide political soundings" meant that he would organize a Draft Reagan movement, Reagan answered, "No."[89] Would such a Draft Reagan movement begin soon? Reagan was coy, answering, "I don't think such a thing is going to happen...But we'll have to wait and see."[90]

Newsweek gave its analysis a few days later in an article by their Los Angeles bureau chief entitled, "Reagan for President?" Reagan, as noted, was curtailing his out-of-state campaign travels to concentrate on the upcoming legislative session. Reagan boosters saw "Nixon as the only man between Reagan and the White House— and not a soul close to Reagan" believed that Nixon could win the nomination.[91] Reagan supporters felt that Reagan's best upcoming chance would be in Oregon, where "the strongest of Reagan's 60-odd Citizens for Reagan groups plan a well-heeled TV and billboard campaign."[92] Reagan supporters did not want to antagonize Nixon. Rather they hoped his support would "melt away" and Reagan troops would then swoop in to grab "every delegate he has."[93] Other Reagan supporters were convinced that Reagan had "the ability to handle" the presidency, but others worried that Reagan's own view, "If God wants him to be President, so be it, and if not, fine," might impact his ability to put in the required long hours that the highest office in the land demanded.[94]

Despite the upbeat press analyses, in fact the campaign insiders knew otherwise. At a February 11 meeting at the Reagan Los Angeles residence with Reagan, Reed, Nofziger, White, Clarke, Smith and Spencer, their internal conclusion was somber: the votes just were not there.[95]

February ended with Reagan being interviewed by *Look* magazine. Reagan reiterated his prior positions on Vietnam: that he wanted to see the mining of Haiphong Harbor and that an enemy population should suffer. These were Reagan's continued advancings of his and Eisenhower's military planning: enemy civilian populations, in addition to their soldiers, should fear the threat of America's military.[96] The Johnson administration had refused to mine Haiphong Harbor, worrying that such an act might enlarge the war. Just as earlier when Ike had been asked about a bombing pause and had answered, So what?!," similarly Reagan answered about the mining, "So what?!" Reagan, like Eisenhower, continued urging that North Vietnam feel the same pain that their invasion of the South had created.

Two additional lessons from Eisenhower appeared again. At press conferences, Reagan stressed he wanted the North Vietnamese to fear the United States' threat of invasion, rather than the Johnson administration policy of publicly stating that it would never invade the North Vietnamese homeland even though the North had invaded the South. Reagan urged that the U.S. Navy should assemble a fake invasion fleet to further scare the North, just as Eisenhower had recommended for North Korea.[97] Reagan was so upset that the Johnson administration had tried to fight a war using only half-measures. He did not want a policy of "guns and butter" but ended by stating that he wanted the administration to declare a war footing by putting "guns come first."[98]

As the nation rapidly was becoming eager to replace Johnson, fervor increased on the Democratic side when a relatively unknown Eugene McCarthy was set to challenge Johnson in the New Hampshire primary. Plus there was growing speculation that Robert F. Kennedy might declare his candidacy too. On the Republican side, the four R's remained: *RN*, *R*omney, *R*ockefeller, and *R*onald *R*eagan.

In Reagan's camp, despite the somber analysis from Reagan's campaign team in California, there was rapidly growing Reagan for President activity throughout the nation: besides the three opt-out states of Wisconsin, Nebraska, and Oregon where Reagan offices and staff were set to open; there were two new Reagan groups in the nation's capital; a pro-Reagan faction was attempting to send a Reagan-majority delegation from Washington state; a national Reagan campaign office was about to open in Kansas; Reagan grass roots groups had formed in Texas and Colorado. And in Washington, D.C. the newest group was about to join the growing choruses of Reagan grass roots activists to make their collective voices heard shouting: Ronald Reagan for President in 1968.

Endnotes

1.   *Newsweek*, January, 8, 1968, p. 22
2.   ibid
3.   Ross, p. 370
4.   Pearson, Drew, "Washington Merry Go-Round, 1/1/68, p. 3
5.   Evans, R and Novak, R, "The Road to Miami Beach," *Harpers*, January 1968, p. 21-26
6.   Evans, p. 21
7.   ibid
8.   Evans, p. 22
9.   ibid
10. ibid
11. ibid
12. ibid
13. ibid
14. ibid
15. Evans, p. 23
16. ibid
17. Evans, p. 23
18. ibid
19. ibid
20. Evans, p. 24
21. ibid
22. ibid
23. ibid

24. ibid
25. ibid
26. Evans, p. 25
27. Evans, p. 25
28. Evans, p. 25
29. ibid
30. Evans, p. 26
31. Weaver, Warren Jr, "GOP Leaders Say Only Rockefeller Can Beat Johnson," *NYT*, 1/1/68, p. 1
32. ibid
33. ibid
34. *Newsweek*, 1/8/68, p. 17-22
35. *Newsweek*, 1/8/68, p. 18
36. *Newsweek*, 1/8/68, p. 22
37. ibid
38. ibid
39. ibid
40. ibid
41. ibid
42. *Newsweek*, 1/8/68, p. 21
43. Davies, Lawrence, "Reagan Disavows Primaries Plan," *NYT*, 1/11/68, p. 23
44. Reagan-Reed, 1/2/1968-1/10/1968, Sacramento
45. See Illustrations
46. Reed, *Reagan Enigma*, p. 127
47. Reagan, Ronald "Top-Heavy Government Or…A Creative Society", speech delivered at the New York Economic Club, 1/17/68, courtesy Students for Reagan
48. Reed, *The Reagan Enigma*. p. 132
49. Reagan-Reed, 1/17/1968
50. Reagan-Reed, 1/18/1968
51. "Republicans: Waiting for Rocky," *Time*, 1/19/68
52. Johnson, Lyndon. State of the Union Address. 1/17/68
53. White and Gill, p. 95
54. White and Gill, ibid
55. RRL, Tape 316
56. RRL, Tape 317
57. White and Gill, p. 96
58. White and Gill, ibid
59. Johns, p. 185
60. Reston, James : Washington: Clifford and the Strategy of 1948 and 1968," *NYT*, 1/21/68, p. E14
61. Thomas, Ikes Bluff, p. 295
62. Eisenhower, Dwight. 1968 Diary. 2/7/68
63. RRL, Tape 315
64. ibid
65. Reagan-Reed, 1/20/1968
66. Eisenhower, Dwight. 1968 Diary. 1/25/1968 and 1/27/1968
67. Cheevers; http://nsarchive.gwu.edu/NSAEBB/NSAEBB453/
68. "North Korea to Put Captured US Spy Ship on Display" AP, 7/25/2013
69. for a complete analysis of Tet as an American military triumph but a public relations disaster, see Hanson, *Carnage and Culture*
70. Eisenhower, Dwight. 1968 Diary. 1/25/66; 1/27/66
71. Gilroy, Harry, "Macmillan, Here, Urges New U.S.-Soviet Talks," *NYT*, 1/12/1968, p. 12
72. "Macmillan Gives War View," *NYT*, 1/13/1968, p. 19
73. "Macmillan and Johnson Confer at White House," *NYT*, 1/16/1968, p. 18
74. Eisenhower, Dwight. 1968 Diary. 2/8/68; 2/14/68; 2/15/68; 2/22/68
75. Goodpaster and McCone each would be given a Presidential Medal of Freedom by President Reagan
76. Ambrose, p. 563
77. Eisenhower, Dwight. 1968 Diary. 2/19/68
78. Hill, Gladwin, "Reagan Finishing National Swings," *NYT*, 1/21/68, p. 41
79. ibid
80. ibid
81. Steffgen, p. 158
82. Lubasch, Arnold, "Bliss Supported as GOP Chairman," *NYT*, 1/28/68, p. 34
83. Kempton, Murray, "Ronald Reagan," *NY Post Magazine*, 2/2/68
84. ibid

85. ibid
86. ibid
87. ibid
88. "Some Help Reagan Can Do Without," *Los Angeles Times*, 2/20/68; "Strategist's Hiring Unknown to Reagan," *Los Angeles Times*, 2/20/68
89. ibid
90. ibid
91. Fleming, Karl, "Reagan for President?," *Newsweek*, 2/26/68, p. 24
92. ibid
93. ibid
94. ibid
95. Reagan-Reed, 2/11/1968, Los Angeles residence
96. Thomas, *Ike's Bluff*
97. Thomas
98. RRL, Tape 326

CHAPTER 16: DILBECK IN D.C.

"I think that if he gets enough backing, he'll come out. I think that's what he's waiting for…I'm trying to get the people to show enough strength that the Republicans will have to draft him."

~ Walter Dilbeck, Jr.[1]

Reagan's increasing pronouncements on world affairs were being noticed not only by his supporters and by the media, but also by a major political operative of the kind whom Eisenhower had mentored Reagan to attempt to attract: a disaffected Democrat. As the new year began, business entrepreneur Walter Dilbeck, Jr., a life-long Democrat, was busy setting up a Reagan-for-President grassroots campaign office in the nation's capital. And it was Reagan's hawkish stances on Vietnam that had persuaded Dilbeck to switch allegiances and start pushing hard to propel Reagan into the White House.

Dilbeck had been used to fighting difficult battles with the odds stacked against him. On April 6, 1945, when young Seventh Army private Dilbeck's F Company of the 253rd Infantry Regiment had been advancing near Buchhof, Germany, suddenly they had been attacked on both sides by over two hundred German SS troops. Most of the American soldiers had panicked and as they had scampered, the Germans had mowed down the fleeing soldiers. But not Walter Dilbeck, who had run up a bare hill and had started returning fire as quickly as possible. Dilbeck had reloaded time and time again amidst heavy enemy fire. Dilbeck's bravery and persistence had paid off for the U.S. Army that day as the Nazi attack had stalled. By then Dilbeck single-handedly had wounded or killed over sixty SS troops for which he was awarded the Distinguished Service Cross, America's second highest medal for gallantry in action.

After the war, Dilbeck went on to build a successful real estate business. Described as "loud and ostentatious," he was a generous man and gave each of fifteen friends and family members a brand new Oldsmobile.[2] Once he spent $120,000 to fly sixty friends back to Buchhof to place a plaque where his heroism had begun two decades earlier. In the mid-1960s, Hollywood producer John Beck was attempting to make a movie about Dilbeck's heroism, and Charles

O'Neal, the father of actor Ryan O'Neal, had written a screenplay called, *The Private War of Walter Dilbeck*.[3]

Disenchanted Democrat

Dilbeck then had become concerned about world affairs and had proposed a partial solution via baseball. A life-long Democrat who had voted twice for Stevenson in the 1950s, Dilbeck first had toured Vietnam for two weeks in 1966 as a writer and observer. He had soured on the policies of the Democratic administration. Another newcomer to politics, Reagan friend actor Charlton Heston, similarly had toured Vietnam at this same time and similarly was in the midst of changing from Democrat to Republican.[4]

Dilbeck had felt that America could win the war easily if the Johnson administration would let the troops fight to win, and he also had concluded that "Asians saw Americans as soft."[5] Such softness helped communism to spread. Dilbeck, who recently had purchased a professional baseball team in the Southern League, had concluded that in order to foster "mutual respect between nations," he would form an international baseball league.[6] So in October, 1966, Dilbeck had formed the Global League[7] to rival the American League and National League. After additional financings of teams in 1967, opening day was announced for April 20, 1968.[8]

But Dilbeck and the Global League remained quietly in the background during the remainder of 1967 and well into 1968 because Walter Dilbeck had a more important, more pressing and more immediate goal: to send Ronald Reagan to the White House in 1968.

Governor Reagan for President Committee

Walter Dilbeck was busy during 1967 setting up his own grass-roots Reagan presidential campaign office in the nation's capital and gathering signatures from Reagan supporters. That fall he announced to the press that his Reagan campaign office was ready officially to open. Dilbeck set up a "six-room suite in a distant corner of a 50-year old hotel" at the "far end" of Washington D.C.'s embassy row.[9]

Reagan's Foreign Policy

In 1967, Dilbeck made a longer, return visit to South Vietnam, and this time adopted four South Vietnamese children.[10] By then Dilbeck fully had soured on the Johnson administration's handling of the Vietnam War and felt that Reagan's aggressive policies—actually to try to win the war—was his second major reason for becoming another early Reagan Democrat for 1968. He told the press that he had never met Reagan and only had seen him on television. But it was Reagan's hawkish views on Vietnam that had been the clincher.

Dilbeck explained, "I think that if he gets enough backing, he'll come out. I think that's what he's waiting for."[11] By the time the campaign office opened that week, Dilbert had gathered some "22,000 signatures of supporters in Indiana." He said he would staff the Reagan campaign office with eleven workers, who would begin a "massive mailing to veterans groups, professional groups, and churches" with the eventual goal of one million signatures.[12] Dilbeck then would send the petitions to Republican Party national headquarters.

Dilbeck himself spent $60,000 in Indiana for the Reagan campaign. "I'm trying to get the people to show enough strength that the Republicans will have to draft him," he added.[13]

Dilbeck's announcement did not go unnoticed in far away Sacramento. The governor's office issued a rebuttal to Dilbeck, saying, "Govenor Reagan is not a candidate for President. He has not authorized Walter J. Dilbeck, Jr., or anyone else to open headquarters on his behalf or to work in any way to promote his candidacy."[14] More forceful words were yet to come from Reagan's office.

Dilbeck, hero of World War II and successful businessman and baseball owner, was not deterred. The following month, Dilbeck targeted Republicans in Iowa. Prior to Reagan's planned visit to Washington D.C. in mid January 1968, Dilbeck had mailed out engraved invitations to Iowa Republicans inviting them to attend a reception and cocktail party. But having a solo grass roots campaign operative in the nation's capital, which now was pushing for votes in Iowa, did not sit well with the decision makers in California once again. This time, the Governor's office in Sacramento issued an uncharacteristic sharp rebuttal to Dilbeck's engraved invitations. Tom Reed reflected that at this time Reagan was less optimistic about running for the presidency, and likely Reagan's staff had asked him if a solo operative such as Dilbeck should be disavowed to which Reagan most likely had agreed.[15]

Up to that point Reagan in many, many press conferences indeed had denied his presidential campaign's existence, and also he had disavowed the actions of Reed and others at various points as we have seen. Reagan would say later that spring that he had no knowledge and would not encourage grass-root activists in Wisconsin, Nebraska, Oregon and in other states. But rarely was the wording as sharply rebuking as it was that January day from Sacramento when the press read: "The proposed opening of a so-called 'Reagan for President' headquarters on January 19 in Washington D.C. is ridiculous...Walter

J. Dilbeck, Jr., who has formed the committee and who apparently has sent out engraved invitations to the opening, is wasting his time and his money, and also is doing a disservice to Governor Reagan."[16] The Governor's office went on to say that Dilbeck had "no connection with Reagan or anyone on his staff."[17] At the same time that this message from the Governor's office was made, Reagan for President offices and activities in Wisconsin, Nebraska, and Oregon---all having begun at the impetus of Tom Reed or his team---were gearing up for the spring 1968 primaries.

Dilbeck's direct campaign activities on behalf of Ronald Reagan during the remainder of 1968, including if he ever succeeded in getting a million signatures dropped off at Republican Party headquarters, are lost to history. There was one newspaper report however that revealed more details of the Dilbeck office in Washington D.C. The office was described as an "unmarked suite in the Alban Towers, an apartment hotel at Massachusetts and Wisconsin Avenues" and was manned by 23-year old Alan Lipscomb from Louisville, KY.[18] The Alban Towers address of the committee, 3700 Massachusetts Avenue NW, was the same apartment building where Frank Sinatra and Betty Davis had stayed during President Kennedy's inauguration. Lipscomb's comments confirmed what Dilbert had said earlier—that a Reagan campaign staff director and ten others would move in soon "to launch a nation-wide campaign to boost California Gov. Ronald Reagan for the Republican nomination for President."[19] Lipscomb elaborated saying that his office planned to set up Reagan organizations "in each state and then coordinate their independent activities."[20] Lipscomb added that Dilbeck had chosen the out-of-the-way location for the office because Reagan was not a candidate yet, but added hopefully, "If he announces his candidacy, we'll move downtown."[21]

For World War II hero Walter Dilbeck, who did not flee in the face of overwhelming Nazi SS troops and fought back to destroy them, certainly two negative pronouncements from Sacramento could not deter his wish to see Ronald Reagan as president in 1968. Indeed he was not deterred. So besides Dilbeck having donated the $60,000 to fund the obtaining of the 22,000 Indiana signatures for Reagan, Dilbeck did end up donating another $80,000 to the 1968 Reagan campaign for a total of $140,000.[22]

In the Dirksen Center files is an invitation inviting the Dirksen's to attend Dilbeck's January 19 reception and cocktail party for the Governor Reagan for President Committee, which would be held at the Shoreham Hotel in Washington D.C. Senator Dirksen phoned in his regrets on January 15.[23]

On January 17, just prior to the Reagan grass roots office opening, Reagan was special guest at the 158th Republican Leadership meeting, held at Dirksen's office. The press conference on this day, when Reagan had discussed Eisenhower, Korea, and Vietnam, was mentioned earlier. Republican National Chairman Ray Bliss was present at the leadership dinner, as was Congressman Gerald Ford. Ford spoke of the unselfish service, which Reagan had given the party. Reagan spoke about California's dire finances, given the budget problems his predecessor, Pat Brown, had created before Reagan's inauguration. Based on his recent travels, Reagan told the group that Republicans across the nation wanted unity.

Reagan then spoke of increasing political activity by young people, which he characterized as a "fresh air" approach.[24] And Dilbeck used his remaining monies to help fund in 1968 another Washington, D.C.-based organization, besides his own Reagan campaign office there, an off-shoot of Young Americans for Freedom, called Students for Reagan.

Endnotes

1. "Millionaire Fan to Finance 'Reagan for President' Push," *Corpus Christi Times*, 12/11/67, p. 8
2. McKenna, p. 2
3. McKenna, p. 4
4. Ross, p. 288-290
5. McKenna, p. 2
6. McKenna, p. 2
7. At a maiden meeting in Evansville, representatives met from thirteen cities Manila, San Juan, Indianapolis, St. Paul, Portland, Long Island, San Diego, Phoenix, Akron, Chicago, Seattle, Cincinnati, and Milwaukee.
8. "Louisville is 8th Member of International League," *NYT*, 10/19/67, p. 61
9. "Millionaire Fan to Finance 'Reagan for President' Push," *Corpus Christi Times*, 12/11/67, p. 8
10. Witcover, Jules, "Agnew Benefactor: High Roller, Mystery Man," *Washington Post*, 1/5/75, p. A4
11. "Millionaire Fan..." op.cit.
12. ibid, "Millionaire Fan"
13. ibid, "Millionaire Fan"
14. "Gov. Reagan Disavows Booster's Office Here," *NYT*, 12/15/67
15. Reed, pers comm. 3/10/13
16. "Invitation," Cedar Rapids Gazette, 1/22/68, p. 4
17. ibid
18. "Reagan Headquarters Opened Here," *Washington Post*, 1/6/68
19. ibid, "Reagan Headquarters"
20. ibid, "Reagan Headquarters"
21. ibid, "Reagan Headquarters"
22. "Walter Dilbeck Claims Partner Spiro Agnew is Worth 'Millions,'" *People*, 12/23/74
23. Dirksen Congressional Center, EMD Papers, Alpha 1968, Reagan
24. Minutes of the 158th Meeting of the Republican Leadership of the Congress, 1/17/1968, 10:00 AM, courtesy Dirksen Congressional Center, EMD Papers, Republican Congressional Leadership Series, F. 77

CHAPTER 17: STUDENTS FOR REAGAN

"It was palpable; it was exciting. We were trying to introduce something completely new to the world. What higher calling?"

~ Kathryn Forte[1]

"Reagan gave voice to the idea that free people made better decisions than government."

~ Pat Nolan[2]

Reagan's idealistic visions of victory over communism in Vietnam were taking hold in idealistic Americans. As Dilbeck got out his checkbook to fund his new baseball team and his Reagan for President campaign office, he also donated money to another brand-new Reagan organization: Students for Reagan (SFR).

America's collective memory may regard the 1960s as a time when many of America's youth turned to radical left politics and culture. But as recounted in *The Other Side of the Sixties* by John A. Andrew III and *A Generation Awakes* by Wayne Thorburn, some youth actually turned towards conservatism. Clif White himself had been instrumental in shifting the Young Republican National Federation towards conservatism.[3]

One recent historian felt that because in the late 1960s the GOP did not have candidates strongly against the Vietnam War, it had become "increasingly irrelevant" to most young people.[4] But conservative youth who wanted to *win* in Vietnam did not feel marginalized, for they had one candidate who also wanted to win: Ronald Reagan. And Reagan's hawkish foreign policy was one decisive element in this swing to the right. Almost all of the leaders of SFR were strong anti-communists, who saw Reagan as a conservative American leader and future president with decisive foreign policy goals.

Students who would support Reagan in 1968 had role models, some mentioned previously, to follow earlier in the decade and even beforehand: Youth for Eisenhower,[5] Youth for Goldwater, YAF, YAF's *The New Guard* magazine, Young Republican National Federation, *National Review*, and *Firing Line*.[6]

Reagan's role on the National Advisory Board of YAF was an inspiration. And one year after the YAF poll, which had shown their huge preference for Reagan to be president, the YAF leaders read Reagan's letter of good wishes. Then they acted. At the September, 1967 YAF convention, the formation of a brand-new YAF-offshoot organization had been announced. It would be dedicated specifically to promote Ronald Reagan for president in 1968: Students for Reagan.[7]

Students for Reagan

The *SFR Chapter Organizational Manual* introduces SFR as "an organization formed to stimulate and demonstrate support among American students for Governor Ronald Reagan—his ideas, his ideals, and his nomination for the Presidency."[8] The manual went on to explain why generating student support for Reagan was so important in 1968:

1.   "Such a display can have a major psychological impact on the people of America—and particularly on the delegates to the Republican National Convention in Miami Beach
2.   Almost half of the students in college today will be able to vote for the first time this year; now is the time to begin promoting Governor Reagan
3.   Student enthusiasm, aroused at this time, will carry over into the November election, when student work will be most vital to a Reagan victory"[9]

What follows is an examination of the important individuals of SFR at the national level and an in-depth review of one of the group's Executive Committee meetings to shed light on what it was attempting to accomplish on a practical level in 1968 to get Ronald Reagan elected president that year. These young idealists saw in Reagan the only leader in 1968 who was standing up against communism and pushing for smaller government just as they were.

The East Coasters
David R. Jones

David Jones taught high school in the Tampa, Florida area for several years before pursuing a career in politics. In 1967 he was recruited by Charles Edison, son of the inventor, to help run the newly formed Fund for American Studies whose purpose was to educate youth about American freedom and free markets. Jones became involved with YAF in 1961 and rose from Florida State Chairman to Southern Regional Chairman to Executive Director.[10] In the 2008 YAF Alumni Survey, collated by Randal C. Teague, he observed, "Next to Bill Buckley, no single individual contributed more to the development of YAF than David R. Jones."[11]

Once SFR came into being, YAF leader Jones became an ad hoc advisor to the new SFR group, attended the meetings run by Bruce Weinrod, whom we will meet shortly, and participated thoughtfully and actively. Jones would attend the Miami Beach convention, where he would play a prominent role in the last possible effort to get Reagan nominated before the first ballot voting would commence. When Jones had been teaching high school, one of his students was Randal Teague.

Randal C. Teague

Randy Teague grew up in a "politically-involved family" in both North Carolina and Florida, and it was in Tampa where Jones had been one of his high school teachers.[12] Six months after YAF had been founded, he joined in March, 1961. In 1964 Teague came to Washington D.C to attend American University, to work for his congressman, to help the Goldwater campaign and then to attend law school. Teague had been YAF's Florida Chairman, Southern Regional Chairman, and a member of YAF's National Board of Directors. He also worked closely with his former teacher, David R. Jones, at the nascent Fund for American Studies.

Teague recalled that he, Jones, and the other YAF leaders wanted to create a separate organization to help Ronald Reagan in 1968. The rationale for the new group was to "give publicity on university campuses to a Reagan boomlet for the GOP nomination." Because there was not enough time to build either membership or chapters throughout the country, they were there primarily to perform foot-soldiering work and to set up "Instant Demonstration I.D. groups"[13] at the convention. The I.D.'s were to accompany Reagan in Miami Beach as pro-Reagan student demonstrators and to counter-demonstrate against Nixon, Rockefeller, and their supporters. They would meet delegates to convince them to vote for Reagan and carry pro-Reagan signs.

The group often used the conference room of YAF and preliminary organizational meetings were early in 1968, many months after the announcement at the YAF convention. They used the YAF infrastructure, its 60,000 membership and local chapters, to educate YAF members about Reagan and to heighten awareness of the new SFR. SFR sent out memorandum to YAF members and placed articles, notices and advertisements in YAF's magazine *The New Guard*.

There was no direct contact of any kind between SFR and Reed in California, Don L. Taylor in Wisconsin or any grass roots Reagan activists such as Dale Young's in Nebraska or in Oregon. YAF contributed to SFR's organizational finances, as did Walter Dilbeck, Jr.[14][15] We will see shortly that donated funds also were sent to SFR from Henry A. Bubb's and John Kerwitz's Citizens for Reagan National Information Center in Topeka.

Teague and Jones needed an enthusiastic and energetic young conservative to run SFR. They found the perfect candidate.

W. Bruce Weinrod

Weinrod's fascination with Reagan began "at an early age," when he used to watch Reagan as host of *Death Valley Days* and his twenty-mule team Borax commercials.[16] In those days before politics had begun for Reagan, Weinrod recalled, "There was something that drew you in" about him.[17] Later, as Weinrod had watched Reagan deliver *A Time for Choosing*, Weinrod thought, "Reagan would be so much better a candidate than Goldwater."[18] Then in a flash, Weinrod realized, "This guy should be President now."[19]

In 1967, Weinrod had met biographer Lee Edwards who, as we have seen, was about to write the first political biography of Reagan and was about to edit Thurmond's autobiography, and Edwards asked Weinrod if he was interested in becoming his only researcher. Weinrod jumped at the chance. Indeed in the acknowledgements of Edwards' early classic, *Reagan: A Political Biography*, Weinrod was thanked. Weinrod worked by establishing contact with many Reagan supporters and grew to admire Reagan as much more than a movie actor. The enthusiastic and energetic Bruce Weinrod would become Executive Director of the Washington D.C.-based SFR.[20] But SFR was not limited only to the nation's capital.

Ronald Docksai, Sr.

Ron Docksai was in high school in New York when, watching on an old black-and-white television, he first had seen and heard Reagan deliver *A Time for Choosing* in October, 1964. Reagan had appealed to his "embryonic verities: common sense, patriotism, and fairness."[21]

He wrote to Reagan in 1966, urging him to run for governor of California and wrote again in 1967 urging him to run for president.[22] While attending college at St. Johns University, he organized "Young New Yorkers for Reagan." Docksai's group affiliated with YAF.[23] Once SFR formed, it became the New York chapter of SFR.[24]

Late in 1967, Jones sent Docksai on a special fundraising mission: to ask Jones' old friend, wealthy conservative Democrat and former governor of New Jersey, Charles Edison, for a contribution. Edison's private residence occupied an entire floor atop the Waldorf-Astoria Hotel in Manhattan, which Docksai recalled as a being comprised of a cavern-like series of hallways of polished dark wood—a "walnut forest—which led to Edison himself seated at a desk with a huge portrait of his father, the famous inventor, peering down.[25] Edison said if Docksai would do something for him, he would contribute a check. Edison barked, "I want you to stand over there and I want you to give me a speech about freedom. I want you to tell me what it means to you personally when you hear someone talk about freedom."[26] Docksai gathered his courage and spoke to Edison about his step-father's migration from Bavaria to America and his love for his new country. Edison liked what he heard and wrote a check for $10,000. Docksai was elated and forwarded the check to Jones YAF headquarters.[27]

Docksai would send a "contingent" to the convention amongst whom was Christopher Buckley, the son of William F. Buckley, Jr.[28] Charles Edison in the interim was making arrangements to travel to the convention by special train and had booked a set of rooms at the Fontainebleau Hotel. Docksai especially was looking forward to working with Weinrod, as "Bruce was legendary for having the largest collection of 50's records one would ever encounter."[29]

Kathryn Forte

Growing up in Pennsylvania, Kathryn Forte had been inspired by a conservative father and by watching Buckley on television. In high school she wrote conservative editorials for the school newspaper and attended Dunbarton College in Washington D.C.[30] Forte held prominent offices in the Dunbarton YAF chapter, Dunbarton's Young Republican chapter, the D.C. Young Republicans and the D.C. YAF chapter.[31] As an active, idealistic young conservative, she had joined YAF picket lines against the Soviet Union and communism, and then against IBM when she had protested east-west trade. She was chosen Miss YAF 1968.[32]

Then in 1968 she became National Secretary for SFR. She recalled the group was "so idealistic about what could be accomplished through political activism and the possibility of a Reagan presidency and a free market/freedom agenda."[33]

Robert Schadler

Because his parents had fled Eastern Europe after World War II and settled in America, young Bob Schadler grew up in a church-going household emphasizing fiscal responsibility and anti-communism. At Georgetown University, he founded an Intercollegiate Studies Institute chapter. Schadler had learned shorthand, had mastered skills as a typist, and had worked at the nascent John F. Kennedy Presidential Library, whose archives were housed in the nation's capital prior to their eventual move to Columbia Point in Boston. Because of his shorthand and typing skills, Schadler was hired by Weinrod to help SFR, and thus Schadler and Forte took and typed the minutes of the Executive Committee.[34]

The West Coasters
Arnold Steinberg

Steinberg had campaigned door to door for Goldwater in 1964 in the hugely Democrat congressional district represented by Jimmie Roosevelt, FDR's son. Steinberg, a leader of Youth for Goldwater, had worked to transform many of those leaders and activists into Youth for Reagan YR in 1966, where he had worked closely with Jack Wheeler, Ronald Reagan's personal choice to head YR.

Steinberg ran California YAF along with Shawn Steel. In 1967 Steinberg wrote the cover article, about Ronald Reagan as California's new governor, for *The New Guard*. He transferred from UCLA back east to George Washington University for his third year of college. When a newly hired editor for *The New Guard* did not work out, Steinberg at age 19 was chosen as his replacement.[35]

He and Weinrod were college roommates—Steinberg at GWU and Weinrod at American University—and shared a tiny apartment within walking distance of the YAF office. It was here where both worked: Steinberg as editor and Weinrod as chief researcher for Lee Edwards. Steinberg later would arrange that the summer 1968 special convention issue of *The New Guard* would have its cover article about Reagan for president and would be written by Weinrod.[36]

Dana Rohrabacher

Well before Ronald Reagan had been elected governor, future Congressman Rohrabacher (R-CA) had begun organizing conservatives. In 1964, he had organized 120 fellow high school students as Goldwater supporters. By 1966 he was a member of YAF and was recruited by Shawn Steel to head the Los Angeles County High School Youth for Reagan during the run for the governorship. Rohrabacher worked closely with both Steinberg and Steel at the time.

During the Reagan gubernatorial campaign, a dispute arose and Spencer-Roberts, running the campaign, wanted to shut down Youth for Reagan. Rohrabacher wanted to save it and knew that if Reagan were aware of the Spencer-Roberts plans, that he would not permit it to be closed down. So Rohrabacher camped out on the Reagan's front lawn until Reagan himself came out to see what was going on. Nancy initially did not want her husband to speak to the young stranger, saying that Reagan was very busy. But eventually Reagan, still in the midst of shaving, ran after the enthusiastic youth until Rohrabacher could tell his idol all about Youth for Reagan. Reagan said, "If you can spend the time waiting for me, I can spend the time listening." It was not shut down.[37]

In early 1968, Rohrabacher was in Prague observing first-hand the nascent anti-communist movement and was unable to participate directly with Weinrod or Steinberg or the others in Students for Reagan. But Rohrabacher would manage to fly back to the Miami Beach convention just in time.[38]

Shawn Steel

Shawn Steel, future attorney and Republican National Committeeman from California in 2013, found his life's purpose as a teenager. He had watched on television when the Soviet Union had invaded Hungary in 1956 and it had left on the young impressionable eleven-year old a "memory scar" that has not faded to this day.[39] Five years later he saw John Wayne and Ronald Reagan speak at the World Christian Anti-Communist Crusade. There, some sixteen thousand enthusiastic attendees also saw celebrities Roy Rogers, Dale Evans, and Pat Boone.[40] Steel was hooked. Hearing the stories of ex-communists inspired him to become a staunch anti-communist himself. Steel recalled that Reagan had been instrumental in helping Steel to "find my purpose" in life.[41]

In high school, Steel found that his conservative point of view left him isolated from most of his peers. But in 1964 he found other youth of similar ideals. Steel founded the San Fernando Valley Youth for Goldwater in 1964 and established chapters in every single high school, more than 30, in the valley. Steel recalled that he had been invited to hear the taping of Reagan's "The Speech", but he did not attend. In 1965 at age 19, he formed chapters of YAF in Los Angeles, which were comprised of the same people as he had recruited the prior year for Goldwater. His Pacific Action Council, the chapter name he had chosen, had more than 500 members. The group brought in conservative speakers and "fought established Republicans."[42]

By 1966 Steel became statewide Chairman of Youth for Reagan for high school students and recruited Dana Rohrabacher to run the Los Angeles chapter as we have seen. Steel worked on behalf of Reagan during the primary but by the time of the general election, he was brought directly to work at Reagan headquarters. Steel recalled that his job was to get high school students to attend rallies and to set up counter-demonstrations against Democrat Governor Pat Brown.

After Reagan became governor, Steel moved up from Youth for Reagan and became State Chairman of YAF. He also became a member of the national YAF board and met national YAF Chairman David Jones, whom Steel felt was his "mentor."[43] Steel attended many national YAF meetings in Washington D.C. during 1967-1968, at which a number of SFR board meetings were held in the next room. He was not an official member of the national Executive Committee of SFR in 1968 but he would attend the Miami Beach convention as a Reagan supporter as we will see.[44]

Pat Nolan

Pat Nolan, a fifth generation Californian, became an avowed anti-communist at a young age. His older sister had known local Hungarian refugee families who had escaped from the failed 1956 revolt. A Polish family, which had fled communism, had been taken in by Nolan's local church. He was at the same anti-communist crusade meeting in 1961 as was Steel, when Nolan heard Ronald Reagan speak for the first time other than on *Death Valley Days*. Nolan recalled that he was "so impressed by Reagan," because he found Reagan to be "disarming and very articulate."[45] Reagan was "so relaxed in his manner, so forthright and spoke so that the common man could understand."[46]

Attending catholic high school in Burbank, Nolan recalled that to the "great chagrin" of his liberal honors social studies teacher, a majority of the honors students were for Goldwater.[47] Late in the campaign, Nolan and his family watched *A Time for Choosing* on their tiny black-and-white television. Nolan nodded vigorously as he watched, thinking Reagan spoke "such straight-forward truth."[48] Nolan recalled how active Reagan had been as a board member with the California YAF. Reagan was not just a passive board member or donor. Reagan spoke at California YAF events, contributed to the newsletter, and headlined banquets. Nolan was hooked on Reagan.

In 1966 he had founded the Burbank chapter of Youth for Reagan. Nolan reported to Steel, who was Los Angeles County director. At his chapter's first meeting, Nolan had forty-two members in attendance and they began by distributing Reagan flyers. Through YAF, his Youth for Reagan chapter obtained a film copy of Reagan speaking at the University of Southern California. Nolan's group showed the film at local Republican meetings.

Nolan recalled how once Reagan had won the 1966 primary, students from Youth for Christopher were brought into the Reagan fold. And at the state convention in Sacramento, Nolan met Reagan personally for the first time. Nolan was at the Biltmore Hotel on Election Night 1966 when Reagan won and saw the unfurling of the Reagan-for-President banner as discussed earlier.

By 1967 Nolan was on the California State Board of YAF. During this first year of Reagan's governorship, Nolan had little to do directly with the presidential campaign but he did help organize YAF rallies and demonstrations, which supported Reagan's policies of fiscal restraint and budget cuts. At this time, Jones was making visits to California to see the local YAF leaders. When Nolan asked about Reagan's running for president in 1968, Jones told him, "Just you wait!"[49]

In the spring of 1968 as the convention approached, YAF was attempting to get as many members as possible to go to Miami Beach. Nolan sent a letter to YAF donors asking them to sponsor YAF students' travel expenses, and Nolan became one of several scholarship winners. Pat Nolan, who had never flown before, prepared to leave for the Republican convention.[50] He did not know it at the time, but Nolan would be the first to hear Reagan looking towards a brighter future after Miami Beach.

Passion for a President Reagan in 1968

What drove these students not only to want to see Reagan as president in 1968 but to put their ideals into action by forming a brand-new political organization: Students for Reagan?

It was Reagan's views on world affairs. At the top of the list were Reagan's forceful stances against communism in Vietnam. But by this time Reagan also had spoken about negotiations with the Soviets and with Red China during the Kennedy debate and had called for the tearing down of the Berlin Wall several times. Reagan's idealism was at the top too.

Kathryn Forte recalls her answer: "The passion we all had" to see Reagan elected in 1968 was "driven by our lofty ideals. That inspiration was the underpinning of everything we did."[51] SFR and each individual officer felt that their shared excitement for Ronald Reagan's attainment of the White House in 1968 was "palpable; it was exciting. We were trying to introduce something completely new to the world. What higher calling?"[52]

Second on the list was what would be called later "The Great Communicator." For Pat Nolan, his enthusiasm stemmed from what he had perceived to be Reagan's Ike-inspired gubernatorial election theme—common sense solutions—and those same solutions now to be applied at the national level.[53] Plus for Nolan, Reagan was "very articulate, disarming, so relaxed in his manner and so forthright; he spoke so the common person could understand."[54] Reagan had his "pulse on the people before the polls" and that is why Nolan believed in Ronald Reagan and his ideals: Reagan "gave voice to the idea that free people made better decisions than government."[55]

For Weinrod, Reagan's ability to articulate conservative views, think on his feet, appeal to the man on the street, and his practical ability to solve problems by working with the Democrat opposition in Sacramento were critically important. But Reagan was "tough when he needed to be."[56] Weinrod recalled one particular Reagan sentence at a speech when he had invoked the phrase about Republicans flying their banners high. Weinrod reflected that Reagan was practical. Reagan had understood the limits of how far he could go without alienating those Democrats and Independents he had sought to attract when he had said, "We don't want to jump off the cliff with our flags flying." For Weinrod, Ronald Reagan had "the whole package."[57]

SFR Attains Legitimacy

SFR had official office stationery for which Bruce Weinrod still proudly has a few copies. The organization's address was listed as 1104 Vermont Avenue, Northeast, Suite 102. Co-Chairmen were Michael Thompson then at the University of Missouri and Charles L. Williams, Jr., at North Carolina State University. Chairman of the National Committee was Hugh L. Henry of the University of Virginia Graduate School. Randal Teague at George Washington University Law School was Treasurer, and finally Bruce Weinrod of American University was listed as Executive Director. Members of Students for Reagan received official membership cards signed by Co-Chairman Williams.[58]

Weinrod sent out a memorandum to instruct new members on how the push to elect Reagan in 1968 was to be made. SFR was to serve as an "organizational outlet" to centralize all campus pro-Reagan activities throughout the nation. SFR would familiarize other students about Reagan's programs, would assist local members attending mock conventions to assure Reagan victories, would coordinate campus efforts to achieve a Reagan victory at the Choice '68 National Collegiate Presidential Primary, and would send "hundreds" of pro-Reagan students to the convention.[59]

From February 26 through March 1, SFR was asked to make Reagan's presence known at a leadership training school run by the Young Republicans. Weinrod quickly got to work. With less than three days notice, he printed and prepared Reagan campaign materials, rented a room for an SFR-sponsored party—including hiring a rock band and having an open bar—and made sure to bus in students from area colleges. Weinrod manned a Reagan campaign materials display.[60] The party "was packed," resulting in Reagan getting "real visibility."[61]

SFR Planning: Executive Committee Meeting March 24, 1968

But SFR was a serious organization, and a perfect example of its serious nature and steadfast purpose in getting Ronald Reagan nominated and elected in 1968 are the detailed minutes of the group's Executive Committee meeting held at 3 PM on Sunday March 24, 1968; the author is indebted to Bruce Weinrod for sharing the 45-year old document and to Kathryn Forte who shared her collection of SFR and YAF documents and memorabilia.

Present at the meeting were Williams, Thompson, Henry, Teague, Weinrod and Jones. The first order of business was selecting a secretary of the Executive Committee and Teague nominated Forte, who was voted in unanimously, accepted and joined the group as a voting member.

The next topic was recruitment of SFR contacts and members amongst college Republicans in West Virginia, Kentucky, Washington D.C. and Virginia plus a young Gary Bauer in Kentucky.

Nixon had strong support on certain campuses in the Northeast, so SFR adjusted its sights. For example, SFR bypassed directly contacting campuses in the Northeast directly, and instead would send one member to the upcoming Republican Student Conference in Boston. And rather than targeting directly the Young Republicans or YAF at Purdue University, SFR targeted their mock convention instead. Other targeted events included mock conventions at Oberlin College and the Young Republican convention in Ohio.

Reagan's prospects looked better in the Midwest. In Michigan, two or three of the five regional College Republican chairmen were for Reagan. The Michigan Chairman of YAF would join SFR as well. In Wisconsin where Don Taylor had been recruiting, the College Republican chairman came out for Reagan, and Milwaukee's Concordia College was targeted also. At Kansas State University where Reagan had delivered the Landon Lecture at the behest of Henry A. Bubb, the head of the Reagan for President Campaign Committee would be running their mock convention.

In the West, contacts were made at Arizona State University, the University of Arizona, the University of Hawaii, and at other colleges in Colorado and California. In Oregon where Reagan would be on the ballot in his most important primary, the chairman of the Reagan for President Committee at Willamette University would hold in April a mock convention for college delegates from many Western states: Oregon, Washington, Idaho, California, Alaska and Utah. The SFR Executive Committee thus made Oregon a major target and devoted the resources to achieve a Reagan victory.

In Mississippi, two college Reagan supporters decided to form a competing organization, Americans for Reagan. In Texas two Reagan supporters were running for state committeemen for College Republicans. Randy Teague promised to look into leads in other Southern states.

David Jones then spoke to the committee about membership, including creating a steering committee and appointing 50 SFR national committee men. Jones emphasized the urgency of the approaching convention in Miami Beach and that SFR should "check the pulse of each school" prior to possibly wasting time on college campuses with little potential for Reagan support in 1968.

The Executive Committee then prioritized campuses for the forthcoming mock conventions. At the top of their list was Washington and Lee University, where a Reagan victory was anticipated and for which Thompson and Williams would attend and Henry would make advance arrangements. Second in priority was Kansas State University, where Reagan support was "substantial" and Williams was to visit a month before the convention to assure success. The Vanderbilt University Mock Convention in mid April was targeted next and Williams was to be in charge there for SFR. The major multistate participation in Oregon was discussed as was an early April mock convention at the University of South Florida, where eleven colleges and universities were to send representatives. Potential other schools to target included Princeton, Northwestern, Purdue, and Ohio State.

Funding

There was no coordination or communication with Tom Reed or Clif White in California or with Reagan grass roots efforts in the three targeted opt-out states. SFR did exert control of its and its chapters' finances. Money was tight. The SFR Executive Committee created an official fund raising manual. Each SFR local college chapter was to collect its own monies, but the national organization was going to target national funds to Washington and Lee's Mock Convention and any other campus chapter, where a few hundred dollars might make the critical difference in success or failure. If a campus wanted funds from national SFR, that chapter had to send in a detailed budget to undergo scrutiny by the SFR Executive Committee. In addition to a budget, the local campus chapter seeking funding had to submit plans, expectations, and strategy.

But Weinrod was contacted by one national Reagan organization. John Kerwitz and Henry A. Bubb of the Citizens for Reagan National Information Center in Topeka told Weinrod that SFR was to receive financial assistance for an upcoming national Young Republican convention to be held in Washington, D.C. Kerwitz sent a $25,000 check to SFR telling Weinrod, "Do something that makes a splash" for Reagan for president.[62] Weinrod rented a room at the hotel and arranged for a bar and a band at the Reagan presidential hospitality suite. Arrangements again were made for young co-eds from local colleges to be bussed in. The Reagan suite was "jam packed" and was such a success that someone else in the hotel called the police so as to quiet the pro-Reagan crowd.[63] Weinrod also had arranged for pro-Reagan literature, bumper stickers and signs to be distributed throughout the convention. He recalled that this was a "serious SFR event to see Reagan elected president."[64]

The reason national SFR seemingly was so tight with funds is that they themselves did not have much to dole out to local chapters. Depite the initial $25,000 donated check, Weinrod recalled that Bubb's citizens group did "not live up to our expectations"[65] The Executive Committee minutes noted that "our organization is not getting funds which have already been promised." Teague did recall that one of their main contributors was Walter Dilbeck Jr, but it is not clear if the likely $80,000 he donated beyond his own Indiana campaign cited earlier all went to SFR or to other Reagan grass roots organizations such as Bubb's or to other targeted states such as the Reagan campaign offices in Wisconsin, Nebraska, and/or Oregon.

Tactics

But Citizens for Reagan National Information Center had two other campaign tools of perhaps even more value to SFR than funding. As will be seen, the campaign film *Ronald Reagan, Citizen Governor* had been sent to Bubb for distribution. Plus there were copies of the Reagan-Kennedy debate *Town Meeting of the World*. SFR, sometimes with the help of parent YAF, distributed both.

That spring, Weinrod and his group continued to work diligently to raise the fervor for Reagan for president on campuses throughout the nation. The available pro-Reagan materials that SFR mailed out to members and chapters consisted of: Reagan bumper stickers 10/$1, buttons 15/$1 and 12in x 18in Reagan posters 3/$1; books Lee Edwards biography of Reagan $1 each; and various Reagan speeches such as his speech in Omaha to the Young Republican National Federation, where he had first used the words *sickly pastels* 20/$1.[66] SFR manned a hospitality suite at each mock convention. Individual SFR members then were mailed an invitation to attend and work at the Miami Beach convention.

SFR was successful due to the hard work of Weinrod, his Executive Committee and Jones. Within two weeks of the SFR office being opened in early March, "all necessary equipment and arrangements for a full-scale operation had been obtained and completed."[67] They recruited many College Young Republicans (CYR), had sent Reagan materials to 42 mock conventions, and Williams had attended the top three.[68] Unfortunately there was scant follow-up information as to how Reagan did.

But former President Eisenhower also had been paying attention to these activities of SFR, for his diary entry on March 2—a week before his next meeting with Reagan—shows he watched on television a tape of one of the mock conventions.[69]

By the end of May there were 115 SFR campus national committeemen and 17 high school national committeemen. Over 500 members of CYR joined SFR.[70] SFR processed over 300 orders for Reagan materials, with the resultant number of Reagan bumper stickers and buttons "in the many thousands" and Reagan literature pamphlets, speeches, etc as cited earlier "in the hundreds of thousands."[71] Thompson, in charge of national meetings, arranged for SFR to have membership displays and hospitality suites at state CYR meetings "around the country," as well as had SFR show both Reagan films.[72]

Reagan on Campus

Not all activities of SFR had been done at the Washington D.C. headquarters or on college campuses. SFR would send members to participate in pro-Reagan demonstrations when Reagan would appear that spring in Washington, D.C., Albuquerque, Denver, Phoenix, and Boise. Weinrod reported that SFR had been mentioned in the press for its pro-Reagan activities in the *New York Times*, *Los Angeles Times* and the *Washington Post*.

Prior to SFR's existence, Reagan, as discussed, had been received well by student crowds in Omaha, at Hiram Scott College, Eureka College, the University of Kansas, and at Yale. Once SFR got involved directly, Reagan's ability to draw large, enthusiastic crowds of college students grew. In January, 1968, Reagan had visited the University of Pittsburgh when he addressed morality. A few months later, when Reagan would visit Boulder, Colorado on April 27, 1968 on another campaign and fundraising trip, he would speak to "a crowd of 3,000 applauding students at the University of Colorado."[73] Discussing student riots, he would draw "cheers from a midday student audience."[74] At Tulane University on May 19, he would address "a cheering crowd of 4,000 at a Republican rally in the Tulane University gymnasium."[75] Not all SFR crowds were large. As will be seen, at a Topeka barbecue in June, Reagan would be greeted by a small three-person SFR contingent. By having its local chapters and members get to these Reagan events, this was SFR at its finest.

At local events, Weinrod continued running his Reagan campaign display for SFR, which showcased the organization and the candidate.[76] Finally, SFR had 20,000 Reagan for President ballots printed and distributed to be used to vote for Reagan. There were campaign buttons and placards[77] Weinrod ended his report stating that SFR's next goal was to plan for the Miami Beach convention.

SFR at the local college level

One could be an active Young Republican and an active member and leader of Students for Reagan. Peter H. Burr attended Nasson College in Kennebunk, Maine. Besides being regional director of the New England Young Republican College Federation, member of the Kennebunk Republican Town Committee, and delegate to the Maine GOP convention, Burr also was a member of the SFR National Steering Committee. In the spring of 1968 he formed a Maine Students for Reagan Committee.

In one instance, SFR took over the entire statewide duties of Reagan grassroots activists. Burr told the press that because there was no Reagan for President Committee in Maine, his Maine SFR committee would assume those actions. The goals for Maine SFR were two-fold: to establish SFR clubs on campuses throughout Maine, and to "see that Governor Reagan's beliefs in government and economy are represented in the Maine delegation to Miami."[78]

Specific SFR tactics included:

1. having students on campus, as well as townspeople, sign printed "ballots" urging Reagan to run for president; the ballots would be tabulated in Washington D.C. at the national office.
2. having campus "mass sell" meetings with a speaker or showing of one of the Reagan films, plus have the membership table outside and distribute ballots again
3. canvassing dormitories in person with detailed suggestions to succeed
4. promoting the attending of the Miami Beach convention, but one must be a member of SFR
5. selling Reagan materials at membership tables books, posters, bumper stickers etc but campaign literature was free
6. involving local media including campus newspapers, radio and posters
7. how to use and improve upon the SFR campaign materials sent to each chapter

The manual also mentioned that new SFR members had to pay $1 national membership dues that went to the national office, but each chapter had the option of asking for chapter dues and/or donations as well.

High School Students for Reagan

Given the personal experiences above of some SFR leaders in themselves having begun their conservative political activities in high school—Steinberg, Weinrod, Rohrabacher, and Steel, it is not surprising that the SFR campus chapter manual had a section on how to start SFR/Reagan for President chapters in high schools. The major idea to present to a high school principal was to advocate for a straw vote amongst the students. A faculty sponsor was needed, and a membership table was encouraged which could be used outside of school as well. Indeed if door-to-door canvassing by high school students could be arranged, it would be received much more favorably by local townspeople because there were local high school students doing the canvassing rather than mainly out-of-town college students.

Other than having SFR high school national committeemen as cited earlier, unfortunately, there is no follow-up information on the success or failure of the SFR program for high schools. As one specific example, when Reagan made one notable campaign visit to Great Falls High School in Montana, there was no evidence of a high school SFR group at the event.

SFR's Problems

SFR had noble goals. But to have begun a nationwide Reagan for President campus organization in the early fall of 1967 with the hopes of achieving success was daunting. Despite announcing SFR's formation at the YAF convention in Pittsburgh on Sept. 1, 1967, SFR did not open its office in the nation's capital until early March, 1968. Thus six crucial months were lost at almost the worst possible time as Reagan made his visits to Kansas State and Yale then as discussed above.

The leaders attempted to establish campus chapters in order to get out the vote for November 1968 because many members and their friends would be voting for the first time. Yet Reagan first had to be nominated. As we will see, a number of SFR members, from local chapters and from the National executive Committee, would play important roles at the Miami Beach convention. But time was the crucial factor. Hoping that less than a year's worth of effort, and in reality SFR had only March through the early August convention with which to be successful, would make an important difference may have been naïve.

The second problem was financial. Due to severely limited funds, SFR could send those few additional dollars to a very few, select chapters and mock conventions. SFR met in the offices of YAF and was dependent upon the parent organization's office space and staff, even though SFR was established as a separate entity. Plus not everyone at YAF was a Reagan supporter, yet how any non-Reagan supporters who worked at YAF viewed SFR is not clear.

The third problem that SFR faced was lack of information. For each of the SFR leaders with whom the author interviewed, none ever communicated with Reagan campaign director Tom Reed at the time and all admitted that at the time, they did not know who he was. SFR did have limited contact with Henry A. Bubb's Citizens for Reagan National Information Center in Topeka, asked Bubb for monies and the two Reagan films, and used some of Bubb's membership pamphlets as adapted for SFR membership use. But Bubb was never asked to ship Reagan campaign materials to any campuses beyond the tiny amounts of buttons and posters cited earlier.

Lack of communication was key. Both Reed and Clif White and the Reagan campaign team were not aware of the existence of Students for Reagan and thus made no effort to reach out to them directly.[79] Plus Bubb never mentioned the existence of SFR to Reed either.[80]

Eureka '68: Beyond SFR

Not all advocacy groups pushing for Reagan in 1967-1968 were affiliated with SFR. Previously, we have seen how Morton Blackwell had been national executive director of the College Republicans. Blackwell had been at Reagan's Louisville campaign visit to aid Nunn and had seen how much pro-Reagan enthusiasm there had been. Soon Blackwell would return home to become a Reagan supporter in Louisiana.

A unique combined student-faculty organization was formed at the University of Illinois in Champaign, Illinois. The grass roots effort was called the University of Illinois Draft Ronald Reagan for President Committee and was formed in late 1967. It combined members from the undergraduate college, the graduate school and faculty. The President of the Committee was Henry Karlson, a senior at the Law School, and the head of advertising was undergraduate senior John Hanke.

In mid December, 1967, the Committee held a press conference to announce the creation of a unique Ronald Reagan campaign button. Called "Eureka '68," the button was bright blue and gold and measured one and three-quarters inches in diameter. The button was named after Reagan's Illinois alma mater, his recent speech there for the library dedication, as well as the fact that "eureka" was California's battle cry and meant in Latin, "I have found it." Karlson told the press that their committee "found in Governor Reagan a proven winner for the 1968 election."[81]

Karlson told the press that the organization would "lay the foundation for an aggressive, constructive effort to encourage Governor Reagan's entrance into the race for the Republican nomination."[82] Karlson planned Reagan advertisements on the campus radio and in the campus newspaper, a campus membership booth, to disseminate pro-Reagan campaign material, and to inaugurate a campus-wide petition to draft Reagan for the nomination.[83]

The press was given four succinct reasons for the formation of the University of Illinois Draft Ronald Reagan for President Committee:

1. Governor Reagan has proven by his overwhelming victory in California that he is able to draw support from all segments of society. He is a proven winner in a state which four years earlier had solidly rejected the Republican choice.
2. Governor Reagan has proven his ability as an able administrator in California, and as a shrewd diplomat at the recent Governor's Convention.
3. Governor Reagan's basic concern is with the welfare of his constituents. The U. of I. Draft Reagan Committee feels that the underlying conservatism of his politics will best serve the nation's interests. Governor Reagan's approaches to dealing with such problems as California's educational system particularly at Berkley sic and deficit spending have shown his ability to deal with the problems facing America today.
4. Governor Reagan is a realistic politician. While he is basically conservative, he has shown willingness to compromise for the sake of unity and yet he has shown the courage to hold his ground in what he definitely believes is right and necessary for the welfare of his constituents. He is a true moderate who will better fulfill the American people's need for establishing a more constitutional

administration in Washington than such Democrats as Governor Wallace on the right or Senator Robert Kennedy on the left.[84]

Clearly this organization of political novices saw what most seasoned professionals did not see about Reagan in 1968: that his track record even after just a year in office qualified him to be not just president, but the same track record and the same man would be an excellent president.

Karlson expanded the outreach of his Draft Reagan committee from just the campus to all of Champaign County. In late 1967 he had sent a formal invitation to Governor Reagan, inviting the Governor to speak at the group's 1968 Lincoln Day Dinner in February, 1968. Karlson's grass roots campaign activities for Reagan for President drew the interest of the Illinois State Republican Party and Senate Minority Leader Everett Dirksen. Dirksen wrote to Reagan asking Reagan to speak at the Lincoln Day dinner.[85]

The intercession of Dirksen asking Reagan to speak, the formation of a unique undergraduate-graduate-faculty Reagan for President Committee, and the expansion to generate county-wide excitement for Reagan into the Young Republicans, all demonstrate what one committed pro-Reagan grass roots activist could accomplish.

Reagan Meets with Students

Reagan did not shy away from students, a group often associated with liberal causes and in 1968 with the liberal icons Robert F Kennedy Jr. and Eugene McCarthy. Yet Reagan not only did not write off the student vote, he actively pursued their votes. At each of the multiple campuses he visited during his presidential campaign, he spoke to student audiences, often met with students in small groups and answered their sometimes hostile questions, and in the case of Yale spent a week with students when he taught classes, spoke at the Yale Political Union, and discussed politics in small groups even when he was being filmed by public television.

As will be reviewed shortly, only four days after a student takeover at Columbia University, when meeting with students at the University of Colorado at Boulder only four days later on April 27, 1968 for a twenty-minute question-and-answer session and press conference, Reagan would not hesitate to participate, saying, "I may be foolish, but I'm brave."[86] Reagan almost never got angry when he encountered hostile questions and in the end got good reviews from students after he had gone.

SFR Prior to Miami Beach

As SFR members and leaders campaigned for Reagan in the spring of 1968, they started to prepare for the convention in Miami Beach.

Four years after having observed carefully all the techniques used by, and events planned by, the college students who had campaigned so actively for Barry Goldwater, William A. Rusher would send a memo to David R. Jones on June 3, 1968 outlining his recommendation that SFR be given "authority and necessary financial support" to establish a Student Activation Center at the Miami Beach convention.[87] Rusher would want the center to handle housing assignments in Miami Beach for the students and Rusher already had reserved 100 motel rooms. Rusher would suggest that if students wrote to Miami area YAF contributors, then they might be able to obtain free housing.

Then Rusher would get specific in emulating for 1968 what he had seen four years earlier. He would want a pool of at least 100 volunteers, as he had arranged for Goldwater in 1964, who would be called upon for "every imaginable purpose"…and usually "at the last minute."[88] Rusher would propose that SFR could decorate a flat-bed truck which would be in continuous use for pro-Reagan rallies and that SFR should have a band, with pro-Reagan outfits and banners, "at all rallies."[89] Rusher would want the rallies at the airport, hotels, and the convention. SFR should distribute pro-Reagan campaign materials to each state hospitality suite so delegates could see them as part of the growing Reagan strength. If there were any high school students, or even younger children at the convention, Rusher wanted at least one Youth for Reagan rally as well. Rusher would end his memo suggesting that the minimum budget for his center was $5,000 and that if Jones and Weinrod found this idea acceptable, then Rusher wrote that he would work on a detailed budget. He would add that an advance time of at least 45 days before the convention was needed, as was time to arrange for Hollywood celebrities to appear at student events.

The Great Communicator—in 1968!

But SFR had one more major tactic to use for Ronald Reagan prior to the Miami Beach convention. As mentioned earlier, Arnold Steinberg, editor of YAF's *The New Guard*, would arrange that the summer 1968 issue be devoted to the Miami Beach convention. The cover would feature campaign signs and balloons under "1968: Which Way America?" Of the various names of Republican candidates seen at the bottom as signs, Reagan's name would be displayed five times to three for Nixon and one for Rockefeller.

The article for Reagan, entitled, "The Conservative Case for Ronald Reagan" would be written by Weinrod and would begin "Strategically, Reagan is the one man who can capitalize upon the serious split within the Democratic Party and, at the same time, retain his Republican base. In 1966, Reagan proved in California that he could attract the Democratic and Independent votes necessary for a Republican victory."[90] After winning the Republican nomination, Weinrod foresaw that Reagan "would go on the offensive from the start" with a "new approach to the nation's problems."[91]

Weinrod would continue that Reagan had "the ability to present the conservative view in an extremely smooth manner. His greatest virtue, perhaps, is his unparalleled ability to explain conservative positions in a way which is appealing to the average voter...His explanations were always masterpieces of clarity...Along with his ability to explain is a similar ability to present the conservative case in the most *positive* light possible."[92]

Weinrod would make an exceptionally clear case that Ronald Reagan indeed was "The Great Communicator" already in 1968— more than a full decade before the term became synonymous with President Reagan.

Weinrod's prescience did not stop there. As if Weinrod knew in advance of how Reagan would defeat Carter due in no small part to America's loss of standing in the world due to the Iran Hostage Crisis and loss of confidence at home with stag-flation and Carter's ill-fated term malaise, Weinrod would write this about candidate Reagan in 1968:

> "The moral authority of the President is a legitimate consideration in choosing a Presidential nominee. The Republican nominee must be a man who can restore confidence in the legitimacy of authority at home and confidence in our resolve abroad. The next President must be able to communicate integrity and sincerity to the people of America."[93]

As Weinrod had declared two years earlier, the nation should see a President Reagan *now*!

Student Polls

Ultimately, SFR must be judged, at least partially, on what either Republican students or students nationally, thought of Ronald Reagan as president in 1968 before and after SFR played any role. As noted earlier, Reagan had been a huge hit at the YAF convention in September 1967 just as SFR announced its existence. Then a full six months elapsed between the announcement of the formation SFR and the opening of its office. A frenzy of activity occurred between March and May 1968, as evidenced by Weinrod's summary memo and the additional SFR activity, which took place across the nation up to the August convention. But did SFR make a difference? The data is meager at best.

Published polls of students or youth during the 1967-August 1968 era tended to highlight the Democratic candidates, specifically the McCarthy versus Kennedy choice, and almost ignore what was happening on the Republican side. A February, 1968, poll at the University of Oregon at Eugene showed Reagan in last place.[94] The next month, the *New York Times* would publish a survey of college students' political preferences on its front page. It was not a poll but rather was report of what student leaders at some colleges, telephoned by the newspaper's reporters, had said. In California, "Governor Reagan's favorite-son candidacy has discouraged student activity among Republicans" but provided no details and no explanation.[95] At about the same time, 1.1 million college students from 1,470 colleges and universities participated in a nationwide straw poll. The poll was sponsored by the Univac division of Sperry-Rand and *Time* magazine, but how it was conducted—to ascertain bias in sampling— was not reported. This represented about one-sixth of America's 7 million college students at the time. Amongst Republicans, the Nixon/Rockefeller/Reagan tallies were 196,870/115,783/28,151 respectively.[96]

The only direct evidence to ascertain the efficacy of SFR's efforts at the mock conventions was a report that at the University of Denver mock convention held two weeks earlier, Rockefeller had only won on the third ballot with Reagan finishing second and Nixon third.[97] The details of that mock convention were not described further to determine exact vote numbers on each ballot, but the fact that actually Rockefeller was not running, and that Reagan had bested Nixon, is the only documented evidence that SFR indeed may have been very effective in getting out the student vote that spring for Ronald Reagan's 1968 presidential campaign.

During the spring of 1968, SFR members had no direct role in any of the primaries and focused on the forthcoming convention. Weinrod recalled, "We thought he had a chance," with "Nixon and Rockefeller dividing up the vote."[98] Docksai was gathering his New Yorkers, including William F. Buckley's son Christopher. Docksai knew that former Governor Charles Edison, from whom Docksai had received the $10,000 donation some months before, was making final arrangements for his special train to travel south to Miami Beach and had already pre-paid for his group of hotel rooms at the Fontainebleau Hotel.

As Bruce Weinrod, David R. Jones, Bob Schadler, Ron Docksai and the rest of SFR prepared for Miami Beach to help Ronald Reagan become the 1968 Republican nominee for the presidency, they kept in contact with—and continued to receive supplies and donations from—the newly formed Reagan national information center in Topeka, Kansas.

Endnotes

1.   Kathryn Forte, personal communication, 4/26/2013
2.   Pat Nolan, pers int 6/8/13
3.   Jones, Boisfeuillet, "The Young Republican Plight," *Harvard Crimson*, 7/11/67
4.   Kabaservice, p. 231
5.   Selinske, Charles, "'Youth for Ike' Group Formed on CU Campus" *Columbia Spectator*, 12/6/1951
6.   Andrew, p. 64
7.   SFR is not mentioned by historians Cannon Governor Reagan or Andrews The Other Side of the Sixties and only briefly on two pages by historian Thorburn A Generation Awakes
8.   Weinrod, pers comm. 1/23/13
9.   Weinrod, ibid
10.   Thorburn, p. 105-106
11.   Thorburn, p. 106
12.   Teague, pers int 12/27/12; Weinrod, pers comm 7/23/2015
13.   ibid
14.   ibid
15.   Teague, pers int, 12/27/12
16.   Weinrod, pers int 12/27/12
17.   ibid
18.   Weinrod, pers int 12/27/12
19.   Weinrod, pers int 5/21/13
20.   Weinrod, pers int., 1/23/13
21.   Docksai, pers comm. 7/19/13
22.   Docksai, pers int 3/15/13
23.   Thorburn, p. 114
24.   Docksai, pers comm. 7/18/13
25.   Docksai, pers comm. 7/16/13
26.   Docksai, ibid
27.   Docksai, Ibid
28.   Docksai, pers int 3/15/13
29.   Docksai, pers comm. 7/18/13
30.   Forte, pers comm., 1/3/13
31.   Forte, pers comm. 4/26/13
32.   "Miss YAF Summer 1968", *The New Guard*, summer 1968 edition, p. 25
33.   Forte, pers comm., 1/3/13
34.   Schadler, pers int 5/21/13

35. Steinberg, pers comm. 3/10/13
36. Steinberg, pers int 1/17/13
37. Rohrabacher, pers int 1/8/13; Nolan, pers int 5/18/13
38. Rohrabacher, pers int 1/8/13
39. Steel, pers int, 1/16/13
40. Ross, p. 163
41. Steel, ibid
42. Steel, ibid
43. Steel, ibid
44. Steel, ibid
45. Nolan, pers int 5/18/13
46. Nolan, ibid
47. Nolan, ibid
48. Nolan, ibid
49. Nolan, ibid
50. Nolan, pers int 6/8/13
51. Forte, pers comm. 4/26/13
52. Forte, ibid
53. Nolan, pers int 6/8/13
54. Nolan, pers int 5/18/13
55. Nolan, pers int 6/8/13
56. Weinrod, pers int 5/21/13
57. Weinrod, ibid
58. See Illustrations
59. Weinrod, Bruce "Memorandum", Students for Reagan, courtesy Kathryn Forte
60. See Illustrations
61. Weinrod, personal communication, 12/16/2014
62. Weinrod, pers int 5/21/13
63. Weinrod, ibid
64. Weinrod, ibid
65. Weinrod, pers comm., 1/23/13
66. "Materials Order Form", Students for Reagan, courtesy Kathryn Forte
67. Weinrod, Bruce, "Executive Director's Report", Students for Reagan, May 1968, courtesy Kathryn Forte
68. ibid
69. Eisenhower, Dwight. 1968 Diary. 3/2/68
70. ibid
71. ibid
72. ibid
73. Hill, Gladwin, "Reagan Completes Tours of Two States," NYT, 4/28/68, p. 52
74. ibid
75. Hill, Gladwin, "Reagan Condemns College Protests," NYT, 5/20/68, p. 39
76. Weinrod, pers int 12/27/12
77. See Illustrations
78. "Nasson Junior Launches State Group for Reagan," undated newspaper article, courtesy W. Bruce Weinrod
79. Reed, pers comm. 3/10/13
80. Reed, ibid
81. University of Illinois Draft Ronald Reagan for President Committee, 12/12/67, Dirksen Congressional Center, EMD Papers, Alpha 1967, Reagan
82. ibid
83. ibid
84. ibid
85. Rainville letter to Governor Reagan, 11/17/67, Dirksen Congressional Center, EMD Papers, Alpha 1967, Reagan
86. Hill, Gladwin, "Reagan Completes a Tour of 2 States," NYT, 4/28/68, p. 52
87. Jones, David R., "Memorandum to William A. Rusher", 6/3/68, courtesy Kathryn Forte
88. ibid
89. ibid
90. Weinrod, Bruce, "The Conservative Case for Ronald Reagan," The New Guard, summer 1968 p. 8-9
91. ibid
92. ibid
93. ibid
94. "U. of Oregon Poll Rejects Johnson," NYT, 2/9/68, p. 21

95.   Van Gelder, Lawrence, "Survey Shows College Students Back McCarthy Over Kennedy," *NYT*, 3/17/68, p. 1
96.   "McCarthy Leads Poll at Colleges," *NYT*, 5/3/68, p. 27
97.   ibid
98.   Weinrod, pers int 5/21/13

CHAPTER 18: CITIZENS FOR REAGAN NATIONAL INFORMATION CENTER

"Reagan is the kind of conservative-minded occupant of the White House the country needs."

~ Henry A. Bubb[1]

Paul Harvey, nationally known ABC commentator and future radio host, announced in late January 1968 the opening of a national information center to be based in Topeka, Kansas to supply information promoting the candidacy of Ronald Reagan for president in 1968. Its national chairman, Henry A. Bubb, was president of the Capitol Federal Savings and Loan Association and past president of the U.S. Savings and Loan League. Bubb may have been lost to history had he not decided to promote the 1968 presidential candidacy of Ronald Reagan.

Bubb had become interested in politics "during a campus election while a student at the University of Kansas in 1928." He had founded the Kansas Young Republican Confederation. By 1937 he had headed the National Young Republicans and held various advisory roles in Republican politics afterwards. Bubb had supported Wendell Willkie at the 1940 convention and had "helped see to it that the galleries were packed with people who chanted, 'We Want Willkie.'" In 1968 Bubb was age 61 and was described as "an angular six-footer with a radio announcer's voice and wavy gray hair." When speaking to reporters, Bubb's "responses were candid, his language salty." He was asked if bankers should shy away from politics. Bubb's answers were the exact opposite. He said that a banker's fears that taking a political stand might hurt their business were "no excuse." He added, "If you don't care enough to stand up for America, you don't deserve the business."[2] He was a man Reagan could like. The feeling was mutual.

Bubb first had heard Reagan speak at a General Electric speech about ten years before and commented, "I must say he impressed the hell out of me." Bubb had supported Goldwater in 1964 but told friends, "We would have been better off with Ronald Reagan at the time."[3] Bubb recalled the enthusiasm of Willkie in 1940, who had "talked to some delegates just after he jumped out of a shower." If he assumed Reagan would court delegates eagerly and openly before the convention as had Willkie, Bubb was to be disappointed.[4]

Ever since Bubb had invited and then appeared with Reagan on the dais for the 1967 Landon Lecture, Bubb had "talked with Reagan on several occasions" about his idea to open a national campaign information office based in Topeka. Reagan had "not been asked for his approval of the national movement," and Bubb added that he "did not know whether Reagan approved of the idea."[5] Bubb had visited California because of Governor Reagan's "great accomplishments." Friends then encouraged him finally to take personal action by opening the office.[6]

In late January, Kansas Republicans gathered for a three-day program during which two Reagan-for-President organizations came into being.[7]

Kansas Citizens for Reagan

Newspaper publisher Charles F. Scanlon announced the formation of Kansas Citizens for Reagan. It was described as an "off shoot" of Bubb's national office. Scanlon had assembled a small cadre of Reagan supporters to become the executive committee, including State Senator Charles Arthur (R-Manhattan). The Reagan grassroots group was the first official group formed in Kansas on behalf of any of the Republican contenders. The formation of Scanlon's group sprang "from a vacuum of similar activity on behalf of any other GOP presidential hopefuls," as no other groups had formed for other candidates. Scanlon made it clear that Kansas Citizens for Reagan was "independent of the official Republican state committee apparatus," which had committed previously to vote on the initial ballot for state favorite son Senator Frank Carlson.[8]

Bubb

Chairman Bubb told the press all about his new national Reagan office: Citizens for Reagan National Information Center. The group's purpose was to be different than Scanlon's Kansas group for Reagan. Bubb's group would be national in scope to "function as a rallying point for Citizen for Reagan groups over the country, serving as a distribution center for information about the California Republican and a clearing-house for correspondence." Bubb added that he hoped other national Reagan grass roots groups "will work through our

Topeka office." He emphasized that his information center would only be an information clearing-house and "it will not be our policy to solicit delegates nor work against any Republican candidate. We will just inform the electorate about this able administrator of our largest state."[9]

Yet Bubb admitted that the "need for a Republican Presidential win in 1968 is urgent." He added that he and others felt that "the present leading Republican candidates were not as strong as they should be." An op-ed columnist lauded the announcement by Bubb as "good and it is music to our ears."[10]

As Scanlon had done for the Reagan Kansas campaign group, Bubb formed an executive committee. But his national information office had national officers some of whom were quite prominent. The officers were from the Midwest, South and West and consisted of William Boeing of Seattle, a known Reagan supporter,[11] brewer Joseph Coors of Golden CO, engine manufacturer James L. Paxton Jr. whose company, Paxton-Mitchell had manufactured the engines of the World War II Liberty ships, Carl Halvorsen of Portland soon to become financial chairman of the Oregon Reagan campaign, Mrs. Marquita Maytag of La Jolla an acquaintance of Reed, and others from TX, KY, IN, NE and LA.[12]

Bubb opened the national office at 822 Kansas Street in the former Senate cafeteria building. Then Bubb announced the hiring of a full-time National Executive Director, Topeka attorney John Kerwitz. Kerwitz had been a supporter of Barry Goldwater in 1964 and had been "closely allied with the conservative wing of the National Young Republicans."[13] As noted earlier, in 1965 when several of Clif White's associates had formed a nationwide consulting firm, Kerwitz had joined the firm's regional office in Topeka.[14] Kerwitz told the press that the building housing the new Reagan national office was "being remodeled, communications are being installed and files established." The office would not open officially until mid-February and Kerwitz's second job would be office manager.[15]

As soon as it was operational, Bubb's center began "printing and distributing leaflets containing information about the California governor."[16] A February 15 Gallup poll showed that Reagan had regained much of the loss of support that had occurred the month before: his support amongst Republicans rose from 8 percent to 11 percent.

By March, grass roots Reagan campaign offices were thriving in five states, led by Colorado. Bubb explained to the press, "We're not going to oppose Nixon." But Bubb added that if neither Nixon nor

Rockefeller had gotten the nomination in early balloting in Miami Beach, his conversations with "a lot of Richard Nixon leaders around the country" had told him they "would come over to our side." Bubb added that Reagan was "the one person, Republican, who can win the presidency." Kerwitz and Bubb and their staff were "distributing publications and pamphlets." In mid March the center had sent out its "first mass mailing" to "VIP Republicans in key states". Kerwitz explained that those VIPs included Republican county chairmen, office holders, and others prominent in the party." He added that mailings were made to "several states including Nebraska where Reagan's name will appear on the primary ballot."

Thus far the response to Bubb and Kerwitz's mailings had been quite encouraging. Kerwitz explained that even though the mailings just had been made, "We've already received several hundred letters back as a result of the mailing."[17] One of those who received the letter was banker Dale L. Young whose story will be recounted later.

In early April, the press reported that besides his information center, Bubb had formed an additional national "organizing committee" to lend support to the center and its officers.[18] During the rest of April, Bubb would start to get involved directly in Reagan state campaigns beyond Kansas. When the Portland, Oregon office opened, Bubb would call by telephone saying, "Reagan represents all of us who believe Nixon cannot win and that group represents all factions of the party...I hope you will work hard to show Gov. Reagan that the people of Oregon want him as the candidate of all factions of the party."[19]

But Bubb would do more than just phone encouragement to other Reagan grass roots groups. He would spearhead a Reagan national finance committee in June and got involved directly at the local state level as well. For example, he would make a two-day visit to help Don Taylor in Wisconsin. Looking ahead to the upcoming major primaries in adjacent Nebraska and in Oregon, Bubb predicted, "We probably won't do much in Nebraska but we'll do our best to get him before the people of Oregon." Bubb would distribute a critical Reagan campaign film that was being produced.

Commenting on how support for Reagan was in his beloved Kansas, Bubb said there was "sizeable support" adding, "I just don't believe the majority of Kansas delegates to the national convention are sold on Nixon as a man who can win."[20]

Bubb's pro-Reagan efforts and comments were beginning to attract the attention of the national press. Indeed the press regarded him as a major Reagan campaign spokesman, as when Bubb would comment on the primaries in Wisconsin, Nebraska and Oregon.[21] "The statements put out by Henry Bubb of Topeka, Kansas, the national Chairman of Citizens for Reagan, become more and more confident."[22] Another reporter from Washington D.C noted that Bubb's efforts from Topeka were "gathering steam."[23] Even the *New York Times* saw fit to report on Bubb's efforts.[24]

In May as the Oregon primary would approach, Reagan would discuss his friend Bubb's group: "It is my understanding that this group in Kansas set itself up as an information kind of bureau to furnish information—this film that I understand will be shown in Oregon, to furnish these things to groups of this kind that are campaigning. So they obviously must be in the business of contacting and coordinating with wherever there are such groups."[25] Bubb hoped and predicted, "A strong showing there could start the Reagan bandwagon rolling." But Bubb would admit, "It's still tough to convince people they ought to vote for somebody who says he's not going to run."

Yet when asked why Reagan would not declare his candidacy openly, Bubb would answer, "I think he will come out, if he has a good showing in this primary."[26] Concluded Bubb, "Reagan is the kind of conservative-minded occupant of the White House the country needs."[27]

Bubb and Kerwitz would commit major financial resources directly to the Oregon effort that spring. They each donated $10,000. Plus Bubb and Kerwitz sent donation monies from their National Information Center to the Oregon campaign in the forms of two much larger checks: $35,000 to the advertising firm the Reagan Oregon team had hired and $37,000 directly to the Oregon Reagan committee.[28] Indeed Bubb was seeing that the country was starting to write checks to Reagan's campaign. Contributions were flowing in at the rate of "thousands of dollars a week." He reiterated that he had no direct contact with Reagan but had "communication through intermediaries." Kerwitz then announced a large expansion of affiliates to include nine states: Colorado, Wisconsin, Indiana, Kansas, Nebraska, Oklahoma, Oregon, Washington, and Idaho, with "more pretty quick."

"In the old days it took a guy with a radio voice to win," reflected Bubb. "Now its television appearance and Reagan has no peer there." Bubb, recalling Reagan's visit to Kansas State University to deliver the Landon Lecture the prior fall, noted, "I saw him captivate those kids." Bubb and Kerwitz continued to work hard to see Ronald Reagan elected president in 1968. Soon Bubb would invite Reagan to return to Kansas in person and later they would exchange an important series of telegrams. As Bubb and Kerwitz expanded their

Reagan outreach, other local Reagan grass activists were busy in the state with the first primary, New Hampshire.

Endnotes

1. "Bubb Sees GOP Bid Campaign by Gov. Reagan," *Junction City Union*, 5/23/68
2. Hutnyan, Joseph, "Kan. S&L Man, Advocate of Businessmen's Political Activity, Stirs GOP Convention," *American Banker*, 8/5/68
3. Meyer, Philip, "Reagan Success Key in Oregon," *Kansas City Star*, 5/12/68
4. O'Connor, Mike, "Millionaire Boosts Reagan Candidacy," undated newspaper article, scrapbook, Henry A. Bubb Collection, University of Kansas
5. Myers, Roger, "Reagan Will Have Center in Topeka," 1/27/68 newspaper article, scrapbook, Henry A. Bubb Collection, University of Kansas
6. "Reagan Office Opens in Topeka," *Kansas Parsons* Sun, 1/27/68, p. 1
7. Morgan, Ray, "Topeka Office to Aid Reagan," *Kansas City Star*, 1/27/68
8. "Kansas group Backs Reagan," undated newspaper clipping, scrapbook, Henry A Bubb Collection, University of Kansas
9. Myers, Roger, op.cit.
10. Waggin, Chuck, *Fredonia Daily Herald*, 1/29/68
11. Kopelson, Gene 2016
12. "Pro-Reagan Committee Is Formed," *Topeka Star Journal*, scrapbook, undated newspaper article, Henry A. Bubb Collection, University of Kansas
13. "Lawyer Heads Reagan Center," undated newspaper article, scrapbook, Henry A. Bubb collection, University of Kansas
14. Steffgen, p. 171
15. "Lawyer Heads Reagan Center" undated newspaper article, scrapbook, Henry A. Bubb Collection, University of Kansas
16. "Pro Reagan Committee Is Formed" op.cit.
17. "More Boost for Reagan," 3/15/68 unnamed newspaper article, scrapbook, Henry A. Bubb Collection, University of Kansas
18. "Reagan Men Push 'School,'" *Omaha World-Herald*, 4/1/68
19. Greenburg, Carl, "Reagan 'No' Is Too Mild To Suit Nixon Faction," *LA Times*, 4/1/68
20. Myers, Roger, "Reagan Vote in Wisconsin Pleases Bubb," *Topeka Daily Capital*, 4/4/68, p. 10
21. "Ron's Vote Just Great," *Kansas City Star*, 5/12/68
22. Chamberlain, John ,"Reagan's Candidacy Is For real," *Richmond Times-Dispatch*, 4/27/68
23. "Reagan Men Push 'School,'" 4/13/68, unnamed newspaper article, scrapbook, Henry A Bubb Collection, University of Kansas
24. "Reagan Committee Formed," *NYT*, 4/17/68
25. RRL, Tape 340
26. "Bubb Sees Reagan Bid After Oregon," *Amarillo Daily News*, 5/24/68, p. 41
27. "Bubb Sees GOP Bid Campaign by Gov. Reagan," *Junction City Union*, 5/23/68
28. "Big Reagan Gifts from Kansas," *Kansas City Star*, undated newspaper article, scrapbook, Henry A Bubb Collection, University of Kansas

Chapter 19: New Hampshire— Watergate on the Merrimack

"It wouldn't matter if Reagan ran third in New Hampshire as long as he made sure Nixon ran second. Nixon would be dead, but Reagan would be very much alive."

~ Republican leader[1]

"Use your imagination."

~ George Romney[2]

"The greatest pseudo-noncandidate in history."

~ George Romney[3]

Watergate was still years in the future, but an alleged break-in in Concord, New Hampshire, during the Reagan presidential campaign could have rivaled the future burglary, had it not been successful and thus been shrouded in secrecy for decades.

None of the four Northeastern state Republican primaries would play major roles in Reagan's 1968 campaign for the presidency. The previous September, a group called Republicans for Ronald Reagan had formed in New York State; it was reported that they were part of a larger national group but the New York Reagan grass roots group was never heard from again.[4] By January, the Northeast Conference of Republican State Chairmen reinforced their complete official neutrality in the upcoming primaries by noting there was support for the "whole gamut" of Republican candidates including Governor Reagan. Howard E. Russell from Rhode Island, chairman of the group, told the press that if Reagan became an active candidate, "there were indications of support."[5] In New Hampshire, a candidate's name could be placed on the ballot by petition, even without his or her consent.[6] This peculiarity would have major ramifications for Reagan in the granite state.

Reagan's role in the March 12, 1968 New Hampshire primary started to receive coverage from the national press almost a year beforehand. In April 1967, a Massachusetts advertising man, Richard Jennet of Sherborn MA, had announced he was starting a petition drive for Reagan's primary in New Hampshire for 1968. Jennet told the press he had obtained petition forms from the New Hampshire secretary of state's office.[7] We have seen earlier how the CBS documentary *What About Ronald Reagan?* had shown film clips of grass roots activists opening the Reagan campaign office in Concord. Likely this was Jennet's group.

According to historian and blogger John Di Stasio, former New Hampshire state senator Russell Carter formed a Reagan for President Club in June, 1967.[8] At month's end, on June 25, when Reagan had attended the Western Governors Conference in West Yellowstone, Montana, we have seen how cryptically he told reporters that he "had taken steps to stop the formation" of a grass roots campaign group which was supporting his candidacy for the presidency in the New Hampshire primary.[9]

New Hampshire was not only not part of the Reagan campaign plan, Reagan did not even want his name to appear on the ballot. Unlike the three opt-out states, where a committee or a secretary of state would place his name on the ballot, in New Hampshire each candidate had to declare a candidacy in order to be listed unless his supporters filed the petition. Reagan, fearing backlash amongst his California constituents, wanted no part of it. Plus Reagan was putting no resources into New Hampshire. It was to be the first opt-out state, Wisconsin—where Reagan had no direct control that his name was to be listed—where he wanted his candidacy first to be viable. But Carter had formed the Reagan club and Jennet's group had started the petition drive and had obtained filing papers. What could Reagan do?

Exactly how Reagan and/or Reed's team had arranged to stop the New Hampshire campaign's formation has never been made clear. But some insight may have been provided by Jim Ince, who owned a public relations firm in the late 1960s.

Ince had become a fan of Reagan from his own high school days in Des Moines, Iowa, where he was an usher at high school football games. One day at local Drake Stadium, Ince was told to bring some hot dogs to the game's announcer in the booth—one Ronald Reagan. Of course Ince was thrilled to make the delivery to Reagan because Ince had heard Reagan announcing games over the radio for many months, and Reagan had by this time become somewhat of a local legend amongst Ince's friends. As Ince handed the hot dogs to the local celebrity, Reagan was very kind to him and seemed to enjoy the hot dogs. Decades later, when Ince would own a public relations firm, he would meet Reagan again at a private Eureka College reception arranged by Ince; Reagan still would relish the memories of those hot dogs.[10]

Ince still kept in contact with an old friend from California, Kay Valory. Valory, the chauffeur and assistant to Reagan when Reagan had volunteered to campaign for Goldwater in California in 1964, in 1976 would befriend a recent college graduate student who was an ardent conservative. When the student was looking for employment, Valory would recommend and arrange for the student to move to the east coast and intern for Ince in the mid 1970s.[11]

A few years later, the student, by then working for Ince's public relations firm, would tell Ince and Valory an intriguing tale from the spring of 1968. The worker—and former student—told both Ince and Valory that he had been the person who had "unfiled" Reagan's campaign filing papers in New Hampshire in the spring of 1967. Nobody recalled who had filed the Reagan primary papers initially, but the worker recalled that when he had been a student and had heard that the Reagan filing papers needed to be retrieved, he volunteered for the mission. It is not clear whether someone from Reed's team, or someone else, let it be known that the retrieval of the papers was to be a goal of the Reagan campaign at that point.[12] Indeed the student may have planned the break-in by himself without any direct involvement from Reagan's campaign. Reed did not recall ever hearing or knowing of the episode but thought it not impossible that Clif White may have known of it.[13]

The graduate student then told Ince and Valory that he had proceeded to fly east, broke into New Hampshire state governmental offices in Concord by crawling into an upstairs window, found the Reagan filing files, and took them with him. What happened to the Reagan filing papers is not known but one must assume that if the story is true, they were destroyed by the student before he returned to California. Unfortunately, the person's identity has not been recalled by either Ince, age 89, or Valory, in her 90's, when interviewed by your author in 2013. But Ince recalled quite clearly what his student had told him.[14]

If true, the episode, quite Watergate-like in its burglary method, demonstrated the zeal of one young Reagan devotee during the 1968 campaign. Certainly such alleged action would have been criminal. Your author must emphasize that there are no facts or corroborating recollections to substantiate any aspects of the supposed break-in, and certainly—given the lack of any known publicity at the time about such an event—it is highly likely that it never happened. Indeed

Reagan's earlier comments, that he had stopped the formation of the grass roots effort, may indeed have referred to something else entirely.

Nixon Fears Reagan Presidential Threat

The alleged retrieval of Reagan's filing papers, or at least Reagan's stoppage of his official efforts in the granite state, was not the end of Reagan's possible New Hampshire campaign. On September 21, 1967, columnist Drew Pearson reported on a secret initial meeting of Nixon's campaign brain trust held in Washington D.C. Pearson was no friend of Nixon, although Patrick Buchanan relates an episode when Nixon had tried to stop Senator Eugene McCarthy from physically beating up Pearson.[15]

Even though by then Reagan's filing papers allegedly had been destroyed, or at least any official campaign had ceased, there still could be a strong write-in vote for Reagan in conservative New Hampshire. Indeed Nixon's staff felt the "biggest danger to Nixon, it was decided, is that in the early primaries, especially New Hampshire, supporters of Ronald Reagan would write his name in." Such a write-in effort for Reagan "could take conservative votes away from Nixon."[16]

At that time, Reagan was viewed as holding the "balance of power" between Nixon and Romney in New Hampshire. Reagan could stop the Nixon presidential drive at the gate. The Reagan campaign in New Hampshire, which was "officially unauthorized," could "severely handicap Mr. Nixon…and ultimately produce the major benefit for Mr. Reagan himself." It was reported that if Reagan's supporters entered with a second petition, Reagan would "ask that his name be withdrawn from the ballot." But such a Reagan withdrawal would "not prevent the organization of a write-in campaign." Leland Kaiser, a California manufacturer, recently visited New Hampshire to "quash" any such Reagan write-in effort, yet upon his return from New Hampshire, Kaiser reported, "A genuine Reagan groundswell" existed in New Hampshire and the support for Reagan "might prove uncontrollable."

The major beneficiary of Reagan momentum would be Romney, as "a well-organized Reagan campaign, even minus the candidate, would almost certainly cut into the potential vote being sought by Mr. Nixon since both men appeal to the conservative side of the party." Reagan could "strike a possibly fatal blow at Mr. Nixon and pre-empt the conservative field in one sweep" by blocking Nixon there. One unnamed Republican leader added, "It wouldn't matter if Reagan ran third in New Hampshire as long as he made sure Nixon ran second. Nixon would be dead, but Reagan would be very much alive.[17]

On September 29, a second Reagan grass roots effort appeared. A New Hampshire Draft Reagan Committee announced that their new office would open in mid October. It was to be run by Robert Robinson of Manchester and others.[18] From Sacramento, Nofziger told the press that "Reagan was not a candidate, had no intention of appearing or running in New Hampshire or seeking New Hampshire primary delegates."

Yet a third Reagan campaign office was opened in Concord on the same day. Manchester advertising executive John A. MacDonald announced the movement to draft Reagan by saying "a significant write-in campaign might induce Mr. Reagan to run for President." Macdonald predicted that if Reagan did not win the primary, he would "come in second." Macdonald told the press that he had not spoken to Leland Kaiser, and the headquarters had opened "without Reagan's blessing."[19] Besides there being no connection to Kaiser, there was no apparent connection between MacDonald's initiative and the prior petition drive announced by Jennet the prior April.

A private poll of Strafford County New Hampshire done by Political Surveys and Analyses of Princeton N.J. was released at the end of the month. This county, in central New Hampshire, was considered a bellwether county. The results showed that Reagan would lose to Johnson, 47 to 30.[20]

Reagan's name was not listed on the New Hampshire ballot.[21] On February 9, the New Hampshire Supreme Court ruled that a state campaign committee for a candidate could conduct a write-in campaign without the permission of the candidate. But the next day, Reagan write-in groups abandoned their efforts.[22]

Romney Withdrawal

On February 28 Romney dropped out of the race. Once he heard of Romney's decision, Reagan called a press conference in Sacramento telling the press it had "no effect on his own noncandidacy stance." When asked if Romney's withdrawal meant now that Nixon had the election sewn up, Reagan replied, perhaps cryptically, "Only an 'overt stop-Nixon movement' could prevent it."[23] Oregon Reagan Chair Robert Hazen, who we will meet later, said that the unexpected Romney withdrawal indicated that "anything can happen in American politics—and certainly no one has the Republican nomination sewed up."[24]

Nixon was "caught by surprise" by Romney's announcement, and Nixon's aides worried privately that they now "expected a stronger challenge" from Reagan. The aides felt that if Rockefeller then started to campaign in place of Romney, "Reagan's chances would also improve." The *New York Times* felt the Romney announcement would have "the greatest impact on what is done for Reagan."[25]

Romney Refuses to Endorse Reagan

When Romney withdrew from the race, he was asked if he could support all of the remaining Republican candidates for party nominee. He declined to endorse any other Republican candidate, even Rockefeller, who had been his supporter.[26]

But then Romney qualified his answer. Romney said that he could not support one particular candidate. When asked who that was, Romney replied, "Use your imagination!" and the reporters found out quickly that Romney had meant Ronald Reagan. In Sacramento when told about Romney agreeing to endorse anyone but him, Reagan answered ruefully, "I had hoped he had learned the lesson of 1964."[27] In mid July, reporters would ask Romney five times whether he would support actively a Reagan candidacy, and he would refuse to answer other than calling Reagan the "greatest pseudo-noncandidate in history."[28]

Despite their possible reconciliation in Pacific Palisades along with Ronald Reagan's defense of him, George Romney had never learned the lessons that Ronald Reagan and Dwight Eisenhower had attempted to teach about party unity. Maybe at some point indeed he had been brainwashed.

Election Results

History will never know who exactly had the privilege of being the very first person ever to vote for Ronald Reagan for president. Reagan received 362 write-in votes in that first 1968 primary. Whoever it was had written Reagan's name on the ballot that day, March 12, 1968, somewhere in the tiny state of New Hampshire.

Nixon won a resounding victory with 80,666 votes. In a motel near Fresno as election results came in, when White told Reagan that Johnson's days were "numbered" and that RFK likely would run, Reagan smiled.[29] It was time for Reagan to turn on the key of his campaign engine and switch from "search for delegates" gear into high "real campaign" gear. It would be another chance to defeat RFK.

Reagan called Nixon's victory hollow, "since he faced no real challenge."[30] Reporters concurred, asking, "Did this really mean he had shed his loser's image? He was, after all, without opposition."[31] Nixon retorted about the invisible Reagan, "The people of this country don't like absentee candidates."[32]

Later that spring when reflecting back on his not having run on the New Hampshire ballot, Reagan would recollect his stopping of his own candidacy, commenting on "how successful we were in shutting off our operations in New Hampshire."[33]

After the Nixon victory in New Hampshire, did Nixon have the nomination sewn up? One historian observed that after New Hampshire, "Nixon's most serious rival was still the unannounced Ronald Reagan."[34]

Nixon's victory became inconsequential compared to the political earthquake that had occurred on the Democratic side. For when little-known anti-war candidate Eugene McCarthy's strong showing against unpopular incumbent Democrat Lyndon Johnson was tallied, suddenly it seemed that not only might a Republican defeat Johnson, but perhaps Johnson might not even be the Democratic candidate.

The eyes of the nation turned onto one Democrat who had not entered the fray in New Hampshire but who now was reconsidering: Reagan's old nemesis, Robert F. Kennedy. Reagan met with Reed, Smith and Clarke at the Reagan residence on March 15 to discuss the likely Kennedy candidacy.[35] But Reagan was busy in California helping a constituency that might be crucial in the fall general election should he win the nomination.

Endnotes

1. Weaver, Warren Jr ,"GOP Sees Reagan Playing Key Role In Two Primaries," *NYT*, 10/15/67, p. 1
2. Weaver, Warren, "Rockefeller Says That He Will Run If Asked By GOP," *NYT*, 3/2/68, p. 21
3. "Bid by Reagan July 21 Denied," *Washington Post*, 7/12/68, p. A2
4. "Reagan Backers Open a Branch to Seek '68 Delegates in State," *NYT*, 9/1967, undated
5. Lubasch, Arnold, "Bliss Supported As GOP Chairman," *NYT*, 1/28/68, p. 34
6. Chester et. al., p. 204
7. "Reagan Primary Drive Set," *NYT*, 4/19/67, p. 28
8. http://www.freerepublic.com/focus/f-news/1148438/posts; accessed 3/7/2015
9. Turner, Wallace, "Reagan Denies Advance Man Seeks Support for Race in '68,'" *NYT*, 6/26/67, p. 20
10. see Afterword.
11. Ince, pers int 1/18/13
12. Ince, pers int, 1/18/13
13. Reed, pers int 2/25/2013
14. Ince, pers int 1/18/13; Valory, pers int 1/20/13
15. Buchanan, p. 143
16. Pearson, Drew, "Washington Merry Go-Round," 9/21/67
17. Weaver, Warren Jr, "GOP Sees Reagan Playing Key Role In Two Primaries," *NYT*, 10/15/67, p. 1

18. "New Hampshire Office," *NYT*, 9/30/67
19. "Reagan Unit Hopes For 'Groundswell,'" *NYT*, 10/16/67, p. 25
20. "Bellwether Poll Favors Nixon," *NYT*, 10/28/67, p. 10
21. *Congressional Quarterly*, 2/2/68, p. 162
22. Krim, Robert, "Rockefeller Write-in Cuts Romney's Support in N.H.," *Harvard Crimson*, 2/19/68
23. "Reagan Unaffected," *NYT*, 3/3/68, p. E2
24. Hazen's comments appear later in Hughes, Harold "Rocky's Oregon Supporters Express 'Shock,' 'Dismay' After Withdrawal," *NYT* 3/22/68, p. 1
25. Ripley, Anthony, "Nixon Surprised By Romney News," *NYT*, 2/29/68, p. 22
26. McCall, p. 97
27. Weaver, Warren, "Rockefeller Says That He Will Run If Asked By GOP," *NYT*, 3/2/68, p. 21
28. "Bid by Reagan July 21 Denied," *Washington Post*, 7/12/68, p. A2
29. Reed, *The Reagan Enigma*, p. 137-138
30. "'Hollow Victory' For Nixon, Reagan Tells Reporters," *Seattle Times*, 3/13/68, p. A
31. Chester et. al., p. 101
32. Perlstein, Rick, p. 241
33. Hill, Gladwin, "Reagan Jocular on Noncandidacy," *NYT*, 3/29/68, p. 28
34. Gould, p. 39
35. Reagan-Reed, 3/15/1968, Los Angeles residence

CHAPTER 20: AMERICANS OF MEXICAN DESCENT AND OTHER MINORITIES

"The cities where we have had some of the worst uprisings and disturbances are cities that happen to be run by Democrat political machines...The other side has failed in solving those problems. It ought to be time to give Republicans a chance."

~ Ronald Reagan[1]

Reagan wanted the party's 1968 platform to "provide new solutions to the problems of social minorities."

~ *New York Times*[2]

While March was about to change from a month of few Reagan campaign activities to an as-yet unforeseen whirlwind, Governor Reagan had been busy helping a constituency which had helped him win election as governor some 17 months earlier. In 1966, Reagan had won against incumbent Brown by almost a million votes, and votes from normally Democratic Mexican Americans had been a significant portion of Reagan's success.[3] The upper ends of Reagan's estimated percentage of the Mexican American vote varied from 40 percent[4] to as high as 50 percent,[5] indicating he "ran more strongly in this community than any Republican had ever done."[6]

Your author will use the more generally-used term "Mexican-Americans" in this analysis, although as pointed out by historian Curtis Patrick, Reagan had told his political advisors in 1966 only to use the term "Americans of Mexican Descent." Reagan was staying consistent with his own ideals, as discussed previously, which followed the ideas of Theodore Roosevelt and of Eisenhower: to avoid placing Americans into hyphenated sub-groups.

Governor Reagan had involved the Mexican American community from the very beginning at his Inauguration. Wanting an inaugural program that "must be dignified and in good taste, it must be nonpartisan and it must establish some traditions," Reagan had emphasized California's Spanish beginnings. For his oath taking in the rotunda, he had placed his hand on the oldest Bible found in any of California's missions, a "400-year-old Bible that was brought to California by Father Junipero Serra." The three day celebration had included concerts, a prayer breakfast, and mariachi bands.[7]

Dr. Francisco Bravo and J. William Orozco had led the "Mexican American Democrats for Reagan" committee to Reagan's massive 1966 election triumph, and a major campaign theme against the incumbent Democratic governor was that far too few Mexican Americans had been hired during his tenure.[8] Reagan would be different. The brief analysis below on Governor Reagan and minorities, not reviewed in other works on Reagan's gubernatorial years and deserving of further scrutiny by historians, serves as an example of how, should Reagan be chosen as party nominee, Reagan's domestic programs for California's minorities would have national implications.

One month after his inauguration, Reagan had sent to the State Assembly and Senate on February 9, 1967 a combination of proposed legislation and executive action in the area of agriculture, which had direct impact on the Mexican American community. Reagan sought increased housing for migrant farm families, the establishment of a mediation service for disputes between farmers and farm workers, and a new farm-labor placement service.

Reagan had seen the need for 600 more family housing units and asked the federal government for $5.5 million in funding. In regards to farm labor disputes and attempts at unionization, he would appoint conciliators with agriculture and labor knowledge, so as to "bring the parties together and recommend a disposition of the problem for the good of the public interest." Due to the ending of the Bracero program, which initially had permitted temporary migrant farm workers into the country to help with field work, and the resultant new need for more farm labor, Reagan had proposed a Citizens Committee be established to review the organization and function of the State Farm Labor Service. He had pushed for quick action for his Mexican American constituents and wanted the committee set up, at the latest, by the following January. He had streamlined governmental bureaucracy by transferring the Farm Labor Technical section, along with regional and local placement bureaus, into one new placement service.

Reagan wanted California to lead the nation in "developing a modern, stabilized workforce" and had proposed that permanent agricultural workers be given state unemployment insurance coverage. One partial solution to the state's need for part-time farm labor was to recruit California's unemployed youth.[9] Later Reagan had authorized the use of prison inmates and welfare recipients as well.[10] In his first eighteen months in office, Reagan had appointed 19 of the top 100 state jobs to minority applicants.[11]

Democratic Disarray

In the spring of 1967 as Reagan was unveiling his new programs for minorities and appointing minorities to state government as he had promised, new problems had arisen back in Washington, D.C. for President Johnson, just as Johnson was gearing up for his reelection campaign for 1968. Fed up with administration delays to create a conference of Hispanics in the nation's capital, the presidents of major Mexican American organizations in California had issued a press release, stating that due to "unanimous frustration, disappointment and impatience over long delays, inaction and indecisiveness on the part of the President Johnson," that they would hold their own "White House Conference." When several Mexican American leaders met with White House Special Counsel Harry McPherson to discuss the problem of the meeting, and then McPherson told Johnson that he should hold their conference to avoid losing Mexican American votes, Johnson told him to "keep this trash out of the White House." The next week Vice President Humphrey flew to California to meet with two other farm activists. Humphrey asked them to stop their picketing and then had the nerve to ask them for their support for Johnson's reelection. The Mexican Americans leaders said such an endorsement would be "premature." When Humphrey asked what it would take to win their endorsement for Johnson's reelection, they told him to support the farm workers strike. Humphrey refused.[12]

Security and Violence

On May 5, 1967, while preparing for the Kennedy debate, Reagan had been planning his second appearance for Mexican Independence Day. The year before, he had appeared on horseback while campaigning for governor.[13] But this time his security forces had voiced concern when the plan was to ride in an open convertible. There were concerns about potential violence from an informant who told of a barrage of garbage to be thrown at a certain intersection. So Reagan had offered to ride again on a horse and was given a local championship horse to ride. Reagan had once again won "many hearts" of the residents of East Los Angeles.[14]

Vietnam

Foreign affairs was never far from the hearts of politicians that year, and the war's impact on minority communities was no different. As reviewed by historian Julie Pycior, the Vietnam War began to intersect the problems of Mexican Americans in California. Concern about possible abnormally high casualty rates by Mexican Americans had prompted the office of California Congressman Edward Roybal to investigate and it turned up numbers suggesting an over-abundance of casualties yet an underrepresentation of officers by Mexican Americans. Roybal's initial attitude about the war had turned out to be quite similar to Reagan's, i.e., that since we were in the war we should try to win. Roybal also had served as an advisor to a study prepared at the University of California, Los Angeles, which showed that less than one percent of students at the University of California system were of Mexican descent.[15] Opposition to the war, by groups such as the Brown Berets, the United Mexican American Students, and the Mexican American Student Confederation, had increased.[16]

Based on the study by Roybal of low minority representation at state colleges and universities, it may well have been Ronald Reagan who was the only political figure offering concrete ideas on how to help. Indeed the daughter of Dr. Francisco Bravo recalled, "Democrats were not providing what California needed."[17]

That fall, Reagan had expounded his position on civil rights for minority groups when he had been interviewed on William F. Buckley's *Firing Line* on October 12, 1967. After coming to Eisenhower's defense related to dismantling the New Deal, and during a subsequent discussion about minority rights and their enforcement, Reagan had stated clearly and precisely, "Where the constitutional rights of the human being, the rights guaranteed by that document to all of us, where those are being violated then I believe the federal government has a responsibility to go in and enforce those rights at the point of bayonet if necessary."[18]

Trip to Mexicali

That fall, Reagan had gone to Mexicali, Mexico to attend a meeting of the Commission of the Californias.[19] Later as president he would return to Mexicali and also would visit Tijuana, Cancun, La Paz Baja and Mazatlan. Governor Reagan's trip abroad—admittedly not very far—served as one of the few venues for the domestic governor and presidential candidate to act officially in the arena of world affairs. His

Mexican visit occurred just as he visited Lawrence-Livermore, where he had enlarged his knowledge of America's anti-missile defense, and just prior to his Seabee presentation.

Upon leaving Mexicali, on November 7, 1967, he wrote a letter to a man from Mexicali who had asked his help in bringing their nephew home from Vietnam. Reagan wrote in part, "I'm not a candidate for any other office so won't be in a position to help."[20] Reagan expanded his world affairs *bona fides* whenever he had the chance.

In early December at his Yale University Chubb Fellowship visit, during a question-and-answer session, students had pressed Reagan about black unemployment. Reagan interrupted, explaining that the group that was "an even greater minority" in California, the group that had the lowest education, the highest drop-out rate and the lowest employment, were the Mexican Americans.

Reagan explained to the all-white Yale students that besides having hired California's first black director of Veterans Affairs, his administration had initiated a new program for bilingual teachers for Mexican American students. Reagan explained that Mexican American students often were falling behind in school because the only language they heard at home was Spanish but at school all they heard was English. Reagan explained his new policy was bringing in bilingual teachers to discern what problems Mexican American students had been having in order to improve teaching and hone in on what specific academic areas the students were having difficulties.[21] Reagan was not bringing in bilingual teachers to let Hispanics remain speaking Spanish. He did not want them to be isolated. Reagan wanted them to be complete Americans, and learning English was a critically-needed skill. He wanted them to become Americans of Mexican descent.

As 1968 began, the Mexican American community was being courted by four separate political groups: Democrats President Lyndon Johnson, Senator Eugene McCarthy, and Senator Robert F. Kennedy plus Republican Governor Ronald Reagan.

By early January 1968, some 700,000 to 750,000 Mexican Americans in California and some 40,000 in East Los Angeles alone had been registered to vote. Bravo cautioned, "Johnson should not take these voters for granted."[22] Roybal still supported Johnson but was becoming disheartened about the president's policy in Vietnam.[23] Johnson's campaign together with the Democratic National Committee produced a bilingual brochure called *Bien Hecho* Well Done, *Sr. Presidente!*, which showed numerous Mexican American appointees to the Johnson administration and programs for them.[24]

Clearly, the Democrat machine was worried. Dr. Francisco Bravo, who had charged the Brown administration with failing to appoint Mexican Americans to office in 1966 and then helped elect Reagan to the governorship, might help Reagan again in the 1968 fall election.

Meanwhile Cesar Chavez's union announced his national boycott of one large grape grower, and his supporters visited many distribution centers across the country looking for support of the boycott. Chavez's initial tactics failed when the grower started to ship grapes under many different labels, so Chavez then announced a boycott of all California table grapes.[25] Chavez began a hunger strike. Reagan felt throughout 1968 that Chavez's union's boycotts, as well as their secondary strikes against stores selling California grapes, were illegal.[26]

At the same time, Robert F. Kennedy, seeing what McCarthy had accomplished in New Hampshire, was considering his run for the presidency against Johnson. On March 10 RFK returned to Delano to attend mass with Chavez, who had just ended his hunger strike. Kennedy stopped in East Los Angeles, wore a "Huelga" Strike! button and met with Chicano students. On the flight back east he told aides he had made his decision and would seek the presidency. A new "Viva Kennedy" organization was started, but some activists were working for McCarthy. McCarthy not only had come out against the war prior to Kennedy but had been "calling for improvements in farm worker conditions for years." Some recalled Kennedy's vigorous anti-communist crusades in the prior decade and were torn. Some realized that McCarthy was an intellectual, who did not appeal to poor minorities, whereas Kennedy had visited and made a difference. Chavez's union might have to alienate the American Federation of Labor, which had supported Johnson. Chavez's activists would continue their voter registration drive. Chavez's union ultimately decided to endorse Kennedy. Kennedy's eventual victory in the Democratic primary in early June, just a few minutes before his assassination, would be won by a tiny margin made possible by the Mexican American vote.[27] Chavez later would attend the Democratic convention as a Kennedy delegate.[28]

Reagan's Campaign

Although clearly most Mexican American voters were firmly in the Democratic camp and changed their loyalties from Johnson to McCarthy to Kennedy and eventually to Humphrey, "Ronald Reagan did not write off the Mexican American vote."[29] Reagan's true forceful direct involvement with Mexican American voters in 1968 did not begin until March, as Kennedy was entering the race, as he had not been thinking about getting the 1968 Hispanic vote until this time.[30] After all, few Mexican Americans were Republican, and very, very few lived in Wisconsin, Nebraska or Oregon at the time. But if Reagan won the nomination and then ran in the general election, there would not be enough time to set up a new grass roots campaign for Hispanics. Just as disaffected Democrats had protested RFK's campaigning in California on behalf of Brown in 1966, and with all the hurts RFK had created for him over the years, Reagan relished the thought of defeating RFK again next fall.

Reagan's niche was to court the same conservative Mexican American business sector as he had done successfully in his gubernatorial race.[31] Reagan's presidential campaign set up the same small nucleus of Dr. Francisco Bravo and J. William Orozco, whose efforts had been so successful two years before in convincing a sizeable number of California Mexican Americans to vote for Reagan. Also Reagan realized that not all Mexican American Democrats were in favor of Chavez, because some Democratic donors liked the growers and Chavez scared them. Reagan "exploited whatever differences could be found."[32]

Reagan approached the California Mexican American community differently than he did with his grass roots campaigns outside of California. Rather than show a Reagan film on television, acknowledged to be an ideal medium at the time for Reagan, the Mexican American community often was poor without television.[33]

As we will see, Reagan frequently would mention his concerns about Mexican Americans during campaign trips across the country. During March, 1968, Reagan was about to concentrate on running special community meetings in California. Plus he already had his established programs which already were helping Mexican Americans: increased worker housing, higher education scholarships, bilingual school teachers, farm placement service, mediation service and unemployment insurance. Reagan would build upon these by adding new programs.

But why would Reagan court the Mexican American vote in California if he were going to win the state primary as a favorite son regardless? Reagan's continued success with California's Mexican Americans could be transferred to other Hispanic constituencies such as Puerto Ricans and Dominicans in the East. But also if he were not the nominee later that fall, but if he decided to run for reelection as governor in 1970, he would need their support once again then.

But of most importance, Reagan cared a great deal for his minority constituents and wanted to help.

Reagan attended a $100-per-plate Republican fundraiser in Fresno on March 13, 1968 and also visited a farm labor housing project with housing officials. He was checking first-hand on the progress of the new program he had instituted to help the Mexican American community.

Reagan's Meetings with Minority Leaders

From March 20, 1968 through March 29, 1968, Reagan held a series of extraordinary private meetings with minority leaders, both Mexican American and black, in East Los Angeles, Los Angeles, Vallejo, Richmond, San Francisco, Oakland, Fresno, San Bernardino, Santa Ana, Riverside, Stockton, and Sacramento.[34]

Reagan's office had left his official calendar blank for the first two full days of meetings. The national press characterized the meetings as "unusual" and "semi-secret." Reagan told the press that the meetings "concerned long-term Negro and Mexican American problems" and had nothing to do with concerns about rioting. When asked if militants were to be included, Reagan answered, "No, I don't think they have anything to contribute…Their approach is not toward solving problems. In their view, the problems are insoluble without their brand of militance." Here Reagan was defining himself away from Chavez to appeal to those Mexican Americans, who as we have seen, might not have been in favor of Chavez, the strike and boycott or Chavez's endorsement of Kennedy.

Reagan explained that he did not put specifics on his schedule because he did not want it to appear "that we were trying to create a circus or get press coverage."[35]

One of those who attended all the meetings of the Mexican American community was Dr. Bravo. His daughter recalled that her father had told her, "Reagan was good" at the meetings and had listened to the concerns of the Mexican American community and proposed solutions to their problems.[36] Without any press fanfare, Reagan met quietly for many hours over many days listening in close, personal sessions with minorities. He cared deeply about Americans of Mexican descent, heard their problems dealing with the state and federal bureaucracies, and offered concrete solutions.

Throughout the audiotapes of the many meetings, one hears Reagan speaking in clear English, as do the Mexican Americans and others who attended and voiced their problems directly to their governor. Reagan did not attempt to speak Spanish. He knew better than try to pander. He respected them, they had shown their respect for him in the 1966 election, and he again was following through on his sincere desires to help—mainly by cutting through the massive federal bureaucracies. He was again demonstrating that following the policies of big government Democrats was not the answer for Mexican Americans; indeed they were the continuing source of the problems. Reagan was demonstrating that conservative Republican ideals—small government and individual freedom and individual responsibility—were the solutions. He told them, and they saw, that he wanted to help get big government off their backs. Or as he famously would say later, "Government is the problem!"

After the series of meetings had finished, Reagan continued to discuss the issues brought up at the meetings and continued to voice concern about the problems of minorities.[37] The fact that Reagan had had a number of meetings in minority communities was credited for "helping keep California cities cool after the death of Martin Luther King."[38] Reagan's reaction to the tragedy, to be discussed shortly, would be another major factor in cooling off reactions to the tragedy.

Outreach to Minorities Nationally

Reagan did not speak to minorities only in California. Reagan's presidential campaign continued, and immediately after the King tragedy, he kept his appointments on April 5 to meet with black leaders and the Women's National Press Club in Washington D.C.[39]

Candidate Reagan was not afraid to be at the forefront of establishing his party's 1968 policies on racial issues, and he would carry his concerns about the Mexican American community to the Republican Governors Association Taskforce which would meet in San Francisco on May 8. In an opening statement, he would tell the group not to use methods which were "tried formulas of days gone by" but wanted the party's 1968 platform to "provide new solutions to the problems of social minorities."[40] The Task Force, visiting twelve cities gathering information, which the GOP governors hoped would be used to determine party platform specifics, would be hosted by Reagan during their brief California visit. Many subjects would be discussed, and Reagan would bring in the chief economist of Bank of America to discuss a "viable partnership" between government and business to reduce poverty. Reagan would tell the press 'he wanted it understood that the GOP governors recognize the importance of dealing with minority problems in the platform.'[41]

Clearly Reagan thought his success in attracting the support and votes of the Mexican American community in 1966, and which was continuing in 1968, could be applied both at the national level for his own 1968 run for the presidency, as well as serve as models for other Republicans nationwide on how to attract support from minorities by breaking the grip the Democrats held on them.

Reagan would follow up the remarks he had prepared at the GOP Taskforce by an official announcement the following week of a "Work, Learn, and Build" program, which would bring together business, labor, and government to "mount a meaningful attack on the problems of the poor in California."[42] "Handouts will be replaced with pay-checks," would be the first of its kind in the country—a clear expansion of Reagan's earlier initiatives when he had first become governor. Reagan never saw government as the sole solution to problems. At most he wanted government to play a minor role compared to the people and business.

The Black Vote

As noted, Reagan did meet in some black communities and with black leaders on the east coast during this period but did not recruit specific members of the black community to help run a portion of his campaign as he had done with Dr. Bravo and Mr. Orozco. Although he did tell the press that "more Negroes hold decision-making positions" in his administration than ever before, he most likely felt that the chances to garner votes in the Mexican American community were much higher.[43]

One reason may be that Reagan had had some difficulties with the black community during his 1966 gubernatorial campaign, as chronicled by historian Lou Cannon. Reagan had been ill when he had appeared at the National Negro Republican Assembly and had been attacked by George Christopher, his Republican opponent in the primary, for having opposed the 1964 Civil rights Act. Reagan was infuriated at the charge and had walked out of the meeting, only to return later and as he apologized to delegates, Reagan had "reiterated his personal abhorrence of discrimination, and declared that his opposition to the Civil Rights Act was based on constitutional grounds."[44]

Was Reagan prejudiced against blacks, as has been charged? Liberal columnist Mark Shields interviewed Reagan's old college football teammate, Dr. William Burghardt. In 1931, the Eureka College football team had been refused entry at a hotel because the team had two black members, one of whom was Burghardt. Reagan brought the two black team members to his home in Dixon, where they were all warmly welcomed. Burghardt reflected, "The Gipper was free of racial prejudice."[45] But on the political front, in 1966, Reagan indeed had made "minimal effort to attract black voters," because he felt they were "irretrievably tied to the Democrats."[46]

But there were a few blacks who had supported Reagan and one had the courage to make his views known nationally. During the gubernatorial campaign and continuing into his presidential campaign, Reagan attacked welfare programs because they had not succeeded in their goals, had created poverty-stricken individuals and families whose reliance on welfare had continued into several generations, and decried vociferously the resultant loss of dignity that the programs had forced upon the black and other minority communities.

Often in campaign speeches in 1967-1968 he would cite the medieval Jewish sage Maimonides, who had taught that the way to help the poor was not to give out handouts but to teach each poor person how to care and feed and clothe himself. In early 1967, a man who identified himself as a Negro from Brooklyn, New York, had written a letter to the *New York Times* defending Reagan's position on welfare and human dignity. He wrote that that he gave his "hearty endorsement" to Reagan's recent Inaugural Address when he had observed, "there is no humanity or charity in destroying self-reliance, dignity, and self-respect." The writer had attacked these same governmental welfare programs, which had ignored "self-esteem and dignity," were "playing cheap politics" and were "unworthy of considering itself truly humanitarian."[47]

We will examine shortly the eloquent speech Reagan would deliver a few hours after the assassination of Dr. Martin Luther King, Jr. Reagan would call for racial justice and equal opportunity and would assail bigotry as well as law breaking. But Reagan would discuss an issue that he would reiterate several times during the 1968 campaign: that blacks and Hispanics were being ill-served by the Democratic Party and that a natural home for them could be the Republican Party due to its reliance on individual freedom. Towards the end of his address in Washington, D.C. after the King tragedy, Reagan would bring up how unions, traditional Democrat allies, were treating blacks and Mexican-Americans:

"I know that only 3 percent of the membership of organized labor in California is Negro and that union apprenticeship programs are slow to take in those with dark skins and Spanish surnames."[48]

Reagan then would cite a California state legislator, a Democrat, who had said, "California and the nation have begun to realize that the black community and the conservative community are coming much closer together."[49]

Federal Plantation

During the presidential campaign, he would not ignore the issue of the lack of blacks in the Republican Party and would continue the ideas he had spoken after the King tragedy. In Chicago on May 21, he would tell an audience at the Hilton Hotel that the Democrat Party had "betrayed Negro American citizens by taking their votes and then breaking promises to them." In Miami when a black woman would charge that the GOP was only for white people, Reagan would counter saying that blacks had stayed out of the Republican Party of their own choice but should come back in as the Democrat Party was the party of the "federal plantation system."[50]

Reagan understood that long after Lincoln had freed them, the blacks had re-enslaved themselves to the Democratic Party and its failed policies. Reagan was trying to educate blacks as to the individual freedom ideals and smaller government policies of Republicans, so that blacks—and everyone else—would be lifted economically to better lives. Even in the second decade of the twenty-first century, it is the rare and brave black spokesperson who in public would utter Reagan's theme.[51]

Although Reagan had held meetings with members of the black communities in Los Angeles, Vallejo, Richmond, Oakland, and San Francisco as part of his late March, 1968 outreach program and later with black leaders after the King assassination as cited earlier, clearly Reagan's major effort continued to be targeting an increasing vote share amongst the Mexican-American community.

Ronald Reagan's overall relationship with the black community is well beyond the scope of this work. Yet even in 2013 with the release of the film *The Butler*, in which President Reagan was portrayed as racially insensitive, four well-known Reagan historians had to point out Reagan's life-long advocacy against discrimination.[52]

On May 11, 1968, Reagan would speak from the heart about his feelings for the poor and minorities and how he thought best to help them. Reagan would wonder,

"Why have we as Republicans allowed our opponents to pre-empt this whole field of human misery and unequal opportunity? All they've offered, and offered it for three decades now, is a kind of federal plantation, a kind of mass therapy, when in truth we're dealing with human beings. Each one is as unique as we are unique. Each one asking only for the dignity to being treated as an individual. Well, ours is a party whose philosophy is based on a belief in individual freedom and individual rights. Ours is the party of the individual. We can't match our opponents in promises. But let us simply say to these people that we'll do whatever is necessary to save human beings, to restore their independence, and their self-respect, but were going to stop destroying them."[53]

After the assassination of Robert F. Kennedy, in mid June 1968 Reagan would be asked by a reporter if any Republican could hope to replace Kennedy as the spokesman of the Mexican Americans and other minority and poor groups? Reagan would reply with caution that he was not meaning to speak of a replacement so soon after Kennedy's death, but that he thought any Republican had good solutions to the problems of minorities and the poor. Reagan would add to the comments he would make on May 11 in stronger terms, saying it was "high time the minority communities in America recognize that they have been subsisting on promises for a great many years from the party now in power. I, for the life of me, can't see any reason why a Negro or an American of Mexican descent or any of our other minorities would continue swallowing the promises. The cities where we have had some of the worst uprisings and disturbances are cities that happen to be run by Democrat political machines...the other side has failed in solving those problems. It ought to be time to give Republicans a chance."[54]

Minorities would continue their entrenched Democratic voting preferences for at least another five decades. Reagan's astute observations—that cities with the worst problems impacting minorities had had Democratic administrations for years—could apply with even more force to urban life in the twenty-first century.

Boycott

The grape boycott that Chavez had organized gained steam in the late spring of 1968 as his group targeted cities, where most grapes were sold, and as a result some cities and some politicians across the country boycotted grapes. Indeed grape shipments had declined some 42 percent in Boston and 98 percent in New York City.[55] To counteract the boycott, the Reagan administration began a new nationwide publicity "counteroffensive," using new slogans in advertisements.[56]

Reagan would be drawn into the controversy directly when notified that New York City's deputy mayor had the city officially join the boycott. Reagan complained that deputy mayor had instructed citizens to boycott all California grapes and not just those picked by non-union farm workers.[57] Reagan felt that the boycott was illegal, as the California grape growers had filed charges against Chavez's union with the National Labor Relations Board. There were also investigations of violations of anti-trust laws.

Lindsay and Rockefeller

Reagan would end up sending telegrams on July 2, 1968 to two of his major 1968 Republican opponents: Mayor Lindsay in Manhattan and Governor Rockefeller in Albany. Reagan would let each know that if the New York City policy was not withdrawn, California was considering retaliatory legislation.[58] Grape purchases would fall some 98% and Mayor John Lindsay would support the boycott publicly.

At a June 6 press conference, initially Reagan would try to downplay Lindsay's involvement, citing that the initial announcement had been made by Lindsay's deputy. But "to the chagrin of Reagan, Lindsay never disavowed the action."[59]

New York Governor Rockefeller would not get involved publicly. "Rockefeller met Reagan's threats and criticism with the calculated strategy of silence."[60] Lindsay's support of the boycott "helped the union's cause exponentially" and this would please pro-union, and anti-Reagan, Rockefeller. Rockefeller's silence, analyzed historian Holmes, would be a planned political move to differentiate himself from the more vocal Reagan.[61] During the subsequent fall presidential campaign, Reagan and Nixon would eat grapes together calling the boycott immoral and illegal.[62]

Native Americans and Asians

Back at the March 1968 community meetings, one Native American woman made a statement of principle that, as discussed earlier, had originated as far back as President Theodore Roosevelt's comments when he said he was against the idea of hyphenated American names such as Italian-American. Classifying Americans in this manner also had been abhorrent both to Reagan and to Reagan's mentor Eisenhower who, as we have seen, were against the use of hyphens, were convinced that the idea of having hyphenated Americans was a Democratic idea to gain votes, and Reagan had confirmed their discussion via the 1966 letter cited earlier and at his January, 1966 announcement of running for office.

Reagan continued the same theme throughout his 1968 campaign by stating at virtually every speech, or when asked by the press, that he did not like the term conservative-Republican or liberal-Republican; he said to his audiences that they were all just Republicans. This was a principle the exact opposite of what the Democratic Party, in its constant breaking down people into groups and subgroups, stood for. This unnamed native American said in frustration to Governor Reagan, "I submit to you that sectionalizing these questions, Japanese, Philippino, Negroes, American Indians, Jews, Italians, is not gonna help...This is a philosophical question involving the whole community." Reagan agreed completely and closed by suggesting that minority appointees should be cognizant of other minorities as well as their own.[63]

Unmentioned by Reagan were his interactions with Japanese-Americans during World War II, cited earlier, when he had convinced a store owner to rehire five Japanese-American workers and Reagan's remarks on America's unique multi-ethnic society.

In 1966 Governor Reagan had made a "conscious effort" to hire Mexican Americans and other minorities. But paradoxically, Reagan, Reed, and Haerle went out of their way to seek to appoint to all positions only those expert and qualified individuals who had not applied for the position. They wanted people who had not sought out governmental jobs but rather needed to be persuaded to serve the people by joining the Reagan team.[64]

One such special individual was Moon Lim Lee of Weaverville. Reagan confirmed Lee's appointment as California's first Chinese American Highway Commissioner. When Lee would die in 1985, President Reagan would call his widow, fondly recalling Lee as "a quiet, mild-mannered man who got the job done and loved people."[65]

Enlarging the Republican Tent

By the time the 1968 Republican convention would approach, Reagan had followed through on his 1966 campaign promises to Mexican Americans. Reagan was attempting to enlarge the tent of the Republican Party when he called for disaffected Democrats and Independents to join his new Republican banner. Indeed he made that call at the end of most of his campaign speeches in 1967 and 1968. Reagan added to his call by hoping to attract those same Mexican

Americans who had voted for him in 1966 to his enlarged tent in 1968. Reagan appointed significant numbers of minorities to important posts, spent time to visit minority communities, held special meetings with their leaders, and listened to their concerns. Reagan received new information that he could use to modify prior policy initiatives. He then expanded his ideas to help minority citizens across the country while he campaigned for the presidency. While candidate Reagan was busy in California and elsewhere fulfilling his promises by proposing innovative programs to help minorities, Reagan's old nemesis was preparing to run for the presidency too.

Endnotes

1.   RRL, Tape 348
2.   "Reagan Urges Republicans To Aid Minority Problems," *NYT*, 5/9/68
3.   Kopelson, Gene. 2014C
4.   Cannon 2003, p. 152
5.   Pycior 1977, p. 222
6.   Cannon 2003, p. 152
7.   "The Inauguration: Hollywood With Spanish Accent," *NYT*, 1/6/67, p. 18
8.   Kopelson, Gene 2014C
9.   "Statement of Governor Ronald Reagan on Agriculture," Office of the Governor, Sacramento, 2/9/1967
10.   Holmes, *The Economic Roots of Reaganism*, pp. 67-68
11.   Cannon 2003, p. 177
12.   Pycior, p. 194-195, p. 205
13.   Kopelson, Gene. 2014C
14.   Patrick, Curtis vol 1, p. 24-25
15.   Pycior, p. 190-193
16.   Pycior, p. 194-195, p. 205
17.   Pumphrey, pers int 8/3/12
18.   RRL, Tape 289
19.   Jennifer Mandel, archivist, Ronald Reagan Library, personal communication, 6/13/12
20.   Author copy
21.   Hoyt, Austin, Ronald Reagan at Yale
22.   Pycior, p. 215
23.   Pycior, p. 221
24.   Pycior, p. 221
25.   Holmes, op. cit., p. 68
26.   Holmes, op. cit., p. 69-70
27.   Pycior, p. 225
28.   Pycior, p. 220-221
29.   Pycior, p. 222
30.   Reed, pers comm., 10/20/13
31.   Pycior, p. 222
32.   Pycior, p. 222
33.   Clarke, *The Last Campaign*, p. 243
34.   RRL, Tapes 330-334
35.   Hill, Gladwin, "Reagan Consults With Minority Group Leaders," *NYT*, 3/27/68, p. 33
36.   Francine Pumphrey, pers int 8/3/12
37.   Hill, Gladwin, "Reagan Believed Waiting in the Wings," *NYT*, 4/7/68
38.   Large, Arlen, "California's Governor Propounds a Tough Line In Bid For GOP Backing," *Wall Street Journal*, 5/22/68, p. 23
39.   RRL Tape 337
40.   "Reagan Urges Republicans To Aid Minority Problems," *NYT*, 5/9/68
41.   Lembke, Daryl, "Reagan Urges GOP To Offer Plans For Minority Aid," *Los Angeles Times*, 5/9/68

42. "Exciting 'Work, Learn and Build' Plan Announced," Capitol Report from the Office of the Governor vol 1, No. 13, 5/14/68, p. 1
43. Naughton, James, "JFK's Missile Gap Now Exists—Reagan," *Cleveland Plain Dealer*, 5/23/68, p. 5
44. Cannon, Governor Reagan, p. 142-143
45. http://www.creators.com/opinion/mark-shields/a-personal-anecdote-in-defense-of-ronald-reagan.html
46. Kabaservice, p. 176
47. "Reagan on Welfare," *NYT*, 1/15/67, p. E17
48. "Reagan Pictures the American Dream: Nashville Banner," 4/16/68, p. 1
49. ibid
50. Corrigan, Richard, "Reagan Stars in Screen Test," *Washington Post*, 5/26/68, p. A8
51. former basketball star Charles Barkley would, http://thehill.com/blogs/blog-briefing-room/news/252181-barkley-voting-for-dems-hasnt-helped-blacks
52. Hayward, Steven et. al., "What 'The Butler' Gets Wrong About Ronald Reagan and Race," *Washington Post*, opinions 8/30/2013
53. RRL, Tape 341
54. RRL, Tape 348
55. Holmes, *Economic*, p. 70
56. Holmes, *Economic*, p. 70
57. RRL, Tape 355
58. Rockefeller Archive Center, Graham Molitor Papers, IV 3A 18, Agriculture and RWR, Box 27, Folder 656, July 2, 1968
59. Holmes, *The Ever-Shrinking Middle Ground*, p. 12-13
60. Holmes, p. 13
61. ibid
62. Holmes, p. 14
63. RRL, Tape 355
64. Reed, pers int 10/17/12
65. Greenberg, Bruce, "Moon Lim Lee's Legacy," *Enjoy Magazine*, 2/11 edition

CHAPTER 21: REAGAN RISES TO FIGHT RFK

"The only one who can stop us is Reagan."
                    ~ Richard Nixon[1]

"From the moment Bobby Kennedy announced, Reagan became a thoroughly motivated candidate."
                    ~ Clif White[2]

"I'm in!"
                    ~ Ronald Reagan[3]

"Ronald Reagan—I'll get even with you!"
                    ~ Robert F. Kennedy[4]

For Reagan and his presidential campaign, March came in like a lamb: he had no campaign trips planned for the whole month, as he was busy in California on state matters including his meetings with minorities. By month's end, March would be transformed into a full-fledged political lion. Robert F. Kennedy would be entering the Democratic race and then Vice-President Humphrey would be on a trip carrying a political secret of such monumental historical importance that he would become physically ill trying to keep the secret.[5]

As March began, Reagan's support amongst Republicans reached its nadir with a March 1 Gallup poll showing only 6 percent support. Coupled with Reagan's repeated denials to the media that he was a candidate, other than as California's favorite son, the Reagan candidacy seemed to be sputtering. Although it was not yet dead in its tracks, there were worrisome signs. By the time of an early March Republican gala, Reagan "was not invited to speak at all."[6] At the first winter meeting of the National Governor's Association, Reagan did not attend.[7]

After the Romney withdrawal, reporters asked Reagan on February 29 about the effect of the withdrawal on his own campaign. The Romney withdrawal was expected to put "greater pressure" on Reagan to actively campaign for delegates in the three opt-out primaries.[8] But an unnamed Reagan friend countered that Reagan was not going into a "delegate-seeking confrontation" with Nixon.[9] The supposed theory from Reagan advisers was that if Reagan "became an active candidate and campaigned in states like Wisconsin, Nebraska, and Oregon, where his name will be on the primary ballots, he would have to win all of the Presidential primaries or his candidacy would backfire."[10] But the trouble with this rationale, if this indeed ever even were the opinions of unnamed Reagan advisors, was that Reagan already had campaigned—sometimes more than once as in Oregon— in each of those states in 1967. So why not return to those three states to invigorate the Reagan grassroots activists who were working so hard?

Reagan had used the rationale of combined fund-raising and campaign trips to great success so far. Plus, Reagan's original approach for the primaries never had the expectation of victories in all three states. Rather it was to be an incremental rising tide of increasing vote tallies in Wisconsin and Nebraska, culminating in an Oregon victory, which would provide the thrust to have the Reagan victory payload splash-down in Miami Beach.

As the press conference ended, Nofziger was asked about any future Reagan trips in the spring and answered that the only planned ones in the spring were to Arizona, New Mexico and Nevada.

Reagan held a campaign meeting on March 3 to review the upcoming Wisconsin primary and Nixon's delegate strength. Reagan, by no means stopping his campaign, wanted a new poll done for Wisconsin.[11] James Reston of the New York Times interviewed Reagan that same weekend, and the resultant front-page report indicated that Reagan still called for new political leadership in the nation's capital. When asked if he would accept his party's nomination, Reagan answered, "You know I won't make the Sherman statement because I've often quoted General Eisenhower when he said that it was 'an arrogant, stupid statement and Sherman shouldn't have made it in the first place.'"[12] Reagan made no specific mention of having first discussed the Sherman statement—and likely the presidency as well—with Ike at their prior golf day: their previously-discussed third meeting.

With Reston then asking Reagan about Vietnam, Reagan continued by once again unhesitatingly citing Eisenhower, and other generals from World War II, who "have spoken of stopping the entrance of supplies into Haiphong Harbor."[13] Reagan again was aghast why Johnson had not followed what Eisenhower and the military had recommended to Johnson in 1965. Reagan reiterated and used the term "sudden surge" as his preferred military tactic rather than the slow build-up under Johnson over the prior years.[14]

On March 10 at the Reagan residence, Reagan's financial backers declared that the campaign was finished. But Reagan's team went ahead with Reagan's Wisconsin poll anyway.[15]

The *Newsweek* delegate count on March 11 showed that Reagan was second in both Florida and Indiana and had gained in Louisiana. Reagan remained first choice in Mississippi, yet his total delegate count dropped to 198 from the 201 he had had in early January.[16] It was not a major change, but the tally showed that despite Clif White's best efforts, Reagan clearly was losing momentum.

Fourth Meeting with Ike

There was no known personal correspondence or telephone calls between Reagan and Eisenhower during the late winter of 1967 through early January, 1968. Then on January 22, as seen earlier, Eisenhower's diary entry revealed that he had spoken to Reagan. This was the time period in which Eisenhower was being briefed on the Tet offensive and the Vietnam War, the *U.S.S. Pueblo* and Soviet missiles. Eisenhower had observed Johnson's failure to send Westmoreland the requested American troop reinforcements, Johnson's over-riding political concerns and fear of a Kennedy challenge. Then in early March Eisenhower had watched a mock Republican convention program and saw the strong support Reagan was achieving across college campuses via Weinrod's Students for Reagan. This was also the time period when Eisenhower had conferred with Harold MacMillan, likely about hostage-taking and the solutions Reagan had offered, should any future hostage crises occur. As will be discussed later, at some soon point thereafter, someone, likely Eisenhower as intermediary, would tell Reagan of Macmillan's approval of how Reagan planned to deal with any future hostage crisis.

As the Democratic race was heating up, on March 9 Eisenhower and Reagan did meet again in Palm Desert. Initially, the former and future presidents golfed together, along with a group of Eisenhower's golf friends, who had wanted to attend the convention.[17] Eisenhower "asked Reagan if he could make this happen."[18] For several hours playing golf together, the two men chatted as Reagan drove Eisenhower in their shared golf cart.[19] Afterwards, the two men held a private luncheon-meeting as well at the Eldorado Club.[20]

Upon returning to Sacramento, Reagan told the press, "The conversation did not involve Mr. Reagan's favorite-son candidacy."[21] Most assuredly this was true, but in fact Reagan had told the press very little of what the men had discussed, other than the fact that Reagan told Eisenhower he would not accept the second spot on a ticket headed by Nixon or anyone else.[22] But in fact, according to Reed, much of importance had been discussed.

Eisenhower now had a broader historical perspective with which to impart to Reagan this time. The general no longer seemed to be advising Reagan on political issues or domestic politics. Eisenhower looked well beyond the past of Korea and the present of Vietnam. Eisenhower seemed to look ahead to a Reagan White House. Eisenhower urged Reagan to grow the American economy as the best way to defeat America's enemies such as the Soviet Union, and the general also tutored Reagan on defense spending.[23] The former president was handing his political baton to Reagan. Indeed as Reagan would reveal to the press only more a decade in the future during his third campaign for the presidency, during their golf outing that day (or possibly during another undocumented golf outing they shared prior to Ike's death) Eisenhower had discussed the Panama Canal with Reagan: the revamped treaty which Ike had orchestrated during his administration and what he foresaw as a new method of administering the canal. Reagan would store those 1968 Eisenhower discussions in his encyclopedic mind and put them to good use, as will be seen later.

Given the number of important geopolitical events that were transpiring, let alone the rising political heat on both Democrat and Republican sides, it is difficult to imagine that they did not discuss many other issues as well. After all, the two men spent a full half day together: sharing a private golf cart, golfing together on the golf course, and at their luncheon-meeting itself. Besides the Pueblo crisis and Tet and the challenges to Johnson, critical Republican primaries loomed immediately ahead. Johnson's unpopularity was soaring. RFK was thinking of entering the race. Both Reagan and Eisenhower despised Kennedy. It is highly likely that the two discussed the Democrats and RFK in particular.

Did they also discuss nuclear weapons? Clearly the two had discussed the critical choice: of whether the U.S. should try to live with communism or should the U.S. try to defeat communism in ways other than by war—i.e. by a strong economy. Was it a prelude, or indeed perhaps one important piece of the origin, of the contrast between Nixon and Kissinger's détente in the 1970s versus Reagan's plans to defeat communism—of course ultimately successful—in the 1980s?

Also, further discussions of the parallels between the Korean and Vietnam wars likely occurred, given the extensive mentoring Eisenhower had given Reagan previously, coupled with the world's headlines on the Pueblo and the psychological effects in America of Tet.

Soon would be the one-year anniversary of the Six Day War and Israel's twentieth birthday. Reagan was going to speak once again at the Salute to Israel in less than two months. Might a discussion of how the Soviets were rearming Arab nations have ensued?

Two days after meeting with Reagan, Eisenhower again golfed with friends, who also were confidants and backers of Reagan, including Gosden. It is highly likely that items discussed were Reagan, current events, and the 1968 nomination, with full knowledge and permission that any additional Eisenhower thoughts got transmitted back to Reagan.[24] Eisenhower concluded the Gosden golf match with, "Nixon would probably make the best president."[25] This was hardly an enthusiastic, ringing endorsement. Electability remained the key for the general. Was Eisenhower, only a few months after his "golf buddy" interview with one reporter, now wavering to friends and starting to admit to them that a nominee Reagan would more likely win the general election?

Shortly thereafter, Nixon campaign staff member Robert Ellsworth met with Eisenhower and discussed the state of the race. Ellsworth later commented that Reagan "continued to intrigue the General." Ellsworth reported, "He (Eisenhower) keeps telling Reagan that he has to stay as Governor for four years to prove he is not a right winger. His (Reagan's) people are always bringing him (Eisenhower) proof to show that he (Reagan) is not a right winger…The Reagan people tell Eisenhower that the Rocky-Reagan ticket would be the best…He (Eisenhower) says that his response to them is that this is not a ticket that would appeal to anyone of any political principle."[26] If anyone from the Reagan campaign ever actually was pushing a Rockefeller-Reagan ticket to Eisenhower, that person has not come to light.

But for Eisenhower, who had been despondent in November 1960, feeling that his eight-year term had been for naught, yet who now was looking at his legacy by continuing to implement the rebuilding of his party with new faces, perhaps he was thinking of a Republican ticket headed at some soon point by Ronald Reagan. Perhaps he was thinking that his interview earlier in the year via his "golf buddy," in which he seemed to favor Reagan for the nomination, soon might receive more publicity. If there was one Republican contender who was speaking almost daily of carrying on Eisenhower's common sense domestic programs, as well as taking the same hard line on Vietnam that Eisenhower was espousing because those policies had worked so well in World War II and in Korea, it was Ronald Reagan.

In this fourth and final meeting with Reagan prior to his death in 1969, Eisenhower, ill but still enjoying life, clearly had looked past the Republican convention to a time when Reagan would be president. Eisenhower was mentoring Reagan to follow the strong leadership Eisenhower had demonstrated. In the 1940s Eisenhower had defeated the Nazis. In the 1950s Eisenhower had stopped the North Korean and mainland Chinese communists. Eisenhower was looking to a future time when his protégé Reagan would finish the job altogether and see world communism defeated and dumped upon the "ash heap of history."

RFK Enters the Race

But events outside of Reagan's control suddenly reignited the engines of the flailing Reagan campaign for the presidency. One day after the surprisingly strong showing of Eugene McCarthy in the New Hampshire primary, just as White had predicted to Reagan, Robert Kennedy said he was reassessing his plans. And on March 16th RFK officially announced he was entering the race for the presidency.

Reagan watched Kennedy's announcement with "intense interest," analyzing every statement and rebroadcast.[27] In private, Reagan was furious. Here was ruthless RFK stepping over the brave Eugene McCarthy. Reagan despised Kennedy and detested his policies. Reagan's mind was already racing many political steps ahead, analyzing the implications. If he were the nominee and if RFK were his opponent, Reagan would relish another debate with his old nemesis.

Nixon, in Oregon, watched the Kennedy announcement on television too. Nixon "sat and looked at the blank screen for a long time, saying nothing. Finally he shook his head slowly. 'We've just seen some terrible forces unleashed. Something bad is going to come of this. God knows where this is going to lead.'"[28] Nixon surmised that Johnson could easily defeat RFK for the nomination. But if somehow RFK got the nod from the Democratic Party, "We can beat that little S.O.B."[29] But Nixon's bravado against RFK as an opponent was not shared by his own staff. In the Nixon camp, "Fear spread quickly among the old Nixon hands from the '60 campaign when Robert Kennedy announced."[30] In reality, for Nixon, another Kennedy-Nixon debate would be a new debacle. Unlike 1962, it not only might cripple him politically permanently, after such a loss there would be no viable Nixon for the press to kick around this time.

The same analysis spread quickly to the rest of the GOP and to the national media. Reagan was seen as the Republican savior. Reed reflected that once Kennedy announced, "Republicans were jolted from their Nixonian slumber by visions of another Kennedy-Nixon election struggle. They needed a more telegenic candidate."[31] The national media quickly reached the same conclusion about the role of television if Robert F. Kennedy were to face Ronald Reagan. One op-ed reporter wondered if "the reputation of TV as the register of campaign potency" would be validated and speculated that due to the media blitz before the Democrat Indiana primary, which would pit Kennedy against McCarthy, "Ronald Reagan, who once beat Bobby Kennedy all hollow in a Telstar TV encounter, could very well be a Republican beneficiary of the Indiana fallout."[32]

Rocky Out

Meanwhile, political events snowballed quickly between the RFK announcement and the end of March. The events on the Democratic side between the RFK announcement and the end of March are chronicled by Schlesinger and Chester et al. On the Republican side while Reagan quietly was relaunching his campaign, the focus shifted to Rockefeller's waffling—especially for the Oregon primary—on whether to stay in the race. Nixon's camp feared that Reagan could in fact prevent a Nixon first-ballot victory if Rockefeller delegates and several favorite son candidates had sufficient votes.[33] After much dithering, on March 21, Rockefeller announced he would no longer be a candidate.[34] Buchanan revealed that the decision may in part have stemmed from a private Pearson report of an extra-marital affair, although in the end it likely was a false rumor started by Pearson himself.[35]

Upon hearing the news of Rockefeller's exit, Nixon phoned an aide saying, "The only one who can stop us is Reagan." [36]Reagan was not pleased that another *R* had dropped out. With only Nixon in the field, Reagan again pondered Eisenhower's main worry: Nixon's electability.[37]

Reagan Takes Control

Ronald Reagan decided firmly to reignite his presidential campaign immediately. Of course the campaign itself never had stopped. Rather it had continued under the direction of the major grassroots activists in Wisconsin, Nebraska and Oregon, Bubb's national center, and the smaller Reagan campaign offices across the country. But the threat of a Robert F. Kennedy presidency so infuriated Reagan, that Reagan called a special meeting on March 25, 1968.

Reagan had a clear purpose from the beginning as to why he was seeking the nation's highest office. He was not in it for personal glory or as the next political step. Indeed he continued to say it still was up to the people to decide if they wanted him as their candidate. Reagan ran because of the policies and the candidates who represented widely different perspectives on America. First, he had detested Johnson's expansionist, big government programs and the mismanagement of the Vietnam War. But with RFK in the race, not only did all the former reasons still apply, but now for Reagan it was personal. He despised his nemesis, and in Vietnam, RFK wanted to cut and run. Reagan had told many press conferences that America was in Vietnam for its own national interest: to preserve freedom for an ally. If RFK were elected, heaven help us!

"I'm In"

As Reed recalled, Reagan told the Los Angeles elders firmly that Reed and White were to "resume command."[38] Reagan told Clark, "I'm in!"[39] Reagan now clearly was in charge.[40]

Critical issues were analyzed and new campaign tactics were needed, because what was needed for America in the spring of 1968 was different than in 1967. No longer could Reagan speak only about his numerous successes on the domestic front in California and address Vietnam briefly. Reagan "needed to articulate his views on the national issues now gripping and ripping the country: Vietnam, inflation, civil disturbances, national priorities and defense."[41]

Statesman

The campaign strategy and tactics needed new direction, but Reagan himself did not need any new preparation in world affairs. He had delivered the Landon Lecture at Kansas State University and had been Chubb Fellow at Yale. He had delivered economic speeches to international financiers in Detroit and New York City. Through his tutoring from Eisenhower, his advocacy of an anti-ballistic missile defense, his visits with veterans, his visit to Lawrence-Livermore, his Seabee ceremony, his visit in Mexicali, and via his first major speech on foreign policy in Albany, Oregon, he was prepared. In fact he already was a statesman and rightful contender for the highest office in the land. And now for Ronald Reagan, the campaign had become quite personal.

New Strategy

Reagan turned to his original supporters for advice on the new campaign direction. There was precious little time left to correct any mistaken new tactics. Bill Rusher, the pro-Reagan conservative stalwart, was contacted. Rusher and William F. Buckley, Jr., the "Two Bill's," had continued to disagree on whom to support for 1968. In Reagan's corner from the start, Rusher had continued to hold meetings of his Hard Core. Rusher, Reed, and Whetstone met in St. Louis on March 23-24, along with twelve other Hard Core members to strategize about the renewed Reagan campaign effort.[42]

Rusher made a proposal that he formalized into a memorandum for discussion. He said that to maximize Reagan's influence in Miami Beach, their strategy had assumed it would be a brokered convention. In order to prevent a Nixon stampede, Rusher recommended that it was not "going to be enough to escalate the Reagan movement only imperceptibly."[43] Rusher wanted a "big splash," which would be on par with other big events of the campaign, such as Romney's withdrawal and Kennedy's entrance.[44] Rusher accepted that Reagan could not declare, but he recommended that Reagan hold a press conference. To the media and the nation, Reagan should state that due to the Kennedy candidacy, he felt it his "obligation to outline, in depth and detail, my differences with Senator Kennedy."[45] Because Rockefeller had stated that although he was no longer a candidate, he would be available for a draft and would continue to speak out on the issues, Reagan similarly should state that he was open for a draft and also would speak out on the issues so that the conservative point of view would be voiced as well.[46] Rusher's plan was rejected by the Hard Core. They were still fearful of an open declaration. So Reagan continued to work on his new campaign plans with White and Reed.

Reagan's original campaign plan, to gain support from the Republican leaders, was long gone. Reagan had squandered the chances to get Tower and Thurmond onto his bandwagon as part of his Southern Strategy. Goldwater always had been just a slight glimmer of possibility because he had been for Nixon since 1965. Even though at the Omaha convention of Young Republicans the prior June, Goldwater had expressed a mild possibility of joining the Reagan bandwagon, he remained for Nixon. Dirksen still was a possibility. Even though the Reagan-Dirksen meeting in Eureka had not culminated in an endorsement, Dirksen had pushed for Reagan a few times. But for all practical purposes, the original campaign plan needed to be replaced.

The possibility of another Kennedy-Nixon debate frightened not only Republican leaders but the grass roots activists as well. Reagan's grass roots activists, who we will meet, had been active since 1964. But they did not occupy the highest priority in the original presidential campaign plan from 1966. Now in March, 1968, the grassroots activists became the campaign's centerpiece. To this plan, "Ron and Nancy Reagan agreed; they authorized an escalated travel schedule and a serious television campaign in our target primary states."[47]

RFK : The Spark That Reignited Reagan

Reagan did not view an RFK candidacy as a potential new, ordinary political challenge. "Reagan considered Kennedy a 'really appalling' prospective President."[48] For Ronald Reagan, the prospect of RFK as the Democrat nominee created a huge shift in momentum for the 1968 Reagan campaign. According to Clif White, "The President's abject surrender to Bobby Kennedy galvanized our Reagan camp, and particularly Governor Reagan."[49] Bill Rusher concurred, using almost the same language, feeling that Johnson's announcement and then Kennedy's official candidacy "had the effect of galvanizing Reagan."[50] Reed saw that immediately after the RFK announcement, Reagan had a sudden "new outlook."[51] Kennedy's ascendancy had forced Reagan "to make a decision as to whether he wanted to launch a real campaign for the nomination and for the Presidency."[52] And Reagan answered with a resounding Yes!

Of course we have seen that Reagan by no means had been just going along for the ride, as White incorrectly had recalled.[53] Reagan had travelled thousands of miles almost every weekend, taking multiple hated airplane flights, and criss crossing the country. But after Reagan's earlier announced curtailment of out-of-state travels in early 1968, even though the grass roots activists were marching full steam ahead, the national campaign had been somewhat in limbo. White continued, "I don't think Ronald Reagan ever hesitated after that. He knew that a Kennedy victory would be a victory for all the forces he had fought against for so long" emphasizing that Kennedy would worsen Johnson's "free-spending social programs" and bring into power "the forces of appeasement."[54] White continued, "From the moment Bobby Kennedy announced, Reagan became a thoroughly motivated candidate."[55] Rusher observed, "Reagan, who thought Kennedy would win the nomination … sincerely believed his election would be a disaster".[56] White concluded, "It was his conscience that made Reagan run in earnest for President after Robert Kennedy tossed his hat in the ring in March 1968".[57]

Reagan's prior run-ins with Robert Kennedy likely provided the final spark to ignite his 1968 campaign in earnest once RFK had made his announcement.

Reagan commented publicly for the first time about the Kennedy official candidacy at a mid month news conference. He said Kennedy had a "very good chance" of winning the Democrat nomination but said it was a "ruthless and cynical act of opportunism." (author's emphasis) Contrasting McCarthy and Kennedy, Reagan said that for Kennedy, "it was like jumping in after someone else has done the spadework."[58] Reagan, the recipient of RFK's ruthlessness for two decades, finally got the chance publicly to use the term so many had ascribed to Kennedy's personality.

Reagan sent to Human Events a detailed campaign staff list, which immediately appeared in print.[59] It was reported that Reagan was stepping up press interviews, including those with the *New York Times* and *Chicago Tribune*. Reed was described as the "buffer" between Reagan and his grass roots activists across the country as well as Reagan's out-of-state travel planner. White was still seeking out delegates. Bubb was distributing campaign materials to Reagan's state campaign offices, as well as serving as a "financial conduit" between the grass roots activists and Reagan's team in California. SFR was opening a full-time office in the nation's capital. All this activity aimed to have Reagan "favorably positioned for a place on the GOP ticket."[60] And Reagan was not aiming for second place!

Meanwhile, Kennedy offered, if Johnson would appoint a Kennedy-approved commission to reassess American policy in Vietnam, to stay out of the Democratic race. When asked about Kennedy's offer, Reagan told the press that Kennedy's deal was "an affront to the very office of the Presidency." Reagan predicted that if

Kennedy did enter the race, the "deep, personal animosity" between Kennedy and Johnson would be exposed to the nation.[61]

Eisenhower continued evaluating the political tsunamis on the Democratic side. As historian Arthur Schlesinger, Jr. revealed, on March 26 Eisenhower wrote a friend about RFK's entrance into the race: "It is difficult for me to see a single qualification that man has for the Presidency. I think he is shallow, vain and untrustworthy—on top of which he is indecisive."[62]

The next day in his diary, Eisenhower made one of his few detailed observations of the Republican scene when he wrote, "It now appears that there is no serious contender left for the Republican nomination except Dick."[63] Was this comment one of relief for front-runner Nixon or disappointment that Reagan's delegate count had not increased further? Likely Eisenhower was happy that his former vice-president seemingly had no major competition, but his comment just as well could have indicated that was he disappointed that Reagan had not developed into more of a challenger. Clearly Reagan never told his coach what he had been doing—campaigning for the presidency— ever since November, 1966.

Exit Johnson

Hubert Humphrey, vice-president of the United States, had a political secret of such earth-shattering political importance that he became physically ill trying to keep the secret. And poor Humphrey could not share the secret with a single soul. He was very quiet on the flight south, and on March 31, 1968, he was in Mexico for a short visit representing the United States at the signing of the Treaty of Tlatelolco, in which nuclear weapons were to banned from Latin America. But it was not Montezuma's revenge that bothered him, for he did not have any diarrhea at the formal dinner, which ended the signing. And it was not the terms of the treaty that bothered him, for he was in favor of its ideals. Suddenly as dinner finished, there was a buzz and uproar. Then Vice-President Humphrey was told that President Lyndon Johnson had made a surprise announcement, to a stunned world-wide audience, that he was not seeking re-election.

Humphrey's "face turned ashen," observed one attendee.[64] Even though everyone in the room was stunned, Humphrey told the group that he had already known. The secret was out. At last Humphrey was not the only one who knew Johnson would not seek re-election. On the flight home, Humphrey stayed in his cabin. Whether he then felt better now that the secret was out, or whether he felt worse---because now he would have to decide if he was going to become a candidate himself in 1968—was never made clear.[65]

Johnson had made his bombshell announcement that he would not seek reelection at the end of a speech in which he told the world that he would unilaterally stop the bombing of North Vietnam. It suddenly seemed as if Robert Kennedy had won the Democratic nomination by default.

Nixon gave a quick assessment: "This is the year of the dropouts. First Romney, then Rockefeller, now Johnson."[66] RFK likely would be unable to unite his party. The worry now was that if Humphrey were the nominee, he could unite the Democrats.[67]

Eisenhower gave his candid assessment in his diary. Johnson's unilateral concession, "without any quid pro quo from Hanoi," would "further bewilder" America. Johnson was contradicting his own prior determination and clearly was capitulating to the "peace at any price" group. Eisenhower felt that the "most puzzling" part of the speech, Johnson's decision to not seek reelection, meant that he wanted to "be excused from the burden of office to which he was elected" and that he was "unwilling to remain personally in the fight" to win the war.[68]

One of the purposes of Johnson's speech, wrote Eisenhower, might have been to discredit Kennedy and McCarthy by Johnson appearing to be the "self-sacrificing patriot." Then Eisenhower, who as we have seen had asked new President Johnson in 1963 to curb Kennedy's harassment of his political enemies, again revealed his true opinions of Johnson's likely successors: he wrote that McCarthy was a "visionary" but that Kennedy was a "sheer opportunist."[69] Reagan couldn't have agreed more. And it is not inconceivable that Eisenhower and Reagan discussed the implications of Johnson's announcement. Eisenhower, as had Churchill and Reagan, had kept the nation above party. But surely Eisenhower, the astute politician whose main political concern for the GOP always had been electability, surely could foresee another Nixon-Kennedy debate fiasco down the road.

Eisenhower made a public analysis of Johnson's withdrawal by writing an article, "Let's Close Ranks on the Home Front," for Reader's Digest.[70] Eisenhower justified the war to the American public by writing that it would be immoral not to resist communist tyranny, which had been trying to subjugate a "brave little country" which America had promised to help.[71]

Eisenhower continued to be briefed on Vietnam and the Pueblo with Generals Westmoreland and Goodpaster and from President Johnson personally. After another heart attack, Eisenhower was flown to the nation's capital for further medical care.[72]

Meanwhile Reagan and his team sprang into action. The center-piece of the planned Reagan media blitz, the campaign film *Ronald Reagan, Citizen Governor*, which would be shown in Wisconsin, Nebraska and Oregon, needed to be finalized. Reagan's communications and planning with the Citizens for Reagan National Information Center headed, by Henry A. Bubb in Topeka, continued. The major Reagan grassroots campaign offices, which had been established already in Wisconsin, Nebraska and Oregon, got into high gear. Other grassroots Reagan campaign activists, such as Walter Dilbeck, Jr., in Washington, D.C., those in many Western states, and the national Students for Reagan, continued pushing Reagan's candidacy.

Clif White was part of Reagan's team again but Spencer-Roberts by then had joined the Rockefeller team. A prior Reagan speechwriter, "horrified at the prospect of a Bobby Kennedy presidency," returned.[73] The reader is referred to Reed's personal recollections of the campaign's reset.[74]

Reagan's New Campaign Speeches

As discussed earlier, Reagan's previous standard campaign speech had been some 40 minutes with four distinct parts: rapid fire quips, then a "serious attack on Federal centralism under the Democrats," then his continually-updated report on his gubernatorial accomplishments, ending with a "flowery finale" about those "sickly pastels:"

"It's become the destiny of our Party to raise a banner to which the people of all Parties can repair—a banner that rejects the sickly pastels of expediency, the cynical shade of those who would buy the people's votes with the people's money."[75]

What is little known is that much of the initial political humor in Reagan's speeches had been provided by comedic actor Pat Buttram. Buttram was a well-known actor during the mid-to-late 1960s, appearing on the hit television show *Green Acres* as the neighbor of the main characters, played by Eddie Albert and Eva Gabor. Buttram, who would have a cameo in the third installment of President Reagan's favorite *Back to the Future* trilogy, died in 1994, and was remembered as a "staunch Republican who often helped Ronald Reagan spice up his speeches with well-targeted political quips."[76] But Reagan's theme now became deadly serious and Buttram was not needed.

Reagan's speechwriting process was similar to what had transpired throughout the campaign: after initial drafts were created and edited,

Reagan reviewed, added, and modified the drafts as he saw fit. Reed reflected, "Reagan enjoyed the process, the product, and the man."[77]

Reagan would not let RFK escape the cascading foreign policy disasters which his and his brother's policies had created. These would be "Robert Kennedy's chickens coming home to roost."[78] Of these new campaign speeches, "The Reagan touch was obvious in the final product."[79] The first of five anti-RFK White Paper speeches would premiere on May 11 in Hawaii.

Ronald Reagan's speeches, given over many decades, have been well analyzed by historians, but scant attention has been paid to 1967-1968. Historian Kurt Ritter concentrated mainly on Reagan's presidential speeches in a classic analysis from 1992. Shortly thereafter, Ritter did analyze Reagan's Southern speeches during the time of Reagan's first presidential campaign and noted it was Reagan's softer tone that made him more acceptable than Goldwater or Wallace.[80] Historian Kiron Skinner and her group felt that Reagan's 1968 speeches lacked the needed "persuasive qualities" and thereby did not generate sufficient fear to make voters support him.[81] Reagan, they felt, was "not a major rhetorician," as his message "did not reach out beyond his core constituency."[82] Other historians disagreed. Lewis Gould noted that Reagan's rhetoric "stirred the blood of the party faithful."[83] Chester et. al. agreed that Reagan was a master of rhetoric; it was the kind of rhetoric many people, unnerved by black militancy and violence in society, wanted to hear."[84] But in fact Reagan's message was broad, constantly was asking for independents and disaffected Democrats to join him. His speeches were uniformly stirring, typically with many standing ovations. His gubernatorial triumph, having attracted so many normally Democratic voters, is what Reagan was duplicating now in preparation for the fall election.

During his presidential campaign thus far, foreign affairs had dominated Reagan's press conferences. Thus far, he only had devoted one speech entirely to world affairs: his Albany, Oregon, Veteran's Day speech. Now Reagan was prepared to enter the arena of world statesmanship on his own terms. He was set to deliver five campaign speeches addressing the most critical problems facing the country and the world. And the way to do it was to attack his old nemesis, the likely Democratic candidate, RFK.

Reagan's Speeches Zero in on RFK

In his new speeches, Reagan began to target Kennedy specifically. Prior to the start of his presidential campaign, Reagan had mentioned Kennedy hardly at all. For example in his first Seattle speech, while running for governor in 1966, he vigorously had attacked the Johnson administration but just had mentioned Kennedy briefly.

Then when his presidential campaign had begun, Reagan's standard campaign speeches, which he gave across the country starting in February 1967 in Eugene Oregon, used four standard jokes in regards to RFK. For example he made these comments in Portland on November 10, 1967. After joking about Johnson, Reagan wisecracked that the audience should feel sorry for LBJ because:

> "Bobby's got the President so nervous that before the convention, he's thinking of putting the country in his wife's name."

> "But Bobby, I'm sure, he's just trying to be helpful; just the other day he announced he wants a Johnson-Humphrey ticket. But he didn't say where to."

> "Every time he offers to help, you can hear a little voice come out of the White House saying 'please Bobby we'd rather lose it ourselves.'"

> "Sometimes I think Bobby gets so excited about poverty because he never had any as a kid."[85]

In his many presidential campaign speeches thus far in 1967-1968, Reagan always had attacked Johnson's Great Society programs but had been supportive, for the most part, of his Vietnam policy objectives; Reagan indeed wanted Johnson to win the war and was critical that Johnson had been too timid to win. But after Kennedy's entrance into the race, Reagan not only planned to assail Kennedy's domestic plans, he also would tell the public how Kennedy was a foreign policy appeaser, whose criticism was undermining the nation at a time of war.

Reagan's sudden newly escalated travel schedule meant first that Reagan would have a busy April—as it had been in the fall.[86] Reagan would concentrate on visiting the West. As we have seen, although he would speak first in the nation's capital to the Women's National Press Club the day after the King assassination while accompanied by some of his SFR supporters, his campaign visits to the West would include New Mexico, where Carter Anderson had arranged his visit. On his second campaign swing to the West that month, this time in Idaho, his campaign team from Oregon would fly in to meet him and beg for him to return to their adjacent state for a third campaign visit. He would end his second trip by speaking in Colorado. But meanwhile Reagan began to attract renewed interest from the press as his campaign began anew.

Many of the national news media articles, which had speculated on Reagan as a presidential candidate ever since 1966, had either accompanying cartoons showing a laughing or smiling Reagan or had photographs of his old movies. Yet the cover story of *U.S. News and World Report* had four photographs, each showing a serious and forceful Reagan. It was a detailed seven-page exclusive interview. After reiterating, "I'm not a candidate,"[87] Reagan was asked the typical gamut of questions about his domestic and foreign policies to which he had answered elsewhere many times before. Reagan pushed for union workers to have secret ballots. He felt that race relations in America had improved dramatically. and that there had been tremendous progress in civil rights. Reagan declared, "To talk about prejudice as if there's been no change in it, no progress made in the hundred years since the Civil War—that is to ignore reality."[88]

When discussing Vietnam tactics, again he cited the policies of Eisenhower, including the threat of invasion and the closing of Haiphong Harbor. Reagan said defiantly, "We should close Haiphong Harbor...If we don't actually invade North Vietnam, at least we should pose the threat."[89]

But now Reagan began to change direction and no longer advocated just a reactive American foreign policy. Reagan was tired of America constantly having to fight against communist insurgencies and wars throughout the world. He declared that America should "give the enemy something else to worry about," by fomenting "some unrest in some corner of his realm to worry about."[90] Reagan wanted world communism to get a taste of its own medicine. Those pro-active anti-communist plans, clearly advocated by presidential candidate Reagan in 1968, would have to wait until the President Reagan of the 1980s.

Reagan then was asked if he were elected president in 1968, what would he do to end the war? He answered, "Ask the people to do away with some of the things that are so pleasant in today's living until the war is over. We should mobilize the power of this nation on a war footing to bring the war to an end. I don't believe in the policy of gradualism in fighting a war."[91] The latter of course was one of the key lessons that Reagan had learned from Eisenhower. Eisenhower and he together had made *Let's All Back the Attack* in 1944, by asking Americans to sacrifice and buy war bonds. It was a direct and personal way for Americans to feel involved. And Reagan was adding that the push for the self-sacrifice he had witnessed during World War II, now in 1968, be applied to Vietnam. He wanted to win. And he wanted all Americans to feel that same urgency and patriotism by jointly sharing and sacrificing in that victory.

Reagan's honoring of his mentor then extended beyond Vietnam. When asked what he would do to help the Middle East, Reagan answered that he would propose help in solving the "greatest problem" in the region: water. Reagan clarified: "This is similar to the proposal made by President Eisenhower," referring to Eisenhower's October, 1953 plan to establish a comprehensive water plan for the Jordan River, as mentioned earlier.[92]

While Reagan's reinvigorated campaign was being noted by the press, and as Reagan set about restructuring his campaign staff in California and writing his new anti-RFK speeches, his national grass roots activists had been busy as well. Nixon noticed.

Nixon's people let it be known that they were not happy that Reagan was not more forceful in discouraging his grass roots activists in opt-out Wisconsin, Nebraska and Oregon. Reagan said of Nixon and Nixon's displeasure, "I've always had good relations with him, going back many years. I'm sure he knows how successful we were shutting off our operations in New Hampshire." When asked why he was not endorsing Nixon, he answered that as California's favorite son, he was obligated to wait until the California delegation met to consider candidates."[93]

At the same, Nixon had a private conversation with the *Los Angeles Times*, noting, "Many thousands of dollars, possibly into the six-figure bracket," were being collected to "boost Reagan for the nomination," and Reagan's continued denials of his candidacy had "baffled " Nixon. Nixon felt that Reagan's efforts to discontinue the grass roots activities had been "comparatively mild," causing Nixon to "look askance at Reagan's professed non-candidacy." Nixon theorized that Reagan's plans were either to keep Nixon firmly in the conservative fold as a "sort of ransom," or were escalating just in case Nixon stumbled. Either way, the Nixon camp felt "confused." It had been Nixon's major worry—that he could not win—at his January 1967 inner circle campaign planning meeting that was now coming back to haunt him in the form of Ronald Reagan.[94] Indeed all along, Nixon "knew, however, that his real opposition might come from Ronald Reagan."[95]

Nixon's exasperation with Reagan and his growing presidential campaign found a partial outlet with a letter Nixon wrote to Reagan a few days later. On April 4, 1968 Nixon wrote, "I just want you to know how much I have appreciated your using your influence to discourage some of your very enthusiastic supporters who understandably wanted to launch a major campaign on your behalf in those states." Nixon added that he understood Reagan would maintain his California favorite son status and closed, "We shall all be working together for victory in November."[96] Nixon still was worried both Republicans might end up campaigning together for Reagan for president that autumn instead of for Nixon for president.

Nixon staffer Patrick Buchanan, who the prior November had felt that Nixon and Reagan had a secret agreement to allow Nixon to run in New Hampshire and Wisconsin without Reagan opposition, felt the letter showed that Nixon was thanking Reagan for following through.[97] On the other hand, Reagan, who had met personally and set up his Wisconsin campaign with Don Taylor, was kept updated by Taylor on the progress of his Wisconsin Reagan club.

Of course Reagan was not discouraging his supporters at all. If Nixon hoped that Reagan might officially bow out, such a possibility immediately was shot down by Reagan, when he wrote back to Nixon on April 10 to congratulate him on his victories in New Hampshire and Wisconsin. Reagan added that he, like Nixon, wanted a united party to stand behind "our candidate."[98] Buchanan again interpreted this letter as evidence of a true Reagan-Nixon detente. Another interpretation is that Reagan wanted to be that candidate.

Or perhaps did Nixon actually welcome the Reagan campaign? As the 1968 presidential campaign of Reagan gained steam towards those two last primaries, *Newsweek* reported, "The Nixon people scarcely seemed depressed." The Nixon campaign would welcome "almost anything that would infuse the Nixon drive with some visible vitality." They did not want to sew up the election too soon and wanted to "avoid sapping the Republican contest of its last shred of excitement." Nixon's team saw Reagan as a "made-to-order patsy," thinking that if Reagan got as far as the nomination race, Nixon would "look pretty good running against the far right."[99]

RFK Debates Reagan by Proxy

Meanwhile Reagan never crossed paths directly with many Kennedy supporters or Kennedy himself. But Robert Kennedy did seem to run across Reagan supporters not infrequently. And in one instance, it was almost a repeat of the CBS Town meeting debate, eleven months earlier, when Reagan had triumphed and RFK had failed miserably.

On April 26 at the University of Indiana Medical School, Kennedy spoke to a hostile group of medical students. This speech is well known to RFK historians and supporters. But what is not well known is that Reagan's unseen presence was a major source of the antagonism. The medical students responded to RFK with "groans and some hisses."[100] Kennedy spoke for some twenty minutes without any applause. Instead of leaving, Kennedy started a question-and-answer session, "by calling on his obvious antagonist, a gangly young man in the balcony holding a blue Reagan balloon." News reporters, and RFK, clearly saw the Reagan balloon. Could RFK not help himself and just had to continue his attacks?

So Kennedy and the student with the Reagan balloon, in effect Reagan's proxy, proceeded to argue about healthcare. Then other medical students joined in and asked more heated questions, demonstrating all of their objections to Kennedy's ideas. After another student asked Kennedy from where the money was coming for Kennedy's proposed massive spending plans, an exasperated Kennedy "pointed at the youth with the Reagan balloon and said "From you!""[101] Had RFK yelled at the student or at Ronald Reagan? Along with the Reagan debate triumph in 1967, this episode can be interpreted as another portent that had Ronald Reagan faced Robert Kennedy in the autumn of 1968, Ronald Reagan likely would have entered the White House in early 1969.

Kennedy did make two comments about his proposed healthcare plan that bears repeating in the second decade of the 21st century. The medical students did end applauding RFK when he had said that medical "decisions should be decentralized and put on the local level" and "you cannot increase the effective demand for medical services and ignore the effective supply of those services, without causing a real inflation in the cost of medical services for all."[102]

Later in the campaign, in the midst of RFK speaking at San Jose State in California, the campus chimes rang out and interrupted him. Kennedy yelled out, "Ronald Reagan, I'll get even with you."[103]

Reagan formulated specific position papers on domestic subjects different than the world affairs white paper speeches he was working on. The former were mailed to voters and the media with clear statements: "not mailed at the taxpayer's expense" and were financed by monies "left over" from Reagan's speaking engagements. Reagan was "committing himself to review the needs of every issue of national politics."[104]

Reagan's re-energized presidential campaign was accelerating on its new trajectory towards an autumn confrontation and election showdown with the Democrat target of Robert F. Kennedy. Republicans were starting to see that only Reagan and his proven track record could win more debates with Kennedy, as well as a fall election. As March ended, a busy Reagan prepared his speeches and position papers and was preparing to leave on his new national campaign tour. Meanwhile, Taylor's grassroots Reagan team in Wisconsin—the first of the three opt-out primaries—had been busy as well, no matter whether Reagan had agreed with Nixon to make no effort there.

Endnotes

1. Gibbs and Duffy, p. 214
2. White, p. 101
3. Reed, *The Reagan Enigma*, p. 139
4. Clarke, p. 53
5. Pycior, p. 222-223
6. Reed, p. 21
7. National Governors Association homepage website meeting minutes, 2/28/68-3/1/68
8. Davies, Lawrence, " Reagan Expected to Remain Aloof," *NYT*, 3/1/68, p. 17
9. ibid
10. ibid
11. Reed, *The Reagan Enigma*, p. 134
12. Reston, James, "Reagan View: Fresh Leader Wanted," *NYT*, 3/4/68, p. 1
13. ibid
14. RRL, Tape 321
15. Reed, *The Reagan Enigma*, p. 136
16. *Newsweek*, 3/11/68, p. 29
17. See Illustrations
18. Eisenhower, David, p. 236
19. See Illustrations
20. Eisenhower, Dwight. 1968 Diary. 3/9/1968
21. "Eisenhower, Reagan Meet In California," *NYT*, 3/11/68, p. 30
22. "Reagan Bars Race for Vice President," *NYT*, 3/13/1968, p. 34
23. Reed, *Reagan Enigma*, p. 49
24. Eisenhower, Dwight. 1968 Diary. 3/11/68
25. Ambrose, p. 566
26. Eisenhower, David, p. 238
27. Reed, *The Reagan Enigma*, p. 140
28. Clarke, Thurston, The Last Good Campaign, *Vanity Fair*, 6/2008
29. quoted in Schlesinger, p. 922
30. Ambrose
31. Reed, p. 22
32. Chamberlain, John, "Reagan's Candidacy Is For Real," *Richmond Times-Dispatch*, 4/27/68
33. Buchanan, p. 221
34. Kopelson, Gene, 2014D
35. Buchanan, p. 222, p. 227
36. Gibbs and Duffy, p. 214
37. Hill, Gladwin, "Reagan Dissatisfied That Nixon Has No Opposition in the GOP," *NYT*, 3/26/68, p. 23
38. Reed, p. 22
39. Reed, *The Reagan Enigma*, p. 139
40. Reed, p. 22
41. Reed, p. 22
42. Rusher, *The Rise of the Right*, p. 210-211
43. Rusher, p. 211
44. ibid
45. ibid
46. Rusher, p. 212
47. Reed, p. 22
48. Frisk, p. 226

49. White, *Why Reagan Won*, p. 100.
50. Rusher, p. 213
51. Reed, *The Reagan Enigma*, p. 140
52. White op.cit., p. 100
53. op.cit., p. 100
54. op.cit., p. 100
55. White op.cit., p. 101
56. Rusher, p. 213
57. White, "Why Reagan Won," p. 104
58. "Reagan Says Kennedy Race Would Be a 'Ruthless' Act," *NYT*, 3/16/68, p. 16
59. Human Events 3/16/1968, p. 4-5
60. ibid
61. Goff, Tobi, "Reagan Calls Kennedy's Offer of 'Deal' Affront to the Presidency," *LA Times*, 3/20/68, p. 3
62. Schlesinger, p. 921
63. Eisenhower, Dwight, *1968 Diary*, 3/ 27/68
64. Pycior, p. 222-223
65. Pycior, p. 222-223
66. Buchanan, p. 232
67. Buchanan, p. 233
68. Eisenhower, Dwight, *1968 Diary*, 4/1/68
69. Eisenhower, Dwight, *1968 Diary*, 4/1/68
70. Johns, p. 200
71. Johns, p. 201
72. Eisenhower, Dwight, *1968 Diary*, 4/7/68; 4/8/68; 4/18/68;4/23/68
73. Reed op.cit., p. 23.
74. Reed, *The Reagan Enigma*, p. 139-145
75. Hill, Gladwin, "Reagan's Speeches at Dinners Crafted for Cheers and Laughs," *NYT*, 10/29/67, p. 54
76. Pace, Terry, "Pat Buttram," *LA Times*, 3/1/2001
77. Reed, p. 23
78. Reed, p. 23
79. Reed, p. 23
80. Ritter and Henry; Ritter
81. Skinner et. al., *The Strategy*, p. 61-61
82. ibid
83. Gould, p. 100
84. Chester et. al., p. 200
85. RRL, Tape 306
86. Reed, p. 22
87. *US News and World Report*, 3/25/68, p. 56
88. *US News and World Report*, 3/25/68, p. 59
89. *US News and World Report*, 3/25/68, p. 60
90. *US News and World Report*, 3/25/68, p. 61
91. *US News and World Report*, 3/25/68, p. 58
92. *US News and World Report*, 3/25/67, p. 62
93. Hill, Gladwin, "Reagan Jocular On Noncandidacy," *NYT*, 3/29/68, p. 28
94. Greenburg, Carl, "Reagan 'No' Is Too Mild To Suit Nixon Faction," *Los Angeles Times*, 4/1/68
95. Gould, p. 58
96. Gibbs and Duffy, p. 214
97. Buchanan, p. 234-235
98. Gibbs and Duffy, p. 215
99. *Newsweek*, 4/15/68, p. 50
100. Carroll, Maurice, "Kennedy Chides Future Doctors," *NYT*, 4/27/68, p. 17
101. Clarke, p. 187-188
102. Carroll, Maurice, "Kennedy Chides Future Doctors," *NYT*, 4/27/68, p. 17
103. Clarke, p. 53
104. Cooke, Alistair, "It's Reagan's Turn to Play It Cool," *Seattle Times*, 5/19/68, p. 92

CHAPTER 22: WISCONSIN—APRIL 2 1968, AND THE KING ASSASSINATION

"A vote from people who are looking for someone who can win in November."

~ Henry A. Bubb[1]

"I'm conservative enough to reassure conservatives, but not so conservative that liberal Republicans couldn't bring themselves to vote for me in a pinch."

~ Ronald Reagan[2]

"The American dream that we have nursed so long is not that every man be level with every other man, but that every man may be free to become whatever God intended."

~ Ronald Reagan[3]

While Reagan was busy back in California, Don Taylor, who had masterminded Reagan's hugely successful campaign visit to Milwaukee, had remained busy. Following his own detailed campaign plan which he had sent to Reagan, he had continued building grass roots support for Reagan during the fall and winter of 1967-1968.

Specifically, over the six months between Reagan's visit and the Wisconsin primary, Taylor traveled "thousands of miles," in his airplane or by automobile throughout Wisconsin, giving speech after speech on behalf of Reagan's 1968 presidential campaign. An unscientific survey had been done of 1,847 people in eight Wisconsin shopping centers during five days starting October 18. In early November, Taylor had received the survey results, which had showed Reagan at 28%—not far behind first-place Nixon at 34% but ahead of Romney at 24% and far ahead of Rockefeller at 12%. A typical Taylor appearance for Reagan was the one Taylor gave on November 30, 1967 in Appleton, where he had been invited by the Outagamie County Young Republicans. Taylor described Reagan's capabilities, his abilities to explain the issues and solutions to ordinary citizens and added, "Reagan is the proven unity candidate to lead the 1968 citizens' revolution."[4]

In the audience that day was the local Young Republican chairman, and future congressman, Toby Roth. Taylor and Roth planned subsequent campaigning by young Wisconsin Republicans throughout the Fox River Valley.

After New Year's of 1968, Reed notified Taylor, confirming Taylor's assumption and fear, that Reagan would not return to Wisconsin prior to the April primary. Taylor realized his task had become a vexing problem. On February 5, Taylor told Reed, "It was impossible to get leading Republicans to openly support a non-candidate." One prominent colleague told Taylor his heart was with Reagan, but that because he wanted to go to the convention, he had to support Nixon. The Wisconsin speaker of the Assembly said that if he could be convinced that it was not "too much of a risk," he would "probably" be willing to endorse Reagan.[5]

While Taylor was dealing with the difficulties of campaigning for an absent Reagan, who continued to deny he was a candidate, the national press finally began to focus on the upcoming Wisconsin primary and the role that the new rising national star, Ronald Reagan, would play as the Republican primary intensified. We saw earlier how in the January issue of Harper's, columnists Evans and Novak had viewed Wisconsin as a microcosm of the country. The initial support for Nixon was starting to ebb in favor of the charismatic Reagan, especially amongst grass roots party volunteers and activists who were far more attracted to Reagan.

In early February 1968, Nixon still was thought to be far ahead, yet Nixon faced "the threat, though, that Mr. Reagan's name on the ballot will siphon off Nixon votes."[6] But at the same time, discussions of polls in Wisconsin, for the most part, did not include Reagan.[7] By mid February, the threat Reagan had posed to Nixon was thought to have lessened. The assessment of The New York Times was that Reagan was not "expected to have much influence on the outcome." Indeed the prior fear of the Nixon team, "that there would be an active Reagan campaign to cut into Mr. Nixon's vote and threaten his strong early lead," had passed. Reagan's campaign at that point was described as "no more extensive than the distribution of $2,000 worth of buttons and bumper stickers. Governor Reagan may receive some 75,000 votes-perhaps 10 percent of the Republican total-but not enough to endanger Mr. Nixon."[8] Some Wisconsin polls predicted only a 3-6 percent tally for Reagan.[9] Clearly the national media had missed completely the hundreds of Reagan volunteers throughout the state who were working on behalf of Reagan via Taylor's club.

Yet at the same time, Taylor did come to the sober realization that despite his own efforts and the work of those hundreds of volunteers, including his Young Republicans, "Reagan's non-campaign had not caught fire."[10]

Romney's surprise withdrawal from the race for the presidency on February 28 led to an unexpected small but symbolic gift for Taylor: a Romney field director gave Taylor all of his leftover Romney buttons. But Taylor did not get discouraged when Nixon's main acknowledged opponent, Romney, now had dropped out. When Taylor pressed one congressman to endorse Reagan publicly, he told Taylor that he was indeed for Reagan. But "after it became apparent that Governor Reagan would not personally campaign for delegates,"[11] he accepted instead a delegate spot for Nixon. This was another example of what Taylor had given to Reed on February 5: a likely Reagan endorsement going to Nixon because of Reagan's lack of campaigning. If only Reagan would take an active role, declare he was a candidate, or visit Wisconsin again, then his supporters would come out of the woodwork to lend support to a Reagan presidential candidacy. It was not to be.

The same day that Romney had withdrawn, February 28, in Sacramento Reagan met with Reed to discuss the plans for Wisconsin.[12] The long-standing plans were reconfirmed: there would be no Reagan campaign visit to Wisconsin in the spring of 1968, despite the successful Milwaukee trip the prior fall.

After the New Hampshire primary vote showed a Nixon landslide on March 12, Taylor knew that "Nixon would sweep the Wisconsin primary too." Yet Taylor and his Wisconsin Reagan for President Club volunteers "never lost heart." In fact Taylor renewed his efforts in one final campaign push for Reagan that spring. Taylor distributed thousands of REAGAN buttons, reprinted thousands of copies of a report on Reagan's first eight months as California governor, and those reports were mailed throughout Wisconsin with extra lots sent to neighboring states. In early March Taylor aligned his club with Henry A. Bubb's Citizens for Reagan National Information Center in Topeka. Once Taylor distributed Bubb's Reagan campaign materials throughout Wisconsin, the renewed energy of Taylor's campaign and resolve helped the Reagan momentum. There was even a new Reagan campaign film to be shown to the public.[13]

But then tragedy struck. Taylor went bicycling near home on March 16 when he was struck from behind by a speeding car. His seven year-old daughter was on her own bike in front of Taylor as they pedaled to an ice cream stand. Taylor's careening bike hit his daughter's, and she fell into a ditch and lost two front teeth. Taylor spun and flew through the air, hit the speeding car's windshield, and landed in the road behind the car. Taylor's scalp was gashed open and his left leg was shattered. Taylor ended up hospitalized for a week and had to cancel his Reagan club campaign appearances in Milwaukee, Racine, and Wauwatosa.

Time was running short for Taylor but there was not much he could do in the hospital. A *New York Times* reporter noted that the only impediments to a Nixon victory would be a verbal or strategic blunder or "the sudden emergence of Gov. Ronald Reagan of California as an active candidate…Nixon's aides believe the prospects of an active candidacy by the Governor himself remain dim."[14] Taylor felt the same.

Taylor's horrific accident did in fact leave him immobile for a week. But although those three Reagan campaign visits had to be cancelled, Taylor would not be stopped in his efforts to see Reagan elected president in 1968. He wanted his beloved Wisconsin to give Reagan his first thrust forward onto the national stage as a presidential contender. After being released from the hospital, Taylor arranged to be driven to a Milwaukee television station for the one last Reagan campaign blitz before primary election day.[15]   The *New York Times* reported that Taylor had announced that his Reagan club had purchased four half-hour periods to show the brand new Reagan campaign film, *Ronald Reagan, Citizen Governor*.

The announcement of Reagan's last-minute television media foray generated marked concern in the Nixon camp. At this point at the end of March, 1968, Nixon was being threatened from several directions simultaneously. Initially, Nixon worried that Republican voters might cross over and vote in the Democratic primary for Eugene McCarthy, as a way of voting against President Johnson. But those worries evaporated with Johnson's March 31 announcement that he would not seek re-election. Suddenly Nixon was without his presumed opponent in November. Nixon faced the real possibility that he might have to face yet another Kennedy brother. And now Republican challenger Reagan announced he would use his prime weapon—his personality and issues—both to be seen by the public on Reagan's own turf: a television film. Nixon's state director was worried enough to warn Wisconsin Republicans, "Any last-minute drive for the California Governor could hurt Mr. Nixon in some conservative areas of the state." The *New York Times* article headline ran, "Nixon Faces Threat from Reagan Camp in Wisconsin Voting."[16]

Indeed Bubb had sent *Ronald Reagan, Citizen Governor* (to be discussed in detail later) to Taylor to be shown on television stations in Milwaukee and Green Bay.[17]   Then Bubb flew to Wisconsin to campaign for two days just prior to the vote.[18]

Wisconsin Election Results: April 2, 1968

Ronald Reagan, in his first test as a national candidate for the presidency, on the ballot for the Republican nomination in Wisconsin, received 50,727 votes (10.4 percent). Taylor recalled that although he was hoping for more, the vote was "pretty respectable for a non-candidate."[19] The following day Taylor filed his final Election Financial Statement, which showed that his Wisconsin Reagan for President Club had raised $6,516.70 and had spent $6,512.55.[20] Taylor reflected decades later that there was no way a conservative banker such as he ever would have allowed a campaign which he had controlled to run in the red! With this campaign surplus of $4.15, the Reagan primary campaign in 1968 may go down in history as the smallest surplus ever recorded. The Nixon campaign had spent almost a hundred times as much.

The final county-by- county tabulations showed Reagan totals had been better than his statewide average in the counties of Brown (2,406 or 13.6 %), Kenosha (1,159 or 11.3%), La Crosse (1,196 or 12.3%), and Milwaukee (12,797 or 12.2%). In Taylor's home base of Waukesha County, Reagan also did better than average (3,673 or 12.9%), yet in Outagamie County where Toby Roth and his Young Republicans had worked so hard, results were below average (1,558 or 9.6%) When totals were tallied based on congressional district, Reagan did the best in the Fourth District, which comprised part of Milwaukee, where he received 5,152 votes (14.0%).[21]

Reagan's success in the Fourth District may indeed indicate that his visit to Milwaukee the prior fall had succeeded in generating the required enthusiasm in Republican primary voters. Had Reagan visited Wisconsin more times in the spring of 1968 as Taylor had hoped, one may surmise that his final vote tally indeed may have been larger.

When the early Wisconsin returns started to come in, Governor Reagan, in Sacramento, "interrupted a dinner party for some state senators." Those initial returns indicated that he might win 12 percent of the Wisconsin vote, and he commented to reporters that as in Nebraska and Oregon, he had attempted to discourage any "volunteer Reagan for President movements." Reagan continued by telling the reporters that because he was not a candidate, the Wisconsin results "can't give me any joy in that regard. But anyone would have to be flattered. I'm appreciative and honored, but it can't change my position."[22]

Reagan returned home to watch the final results and then, in a celebratory mode, he called Reed.[23] Realizing he just had replaced Rockefeller as Number Two with Republican voters, Reagan laughed, "That's progress?"[24] Reagan's team immediately upped the ante, now aiming for 22 percent in Nebraska and 44 percent for Oregon. Oregon still even offered the chance for a victory, which would "blow the game wide open."[25] It was a "nice beginning."[26] The first step in the original Reagan plan for increasing vote tallies in the three opt-out primaries had been achieved.

And to top it off, RFK had failed miserably in Wisconsin, garnering only six percent. RFK would have no easy time getting the Democratic nod. He no longer was the default candidate.

The next morning, an erroneous report circulated that Reagan was going to retire from politics, prompting his Sacramento office to deny the rumor promptly. One reporter noted that the quick denial erased "any doubt that Governor Reagan's sights reach beyond the governorship of California."[27]

Bubb told reporters that Reagan's goal of ten percent had been topped. Of course not mentioned was Reed's original goal of fifteen percent. Bubb said that Reagan's showing in Wisconsin was "a vote from people who are looking for someone who can win in November." Bubb added that the Reagan forces did not spend "a lot of money" in Wisconsin and ended agreeing completely with Taylor's assessment that the big problem for Reagan's team in Wisconsin was that they did not "have an announced candidate to tout."[28]

Newsweek felt Nixon's victory in the Wisconsin Republican primary "should have given his campaign another tremendous boost," but Nixon's closest aides admitted that the Wisconsin vote was "nearly meaningless," as Ronald Reagan "had not actively campaigned."[29] With Reagan having achieved almost 11 percent in Wisconsin as the first step in Reagan's master plan, the second part lay next in Nebraska. And perhaps the Reagan campaign film, only shown briefly at the end of the Wisconsin campaign without any major publicity, could be put to more substantial use in Nebraska and then later in Oregon. Unfortunately, the lesson that Reagan's personal campaign visit had played a critical role went unlearned by Reed.

For Taylor, back home in Waukesha County nursing his scalp wound, in a cast from his broken leg and unable to fly his plane,

Reagan's loss to Nixon caused him to face "the future with an uncharacteristic attitude of uncertainty. Reagan was through...too old." Later that fall, Governor Reagan would send a thank you letter to Taylor on October 14. Taylor reflected years later that in 1968 as Reagan's first campaign for the presidency had ended, he "couldn't envision the greatness of America under his principled leadership which awaited us just a dozen years ahead!"[30] But that would be in the future. More tragedy awaited America in early April, 1968.

Reagan, SFR, and the Assassination of Dr. King

April 4, 1968 is remembered as the day Dr. Martin Luther King, Jr., was assassinated. But few know it is also a milestone date for Reagan and for the freedom of Eastern Europe. After he had finished with his private meetings with minorities in California, and while he savored the Wisconsin vote tally, Reagan was to speak in the nation's capital on April 4 to the Women's National Press Club and then meet with congressional Republicans. But prior to departing Sacramento, Reagan met with a group of Croatian-Americans and signed a proclamation marking Croatian independence. Reagan's actions that day in regards to the freedom of Eastern Europe will be reviewed in detail later.

Meanwhile in anticipation of Reagan's arrival, Weinrod had organized a pro-Reagan SFR rally at the Baltimore airport to greet Reagan. There was to be a second pro-Reagan rally the next day.

As Reagan was flying east, an hour before landing, the captain came back to tell Reagan personally of the King assassination. William Clark Jr. observed Reagan with a "sorrowful facial expression," and for the duration of the flight, Clark observed Reagan "looking down toward his feet, his lips silently praying."[31]

After landing, Reagan did deliver his planned speech at the Hilton Hotel. Historian Lou Cannon felt that the King assassination had reminded Reagan of the potential for California to experience renewed riots as had occurred previously in Watts.[32] Another review of Reagan's reaction cited that Reagan had only issued a statement "blaming King's assassination on his philosophy of nonviolent disobedience," in which Reagan called his death "a great tragedy that began when we began compromising with law and order and people started choosing which laws they'd break."[33]

But in fact Reagan's reactions were more than just terse statements issued from Sacramento. What has not been reported is what Reagan said immediately after the tragedy at the hotel where Nofziger, Weinrod and Schadler heard him. Reagan said:

> But one problem overshadows all the others and the cowardly hand of an assassin laid that problem on America's doorstep...Our nation died a little, too. It started dying and his murder began with our first acceptance of compromise with the laws of the land. That compromise ranges from our indifference when some would apply the law unequally to those today, black or white. ...We know there are those today who spread the poison of bigotry. And we can't ignore them any more than we should overlook those others who are determined that no American should ever again have to tell his child he is denied some of the blessings of this land because he is in some way different....We can make the difference. We can insure equal rights and equal opportunity and equal treatment for all our citizens"[34]

Reagan's speech, delivered only hours after the assassination, was given front-page coverage only in a few national newspapers. In it, Reagan did voice his continued disapproval of the tactics of King and others for having broken the law. But Reagan extended his analysis by condemning not only the law-breaking assassin, but also by condemning bigots who denied equal treatment, rights, and opportunities for blacks. Reagan also preached for citizens to become involved to overcome prejudice. He ended by proclaiming that the American dream was not to provide equal outcomes but rather to provide equal opportunities:

"The American dream that we have nursed so long is not that every man be level with every other man, but that every man may be free to become whatever God intended."[35]

Reagan's eloquent optimism about racial justice and equal opportunities for all, delivered within hours of the terrible King tragedy, were one of the finest he espoused during his 1968 campaign.

When Nofziger, Weinrod, Schadler and Reagan left the hotel, they could see smoke in the distance from "fires and burning buildings" due to riots amongst the distraught black populace. Weinrod recalled that everyone around them was trying to leave the city. There was gridlock.[36]

Immediately after the speech, Reagan and his group headed for Southeast Washington to calm local black militant leaders. As Reagan chatted with them for just a few minutes, a police officer came in and asked them to leave the area. Stuck in gridlock, Nofziger, Reagan, and his security team abandoned their car and started walking. His security team wanted Reagan to wear dark glasses, but Reagan yanked them off.[37] As noted earlier, his speech was credited with keeping California relatively calm unlike elsewhere.

As Reagan flew west, he, Nancy Reagan, Reed and Nofziger discussed the political ramifications of the King tragedy.[38] Reagan did not attend the King funeral.

As the nation was dealing with the violence that accompanied the King assassination, politics remained at the forefront as the critical next primaries loomed. The implications of Reagan's strength in Wisconsin, after the multiple showings of the campaign film and Taylor's efforts, was assessed. Johnson was out on the Democratic side. With Romney and Rockefeller out on the Republican side, did Nixon have the nomination sewn up by default?

Reagan's office started receiving a "300 percent increase in telegrams and letters urging him to run for President," and they now numbered some "200 a day," including many from Nebraska where Reagan was next to appear on the ballot.[39] Bubb explained, "When Rockefeller was in, our aim was for Rockefeller and Nixon to knock each other off. Then Reagan would be the logical person to turn to. Now our aim is for there to be enough favorite sons to hold it off for a couple of ballots and then turn to Reagan."[40]

With the Wisconsin first step accomplished, the chairman of Texans for Reagan, J.R. Butler of Houston, noted, "We think Nixon would make a good President. We think Reagan would be a better one."[41] The Wisconsin vote started a ripple effect. New grass roots activists were "quietly putting together organizations" for Reagan, and Bubb's clearing house continued "sending campaign materials to other states."[42]

Reagan himself was asked on April 5 if Nixon's nomination was inevitable. He told the press, "The great majority of the people are keeping an open mind." Thus Reagan "refused to concede" that Nixon had it all sewn up.[43] The next day, a press analysis saw Reagan as "waiting in the wings" and so far this strategy had "worked well."[44]

With the upcoming Easter lull in Sacramento, Reagan was preparing his trips West to New Mexico, Arizona, and Nevada. Of his own chances, Reagan said, "I'm conservative enough to reassure conservatives, but no so conservative that liberal Republicans couldn't bring themselves to vote for me in a pinch."[45] The busy autumn that Reagan had had was about to be repeated. Wisconsin had shown that Reagan had become a true national candidate beyond California; he had attracted the critical first votes from another state. Reagan the candidate was on the map. Reagan held campaign meetings at his Los Angeles residence on April 14 and 21 to review overall campaign plans, the organization and finances in Nebraska, and his support from other governors.[46] Reagan forged ahead.

Endnotes

1. Myers, Roger, "Reagan Vote In Wisconsin Pleases Bubb," *Topeka Daily Capital*, 4/4/68, p. 10
2. Hill, Gladwin, "Reagan Believed Waiting in the Wings," *NYT*, 4/7/68, p. 45
3. "Reagan Pictures the American Dream," *Nashville Banner*, 4/16/68, p. 1
4. Taylor, p. 14-15
5. Taylor, p. 16
6. Janson, Donald, "Rockefeller Put In Wisconsin Race," *NYT*, 2/7/68, p. 21
7. Ripley, Anthony, "Polls Deceptive, Romney Aide Says," *NYT*, 2/3/68, p. 30
8. Weaver, Warren Jr, "Wisconsin Awaits Nixon and Romney," *NYT*, 2/18/68, p. 49
9. Reed, p. 25
10. Taylor, p. 17
11. Taylor, p. 18
12. Reagan-Reed, 2/28/1968, Sacramento office
13. Taylor, p. 18-19
14. Semple, Robert Jr, "Nixon Has Field To Himself-Almost," *NYT*, 3/24/68, p. E1
15. Taylor, p. 19-20
16. "Nixon faces Threat From Reagan camp In Wisconsin Voting," *NYT*, 3/30/68, p. 17
17. Greenburg, Carl, "Reagan 'No' Is Too Mild To Suit Nixon Faction," 4/1/68, *Los Angeles Times*, 4/1/1968
18. Myers, Roger, "Reagan Vote In Wisconsin Pleases Bubb," *Topeka Daily Capital*, 4/4/68, p. 10
19. Taylor, p. 20
20. Taylor, pers comm., 3/8/13
21. The State of Wisconsin Blue Book 1970, Document Sales, State Office Building, Madison, p. 827-828
22. "Reagan Still 'Noncandidate,'" *NYT*, 4/3/68, p. 30
23. Reed, *The Reagan Enigma*, p. 147
24. Reed, ibid, p. 147
25. Reed, *The Reagan Enigma*, p. 147
26. Reed, p. 25
27. Hill, Gladwin, "Reagan Believed Waiting In the Wings," *NYT*, 4/7/68
28. Myers, Roger, "Reagan Vote In Wisconsin Pleases Bubb," *Topeka Daily Capital*, 4/4/68, p. 10
29. Taylor, p. 26
30. Taylor, p. 26
31. Patrick, Curtis vol. 1, p. 27
32. Cannon, p. 262-263
33. Clarke, p. 123
34. "Reagan Pictures the American Dream," *Nashville Banner*, 4/16/68, p. 1
35. ibid
36. Weinrod, Schadler, pers int 5/21/2013
37. Nofziger, p. 70-71
38. Reagan-Reed, 4/5/1968, commercial air trip
39. "Support for Reagan As GOP Presidential Candidate Growing" undated and unnamed newspaper article, Henry A. Bubb Collection, University of Kansas Archives
40. ibid
41. ibid
42. ibid
43. "Reagan is Doubtful on Nixon's Future," *NYT*, 4/6/68, p. 36
44. Hill, Gladwin, "Reagan Believed Waiting in the Wings," *NYT*, 4/7/68, p. 45
45. ibid
46. Reagan-Reed, 4/14/1968-4/21/1968; Los Angeles residence

CHAPTER 23: THE PERI-PATETIC CANDIDATE

"If they should want me, in Miami, I'll be ready."
~ Ronald Reagan[1]

"In the last couple of weeks there has been a rather significant increase in the number of self-generated state and local citizens-for-Reagan committees in such states as Minnesota, Kansas, Colorado and Idaho."
~ Clif White[2]

"You can't stop us."
~ Texas Reagan for President grass roots activist[3]

"Wouldn't she be a beautiful First Lady of the Land?"
~ Phoenix newspaper[4]

In early April, after the horror of the King tragedy, the encouraging tally in Wisconsin, and Reagan's signing of the Croatian proclamation (to be detailed later), he refocused his presidential plans on activating and energizing his grass roots activists who already were hard at work. But he still wanted the people—the delegates and voters—to decide. He told one of his financial backers, "I've only been here less than two years. I don't have the courage or immodesty to tell the American people to vote for me. If they should want me, in Miami, I'll be ready."[5]

One of the few times Reagan expounded in detail and offered his opinion of the Reagan grass roots efforts was at a mid-spring press conference. When asked what instructions he was sending to the grass roots campaign offices across the country, Reagan explained:

"Whenever these movements sprang up, and they did throughout the country, I couldn't help but be aware of them, I tried to turn them off. We were very successful in New Hampshire…There are some of them that have just told us to mind our own business. 'This is the way we feel and we're gonna do it.' Some told us this in person. Some came here for that purpose. A man from Texas said, 'We feel that this is the way a lot of people from Texas feel and we're gonna find out how many feel that way. And you can't stop us."[6]

Reagan was then off on his Western campaign trip previously announced by Nofziger. With the remaining opt-out primaries in Nebraska and Oregon next, followed by the California primary, it was natural for Reagan to campaign in the West again. Reagan's strongholds in 1968 were the West and South. Reagan reflected on the importance of the West to his thinking. At a press conference in Amarillo, Reagan became philosophical and said from the heart "I think those of us in the West perhaps have a pause and have a message. For part of the country they have accepted the doctrination for too many years that we're no longer capable of managing our own affairs and that we must accept the government answer to all our problems."[7]

As discussed earlier, Nofziger reveled in recalling how he had sent Frank Whetstone and Anderson Carter out on Reagan's campaign trail to round up more Western delegates and stir grass roots activists. Whetstone, of Cutbank, Montana, was second in command in Reagan's campaign and was in charge of Montana as well. Whetstone was an oil and gas executive, newspaper editor and owner of radio station KLCB in Libby, Montana. An active Republican, Whetstone was described as a "gigantic frontiersman who had accidentally put on a business suit." At one of White and Rusher's meetings in 1961, when the group had been plotting Goldwater's ascendancy, Whetstone had stood up "glowering at the others" and mused that they all would be "on the firing line in a national convention." Next he wondered, "where the rest of you s.o.b.'s will be when we get down to that final ballot?"[8]

Carter was Western campaign director. Carter, a New Mexican rancher and farmer, as well as an oil and gas businessman, was a life-long conservative Republican. As noted earlier, during the campaign when Carter became ill and could not cover all of Reagan's Western targets, Fred Van Natta of Oregon took over the role as Western Regional Director in those states from which Carter would be absent. Thus the states in which Van Natta was in charge were Washington, Oregon, Idaho and Utah.[9]

Van Natta recalled two 1967 campaign planning meetings in Wyoming and Nevada he had had with Whetstone and other Reagan western campaign workers.[10] Van Natta had attended the Reagan events in opt-out Oregon in 1967 and had helped create Reagan's initial campaign teams there. But not every Western state would hold a primary. So Van Natta also would work with conservative Reagan supporters and delegates in non-primary states. Thus while Van Natta also was busy, along with Whetstone and Carter, in directly managing some 1968 Reagan Western state campaigns, Van Natta also kept in close contact with Ken Rogstad in Washington, who originally had invited Reagan to speak in Seattle in 1966. Reagan's first stops in April were to the Southwest.

New Mexico and Arizona

Reagan flew to Albuquerque to continue his "non-campaigning."[11] In front of over 2,000 cheering Reagan supporters who had paid $10-per-person, liberal Republican Governor David Cargo introduced him as, "a man we could all support if he should get the nomination."[12]

In Arizona, the Reagan's visited their daughter Patty for Parents Day at the Orme Ranch School, and they also relaxed a bit with Nancy's parents, who had retired near Phoenix. One Phoenix newspaper did a one-page story on Nancy Reagan, which began, "Wouldn't she be a beautiful First Lady of the Land?"[13]

Even though the campaign's thrust was now directed at grass roots activists, Reagan had not given up trying to garner the support of Goldwater, despite his continuing support for Nixon ever since early 1965. The Reagan's attended a "big cocktail party being given by Republican leaders" at the Goldwater home.[14] Later, after speaking to 1,300 people at a $50 dinner in Phoenix, Reagan was "warmly welcomed by Goldwater."[15] After all, Reagan had been Goldwater's California Co-Chairman, had delivered *A Time for Choosing*, and after the 1964 election loss had expressed harsh outrage by the lack of support of Goldwater by Rockefeller and Romney at the time. As discussed, in Nebraska in June, 1967, Goldwater had expressed a potential change in heart after having seen the support for Reagan amongst the party's youth. Perhaps Goldwater at least could be persuaded to switch from Nixon to being neutral?

But Goldwater shot down Reagan's hopes, telling Reagan that by mid June, the Republican nominee would be known. There was no pledge of Goldwater neutrality.[16]

Reagan told his campaign team about the discouraging conversation with Goldwater. In fact, Goldwater wanted Reagan to stop campaigning altogether and to send all California delegates to Nixon early in the roll call.[17]

Despite what Reagan had heard from Goldwater in private, with Reagan's new and quite public campaign visits, press speculation about Reagan's candidacy grew again. During the inactive time in early 1968 after Reagan had told the press that his out-of-state trips had ceased, things were relatively quiet for Reagan, as we have seen. But after the excitement of Kennedy's entrance and Johnson's departure, Reagan was busy during late March quietly planning his new strategy and writing his White Paper speeches. But the new trips West in early April fueled new speculation about what Reagan planned. It was noted by the national press that Reagan's campaign activities had "continued to gather impetus," as had "the disavowed Reagan-for-President movement."[18] Reagan was noted to have been "hardly back from his southwestern swing when his office in Sacramento disclosed a tentative touring schedule that could take him into a half-dozen states."[19] Reagan's reappearance into the campaign limelight was succeeding. He reiterated to the press again that he still was open to a draft.[20]

Officially, Reagan's aides, when asked about the campaign plans, said that Reagan's new schedule was due to "unexpected word" that the Legislature might recess from mid-May through early June and denied that the "step up in activity resulted from the somewhat altered shape of the Republican competition."[21] Reagan would not visit either Nebraska or Oregon, where "local booster groups are fervently pushing his cause."[22]

The national press then saw what Reagan had planned from the very beginning. Reagan, while outwardly discouraging any campaigns in his behalf, "had progressed from a showing of less than 1 percent in the New Hampshire primary to 11 percent in the Wisconsin primary."[23] In Nebraska, he "might draw something like 23 percent."[24] And in Oregon where his supporters "are staging a full-dress campaign supposedly with no encouragement from Governor Reagan, hope to corral as much as 40 percent of the vote."[25] After that, Reagan will win California with "practically a 100 percent showing."[26] The national press finally started to see that these step-wise increasing vote tallies, which Reagan originally had envisioned in late 1966 to win in Miami Beach in the summer of 1968, might in fact become a reality.

Colorado

Reagan had traveled to Colorado in December 1966 to the Republican Governors Conference. This was the meeting where he had discussed economic ideas with Ohio Governor Rhodes prior to Reagan's inauguration. But this was also when Reagan had appointed his campaign team and likely began to think of Rhodes as a fellow conservative who might make a good running mate for the 1968 fall general election. And establishing preliminary Colorado contacts for his presidential campaign was a natural agenda item during that trip.

West of Denver in Golden, Colorado, sits Coors Brewery. Joseph Coors officially was recruited to be the 1968 Reagan campaign chair for Colorado during a visit Coors made to Sacramento, when he was elected to the Board of Regents of the University of California.[27] Van Natta and Whetstone subsequently met with Coors to plan Reagan's campaign plans to search for Colorado delegates.[28] But Colorado's Republican leadership was not particularly welcoming to conservatives.

Governor John Love of Colorado, who later would become President Nixon's first energy "czar," was chairman of the Republican Governors Association in 1967. In 1964, Love had been the leader of the state delegation, which had voted overwhelmingly for Goldwater, even though Love had been opposed. In early 1967, vowing, "I'll not be in that position again," he had started to purge party conservatives.

One such target was Jefferson County Republican chairman Arthur H. Davis Jr. Jefferson County was a heavily Republican suburb west of Denver and Love placed his administrative assistant to run against Davis at the county central committee meeting. Davis had complained, "The liberals have been trying to purge the conservatives," in order that liberals would "control the delegation to the Republican National Convention." In El Paso County, where Colorado Springs is, conservative Weldon Tartar had been Republican chairman for nine years and was facing a similar fight. Tartar had told the press that his county would vote for Nixon, because he doubted "there is sufficient stature yet in the public mind to support Gov. Ronald Reagan."

Love said that his rationale for getting rid of conservatives was that he had wanted his delegation to remain uncommitted until a "moderate candidate surfaced." Yet Love and his delegation did "want a winner." Love did admit that he "found considerable interest in Governor Reagan as a dark horse."[29]

By May, 1967, a new Colorado Reagan-for-President grass roots organization had been formed. The group had planned to "capture the state's delegation to the Republican national convention in 1968," because Reagan was "the most potentially electable candidate in America today."[30]

When they had attended the Western Governors Association meeting in late June, 1967, Love and New Mexico Governor David E. Cargo had remained uncommitted.[31] It was at this meeting where Reagan first had said he would accept a draft. Thus not unexpectedly, both Governors Love and Cargo were asked about the campaign of Reagan. When asked about Reagan, Love reflected, "The more you talk to him, the more he sounds like a candidate. He's very willing to travel and very willing to speak outside his home state, which is what governors do when they run for President."[32]

By the time the summer began, Love had succeeded in ousting the conservative party county chairman in the Denver suburb, Arthur H. Davis. But pro-Reagan Davis took matters into his own hands. Davis, a Colorado public relations firm officer, shopping center executive and meteorologist, started a Reagan "boomlet." Davis and 32 others formed a grass roots Colorado Reagan for President club which by mid summer had over 2,000 members. Davis charged each member $1. Love was not pleased with Davis for either his conservative views or for the new Reagan campaign in Colorado. Love's intentions of bringing an uncommitted delegation to Miami Beach now might be thwarted in part by the "diversion" of the "Reagan boomlet."[33]

Davis had continued his grass roots Reagan campaign throughout the remainder of 1967. When the Western States Republican Conference had been held in Denver, Davis and his Reagan team were seen "serving coffee and cookies". *Time* just had pictured Reagan on its cover. Reagan sentiment in the West was noted to be "high."[34] Davis recalled that his group, Coloradans for Reagan, needed three co-chairmen because of their shared enthusiasm for Reagan.[35]

In late April, 1968, Reagan insisted his Colorado trip was for fundraising. But when asked if he would be available for the Republican nomination, Reagan reflected his and Eisenhower's view that the Sherman statement had been wrong: "I think any citizen of the United States is, if his fellow citizens decide they want him." But he again brought out his basic philosophy when he cautioned, "I always think the job seeks the man. I can't conceive of myself soliciting it."[36]

On Saturday April 27, 1968, Reagan flew to the University of Colorado in the liberal bastion of Boulder.[37] As Reed recalled, towards the top of Reagan's national campaign finance committee remained Coors, and Reagan stayed at the Coors' home.[38] After a private breakfast with Governor Love and Coors at the Coors residence, Reagan met with forty Colorado Republican leaders in the Boulder Harvest House Motel.[39]

Four days earlier, back east at Columbia University, student radicals had taken over the school administration building to protest Vietnam. There was no quick reaction from the university or from the police. As will be seen, Reagan took sharp notice of those events, especially the lack of any quick response to the radicals' take-over. Not knowing exactly what to expect in Colorado, at a packed MacKay Auditorium, Reagan beamed when looked out and spoke to 3,000 cheering and applauding students.[40]

Reagan wondered how students of their generation would view what the members of Reagan's generation had accomplished. He answered that seldom had any generation served America for freedom as much as did his generation, which had fought in two world wars and two subsequent wars. He ended by telling the students that they should be optimistic about the future, because America had given the world "a golden shining hope."[41]

Prior to the question and answer question session, Reagan was asked how he felt about meeting with possible hostile students, based on the news from Columbia University. Having shown his steel at hostile Yale University students (and faculty) only a few months earlier, Reagan quipped, "I may be foolish, but I'm brave."[42] The Colorado students cordially asked about the draft, but then asked about the Reagan vice-presidential rumors. He answered that he found a "greater opportunity" to prove that his policies were correct by continuing as governor rather than as vice-president. The final student asked him if he was running for president, and Reagan answered with phrases he had used throughout his campaign: "The job seeks the man," "I don't anticipate that they will select me," and "I don't believe in the Sherman statement."[43]

Reagan had never hesitated about speaking in liberal Boulder to a presumably liberal student audience. Yet his warmth and openness in answering questions may have opened the eyes of some students. And as noted, there was good evidence in the audiences of support for him for president. Reagan extended the original time of the student questions from a half-hour to one full hour. Historian Lou Cannon called Reagan's speech and his extended, impromptu question-answer session as, "one of his best political performances."[44] Reagan did not discuss much more about the crisis at Columbia, in which a dean and two administrators had been held hostage for 24 hours. But with the Pueblo hostage crisis still making the news daily, and Reagan continuing to make statements on the poor handling of the U.S.S. Pueblo by the Johnson administration, Reagan began to plan how to deal with future hostage crises. Reagan then left Boulder.

It would take another 45 years for the University of Colorado at Boulder specifically to include a conservative, when noted Reagan scholar Steven Hayward would be appointed the school's first Visiting Scholar of Conservative Thought and Policy in 2013.[45]

While preparing to leave Colorado, at Stapleton Airport, Reagan spoke to a crowd of several hundred supporters, who had braved the rain and snow. There were "Reagan for President" banners. Talk of him being president in 1968 "sprouted like the spring verdure at all his stops." When Reagan saw the campaign slogans, he "took appreciative cognizance" but continued to deny his candidacy. But when asked what he would do if offered the nomination, he said he would "not refuse," because "no citizen" should renounce such "national service."[46]

Increasing Grass Roots Support

At mid-month White told the press, "In the last couple of weeks there has been a rather significant increase in the number of self-generated state and local citizens-for-Reagan committees in such states as Minnesota, Kansas, Colorado and Idaho."[47]

When asked what he thought about White's revelation of this increasing grass roots support across the country for his candidacy, Reagan said, "Naturally I was interested in hearing that. I'm not going to run away and pretend it isn't happening. Obviously I'm going to try and make an assessment."[48] Reagan said afterwards once again that "the job seeks the man" and that he was well aware that his close friends and advisors were "hoping" he would become declared candidate for the presidency.[49]

At this point Rockefeller was reassessing his prior March 21 decision to drop out. Reagan insisted that the nomination "is going to be made at the convention" and neither Nixon nor Rockefeller had the nomination sewn up.[50]

Regaining Lost Luster

Because of the constant stream of denials—which he made at every press conference denying that he was a candidate—the fervor for Reagan, which had been evident the prior June at the meetings of the governors in West Yellowstone, had diminished. Reagan's fellow Western governors felt Reagan had "lost much of the Presidential luster that bedazzled them eight months ago." But "events could restore the sheen." Governor Hathaway, who had previously thought Reagan had been a "strong possibility for the Republican Presidential nomination," now thought, "Only the withdrawal of Richard M. Nixon could give life to a Reagan candidacy." Governor Timothy Babcock, who the prior summer had been "the most outspoken in suggesting

Mr. Reagan for President," now was for Nixon. Governor Paul Laxalt of Nevada, who would play major roles in Reagan's future attempts to be president, thought that in early 1968 Reagan's dimmed luster was "of his own doing. He's downplayed it. This unavailability is the best strategy in the world."[51]

But by April, Reagan had turned the corner and was on the upswing. After the surprising Johnson withdrawal announcement, Laxalt told the press that Republicans "should think in terms of a winner," saying now he "could support Mr. Reagan." In Wyoming, "some support," not specified further, had developed for Reagan, which was described as a "back up" effort to nominate Reagan if Nixon faltered.[52]

Nixon was getting exasperated with Reagan and in early April had had the interview with the *Los Angeles Times*, where he had complained about Reagan's fund-raising and refusal to stop his grass roots activists. To shore up his bulwarks against Reagan's rising strength in the West, Nixon went on a week long tour of major Western states. Nixon claimed that "every Republican leader," including those in Wyoming and Montana, had told him that he could carry their state in November. Nixon declined to tell reporters his delegate count from the Western states but thought that by the time of the convention in Miami Beach, he would have a "substantial bloc of delegates from Western states." Whether those unnamed Republican leaders included Hathaway or Babcock was not mentioned nor whether those same leaders thought Nixon would win the nomination first.53

A few days later, Nixon confidant Martin Feldman, a New Orleans attorney, called John Mitchell at Nixon's national campaign office and urged the Nixon leaders to stop worrying about Rockefeller. British historians, observing the scene, felt that "Feldman was right. It was Reagan, not Rockefeller, who in the end constituted the more direct threat to Nixon's power base."[54] Reagan would continue to pressure Nixon in the West by returning to Wyoming in mid June.

A Missed Opportunity in the Northeast

On April 23, Pennsylvania held its primary. It was not an opt-out state. It was entirely a write-in primary. No candidate's name was on the ballot. Thus Pennsylvania was a lost opportunity for Reed. He might have scheduled Reagan to speak there and to seek out conservative activists to start a Reagan grass roots write-in campaign as in the three opt-out states.

Reagan was no stranger to Pennsylvania. On the same day in 1966 that Reagan had obtained the gubernatorial endorsement and presidential timbre comment from Eisenhower in Gettysburg, Reagan and Reed had met in Pittsburgh with a group of wealthy industrialists representing the Mellon family, the H.J. Heinz Company, and others from metal factories.[55] Pittsburgh was where Reed had been in 1964 when he had heard Reagan deliver "The Speech." And possibly Reed, via his industrialist father, had additional conservative political contacts in the area. Plus Reagan did speak in Pennsylvania twice on January 18, 1968 as we have seen.

The Pennsylvania primary was characterized as showing an "unusually small turnout."[56] Columnist Drew Pearson noted that the Republican Party had only one-tenth of their registered members vote.[57] The final state tabulation showed that amongst the top three candidates (Nixon, Rockefeller and Reagan), Reagan garnered 7,934 out of 232,664 write-in votes (3.4%).[58]

Had any kind of reasonable effort been made, possibly by having Reagan visit the state at least once in 1967 more than a quick visit in early 1968, it is not unreasonable to assume that Reagan could have achieved at least the 10-11 percent of Wisconsin. The Wisconsin vote could have been followed by a good showing in Pennsylvania to help aid the bandwagon effect for upcoming Nebraska and Oregon. Pennsylvania could have been one more state to add to the growing chorus of "Reagan for President." Working hard for a write-in campaign was a lost opportunity that was about to work further north for Reagan's opponent, Rockefeller.

Massachusetts held its primary a week later, on April 30. By late 1967, Massachusetts Republican Governor John Volpe had thought of becoming a favorite son and had also let it be known that he was open to being Reagan's vice-president.[59] Reed had made no effort in Massachusetts and unlike in neighboring New Hampshire, there was no organized Reagan grass roots effort either. Rockefeller, who had dropped out of the race on March 21, had re-entered it on the day of the Massachusetts primary. Rockefeller won with a surprise write-in victory. Reagan, not surprisingly, received only 1,826 votes (1.5 %).[60] But Nixon had lost his first primary in 1968. His loser image was not eradicated. Could the trend continue?

As April ended and May began, a poll by the *New York Times* indicated Reagan had 206 delegates. Nixon still led but more Reagan threats started to emerge in unlikely places. For example, Nixon "averted a Reagan threat in Virginia by publicizing Mr. Nixon's party work in the state." What the cited Reagan threat in Virginia was is not clear, as Virginia was not a part of Reagan's master plan. But certainly some Reagan grass roots activists there obviously made their presence known. Of the remaining primary states, Reagan had 98 delegates.[61]

The Peri-patetic Governor

Reagan would remain quite busy in May and June. Nancy Reagan was busy too and attended the Republican Women's conference along with the wives of the other contenders.[62] Nebraska and Oregon would have their all-important primaries, but Reed would stick to his fateful decision not to have Reagan revisit either of those two remaining opt-out primary states.

Reagan honed and finalized his White Paper speeches, as his jousting with RFK was about to begin in earnest. White ramped up his delegate hunting. Reagan's team sent out the first of several position papers on domestic policies.[63] Reagan would deliver his major foreign policy addresses during visits to Hawaii, North Carolina, Florida, and Illinois, and would finish with a whirlwind tour of Ohio in Columbus and Cleveland followed by his ultimate masterpiece address in Amarillo.

Lest one think that Reagan was off on vacation the rest of the time, the above schedule does not list the numerous in-state speeches he made in California—often several a day. With all the thousands of miles he had traveled, Ronald Reagan certainly had become, in the words of British historians, the "nation's most peripatetic governor."[64]

Political scientist Robert Kaufman assessed Reagan's accomplishments as governor and his presidential chances in the academic literature at that point. Citing Reagan's initial 1966 coattails and his subsequent successes in helping to foster Republican wins in several special elections, Kaufman added that Reagan's "political acumen" had left the Democratic majorities in the California legislature "thoroughly checkmated," such that the Democrats had been unable to mount any major attacks on the governor. The support Reagan had received during the cross-country speechmaking and fundraising trips during 1967 and 1968 had gotten Reagan growing support amongst the Republican "leadership cadres and financial angels," which culminated in his "strategically well calculated 'non-candidacy.'"[65]

Reagan now fixed his eyes upon the second planned step of his master campaign strategy: the all important Nebraska primary and preparing for his first major White Paper address.

Endnotes

1. Willis, Doug, http://www.apnewsarchive.com/1987/Confidants-Say-Reagan-Barely-Missed-Republican-Nomination-in-1968
2. Hill, Gladwin, "California GOP Briefed by White," *NYT*, 4/16/68, p. 18
3. RRL, Tape 340
4. Mackley, Mona, "Nancy Reagan In a Big Job," *Phoenix Gazette*, 4/9/68, p. 41
5. Willis, Doug, http://www.apnewsarchive.com/1987/Confidants-Say-Reagan-Barely-Missed-Republican-Nomination-in-1968
6. RRL, Tape 340
7. RRL, Tape 356 Part I
8. Frisk, p. 155
9. Van Natta, pers comm. 6/19/12
10. Van Natta, pers comm. 9/4/12
11. Hill, Gladwin, "Reagan Believed Waiting in the Wings," *NYT*, 4/7/68, p. 45
12. Hill, Gladwin, "Reagan Steps Up a 'Noncandidacy,'" *NYT*, 4/14/68, p. 50
13. Mackley, Mona, "Nancy Reagan In a Big Job," *Phoenix Gazette*, 4/9/68, p. 41
14. ibid
15. Hill, Gladwin, "Reagan Steps Up a 'Noncandidacy,'" *NYT*, 4/14/68, p. 50
16. Cannon, p. 260
17. Reed, *Reagan Enigma*, p. 150
18. Hill, Gladwin, "Reagan Steps Up a 'Noncandidacy,'" *NYT*, 4/14/68, p. 50
19. ibid
20. Reed, *The Reagan Enigma*, p. 150
21. ibid
22. ibid
23. ibid
24. ibid
25. ibid
26. ibid
27. Reed, pers comm. 10/17/12
28. Van Natta, pers int 8/30/12
29. Turner, Wallace, "Gov. Love Seeking GOP Shift," *NYT*, 3/5/67, p. 52
30. "Reagan Drive in Colorado," *NYT*, 5/19/67, p. 19
31. Turner, Wallace, "Reagan Denies Advance Man Seeks Support for Race in '68,'" *NYT*, 6/26/67, p. 20
32. Turner, Wallace, "Reagan Doubts He'll Be Drafted," *NYT*, 6/27/67, p. 24
33. Turner, Wallace, "Colorado's GOP Confident On '68,'" *NYT*, 8/6/67, p. 43
34. Kneeland, Douglas, "Confidence Noted at Parley of GOP," *NYT*, 10/30/67, p. 16
35. Davis, p. 2
36. Hill, Gladwin, "Reagan Adheres to Noncandidacy," NYT, 4/25/68, p. 26
37. Hoover Archives, courtesy Jenny Fichman
38. Reed, *The Reagan Enigma*, p. 151
39. Reagan-Reed, 4/27/1968, Coors residence
40. Hill, Gladwin, "Reagan Completes a Tour of Two States," *NYT*, 4/28/68, p. 52
41. RRL, Tape 338
42. Hill, op.cit.
43. RRL, Tape 338
44. Cannon, Ronnie and Jesse, p. 268
45. Belkin, Douglas, "Colorado School Names Conservative-Studies Professor," *WSJ*, 3/14/2013, p. A5
46. Hill, Gladwin, "Reagan Completes a Tour of Two States," *NYT*, 4/28/68, p. 52
47. Hill, Gladwin, "California GOP Briefed by White," *NYT*, 4/16/68, p. 18
48. Gillam, Jerry, "Reagan Reassessing Chances in View of Increasing Support," *LA Times*, 4/17/68
49. "Reagan Hints Reassessment of His '68 Plans," *Washington Post*, 4/17/68
50. Davies, Lawrence, "Reagan Admits He's Interested in Reported 'Grass Roots' Drive," *NYT*, 4/17/68
51. Turner, Wallace, "GOP Governors Shift On Reagan," *NYT*, 2/18/68, p. 43
52. Turner, Wallace, "Mountain State Query," *NYT*, 4/2/68, p. 33
53. Clarity, James, "Nixon Confident of West's Votes," *NYT*, 4/27/68, p. 16
54. Chester et. al., p. 189
55. "Guest of Industrialists," *NYT*, 6/16/66, p. 30

56. Franklin, Ben A.,"Pennsylvania Vote Favors McCarthy And Senator Clark," *NYT*, 4/24/68, p. 29
57. Pearson, Drew, "Washington Merry-Go-Round," 4/28/68
58. 1969 Pennsylvania Manual, p. 664
59. White, p. 135
60. "Rockefeller Wins Mass. Primary," *Seattle Times*, 5/1/68, p. 13
61. Semple, Robert Jr, "Survey Shows 725 Are Leaning or Committed to Ex-Vice President," *NYT*, 5/5/68, p. 1
62. *Newsweek*, 5/6/68, p. 64
63. "First of Reagan's 'Position Papers' Out," *Seattle Times*, 5/2/68, p. 13
64. Chester et. al., p. 199
65. Kaufman, Robert W., "Ronald Reagan: A Republican Messiah?," *North American Review*, 253 (May-June 3, 1968), p. 10-12.

CHAPTER 24: REAGAN'S FIRST WHITE PAPER SPEECH

"Does Bobby now deplore his own judgment? Those were his words."
~ Ronald Reagan[1]

"The seizure of the Pueblo and the kidnapping of our men is a humiliation we will not endure."
~ Ronald Reagan[2]

"A great, incisive, firm speech." ~
Senator Hiram Fong[3]

In commemoration of the upcoming one-year anniversary of Israel's victory in the Six Day War, Reagan spoke at Salute to Israel, again—as eleven months earlier—at the Hollywood Bowl. He warned that the real "enemy," sitting in Moscow, had rearmed Israel's foes. He proclaimed that America should no longer remain neutral and should rearm Israel. But Reagan looked ahead to a time when America could aid the Jews and Arabs in peaceful endeavors. Following up on his recent reference to Eisenhower's Jordan River irrigation project proposed some fifteen years earlier, Reagan was more specific this time and called for the construction of nuclear-powered desalinization plants in the Mideast.[4]

Then Governor Reagan flew to Hawaii to attend the afore-mentioned governors conference and to deliver the first of his five White Papers, which he had been preparing since March.[5] Finally it was time to attack his old nemesis, Robert F. Kennedy. It was a full year since the Reagan debate triumph over Kennedy. Now Reagan would attack directly the failures of RFK. But first the candidacy of Rockefeller interfered.

Rockefeller had dropped his bombshell, "I am not and will not be a candidate for the Presidency," on March 21.[6] This was certainly consistent with what he had told the press during the October governors' cruise. But after President Johnson's March 31 surprise announcement that he would not seek reelection, and the King assassination a few days later, as well as from urgings of some

Republican leaders, Rockefeller began to reassess his thinking. On April 30 on national television, Rockefeller announced he was re-entering the race once again.[7]

As had occurred seven months earlier with the *Time* magazine cover, suddenly there was renewed speculation about a Rockefeller-Reagan ticket. Just before making his announcement of re-entering the race, Rockefeller had called Reagan; Reagan wished him good luck. A Reagan campaign operative thought that Rockefeller's entrance had assured that "nothing will be settled on the first ballot, and if it goes to a second or third ballot, the delegates may just fall back on Reagan."[8] California Speaker of the House (and future gubernatorial opponent to Reagan in 1970), Democrat Jesse Unruh, sought to undermine Reagan in any way he could and added, "Because I don't think he really enjoys being Governor," that Reagan would accept the second spot on a Rockefeller-Reagan ticket and this would "be the best way Rockefeller could win the support of the California delegation."[9]

Rockefeller was not thinking of a running mate quite yet after all the press speculation the prior October; it was too early. But having a combination of a liberal and a conservative on the same ticket had helped Kennedy-Johnson, as well as Rockefeller's own gubernatorial campaigns when he had run successfully three times with conservative Lieutenant Governor Malcolm Wilson. Reagan being on the ticket would assure the 86 votes of California going to a Rockefeller-Reagan ticket and perhaps also the votes of other conservative delegations such as Texas. But would placing Reagan on the ticket win the Republican nomination but only end up losing the general election? Rockefeller was keeping his thoughts to himself. Plus as Reagan knew, Eisenhower on multiple occasions was against such a ticket headed by Rockefeller. The former president never had been asked for his thoughts on a Reagan-Rockefeller ticket.

During the conference, reporters observed that Clif White, nominally in charge of the California delegation but in reality Reagan's national delegate hunter, had met several times with Rockefeller supporter Leonard Hall.[10] Both had "brief meetings" with Reagan as well. The conclusion of the two staffers was that Nixon had not yet wrapped up the nomination.[11]

It was then rumored that Reagan had a private deal with Rockefeller to run as his running-mate—supposedly confirming the *Time* magazine speculation from six months earlier, at the time of the governors cruise to the Virgin Islands, which was when Rockefeller had said he did not want to be president. The rumors reportedly "were cutting off the flow of money to Reagan-for-President volunteer organizations."[12] After a press conference, at which no reporter asked Reagan about the rumors, late in the evening Reagan issued a formal unequivocal statement denying any such deal with Rockefeller and denying he would accept the vice-presidency no matter who the Republican nominee was.

The purpose of Reagan's formal statement of denial was "to assure nervous pro-Reagan conservatives around the country that (he was) not about to become a political bedfellow of the liberal New York governor."[13] Shortly thereafter, when campaigning in Ohio, Reagan would see a sign promoting him for president and protesting any Rocky-Reagan ticket. Reagan would yell: "You can quit carrying that sign. I'm not going to make a deal with anyone."[14]

First White Paper

The recent news in Honolulu, besides the continued lack of American response about the captured crew of the *U.S.S. Pueblo* by North Korea, was a just completed meeting between the United States and the Republic of Korea, which had established the first Security Consultative Meeting between the two nations. Thus as Reagan arrived in Hawaii, the multiple world hotspots in Asia—of Vietnam and the Korea's—were at the forefront of everyone's concerns. At the Royal Hawaiian Hotel on May 11, 1968, Reagan delivered his first White Paper presidential campaign speech.[15] Like the Veteran's Day speech in Albany, Oregon, the prior November, the topic was world affairs. But now he zeroed in on RFK. The evening before had been a $500 per couple private cocktail reception with Reagan, which 50 people had attended, and for his formal speech, some 1,000 people paid $100 each.[16] Entitled *The History and Significance of the U.S. Role in the Pacific*, Reagan finally had the chance to return the fire, which RFK had directed at him for so many years.[17]

Candidate Reagan laid the blame for America's foreign policy ills clearly and directly at the foot of Robert F. Kennedy. He lashed out at critics of the Vietnam War and specifically asked how the recent Tet offensive, which the U.S. and South Vietnam decisively had won militarily, could have been turned into such a "smashing catastrophic" psychological defeat? He answered his own question by saying the fault directly was attributable to Robert Kennedy. Reagan explained that America had "listened too closely to the new isolationists, to voices of defeat and retreat" citing that the "fiercest assault" came from "within the party, which made the intervention necessary." At the same moment, the Democrats were attacking President Lyndon

Johnson's policies. However Reagan clearly blamed Robert Kennedy by directly tying RFK to the policies RFK had established under his late brother's administration:

"The so called Johnson policy so violently attacked by some Democrats nearly all stemmed directly from the very policies which were developed by the late President Kennedy when these same critics were advisors close by his side. The junior senator from New York has lately said that he was wrong about Vietnam in the beginning. But he hasn't told us where he thinks he went wrong."[18]

After detailing two of President Kennedy's public commitments to Vietnam, Reagan asked if RFK disavowed his brother's commitments? Then Reagan got quite specific when he lanced directly into RFK by citing the latter's 1962 comment in Saigon, "We are going to win in Vietnam—we will remain there until we do." Asked Reagan in follow-up after citing Kennedy's quote, "Does Bobby now deplore his own judgment? Those were his words."[19]

Reagan reviewed that General Ngo Dinh Dhiem had been assassinated with the cooperation of the Kennedy administration and that afterwards, the Viet Cong and North Vietnamese could not believe that the Americans had been so foolish for having encouraged the assassination of South Vietnam's major unifying figure. Reagan ended by citing Kennedy's inaugural trumpet call, to bear any burden in the pursuit of liberty, but Reagan was ashamed that Kennedy's brother and other Democrats "not longer hear that trumpet."[20]

Reagan did not hesitate to speak off the cuff after his formal White Paper speech. After all, ever since he first had announced he was touring California in September, 1965 to assess whether he should run for governor, he had held many impromptu press conferences and was adept at speaking without the need of a teleprompter. That evening he addressed the Pueblo incident again, as he had many times ever since the ship had been seized four months earlier. Reagan stated that the American people wanted to tell the Johnson administration, "The seizure of the Pueblo and the kidnapping of our men is a humiliation we will not endure."[21] Reagan was commenting from afar about the continuing January hostage crisis, wherein Americans still were being held in the hostile country of North Korea. As will be discussed, the North Korean-Pueblo hostage crisis of 1968 would prepare Reagan for two future hostage crises: the Iran hostage crisis of 1979-80, whose eventual successful outcome would culminate on Inauguration Day for President Reagan in 1980; and the hijacking of the *Achille Lauro* during his presidency.

Hawaii Republican Senator Hiram Fong, a Nixon supporter, told the press that Reagan had delivered a "great, incisive, firm speech," which Fong had wished "all Americans could have heard."[22] Fong would remember Reagan's speech at the upcoming national convention.

Reagan indeed did want to speak to the nation. He continued transforming into a world statesman. The press noted and spread the word. The Associated Press quoted John F. Kennedy's inaugural pledge to "pay any price, bear any burden" for the defense of liberty and headlined Reagan's scorn for RFK—"who inherited the power but who no longer hears that trumpet nor recognize its grand notes."[23] United Press International cited Reagan's call not to bargain away what America had won.[24]

After the questioning about his meetings with Hinman, Clif White met with the press again, as the reporters characterized the Reagan campaign as undergoing a "reassessment."[25] The press thought that White was not using the conference to "drum up new campaign support."[26] White corrected their mistaken impression, noting that Nixon had not wrapped up the nomination yet, described the status as "still an open situation," and revealed that his travels across the country had demonstrated "increased interest in Reagan as a potential Presidential candidate...the people were showing more interest."[27]

Reagan's first White Paper speech had been a great success. More would follow. But meanwhile, while in Hawaii, Reagan kept close track of what was happening in Nebraska, the second opt-out primary state.

Endnotes

1. Greenberg, Carl, "Rumor of 'Deal' With Rockefeller Hurting Reagan," *LA Times*, 5/13/68, p. 3
2. Greenberg, ibid
3. Greenberg, ibid
4. RRL, Tape 340
5. See Illustrations
6. Persico, p. 67-69
7. White, p. 232
8. *Newsweek*, 5/13/68, p. 31
9. "Reagan as Running Mate With Rocky," *Kansas City Star*, 5/10/68
10. "Rockefeller, Reagan Aides Discuss Tactics," *Seattle Times*, 5/13/68, p. 6
11. "Governors Weigh Problems, Politics," *Seattle Times*, 5/13/68, p. 6
12. Greenberg, Carl, "Rumor of 'Deal' With Rockefeller Hurting Reagan," *LA Times*, 5/13/64, p. 3
13. ibid
14. "Rocky's Name Haunts Reagan on Stop Here," *Cleveland Plain Dealer*, 5/23/68
15. See Illustrations
16. Greenberg, Carl, "Rumor of 'Deal' With Rockefeller Hurting Reagan," *LA Times*, 5/13/68, p. 3
17. "First of Reagan's 'Position Papers' Out," *Seattle Times*, 5/2/68, p. 13
18. RRL, Tape 341
19. Greenberg, Carl, "Rumor of 'Deal' With Rockefeller Hurting Reagan," *LA Times*, 5/13/68, p. 3
20. ibid

21. Greenberg, ibid
22. Greenberg, ibid
23. Reed, *The Reagan Enigma*, p. 153
24. Reed, ibid
25. "Governors Weigh Problems, Politics," *Seattle Times*, 5/13/68, p. 6
26. ibid
27. Greenberg, Carl, "Rumor of 'Deal' With Rockefeller Hurting Reagan," *LA Times*, 5/13/68, p. 3

CHAPTER 25: NEBRASKA—MAY 14, 1968

"Mr. Nixon can almost feel the hot breath of California's Gov. Ronald Reagan on his neck."

~ Reporter in Nebraska[1]

"He could beat Nixon."

~ Dale L. Young[2]

"The grass roots popularity of this man is unbelievable. Just today, we have had teams of students supporting Governor Reagan come to Omaha from Illinois, California, and Kansas State University wanting to work for Mr. Reagan here in Nebraska."

~ William H. Thompson[3]

"Personally of course I have to be very thrilled that that many people would hold me in that regard."

~ Ronald Reagan[4]

"Reagan did very well."

~ Richard Nixon[5]

"The question for the party is which man is best equipped to meet Senator Kennedy."

~ William Sherwood[6]

Nebraska was the second stepping-stone in Reagan's plan. After Reagan had achieved almost 11 percent of the Wisconsin vote due to a combination of Don Taylor's campaigning, Reagan's 1967 visit to Milwaukee, and the brief showing of Reagan's new campaign film, more effort was needed next in Nebraska.

Reagan first had visited Nebraska in 1961 and had spoken in Grand Island. In Lincoln in 1966, he had addressed a large gathering at the Republican Founder's Day.[7] Later that year when Nebraska

Secretary of State Frank Marsh had discussed the new Nebraska opt-out primary law, he noted, "Very much on the scene" in everyone's mind was Governor-elect Ronald Reagan.[8] The details of the new law, and the campaigns of Reagan's opponents, are discussed by your author elsewhere.[9]

In June, 1967, Nebraskans had been seen Reagan as the "rising star" of the party, and Reagan's Nebraska candidacy was seen as a threat to Nixon by splitting off conservative votes, which might lead to a Romney win. This was prior to Romney's brainwashing comment, so at that time, it was theorized that in 1968, if Romney were to do well against Nixon in New Hampshire, then in "Nebraska he almost surely will have the opportunity to meet Reagan head-on, no holds barred."[10]

It was late that month at the Young Republican National Federation convention in Omaha when Reagan had delivered his speech where he first had uttered "sickly pastels" and had received the tumultuous reception. It was here where Nixon had almost no convention presence and had refused to attend and suffer a likely dramatic convention defeat against Reagan. Sure enough, Reagan had won the straw poll decisively over all other candidates, and Goldwater had thought he might reassess his support for Nixon. After Reagan had campaigned in Douglas County and Scottsbluff, the media had concluded, "Ronald Reagan is going to be a formidable candidate in the next Presidential primary here next May." But at each locale, Reagan had "denied again, as he does almost daily, that he is a Presidential candidate."[11] It was here that the *New York Times* reporter was reported to have blurted out impulsively, "I've never seen anything like it…There isn't anybody who can touch Reagan."[12]

A month later, Governor Norman Tiemann and most state GOP party leaders had predicted that Reagan was "expected to pull votes away" from Nixon. Asked by the press what they thought of Nixon having to face Reagan in Nebraska, the Nixon troops said they would "be delighted to face Mr. Reagan in Nebraska." A sample of Nebraska Republican voters, none of whose details were specified, indicated that Reagan was 'popular." But at that point in the summer of 1967, he was "not regarded too seriously as Presidential timber." The analysis concluded, however, "This could change with an open Reagan effort."[13]

As we saw earlier, Reagan had stopped in Grand Island on October 1. Clif White had arranged for Reagan's brief refueling stop in order to meet Nebraskan supporters at the airport. White was organizing those volunteers as the future Reagan campaign teams for the

Nebraska opt-out primary. There was a mini-rally and meeting, but at the time Reed felt Reagan gave "no encouragement to the would-be campaign workers."[14] Yet as we will see, despite Reed's somewhat pessimistic analysis—possibly because this was the beginning of the time period when he was no longer in charge of the campaign and had been demoted to the role of out-of-state travel planner—in fact grass roots efforts for Reagan were about to begin in earnest. In November, analysts felt that in Nebraska, "Mr. Nixon can almost feel the hot breath of California's Gov. Ronald Reagan on his neck."[15]

As 1968 began, while deciding upon which names to list on the ballot, the Nebraska secretary of state had to deal with several notable third parties and fringe candidates, the latter of which included a Republican cowboy candidate, Americus Liberator.[16] The secretary of state had said that Reagan was a "cinch" to be listed on the ballot.[17] *Newsweek* reported that Nixon easily would "win in Nebraska against anyone but Ronald Reagan." Yet at the time, "Reagan has refused to give his Nebraska supporters a word of encouragement."[18]

In mid February, Reagan had been informed, via telegram, that his name was entered on the Nebraska ballot.[19] Seemingly that was the only important news about the Reagan campaign in Nebraska that month, for "the only signs of real competitive activity, on behalf of Governor Reagan, are far below the political surface and tentative at that." Reagan forces were described by the national media as "relatively inactive in preparing for the May 14 primary." Indeed Republican Party leaders had agreed that unless Nixon stumbled in New Hampshire or Wisconsin, "no Reagan effort will probably develop" in Nebraska. But at the same time, a cryptic report mentioned that "key party people" were approached by "Reagan representatives" and asked to "remain on the alert" if a Nebraska campaign for Reagan "should appear worthwhile."[20]

In fact, grassroots Reagan campaign activity was stirring in Nebraska. Reagan operatives have been detected "taking a Nebraska poll testing the Governor's potential strength in the state." Such a poll would be helpful "only in deciding whether to activate a primary campaign."[21] Indeed the formal Reagan campaign in Nebraska for the 1968 Republican nomination was about to begin full steam.

The filing deadline arrived, with filings having poured into the secretary of state's office with "unprecedented numbers," because delegates would be chosen via the primary vote. Nixon had the support of sixteen regular delegates and nine alternates, whereas Reagan had six delegates and one alternate. But although amongst the 37 Republicans seeking ten at-large delegate seats, seven were for Nixon, yet fully five were for Reagan—without Reagan having had virtually any noticeable campaign apparatus in place.[22] The final Republican ballot in Nebraska showed the names of Ronald Reagan, Richard Nixon, and perennial candidate Harold Stassen.[23] By the end of March, well before the Nebraska primary, both Romney and Rockefeller had withdrawn.[24] In reality, the Nebraska Republican race had become a contest between Nixon and Reagan.

Dale L. Young

On March 25 in Lincoln, less than two months before the Nebraska primary, banking executive Dale L. Young opened his mail in and inside was a letter from Citizens for Reagan National Information Center postmarked from Topeka, Kansas. Young had been one of the enthusiastic attendees at the 1964 convention but that fall had not watched Reagan deliver The Speech.[25] Young's parents in California had become enthusiastic supporters of Governor Reagan, and during 1966 and 1967 Young had learned about his party's rising new conservative hero. By 1968 he was treasurer of the Nebraska State Republican Party as well as a member of the State Republican Executive Committee.[26]

The letter invited Young to join the "Reagan for President campaign for Nebraska" and was signed by John Kerwitz, Executive Director of Citizens for Reagan National Information Center.[27] Kerwitz and Bubb's Topeka office had disseminated Reagan campaign materials across the country, to grass roots activists as well as the three Reagan campaign offices in the opt-out states of Wisconsin, Nebraska, and Oregon.

Young immediately called both Kerwitz and Bubb, saying that if Reagan would come to Nebraska, "He could beat Nixon."[28] Young said he wanted to help and would be happy to establish a Reagan for President campaign office in Lincoln.

Reagan's Campaign Offices

Bubb and Kerwitz sent two staff workers to Lincoln. Young and the two workers rented a storefront office in Lincoln. Young then hired the Omaha advertising firm Bozell and Busch to plan the Reagan media campaign in Nebraska. Young hired college students to man the office and to help send out mailings to Republican Party members in eastern Nebraska. There was no formal newspaper or radio advertising initially, but that would change.

One day, Young was in his office at the bank in Lincoln when a fellow banker from one of their correspondent banks in New York City arrived for some financial business. The New Yorker noticed the Reagan for President material in Young's office and asked Young, "Are you working for Dutch Reagan?" When Young answered that indeed he was, the New Yorker proceeded to tell Young that he knew Reagan quite well years ago in Hollywood. Apparently the banker, Reagan and a third man were all roommates in California at a time when Reagan did not have steady acting work but had started to date Jane Wyman. The banker recalled that he himself was the only steadily employed roommate, as he had a job at Bank of America; so he helped support Reagan by paying most of the rent. Reagan and the third man were not slouches however. The latter two got part-time jobs in Hollywood signing autographed pictures that would be mailed out to fans. But the photos were of other stars, not Reagan, and the two men had been hired to sign the other pictured stars' names!

Young related that he had no contact with any other Nebraska campaign office for Reagan. Also he had no direct contact with Tom Reed. He said his support of Reagan was "respected" by his Republican Party colleagues in Nebraska. He experienced no animosity but he also received no particular support or encouragement.[29]

Young ran the major Reagan campaign office in Nebraska. But Dr. William H. Thompson, a retired dean at the University of Omaha and whose daughter had married investor Warren Buffett, opened a Reagan-for-President headquarters in Omaha, calling his grass roots team the "Nebraskans For Reagan Committee."[30] Thompson's official stationery listed James L. Paxton Jr. as Vice-Chairman and Bruce Barton as Finance Chairman and bore the slightly modified title of "Nebraskans For Ronald Reagan." The Committee headquarters was at the southeast corner of 16th Street and Harney.

A third Reagan campaign office in Nebraska was started by Oxford attorney William H. Sherwood. Sherwood's office was also in Omaha but it is not clear if he and Thompson worked together or separately; they are each deceased and Young did not interact with either as noted.

Thompson sent out a letter to Nebraska Republicans, asking them to read an enclosed Reagan brochure: if Reagan were to receive a "significant vote in Nebraska, we believe he will respond to the call."[31] Thompson had received the brochures from Bubb's Topeka center. In his cover letter, Thompson then mentioned a forthcoming television campaign, in which he would help launch the major media innovation of the entire Reagan presidential campaign in 1968. The brochure itself had a cover of Reagan, with captioned words of his appealing to Democrats and Independents to join him, because "the issues of our time override party considerations." The second page was a Reagan biography with both Thompson's Nebraska Committee and Bubb's Topeka center listed.

The Reagan Threat

By April, although Governor Tiemann said the Republican race was "kind of a dull affair,"[32] the inroads the Nebraska Reagan campaign was making against Nixon were starting to be noticed. "What once appeared to be a no-contest Republican election for Richard M. Nixon may become a battle." Reagan's campaign was attracting donations, prompting a media comment, "There is ample money in Nebraska and elsewhere for a Reagan campaign." Actually, some Nixon leaders "received letters from Reagan friends soliciting contributions."[33] Nixon could not help but notice what was happening from his political right, just as he had predicted and feared more than a year earlier when he had met with his aides to plan his 1968 campaign.

Previously the Nixon campaign had announced that Nixon did not need to campaign much in Nebraska any longer because he had such strong support. But now Nixon's team in Nebraska issued no further boasts of achieving sixty percent of the vote. Indeed there was no further talk of Nixon not needing to visit Nebraska. Because of the Reagan threat, suddenly on April 9, Nixon announced an about-face. Nixon was making a return trip to Nebraska and he would visit each congressional district. Nixon needed to shore up his campaign in every part of conservative Nebraska.

The threat to Nixon was real, it was from Reagan, and the Nixon campaign had admitted it publicly. The big guns from the Nixon national effort, national director Robert Ellsworth and general counsel Thomas Evans, were brought in. Ellsworth used the term "crucial" to describe the Nebraska primary, because Nixon would face "on-the-ballot competition" from Reagan. Ellsworth admitted there were "substantial efforts made on behalf of Mr. Reagan in Nebraska," and expected Reagan would make a "strong showing."[34] What "strong" meant was not clear, and likely Ellsworth had hoped his comments had set the bar too high for Reagan, so that whatever vote Reagan achieved, the Nixon campaign could claim that Reagan had under-achieved. Nixon planned a media offensive, targeting newspapers, billboards, radio and television advertisements, to try to stop Reagan's momentum.[35]

From his campaign office in Lincoln, Young arranged for neither radio nor newspaper advertisements,[36] and Thompson, as noted, had sent out the donation letter and brochures. But Bubb kept the third Reagan campaign office, that of Sherwood, busier. Sherwood told the press that once Bubb had sent the literature, "all we had to do was stuff the envelopes and pay the postage." Bubb sent bumper stickers as well. Sherwood reflected later about his Reagan campaign staff, "There wasn't a politician in the whole bunch. We had a group of amateurs with neither money nor public relations firms to tell us what to do."[37]

Finances

The original Nixon budget for Nebraska had been $75,000. But by early April, it had been cut to only "about $50,000."[38] It had undergone a "substantial cutback" because Nixon was "doing real well in Nebraska "and the Nixon team did not "want to spend any more" than they had to."[39] But due to the Reagan threat, the Nixon national coffers suddenly had to send more monies to shore up Nixon. A month later, Nixon's Nebraska campaign grew from $50,000 to $68,000.[40] By Election Day it would mushroom to $100,000 to counter the Reagan threat.

Meanwhile the Reagan campaign in Nebraska had to manage with one-third that total. Young recalled that his Reagan campaign office in Lincoln had received $20,000 in total contributions that spring. Several checks were sent from Bubb's center in Topeka, for which Young opened a campaign bank account. Reed in Sacramento forwarded a campaign check signed by Marquita Maytag. Reed related that he had personally convinced the appliance heiress to send the check.[41] Young sent your author a photocopy of Maytag's note, which read "Am sending this to you via Tom Reed's instructions" along with her check.[42]

Sherwood told the press that his Reagan campaign office in Omaha "couldn't have cost more than $10,000," adding that the Nixon campaign "would probably spend more" at their election-night party than would the entire Reagan campaign.[43]

Thompson's committee reported its final financial numbers to the secretary of state's office after the election. Treasurer Barton reported expenditures of $7551, which included $2787 for television, radio and newspaper advertising and more than $2500 for stamps.

Collections in amounts greater than $25 added up to $6290, with the largest donation, of $1000, from the president of the Union Pacific railroad.[44] *Newsweek* reported that the Reagan campaign in Nebraska spent "between $15,000 and $30,000 on literature and on TV time."[45] But *Time* claimed the amount as only costing $13,500.[46]

Ronald Reagan, Citizen Governor

With Nixon concentrating on countering the Reagan threat with conventional media advertisements, the Reagan campaign was about to inaugurate for Nebraskans a brand new campaign innovation that would send Nixon's staff into a tizzy. In late April, Young—who had created no radio or newspaper advertisements for Reagan as discussed—met a *New York Times* reporter, who then reported that the Reagan presidential campaign in Nebraska instead "would concentrate mainly on television presentations concerning Mr. Reagan."[47] These would not be conventional commercials as Nixon was using. Indeed Reagan's unique television campaign, begun briefly in Wisconsin just as Taylor had had his bicycle accident, would be so successful in Nebraska that it would serve as the template for the Oregon primary.

The Reagan campaign made a tactical decision to expand a typical political campaign's use of newspaper and radio advertising into the new medium of television via a new Reagan campaign film. Reagan did not want to visit the three opt-out primary states to campaign there directly in 1968 because it was felt this would be arrogant. Exactly who made the decision for Reagan to avoid Nebraska in 1968 was not clear, for his 1967 visit had been an overwhelming success as seen earlier. Although Reed claims that "for reasons not clear, Reagan did not wish to visit the state,"[48] one may not unreasonably suppose that if campaign director Reed had wanted Reagan to go to Nebraska, Reagan would have agreed and gone. On the other hand, based on Reed's recollection above, Reagan may have felt that such a visit would alienate too many Californians.

So showing Reagan to voters on their television screens might be a good substitute. Regardless, as had occurred weeks earlier in Wisconsin, in the absence of Reagan in person in Nebraska, Reagan on film would have to do.

Reed had used some Reagan footage during the 1966 campaign. Reed recalled that he and Reagan's brother Moon, an advertising executive, had hired San Francisco commercial producer Greg Snazelle to create short television advertising spots for Reagan. Reed had wanted separate commercials for Reagan being portrayed as more conservative for southern California television audiences and more moderate for northern California audiences—which was Reed's 1966 campaign territory.[49] The problems with the resultant films were that Reagan was seen just in full frontal view as a "talking head," and the shots of the audience had been old, stock, black-and-white movie footage from the 1930s and 1940s, which showed them wearing clothing in style from decades before. Reed wanted something new for 1968.[50]

Reed hired Snazelle once again, now with San Francisco advertising executive John Mercer, to create a new 1968 campaign film. But rather than just having short clips as in 1966, the 1968 film was to be a half-hour biographical mini-documentary planned to appeal to audiences in Wisconsin, Nebraska and Oregon. Reed recalled he went through hours and hours of watching old Reagan speeches from his pre-gubernatorial and gubernatorial days including whatever was available from his campaigns on behalf of Nixon in 1962 and Goldwater in 1964 (the latter of course including "The Speech").[51] He worked closely with Mercer and Snazelle to create the final thirty minute film. Snazelle recalled, "Reagan was the first politician to come along literally tailor-made for the media."[52]

During Reed's research, he came across what a group of British historians described as his "prize find," the entire broadcast of Nixon's press conference after his 1962 loss to Governor Brown—when Nixon had declared, "You won't have Dick Nixon to kick around anymore."[53] Reed would use the footage later to convince the Nixon forces not to challenge Reagan in the California primary.

The final film, *Ronald Reagan, Citizen Governor*, offers a glimpse of pre-presidential Reagan at his best. Plus in it the "pastels" phrase would be refined into the exact wording with which readers are familiar and he would use years later in 1975. Reed sent the completed film to Bubb in Topeka who, as chairman of the Citizens for Reagan National Information Center, would distribute it to the Reagan campaign offices in Wisconsin, Nebraska and Oregon.[54]

The film acknowledges Bubb's committee and begins with Reagan's swearing-in ceremony and him citing Benjamin Franklin's admonition to do one's best, and then Reagan affirms he will follow "the precepts of the Prince of Peace."

The film traces chronologically Democrat Governor Brown defeating his Republican opponent in 1958 followed by Brown defeating Nixon in 1962 and Nixon's saying the Republican Party "needs a new leader" with a "new birth of freedom." The clear inference is that Nixon is finished politically and the party should turn to Reagan. California Republican Party state chairman at the time, James Halley, says that Ronald Reagan is a uniter of Republicans.

Reagan's career is then summarized: giving congressional testimony at the House Committee on UnAmerican Activities where he had met Nixon, factory speeches for General Electric, president of the Screen Actors Guild, and his refusal to run for congressman or senator in 1962 or 1964 despite the pressure exerted by California Republican leaders.

Reagan's 1966 gubernatorial triumph is detailed including that despite California Democrats having outnumbered Republicans by 3:2, Reagan wins by almost one million votes. Reagan is seen at the podium upon hearing the news that he won and thanks "many good friends from the other party and independents" for his victory.

This initial segment of the film—Brown beats Knowland, Brown beats Nixon, Reagan beats Brown—was characterized by one critic "like the children's game, rock-scissors-paper" with the clear conclusion, Reagan beats Nixon.[55]

Reagan ends by exhorting Republicans to raise a banner to attract all Republicans as well as those Democrats and independents who want to join him. But he cautions not to color the banner with "the **pale pastels** of political expediency."(author's emphasis) The wording from his June 1967 speech to the Young Republican National Federation convention thus had changed from "sickly" to "pale," where it would remain fixed in history.[56]

The film ends asking the question addressed to the viewer: "Ronald Reagan, where does he go from here?" Reagan's master stroke was completed. Nofziger approved it. Nancy Reagan had wanted to see it too but was "turned down." Reagan himself did not wish to see this first film version but would see a revised version to be used in Oregon.[57]

The film, completed and shown briefly just before the earlier Wisconsin primary—when Taylor had had his bicycle accident— would now be seen by a much bigger audience in Nebraska. Reagan's team hoped the unique film would fix the attention of Republican voters upon Reagan just before the critical primary.[58] The film shown in Wisconsin and Nebraska featured Reagan speaking on domestic themes. By the time of the later Oregon primary, a new version would be created in which Reagan's mastery of world affairs would shine through as well.

The Ambition of the Citizen-Candidate

The issue of Reagan's ambition to be president in 1968 was discussed earlier from the perspective of Stu Spencer and historian Lou Cannon's observations that Reagan's fear of flying, coupled with constant campaign and fund-raising trips during almost every weekend, demonstrated his true ambition to be president.

But there was also a second aspect to Reagan's ambition according to Cannon. Reagan's ambition often was "hidden."[59] Reagan not only was modest, he did not see himself as someone who "compromised and cut corners" as did other politicians. He was a citizen-politician, and now in 1968 was a citizen-governor, who "did not make deals," and because he saw himself as someone who was "never motivated by political considerations," he denied he had a political strategy because that revelation would "be giving away the game." Reagan's genuine belief that he was not a politician was the "secret of his political success." What Cannon likely had not realized was that the origin of Reagan's belief and slogan was from his own analysis of Eisenhower prior to 1952 and then Ike's mentoring of him.

Cannon's thoughts are corroborated by Reagan's statements to the press during the entire campaign. At almost every press conference, he would deny that there was a strategy to get him nominated except as California's favorite son. The clear inference from Reagan's new film was that the citizen-politician, who had changed into the citizen-governor and now would become the citizen-candidate if the public wanted him to be, hopefully soon would be elected the Citizen-Nominee in August followed by the Citizen-President in November.

Overwhelming Success

After Bubb received the film from Reed, he sent one copy off to Young in Lincoln. As noted, Young, via his local advertising firm, arranged for *Ronald Reagan, Citizen Governor* to be shown on Nebraska television.[60]

Young recalled at the time another encounter with a reporter from the *New York Times*, whose questioning about the film apparently never appeared in print. Young recalled that the reporter asked Young how much the planned television showings of the Reagan film would cost; Young recalled telling him less than $20,000. When the reporter then asked how many times the film would be shown, Young answered 18. The reporter could not believe the answers and badgered Young about his honesty. Young recalled being fairly perturbed that his integrity was being challenged by a reporter from the elitist eastern press, so he asked the reporter if he knew how much it cost to show a half-hour film on Nebraska television. When the reporter admitted he did not, Young told him "just $70."[61] Young arranged to show the Reagan film throughout the Nebraska television market.

Young recalled that he never saw any local press reaction to the Reagan film. But Dr. Thompson, who spoke at the Omaha headquarters of Nebraskans For Ronald Reagan Committee on May 10, told the press that the response to the Reagan film in Nebraska was "overwhelming." Thompson added, "The grass roots popularity of this man is unbelievable. Just today, we have had teams of students supporting Governor Reagan come to Omaha from Illinois, California, and Kansas State University wanting to work for Mr. Reagan here in Nebraska."[62]

Other Reagan Supporters

Besides the campaign offices established and run directly by Young, Sherwood, and Thompson, there were other Nebraskans involved in the 1968 Reagan campaign. Donald Ross, in 2012 a Federal Judge on senior status for the Eighth Circuit Court of Appeals, served as vice-chairman of the Republican National Committee under Ray Bliss at the time. After the 1964 Goldwater defeat, Ross and Bliss had arranged a series of 25 Republican speakers, including Eisenhower, to go on educational-political tours. Judge Ross helped Reagan in Nebraska in 1968 along with Charles Thone, future congressman and Nebraska governor, as well as William E. Barrett, future Nebraska Republican state chairman and five-term congressman. Thone was a friend of Clif White and had been contacted by White and Reed when Reagan had made his June, 1967, visit to Nebraska.[63]

There was little, if any, interaction between the Reagan campaign and the campaigns of the Democrats. Yet the conservative nature of Nebraskans was not unnoticed by the Kennedy campaign that spring. Recently, blogger Moe Lane found a video showing RFK warning young students in Nebraska that in a few decades, they might need to wear gas masks due to air pollution.[64] When Kennedy spoke to students at the University of Nebraska decrying the use of military weapons in Vietnam and suggested that America should fight the war with "exemplary action at home and abroad," he was booed. When Kennedy added next that he favored stopping bombing of North Vietnam, he was booed again.[65] As historian Victor Davis Hanson has observed, during this time "most Americans were still willing to support a war they thought could be won outright."[66]

Nixon's campaign team had seen how the minimal showing of the Reagan film had helped lead to Reagan achieving almost eleven percent of the Wisconsin vote. Now in Nebraska, the same film would be shown much, much more. Nixon certainly remained the front-runner, yet any increase in Reagan's expected vote would be seen as momentum shifting to Reagan and away from Nixon. In conservative Nebraska, Republican voters might give Reagan an unexpected push towards Miami Beach.

So Nixon, who had had to return to Nebraska in early April to thwart the growing Reagan threat by visiting every congressional district, now in May had to return again to thwart the Reagan television campaign film that was flooding Nebraska living rooms. Newsweek confirmed that Nixon's only "real" opponent was Ronald Reagan.[67]

Just before primary day, the *Omaha World Herald* ran a full-page election article with caricatured drawings of the major candidates from each party. Reagan was drawn as smiling with a full head of hair but certainly the most wrinkles of any of the candidates. The analysis pointed out all the Reagan campaign media efforts, which had included "tapes of the California Governor's speeches, mailings and advertisements to rally the conservatives." Reagan's series of radio commercials was seen as extending "an open hand" for "Democrats to write in Mr. Reagan on their ballots." Despite the Nixon Nebraska team's publicly stated goal of obtaining "51 per cent," others said that Nixon had to win "at least 65 to 70 per cent" in order to combat the "Nixon can't win talk." A newspaper editorial had upped that percentage to "67 to 75 percent," which prompted one Nixon supporter to complain that the newly raised expectation was "ridiculous." But just before Election Day, the Nixon campaign in Nebraska, threatened by the Reagan campaign since April, attempted to counter Reagan's appeal to disaffected Democrats by sending its own letter to Nebraska Democrats, asking them to write in Nixon's name. Reagan's goal was to "keep Mr. Nixon from waltzing off with the Nebraska prize" but needed to "run a strong second" in order to "gain prestige."[68]

In Hawaii at the governors conference and about to deliver his first White Paper speech, at a press conference, Reagan downplayed his chances, saying that he heard his upcoming vote projection "might be 10 percent."[69]

Primary Day

For a few fleeting days in mid May, 1968, Nebraska became the center of the political universe. NBC basically took over the Sheraton-Fontenelle Hotel in Omaha, which "rented the ballroom, mezzanine, one hundred sleeping rooms and ten first floor rooms to cover the primary." NBC had planned originally to send 110 people to cover the event but scaled the number back to 75 due to having to cover the upcoming Paris peace talks as well. Heading the NBC team were veteran broadcasters Chet Huntley and David Brinkley, who had "four rooms each" plus "four telephones." The plans for ABC and CBS were described as much less extensive.[70]

But within a week, plans changed. Brinkley and Huntley were sent off to Paris so NBC brought in Frank McGee and Sander Vanokur instead. NBC did station one hundred staffers throughout Nebraska precincts to help make projections. The NBC producer announced that their Nebraska election coverage would "include the first use of a communications satellite in the 1968 campaign." This was needed because when the results would be announced, Governor Reagan would be in Hawaii attending the fore-mentioned governor's conference. By using the satellite, Reagan's reaction would be broadcast live across their network. CBS and ABC decided to have election night coverage from their New York City studios headed by Mike Wallace and Howard K. Smith, respectively along with local correspondents in Nebraska, which included Roger Mudd for CBS and William H. Lawrence for ABC. Fully 150 domestic and foreign correspondents had registered for covering the Nebraska primary.[71]

Within hours of the upcoming primary, Nixon national director Ellsworth told the press again that the Reagan campaign was "substantial." Nixon's Nebraska chairman George Cook admitted that to counter the Reagan campaign and its media blitz, Nixon had to up their spending to $100,000, adding, "The ball game has changed in the last two weeks. I'll be satisfied with 51 percent."[72] Clearly, Nixon was worried about the Reagan threat in Nebraska until the very last minute.

The *New York Times* led its primary preview by saying that Reagan had staged "the nation's first all-television campaign" and that the main Reagan tactic had been to "drench Nebraska" with the Reagan film.[73] Would it work? Would Reagan best his tally in Wisconsin?

Election Results

When 1,979 of the 2,133 precincts had reported, Reagan had won fully 39,044 votes. The initial tally suggested Reagan had won almost 22 percent of the Nebraska Republican vote.[74] The final tallies from the secretary of state's office, released in late June, would show Reagan had received 42,703 votes or 21.28 percent.[75] Appeals for Democrats to vote Republican yielded 1,905 for Reagan.[76] Eisenhower's original suggestion for Reagan to work to attract disillusioned Democrats, which had worked in 1966, now was starting to work at the national level in Nebraska.

Young said he and his co-workers in the Reagan for President campaign office in Lincoln "were thrilled."[77] And what did Reagan think of his grassroots teams in Nebraska? On May 19, he told the press, "I wasn't in Nebraska...There was a group of people who were amateurs in the sense of not being political pros...It was a very low gear and low financed effort. Personally of course I have to be very thrilled that that many people would hold me in that regard. But I have no way and no means to base any assessment on what it means."[78] He would say more shortly.

Once the Nebraska primary was tallied initially and Reagan had seemingly won 22%, Bubb acknowledged that Reagan was "not a candidate, he did not campaign in Nebraska, and he still got nearly 25 per cent of the vote." Indeed Bubb was elated and told the press, "Reagan's showing was absolutely great."[79]

Reagan's competitors had to face the reality of the Reagan steamroller. The cowboy candidate Americus Liberator, who had mocked Reagan's idea that "he could win Nebraska by merely airing a few commercials on TV," experienced the first of what would amount to three losses (1968, 1976, and 1980) to Reagan.[80]

Nixon admitted Reagan "had made a good showing, just about what we'd thought he'd do there and what we think he'll do in Oregon."[81] Nixon admitted begrudgingly that his own win came "despite a major effort on the part of Reagan forces."[82] Then when asked if Reagan should be taken more seriously now, Nixon—possibly torn between Reagan having campaigned for Nixon in 1960 and 1962 yet was now a competitor gaining ground on Nixon—answered, "I think all of the Republican Governors that want to be President should be taken seriously."[83] But possibly the most honest of Nixon's opinions about Reagan's 22% was reported by *Time*, which noted, "Nixon was forced to admit that the Californian did 'very well.'"[84] Buchanan confirmed at the time that Reagan, not Rockefeller, remained Nixon's biggest problem.[85] In fact, the press was so laudatory towards Reagan, Nixon's frustration showed. One reporter noted that Nixon was the country's only politician who could win 70 percent of the vote and have the analysts talking about his opponent's 23 percent. "Yet it happened in Nebraska with Gov. Reagan."[86]

The local Nebraska press felt that besides winners Nixon and Kennedy, the only backers who "could find any comfort in the verdict" were those who had supported Reagan. Reagan's good showing was "certain to mean more activity on his behalf—and possibly more by the Californian in his own behalf."[87] When viewed by the press in Oregon, whose own primary election would be in two weeks, Reagan "surprisingly polled nearly a quarter of the GOP vote." The Oregon press speculated that finally Rockefeller and Reagan "might join forces" to stop Nixon.[88]

At the national level, the *New York Times* said that Governor Reagan "made his best showing of 1968 with more than one-fifth of the total. That was almost double his showing in the Wisconsin primary." The newspaper did not know it, but Reagan's plan was falling into place. The newspaper acknowledged Reagan's television campaign once again plus Reagan's appreciation when he said, "I am grateful to the people of Nebraska." The *Chicago Sun-Times* reported, "Reagan's methodically planned campaign by remote control for the Republican presidential nomination "received a "timely push forward." Reagan's vote tally was "impressive" and "perfectly timed."[89] San Francisco KPIX-TV 11's reporter Mike Lee commented tersely, "Reagan pulled a strong vote." [90]

Time said that with the Nebraska vote, Reagan's "fortunes were on the rise." Governor Tiemann said Reagan's tally was "amazing and significant" especially because Reagan had made no personal appearances there.[91] Newsweek said that Reagan's approximate 22% was "on the strength of a direct-mail and television campaign." Although Nixon had beaten Reagan in nearly all sub-groups of Republican voters, "Ronnie did reasonably well among the affluent."[92] The official *Newsweek* delegate count showed Reagan at 192, still well behind Nixon and Rockefeller. Rockefeller had just won the Massachusetts primary via write-in, which had caused "some conservative pro-Reagan Republicans" in Louisiana, Mississippi, and South Carolina to move to Nixon to guarantee the defeat of Rockefeller.[93]

One historian later characterized the Nixon win in Nebraska as creating the "near-inevitability of Nixon's nomination" and that "wishful thinking, in and out of the Reagan camp, conjured up prospects, however, that reality could not."[94] But that analysis missed the point. Reagan never expected to win in Nebraska. But he achieved his goal of rising momentum. In New Hampshire, Reagan had made no campaign effort (plus the filing papers had been retrieved and had never been seen again) because it was not an opt-out state and the new governor could not appear to be running for higher office overtly at that point; he had obtained a few hundred write-in votes. In Wisconsin, the first of the opt-out primaries, Reagan had relied on Taylor and his core of 400 volunteers plus minimal use of the new campaign film. Reagan had achieved almost eleven percent of the Republican vote and emerged as a national candidate. But it was in Nebraska where Reagan had doubled his vote from Wisconsin, and the true national appeal of Ronald Reagan was confirmed with his impressive 22 percent of the vote. It was achieved with the combined efforts of Reagan, Reed, Bubb, Young, Thompson, Sherman, their Nebraska grass roots Reagan campaign workers, the Nebraska Young Republicans, and the critical use of *Ronald Reagan, Citizen Governor.*

It was Reagan's campaign plan all along that foresaw him sailing into the 1968 convention with a sizeable number of delegates in order to prevent a Nixon first-ballot victory and then have the delegates turn to him to become their nominee. For Ronald Reagan, who would not win in 1968, and who would challenge President Ford in 1976 and lose again, his election to the presidency in 1980 in no small part can be traced to the voters of Wisconsin and Nebraska in 1968.

After again speaking to the press in Hawaii about his initial reactions to the Nebraska results, Reagan—just three days after delivering his triumphant first White Paper speech—was asked if he would accept the party's nomination. If he were offered the nomination, "he would not refuse it." But asked once again about him starting to campaign actively, he demurred once again answering, "I could not now foresee myself soliciting the job. It's a job that seeks the man." Reagan said he had been told only to expect ten percent of the vote, and the showing of approximately 21-22% was "very thrilling, very gratifying."[95] Reagan then added that he had "no idea what it means" and it made no change in his being a "noncandidate."[96]

Governor Tom McCall of Oregon, the Rockefeller supporter who in 1967 had met Reagan in Eugene and later in Portland, stood next to Reagan at the press conference and used it as an opportunity to follow-up on the unexpected good news about the 1968 Reagan campaign by inviting him to campaign in person in the next opt-out state of Oregon. Politely, Reagan declined the invitation.

With speculation swirling about what the Nebraska results would mean further down the road, the news media and the Reagan campaign team in Nebraska then turned its attention away from Nebraska and gazed west towards Oregon. Sherwood reflected that if Reagan's momentum from Wisconsin and now Nebraska could continue into Oregon, his chances of getting the GOP nomination would be "pretty good." Sherwood added, "The issue is which candidate can beat Bobby Kennedy next fall. The question for the party is which man is best equipped to meet Senator Kennedy." Sherwood emphasized that the Reagan campaign had not run "against Richard Nixon" and indeed would support Nixon if he won the nomination. Rather the Reagan grass roots activists felt Reagan was "better all the way around." He was pleased at the Reagan accomplishment in Nebraska believing that Reagan's achievement was "the beginning of something...a wave of the future—a new force which will grow incredibly in the next few weeks until it sweeps everything before it."[97] *Newsweek* concurred: "Reagan's electronic effort in Nebraska was a warm-up for his TV drive in Oregon."[98]

Reed felt that the Reagan campaign was "on track," yet Kennedy had won the Democratic side with 52 percent.[99] But overall, the significance of Nebraska for Reagan cannot be overstated. Reagan had achieved his second step: 11 percent in Wisconsin and now 22 percent in Nebraska. It was onward to Oregon where Reagan's largest campaign organization for 1968 was getting into high gear.

With RFK again as the likely Democratic nominee, Reagan "savored" the forthcoming battles with his nemesis.[100]

Reagan's grass roots supporters in Nebraska were not done. As the Miami Beach convention would begin, they would continue their pro-Reagan efforts by trying to convince fellow Nebraskan delegates who were for Nixon instead to cast their votes for Reagan.

While all the analysis of Reagan's strong showing in Nebraska was underway, Reagan had been in Hawaii delivering his first White Paper. After the Nebraska primary triumph, it was time to deliver the second White Paper attacking his old nemesis.

Endnotes

1.   Jarrell, John, "Key Primary In Nebraska?," *Omaha World Herald*, 11/22/67
2.   Dale L. Young, pers int 10/6/12
3.   'Reagan Story' A 'Smash Hit,'" *Omaha World Herald*, 5/11/68
4.   RRL, Tape 342
5.   *Time*, 5/24/1968, p. 27
6.   Wilson, Larry, "Reagan Man: Cost Less Than $10,000," *Omaha World Herald*, 5/18/68
7.   Walton, Don, "Nebraska Was Reagan Country," *Lincoln Journal Star*, 2/6/2011
8.   "New Primary Law Rigid In Nebraska," *NYT*, 12/11/66, p. 52

9.   Kopelson, Gene. 2014A
10.   Wicker, Tom, "In the Nation," *NYT*, 6/29/67, p. 42
11.   Weaver, Warren, " Reagan Wins Cheers In Omaha Again," *NYT*, 6/25/67, p. 40
12.   Buckley, William F., "Reagan and California," *National Review Online*, 1967200511170828. asp
13.   Wilson, Larry, "Nebraska, 3 Others to Offer Top Presidential primaries," *Omaha World Herald*, 7/24/67
14.   Reed, p. 20
15.   Jarrell, John, "Key Primary In Nebraska?," *Omaha World Herald*, 11/22/67
16.   Kopelson, Gene 2014 B
17.   Wilson, Larry, "Rocky Won't Be a Candidate in Nebraska," *Omaha World Herald*, 1/17/68
18.   *Newsweek*, 1/22/68, p. 13
19.   Kneeland, Douglas, "Rockefeller's Name Entered on Nebraska Ballot," *NYT*, 2/15/68, p. 17
20.   "Nixon Far Ahead In Nebraska Race," *NYT*, 2/25/68, p. 37
21.   Ibid
22.   "McCarthy Backers Stage Filing Rush," *Omaha World Herald*, 3/15/68
23.   "Nebraska Deadline Passes," *NYT*, 3/16/68, p. 14
24.   Kopelson, Gene, 2014A
25.   Young, pers comm., 7/16/13
26.   Young, personal interview 6/15/2015
27.   See Illustrations
28.   Dale L. Young, pers int 10/6/12
29.   Dale Young pers int 10/6/12
30.   Wilson, Larry, "GOP Primary Catching Fire With Write-Ins," *Omaha World Herald*, 4/7/68
31.   See Illustrations
32.   "Tiemann Says Wallace to Blame for Omaha Civil Disorder," *Omaha World Herald*, 4/25/68
33.   Wilson, Larry, "GOP Primary catching Fire With Write Ins,'" *Omaha World Herald*, 4/7/68
34.   Pieper, Don, "Nixon: Nebraska 'Crucial,'" *Omaha World Herald*, 4/9/68
35.   Kopelson, Gene. 2014A
36.   Young, pers int 10/6/12
37.   Wilson, Larry, "Reagan Man: Cost Less Than $10,000," *Omaha World Herald*, 5/18/68
38.   Pieper, Don, "Nixon: Nebraska 'Crucial'; Will Visit All 3 Districts," *Omaha World Herald*, 4/9/68
39.   Pieper, Don, "Nixon Backers Put $67,000 In Coffers," *Omaha World Herald*, 5/5/68
40.   Ibid
41.   Reed, pers comm. 10/17/12
42.   Dale Young, pers comm. 10/9/12
43.   Wilson, Larry, "Reagan Man: Cost Less Than $10,000," *Omaha World Herald*, 5/18/68
44.   "Reagan Backers Exceed Income," *Omaha World Herald*, 5/27/68
45.   *Newsweek*, 5/27/68, p. 33
46.   *Time*, 5/24/68, p. 27
47.   "Reagan Drive in Nebraska," *NYT*, 4/27/68, p. 16
48.   Reed, p. 25
49.   Chester et. al., p. 204
50.   Reed, pers int 10/17/12
51.   Reed, pers int 10/17/12
52.   Chester et. al., p. 204-205
53.   Chester et. al., p. 205
54.   Reed, pers int 10/17/12
55.   Diamond, Edward and Bates, Stephen p. 154
56.   Ronald Reagan, Citizen Governor, videotape available at Ronald Reagan Presidential Library, and an abridged version at www.reagan68.com
57.   Chester et. al., p. 206
58.   Reed pers int. 10/17/12
59.   Cannon, p. 324
60.   Dale Young, pers comm. 11/1/12
61.   Dale L Young int 10/6/12
62.   'Reagan Story' A 'Smash Hit,'" *Omaha World Herald*, 5/11/68
63.   McCollister, pers int 9/17/12
64.   http://moeticae.typepad.com/countup_from_dystopia/2011/10/old-rfk-ad.html
65.   Clarke, *Last Campaign*, p. 53
66.   Hanson, p. 403
67.   "Republicans: The Road to Nebraska," *Newsweek*, 5/20/68 p. 40
68.   Wilson, Larry, "Nebraska's Primary Develops Into a Key Test," *Omaha World Herald*, 5/12/68, p. 1

69. RRL, Tape 340
70. Thomas, Fred, "Hotel Whirls With Activity For Election," *Omaha World Herald*, 5/6/68
71. Garson, Arnold "Newsmen Preparing To Tell Vote Story," *Omaha World Herald*, 5/11/68
72. Wilson, Larry, "Within a Few Hours Now Primary Goes To Voters," *Omaha World Herald*, 5/13/68
73. Wicker, Tom, "In the Nation," *NYT*, 5/14/68, p. 46
74. "Voting By Counties," *Omaha World Herald*, 5/15/68
75. "Official Report of the Board of State Canvassers of the State of Nebraska" compiled by Frank Marsh, Secretary of State, compiled 6/26/68
76. "Governor Assists In Certifying Loss," *Omaha World Herald*, 6/27/68
77. Dale L Young pers int 10/6/12
78. RRL, Tape 342
79. "Ron's Vote Just Great," *Kansas City Star*, 5/12/68
80. Kopelson, Gene. 2014B
81. Weaver, Warren, "Nebraska Gives 53% to Kennedy," *NYT*, 5/15/68, p. 1
82. Janson, Donald, "'Freedom Budget' Approved by Nixon," *NYT*, 5/15/68, p. 33
83. "Nixon Pleased," *Omaha World Herald*, 5/15/68
84. *Time*, 5/24/68, p. 27
85. Buchanan, p. 258
86. Buchanan, p. 261
87. Olofson, Darwin, "Three Candidates Derive Comfort From State Vote," *Omaha World Herald*, 5/15/68
88. Bell, Jack, "Nixon Far In Front Of Reagan," *The Oregonian*, 5/15/68, p. 1
89. Littlewood, Tom, "Reagan Ducks Limelight But Scores A Hit," *Chicago Sun-Times*, 5/16/68, p. 24
90. https://diva.sfsu.edu/collections/sfbatv/bundles/201657
91. Time, 5/24/68, p. 27
92. Newsweek, 5/27/68, p. 33
93. Newsweek, 5/13/68, p. 29
94. Witcover, p. 295
95. "Reagan Is Surprised at Nebraska Showing," *Omaha World Herald*, 5/15/68
96. "Nebraska Vote Gratifies Reagan, 'Noncandidate,'" *NYT*, 5/15/68, p. 31
97. Wilson, Larry, "Reagan Man: Cost Less Than $10,000," *Omaha World Herald*, 5/18/68
98. *Newsweek*, 5/27/68, p. 33
99. Reed, p. 25
100. Reed, *The Reagan Enigma*, p. 153

CHAPTER 26: REAGAN'S SECOND WHITE PAPER SPEECH

"Bobby, I don't know, I watched him in Indiana and when he appears before the chamber of commerce he plays Calvin Coolidge."

~ Ronald Reagan[1]

Reagan did not have much time to assess his triumph in Nebraska. Nixon had won and was still the clear leader in delegates. But Governor Reagan, after leaving Hawaii, prepared for his next campaign swings. The press was elated. After Reagan's Nebraska showing, fully forty members of the press planned to accompany Reagan from then on.[2] Meanwhile Reagan was about to deliver the second of his five White Papers attacking RFK. But was this the same liberal RFK?

RFK's Turn Right

Back In California after the Hawaii meeting, Reagan continued his attacks on RFK but now turned to domestic themes. As discussed earlier, Reagan always tried to include humor in his speeches, especially as warm-up comments at the beginning of his talks. Besides attacking Robert Kennedy's record and his policies, Reagan also did add humor. Reagan began to comment about some new incongruous Kennedy remarks, which surprisingly had favored smaller government and had admitted some failures of big government solutions. It was not just Reagan who noticed the change in Kennedy's comments, which now had "conservative-sounding themes at times.[3] Even the *New York Times* realized that RFK was "emphasizing criticism of Federal Government as a bureaucracy, he is championing local autonomy, and endorsing the old Republican slogan: 'the best government is a government closest to the people'…The Senator is harshly critical of the…execution of welfare." Kennedy's comments also had included warnings that federal aid for education was "not a substitute for the efforts of states and local communities."[4]

RFK's turn to the political right was thought to be due to the more conservative leanings of Indiana Democrats, where he was campaigning at the time. But even more likely, RFK may have begun to realize that his most fearsome opponent in the general election would be the conservative who had triumphed over him in their 1967 debate: Ronald Reagan. None of RFK's subsequent major biographers mention this rightward shift of RFK at this time.

Was RFK learning from Reagan? As was true with the lack of files about the debate, the RFK files at the John F. Kennedy Presidential Library contain no record of RFK's conservative words during this time. The only instance of the library's acknowledgement of RFK's new found conservatism in the spring of 1968 was during their November 18, 2000 RFK symposium held at the library.[5] Historian Jeff Shesol told those attendees that in 1968, RFK "had also begun to voice his suspicions about bureaucracy and the effectiveness of heaping federal money onto these problems. He felt that there was an important role for the private sector in lifting lives and helping the cities around the country and in rural areas as well. This doesn't strike us today as a particularly radical idea. Except that there has to be some marriage of public and private efforts to solve any of those problems. Right at the time, it earned Robert Kennedy comparisons to Ronald Reagan. It was seen as something approaching heresy from the Democratic Party of that day. It was a real break from tradition."[6]

Kennedy had not just changed his emphasis to the smaller government favored by Reagan. RFK was now mirroring Reagan's themes of law and order. "Kennedy had caught the strange, shapeless fear of violence in the American mind. Kennedy had thus re-oriented his campaign to stress his record as chief law-enforcement officer at the Department of Justice (and) as Attorney-General".[7] Except that like Eisenhower, Reagan had been outraged that the former attorney general's 1965 proclamation that blacks did not have to obey the law.

Reagan noticed RFK's new "conservatism" in April and May, 1968. Reagan began to hammer home these Kennedy inconsistencies in virtually every speech he gave that spring. For example at his press conference in New Orleans on May 20 before flying off to Washington, D.C, Reagan listed those recent brand new Kennedy conservative campaign themes, telling a reporter: "He is advocating states' rights, local autonomy, turning the government back to the people; big government has failed; welfare has failed; we must turn to the private sector. This does sound a little strange you've got to admit."[8]

As will be detailed later, at a future June 1981 Rose Garden ceremony wherein President Reagan would give to the surviving Kennedy family the Congressional Medal of Honor in remembrance of RFK, Reagan would reference these 1968 RFK speeches by saying, "I remembered...the closeness that had developed in our views about the growing size and unresponsiveness of government."[9] The 1981 *New York Times* reporter then would comment derisively, "A bit of politics did creep into the ceremony. The President managed to mention smaller government while Senator Kennedy talked of looking after the needs of the forgotten."[10] Yet clearly as discussed by the earlier *New York Times* reporter from 1968 cited here, it was in fact RFK whose views were evolving towards the political right, coming closer to the conservative views of Reagan.

Second White Paper

With the first Reagan White Paper having been delivered a week earlier in Hawaii, the second speech, *Rising Expectations and the Tinderbox*,[11] was delivered on May 17 in Los Angeles to the National Newspaper Association. Likely Reed and his speechwriter had borrowed heavily from Milton Friedman's December 17, 1967 letter to *Newsweek*, in which Friedman showed that liberals had encouraged "unrealistic and extravagant expectations" within black communities, which later erupted in violence when progress was slow.[12] But the hidden hand of Reagan's mentor was about to carry forth as well.

Reagan began with the usual humor aimed at RFK by reminding the audience that recently, Kennedy had "wanted a Johnson-Humphrey ticket, and now we know where to (laughter). Jesse Unruh says his candidate Bobby Kennedy needs money...Bobby, I don't know whether you've been listening to television or if you've been watching him on the Indiana campaign trail, but for a minute it sounds an awful lot like us. You know he wants to turn the government back to the people! He wants to turn to the independent sector and to private business because big government has failed! The only difference between them and us is, we say it when its not an election year. Bobby, I don't know, I watched him in Indiana and when he appears before the chamber of commerce he plays Calvin Coolidge."

There was large applause.[13]

Reagan then became serious. Reagan then referenced the public spat between Eisenhower and RFK after the 1965 Watts riots, when Eisenhower had called for citizens to obey the law and RFK quickly had said the opposite. Reagan reminded his listeners that Kennedy---the former Attorney General—had stated that there was "no need to tell Negroes to obey the law," and Reagan—replying to RFK's lashing out at Ike—concluded that "civilization cannot afford demagogues in this era of rising expectations."[14] Later in the speech, Reagan did make a noted change to being in favor of California's open housing law.

The international press, picking up only on the last Reagan theme, commented mildly that Reagan was a "dark-horse candidate" and issuing such new white papers took the place of major speeches. Yet Reagan had been delivering major speeches out-of-state ever since his first in Seattle almost two years earlier.[15] Reagan's second White Paper was termed "a milestone in the public's progress of Ronald Reagan" for it marked "a noticeable swerve to the left."[16] This was one reporter's interpretation of what Reagan was attempting to achieve. Reagan had stated that he would veto any repeal of California's open-housing law because minorities had "legitimate grievances."[17] But this was no sudden swerve to the left for political expediency. For by this time, Reagan had had the many lengthy, private meetings with minority communities discussed earlier, and these meetings—unattended by the press—had convinced him of the law's importance. But the added importance of Reagan's second White Paper speech was his having publicly seconded Eisenhower's 1965 call for respect for the law and attacking RFK's 1965 call that blacks did not need to obey the law because of their grievances against society.

With two successful speeches attacking RFK under his belt, Reagan prepared for a hugely important campaign swing to the South both to add to his delegate count and to deliver his next White Paper speeches.

Endnotes

1.   RRL, Tape 340
2.   Reagan-Reed, 5/19/1968, chartered jet
3.   Weaver, Warren, "Kennedy: Meet the Conservative," *NYT*, 4/28/68, p. E1
4.   Weaver op.cit.
5.   Your author in attendance
6.   Shesol, Jeff, Comments. Robert F. Kennedy Conference, John F. Kennedy Presidential Library, November 18, 2000, p. 20
7.   White Theodore, p. 136
8.   RRL ,Tape 342
9.   Reagan-Reed, 5/19/1968, chartered jet
10.   Ayres, op.cit. at top of chapter
11.   Reed, p. 24
12.   Buchanan, p. 252
13.   RRL, Tape 340
14.   Reed, p. 24
15.   Cooke, Alistair, "It's Reagan's Turn to Play It Cool," *Seattle Times*, 5/19/68, p. 92
16.   ibid
17.   ibid

CHAPTER 27: REAGAN ATTACKS—SOUTHERN SOLICITATION, PART ONE

"The man to really worry about was Ronald Reagan."
~ Martin Feldman[1]

"Had he asked for support in the atmosphere of the occasion, charged with his presence, the Californian would have received it from us then and there."
~ Harry Dent[2]

"He says he's not a candidate now, but the reason we asked him is that we thought it possible he might become one."
~ Texas Republican State Chairman Peter O'Donnell[3]

"I can't even describe the excitement."
~ Jim Gardner[4]

"I think the GOP should neither write off nor take for granted the South...The Republican Party must come in... and actively seek its votes."
~ Ronald Reagan[5]

"If Russia needs our wheat to satisfy the hunger of her people...the wheat could be delivered easier if there were no Berlin Wall."
~ Ronald Reagan[6]

The South in the Spring of 1968

Reagan had much work to do in the South. By early 1968 as we have seen, Peter O'Donnell in Texas still was for Reagan. In South Carolina, Harry Dent did not think that Reagan could win, but his boss, Senator Strom Thurmond, was telling his audiences to work hard to elect candidates whose political philosophy most closely matched those of Reagan.

Grass roots Reagan groups in the South were growing too. Previously, Bob Dent had formed Citizens for Ronald Reagan in Fort Worth, and by the spring of 1968 another Texas grass roots group, Texans for Ronald Reagan, had formed under the leadership of J.R. Butler of Houston. Richard Nixon was aware of the pro-Reagan forces in Texas and complained publicly that Reagan had not stopped the grass roots activists.[7] Obviously, in addition to the Reagan threats in Wisconsin and Nebraska, Nixon felt threatened that Reagan had had his own Southern Strategy too.

In early May, Martin Feldman, a Nixon advocate who was general counsel to the Republican Party in Louisiana, called Nixon's campaign manager, John Mitchell. Feldman felt that the whole Nixon strategy was wrong. The Nixon headquarters was "hypnotized by Rockefeller," yet Feldman knew from his contacts in Louisiana and other Southern states, "The man to really worry about was Ronald Reagan."[8] Mitchell answered complacently that Feldman should not worry because at Nixon headquarters, they had the "broad picture" especially because Reagan "was still, officially at least, not a candidate."[9] Historian Chester felt that Feldman had been correct: "It was Reagan, not Rockefeller, who in the end, constituted the more direct threat to Nixon's power base."[10] Mitchell's comments seem at odds with Nixon's own thoughts throughout the campaign that Reagan was his most direct threat.

After his prior visits to South Carolina in September and Texas in October, it was in May, 1968, that Reagan began his third major campaign swing to the South. It was during this hectic trip that Reagan would deliver the third and fourth of his White Paper speeches, in which he planned to tie Robert Kennedy to the failures of the Kennedy-Johnson administrations. But the major purpose of the visit to the South, beyond attacking his presumed opponent in the fall, was to gather delegates in the South to win the nomination. Reagan still needed delegates to stop Nixon's drive for a first-ballot victory.

Kicking the Devil

At a press conference just before leaving California, when the inevitable subject of Vietnam arose, Reagan declared that America should set a firm deadline for the peace talks with North Vietnam to begin, and if they did not, we should "kick the devil out of them."[11] Not all those listening took Reagan's foreign policy advice seriously. Humorist Art Buchwald, after hearing Reagan, decided to attack Reagan by gently poking fun at the governor. Buchwald's column, in which Johnson administration officials wondered why they themselves had not thought of Reagan's suggestion, clearly was intended to attack Reagan because of his supposed naivete.[12]

From a conservative perspective, had the military at that point been given orders to follow Reagan's constant suggestions—developed closely with Eisenhower: mining Haiphong Harbor, not telling the enemy that there would be no invasion, staging practice naval-marine amphibious landing exercises, having a rapid surge in military strength, and threaten to use nuclear weapons, the Vietnam War might have ended with an American triumph years before America fled the country in defeat in 1975. Buchwald's derision of Reagan would not be the humorist's last entrance into the Republican race that spring.

New Orleans: The Third White Paper

Reagan's whirlwind trip was planned as a visit to five states— Louisiana, North Carolina, Florida, Illinois and Ohio—whose combined delegates of 202 was nearly one-third the total needed to win.[13] There had been a last-minute change for Reagan to attend a Republican Congressional strategy meeting in the nation's capital as requested by Senator Tower.[14] Perhaps Tower was not so firmly in the Nixon camp as thought previously.

The national press noted the marked increase in Reagan's travel entourage and what it meant. Previously the press had to follow Reagan as best it could by commercial jet. But now with his American Airlines chartered jet hauling "his staff and some 40 reporters and TV crewmen," Reagan, who previously "had resisted these symbols of grand ambition," had the new status of a "national candidate."[15] Reagan's staff included policy staff, tour managers, security aide, and communications director. There was no doubt that Reagan openly was "seriously pursuing the presidency."[16]

Reagan was met at the New Orleans airport by state Republican officials and 50 Reagan supporters, who waved "Reagan-for-President placards."[17]

The first question at the press conference was about foreign affairs and Reagan's prior comments in Sacramento. Reagan forcefully brought up what Eisenhower had done the decade before. "Based on our experience in Korea, where negotiations had dragged on for two full years, and during those two years more than 20,000 American soldiers were killed during the negotiations, you must set a time (limit):" that if the enemy were not negotiating in good faith, "such that if you have not made progress…you must not be afraid of the threat of force."[18] As Eisenhower had threatened, upon taking office, to the North Koreans, Reagan wanted to threaten now to the North Vietnamese. He wanted the enemy to know that once a new Republican entered the White House, "You are going to review all your options" including the threat, "You are going to fight the war on their soil and not on your own."[19]

What basis did Reagan have for critiquing the skills of the negotiations of the administration? As is well known, Reagan had been president of the Screen Actors Guild and his biographers uniformly have cited his skills as a negotiator. Indeed fellow actor and later SAG leader, Charlton Heston, in 1960 had been "stunned" and "awed" by Reagan's tough negotiating skills.[20]

Reagan was asked about his new, chartered airplane and the press entourage. Reagan explained because there was not good commercial air service into North Carolina for his exact itinerary, that the press had asked his campaign staff to arrange for the chartered jet and the press said they would pay for it. For what seemed like the thousandth time, he denied that he was a candidate and when asked about Oregon, Reagan answered, "I am not a candidate. If I were trying to do something in regard to a presidential campaign, I wouldn't be heading east, I'd be heading to Oregon, wouldn't I, where there's a primary next week."[21] And when asked if he would be running in Oregon, Reagan declared, "No I will not."[22] Reagan predicted that no matter how much infighting might have occurred, ultimately the Democrats would choose a "Humphrey-Kennedy ticket."[23]

Again Reagan brought up the apparent turn to the right that RFK recently had made in some speeches by joking:

"Bobby Kennedy? I can't keep up with his material. I want to tell you on this speaking tour I've made an inquiry as to whether he's going to be in any of the towns ahead of me because he's making speeches lately that sound so much like mine, I'm going to have to change my material."

This drew large laughs from the press. Reagan continued:

"I heard him out in California the other day… He was standing up in front of a cheering crowd…They were cheering their heads off as he said we must give the government back to the people. We must restore local autonomy. He said big government has failed. We must turn to the independent sector, to private enterprise to solve the problems of welfare and give the people jobs… He's gotten me afraid any more to even quote the founding fathers because I'm afraid if I do he'll think I'm talking about his old man," which drew loud laughs.[24]

Rockefeller

The Rockefeller forces had a small contingent in New Orleans headed by a history graduate student named Newt Gingrich. Gingrich was remembered at the time as a clever learner. Gingrich loved to tell friends about history and even while trick or treating with his family, Gingrich lectured throughout. At the time, despite trying to establish roots in the Georgia Republican Party, he had taken on the Republican establishment by supporting Rockefeller over Nixon.[25] Another Rockefeller operative was Tanya Melich, a former director of political research for ABC News and now on Rockefeller's paid campaign staff. She and Gingrich would attend the Miami Beach convention.

Next was a party at the Ponchartrain Hotel, where Reagan spoke to 400 Republicans and others who had paid $100 each to hear him. He said that the vast majority of working Americans finally had discovered that they "were not the beneficiaries of the Great Society but they were paying for it."[26] Reagan explained that despite being called by the Democrats as unwilling to help the poor, Republicans in fact would gladly contribute for programs to help the poor find jobs and educate their children *if* the programs were working.

Addressing any Democrats in the audience, he defied anyone who could say that "the Party of Jefferson and Jackson" bore any resemblance to the "present leadership" of the Democrats of today, which generated considerable applause.[27] Then a questioner asked if there would be room in a future Reagan administration for any Southern Democrats, as there "were a few here in this audience."[28] Reagan clearly was succeeding in attracting members of the opposition and apparently it was not just rank and file party members but actual elected officials who were willing in public to support his presidential efforts in the fall. As he had done throughout his 1968 campaign, Reagan was appealing to Democrats and Independents not by modifying his conservative positions and changing them into liberal ones, but rather by educating the Democrats that their views were in fact Reagan's own conservative principals all along. He did not appeal to them by moving to the left; he made them realize they were on the right.

Third White Paper and Silent Majority

At the major event, a Republican rally at the Tulane University gym for 4,000 cheering students who had paid $2 each, the national press noted that Reagan was "looking more and more like a candidate for the Republican Presidential nomination."[29]

Reagan delivered *National Priorities and the Negotiations in Paris* that same day, May 19. Reagan began by making the standard four jokes at Kennedy's expense. The essence of the serious portion of his speech was that there needed to be "hard choices between guns and butter, since trying to have both was fueling inflation," and that nobody in the Johnson administration seemed to be in charge of "national priorities."[30] To wild applause, he called the *U.S.S. Pueblo* incident a "humiliation this nation will not endure."[31] Reagan discussed student riots and administrators who had refused to condemn the students by stating, "The great **silent majority** (author's emphasis) of teachers and students who want order must come to the administrators."[32]

Richard Nixon has been linked forever with "silent majority," the term which he would use in November, 1969. Although the term had been in political usage occasionally previously—it was a term used in the 1800's to describe the dead—and the term had been used in John F Kennedy's *Profiles in Courage,* here is clear evidence that Reagan, while campaigning in 1968, used the term well before Nixon.

The *Los Angeles Times* devoted extensive coverage to praising Reagan's speech. The *Washington Post* noted accurately that Reagan had "invoked Dwight Eisenhower's name to justify a threat to invade North Vietnam if peace talks fail."[33]

Hanging Loose

Reagan was photographed signing autographs at Tulane,[34] and after Reagan had finished at the Tulane rally, he went to a special private chairman's dinner with representatives from eleven Southern States: Louisiana, Texas, Alabama, Mississippi, North Carolina, South Carolina, Virginia, Tennessee, Kentucky, Arkansas and Florida. Texas Republican Chairman Peter O'Donnell officially had arranged the dinner and Senator Tower of Texas was a special guest at the dinner.[35] But as we will see, it was Harry Dent on behalf of Strom Thurmond who was the true behind-the-scenes driving force for the invitation to Reagan.

The chairmen actually were the Southern Association of Republican State Chairmen. Reagan's team had pulled out all the stops as Reagan searched for Southern delegate support, plus it appeared superficially as if both O'Donnell and Tower's support still were up for grabs. Indeed the press noted that O'Donnell, Tower, and the other Southern Republicans were "sounding out the Governor's views on strategic possibilities."[36]

While the latter was true, the private meeting with Reagan and the Southern Republican state chairmen was in reality the brainchild of Thurmond's advisor Harry Dent. Dent recently had hosted Nelson Rockefeller at a private luncheon in Columbia, South Carolina to discuss the political situation, but nothing much had transpired.[37] Nixon was still out-polling Reagan, so Dent proposed that the three major candidates, Nixon, Rockefeller, and Reagan, be invited to meet with the Southern chairman to discuss their platforms. But Dent's motive was more self-serving than only learning about policy differences. According to historian Rick Perlstein, by this time Dent had "organized his fellow Southern Chairmen in a scheme to vote their delegations as a bloc," but first "they would play hard to get."[38]

Besides Tower and O'Donnell, who Dent recalled decades later in reality were in New Orleans "trying to line up Republicans for Nixon,"[39] Fred La Rue of Mississippi was there doing the same thing. Dent on the other hand wanted to "hang loose—as he phrased it[40]—by being less committal, as did William F. Murfin, the Florida chairman and Clarke Reed of Mississippi, the chairman of the association.[41]

Dent had hosted a pre-New Orleans planning meeting in Greenville, Mississippi with Murfin and Clarke Reed, where they determined that indeed they would be "hard to get."[42] They planned to give Rockefeller every courtesy but his chances in Dixie were two: "slim and none."[43] The cabal decided to keep their pact until they had decided between the two realistic choices: Reagan or Nixon.

Dent and his "Greenville Group" wanted the South to exert maximum leverage on whomever would become the Republican nominee. Certainly the probabilities favored Nixon. Indeed when Dent and Thurmond had had their private meeting with Reagan the prior fall in Columbia, Reagan expressed no fervor to become an avowed candidate. Yet if Nixon sailed without major competition to win the convention, the South would have no leverage at all. Thus they needed to keep the Reagan candidacy alive as a threat to Nixon so that Nixon would have to turn to Thurmond for help to thwart Reagan. And then Thurmond would go in for the political kill by exacting his price.

Of the members of the Greenville Group, only Clarke Reed of Mississippi, no relation to Tom Reed, "took real pleasure in the prospect of double-crossing Reagan."[44] In 1966 Clarke Reed, in the midst of a tough election to become governor of Mississippi, had asked for Reagan's help but there had been no response. Nixon then was asked and came to help Reed.[45] Reed did not forget and would seek his revenge against Reagan through to completion at Miami Beach and beyond into the 1970's.

Reagan and Rockefeller's teams accepted Dent's proposal, officially via O'Donnell and Tower of Texas,[46] although Reed recalled the invitation came via Murfin,[47] to come to New Orleans. But Nixon, whose advisors "seemed chagrined to have to court something they thought was already available," insisted that Nixon's visit be held later in Atlanta.[48]

Dinner With Reagan

Reagan was the first supplicant to have his meeting, which was described by Dent as a dinner in Reagan's suite at the Roosevelt Hotel,[49] named the Rendezvous Room,[50] although Reed recalled it was at Antoine's Restaurant.[51] Dent recalled, "A full course dinner was prepared with all the trimmings," and that it was "grand and very intimate."[52] These men were "Reagan fans," but wanted to win and dreaded a Rockefeller candidacy.[53]

Reagan told the group he would not be a candidate. Dent remembered, "Had he asked for support in the atmosphere of the occasion, charged with his presence, the Californian would have received it from us then and there."[54] For Thurmond, although Reagan did not commit to running, "his personality and his conservatism made hearts throb."[55] O'Donnell from Texas left the Reagan meeting, and his comments made front page news when O'Donnell told the press, "He says he's not a candidate now, but the reason we asked him is that we thought it possible he might become one."[56]

It seemingly was another blown opportunity. Had Reed and Reagan discussed what Reagan should say ahead of time? Decades later, Reed told your author that he had not had any discussions with Reagan on what to say; indeed Reed felt it would be presumptuous of him as campaign director to entertain any such thoughts,[57] even though the same thing had happened with private meetings earlier with Tower and O'Donnell at the Texas Summit in California and with Everett Dirksen in Eureka—i.e. no firm declaration of his candidacy, as we have seen. One group of historians characterized the dinner as "the moment Reagan did (the) most damage to his chances to be President."[58]

Did Reagan expect that they would offer him the support first without him having to ask for it? It turned out that Reagan was not a supplicant after all, but as we will see, many members of the group who met and heard Reagan in New Orleans would not automatically change to Nixon. The Southern door for Reagan was not closed yet, but with his refusal once again to declare privately that he was running for the presidency, the door was closing fast.

What did not help matters, as Dent recalled, was that Reagan's group handing of the bill to Dent was "typical of the style of Reagan's staff."[59]

Thurmond, Reagan, Nixon, and the ABM

The recollections of those involved at the Reagan-Dent dinner clearly emphasized whether Reagan would become a candidate. But lost in the fog of memory may have been an even more important part of their conversation. As we saw earlier, Thurmond had published his new autobiography and in it he had reflected that since 1957 he had "consistently urged the development of an effective U.S. ABM defense."[60] And Reagan, shortly after the September, 1967 meeting with Thurmond in South Carolina at the same time as the *Life* cover story on the ABM had appeared, had become a firm advocate of an anti-missile defense shield when he had visited Lawrence-Livermore a few weeks later.

In his book, Thurmond had traced the history of the funding of the anti-ballistic missile (ABM) program beginning in the mid 1950's when Congress had funded early research and development; in 1963 in a secret Senate session, the new prototype ABM system of the Soviet Union was revealed; Congress approved $196 million in 1963 and $167.9 million in 1966; later in 1966 the Soviets had begun deploying their system; in January, 1967 Johnson stopped development pending nuclear arms control discussions with the Soviets followed by McNamara's arguments against an American system even though the Chairman of the Joint Chiefs of Staff disagreed.[61] And in September, 1967, just as Reagan had landed in South Carolina to meet Thurmond as seen earlier, McNamara had espoused in *Life* his deployment of a "thin" system—Sentinel—against Communist China which had detonated its first nuclear bomb in June.

Thurmond ended his book analysis stating, "The Soviet danger is the major threat, and it must be faced resolutely. The Sentinel system is only the beginning, but a step in the right direction...For our future peace and security, our ABM defenses should be expanded."[62]

For Thurmond at this point in 1968, when he was evaluating Reagan through Dent, even though many other issues were important, very likely Dent would bring up how important national defense was to obtaining Thurmond's support.[63] To Thurmond, shortly to meet with Nixon in Atlanta, two items were paramount: getting Nixon to owe him, Thurmond, a huge political debt and to continue his cherished anti-missile defense.

Historian Jules Witcover reported that when Nixon would go to Atlanta to visit the Greenville Group, the emphasis would not be on the Supreme Court or civil rights or the selection of vice-president. Indeed the topic of Reagan as a threat to Nixon did not even come up. The main political discussions would involve the candidacy of George Wallace as a threat to Nixon.[64] This had been Nixon's main concern when he first had chatted with Dent in the car.

One historian felt that Thurmond's concealment of the Reagan threat to Nixon was "a major reason for Nixon's comparative ignorance of Reagan's potential threat."[65] Yet in fairness to Nixon's political acumen, we have seen how years before he correctly had perceived that Reagan would be the major threat to himself for 1968. And with Nixon having to shore up his support in the three opt-out state primaries by revisiting Wisconsin, Nebraska and Oregon before the voting because of the rapidly ascending Reagan strengths, Nixon knew quite well who his major competitor was.[66]

At the meeting, Nixon would become agitated when he would realize that indeed Wallace would siphon off Southern votes in the general election, so he would ask the Greenville Group who could help him? The answer of course would be Thurmond, who dutifully would fly to Atlanta the next day for an additional meeting with Nixon. Thurmond was set to exact his price.

But before committing his support, during the drive back to the airport, Thurmond suddenly would change subjects with Nixon. "Thurmond delivered a long and frank monologue on what he needed to see in a nominee he could support," and "if that candidate could support him on national defense, he could go along."[67] Witcover admits that there are no confirmatory written notes, but at the Nixon meeting, "Everyone knew the ABM was dear to his heart."[68] A second group of historians reported, "According to authoritative accounts, Nixon's specific promise of support for the development of the ABM system...convinced Thurmond to support his candidacy."[69] A third group of historians declared that for Thurmond to support Nixon and to create an alliance, this was the "clincher."[70] Indeed after their meeting, Nixon would send Thurmond a letter about how impressed he had been about Thurmond's new book.[71]

Since Thurmond would ask Nixon to support the ABM, and this may have been one of the most important prerequisites to Thurmond for his support, it is highly likely that similarly he would have asked Reagan the same question, or at least brought the subject up via Dent, during this earlier Reagan-Dent dinner. If anyone attending the dinner had those recollections, they have not been recorded. If Thurmond brought up the subject with Reagan later, he would have found that they indeed were soulmates on national defense. Reagan would become more involved with the ABM controversy once again a few months later.

Reagan and Rockefeller Breakfast

After the dinner with the Southern Republican leaders, Reagan learned that Governor Rockefeller would be meeting with the same group the next day. Because of the renewed talk about a possible Rockefeller-Reagan "deal" earlier in Hawaii, Reagan did not want to be anywhere near Rockefeller. He told the press that he did not intend to see Rockefeller. But a chance coincidence spoiled Reagan's plans.

The Reagan and Rockefeller staffs had, by chance, arranged that the two likely opponents and unlikely partners were booked at the same hotel, the Roosevelt, on the same day. Reagan did not know it yet, but the forceful actions taken by Republican President Theodore Roosevelt many decades earlier would play an important part in Reagan's thinking later during this trip down South.

And despite Reagan's stated intentions not to meet Rockefeller, Reagan and Rockefeller did meet privately. Rockefeller contacted Nofziger asking to meet Reagan, but Nofziger said, "No."[72] Early the next morning, Rockefeller, unannounced, stopped by Reagan's room. Reagan was annoyed, but he could not turn Rockefeller away. So Reagan let Rockefeller in and the two men chatted briefly. Buchanan reported that when Rockefeller wanted Reagan to join him in an all-out Stop Nixon movement, "Reagan put him off more abruptly."[73] But what seemingly was most important to Reagan to tell the press was not that they discussed the Republican nomination or any thought of a pact between them to stop Nixon. Rather Reagan had chosen to discuss with Rockefeller the candidacy of his nemesis, Robert F. Kennedy.[74]

Both Reagan and Rockefeller did however tell the press platitudes about having discussed problems common to each of their states. Rockefeller emerged from the meeting and told the press that there was "no ideological gulf between them." He said they had discussed mutual problems of big states and, when asked if he had discussed the vice-presidency with Reagan, Rockefeller answered, "I haven't given any thought to a running mate."

When Reagan came out a few minutes later and was asked if he would accept the vice-presidential nomination, he repeated what he had said so many times previously that spring and prior year: "I'm not interested in the second spot,"[75] and further clarified that he disavowed "any interest in running for President" as well.[76] Both men denied the formation of any Rockefeller-Reagan "dream ticket."[77] As noted, it had been Robert Kennedy's recent swing to the political right, which Reagan had seen fit to discuss in the few precious minutes the two men had met.

Then nationally-syndicated humorist Art Buchwald once again aimed his typewriter at the Republicans by devoting an entire column to the Reagan-Rockefeller meeting. He set the scene in the hotel's sixth floor where Rockefeller tip toed down the hotel hallway to knock on Reagan's door. Reagan did not want to let Rockefeller in nor have any contact with him for fear it would like they were making a deal. Buchwald ended the column facetiously by writing that Rockefeller had met Reagan only in order to get an autograph of the former actor for his wife![78]

Buchanan felt the short Reagan-Rockefeller meeting and Reagan's strong rebuff of Rockefeller were further evidence that Reagan was attempting to prove to Nixon that there was no collusion between Reagan and Rockefeller to stop Nixon.[79]

After the early morning bite to eat with Reagan, Rockefeller did meet with Dent's group for a two hour lavish breakfast in the hotel's Rendezvous Room and according to legend attempted to put sugar onto his steak and grits, thereby disqualifying himself.[80] But in reality Rockefeller was not in the running regardless—as Dent had declared beforehand in Greenville.

Louisiana delegation

Given the three-way Nixon vs. Reagan vs. Rockefeller contenders, strange political bedfellows sometimes emerged. In some black areas in Louisiana after the Rockefeller visit, Rockefeller was showing growing strength, and in response, Nixon forces "enlisted Reagan supporters" to squelch it. Nixon representatives ended up calling local registered Republicans and encouraged any Nixon or Reagan supporters to attend the upcoming district conventions. Although this was done to thwart Rockefeller, Reagan forces "got a firm foothold" in the Louisiana delegation. At the same time, Clif White had had an agreement with a Rockefeller delegate hunter, who fed information back to White as to what was going on.[81]

Louisiana had growing delegate strength for Reagan. Morton Blackwell was elected at-large delegate—committed to Reagan for president—as were others from Louisiana. Blackwell and the other Reagan delegates started to convince those uncommitted delegates that Reagan was the GOP's best choice. Blackwell recalled that even before he would depart for Miami Beach, he had obtained commitments from a number of fellow delegates to vote for Reagan on the second ballot.[82]

In D.C.

On May 20, Reagan was to fly to Washington, D.C. for the planned meeting with congressional Republicans. Just before leaving, Reagan met a group of conventioneers from a Georgia automobile association and greeted the crowd warmly, shaking hands with many.[83] Asked by the press how he felt about the South, Reagan answered: "I think the GOP should neither write off nor take for granted the South...I think the Republican Party must come in and...actively seek its votes."[84]

And how was the idea of a possible Rockefeller-Reagan ticket received in the South? One reporter felt, "If Governor Reagan of California has a nucleus of strength in his unannounced campaign for the GOP nomination, it is in the South—And he was careful not to jeopardize it" in New Orleans.[85] But William Murfin, state GOP chairman of Florida, warned that "if Reagan starts playing around with Rockefeller, then he's going to have trouble in Florida."[86] And with all the Rockefeller and Reagan intrigue in New Orleans over the past day, Harry Dent added: "Our delegates like this man Reagan, but they're in love with Nixon."[87] Others would feel the opposite.

At his press conference after landing in Washington D.C., Reagan hit RFK again about his recent apparent swing to the right: "Bobby Kennedy in California is campaigning on the Barry Goldwater platform." Then after being asked about what he thought of Kennedy as the nominee, he continued his thoughts of the prior day when he had questioned whether Kennedy's recent statements---favoring the free enterprise system and admitting that big government had failed— would be remembered by Kennedy later on. A reporter then asked Reagan what he thought of the upcoming Democratic primary race in California on June 4. Reagan explained that President Johnson's name still technically was on the ballot even though he had dropped out of the race. With the remaining names listed as Eugene McCarthy,

Hubert Humphrey, and RFK, Reagan opined, "This is a very mixed up race out there and I think Bobby Kennedy could very likely take it and be the winner with 30% of the vote."[88]

The reporters returned again to ask Reagan about Kennedy's recent speeches. To let other reporters understand what he had just been asked, Reagan paraphrased a reporter's question saying he just was asked if I thought Kennedy "was speaking with a forked tongue saying one thing to the poor people and one thing to the business people," explaining further that he found it inconsistent that Kennedy was pledging to triple or quadruple some social security payments but at the same time admitting the failure of big government to solve social problems. Quipped Reagan, "If this marks true conversion, I'll be the first to hold out a hand to welcome him to our ranks."[89]

Reagan denounced a group of student demonstrators who were protesting the Institute for Defense Analysis, a Pentagon strategy advisor. Reagan was about to deliver two more White Papers including his major address on defense policy in Cleveland in two days and thus was well attuned to these issues. He deplored "eliminating this legitimate participation by the academic community in our national security."[90] Reagan had faced similar questioning about ties between academic and military institutions when he had been at Yale for his Chubb fellowship six months earlier.

Reagan met with 18 Republican senators and eight Republican representatives for lunch in a Senate conference room. Senator Tower, who had asked Reagan to change his travel plans in order to attend the gathering, said that the conservative group was "uncommitted," and afterwards Reagan told the press that the group had discussed "national issues."[91]

At his press conference at the Rayburn House Office Building, his second on Capitol Hill in four months, Reagan "depreciated the significance" of a recent poll showing Nixon a 56 percent favorite amongst California voters.[92] He reiterated that his touring was "simply to help Republican fund raising efforts."[93] Reagan prepared to leave the nation's capital to meet one of his most ardent supporters, a young congressman from North Carolina, Jim Gardner.

Congressman Gardner

Jim Gardner, at age 80 so busy still in Republican Party politics in 2013 that he had to postpone an interview with your author because of important work in the state capital with North Carolina's new Republican governor, recalled that although he grew up in a non-political atmosphere at home, after he had started a fast-food restaurant business for himself in 1961 in Rocky Mount and then had joined the junior chamber of commerce, he started to see that Democratic policies were wrong. He and several other businessmen went to hear Barry Goldwater speak and were so taken by Goldwater's words that all ten, all registered Democrats—because at that time "there was almost no Republican Party in North Carolina,"—went to the county seat and told the clerk that they wanted to change their party registration.[94] The clerk asked, "What do you mean?" and when they answered that they all wanted to change to Republican, she "looked at them like they were crazy."[95] They were sent to the county chairman, who asked the men why they wanted to change and they said they just did. The administrator did change their registration but Gardner recalled he "couldn't even spell the name Republican."[96]

Gardner then had formed the county Republican Party. At age 29, he was asked to run against a powerful multi-term Democrat congressman who was the chairman of the House Agriculture Committee. Gardner's entire family thought he was crazy, but with the support of his business partner, they raised money and campaigned and received fully 48 percent of the vote. Gardner went to his opponent's campaign victory and venue and when he stuck out his hand to congratulate the victor, Gardner's Democrat opponent—the victor—would not shake his hand. At that instant Gardner knew he would run again. Gardner's near victory so terrified the Democrat-controlled legislature in Raleigh that they gerrymandered Gardner's district by removing the two counties that Gardner had won.

Gardner became state Republican chairman, the first time an eastern North Carolinian was so honored as previously the party, what little there was, had been based out of Charlotte in the west. In 1966, political newcomer Gardner won decisively by a 13-point margin and went to Congress the same year as Ronald Reagan first had been elected to public office.

In 1968 Gardner was running for governor, and despite having felt some loyalty to Richard Nixon who had traveled to North Carolina to help in 1966, Gardner wanted to see if Reagan would come to help. Gardner had followed Reagan's political career since Reagan had become governor, so he contacted Reagan's office. Gardner and North Carolina were made part of Reagan's Southern Solicitation.

North Carolina

Winston-Salem was Reagan's first stop in North Carolina, recalled Gardner. Gardner planned to have a rally at Wake Forest University's coliseum, which seated 6,000 people plus a fund-raiser. At the airport, Gardner recalled, "I can't even describe the excitement" when Reagan greeted the crowd.[97] Reagan did a "fantastic job" at the coliseum and then the group went to the fund-raiser. Between venues at a private meeting, Clif White told Gardner, "We think Nixon's support is very thin…Would you support us?…Would you fly down to Miami with the governor?…We want to test the waters down there."[98] Gardner answered, "Absolutely!"[99]

Reagan arrived at the Charlotte airport on May 20 to a welcoming crowd of 200 people armed with "'Reagan for President' banners and placards."[100] Charlotte was where in his speeches he was to be most derisive of Kennedy. At the airport rally he again addressed Kennedy's new-found conservatism by telling the crowd, "The junior Senator from New York, what he's saying now in this election year doesn't match very well his voting record in the Senate."[101]

At the White House Inn, he addressed a crowd of 400 who had paid $25-a-plate to see him.[102] Reagan shared the dais with Gardner.[103] His attacks on Kennedy's turn right continued, saying that Kennedy had "picked up Barry Goldwater's old speeches."[104] Reagan did some historical reflecting next. Decades earlier, Reagan had been taken by Franklin Roosevelt's 1932 speech which, unbelievable as it sounds given the massive expansion of the federal government that then ensued, had called for smaller government. Reagan had become an FDR Democrat based on that unfulfilled speech, and he reflected ruefully that Republicans in 1968 could run on that same 1932 speech in which FDR had promised to "return the constitutional authority to the states," to "reduce federal spending by 25 percent," and "to do more to reduce the size of government and give more freedom to individual people."[105] Whether Reagan idolized FDR, as historian Doug Brinkley and others have felt, will be discussed later in the context of the Eisenhower-Reagan relationship.

At a press conference at the Inn, he joked about the name of the Inn, saying he could always see he had slept at the White House![106] Reagan predicted that for the first time in decades, the convention would be "multiple ballot…before the decision is made."[107] Clearly the long-ago plans of Reagan and his team were at last being revealed to the public and here was the mechanism by which Reagan hoped to win in Miami Beach.

Reagan then told the press that he would not be surprised if Johnson just would resign so that Humphrey could run in the fall as an incumbent.[108] Saying, "There's a very good chance the ticket on the other side could be Humphrey and Kennedy," Reagan felt that Humphrey had three factors going for him that would lead to his win over Kennedy: the South, big labor, and the power of the administration.[109]

The *New York Times* commented that in Charlotte, Reagan's "most pungent remarks of the day were focused on…Senator Robert F. Kennedy." [110] Reagan ended his North Carolina campaign stops noting that many Kennedy family members were in California campaigning on behalf of RFK. Reagan specifically noted that the family matriarch Rose Kennedy was there responding to criticism about how much money their family was spending on the campaign by answering her critics that it was their money and they were free to spend it as they chose. Reagan added that he had no problem how the Kennedys chose to spend their own money but rather was concerned that what "I'm worried about is the way they want to spend ours!"[111]

Reagan then flew off further south to Florida, and now was accompanied by Gardner. On the flight, Gardner sat with Reagan, Reed and White; White told him "We're gonna take a run at this thing."[112] Gardner was asked to second Reagan's name being placed in nomination at the convention.[113]

Before Reagan had arrived in Florida, Rockefeller, who had had his private New Orleans breakfast meeting—the sugar on the grits episode, immediately had flown to Florida seeking support. But Rockefeller was in for a rude awakening. Although he did meet with Governor Claude Kirk in Tallahassee, Rockefeller then "received a snub from three top Florida Republicans," when State GOP Chairman William Murfin, Congressman Ed Gurney and William Cramer all "said they had more pressing business elsewhere."[114] Rockefeller held a joint press conference with O'Donnell, but the questions focused on Reagan. When O'Donnell said, "I think we'll have an open convention at Miami and the decision on a nominee will be made there," the press interpreted the comment indicating, "Neither Rockefeller nor Reagan swayed many" of the Southern state chairmen.[115] A follow-up questioner asked if the situation was still fluid, and O'Donnell answered, "I think a majority of the delegates will go in uncommitted."[116]

If this were true, then Reagan still had time to add another new strategy for the presidential campaign besides the attacks on likely general-election opponent Kennedy. Although all along Clif White had been hunting for delegates, if despite the Southern party leaders' probable support for Nixon, the delegates themselves possibly could be swayed individually, then there still was time. But time was running short.

When asked what he thought Reagan's overall position was, Rockefeller answered, "I would say under pressure of a draft he would be available."[117] Rockefeller told the press that he did not see "any ideological gulf" between himself and Reagan on the direction "the Republican Party should take."[118] This may have been partially true when both men had spoken for *Mr. Lincoln's Party Today* in 1962. But certainly in 1968, with big-government Rockefeller and small-government Reagan, and dovish Rockefeller on Vietnam versus hawkish Reagan, this was no longer true.

Fourth White Paper

Compared to Rockefeller's disastrous reception in the Sunshine State, Reagan was about to experience cheering crowds eager to see him as president. He flew on to Fort Lauderdale later in the day on that busy May 20 and was greeted by a supportive airport rally. The first comments he made were about Robert Kennedy. He questioned again Kennedy's inconsistencies saying, "The junior senator from New York, what he's saying now in this election year, doesn't match very well his voting record in the Senate." His brief airport appearance ended as he joked with a well-wisher who asked Reagan if he could keep Bobby Kennedy out of California.[119]

To the airport crowd of more than 500 who cheered him, Reagan declared, "If Vietnam is a symbol of the foreign policy of this administration, and Newark and Detroit are symbols of the domestic policy of this administration, then you and I have been pouring our money down a rathole."[120]

Then off to Tampa, Reagan's speech onslaught against Kennedy continued with *Atlantic and Caribbean Foreign Policy* late on May 20. Reagan reviewed President Kennedy's foreign policy on Cuba from the Bay of Pigs fiasco through the Cuban Missile Crisis, and Reagan detailed how Kennedy had not acted when the CIA first had reported the Soviet missile buildup during the summer of 1962.[121] Reagan "decried the fact" that only after the U-2's photographs were analyzed—conveniently only "a few weeks before the mid-term elections"—had Kennedy acted.[122] The *Los Angeles Times* told the public that Reagan had cut clearly through to the heart of the matter by "saving some of his sharpest barbs for Sen. Robert F. Kennedy."[123]

On May 21, Reagan and Reed met with Fort Lauderdale and Miami area financial supporters.[124] At his first press conference, Reagan complained about domestic policies that had been established by a "little collection of intellectuals" back East, which claimed it knew better how individuals should run their lives than the individuals themselves.[125] But Reagan's big guns were aimed at foreign policies of the Kennedy-Johnson years.

In Miami on the same day, Reagan began by protesting at the humiliating treatment of the *U.S.S. Pueblo*. With background information likely garnered from Eisenhower, Reagan reminded the public that in World War II, the allies had mined Haiphong Harbor—successfully against the Japanese—via 43 mines, as it was a shallow-draft harbor, with the unstated but obvious conclusion that the harbor should have been mined a long time ago. He again wanted to threaten the North Vietnamese that the war should be fought on their land for a change.

Then as he had done during the Kennedy debate exactly one year earlier, Reagan again called for wise bargaining with the communists. Rather than offering free gifts, once again in public Reagan wanted to see a huge major Soviet concession. As historian Paul Kengor noted, Reagan once again offered: "If Russia needs our wheat to satisfy the hunger of her people…the wheat could be delivered easier if there were no Berlin Wall."[126]

Reagan also held another press conference, where he was asked about what he had promised the press before the campaign trip had begun, namely that he had wanted to assess the grass roots efforts that had been created to see him elected president. Asked what his assessment was, Reagan reviewed that White's earlier statement—about increasing grass roots support for Reagan across the country—had caught him by surprise and he was going to assess it. He told the press in Miami that even though he had seen very enthusiastic crowds at every stop over the past few days in the South, "It would be awfully easy to delude yourself into thinking that there was something there that wasn't."[127]

Reagan and his team left Florida and flew off to Chicago for a brief stop with financial backers.[128] Then it was off to Ohio for a short governors conference and to deliver his fifth White Paper.

Endnotes

1.   Chester et. al., p. 189
2.   Dent, p. 80
3.   Large, Arlan, ""Reagan on the Road," *WSJ*, 5/22/68, p. 1
4.   ibid
5.   Atkinson, Paul, "Rocky, Reagan" unidentified newspaper article, 5/20/1968, Omaha Nebraska Public Library File on 1968 Presidential Election
6.   Kengor, p. 36
7.   Greenburg, Carl, "Reagan 'No' Is Too Mild to Suit Nixon Fashion," *LA Times*, 4/1/68
8.   Chester et. al., p. 189
9.   ibid
10. ibid
11. "Parley Deadline Urged," *NYT*, 5/19/68, p. 47

12. Buchwald, Art, "Well, Somebody Ought to Threaten to Kick Somebody," *Seattle Times*, 5/30/68, p. 12
13. Hill, Gladwin, "New Reagan Tour Will Begin Today," *NYT*, 5/19/68, p. 47
14. ibid
15. Large, Arlan, "Reagan on the Road," *WSJ*, 5/22/68, p. 1
16. Reed, *Reagan Enigma*, p. 154
17. Hill, Gladwyn, "Reagan Condemns College Protests," *NYT*, 5/20/68, p. 39
18. RRL, Tape 342
19. ibid
20. Ross, p. 289
21. ibid
22. ibid
23. ibid
24. RRL, Tape 342
25. www.pbs.org/wgbh/pages/frontline/newt/interviews.html
26. Hill, Gladwyn, "Reagan Condemns College Protests," *NYT*, 5/20/68, p. 39
27. ibid
28. ibid
29. Hill, ibid
30. Reed, p. 24
31. RRL, Tape 342
32. ibid
33. Reed, *Reagan Enigma*, p. 155
34. See Illustrations
35. Hill, ibid
36. Hill, ibid
37. Dent, p. 79
38. Perlstein, Rick, "The Southern Strategist," *NYT Magazine*, 12/30/2007
39. Dent, p. 79
40. ibid
41. ibid
42. Dent, p. 80
43. ibid
44. Chester et. al., p. 439
45. Chester et. al., p. 439-440
46. ibid
47. Reed, pers comm., 10/20/13
48. Dent, p. 80
49. Dent, p. 80
50. Chester et. al., p. 445
51. Reed, pers comm., 10/20/13
52. Dent, p. 80
53. Reed, *Reagan Enigma*, p. 155
54. Dent, p. 80
55. Bass and Thompson, p. 224
56. Large, Arlan, "Reagan on the Road," *WSJ*, 5/22/68, p. 1
57. Reed, pers comm., 10/20/13
58. Chester et. al., p. 444
59. ibid
60. Thurmond, p. vi
61. Thurmond, p. 70-71
62. Thurmond, p. 71-72
63. Witcover, p. 310; Chester et. al., p. 447
64. Chester et. al., p. 446
65. Chester et. al., p. 446
66. Kopelson, Gene. 2014D
67. Witcover, p. 310
68. ibid
69. Skinner, Kudela, et. al., p. 70
70. Chester et. al., p. 447
71. Skinner, p. 70
72. Buchanan, p. 235
73. Buchanan, p. 236
74. Hill, Gladwin, "Reagan Derides Kennedy Stands," *NYT*, 5/21/68, p. 29
75. "Reagan, Rockefeller Confer," *Seattle Times*, 5/20/68, p. 9

76. Atkinson, Paul, "Rocky, Reagan" unidentified newspaper article, 5/20/1968, Omaha Nebraska Public Library File on 1968 Presidential Election
77. ibid
78. Buchwald, Art, "When Rockefeller called on Reagan in New Orleans," *Seattle Times*, 5/26/68, p. 12
79. Buchanan, p. 236
80. Dent, p. 81
81. Chester et. al., p. 440-441
82. Blackwell, Morton, personal communication 11/19/2015
83. Atkinson, op.cit.
84. Atkinson, ibid
85. Gould, Geoffrey, "'Supreme Ticket' Far from Reality" unidentified newspaper article, 5/22/68 sec 1 p. 2, Omaha Nebraska Public Library File on 1968 Presidential Campaign
86. Gould, ibid
87. Gould, ibid
88. RRL, Tape 342
89. Hill, Gladwin, "Reagan Derides Kennedy Stands," *NYT*, 5/21/68, p. 29
90. Corrigan, Richard, "Reagan Stars in Screen Test," *Washington Post*, 5/26/68, p. A8
91. Hill, Gladwin, "Reagan Derides Kennedy Stands," *NYT*, 5/21/68, p. 29
92. ibid
93. ibid
94. Gardner, pers int, 3/27/13
95. ibid
96. ibid
97. ibid
98. ibid
99. ibid
100. Hill, Gladwin, "Reagan Derides Kennedy Stand," *NYT*, 5/21/68, p. 29
101. RRL, Tape 342
102. Hill, ibid
103. See Illustrations
104. RRL, Tape 342
105. RRL, Tape 342
106. RRL, Tape 342
107. RRL, Tape 342
108. RRL, Tape 342
109. ibid
110. Hill, Gladwin, "Reagan Derides Kennedy Stands," *NYT*, 5/21/68, p. 29
111. RRL, Tape 342
112. Gardner, pers int 3/27/2013
113. Reed, *The Reagan Enigma*, p. 156
114. Atkinson, Paul, op.cit.
115. Atkinson, Paul, op.cit.
116. ibid
117. Atkinson, op.cit.
118. Atkinson, op.cit.
119. Hill, Gladwin, "Reagan Derides Kennedy Stands," *NYT*, 5/21/68, p. 29
120. Large, Arlan, "Reagan on the Road," *WSJ*, 5/22/68, op.cit., p. 1
121. Reed, *The Reagan Enigma*, p. 156
122. Reed, *The Reagan Enigma*, p. 24
123. Reed, *The Reagan Enigma*, p. 156
124. Reagan-Reed, 5/12/1968
125. RRL, Tape 342
126. Kengor, p. 36
127. RRL, Tape 342
128. Reagan-Reed, 5/12/1968

"Many were closer to going with Reagan, the noncandidate."
~ Harry Dent[1]

Reagan did a "candidate-like job of slashing at the Democrats' foreign policy and defense spending...Reagan had all the trappings of a man at least willing to let the lightning strike him, if the Republican Party aims it in his direction."
~ *Cleveland Plain Dealer*[2]

Landing in Columbus, Reagan and his team met with Ohio Governor Jim Rhodes, and Rhodes continued to be viewed as a likely choice for Reagan's running mate.[3] But what bothered the Reagan team was not the thought of a Reagan-Rhodes ticket. It was the pairing that Eisenhower had disliked so greatly and which never seemed to be able to be swatted down: a Rockefeller-Reagan ticket. Then Reagan was off to Cleveland.

The persistent rumors of collusion between Rockefeller and Reagan not only did not disappear, they intensified. On May 22, Reagan landed at Cleveland's Burke Lakefront Airport and saw a sign: "Reagan-Yes. Rocky-Reagan No." Reagan assured the crowd with, "You can quit carrying that sign. I'm not going to make a deal with anyone."[4]

At an outdoor downtown rally, Governor Reagan was greeted by many large banners and signs of welcome from the local Croatian American communities in the region. Reagan's relationships with this group of Americans of Croatian descent, who yearned for freedom in the land of their fathers, will be explored shortly. At the rally, Reagan again distanced himself from Rockefeller by saying that Rockefeller turned "more to government to solve our problems."[5]

Then came Reagan's piece de resistance—the hard work since eight weeks earlier when RFK's announcement had sent shock waves through the Reagan campaign and Reagan had regained full control and reenergized his campaign. Reagan's many hours of work on perfecting his five White paper speeches would now culminate in his final attack on his likely Democratic opponent in the fall general election.

Reagan's final white paper, *Defense Preparedness*, was given in front of 2,300 Republicans at a $150-per-plate dinner at the Cleveland Sheraton. Afterwards Reagan would speak briefly to 2,000 people at a rally at Public Square, and then later at a $1,000 per person private cocktail reception.[6]

Reagan's speech would be reprinted and distributed by Bubb's Topeka center.[7] Reagan was set to deliver an even more nuanced and detailed critique of the Kennedy-Johnson years than he had delivered six months earlier in Albany, Oregon. Reagan was about to mention his mentor, Eisenhower, fully five times in the speech.

Reagan began by attacking John Kennedy's repeated false accusations in 1960 of a supposed missile gap that Eisenhower supposedly had allowed to develop. Reagan informed his audience of the flourishing partnership between industry and the American military during the Eisenhower years. All the truly commanding revolutionary weapon systems in America's inventory, which were without precedent in history—including ballistic missiles, miniaturized nuclear warheads, reconnaissance satellites, nuclear submarines, over-the-horizon radar and supersonic jets—"were all developed or brought forward during the eight Eisenhower years."

Reagan lambasted the neglect during the Kennedy-Johnson years, to such a point that America was powerless when the *U.S.S. Pueblo* had been captured. Reagan brought up the incompetence associated with the capture, saying that the Americans had been unable to respond because, "the only fighter-bombers in striking distance were equipped only for a nuclear response."[8] Johnson's only solution was to offer a ransom because the American military was unable to respond to the capture.

Reagan then had his chance to summarize in public what his private mentoring by Eisenhower had taught him. Reagan said things were different a few years back under the strong but steady leadership of Eisenhower. "Twice during the eight years when Eisenhower directed the strategy, menacing Soviet movements against Berlin were disposed of without the call up of a single reinforcement, simply by a show of calm, unwavering resolution." Then Reagan cited Eisenhower's firm stand when Communist China had threatened the off-shore islands of Quemoy and Matsu. Reagan remembered, "A voice spoke in our nation's capital—with a tone we haven't heard for too long a time. Dwight D. Eisenhower said: 'They'll have to climb over the Seventh Fleet to do it.'" Reagan reminded his listeners that Ike had given Nationalist China the Sidewinder missile for its defense. He cited Eisenhower's firm stand against the Soviet thrust toward Syria and Lebanon when he brought American forces to the region. And when twice the Soviets menaced Berlin, Eisenhower had shown calm, unwavering resoluteness. Reagan contrasted Eisenhower's record with the Kennedy-Johnson failure in Vietnam. Reagan denounced Khrushchev's "contemptuous raising of the wall around Berlin."[9] As he had done in the RFK debate and in Albany, Oregon, and in Miami, Reagan again pushed loudly and clearly to tear down that wall.

Reagan concluded by warning of the Democratic administration's own report that the Soviets were succeeding in a "massive drive toward strategic military superiority," just as the United States was slowing down due to Kennedy-Johnson policies. The Soviets were achieving nuclear parity in 1968 and that the true missile gap—of U.S. *superiority* in the Eisenhower years—had been allowed to close during the Kennedy-Johnson years. Due to mismanagement of the Kennedy-Johnson years, a true missile gap—now about to favor the communists—"has become a reality."[10]

The *Cleveland Plain Dealer* reported that Reagan's charges were the "strongest assault made" so far by Reagan, who was seen clearly as "a man on the stump seeking popular support." Vietnam was "whipped...as a key issue." Reagan did a "candidate-like job of slashing at the Democrats' foreign policy and defense spending... Reagan had all the trappings of a man at least willing to let the lightning strike him, if the Republican Party aims it in his direction."[11]

With the Oregon primary only two days away, *The Oregonian* noted that Reagan had handled all press conference questions "nimbly," and if after a long hot summer and a possible convention deadlock between Nixon and Rockefeller, "If that is what Republican delegates wanted, he is inviting that lightning."[12]

Reagan and his team flew back to California to await the results of Oregon. Meanwhile his campaign swing into the South was analyzed by both the *New York Times* and the *Wall Street Journal*. The former reported that after some 7,000 miles of travel, Reagan and the members of his team "wore satisfied smiles" as they landed in California.[13] Reagan had raised $750,000 for Republican coffers during his April-May campaign swing but more importantly, it had "brought off smoothly a major transition in the 57-year old state executive's political stance."[14] Almost imperceptibly, Reagan had changed from the "man from California to the man bound for Miami Beach."[15] Just as Reagan and his team had wanted, because of the

Kennedy announcement and the resultant new campaign plan in place, Reagan was no longer retelling his accomplishments in Sacramento, important as they had been. Rather now Reagan was using the "common sense" approach to national and international problems.[16] Reporter Hill did not know that Reagan's use of "common sense" had originated with the careful political instructions Eisenhower had first given Reagan some three years before. Reagan had succeeded in changing the entire thrust of the campaign. World affairs now had become the major thrust and theme of the campaign. Reagan, the world statesman, was telling America and the world what to expect from a Reagan presidency. But would the voters join Reagan?

Reporter Hill, who was part of the Reagan press entourage and had accompanied Reagan throughout the grueling trip, had noted the audiences which were "under thickets of placards and banners reading 'Reagan for President,' 'Reagan in '68,' and 'We Want Ronnie.'"[17] And then Reagan no longer said, "I am not a candidate," but "shifted his theme" to declaring that he would refrain from declaring his candidacy until the point when his name would be placed in nomination as California's favorite son.[18]

And when the combined crowd of some 15,000 in Charlotte and Fort Lauderdale and Miami Beach and the other stops he had made heard this, the crowds "responded with enthusiastic applause punctuated by cheers, yells and standing ovations."[19]

So here for sure was that support from the people that Reagan was awaiting. Reagan had received the same tumultuous enthusiastic cheers and applause when he was awakened after delivering The Speech in 1964; he got the same calls for him to run for president in Seattle in 1966, in Eugene and Omaha and at Kansas State and at Corvallis and Albany and Hiram Scott College and at Yale in 1967.

Hill noted that the crowds had reflected the activities of "local fund raising groups," as well as with the help of Henry Bubb's Citizens for Reagan National Information Center in Topeka. And Reagan's initial strategy of "eschewing open candidacy, and of stepping on the toes of no one already in the race" had gained him "cordial entrance" into the highest echelons of party councils.[20]

Reagan had changed officially into an announced, open candidate for the presidency. Yet despite reporter Hill's assessment of the apparent change, Reagan had been telling everyone who had asked him that he would indeed be a candidate—a favorite son candidate. That was the whole rationale for not withdrawing his name from the ballots in the three opt-out states. And it was the same approval that Eisenhower had given to Reagan: he was indeed to be a candidate for the presidency as California's favorite son. So had anything really changed?

But not only was Reagan an announced candidate. He was a statesman on the world stage—a plausible future president now espousing difficult policy decisions ranging from Vietnam to Cuba to Berlin.

The *Wall Street Journal* reporter had similar reflections after the trip. Reagan's trip to the South was "Presidential in trappings and timing."[21] At this point in the campaign, Reagan was "most menaced" by Nixon. The plan still was to "prevent a first ballot nomination for Mr. Nixon," and then a deadlock between Rockefeller and Nixon would "turn the convention to Gov. Reagan."[22] Reagan's trip to the South "made a hit with conservative Southerners," who still feared Nixon's image as a loser.[23] Then Charlton Lyons, former state chairman in Louisiana, managed to say the exact opposite of what Harry Dent had professed so recently: "Our Republicans are for Nixon, all right, but they love Reagan."[24] Unfortunately for Reagan, whether it was Dent or Lyons, in the end the support was still going for Nixon. Lyons concluded by saying that the Louisiana delegation "probably will go uncommitted" to Miami Beach.[25] So there was still hope and time to try to sway delegates to Reagan. And Jim Gardner started work on convincing his North Carolina delegation that it wasn't "Nixon's the One" but "Reagan's the One."

Antidote to Wallace

Segregationist Democrat and third-party candidate Wallace still had strong support in the South, and there was continued speculation that the third party vote for him could throw the general election, if Rockefeller or Nixon were at the top of the ticket, into the House of Representatives. Reagan was seen as the only candidate who could "chop Wallace back to size" as he was the "natural Republican antidote to Wallace."[26] Thus speculation about Reagan as vice-president under Rockefeller continued. Of course those analyzing that possibility failed to realize that since Reagan was the antidote to Wallace, then Reagan could just as well be at the top of the ticket.

Nixon in Atlanta

Two weeks after Reagan and Rockefeller had met with Dent's group of Southern Republican state chairmen in New Orleans, Nixon met with the group in Atlanta, as discussed briefly earlier. The Nixon staff had been convinced that the South was his, but Dent recalled, "They were incorrect. At that time, many were closer to going with Reagan, the noncandidate."[27] So Reagan's failure to ask for their support forcefully in New Orleans had not been a fatal mistake after all.

Dent held an initial meeting with Nixon, his new campaign manager John Mitchell, and advisor H.R. Haldeman, at which Nixon said his prime goal as president would be to appoint "conservative appointments only."[28] Nixon did well at this preliminary meeting, so Dent called Senator Thurmond, who flew to Atlanta for the second meeting with Nixon the following morning. It was at this meeting where Thurmond had asked Nixon about missile defense, as mentioned earlier. But Thurmond had other items to discuss with Nixon too.

Dent recalled that Thurmond was "particularly pleased" at what Nixon repeated about the Supreme Court nominees.[29] On the question of the vice-presidency, Nixon declared that he did not want to balance the ticket philosophically but would "seek someone who would share his philosophy."[30]

Nixon and Thurmond rode to the airport together, but Dent claimed that no "sinister deals" had been made.[31] Yet the deal that sealed it for Nixon was his pledge to Thurmond that his running mate would be "acceptable to all sections of the Party," meaning that Thurmond had veto power over Nixon's choice.[32] The Southerners within the Republican Party were now "calling the tune."[33] Thurmond would go to Miami Beach "fully committed" to Nixon.[34]

In his autobiography *RN*, Nixon told a completely different tale of what had transpired with Thurmond and Dent. Nixon wrote that he was the one who had invited Thurmond, that Thurmond's main concern was that America be the first in the world militarily (Nixon mentioned nothing about missile defense specifically), and the second criteria was that Thurmond had wanted tariffs to protect South Carolina against textile imports.[35] Clearly, just as some eighteen minutes of tape had been erased from Nixon's secretary's tape recording of Watergate, apparently critical meetings that garnered for Nixon the 1968 nomination were erased in his mind too. But one item Nixon did not fake in his memoirs: Thurmond's pledge of support "would become a valuable element in my ability to thwart any moves by Reagan on my right."[36]

As a result of the two meetings, Thurmond, as well as a "majority of the southern chairmen," decided to go with Nixon, as had Tower previously.[37] Dent called Tom Reed with the news about the decision of the Southerners, in the hopes that Reagan would "follow suit and join in a Nixon bandwagon."[38]

Reed and Reagan, having settled back in California after the fifth White Paper, awaited the results of the Oregon primary.

Endnotes

1. Dent, p. 81
2. "Reagan Not Running But Ready," *Cleveland Plain Dealer*, 5/23/68
3. Reed, *The Reagan Enigma*, p. 156
4. "Rocky's Name Haunts Reagan on Stop Here," *Cleveland Plain Dealer*, 5/23/68
5. "Reagan Not Running But Ready," *Cleveland Plain Dealer*, 5/23/68
6. Naughton, James, "JFK's 'Missile Gap' Now Exists---Reagan," *Cleveland Plain Dealer*, 5/23/68, p. 1
7. Reagan, Ronald, "Defense Preparedness", 5/22/68, reprinted by Citizens for Reagan National Information Center, Topeka, Henry A. Bubb, Chairman
8. ibid
9. Kengor, p. 36
10. Naughton op.cit.; Reagan op.cit.
11. "Reagan Not Running But Ready," *Cleveland Plain Dealer*, 5/23/68
12. "Reagan Caps 4-State Swing By Attacking Demo Defense Record," *The Oregonian*, 5/23/68, p. 7
13. Hill, Gladwin, "'I Am Not a Candidate' Stance Dropped by Reagan on His Tour," *NYT*, 5/24/68, p. 16
14. ibid
15. ibid
16. ibid
17. ibid
18. ibid
19. ibid
20. ibid
21. Large, Arlen, "Reagan on the Road," *WSJ*, 5/22/68, p. 1
22. ibid
23. ibid
24. ibid
25. ibid
26. Cunningham, Ross, "Wallace May Force Unlikely GOP Ticket," *Seattle Times*, 5/26/68, p. 12
27. Dent, p. 81
28. Dent, p. 82
29. ibid
30. ibid
31. ibid
32. Perlstein, op.cit.
33. ibid
34. Bass and Thompson, p. 225
35. Nixon, p. 304-305
36. Nixon, p. 305
37. ibid
38. Dent, p. 83

CHAPTER 29: OREGON—MAY 28, 1968

"There is a snowball here. We don't know whether it will evaporate when the heat is put on it—but we are going to try and roll it!"

~ Fred Van Natta[1]

"In Oregon he was faced with real opposition from the Reagan forces."

~ Theodore H. White[2]

Reagan was "the only candidate who can unite the Republican Party and defeat the New York Senator."

~ Robert Hazen[3]

"The nation's first all-television" campaign.

~ Tom Wicker[4]

"We're not against using Kennedy money for the Reagan campaign."

~ Oscar Funk[5]

"Reagan Tops Kennedy in Pre-Primary Tiff."

~ *Siuslaw News*[6]

When Reagan had been in Hawaii at the governors conference and had commented on his surprise 22 percent plurality in Nebraska, Oregon Governor Tom McCall had stood next to Reagan and invited him to come north to campaign in Oregon. Politely, Reagan had refused. Whether to campaign in Oregon in 1968 was not an easy decision for Reagan or for Reed.

The major issues which encapsulated the dilemmas facing Reagan in the critical Oregon primary were asked of him in four cogent and precise questions when he would appear on NBC's *Face the Nation* on May 26, just prior to the primary. Reagan was in Burbank and panelist Lawrence E Spivak was in the program's Washington, D.C.

studio.[7] The show's moderator, Edwin Newman, observed, "Reagan-for-President activity continues across the country."

Spivak asked if there were any chance Reagan would announce his candidacy before the Oregon primary? Reagan replied, "There will be no change in my present position...nor have I any plans for going to Oregon." And would he announce before the convention? Reagan answered, No." Spivak asked why a voter in Oregon should vote for him, and Reagan mused, "I don't know that I would have any answer. I have said repeatedly this is to be an open convention. I believe that the grass roots Republican sentiment is for waiting until the convention when all the issues are in, all the information is in, then a decision is going to be made on. I believe a great factor will be the winnability of the candidate. And I would think that part of the factors would be the sentiment of the grassroots, and if someone should be voting on the basis of what he actually believes, he has to be voting his own conscience." And when asked if and why he wanted to win in Oregon, Reagan replied, "No, let me simply say those people in Oregon, who have been doing this on their own, a few of them came over to see me in Idaho where I was speaking a short time ago. They told me they would be gratified by fifteen percent of the vote. Because of the fact that I was not campaigning, and they were doing this on their own. I would have to be frank and say this. Naturally anyone would be gratified and very proud to find that a sizable group of citizens held him in that regard. Also I would have to say that anytime you are injected into a contest in this way, in this business, it has a bearing on my own job here in California....For that reason, for pride alone, make me now that I have been injected in the race, want to at least hold my head up." And finally, when asked why he continued to deny he was a candidate despite all the grass roots activity across the nation, Reagan answered, "Because I am not. I have no intention of declaring. I am not campaigning."[8]

To potential Oregon Republican voters, and to those hard-working grass roots Reagan campaigner workers, some of whom had been working for Reagan for a year and a half, these must have been discouraging comments indeed. After all, Reagan had competition in Oregon, and during the spring of 1968, in-person visits were planned by Nixon, Romney, Rockefeller and even Rockefeller stand-in John Lindsay, mayor of New York City.[9]

Yet Reagan's answers were consistent with the tightrope walking Reagan had been doing for a year and a half: denying in public that he was a true candidate, acknowledging that he would be a favorite-son candidate from California, yet knowing that his behind-the-scenes presidential campaign was gaining steam with the growing sequential votes in Wisconsin and then in Nebraska.

The greatest effort in the 1968 Reagan-for-President campaign took place in Oregon. Many of those important participants are still alive today in 2012-2016 to tell this history, which has not been told until today.[10] The hard work on behalf of Reagan, his boots on the ground, came from the loyal grass roots activists who wanted to see a President-Elect Ronald Reagan in 1968.

Oregon was the last of the three "opt-out" primary campaign states.[11] As in Wisconsin and Nebraska, the Oregon opt-out law forced the secretary of state to put all "serious presidential candidates" on the ballot.[12] Thus those seeking the presidency had to compete in Oregon. Republicans were choosing eighteen total convention delegates, in which voters were asked to pick ten at-large state delegates and then to choose two more delegates in each congressional district. However a candidate could sign an affidavit stating that he wished to have his name withdrawn because he was not in fact running for president. Reagan, as planned from the start of the campaign, had availed himself of this potential conflict. Because he was a favorite son candidate from California, he could not sign the Oregon withdrawal affidavit for fear of perjury.[13]

Oregon was the third leg, actually the lynch-pin, in Reagan's master plan. Before the Oregon primary, the plan had succeeded---"a noticeable showing in Wisconsin—with no campaign; a better-than-expected result in Nebraska—with only local support." And Oregon would be the finishing triumph: "a victory in California's neighboring Oregon."[14] But long before the Oregon primary approached, Reed's initial lofty hope of a victory had been tamped down to the expectation of bettering the percentage achieved in Nebraska. Reagan needed his biggest grass roots team in Oregon.

Don Hodel

In early 1967, young attorney Don Hodel had been chairman of the Oregon Republican Party. In October, 1964 when he had been secretary of the Clackamas County Republican Central Committee and liaison to the state Goldwater campaign, he had watched, on television, Reagan deliver The Speech. Hodel recalled, "It resonated with me tremendously."[15]

In 1967, the Oregon Republican Party was still "a state divided along Rockefeller-Goldwater lines from four years earlier."[16] Because the state party was in such disarray, the "lowly position" of state chairman was "unfillable…No one with any stature was willing to take the job," recalled Hodel. Finally, Hodel, at age 31, took the job. The real power, in part, was provided by others, such as former Governor Mark Hatfield—running for Senate in 1968, House Majority Leader Monte Montgomery and Governor Tom McCall.[17]

Tom McCall: Unfriendly Northern Neighbor

Governor Tom McCall has been mentioned briefly before, when he had attended some of the governors conferences with Reagan. McCall officially had invited Reagan for the Eugene visit in early 1967. That November, McCall and Reagan first had greeted the Dairy princess and later, each on horseback during the Veteran's Day Parade in Albany, were driven to Corvallis at top speed to watch O.J. Simpson's football loss in the rain. That evening, Reagan had delivered his first address devoted to world affairs.

McCall's parents had moved to Portland, Oregon, from Massachusetts in 1909, but their baby Thomas was born during a 1913 return visit East in the tiny hamlet of Egypt, Massachusetts. Egypt, now a section of Scituate, is between Boston and Cape Cod. Around the time of Tom's birth, members of the Massachusetts government rode the train to have their mail stamped being sent from Egypt, Massachusetts. Today the old post office is a country store still nick-named, "Postie."

Lyn Nofziger told one story about McCall and his mother, who still lived in Boston in the 1960s. His mom thought that Tom was neglecting her, and as she could not get through to her son in Oregon, she called the White House. Somehow, Lyndon Johnson got on the phone, and when he heard what she had said, the president immediately called McCall in Salem. When McCall answered the phone call, Johnson ordered, "Tom, this is Lyndon Johnson. Call your mother!"[18] In his memoirs, Nofziger also related that he and McCall "got to be pretty good friends." At one point while they both attended a national park opening, McCall gave Nofziger a present of a rock on which McCall had written, "Genuine Oregon Petrified Turd," which an amused Nofziger kept for many years.[19]

McCall had spent his youth in both Oregon and Massachusetts, and after graduating from the University of Oregon with a degree in journalism, he became a newspaper reporter, radio news announcer, and war correspondent in the Pacific. After the end of World War II, he returned to radio to do a nighttime radio talk program. After joining the Young Republicans, he became an assistant to the governor. Eventually he was elected Oregon secretary of state in 1964 and governor in 1966 at the same time as Ronald Reagan.

A few days after being elected, Governor-Elect McCall wrote a letter to Governor-Elect Reagan. In it he urged Reagan to expand his thoughts beyond right-wing magazines. McCall's secretary, a Reagan admirer, refused to type it, scolding McCall, "You'll destroy the relationship between two states, and he's more right than you are!"[20] That particular letter was never sent.

But as noted earlier, McCall did end up inviting Reagan to visit Eugene. After McCall had introduced his secretary to Reagan, McCall brought Reagan into his office. McCall then quickly returned to the secretary's desk with a mischievous smile saying, "I just want you to know that as we speak, Governor Reagan is going to the bathroom!" McCall had found it "hilarious" that Reagan did such human things.[21]

McCall's biographer notes, "McCall had little respect for the former actor. He disliked Reagan's strident rhetoric, and bristled at any suggestion that the two shared a history because they had gained fame in the same way—through television."[22] Reagan had arrived in Eugene "with a fleet of aides and bodyguards."[23]McCall "could not understand politicians who surrounded themselves with pomp."[24]

As we saw earlier, in March 1967 shortly after Reagan's Eugene visit, Governor McCall wrote a letter to other Republican governors asking them to stay uncommitted. But McCall had been rebuffed. Two sequential governors' meetings then took place, in which his thoughts about Ronald Reagan, as well as the thoughts of other governors, became evident.

The Western Governors Conference, in which fully eleven of thirteen were Republicans, had opened at West Yellowstone MT on June 25, 1967. We have seen already how Reed, Clif White, and Frank Whetstone had accompanied Reagan on the trip and how the press had asked Reagan about Reed's role and how Reagan had announced he was open for a draft from the party. Although the press noted the growing support for Reagan amongst some Western governors, McCall had his own observations about Reagan to share with the press. He called Reagan, "the hottest piece of political property the Republican Party has going." About Reagan's activities at the conference, McCall said, "It's a terribly heady diet he's having."[25] With some jealousy, he added, "There are just plain governors and then there's Reagan." McCall's dislike of Reagan's pomp seemingly got the better of him. Perhaps it was jealousy of Reagan's popularity or stardom. Perhaps it was McCall's thinking that Reagan's conservative philosophy, carefully thought out for many years by 1967, was just right-wing extremism.

Indeed when McCall then was asked what he thought of Reagan becoming president in 1968, McCall said Reagan "lacked experience" and although McCall did admit to being "impressed with him, but that still doesn't make him Presidential material."[26] Later McCall admitted that he "disagreed with Reagan's political philosophy."[27] At the conference, and still supporting Rockefeller, McCall suggested that Republican moderates should join together in a formal agreement, which would name one agreed-to candidate "at a strategic time." Most other Republican governors objected, so McCall dropped the proposal.[28]

McCall later remembered that his comment about Reagan being "the hottest political property" had made national headlines.[29] The reaction of the national press in this manner had surprised him, as it had been his first experience with the press corps in a national setting. He remembered the meetings as "twelve faceless souls...twelve nobodies, plus very much of a somebody, regionally and nationally, Governor Ronald Reagan of California."[30]

Over the summer of 1967, McCall had remained busy praising Rockefeller. When asked about Reagan, McCall answered, "Probably Reagan has come up somewhat in the last two or three months, but I don't know where he was to begin with."[31][32] Yet McCall may have tempered his thinking about Reagan at least a little, because that summer during a conversation with Hodel, McCall said words to the effect, "I really like this fella, Reagan. He might make a good president."[33] Hodel noted that McCall, knowing of Hodel's conservative reputation may have expressed his opinion in more glowing terms than he felt. Certainly, Hodel did not think McCall was a potential supporter of Reagan.[34] McCall then added, "You know who else likes him? Bob Hazen."[35] Whether he realized it or not, McCall had done a major service for the presidential aspirations of Ronald Reagan.

Robert Hazen

Once the Albany Veteran's Day parade and Corvallis football game were over that fall, Hodel had fulfilled his promise to recommend a candidate for Oregon State chairman for Reagan '68.[36] Hodel and other colleagues, who we will meet shortly, agreed that Hazen was an excellent choice to head Reagan's most important primary campaign organization because he was prominent and partly because he had a moderate image offsetting in liberal Oregon efforts to paint Reagan as "too conservative."[37] Hodel recalled that he had no difficulty contacting Hazen, because their fathers had been friends.[38]

Hazen, president of a local savings and loan, was described by his children as, "always a leader." His high school class president photograph shows him as a handsome young man in dark suit and tie with a serious expression. Hazen was also a "Yell King—a male cheerleader—and "never grew out of that phase."[39] His daughter recalls, "He was the president of almost every organization in Portland... President of the Rose Festival, Kiwanis, American Savings and Loan Institute, Toastmasters" and was active in the American Legion.[40] Hazen's son described him as a conservative Republican who was a "do-er," that "he could raise funds like nobody's business."[41] Hazen was called "Mr. Portland," as "people would stop to talk to him on the street or sit with him in restaurants."[42]

Hazen was "exuberant" and "he loved to be interviewed."[43] Hazen in fact was savvy with media. He had a fifteen minute morning radio show on KEX, and later on KOIN, as marketing vehicles for his savings and loan. Hazen also did television spots and his son recalls, "I got a lot of stick from kids at school because he had a fairly high voice."[44]

Hazen had been Multnomah County chairman of Nelson Rockefeller's successful 1964 primary campaign against Barry Goldwater, and his prior support of Rockefeller would follow him during Reagan's campaign. Hazen insisted that Hodel be his back-up. Hodel asked Reed in California officially to offer Hazen the job.[45] Hazen immediately accepted the state chairmanship. At that point, recalled Hodel, "We were off and running."[46]

Although Hazen was media savvy, sometimes Hazen's comments drew consternation from both Hodel and Reed. Hodel recalls that Hazen "was an optimist and spoke from the heart" and was a "genuinely outgoing, friendly person." But sometimes such forthrightness created problems, which "made Reed wince."[47] Hodel recalled one phone call in the middle of the night while he had been trying to catch up on work for his regular job as a lawyer. It was Reed complaining, "I decided I didn't need to sit here and worry about this all by myself" and proceeded to voice concern to Hodel about something Hazen was quoted in the press as having said. What Reed had not understood from California, but what Hodel understood as a Portland native, was that Hazen was "such a well-liked local and statewide personality that he had become accustomed to speaking his mind; if he said something a little startling, nobody held him accountable. Out of exuberance, he sometimes said things about the campaign and about the candidate that could be abused by the national media."[48]

But it was not just Hazen's comments that annoyed Reed and perplexed the media. Indeed as we shall see, Hazen would continue to campaign for the Reagan presidency well into June and July 1968, which would prompt *The Oregonian* to write an editorial asking Hazen to cease and desist from his strong support and continued campaigning for Reagan.

Reed became Hodel's "main and frequent contact during the Oregon primary campaign."[49] Now that the Reagan 1968 Oregon campaign had an overall state chairman, then additional mid-level campaign workers, to become local-regional office heads, were added. Spencer flew to Eugene in early 1968 and met with conservative radio station owner Hobie Wilson and local Reagan supporter Peter Murphy. Murphy became Lane County chairman, and his reach for Reagan extended into adjacent counties. Murphy was realistic about Reagan's chances: "It would be an uphill battle," as all prominent Republicans he knew were for Nixon.[50] We will meet Murphy in detail shortly.

Fred Van Natta: Rock Star Lobbyist

At your author's summer 2012 interview/reunion of Reagan's Oregon 1968 team, the clear leader was Fred Van Natta. He remains a lanky individualist whose knowledge of local and national politics is expansive. With a reputation as a "rock star lobbyist," but recently retired from the firm that bears his name, his recollections were crisp, detailed, and his enthusiasm for the 1968 Reagan campaign was quite evident.

Van Natta, a native Oregonian with a master's degree in politics, interned for the Oregon Republican state committee and in 1964 was assigned to work in Pennsylvania for Bill Scranton's brief presidential campaign doing nationwide delegate work. Van Natta heard Reagan's 1964 speech, recalling, "It was the best speech I had heard in the campaign. It clearly placed him on my list."[51]

One of the few bright spots after the 1964 Goldwater debacle was the change in the Oregon House of Representatives to a Republican majority. After returning to Oregon, Van Natta applied for work and became assistant to the speaker of the Oregon House.[52] By June, 1967 Van Natta had decided to form his own campaign management firm and rented the Salem office and house of Travis Cross, who initially had gone back to Michigan to aid the Romney campaign.

Van Natta was offered contracts with the Romney and the Nixon campaigns. While mulling over which team to join, Van Natta got a 2 A.M. phone call from Tom Reed in California with an offer to join the Reagan campaign. Van Natta realized that he would never be at the top of either the Nixon nor Romney campaigns in Oregon, but if he took the job with Reagan, he could be potentially not just be the head consultant of the Reagan 1968 Oregon campaign, but he could also be a major organizer of all Western states. So Van Natta happily declared to Reed, "Yes!" Van Natta reflects back and commented that he was "more a mercenary than an ideologue and I still am."[53]

Hodel recalled that he had been asked in 1968 about the possible lack of loyalty of Van Natta to Reagan. Van Natta could be viewed as a political professional who came for the money and did not care if Reagan won. But each time he had been asked this question, Hodel came to Van Natta's defense immediately. Hodel recalls his answer was, "Fred is a professional. He has signed on to do his best to help Reagan win Oregon and he is doing that. We can trust him fully so long as he remains engaged by us."[54]

Before there was any official Oregon Reagan 1968 presidential campaign office, Van Natta discussed with Hodel what had to be done. Hodel brought along two conservative attorneys, Don Pearlman and Diarmuid O'Scannlain, and all four met regularly in a Lake Oswego restaurant to plan how Reagan could win the Oregon primary. During these meetings, Hodel's recommendation of Robert Hazen was discussed and approved. Once Hazen had accepted overall state chairman role, of course he attended the meetings as well.

Pearlman and O'Scannlain

Don Pearlman and Don Hodel went way back. The two Oregonians had become roommates at Harvard, and would work closely together during the Reagan administration in the 1980's, when Hodel would serve in the Reagan cabinet.[55] Hodel recalled fondly that Pearlman, who had a flair for political operations, had worked hard to see that Hodel had been elected president of the Harvard Young Republicans ten years after Rusher was. With a degree from Harvard in economics and his law degree from Yale University, Pearlman returned West and joined a law firm in Portland. Reagan supporter Sally Gram laughs when she reflects on her working with Pearlman during 1968 because, "He looked so sinister...but I liked him a lot" and Van Natta recalls that his manner "was more lawyerly." Diana Evans, another major

Reagan supporter, sparkled when she recalled him fondly as a "droll troll."[56]

Pearlman was committed to continuing his conservative Republican political activities after returning to Portland. Pearlman, like Hodel, was introduced by Rusher to Diarmuid O'Scannlain and eventually Pearlman and O'Scannlain for a time would become law partners.

The Honorable Diarmuid O'Scannlain of the IXth Circuit of the United States Supreme Court was born in Manhattan. After graduating from St. John's University, he met Bill Rusher, the publisher of *National Review*. Rusher introduced O'Scannlain to Youth for Eisenhower and he served on the National Board of the Young Republican National Federation. At Harvard Law School he became president of the Harvard Law and Graduate Schools Republican Club. Rusher was best man when O'Scannlain married his wife in her hometown of Tacoma. He then joined the board of Young Americans for Freedom.[57] O'Scannlain returned West to Portland and Rusher advised O'Scannlain to meet Don Hodel and Don Pearlman. Hodel, newly at Georgia-Pacific's legal department, had just left the same law firm that O'Scannlain just joined.

O'Scannlain joined a Republican group founded by Senator Bob Packwood called "The Trumpeters," which was a state-wide network of Republicans that met every Friday morning for breakfast in downtown Portland. O'Scannlain characterized the group as having both liberal and conservative Republican members. Hodel had already been a member.[58] O'Scannlain sponsored prominent conservative John Gram for membership.[59]

By 1967 Hodel and Pearlman's contacts with Reed and Haerle involved O'Scannlain, who recalls being "swept into what Hodel and Pearlman were doing." Although O'Scannlain did not attend either of Reagan's 1967 Oregon visits, he became a full-fledged member of the Oregon Reagan 1968 presidential campaign team.[60] Hodel described O'Scannlain at the time as being "very able and earnest, yet still having a good sense of humor." The Reagan campaign in 1968 in Oregon benefited from O'Scannlain's "good judgment and excellent political connections with people like Bill Rusher."[61]

Judge O'Scannlain recalled updating Rusher about Reagan's 1968 Oregon campaign, saying, "We're encouraged and we're working hard." Although Rusher was in contact with Reagan's campaign via Sacramento, he was not involved with the Oregon campaign directly.[62]

The Grams

John and Sally Gram hosted the previously-noted mini-reunion of the Oregon 1968 Reagan campaign team in their home in Lake Oswego, Oregon, in the summer of 2012 with your author present. Sally is a vivacious and energetic, petite woman, whose memory of those events some 45 years ago remains phenomenal. She clearly was as involved with the 1968 Reagan campaign as was her husband, John, a soft-spoken congenial man who recalls those days fondly. Hodel remembers them in 1968, describing John as a "selfless team player who was dedicated to trying to win and guileless." Sally was "very earnest and was always upbeat even when things were not going well."[63]

John Gram, age 86 in 2016, won a high school writing contest as a conservative student. The contest sponsor, the AFL-CIO, was "mortified and tried to squelch it." After marrying Sally, they moved to California to work in the garment industry. There he became president of the North Valley California Young Republicans, the largest such group in the United States at the time.[64] One of their speakers was Ronald Reagan. Hearing Reagan in person for the first time, Gram was "very impressed. He fired me up more."[65] In 1964 when they drove back to Portland, their "Goldwater" car bumper stickers "caused a little stir." By 1966, they were staunch Reagan supporters. When they were transferred back to Portland and sold their car, the "last thing we did is we had to take the Reagan sticker off" their car. That was their good-bye to California. Just before leaving, Sally received a questionnaire asking who she thought would be the best candidate for the presidency in 1968 and she answered "Ronald Reagan."

Once back in Portland, Gram received a phone call from Don Hodel, asking him to help with the Reagan Oregon office and Gram accepted immediately. Hodel confirmed that he made the call, rather than Bob Hazen, because "Bob was a little less involved with the day-to-day stuff."[66]

Diana Evans

Diana Evans and her family raised cattle in rural Oregon and were always conservative Republicans. Diana, 84 years young in 2012, worked for her local congressman in the nation's capital before returning to Lake Oswego, Oregon, in 1964. Her work for Reagan's multiple campaigns was highlighted in *Time* in 1980. She had watched Reagan's 1964 speech on behalf of Goldwater and became "an instant believer."[67] Evans had created a local Oregon group of Goldwater activists, and there, Hodel first had met her when he had been liaison from the Clackamas Republican Central Committee to the Goldwater campaign.[68]

In February 1967 she saw Reagan at the Eugene visit and thought Reagan was "great" and "down to earth and attractive to people who were down to earth."[69] Diana describes herself as a "grass roots type of person." Diana had been president of the Lake Oswego Republican Women's Club, but it became too liberal for Diana, so she founded a new competitor Republican Women's Club. She needed no further convincing to join the Reagan 1968 campaign team.[70] Her job was to recruit volunteers.[71]

Hodel described Evans at the time as "entirely selfless in that she wanted to improve America's leadership. She had no personal political ambitions." Evans was "smart, quite knowledgeable, very supportive, and willing to give good, solid advice." In an era with less involvement in politics by women than in the 21st century, Evans always introduced her good ideas "in a way calculated not to offend the men involved."[72]

Thus Reagan's team of dedicated, enthusiastic grass roots Oregonians was complete. Van Natta was the director of Western States, Hazen was state chairman working with, and having back-up from, Hodel. The Portland campaign office was run by the Grams. O'Scannlain, Pearlman, and Evans were general campaign activists. Murphy ran the mid-Oregon office. Goode had helped initially with his critical decision to ask Governor McCall to invite Reagan to visit in late 1967, even though he played no further role in 1968. One area without direct political coverage was the rural section of far eastern Oregon, which was closer to the Idaho border than to Portland. That deficit would be corrected later. Van Natta recalled that the names, "Citizens for Reagan," "Draft Reagan," and "Reagan for President" were used at various times by the media. But as far as the grass roots campaign workers themselves were concerned, they all meant the same thing.[73] Now they all got to work with one goal: to see Reagan win the White House in 1968.

Reagan's Oregon Campaign Office

When the Reagan 1968 Oregon presidential campaign office opened officially, Henry A. Bubb from the Citizens for Reagan National Information Center wished the Oregon staff good luck: "We do not expect to win in Oregon as we do not have a candidate campaigning but I hope you will work hard to show Gov. Reagan that the people of Oregon want him as the candidate of all factions of the party."[74] The Grams recalled that because of all the media attention on the Democratic primary of McCarthy versus Kennedy, "We were not overwhelmed with volunteers."[75] McCarthy's Oregon headquarters was directly across the street from the Reagan headquarters. The Reagan office, which Van Natta had rented at SW Fourth Avenue and Stark streets in downtown Portland, was on two floors and was furnished sparsely. John Gram, unpaid, was there almost every day. Sally was the actual office manager and Evans worked hard too. Both made phone calls and stuffed envelopes.[76] [77]

As noted, Evans was in charge of volunteer recruitment. *Time* reported that she ran up "monthly $200 phone bills" campaigning for Reagan and that "her banker husband bought her an extra long cord so she could cook while she talked." Evans added, about her long hours working for Reagan: "My children never went hungry."[78] Van Natta created several different versions of Reagan-for-President campaign buttons specific for Oregon, including one, which combined "Oregon" and "Reagan" into "OReagan" superimposed upon the state map.[79]

"It was not a neatly planned campaign like in the textbooks," recalled Van Natta. It was a "guerilla effort" put together by volunteers and paid staff. The behind-the-scenes team in California and the on-the-ground team in Oregon had to react quickly when money came in and to events and "opportunities" as they unfolded.[80] Judge O'Scannlain characterized the Oregon Reagan campaign as very "ad hoc" locally within Oregon, with no "officially public" campaign that could be traced back to Sacramento. The emphasis was "entirely Oregonians thinking good things about their neighbor." O'Scannlain reflected back on why Reagan did not visit Oregon personally in 1968 and surmised that it was in part a way "not to tip off the Nixon people." The key was that the Oregon effort was to be seen as "home-grown," even though it was funded in part and directed by Reed and Spencer. O'Scannlain recalled his many trips to the headquarters to help stuff envelopes and attend numerous planning meetings: "We were doing everything we could to develop support for him."[81]

Beyond Portland, there were Reagan for President headquarters in ten of the thirty-six counties in Oregon.[82] Most were just small office spaces manned by one or two supporters, but two would make national news: the Lane County office run by Peter Murphy and the coast office in Florence run by Oscar Funk, which will be described later.

Oregon was Reagan's most critical primary, yet Reed kept his distance, and as noted, Reagan never returned to Oregon in 1968 despite his several prior campaign stops in 1967. Delegate hunter Clif White told Hodel that he was working closely with Reed.[83] Van Natta recalled that many times, he reviewed with Reed Reagan's progress from Wisconsin to Nebraska and that for the most important primary, "We're gonna do a bunch in Oregon."[84] Reed told Hodel that from the very beginning that Reagan would not come to Oregon because they "did not want him to be seen as an active candidate for president." Yet "it was alright for him to be drafted but not to go out and seek it. The goal was to establish his electability first, then draft him."[85] Reed still felt at that early time, "We hoped to win" in Oregon and shortly thereafter to win in his home state of California.[86]

Late 1967: Media Recognition

Speculation about Reagan's Oregon plans had surfaced during his 1967 Eugene visit in February and his Portland/Corvallis/Albany visit in November. As discussed earlier, just before Christmas *The Oregonian* had reported that Travis Cross, the Oregon press aide from whom Van Natta was renting his house, was bolting the Romney campaign for Reagan's. The article brought some details of the Oregon Reagan effort to light for the first time. Van Natta handled press relations, Hazen was identified as chairman, and the campaign's two financial officers were mentioned.

Portland contractor Carl M. Halvorson was financial chairman, and Salem sand and gravel dealer Harold Wallings was treasurer. Van Natta recalled that Halvorson had been president of Associated General Contractors in Portland and "knew how to raise money." Halvorson and Van Natta soon would meet privately with Reagan. Wallings was "wealthy in his own right" recalled Van Natta.[87]

Van Natta then had been asked about the level of support for Reagan in Oregon and answered, "There is a snowball here. We don't know whether it will evaporate when the heat is put on it—but we are going to try and roll it!" The overall assessment in late 1967 of the Reagan effort in Oregon was that Reagan had a "knowledgeable and able" campaign staff, "at work seeking to win the May primary."[88]

The very next day after the Hughes article appeared, the *New York Times* ran a long article highlighting Reagan's Oregon presidential campaign efforts to that point. Reagan's 1967 visits to Eugene in the spring and to Albany and Corvallis in the fall were ignored, but the thrust of the article was that many of those newly supporters who were campaigning in Oregon on behalf of Reagan had been part of Rockefeller's 1964 team. "A draft Reagan movement, officially called 'Citizens for Reagan,'" was confirmed by the reporter and "its first coup" was the acceptance of Bob Hazen to be chairman. When asked why he switched from Rockefeller in 1964 to Reagan in 1968, Hazen answered that he liked Reagan's speeches and "because he has ideas...(and)...he is willing to put them in effect.[89]

One Rockefeller supporter had watched the growing Reagan campaign in Oregon with "misgivings, even alarm" but had a similar explanation of the Reagan boom in Oregon: "These fellows who worked enthusiastically for Governor Rockefeller in 1964 are party activists; they want to do something now. Rockefeller is not giving them the chance. Reagan is."[90]

Oregon House Speaker Monte Montgomery had been co-chairman of the Rockefeller 1964 primary campaign, but in 1968 quietly was supporting Reagan. Montgomery had given campaign advice to Rockefeller in 1968, suggesting that Rockefeller stay away from Oregon because he likely would lose.[91] Van Natta, who had worked for Monte for two years and still was close with him, recalled that Monte did not endorse any Republican candidate during the primary but was definitely for Reagan "in private."[92]

The office of the Oregon secretary of state contained files of letters written by voters advocating various Republican presidential candidates. Besides Nixon and Rockefeller, the "thickest" were for Reagan. Of the candidates listed for vice-president, and Reagan was listed for both spots on the ballot, Reagan's file of letters from Oregon supporters was "the bulkiest."[93] Although Reagan would withdraw from being listed for vice-president, Reagan's press office in Sacramento would reiterate that Reagan could not withdraw from the presidential ballot in Oregon because he was going to be a favorite son candidate from California.[94]

Van Natta's Meeting with Reagan

In late 1967, Western Regional Director Van Natta and potential Oregon Financial Chairman Halvorson had flown to California to meet privately with Governor Reagan in a hotel suite. Halvorson wanted assurances from the governor himself that the governor "was serious, that it was a serious venture, because he was going to go out and raise money for him." Reagan previously had met Van Natta for several days just a few weeks earlier at the Corvallis-Albany Veterans Day weekend events as we have seen. Van Natta took no notes at the meeting but recalled that Reagan chatted with them about his political philosophy. Although Reagan never said if he was or was not going to run, he "showed enough interest in the race and said enough things that Halvorson liked" so that Halvorson agreed to be the financial chairman. Van Natta also recalled that the trip had marked a traumatic experience for Halvorson who had been calling back to Oregon a number of times during the visit without success, only to discover upon his return to Oregon that his business had burnt down.[95] Halvorson also would join the Executive Committee of Bubb's Citizens for Reagan National Information Center.

January 1968

In early 1968, columnists Evans and Novak had noted that perhaps problems were starting to develop in the Reagan campaign in Oregon. They felt that the constant denials of Reagan that he would visit Oregon were starting to take a toll. They felt that there was a "deceleration of the boom" for the Reagan effort and that Reagan's chances in Oregon were not "nearly so bright as they seemed last September."[96] Unmentioned were Reagan's visits to Oregon in 1967, one of which had occurred just six weeks before.

The very next day at his weekly news conference in Sacramento, Reagan had confirmed his plans to avoid returning to Oregon in 1968. Based on the "setting up of a Reagan campaign organization by his supporters in Oregon," a reporter asked him if there were any conceivable circumstances that would lead him to "campaign in your own behalf...in Oregon?" Reagan answered, "No, I can't. I have no such intention."[97] Not mentioned was that Reagan's Oregon campaign was just starting in earnest in Oregon even if the candidate himself had no specific plans to return. What remains unclear if the force behind the decision to avoid visiting Oregon in person during 1968 had originated with Reed or with Reagan himself. Just as had occurred in Wisconsin and in Nebraska, that decision would cost Reagan dearly.

By month's end, rumors began to spread that Reagan might come to Oregon after all. Unnamed "ranking Republican leaders" were telling reporters that Reagan "will campaign for the Republican presidential nomination in the Oregon primary next May." One of Oregon's "best informed Republicans has intelligence," indicating that Reagan would announce in May that he was no longer a favorite son from California and that he would "campaign personally and intensively in the state for two or three weeks before the primary." It was mentioned that a "number of Oregon businessmen" were asked to contribute to such a Reagan campaign but with the "clear understanding" that Reagan would "make a major effort." This unnamed source may have been Halvorson, as it is consistent with what Van Natta had recalled of their private meeting with Reagan. Workers for Reagan already had "blocked out substantial segments of local television time for the last weeks before the voting on May 28." The Oregon Rockefeller camp was pleased by these indications of an accelerating Reagan effort in Oregon, feeling Reagan's campaign "would divide the conservative opposition" to Rocky amongst Reagan and Nixon. The opposite was true in the Oregon Nixon camp, which greeted the news of "multiplying Reagan activity in Oregon" as "less than welcome." For "nearly every vote produced by an active Reagan campaign would mean one less for Mr. Nixon." Reagan continued to deny his intentions to return to Oregon, and "leaders of the Citizens for Reagan" denied that the Governor had either directed or encouraged them.[98]

February

In February, Reagan's Oregon staff felt that "even without campaigning, Reagan and Rocky (with a write-in effort) will run 1-2 in Oregon." *Newsweek* called Reagan's Oregon campaign as the "strongest of Ronnie's 60-odd Citizens for Reagan groups" because of its planned media blitz.[99] A student poll from the University of Oregon at Eugene showed Reagan trailing Nixon and Rockefeller but ahead of Romney.[100] McCall, previously in June, 1967, having called Reagan, "the hottest political property around," now gleefully declared that Reagan was not "sizzling anymore."[101] Of course McCall may have said the latter during the prior June so he could make a future negative comparison, in 1968, to aid Rockefeller.

When Romney had withdrawn in late February, one *R* was gone. Hazen said that no candidate had the Republican nomination sewed up. Liberal Republican Governor McCall, with fellow liberal Rockefeller as his first choice, was quite happy that Romney had withdrawn.[102] But first Rockefeller would still have to decide whether to enter his name in Oregon. While deciding what to do about Oregon, Rockefeller even contemplated challenging Reagan in California. Rockefeller could follow up the Oregon race with a direct entrance into the California primary, "if circumstances then seemed to warrant a bold challenge to Gov. Ronald Reagan in his home state."[103] Rockefeller's supporters had to suffer through constant Rockefeller waffling, as their candidate dithered, unable to make a firm decision whether to sign a withdrawal affidavit, encourage the petition drive, or officially enter the primary once his name was put on the ballot.[104] [105] [106] McCall applied more pressure.[107]

March

On March 11, the Oregon secretary of state had announced that Reagan's name would be placed on the Republican primary ballot for president. A new feature of the law was that vice-presidential names were to be listed also, and Reagan was listed for that office too. Reagan quickly withdrew from the ballot for vice-president. Three late Oregon straw polls found Reagan "trailing far behind" both Nixon and Rockefeller.[108]

The next day, March 12, 1968, Nixon had won the New Hampshire primary, and this result was interpreted as pushing Rockefeller to enter into the Oregon primary so he could then "do battle openly with Mr. Nixon and possibly Gov. Ronald Reagan of California."[109] Nationally syndicated columnist James Kilpatrick wondered why Rockefeller did not enter primaries other than in Oregon, as "With the name of Ronald Reagan also on the ballot, conservative votes will be divided."[110]

Meanwhile Reagan continued to frustrate his grass roots activists. Just as his mid-January Sacramento news conference had made national headlines when he had said he would not go back to Oregon, so did Reagan's mid-March news conference, when he announced that he would "do all he could to discourage his Reagan-for-President fans" in Oregon. A few days after Kennedy announced he would enter the race, Reagan reiterated that he could not "take my name out of the Oregon primary," citing the conflict with his California favorite son status. Reagan was staying in the race.[111]

As had been surmised by columnists Evans and Novak earlier, this continuing denial by Reagan that he was a candidate was starting to take its toll on his enthusiastic Oregon campaign team. As noted, the major reason for the Oregon opt-out law was that Oregonians had felt slighted in prior elections by candidates who had skipped Oregon to campaign in California. Oregonians wanted candidates to campaign in person in their state. But with Reagan still not coming in 1968, as the primary approached despite his two major visits in 1967, "contributors and voters held back for lack of a real candidate."[112]

After Nixon's campaign manager charged that Reagan had a "full blast" campaign in Oregon, Reed then joined the fray. Reed, described as Reagan's "eyes and ears," was accused of making frequent trips to

Oregon to run the Reagan campaign. Reed said those charges were "totally erroneous," as he had only made the one trip to Oregon for the Portland-Albany Veteran's Day parade-Corvallis football game visit the prior November. This was in fact true. In 1968, neither Reagan nor Reed were in Oregon prior to the primary. Reed was accused of sending money to Oregon, to which he said such accusations were "similarly wrong."[113]

During the time that Rockefeller was waffling in indecision, Nixon predicted that if Rockefeller entered and the race became three way including Reagan, that Rocky would win. Nixon clearly felt that Reagan and he would split the conservative vote.[114]

Rockefeller made his decision on March 21 to withdraw from the Oregon primary and the national race altogether. In the 21st century, one might say that Rocky was for running for president before he was against it. Now two *R*'s were gone. This is when Nixon had admitted, "The only one who can stop us is Reagan."[115] Nixon told the media this would "enable him to reduce the amount of campaigning he had planned for...Oregon."[116] One reporter thought that Nixon had sewn up the nomination, unless Nixon faced "the sudden emergence of Gov. Ronald Reagan of California as an active candidate."[117] The reporter noted there was more Reagan activity in Oregon than Wisconsin, but Nixon's aides said they viewed the chances of an active Reagan candidacy in Oregon as "dim."[118]

The reaction to Rockefeller's withdrawal from the Reagan Oregon campaign came through Chairman Hazen. Hazen said that although Rocky's withdrawal was a surprise, the Rockefeller move has "not changed our position at all."[119] With Rocky out of the race, Hazen claimed the withdrawal actually "puts us in a stronger position." At this time, the Reagan campaign in Oregon was "gaining momentum (and) was expected to take votes away from Nixon, perhaps seriously crippling him if Rockefeller had stayed on the Oregon ballot." Reagan privately was "encouraging the Oregon effort on his behalf."[120]

April: Nixon Feels the Reagan Threat

After Reagan's strong almost eleven percent tally in Wisconsin on April 4, his Oregon supporters "took heart." After discussions with Van Natta and Reed, Hazen addressed the press.[121] Hazen applauded the results noting, "Reagan's vote with virtually no campaign clearly shows the nation sees in Governor Reagan new leadership for possible action" and added that support for Reagan in Oregon was "increasing, particularly since President Johnson's withdrawal."[122]

Then in mid April a full-fledged analysis of the Reagan versus Nixon contest in Oregon appeared in the Northwest press under a UPI byline. Nixon was about to "put his political prestige on the line" against Reagan, as it would be the "only test of Nixon's popularity with West Coast voters" prior to the convention. Nixon's Oregon team was described as "waging a vigorous campaign…that would help erase nagging doubts" that Nixon could win. The Reagan team was "convinced Reagan can win-but only if he becomes an active candidate and campaigns in person in Oregon." Van Natta was quoted in the article as saying, "Without an active campaign, we're not going to win in Oregon. We recognize that. We have provided the groundwork so he could come in here and campaign and win."[123]

The national press took notice of what Reagan was doing in Oregon too. The New York Times noted a "growing feeling" amongst Oregon political pros that Reagan would achieve "a greater prospective vote… than they had foreseen." A certain "highly placed Republican liberal," possibly Governor McCall, suggested Reagan might achieve "more than 40 percent," because "a lot of liberals and moderates" felt that the only way to stop Nixon's string of victories before Miami Beach was to vote for Reagan in Oregon. Nixon's campaign estimated Reagan's chances at "30 percent," in contrast to Hazen who was described as "more optimistic" than three weeks earlier, when he had told a visitor to the Reagan campaign headquarters that 20 percent would have made the campaign "a success" at that point.[124]

The back-and-forth overestimates and underestimates by both the Nixon team and Reagan team were recalled years later by Van Natta, who reflected, "We were outfoxed and outsmarted and outtalked" by the Nixon team.[125] Hodel discussed a reasonable bar over which the Reagan campaign could claim victory as 15%, but that Hazen's 20% was "off message" and was another instance of Reed in California being exasperated about Hazen and complaining to Hodel.[126] Neither Reed or Van Natta or Hodel had wanted any public comment setting too high a bar, in case Reagan did not do as well. Van Natta considered "anything over 15 percent of the total to be a victory."[127] Years later Van Natta would admit that he purposely had underestimated, so that anything above this 15 percent would appear to be an unexpected Reagan surge. This would serve to counter any purposeful overestimate of Reagan's vote expectations by the Nixon team.[128] Indeed in mid April, Nixon's team suddenly said that they would consider a victory "anything more than 51%."[129] But Nixon spokesman Robert Ellsworth eventually would tell the press that Nixon would be "doing well if he received 33 per cent of the vote," adding if he achieved 40 per cent, it would be an "exceptionally strong" Nixon showing.[130] If Nixon did better than what the Nixon spokesman had told the press, then these purposeful vote underestimates would lead to feelings of a Nixon landslide.

The significance of the Oregon Reagan versus Nixon contest was not thought to be just of regional importance however. Because Oregon was the "last major test of GOP voter sentiment before the convention," it held national implications. Indeed "Oregon could hold the key to a possible Reagan draft" at the Miami Beach convention. Reagan's denials continued, as he "disavowed Hazen's group" and confirmed again he "will not campaign actively in Oregon or elsewhere." Yet Reagan "refused to ask Oregon voters not to vote for him."[131]

In mid April, Nixon's state chairman said that Nixon would get a "2-to-1 victory in Oregon" over Reagan.[132] Yet the Republican fears of what a Robert Kennedy Democrat nomination would mean to Nixon as the Republican nominee—with the fears of a new Nixon-Kennedy debate fiasco compared to Reagan's May debate triumph over RFK— resurfaced, as discussed earlier. Thus "talk of a stop-Nixon drive" was on the rise.[133] Reagan backers denied this, saying that their campaign was "positive, pro-Reagan and not anti-Nixon."[134] But as we will see, Reagan was almost set with the finishing touches on a new, updated version of *Ronald Reagan, Citizen Governor*, which again devastatingly would portray Nixon as a loser. Once again, in the last of the opt-out states, Nixon needed to shore up his defenses against the emerging shift to Reagan. Whereas earlier Nixon had said he no longer needed to campaign in Oregon, Nixon had to shift gears quickly before Reagan's grass roots activists gained even more ground.

So Nixon began a new eight-state trip to "start closing the door" on Reagan's campaign.[135] With many of the governors leading uncommitted slates to Miami Beach, it "reduced the possibility that Reagan could demonstrate enough out-of-California support to get his campaign off the ground."[136] Oregon had emerged as "without doubt the last obstacle in Nixon's way to the nomination."[137] If Nixon were to be stopped, "it would have to be there."[138]

The third week in April saw the results of one of the very few Oregon Republican polls. Daryle E. Lempke of the *Los Angeles Times* released a poll showing Nixon 47.6 percent, Rockefeller 15.8 (he was not on the ballot) and Reagan 12.6 percent. The poll was analyzed as "not a professional poll." Lemke apparently had sampled voters in Portland, Salem, Eugene and Roseburg and had "large numbers of uncommitted voters" and "no independent voters were counted." Further details of the poll were not available. An earlier unnamed poll apparently showed Reagan at 8 percent. The Nixon campaign again predicted Reagan would achieve around "30 percent," with Van Natta commenting again that this prediction was "just setting us up for the kill." Van Natta reflected on the bias in the Lemke poll, noting its sample included only the liberal Republican bastions of the western Oregon large cities and completely ignored the conservative Republican strongholds of Bend and Pendleton and most of rural southern and all of eastern Oregon; plus it was a completely non-random sample.[139]

Nixon took no comfort in the latest poll, for in late April he made a second campaign swing to the Western states, including Oregon and Idaho, to fend off Reagan. In Boise he had to acknowledge Reagan's growing success, noting that he expected Reagan "would gain additional support for the Republican nomination in both Idaho and Oregon."[140] Nixon was concerned about Reagan's ability to attract Western, conservative Republican voters and "it was only in Oregon that law-and-order became the prime theme of the Nixon campaign."[141] Nixon hoped to outflank Reagan on the political right, with a similar campaign speech emphasis just as Reagan was doing.

As seen, this was the same time period when RFK similarly had changed his campaign theme to much more conservative, pro law-and-order stances and in addition he even modified his appearance to becoming more conservative as well. Both Nixon and Kennedy were feeling the pressure from Reagan.

Nixon Analyzes the Reagan Threat

Nixon remained the odds-on favorite to win, yet as we have seen earlier he always felt that the greatest threat to his nomination was Reagan. Reagan's greatest effort at challenging Nixon was waged in Oregon. Although historian and Nixon advisor Patrick Buchanan barely mentions the Reagan threat to Nixon in Oregon,[142] Nixon knew he must stand his ground. As historian Theodore H. White correctly observed, "In Oregon he was faced with real opposition from the Reagan forces."[143]

During that same spring of 1968, another Nixon advisor, Harry Treleaven, who later would be credited with creating the slogan "Nixon's the One!" wrote a confidential memo to Nixon analyzing the threat that Reagan posed in Oregon. Author Joe McGinnis was granted access to those private Nixon staff memorandums. Treleaven's specific points to Nixon about Reagan included: Reagan's $350,000 estimated budget and Reagan's emphasis on small government, fiscal responsibility, and his ability to win. Treleaven added that the emotional appeal amongst Democrats for Kennedy and McCarthy could lead to GOP voters, for "impractical, emotional reasons," similarly to swing away from Nixon to Reagan. Under strategy, Treleaven had only one recommendation for Nixon: "We should not let Reagan pre-empt the anti-big government position."[144]

After Reagan's great achievements in Wisconsin and Nebraska, the Nixon camp felt threatened that "Reagan forces would be able to fan the brushfire higher in Oregon." Reagan backers were seen as "pouring money and effort into Oregon." Nixon was seen as "constantly aware of heightening efforts" to "woo the same delegates by well-heeled and politically astute representatives" of Reagan in Oregon.[145]

The Reagan and Nixon camps dueled again about other polls. The Nixon campaign circulated a new poll by Don M. Muchmore, which showed Reagan "easily defeated" by any of the Democrats. The Reagan team said they would not "take these tactics without a fight" and threatened to retaliate by showing that Nixon delegates would not have gotten "enough signatures to get on the California ballot."[146]

Finances

Some Reagan campaign budget numbers appeared in the press. Reagan's Oregon staff was reported to have hoped "to get $300,000 from the national organization, much of the money coming from California" and hoped to "raise $50,000 in Oregon."[147] Van Natta recalled that the $300,000 figure was from an "overly enthusiastic" Chairman Hazen, saying what he had hoped would occur but not likely to happen. Indeed Van Natta recalled they were "ruffling their feathers" towards the competition to "appear bigger" than they truly were. Van Natta recalled that they never "believed we had $350,000 to spend."[148] Van Natta received checks from private individuals, from Bubb's center in Topeka, and forwarded from Reed and Spencer in northern California. No money ever was borrowed. Van Natta recalled that the budget was extremely "tight" and by the end of the campaign, all funds had been expended.

The final tabulations from the Oregon secretary of state's office would show that a total of $123,310.34 was contributed and a similar amount expended. The "Citizens for Reagan," of which Van Natta was shown as director, had received $118,438.50, of which the largest contributors were: Citizens for Reagan ($37,000), Bubb's "National Citizens for Reagan" of Topeka KS ($35,000) and two individual contributions of $10,000 each. "Lane County Citizens for Reagan," headed by Peter Murphy, raised $2,185. Carl Halvorson donated $720 individually and $1000 to the Citizens for Reagan. William E. Boeing of Seattle did follow through and donated $1,000.[149] Hazen, Van Natta, and Murphy all had individual contributions. [150]

Van Natta gave a mid-spring financial update, noting that of the $350,000 budgeted for the Reagan Oregon campaign, he had raised "only $100,000, about half of it out of the state." Van Natta suggested that the campaign might spend another $100,000 even before donations arrived and might even resort to borrowing money for that purpose.[151] The national press still would be reporting, inaccurately, at the end of May that the Reagan campaign spent "considerable sums—perhaps as much as $400,000—on television advertisements."[152]

McCall's Invitation to Reagan

Rockefeller had re-entered the race at the end of April, and a few weeks later his Oregon team admitted they were up against a Reagan campaign team that was "well organized and well financed."[153] A new NBC Oregon poll showed Reagan was surging and was now ahead of Rockefeller: Nixon 55%, Reagan 20% and Rockefeller 16%.[154]

At this time, Rockefeller-supporter McCall was still listening to Reagan deliver his First White Paper address at the governors conference in Hawaii and had not given up on his invitation to Reagan to come north to campaign in Oregon. McCall publicly urged Reagan to officially announce his Oregon candidacy and "give Mr. Nixon a good race," agreeing with Van Natta's assessment that "Reagan would have to campaign in person if he wants to make a good showing." McCall emphasized that because Reagan was only an hour away from Oregon by jet, it would be "unusual" if he won without personally campaigning in the state. McCall hoped that, for the good of the party, Reagan would campaign actively in person to prove the result "comes from winning a tough primary...that it would be a vigorously fought contest between the two of them." McCall still planned to write in Rockefeller's name on his own ballot. [155]

McCall followed through by calling Reagan directly and offering "to help him if he would campaign in Oregon." McCall ostensibly would help Reagan, but only if it helped Rockefeller: "The only way Rocky can win is to keep the convention open and the only way to do that is to have Reagan raise hell in Oregon."[156]

McCall's invitation created an immediate quandary. Hodel and Reed analyzed McCall's public admission that he wanted to use Reagan to stop Nixon so Rockefeller could then triumph. Yet Reed and Hodel hoped initially that McCall's invitation would entice Reagan to fly north. Hodel and Reed debated strategy. McCall was "such a wild card that it was high risk strategy to rely on him for anything," recalled Hodel. So if Reagan did come to Oregon at this point, it would cast Reagan as a "stop-Nixon person rather than a genuine candidate." Even if Reagan did arrive at this late date, key players and contributors who had signed up with Nixon could not be unhooked now. Indeed that unhooking "had to have been done months earlier." Then Hodel and Reed discussed a potential worst-case scenario. Reagan might arrive in Oregon at McCall's invitation, McCall reiterates that he is not supporting Reagan but just trying to stop Nixon, and Reagan then gets only 15% of the vote. That would have been a "huge setback and Reagan would have gotten the label as 'spoiler' rather than full-fledged candidate." In the end, Hodel and Reed decided they could not risk having Reagan return to Oregon at McCall's behest, and Reagan did not push to change their minds.[157]

Reagan-Lindsay?

Rockefeller's team decided to bring in New York City Mayor John Lindsay as a surrogate for Rockefeller. In late 1967 Lindsay had visited California and met Reagan for the first time in Los Angeles at Reagan's Biltmore Hotel suite for a half-hour meeting. They had discussed the "pressures" they each had experienced when governing. When he was in the city that day, Lindsay had seen his first "Lindsay for President" signs and was "euphoric." When Reagan was asked what he thought of Lindsay as a possible Republican contender in 1968, Reagan told the press, "The Republican Party is rich in talent, and traditionally the Mayor of the largest city should be considered." Reagan planned to meet with Lindsay in Manhattan in January.[158] Reagan did add that Lindsay should be considered "a possible nominee for President or Vice-President in 1968," adding that he did think Lindsay was "qualified and capable" to be president. When Reagan had been asked about a potential Reagan-Lindsay ticket, Reagan laughed saying "That's not a dream ticket, it's a nightmare."[159]

Lindsay's brief campaign swings to Oregon are reviewed by your author elsewhere.[160] In Corvallis and Eugene, students listened politely as Lindsay extolled the virtues of Rockefeller. But "what really turned them on was the evil prospect of a Rockefeller-Reagan ticket."[161]

Mayor Lindsay did not say anything directly about Ronald Reagan's Oregon candidacy for the presidency. But when asked if he had any reservations about Mr. Reagan as vice-president, Lindsay's reservations about Reagan were "anything but mild." The press reminded Lindsay of Rockefeller's comments, cited earlier, that there was no ideological gulf between them. Asked directly if he had any ideological differences with Reagan, Lindsay shouted, "I sure do."[162]

Would he consider being Ronald Reagan's vice-presidential running mate? Lindsay "said both publicly and privately that he would not run with a conservative Presidential candidate like Reagan."[163] As noted above, even Reagan could not conceive of such a Reagan-Lindsay ticket.

Ironically, the reporter noted that although Lindsay's comments had "brought down the house," the "direct slap" at Reagan probably had cost him the vice-presidency.[164] The reporter reminded his readers that both Nixon and Rockefeller were New Yorkers, and the Constitution forbade both the president and vice-president from being from the same state. Thus amongst major Republican contenders in late May, only Reagan from California could have chosen Lindsay to be his running mate.

The possibility of a Reagan-Lindsay ticket, as a ticket that would be balanced geographically and ideologically, had been mentioned in the national press the prior September.[165] Thus the potential idea of a Vice-President John Lindsay had evaporated, due to the Mayor's self-inflicted quick comment as he had attempted to ingratiate himself with his liberal, student audience. Reagan may have gotten the last laugh however. After Lindsay had told the press that he had the second toughest job in America, Reagan, "always quick to turn a memorable phrase, agreed that it probably was the second most difficult job in the world—'the way he does it.'"[166]

Reagan's last dealing with Lindsay prior to the convention would occur in the early summer when Lindsay's deputy mayor would announce a city-wide boycott against California grapes because of perceived stances of Reagan and California farmers against farm worker attempts to unionize. At an early summer press conference, when asked if he would intercede between the farmers and grape workers now that New York City had instituted a boycott, Reagan would reveal that he had called Lindsay earlier in the day and that Lindsay had no idea what his deputy mayor had done. Reagan's Executive Secretary, William Clark, would send Lindsay a telegram saying that it would "highly unwise" for governmental entities like New York City to get involved with the boycott and Reagan had hoped that "retaliatory legislation on the part of the California legislature" would not occur.[167] Rockefeller's response of silence would be a calculated political maneuver to differentiate himself from Reagan.[168] The following month at the platform committee meeting of the party in Miami Beach, as will be seen, Lindsay and Reagan would have clearly differing views.[169] At the convention, Lindsay would get one official vote, from Minnesota, in the first round.[170]

The Media

Reagan's campaign team pioneered many innovative media techniques, which reached their peak in Oregon. During much of latter March and April, because of the success of its media campaign as well as the reactions of Reagan's Oregon opponents, the Reagan 1968 campaign in Oregon made news. Not only was the Reagan staff interviewed by newspapers as noted, but the campaign expanded their public outreach to radio and television. Reagan's media efforts in Oregon "had plenty of muscle and money" and its "media budget was virtually open-ended."[171] Reagan's team's efforts consisted of "an impressive advertising drive, highlighted by television film clips, radio spots, newspaper ads, and an eight-page tabloid that will be mailed to nearly half a million Republicans."[172]

Hazen, Gram and Van Natta arranged for local radio spots in the large Portland metropolitan market. Gram arranged for the radio stations to interview Hazen whenever events occurred that might impact the Reagan campaign. Nearby Oregon City had an all-news radio station and one of their radio reporters was at the Reagan office frequently to report on the local Reagan campaign.[173] Gram recalled that whenever reporters stopped by, which was every few days, he and Sally would fill in the details of the Reagan-for-President efforts then underway.

The Reagan campaign expanded into television. A television reporter from Los Angeles' KNBC interviewed Gram for a full hour about Reagan's Oregon campaign.[174] As will be discussed, similarly young Tom Brokaw would fly in from Los Angeles to report on a conflict on the Oregon coast between the Reagan and RFK campaign teams. Sally Gram recalled that when anything newsworthy happened, John Gram had Hazen appear on the Portland 11 PM news shows. Hazen thus appeared on local Portland television news programs one evening to three evenings per week from March 1968 through the primary in late May.[175] Then came the onslaught from the national news media celebrities.

Pierre Salinger, former press secretary to President Kennedy, and who had lost to Reagan's friend George Murphy in 1964, came to Portland to campaign for Robert Kennedy. At one point, Salinger went to the Portland Rose Garden, overlooking the city with vistas of Mount Hood. John and Sally Grams' daughter had a "confrontation" with him when she had "tried to hand him a Reagan bumper sticker."[176]

CBS network anchor Walter Cronkite hosted a cocktail party for members of all Oregon presidential campaigns at the Benson Hotel. The party was "clearly aimed" for the McCarthy and Kennedy people, and the latter included long-suffering press secretary Frank Mankiewicz. The Grams recalled that the Benson had been chosen because it had a Presidential Suite for Kennedy and was considered safe because it had a heavy cement cornerstone to protect the building from earthquakes.[177]

As local leaders of Citizens for Reagan, the Grams were invited to attend the party also. Both John and Sally each recall Cronkite's surprised reaction when they were introduced to him as the Portland chairman and office manager for the Reagan campaign, respectively. John recalled that he spoke to Cronkite "for perhaps seven minutes." Cronkite was "amazed" that there was someone in Oregon as conservative as John was. He asked why, as conservatives, John and Sally were actively supporting Reagan in a "progressive state" like Oregon. Cronkite then seemed to understand their reasons after explaining why they were on Reagan's presidential campaign team. John Gram recalled how kind Cronkite was to both of them that evening. Cronkite went out of his way to introduce them to others, as he recognized they were "the amateurs amongst the professionals."[178] After his professional duties were done, Cronkite went fishing on the Deschutes River. This episode is not mentioned by Cronkite's biographer.[179]

But the reaction of Kennedy supporter Frank Mankiewicz was altogether different. John and Sally Gram remember their conversation as "spirited," because Mankiewicz was trying to "run down the Reagan campaign." They remembered him as "patronizing and not pleasant." Mankiewicz was not happy that anyone from the Reagan campaign had been invited by Cronkite or CBS News, because in Mankiewicz's mind, "Reagan was not a candidate."[180] Mankiewicz still was reeling from Kennedy's devastating loss to Reagan a year earlier in the *Town Meeting of the World* debate and the fact that Kennedy, who had told Mankiewicz and others that he never wanted to debate Reagan again, over the ensuing year constantly had been needling Mankiewicz that he had been the one who had arranged for Kennedy to debate Reagan in the first place.

At Reagan campaign headquarters, young CBS reporter Mike Wallace showed up and was greeted by Van Natta. Wallace wanted to know all about the Reagan campaign. Van Natta updated him on the ten functioning county offices and the central headquarters in Portland. Wallace asked how much money was to be spent and was told that they expected to spend about $100,000. Van Natta then recalled that Wallace then acted as he would in the future on 60 Minutes and "flared and jumped all over me" saying, "Don't lie to me. I know better than that; I know what it takes to run a campaign headquarters." Van Natta then somewhat naively asked Wallace what he thought it took to run a campaign. Wallace answered that he knew it would cost $10,000 to $20,000 for each county office. Van Natta cut off Wallace triumphantly rejoining, "Not in Oregon!" Van Natta reflected that Wallace's abusive and adversarial relationship with those he would interview in the future had been practiced on him that day. Van Natta said that although he was not prepared for Wallace's interrogatories, he "held his ground" and never forgot that personal encounter with a young Mike Wallace.

Later when he spoke at the annual dinner of the City Club of Portland at the Portland Hilton ballroom, Wallace reported on the Reagan campaign efforts in Oregon. Wallace emphasized that his remarks were personal and not those of CBS. He told his audience that the Reagan effort in Oregon was "one of the most interesting to watch" and estimated that Reagan was spending "$300,000 to $350,000 on his primary campaign in Oregon." Wallace analyzed the television campaign as "highly effective" and thought Reagan would get 25 to 30 percent of the Republican vote. He told the audience that although Reagan would then get "100 percent" in California, "his only chance for the nomination would be for a Rockefeller-Nixon deadlock."[181] Up to then Reagan's Oregon media campaign was fairly standard. Now Reagan would use his newly-updated secret weapon.

Ronald Reagan, Citizen Governor

Reagan's secret weapon, which had helped him so much in Wisconsin and Nebraska was the specially-made campaign film, *Ronald Reagan, Citizen Governor.* Its use became virtually mandatory in the final, all-important primary in Oregon.

As described by historians Chester, Hodgson and Page, the "prospect of the Oregon primary produced a flurry of extra work," because the Reagan biographical film had to be updated. Since the initial creation of the film, the *U.S.S. Pueblo* had been captured and King had been assassinated. Reagan's concluding segment for the initial film, as shown in Wisconsin and Nebraska, now looked "dated."[182]

Tom Reed got busy with Snazelle and Mercer once again. Reed thought that Reagan should make a new speech thus permitting substitutions of new parts of the talk in place of the now outdated segments. Reagan agreed with these revised plans for his presidential primary campaign in Oregon and at his next appropriate venue, an Oakland fundraising speech, a camera team filmed the candidate anew. But there was a major stumbling block to the new film footage: the audience was somewhat inebriated, causing Reagan some difficulties in delivering his talk to an audience which did not respond as other more attentive audiences usually did. Reagan was "very unhappy" about the Oakland speech and the resultant film footage.[183] But Snazelle was able to edit the new film footage, added the sounds of applause where appropriate, and thought Reagan would be pleased with the new composite campaign film for Oregon—the most important non-convention part of his 1968 campaign. But Reagan "was still worried" and according to Chester et. al. "broke the original ground rules" of not directly seeing the film. Reagan, who had never seen the version first used in Wisconsin and Nebraska, "saw the film himself before giving it the final O.K."[184]

Hazen and an advertising agency hired by Van Natta planned how the film would be used.[185] At that time the large television markets in Oregon were Portland, Eugene, and Boise, which covered eastern and northern Oregon. Gram proudly told "anyone who came by the office" about the new film.[186] On April 6, the *New York Times* confirmed, "Oregon backers of Gov. Ronald Reagan of California have started a statewide television and radio campaign." The 30-minute color film was described as Reagan's "main campaign vehicle."[187]

The updated version of *Ronald Reagan, Citizen Governor* initially was shown some six times on local-regional Portland television.[188] It won "critical acclaim and good ratings."[189] Reagan's campaign was buoyed by the acclaim for the movie, and Reagan's team purchased additional airtime and showed the film in Medford, La Grande, Eugene, and Klamath Falls.[190] The media reported that Van Natta had paid $50,000 each for two initial showings in late April and early May.[191] By April 6 the film had "already been shown in every television market in Oregon" and would be "repeated as often as money allows."[192]

The Grams were one of several host families and invited friends and potential Reagan voters to watch the film. Sally recalled that because showing such a campaign film was so novel, never having been broadcast previously in the state, a local television station sent a film crew to their home to film Sally, John, and her friends watching the Reagan film. Sally said her reaction to the film was, "It was terrific."[193] Indeed it was mentioned later in the local press that CBS had had "camera crews filming the Reagan" film.[194]

The newer version of the film had added domestic updates including: Reagan's reaction to the assassination of Martin Luther King—when he is accompanied by Students for Reagan—and Reagan is seen admonishing his fellow Republicans not to cede the areas of unemployment and poverty to the Democrats because their policies have been "colossal failures."

But the major film updates were about Reagan's growth into a world statesman and presidential contender. Eisenhower's coaching shines through, as Reagan is seen addressing the Vietnam War by tying together the Kennedy and Johnson administrations and their failed policies in Southeast Asia. Reagan traces the "floundering of purpose and loss of nerve" from the Bay of Pigs incident to the *U.S.S. Pueblo* incident. He castigates the foreign policy tactic of "flexible response," which had been started by Kennedy and continued by Johnson, instead of the threat of massive nuclear retaliation, which was the major successful tactic of Eisenhower. Reagan describes how the failure of the United States to do anything about the U.S.S. Pueblo indicates it was indeed a policy of "no response."[195]

Reed, Snazelle and Mercer then created a brand new "TV barrage with a series of sixty-second commercials," featuring interviews with local Oregonians who were shown praising Reagan.[196] *Time* reported that the Reagan campaign team also created "20-second Reagan spots, 60-second plugs, (and) five-minute shows" for Oregon television.[197] In two such preplanned interviews, Don Hodel was shown saying, "We need a winner" and in another, "He's the one who can unite the people."[198]

The regional press explained that the film was additional evidence that "a major campaign for Gov. Ronald Reagan" was underway in Oregon. Referring to Reagan's old Borax show, the updated campaign film was described as "hotter than Death Valley," featuring "dramatic shots of Reagan speeches in California and Oregon." The effectiveness of the film in Oregon was noted as "politically potent" and "quite a voter persuader."[199] But was it enough?

Hazen mentioned that more films were planned. The Reagan team tried initially without success to get CBS to release footage of the 1967 Reagan-RFK *Town Meeting of the World* debate in the hopes that Oregon television audiences would compare Reagan's recent debate win against RFK versus the memory of Nixon's loss to John F. Kennedy in the 1960 presidential campaign debates. But at this point CBS, which had tapes of the debate, "will not make them available."[200] Was this due to direct pressure from RFK, who, campaigning in Oregon himself, knew of the Reagan campaign's request? CBS officially claimed their refusal was due to "copyright privileges."[201] Eventually CBS would relent and give permission for Van Natta to edit the original debate into a shorter version to be shown on Oregon television, and at about the same time, CBS would give permission for Bruce Weinrod's Students for Reagan office in the nation's capital to distribute copies to its members as well.

The Reagan film broadcasts along with the other media blitzes were having major impacts. *The Oregonian* reported that now there were "strong pockets of Reagan supporters" in Oregon overall. Specifically in Lane County (see later), "as many as 80 percent…of the precinct and Central Committee workers" were Reagan supporters.[202] If more money flowed into the Reagan Oregon campaign, more films and film clips could be shown, which would "pump real life into the Oregon Republican primary that appeared headed for Dullsville after…Rockefeller withdrew."[203]

The national press also made their assessment. The *New York Times* reported that Reagan's campaign staff "started a statewide television and radio campaign," which "has already been shown in every television market in Oregon and will be repeated as often as money allows."[204] Reporter Tom Wicker commented that Reagan was staging "the nation's first all-television" campaign, which though done on a "small scale" in Nebraska, would be used "more extensively in the Oregon primary." Wicker seemingly disdainfully characterized the strategy to use the film as "Reagan's ploy…to flood Oregon." If Reagan does well then Reagan's vote-getting reputation would be "enhanced." But "if it flops, Reagan can always point out that he never set foot" in Oregon.[205]

Time felt that the Reagan film was "expertly produced" and had caught Reagan in a "wide assortment of moods." The Reagan campaign had made "the most of their leading man's telegenic appeal."[206] *Newsweek* commented, "If the heavily bankrolled Reagan TV campaign in Oregon can seriously wound Nixon," then a "Rocky-Reagan ticket might still seem a plausible possibility."[207]

Nixon Still Feels Threatened

The Oregon Nixon campaign chairman was not pleased by the Reagan media blitz, complaining that he did "not take the Reagan effort lightly" and estimating that Reagan might take "more than 30%" of the Oregon vote.[208] Van Natta felt this was another clear effort to raise expectations that could not be met.[209] Nixon's spokesman charged that the film "violated" the 11th commandment, adding, "The Reagan people sanctimoniously put up Parkinson's law in their headquarters and then showed this film." The Nixon chairman did clear Reagan of personal responsibility for the film but added that he thought Reagan could stop his Oregon campaign if he had wanted.[210]

But Reagan's film did not attack Nixon. It showed clips of what truly had happened: Nixon first had lost the presidency to Kennedy and then the California governorship to Brown; then four years later Reagan defeated Brown by almost a million votes. The Reagan film left it to the viewers to draw the obvious conclusion: Nixon was a loser; Reagan was a winner.

After sensing this increasing worry in the Nixon camp, Van Natta decided to respond by increasing the Reagan threat: "I'm going to buy every dime's worth of TV time I can."[211] Van Natta increased fundraising targets for Reagan, telling the press that he was trying to raise another $50,000.[212] A week later it was reported that the Reagan forces "hiked their ante to $370,000 for television time alone."[213] As Reagan was becoming an Oregon political celebrity, his support was about to increase from the world of sports. O.J. Simpson, who had played in front of Reagan in Corvallis the prior November, would be upended by an even more famous football player at the time.

Y.A. Tittle

In 1968, sports celebrities endorsed many candidates. RFK had Roosevelt Grier and Rafer Johnson. Months after O.J. Simpson's loss in Corvallis while Reagan had watched, the football star endorsed Hubert Humphrey. On the Republican side, Rockefeller was endorsed by Hank Aaron and Howard Cosell. Nixon was favored by Wilt Chamberlain, Bart Starr and Ted Williams. And Ronald Reagan had Y.A. Tittle.[214]

Tittle had played for the Baltimore Colts, San Francisco 49er's and New York Giants and was then quarterback-coach for the 49er's. A famous photograph of Tittle, now hanging in the Pro Football Hall of Fame, showed him on Sept. 20, 1964, having suffered a broken sternum and a concussion as he knelt, helmetless and bloodied, after having been tackled to the ground and having thrown an interception. Tittle previously had campaigned for Reagan's gubernatorial campaign.[215]

In May, Van Natta was attempting to get national Reagan supporters to visit Oregon to speak, and he mentioned that although no movie stars were being sought, some "professional football stars" might visit.[216] Reed arranged the visit of the famous gridiron star.[217] Tittle's appearance, "as part of the Ronald Reagan presidential primary campaign," was accompanied by a "high school press conference" at Reagan headquarters.[218]

Gram arranged for several media interviews of Tittle. After an hour-and-a-half session, the sports editor of *The Oregonian* wrote, "To our surprise," Tittle took a "deep interest in politics and especially in one presidential candidate, Gov. Ronald Reagan." Tittle had come to Portland "at his own expense to help the 'Citizens for Reagan' committee in Portland." After listening to Tittle's speaking about why he was endorsing Reagan for president, the editor concluded, "We don't doubt that his political arguments are good."[219]

At Reagan's Portland headquarters office, "more than twenty" of the campaign staff came to meet Tittle and to have his autograph. Gram recalled that Tittle had told him he had known Reagan for a number of years.[220] Tittle's pro-Reagan comments were heard on local radio, and Tittle was seen on local television endorsing Reagan. Gram reflected that Tittle's visit was "the best" of any visiting Reagan supporter, because "it worked the best."[221] Tittle, still working part-time in the family insurance business in California, declined to be interviewed by your author.

Reagan Meets His Oregon Team...in Idaho

Despite the earlier McCall invitation to campaign personally in Oregon, Reed did not want Reagan to go, even though Reagan had been there twice in 1967. So if Reagan would not come to Oregon, then his campaign staff would come to him via Boise, Idaho. The rationale was simple: northeastern and eastern, rural Oregon was focused on Boise for their newspaper, radio and television coverage. Idaho's main television station, KTVB, had a feeder station, KTVR, in LaGrande, Oregon, which covered most of northeastern Oregon.[222]

The Oregon Reagan campaign purchased advertising time and persuaded Idaho Secretary of State Pete Cenarrusa to head an Idaho Friends of Reagan Committee. Cenarrusa told the press that he had been approached by Young Republicans, as well as senior members of the party, to head the committee. When he decided to accept the Reagan campaign chairmanship in Idaho, he said, "It is more healthy to have more than one candidate at the convention. We want to give the convention another choice. Reagan may actually be stronger than Nixon."[223] The organizers of the new Reagan campaign in Idaho were Frank Whetstone and Clif White. Whetstone told the press, "A definite group is working for Reagan. In case Nixon falters, we want somebody who can step in."[224]

Reagan's team booked television slots on Boise's KTVB for the weeks of April 28, May 5, May 12, and May 19, ending with a "half-hour in prime time Monday May 27," the night before the primary.[225] The bookings were arranged via the advertising firm hired by Van Natta.[226] The purchased slots were described as a "heavy schedule of 20- and 60-second announcements," because of its "large audience in northeastern Oregon" watching at home via La Grande's KTVR.[227] Van Natta was duplicating the same media thrust that he was orchestrating for Oregon now into Idaho with the dual targets of reaching rural Oregon Republican voters as well as Idaho Republicans simultaneously. It was to be the same combination of shorter spot campaign ads, culminating with showing *Ronald Reagan, Citizen Governor* for that May 27 prime time slot the evening before the primary in Oregon.

Idaho itself was not holding a primary. As early as March 1967, Idaho Governor Don Samuelson was noted to be a "new passenger on the Reagan bandwagon."[228] And at the June 1967 Western Governors Conference, he was "known to feel warmly toward" Reagan.[229] But by February 1968, Samuelson remarked that Reagan only was being touted for vice-president.[230] By April, Cenarrusa had succeeded in generating "some support" for Reagan in Idaho, but it was characterized as "backup" support if Nixon faltered.[231]

Just hours prior to Reagan's visit to Boise, Nixon was there to shore up his defenses against Reagan. The Reagan threat to Nixon, begun in Wisconsin and then Nebraska, now was expanding beyond Oregon into Idaho. Nixon acknowledged Reagan's increasing support due to the Reagan media campaign and now Reagan's personal appearance.[232]   One group of historians analyzed the Reagan and Nixon appearances in Boise as having opposite purposes: "Reagan was in Boise to rally the rank and file to his side; Nixon was there to hold the line."[233] As Nixon was leaving Boise, Samuelson called Reagan the "new dynamic voice in the Republican Party." Nixon's attempt to keep Samuelson in line had not succeeded.[234] The Reagan threat was growing daily.

The same day—April 26—Van Natta, Hazen, the Grams, O'Scannlain, Pearlman, and Hodel headed a group of 33 Reagan supporters who flew, in a rented DC-3, which Sally Gram remembered as lasting "four to five hours to fly there and back."[235]

Meanwhile Reagan departed Sacramento and upon arrival at the Boise airport held a press conference. Reagan was asked immediately if he would be amenable to being Nixon's vice-president and he said, "No." After discussing the growing grass-roots efforts in Oregon, he was asked about Nixon having just departed Boise. Reagan quipped, "If I had been competing with him, I would have been here for breakfast," which drew laughter. He elaborated that he had been holding off for several months on an invitation from Governor Samuelson to speak at a Boise fundraiser. He was then asked if the group flying into Boise from Oregon were there to ask him to officially run for president and he answered, "I don't know....I'm not campaigning there. I know there is quite an effort being made there... I doubt if a single primary is going to have a great effect on the race."

Foreign affairs came to the forefront when he was asked about the capture of the *U.S.S. Pueblo*. He admitted he didn't know all the options as a non-insider, but he declared that the Johnson administration was "derelict" in letting it happen. Reagan said the U.S. should use "whatever options" were needed to get the ship and crew back from North Korea. As we will see later, Reagan would formulate a specific plan to deal with future hostage crises.[236]

That evening at the Boise college gymnasium, after a brief number by a rag-time band, Reagan addressed more than 1500 people at the $50 per plate Republican fundraising dinner, which was described as "the largest party fund-raising event in Idaho's history."[237]

Reagan delivered his standard campaign speech, initially joking about Johnson and RFK. He attacked the falling dollar and Johnson's proposed restrictions on foreign travel by saying, "We're the only people whose money can go to Europe but we can't." He paraphrased Churchill when he mocked Humphrey, saying the vice-president "was a modest fellow and he has a lot to be modest about." Changing to a somber tone, Reagan addressed the recent King assassination: "something of America was assassinated also with his death."

Reagan turned to world affairs, pushing for negotiations with the enemy in Vietnam only if they first stopped hostilities. Then Reagan came to the *U.S.S. Pueblo* incident. He assailed the Kennedy-Johnson policies of going from a primarily nuclear navy to a "flexible response" strategy, decrying that when the ship was attacked, there "was no response." This was only a warm-up for how Reagan would criticize the Kennedy-Johnson military priorities in his last White paper speeches and later in Amarillo.[238] Reagan was filmed during his speech, and segments were used for the new version of *Ronald Reagan, Citizen Governor* that was still in production at the time.[239]

Reagan and His Team

At the later private meeting, his Oregon supporters "urged him to campaign actively" in their home state. But Reagan told them he was "sticking to his status as a non-candidate."[240] Hazen told Reagan that he "would sweep the state if he campaigned here," adding that since Kennedy's entrance into the Democratic race, there was an "upsurge of interest" in Reagan because Reagan was "the only candidate who can unite the Republican party and defeat the New York Senator." The visitors from Oregon were "happy that he has not closed the door on an Oregon visit before the May 28 primary."[241]

Sally Gram recalled that the personal visit with Reagan was "very exciting" and that he was "very magnetic." The visit with Reagan in-person was in a room with a small table attended by some nine to twelve of the Oregon team. Reagan gave them "a little pep talk."[242] Van Natta recalled that they were each given small bottle sets of bourbon as gifts from Tom Reed and Ronald Reagan, and Van Natta still has two small bottles in his office in 2012.[243]

For Van Natta, the chance to visit with Reagan once again was quite special. Van Natta remembered that when Reagan was looking and speaking with you, "You're the only person in the room…He had an effect on me that doesn't happen very often…I came away energized."[244] For O'Scannlain, the Boise trip would be his first meeting with Reagan in person. He recalled Reagan's talk as "warm and inspiring" and that Reagan clearly told them that he appreciated what the group from Oregon was doing on his behalf. It was clear to all in the room that Reagan was running for president. But the strategy was to create a "strictly local operation." Reagan's Oregon friends hoped for more: that he would throw his hat in the ring while at the same time he would not be "overrun by the Nixon juggernaut."[245]

As Reagan flew off, for Cenarrusa and Samuelson, a plan emerged to have Senator Len Jordan as favorite son with the delegation being pro-Nixon. But most of the 14 delegates would "swing comfortably into the Reagan camp if and when the time comes—maybe on the second or third ballot at Miami Beach."[246] Long afterwards, Reagan would continue to receive support in Idaho. At the mid-June Idaho State Republican Assembly meeting in Coeur d'Alene, a "Nixon-Reagan oriented delegation" would be chosen to go to Miami Beach. Although the fourteen delegates "were reported to favor" Nixon, they "could easily swing to Gov. Ronald Reagan of California."[247]

The Reagan Juggernaut

Less than two weeks before the primary, Nixon again protected his right flank, this time by visiting Reagan strongholds in rural eastern Oregon.[248] In Pendleton, Nixon mimicked Reagan by attacking the student takeover of Columbia University.[249] Reagan, who had attacked student demonstrators starting with his attacks on Berkeley demonstrators while running for governor, had continued during 1967 and 1968 as we have seen. These were themes he had used to great effect at Hiram Scott College, Yale University, the University of Kansas, and the University of Colorado. Clearly, Nixon had started to use the same themes feeling pressure from the right from Reagan, just as Nixon had foreseen at his early campaign planning meeting at his Manhattan apartment. As we will see later, Reagan would use the example of the Columbia University takeover when he would discuss his solution to dealing with hostages.

During this campaign swing, although Nixon was smiling, "beneath the confidence there was a note of concern in the Nixon camp," which "stemmed from the pronounced popularity displayed" by Reagan's recent strong 22 percent showing in Nebraska. Nixon's campaign was worried that Reagan's team "would be able to fan the brushfire higher in Oregon."[250] If Reagan did well in Oregon, it "could tarnish the winner image Nixon has sought to build…It would do nothing to diminish mounting talk of a Rockefeller-Reagan combination to stop Nixon."[251] In addition, observed historian Theodore H. White, for Nixon "Oregon was critical; a strong showing by Reagan here would enlarge Reagan, in Southern eyes, to a southern-oriented candidate with national potential."[252] Although Nixon was "outwardly unconcerned about the Reagan vote in Nebraska," amidst all the Reagan campaign activity in Oregon, it was obvious that "no other primary state has received this much Nixon attention."[253] Appling confirmed Nixon's worry about the growing Reagan threat, stating that Nixon had increased his financial commitment to Oregon now to "$500,000 on the primary."[254]

Nixon, seeing the rise of Reagan along the Wisconsin-Nebraska-Oregon trajectory, himself began to tamp down expectations, telling reporters that in Oregon he no longer anticipated the 70%-80% he had received in Wisconsin and Nebraska. His goal now was "anything above the combined total for Reagan and Rockefeller."[255] Of course such a comment by Nixon could very likely have been made so that if he did better than this, he could claim new additional support. In a similar vein, just after his Nebraska victory, Nixon had "predicted a Reagan vote of 20-30 per cent in Oregon. Now the latest Nixon leaders have raised this to 35 per cent."[256] As discussed, by Nixon raising falsely high expectations for Reagan, any Reagan vote tally less than this would be claimed as a more intense Reagan defeat than otherwise and could be used easily to lessen any Reagan momentum. Simultaneously, the Nixon forces made public vote estimates for themselves that were "deliberately pessimistic" of 33 percent, then claiming a vote of 40 per cent would be "exceptionally strong," so that any ultimate higher vote would be seen as a Nixon landslide.[257]

As the primary date approached, Nixon had to fight off the Reagan threat yet again: Nixon once more was back campaigning in Oregon.[258] He flew to Klamath Falls. At the Oregon Technical Institute, he made a direct reference to Reagan, noting sarcastically, "These are not times for absentee candidates."[259] Reagan's conservative campaign themes still loomed in the forefront of Nixon's thoughts, because it was noted that Nixon emphasized national defense and fiscal responsibility "in an apparent effort to protect his right flank."[260]

Gov. McCall saw the handwriting on the wall and understood that his support for Rockefeller was a lost cause. McCall wrote that he would support, "work, and fight" for whoever would win the primary.[261]

Beyond Portland

Reagan's grass roots activists were not confined to Portland. There were Reagan-for-President offices in ten of Oregon's counties.[262] But the busiest outside of Portland was in Lane County and was headed by Peter Murphy. As noted earlier, Murphy had attended Reagan's 1967 Veteran's Day football game in Corvallis so he could see "The Gipper" in person and to see him ride a horse; later he had been recruited by Reed, Spencer and conservative radio owner Hobie Wilson to run Lane County even before Van Natta had been recruited. Murphy's official title was chairman of the Lane County Citizens for Reagan Committee. Hodel recalled that Murphy "was an enthusiast about anything he undertook" and was "congenial and earnest."[263]

Murphy set up his Reagan-for-President county headquarters out of his own office in Springfield. He recruited a number of local volunteers to help. Receiving no money from California or Topeka or Portland, Murphy raised all campaign monies locally himself via telephone. Murphy did receive handouts and pamphlets from Reed and Spencer. Murphy used them when he and his staff set up many social meetings of Republican Women's groups in Lane, Coos, and Douglas counties, plus his volunteer office staff sent out mailings to local Republicans. Usually some twenty-five Republican women attended the meetings, and they "listened courteously." Murphy succeeded "slightly" in changing their minds towards supporting Reagan.[264]

Although all local prominent Republicans were for Nixon, Murphy did feel he made headway by the group meetings and the mailings of the Reagan literature to general party members and to the Lane County Republican Party office. When *Ronald Reagan Citizen Governor* was to be shown on television those six times, Murphy had his staff contact as many people as possible to watch the film. The local newspaper, the *Eugene Register-Guard*, had some short articles about the Lane County Reagan campaign.[265] By then Murphy's grass roots movement caught on, and many people started calling Murphy's office asking for information about Reagan's presidential campaign and/or voicing their support for him.[266]

The Reagan Bus

Murphy's company had a veneer mill on the Oregon coast two miles east of Florence in Cushman, so he sometimes worked there on behalf of Reagan too. But in Florence was another staunch Reagan supporter, restaurant owner Oscar Funk. Murphy supplied pamphlets and handouts to Funk, whose unique campaign technique was his Ronald Reagan bus. Funk soon would butt heads with a vocal RFK supporter: his own brother Ernie. Ironically, their internecine quarrel would lead to the most unique way ever found to fund a Ronald Reagan campaign: rental money from Robert F. Kennedy's campaign.

Oscar Funk outfitted an old school bus into a Ronald Reagan for President campaign bus, with Reagan signs on the sides and pamphlets and brochures to hand out. Murphy recalled that Funk traveled north and south along the Oregon coast to major towns such as Reedsport, Coos Bay and Newport. Others reported that Funk actually traveled "throughout the state."[267]

Murphy rode with Funk in the Reagan bus.[268] Another rider was a young budding journalist, Francis Rothauge. Rothauge recalled that Van Natta hired him as a Reagan field man. As the bus traveled from Portland west to Astoria and then down the coast to Coos Bay and then turned back east to traverse the north-south Willamette Valley, Rothauge stopped at every radio and television station and high school he could find to hand out Reagan campaign materials and speak about Reagan. Over a period of some seven to ten days, as the primary approached, Rothauge and four others manned the bus as Funk drove, with their reception from the crowds recalled by Rothauge as good.[269]

Reagan Tops Kennedy

Meanwhile Funk realized that in addition to Murphy's coastal Reagan office in nearby Cushman, and besides the bus, he needed his own Reagan campaign office. He chose a building he owned in "Old Town" Florence. But he had not known who else was interested in the same building. Kennedy's campaign staff had found the same empty building, previously an electric repair shop, and, via a local realty agent, was directed to one Ernie Funk. Ernie "gave Kennedy workers permission to occupy the building," but only afterwards did Ernie decide it might be a good idea to tell his brother Oscar—the owner—what he had done.

Oscar, the "staunch Reagan backer," nearly "had apoplexy when he heard about his new tenants." Oscar had wanted the building for Reagan headquarters. Oscar then told his brother Ernie in no uncertain terms to "get the Kennedy forces out." So Ernie dutifully went to the Kennedy people, asking them to move out and even "offered them $35 to help them move." But the Kennedy staff refused.

The standoff led to a showdown on the next Saturday during the 61st annual Florence Rhododendron Festival. As the town was filled with people, Oscar Funk and his Reagan campaign staff—including Murphy—all arrived in Oscar's Reagan-for-President bus and parked right in front of Kennedy headquarters. Oscar and his staff got into a verbal dispute with the Kennedy staff, and a county deputy sheriff had to come to arbitrate. Rothauge recalled that the sheriff told both brothers that nobody wanted any trouble, so couldn't they reach an equitable solution?

Ernie offered Oscar $50 as monthly rent but Oscar refused the offer. When asked what he thought a good rent payment would be, Oscar answered $500 and Ernie agreed on the spot to pay. So Murphy announced the settlement. "We're letting the Kennedy workers stay there until Monday when they can look for quarters elsewhere. We want to keep our campaign clean." But Murphy added with a grin, "We're not against using Kennedy money for the Reagan campaign. From the rental we are getting, we will be able to buy a couple more TV 'spots'."[270]

The headline in an article for the Siuslaw News read, "Reagan Tops Kennedy in Pre-Primary Tiff."[271] This newspaper reported that the agreed-to rent was only $37.50 for two weeks, but regardless, had RFK lived to become the Democratic nominee and had Reagan won in Miami Beach, the headline might have presaged the election results the following November.

Watching and reporting on the events in Florence was a small film crew from the NBC News office in Los Angeles. One of the reporters was a young reporter named Tom Brokaw. Rothauge recalled that Brokaw had heard of the excitement and flew to Oregon to see what was going on.[272] Brokaw's crew took a photograph of Reagan's fieldmen welcoming Funk's bus to Florence, and Brokaw had a 5-minute segment on his nightly news program. In 2014, Brokaw did not return calls from your author for his recollections.

RFK Helps Fund Reagan for President

Meanwhile, the excitement about the Reagan-RFK brouhaha was not over. Oscar Funk took out an ad for Reagan for President in the *Siuslaw News* and added at the bottom that the ad was "paid with funds from Western Lane Kennedy for President Committee" as well as Oregon Citizens for Reagan.[273] When local high school students read the ad, they were outraged and picketed the newspaper. But the newspaper had the check,[274] and the principal called the students back to class. Besides RFK's direct sparring with the pro-Reagan medical students in Indiana, this only other major interaction between the Reagan and Kennedy forces in 1968 had come to a peaceful end.[275] Ever since both Kennedy's had sent checks to Nixon's senatorial campaign against Reagan's friend Helen Gahagan Douglas, this may have been the only other documented instance of funds from a Kennedy campaign being used to support a major conservative candidate.

Funk's new Reagan office on the Oregon coast had volunteers helping with the Reagan effort.[276] During the final days of the primary campaign, Murphy did stay in intermittent contact with Reed to report in.[277]

No Help From The Oregon Republican Party

The heroic efforts of the Reagan team in Oregon were accomplished in isolation, as the vast majority of established and official members of the Oregon Republican Party were for Nixon, or in the case of McCall and Hatfield, were for Rockefeller.[278] Virtually all the leadership of the Republican State Central Committee of Oregon either "did not participate in the campaign,"[279] or "were for Nixon."[280] The sole exception was Secretary Shirley Shay who passed away in 2012. O'Scannlain recalled that she was for Reagan but was not certain "how public she was about it."[281] At the county or precinct level, Hodel recalled, "Individual county party officials may have supported Reagan, but they would have been the minority... The 'regular party' people were for Nixon...It was his turn."[282] Hodel recalled that the party leadership stayed out of the presidential primary. The party would be damaged if party officials took sides in a primary. Any official who was for Nixon or Reagan did so privately and did no active campaigning for any one candidate before the primary.[283]

Would it have made much difference had more state or county or precinct Republican party officials been for Reagan? Hodel thinks not. "The reality is that the party was terribly weak and ineffective in Oregon at that time so what these people did, or did not do, made little difference in the outcome."[284]

Culmination: May 1968

May 14, the day of Y.A. Tittle's arrival in Portland, was the day Reagan had garnered the unexpectedly high 22% in Nebraska. Nixon's campaign was then forced to reassess vote projections in Oregon. They upped Reagan to some "six percentage points better in Oregon" than in Nebraska, due to the television campaign of Reagan. Nixon would spend $300,000 and Reagan's campaign would spend "nearly as much." Van Natta admitted the true figure would be "less than $100,000," although additional out-of-state money was financing his distribution of a Reagan biographical paperback book.[285] As noted earlier, Reagan was in Honolulu, attending the Western Governors Conference and delivering his first White Paper speech attacking RFK, when he learned of the Nebraska results.[286]

Van Natta reflected, "In one sense we were surprised at the Nebraska outcome; in another sense we were distraught." The Oregon Reaganites were surprised but very happy that Reagan had done so well in Nebraska, as they had doubled the vote from

Wisconsin. None of them thought Reagan would go from 11% to 22%. But now they were distraught with the knowledge that they had to beat what Nebraskan voters had just accomplished for Reagan. The entire campaign strategy of Wisconsin-Nebraska-Oregon was the incremental effect of an increasing percentage for each sequential primary. After Nebraska, Van Natta had "never believed we would beat the 22% number; we didn't think we were going to do that well" in Oregon. The entire Reagan plan to create a cascading tidal wave— of increasing numbers as the primaries moved west, with Oregon planned to do best at the end before California's expected 100 percent vote for Reagan—had been "substantially damaged" by the "good turnout of votes in Nebraska."[287]

Gram arranged for Hazen to be interviewed at three different Portland television stations.[288] Gram was quite excited as to how well Reagan had done.[289] He issued a press release saying, "Wow! How about the Reagan Nebraska vote?... (it) demonstrated a vote of confidence... (and is) a challenge that the Oregon Citizens for Reagan intend to match and beat."[290]

Reagan's Nebraska success was infectious. The entire Portland campaign headquarters for Reagan "buzzed with new enthusiasm." Van Natta's official comment to the press, more circumspect than what he had thought privately above, admitted that the final 22 percent Nebraska vote for Reagan set a new bar and that the Oregon team now had to "shoot for bettering Nebraska."

Everyone sprang into action. Other Reagan workers promised to work "like dam-building beavers" to win Reagan a "big share" of the upcoming May 28 primary vote.[291] Reagan commented, "In Oregon I understand the people there are putting up a bigger effort; again I've not been there. I'm not going there. Some of them came over to see me at a speaking engagement in Idaho and told me that they would be ecstatic if they managed to come up with fifteen percent of the vote in Oregon."[292] Reagan neglected to mention his two major visits to Oregon in 1967. Unspoken was Reed's original goal of winning in Oregon.

At this time, there was renewed talk of a Reagan and Rockefeller ticket after they had met briefly and unexpectedly in New Orleans. The growing Reagan enthusiasm in Oregon did not need this news at this time. In all the Reagan county offices, "telephones...were kept busy" because "a lot of little old ladies called," asking if the Reagan team was aware of the meeting. Van Natta put out the fires. "Talk of a Rockefeller-Reagan ticket has caused us a lot of trouble in Oregon. Great droves of Reagan supporters would vote for Richard Nixon at the thought of Rockefeller skulking around anywhere." Van Natta then accused the Nixon campaign of fanning those flames of concern by saying that "Nixon backers have been saying that Robert Hazen, Chairman of Oregon Citizens for Reagan, and Mr. Van Natta actually want to see Mr. Rockefeller nominated." Van Natta wanted the press and public to know what Nixon's team was doing to undermine the Reagan vote.[293]

New Poll

Then Van Natta received a new campaign tool arrived from Reed, which was a detailed Merrill/Wirthlin Associates Oregon public opinion poll, commissioned from Sacramento, with Reed and Spencer having analyzed it in California. They used it to "guide" the Oregon staff of what to say about issues.[294] Van Natta donated a copy of the poll to the Willamette University Library in 2012, where it sits on a lonely shelf.

The poll was done door-to-door but unfortunately who was polled, how they were selected, and who the identification of the pollsters is not recorded. Similar to the earlier poll critiqued by Van Natta, those polled in this new poll were from Portland, southern Oregon and the central valleys. Once again, conservative Republican strongholds of northeastern and eastern Oregon were not included. There were fifty-six questions on hot topics of the day, and those polled were asked to choose from a list of ten responses what they liked and then disliked about Nixon, Rockefeller, and Reagan. They were also asked to rate the three, along with rating RFK, on a sliding scale of liberal to conservative. The poll also then asked their choice if they had to send a sealed ballot today for their specific choice for president and vice-president.

Van Natta reflected that the poll was taken because Oregon was one of the few states in 1968 that had a primary system.[295] Thus voting by registered party members was the determining factor, rather than a state such as neighboring Washington, wherein party caucuses and conventions determined the delegates to Miami Beach.[296] Van Natta started using the poll results to plan his final campaign jewel, his brand new newspaper advertising tabloid.[297] Meanwhile an old Reagan media triumph was about to resurface.

RFK Debate Film Redux

At long last, efforts to unearth and show to the public the 1967 *Town Meeting of the World* debate, refused initially by CBS possibly due to Kennedy pressure, finally came to fruition. CBS relented and licensed Van Natta to show an edited version of the debate to private and public audiences. Van Natta cut the one-hour debate down to 29-minutes. The entire Portland campaign office staff sent out teams of "action squads" to pass out bumper stickers and literature throughout Clackamas, Multnomah, and Washington counties announcing the showings.[298]

One private showing occurred on May 20 at a luncheon meeting of the Tri-County Republican Club at the Hoyt Hotel.[299] Evans recalled the event quite clearly. There were forty Republican women who saw the debate and they were from Multnomah, Washington and Clackamas counties. There were mainly Reagan supporters and Evans recalled they all felt Reagan had done well against Kennedy.[300] In Southern Oregon, Francis Rothauge, no longer manning the Reagan campaign bus, took a copy of the film to the Jackson County Republican Women's Association in Medford, where he recalled, some 20-30 enthusiastic women watched the debate.[301]

Of course everyone there was well aware that Kennedy was in Oregon campaigning in the Democratic primary and was the likely nominee to face Reagan or Nixon. The hidden message of course was that while everyone knew that Nixon had lost the debate and the general election to John Kennedy in 1960, they were watching how Reagan had defeated RFK in their debate a year earlier. Showing the debate served as a complement to the Reagan film: both sending the clear message that if they wanted to beat RFK in the fall, they had better vote for Reagan in Oregon and then nominate Reagan in Miami Beach.

Van Natta's Home Grown Newspaper Tabloid

By this time, media-savvy Van Natta had arranged that copies of Lee Edwards' Reagan biography, for which Bruce Weinrod had been principal researcher as we have seen, was mailed to some 447,000 registered Oregon Republicans. Van Natta now was set to unveil his crown jewel for the campaign: a mass advertising tabloid newspaper supplement. With a fine tooth comb, Van Natta had gone over the Oregon voter poll that Reed had sent, looking for trends to exploit in the last few days before the election. Van Natta still takes special pride in the tabloid he had created in 1968, because "the tab was our home grown effort."[302]

On May 19, the Reagan advertisement arrived on newsstands: an eight-page, color supplement appearing in *The Oregonian* and *The Oregon Statesman*.[303] Van Natta characterized it as "our major campaign piece."[304] Time reported that the tabloid was mailed out to 750,000 people.[305]

The front page photo showed a smiling Reagan under the banner, "Reagan for New Leadership" and the title was, "The <u>Winning</u> Republican for President." The initial article was a brief biography, which ended with his huge gubernatorial victory in California because the Republican Party had decided "they needed a man who could win." "The Reagan Record," at the top of page 3, spoke of his lowering property taxes, cutting the budget deficit, streamlining state government, using modern business practices and was accompanied by pictures of Reagan. There were photographs and comments from Hodel, Gram, Evans and Murphy. Van Natta shrewdly also had photos and comments from members of different segments of Oregon society, including two college students, a lumberman, a hotel manager, a farmer, a corporal serving in Vietnam, an automobile dealer and a businessman. Photos of Reagan visiting Oregon in 1967 reminded the reader that indeed Reagan had been there twice in 1967, most recently the prior November, even if he had not been there in 1968. "Reagan the Winner" showed the governor as a skilled fundraiser, next to a smiling Dwight Eisenhower, and "as a winner wherever he goes." Quotes from local newspapers abounded: *The Oregonian* "Reagan Proves Able Politician" and "New Flurry Noted in Reagan Drive"; *Medford Mail Tribune* "Hatfield Foresees Boom Developing for Governor Reagan"; Salem *Capital Journal* "Ike, Reagan Talks Spark Speculation" and "Reagan Builds Up Fast As '68 Prospect"; Eugene *Register-Guard* "Reagan's National Image Very Good." National magazine headlines were also recorded: *Atlantic Monthly* "Predict Fight By Reagan For GOP Bid" and *Fortune* "Ronald Reagan-Rising Star of the West." The back page proclaimed, "The Republican Party needs a Candidate who can WIN!" with a letter from Chairman Hazen.

In addition to the tabloid, distributed via newspapers, Van Natta indeed had created a full media blitz for the final days before the primary vote. The national press took note of Van Natta's television and radio tactics. *Time* said there were "20-second Reagan spots, 60-second plugs, five-minute shows, and a full half-hour program," and the Reed film, which was an "expertly produced program."[306] The *New York Times* saw that "Reagan backers are pouring money and effort into Oregon." Van Natta's tabloid promoted Reagan as "a winner in November" and was an "undisguised allusion to Nixon's greatest handicap with faithful Republicans, his losses as the party's nominee for President and Governor of California."[307]

Nixon Panic?

Just days before the primary election, the *New York Times* confirmed the success Reagan's all-out multimedia campaign was having against Nixon: Oregon would be Nixon's "last and most difficult primary because a strong drive for votes has been mounted for Gov. Ronald Reagan,"[308] and reiterated, a few days later, that Nixon faced "the only real challenge of his six-primary run" for the nomination.[309] How serious a threat was Reagan to Nixon? Citing the 20 percent figure projected by the Reagan campaign staff, the reporter noted, "This would be a comedown" from the 22 percent in Nebraska after "an expenditure…for television alone eight times as large."

Nixon was feeling the heat from Reagan, admitting to the press they had now increased their Reagan vote projections to 35 percent, because Reagan had upped projected campaign budget forecasts to $400,000.[310] Of course Nixon was setting Reagan to too high a bar; it was unlikely at this point that Reagan would achieve 35 percent. Thus any tally below this would be declared by Nixon to be a Reagan failure. Nixon himself claimed to have scaled back his own vote projections, because "his winning percentage may be reduced by the Reagan drive."

Yet Nixon took action and as seen upped his budget to $500,000 to battle Reagan. Privately, he likely felt even more threatened. Nixon was noted to be "constantly aware" of Reagan's growing activity. So to shore up the falling bulwarks against the Reagan onslaught even further than just adding money, Nixon also increased his visits to Oregon. For "no other state has received this much Nixon attention." A strong Reagan showing could "tarnish the winner image" Nixon had sought.[311] That was exactly Reed and Spencer's plans all along.

The same day, the regional press analyzed the situation in the closing days as that "the Reagan forces (were) more strongly organized in Oregon than in any other primary state outside California." The Oregon Reagan team said they would "claim a victory of sorts if their man gets 20 percent or more" of the vote. Clearly Hazen, Van Natta and Gram were tamping down expectations in case their goals eluded their hopes.[312]

A final Oregon Republican poll was released by Oliver Quayle of NBC, which gave Nixon 55 percent and Reagan 20 percent, which was interpreted by Oregon political leaders as showing "the bulk of the undecided vote" would go to Reagan.[313] Nixon's campaign worries about Reagan's media blitz culminated by showing their own $100,000 pre-recorded campaign documentary film, *Nixon Now*, on nationwide television the evening before the election. Nixon had had to copy Reagan by creating his own film.[314]

Hazen countered, "Oregon Republicans were showing little enthusiasm for Nixon" and "supporters of ... Nixon ... were showing signs of panic."[315] National columnist Drew Pearson wrote that Reagan "has been spending money as if he meant business" and then cited Hazen's buying large blocks of media time as "pulling all the stops to elect his candidate." Pearson added that Reagan was serious about running for president. "Reagan is spending money all-out for a showdown with Nixon."[316]

Then the Reagan staff ran out of campaign buttons. Hazen appealed to the public via the local press, pleading that although some 20,0000 buttons had been made, "there is a shortage" and "they didn't have money for more buttons."[317] That day, Clif White arrived in Portland to "watch the action in the closing days of the Oregon primary." White analyzed the race at this point saying, "I have never seen a time when the delegates and the party leadership has (sic) been as anxious to remain uncommitted as this year." He predicted a three-ballot convention in Miami Beach.[318] Sally Gram recalled White wore an unexpected eastern bow-tie and hosted a pep-talk breakfast at Hazen's office for fifty Reagan supporters.[319]

The Final Oregon Vote

The raw election data was tabulated and disseminated by a new News Election Service operated by the Associated Press.[320] Write-in votes for Reagan for vice-president had begun, even though he had withdrawn from the vice-presidential race as noted earlier. Via a new "Early Counting Board," votes started to be counted at 4 PM with an early report at 8 PM, so as to give the east coast viewers some indication as to what had happened.[321] The national television news media descended into Portland, including Walter Cronkite, Mike Wallace, David Brinkley, Frank McGee, and Bill Lawrence. Bill Stout was assigned to be in La Jolla to "report on Gov. Ronald Reagan's reactions."[322]

The Northwest media had been impressed by Reagan's Oregon grass roots campaign. From Seattle, where Reagan had first spoken as a national candidate in 1966 and from where their poll had found that voters had no problems with an actor running for public office, came the analysis that via "television and a deluge of campaign advertising," Reagan "acts like a man who wants the assignment."[323]

But from back East, the liberal *New York Times* editorial board chimed in with a last-minute attack on Reagan. Entitled, "The GOP's Missing Men," the editorial thought that any possible Rockefeller-Reagan alliance to stop Nixon was "illogical both in principle and in practice." The board then wondered about the supposed "grave question of personal capacity. Mr. Reagan has yet to demonstrate that he is a competent Governor or that he is qualified to be an architect of the nation's foreign policy and commander in chief of its armed forces and nuclear power."

Had the editorial board ever actually listened to any of Reagan's numerous campaign speeches addressing winning the Vietnam war, Cuba, dealing with communists, calls to tear down the Berlin Wall, and the *U.S.S. Pueblo*, they would have found that his audiences had enthusiastically agreed with his world view and that his views had been carefully thought out since the 1950's; and unbeknownst to the newspaper, had been refined and expanded by Eisenhower's continued guidance. Indeed with hind-sight from the early 21st century, the *New York Times* conveniently never asked those same questions in 2008 of a candidate whose experience in governing would be much less than what Reagan had had by 1968. But for Ronald Reagan in 1980 and 1984 and his role in world history, he was in fact the same man as in 1968. In 1968, Ronald Reagan had become a world statesman and true contender for the presidency. Conservatives had seen his transformation but the liberal elite could not see.

The final word came from a reporter rather than their editorial board. "Enthusiastic backers of Ronald Reagan have conducted the most ambitious campaign yet attempted for the California Governor in a primary state." There was still last-minute hope that a strong showing in Oregon "will persuade him to become an active candidate for the Republican nomination."[324] It was reported that "most impartial observers here feel that Mr. Reagan would have to get more than 30 percent to build the momentum necessary to justify an active candidacy."[325] But one also may question whether the reporter also was inflating Reagan vote tally projections so as to negate the actual Reagan vote.

Hazen and Van Natta and the rest of the entire state team in Oregon knew Reagan would not win Oregon, but still they hoped to best Nebraska's 22 percent. Van Natta and Hazen made one last attempt by showing *Ronald Reagan, Citizen Governor* one last time at 7:30 PM on KOIN-TV Portland on election eve.[326][327]

During the week leading up to the Oregon primary, Reagan was in the midst of his whirl-wind Southern Solicitation, delivering his five White Papers attacking RFK and Kennedy-Johnson domestic and foreign policies. After Reagan's appearance on *Meet the Press*, cited earlier, Rockefeller told ABC's *Issues and Answers* it was clear to all that "Reagan was now aiming for the top spot himself."[328] But some national observers cautioned that Reagan and Rockefeller needed each other in order to stop Nixon.[329] Reagan's final words before the vote were that "pride alone" made him want to receive a "good vote." He reiterated that he wanted the convention delegates to consider "all men placed in nomination," including himself, because a great factor will be "the winnability of the candidate."[330]

Election Day

On May 28 fully 75.6 percent of eligible Republicans voted.[331] At 8:07 PM, Chet Huntley of NBC-TV declared Nixon the winner just as David Brinkley had just called Reagan "the biggest-spending non-candidate in history." Reagan came in second with 63,707 votes—way ahead of Rockefeller at 36,306.[332] Amongst Democrat write-in votes, Reagan at 3,082 beat Nixon (2,974) and Rockefeller (2,841) confirming his appeal to disaffected Democrats.[333]

Reagan was interviewed from La Jolla, in which he said Nixon was "doing quite a bit better than the polls indicated." Reagan continued, "I don't have any strategy. A few people from Oregon came over to see me in Boise and told me they'd be ecstatic, that was the word they used, if I got 15 percent of the vote."[334]

But the behind-the-scenes story of Richard Nixon's Oregon victory was not over. Nixon and Kennedy had been at the same hotel, and the press, of course, swarmed Kennedy in defeat and virtually ignored Nixon in victory; Nixon and Kennedy did not speak with one another.[335]

At the hotel bar after the results were known, Van Natta recalled seeing Nixon's campaign manager at a darkened table in the corner and went over to congratulate him on running the successful Nixon primary campaign victory. But "there was someone sitting with him in the dark." When he finally realized that it was Nixon at the table in the shadows, Van Natta felt somewhat embarrassed for having interrupted their conversation.[336] Even some forty-five years later, Van Natta remains somewhat mystified as to why victorious Nixon felt compelled to remain hidden away from public view after having achieved what may have been his most important victory in the Republican primary season in 1968 that night. But Van Natta was not the only outsider to see Nixon that evening. Presidential historian

Theodore H. White also saw Nixon later that same evening in the hotel's London Grill Restaurant. By this time both Nixon and his manager had been joined by their wives and with "no one else even close, or watching," White was perplexed. On such an election night when the victor normally would be "overwhelmed and pestered to death by the gawkerie of people," Nixon "sat entirely alone with his little group."[337] Nixon was staying at the same hotel as Robert F. Kennedy, who just had lost his first election. But at the Benson Hotel, Kennedy in defeat garnered more press attention than Nixon in victory.[338]

White and Nixon discussed what the results meant for both the Democrats and Republicans. White observed that what was most important for Richard Nixon was "Reagan's poor showing. Reagan had made a massive TV effort. Defeat had now eliminated him as a viable national candidate."[339] How wrong White was.

Aftermath for Reagan

The *New York Times* page 1 headline on May 29 was, "Nixon Is A Strong Winner," with the sub-heading ,"Reagan Runs Second but Trails Badly," at a point where 1,518 0f 2,599 precincts had reported and at that time Reagan had 22 percent of the vote. A half-hour after the polls had closed, Reagan said at the time that his very early share count of 20 percent was "quite a bit better than the polls indicated and quite a bit better than had been expected by persons working on the campaign in Oregon. They told me they would be ecstatic if I got 15 percent." Reagan ran strongest in rural areas, where "his government economy views" and "hawkish stand on Viet Nam" were "well accepted" according to NBC.[340]

But here Reagan finally acknowledged in public that the team in Oregon was not just a group of independent pro-Reagan workers from whom he had distanced himself, but rather they were indeed his presidential campaign staff in Oregon. Reagan also had compared the vote with the *Los Angeles Times* pre-election poll of 8 percent cited earlier but ignored the NBC poll whose 20 percent Reagan projection seemed right on target. His reaction was described as "not unhappy." Then Reagan admitted "Yes, of course, it would be different," in hindsight "if he had campaigned" in person in Oregon. But when a newsman immediately followed-up with a second question asking if he would now announce as an active presidential candidate, Reagan answered, "No, nor would I had the results been reversed."[341]

Hazen, Van Natta, and Rothauge watched the returns from the downtown Portland headquarters office of Citizens for Reagan. They sat in the second floor portion of the office, while the staff and supporters "munched jelly beans" in front of the first floor television sets. Van Natta summed up their reaction: "Governor Reagan said he would be pleased with 15 percent of the Oregon vote. We are delighted with what now looks like 22 percent or more." He called the Oregon campaign "almost a carbon copy of the Nebraska campaign," adding "We not only equaled Reagan's surprising large Nebraska percentage, but are drawing a greater number of total votes in Oregon."

After telling the media that the Reagan campaign had spent between $100,000 to $110,000 in Oregon, Van Natta summed up the results, noting, "Particularly in view of the intensive, blitz campaign waged by the professional staffs of the other candidates during the last two weeks of the primary, we are very proud that such a large number of Oregonians voted for Governor Reagan."[342] Hazen spoke to the press also.[343] Van Natta and Reagan were putting as best a face forward to the media as they each could muster. Both Reagan and Van Natta cited each other's supposed 15 percent pre-election projection as having been surpassed by the actual vote, when in reality as seen earlier, the plan of the campaign was to beat Nebraska's 22 percent. They failed to do so.

Nixon's analysis of Reagan's vote tally in Oregon was, "I don't think Reagan did so badly here. It's just that we did so well. We didn't spend as much the last two weeks on television, but our campaign effort on television was more successful." Rockefeller's chairman said, "I was disappointed in Reagan. I expected him to get 25 percent or more."[344]

The Oregonian concluded, "Governor Reagan's showing was not nearly as good as expected by those who spent a small fortune in advertising the absentee candidate" and continued that for "Reagan or any combination of anti-Nixon delegates to stop Dick Nixon" would be "difficult."[345]

A post-primary gathering was held by O'Scannlain, in his Portland home, for the Pearlmans, the Grams, Diana Evans, and the Hodels. Suddenly the phone rang. A very familiar voice said, "I hear you're having a wake...This is Ronald Reagan." He said he knew everyone had gathered and had wanted to thank them all and how much he appreciated their hard work. Reagan's greeting and call would not be the only time he would call the Oregon supporters to attempt to allay their disappointment during the 1968 campaign. Afterwards, in public Gram put his "best face on it" now that Reagan had lost."[346]

O'Scannlain recalled, "I don't know that any of us really expected to pull it off. We were hoping to make it as close as we could." He noted that people had been "happy" that they had come close.[347] Hazen gave a silver medallion present to all the major campaign workers.

In Lane County, Peter Murphy gathered his Reagan committee for a social get-together at the courthouse to see the returns. Everyone "took it hard." Murphy had been in contact with Tom Reed during the evening, who told Peter they had done "better than we expected." Afterwards he spoke to Reed "a few times" so he would feel involved somehow with the Reagan national campaign until Miami Beach. To Murphy's surprise, a Nixon delegate who had seen Murphy's enthusiasm, "out of the clear blue," invited Murphy to be an alternate and he accepted on the spot. Murphy prepared to fly to Miami Beach.[348]

Over the next few days, the *New York Times* gave their final assessment of the Oregon Republican primary results. Oregon voters had "rejected the campaign of Governor Reagan." Although acknowledging that indeed Reagan "did considerably better" than Rockefeller, Reagan "could hardly be said to have thrown a scare into the Nixon camp." Reagan's supporters were noted to have said Reagan would "be happy to equal his Nebraska showing of 22 percent." At this time, Reagan's 23 percent in Oregon was deemed a "modest upsurge" compared to Nebraska but this was achieved "at a campaign expenditure at least ten times larger than the Nebraska total." It was felt that Reagan still could be the Republican nominee, if Nixon "faltered" or if the convention became deadlocked, but the "Oregon primary provided not a shred of evidence that either of those events was likely."[349] Reagan's strength remained only with "the Goldwater Republicans in the south and in the Mountain States."[350]

The final vote tally from the Oregon secretary of state showed that Reagan had received 63,707 votes in the Republican party for president, 3,082 write-in votes for president in the Democrat party tally, 13,464 write-in votes for vice-president on the Republican side and 1,048 write-in votes for vice-president on the Democrat side. Despite the earlier 23 percent, Reagan's final percentage of 20 percent not only failed to best what Nebraska had produced, indeed it did not even equal Nebraska.

Analyzing results by county, Van Natta observed that the Reagan vote in Malheur County (1,115 or 36%) was the number one Reagan county in the state. Malheur was near Boise where in fact at that time many Oregonians from there "shopped and got their news." Van Natta felt that although Reagan did not visit Oregon during the Boise trip, their vote was "a direct result of the Boise visit."[351] The other

Oregon counties with the largest percentage votes for Reagan—all 30 percent or higher—were Douglas, a timber-based economy at 35 percent; Lake, a small county in eastern Oregon at 32 percent; Jackson, adjacent to the California border with the city of Medford at 31 percent; Curry, another county adjacent to California but on the coast at 31 percent; and Josephine, another timber-based economy at 30 percent. Van Natta's final conclusion was that "our big picture scheme of climbing the mountain the closer to the convention it gets, the more people like Reagan, didn't happen."[352]

Back in California, Reed watched the returns. "A deathly silence filled the room. The faces of the youngsters and old pros gathered around me all turned to stone."[353] Reed felt it was all over: "We were dead in the water."[354] Reed had failed in his original goal of directing a Reagan victory in Oregon. Now his lesser goal, of at least beating Nebraska, had failed too. On May 29 Reed met with Reagan "to tell him that in our collective opinion, his presidential campaign was over....There was no chance of victory."[355] Yet Reed reflected later, "To this day, I am not sure if he heard me or if the message sank in."[356]

Reagan turned back from staring out a window. "Too bad," were his only words as an "aggrieved scowl" crossed his face.[357] Reed then mentioned that the loss RFK had just experienced on the Democratic side meant that RFK and McCarthy would duel it out for the big prize in California, only six days away. Reagan was cheered by the realization that his old nemesis, RFK, might not succeed to the presidency after all. And Reagan soon would gain all the delegate votes from California on the Republican side. Reagan later would reflect to Reed, "Oregon was good. The people were just not ready for me."[358]

The Oregon primary was the second time that the Reagan campaign seemed to be over in the mind and comments of Reed. The first time had been some six months earlier when the campaign shake-up had resulted in Reed's demotion and the resultant slow nose-diving of the campaign. Now for the second time Reed declared to Reagan that all was lost. But Ronald Reagan did not give up on his first attempt at the presidency.

The decision to avoid having Reagan visit Oregon in 1968 may have been the decision that created the fatal flaw in the entire campaign for the presidency in 1968. As he had two successful visits to Oregon in February 1967 and as recently as November 1967, certainly a reason could have been found—even if such a reason were required to provide cover for his campaign—for a return visit a few months later in the spring of 1968. Reagan's Oregon campaign team, especially

Van Natta and Hodel, had discussed the plan—to keep Reagan away while building enthusiasm and hoping for a draft in Miami Beach—many times with Reed. Had Reagan visited Oregon, perhaps even just once in the spring of 1968, he could have had his own new motto: "Reagan Cared Enough to Come to Oregon in 1968." Such a visit might indeed have convinced enough Oregon Republican voters that not only was his candidacy the "real deal" but also convince them to vote for him in sufficient numbers to hit the goal of approximately thirty percent. Real momentum could have been created in Oregon, and later the entire convention could have turned out differently.

Ruefully, Tom Reed reflected forty-five years later with your author that this analysis "hit the nail on its head," agreeing that this was the fatal flaw in his own strategy and tactics back in 1968.[359] Even though *Ronald Reagan, Citizen Governor* had succeeded in generating growing tallies in Wisconsin and then in Nebraska, the film was not effective, where it had counted most, by getting Reagan to that 30 percent. Indeed Reed concluded, "We lost Oregon big time."[360] But the fault lay not in the film. It was Reagan's not showing up in person that likely was the critical factor.

Hodel added an important caveat in 2015. Even had Reagan accepted McCall's original invitation and had campaigned in Oregon in person, Nixon would have continued his claim that all Reagan's candidacy meant was to increase the likelihood of a Rockefeller victory. Hazen's support for Rockefeller in 1964 did serve to counter the arguments that Reagan was just a right wing ideologue. But it still gave Nixon much ammunition that a vote for to Reagan was a vote for Rockefeller. And mainstream party members remained "spooked" that Reagan's candidacy might just open the door to the hated New York governor who had refused to back Goldwater in 1964.[361]

More than four decades after those events in 1967 and 1968, the Reagan 1968 Oregon campaign team still gets together occasionally. Besides the mini-reunion/interview with your author in 2012 mentioned earlier, Hodel recalled that the group's last official reunion was in 2006 when these life-long friends, even though now separated by a thousand miles in some cases, met for dinner once again. The Hodels, Grams, O'Scannlains, and Diana Evans took much-deserved pride that the Reagan campaign for the presidency had begun in 1968 and that they had all played major roles. These old friends reminisced about the now-gone but ever-present Pearlman's, Hazen's, and of course hovering over them all was the memory of Ronald Reagan.[362] Little did any of them realize that most would be hard at work once again for Reagan in 1976—dealing with disappointment again—but to ultimate triumph in 1980 and 1984. Indeed some would then play very prominent roles in those future campaigns and in the Reagan administration.

One man who would not give up the fight to see Ronald Reagan elected president in 1968 was Hazen, who we will meet again in late July. At the same time as the Oregon results were coming in, Van Natta had been in close contact with Ken Rogstad in Seattle. Van Natta informed Reed that there was an ongoing fight with the credentials committee there and it still was possible that 15 Reagan delegates from neighboring Washington might make a Reagan majority delegation. But something else loomed on the immediate horizon: the California primary was only days away.

Endnotes

1.   Hughes, Harold, "Rumors Persist That Travis Cross Will Bolt Romney Camp, Join Reagan," *The Oregonian*, 12/22/67, p. 29
2.   White Theodore, p. 136
3.   Wicker, Tom, "Reagan on the Move," *NYT*, 4/28/68, p. E19
4.   Wicker, Tom, "In the Nation," *NYT*, 5/14/68, p. 46
5.   "Political Rhubarb Mixes Kennedy, Reagan Funds," *The Oregonian*, 5/19/68, p. 24
6.   article headline from Siuslaw News, 5/19/68
7.   See Illustrations
8.   RRL, Tape 393
9.   Kopelson, Gene. 2014D
10. Reed, *The Reagan Enigma*, p. 160; Skinner et. al.
11. Hughes, Harold, "Nixon, Kennedy Oregon Primary Favorites," *The Oregonian*, 5/19/68, p. 111
12. Walth, p. 218
13. Kopelson, Gene, 2014D
14. Reed, Thomas, p. 12
15. Hodel, pers comm. 7/14/13
16. Hodel, pers comm. 8/25/12
17. Hodel, pers comm. 10/7/12
18. Nofziger, p. 69
19. Nofziger, ibid
20. McCall, Tom, "Maverick," p. 74
21. Walth, p. 202-203
22. Walth, p. 202
23. Walth, p. 202
24. ibid
25. Walth, p. 202
26. ibid
27. McCall, Maverick, p. 149
28. Weaver Warren Jr, "'68 Road Baffles GOP Governors," *NYT*, 6/28/67, p. 8
29. McCall Maverick, p. 14
30. ibid
31. ibid
32. Davies, Lawrence, "Oregon Prepares for 1968 Primary," *NYT*, 8/20/67, p. 31
33. Hodel, personal communications 8/22/12 and 3/25/2015
34. Hodel, pers comm. 10/7/12
35. Don Hodel, pers comm. 8/22/12
36. Hodel pers comm. 8/25/12
37. Van Natta, pers int 7/30/12; Hodel pers comm. 3/25/2015
38. Hodel, pers comm. 10/7/12
39. Fred Van Natta int, 7/30/12
40. Syd Willett, pers comm. 6/15/12

41. Deck Hazen, pers comm. 6/15/12
42. Syd Willett op.cit.
43. John Gram int, 7/30/12
44. Deck Hazen ibid
45. Hodel, pers comm. 9/2/12
46. Hodel, pers comm. 8/25/12
47. Hodel, pers comm. 10/7/12
48. Hodel pers comm. 10/7/12
49. Hodel ibid
50. Murphy pers int 8/16/12
51. Fred Van Natta, pers comm. 11/13/12
52. Van Natta, pers comm. 11/11/12
53. Van Natta int, 7/30/12
54. Hodel pers comm. 10/7/12
55. see Afterwards
56. Sally Gram pers int, Fred Van Natta pers int, Diana Evans pers int all 7/30/12
57. Diarmuid O'Scannlain pers int, 8/23/12
58. Hodel pers comm. 10/7/12
59. John Gram, pers comm. 11/12/12
60. Diarmuid O Scannlain op cit
61. Hodel, pers comm. 10/7/12
62. OScannlain, pers int 8/23/12
63. Hodel, pers comm. 10/7/12
64. John and Sally Gram int 7/30/12
65. John Gram int, 7/30/12
66. Hodel, pers comm. 9/2/12
67. "The Long March," *Time,* 7/28/80, p. 30
68. Hodel, pers comm. 10/7/12
69. Diana Evans pers int, 7/30/12
70. Evans, pers int 7/30/12
71. Time op.cit.
72. Hodel, pers comm., 10/7/12
73. Van Natta, pers int 7/30/12
74. Greenburg, Carl, "Reagan 'No' Is Too Mild To Suit Nixon Faction," *Los Angeles Times*, 4/1/68
75. John Gram, pers int, 7/30/12
76. Diana Evans, pers int 7/30/12
77. Sally Gram, pers int, 7/30/12
78. *Time* op.cit.
79. See Illustrations
80. Van Natta pers int 7/30/12
81. O'Scannlain, pers int 8/23/12
82. Van Natta pers int 7/30/12
83. Hodel, pers comm. 10/7/12
84. Van Natta, op.cit.
85. Hodel, pers comm. 10/7/12
86. Reed, p. 25
87. Van Natta, pers comm. 9/4/12
88. Hughes, Harold, "Rumors Persist That Travis Cross Will Bolt Romney Camp, Join Reagan," *The Oregonian*, 12/22/67, p. 29
89. Davies, Lawrence, "Reagan's Backers in Oregon Seek to Enlist Rockefeller's '64 Supporters," *NYT*, 12/24/67, p. 33
90. ibid
91. Kopelson, Gene. 2014D
92. Van Natta pers int 7/30/12
93. Van Natta ibid
94. "Reagan Off Ballot for Vice President," *NYT*, 3/15/68, p. 25
95. Van Natta, pers int 7/30/12
96. Evans and Novak, "Monte Advises Rocky to Stay Out of Oregon," *The Oregonian*, 1/9/68, p. 18
97. Davies, Lawrence, "Reagan Disavows Primaries Plan," *NYT*, 1/11/68, p. 23
98. Weaver Warren Jr, "Oregon GOP Sure Reagan Will Run," *NYT*, 1/28/68, p. 37
99. Fleming, Karl, "Reagan for President?," *Newsweek*, 2/26/68, p. 24
100. "U. of Oregon Poll Rejects Johnson," *NYT*, 2/9/68, p. 21
101. Turner, Wallace, "GOP Governors Shift on Reagan," *NYT*, 2/18/68, p. 43
102. McCall, p. 97
103. Weaver Warren Jr, "Rockefeller's Aides Plan Write-In Drive in Oregon Primary," *NYT*, 1/31/68, p. 1
104. Semple, Robert Jr, "Nixon Announces for Presidency, *NYT*, 2/2/68, p. 1

105. Weaver Warren Jr., "Rockefeller Says That He Will Run If Asked by GOP," *NYT*, 3/2/68, p. 1
106. Witkin, Richard, "Rockefeller Open to Oregon Race," *NYT*, 3/8/68, p. 1
107. Weaver Warren Jr, "Rockefeller Bloc Loses Early Bid in GOP Canvass," *NYT*, 3/1/68, p. 1
108. Davies, Lawrence, "Two New Yorkers On Oregon Ballot," *NYT*, 3/12/68, p. 23
109. Wicker, Tom, "Effects of Primary," *NYT*, 3/13/68, p. 1
110. Kilpatrick, James, "Rockefeller Magic—In Oregon Only?," *Seattle Times*, 3/18/68, p. 12
111. "Reagan Is Staying In Race In Oregon," *NYT*, 3/20/68, p. 33
112. Hodel, pers comm. 10/7/12
113. Greenberg, Carl, "Reagan Link with Oregon Unit Denied," *LA Times*, 3/27/68
114. Davies, Lawrence, "Nixon Accuses Administration Of Causing Stampede for Gold," *NYT*, 3/16/68, p. 15
115. Perlstein, Rick, p. 268
116. Knowles, Clayton, "Confident Nixon Declines to Say He Has Won GOP Nomination," *NYT*, 3/22/68, p. 33
117. Semple Robert B Jr, "Nixon Has the Field to Himself-Almost," *NYT*, 3/24/68, p. E1
118. ibid
119. Hughes, Harold, "Rocky's Oregon Supporters Express 'Shock', 'Dismay' After Withdrawal," *NYT*, 3/22/68, p. 1
120. Hughes, ibid
121. Van Natta, pers int 7/30/12
122. Hughes, Harold, "Two Interpretations Placed On Demo Vote," *NYT*, 4/3/68, p. 6
123. Kempster, Norman, "Nixon Vs Reagan in Oregon Primary," The Seattle Times, 4/11/68, p. 16
124. Davies, Lawrence, "Drive in Oregon to Stop Nixon Attributed to Reagan Backers," *NYT*, 4/14/68, p. 49
125. Van Natta, pers int 7/30/12
126. Hodel, pers comm. 10/7/12
127. ibid
128. Van Natta, pers int 7/30/12
129. Kempster op.cit.
130. Semple, Robert B. Jr., "Nixon Criticizes 'Absentee' Rivals," *NYT*, 5/26/68, p. 44
131. ibid
132. Davies, Lawrence, "Drive in Oregon to Stop Nixon Attributed to Reagan Backers," *NYT*, 4/14/68, p. 49
133. ibid
134. ibid
135. Witcover, p. 289
136. Witcover, p. 290
137. Witcover, ibid
138. ibid
139. Van Natta, pers int 7/30/68
140. Clarity, James F., "Nixon Confident of West's Votes," *NYT*, 4/27/68, p. 16
141. White, Theodore, p. 136
142. Buchanan, p. 263
143. White Theodore, p. 136
144. McGinnis, Joe, "Selling of the President," p. 228-229
145. Hughes, Harold, "Reagan Leaves Door Ajar in Oregon Race," *The Oregonian*, 4/28/68, p. 29
146. Hughes, ibid
147. Hughes, ibid
148. Van Natta pers int 7/30/12
149. Kopelson, Gene. 2015A
150. "Official Abstract of Votes Primary Election 1968" and the "Summary Report of Campaign Contributions and Expenditures: 1968 Primary Election" compiled and published by Elections Division, Secretary of State's Office, Salem OR
151. Semple, op.cit., *NYT*, 5/26/68 p. 44
152. ibid
153. "Mail Effort Backs Rocky," *The Oregonian*, 5/19/68, p. 120
154. Davies, Lawrence, "Rockefeller Backers in Oregon Open Campaign for Write-Ins," *NYT*, 5/23/68, p. 24
155. Kempster, Norman, "Nixon Vs Reagan in Oregon Primary," *The Seattle Times*, 4/11/68, p. 16
156. Hughes, Harold, "Reagan Leaves Door Ajar in Oregon Race," *The Oregonian*, 4/28/68, p. 29
157. Hodel, pers comm. 10/7/12
158. Blumenfield, Ralph, "Reagan Plans to return Lindsay's Visit," *LA Times*, 12/12/67
159. Reeves, Richard, "Lindsay Confers with Reagan As He Begins Los Angeles Visit," *NYT*, 11/17/67, p. 1
160. Kopelson, Gene. 2014D
161. Wicker, Tom, "In the Nation: On the Stump in Oregon," *NYT*, 5/26/68, p. E19
162. Wicker op.cit.
163. Reeves, Richard, "Lindsay's Future in Dark," *NYT*, 5/13/68, p. 38

164. Wicker, op. cit.
165. *US News and World Report*, 9/18/67, p. 52
166. Richardson, p. 273
167. Rockefeller Archive Center, Graham Molitor Papers, IV 3A 18, Agriculture and RWR, Box 27, Folder 656, Item 7/2/68
168. Holmes, *The Ever-Shrinking Middle Ground*, pp.12-14
169. Finney, John W., "Nixon and Reagan Ask War on Crime," *NYT*, 8/1/68, p. 1
170. White, Ted, Appendix B
171. Chester et. al., *An American Melodrama*, p. 207-208
172. Hughes, Harold op.cit., 3/28, *The Oregonian*, p. 24
173. John Gram pers int 7/30/12
174. John Gram, pers int ibid
175. Gram, pers int 11/12/12
176. Sally Gram, pers int 7/30/12
177. John and Sally Gram, pers comm. 9/11/12
178. John and Sally Gram pers int, 7/30/12 and pers comm. 9/11/12
179. Brinkley, Douglas. Cronkite
180. John and Sally Gram, pers comm. 9/11/12
181. Murphy, Francis "Behind the Mike," *The Oregonian*, 5/23/68 sec 2 p. 19
182. Chester, *Am Melodrama*, p. 207
183. Chester, ibid
184. Chester, ibid
185. John Gram, int op.cit.
186. John Gram, ibid
187. "Reagan Supporters Use Film in Oregon," *NYT*, 4/7/68, p. 38
188. Richardson, *A Nation Divided*, p. 253
189. Chester, et. al., p. 208
190. Greenberg, Carl, "Reagan Link with Oregon Unit Denied," *LA Times*, 3/27/68
191. Human Events, 3/16/1968, p. 4
192. "Reagan Supporters" op.cit.
193. Sally Gram, ibid
194. Hughes, Harold, "Reagan Forces To Use Telstar Show to Boost Oregon Primary campaign," *The Oregonian*, 4/21/68
195. Film available from Reagan Presidential Library and www.reagan68.com
196. Chester et. al., op. cit.
197. *Time*, 5/24/68, p. 27
198. Hughes, Harold, "Reagan Forces To Use Telstar Show to Boost Oregon Primary Campaign," *The Oregonian*, 4/21/68
199. Hughes, Harold, "Film Adds Impetus To Oregon Reagan Drive," *The Oregonian*, 3/28/68, p. 24
200. Hughes op.cit.
201. Time, 5/24/68, p. 27
202. Hughes, Harold op.cit., 3/28, p. 24
203. Hughes, ibid
204. "Reagan Supporters Use Film In Oregon," *NYT*, 4/7/68, p. 38
205. Wicker, Tom, "In the Nation," *NYT*, 5/14/68, p. 46
206. *Time*, 5/24/68, p. 27
207. *Newsweek*, 5/27/68, p. 33A
208. Hughes, Harold, "Film Adds Impetus To Oregon Reagan Drive," *The Oregonian*, 3/28/68, p. 24
209. Van Natta, pers int 7/30/12
210. Davies, Lawrence, "Drive in Oregon to Stop Nixon Attributed to Reagan Backers," *NYT*, 4/14/68, p. 49
211. *Newsweek*, 4/8/68, p. 43
212. Greenberg, Carl, "Reagan Link with Oregon Unit Denied," *LA Times*, 3/27/68
213. *Newsweek*, 4/15/68, p. 50
214. *Sports Illustrated*, Vault: Scorecard, 7/29/68
215. Reed, pers int 10/17/12
216. Semple op.cit., *NYT*, 5/26/68, p. 44
217. Van Natta, pers int 7/30/12
218. "Primary Race Draws Tittle," *The Oregonian*, 5/14/68, p. 30
219. Gregory L.H., "Greg's Gossip," *The Oregonian*, 5/22/68, sec 3, p. 1
220. John Gram pers int 7/30/12
221. Gram pers int 7/30/12
222. Clarity, James, "Nixon Confident of West's Vote," *NYT*, 4/27/68, p. 16
223. Turner, Wallace, "Reagan Backers Open Idaho Drive," *NYT*, 4/7/68, p. 38
224. Turner op.cit.

225. Turner, ibid
226. Van Natta, pers int 7/30/12
227. Turner, ibid
228. "Another Opinion," *NYT*, 3/26/67, p. 155
229. Turner, Wallace, "Reagan Denies Advance Man Seeks Support for Race in '68," *NYT*, 6/26/67, p. 20
230. Turner, Wallace, "GOP Governors Shift on Reagan," *NYT*, 2/18/68, p. 43
231. Turner, Wallace, "Mountain States Query," *NYT*, 4/2/68, p. 33
232. Clarity, James, "Nixon Confident of West's Vote," *NYT*, 4/27/68, p. 16
233. Skinner, Kudella et. al., p. 64
234. Wicker, Tom, "Reagan on the Move," *NYT*, 4/28/68, p. E19
235. Sally Gram pers int 7/30/68
236. RRL, Tape 338
237. Hill, Gladwyn, "Reagan Completes a Tour of 2 States," *NYT*, 4/28/68, p. 52
238. RRL, Tape 338
239. Wicker, op.cit., *NYT*, 4/28/68
240. Wicker, ibid
241. Wicker, ibid
242. Sally Gram pers int 7/30/12
243. author's note: Van Natta gave the remaining two bottles to your author as a gift in the fall of 2012 as the author left Salem to drive to interview Tom Reed in California; your author then returned one of the bottles of bourbon to its original owner, Reed, the next day.
244. Van Natta pers int 7/30/12
245. O'Scannlain, pers in 8/23/12
246. Wicker op.cit., *NYT*, 4/28
247. "Idaho GOP Uncommitted," *NYT*, 6/16/68, p. 18
248. Janson, Donald, "Nixon: Still in Front," *NYT*, 5/19/68, p. E3
249. *Newsweek*, 5/27/68, p. 33
250. Janson op.cit.
251. Janson, ibid
252. White, Theo, *The Making*, p. 136
253. Janson op.cit.
254. Janson op.cit.
255. Janson op.cit.
256. Weaver Warren Jr, "Nixon's Only Primary Hurdle Is Reagan in Oregon," *NYT*, 5/20/68, p. 38
257. Semple, Robert B. Jr., "Nixon Criticizes 'Absentee' Rivals," *NYT*, 5/26/68, p. 44
258. Mears, Walter, "Oregon Vote Nears; Kennedy Worried," *Seattle Times*, 5/26/68, p. 8
259. Hughes, Harold, "Nixon Delivers Blast At Absent Candidates," *The Oregonian*, 5/26/68, p. 2
260. ibid
261. Semple, Robert B, "Nixon Telethon Ends Drive in Oregon," 5/27/68, p. 26
262. The final tabulation by the Secretary of State's office showed specific named individuals as Reagan county chairmen or Reagan county finance chairmen for Benton County, Clatsop County, Jackson County, Josephine County, Klamath County, Wasco County, and Yamhill County.
263. Hodel, pers comm. 10/7/12
264. Peter Murphy, pers int 9/14/12
265. Peter Murphy, pers int 9/14/12
266. Peter Murphy, pers int 8/16/12
267. "Political Rhubarb Mixes Kennedy, Reagan Funds," *The Oregonian*, 5/19/68, p. 24
268. Peter Murphy, pers int 9/14/12
269. Rothauge, pers int 11/14/14
270. Oregonian, ibid
271. *Siuslaw News*, 5/23/68
272. Rothauge, pers int 11/14/14
273. See Illustrations
274. In 2015, your author was unable to locate the check copy in the files of the newspaper.
275. *Siuslaw News*, 5/29/1968
276. Peter Murphy, pers int 9/14/12
277. Peter Murphy pers int 8/16/12
278. Kopelson, Gene. 2014D
279. Fred Van Natta, pers comm. 9/19/12
280. Diarmuid O'Scannlain, pers comm. 9/19/12
281. O'Scannlain, op.cit.
282. Hodel, pers comm. 9/19/12
283. Hodel, pers comm. 10/7/12
284. Hodel, pers comm. 9/19/12
285. Janson, Donald, "Freedom Budget Opposed by Nixon," *NYT*, 5/14/68, p. 33
286. "Nebraska Vote Gratifies Reagan, 'Noncandidate,'" *NYT*, 5/15/68, p. 31

287. Van Natta pers int 7/30/12
288. John Gram, pers int, 7/30/12.
289. John Gram, pers int 7/30/12
290. "Backers See Hope In Vote," *The Oregonian*, 5/15/68, p. 21
291. "Reagan Backers Plan 'Beaver' Effort," *The Seattle Times*, 5/16/68, p. 23
292. RRL, Tape 342
293. "Parley Disturbs Reagan Backers," *NYT*, 5/21/68, p. 27
294. Van Natta in 7/30
295. Fred Van Natta, pers comm., 7/30/12
296. Kopelson, Gene. 2016
297. Van Natta pers comm. 9/18/12
298. Hughes, Harold, "Reagan Forces To Use Telstar Show to Boost Oregon Primary Campaign," *The Oregonian*, 4/21/68
299. "GOP Group Planning Film," *The Oregonian*, 5/17/68, sec 2, p. 3
300. Diana Evans, pers int 7/3012
301. Rothauge, pers int 11/14/14
302. Van Natta pers comm. 9/18/12
303. See Illustrations
304. Van Natta, pers int 7/30/12
305. *Time*, 5/24/68, p. 27
306. *Time*, 5/24/67, p. 27
307. Weaver, Warren, "Nixon's Only Primary Hurdle Is Reagan in Oregon," *NYT*, 5/20/68, p. 38
308. Janson, Donald, "Nixon Bids Columbia Oust 'Anarchic students,'" *NYT*, 5/16/68, p. 22
309. Weaver, Warren, "Nixon's Only Primary Hurdle Is Reagan in Oregon," *NYT*, 5/20/68, p. 38
310. Weaver, ibid
311. Janson, Donald, "Nixon Still In Front," *NYT*, 5/19/68, p. E3
312. Hughes, Harold, "Nixon, Kennedy Oregon Primary Favorites," *The Oregonian*, 5/19/68, p. 111
313. Weaver op.cit., 5/20/68, p. 38
314. Witcover, p. 299
315. Lahr, Raymond, "GOP Harmony Cracking in Oregon," *The Seattle Times*, 5/21/68, p. 10
316. Pearson Drew and Anderson Jack, "Reagan Is the Man to Watch in Oregon," *Washington Merry-Go-Round*, 5/22/68
317. Hughes, Harold, "Kennedy Alone for the Day," *The Oregonian*, 5/24/68, p. 1
318. "Republican Convention Likely to be 3 Ballots," *The Oregonian*, 5/24/68, p. 38
319. Sally Gram, pers int 7/30/12
320. Hughes, Harold, "Nixon, Kennedy Oregon Primary Favorites," *The Oregonian*, 5/19/68, p. 111
321. Murphy, Francis, "Behind the Mike," *The Oregonian*, 5/24/68, sec. 2, p. 5
322. Murphy, Francis, "Behind the Mike," *The Oregonian*, 5/24/68, sec. 2, p. 5
323. Mears, Walter, "Oregon Vote Nears," *The Seattle Times*, 5/26/68, p. 8
324. Weaver, Warren, "Stiffest Test for Kennedy Is Due In Oregon Tuesday," *NYT*, 5/26/68, p. 1
325. Weaver, ibid
326. Ad, *The Oregonian*, 5/27/68, sec. 2, p. 19
327. See Illustrations
328. "Rockefeller's Mind 'Open' About Reagan," *NYT*, 5/30/68
329. Cunningham, Ross, "Wallace May Force Unlikely GOP Ticket," *Seattle Times*, 5/26/68, p. 12
330. "Reagan Hopes for Good Ore. Vote," *The Seattle Times*, 5/27/68, p. 6
331. Allman, pp. 517-525
332. Allman, p. 519
333. Allman, p. 519
334. Murphy, Francis, "Behind the Mike," *The Oregonian*, 5/29/68, sec 2, p. 3
335. Witcover, p. 304-305
336. Van Natta, pers int 7/30/12
337. White, p. 137
338. Witcover, p. 304-305
339. White, p. 137
340. Davies, Lawrence, "Nixon Is A Strong Winner," *NYT*, 5/29/68, p. 1
341. "Gov. Reagan Not Unhappy," *The Oregonian*, 5/29/68, p. 9
342. "Nixon Likes Sound of Voices Heard in Oregon Primary Vote," *The Oregonian*, 5/29/68, p. 1b
343. *The Oregonian*, 5/29/68, p. 20
344. "Nixon Likes Sound of Voices Heard in Oregon Primary Vote," *The Oregonian*, 5/29/68, p. 1b
345. "Oregon Wants McCarthy, Nixon," *The Oregonian*, 5/29/68, p. 26
346. John Gram, pers int 7/30/12
347. O Scann pers int 8/23/12
348. Peter Murphy int 8/16/12
349. Weaver Warren, "Outlook After Oregon," *NYT*, 5/30/68, p. 1
350. "The GOP After Oregon," *NYT*, 5/31/68, p. 28

351. Van Natta pers comm. 8/1/12
352. Van Natta pers int 7/30/12
353. Reed, *The Reagan Enigma*, p. 159
354. Reed, p. 25
355. Reed, p. 26
356. Reed, ibid
357. Reed, *The Reagan Enigma*, p. 161
358. Reagan-Reed, 6/5/1968, Sacramento office
359. Reed, pers comm., 3/10/13
360. Reed, pers comm., 10/20/13
361. Hodel, pers. comm. 3/25/2015
362. Hodel, pers comm. 10/7/12

CHAPTER 30: CALIFORNIA—JUNE 4, 1968, FAVORITE SON, AND THE RFK ASSASSINATION

"Reagan's is the power to change men's minds."
~ Reagan activist[1]

"More than any other single factor for which Governor Reagan is known throughout the nation is his ability to establish party unity."
~ Gardiner Johnson[2]

"The freedom of the world is at stake in the Middle East. But who defends that freedom? Only that one tiny nation born of a hunger for freedom and inspired by two decades having the taste of freedom...Those who made the desert flower have been forced to lay aside the tools of peace and they have stood manning the ramparts as armed guards. They deserve better from us. They must be provided the weapons to match the Soviet arms now aimed at their nation's heart."
~ Ronald Reagan[3]

"The enemy sits in Moscow. I call him an enemy because I believe he has proven this, by deed, in the middle east which led to, precipitated, the tragedy of last night.... This same Soviet power... has impressed upon the world its belief that the end justifies the means and there is no morality except what furthers the cause."
~ Ronald Reagan[4]

"We defeated them by opposing what they were trying to do. And I'd suggest that to anyone who's interested in opposing communism."
~ Ronald Reagan[5]

"With Bobby Kennedy's assassination, the whole political scene had shifted once again...I knew that Richard Nixon was going to be much more difficult for us to beat with Bobby Kennedy gone...Nixon...could not beat another Kennedy in 1968."

~ Clif White[6]

"The man who lost it for us was Sirhan Sirhan."

~ Michael Deaver[7]

The American people forever will recall with horror the 1968 California Democratic primary, for in the early morning hours of June 5, 1968, a few minutes after declaring victory on the Democratic side, Robert F. Kennedy was assassinated. The same day in New Jersey, with no grass roots campaign and no personal visits, Reagan received 2,737 votes of 87,970 (3.1%). For Reagan, California was to be the apex of the primary season.

The Republican California Delegation

William French Smith was chairman of the delegation, recalling that the delegation had Reagan, Rockefeller and Nixon supporters within it.[8] As discussed earlier, Stuart Spencer had been put in charge of putting the delegate slate together.[9] Spencer recalled that Reagan's financial backers had their favorites for people to be chosen as delegates and Spencer complied with their requests. But Spencer also made certain that if in fact Reagan was to be favorite son and chosen on first ballot, that Nixon would be chosen on the second ballot. So ironically Reagan's and Nixon's plans for California and the rest of the nation were mirror images: Reagan was to be the choice for all the other states at Miami Beach after the first ballot, while Nixon was to be the choice for California after the first ballot.[10]

Paul Haerle recalled that along with Spencer, the steering committee was composed of Reed, William Clark, Nofziger and a few others and met weekly at the Comstock Club. Haerle recalled that the delegation was composed of legislators, long-time Reagan supporters, as well as a few former George Christopher supporters, plus donors from wealthy sections of San Francisco and Los Angeles. Haerle recalled that because there could only be two delegates and two alternates per congressional district, plus some delegates-at-large, there was intense scrambling and jostling for positions. As many of the wealthy donors who wanted to be delegates were from the same district, some could not attend. Haerle thought all the in-fighting was quite funny to watch. He recalled that in San Marino, there were fifteen millionaire donors all fighting for the same two seats. Haerle and Reed made most of the choices based on political calculations and then let Reagan financier Holmes Tuttle get stuck having to decide how to divvy up the remaining delegates amongst the other wealthy donors he knew.[11]

Lieutenant Governor Robert Finch was of course included in the delegation too. Finch was in a delicate position as both a long-time Nixon supporter and adviser, who at the same time had to stay somewhat loyal to Governor Reagan. Finch was described by historian Theodore H. White as "tall, craggy-faced, sandy-haired, a chain smoker," who also had been an Eagle Scout. He had won a National College Speech Contest speaking on President Andrew Jackson and had a "vivid concern for people," especially for blacks, having grown up in Inglewood, California.[12] Finch, who would become Nixon's first choice for vice-president and eventually become secretary of Health, Education and Welfare under President Nixon, had befriended Nixon in the late 1940s and worked on all Nixon campaigns. Shortly before the 1964 convention, when Finch was discussing Nixon's perception that Goldwater would lose badly yet Nixon had to help the party—in order "to have any future claim" on Republicans—Finch had realized that Nixon was deciding to run for president again.[13]

In 1966, Finch had run for lieutenant governor and California law required that governor and lieutenant governor be voted upon separately. During the fall 1966 gubernatorial campaign, Reagan's team offered to help Finch. Finch had stayed out of the spring Republican gubernatorial primary between Reagan and Christopher. In the fall, Finch "was by himself much of the time, always trailing the incumbent," Democrat Glenn Anderson.[14] Reagan started to make joint appearances with Finch. Nixon also helped Finch by spending several hours advising him, appearing on television, and attending a Finch fundraiser.[15] In the end, Finch had received more votes than did Reagan. But Finch was never welcomed into Reagan's inner circle in Sacramento, because he was more liberal than Reagan and "his old ties to Nixon made him suspect by Reagan men looking toward the Presidency."[16]

Finch's attitude toward Reagan's favorite son status was described as a "formality," which was subject, "like all such candidacies, to withdrawal on later ballots or even, if the situation warranted it, before the balloting began."[17] Via the letter described earlier, Nixon had accepted Reagan's role as California favorite son.[18] Finch had been present in early January 1967 at the initial Nixon campaign strategy session, when he had made suggestions to Nixon about

Reagan. During the spring of 1968, Finch remained Nixon's "chief confidant and closest friend," who had "long and constant telephone conversations" with Nixon in New York and whose cross-country flights from Sacramento to the east coast to meet with and advise Nixon went "unnoticed."[19]

Reagan's Coat-tails and Party Unity

The California system of having a delegation chosen by delegates via congressional district, rather than by primary election, came under challenge the summer of 1967, when legislation was proposed to establish an Oregon-style primary in California. As Reagan wanted to claim the delegation as favorite son because that status was critical for his presidential campaign, he threatened to veto the bill if it arrived on his desk.[20]

As discussed earlier, Reagan's favorite son status served as the mechanism by which Reagan would gain 86 delegates to add to those he had hoped to garner from the initially-planned win in Oregon as well as from other states. But the second motive was not only to heal the old political wounds within the state party; it was for Reagan to have long coattails to benefit other conservative Republicans.

This is one area where neither Eisenhower nor another of Reagan's heroes, Churchill, had provided a positive example. It was widely known that during Eisenhower's two terms, the national Republican Party had suffered with huge gradual losses in Congress. Similarly, Churchill during both of his two terms as prime minister had neglected increasing his party's representation in Parliament.[21]

Reagan's political success in California had national implications for 1968. First, his coat-tails in 1966 had been far-reaching. Reagan's election "won Republican control of all but one state-wide office, increased the state's Republican representation in the U.S. House and significantly bolstered the party in the state Senate and Assembly."[22] A memo was to be circulated at the Miami Beach convention, which would analyze Reagan's coat-tails in 1966 in California versus those of Rockefeller. By comparing the net change in the state houses and U.S. House in 1966 for New York versus California, complied from the *Congressional Quarterly*, a Reagan activist found that there had been little change in the makeup of those elected officials in New York despite a Rockefeller victory. But in California in 1966, there had been "sharp Republican gains over the whole ticket, despite the ticket-splitting tendency of the California voter." In fact, the gains under Reagan in 1966 were not just a recovery of seats lost in 1964, but these were "advances into previously Democratic territory." The activist concluded that New York Democratic liberals voted for liberal Republican Rockefeller but not for other Republicans, whereas Reagan's assault on the entire Democratic philosophy had wide appeal to Independents and Democrats, and the latter had continued to pull Republican levers at the polls in 1966. The analyst concluded, "Reagan's is the power to change men's minds." The pro-Reagan memo would be sent to delegates on August 1, 1968.[23]

Second, Reagan's coat-tails continued during his governorship. In August, 1967, the Republicans "reclaimed a seat in the state Senate which in effect gave them political control over that body," followed by a second off-season election victory in the U.S. House, which gave the correct impression that a "wave of Republicanism is sweeping the state. The party credits much of this success to Ronald Reagan."[24] Third, Reagan's political judgment was astute. "Reagan's political acumen in the office of Governor has left Democratic majorities in the legislature thoroughly checkmated. It was not only the subtle appreciation of his personal popularity, but also his tactics which made it difficult for the Democrats to mount an attack on the Governor."[25]

Unfortunately, the proven vote-getting results of Reagan's political coat-tails were never exploited by Reed or White as another reason delegates and voters should choose Reagan. Ultimately Nixon would prove to have few, if any, coat-tails in 1968. Had Reed and White chosen to make Reagan's coat-tails a major campaign theme, things might have turned out differently.

Reagan had been able to unify the California Republicans, which had permitted his "dramatic entrance into national presidential politics."[26] Within two months of becoming governor, Reagan was praised for his efforts at achieving unity when the California Republican State Central Committee met on March 4 in San Francisco. "Party moderates and conservatives vied with one another to praise the Governor as having brought unity to California republicanism." The state chairman told the group he had been "besieged" at a recent National Committee meeting by Republicans across the country wanting Reagan to speak. Gardiner Johnson, California's Republican National Committeeman noted, "More than any other single factor for which Governor Reagan is known throughout the nation is his ability to establish party unity." At the meeting, some Republicans did acknowledge that if Nixon or Romney faltered, Reagan would emerge as a "possible compromise candidate." Reagan's office announced that after he had proposed budget cuts and a new policy for students having to start to pay a small portion of their tuition at state-run colleges, Reagan's approvals hit 67.8 percent.[27]

Liberal California Republican Senator Thomas Kuchel, who had fought against the Owosso group after making disparaging remarks about Reagan, took a long time to support Reagan. In 1966 Kuchel had backed Christopher and then refused to back nominee Reagan in the general election. Yet whereas some observers thought in 1967 it might seem natural for Reagan to stir up trouble for Kuchel in 1968, when he would be seeking re-election, at that point Reagan and Kuchel reached a working relationship without overt hostility. Their two staffs worked together and Reagan's team suggested to Kuchel that he use "look-what-I've-done-for-California" as a campaign theme in 1968. Kuchel needed Reagan not to mount an opposing candidate to him in 1968, and Reagan wanted a cohesive California delegation in 1968. Reagan also pledged neutrality if there were a senatorial primary fight and also pledged to support whoever became the party nominee for Senate in 1968.[28] In the end, Kuchel decided to work with Reagan.[29] Later that fall, Reagan made his views even more clear by holding a private meeting with Kuchel supporters. He told them that not only would he remain neutral, he had told his staff and aides to do so as well. Conservatives "who had thought about running against Mr. Kuchel suddenly found that money for the campaign was hard to find. Big contributors did not care to offend the Governor." Reagan had achieved "a larger degree of unity than California Republicans had seen in years."[30]

Had Reagan won the nomination in the summer of 1968, likely he would have followed through on the many promises he had made while campaigning: he would emulate his success in California by seeking unity with his opponents for the presidency (Nixon, Rockefeller, Romney, Lindsay) as well as campaigning hard for other Republicans in the fall of 1968. In reality, what would happen is that Nixon would have no coattails at all.

Favorite Son

Reagan was not always assured smooth sailing to win easily the California delegation as favorite son. In early 1968 it was reported that Rockefeller forces, if circumstances then seemed warranted, were "preparing a position" which would allow Rockefeller to enter the June 4 California Republican primary to challenge Reagan in his home state.[31]

Then a new problem arose the next month. The Committee for a Free Delegation, headed by James Wilcox of Los Angeles and general counsel for Signal Insurance Company, announced that they were going to file an 86-member opposition slate of delegates with the California secretary of state. Wilcox said his group wanted a candidate who had different views on Vietnam than did Reagan, but his group had to collect 18,000 signatures by a mid-April deadline.[32] By mid April, despite going to several college campuses to get the requisite number of signatures, Wilcox's group did not get enough signatures and the filing failed. The failure of any California opposition was interpreted as having Reagan in a position to "make an impressive showing of surging support in advance of the August national convention."[33] This would not be the last time that Reagan would have to deal with signatures of opposition constituents.

In the meantime, Reagan sent Robert C. Walker, a San Diego public relations man, to Miami Beach on March 25 to "open a California delegation headquarters office." His job was to make "mechanical arrangements" such as housing for the 86 delegates and 86 alternates.[34]

On April 15, the first of two formal meetings of the California delegation was held at the Los Angeles Airport Marina Hotel under the chairmanship of Governor Reagan. Of the 86 delegates and 86 alternates, 120 met in closed session with Reagan and Clif White for eighty minutes. The media noted that Reagan's presidential poll numbers in California, which had started to drop the prior fall, continued to do so. Reagan had garnered 19 percent of the California Republican vote in September 1967, 12 percent in January 1968 and had dropped down to only 8 percent in the poll done by the *Los Angeles Times*. In that freshly-released poll, Nixon had 54 percent and Rockefeller 35 percent and each had been steadily climbing versus Reagan's steady decline.[35]

Other similar polls late that spring showed Reagan not achieving more than 11 percent support amongst California Republicans when they were asked their preference for president. But those same polls showed that a majority preferred "to send unpledged delegates to the convention." But Reagan's name was the only one listed and one observer noted that on the ballot beneath Reagan's name was a blank, which had "been carefully inked out to discourage write-ins." If Reagan wanted to run for re-election in 1970, Californians might not take kindly to him if he ran for president so quickly and was using the governorship for less than one full term only as a stepping stone.

Once Reagan had lost in Wisconsin, Nebraska, and Oregon, some viewed a potential continuing Reagan presidential candidacy as useless. But Reagan—as possible vice-president for Rockefeller—was viewed by some as an ever-present possibility. And as California Republicans voted on June 4, it was noted by some that "Rockefeller is more eager for Reagan's delegates than Reagan."[36]

Pat Nolan, as we will see who was a Student for Reagan from California, has provided some additional insight, as he was steeped in California Republican politics at the time. Nolan would attend the Miami Beach convention and spent much time with his home state delegation. He observed that there was a clear division between the hard-core Reaganites versus those delegates loyal to Nixon. Indeed Nolan felt that a number who may have said they were for Reagan "loved to touch the royal purple" and thus secretly felt Nixon would win and wanted to be part of that winning team.[37]

Just prior to the California primary, the New York Times analysis consisted of mere notice that Reagan once had been a Democrat and cited the comments of a San Francisco trial lawyer, who was a member of Democrats for Reagan and who said, "If the election were held today, I think the whole country would throw the Democrats into all the rivers and lakes. People are tired of them," by citing disorder and crime as major issues.[38] The liberal Republican Ripon Society, not a friend of Reagan as discussed earlier, released a new report claiming Reagan was "ill-equipped to handle foreign policy" and lacked managerial skills to control governmental bureaucracy with the final opinion that he was unqualified to be president or vice-president.[39]

Israel

Reagan's in-state appearances have not been discussed here in much detail, for they reflected concerns of Reagan as governor even if at times he did address issues outside of California. He did answer questions at Sacramento press conferences about his presidential campaign travels and plans. But occasionally in California, as he had done vociferously across the country especially in his White Paper speeches, he did speak of foreign affairs beyond Vietnam.

On May 5, 1968, Reagan spoke at the Salute to Israel event in Los Angeles, which commemorated both Israel's birth twenty years earlier and its stunning victory in the Six Day War almost a year before. In 1948 when Israel was created despite the Arab invasion to destroy it, Reagan who had been horrified at the Holocaust as discussed earlier, had "rejoiced" because the victims of the Holocaust "deserved a country of their own."[40] Eisenhower had advised Reagan on confronting charges of anti-Semitism in 1966, and as theorized before, likely Eisenhower and Reagan had discussed Israel at their meeting two months earlier. And eleven months earlier, Reagan had spoken at a Hollywood Bowl rally to support Israel in the midst of the Six Day War and had followed-up his brief remarks there with more specifics in Omaha, as discussed.

Reagan said to the audience, composed mainly of Jewish Americans of California, "If you're to survive as a nation yourselves and to fulfill God's purpose in the world, they should always remember that man is not animal, he is a creature of the spirit. And there are things for which men would be willing to die."[41] Reagan reflected that in the year since he had last spoken to the same group shortly after Israel's victory eleven months earlier, the Egyptians and Syrians had been rearmed by the Soviet Union, which "relentlessly pursues its goal of world domination."[42] He continued his admiration for the young democracy saying, "The freedom of the world is at stake in the Middle East. But who defends that freedom? Only that one tiny nation born of a hunger for freedom and inspired by two decades having the taste of freedom."[43] But "Those who made the desert flower have been forced to lay aside the tools of peace and they have stood manning the ramparts as armed guards. They deserve better from us. They must be provided the weapons to match the Soviet arms now aimed at their nation's heart."[44]

There was much cheering and applause at that point. Reagan wanted to bring Israel and her neighbors to the peace table, but he said "I do not suggest bringing these nations to the table by reason of our power or threats of force." Hearkening back to President Eisenhower's Jordan River project, Reagan proposed that joint desalinization projects headed by the U.S. could start the peace process. But Reagan was firm that the goal for Israel would be the "guarantee of their borders and the sovereignty of their nation."[45] Reagan, who previously had forcefully declared that America should clearly not remain neutral but should be on Israel's side, again was extending his foreign policy bona fides beyond Vietnam into this other cauldron of the world—the Middle East.

Perhaps future President Ronald Reagan, who would only be in office for less than five months in early June, 1981 when a surprise Israeli raid—Operation Opera—would destroy Saddam Hussein's Osiraq nuclear reactor, might have recalled his 1968 words: about fragile Israel as the Middle East's only democracy and its need to defend itself against existential threats. Not only would he regard

America's protection of Israel what "was owed the survivors of the Holocaust," but he would tell all that Israel was a "strategic bulwark against Soviet intervention in the Middle East."[46] Clearly some of the future policies of President Reagan towards Israel had been espoused by Reagan several times during his 1968 campaign. Clearly Reagan was on the world stage as a world statesman.

West coast political reporter and columnist Bill Boyarsky had just published his Reagan political biography, The *Rise of Ronald Reagan*.[47] He was interviewed about his book and about Reagan. Boyarsky praised Reagan's television skills by stating, "Nobody can touch Reagan's technical ability....Reagan is not only better than Senator Robert Kennedy on the tube, but is as good as the late Jack Kennedy was."[48] And that is what Reagan was aiming to accomplish: to defeat his nemesis, Robert Kennedy, in the general election.

Reagan's travels during these two weeks—between the Nebraska and Oregon primaries—included Hawaii for the governors conference, as we have seen, and preparing for a hectic new campaign visit to the South, which we will explore in detail shortly. During this time, Reagan also returned to his native Illinois.

Dirksen Reappears

When we last discussed Senator Dirksen, he had wanted his delegation to go to Miami Beach unpledged and he had noted the increasing support for Reagan in Illinois. Reed had been disappointed that Reagan had not been more forceful with Dirksen at their meeting at Eureka College the prior year, but perhaps Reagan could not speak openly at the time. Reagan had been asked to attend several speaking engagements in Illinois as well. Dirksen had been invited to Walter Dilbeck Jr.'s Governor Reagan for President Committee in the nation's capital but had been unable to attend.

Regardless of how much true support Dirksen felt for Reagan, there was a growing correspondence between Reagan and Dirksen in 1967, which turned personal and personable in 1968. The theme of the communications between them changed, from requests for Reagan to speak to Illinois Republican Party groups in general, or related to matters of federal governmental policies and their impact upon California, to very specific information flow about the 1968 race for the White House.

Senator Dirksen usually addressed his letters to Reagan with "Dear Governor" and occasionally "Dear Ron." Similarly throughout 1967 Governor Reagan's letters to Senator Dirksen always began

"Dear Senator." But in early 1968 Reagan started to address Senator Everett Dirksen with the more personal greeting, "Dear Ev."

The request that Dirksen had made of Reagan to speak to the United Republican Fund of Illinois, discussed earlier, was fulfilled on May 21, 1968 at the end of his whirlwind campaign visit to the South. Arrangements were confirmed via an April 15 telegram from Reagan to Dirksen.[49] On April 29 Dirksen wrote Reagan that he might not be able to attend. Reagan answered on May 7, "My trip to Chicago will not be complete without seeing you."[50] Dirksen replied on May 13, "I will kill all the cows in the barn to be on hand."[51]

After Reagan's May 21 speech, the national media reported that one Reagan supporter had likened the candidate to Winston Churchill, whose own years in the political wilderness had ended when the invasion of Poland by Germany had proved Churchill's prescient warnings correct all along. To be compared to Churchill was almost as high an honor as to be compared to Eisenhower. The reporter thought the comparison of Reagan to Churchill was "strained," but if by convention time the cities were ablaze again and if the Vietnam negotiations appeared to be an American sell-out, "Delegates would turn to the Republican who has been taking the most hawkish line on both domestic rioters and foreign Reds."[52]

Dirksen did attend the Reagan speech. Dirksen would play a prominent role at Miami Beach, and despite the lack of an endorsement from Dirksen in Eureka the year before, or of any commitment at the time from Reagan to be a candidate, the last of the Republican leaders was still a possible Reagan supporter-to-be.

Triumph and Tragedy

May 1968 ended with the Democratic candidates finishing their California primary campaigns and June 1968 began with Reagan awaiting the final Republican California primary vote tally. Reagan and his presidential team seemingly successfully had changed course after Kennedy had entered the race, with the March 25 meeting having been the turning point. Hopes were high on the Reagan side that if Kennedy then would win in California, the likelihood of a future final nomination of RFK as Democrat nominee in Chicago would lessen Republican enthusiasm for Nixon on the first ballot in Miami Beach and thus catapult Reagan to the Republican nomination on the second ballot.

On June 4, Ronald Reagan won on the Republican side. On the Democratic side, voting results stretched into the early morning hours of June 5. History recorded that a few minutes after declaring victory, Robert Kennedy walked into the hotel kitchen, where he was gunned down by the assassin, Sirhan Sirhan. It is beyond the subject of this book to delve into the motives of RFK's killer, but it should be noted that his diary had entries, which called for the overthrow of the United States government as well as praise of communism.[53] Some historians have speculated that as a Palestinian, the killer was incensed over RFK's support for selling fighter jets to Israel, thus making RFK's assassination on American territory in 1968 possibly the first preamble or preview of the War on Terrorism, a full third of a century before the tragic events of Sept 11, 2001.

Reagan's Offer to Help is Refused—Reagan's Public Statement

Kennedy was brought to Good Samaritan Hospital, where Reagan's security personnel "offered every assistance…but they were told to 'get out; we don't need Reagan's help.'"[54]

Shortly after news of the assassination reached him, Reagan made a brief public statement offering condolences to Mrs. Kennedy and the Kennedy family and offering to help in whatever way he could:

"The people of this nation feel as we do here in California that there is no place in America for the atmosphere of violence that seems to pervade our land. We are determined to replace this with sanity and order, and I hope that all who are praying for the Kennedys and Senator Kennedy as we all are, I hope at the same time we will add a vow, a pledge, that we're not going to rest, any of us, in or out of government, until we end this lawlessness, that seems to be so prevalent in our society today."[55]

The official Reagan tribute appeared shortly thereafter in the *New York Times*: "The tragic, senseless death of Senator Kennedy affects all Californians and all Americans. My sympathies go out to Mrs. Kennedy and the Senator's children as well as his parents and other members of his family. Prayers of all Americans are with them."[56] Reagan had not met Ethel Kennedy up to that point, but future President Reagan would deliver a moving tribute in honor of his former adversary to Ethel and her family at the White House Rose Garden, as we will see.

Reagan had lived through the Kennedy assassination in the fall of 1963 and both the Martin Luther King Jr. and now Robert F Kennedy assassinations in the spring of 1968. He hoped to end such lawlessness, yet in a major irony that only perhaps someone in the theatre like Reagan perhaps could appreciate, Reagan himself was to be the next target of American political assassination only a little more than a decade in the future. Of those four political assassination attempts in America during the second half of the twentieth century, only Reagan would survive. Nancy Reagan had "panicked" when she heard the news of RFK, fearing for the safety of her husband.[57] But was it just random acts of violence that now had silenced a second Kennedy? Or was there more behind it?

Ronald Reagan reacted to the assassination not calling to repeal the Second Amendment, not calling to outlaw guns, and not claiming that American society was sick. He remained firm in not leading the Blame America First crowd on the political left. Reagan placed the blame squarely on the individual who had committed the crime. Reagan wanted individuals to accept responsibility for the good or ill each created. And Reagan remained appalled by those who broke the law. But in the case of Sirhan Sirhan, his communist ties, like those of Lee Harvey Oswald in 1963, would get special scrutiny from the ever-watchful anti-communist candidate Reagan.

Reagan's Personal Reflections

Immediately after the RFK assassination, comedian Joey Bishop asked his friend Governor Reagan to appear that night on his nightly talk show on June 5 to discuss the assassination. Reagan cut short a staff meeting to speak live on the program. Reagan explained that the Jordanian-Palestinian assassin's motive was revenge for Kennedy's support for Israel. Reagan then decried the lawlessness in society. Reagan harkened back to the 1965 verbal spat between Eisenhower and RFK, when the former attorney general had proclaimed that blacks did not have to obey the law. Reagan reminded the listeners that some leaders had urged citizens that they could choose which laws to obey. Reagan placed full responsibility on Sirhan Sirhan: "We must return to a principle that the individual is responsible for his misdeeds and must pay the price."[58]

Then Reagan mentioned the recent campaign slogans that Kennedy had used, about returning governmental power to the people, and about which Reagan had joked on the presidential campaign trail, and Reagan turned these into their finding of a common bond even though they had been political opponents.

Then Reagan once again quoted the medieval Jewish philosopher Maimonides, who had observed that the worst way to help a poor person was to give him a handout but the best way was to teach him how to help himself. Reagan proceeded to quote the Jewish *Talmud* and its teaching that a man must be taught how to make a living or else he will become a thief. Reagan last had mentioned Maimonides in a public speech when he had spoken the prior September in Eureka IL. Host Joey Bishop interrupted Reagan asking if the *"New Testament could get some equal time?"* This lightened the tense atmosphere and Reagan did then mention Jesus' teachings on individual responsibility. Reagan stressed that he did not want Americans to feel that RFK's death signaled that there was something wrong with American society. Reagan cautioned, "America is not to blame" and again stressed that the individual assassin was at fault.[59] Not to blame America first, a future famous phrase of President Reagan's United Nations Ambassador Jeane Kirkpatrick, might be traced to Reagan's thinking here.

Although his famous "Evil Empire" speech was to be some fourteen years in the future, Reagan then tied together directly RFK's death by a Jordanian-Palestinian, because of RFK's support of Israel, with Soviet communism and the latter's role in the Mideast. Reagan had just spoken about Israel's independence as he continued to burnish his expertise in world affairs. The 1967 Six-Day War had occurred exactly one year before.

> The enemy sits in Moscow. I call him an enemy because
> I believe he has proven this, by deed, in the middle east
> which led to, precipitated, the tragedy of last night....
> This same Soviet power... has impressed upon the world
> its belief that the end justifies the means and there is no
> morality except what furthers the cause.[60]

Historian Paul Kengor analyzed a portion of the show to prove that Reagan's views on the Soviet Union had remained steadfast.[61] Kengor shows how Reagan tied the Soviet's having fed false intelligence to Egypt to induce the conflict as its primary cause, one of whose end results was the death of Robert Kennedy.[62] Kengor shows how Reagan's conclusion, that for the Soviets the end justifies the means, would be the exact same words President Reagan would use at his first press conference.[63]

Unmentioned yet by Reagan was that Lee Harvey Oswald, the killer of President John F. Kennedy only five years earlier, had lived for some time in Moscow before going to Dallas. One theory was that he was in fact a Soviet assassin. With RFK having been murdered less than twenty-four hours ago, here was Reagan tying in the Soviets possibly to the murder of another Kennedy brother. Was

Sirhan Sirhan a Soviet agent too? Who might be next? Joey Bishop interrupted by mentioning that due to the assassination, President Johnson had ordered that all presidential candidates be given Secret Service protection. When asked by Bishop if he had gotten this added security, Reagan said, "No. I'm not a declared candidate."[64] Reagan eventually would get the added protection and in Indianapolis would tie in Oswald's communism to the murdered president.

Bishop and Reagan discussed briefly other assassinations in American history and Bishop asked if it was just a sign of the times. Reagan answered that political assassins could always be around. In another ironic prophetic comment, which would apply to himself when John Hinckley would try to assassinate him a decade-and-a-half in the future, Reagan surmised, "Anyone serving in public office today…is a potential target."[65]

Bishop asked Reagan what he thought the rest of the world was thinking. Reagan answered that although he was sure that some foreign writers were gleefully about to write stories attacking America, Reagan reminded his listeners that since World War II, America had put a military presence "between them and the barbarians" to preserve their right to write freely. Reagan's comments drew sustained applause from Bishop's studio audience.[66]

Rockefeller's Reaction

After RFK's death, Nelson Rockefeller "sensed a void in the political center" and told his staff that he thought "the people who supported Bobby Kennedy are going to come to me now" and would move his campaign politically to the left. Rockefeller was the first candidate to start campaigning after the assassination and planned not just a symbolic shift to the left but an actual trip to the "left" coast to visit Watts in June.[67]

During the spring of 1968, Rockefeller's political researcher Molitar had been busy assessing the Reagan threat to Rockefeller. Rockefeller now needed Molitar's analyses to formulate policies. And although much of what Molitar had read and analyzed for Rockefeller was about Nixon, there was a good deal he had written about Rockefeller's competitor Ronald Reagan. But another Rockefeller advisor was studying Reagan's foreign policy too.

Rockefeller advisor Dr. David Barshatky had sent a confidential memo to Rockefeller in May entitled, "Rockefeller and Reagan On Vietnam." What role Kissinger had had in the analysis is not clear from the files. Regardless, the summary began, "Governor Rockefeller and Governor Reagan publicly differ on the crucial issue of Vietnam by about the same magnitude as the difference in their experience in foreign affairs," Rockefeller having been a United States emissary to Latin American decades earlier. Citing recent Rockefeller speeches compared to Reagan 's interview with *U.S. News and World Report* on March 25 and a recent Reagan press conference, Barshatky compared the views of the two candidates on the war adding his own commentary. Seen from the hindsight of four and a half decades later, the memo makes interesting reading.

On the Americanization of the conflict, Rockefeller advocated a policy of "de-Americanization," whereas supposedly Reagan favored Americanization. Barshatky felt that Reagan was naïve in seemingly ignoring the Soviet Union and China but he did note that Reagan wanted "a stiffer attitude toward the Soviet Union," citing the Reagan comment noted earlier when Reagan was advocating that the U.S. should stir up trouble for the communists rather than just always trying to put out fires around the globe that had been started by the communists. Reagan wanted "to give the enemy something else to worry about in another corner of the world."

Then Rockefeller was praised by his own analyst, when he had said that the objective of the enemy in Vietnam "has not been to seize terrain but to disrupt orderly government" and that one could not talk of "total military victory in Vietnam." Reagan of course was criticized severely by the Rockefeller analyst when he had advocated a policy of "rapid military escalation," which if it "had been very intense in a short period of time, the conflict might well have been over." Reagan's advocating the mining of Haiphong Harbor and using the threat of invading North Vietnam ("Hanoi should be given 'a taste of war on Vietnam soil'") were ridiculed.

Finally, Reagan's ideas about the use of atomic bombs in Vietnam were ridiculed and misinterpreted completely. Reagan had said clearly that he did not advocate using them in the conflict. As discussed earlier via historian Evan Thomas' analysis of Eisenhower's use of threats, which the general had passed onto his protégé Reagan during their private meetings, many times Reagan subsequently told the public that he wanted the Johnson administration to threaten to use them. Reagan was quoted: "The last person in the world who should know we wouldn't use them is the enemy. He should go to bed every night afraid that we might."[68]

Of course in retrospect, Reagan was dead on. The North Vietnamese indeed were after total military victory and a complete seizure of the entire territory of South Vietnam, as the events of 1975 would prove. Whether Reagan's policy of a surge in rapid military deployment would have worked, rather than the gradual escalation used by the Johnson administration, is of course not known. However such a policy would work quite well for General David Petraeus at the beginning of the 21st century in the Iraq War.

Rockefeller advisor Molitar sent Rockefeller a different Vietnam analysis. Rockefeller needed it in case he might be asked to distinguish his own views from those of Reagan. Whereas Reagan had advocated blocking Haiphong's harbor, Rockefeller had stated, "Escalation in the north is not the answer." Whereas Reagan said he wanted no coalition government with the Viet Cong, Rockefeller said it was possible. Whereas Reagan wanted no negotiations unless a cease-fire were "rigidly enforced," Rockefeller had said nothing thus far about a cease-fire.[69]

Rockefeller used several political researchers and advisors at once. Besides Barshatky and Molitar, Rockefeller's main advisor was his executive assistant, George Hinman. As we have seen, once Reagan had been elected governor in 1966, Hinman had voiced his and Rockefeller's mixed feelings about Reagan's victory. Hinman added that he and Rockefeller had hoped that the realities of governing a complex state like California would "have a moderating effect…at least I very much hope so."[70]

Hinman chronicled and summarized Reagan's positions on numerous issues, as had Molitar and Barshatky. Hinman distrusted Reagan's policy of "firm and swift repression" for riots and student protests and praised his boss Rockefeller's "call for peaceful demonstrations and a more nuanced understanding…regarding the arguments and root causes of such dissent."[71] Yet Reagan was correctly reading the minds of the majority of American citizens, who felt that laws should not be broken whenever and wherever someone wanted to break them and that individuals must be held accountable for their actions rather than society being blamed when crimes had occurred.

Another problem that surfaced in the spring of 1968, highlighting the differences between Reagan and Rockefeller on domestic issues, was the national boycott of California grapes orchestrated by Cesar Chavez's farm workers union. This issue had turned into a dispute between Governor Reagan and New York City Mayor John Lindsay who supported the boycott. While Reagan and Lindsay exchanged messages and threats, New York Governor Rockefeller did not get involved publicly. "Rockefeller met Reagan's threats and criticism with the calculated strategy of silence."[72] Rockefeller's silence, analyzed historian Todd Holmes, was felt to be a planned political move to differentiate himself from the more vocal Reagan.[73]

Kissinger and the Politics of Weariness

A complete reassessment of the Rockefeller campaign then was sent to Rockefeller from Henry Kissinger on June 9, 1968 and was entitled, "Where Are We Now In The Campaign?" Kissinger wrote that he felt that the pundits who thought that Nixon and Humphrey had wrapped up the campaign were wrong. Kissinger was not shy about expressing his opinion of that choice for president, but of course had no inkling he was writing about his future employer—when he would become national security advisor and secretary of state for President Nixon—"Many people will gag at the choice of Nixon and Humphrey." He thought that with the two assassinations and Johnson's re-election announcement, "This is no year for experts because traditional rules simply do not apply...Anybody who can appeal to idealism and the desire for commitment may start a groundswell which is bound to express itself in public opinion polls." Kissinger clearly was thinking of Rockefeller's possible new chances, but his words applied just as well to Reagan's grass roots campaign, which was ongoing at exactly the same time. Kissinger apparently did not conceive that idealism and commitment could also apply to conservatives and not just liberals. Kissinger advocated the new Rockefeller approach to be called "the politics of weariness."[74]

At the time Rockefeller read the Kissinger memo, the governor was planning a Los Angeles dinner for June 12, 1968 during the trip to Watts. On the typed guest list, attached to the memo in the files, were a number of known Reagan financial supporters and former Reagan campaign director William French Smith. Three Reagan Hollywood friends included were Bob Hope, Jules Stein and Jack Warner. Other notable people invited were Norton Simon, Rockefeller's own George Hinman, and Freeman Gosden, the man who was the go-between Reagan and Eisenhower. Rockefeller wrote in a few additional names to the invitation list, including known former Kennedy supporters Roosevelt Grier, Frank Manciewicz, Ted Sorensen, Arthur Schlesinger, Mac Bundy, Adam Walinsky plus actor Kirk Douglas and Tom Watson of IBM.

Shaken, Not Stirred

That Rockefeller was not attuned fully to common American culture was related by speechwriter, and future Rockefeller biographer, Joseph Persico. During the flight to California, Secret Service agents were on the plane being newly assigned after the Kennedy assassination. As Rockefeller moved down the aisle to greet the reporters, one kidded the governor, by saying they were "traveling now like James Bond." Rockefeller asked blankly "Who?" The reporter answered, "You know, James Bond. 007. Sean Connery." Rockefeller wondered with a blank stare, "How many delegates has he got?"[75]

What was said eventually at the Los Angeles dinner was not revealed. But clearly Rockefeller saw himself not just as a candidate moving to the left but possibly as a new candidate of the center who could attract both Reagan supporters and former Kennedy supporters. Rockefeller indeed was following the advice of Kissinger and his team.[76] But to stop Nixon, Rockefeller still would need the help of Reagan.

Reagan Continues to Speak About RFK

A week later, Reagan brought up the Robert F. Kennedy assassination when he spoke in Indianapolis on June 13, 1968, prior to leaving for the Republican Governor's Conference. Reagan was continuing his theme, first expressed on *The Joey Bishop Show*, to tie both Kennedy assassinations to world communism. Historian Paul Kengor reviewed part of his Indiana speech recently in an online article.[77] Earlier in the day Reagan had spoken briefly after landing at the municipal airport[78] and when discussing violence in American society and the death penalty in the context of "our Judeo-Christian tradition," Reagan again quoted Jewish sources, this time citing the Ten Commandments. He reminded his audience, "The term 'Thou Shalt Not Kill' as translated from the ancient Hebrew, the phrase actually is 'Thou Shalt Not Murder.'"[79]

It is not clear if Reagan's quoting of Maimonides, the Jewish *Talmud* and then the Jewish *Torah* (Old Testament) and its Ten Commandments in important speeches just a few days after the RFK assassination indicate he had re-read some of these texts while thinking about the recent tragedy, whether they were just part of Reagan's religious training throughout his life, or he was recalling his exhortations the prior September in Eureka.

That evening he spoke for forty minutes at the manufacturer's building at the Indiana State Fairgrounds at a dinner-fundraiser,[80] in which 2500 Republicans had paid $100 per plate.[81] Reagan began by telling his audience he was going to put away his prepared political text, "because I can't find it within myself to deliver those remarks tonight.. ..Our minds are still on the senseless tragedy of a week ago… We're sick with grief, sick with anger." Reagan described the death of RFK as an "act of senseless savagery and it was just that."

Even though Reagan was one of RFK's opponents that year for the presidency, and indeed as seen above he had many years' worth of entanglements with RFK for which to be resentful and angry, he described the killing as "utterly senseless and bearing no relationship to the causes articulated by the Senator or by his opponents…The Senator had been speaking of unity among our people—the healing our wounds…I think it would be well if we continue that talk".

Then Reagan transitioned into connecting the assassinations of the two brothers with a common source of evil. For RFK "allegedly it was the violence of the war in the middle-east imported to this country by an alien," and Reagan then reminded them that just "five years ago, a President was murdered by one who renounced his American citizenship to embrace the godless philosophy of communism." Reagan then charged that "at the highest level of government", a decision was made to conceal Lee Harvey Oswald's communist ties for fear of upsetting the Soviet Union. Reagan's outrage was clear. As historian Kengor has summarized, "Moscow's nefarious ways had led, directly or indirectly, to the murders of two of America's most cherished political figures-the Kennedy boys."[82] One observer commented that the solution to the violence, to the three assassinations of John F. Kennedy, Martin Luther King Jr. and Robert F. Kennedy, was clear: "Ronald Reagan…was needed in the White House, speedily."[83]

The next day in Cheyenne Wyoming at a fundraiser, Reagan spoke about the Kennedy's one last time before he was to fly to Tulsa for the Republican Governors Conference. A reporter asked him if he thought the recent wave of assassinations might be due to a communist conspiracy. "You'd be very naïve not to think that communists had a hand in it."[84] Reagan explained and then amplified that he didn't necessarily think they had a direct role but reiterated the communist connections of Oswald and Sirhan, which he had mentioned the day before. When telling of his annoyance that the U.S. government had ordered that the communist ties of Oswald be ignored for fear of upsetting the Soviets, this time Reagan added, "I'm not too concerned about whether we offend the Soviet or not." He then proceeded to elaborate on his personal experience of how the communists had tried to "take over the economic control" of the motion picture industry. Reagan explained that the communists weren't defeated by "pointing fingers or naming names or calling people communists. We defeated them by opposing what they were trying to do. And I'd suggest that to anyone who's interested in opposing communism."[85]

After the RFK assassination, as alluded to above, security was heightened for all presidential candidates, and security preparations for the convention increased as well. Reagan himself reported that there were "reports that foreign agents were plotting to kill other American officials."[86] During his Indianapolis speech noted above, body guards for Reagan were photographed allegedly manhandling a press photographer who had attempted to photograph candidate Reagan[87] Reagan's two main Secret service agents were Edward Hickey and John Simpson, both of whom would have prominent roles with Reagan in the future.[88]

In his autobiography *An American Life*, Reagan made scant reference to Robert F. Kennedy—only mentioning the heightened security after RFK's assassination (see above), and he did not mention the latter's roles in Reagan's testimony, the Gridiron Dinner, the *Town Meeting of the World* debate, their campaigning against each other in 1966 and 1968, the firing from GE and resultant unemployment, nor the 1981 memorial ceremony at the White House. Perhaps indeed Reagan had forgiven RFK, who by the 1990 autobiography had been dead more than twenty years, or he didn't want to speak ill of the dead, or perhaps all of his interactions with RFK over the 1950s and 1960s were memories just too painful for Ronald Reagan to relive in writing.

Reagan Campaign Over?

With the assassination of Robert F. Kennedy, Tom Reed reflected, "The mood of the Republicans became one of despair. The stage was now set for two stodgy former Vice Presidents, Nixon and Humphrey, to slug it out in the fall."[89] Clif White observed, "With Bobby Kennedy's assassination, the whole political scene had shifted once again...I knew that Richard Nixon was going to be much more difficult for us to beat with Bobby Kennedy gone...Nixon...could not beat another Kennedy in 1968."[90] This had been one of the arguments for a Reagan candidacy in the first place.

Reed, as head of the 1968 Reagan presidential campaign, had to tell candidate Reagan the new, grim political situation. So during that week, Reed met with Reagan and speaking on behalf of himself and the other Reagan-for-President close advisors, Reed recalled telling him "that in our collective opinion, his presidential campaign was over...There was no chance for victory...I am not sure if he heard me or if the message sank in."[91]

Reed reviewed a heated and contentious meeting on June 9, which he termed a 'civil war" amongst Reagan's campaign staff.[92] Again the campaign was in disarray. It was in "meltdown mode" and was a "headless juggernaut."[93]

Yet for Ronald Reagan, who had been told first that his 1968 presidential campaign was over when Reed was demoted and as a result had put the campaign on a slow tailspin, and who had been told for a second time that the campaign was over after the Oregon primary, and now for the third time was told the campaign had no chance and was over, this time because Robert Kennedy was dead, there were still two months before the Republican convention in Miami Beach.

There was still a detailed campaign plan as well as all the additional planned speeches, trips, press conferences, appearances and more governor meetings still ahead. The Reagan finance committee was intact and was paying for the huge Reagan effort at the convention. Nixon still held less than 600 of the needed 667 delegates.[94] Who knew what else could happen between early June and early August? Ronald Reagan was no quitter.

The second and final pre-convention meeting of the California delegation took place on June 22 in Los Angeles. Reagan's chairmanship of the delegation was formalized, and the two new Republican national committeemen were announced. Tom Reed was selected as one and had achieved his long time personal goal. Reagan, Finch and California Senator George Murphy joined together to exhort the delegates to maintain unity behind Reagan as their favorite son and also not to commit to any candidate for second-ballot.[95]

Robert F. Kennedy had been an antagonist to Reagan for many years: the two lawsuits with GE, the SAG-MCA testimony, the cancellation of *General Electric Theatre*, the Gridiron Dinner, the *Town Meeting of the World* debate, and the many Reagan speeches joking about—and then attacking—RFK. Robert F. Kennedy had been directly or indirectly the force opposing him for each one. And since March 1968, when RFK had announced his own candidacy, if Reagan could win the Republican nomination, RFK seemingly was going to be his final opponent for the Presidency in the fall. Yet although RFK now was dead, Reagan's comments and speeches about RFK's death had showed "the grace that Ronald Reagan showed toward his political opponents".[96]

But despite the death of RFK, Ronald Reagan did not stop his 1968 campaign for the presidency. Reagan prepared to fly off to Topeka for a critical financial meeting and barbecue with Henry A. Bubb's Citizens for Reagan National Information Center. Meanwhile

Reed was updated by Western States Director Fred Van Natta that a credentials fight was brewing that could determine whether Reagan might actually win a majority of delegates in Washington State.

Endnotes

1. Williams, David C., untitled memo, 8/1/1968
2. Davies, Lawrence, "California GOP Praises Reagan," *NYT*, 3/5/67, p. 40
3. RRL, Tape 339
4. RRL, Tape 347
5. RRL, Tape 348
6. White, Why Reagan Won, p. 106
7. Deaver, oral history, p. 19
8. Smith, oral hist, p. 40
9. "Some Help Reagan Can Do Without," *Los Angeles Times*, 2/20/68; "Strategist's Hiring Unknown to Reagan," *Los Angeles Times*, 2/20/68
10. Spencer, oral history, tape 4 of 13, p. 35
11. Haerle oral hist, p. 25-26
12. White, p. 140
13. White, p. 48
14. Boyarsky, p. 153
15. Chester, et. al.
16. Boyarsky, p. 154
17. Chester, et. al.
18. Jonas op.cit.
19. White, p. 141
20. Weaver, Warren Jr, "Republicans Face Four Key Primaries," *NYT*, 7/9/67, p. 29
21. Leaming
22. Kaufman, Robert W., "Ronald Reagan: A Republican Messiah?," *North American Review* 2533, 1968, p. 11
23. Williams, David C., untitled memo, 8/1/1968
24. ibid
25. Kaufman, op.cit., p. 12
26. ibid
27. Davies, Lawrence, "California GOP Praises Reagan," *NYT*, 3/5/67, p. 40
28. "Welcome to the Fraternity," *Time*, 5/19/67, p. 30
29. Duscha, Julius, "Reagan Gives Surprising Performance: Not Great, Not Brilliant, But…" *NYT*, 12/10/67, p. 296
30. *U.S. News and World Report*, 10/30/67, p. 62
31. "Other GOP Developments," *Congressional Quarterly*, 2/2/68, p. 163
32. Hill, Gladwin, "Reagan Dissatisfied That Nixon Has No Opposition in the GOP," *NYT*, 3/26/68, p. 23
33. Hill, Gladwin, "Reagan Steps Up Non Candidacy," *NYT*, 4/14/68, p. 56
34. Hill, op.cit. 3/26; as best as can be determined, this Walker is different than Reagan's Southern director
35. Hill, Gladwin, "California GOP Briefed by White," *NYT*, 4/16/68, p. 18
36. Bartlett, Charles, "Reagan Candidacy Loses Luster," *Western Star*, 6/4/68
37. Nolan, pers int 6/8/13
38. Curtis, Charlotte, "California Primary: A Political Test of Newness," *NYT*, 6/2/68, p. 1
39. Kabaservice, p. 240
40. Cannon, President Reagan. p. 340
41. RRL, Tape 339
42. ibid
43. ibid
44. ibid
45. ibid
46. Cannon, Pres Reagan, p. 340-341
47. Boyarsky
48. Humphrey, Hal, "Book Rates TV Image of Politicians," *The Oregonian*, 5/31/68, sec2, p. 13
49. NFD003 SPOBO20, 1968 Apr 15, Dirksen Congressional Center, EMD Papers, Alpha 1968, Reagan
50. Reagan to Dirksen, 5/7/1968 letter, Dirksen Congressional Center, EMD Papers, Alpha 1968, Reagan
51. Dirksen to Reagan, 5/13/1968 letter, Dirksen Congressional Center, EMD Papers, Alpha 1968, Reagan

52.   Large, Arlen, "Reagan on the Road," *WSJ*, 5/22/68
53.   Hayward, p. 213
54.   Reed, p. 26
55.   RRL, Tape 346
56.   "National and International Figures Offer Tributes to Kennedy," *NYT*, 6/7/68, p. 29
57.   Colacello, Bob, "Ronnie and Nancy," *Vanity Fair*, 7/98, p. 136
58.   RRL, Tape 347
59.   ibid
60.   ibid
61.   Kengor, p. 36-38
62.   Kengor, p. 37
63.   Kengor, ibid
64.   RRL, Tape 347
65.   ibid
66.   RRL, Tape 347
67.   Persico, p. 75
68.   Barshatky, David, "Rockefeller and Reagan on Vietnam", Rockefeller Archives, Graham
      Molitar papers, F 862 Reagan, IV 3A 18, Box 32, Folder 862
69.   Molitar, Walter, "Rockefeller-Reagan Differences" Rockefeller Archives, Graham Molitar
      papers, IV 3A 18, Reagan NAR, Box 32, Folder 862, 6/3/68
70.   Holmes, p. 9
71.   Holmes, p. 11
72.   Holmes, p. 13
73.   ibid
74.   Kissinger, Henry A., "Where Are We Now In The campaign?", memo to Rockefeller,
      Rockefeller archives, NAR RG-15 Gubernatorial Collection, Presidential Campaign 1968
      Series, Box 4, Folder F149, 6/9/68
75.   Persico, p. 76
76.   Kissinger, Henry A., "Where Are We Now In The campaign?", memo to Rockefeller,
      Rockefeller archives, NAR RG-15 Gubernatorial Collection, Presidential Campaign 1968
      Series, Box 4, Folder F149, 6/9/68
77.   Kengor, Paul, "Reagan-RFK 1967," *National Review Online*, 6/5/08, p. 4
78.   Papers of Kathryn R. Davis, Hoover Institution Archives, Box 2
79.   RRL, Tape 348
80.   Papers of Kathryn R. Davis, Hoover Institution Archives, Box 2
81.   Chester et. al., p. 363
82.   Kengor op.cit., p. 4; Reagan's speech is available online at www.reagan68.com.
83.   Chester, et. al.
84.   RRL, Tape 348
85.   RRL, Tape 348
86.   Reagan, *An American Life*, p. 172
87.   See Illustrations
88.   Nofziger, p. 72
89.   Reed op.cit., p. 26
90.   White, *Why Reagan Won*, p. 106
91.   Reed, p. 26
92.   Reed, *The Reagan Enigma*, p. 164
93.   Reed, *The Reagan Enigma*, p. 165
94.   Reed, *The Reagan Enigma*, p. 165
95.   Hill, Gladwin, "Reagan Asks California Delegation to Shun Second Ballot Commitments for
      Convention," *NYT*, 6/23/68, p. 49
96.   Kengor op.cit., p. 4

CHAPTER 31: WASHINGTON STATE[1]

"Yes. The thing we've got to have in a President is leadership."
~ Governor Dan Evans[2]

"He was pretty damn smart when you got down to it."
~ Governor Dan Evans[3]

In 2012, retired attorney and conservative Republican activist Dick Derham sits comfortably at his local Starbucks, his white goatee glistening off the reflection of Seattle shining through the window after a downpour. He regales with an intricate story of how Ronald Reagan almost won Washington State in 1968. The behind-the-scenes story and intrigue has not been told before. Reagan's campaign had concentrated on the three opt-out primary states, holding together his California delegation, and the attempts to gain delegates from Southern states. Yet the structure of those three opt-out primary states, in which the secretary of state or a committee made a list of likely national candidates and then state Republicans voted in a primary, was a distinct minority in 1968 politics. Most states in 1968 had the structure that Washington had: precinct caucuses, county or district meetings, and then state conventions determined the delegates to be sent to Miami Beach rather than via a direct primary election.

The story of Washington in 1968 is that, had three conservative counties been seated at the Republican State Convention that year, fifteen delegates would have been in Reagan's camp in Miami Beach, and this could have persuaded just a few other delegates to vote for Reagan—thus denying Nixon a first ballot nomination. But instead, just six Reagan delegates emerged from the political maneuvering. The story of Washington State's conservative Republicans in the mid 1960's illustrates the difficulties facing a conservative group when the higher powers in the party pushed a different, liberal, agenda. The role of Washington State in Reagan's 1968 presidential campaign is a prime example of these issues. This story was one battle in the decade-long struggle between liberal Republican Governor Dan Evans and conservative King County Republican Chairman Ken Rogstad.[4]

At Harvard, Derham had been president of Students for Nixon, and along with future 1968 Oregon Reagan activist Diarmuid O'Scannlain, had joined the Harvard chapter of YAF.   After graduating Columbia Law School, Derham served in the U.S. Army in West Germany. Being stationed abroad, he only had limited contact with all the political developments back home. He had seen movies starring Reagan, as well as The Speech in 1964, but Derham never had thought of Reagan as a presidential candidate. He had not known much about Reagan's campaign for governor nor Reagan's first year in office. Derham remained a conservative Republican for Richard Nixon. Thus upon his return to Seattle (King County) in November 1967, his prior participation in conservative causes in college and law school meant that he was viewed as a reliable conservative by the local King County conservative Republican establishment—headed by Ken Rogstad.

Ken Rogstad, a Boeing engineer recruited by Frank Whetstone to become active in the Draft Goldwater movement, and Jim Munn, a POW in World War II after his plane was shot down over Germany and an attorney in Seattle, had been part of a team of young conservatives to work for Goldwater in 1964. This group of young conservatives had dominated the Washington State Republican convention that year and sent a solid pro-Goldwater delegation to the national convention in San Francisco. After the Goldwater landslide loss, the team had wanted to try again in the future. In a state like Washington where the Republican delegate selection process was based on a caucus system, it was relatively easy to reassemble the conservative team to look for other conservative candidates.

Shortly after his successful maneuver in 1964 not to be photographed next to Goldwater, newly elected liberal Republican Governor Dan Evans of Washington State had declared that he wanted to be a hands-on head of the party and to formulate its direction. As reviewed by your author, over the next several years, Evans and Rogstad had fought back and forth for dominance of the Republican Party in Seattle.[5]

By the time Rogstad had arranged for Reagan's 1966 state party convention speech in Seattle, although Rogstad's conservative forces were dominant, wounds within the party were not healed. Despite the well-publicized poll, which had shown strong public support for an actor to enter politics, neither Governor Dan Evans "nor any of his official staff attended the convention;" he had said he had a "prior commitment." Perhaps he did, or perhaps he did not want to hear very clearly the conservative views of candidate Ronald Reagan.[6]

After Reagan's stirring speech in June, and later despite clear opposition from Evans during the fall elections, Rogstad won.[7] Unlike the eight-vote margin achieved by Rogstad two years earlier, this time he won by 778-658, handing the governor a "crushing defeat."[8] For Governor Evans, the defeat of his personal choice was an "undeniably hard blow."[9]

Edward Lange, attorney for the Washington State Republican Party at the time, recalled in 2014 that subsequent rules were adopted to prohibit any appointed party officers being made delegates automatically, rather than via elections by precinct caucuses.[10] The new rules would have major importance for 1968.

During early 1967, Rogstad and Evans had tried to mend fences.[11] In October when Reagan had appeared on the cover of *Time* and speculation focused for awhile on who might be the Republican vice-presidential nominee, Evans was cited as having been "frequently mentioned." But when asked, Evans replied, "If I had to make my choice between the two Washington's, I would select Washington State any time."[12]

Reagan returned to Seattle to campaign and had spoken on November 10, 1967, just prior to Reagan's Veterans Day stops in Portland, Albany, and Corvallis, Oregon. To a cheering crowd of 1,100 at the Olympic Hotel's Grand Ballroom and an overflow crowd watching on closed-circuit television in an adjacent room, this was where Reagan had enthralled his listeners, with Reagan's visit being described as "the biggest political fund-raising luncheon" ever held in Seattle.[13]

Conservative Washington State in 1968

Rogstad and other conservative Republicans spread their message in those years, so that by the time of the 1968 local, county and state Republican conventions, fully the four most populous counties in Washington (King—Seattle, Spokane, Pierce-Tacoma, and Snohomish-Everett) were in conservative Republican hands. Rogstad and other colleagues were solidly for Reagan in 1967-68. Evans was for Rockefeller. High political theater was about to commence, with the stage being set for the high expectations, major disappointments, and political machinations all of which unfolded in front of Derham. At this point, however, as a newcomer to Washington State Republican political activity, Derham had assumed the contest would be between Rockefeller and his own choice, Richard Nixon.

The Washington State Republican Party elected its national delegates through a three-level "caucus-convention" process: precinct caucuses, which elected delegates to legislative district conventions, which in turn elected delegates to the state convention where the state's 24 national delegates would be selected.

The first part of the process was the precinct caucus. In Washington, a voting precinct comprised about 300 voters—equivalent to a few city square blocks in Seattle. On the first Tuesday of March 1968, at 8 PM, in living rooms across the state, voters who had identified themselves as Republicans gathered. Washington had no party registration. Each caucus then discussed issues and completed a poll for use in the county and state platform committees. Crucially two precinct delegates were elected to the next level up. These higher levels were either legislative district caucuses for the larger counties or county conventions for smaller counties. At those higher level caucuses or conventions, delegates to the Washington state convention would be elected. Derham was elected as one of the delegates representing his Seattle precinct. In the weeks before the legislative district convention, the district leadership prepared a slate of recommended delegates to represent the district at the state convention. All were reliably conservative. Derham was asked to serve as an alternate delegate, meaning that he would be seated at the state convention if some delegates could not attend.[14]

Prior to the district convention of April 4, a "pre-meeting" was held, at which the district chairman gave an orientation on how the district convention would be conducted. One key element of the briefing was the advice that, when candidates were nominated for delegate or alternate, they would be asked to state their candidate preference. Those on the district slate were advised to state that they were for Nixon. In looking back on these events some 45 years earlier, Derham has this interpretation. The district was closely split between conservatives (those who had backed Goldwater in 1964) and Evans-Rockefeller liberal Republicans. It was important not to split the vote for the district slate. While Derham had known of no public campaign for Reagan in Washington at this point, no doubt some of the 1964 Goldwater supporters were, at least privately, hoping Reagan would run. Had a candidate for state delegate announced, "I am for Reagan," he would have forfeited the votes of both Rockefeller and many Nixon supporters; thus such a delegate candidate would have risked losing election as a delegate. Therefore everyone was advised to state their preference was for Nixon. Derham now is certain that some would have identified for Reagan and some for Nixon.

But there was a grass roots effort for Reagan in 1968. According to conservative Republican State Chairman C. Montgomery Johnson on March 13, Nixon at that point was only slightly ahead of Rockefeller, with Reagan "far behind." The supporters of a Draft Rockefeller movement accused Reagan supporters of "using Nixon as a stalking horse and infiltrating the Nixon campaign." Reagan grass roots chairman William E. Boeing denied any infiltration and countered that in the four major conservative-oriented party organizations in the four largest counties, there was "much support" for Reagan.[15]

So the next month, on April 4, 1968, Derham dutifully went to a local junior high school where the legislative district convention was held. The district-recommended slate was duly elected. People's minds were preoccupied with the tragic news of the King assassination.

The King County Republican party convention was held in early May and the major business was to set the party platform. The 2,095 delegates rejected one of the governor's major liberal initiatives when they adopted a plank calling for an amendment to the state constitution "prohibiting a state income tax of any type."[16]

At the meeting, Ken Rogstad had appointed more than 400 delegates-at-large, and Edward N. Lange, an Evans supporter, protested Rogstad's action by claiming the bylaws did not permit such an action. Jim Munn, by then Rogstad's party attorney, had been chairman of the bylaws committee and reiterated that the rules were written not to be "exclusionary" but to be "inclusionary." More than 2,000 delegates agreed with the conservative rationale and rejected the liberal protest.

In another critical decision, the delegates approved the use of a "unit-rule," under which the choice for president of the majority would bind the same choice to all members at the upcoming state convention. The unit-rule, critical for Reagan's supporters in Washington State, would turn out to be even more important for Reagan later in Miami Beach. At the King County convention, some members felt that this maneuver would force some delegates who had been in favor of Nixon to "swing behind Governor Ronald Reagan, should he become a candidate." Not everything went Rogstad's way however. The State Central Committee determined that financial allocations to each county were to be determined by the 1964 Republican vote. Rogstad felt that calculation was "devised to reduce the delegate strength of King, Pierce, Snohomish and Spokane counties."[17]

Between the times of the King County convention in early May and the state convention in late June, Governors Reagan and Evans had attended the Western Governors Conference in Hawaii, where Reagan had delivered his first White Paper speech. Reporters asked Governor Evans if Richard Nixon, Governor Nelson Rockefeller and Governor Ronald Reagan would be acceptable Republican nominees for president, and he answered that they would indeed be acceptable by stating, "I don't know of any governor who would not support any of the three."

When pressed further specifically being asked if he considered Ronald Reagan qualified to be president, Evans replied, "If he can be selected as the nominee, I think yes. The thing we've got to have in a President is leadership. We have not been getting any." Evans thought Reagan had strong leadership qualities and indeed was presidential timbre. Evans quickly added however that he was maintaining "personal neutrality on the three potential presidential candidates."[18] Former Governor Evans did not return phone calls from this author for his recollections.

Yet on a more personal level, Evans heaped additional praise on Governor Reagan in Honolulu. Even though it was known generally that Evans was "no Reagan fan," Evans said about Reagan, "He's got that thing that makes a man into a figure. He knows how to communicate with people, without opening his mouth."[19] Perhaps Governor Evans was searching for a word used in later times, charisma. Evans praised Reagan further admitting, "He was pretty damn smart when you got down to it."[20]

State Convention

Two and a half weeks after the RFK assassination and while Reagan was revamping up his campaign plans to emphasize law and order, at an arena at Seattle Center, site of the 1962 World's Fair, the Republican state convention was held June 21-22, 1968. It is not clear if anyone thought of themselves as "The Man in the Arena"— the speech delivered by Republican Theodore Roosevelt some six decades earlier. Derham was about to receive a first-class education in political chess gamesmanship.

As experienced politico Clif White could testify, as could Dwight Eisenhower—recalling what had transpired at the credentials committee during the 1952 GOP convention,[21] at any political convention, the first order of business is to determine who, in fact, is entitled to participate and vote in the convention. That is achieved by the adoption of the report of the Credentials Committee. In many conventions, approval of the credentials committee report is a minor formality and not subject of contention. In 1968 in Seattle, that was not to be the case. The lack of coordination between White and Reed with the local grassroots activists like Rogstad would be a first critical error.

The four largest counties in Washington in 1968, King, Pierce, Snohomish, and Spokane, had in aggregate a majority of the state population and a majority of delegates elected to the state convention. As we have seen for King County, but similarly for the other three, all four were under the control of the conservative wave of Republican Party activists headed by Rogstad. Thus all four counties elected solid conservative slates of delegates to the state convention. Amongst them, if seated, they would be a majority of the state convention. But if some or all were not seated, control of the convention would shift to the more liberal elements of the party. As the state convention opened, challenges were duly made to the seating of all four counties, thus bringing each before the Credentials Committee.

The critical level of power was at the Credentials Committee itself. In Washington, each of the 39 counties was given one vote on the Credentials Committee, and thus the four most populous counties (all four were firmly conservative as noted earlier) only had those four votes. The Credentials Committee had the all-important power to determine whether a county delegation would be placed on the temporary roll of the convention, and thus seated on the floor of the convention while the report of the Credentials Committee itself was debated and adopted. Counties not placed on the temporary roll were "off the floor" and not in a position to participate or vote on decisions on what delegations should be seated.

The related issue was which county delegations got to vote on the seating of other county delegations. Specifically, delegates on the convention floor decided the outcome of all credential challenges. Separately, the state party platform and national delegates were voted on by all those delegates seated at the convention, and not by equal voting per county.

Most of the 35 other counties were controlled by the liberal wing of the state party, headed by Governor Evans. As noted, at the onset of the convention, the Credentials Committee proceeded to challenge the credentials of the four conservative counties. Had they been seated, those four conservative counties—which had a majority of the state Republican Party members—would control both the subsequent votes on the party platform and the composition of the delegates to the Miami Beach convention.[22]

The Credentials Committee placed none of the four challenged county slates on the temporary roll, so none was permitted to participate in the debate that ensued. Then the Credentials Committee arranged its report so that King County, having one-third of the entire total convention votes, would be voted upon last.

The convention then proceeded to adopt the report of the Credentials Committee, paragraph by paragraph, seating "alternative" delegations for two of the three counties other than King County and a split delegation for the third. Only after those county delegations had been seated and the liberal Republicans, having achieved solid control of the convention, did the convention reach the recommendation of the Credentials Committee, whereupon it proceeded to seat King County.

Derham then saw and understood that the King County delegates were not able to vote to seat their fellow-conservative delegations from Pierce, Snohomish, nor Spokane counties.

But the high drama was not over. Prior to the challenge to King County, the three unseated conservative county delegations from Pierce, Spokane, and Snohomish then met separately with Ken Rogstad and his team to decide what to do next. One option was just to go home. Another idea was to hold a separate renegade party convention just for those four counties. A convention hall had even been arranged for that purpose. However Ken Rogstad and others from the King County delegation decided to stay in the official convention so that they could at least send six Reagan delegates to Miami Beach. This decision may have been the second critical error.

Ultimately, the convention decided to seat the King County delegation, fearing that holding a state convention without representatives from Seattle would delegitimize the entire proceedings. Had King County participated in the alternative state convention, the resulting slate of national delegates would have claimed to represent a majority of the delegates elected to the state convention. They thus would have been in a position to make a serious challenge to the official delegation at the national convention in Miami Beach having had a full slate of delegates of a more conservative bent. But by seating King County, the convention posed the King County leadership with this challenge: participate in the official convention and elect six conservative national convention delegates or participate in the alternative convention and potentially end up with none.

Rogstad was aware that there might be national implications of the events going on in Seattle, and he arranged that Van Natta, Reagan's Western Regional Director, who was staying at an adjacent hotel, be let into the convention at various times by a friendly security guard by using a special code. Van Natta kept Reed fully informed with current information about the Seattle convention.[23]

Since King County had two congressional districts located completely or almost completely within its own boundaries, the King County delegates to the state convention were able to elect three delegates and three alternates from each district. Both districts were under the control of Ken Rogstad and his leadership team. All six delegates were solidly for Reagan.

Thus the 1968 state Republican Party convention was held without the regularly-elected and conservative delegates from Pierce, Snohomish nor Spokane counties in attendance. Rogstad's six Reagan delegates held firm and eventually would vote for Reagan in Miami Beach in the first round of balloting.

To this day, Derham fully believes that had those three additional conservative counties been seated, a majority of Washington state delegates would have voted for Reagan in Miami Beach. Instead of the 15 Nixon/3 Rockefeller (including Governor Evans)/6 Reagan (all from King Co. including Ken Rogstad and Jim Munn) vote tallies as occurred, the balance would have been tipped firmly for Reagan.

Considering Nixon would get 692 votes on the first ballot in Miami Beach, only 25 more than the majority required for nomination, had 15 Washington state votes shifted to Reagan, only a few more delegate shifts would have required the national convention to move to a second ballot. As we will see later, many of the Nixon delegates were only pledged to him on the first ballot and many shifts to Reagan would have occurred on the second ballot. And with Reagan thus having shown strength outside California by winning Washington State (besides North Carolina and at a point when Utah was still deciding to whom their delegates should support), this could conceivably have shown many other state delegates in Miami Beach that Reagan was a challenger with national stature, and that those Miami Beach delegates had a choice besides Nixon. Alas it was not to be in 1968.

Inferring from what he saw and his later knowledge of the people involved, Derham believes that the original Draft Goldwater coalition within Washington State, as well as outside, wanted to stay together to work for a new conservative candidate. He thinks it likely that at some point Frank Whetstone and William Boeing spoke to Ken Rogstad and said something like, "We're going to do it again."And that idea stimulated Rogstad and other members of the conservative leadership in Washington State to attempt to put together a conservative majority. Derham firmly believes that they were working for a Washington State delegation pledged to Ronald Reagan, whether or not Governor Reagan had made a public declaration to run at that point...And they almost pulled it off!

Two important political links never used by Reed, Rogstad, Van Natta or other Washington grass roots Reagan conservatives were the important previous convention experiences of Clif White and Eisenhower, as alluded to above. White's initial political career had been founded on his expertise in handling credentials committee problems. In 1952, Eisenhower had more popular delegate votes in Texas than his Republican opponent, Senator Robert Taft. Shortly thereafter, Taft's forces regained control of the Texas delegation. The Eisenhower delegates from Texas bolted and elected their own slate of delegates. Both presented themselves before the Credentials Committee at the national convention in Chicago, as cited above. A speech by Massachusetts Senator Henry Cabot Lodge ended up swinging the decision to seat Eisenhower's Texas delegation. The rest is history.[24]

Thus if anyone from the Reed's team or Rogstad's team might have spoken to White or had contacted Eisenhower, it is not inconceivable that through various political maneuvers, Rogstad's conservative Reagan slate would have been seated—thus resulting in another state for Reagan in 1968. But as it was, Rogstad and the other dejected Reagan delegates made preparations for the Miami Beach convention. As the machinations in Washington State came to a conclusion in late June, Reagan prepared for a busy July on a renewed quest for delegates from the South.

Endnotes

1.   portions of this chapter appear in Kopelson, Gene. 2016
1.   Portions of this chapter appear in Kopelson, Gene. 2016
2.   "Evans, McCall at Odds Over Primaries," *Seattle Times*, 5/14/68, p. 11
3.   Kabaservice, p. 241
4.   Kopelson, Gene. 2016
5.   Kopelson, Gene 2016
6.   Lyle, Burt, "Conservative-Minded GOP Convention Cheers Reagan," *Seattle Times*, 6/19/66, p. 17
7.   Robinson, Herb, "Republicans Fight It Out In County," *Seattle Times*, 11/2/66, p. 2; Robinson, Herb, "Evans Shows New Skill As Politician," *Seattle Times*, 11/25/66, p. 2; Robinson, Herb, "Evans Lauds and Raps GOP Foe," *Seattle Times*, 11/20/66, p. 41
8.   "Republicans Re-elect Rogstad," *Seattle Times*, 12/10/66, p. 1
9.   Robinson, Herb, "Ken Rogstad Had Broad Support," *Seattle Times*, 12/11/66, p. 57
10.   Lange, personal communication, 5/5/2014

11. "Harmony Sought," *Seattle Times*, 1/27/67, p. 2
12. *Time*, 10/20/67, p2. 0
13. Burt, Lyle, "Reagan Blasts Welfare Programs," *Seattle Times*, 11/11/1967, p. 15
14. Derham, personal interview 8/12/2012
15. Davies, Lawrence, "Seattle Backers Push Rockefeller," *NYT*, 3/14/68, p. 29
16. "County GOP Rejects One of Evans' Major Programs," *Seattle Times*, 5/5/68, p. 39
17. "King County GOP Sets Stage for Delegation Challenge," *Seattle Times*, 5/5/68, p. 39
18. "Evans, McCall at Odds Over Primaries," *Seattle Times*, 5/14/68, p. 11
19. Lewis Flora, "Reagan Has 'That Thing' Says Dan Evans," *Seattle Times*, 5/22/68, p. 12
20. Kabaservice, p. 241
21. Lawrence, W.H., "Committee Backs Taft Georgia Bloc; Floor Fight on Credentials Up Today," *NYT*, 7/10/1952
22. Lange, personal communication 5/5/2014
23. Fred Van Natta, personal communication, 6/10/2013
24. Jacobs, p. 280-282

CHAPTER 32: REAGAN ASCENDANT— SOUTHERN SOLICITATION, PART TWO

"Maybe the other side thought that this might soften those who want that anti-missile defense, and might stiffen the resolve of those who are opposed, and we might end up with no anti-missile defense; At the same time we do have information in the press that the enemy does have such an anti-missile defense."

~ Ronald Reagan[1]

"If you try to out do us and become stronger, you haven't got enough people and you haven't got enough money because we're going to do what ever we have to do to stay stronger than you are."

~ Ronald Reagan[2]

"We could deliver it better if the Berlin Wall wasn't there."

~ Ronald Reagan[3]

"The truth is the Great Society has brought forth little that is great and nothing that is new. Practically all of the truly commanding weapons systems now in the American inventory were developed or brought forward during the Eisenhower years…But where are these men with their drive and determination now? Having pulled America's chestnuts out of the fire in the '50s, what do they have to say about American technology in this decade?"

~ Ronald Reagan[4]

"I'll run like hell."

~ Ronald Reagan[5]

"An approaching political cyclone."

~ *Los Angeles Times*[6]

"When we went to Miami, we knew the North Carolina delegation was going to be for Reagan."

~ Jim Gardner[7]

"He was the inspiration for it."

~ Ronald Reagan[8]

"Don't worry about Rockefeller and Wallace; it's either Nixon or Reagan."

~ Ronald Reagan[9]

By late June and early July, Robert F. Kennedy had been dead for nearly one month, and seemingly the Reagan presidential campaign had died in that instant also. Yet the Reagan campaign had arisen from its ashes before: after Reed's demotion, after RFK's entry into the race, after the failure for Oregon to significantly top Nebraska, and now the death of Reagan's anticipated opponent in the general election.

But Reagan himself never agreed with the defeatism—no matter how temporary. He personally had campaigned hard after Reed's demotion, and after the Kennedy announcement, it was Reagan personally who told his financial backers to butt out and that the campaign officially was reactivated. Even with the Oregon disappointment, Reagan had demonstrated increasingly good results beforehand in Wisconsin and Nebraska. There was growing student support and minority community support, at least from the Mexican Americans in California, whose numbers might be expanded to other states in the fall. Many states had grass roots Reagan campaign organizations and offices besides those in the three opt-out states.

Plus the Miami Beach convention loomed ahead and White still was hunting nationwide for delegates. That pathway for Reagan to win the nomination, by winning delegates, was always at the top of the list. With no more primaries left, continued efforts at delegate hunting became crucial. And the main place that Reagan knew he had the possibility still to win was in the South. After Reagan's May visits to the South, Reagan now planned a return visit.

New Strategy

Reagan once again showed his resilience. At this point White estimated that Reagan had 250 votes and that Nixon still did not have the nomination sewn up. White and Reed met Reagan at the Reagan residence in early July. After debating different campaign strategies,

Reagan decided to stand firm and not split the party. He would continue hunting delegates and stop a first ballot Nixon victory.[10]

Reed called back Harry Dent with the news that Ronald Reagan had not given up his campaign to be president. Reed told Dent, "Reagan's number one issue, law and order, would catapult him into a much stronger position nationally."[11] Besides hunting nationally for delegates emphasizing the law and order theme, Reed, White and Reagan would make the hunt for individual Southern delegates their next priority now that the Southern leaders for the most part had gone for Nixon. Plus both Thurmond and Reagan would learn that not all Southern Republican leaders and delegates needed convincing to push for Reagan's election, no matter what Ol' Strom said.

Thurmond and Dent announced their official support for Nixon shortly after Reed's call. Yet Thurmond did not have an easy time of it by supporting Nixon. Reagan's strength in the South ran deep. At a meeting of the South Carolina delegation in early June, all 22 delegates were "unanimous for Reagan."[12] It took all of Thurmond's cajoling to convince them otherwise. Thurmond told the delegates that they must "quit using our hearts" because a vote for Reagan was really a vote for Rockefeller; their only choice was Nixon.[13] So the delegates had their arms twisted and shifted to Nixon, although some of those arms would get untwisted at Miami Beach.

Another bastion of Reagan support remained in Texas, where "Butch" Butler had been campaigning for Reagan after State Chairman O'Donnell had selected him the prior December. Another pro-Reagan effort was spearheaded by Ronald B. Dear, who would help Reagan gather fifteen Texas delegates.[14] The Texas state convention also was held in June, in Corpus Christi, and the pro-Reagan forces held a wild demonstration supporting Reagan when they all sang, "California, Here I Come."[15] When a resolution arose which urged Reagan to become more active nationally, those Texan Republicans who, like Tower, were for Nixon decided not to challenge it. The Texans indeed remained split between Reagan and Nixon. Tower was voted favorite son, and this maneuver greatly pleased Butler and the Reagan forces, because votes for Tower would take away votes for Nixon on the critical first ballot.[16] But at Miami Beach, Nixon would force a change in Tower's plans.

Individual Delegates

The final weeks before the Miami Beach convention saw the last strategy of Reagan come to the forefront. The original plan, to get the help of the GOP leaders, was gone, even though Dirksen was still a remote possibility. The second strategy, to attack Kennedy, was lost with the assassination and with it the fear of another Nixon-Kennedy debate fiasco to have been replaced with a new Reagan-Kennedy debate triumph. The final strategy—hunt for individual delegates via the theme of law and order—was now on. Nixon still did not have the nomination locked up.

In mid June after the shock of the assassination started to subside, Reagan began his travels anew. Some of these speeches have partly been reviewed earlier when Reagan had commented about Kennedy and the assassination.

Indianapolis

Reagan visited Indianapolis on June 13 and after landing at the airport, he proceeded to the Narott Hotel's grand ballroom for a press conference followed by a reception. Later he went to the manufacturer's building at the Indiana State Fairgrounds for a Republican fund-raising speech.

The Poor People's March had occurred at this time and because Reagan had questioned the methods of the governmental programs as well as the definition of poverty, he had been attacked. Reagan issued a statement on June 13, which was handed out to the press in Indianapolis. What Reagan said then equally could be applied to poverty programs in the second decade of the 21st century, wherein the poor usually have color television, cell phones, and at least one automobile. Indeed when the definition of poverty remains as being below a certain, lowest income percentile, this means that by definition no matter what possessions that lowest percentile has, they will always be "in poverty." In his statement Reagan declared, "We have done a pretty good job of eliminating poverty...Poverty in most of the world is taken to mean those people who cannot provide necessary food, shelter and clothing for themselves. In our country now, many people are being considered poor simply because they can't afford what someone with a little higher income has."[17] Reagan did not think it necessary to hold a march to "convince Americans that they must be compassionate and generous."[18] Reagan concluded that if the purpose of the march had been to point out governmental program bureaucracy and inefficiency and political mismanagement of program funds, "I might join the march myself!"[19]

For his main 40-minute speech, Reagan decried corruption in Vietnam and cited examples of how food and medicines sent from

America had fallen, in part, into the hands of black marketers. Plus American military arms were in the hands of the Viet Cong and North Vietnamese and were being used to kill our troops. But his main criticism was directed at Johnson administration officials, who had told the press that they could do nothing about the corruption because we were "guests in their country."[20]

Reagan, purposely mimicking Kennedy's 1961 Inaugural Address, whose lofty words had been abandoned by the Democrats, then said firmly that it was "time to tell friend and foe alike" that "We are in Vietnam because it is in our national interest to be there, and whether it offends friend or foe, we're going to do what has to be done beginning now."[21] There was tumultuous applause. The next loud applause was when he told the audience that he wanted the government to tell young people that they would be allowed to fight to win in Vietnam and, "Stealing the Pueblo and kidnapping our men was a humiliation this nation will not tolerate."[22]

At his press conference, he added, "It's high time the minority communities recognize that they have been subsisting on promises for a great many years from the party now in power. I for the life in me can't see any reason why a Negro or an American of Mexican descent or any of our other minorities would continue swallowing their promises."[23] Reagan's Southwestern Strategy was continuing and clearly he still was hoping for inroads in the fall into the black population as well.[24] As discussed earlier, the same opinion held by Eisenhower—on the high expectations that had been created by Democrats[25]—remained another example of Eisenhower and Reagan likely having discussed the issue during one of their conversations or personal meetings.

Tulsa

His second stop was Tulsa, for the Republican Governors' Conference. Reagan and Reed discussed the formation of a national finance committee on June 14 and plans were confirmed the next day.[26]

On June 15 on CBS's *Face the Nation*, filmed in Tulsa, Reagan was asked to choose which other Republican contender, Nixon or Rockefeller, he felt more aligned politically; he chose Nixon.[27] When asked if he shared the same political philosophy with either man, Reagan answered that in the area of Vietnam and the involvement of the government in domestic affairs, he was "closer to Mr. Nixon."[28] Reagan offered two final thoughts on the Nixon candidacy in the late spring. He said that Nixon would face a tougher race for the presidency from McCarthy than from Humphrey because Humphrey was carrying so much political baggage from Johnson and he also thought that in the fall Nixon would have an easier time carrying California than would Rockefeller.[29]

At a press conference, Reagan cited economist Milton Friedman's recent statement, termed a "negative income tax," that the government might just send a check out to each taxpayer so they could make their own individual choices for healthcare and other services.[30]

Reagan called the governors conference, "one of the most productive" of all the conferences he had attended since his inauguration.[31] The main purpose of the meeting was to prepare gubernatorial recommendations for the official Platform Committee of the party to consider. These were to be in the areas of welfare reform where they wanted governmental programs changed from giving out handouts to creating jobs, gun control, law enforcement, and reducing the size of the federal government.[32]

In Tulsa, Reagan and his team shored up support amongst the governors. Many were running, like Reagan, as a favorite son. Reagan hoped to have each commit that they would control their delegates. If there were to be any delegates who would vote independently, Reagan wanted to make sure they voted for him and not for Nixon. Governors Rhodes, Romney, Rockefeller, and Shafer retained almost all their delegates. Volpe of Massachusetts had lost his delegates to the Rockefeller write-in primary vote. If Nixon did not win on the first ballot, the three governors of the opt-out primaries still might be of help in Miami Beach. As Reed recalled, Reagan left Tulsa pleased that there was no evidence of a Nixon stampede.[33]

Cheyenne

Reagan's next stop on his mid-June swing was to Wyoming. Despite the strong initial support Reagan had received from many fellow Western governors in 1967, as we have seen, his support had started to fade in early 1968.

At his Cheyenne press conference, when asked if Nixon would falter on the first ballot, would he then be an official candidate, Reagan answered that there was "no way" prior to the convention that he would "solicit for or ask for the job."[34] He explained what he had said repeatedly: that the convention was still open because nobody had it sewn up yet but that if the delegates came to him as California's favorite son and wanted him then, "I am a candidate."[35] When asked if he could support Nixon he said emphatically, "Yes!" He reminded the reporters that he had supported Nixon in prior elections and that unlike 1964, in 1968 there would be Republican Party unity.

Actor

Then he was asked a question about his past as an actor, which he might have thought had been resolved by the poll taken in 1966 prior to his first national speech in Seattle. When asked if his background as an actor was appropriate for someone seeking the presidency, he first joked that equal opportunity applied to actors. When discussing the role of television in a campaign, he first stated that the idea that "maybe just a personality can win because of television" was incorrect. Reagan then reflected from decades of experience by pointing out the one important fact, which many in the media had ignored: "You can't lie to that camera."[36]

At his formal campaign and fund-raising speech with Governor Hathaway, he again referred to the "great forgotten Americans"— clearly another synonym of the term he had used—Silent Majority— who were generous in helping their neighbor and that those forgotten Americans were white and black and might not have been born here. At his press conference afterwards, when asked why he doesn't run officially for president now, he gave his standard answer, "The job seeks the man and not the other way around."[37] Once again, if the delegates voted him as their nominee, he would accept. He said he did not start out in politics but entered the field only after realizing what government should be. As Eisenhower had been reluctant prior to being a full-fledged candidate in 1952, Reagan would be so in 1968.

Détente, Evil Empire and the Fall of Communism

When the reporters turned to foreign affairs, Reagan broadened his foreign policy recommendations. He explained that Vietnam should not be looked at in isolation but should be thought of as part of a concerted, world-wide effort of communism. Not masking any words, Reagan again stated flatly, "The enemy is in Moscow where he's always been."[38] The reporters, and others present hearing Reagan, burst into spontaneous applause. Reagan clearly was saying in public in 1968 what would become the term "evil empire" during his presidency.

He reiterated points he had made before—especially in the 1967 debate with RFK and which student Bill Bradley had reiterated—that American was peaceful and did not "gain land for ourselves in this way."[39] But he then cautioned, "Our philosophy should be based on strength and not fear." Reagan was using Eisenhower's philosophy of peace through strength, and Reagan often would use that same quote as president.

He was against those whose philosophy was, "If we stall long enough, if we appease long enough, if we don't have a confrontation the enemy, eventually will soften and learn to love us." He was broadening his foreign policy statements into Soviet relations. Here was Ronald Reagan in 1968 clearly and firmly stating that accommodation with the Soviets was the wrong approach; in 1976 he would run against President Ford in large part due to his own feeling that détente under Nixon-Kissinger-Ford was the wrong approach.

Reagan wanted the Soviet Union to understand, "If you try to out do us and become stronger, you haven't got enough people and you haven't got enough money because we're going to do what ever we have to do to stay stronger than you are."[40] Reagan clearly was forming his plans to win the Cold War. And it had been Eisenhower who had mentored Reagan on how to do it. Plus Reagan did not know it, but in 1968 he was laying out the exact framework he would follow in the future: when the American military build-up under future President Reagan could not be matched by the Soviets and would be an integral reason for the collapse of communism.

Reagan ended on a conciliatory note, stating that although he was in favor of building bridges to Moscow. But those bridges had two ends. When the Soviet citizens were hungry and needed to buy American wheat, America should say, "We could deliver it better if the Berlin Wall wasn't there."[41] Reagan continued once again to call for the tearing down of the Berlin Wall during his campaign.

Presidential candidate Reagan, who initially had devoted the majority of his campaign speeches to his domestic accomplishments as governor, had come a long way since his first tentative criticisms of Vietnam policy back in New Haven in 1965 and in Seattle in 1966. Reagan's March, 1968 plan to emphasize foreign policy expertise clearly was succeeding. But would it gain Reagan more delegates?

Reagan's financial backers by this time had adopted a campaign budget of $440,000, had already raised $366,557 of it, and had told the California delegation that their budget was going to be reduced so as to devote more monies to Reagan's national candidacy.[42]

Reagan left the Republican barbecue in Cheyenne and made a quick visit to Salt Lake City for a dinner with supporters prior to the Utah Republican Party state convention in July.[43] A bigger barbecue came next.

The Baleful Campaigner Meets Bob Dole and Alf Landon

June 1968 was the busiest month for the Reagan information center in Topeka and Reagan committee that Bubb had founded. Bubb and Kansas Republican National Committeeman McDill Boyd invited Reagan to visit Kansas. Here was the opportunity for Reagan to thank the man who virtually single-handedly had not only opened Reagan's national information center, but had been hugely successful in sending Reagan's film, *Ronald Reagan, Citizen Governor*, to the three opt-out states where the film had been decisive in helping Reagan as well as supporting Students for Reagan and all the other grass roots Reagan campaign offices across the country. Plus as Reagan and White were now hunting delegates in earnest and emphasizing law and order, the Topeka visit could provide more momentum towards Reagan with the convention now only six weeks away.

After Reagan authorized the formation of his national finance committee on June 15, Bubb and Reed arranged for a group of wealthy pro-Reagan financiers and donors to fly in to Topeka for a meeting just before the governor was to arrive. Seventeen wealthy Reagan backers met for thirty minutes in Bubb's midtown office.[44] Besides Bubb, the Republican donors were from Houston, St. Louis, Louisville, Los Angeles, Palm Beach, and Omaha.[45] Governor Reagan made sure to include young Kansas Congressman Republican Robert Dole—future Senate majority leader and party nominee for president in 1996—in the preplanning by sending him a letter of invitation.[46] The author believes it is the first official correspondence between the two men.[47]

Governor Reagan arrived via a "sleek $1.5 million" chartered French-built twin-engine executive jet aircraft owned by Pan American Airways' business division. Bubb was at the airport to greet him along with Alf Landon, former GOP candidate for president in 1936 plus 750 others. The year before, Reagan had delivered the Landon Lecture, with Bubb sitting nearby, as we have seen. Reagan's second campaign visit to Kansas, in June, now was accompanied by heavy security after the Kennedy assassination earlier in the month. Secret Service agents directed the security, and present were Topeka policemen, Kansas Highway Patrolmen, and agents of the Kansas Bureau of Investigation.[48]

The enthusiastic Reagan fans "pushed against restraining ropes at the edge of the runway." Reagan stepped out of the jet to the strains of "California Here I Come," signed autographs and then "jumped on a portable bandstand" to speak to the group. A reporter noted signs proclaiming, "Nominate the Citizen Governor"—a reference to the Reagan campaign film; "Welcome Dutch"—Reagan's nickname from birth; and "Please Say Yes, We Need You." Yet when Reagan saw a group of McCarthy backers, he reminded the audience that at one time he too had been a Democrat and urged the McCarthy supporters to become Republicans. Reagan urged them to switch parties: "Come on over; the water's fine."

Reagan then went into an airport hangar for a planned press conference. Although the temperature was 91 degrees outside but even more hot inside the hangar, Reagan "appeared cool." He was asked about his thoughts on the security and he quipped, "Nancy is very pleased." But the comments of Reagan's that made national headlines were when he said if he were made the nominee at the convention, "I certainly could not refuse my Party or my country."[49] After the press conference, Reagan left via motorcade accompanied by Bubb and other prominent Republicans, including Congressman Dole.[50]

Reagan, Bubb and the other officials met for thirty minutes at Bubb's private offices in downtown Topeka. Each of the seventeen donors updated Reagan on the delegate count and future status of their own state delegations plus gave him "future budgets for efforts boosting the California Republican for the GOP nomination." None of these seventeen wealthy backers and donors seemed to have any doubts he was running, yet an agreement was reached at the meeting, stating, "Reagan should continue as an unannounced candidate." Not all of the seventeen agreed with this approach however. But the latter group felt "it was better than running the risk of splitting the party with a formally announced candidate and an aggressive attempt to win delegates." The private talks also involved discussions of the candidacies of Nixon, Rockefeller and George Wallace.[51]

Reagan then was brought to Fairvalley Farm, owned by wealthy grocer Ned Fleming, for a $100-a-plate Republican fundraising barbecue. Topeka banker and Bubb's son-in-law John C. Dicus attended the barbecue and remembered it well. Dicus chuckled when recalling, "It was a good Kansas windy day" and was "a very special occasion for Topeka."[52]

When Reagan reached the barbecue, he took off his suit coat and started shaking hands again. One reporter noted a "small measure of bipartisanship" to the event, because the meat for the barbecue had been specially prepared by Walter Jetton, local master barbecue chef, who was also a chef for President Johnson. The Kansas beef had been purchased in Kansas City, shipped to Fort Worth for the barbecuing at Jetton's farm, and then sent on to Topeka in a special van.[53]

Reagan used a farm wagon as a platform and a bale of hay as a lectern while some listened on horseback. Reagan was "The Baleful Campaigner."[54] In your author's opinion, it remains the most iconic of the photographs of any of candidate Reagan's four presidential campaigns.

Then Reagan and Bubb flew off to Washington D.C.[55] On June 28, Reagan wrote Bubb a thank you note, citing Bubb having "acquired and distributed a great deal of information about what we are trying to accomplish."[56]

Some 45 years later in 2013, Bob Dole, former congressman and senator and 1966 Republican nominee for president, recalled fondly Reagan's visit to Topeka. Dole reflected for your author that Reagan "was obviously campaigning and did very well in Kansas."[57] After the Topeka barbecue, Reagan traveled with Bubb, Nofziger and Reed to the nation's capital and met with other Republican candidates.[58]

Bad News

In late June, *Newsweek* reported its updated projected delegate count. Reagan had dropped to 146 but the analysis indicated, "Nixon's followers are nervous about his convention staying power."[59] If Reagan and Rockefeller held their delegates firmly for two ballots, by the third ballot, "Many Nixon delegates would scatter...Ronald Reagan... would inherit more than 300 Nixon votes."[60]

Besides the bad news of the declining projected delegate count, Reagan was under attack back home. Drew Pearson reported with glee that a California grass-roots effort to recall Reagan was "beating the bushes" and had "rolled up a total of 650,000 signatures" of the required 780,000 required.[61] At his weekly press conference, Reagan confirmed that such a recall, with a signature deadline of August 1—less than a week before the convention was to open---could be "embarrassing."[62]

1980's De Ja Vue Early?

In July, several events occurred that in hindsight one may be forgiven if one thought one suddenly was reading about crucial events from the future Reagan presidency. History was about to be set in 1968 that would repeat uncannily some fifteen years later.

Strategic Missile Defense

In a little-noted press conference on July 2, Reagan again would bring up a subject that would lay dormant for almost 15 years, until it would resurface in the early years of the Reagan administration: anti-missile defense.

As we have seen, it was in Seattle the prior November (two months after meeting Thurmond, the time of the *Life* cover story on missile defense, and Thurmond's forthcoming book with an important section on missile defense) where Reagan had told the public and the press for the first time that he had been reading all he could about a defensive missile shield. And in late November, Reagan personally had spent a day with Dr. Edward Teller at Lawrence-Livermore seeing in person all the cutting-edge developments.

In front of the Senate in July, 1968, when nuclear negotiations with the Soviets had been stalled, was the question from the *Life* cover story some nine months earlier: of whether America should continue working on the anti-missile defense system—called Sentinel—to defend itself against Red China. As seen, Thurmond clearly wanted the system to protect against a Soviet attack as well. Major political consideration for the Democratic-controlled Senate was not whether the nation should pursue such a defensive system, but whether funding and deploying the system would "deny the Republicans a 1968 campaign issue."[63]

On June 29 in Moscow, Soviet leaders announced suddenly that they would re-enter nuclear talks. The *New York Times* analysis was, "The burden of diverting billions of rubles…would severely strain the economy for the next decade, compelling the leadership to shelve or sharply curtail urgent projects to modernize industry and agriculture and to raise living standards."[64] The Soviets had constructed a missile shield around Moscow early in the 1960s, as reviewed in Thurmond's book, but the reporter's analysis felt that Moscow had decided to enter talks and stop any efforts for a missile shield because "attempts to build such defenses would be folly."[65] Almost all American politicians and the press agreed with the Soviets and the idea of a protective Sentinel missile shield for America was shelved.

But one prominent American nuclear physicist who did not want the missile shield shelved was Dr. Edward Teller, the man who personally had given Reagan the tour of Lawrence-Livermore and who had taken the time to answer all of Reagan's probing and thoughtful questions. Later, testifying at the Senate Foreign Relations Committee on July 17, Teller would tell the Committee that what needed to be excluded from any treaty to stop the spread of nuclear weapons were "defensive systems."[66]

Trust But Verify?

Ronald Reagan was the only presidential candidate in Teller's camp. At a July 2 Reagan press conference during a quick pre-Independence Day campaign stop in South Carolina, Reagan and a reporter were discussing the slight lessening of tensions between America and the Soviet Union that the Soviet announcement might have created. Reagan cautioned the reporter saying,

"I think it would be wonderful it is true. **But we have been burned a few times in the past...We ought to keep our guard up and not be willing to show our hands yet on these.**"[67] (author's emphasis)

Reagan was suggesting that the Johnson administration use the negotiating skills Reagan had mastered long ago, as president of the Screen Actors Guild, and for which he had been urging on Johnson about the proposed Vietnam peace negotiations. Reagan wanted Johnson to be a good negotiator about America's missile defense possibilities and not to lay all of his hand on the table. Of course Reagan was telling the world that he would be a much better negotiator with the Soviets than the Democrats. Reagan had said as much ever since the Kennedy debate. And here was the inkling of what later would become President Reagan's "trust but verify" policy towards any treaties with the Soviet Union, the final direct link after Eisenhower's "Open Skies."

Reagan continued, **"Maybe the other side thought that this might soften those who want that anti-missile defense, and might stiffen the resolve of those who are opposed, and we might end up with no anti-missile defense; at the same time we do have information in the press that the enemy does have such an anti-missile defense."**[68] (author's emphasis) One can imagine in Reagan's mind, by again calling the Soviet Union "the enemy," the early beginnings again of future President Reagan's term "Evil Empire."

But one can imagine a bit more. Clearly Reagan did want a missile shield back in 1968 and likely knew that Senator Thurmond and a few others would support him. The Soviets admitted that their system could not compete. America had no idea if it might work, but following the Soviet's statements that it was folly, the Johnson administration, in the midst of spending billions on the Vietnam War and Great Society programs, gladly abandoned the idea, without devoting any significant resources to see if it even were possible.

In the 1980s, future President Reagan would take the opposite approach and would make his own Strategic Defense Initiative a top priority, as evidenced by his walking out of his summit with Gorbachev in Iceland. Later, when Gorbachev would see that the Soviet Union could not compete, faced an American build-up in missile defense and in all military areas, plus a surging American economy all due to Reagan—and originally suggested to him by Eisenhower as discussed and even confirmed by the June 29 newspaper analysis above, the handwriting would be on the wall, presaging the imminent collapse of communism.

So what might have happened if Reagan were elected in 1968? It is not inconceivable that Reagan as president might have resurrected the anti-missile shield upon taking office, mobilized public opinion along with Thurmond and Teller and devoted the country's resources to develop it, just as John Kennedy had done for the moon landing. Such an earlier President Reagan in the late 1960s or early 1970s might have created the same future collapse in communism almost two decades earlier than was to occur.

Flight 007?

Students of history may also point to another episode that would herald and contribute to the fall of communism under President Reagan's future watch. Korean Air Flight 007 would stray into Soviet airspace and would be shot down with a congressman aboard. Future President Reagan would lead the world-wide condemnation of Gorbachev's communist society and system falling farther and farther behind the West. Indirectly, that incident also would contribute to the demise of communism shortly thereafter.

But back in 1968, just as the Soviets admitted that their socioeconomic system could not compete with the West if it had to create an anti-missile shield and also simultaneously help its citizens improve their standard of living, here was the front-page headline of the *New York Times* on July 1: "Jet with 214 Servicemen Intercepted by Russians, Forced to Land in Kuriles."[69] Fortunately in this case when a passenger jet strayed off-course, it was not shot down by Soviet pilots as would occur in the future, but rather it was escorted to an airbase. Would President Ronald Reagan recall that 1968 incident when he would deal in the future with Korean Air Flight 007 after a Soviet pilot would shoot it down?

The parallels between events in 1968 and the future times of President Reagan are worthy of further analysis: the off-course jet in 1968 versus Flight 007, the anti-missile shield in 1968 versus the Strategic Defense Initiative, and the commonality of the Soviet Union admitting that it had a social and economic system that could not compete with the West, especially if it were to be put under the stress of building a highly technologically-complex missile defense shield. But the strangest parallel was to be the *U.S.S. Pueblo* and Reagan's news conference a few weeks hence. Meanwhile, Reagan and his campaign took a break for July 4th—almost.

Reagan Meeting with Rockefeller's Surrogate

After re-entering the race in late April, Rockefeller was back at campaigning and finally had gone to Oregon for the July 4th weekend.[70] Shortly thereafter, New York Republican Senator Jacob Javits was asked if he would endorse Reagan as Rockefeller's running mate, he said would "swallow hard" and support it.[71] After Rockefeller calculated that he had gotten perhaps 300-400 first ballot votes prior to the convention, "Only if Ronald Reagan, of California, were also going to break into the contest could those 300 or 400 Eastern votes be enough to deprive Nixon of the nomination and make the Republican convention a free-for-all."[72]

Thus for Rockefeller to have any chance at obtaining the nomination, he needed the help of Reagan to help stop Nixon's first ballot victory. Could an official agreement be reached formally or informally between Rockefeller and Reagan? Candidate Reagan had finished his stop in South Carolina and had flown home for the holiday. Historian White reported that on the July 4th weekend while Rockefeller was in Oregon, his "chief surrogate," Emmet Hughes, had a private visit with Reagan at Reagan's home in Los Angeles. One Reagan Secret Service agent, who knew Hughes, was shocked to see him with Reagan. The meeting lasted an hour and a half. Although no formal or informal deal was made, Reagan told Hughes to tell Rockefeller the "one certainty that was necessary to give the Rockefeller campaign validity." The message to Rockefeller, which

"Rockefeller could rely on," was crystal clear: "Reagan was in this race for keeps."[73]

Owosso

I. Walter Jorgensen and Robert M. Smith made one more documented effort to help Reagan. After all, they had started it all back in 1964 as they had watched The Speech. They wrote a letter to Minority Leader Dirksen and pleaded with the senator to review his positions, to note Reagan's unchanged Republican views and to, "Phone him...do SOMETHING, NOW." They reminded Dirksen of Nixon's 1960 debate loss to Kennedy. Because the press did not "give Reagan backers the opportunity to be heard," history would record Dirksen as the "Patrick Henry of our time" if he would endorse Reagan.[74] Dirksen was not swayed.

Security concerns came to the forefront again. On July 9, two black men approached the Reagan residence carrying homemade firebombs, which fortunately did not explode. Reagan's Secret Service agent sent off a warning shot. Reagan commented that he hoped such hoodlums should better themselves by looking for jobs.[75]

Anti-Semitism Again

A week later at his weekly press conference, Reagan was asked, "Do you believe that any man who aspired to be the leader of all the people should be a member of any organization that discriminates against any group on the basis of race or religion?"[76] That Ronald Reagan was not an anti-Semite was discussed earlier when he had been accused falsely of anti-Semitism, which had been brought to the attention of Dwight Eisenhower. As we have seen, Eisenhower vigorously had defended Reagan twice against those charges: by making suggestions to Reagan on how to fight the charges at a future press conference and later by communicating with Samuel Goldwyn. Now in 1968, Reagan explained to the reporter that he did not favor any such organization with those policies and explained that the only time he had ever belonged to such an entity, a southern California country club, as soon as he knew the details of its discriminatory policies, "I withdrew."[77]

At the same press conference, Reagan had to defend his campaigning against recent charges from Rockefeller, who had charged that Reagan was "working hard" for the nomination.[78] Reagan retorted that he was working hard—for the Republican Party.

Bubb's Telegrams

In July speculation mounted about an official declaration from Reagan that he was an open and avowed candidate other than that of favorite son. Private telegrams exchanged between Henry Bubb and Reagan then made national headlines and impacted the race for the Republican 1968 nomination.

Some confusion apparently had arisen at reports that Reagan might have thought Nixon had the election sewn up and thus would not permit his name to be placed in nomination and would release his 86 California delegates. Bubb sent an urgent telegram to Reagan saying in part, "Please give the hundreds of thousands of Republicans now supporting your candidacy the opportunity to keep the convention open...We believe the nomination will be yours unless you turn aside our efforts"[7980]

Reagan then did something very unusual—he released the Bubb telegram to the national press along with his response. Up to that point during the 1968 presidential campaign, Reagan had disclosed private correspondence "in one or two instances," only to thank loyalists and reiterate he was not a candidate or "where he disavowed pro-Reagan activity." Reagan's telegram answering Bubb's concerns, and invoking what he had discussed with Ike about the Sherman statement, was sent the next day to Bubb and released to the press. "I do not believe the nomination is locked up for any candidate and I do believe it will be an open convention." Reagan then dropped his bombshell: "My name will be placed in nomination. Obviously at that time I can be considered a candidate by delegates so inclined. I am well aware of and greatly honored by the activities in my behalf. While it would be impossible for me to present myself as a candidate prior to the convention, I have never subscribed to the Sherman statement. Indeed, it is my belief that any citizen's response should be the direct opposite."[81]

But why did Reagan release the telegrams to the press when almost all prior correspondence about his 1968 presidential campaign had remained private? As Bubb had known Reagan's plans in detail for many months, the release to the public "served to notify Reagan supporters in other states that he still believes he has a chance and will be placed in nomination on the first call of the states to make nominations."[82]

Once Reagan released both telegrams, the national press had a field day. Besides the report by the *Los Angeles Times* reporter above, the *Washington Post* headline ran, "Reagan Plans Bid for Nomination" and the Washington Times had, "Reagan Won't Pull Out, Calls Self Candidate."[83] Back in Bubb's hometown of Topeka, an editorial in the *Topeka Daily Capital* praised Bubb's hard work on behalf of Reagan. If the Republican Party nominated Reagan, Reagan "will be indebted to Henry A. Bubb of Topeka." Then should Reagan be elected president, Bubb "should be in line for appointment as secretary of the treasury or some other position in the Reagan administration."[84]

Declaration of Candidacy in July?

Building on the momentum of the national spotlight having been fixed firmly on the Reagan candidacy, Bubb announced that his Citizens for Reagan National Information Center had purchased television air time to show *Ronald Reagan, Citizen Governor* to be broadcast on the CBS television network at 7:30 PM on Sunday July 21.[85] This would be a little more than a month since Reagan had appeared on CBS television's *Face the Nation*. Bubb provided more details, saying the television film actually would be a rebroadcast of a Reagan speech he had given recently in Indiana, and Bubb characterized the speech as of "major importance to the American people." He added that his center had set up a special fundraising committee to raise funds to pay for the air time and then specified that "individuals and Reagan booster-groups in all 50 states have joined in the effort. Gov. Reagan is aware of our plans."[86] Reed's list of meetings confirms that he had taped the June 13 Indianapolis speech in preparation for a July 21 nationwide broadcast.[87]

The *Boston Herald Traveler* reported that Reagan would announce his candidacy during the July 21 broadcast. Nofziger denied it saying, "I'll tell you positively it isn't going to happen."[88] Reagan himself denied it on July 11 saying, "There's nothing to it...I have no strategy of that sort...I will become a candidate when my name is placed in nomination at the convention and not before then."[89] The July 21 broadcast was never made.

At the same time, Reagan was telegramming Thomas C. Taylor, Chairman of the Citizens for Reagan Committee in Maine, that it would be "impossible" for him to present himself as a candidate prior to the convention.[90] George Romney called Reagan "the greatest pseudo non-candidate in history" and forgetting the Eleventh Commandment of Parkinson and Eisenhower, as noted earlier, Romney "refused at least five times during a press conference in Detroit to say whether he would actively support Reagan if he were the GOP Presidential nominee."[91]

Afterwards, Governor Reagan sent Bubb a letter of thanks. As mentioned, they had been friends since Bubb had met Reagan for the first time some fifteen years before on Reagan's lecture tours of GE factories. In thanking Bubb for his having arranged the Reagan visits, to deliver the Landon Lecture, and to meet his campaign financiers in Topeka, for having joined him on the trip to Washington D.C., and for his having become chairman of Citizens for Reagan National Information Center, Reagan wrote how much he appreciated all that Bubb had done, especially the work the center had been doing.[92] Henry A. Bubb continued his activities on behalf of the Reagan presidential campaign in 1968 and flew off to Miami Beach for the convention.

Declaration of Candidacy in Early August?

Then it seemed as if Reagan's announcement perhaps would be two weeks later after all. Whetstone was in Amarillo in early July as Reagan's advance man for the upcoming trip. Whetstone was the newspaper publisher, oilman, financier and old friend of Clif White who was part of Reagan's original team. In Texas, Whetstone was "beating the bushes on behalf of Reagan."[93]

Once Reagan released the Bubb telegrams, Whetstone was quoted by U.P.I and A.P as saying Reagan would announce "as an active candidate for the GOP nomination probably two days before the Republican National Convention opens August 6."[94] When asked if Whetstone's statement was accurate, Governor Reagan's press secretary Paul Beck referred the reporters to the telegram Reagan had sent to Bubb.

Congressman Price Endorses Reagan

Then West Texas Congressman Bob Price joined North Carolina Congressman Jim Gardner and said he would support "Governor Ronald Reagan as a candidate for the Republican nomination." Price's endorsement of Reagan's candidacy "was seen as obviously undercutting Sen. John Tower's earlier statement" supporting Nixon.[95] Thus not all Texas delegates or Texas party leaders were following the instructions of the state chairman or other important Republicans, and as we will see Price and Gardner would be asked to play critical roles for Reagan at the convention.

In mid July, one concern of the Reagan team, that of the potential gubernatorial recall vote, finally was laid to rest when insufficient signatures were obtained, plus the Reagan team in Sacramento felt that half the signatures were invalid.[96] Pearson must have been greatly disappointed.

Utah Cyclone

The last of the Republican delegates to be decided in 1968 was in Utah. After Reagan had to Salt Lake City for a brief visit on June 15, he returned on July 12 for the state Republican convention. Reagan was the keynote speaker in front of delegates who would choose their delegation the next day.[97] The Reagan's had been victims of the fire-bombing attempt on their home the prior week. In keeping with the new campaign strategy focusing on violence, Reagan told the audience that part of the reason for the political violence was that some candidates chose to "attack on personalities rather than issues."[98]

An initial report after the state party meeting by State Chairman Richard Richards indicated that they would support favorite-son George Romney of Michigan; the Romney family was Mormon. But the support in Utah was to be for the first ballot only" unless another candidate had the nomination sewn up."[99] However a follow-up report indicated that Reagan had more support there than originally thought. In what signaled an "approaching political cyclone," Reagan's backers "staged a minor coup by making Utah the first delegation outside California with a pro-Reagan majority." It was Reagan's law and order speech that had achieved the desired result, as Reagan had hoped.[100] And whether it was Utah or North Carolina which would be the first state to have a Reagan majority outside of California would turn out to be moot. By the time of the first ballot in Miami Beach, the political cyclone for Reagan in Utah would hit a stone wall named Nixon. There would be no first ballot votes for Reagan from Utah at Miami Beach because they would revert back to Romney. When Reagan was done in Salt Lake City, seemingly having gained a new Reagan-majority state to add to North Carolina, he flew home to Sacramento.

Courting Delegates in Sacramento

While Bubb and Reagan were dealing with the telegrams and advance man, Whetstone was in Texas, and Sacramento became the scene of open campaign activity. Harry Dent of South Carolina, who knew that "for Southerners, a struggle at the convention would be between Thurmond and Reagan,"[101] recalled that "Reagan's considerable charm and charisma were exerted upon Southern delegates, many of whom were flown to see the governor personally in California."[102] Nixon confirmed these meetings when he recalled, "Before the convention, Reagan had been flying in Southern delegates to California to meet with him, making ideological appeals that were difficult for them to resist."[103] There are no known records of which delegates went to Sacramento to meet with Reagan as the convention approached. Dent was described as in a "constant state of anxiety" as his delegates continued to be courted by Reagan. Dent said that the Southern delegates were "just about ready to burst their britches for that man."[104] Deaver recalled that at the time, Reagan actually held a Florida delegate majority.[105] Clearly Thurmond's arm twisting for Nixon was unraveling. But Nixon was about to get some critical help—from his old boss.

Ike Endorses Nixon

Throughout the spring and early summer of 1968, Eisenhower still had not decided if he would endorse Nixon. As Eisenhower had commented for so long, electability was the key, regardless of whom he felt might make the best president. Was Eisenhower hoping that the convention would turn to someone other than Nixon—his protégé Reagan? After all, Eisenhower had wanted Reagan to be favorite son. Reagan was the only major candidate who espoused the same foreign policies as did the former president. Plus Reagan clearly had proven himself as a major winner. Reagan had now proven himself to be a true contender for the presidency and a world statesman on the world stage.

And as partial proof that indeed secretly Ike may have hoped the convention would turn to Reagan was the late December-early January "golf buddy" interview cited earlier. Eisenhower—highly likely the secret buddy—never refuted the reporter's conclusion that because of Reagan's strong support for victory in Vietnam, that Reagan—less experienced than Nixon but clearly a candidate who could win—was in fact Ike's choice for nominee.

Eisenhower had been flown east from California after suffering another heart attack while playing golf with Gosden. Eisenhower had continued to keep updated on foreign affairs and the Republican race, as much as doctors would permit. From his hospital bed at Walter Reed Amy Hospital, he met with Johnson, Nixon's representative, an admiral, Generals Westmoreland and Goodpaster, and Ray Bliss the Republican Chairman.[106]

Then on July 15 Nixon arrived. The two men discussed the campaign, but Nixon "found himself unable to ask Eisenhower face-to-face for his support."[107] But on the flight back, Nixon "wrote his former boss a letter formalizing his request for help." Nixon's prime worry always had been Reagan, but Rockefeller was in the background too. Learning of Eisenhower's original plan to endorse Nixon on August 6 just before balloting was to begin, Nixon feared, "This might be too late to render any assistance against the Rockefeller and Reagan forces."[108]

Three days later, Eisenhower spoke to the cameras from a wheelchair at the hospital and finally officially endorsed his former vice-president.[109] Could Eisenhower have said no to his vice-president and endorsed Reagan instead? The quiet understanding between Reagan and Eisenhower was that Reagan would be California's favorite son. Reagan never told Eisenhower of his presidential campaign, which by then had been ongoing for a year-and-a-half and most likely Eisenhower had never asked Reagan if he were running outright in 1968. Yet despite all the successful mentoring of Reagan that Eisenhower had done, likely Eisenhower at the end felt that it was Nixon's turn once again. Plus there was the significant family factor for Eisenhower to consider: the new couple, his grand-son David and Nixon's daughter Julie. What family rift might ensue between him and his grand-son if he would not endorse his grand-son's father-in-law, especially now that Nixon had asked? Thus Eisenhower at the end had the only choice remaining open to him: to endorse his former vice-president, Richard Nixon. Staying neutral until the delegates voted at the convention—as he had done in 1964—and seeing a possible Reagan nomination, was just not possible in 1968. But for shrewd Ike, one thought lingered: if Nixon were stopped on the first ballot, would the man Eisenhower had mentored privately for three years—Reagan, the man who could win in November, and possibly the general's true choice all along—get the nomination?

The next day at a July 19 press conference, Reagan was asked for his reaction to the Eisenhower endorsement of Nixon. Reagan answered that Eisenhower "is a man that's much loved within the party, highly respected, and anyone would be very proud to have his endorsement."[110] Later he added, "I think that anyone would be very proud to have the President's endorsement. I think that a number of other Republicans must have taken great pride in his unqualified statement of approval of all the other Republican leaders who have been mentioned. He is a revered and honored figure in the Republican Party."[111] Reagan was quick to add that he did not think the endorsement would change too many minds of those delegates who either were committed already or those who remained uncommitted.

Of course Reagan hoped from Clif White's delegate analysis that if Nixon would fail to get the nomination on the first ballot, the delegates would turn his way. Eisenhower, by endorsing Nixon, now had demonstrated that no longer would he remain a neutral observer as he had done in 1964. Once the Miami Beach convention would start to turn to Reagan on the second ballot, Reaganknew from their March 13, 1967 meeting that Ike would endorse him as well. After all unlike the lukewarm endorsement Eisenhower had given Goldwater in 1964, Eisenhower in 1966 had endorsed Reagan for governor publicly. Only Eisenhower and Reagan and Freeman Gosden knew the details of all the political mentoring Eisenhower had been giving Reagan over the past years. And as it had been Eisenhower who had urged Reagan to be favorite son, it was natural and fitting that the general would endorse him as party nominee, just as Ike had told the press in March, 1967. And as shrewd a politician as Eisenhower would have known that there was no guarantee Nixon would win. If the delegates turned to Reagan as the party nominee, the general could bask in the fact that he had been Reagan's mentor and then hopefully in January, 1969, begin to see the changes in foreign and domestic policy that both he and Reagan had planned.

In fact Eisenhower's endorsement did not seal the nomination for Nixon, for Reagan continued to threaten Nixon in the West. Colorado held its state convention next. Even stalwart Nixon supporters still were being pressured by voters to change their votes to Reagan. Fred Seaton, the former Eisenhower administration secretary of the interior who was a Nixon supporter, received such a huge stack of letters and telegrams urging him to change his vote to Reagan. The most important was from Reagan Colorado Chairman Joseph Coors, telling Seaton that the press had greatly underestimated Reagan's support in Colorado. Coors predicted that Reagan would end up with fourteen of the delegates. Coors reported to Seaton that at the Colorado Republican State convention, there were more votes cast for Coors, representing Reagan, than for Governor Love, who supported Rockefeller. He asked Seaton to reconsider his support for Nixon.[112] Later at the convention, Seaton would continue to receive letters from Nebraskans and others, urging him to vote for Reagan.[113]

On July 14, Reagan gave a telecast on equal opportunity.[114] The speech, in which Reagan called minorities to have "an equal place at the starting line," while acknowledging their grievances, served as a climax to his prior meetings with minorities, which had begun in March.

Southern Solicitation

On July 15 Reagan announced his final campaign trip plans. He would visit a number of Southern and Border States in a last-ditch effort to woo undecided delegates in the South. Reagan initially told the press that the purpose of the trip was to "offset the strength" of George Wallace and that Southern Republican leaders had asked him to visit.[115] He said that conservative voters should "resist the siren call" of Wallace.[116] As will be seen, it was Reagan's ability to blunt Wallace that would be the primary rationale for Nixon's advisors recommending Reagan as Nixon's vice-presidential choice.

But the press did not buy it. Any concern about Wallace taking conservative Southern votes away from a Republican—as the reason for the trip—conveniently ignored the fact that the first battle was to win the nomination. Reagan was now seen as having "changed his tune" amidst signs that "a drive is building to win him the Republican Presidential nomination."[117] He no longer denied that he was a candidate. He no longer attempted to "publicly discourage efforts" by grass roots activists across the country.[118] Indeed he had given Bubb permission to show the film on television. The cost for showing the film now was estimated at $100,000.[119] The film was to have "a pitch for delegates to vote for Reagan at the GOP convention."[120]

Reagan told the press that he had given up on discouraging his grass roots supporters, because "the movement kept springing up. There were well-intentioned people that insisted on their right to make this effort."[121] Reagan's strategy remained, to "go to Miami Beach unsullied by pre-convention campaigning."[122] After all, Reagan had followed scrupulously Eisenhower's extension of the Eleventh Commandment; his attacks throughout his presidential campaign had been against Democrats. And at the convention, Reagan was to be seen as "the only man who can unify the Party and defeat the Democratic nominee."[123]

By then Reagan had increased the total of what his campaign and fund-raising trips had raised for Republican coffers to some $4 million.[124] But was Reagan finally truly committed? One un-named member of the Republican delegation from California noted, "I don't get the impression that he's very revved up about it himself."[125]

Goldwater

One reason for Reagan's continued low-key posture may have been Barry Goldwater. Goldwater, at whose home Reagan had failed to get a promise of neutrality in early April, was now running for the Senate. On June 19, Goldwater had sent a letter to Reagan reminding him of their conversation in April and reiterating to Reagan that Nixon would win on the first ballot.[126] Reagan, who may have "resented Goldwater"[127] for not supporting Reagan's own 1968 presidential bid of a fellow-conservative, should have realized that Nixon had campaigned heavily for Goldwater in 1964 too. But instead of accepting defeat and withdrawing, as Goldwater wanted, at that point "Reagan knew that Goldwater was telling him to get out of the race, which may have made him more inclined to stay in it."[128] It was but another example of Reagan resisting calls to stop his presidential quest.

Reagan had inched up in the Gallup poll: from his nadir of 6 percent support amongst Republicans in early March now to 7 percent on July 1. As Reed put the finishing touches on Reagan's final presidential campaign trip for 1968, he reflected that rather than a Southern strategy, the trip was more of a "Southern solicitation."[129] After finishing his final meetings in California with Mexican Americans and minority editors, Reagan flew off on July 19 with Reed, White, William French Smith, Holmes Tuttle and the press, on what historian Cannon termed a "far-fetched attempt to win over the South without Goldwater, Thurmond, Tower" or the other state chairmen committed to Nixon.[130] Harry Dent recalled, "The purpose was to meet with as many GOP delegates as possible, especially those who would be Reagan inclined. I considered Reagan's forces sharp in this effort to undo the strategy of Southerners hanging loose. So now the real struggle to keep Southerners linked together behind one man who was electable was facing its first test."[131]

Columnist Robert Novak, invited by Clif White, would accompany the Reagan team on the end portion of the trip as we will see. Novak had authored the major piece on the growing strength of Reagan in Wisconsin earlier in the year. In Novak's autobiography, he confirmed that the Reagan campaign quietly had hired a former Nixon deputy campaign chairman, Bob Walker, to be the campaign's Southern Chairman.[132] Walker had been wooing delegates and most likely had helped White with delegate hunting and may have kept Reed up-to-date on the Reagan campaign in the South as Fred Van Natta of Oregon had been doing in the West. Walker also was sent early to Miami Beach to organize Reagan's convention preparations. Meanwhile, Reagan prepared to deliver an address on world affairs even more extensive than any of his previous White Papers, the culmination of all the teachings from Eisenhower coupled with all he had seen and read and thought through himself.

Amarillo

The July 22 issue of *Newsweek* hit the newsstands with their analysis of the Reagan effort. If Nixon were stopped on the first ballot, he would certainly falter on the second. Then with most votes going to Reagan, he would win on the third or fourth ballot.[133] The Reagan entourage, including forty members of the press, flew in a chartered 727 to Amarillo. It was a far cry from 1966's *Turkey Bird*.

In Amarillo, Reagan first addressed a "fund-raising barbecue and met with pro-Reagan delegates from five states."[134] Indeed the national press noted that Amarillo, where the total number of delegates with whom he met was 50, was the first place since the Reagan campaign had begun in which a stop had been made "solely for the purpose of conferring with delegates."[135] The delegates had been assembled by "the national Reagan-for-President movement."[136]

Reagan was asked what he would do at the convention if he were nominated. Reagan finally gave the answer his supporters had been waiting to hear since 1964: "I'll run like hell."[137] White followed up saying that Reagan was a man with "courage, common sense, and charisma," who was needed sorely in the White House.[138]

At a rally for Texas Congressman Bob Price, Reagan explained that the party was asking those Republican governors who were not running in 1968 to visit those states without a Republican governor in order to rally support to all Republican candidates. Reagan explained that the party had assigned him to Texas, but after the cheers quieted down, he explained seriously the importance of the down-ballot vote by invoking once again the lack of a Republican Congress for his mentor Eisenhower. "We had a Republican President but at the same time he didn't have the rest of the team...This time we not only have to return Bob Price", but Reagan explained that the voters had to elect a Republican majority to "put an end to what's been going on for too many years."[139]

Clearly, Reagan wanted to make it clear that besides winning the presidency, his other major goal was to add Republicans in the House and Senate and in local government. Reagan wanted party unity plus long coattails throughout the nation, just as he had accomplished in California. Did Reagan or Reed or White finally regret not having stressed Reagan's coattails before in order to differentiate himself from Nixon? The answer is unknown.

When asked beforehand what he would discuss with the delegates, Reagan explained that at this point, with the convention looming ahead, it was quite appropriate that "delegates do begin to get together and exchange information and views with those of us who are uncommitted."[140] But at the meeting itself, he was more forceful about openly being an active candidate. Reagan told the Texas delegation that if he were the party nominee, "You bet I'd be active."[141] Reagan reiterated that the delegates had remained "uncommitted" and there was going to be no "coronation" for the un-named front-runner.[142] At the Texas convention, a unanimous resolution passed which had praised Reagan's achievements as governor and which had urged Reagan to enter the national political scene.

Meanwhile, Nixon supporter Fred Seaton knew the importance of mailing out letters of political support. Seaton had been a Nixon supporter ever since he had mailed out letters in 1966 urging Nixon's election in 1968.[143] But in 1968, Seaton was on the receiving end. Indeed Seaton may have begun regretting opening his mail. Not long after receiving the pro-Reagan letter from Coors, Seaton received a letter from Dudley C. Sharp, secretary of the Air Force in the Eisenhower administration. It was another pro-Reagan letter from a highly influential person. Sharp urged Seaton to vote for Reagan based upon Reagan's speech on defense preparedness, which had been delivered in Cleveland on May 22.[144] Seaton would hear about Reagan from his own constituents in Nebraska soon.

1968 or 1979?: Despair or Malaise

As we have seen, Reagan's 1968 campaign would produce so many similarities to events that would occur during his third presidential campaign and his presidency that the word "foreshadowing" has to be invoked. We have seen how Reagan first proposed tearing down the Berlin Wall when he debated Robert Kennedy the prior spring and had mentioned it many times since. As we have seen, a jet would stray into Soviet airspace near Siberia and Soviet jets would intercept it—but this was not yet Korean Air Flight 007; and finally Reagan forcefully would advocate publicly creating an anti-ballistic missile shield to protect the United States—but this was not quite yet Star Wars.

But the most astounding set of similarities to 1979-1980 would occur during his Amarillo speech of July 19. Reagan noted, "The President referred to 'an unease' in our land."[145] Reagan was referring to Johnson's January 17 State of the Union Address where he had used the phrases, "There is in the land a certain restlessness—a questioning," and later uttered the phrase, "I spoke of despair."[146] Would Reagan remember Johnson's speech when in the future he would attack President Carter's speech about national "malaise?"

Hostage Crises: Perdicaris, *U.S.S. Pueblo*, Iran and *Achille Lauro*

At the Amarillo press conference prior to his speech, Reagan was asked what he would do to get the *U.S.S. Pueblo* ship and crew back and he answered that it was admittedly too late for strong military action now. But he proceeded to reveal his specific recommendations for how to handle such a crisis in the future and cited, off-the-cuff, the example of former President Theodore Roosevelt. Reagan then cited what British Prime Minister Harold MacMillan thought about Reagan's plan to deal with such a hostage crisis in the future.

Specifically, Reagan was quick to clarify that it was only President Johnson who knew all the options about the *U.S.S. Pueblo*, but Reagan said:

> I have felt was where we went wrong was in that first hour. The first 24 hours—that's the magic period. That's when this country should have said to them that we wanted the Pueblo and we wanted those men back or we would take whatever action was necessary to secure their return.[147]

Here was Reagan once again using the threat of unspecified military response, as Eisenhower had done in Korea and Reagan himself had updated for Vietnam. But now he was applying it to Eisenhower's old foe, North Korea. Yet there was one additional prior example of how a Republican president had dealt firmly with a foreign power when a hostage had been held.

Reagan then spontaneously cited the example of President Theodore Roosevelt and the Perdicaris Affair. As mentioned earlier, future President Reagan would place a statue of Roosevelt in his private study.[148] Governor Reagan must have studied Roosevelt quite well by this time, for spontaneously he proceeded to give a detailed history lesson to the press. In Morocco, a naturalized American citizen, Perdicaris, had been kidnapped by a Berber chieftain, Raisuli. Roosevelt and his Secretary of State, John Hay, had taken quick action. Reagan reviewed that as American warships had steamed towards Morocco, the famous stern threat had been sent, "We want Perdicaris alive or Raisuli dead!" Shortly thereafter, Perdicaris was freed.[149]

Reagan added to the impromptu history lesson and current events by stating, **"Former Prime Minister Harold MacMillan of England" said, "I was completely right and that 24 hours is the time. Had Britain, in the first 24 hours, made such a statement and taken such an action in the Suez Crisis, there would be no Nasser today."[150] [151] (author's emphasis)** Reagan added that when one of the Columbia University student leaders—who had taken over the administration buildings on April 23 and had held the dean and two administrators hostage for that first day, all immediately prior to Reagan's Colorado visit—later was asked how the university could have stopped the protest, he answered that if they had acted within the first 24 hours, the protest would have collapsed. For Reagan, those first 24 hours were critical to his thinking on solving any future hostage crisis.

So in 1979 when the Iranians would storm the American embassy and would take the staff hostage, would candidate Reagan remember the firm and aggressive solution that he had proposed in 1968? Certainly President Jimmy Carter's future lack of actions indicate that he did not know of Reagan's proposal, backed up strongly by MacMillan, on how to deal with such a crisis. In the future, American students would be threatened by a communist takeover in Grenada. Following the lessons of Eisenhower and his own mastery of military strategy and how to deal with hostages—begun during his 1968 campaign—President Reagan's quick and decisive show of overwhelming military power would culminate in America's first military victory since the loss in Vietnam.[152] President Reagan would take swift action when the Achiile Lauro would be hijacked. And the urgency of such action, being required in the first few hours of such a crisis, makes one wonder if in 2012, when the American consular staff would be under attack in Benghazi, the resultant 3 AM phone call to the White House and secretary of state's office was ever answered.[153]

But Reagan then proceeded to say that the present administration could not give the North Koreans any kind of ultimatum now, when six months had passed by already since the seizure of the ship. But then he added, "I would think that a new president could once again have the option of the 24 hours, that a new president coming in could make this an order of business and say, 'Something is going to be done.' And I don't think it's always necessary to tell the enemy what. I think he ought to spend a few restless hours wondering what you're going to do!"[154]

Not only was Reagan again using Eisenhower's military dictates of threats, but candidate Reagan was looking ahead to January 1969 and the possibility that a new Republican president's arrival would force the North Koreans to hand over the hostages or face unspecified consequences. Eisenhower had charted a new course to end the Korean War when he took office. And Reagan was offering that should he become president in January, 1969, both North Vietnam and North Korea would have to deal with a new more hard-line Republican president—hopefully a new President Reagan. But what Reagan did not realize was that he just had laid out the roadmap that he himself would follow when his own inauguration in January 1981 would trigger a solution to the Iranian Hostage Crisis by the freeing of all hostages within hours of his swearing in.[155]

Reagan knew what he would do if he became commander-in-chief in January, 1969. The Vietnam War was still winnable then, as Reagan had been telling audiences throughout his campaign. Only decades later would Richard Nixon reflect that the first thing in office he should have done was to follow what Reagan had been advocating: to mine Haiphong harbor and bomb the sanctuary sites to win the war in 1969.[156]

Reagan never provided, and the press never asked for, further details on when and how he had learned of MacMillan's comments that Reagan's solution on dealing with hostages was correct. But given that MacMillan had met with Eisenhower in January, and that MacMillan had told the press about the ABM treaty, it is most likely that it had been Reagan's hidden mentor, Ike, who had been the intermediary. It was but another example of Eisenhower using his hidden hand technique to help Reagan in the 1960s, whose ultimate effects would extend well into the 1980s.

Reagan's Finest Campaign Speech

All of Reagan's comments on world affairs were told directly to the press, who ended up not reporting much of what he had said. Reagan's actual speech came next and was a billed as a tribute to Congressman Price, whose public support for Reagan would earn him the role of one of three people to second Reagan's nomination at the convention. But Reagan would end up delivering a much more detailed and nuanced version of the defense preparedness speech he had delivered in Cleveland on May 22.

Reagan told the crowd he was against a "federal plantation" system which held back those who were poor and disadvantaged, yet at the same time Republicans were for recognizing the poor as "individuals" and that Republicans wanted a system that "stopped destroying" the poor by them becoming addicted to governmental welfare programs.[157] Reagan again called attention to Johnson's comment about an "unease" in the land.[158]

ABM and SDI

Turning quickly to world affairs as his main theme, Reagan brought up the ABM Treaty and America's missile defense shield. He noted that in recent days there were "big smiles in the Kremlin," but then asked if they were laughing with us or at us.[159] Any discussion of a new nuclear treaty "would stop us from protecting our cities, as theirs are already protected by an anti-ballistic missile program."[160]

Clearly now in public at a major address rather than just in a press conference, Reagan for the first time in a major venue was sounding a clarion call about the importance of an anti-ballistic missile shield for America. Reagan wanted to protect America from incoming nuclear-tipped missiles in 1968, more than a decade before he would resume his concern when, as president, he formally would begin to research and implement his Strategic Defense Initiative.

And after his presidency, on March 23, 1993, former president Reagan would address the historic success of his Strategic Defense Initiative but would also hearken back to what he had first called for in 1968: " Unfortunately, there is a stubborn contingent of policymakers who insist on abiding by the obsolete ABM Treaty and support only extremely limited missile defenses, or even none at all."[161] Indeed in 2013 after reviewing this author's research with Reed, Reed, who would become one of President Reagan's National Security advisors, reflected that SDI did in fact all begin during the 1968 campaign.[162]

Had Eisenhower discussed the ABM Treaty with Reagan? There is no direct evidence they ever discussed the subject. But it was critically important to Eisenhower. As one recent commentator has noted, the Eisenhower administration had based virtually its entire foreign policy on the threat to use massive retaliation against the Soviet Union. But those threats rang hollow once "the U.S. government renounced plans to defend America against ballistic missiles."[163]

Of course Reagan's ideas, developed later as the Strategic Defense Initiative, would be vindicated when America and its allies such as Israel would base their defenses in part on such missile shields which would prove to be highly successful.[164] Thus it is not unlikely that at some point Reagan and Eisenhower had discussed anti-ballistic missiles.

In his Amarillo speech, Reagan then turned to Vietnam. He wondered why the Johnson administration would enter into any treaty with the Soviet Union, when their weapons were killing our soldiers in Vietnam, and the fact that the Soviets had "broken more than 50 treaties" before.[165] Clearly, future President Reagan's skepticism about negotiating with the Soviet Union and his future "trust but verify" policy clearly were there in 1968.

Reagan Reflects on the Eisenhower Years

Reagan continued to the heart of his speech. It would be his most detailed and personal homage to his mentor Eisenhower, and attack on his nemesis Kennedy, that Reagan ever would make. He told his Texas audience that their state and his, both the homes of large defense industries, can "view with some horror the incompetence of the Great Society in the matter of our nation's defenses." Reagan then proclaimed:

> The truth is the Great Society has brought forth little that is great and nothing that is new. Practically all of the truly commanding weapons systems now in the American inventory were developed or brought forward during the Eisenhower years. The ballistic rockets with their numerous variations; the development—driven to completion by a brilliant young missile man of a new breed General Bernard Schriever—of the miniaturized thermonuclear warhead made possible by the inventive genius of Dr. Edward Teller; the supersonic jet strike force conceived and made operable by General Curtis LeMay—the father of the Strategic Air Command—and one of the greatest air geniuses of all time; the entire Polaris concept, coupling missile and weapon technology with a nuclear submarine, born of Admiral Hyman Rickover's persistence. But where are these men with their drive and determination now? Having pulled America's chestnuts out of the fire in the 50's, what do they have to say about American technology in this decade?[166]

Was even this last line derived directly from Reagan's talks with Eisenhower? Reagan had directly quoted his mentor on many prior occasions. Historian Travis Jacobs points out that Eisenhower had been upset that he had been called upon by Truman to pull Truman's "chestnuts out of the fires" for the mismanagement of the Korean War, via Eisenhower's appointment to return to military duty with NATO and take a leave from the presidency of Columbia University. And later as president of the nation, Eisenhower had used atomic threats to end the fighting. Very possibly Eisenhower had used the term during discussions with Reagan. Thus if Reagan thought that he would have to play the same role in 1969, as new president to win the Vietnam War, Reagan would have to pull America's chestnuts out of the fire anew.

Reagan went on stating that Schriever had reported that the Soviets were achieving military superiority while the United States was "slowing down."[167] Dr. Teller was testifying in front of the Senate Foreign Relations Committee "pointing out the need for an effective defensive system."[168] LeMay confirmed, "There had been no new military technology since the end of the Eisenhower era.... LeMay pointed out that by fighting a land war in Asia without wanting to win, it had so bankrupted America that no new military planning or systems had been considered...Under this administration, it is the civilian bureaucracy that is viewing with the alarm the military ideas of the next generation...They are planning on fighting the next war with the last war's weapons."[169]

Reagan warned, "America is abandoning its defenses."[170] And Reagan wondered why the Johnson administration did not even listen to its own chairman of the Joint Chiefs, whose recent testimony confirmed that America's worst threat was the growing nuclear superiority of the Soviets.[171] Reagan concluded that it was time to turn out the Democrats.

Reagan's earlier campaign speeches devoted to world affairs (in Albany, Oregon, and later his First White Paper speech in Honolulu on America in the Pacific, his Third White Paper speech on Vietnam, his Fourth White Paper speech on Atlantic and Caribbean policies, and then his Fifth White Paper speech on military preparedness in Cleveland) were candidate Reagan's first specific and detailed shots across the bow of the Kennedy-Johnson years. Now in the final weeks before the convention, Reagan had spoken in Amarillo what was the most scathing attack on the Kennedy-Johnson administration's defense policies ever delivered.

As historian Evan Thomas has noted, Eisenhower knew very well Clausewitz's dictum, "Nations relied on old technology and tactics at their peril,"[172] and likely from Eisenhower, Reagan studied that dictum and brought it into 1968 and beyond.

Reagan's Inspiration

Ronald Reagan had written many private letters of thanks to Eisenhower for all the years of guidance his coach, the general, had given his new prize player and student. But despite praising Eisenhower in many speeches and at many press conferences during the campaign, and in Amarillo praising what Eisenhower had overseen in the 1950s, only once in public at that time did Reagan express how very much Eisenhower had meant to him personally and politically. And it was during his Amarillo stop when Reagan had reflected on the technological flowering that had occurred during President Eisenhower's watch.

At the same press conference where he had been asked about the Nixon endorsement, Reagan was asked by a reporter that when Eisenhower had referred to the Republicans as the party of common sense, would that be a great slogan. Reagan had never before been asked about the origin of his 1966 campaign slogan. Reagan for the first time finally had the chance to say what Eisenhower had meant to him. "To tell you, I used it as my slogan in the campaign in California...*He was the inspiration for it.*"[173] (author's emphasis) Reagan would use "common sense" again when running for president in 1980, during his presidency, and again later in his own future Farewell Address.

As the Reagan campaign team left Texas, they said they were "more sure than ever that Reagan has support from a majority of Texas' 56-vote slate."[174] Dent later reflected that White and Whetstone had "produced at least 20 Reagan delegates—twice as many as Nixon forces expected."[175]

Little Rock

The first Reagan event in Arkansas was a rousing evening talk by Clif White to the delegates.[176] When Reagan landed, he saw a number of "Reagan for President" signs and thanked the supporters by saying, "You have done me a very great honor by suggesting such a thing."[177] At a mid-day press conference at the Lafayette Hotel, Reagan predicted that if a first-ballot stand-off between Nixon and Rockefeller were to occur, the delegates might have to turn to one of "the favorite sons," such as himself.[178] Here was Reagan finally telling the nation of what he and Reed and White had planned so long ago. He explained to the press that his stops in Little Rock and other cities were to or from the upcoming governors conference and indeed he had given up potential free days back east to campaign on behalf of the party and groups of delegates who had invited him.[179]

One reporter asked Reagan what the delegates asked him since he remained a professed "non-candidate;" Reagan answered that they "had an exchange of views on the political situation."[180] He then was asked if the delegates were looking for "a new face, these citizen-politicians," but Reagan went on that the delegates were going to remain uncommitted until "the last minute." Reagan may have been flattered that a reporter had used the same term he had used as his gubernatorial campaign slogan (whose model had been derived from Ike) but may have been annoyed that the reporters had pluralized the phrase to indicate that Reagan was not alone in claiming that title. Regardless, he said his previous meetings with delegates typically would end with both them and him agreeing to "stay uncommitted."[181]

Up to that point, the press had failed to mention that almost all of his prior out-of-state trips had been scheduled on weekends. Reagan clarified things by noting, "This so-called tour is a weekend trip to and from the convention."[182] When asked what he thought of the California recall petition, he said it was all politically motivated and the people behind it did not "have anything in mind other than an embarrassment to me."[183]

Reagan and his campaign team met with 17 of the state's 18 delegates. The delegates had been pledged to Nelson Rockefeller's brother, Governor Winthrop Rockefeller, as favorite son on the first ballot. Reagan would need their help on the second and subsequent ballots.[184]

Charlottesville

Lou Cannon, then a reporter, interviewed Reagan on the flight from Little Rock to Charlottesville. Reagan modified his earlier prediction and now thought that there would be more than two ballots at the convention. Reagan also told Cannon that in the general election, he did not want the racist vote from supporters of George Wallace.[185] Reagan was looking beyond Miami Beach and onto the fall general election. He told the press that he was not out to stop Nixon.[186]

With Clif White now having started formal speeches to delegates in Little Rock, the press noted that the Reagan presidential campaign had "entered its most intensified phase."[187] White was being "unleashed" for the first time and was soliciting delegate votes for Reagan quite openly.[188] White's talks were approved by Reagan. The other members of Reagan's campaign team who had made the trip, Tuttle, Smith, and Reed also were seen courting delegates.[189]

At his press conference, when asked if he thought he could carry Virginia, he reminded the reporter that he was not an official candidate yet. But he did return to the Eisenhower theme, saying that he thought whoever the Republican Party nominee was, he could carry the state because of the "common sense thinking of the people of Virginia."[190]

Baltimore: Threats to Reagan

In Baltimore, Reagan was expanding his hunt for delegates to a region that had not been targeted previously by Reed and White. Reagan met "with delegates from a half-dozen mid-Atlantic states."[191]

But with the Kennedy assassination keenly still in everyone's mind, Reagan had concerns other than hunting delegates. Reagan himself was being hunted. Besides the two firebomb attempts noted earlier, now the FBI was investigating "a conspiracy ascribed to black militants" to "kill him."[192] Reagan said that there was nothing much he could do about the threats, but now that he was a "possible Presidential contender," the press noted a "conspicuous" Secret Service detail.[193] As we have seen, in reality Johnson had increased Reagan's security after the Kennedy assassination in early June. And Ed Meese and Curtis Patrick, one of Reagan's security officers from Sacramento, were evaluating the Miami Beach security situation as we will see.

Frankfort

In Kentucky, which Reagan had visited the prior fall as we have seen, Reagan met with Governor Nunn and 23 of the state's 24 delegates. Almost every single delegate took a picture with him.[194] But Reagan had no luck in convincing any of them.[195] The faithful "were shopping but not buying."[196] Unfortunately, Morton Blackwell's youthful Reagan supporters, present at Reagan's prior visit, had not convinced Kentucky's GOP delegates to change away from Nixon.

Cincinnati: Reagan's Running Mate Chosen

Since the out-of-state campaign trips had begun in February, 1967, Reagan had attended every single national and regional governors conference, unless there was pressing business in Sacramento. The final one before the convention was the National Governors

Conference in Cincinnati. The national press noted that Reagan's political fortunes were "on the upswing."[197]

In the hotel lobby of the conference, a gunman was apprehended whose target was Reagan. It was only two weeks earlier when the two youths with the Molotov cocktails had been driven off from Reagan's home in Sacramento and a day since the he was informed of the black militant plot.[198]

One long-time supporter from the Pacific Northwest accompanied Reagan. Bob Hazen, Reagan Oregon state chairman, who we last saw after the Oregon primary was over, had not given up on Reagan, even with the lack of forward momentum that the final Oregon tally had provided. In late June, even though only "three, and not more than five" Oregon delegates supported Reagan, Bob Hazen was described as "the leading Reagan delegate."[199] The still-pro Reagan Oregon faction was comprised of delegates who were "newcomers to convention politics or do not hold public office."[200]

Hazen spoke to the national media as soon as Reagan's jet landed at the Covington, Kentucky airport, saying, "We are on our way."[201] When reporters asked Hazen if Reagan had won any Southern delegates away from Nixon, Hazen answered, "We sure softened them up."[202]

But not everyone back home in Oregon was pleased by Hazen's continued support for Reagan that summer. An editorial in *The Oregonian* said that Hazen's "current labors in Ronald Reagan's vineyard raise a question of political ethics."[203] The editorial then reviewed the Oregon law which stated that each elected delegate must use "his best effort" to support whoever won the Republican primary, until such candidate receives less than 35 percent of the convention vote, releases the delegates, or until two ballots have been taken.[204] The editorial asked, "Is Mr. Hazen using his 'best efforts' for Mr. Nixon by campaigning with Gov. Reagan in the South and making statements to the press about Reagan's gains? Is he using his 'best efforts' by writing a letter to Washington convention delegates touting Gov. Reagan and asserting 'it is the third ballot that's going to count.'?"[205] They concluded, "It looks to us as if Mr. Hazen is in violation of both the spirit and the letter of Oregon law by continuing to campaign for Gov. Reagan."[206]

The crowd of 1,500 cheering supporters at the Covington airport had "stood for more than two hours during a stifling hot, humid afternoon" awaiting Reagan and his party[207] Reagan said that delegates "are going to Miami with a free and open mind."[208]

At a press conference during the governors conference, Reagan's stances on foreign affairs reflected well on his mentoring by Eisenhower. Reagan said that America should tell the communists, "America is reviewing all our options," including battlefields, choice of weapons and targets.[209]

Reflecting Eisenhower and General Bradley's committee report of six months earlier, Reagan reiterated his call to mine Haiphong Harbor. But he now added something new: to consider bombing "the dams that supply water for North Vietnamese crops."[210] Clearly Reagan had continued applying the military philosophy that Eisenhower had taught him personally. Eisenhower had defeated Nazi Germany with using overwhelming military force and by harassing and impacting both the military and civilian populations of the enemy. And as seen earlier, the general had told Reagan directly that this was a tactic America should use now in Vietnam.

This was yet another example of the clear thread of tactics directly from Eisenhower to Reagan. One of the prime reasons that Eisenhower had brought North Korea to the negotiating table, besides the threat of nuclear weapons, was that Eisenhower had ordered air attacks on North Korea's dams and electric plants which had resulted in flooding of the rice fields and resultant famine as discussed by historian Evan Thomas.[211] Reagan had learned his lessons from Eisenhower well. And in final deference to what Eisenhower had taught him about the use of threat and never to reveal one's ultimate decision about using nuclear weapons, Reagan said that by telling the enemy that it would not use nuclear weapons, "The U.S. should not have publicly removed such a possibility."[212]

The national media described Reagan's presidential bid at that point as a "strong, late-hour, lapel-grabbing bid," which by Cincinnati had turned into a "maelstrom of speculation."[213] Clif White said, "I have no doubt Reagan will be nominated."[214] Bob Hazen was pushing for faster and definitive action by Reagan saying, "He's got to come out dramatically. He's not in the ballgame now. And by convention time I am afraid it will be too late."[215] Reed and White were described as Reagan's "key tacticians,"[216] and their delegate estimates were 460 firm for Nixon with another 100 leaning toward Nixon. Rockefeller was thought by the Reagan team to have 375-400.[217] But Nixon still was short of the magic 667 needed to clinch the nomination, and by "keeping delegates loose in the saddle—from going to Nixon now," he might be denied through two full ballots.[218] At that point the delegates would turn to Reagan, or so Reed and White and Reagan hoped.

Look magazine came out with a major story on Reagan the day of the convention in Cincinnati. Reagan's gubernatorial record was reviewed, with emphasis on Reagan's policies of using private business practice to lessen governmental inefficiencies and to lessen California's welfare rolls. Practically unmentioned was Reagan's stature as a world statesman. Reagan's team had sensed "omens of a shift toward conservatism across the country." What were Reagan's chances? One Reagan team member said, "Anything can happen between now and the election," as another noted, "Every candidate this year is standing on a quaking platform of quicksand. Reagan can stand on that platform as well as any of them."[219]

The most important campaign event in Cincinnati during the trip was the meeting that Reagan had with Ohio Governor Jim Rhodes. Reagan had conferred with Rhodes prior to being inaugurated to learn first-hand about Rhodes' successful programs to decrease the size of government. They had seen each other at many of the governors conferences over the intervening two and a half years, and Reed recalled that the decision to name Rhodes was a "team" effort.[220]

Eastern Europe: Croatia and Latvia

A new controversy in the area of foreign affairs arose at this time. Croatia, a tiny country on the Adriatic which would become the newest member of the European Union in 2013, had a checkered past by suffering various forms of government as a part of several European states. It was split into northern (German) and southern (Italian) spheres of occupation during World War II and later became part of Tito's Yugoslavia.[221]

Historian Paul Kengor's *The Crusader* traces Reagan's entire decades-long devotion to seeing the end of communism.[222] Reagan had been introduced to its evils as president of the Screen Actors Guild when he was threatened with acid for speaking against communist infiltration in Hollywood. In Reagan's early autobiography *Where's the Rest of Me?*, Reagan saw that America should not permit the Soviets to keep Eastern Europe captive because of the Soviet threat to use atomic weapons.[223] During the 1968 presidential campaign, Reagan had verbally fought against North Vietnam in almost every press conference and in many campaign speeches. Reagan first had called in 1967 for the Soviets to tear down the Berlin Wall during his town hall debate and again later in Miami and other campaign stops. At press conferences he had brought up North Korea and the *U.S.S. Pueblo*, he had referenced Eisenhower's comments when Red

China had threatened Taiwan's off-shore islands, and he had tied the assassinations of both Kennedy brothers to communism. But on a practical level as a sitting governor on the west coast, what could he do directly other than speaking out on the campaign trail?

At the time, there were on-going tensions between the Soviet Union and Czechoslovakia. Unbeknownst to Reagan, Students for Reagan member Dana Rohrabacher, a future congressman, was in Czechoslovakia to see what was happening first hand. The main issue was whether America should aid Eastern bloc countries in the hopes of lessening tensions or whether America should lessen ties or even boycott Eastern Europe in the hopes of providing hope to the beleaguered and virtually imprisoned populations which were under Soviet domination, even if worse hardships might be created.

Governor Reagan had found several ways to act in an official capacity against communism. At his inauguration, he had greeted a wounded veteran and had placed a California military base flag at the top of the rotunda. In Oregon and in San Francisco, he had visited Vietnam veterans to offer solace. In California, he had warned about the growing menace of Soviet influence in the Middle East when he had attended several events honoring Israel. He had become an honorary Seabee and had accepted their base camp flag from Vietnam. But multi-ethnic California now offered a new way.

The California Croatian-American community had families in their homeland, which had remained under the yoke of the oppressive Tito regime. In America, Croatians had centered historically in the Mid-West but in the recent past had large enclaves in California. Historically, they had leaned Democratic.

Current American community activist of Croatian descent, and retired industrial engineering manager, Dan Rados, who knew most of those involved, recalled that in early 1968, a small group of fellow Americans of Croatian descent, amongst them Tadija "Ted" Pavich,[224] who had served fifteen years in Tito's prisons—and Fr. Petar Topic— who had fled from Tito's troops in 1945—joined other Americans of Croatian descent and, with the help of local Republican assemblyman Earle Crandall, had approached Reagan officials and Reagan in Sacramento.[225] The exact details of the preliminary meetings remain unknown. Croatia and its neighboring state of Slovenia, at that time parts of communist Yugoslavia, in early 1968 had objected to rising taxes.[226]

On April 4, just prior to flying east and hearing the news of the King assassination during descent, Governor Reagan, in a small signing ceremony in his office, signed a proclamation honoring Croatian independence.[227] Reagan's proclamation read in part,

"Whereas Croatia is presently subjugated to force and terror by Yugoslavia which has prevented the election of representatives to the Sabor and has deprived Croatians of the basic human rights of self-determination, free elections, economy, culture, religion, and even language; and whereas more than 150,000 Americans of Croatian descent live in California....and always maintain their vigilance against Communist aggression..."

Reagan was sending a loud and clear message to Americans of Croatian descent throughout the nation, to the nation's capital, and to those under the yoke of communism in Eastern Europe, that he was a man to be reckoned with. Even as a domestic governor and presidential candidate, Reagan found any way he could to sound the clarion call for freedom.[228]

Reagan then expanded his vision for a free Croatia to include all of communist Eastern Europe. Reagan later added to his official Croatian proclamation by invoking Captive Nations Day:

"Each year we observe a Captive Nations Day. At one time, pronouncements on that day here in our own land anticipated the future freedom of those now held captive and enslaved. But more and more we have diluted that theme until now we use the day to speak of peace with no mention of freedom."[229]

One sees the continuing thread, from Theodore Roosevelt to Eisenhower and to Reagan, of using the term, Americans of Croatian descent, rather than the term, Croatian-Americans. All three Republicans, as discussed earlier, despised the use of hyphenated groups by Democrats in order to seek political advantage with such defined subgroups of hyphenated Americans.

Reagan's signature on the proclamation electrified the Croatian communities both in America and in their homeland. Indeed Rados recalled that Reagan's signing of the proclamation was "the pivotal point" in creating a significant change in party allegiance for Americans of Croatian descent.[230] With the preparations for the November general election in full swing, Reagan's proclamation swung the vast majority into the Republican tent. As seen earlier, in May, Reagan had been greeted in Cleveland by crowds waving banners from the Croatian American communities of the Midwest. Reagan had aroused in his supporters the hope that he and his public pronouncements might begin the process of bringing freedom to their homelands from more than two decades of Soviet occupation. Reagan in this initial way was delivering on his carrying forth the ideals of his heroes Churchill and Eisenhower.

The official reaction from communist Yugoslavia was not surprising. According to a State Department document released decades later, Yugoslavian Ambassador Crnobrnja was unhappy that Reagan had proclaimed April 10 as Croatian Independence Day and it was noted that some Americans of Yugoslav origin were unhappy.[231] As will be discussed, the reactions of Croatians would be the opposite.

Columnist Drew Pearson, ever eager to criticize anyone who was a threat to his Democratic allies, wrote a column on July 23 discussing his opinions on Eastern Europe. Columnist Pearson showed his political bent when he declared amazingly, "Actually the Red Army has been a great economic boon to these East European countries," for he believed the occupying forces gave them "protection" and thus they did not have to spend their own money on defense.[232] One can only imagine what he would have written after the Nazi invasion of Poland on September 1, 1939—the cause of World War II—in thanking the Nazi's for alleviating the need of the Polish populace from having to fund their own army any longer?

Pearson then proceeded to attack Reagan's declaration about an independent Croatia. The headline ran, "Gov. Reagan Insults Yugoslavia" and called the policy Reagan was offering the "worst policy the United States could follow."[233] But Reagan was not attempting to honor a Nazi government during World War II. Pearson was misreading the history happening in front of him. Governor and presidential candidate Reagan was trying, as best he could from far away Sacramento, to tell the people of one small section of communist-controlled Eastern Europe that in effect, "America hears you. We know you want independence from the Soviet Union and to be free once again."

Reagan saw the future and wanted to stand up for the freedom of Eastern Europe. By signing the proclamation honoring Croatian independence, and speaking about Captive Nations Day, Reagan was sending another clear message to the Soviet Union of how important freedom was to Reagan now. Rados recalled that those Croatian Americans, as well as those Croatians, who in 1968 learned of Reagan's proclamation were inspired greatly that a President Reagan in 1969 might in some way help them on their road to freedom from communism.[234]

Governor Reagan then welcomed the Latvian Folk Ensemble of New York at his Sacramento office, where the dance group presented

Reagan with their album.[235] It was another way for candidate Reagan to enter the world of garnering freedom for Eastern Europe.

In the future in 1980 at a nationally-televised press conference, shortly after winning the Republican nomination, nominee Reagan would discuss Croatian independence from Yugoslavia.[236] In 1982, future President Reagan would proclaim June 14 as Baltic Freedom Day, commemorating the date that the Soviets began deportations from the Baltic States in 1941. And at the Ronald Reagan Centennial Celebration in Simi Valley in early February, 2011, Latvian Ambassador Andrejs Pildegovics would remind the attendees of Reagan's unflagging support to help captive nations regain their freedom.[237]

And it would be in the Eastern bloc—in which the fall of communism, due to President Reagan's policies, would begin in the late 1980s, but which clearly had begun in 1965-1968—where major monuments and statues to Ronald Reagan (in Warsaw, Budapest, Wroclaw, and the former Soviet republic of Georgia, in Tbilisi) plus major parks, squares and roads (in Prague, Gdansk, Krakow and Wroclaw) proudly proclaim in the 21st century the supreme importance of Ronald Reagan in achieving their collective freedom.

In his first autobiography, Reagan had written about freedom for Eastern Europe. The Croatian proclamation in 1968, which the California legislature later rescinded, and his meeting with the American dancers of Latvian heritage, may be seen as Reagan's first official entrance into the world of Eastern European foreign affairs. Reagan had made two official acts as governor and presidential candidate, which were the first official steps Reagan ever made in the long road to see communism defeated peacefully. After he had signed the proclamation, the Croatian-American community in California and its sister communities in the Cleveland and the rest of the Midwest, and undoubtedly Latvians as well, were proud that, as Rados reflected, Reagan had "done something wonderful."[238]

In the future President Reagan would journey on that long, tortuous road—seeking the end of communism and freedom for Eastern Europe—through the calling of the Soviet Union an "evil empire," would leave a meeting with Gorbachev in Reykjavik where he would insist on not abandoning his anti-ballistic plan—whose origins in Reagan's mind clearly started in 1967, and which would culminate in the tearing down of the Berlin Wall—which he had first called for publicly when debating Kennedy in the spring of 1967.

Reagan's 1968 calls for freedom in Croatia, Latvia, and all of Eastern Europe still resonate in the second decade of the 21st century.

Dan Rados still is active in calling for freedom in his beloved Croatia.[239]

Birmingham

The last stop on the Southern Solicitation was Alabama. On July 24, Reagan reviewed the convention planning with his campaign staff.[240] One party leader flew in eight South Carolina delegates and five alternates to meet Reagan.[241] From Georgia, Republican National Committeeman Roscoe Pickett flew his own plane with more than a dozen delegates to meet Reagan.[242] Columnist Robert Novak recalled that the Reagan team had flown in even more, so that the total was some "ninety delegates and alternates."[243] After a welcoming rally and his customary press conference, Reagan met privately with "ten delegates from Georgia, five from Mississippi, 13 from South Carolina and 10 from Louisiana.[244] Throughout the talks with delegates, held at the Tutwiler Hotel, White was at Reagan's side. Novak, who was present at the time having been invited personally by White, met some Southern delegates who had become so distrustful of Nixon "that they were desperate for any alternative."[245] But others told Novak that it was too late; Reagan should have come to campaign earlier because at that point they had "unbreakable commitments to Nixon."[246] But some were quick to add that if there were a second ballot, "they would bolt to Reagan."[247] Novak asked White if Reagan would consider appearing on CBS's *Face the Nation*, which Novak would host, the day before the convention was to open.[248]

One Georgia delegate provided the Rockefeller campaign with details of what Reagan and White had said. Subsequently based on what the delegate had detailed, Tanya Melich, former director of political research for ABC News, and now on Rockefeller's paid campaign staff, sent out a July 26 memo to fellow Rockefeller staff members.[249] White had made the major presentation, emphasizing to the assembled delegates three major points: that polls proved that Nixon could not win; that their nominee must attract independent and Democratic voters, as Reagan had done masterfully in 1966; and there was a great number of undecided voters who did not like the choice of Nixon or Rockefeller and were "looking for a new leader." When asked if he would agree to become Rockefeller's vice-president, as had been the speculation in the media especially the Time cover from October, Reagan said that he did not think any Reagan or Nixon delegates would shift to voting for Rockefeller. Reagan concluded saying that there was "no chance" of Rockefeller being nominated and added, "Don't worry about Rockefeller and Wallace; it's either Nixon or Reagan."[250]

In his main speech at City Auditorium, Reagan urged his listeners not to throw their votes away by voting for George Wallace. The *Birmingham News* editorialized that Reagan "is a candidate, period."[251] Alabama's 26-member delegation was split almost exactly in half between Reagan and Nixon, but one pro-Reagan delegate told the press that Reagan "would pick up several more votes by convention time."[252] Then Reagan addressed a last reception for 200 Alabama Republicans who had paid $100 per person to hear him.[253]

The Evans-Novak column of July 28 explained the significance of Reagan's visit to Birmingham. They reported that Reagan's trip was a "major breakthrough."[254] Admittedly Nixon forces had persuaded Thurmond to drop his favorite son status and to endorse Nixon. Under the unit rule, Nixon aides were quite confident that Nixon thus would get all 22 delegates. But the unit rule could not be enforced if any delegate objected. And with Reagan's forces working over the Alabama delegation, it looked like even one defection would likely cause a major split and possibly even a Reagan majority. And once another Southern state, besides North Carolina, went to Reagan, who knew how many more would join the bandwagon? Plus would Utah remain a Reagan-majority delegation? At the convention, would Ken Rogstad from Washington State and his Reagan delegates challenge the other slate of delegates, possibly turning Washington into a Reagan majority too?

In Birmingham, Evans and Novak detected a 'pattern of small Nixon losses and small Reagan gains" amongst the 90 delegates and alternates who met Reagan.[255] The most dramatic change was seen in the Louisiana delegation, which in June had seemingly been all for Nixon, yet after the Birmingham meeting with Reagan, Reagan had nearly half the delegation and "may move into a majority."[256] Similarly, in Mississippi, the state's twenty delegates were split evenly with either Reagan or Nixon able to win the entire delegation because of the unit rule.[257]

Threats from John Birch Society

Reagan had one final meeting with representatives of the South. Tanya Melich of the Rockefeller team sent out another memo, this time describing a July 29 private meeting between Reagan and a select committee of members of the John Birch Society. Melich got her information from an attendee the meeting. The society told Reagan to accept the vice-presidency under Nixon and that they would threaten Nixon that unless he chose Reagan, they would not support Nixon on the first ballot. They also threatened Reagan that if he did not accept their demand, that they would not deliver the South to him. Reagan was seen as "not happy" and replied "no man runs for the vice-presidency." Melich concluded that if Reagan accepted the proposal, it would deal a "serious blow" to Rockefeller's chances. If Reagan said No, in order for the society to carry out their double threats, their members would be "forced to vote for Reagan on the first ballot to stop Nixon and to switch on succeeding ballots as is necessary to prevent either Nixon or Reagan from gaining momentum."[258]

Solicitation Success?

As Reagan headed back to Sacramento for gubernatorial activities prior to the Platform Committee meetings in Miami Beach, he may have read in *Newsweek* that his odds were 50 to 1.[259] Reagan made an appearance on ABC's *Issues and Answers*, where he said that hecklers who had disrupted a speech by Vice President Humphrey were "monsters."[260] After a few days' rest before the convention was to begin, signs that Reagan's planned Southern Solicitation was having an effect on Southern delegates were being reported by the national media.

Rockefeller's campaign had circulated a memorandum claiming that Reagan had increased his projected tally to 280 votes. Nixon had "slipped so badly that he will receive no more than 515 votes on the first ballot" was the theme of the memo, because Reagan had "siphoned off much of Mr. Nixon's former strength in the South and some of his support in other parts of the nation" too.[261]

Four delegates from Washington State who previously were pledged to Nixon said they now were "uncommitted."[262] Was Ken Rogstad working hard behind the scenes, as Bob Hazen had been doing as well? Was Rogstad going to push for the credentials fight? Would Utah hold for Reagan? A number of Nixon delegates told the press that they were "increasingly worried about Mr. Nixon's ability to win in November,"[263] which of course was the rationale behind *Ronald Reagan, Citizen Governor*. Further along, the memo projected that after Nixon would falter on the first ballot, Reagan would achieve 310 to 320 second round votes just as Nixon was falling. After that, the convention would be "wide open."[264]

Specific delegate shifts projected by the memo included: Texas, where the prior estimate from Senator Tower of 44 Nixon votes had dwindled to "no more than 30 to 31;" Florida, where State Chairman Murfin's previous projection of 30 Nixon votes was reduced to "fewer than 15" of the state's 34 delegates; and Mississippi, where prior estimates that Nixon would get all 20 votes dropped dramatically to barely "five or six."[265] Of course the Rockefeller team expected that their candidate would beat Reagan if it came to a third ballot, just as Reed and White thought that Reagan at that point would beat Rockefeller. Patrick Buchanan theorizes further of what difficulties the two candidates may have had and concludes the convention would have returned to Nixon anyway.[266]

The *New York Times* however was not as upbeat as the Rockefeller camp had been about the tide turning toward Reagan and Rockefeller. Nixon indeed had lost delegate strength in the South to Reagan, but "not as much as either the Reagan or Rockefeller supporters would like."[267] The newspaper had done a survey of correspondents which showed that "15 to 20" former Nixon supporters had changed to Reagan with additional switching "possible in the week left before the presidential balloting."[268] The Nixon team felt the changes, although real, "did not appear to be large enough to provide a major threat."[269] Southern delegates chose Reagan as a close second choice after Nixon, but if Nixon's delegate count declined further, "much larger numbers of votes would undoubtedly go to Mr. Reagan."[270]

The newspaper's analysis continued that Reagan had made his "principal inroads" into Nixon's strength in Texas and North Carolina, with "smaller losses" in Alabama and Florida.[271] Then Jack Cox, the 1962 Republican candidate for governor of Texas, changed from Nixon to Reagan. The Reagan grass roots groups in Texas had been pushing. Despite the presence of Senator Tower in the Nixon camp, Cox was "actively soliciting other pro-Nixon delegates to join him."[272] Amongst the 56 Texas delegates, Reagan's support had grown to 20 compared to a few weeks earlier when Reagan had had only 12. Cox thought he could raise the Reagan tally to 24 or 25.

The personal visit of Reagan to Alabama was credited for another slight increase. Of the state's 26 delegates, Reagan now had 12 versus 10 before the trip. In Mississippi, Reagan was up to a quarter of the total, but Mississippi was a unit-rule state and thus Nixon would get all the votes. In South Carolina, also a unit-rule state, the 22 delegates were "nearly evenly split."[273] Thus despite Ol' Strom's private and public pronouncements, half his delegation was for Reagan; but the expected pressure from Thurmond was expected to keep all the votes for Nixon. In Florida, some observers felt Reagan had gone only from 8 to 9 delegates, yet Reagan's team felt that it could rise to 18.

With Reagan's growing success in the South, Dent, along with National Committeeman Fred La Rue of Mississippi, were "hurriedly summoned" to Nixon headquarters in New York.[274]

Reagan's team had their own memo and their own analysis too. Bill Clark in Sacramento had received a memorandum from one of Reagan's public relations officials, Russ Walton. In it, Walton felt that the Rockefeller campaign was "desperate" with its only chance as dividing up the conservative vote between Reagan and Nixon.[275] Walton recommended a "hard" delegate count on the convention's opening day, August 5, and if it showed Nixon as winner, then Reagan should urge Party unity and withdraw."[276] Historian Cannon felt that Reagan should have taken the advice, [277]but considering how long and hard Reagan, Reed, and White had come since their first planning meeting, it would have been uncharacteristic for Reagan to have withdrawn until Nixon had actually gone over the needed 667 votes.

Push-back Against Ol' Strom

Jim Gardner, who was with the team on the May trip to the South, had not gone with Reagan and Reed on the Southern Solicitation in July. Gardner's original enthusiasm for Reagan stemmed from his observations that Nixon "was not as conservative as Reagan. I got caught up in the excitement of Ronald Reagan and the contest."[278] He had started to work on the North Carolina delegation as soon as he was back home from having accompanied Reagan, Reed and White to Florida in May. He had called delegates "one by one" and even though some told him that they were for Nixon, as the convention approached, he had convinced a majority of the North Carolina delegation to vote for Reagan. "When we went to Miami, we knew the North Carolina delegation was going to be for Reagan."[279]

The main stumbling block in the South remained Ol' Strom. One rumor was that Thurmond would not support Reagan because he was divorced.[280] Gardner knew that Thurmond had "really worked on the Southern delegations" rooting for Nixon. In July, Congressman Gardner was in Washington, D.C. and went to see Thurmond in his Senate office. Gardner told Thurmond of his and his delegation's support for Reagan. Thurmond said, "I love Ronald Reagan but I am committed to Richard Nixon."[281] Gardner may have been the only delegate or Southern chairman who had the courage to try to convince Thurmond to change his mind.

Gardner, as determined a Reagan supporter in 1968 as ever there was, had one more trick up his sleeve to try to prevent a first-ballot

Nixon victory. When his push-back against Thurmond had failed, the creative Gardner planned one new maneuver. Gardner knew he was going to Miami Beach with a Reagan-majority delegation. But this was no guarantee that if his delegates saw momentum building towards a first-ballot Nixon victory, many might break ranks and vote for Nixon. So to guarantee no late defections to Nixon, Gardner wanted his delegation to declare him their favorite son so as to prevent any first ballot vote to Nixon.[282] Gardner then flew off to Miami in charge of the only Reagan-majority delegation, perhaps with the exception of Utah as discussed earlier, outside of California.

So the final campaign stop of the final campaign trip of Ronald Reagan's first campaign for the presidency had come to an end. Two years earlier in 1966, when he was not yet elected governor, conservative Republicans had paid $1 apiece to see Reagan in Seattle at that first out-of-state appearance. It was there where the voter survey had indicated that people would support an actor running for political office. It ended in 1968 in Birmingham where now for $100 apiece, conservative Republicans could see the man who they hoped would become the next president of the United States. Clearly candidate Reagan's stock had multiplied dramatically. But was it enough?

Endnotes

1. Graham Molitar Papers, Record Group IV 3A 18, Series Arms Control, Box 27, Folder 657, Rockefeller Archive Center
2. RRL, Tape 348 Part II
3. RRL, Tape 348 Part II
4. RRL ,Tape 356 Part I
5. Cannon, p. 266
6. Broder, David, "Reagan Delegates," *LA Times*, 7/18/68
7. Jim Gardner, personal inerview, 3/27/2013
8. RRL, Tape 356 Part I
9. Melich, Tanya, "Ronald Reagan's Trip to Birmingham and His Meeting with Delegates", memo 7/26/1968, Tanya Melich papers, M.E. Grenander Department of Special Collections and Archives, University Libraries, State University of New York at Albany, Series II-Box 3: Folder 3
10. Reed, *The Reagan Enigma*, p. 167
11. Dent, p. 83
12. Chester et. al., p. 447
13. Chester et. al., p. 447
14. http://www.conservativehq.com/article/14264-memoriam-ray-barnhart-and-ronald-b-dear
15. Chester et. al., p. 444
16. Chester et. al., p. 444
17. "Statement by Governor Reagan on the Poor People's March," Indianapolis, Indiana Press Conference, 6/13/68
18. ibid
19. ibid
20. RRL, Tape 348 Part I
21. RRL, Tape 348 Part I
22. RRL, Tape 348 Part I
23. RRL, Tape 348 Part I
24. Kopelson, Gene 2014C

25. Pipes, p. 296
26. Reagan-Reed, 6/14/1968-6/15/1968, Tulsa hotel
27. "Reagan Finds Views Nearer to Nixon's," *NYT*, 6/17/68, p. 33
28. ibid
29. "Reagan Considers McCarthy Hardest Nixon Opponent," *Washington Post*, 6/25/68
30. RRL, Tape 348 Part II
31. RRL, Tape 348 Part II
32. RRL, Tape 348 Part III
33. Reed, The Reagan Enigma, p. 166-167
34. RRL, Tape 348 Part II
35. ibid
36. RRL, Tape 348 Part II
37. RRL, Tape 348 Part II
38. RRL, Tape 348
39. ibid
40. RRL, Tape 348 Part II
41. RRL, Tape 348 Part II
42. Cannon, Ronnie and Jesse, p. 269-270
43. Reagan-Reed, 6/15/1968
44. Randolph, Gordon, "MGIC Chairman Heads Reagan Drive," *Milwaukee Journal*, 8/5/68
45. Myers, Roger, "Key Reagan Backers Agree to Unannounced Candidacy," 6/23/68, unnamed newspaper, scrapbook, Henry A Bubb Collection, University of Kansas
46. See Illustrations
47. Letter to Bob Dole from Ronald Reagan, June 16, 1968, VIP Letters Collection, Robert J. Dole Archive and Special Collections, University of Kansas
48. Clark, Robert, "Reagan Gives Nod to Draft," *Kansas City Star*, 6/23/68 p1A
49. Clark, Robert, "Reagan Gives Nod to Draft," *Kansas City Star*, 6/23/68 p1A
50. Petterson, John, "750 Greet Reagan At Topeka," Wichita Eagle and Beacon, undated newspaper article, scrapbook, Henry A Bubb Collection, University of Kansas
51. Myers, Roger, "Key Reagan Backers Agree To Unannounced Candidacy," 6/23/68, unnamed newspaper article, Scrapbook, Henry A Bubb Collection, University of Kansas
52. Dicus, pers int 12/7/12
53. Clark op.cit., *K C Star*, 6/23/68
54. See Illustrations
55. Dicus, pers int 12/7/12
56. Reagan letter to Bubb, 6/28/1968, Henry A. Bubb Collection, University of Kansas Archives
57. Dole, Robert, pers comm. 8/19/2013
58. Reagan-Reed, 6/22/1968-6/23/1968
59. *Newsweek*, 6/24/68 p31
60. ibid
61. Pearson, Drew, "Washington Merry-Go-Round," 6/29/68
62. Hill, Gladwin, "Reagan Concedes Recall Drive May Embarrass Him in Party," *NYT*, 7/3/68, p. 13
63. Lapp, Ralph E., "China's Mushroom Cloud Casts Long Shadow," *NYT*, 7/14/68, p. SM6
64. Anderson, Raymond, "Soviet Bid Linked to Missile Costs," *NYT*, 6/30/68, p. 5
65. ibid
66. "Washington Proceedings," *NYT*, 7/18/68, p. 20
67. Graham Molitar Papers, Record Group IV 3A 18, Series Arms Control, Box 27, Folder 657, Rockefeller Archive Center
68. ibid
69. Foe, Sylvan, *NYT*, 7/1/68, p. 1
70. Kopelson, Gene, 2014D
71. Knowles, Clayton, "Javits Cautions on Reagan choice," *NYT*, 7/22/68
72. White, p. 236
73. White, p. 236
74. Jorgensen, I. Walter and Smith, Robert M. letter to The Honorable Everett M. Dirksen, 7/8/1968, Dirksen Congressional Center, EMD Papers, Apha 1968, Reagan
75. "Reagan Guard Routs Two Firebombers," *NYT*, 7/11/1968, p.25
76. Graham Molitar Papers, Record Group IV 3A 18, Series Civil Rights, Box 26, Folder 660, Rockefeller Archive Center
77. ibid
78. Hill, Gladwin, "Reagan Says Aim is to Help Party," *NYT*, 7/10/68, p.20
79. "Reagan Urged On," *Topeka Star Journal*, 6/28/68
80. Bennett, Ralph, "Reagan Aides race Time to Convention," *San Diego Evening Tribune*, 7/8/68, p. A-4

81. Bennett Ralph, "Reagan Aides Race Time to Convention," *San Diego Evening Tribune*, 7/8/68, p. A4
82. Greenberg, Carl, "Reagan's Name May Be Placed In Nomination Before Nixon's," *LA Times*, 7/5/68, p. 3
83. The Republican Battle Line, vol II no. 7, 7/15/68, p. 1
84. "Mr. Reagan Is Available," *Topeka Daily Capital*, 7/8/68
85. Republican Battle Line, op.cit.
86. "Reagan Boosters Plan TV Speech On CBS, Sunday" undated unnamed newspaper article, scrapbook, Henry A. Bubb Collection, University of Kansas
87. Reagan-Reed, 6/13/1968
88. "Bid by Reagan July 21 Denied," *Washington Post*, 7/12/68, p. A2
89. "Reagan Denies a Report He'll Enter Race July 21," *NYT*, 7/12/68, p. 34
90. ibid
91. ibid
92. See Illustrations
93. Greenberg, Carl, "Reagan's Name May Be Placed in Nomination Before Nixon's," *LA Times*, 7/5/68, p. 3
94. The Republican Battle Line, vol II no. 7, 7/15/68, p. 1
95. ibid
96. "A Recall for Reagan?," *Newsweek*, 7/15/68, p. 27
97. "Reagan Attributes Violence to Criticism of Personalities," *NYT*, 7/13/68, p. 12
98. ibid
99. "GOP Delegates in Utah Back Romney Conditionally," *NYT*, 7/17/68, p. 18
100. Broder, David, "Reagan Delegates," *LA Times*, 7/18/68
101. Dent, p. 84
102. ibid
103. Nixon, p. 309
104. Chester et. al., p. 448
105. Deaver, p. 20-21
106. Eisenhower, Dwight. 1968 Diary. 6/11/68;6/12/68;6/13/68;7/4/68;7/5/687/14/68
107. Eisenhower, David, p. 256-257
108. ibid
109. Eisenhower, David, p. 256-257
110. RRL, Tape 356 Part I
111. RRL, Tape 356 Part I
112. Joseph Coors to Fred A. Seaton, letter 7/23/68, Fred A Seaton Papers, Post-Presidential Files, Dwight D. Eisenhower Presidential Library
113. Nettie J. Sandritter to Fred A. Seaton, letter 8/3/68, Fred A Seaton Papers, Post-Presidential Files, Dwight D. Eisenhower Presidential Library
114. Cannon, Ronnie and Jesse, p. 271
115. "Reagan Says Swing is Aimed at Wallace," *NYT*, 7/16/68, p. 26
116. "Reagan Calls on Conservatives to Resist Appeals of Wallace," *Sacramento Bee*, 7/17/68
117. "'Candidate' Reagan Changes Tune", undated newspaper article, Henry A Bubb Collection, University of Kansas
118. ibid
119. ibid
120. ibid
121. ibid
122. ibid
123. ibid
124. ibid
125. ibid
126. Cannon, p. 265
127. Cannon, p. 265
128. Cannon, p. 265
129. Cannon, p. 265
130. Cannon, p. 265
131. Dent, p. 84
132. Novak, p. 166
133. *Newsweek*, 7/22/68, p. 20
134. Cannon, p. 265
135. "Reagan Will Meet Eastern Delegates as a Noncandidate," *NYT*, 7/20/68, p. 12
136. ibid
137. Cannon, p. 266
138. ibid

139. RRL, Tape 356 Part I
140. RRL, Tape 356 Part I
141. Greenberg, Carl, "Reagan Drive Enters Intense Stage in South," *LA Times*, 7/21/68, p. A2
142. RRL, Tape 356 Part I
143. Buchanan, p. 101-102
144. Dudley A. Sharp to Fred A. Seaton, letter 7/19/68, Seaton Papers, Post-Presidential Files, Dwight D. Eisenhower Presidential Library
145. RRL, Tape 356 Part I
146. Johnson, Lyndon, State of the Union Address, 1/17/68
147. RRL, Tape 356 Part I
148. See Illustrations
149. Perdicaris later would contribute to Roosevelt-backed relief aid for France in World War I; Thompson, p. 220
150. MacMillan's comments about Reagan and the *U.S.S. Pueblo* hostages do not appear in any MacMillan biography. MacMillan had met with Eisenhower in early 1968 as seen.
151. RRL, Tape 356 Part I
152. Hanson, 2010, p. 185
153. Military historian Victor Davis Hanson explores the pros and cons of quick and threatening reaction to hostage situations; Hanson, 2010, p. 39-41
154. RRL, Tape 356 Part I
155. In 2015, candidate Donald Trump proclaimed that like President Reagan in 1981, if Trump were president in January, 2017, Iran quickly would free the hostages held because President Obama's Iran agreement never addressed that issue.
156. Buchanan p. 95
157. RRL, Tape 356 Part I
158. ibid
159. RRL, Tape 356 Part I.
160. ibid
161. Reagan, Ronald, Statement On The Occasion Of The Tenth Anniversary Of The Announcement Of The Strategic Defense Initiative, March 23rd, 1993
162. Reed, pers comm., 10/20/13
163. "President Rand Paul's Foreign Policy," *The Federalist*, 8/11/2014
164. Boot, Max, "Reagan Vindicated: Missile Defense Works," Commentary 11/18/2012
165. Ibid
166. RRL, Tape 356 Part I
167. ibid
168. ibid
169. ibid
170. ibid
171. ibid
172. Thomas, Ikes Bluff, p. 98-99
173. RRL, Tape 356 Part I
174. Greenberg, Carl, "Reagan Drive Enters Intense Stage in South," *LA Times*, 7/21/68, p. A2
175. Dent, p. 86
176. Hill, Gladwin, "Reagan Looking to Later Ballots," *NYT*, 7/21/68, p. 46
177. RRL, Tape 356 Part I
178. Hill, op.cit.
179. RRL, Tape 356 Part I
180. ibid
181. RRL, Tape 356 part I
182. ibid
183. RRL, Pate 356 Part I
184. Greenberg op.cit.
185. Cannon, p.265
186. Greenberg op.cit.
187. Greenberg op.cit.
188. Greenberg
189. Greenberg
190. RRL, Tape 356 Part III
191. Hill, Gladwin, "Reagan Shrugs Off Plot Report, But His Protection is Increased," *NYT*, 7/22/68, p. 30
192. ibid
193. ibid
194. Gibbs and Duffy, p. 216
195. Cannon, p. 265

196. Gibbs and Duffy, p. 214
197. Myers, Roger, "Reagan Takes Hawkish Stand," *Topeka Capital*, 7/22/68
198. Perlstein, p. 294
199. Hughes, Harold, "Rockefeller Believed Oregon GOP Delegation Favorite If Nixon Falters," *The Oregonian*, 6/28/68, p. 35
200. ibid
201. "Reagan Reportedly 'Softened Up' Southern Vote," *The Oregonian*, 7/22/68, p. 16
202. ibid
203. "A Delegate's Pledge," *The Oregonian*, 7/24/68, p. 22
204. Ibid
205. ibid
206. ibid
207. ibid
208. ibid
209. Myers, Roger, "Reagan Takes Hawkish Stand," *Queen City Capital*, 7/22/68.
210. ibid
211. Thomas, Ike's Bluff
212. Meyers op.cit.
213. Waugh, John, "We're Not Going to Sit Around," *Christian Science Monitor*, 7/23/68
214. ibid
215. ibid
216. ibid
217. ibid
218. ibid
219. Look, 7/23/68
220. Reed, p. 27
221. Dan Rados, personal communication, 9/14/2015
222. Kengor
223. Kengor, p. 31
224. Pavich, pers int—
225. Rados, pers int 11/10/13
226. Eder, Richard, "Aide Challenges Yugoslav Powers," *NYT*, 1/21/68, p. 26
227. See Illustrations
228. Reagan, Ronald "Proclamation of Croatian Independence," April 4, 1968, Office of the California Secretary of State and courtesy Dan Rados
229. Boyarsky, p. 257-258
230. Rados, personal interview, 8/17/2015
231. "Information Memorandum from the Deputy Assistant Secretary of State for European Affairs Springsteen to Secretary of State Rusk, 6/11/1968" Foreign Relations of the United States 1964-1968, vol. XVII, Eastern Europe, Document 189. https://history.state.gov/historicaldocuments/frus1964-68v17/d189
232. Pearson, Drew, "Washington Merry-Go-Round," 7/23/68
233. ibid
234. Rados, personal interview 8/17/2015
235. See Illustrations
236. Palaich, Michael "About the History of Croatian Emigration." www.hrsvijet.net, article ID 15778, 7/25/2011
237. "Ambassador participates in Ronald Reagan Centennial in L.A." Embassy of the Republic of Latvia to the United States of America, 2/2011
238. Rados, pers int, 11/10/13
239. http://dailycaller.com/2015/01/02/is-serbia-controlling-croatia-by-blackmailing-its-president/
240. Reagan-Reed, 7/24/1968, Birmingham hotel
241. Dent, p. 85
242. White and Gill, p. 115
243. Novak, p. 166
244. "Reagan in South to Aid GOP Fund," *NYT*, 7/25/68, p. 22
245. ibid
246. ibid
247. ibid
248. Novak, p. 166-167
249. Melich, Tanya, personal communications 3/25/2015 and 4/30/2015
250. Melich, Tanya "Ronald Reagan's Trip to Birmingham and His Meeting with Delegates", memo 7/26/1968, Tanya Melich papers, M.E. Grenander Department of Special Collections and Archives, University Libraries, State University of New York at Albany, Series II-Box 3: Folder 3

251. Cannon, p 236-267
252. op.cit. *NYT*
253. op.cit. *NYT*
254. Dent, p. 85
255. Dent, p. 86
256. Dent, p. 86
257. White and Gill, p. 114
258. Melich, Tanya memo "Reagan/Nixon-John Birch Society" 7/29/1968, Tanya Melich Collection, M.E. Grenander Department of Special Collections and Archives, University Libraries, State University of New York at Albany, Series II-Box 3, Folder 3
259. *Newsweek*, 7/29/68, p. 15
260. Hill, Gladswin, "Reagan Compares Hecklers to Monsters," *NYT*, 7/29/68, p. 23
261. Apple, R. W. Jr., "Rockefeller Sees Reagan Cutting Nixon's Strength," *NYT*, 7/28/68, p. 1
262. ibid
263. ibid
264. ibid
265. ibid
266. Buchanan, p. 302-303
267. "15 to 20 Nixon Votes in South Shift to Reagan, Survey Finds," *NYT*, 8/1/68, p. 20
268. ibid
269. ibid
270. ibid
271. ibid
272. ibid
273. ibid
274. Dent, p. 86
275. Cannon, p. 267
276. Cannon, p. 267
277. ibid
278. Gardner, pers int 3/27/13
279. ibid
280. Bob Schadler, pers int, 5/21/13
281. Gardner, pers int 3/27/13
282. op.cit. above, *NYT*, 8/1/68

ILLUSTRATIONS

President Reagan and bust of Theodore Roosevelt, courtesy Ronald Reagan Presidential Library.

Eisenhower's hand-written modifications of the script for *Mr. Lincoln's Party Today*, courtesy Dwight D. Eisenhower Presidential Library

Mr. Lincoln's Party Today (front), courtesy, author

Mr. Lincoln's Party Today (back), courtesy, author

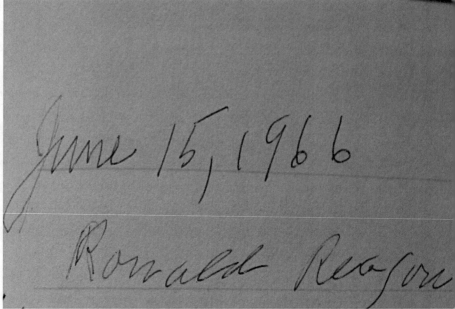

Governor Reagan signs in at Eisenhower home in Gettysburg on June 15, 1966, a required by Mamie Eisenhower of all guests, courtesy National Park Service, Eisenhowe National Historic Site

Dwight Eisenhower, Tom Reed, Ronald Reagan at Eisenhower's Gettysburg office, June 15, 1966, courtesy Thomas C. Reed.

"Ya Basta?!" After Eisenhower advises Reagan to have a broad political tent to attract disaffected Democrats, Reagan creates this 1966 campaign poster to attract American voters of Mexican descent, likely modeled after Eisenhower's in 1952, courtesy Kenneth Burt.

In Seattle as nominee for governor, Reagan makes his first out-of-state campaign speech just three days after meeting with Eisenhower. Reagan makes his first official statement on foreign policy as nominee, June 18, 1966. courtesy www.historylink.org

Governor Reagan at the Hollywood Bowl Rally for Israel's Survival during Six Day War, June 11, 1967, courtesy Ronald Reagan Presidential Library.

Reagan speaking at Western Governors Conference, where Reagan's presidential candidacy overshadows the meetings, June 25-27, 1967, courtesy Ronald Reagan Presidential Library.

Nixon and Reagan reach a short-lived detente at Bohemian Grove, July 23, 1967, courtesy Thomas C. Reed.

Governor Reagan at dedication of Melick Library at his alma mater, Eureka College, Sept. 28, 1967, courtesy Eureka College Archives.

Reagan's old college fraternity, Tau Kappa Epsilon, welcomes it's illustrious member, Sept. 28, 1967, courtesy Ronald Reagan Presidential Library.

In Manhattan just before leaving on the governors cruise, candidate Reagan tapes ABC's *Issues and Answers*, Oct. 15, 1967, courtesy Ronald Reagan Presidential Library.

Bon voyage! on the *S.S. Independence*: Governor and Mrs. Reagan, William Clark, and Tom Reed, Oct. 15, 1967, courtesy Ronald Reagan Presidential Library.

Governor Reagan delivers the prestigious 1967 Landon Lecture, Oct. 26, 1967. Henry A. Bubb (not seen) sat with Reagan on the podium. courtesy Morse Department of Special Collections, Kansas State University Libraries.

Honorary Grand Marshalls California Governor Ronald Reagan and Oregon Governor Tom McCall ride in the Albany, Oregon Veterans Day parade, November 11, 1967, courtesy Paul R. Pritchard and the Albany Regional Museum.

Reagan and McCall arrive to watch famous University of Southern California vs Oregon State University football game featuring star O.J. Simpson, November 11, 1967, from the Oregon State University Libraries Special Collections and Archives Research Center.

Chubb Fellow Governor Reagan answering student question at Yale University student press conference, December 4, 1967, courtesy Ronald Reagan Presidential Library.

The Reagan's, in front of statue of Nathan Hale, enjoy their visit to Yale University, early December, 1967, courtesy Ronald Reagan Presidential Library.

In front of the California State House, Governor Reagan is made an honorary Seabee and accepts the state flag flown over Seabee Camp Barnes in Dong Ha, Vietnam, December 13, 1967, courtesy Ronald Reagan Presidential Library.

Governor Reagan is received warmly at the Economic Club of New York, January 17, 1968, courtesy Ronald Reagan Presidential Library.

The three golf buddies: Eisenhower, Reagan and their mutual friend, Freeman Gosden, Palm Desert, March 10, 1968, courtesy Ronald Reagan Presidential Library.

The two old football players have their fourth and final meeting: Political mentor Ike and protege "Dutch" Reagan again spend many hours together, Palm Desert, March 10, 1968, courtesy Ronald Reagan Presidential Library.

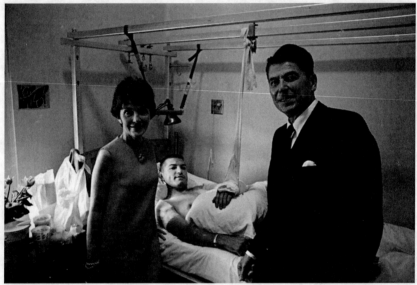

Governor and Mrs. Reagan spend a private moment with a wounded Vietnam War veteran at Letterman Hospital, February 25, 1968. The Reagan's often would visit wounded veterans during the 1968 campaign and long afterwards. Later as president, Reagan tried to bring closure and healing to the nation, courtesy Ronald Reagan Presidential Library.

STUDENTS for REAGAN

Suite 102
1104 Vermont Avenue, Northwest
Washington, D. C. 20005
Telephone: (202) 462-1333

CO-CHAIRMEN
Michael W. Thompson
University of Missouri
Charles L. Williams, Jr.
North Carolina State University

CHAIRMAN, NATIONAL COMMITTEE
Hugh L. Henry
University of Virginia
Graduate School

TREASURER
Randal Cornell Teague
George Washington University
Law School

EXECUTIVE DIRECTOR
W. Bruce Weinrod
American University

Students for Reagan, official stationery letterhead, courtesy Bruce Weinrod.

Bruce Weinrod manning Students for Reagan campaign booth, Spring 1968, courtesy Bruce Weinrod.

Students for Reagan 1968 campaign button, courtesy Bruce Weinrod.

Students for Reagan membership card, courtesy Bruce Weinrod.

Students for Reagan bumper sticker, courtesy Bruce Weinrod.

Governor Reagan signs Proclamation marking April 10 as Croatian Independence Day. Tadija "Ted" Pavic, State Representative Earle P. Crandall, Fr. Petar Topic, Governor Reagan, Nikola Kirigin-Chargin (l.-r.), April 4, 1968. Later that day while flying east, Reagan would learn of the assassination of Dr. Martin Luther King, Jr., courtesy Peter S. Carter and Dan Rados.

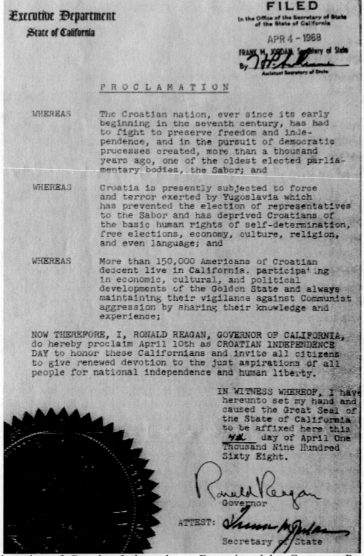

Proclamation of Croatian Independence Day, signed by Governor Reagan. Croatia is "presently subjected to force and terror exerted by Yugoslavia... More than 150,000 Americans of Croatian descent live in California...and (are) always maintaining their vigilance against Communist aggression." April 4, 1968, courtesy Office of Secretary of State of California and Dan Rados

Governor Reagan continues, in whatever ways he can as a domestic governor and presidential candidate, his quest for freedom for Eastern Europe: accepting an album from Latvian dancers, April 1968. courtesy Ronald Reagan Presidential Library.

Since early 1967, candidate Reagan continues campaigning out-of-state almost every weekend. Reagan conquered his aviophobia in order to run for president. Governor Reagan, Tom Reed, Lyn Nofziger (l.-r.), April 1968. courtesy Ronald Reagan Presidential Library.

Candidate Reagan visits his Oregon presidential campaign team while campaigning in Idaho, April 26, 1968. The decision not to have Reagan campaign in Oregon in person in 1968, despite several campaign visits in 1967, likely was a critical error. courtesy Ronald Reagan Presidential Library.

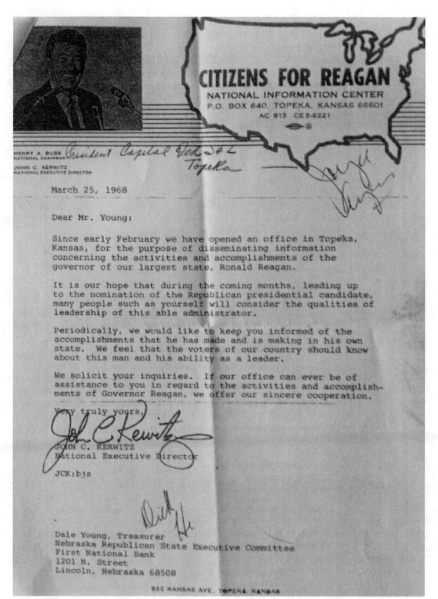

Dale L. Young is invited to chair a Reagan for president campaign office in Nebraska, March 25, 1968. Letter sent by Henry A. Bubb's Citizens for Reagan National Information Center in Topeka, courtesy Dale L. Young.

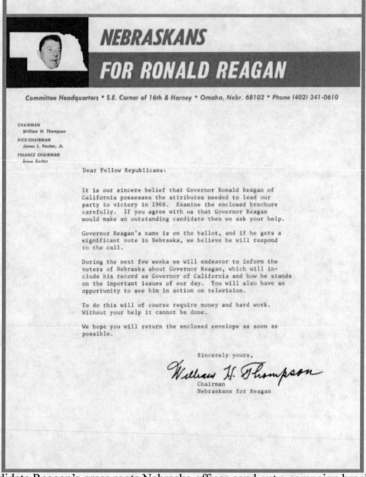

Candidate Reagan's grass roots Nebraska offices send out a campaign brochure and letter. The committees of Young, Thompson, and Sherwood would be critical for Reagan's future success in the Nebraska primary, courtesy Nebraska Public Television.

Candidate Reagan delivers his first White Paper speech, attacking Kennedy-Johnson foreign policy, in Honolulu, May 11, 1968, courtesy Ronald Reagan Presidential Library.

The Reagan's relaxing during the governors conference in Hawaii, May, 1968, courtesy Ronald Reagan Presidential Library.

Candidate Reagan campaigns in Charlotte for Congressman Jim Gardner, who is running for governor of North Carolina. Reagan jokes that he hopes soon to speak from the actual White House in Washington, D.C., May 20, 1968, courtesy Jim Gardner

Reagan 1968 presidential campaign buttons, collected by Fred Van Natta, Reagan's Western States campaign director. Note combination of Oregon and Reagan into OReagan, courtesy Fred Van Natta.

Enlarged

In coastal Oregon, a quarrel between two brothers leads to Robert F. Kennedy's campaign actually paying, in part, for a Reagan-for-president campaign advertisement: fine print, "Paid with funds from Western Lane Kennedy for President Committee and Oregon Citizens for Reagan," May 25, 1968, courtesy Central Coast Publishing and *Siuslaw News*.

On *Meet the Press*, candidate Reagan holds his ground against a press onslaught just prior to the Oregon primary, May 26, 1968, courtesy Ronald Reagan Presidential Library.

Robert Hazen, chairman of Reagan's Oregon state campaign, May 26, 1968, courtesy Fred Van Natta.

PETER C. MURPHY, JR.
Lumberman
Eugene, Oregon

I feel the Republicans can move back into the White House in November. We can achieve this by only putting forth our best vote-getter. That man, I believe, is Governor Reagan.

Peter Murphy, director of mid and coastal Citizens for Reagan, May 26, 1968, courtesy Fred Van Natta.

Front page of 8-page newspaper tabloid, created by Reagan Western States Director Fred Van Natta just prior to the primary; the tabloid is distributed as a newspaper supplement throughout Oregon, May 26, 1968, courtesy Fred Van Natta.

State of California
GOVERNOR'S OFFICE
SACRAMENTO 95814

Boyd, Huck

RONALD REAGAN
GOVERNOR

RECEIVED
JUN 19 1968
BOB DOLE

June 17, 1968

The Honorable Robert Dole
House of Representatives
Washington, D. C. 20515

Dear Mr. Dole:

Just a note to confirm that I am planning
to speak at a fund-raising barbeque in
Topeka on June 22. The original arrangements for this were made through your
National Committeeman, Mr. McDill Boyd,
but I wanted you to know personally of
my plans.

Sincerely,

RONALD REAGAN
Governor

Candidate Reagan invites Congressman Robert Dole to a Reagan campaign barbecue in Topeka, which is the oldest known Reagan-Dole correspondence. Letter to Bob Dole from Ronald Reagan, June 16, 1968. VIP Letters Collection, Robert J. Dole Archive and Special Collections, University of Kansas, courtesy Reagan Foundation

"The Baleful Campaigner": Candidate Reagan's most iconic photograph of his entire campaign. Reagan used a farm wagon for a platform and a bale of hay as a lectern, as cowboys watch and listen to the presidential candidate, June 24, 1968. Reagan sent a copy to Henry A. Bubb. courtesy *The Manhattan Mercury* and Kenneth Spencer Research Library, University of Kansas Libraries.

Campaigning in South Carolina, July 3, 1968, courtesy Ronald Reagan Presidential Library.

Reagan communications trailer at Miami Beach convention, August 1968, courtesy Tom Reed.

Nancy Reagan and son Ron Jr. at Miami Beach convention, with CBS reporter Mike Wallace in background, August 1968, courtesy Ronald Reagan Presidential Library.

Governor and Mrs. Reagan amidst their supporters at Miami Beach convention, August 1968, courtesy Ronald Reagan Presidential Library.

Aircraft carrier *U.S.S. Dwight D Eisenhower* as crew forms "IKE." President Reagan looked down upon the ship from his helicopter on the 40th anniversary commemoration of D-Day, June 6, 1984; Reagan shouted, "I like Ike! I Love Ike!" U.S. Navy Archives and Brinkley, Douglas, *The Boys of Pointe du Hoc*.

Official photograph of President Ronald Reagan and his cabinet. Reagan's mentor, President Dwight D. Eisenhower looks on. Reagan, Eisenhower's protégé, completed Eisenhower's vision to decrease nuclear arsenals, to bring freedom to Eastern Europe, to defeat communism, and to maintain a strong American military as a deterrent. Reagan is Eisenhower's political heir. courtesy Ronald Reagan Presidential Library.

PART FOUR

THE MIAMI BEACH CONVENTION

CHAPTER 33: THE PLATFORM COMMITTEE

"Eight years ago there was no missile gap. Today, there is. Eight years ago, our national security was not in danger. Today it is. Eight years ago our land was not torn by riots and insurrection. Today it is…America cannot risk a nuclear Pearl Harbor…The day will surely come when those who are now young will ask us, 'Where were you when America called out for leadership?'"

~ Ronald Reagan[1]

"The only spontaneous display of emotion for a witness throughout four days of public hearings."

~ Chester et. al.[2]

As soon as Reagan had finished his Southern Solicitation and finished his work in Sacramento, he headed to the convention site at Miami Beach early to attend the platform committee hearings. The California delegation would remain at home until Reagan would fly West again to get them in a few days. A new California poll showed Governor Reagan winning reelection in 1970 by twice the margin of his 1966 triumph, with Reagan winning 2:1[3]

Paul Haerle was still appointments secretary in Sacramento but was sent to Miami Beach before any other Reagan campaign staff. His job had been to set up the Reagan headquarters in the Deauville Hotel and garner the requisite number of hotel rooms and turn them into Reagan campaign staff offices. He was also assigned the task of creating an accurate map of Miami Beach, showing exactly where each delegation was staying and when they would arrive in Miami Beach.[4] Reed and White arrived on July 24 and held their first on-site campaign staff meeting on July 29.[5]

Reagan was the first of the prime contenders to arrive in Miami Beach. Despite the changes in his campaign since November, 1966, nevertheless, Ronald Reagan actually arrived in Miami Beach with more popular votes cast (1,696,632) than Nixon (1,679,443). In those primary states where his name had not been on the ballot and in which virtually no effort had been made, except those small Reagan grass root offices discussed earlier, his name was written-in for 0.35 percent in New Hampshire, 1.66 percent in Massachusetts, 3 percent in both Pennsylvania and New Jersey, and 7.2 percent in Illinois. The Reagan vote percentages in the three opt-out states—where he had appeared on the ballot—were finalized as 10.36 percent in Wisconsin, 21.28 percent in Nebraska, and 20.41 percent in Oregon. And of course in California where he had been favorite son, he won and received 100 percent of the delegates.

On Wednesday, July 31, Reed had breakfast with Ron and Nancy Reagan, and the plans for the week were outlined.[6] Reagan then left for the platform committee meeting. Nixon did not appear in person; rather the front-runner had sent the committee a seven-page position paper. Reagan's in-person testimony was on the platform committee's third day of hearings, which were held at the Fountainebleau Hotel's night-club café, the La Ronde Cafe.[7] That hotel served as the convention's executive and communications headquarters. At this time, Reed and White's count had Nixon at 570, still 107 short of victory.[8]

Senator Dirksen was chairman of the Republican Platform Committee. Reagan had written a congratulatory letter to Dirksen on June 28 in regards to Dirksen being selected as chairman.[9] All hope for Reagan to have gotten Dirksen's support had vanished at the June 29 Illinois Republican State Convention, which went for Nixon.[10] In early July, Dirksen had received a letter from the still-active Owosso group. I. Walter Jorgensen, the founder, and Robert M. Smith, the national chairman, of Republicans for Ronald Reagan wrote to Dirksen asking the minority leader to reconsider his support for Nixon. They asked Dirksen to review Reagan's stances on the great issues of the day as well as to remember how Nixon had lost the 1960 debate and election to Kennedy. They ended by stating that if Dirksen would now support Reagan, history would remember him as the "Patrick Henry of our time."[11] There is no record of Dirksen's reply.

After a Dirksen friend similarly had sent a note of approval about Reagan, on July 23 Dirksen wrote a return letter. Dirksen wrote that Reagan handled himself extremely well and that Dirksen fully shared a high opinion of his talent and attainments, but Dirksen remained in Nixon's camp. Of course Dirksen had not endorsed Reagan at the library dedication the prior fall and Reagan had failed to ask Dirksen's support at their private meeting that same evening. Reagan's subsequent visit to Chicago at the behest of Dirksen, and their continuing personal and official correspondence, all indicated that Reagan had succeeded in cultivating what ended up being a warm, personal friendship between himself and the Senator. Unfortunately, it did not translate into political support.

During the summer, Dirksen had received many more constituent letters urging the minority leader to openly support Reagan, and those letters and then telegrams kept pouring in after Dirksen checked in to the Marco Polo Hotel in Miami Beach.[12]

Those who saw Reagan at the platform committee hearing saw that Reagan "roused this normally somnolent body to a display of enthusiasm."[13] Reagan's appearance was described as, "the only spontaneous display of emotion for a witness throughout four days of public hearings."[14] Even the New York Times noted that for the first time in three days of slow-moving hearings, Reagan's appearance "produced the crowds and hectic atmosphere of a political convention."[15]

Reagan told Dirksen and the rest of the committee that it would be presumptuous of him to offer specific suggestions to the committee. Rather, he wanted to address and answer President Johnson's claim of the "unease pervading our land" in the State of the Union address six months earlier. Of course Reagan had addressed this topic masterfully while on the campaign trail, but now he had the eyes and ears of the whole party watching and listening to him give his rebuttal to Johnson. Reagan would not know it, but it was perfect preparation for his future attack upon future President Jimmy Carter's "malaise" speech a decade later.

Citing his prior gubernatorial campaign theme, which had come from Eisenhower, Reagan told the committee that their nominee would "bring our people back together to restore reason and honor and common sense to our land and its highest office." Reagan knew that rebuilding the republic would not be easy, but Republicans "cannot shrink from controversy." The nation was "agitated by suspicion," filled with fear, and was on an aimless course from "lack of leadership." As Reagan had promised over the past 18 months during the campaign, he wanted to reduce federal power, give power back to local government, and emphasized the role of individual responsibility. A President Reagan in 1969 would restore hope to the nation.

Reagan quickly switched away from domestic concerns and gave his listeners his vision of what the world could expect from a President Reagan in 1969. He summarized his prior speeches—from Albany, Oregon to Cleveland and most recently in Amarillo—now as a true statesman on world affairs. For Vietnam, he again emphasized what he would do as president: finally to give to the military the tools to win the war. Reagan knew where he wanted to lead the country, bemoaning that America's "planes are restricted," reminding his listeners that the "Pueblo is abandoned" with 82 men held in captivity, all while America's treasury was being "squandered."

Invoking the administration of his mentor, Reagan compared 1968 to where things stood when Eisenhower had left office: "Eight years ago there was no missile gap. Today, there is. Eight years ago, our national security was not in danger. Today it is. Eight years ago our land was not torn by riots and insurrection. Today it is." The problems created by the Kennedy-Johnson administrations were "not hallmarks of a great society." Statesman Reagan said firmly that it was up to the Republicans to "repair this damage, to renew the spirit and restore the purpose and pride in America." As the next president, Reagan would defend America via his advocacy for an anti-ballistic missile defense shield; he warned that America "cannot risk a nuclear Pearl Harbor."

Then Reagan, citing what later would become his trust-but-verify but originating with Ike's "Open Skies," said that America's next president definitely should discuss treaties to limit weapons, but only if "effective devices of inspection become available." But whether a President Reagan would sign such a treaty would depend upon America's national security.

Reagan ended by warning the committee, "The day will surely come when those who are now young will ask us 'where were you when America called out for leadership?'"[16] Reagan served notice to America's enemies that come January, 1969, they would have to deal with a brand new occupant of the White House.

During the testimony, the audience and even "the committee of jaded party regulars" frequently broke into applause. As Dirksen pounded his gavel to regain order, he smiled. One reporter confirmed the earlier observation that the Republicans' reactions to Reagan's talk had been the only display of emotion through four days of hearings.[17]

Afterwards at a press conference when he was asked whether he would become a full-fledged candidate once his name was placed in nomination, Reagan answered "At that point, you have no choice in the matter."[18]

The national media noted that the position paper that Nixon had sent to the committee, on law and order, clearly was designed to blunt the Reagan drive. Nixon was "losing some conservative support" to Reagan. One interested person who had arrived early at Miami Beach and had watched Reagan's testimony was Harry Dent. He felt that Reagan's appearance was "superb" and he had stirred both the committee and the delegates.[19] The media noted that Reagan had taken a "stand firm, fight-to-win position in Vietnam, referencing President Kennedy, "It is time to tell friend and foe alike, we are in Vietnam because it is in our national interest to be there."[20]

A second visitor to testify about foreign affairs at the platform committee meeting was John Lindsay. Reagan last had dealt with the New York City mayor during the grape boycott earlier in the year. Lindsay wanted the committee to draft a statement exactly opposite to that of Reagan on Vietnam.[21] Despite both being from New York, Lindsay had been under scrutiny by the Nixon team as a possible vice-presidential choice and had a small team in Miami Beach in case a deadlocked convention might turn to him. In the end, Dirksen's final platform committee document indicted Johnson's policy of gradual escalation, thereby validating the forceful criticisms Reagan had been stating for almost two years.[22]

Afterwards on September 9, Dirksen would write Reagan about his appearance at the platform committee. In it, Dirksen would thank Reagan for his "significant contribution" to the thinking and labors of the committee.[23] After he was done at the platform committee hearings, Reagan flew off to visit a few other states, in order to "drop in" on more delegations which were packing for Miami Beach.[24] The latest recall motion against Governor Reagan had gotten some 440,000 votes but not the required 780,000 needed.[25] As Reagan then flew back to Sacramento to prepare his California delegation for the trip East, preparations continued in Miami Beach and delegates started arriving.

Endnotes

1. Reagan, Ronald, "Speech to Platform Committee," 1968 Republican National Convention, courtesy Ronald Reagan Presidential Library
2. Chester et. al., p. 448
3. *Time*, 7/26/68
4. Haerle, pers int 11/22/12
5. Reed, *Reagan Enigma*, p. 168
6. Reed, *Reagan Enigma*, p. 168
7. Witcover, p. 338; Chester et. al., p. 448
8. Reed, p. 27
9. Reagan to Dirksen, letter 6/28/1968, Dirksen Congressional Center, EMD Papers, Alpha 1968, Reagan
10. Janson, Donald, "GOP in Illinois Adds Delegates Leaning to Nixon," *NYT*, 6/30/1968, p. 41
11. Jorgensen, I. Walter and smith, Robert M. to The Honorable Everett M. Dirksen, letter 7/8/68, Dirksen Congressional Center, EMD Papers, Alpha 1968, Reagan
12. Dirksen Congressional Center, EMD Papers, Politics, F. 642
13. Chester et. al., p. 448
14. ibid
15. Finney, John W., "Nixon and Reagan Ask War on Crime," *NYT*, 8/1/68, p. 1
16. Reagan, Ronald, "Speech to Platform Committee," 1968 Republican National Convention, courtesy Ronald Reagan Presidential Library

17. Evans, *The Education of Ronald Reagan*, p. 187
18. Witcover, p. 338
19. Dent, p. 84-85
20. Finney, John W., "Nixon and Reagan Ask War on Crime," *NYT*, 8/1/68, p. 1
21. Chester et. al., p. 452
22. Chester et. al., p. 452
23. Dirksen to Reagan, letter, 9/9/1968, Dirksen Congressional center, EMD Papers, Alpha 1968, Reagan
24. Chester et. al., p. 449
25. Chester et. al., p. 190

> "One of the most fascinating, closely contested convention
> struggles I ever covered."
>
> ~ Robert Novak[1]

Fully 3,000 radio and television reporters covered the convention.[2] For its convention cover, *Life* highlighted Democrat George Wallace as a spoiler, with Reagan and Nixon trying to slow him down.[3] By the end of the convention, seeing middle-road Nixon trying to out do conservative Reagan, the liberal media would be bored to death. *Life* magazine had found the convention to be "wordy and wearisome."[4] *New York Times* drama critic Clive Barnes could not find much drama.[5] Liberal TV anchorman Walter Cronkite of CBS filled in minutes by discussing the cost of balloons. At one point Cronkite, who had observed Reagan back at the 1964 convention, was caught dozing. Cronkite's biographer, historian Douglas Brinkley, reflected that this was not one of Cronkite's best performances.[6] Cronkite then interviewed humorist Art Buchwald. Buchwald, after having lampooned the Reagan-Rockefeller meeting in New Orleans and his prior attack against Reagan's aggressive policy to win in Vietnam, had not commented recently about Reagan.[7] CBS also had Mike Wallace and Dan Rather as floor reporters. Columnist Jimmy Breslin wrote about John Wayne's visit to a bar at the Fountainebleau.[8] Food critic Craig Claiborne critiqued 6 local restaurants.[9]

Amidst the boredom of the liberal reporters, there was some actual political coverage. Johnson hatchet-man columnist Drew Pearson entered the fray with his last anti-Reagan column on August 6. He called conservative Reagan a political "chameleon" and proceeded to attack Reagan and his policies as best he could.[10]

Presidential historian Theodore H. White was there to write his next book. At the time, White wondered why the Young Republicans had failed to gain control of the GOP.[11] Decades after White would write his masterpiece of 1968, conservative reporter Robert Novak would reflect that White had been wrong about the 1968 Republican convention. Whereas White and the rest of the liberal media characterized the whole affair as "dull," Novak thought it had been "one of the most fascinating, closely contested convention struggles I ever covered."[12]

To enliven their third-place ratings, ABC featured debates between William F. Buckley, Jr., still supporting Nixon, and liberal writer Gore Vidal.[13] Vidal's prior 1964 observation of Reagan—seeing Reagan closely observing Eisenhower—may have been the last time Vidal had seen Reagan up close. Buckley had been asked in December, 1967 by ABC television to cover the event.[14] Buckley made it to the convention via Paul Haerle, who had been at Reagan headquarters as an advance-man. Haerle recalled that when he had been on the phone with Buckley a few weeks before the convention, Buckley had asked him for a ticket. Haerle was able to comply, and that is how Buckley went to the convention.[15] Buckley brought along his son, Christopher.

The *Washington Post* had previewed the Buckley-Vidal sparring as a "dream television match."[16] Vidal had used two research assistants to "prepare for his clash" with Buckley, and during the coverage, Vidal and Buckley would trade insults and invective.[17] The Vidal-Buckley verbal fighting would reach epic proportions at the subsequent Democratic convention. In 2015, the Buckley-Vidal debate coverage was the subject of a documentary, *Best of Enemies*, by the debate firm Intelligence Squared.

In Miami Beach, Vidal made no new observations about Reagan and Eisenhower. Vidal described Reagan as a "well-preserved not young man. Close-to, the painted face is webbed with delicate lines while the dyed hair, eyebrows, and eyelashes contrast oddly with the sagging muscle beneath the as-yet unlifted chin, soft earnest of wattle (sp) soon-to-be…Animated, the face is quite attractive and at a distance youthful, particularly engaging is the crooked smile full of large porcelain-capped teeth. The eyes are the only interesting feature: small, narrow, apparently dark, they glitter in hot light, alert to every move, for this is enemy country—the liberal Eastern press."[18]

Decades later, the one 1968 history that people would remember was that of author Norman Mailer. The famous writer and filmmaker had tried his hand at a new endeavor: journalism. Because of his successful prior exploration of the 1967 march on the Pentagon in his Armies of the Dead, he had been hired by *Harper's* magazine to cover both 1968 political conventions. His resultant masterpiece, *Miami and the Siege of Chicago*, would be written hastily within ten days of the later Democratic convention, yet would become an instant hit. Indeed some four decades later, two laudatory reviews would appear in the national press in 2008.[19]

Mailer did spend time with Reagan in Miami Beach and Mailer would devote several pages to his impression of Reagan, but Mailer made no other comments about Reagan. Mailer's biographer has found no additional personal notes about Reagan in Mailer's papers, which are housed at the University of Texas-Austin. Plus Mailer's children were too young at the time to recall any specifics about their father interacting with, or observing, Reagan at the convention.[20]

As the reporters and writers settled in to prepare for their convention coverage, the eyes of the nation turned toward Miami Beach.

Endnotes

1. Novak, p. 165
2. *Newsweek*, 8/19/68, p. 58
3. *Life*, 8/2/1968
4. *Life*, 8/16/1968 p 36
5. *Newsweek*, 8/19/68, p. 60
6. Brinkley, D., personal communication, 5/6/2015
7. *Newsweek*, 8/19/68, p. 58-59
8. *Newsweek*, 8/19/68, p. 60
9. ibid
10. Pearson, Drew, "Washington Merry-Go-Round," 8/6/68
11. *Newsweek*, 8/19/68, p. 59
12. Novak, p. 165
13. ibid
14. Judis, p. 288
15. Haerle, pers int 11/22/12
16. Judis, p. 288
17. Judis, p. 289
18. Vidal, Gore, "The Late Show," *The New York Review of Books*, 9/12/68
19. Rich, Frank, "How to Cover a Convention," *The New York Review of Books*, 5/29/2008; Hitchens, Christopher, "Master of Conventions," *The Atlantic Monthly*, 8/19/2008
20. Lennon, J. Mike, personal communication 9/9/12

CHAPTER 35: THE SIEGE OF RICHARD NIXON

"The real struggle was between Reagan and Nixon...The rank-and-file delegates wanted to bolt to Reagan, depriving Nixon of a nomination he thought was wrapped up."
~ Robert Novak[1]

"There is nothing more impressive than Ronnie Reagan behind closed doors."
~ Harry Dent[2]

Nixon's nomination "was by no means either certain or even easy."
~ William Rusher[3]

So many delegates wanted to vote for Reagan on the second ballot that further declines in Nixon's fortunes would create "larger numbers of votes (which) would undoubtedly go to Mr. Reagan."
~ New York Times[4]

Despite Mailer's title, *Miami and the Siege of Chicago*, although later that summer Chicago was indeed under siege during the violent Democratic convention, at the earlier Republican conclave, it was in fact Richard Nixon who was under siege. Two weeks before the convention, the *New York Times* reminded its readers that of the 1,333 delegates, only a little more than 100—from about six states—were "legally-bound" to vote for Nixon on the first ballot.[5]

Every August in Miami Beach was hazy, hot and humid with likely thunderstorms. In August 1968, the thunderstorms were political. And one person who was going to sweat the approaching political storm clouds would be Richard Nixon. Perhaps not quite the sweat that had formed on his forehead during his televised 1960 debate loss to John F. Kennedy, where his appearance was visible to millions, but Nixon would be uncomfortable all the same.[6]

Liberal author Mark Kurlansky wrote that Reagan "appeared so unelectable" and "was the butt of so many jokes."[7] But Thurmond's camp knew the truth: it was Reagan who could derail Nixon's candidacy. Harry Dent recalled, "Reagan and his people would work all their candidate's charismatic powers to break our ranks."[8]

Erosion

Could Nixon get to the magic number of 667 delegates to win a first ballot victory? CBS's August 2 final count showed Nixon at 644 votes, still 24 short of victory, which agreed with Reed and White's count.[9] But three days later, *Newsweek's* final pre-convention delegate count showed that Reagan had "picked up at least 40 delegates" and was "gaining much more rapidly than Rockefeller." Their tabulation showed Nixon had lost ground, now fully 76 votes shy of a first ballot victory.[10] Nixon recalled in his memoirs that a new catchword began making the rounds in Miami Beach: *erosion.*"[11]

Rusher recalled that Nixon would be strongest on the first ballot, but after that, Nixon's total would shrink "like a scoop of ice cream" in the hot Miami Beach sun.[12] Fearing his own 1967 prediction—that Reagan was his major threat, confirmed by the threats Nixon had felt in Wisconsin, Nebraska and Oregon—was now coming true in front of his eyes, Nixon tried to shore up the bulwarks against further erosion to Reagan. Nixon forced Texas Senator John Tower to relinquish his favorite son status. Nixon "needed first-ballot votes too badly" to allow Tower to remain and deprive him of critical delegates.[13] It was a tactic Nixon would need again, in the final hours of the voting, to stop a first ballot loss and then likely nomination of Reagan.

There never had been even one debate amongst the three major rivals in 1968. Knowing that Reagan had triumphed dramatically at the RFK debate and at virtually all his campaign speeches in 1967-1968, on August 2 Henry A. Bubb, already at the convention, sent a telegram to GOP National Chairman Ray Bliss urging that since there had been no debates, that all three contenders, Reagan, Rockefeller and Nixon, be allowed at least to speak before the balloting got underway.[14] Mailer, filing the same story, added that Bubb did not consult with Reagan before sending the telegram. Mailer did report that Bubb hoped the additional Reagan speech would "dramatically swing delegations and voters behind him."[15] Bubb told the press, "Each man should be given equal and ample time to present his political philosophy and his solutions for the major problems which confront us today."[16] In no way did Nixon want the convention to see Reagan as an equal. The idea was shelved. But Bubb did arrange for Reagan to meet Bubb's own Kansas delegation on Tuesday.

Clif White met privately with Murfin of Florida right before the convention. Excluding Governor Kirk, who was for Rockefeller, that left a Florida delegation of 33. "If I get sixteen of these thirty three, will you make it seventeen?" Murfin answered, "Yes. I'll do that."[17] White next went to Florida delegate Paula Hawkins, asking if White could get fifteen votes, would she as a fellow conservative, become the sixteenth vote for Reagan? She answered, "Yes."[18] It was looking promising that White could flip Florida. If so, the whole South might suddenly switch en masse to Reagan.

But was not Rockefeller in fact the main worry of Nixon? Columnist Robert Novak in his autobiography, reflected that author Theodore White's chapter on Miami Beach had been entitled, "Rockefeller versus Nixon." Yet throughout the convention, Rockefeller had a subdued presence. He did not seem to go out seeking votes energetically; rather he reassured his supporters, "I haven't got any horns."[19] Novak felt that White's analysis clearly had been wrong. Rockefeller "never had a chance. The real struggle was between *Reagan* and Nixon."[20] A major reason was that Novak, as we will see, had major sources throughout the Southern delegations, which White did not have.[21] As we have seen, long before, Nixon had told his supporters in private that the main threat from the beginning was Reagan. Rockefeller was just a minor distraction. Nixon continued fearing that Reagan would grasp the nomination and leave Nixon in the dust.

Did Nixon feel that Reagan and Rockefeller were ganging up? As discussed earlier, Patrick Buchanan maintains that it was in fact Reagan and Nixon who had the secret agreement and that even as late as New Orleans, Reagan had gone out of his way to show Nixon that he and Rockefeller had no secret deal. But Rockefeller had sent his representative to meet Reagan on July 4 and although no official anti-Nixon agreement was formulated, Rockefeller then knew that Reagan planned to stay in the race. Rockefeller then had sent another agent to talk to Clif White. Bruce Bradley, one of Rockefeller's delegate hunters, had forged the agreement with Clif White to share "useful delegate information," and in May in Louisiana, Bradley had been helpful when Reagan forces had strengthened.[22] Thus as best as can be determined, Reagan and Rockefeller never reached a true agreement to stop Nixon.

The August 1 memo from activist David Williams, which, as discussed, had demonstrated Reagan's much superior 1966 coattails versus Rockefeller, was circulating amongst delegates. But in truth, Reagan and Rockefeller needed each other. Neither man would have enough votes individually to stop Nixon. But if Rockefeller got enough votes, the Reagan forces calculated that Reagan's strength would join Rockefeller's tally in stopping Nixon on the first ballot. And from Rockefeller's point of view, he needed Reagan to do well enough too. Reporter Novak observed that by the time Rockefeller had re-entered the race on April 30, it was too late, as he had missed the primaries. The only rationale Rockefeller had to fight against Nixon was the "candidacy of Ronald Reagan creating a convention deadlock."[23] Indeed others observed that Rockefeller's only chance depended upon "the sweet-talking talents of his ideological opposite, Ronald Reagan."[24]

Reagan and Rockefeller thus planned, independently without any formal agreement, to continue to undermine Nixon by continuing to convince delegates committed to Nixon, or those on the fence, to switch their allegiance. Cliff White and Tom Reed on behalf of Reagan, and Rockefeller's team, worked simultaneously and in parallel. Nixon later recalled that Reagan and Rockefeller forces had continued corralling delegates to show them that Nixon's strength was eroding and Nixon was losing delegates.[25]

But although each team shared the common goal of stopping Nixon on the first ballot, few discussed the inevitable Reagan versus Rockefeller showdown to come afterwards, should they succeed with their initial goal. Rusher recalled that in a final battle between Reagan and Rockefeller, once Nixon had been defeated, Cliff White "was serenely confident as to how that would turn out."[26] As noted, Patrick Buchanan felt that even if Nixon had failed to achieve a first ballot victory, the convention would have turned to Nixon anyway. Yet Rockefeller had commissioned a poll pitting Reagan against Humphrey, which purportedly showed a massive Humphrey triumph. It was to be used against Reagan if Nixon were stopped.[27]

As the convention began, Rockefeller's team was estimating that he had about 300 delegates but realized that Rockefeller needed Reagan to get to at least 277 votes in order for Nixon to be stopped on the first ballot.[28] Some historians recorded that Rockefeller's own vote projections had never been higher than 350 and that his basic strength in committed delegates was realistically around 250, centered in the industrial Northeast states.[29]

As Rockefeller staff, delegates and supporters arrived—including Hillary Rodham, Newt Gingrich, Tanya Melich, and Henry Kissinger—columnist Drew Pearson continued to push Rockefeller's candidacy.[30] The Republicans in the rest of the country did not like his policies—advocating big government programs—and could never forgive his refusal to endorse Goldwater four years earlier. Indeed

Kentucky Governor Louie Nunn, whom Reagan had visited during his Southern Solicitation, when asked about Rockefeller strength within his delegation, joked somewhat seriously no doubt, that if any of his delegates voted for Rockefeller, they "wouldn't be allowed off the plane back home."[31]

According to Kissinger biographer Walter Isaacson, Rockefeller's team had gotten fed up with Kissinger's planning of what Rockefeller's new position on Vietnam should be, so they placed Kissinger on a different hotel floor than their candidate. This infuriated Kissinger. Kissinger was sent out, on his first assignment to talk to average politicians, to the Iowa delegation. Kissinger then worked on compromise convention language about Vietnam. During the convention, Kissinger never spoke to Reagan. Kissinger, of course having no knowledge of his future destiny with Nixon or with Reagan, at this point called Nixon "a disaster," a 'hollow man, and evil," and railed against the "shallowness" and "dangerous misunderstanding" of Nixon's foreign policy.[32] Your author attempted to contact Kissinger for his recollections without success.

Rockefeller's only hope lay with Reagan. If Reagan could derail Nixon's delegate strength in the South and create a first ballot deadlock, then Rockefeller thought he "would be in business."[33] As noted, how Rockefeller planned to deal with Reagan on the second or third ballots was never discussed.

The original plan of Reagan, Tom Reed and Cliff White was for Reagan (after his multi-year stealth campaign) to declare his official, open candidacy in Miami Beach at the "latest possible moment."[34] With a first-ballot deadlock between Nixon and Rockefeller, the delegates could then turn to Reagan. But with Rockefeller's withdrawal announcement in March followed by his late April announcement to re-enter the race, too much time had been lost. A strong Rockefeller challenge to Nixon on the first ballot seemed very unlikely. Thus Reagan himself needed the "momentum" of an active and announced candidacy to prevent the Nixon first-ballot victory.[35] Yet if Reagan announced too soon, Nixon could launch counter-measures.

How many ballots did Reagan think it would take to secure the nomination? Historian Geoffrey Kabaservice cites a private interview of Rusher and White by a member of the liberal Republican Ripon Society, in which the plans were that by about the third ballot, Regan would become the nominee and offer the vice-presidency to Percy with Nixon as secretary of state.[36] In Miami Beach, Reagan would do everything possible to appear progressive and moderate.[37] "White and the Reagan team relied on Rockefeller to withhold 400 first-ballot votes from Nixon. Rockefeller more than met that target, with in excess of 250 votes of his own and about 150 favorite-son votes in his column. Reagan had to hold back another 250 votes if Nixon was to be stopped."[38]

It still would depend upon the South and Thurmond. If either Florida or Mississippi were not secured by Nixon, then in those states—which had the unit rule—Nixon "would lose 54 votes."[39] When White asked Thurmond directly why he was supporting Nixon instead of Reagan, Thurmond answered that Rockefeller might be nominated if the South didn't support Nixon. "White protested that the delegates would back Reagan on a second ballot. 'Well you may be right, son,' Thurmond drawled, 'but we just cain't take that chance and let Rockefeller slip in.'"[40]

What was Reagan's delegate strength as the convention opened? On July 31, the *New York Times* reported that Nixon had lost delegate strength in the South to Reagan, indicating some 15 to 20 had abandoned Nixon to join the Reagan bandwagon. Rockefeller's supporters indicated the true number of delegate switches from Nixon to Reagan was 40.[41] The Rockefeller team's prediction to the *New York Times* on August 3 was that Reagan would hit 300 votes.[42] Yet Clif White never thought Reagan's numbers would be that high. Privately White hoped that Reagan might achieve as high as 250 on the first ballot, which when coupled with Rockefeller, would stop Nixon on that first vote. White rarely told anyone else that Reagan would get more than 180.[43] But whereas Rockefeller's meager attempts to get more votes at the convention likely would meet little success because of the antipathy most of the party members outside the Northeast felt towards him, Reagan at the convention "could expect that his proselytizing among the delegations could be converted into concrete votes."[44]

Dent had been spreading the word up to the convention that Reagan should declare his candidacy and had been meeting privately with various delegations at Miami Beach. As he had observed during Reagan's Southern Solicitation, Dent reflected, "There is nothing more impressive than Ronnie Reagan behind closed doors."[45] As comforting as those words might be for a Reagan supporter, Dent, Thurmond and Clarke Reed were about to complete their double-cross of Reagan because they had cast their lots with Richard Nixon.

Was in fact Richard Nixon's nomination inevitable? Many pundits had been prognosticating about Nixon's guaranteed coronation at Miami Beach for virtually all of 1968. Yet in truth, as reported by those in attendance at the time, Nixon's victory "had been anything but effortless. Nor was it inevitable."[46] Rusher reflected that at the time Nixon's nomination "was by no means either certain or even easy."[47] White said that Nixon's Southern delegates were "ripe for harvest," and counted on grabbing one or two "choice" Southern delegations.[48]

Nixon's team's estimates of his vote tally continued to decline. Weeks before Miami Beach, a first-ballot tally of 850 was bandied about, but just before the convention the number had dropped to 700. Privately, Nixon's head counters admitted that even getting to 700 was not guaranteed. Indeed the "achievement of a simple majority was anything but assured."[49] The New York Times reported with so many delegates wanting to vote for Reagan on the second ballot, that further declines in Nixon's fortunes would create "larger numbers of votes (which) would undoubtedly go to Mr. Reagan." [50]

The switches to Reagan were occurring throughout the South. In North Carolina, delegation chairman Representative Jim Gardner, having committed to Reagan, was in the midst of trying to become the delegation's favorite son to deprive Nixon of any of his state's 26 votes. At a minimum, Gardner had pulled another six votes to Reagan and, as discussed, had made North Carolina the only Reagan-majority state. In Texas, former gubernatorial candidate Jack Cox had switched to Reagan and was "actively soliciting after pro-Nixon delegates to join him."[51] Amongst Texas' 56 delegates, several weeks earlier only 12 had been for Reagan. But the Reagan count had increased dramatically to 20, and Cox predicted he could get a total of 24 to 25. If a few more shifted, Texas would be another Reagan-majority delegation. In Alabama, chairman Goldthwaite clearly was pro-Reagan, and Reagan's personal visit had been credited with increasing his delegate count from ten to twelve or more. In 34-delegate Florida, his strength was described as varying from having risen only from eight to nine but other reports showed that it could be as high as 18. White felt he had been given the previously noted promise from State Chairman Murfin: if White could gain support for Reagan from half of the state delegation, Murfin would vote in caucus for Reagan and thus, based upon the unit rule, all votes would go for Reagan. And with Florida's votes announced early in the alphabetical roll call, Nixon's first ballot plans might indeed fall apart quickly.[52] In Mississippi, Reagan was only garnering about five of the 20 delegates. In South Carolina, the delegation seemed split between Reagan and Nixon. The unit-rule seemed to be helping Nixon, yet Reagan's continued gains coupled with Rockefeller's strength in the Northeast could in fact stop Nixon from getting his critical first ballot victory.[53]

For in order for Nixon to be made king, someone needed to be kingmaker. Someone needed to relieve the siege Nixon was experiencing. And Senator Strom Thurmond fit the bill. For "without Thurmond, Nixon would have been in dire trouble; Nixon knew it, Thurmond knew it," and Thurmond "exacted his price for it."[54]

Thurmond and Dent had encouraged the Reagan candidacy from their first meeting in 1967 in Columbia, South Carolina, wherein their private meeting had failed to elicit the fervor of Reagan to be an avowed candidate. If Nixon sailed to the nomination, he had no need for Thurmond. But if Nixon had major competition—if in fact there was the plausibility that Nixon actually might lose to Reagan—then Thurmond could be Nixon's savior and exact his political price.

So Dent had continued to fan the flames of a Reagan candidacy. It was easy for Dent. Indeed Reagan was "adored by the party's rank and file and by many of its chieftains everywhere below the Mason-Dixon line."[55] Besides Dent and Thurmond, other Southerners outwardly had pushed the Reagan candidacy even though they saw Reagan only as a political pawn.

The Greenville Group, as seen earlier comprised of Dent of South Carolina, William Murfin of Florida, and Clarke Reed of Mississippi, had created their "hang loose" strategy prior to the visits of Reagan and Rockefeller to New Orleans and of Nixon to Atlanta. They knew they did not want to go with a loser, and whoever became the nominee "would have to sweat for it."[56] Thus in its determination to "retain bargaining power," having a true Reagan candidacy was an "essential lever."[57] And during the months preceding the election, the members of the Greenville Group were amongst those "most ardently" pushing Reagan to announce publicly his candidacy.[58]

Clarke Reed, who had met Reagan in New Orleans, but who secretly still wanted revenge for the sleight he had felt Reagan had handed him in 1966, was pushing "anyone who might have Reagan's ear," that Reagan should become an open candidate.[59] Like Thurmond and Dent, Reed did not want Nixon to coast to victory. Reed said, "The harder Nixon had to fight, the more the South stood to gain."[60] Thus the entire strategy of Thurmond, Reed, Dent and the other Southern leaders was to exact a political price from Nixon due to the Reagan threat.

But what if Dent and Thurmond's plan backfired? What if the Southern delegates, whose support of Reagan all three had been pushing, actually turned en masse and voted for Reagan on the first round? One group of attendees calculated that the moment Reagan would declare his candidacy, if emotion ruled the delegates, "at least 300 of the South's 334 convention votes" would have gone immediately to Reagan.[61]

And what if neither Reagan nor Nixon won? Reagan indeed might not win on the first round, and if Nixon as well were destroyed by a first ballot loss, there was a reasonable probability that the convention might instead turn to Rockefeller—whom the South hated.[62] The threat of a Rockefeller victory was the rationale Thurmond and the leaders of the Southern delegations used to keep reminding their delegates to vote for Nixon, for they claimed only Nixon could stop Rockefeller.[63]

And on the other hand if Reagan would win the nomination, what could they extract from him? And could he win in November? These possibilities only served to enforce their true preference for Nixon in 1968.

Yet others observed that if indeed Nixon were stopped on that first ballot, the rank-and-file Southern and Western delegates would "risk everything for the man they really wanted, Ronald Reagan."[64] For indeed Reagan's appeal was not limited to one geographic region. Besides having proven himself able to win election in the West, winning the nation's most populous state with an almost million vote margin in 1966, Reagan had accomplished a great deal since then. His appeal was broadening. And his poll numbers in California had remained high. His huge national support amongst students and youth for Reagan never faltered. His support in the West remained high too. Plus one group of historians described that Reagan also had "a reservoir of affection in the North."[65] Reagan had, in a time of uncertainty and frustration, projected a "promise of new directions," just as Kennedy had done in 1960.[66]

As we will see, growing Reagan support during the convention itself would force Nixon into a final session with Thurmond at which point Thurmond, having extracted some concessions from Nixon in Atlanta, would be able to exact his final price. Then despite the prying eyes and ears of some 6,000 reporters, Thurmond would cajole delegates and would win "many of the crucial skirmishes in the caucus battles" that would occur away from the convention floor. In the end, Nixon's final margin—a scarce 25 votes—would be "agonizingly— almost insultingly—small."[67] And at various points during the proceedings, "many more than this number of Nixon votes" would be in jeopardy.[68] And his victory would not occur until the next-to-last state, Wisconsin, would vote. Had a number of the "wavering votes, some of which were dragooned only a few hours before the balloting, stay loose," Nixon's candidacy would have "crumbled with unnerving rapidity."[69]

While Nixon was losing delegate strength to Reagan, Reagan's campaign staff was preparing for their candidate's arrival.

Endnotes

1.   Novak, The Prince of Darkness, p. 165-167
2.   Chester et. al., p. 455
3.   Rusher, p. 231
4.   "15 to 20 Nixon Votes in South Shift to Reagan, Survey Finds," *NYT*, 8/1/68, p. 20
5.   Weaver, Warren Jr., "Delegates: Theirs is the Power," *NYT*, 7/14/68, p. E4
6.   Nixon was ill at the time also.
7.   Kurlansky, p. 265
8.   Dent, p. 84
9.   Reed, p. 27
10.   *Newsweek*, 8/5/68, p. 22
11.   Nixon, p. 309
12.   Rusher, *The Rise of the Right*, p. 213
13.   Chester et. al., p. 444
14.   "Hopefuls Urged to Speak at GOP Convention," *Rocky Mountain News*, 8/3/68
15.   Mailer, Norman, ""Drive by Reagan Gains Momentum," *Baltimore Sun*, 8/3/68
16.   Lastolie, Joe, "Asks Address by Candidates," *Kansas City Times*, 8/3/68, p. 2B
17.   White and Gill, p. 119
18.   White and Gill, p. 120
19.   Chester et. al., p. 454
20.   Novak, p. 165
21.   Novak, p. 167
22.   Chester et. al., p. 441
23.   Novak, p. 165
24.   Chester et. al., p. 454-455
25.   Nixon, p. 309
26.   Rusher, p. 213
27.   *Newsweek*, 8/19/68, p. 14
28.   Rabbe, Will, "Strange Bedfellows: Ronald Reagan and Nelson Rockefeller at the '68 Convention," hppt://willrabbe.com/microblog/2011/2/16/strange-bedfellows-ronald-reagan-nelson-rockefeller.html
29.   Chester et. al., p. 454
30.   Pearson, Drew, "Rockefeller Prediction," Washington Merry-Go-Round, 8/5/1968
31.   Chester et. al., p. 454
32.   Isaacson, p. 126-127
33.   Chester et. al., p. 454
34.   Chester et. al., p. 448
35.   Chester et. al., p. 448
36.   Kabaservice, p. 241
37.   ibid
38.   Kabaservice, p. 242
39.   Kabaservice, p. 242
40.   Kabaservice, p. 242
41.   "15 to 20 Nixon Votes in South Shift to Reagan, Survey Finds," *NYT*, 8/1/68, p. 20
42.   Chester et. al., p. 455
43.   Chester et. al., p. 455
44.   Chester et. al., p. 455
45.   Chester et. al., p. 455
46.   Chester et. al., p. 434
47.   Rusher, p. 231
48.   *Newsweek*, 8/19/68, p. 23
49.   Chester et. al., p. 456-457
50.   "15 to 20 Nixon Votes in South Shift to Reagan, Survey Finds," *NYT*, 8/1/68, p. 20
51.   "15 to 20 Nixon Votes in South Shift to Reagan, Survey Finds," *NYT*, 8/1/68, p. 20
52.   Evans, *The Education of Ronald Reagan*, p. 186
53.   "15 to 20 Nixon Votes in South Shift to Reagan, Survey Finds," *NYT*, 8/1/68, p. 20
54.   Chester et. al., p. 434
55.   Chester et. al., p. 438
56.   Chester et. al., p. 439

57. Chester et. al., p. 439
58. Chester et. al., p. 439
59. Chester et. al., p. 440
60. Chester et. al., p. 440
61. Chester et. al., p. 438
62. Chester et. al., p. 440
63. Chester et. al., p. 457
64. Chester et. al., p. 457
65. Chester et. al., p. 438
66. Lewis, Joseph, p. 204
67. Chester et. al., p. 434
68. Chester et. al., p. 435
69. Chester et. al., p. 435

CHAPTER 36: FUN AND SNOOPING

The security around each candidate was devised "as much to protect them from political spies as from political assassination..."

~ Drew Pearson[1]

The 1968 Republican convention was the first held south of the Mason-Dixon line. The city of Miami Beach had bid $800,000 to host the convention, calculating that with each attendee spending $35.42 per day, the local businesses would do well.[2] Besides the 1,333 delegates, there were alternate delegates, press, families, and campaign staffs—totaling an expected 20,000 people from August 4 to August 9.[3] At the convention, Reagan had a staff of 80, Rockefeller had 200 and Nixon had 300.[4] The Fountainebleau Hotel was the executive and communications center of the convention. In the lobby was a plaque thanking Frank Sinatra for filming a recent movie there.[5]

Newsweek featured a map of Miami Beach showing where the candidates were staying. Superficially, it seemed as if the three major candidates had equal presences. Nixon was at the Hilton Plaza. Reagan was housed at the Deauville Hotel. It was a $2 taxicab ride from Reagan's hotel to convention hall. There was no preference given to parking space allocation at convention hall, with Reagan, Rockefeller, and Nixon each allotted 25 spaces.[6] The delegates could see live elephants in front of them and then look up to see a helium-filled elephant flying above the convention center.

But except for the equality in parking spaces and cab fare, little else would be done equally. Each candidate had different priorities. It was Reagan's team that was in last place in spending at Miami Beach. Nixon had garnered most of the financial support and his campaign coffers were full. Rockefeller had his own private wealth to spend and he did.

The Rockefeller team was stationed at the luxurious Americana Hotel, which advertised "the spiciest, splashiest, stark-nudest review this side of Paris."[7] Among Rockefeller's paid campaign staff was Tanya Melich, former political research director for ABC News.[8] Rockefeller supporter Newt Gingrich[9] had arrived from New Orleans.

Afterwards, Melich would write Gingrich a thank you note, noting that Gingrich's "little New Orleans group was the only really viable Rockefeller Southern support" they had.[10] Another Rockefeller supporter was a young Republican named Hillary Rodham, who had been a 1964 "Goldwater Girl" as mentioned earlier. She had begun her journey to the far political left. At the convention, she would meet Frank Sinatra and share an elevator with John Wayne.[11]

Nixon and Rockefeller did spend lavish sums to continue to woo delegates outside of Convention Hall. Nixon had two men meet each plane of delegates to offer selected delegates private cars to transport them to their hotels. Nixon and Rockefeller had "mounds of literature" in every hotel lobby. The candidates published a four-page daily newspaper and bought "incessant local television spots" to herald their causes.[12] Nixon had "Nixon's Navy", a flotilla of power houseboats of the wealthy along an adjacent waterway where delegates could be entertained and persuaded "in conditions of luxurious repose."[13] "Nixon's Navy" also ferried Nixonites across the inlet to staff cars, avoiding traffic.[14] Rockefeller had the "gaudiest theatrical display of all," a sternwheeler showboat named Biscayne Belle that went up and down Indian Creek with two deckloads of pretty girls, screaming and waving balloons for their candidate while music blasted in the background.[15] But Reagan, unable to compete in luxurious delegate maritime or land transportation spending, had his own secret weapon: The Reaganettes.

The Reaganettes

Nancy Reagan had transformed her 1966 gubernatorial campaign group The Reagan Girls into 1968's *The Reaganettes*. Mrs. Reagan, present at virtually all the initial 1967 Reed-Reagan meetings to plan the delegate hunting and campaign, was seen in much film footage of the convention. She had not traveled with him for virtually any of the weekend presidential campaign speeches during 1967-1968. During the year and-a-half of the campaign, when asked why her husband was so busy every weekend with speeches if he was not campaigning for president, she answered, "Oh, Ronnie just likes to make speeches."[16]

But she had been with him at Yale in late 1967, in the nation's capital in early 1968, with her husband in Illinois and Arizona, and had joined the other candidates' wives at the Republican Women's Conference in May.[17] She had worried greatly for her husband's security after the King and RFK assassinations, the bombing plot against the Reagan home, and the other plots discussed earlier. Yet she arrived in

Miami Beach and enthusiastically organized her *Reaganettes*. At the convention, she attended many women's luncheons, was available to the press, and recited "only scripted, practiced lines" according to one biographer.[18] In 2015, she no longer grants interviews or answers written questions.[19]

The Reaganettes were led by Dolores "Dee" Mastrangelo, a "leggy Miami music teacher." Besides Mastrangelo, there were 18 other "mesh-stockinged, top-hatted, high-heeled" *Reaganettes*.[20] They dressed in "bright red and white cheerleader-style outfits," equipped with pom-poms.[21]

Nixon had the phrase "Nixon's the One!" Reagan had a song. Jimmy Dixon, a songwriter and husband of psychic Jeanne Dixon, and John Philpott, in the music business, composed what became Reagan's convention campaign song to counter Nixon's campaign phrase, "Nixon's the One!" It was *Ronald Reagan, **He** is the One!* The refrain was "Ronald Reagan is the man to lead the GOP/The man to lead us to VICTORY."[22]

Nixon had 36 teen-age dancers.[23] Reagan had groups of enthusiastic young girls and boys outfitted with Reagan caps, "teen-agers with Reagan signs," and Students for Reagan with bullhorns. All "howled and postured" whenever Reagan emerged from his limousine and then quickly went to the next stop on Reagan's itinerary to greet him anew.[24]

The Reaganettes were seen all over. Before Reagan arrived, they stood and waved pompons and spoke to delegates about Reagan.[25] Anytime Reagan arrived, *The Reaganettes* cheered, "Ron, Ron, he's our man. If he can't do it, no one can!"[26] *The Reaganettes* remained an integral part of Reagan's campaign team's plans to greet Reagan wherever he went.[27]

But there was more to advance planning of Reagan's stops than just arranging for *The Reaganettes*. Tom Ellick was a member of YAF and worked with Art Van Court and Curtis Patrick of Reagan's security team—under the overall direction of Tom Reed—to make a series of planned impromptu mini-press conferences. Henry Bubb's volunteers turned a portion of Miami Beach into a "haven of enthusiastic Reagan backers."[28]

SFR joined the fun. David Jones had given Randy Teague, Bruce Weinrod, and the rest of SFR and YAF, a complete Reagan schedule so they could prepare placards and signs to greet Reagan at each campaign stop by creating "spontaneous" pro-Reagan rallies.[29] According to historian Wayne Thorburn, "hundreds" of students showed up wherever Reagan appeared, held "Students for Reagan" signs and handed out Reagan campaign literature.[30] *The Reaganettes* joined in, cheering a supposedly surprised Reagan. After asking Reagan if he would say a few words, then Reagan would "go into his extemporaneous speech." The entire crew—SFR, YAF, *The Reaganettes*, Bubb's group—then would run off to Reagan's planned next stop to meet Reagan again.[31]

Van Natta had a whole collection of Reagan campaign buttons, including "OReagan."[32] Another button, blue, with a flaming torch in the center inscribed "Ron Turns Me On" was seen all over Collins Avenue.[33] But despite the fun, security for Reagan was deadly serious.

Reagan's Security

Reagan had decades-long experience dealing with personal safety and security. In 1945 during a labor dispute, Reagan had been threatened with acid in his face. He went to Warner Brothers Studio and "convinced them to issue him a .32 Smith and Wesson pistol." Historian Marc Eliot felt the story was apocryphal, but Reagan did have a gun and the police guarded Reagan's home.[34] Historian Steven Ross relates that Reagan carried the gun for several months.[35] Then when he was preparing to board a bus with a group of fellow actors to cross a picket line, the bus was fire-bombed.[36] Author Brad Meltzer in 2015 revealed that Reagan would carry a gun while president.

As a politician, he was used to the presence of security guards. Early in his campaign for governor, he had hired former LAPD officer William Friedman to help with security. The night he was inaugurated, the capitol was sealed off with 30 armed state policemen. Two days later in the inaugural parade, a procession of armed police and highway patrolmen were present. When he spoke from the Capitol steps, police were on rooftops. At the inaugural Ball, 50 National Guard troopers were there along with state police.[37]

When in office, Reagan hired Arthur Van Court, a husky former LAPD officer, who always had a gun and was given the title of travel secretary.[38] Other members of Reagan's security detail also carried concealed weapons.[39] Later a new security training program was created in Sacramento by Ed Meese.[40]

The governmental security agencies, convention attendees, and their families all were well aware of the recent assassinations of Robert F. Kennedy and Martin Luther King, Jr., and that of President Kennedy only five years earlier. As noted earlier, in early June after the RFK assassination, Nancy had panicked. Then Reagan got added security when President Johnson had given Reagan Secret

Service protection. Ed Hickey was included in that group and after the convention, he would retire from the Secret Service and join Reagan's staff. In Sacramento in mid June, Reagan received reports that black militants, protesting new gun laws, had entered the city and were going to storm the State Capitol building.[41] When similar rumors about potential violence spread at the convention, Reagan had his suite doors locked.[42] When Reagan had testified to the platform committee, he had entered and left with six secret servicemen.[43]

Edwin Meese was assigned to be coordinator of Reagan's security, and that of the entire California delegation, at Miami Beach because of his military intelligence experience and active military status. He recalled that he worked closely with volunteers from the Los Angeles Police Department and California Sherriff's office at the time to prepare for the details of the trip to Miami Beach. Meese himself was not able to attend because of military reserve duty during that time.[44] One of those LAPD officers was Chuck Ward. Ward was there in uniform in addition to many LAPD police in plain clothes.[45] Van Court was Reagan's primary security chief, but Ward served as a back-up.

As historian Curtis Patrick relates, most of the Reagan security team had given up their personal vacations to come to Miami Beach and manned the un-air conditioned stairways and stairwells during the entire convention. The fire stairs were used because the regular elevators were jammed with press, delegates and tourists and stopped at almost every floor. Many times Reagan's security staff ran up the twelve or fifteen flights.[46] All there were there because of their dedication to Reagan and Reagan's principles.[47]

Miami Beach's chief of police promised to "provide maximum security with minimum visibility."[48] The British reporters who were there observed that the convention hall looked like an "armed camp," with "gun-toting policemen manning its outer defenses—a six-foot high chain-link fence erected specially for the occasion."[49]

There were more security personnel than delegates, as the city's own two-hundred-man force was supplemented by the Florida highway patrol, public safety departments, one hundred Secret Service agents, military intelligence, the FBI, the Bureau of Narcotics, and the U.S. Army (which provided bomb-control experts).[50] There was not enough housing for all the agents, so many were assigned to live on board a ship.

The agents were kept busy. All city manholes were opened. Cuban exiles living in Miami were checked. The teams of agents had combat vests, Mace, signal equipment, and ammunition. Initially, the plans were for each candidate to sleep at a private home, the identities of which were kept secret.[51]

Besides the presence of myriad security forces, an added layer of security was provided at Convention Hall. The Republican Party security personnel had created tickets, badges, and passes to exclude "gate crashers," and no experienced reporter in attendance "could remember a more exasperating setup."[52] Plus convention tickets were coded with numbers on them being changed frequently.[53]

But the security systems were not fool proof. The night before the convention opened, Mailer followed Reagan's group into the hall. Mailer had no ticket, but mustering a look of concern, he went right in unchecked and unchallenged.[54] Randy Teague confirmed that compared to the 21st century, security in fact was minimal. Many times he and other SFR members were just handed badges so they could enter the hall. Instead of the candidate being led quickly from a van to an entrance door as done today, in 1968 Reagan usually was let out of his car a block away from any entrance door, so he could be greeted by those "spontaneous" SFR members and *The Reaganettes*, who cheered him on.[55]

Protection from Political Assassination

The security teams had a hidden purpose beyond that of physically protecting Reagan. The security around each candidate was devised "as much to protect them from political spies as from political assassination." The rival candidates engaged in espionage. They "intercept one another's radio signals, infiltrate one another's caucuses, inspect each other's trash." Nixon's spy network was the most efficient. Reagan's team did not locate his broadcast bands, whereas Nixon had learned that Reagan was broadcasting on seventeen different broadcast bands ranging from 48.56 to 456.650. Nixon's communications center was atop the Hilton Plaza in a converted woman's sauna. Each Nixon staff member had a plastic identification card with coded boxes telling exactly into which rooms that person could enter. Nixon's suite on the 17th floor was completely sealed off and was described as "better guarded than a nuclear laboratory." All campaign waste---notes, typewriter ribbon, carbon paper---was put into special "burn bags" and incinerated each night. Nixon's rooms were checked repeatedly for electronic bugs.[56]

Communications

Despite Nixon's discovery of the Reagan radio frequencies, Reagan's communication center and networks were impressive. The landlines were extensive. At Reagan's hotel, Reagan's team set up an entirely separately wired telephone system from various rooms to the lobby, in which cables were "hanging out the windows from one floor to another" up and down fire stairs, with a commercial switchboard which was trucked in from California. It looked like an airplane cockpit and worked 24 hours a day. As historian Patrick relates, sometimes delegates abused the private phone system, such as calling for ice and were told politely the private phone was not room service.[57] Also at the Deauville, Bob Tarbet, a close Reagan aide, watched as Lyn Nofziger brought a brand-new teletype machine into the Reagan telecommunications center. Tarbet would type out the words that Nofziger would give him for Reagan's first official public announcement that officially he was a candidate for president.[58]

Besides the extensive landlines and teletype, Reagan made use of new wireless technology. Custom-made high-tech Motorola walkie-talkies had been created for a select group of Reagan floor leaders and delegates.[59] They were designed with secret frequencies at Motorola Labs in Illinois, even though the Nixon team learned the details. In addition, cutting edge communications were set up also via Pacific Telephone and Telegraph, Motorola and Lockheed engineers, so that Reagan's people had "the highest technology, quality and capability of anything in the communications field, anywhere."[60] At the Deauville alone, Reagan's team had 54 walkie-talkies.[61] All communications, landline or teletype or wireless, radio or television, were all linked at the convention center at the central brain of the Reagan campaign at the convention: Reagan's central communications command trailer.

Reagan's Command Trailer

Patrick relates he had created a "high-tech communications command center and clandestine rolling field office, planning room, operations and strategy center," which was housed inside a brand-new 45-foot Mayflower moving van semi-trailer. The van was constructed via select members of Lockheed Aircraft's Skunk Works in Burbank, whose role was to create electronic anti-eavesdropping equipment. The trailer had 20 stations for field commanders who had at their disposal the latest in walkie-talkies, radiophones and hard-wired, secured telephones. To protect against Miami Beach's summer sweltering heat and humidity, it had state-of-the-art air conditioning by the Lennox Corp.

The van itself was the ultimate piece of subterfuge. After it was driven 3,000 miles to Miami Beach, it was positioned against the outside of the convention center against a solid concrete wall. The wall had a "movie-set style loading dock painted on the side of the building." This gave the impression to the opposition that Reagan's supposed true trailer would come in as soon as this moving van would finish unloading its cargo. But of course the moving van in fact was the true Reagan communications trailer.[62] As soon as the disguised van arrived next to the painted wall, as all the wireless equipment was being readied for use, Fred Van Natta helped run phone lines to each delegation that was hooked up to the communications trailer.[63]

The whole goal of the electronic command post and its myriad networks was to "locate key Reagan delegates in the swing states and try to hold them to a second ballot vote for Governor Reagan."[64] Reagan's growing delegate strength was the key.

Endnotes

1.   Pearson, Drew, "Washington Merry Go-Round," 8/7/68
2.   Chester et. al., p. 427
3.   Chester et. al., p. 428
4.   Chester et. al., p. 456
5.   Chester et. al., p. 431
6.   *Newsweek*, 7/29/68, p. 22
7.   Chester et. al., p. 431
8.   Kabaservice, p. 113
9.   Gingrich did not return this author's inquiries for his recollections.
10.   Melich, Tanya, letter to Newt Gingrich 8/12/1968, Tanya Melich Collection, University Archives, M.E. Grenander Department of Special Archives and Collections, State University of New York at Albany, Series II-Box 3, Folder 17
11.   Leibovich, Mark, "In the Turmoil of '68, Clinton Found a New Voice," *NYT*, 9/5/2007
12.   O'Neil
13.   Chester et. al., p. 456
14.   Witcover, p. 341
15.   O'Neil, Paul, "A Correspondent's Observations on the Grand Old Proceedings," *Life*, 8/16/68, p. 26
16.   Kelley, p. 172
17.   *Newsweek*, 5/6/1968, p. 64
18.   Kelley, p. 173
19.   Wren Powell, pers comm. 7/3/2013
20.   O'Neil, Paul, "A Correspondent's Observations on the Grand Old Proceedings," *Life*, 8/16/68, p. 26
21.   Patrick ,vol, 1, p. 44
22.   Dawson, Wainwright Jr. Reagan Campaign Music
23.   Mailer, p. 30
24.   O'Neil, Paul, "A Correspondent's Observations on the Grand Old Proceedings," *Life*, 8/16/68, p. 26
25.   O'Neil, Paul, "A Correspondent's Observations on the Grand Old Proceedings," *Life*, 8/16/68, p. 26
26.   *Newsweek*, 8/19/68, p. 23
27.   Patrick, vol. 1, p. 44

28. O'Connor Mike, "Millionaire Boosts Reagan Candidacy," unnamed newspaper article, Henry A Bubb Collection, University of Kansas Library
29. Teague, pers int 12/27/12
30. Thorburn, p. 167-168
31. Patrick, Curtis vol. 1, p. 43-44
32. See Illustrations
33. *Newsweek*, 8/5/1968, p. 19
34. Eliot, Marc, p. 188-189
35. Ross, p. 147
36. Boyarsky, *The Rise of Ronald Reagan*, p. 81
37. Boyarsky, *The Rise of Ronald Reagan*, p. 16
38. Boyarsky, *The Rise of Ronald Reagan*, p. 15
39. Patrick, vol. 1, p. 39-40
40. Patrick, vol. 1, p. 24
41. Pearson, Drew, "Washington Merry Go-Round," 6/10/68
42. Boyarsky, p. 15
43. Vidal, Gore, "The Late Show," *The New York Review of Books*, 9/12/68
44. Meese, pers int 1/3/13
45. Patrick, vol. 1, p. 273
46. Patrick, vol. 1, p. 241
47. Patrick, vol. 1, p. 240
48. Chester et. al., p. 431
49. Chester et. al., p. 431
50. Chester et. al., p. 431-432
51. Pearson, Drew, "Washington Merry-Go-Round," 8/3/68
52. Chester et. al., p. 432
53. Pearson, op. cit.
54. Mailer, p. 31-2
55. Teague pers int 12/27/2012
56. Pearson, Drew, "Washington Merry Go-Round," 8/7/68
57. Patrick, vol. 1, p. 240-241
58. Patrick, vol. 1, p. 239
59. Patrick, vol. 1, p. 241
60. Patrick, vol. 1, p 241
61. Pearson, Drew, "Washington Merry Go-Round," 8/5/68
62. Patrick op.cit.
63. Van Natta, pers comm. 6/16/2012
64. Patrick, vol. 1, p. 308

An "investment in Reagan's future."

~ Randall Teague[1]

Before the hordes of delegates and media descended upon Miami Beach, much preparatory work had been done by members of Reagan's campaign team, besides those who had been there early for security or communications.

Henry A. Bubb flew in early from Kansas. With help from his team headquartered at his Reagan information center, which had grown to some 600 volunteers by that point, he started arranging meetings for Reagan and targeted delegates.[2] Bubb and Kerwitz arrived with other Topekan grass roots activists and opened their Citizens for Reagan headquarters at the Deauville. Many wore "Ron Turns Me On" campaign buttons. They rented an entire ballroom on the hotel's main floor. Bubb told the press that already Reagan had been booked for twenty-one press interviews that day alone.[3]

Randy Teague, Bruce Weinrod and fellow SFR members also arrived about a week early, accompanied by hundreds of additional members of YAF.[4] Weinrod recalled that some 200-350 total SFR members were in Miami Beach. SFR and YAF comprised a significant presence at the convention, of Reagan youth, and they participated in the airport and hotel rallies.[5] Every delegate and alternate was given a free copy of the Reagan biography in which Weinrod had been the chief researcher.[6]

There had been a joint "On to Miami Committee" headed by SFR Co-Chairman Michael Thompson and YAF Executive Director David Jones, the latter of course having been present at most of Weinrod's SFR activities during the prior six months. Teague recalled that Jones was a perfect choice to be in charge of all SFR and YAF activities at the convention, due to his attention to detail and prior close ties with White and Rusher.[7]

Ron Docksai had gathered his New York SFR group and came down on Edison's train. Docksai was looking forward to meeting Weinrod and his fabled record collection.[8] Meanwhile Shawn Steel flew in from California, as did Pat Nolan. Nolan flew east on his first airplane trip. Each morning, Nolan reported to YAF headquarters for his assignment: picking up delegates at the airport or handing out flyers. On one occasion on a Reagan bus, Nolan sat with William F. Buckley Jr.'s son, Chris, as they visited the Texas delegation. Nolan met two pretty Rockefeller Girls, models hired by their campaign. But they actually were for Reagan. So Nolan convinced them to spend the week campaigning for Reagan.[9] Dana Rohrabacher departed Czechoslavakia[10] to attend the convention. Matt Lawson had graduated Hamilton College and had moved to California. Lawson volunteered for SFR and carried a number of Reagan's campaign materials to the California delegation.[11] Bruce Schadler recalled seeing a "Veterans for Reagan" bus around Miami Beach.[12]

Teague recalled being kept so busy that he got virtually no sleep from Monday through Thursday; because of lack of sleep, at a planned post-convention deep sea fishing trip, for the first time in his life he would get seasick and demand that the captain turn the boat around. Teague recalled that although almost everyone at SFR assumed that Nixon would get the nomination, they all believed in Reagan and gave him their all, because they saw their role at Miami Beach as an "investment in Reagan's future."[13]

SFR and YAF members held a meeting of the national board of directors. Of course SFR was for Reagan 100 percent. But YAF was not far behind. Fully nineteen of YAF's twenty-one directors endorsed Reagan. The young saw and acted when their GOP elders and delegates could not.[14]

Rusher visited delegations that Nixon had kept in line, trying to counter with the reasons that those delegates should vote for Reagan.[15] Others from Sacramento came, including William Clarke, Mike Deaver, and of course, Nofziger, White and Reed, who had arrived earlier.

Then the rest of Reagan's grass roots activists from across the country arrived. The Oregon delegation was led by Senator Hatfield and was legally bound to Nixon. The Oregon delegates "seemed willing to accept Nixon with grace if not enthusiasm."[16] In the group was Don Hodel, having been asked by Bob Hazen to be an alternate. Peter Murphy also came as an alternate; a Nixon delegate who had seen Murphy's enthusiasm for Reagan during the primary campaign had asked Murphy to be an alternate. He remembered being greeted by *The Reaganettes* at the airport.[17] He knew both Governor McCall and Senator Hatfield, and Murphy chatted with them frequently during the proceedings. They all were seated behind the South Carolina delegation. At the convention meetings, although everyone else was for Nixon—who had won the Oregon primary—Murphy recalls he was "encouraged" to hold up a Reagan sign, especially when his name was placed in nomination and was seconded.[18]

Fred Van Natta had been there for almost two weeks, helping with delegate counts and telephone wiring. Van Natta flew in with a group of Young Republicans from Lane County.[19] Bob Hazen came, still cheering and working for Reagan despite the warnings of *The Oregonian*. Morton Blackwell arrived as at-large delegate from Louisiana, along with the rest of his Reagan delegates, and the second ballot commitments he had obtained from many of the rest.

Not all of Reagan's Oregon staff came to the convention. Watching from their home near Portland with a friend, Sally and Bob Gram recalled seeing Senator Hatfield wearing a white linen suit. Her friend remarked that if the senator were nominated to be vice-president, he'd have to "come home and change his clothes!"[20] During the day and evening of Reagan's nomination and the vote, the O'Scannlains and the Pearlmans joined the Grams. It is not known if the feuding Funk brothers in Florence, Oregon, watched on separate televisions.

From Washington State, where the Reagan delegates from the three conservative counties had been excluded and who had decided to toss in the towel, Ken Rogstad came, along with the liberal slate of delegates headed by Governor Dan Evans. Evans was preparing for his keynote address. He knew that Nixon was considering him for vice-president but he still wanted Rockefeller.[21]

From North Carolina, Jim Gardner arrived with his unique but solitary Reagan-majority delegation. Back in Wisconsin, Don L. Taylor watched the proceedings, sitting with his leg in a cast while nursing his scalp injury and comforted his injured daughter. William H. Thompson, one of the three Reagan chairmen from Nebraska, attended. Ronald B. Dear came with group of fifteen Reagan delegates from Texas. Historian Wayne Thorburn tells the story of delegate Harold Herring. Herring later would become instrumental in arranging the first private meeting of Reagan and Jesse Helms, which would become critical to Reagan's 1976 campaign.[22] The California delegation planned a large reception for the Reagan's at the Deauville, to honor the Reagan's with speeches, music, cheers and tears.[23] The months and years of hard work that these grass roots Reagan activists had accomplished now was to see, hopefully, the nomination of Ronald Reagan.

Endnotes

1.   Teague, pers int 12/27/12
2.   O'Connor, Michael, "Millionaire Boosts Reagan candidacy," anonymous and undated newspaper article, Henry A Bubb Collection, University of Kansas
3.   "Bubb Pins Reagan Hope on Late Ballot," anonymous and undated newspaper article, Henry A Bubb Collection, University of Kansas
4.   Teague, pers int 12/27/12
5.   Weinrod, pers int 5/21/2013
6.   Perlstein, p 296
7.   Teague, pers int 12/27/12
8.   Docksai, pers comm
9.   Nolan, Pat, pers int 5/18/2013
10. Shortly after the convention ended, the Soviets would invade.
11. Lawson, pers int 1/28/13
12. Schadler, pers int 5/21/2013
13. Teague, pers int 12/27/12
14. Rusher and Morrow, p. 216
15. White and Gill, p. 121
16. Allman op.cit.
17. Murphy, pers int 8/16/12
18. Peter Murphy, pers int 8/16/12
19. Van Natta, pers int 7/30/2012
20. Gram, pers int 7/30/2012
21. Chester, p. 454
22. Thorburn, p. 169
23. Patrick, vol. 1, p. 45

CHAPTER 38: THE 57 HOUR CANDIDATE

"Gosh, I was surprised. It all came out of the clear blue sky."

~ Ronald Reagan[1]

"I was the most surprised person in the world when it happened."

~ Nancy Reagan[2]

"It's a new ball game. The bases are loaded; Reagan is at bat, and he's a darned good hitter."

~ Henry A. Bubb[3]

"The lightning struck. I have been in politics for I don't know how many years, and I have never seen anything like it."

~ Harry Dent[4]

"There was no question that rank-and-file delegates wanted to bolt to Reagan, depriving Nixon of a nomination he thought was wrapped up."

~ Robert Novak[5]

"Ronald Reagan, if he were in the White House might suddenly in the face of great national challenge rise to it just like Lincoln did, because there *is* some steel in the fellow."

~ Everett Dirksen[6]

Reagan's support in the Florida delegation "almost changed the course of American history by flipping it to Reagan under the winner-take-all unit rule."

~ Robert Novak[7]

Reagan hit the sands of Miami Beach running. But back in South Carolina and then in the nation's capital, Senator Thurmond was busy making phone calls and sending telegrams to Southern delegates, saying what a great candidate Nixon would be. Goldwater and Nixon himself did the same.[8] Thurmond, Dent, Nixon and their allies and teams were taking "no chances" on Reagan's magic[9] Thurmond was scaring the Reagan-leaning delegates, telling them that any vote for Reagan would in reality be a vote for Rockefeller: if Nixon did not prevail on the first ballot, the convention supposedly would turn to Rockefeller.

White recalled that in Miami Beach, "No one worked harder than Ronald Reagan."[10] And there was much work to do. The Reagan's joined Reed and several financial backers at a lavish dinner on the waterways of Miami Beach on Friday evening, August 2.[11] All their hard work for the past 18 months hopefully was coming to fruition.

Saturday, August 3

A *New York Times* story appeared, headlined, "Rockefeller Aides Fear Reagan is Gaining Ground." The inside information was supplied by Rockefeller's floor manager. Yet as discussed earlier, Rockefeller needed Reagan to be gaining strength to stop a Nixon first ballot triumph.[12]

After his final Sacramento meetings cajoling out-of-town delegates, Reagan gathered his delegation in California and flew back east to Miami Beach. Reagan's campaign team was prepared for their hero's arrival. Rally invitations had gone out announcing Reagan's arrival at 8:30 PM at the far end of concourse 1 at Miami International Airport. A Dixieland band began the festivities. One California aide, Sal Russo, had bused in a "truckload of people" onto the tarmac.[13] After a brief Reagan speech, it was off to the hotel on Miami Beach.

SFR and Youth for Reagan members, along with YAF supporters, greeted Reagan when he arrived at the Deauville Hotel, and Reagan spent twenty minutes meeting his young supporters.[14] On a television interview, Reagan said firmly he disagreed with George Wallace's stances on issues.[15] Then Reagan went immediately to a series of "by invitation" meetings with delegates arranged by Van Natta.

After a caucus with the California delegation, one Reagan aide said that between 200 and 300 delegates would vote for Reagan on the first ballot, and Deputy Chairman William French Smith told the press that his delegates were holding firm for their favorite son, Reagan, with "absolutely no" defections.[16]

Governor Nunn spoke to a Reagan contact, telling him that although on the first ballot, his Kentucky delegates were committed to Nixon fully 22 of 24 initially, on a second ballot, the delegation would switch immediately to Reagan.[17] In Texas, 41 were for Nixon and 15 for Reagan, but if there were a second ballot, it would reverse at 41 for Reagan and only 15 for Nixon.[18] Nixon's support was paper thin—was it enough for a first ballot victory? And with enough effort over the remaining days, could Reagan gather enough momentum to stop him?

Sunday, August 4

In their final pre-convention analysis, the *New York Times* included Reagan along with Nixon and Rockefeller as the three major candidates about whom the delegates were wondering and analyzing in terms of who best could solve the nation's problems.[19]

Southern delegates met with Nixon's representative, John Mitchell, who assured them that Nixon would not split his ticket by having a liberal vice-president. But rumors swirled around convention hall that they were about to be double-crossed on this critical point by Nixon.[20] Dent recalled that at Miami Beach he was "picking up the distressing, disruptive rumors…that Nixon was indeed going to balance the ticket."[21] To the Southerners, this meant any of the liberals: Rockefeller, Percy, Hatfield, or Lindsay. The rumors "unnerved" Dent throughout the convention, as delegates repeatedly asked him and Thurmond, "Yeah, but how can you trust Tricky Dick?"[22]

The Reagan's hosted a brunch buffet for the California delegation in Reagan's "towering suite." Former Senator William Knowland proposed that Reagan formally announce his candidacy in "response to a delegation draft," which Knowland would create the next day.[23] Reagan agreed and headed out to meet Thurmond's delegation.[24]

Pat Nolan and his two former Rockefeller Girls were at the hotel of the South Carolina delegation, just as Reagan was to arrive. A Reagan rally was underway and the enthusiasm was strong. As soon as Reagan arrived, he commanded the attention of all. Reagan looked relaxed, tan in his cream colored jacket. Reagan's handsome smile twinkled as he greeted close-by supporters and waved to the throng. Senator Thurmond greeted Reagan. Nolan recalled that one could not tell from Thurmond's "glowing" comments about Reagan that he had been for Nixon. When Reagan took the podium, the crowd shouted, "Reagan! Reagan! Reagan!" The cheers rolled on and on. As the applause continued for several minutes, Reagan's smile grew bigger. Nolan looked over the crowd as Reagan then spoke to gauge their reaction. Nolan saw them "hanging on every word," with their enthusiasm increasing. Reagan was winning them over as the crowd nodded and burst into spontaneous applause. Nolan reflected that many politicians usually leave their audiences yearning for the end of the speech. But not so with Reagan: he left them begging to hear more.[25]

But Nolan did in fact concentrate on what Reagan was saying. Nolan wrote down his thoughts in his notebook. Reagan told the crowd that in the White House, everything he would do would be done as if he were not seeking reelection, and he would pick a running mate of the same conservative political philosophy."[26] Nolan was thrilled.

That day, the South Carolina delegation met with a vocal minority standing firm for Reagan. Slowly, the Reagan group gave way. But Jim Edwards, one of the last Reagan holdouts and outfitted with a Reagan walkie-talkie, finally gave in when the delegation decided they would support Reagan on the second ballot "regardless of Nixon's position at that time."[27] Nixon's support remained paper thin and was almost non-existent beyond that first ballot. Then a formal meeting of the South Carolina delegation was held with the press invited. Reagan's representative was Robert Walker, Southern States Director. Walker asked the delegation to return to an uncommitted position until Reagan arrived, but the delegation decided to nominate Thurmond as favorite son, have him withdraw, and then give all 22 votes to Nixon.[28]

Reagan visited delegations of Alabama, Georgia, Montana, Mississippi, Utah and Wyoming. The Reagan forces were "pushing an all-out attack to pry, convert, cozen, and steal Southern delegates from Nixon."[29] His pitch to the delegates was "brilliantly seductive," where he told the delegates that he hoped they would get the chance to vote for a second, third, or even a fourth ballot: enough for "an open convention, so that all views get a chance to be expressed."[30] This is exactly what Reagan had been telling reporters at his press conferences since early 1967.

Alabama, Georgia and Mississippi were Nixon's weakest states, recalled Dent.[31] Alfred Goldthwaite, the Alabama chairman, clearly still favored Reagan and thus Dent, on behalf of Nixon, was "resigned to taking the hindmost part."[32] Although in Mississippi and Georgia, Nixon and Dent had the loyalty of the delegation leaders, yet Dent was concerned about the growing Reagan minority factions. The pro-Reagan delegates were "doing all they could" to undermine the prior support for Nixon their leaders, such as Clark of Mississippi, had established.[33] Finally in the South, Louisiana turned to Reagan. Fully seven of the 26 delegates were in the Reagan camp.[34]

But Utah provided the major setback that day. After having seemingly achieved an almost unanimous level of support previously in July as seen, which would have made Utah the second state—after North Carolina—with a Reagan-majority delegation, they decided at the last minute to go with their original plans and declared for fellow-Mormon George Romney as a less controversial choice.[35]

Nixon's men encouraged dissent within the California delegation, so Reagan knew he had to "get them in line behind something formal, even if this meant declaring earlier than intended."[36]

At 1 PM, ABC News broadcast *Issues and Answers*, featuring Senator Dirksen and Governor Evans of Washington. When asked if the Illinois delegation would produce two votes for Reagan, Dirksen agreed. When asked what likely would happen if Nixon did not achieve a first ballot victory, Dirksen felt the delegates would turn to Reagan rather than Rockefeller: "There is a reservoir of prospects for Ronald Reagan, no less, and he would gain in the number of votes beyond the first ballot because I have noticed the appeal that he has and that manifests itself…Reagan has made an impression throughout the country."

Then when asked if Reagan had the experience to become president, a question the program would not ask of the Democratic nominee in 2008, Dirksen made the analogy of Lincoln—a one-term congressman and country attorney—to Reagan, a sitting governor with major achievements. When reporter Bill Lawrence tried to change subjects, Dirksen objected, "No, we have to button this up…Ronald Reagan, if he were in the White House might suddenly in the face of great national challenge rise to it just like Lincoln did, because there is some steel in the fellow…Who knows what name will come out of the convention and I want to be proud of any names that come out of there." Dirksen, at long last and not in the manner initially hoped, gave his public support for Reagan, but only as a second choice.

When next Governor Dan Evans was asked if the real threat to Nixon was Governor Reagan, rather than his own candidate, Rockefeller, Evans answered, "I think in stopping Mr. Nixon, yes… The big difference is how much strength Governor Reagan really will have on the first ballot…If he has 260 or 270 votes, then I think it might very well be an open convention." When asked if Reagan would pick up votes as the convention went along, Evans answered, "Yes." When asked if Reagan had appeal to siphon off votes that might go to Wallace in the general election, Evans answered, "There are many other border states in some of the South that Governor Reagan might very well carry." In closing, Evans predicted that the convention would go to a second ballot and at that point the favorite sons would step aside, allowing the delegations the freedom to vote for someone new. He thought that indeed Reagan could beat Nixon. Evans concluded by stating that whoever was the nominee, he would do everything he could to help win the fall election.[37]

Just after the ABC telecast ended, Nancy Reagan was to have a press conference at 2:30 PM but apparently nobody told her, so she did not appear.[38] The next major television interview show again featured Reagan. White had persuaded Reagan to appear on CBS's *Face the Nation*.[39] Reporter Novak was one of the panelists along with Martin Agronsky and Bill Stout. It was filmed at the Fontainebleau Hotel.

Novak asked Reagan if he felt he were qualified to be president, and Reagan answered that it was up to the delegates and people to decide. Novak suggested that a dream-ticket was Nixon-Reagan and asked if Reagan would accept the vice-presidency. Reagan answered, "I would turn it down from anyone."[40] Novak recalled further details of the program in his autobiography:

Novak: How do you square the fact that you have not and say you're not going to announce for President, and yet you have a highly competent, highly professional staff working out of your hotel here in Miami Beach on a full-scale delegate basis?

Reagan: "Once I'm placed in nomination, I am a candidate, if the delegates choose to consider me along with those who have been campaigning, this they are free to do."[41]

Novak reflected that Reagan had "just become a candidate for President, employing the tortuous formula laid out for me by Clif White" so long ago in the late fall of 1966. Novak reflected that Nixon's southern flank was about to become "unhinged."[42]

World affairs occupied a good portion of the questions. Reagan again invoked Eisenhower's prior advice about Vietnam. Reagan made it clear that he planned to use threats against North Vietnam to get them to bargain faithfully at the negotiation table. Those threats did indeed include the mining of Haiphong Harbor and an invasion.

Reagan disagreed sharply as to the manner in which the administration's military escalation had been undertaken. It took two full years which had had allowed the enemy to adjust. Reagan said if they had listened to him earlier, when he had pushed for a sudden escalation—his surge—that the war might have been over.

Reagan was aghast that Johnson's chief American negotiator had taken a year lease on his Paris apartment. Reagan wanted the North Vietnamese to be faced with an American team that demanded quick resolution or they would escalate the war to win. Reagan cited his 25 years experience as a negotiator for the Screen Actors Guild. Reagan knew how to threaten and how to negotiate. Also he was mortified that the American military had laid out their plans openly, so that the enemy had known exactly what was headed their way. For Reagan, this was no way to run a war and was no way to deal with communists.[43]

After the interview, it was Eisenhower's turn to address the convention. During the summer while he was at Walter Reed Army Hospital, Eisenhower kept current on national political developments as the convention approached. After endorsing Nixon, on July 29, Eisenhower met Senator Mark Hatfield, but Eisenhower recorded no comments about the visit in his diary.[44]

But Eisenhower also kept current on what was happening in Vietnam. On July 21, General Goodpaster called him directly from Saigon.[45] Three days later, Ike was visited by Admiral Strauss,[46] on July 26 by General Milton Baker,[47] and on July 30 by Admiral Aurand.[48] Then just as the convention was starting, President Johnson visited on August 2,[49] followed by Tom Dewey two days later.[50]

Eisenhower addressed the GOP convention via closed circuit television from the hospital. After his famous Farewell Address on the military-industrial complex seven years earlier, he did not address any domestic policy or national political issues. This was to be ill Eisenhower's final farewell to his party and possibly to the nation. Ike's last speech deserves further reassessment by historians. His theme was "Communist Danger," and he warned the nation and his party not to fall back complacently and not to accomodate communism's "expansionist tyranny."[51]

Was Eisenhower concerned that Nixon and Rockefeller were too soft on communism, especially since only Reagan wanted to fight and win in Vietnam? Was Eisenhower subtlely telling the delegates to think very carefully about whom to nominate, and only to nominate a candidate who would fight communism to win? Was this farewell Eisenhower speech in fact a follow-up of his January "golf buddy" interview? By being forced in July, by Nixon's request and the engagement of Julie and David, to endorse Nixon, was it his only way to send the message to the nation a second time that Reagan was his preferred choice? It certainly seemed that way from the general's theme and warning. It was almost as if Eisenhower could envision

Nixon's future détente and wanted to push the convention to select his protégé, Ronald Reagan, as the commander-in-chief who would carry forth Ike's prior recommendations to defeat communism via both a growing economy and a strong military.

What Reagan thought about what Eisenhower was saying, watching and hearing his mentor for what would turn out to be the last time, is not known. But as Reagan had been doing since his first mentoring by Ike back in 1965, eventually as president, Reagan would reverse accommodative détente and eventually win the Cold War peacefully. Of the presidents to sit in the White House after Ike, only Ronald Reagan would be able to follow through on Eisenhower's advice to the letter.

The next day Eisenhower would suffer his seventh heart attack, with subsequent ventricular fibrillations fourteen separate times, requiring multiple cardiopulmonary resuscitations. Miraculously, Eisenhower would recover with his mind intact.[52]

Columnist Hugh Sidey penned a tribute to Eisenhower and his convention address. "While all the candidates from Reagan to McCarthy diagnosed in detail the nation's ailments, Ike maintained a hearty belief that it was a fever, and the body was fundamentally sound." Sidey wondered, "Why all the would-be Presidents (and President) who have been frantically searching for some formula to catapult them to the heights of popularity have failed to study the example of Eisenhower."[53]

But Sidey was wrong. Ronald Reagan, mentored by Eisenhower since 1965, truly became Eisenhower's protege in the 1960s. How Reagan would continue the legacy of his mentor will be seen later. Meanwhile the delegates went back to their hotel rooms to prepare for the official start of the convention.

DAY 1, Monday August 5: Reagan Announces and Thurmond Becomes Kingmaker

That first convention day was to be the "day of Nixon's greatest danger," noted *Newsweek*.[54] As the delegates opened their *New York Times*, they read a front-page story that Nixon would choose one of three liberals as his running mate: Rockefeller, Lindsay or Percy.[55] Nixon press aide herb Klein had been the source of the story, when he had been asked about Nixon's choice for vice-president. Hoping to appeal to liberal, Northern delegates, he mentioned only one name: Oregon Senator Mark Hatfield.[56] Thurmond grabbed a copy of the paper and kept it in order to show Nixon upon Nixon's arrival later in the day. The *New York Times* story went through the convention "like wildfire."[57]

One of the final messages that Jim Gardner of North Carolina, who, as noted, already had delivered his delegation to Reagan, told the governor prior to the convention was that unless he declared himself an open candidate, not much could be done.[58] In the California delegation, there were the stirrings of rebellion such that Reagan was told he would have to declare himself.[59] Senator William Knowland called a caucus of the California delegation to mull over what they expected from Reagan.

Reagan arrived for the opening session a few minutes late, just as the invocation and other opening ceremonies were happening, and joined the California delegation at the center of the hall near the front.[60]

Western actor John Wayne, a conservative but a Nixon supporter and whose movie *The Green Berets* just had opened, spoke the first morning and brought up Vietnam, telling the delegates that he wanted his daughter to be proud of his country's fighting men. The delegates cheered enthusiastically.[61]

That morning, Clif White stood outside the Reagan trailer in the broiling August sun, reporting that the Reagan effort was "nibbling away, but we still need one state—one visible switch to Reagan. I need one break—just one break and we've got him....I'm within a few votes of getting a majority in at least two states, but I don't have it yet."[62] [63]

Historian Theodore White visited Clif White at Reagan's seventeenth floor official command headquarters at the Deauville. The historian did not know that the real action was in Reagan's command trailer. Clif was frustrated with delegate loyalty to Nixon on the first ballot, even though their hearts were with Reagan, telling the historian, "I've got to drag people across the line but they've made these half-baked commitments to Nixon, and they wriggle and wriggle and they can't get off."[64] One delegate from Louisiana had just visited Reagan headquarters. There were "tears in his eyes," but he could not get out of his first ballot obligation to Nixon.[65]

As White chatted with reporters hoping for a political miracle, Reagan met with Ohio Governor James Rhodes. Reagan "clearly looked on Rhodes as a friend."[66] Rhodes remained Reagan's choice for vice-president, after the decision made by Reagan a few days earlier during the National Governors Association meeting in Cincinnati, as mentioned.[67] Reagan clearly wanted a vice president of his own conservative philosophy.[68] Likely Reagan recalled Eisenhower's thinking, expressed about the possibility of a Rockefeller-Reagan ticket, that such an alliance of political opposites was ridiculous.

Yet others felt Rhodes was waiting for the convention to turn to him to become its nominee.[69] On the other hand, the Greenville Group felt he was a Rockefeller supporter and that at this Monday morning meeting, Rhodes had convinced Reagan to declare openly for the presidency that same day, in order to generate excitement to conceal the fact that Rockefeller's campaign had "stalled badly."[70] William French Smith similarly felt that Rhodes was for Rockefeller and in urging Reagan to declare, Rhodes hoped to split the conservative vote and thus benefitting Rockefeller.[71]

Meanwhile Nevada decided to give Reagan a first-ballot "courtesy vote," and more votes in the Mountain States were edging towards Reagan.[72] That day, Reagan was to meet with the delegations from West Virginia, North Dakota, Hawaii, Alaska, Kansas, Nebraska, Iowa, Minnesota and Idaho.

One of the Yale undergraduates who had interviewed Reagan the prior December during Reagan's Chubb Fellowship, Tony Dolan, interviewed Reagan at the Eden Roc Hotel. Historian John Judis revealed that Dolan predicted that Reagan would "win the nomination and the election and create a Roosevelt-like change in the country."[73] Dolan's prediction would turn out to be correct—but twelve years too early.

At his suite at the Deauville Hotel, Reagan lunched with the Greenville Group. Also present was Reagan-supporter Alfred Goldthwaite of Alabama, the only Reagan-committed Southern Chairman besides Jim Gardner.[74] Dent tried to talk Reagan out of his candidacy, feeling that they "liked him more than Nixon and did not want to see him hurt."[75] Reagan asked the group if he should announce as a candidate. Dent spoke, saying they felt his main weakness was his ability to win in November, coupled with Thurmond's having given his word to Nixon.[76] Reagan revealed to them that finally he would declare openly that same afternoon.[77] One of Reagan's aides admitted that the impetus indeed had been the earlier meeting with Rhodes.[78]

Knowland came to Nofziger to review the announcement plans made the day before. Then Nofziger and Knowland went to Reagan. The decision from the day before was confirmed by Reagan, "without further consultation."[79] Henry A. Bubb had been pressing Reagan too.[80] Waiting until Wednesday simply was way too late for an official announcement.

Around 3:30 PM, Nancy Reagan, tired of all the questioning she was getting from reporters questioning the viability of her husband's candidacy, called a small press conference and announced that he was not a candidate for the nomination.[81] But in a half-hour, she would be proven wrong.

Lightning Strikes

As a response to Reagan's decision, Knowland proceeded to orchestrate the promised official Reagan draft proclamation.[82] After meeting with his California delegation, Knowland called a hasty press conference at the Napolean Room of the Deauville Hotel and at 4 PM announced that the California caucus had passed a resolution. Weinrod and other SFR members, present at the hotel and not at convention hall, got minimal advance notice; they were told to "get as many people down there as you can."[83] Noting the growing calls for Reagan to become an open candidate, the California delegation "hereby recognizes Governor Reagan in fact is a leading and bona fide candidate for President."[84] For Weinrod and his SFR, it was huge. Everyone was given placards to hold up. They all cheered Knowland and could not wait for Reagan to get to the podium.

At the time of the Knowland official announcement, Reagan had been at the private meeting with the Idaho delegation, accompanied by Nofziger and White. Reagan then met briefly with delegates from Maine, Vermont and New Hampshire. Reagan walked into the room where the reporters awaited.[85] Weinrod reflected decades later that the palpable excitement was "one of the highlights" of his career in politics.[86] Just before Reagan spoke to the press, Lieutenant Governor Finch was hustled away by Deaver, so as to avoid embarrassment to Finch, the Nixon friend, advisor, and loyalist.[87]

Reagan smiled joshingly, "Gosh, I was surprised. It all came out of the clear blue sky."[88] He told the press that he was not at the meeting of the California delegation when its members had voted unanimously to declare him a candidate for president. He joked but added, "It certainly makes life easier…It does clarify the situation. Yes as of this moment…I am a candidate." Weinrod, all the rest of the SFR and everyone else in attendance, applauded loudly as cheers went up.

When asked if the formal announcement of his candidacy would change anything, he answered, "No." He said he would continue meeting with delegations and presenting his approaches to solve problems. He said for the past year and a half he had been answering reporters that he would in fact become a candidate for president as favorite son on Wednesday night but that now the announcement had been made early. He ended by saying he had not been pressuring any of the delegates during his prior meetings and did not expect that to change.[89]

Reagan left the SFR and reporters and proceeded to a meeting with Jim Gardner and the North Carolina delegation.[90] There, future reporter Walter Shapiro was covering the delegation for his college newspaper and became mesmerized by Reagan, later recalling that he "could not resist rooting for him."[91]

The official announcement of Reagan's candidacy produced "more stress" within the California delegation because many delegates, such as Lt. Governor Finch, were for Nixon.[92] But the news of the official Reagan candidacy spread like wildfire. Reagan enthusiasts "appeared out of nowhere."[93] So there it all was. Finally Reagan confirmed to the citizens of the country what he and Nancy and his team first had planned at that first November, 1966 campaign meeting so long ago. What the citizens and reporters had not understood was that, despite the official announcement that day at the convention, Reagan had, in fact, been campaigning steadily for a full 22 months.

Nancy learned of the pending official declaration from the radio.[94] Nancy, who thirty minutes earlier had told the press that he was not a candidate, sank into a chair, exclaiming, "Oh, no. Well, how about that. I am surprised, completely surprised, but I'm very glad if that's what he wants to do…It's so tremendous, so awesome a job."[95] She added, "I was the most surprised person in the world when it happened."[96]

Henry A. Bubb initially told the press that Reagan's announcement was "great, but three months too late." Bubb added that it was a "great psychological lift" for the Reagan campaign team and would help get some delegates in the South. But Bubb reminded the press that ever since the Oregon primary, Bubb had been urging Reagan to declare openly his candidacy.[97] Bubb added that had he announced earlier, Reagan could have had "at least 150 more first ballot votes."[98]

Reagan Juggernaut

After meeting with Gardner and the North Carolina delegation, Reagan went to Bubb and the Kansas delegation. Former Kansas Governor John Anderson, a Rockefeller supporter, analyzed that the Reagan announcement likely would prevent a Nixon first ballot victory. And Philip Kassebaum, one of three state co-chairmen for Rockefeller, said that after Nixon would be stopped, getting Nixon voters to switch to Rockefeller "was going to be tough" due to the enthusiasm for Reagan.[99]

After his meeting with Reagan, Bubb then became much more optimistic. He told the press that the Reagan announcement created a "whole new ball game. The bases are loaded; Reagan is at bat, and he's a damned good hitter." He thought that the announcement would bring the delegations from Florida, Alabama, Louisiana and South Carolina "largely into the Reagan fold." This would prevent a first ballot Nixon victory. It was now a two-man race between Nixon and Reagan, and Reagan would triumph. Bubb admitted that at that point his own Kansas delegation had only 3 firm Reagan votes of 20.[100]

Governor Rhodes, likely hoping to be the next vice-president next to a President Reagan rather than a Rockefeller supporter, mimicked Bubb and also proclaimed, "It's a whole new ball game."[101] Governor David Cargo of New Mexico said: "It's like a woman who's eight and half months pregnant announcing she's going to have a baby."[102] Even months later, Harry Dent reflected: "The lightning struck. I have been in politics for I don't know how many years, and I have never seen anything like it."[103]

At the Reagan telecommunications center at the Deauville, Bob Tarbet typed out the headlines onto the brand-new teletype machine that so many had waited so long to read: Ronald Reagan was running for president of the United States.[104] At the moment of the announcement, the New York Times reported that Reagan had about 200 delegates. Tower of Texas said of the announcement, "It's too late." Nixon's team said it had changed nothing, and Rockefeller admitted that Reagan now "might well" get additional delegates.[105]

The Nixon team was "gobsmacked" by the Reagan announcement and boom.[106] Despite their having been forewarned by Reagan himself, the Greenville Group panicked. Thurmond was sent to work harder, and Clarke Reed, who had his own personal revenge waiting to be taken upon Reagan, panicked—wondering how he ever could return home having "led the battle" for Nixon over Reagan.[107]

Once the New York Times story on the vice-presidency had hit in the early morning, "all day Monday it was just pandemonium."[108] Reagan supporters had been busy spreading the word to now-wavering Nixon supporters: "The fix is on! The fix is on!"[109] Was Nixon going to "sock it"[110] to the South after all?

Thurmond attempted to forestall the switching to Reagan by proclaiming, "I'm standing firm."[111] But by late in the afternoon, as Thurmond was preparing to leave for the airport to greet Nixon, one aide admitted, "It had gotten to the place where, really, just the

Senator's 'standing firm with Nixon' wasn't enough."[112] All Thurmond heard back was, "Tricky Dick! Tricky Dick!"[113]

Then Jim Gardner started spreading the word throughout the convention that he and his North Carolina delegation were a Reagan-majority delegation.[114]

The delegates were realizing that although at times Nixon had claimed he was conservative, in reality there was only one man at Miami Beach who could tap the "surge" of the delegates' call for conservatism in 1968: Ronald Reagan.[115] At a large social event in the late afternoon, Dent and Thurmond socialized with William Rusher and conservative writer Phyllis Schlafly, each of whom was a Reagan supporter. The latter both tried to convince Thurmond and Dent of the error of their ways in following Nixon, even to the point of urging them to get whatever promises Nixon might make to them in writing. Rusher tried repeatedly to persuade them, without success.

At 6:50 PM, Nixon finally arrived, having spent the previous days at Montauk, Long Island, where he was writing his acceptance speech. He had been absent from the scene during the weekend when Reagan and Rockefeller had been "sweat(ing) out the weekend delegate-hopping along the oceanfront hotels."[116] Thurmond greeted Nixon by immediately showing him the earlier story about his picking a liberal running mate.[117] Nixon's motorcade entered the Hilton Plaza, accompanied by dancers singing choruses of "Nixon's the One."[118] If Nixon expected a coronation, he was in for a shock.

Indeed the news of the day was not Nixon's arrival. Rather, the early report of Nixon's running mate, which had been the major topic amongst the delegates, suddenly was replaced. Now the news of Reagan's declaration of open candidacy electrified the convention even as the news was 'still filling the news wires."[119]

When Nixon ascended to his penthouse suite, he voiced some initial concern that Reagan was "operating at full force" with Reagan trying to "breach my Southern flank."[120] But then Nixon dismissed Thurmond's concern from the morning story about the choice of his running mate. Indeed the news of the Reagan candidacy "did not seem to disturb Nixon in the least."[121] Nixon assumed that any move towards Reagan would cause any Rockefeller supporters to move to his, Nixon's way.

Although the delegates listened to the speeches during that first day, the real action remained in the Southern delegations. Reporters Evans and Novak had permanent floor passes and excellent sources within all the Southern delegations. They roamed the convention constantly and concentrated on the South. Novak observed, "There was no question that rank-and-file delegates wanted to bolt to Reagan, depriving Nixon of a nomination he thought was wrapped up."[122]

The head of the Nixon faction in Alabama was "frantic" about the mood within his delegates. Because state chairman Goldthwaite still held steadfast for Reagan, Nixon's man was frantic that he and the rest of the Nixon supporters would have to cast their ballots for Reagan.[123] There were similar "violent tremors amongst the delegations of Florida, Texas, Mississippi and Louisiana.[124] Jim Gardner of North Carolina reiterated his prior announced backing of North Carolina for Reagan, telling Thurmond flat out, "I'm for Ronnie!"[125] The South Carolina delegation "had been forced to concede to the Reaganites" that they would go for Reagan on the second ballot if they permitted the delegation's Nixon supporters the chance to go with Nixon—but only on that first ballot.[126] Dent observed that although the Nixon camp was attempting to show an air of invincibility, "behind-the-scenes members of the camp were deeply concerned whether they could hold off the Reagan raid on their soft underbelly, the South."[127] And Dent added, "Reagan was the real threat."[128]

Prior to the evening session, the delegates watched the network news programs. On ABC's *Evening News*, the lead story with reporter Frank Reynolds was Reagan's announced candidacy. Reagan was shown, declaring he was attempting to stop a first ballot Nixon victory. ABC projected Reagan's delegate count at 209-217, with Nixon still 66 votes shy of a first ballot victory.[129] On NBC's *Nightly News*, reporters David Brinkley and John Chancellor reported that Reagan's candidacy was the "worst non-kept secret." Reagan was reported to have met with six delegate groups on Sunday and twelve delegations on Monday. One Georgia delegate was interviewed, exclaiming that if Nixon were not nominated on the first ballot, it would be Reagan on the second. Reporter Sander Vanocur reported that the Reagan and Rockefeller teams had set up a "communications system" between the two campaigns and that once Nixon was stopped, they would "start carving on each other."[130]

At 7 PM, Reagan held a fifteen-minute meeting with delegates from Nebraska and Kansas at the Sea Gull Hotel. Besides Henry A. Bubb, William H. Thompson from Reagan's Omaha campaign office was there as well. Fred Seaton attended too and undoubtedly received even more pressure from Nebraskans and Coors to switch his vote to Reagan.[131]

On the way over to the evening session, Dent ran into Jim Gardner. Dent had not known of Gardner's North Carolina delegation being pro-Reagan, and Dent was "incredulous."[132] Dent couldn't believe it.

How dare anyone from the South stand up, defy Ol' Strom, and vote for Reagan? Upon arrival at convention hall, Dent immediately spoke to other members of the North Carolina delegation, who confirmed that indeed North Carolina, thanks to Gardner, now in fact had a Reagan majority delegation.

This news was critical. Dent picked up the nearest phone and called John Mitchell at Nixon headquarters, saying he needed to meet Nixon immediately—not tomorrow as planned. "Things are taking a turn for the worse."[133] Ever since Reagan had announced in the afternoon, the Reagan passions had been "stirring" in Miami Beach.[134] The Gardner and North Carolina support for Reagan had created "the most traumatic shock wave" the Nixonites had felt.[135] Dent saw and heard that delegates from all over the convention "were telling of more and more possible defections from Nixon to Reagan."[136]

By 9:30 PM, the news that was spreading like wildfire throughout the hall, that Reagan was gaining ground, was confirmed by the press. CBS just completed its first delegate count since Reagan had announced his open candidacy earlier in the day. Nixon was still short of the nomination at 626, Rockefeller steady at 243, but Reagan had gained 16 to 192. The remaining votes were for favorite sons and others.[137] Reagan was gaining. But was it enough?

Dent, on the convention floor, could feel more slippage for Nixon.[138] Dent was told that rather than remaining favorite son, Ohio Governor Rhodes "planned to throw Ohio's support to Reagan, with Rhodes to become his running mate."[139] Now Thurmond himself was extremely worried, even if Nixon seemingly was complacent.

On the podium, it was Barry Goldwater's turn to speak. At 10 PM Goldwater began and received "thirty-three bursts of riotous applause."[140] This indicated clearly that the delegates still were conservative and still with him in their hearts. Who could channel this residual 1964 Goldwater energy into 1968 delegate votes? Rockefeller's love of "big-government-spending" was not the GOP way; only if he could convince the delegates that only he could win in November was Rockefeller likely to succeed.[141] Reagan's musical team of Dixon and Philpott had been singing, and Nixon was not the one. As Nixon had confirmed earlier, it was Reagan who set the delegates' hearts aflutter. Nixon was incapable of exciting "that kind of fervor."[142] Nixon was the unexciting consensus candidate.

It was Reagan—the articulate conservative of 1968—for whom they were cheering. Reporters noted that the applause for Goldwater indeed was a sure sign of "latent Reagan strength."[143] Thurmond needed to act and act fast. The dam for Reagan was about to break wide open, sending Nixon and Thurmond down river grasping for political life preservers.

While Goldwater was at the podium eliciting conservative fervor, which he did not realize was being funneled to Reagan, Thurmond and Dent arrived at Nixon headquarters at the Hilton, just as Dent frantically had requested. Ahead of time, Dent had planned to do most of the speaking. John Mitchell met them, and after taking the elevator to the fifteenth floor, they walked up the final three flights to Nixon's suite. Haldeman and Ehrichman were there too.

Nixon and Thurmond initially chatted socially as if nothing were amiss. Dent could not understand Nixon's continued non-chalance. Dent was fearful that Nixon had not understood "how far out on a limb" Thurmond had gone to bat for him.[144] Dent had heard reports that Nixon was planning to court the urban Northeastern vote and to forget about the South. Maybe Reagan in fact deserved their loyalty for 1968.

First Dent told Nixon again about the *New York Times* article earlier in the day and the damage it had created. Dent then told Nixon about Reagan's announcement and that numerous defections to Reagan within the Southern delegations had occurred all day.[145] Dent proceeded to tell Nixon the news that Jim Gardner's North Carolina delegation now had a Reagan majority. Dent recalled that Nixon was "startled" by the Reagan gains.[146] Others in the room similarly felt Nixon truly was "stunned" by the news of the onslaught of more and more defections in the South, and then the meeting suddenly became "panicky."[147] One group of historians claimed that Nixon had been viewing Rockefeller as his main enemy,[148] but long ago and throughout the campaign trail, Nixon knew it was Reagan.

And Nixon knew that he had been threatened by Reagan before. In Wisconsin, Nixon felt threatened when Reagan and his grass roots team headed by Don Taylor had first shown *Ronald Reagan, Citizen Governor*. Here Reagan first had emerged as a national candidate by showing strength outside California. In Nebraska, the three grass roots offices of Young, Thompson and Sherwood had made significant inroads prior to the primary. Nixon felt threatened by Reagan and had to return to Nebraska early in April and again in May to shore up support. The Reagan film was shown more often in Nebraska, and Reagan had shot up to almost 22 percent.[149] By the time of Oregon, Reagan had his largest grass roots teams who had given their greatest effort, and Nixon again had been forced to return again and again to campaign to thwart the Reagan threat.[150]

Although in each opt-out primary Nixon had ended up winning, Reagan was not an avowed candidate in any; despite multiple appearances in those states in 1967, Reagan had not campaigned in any of those states in person in 1968. But now things were different, for Reagan was an avowed candidate—literally just for a few hours—and already the fact that he was an open candidate had thrown the convention on its head.

Nixon told Dent and Thurmond that in fact now he did plan to campaign for Southern votes. So Dent and Thurmond wanted to know more specifics, picking up on their earlier meeting in Atlanta. So next, Thurmond probed Nixon about forced school busing. But of critical importance was the vice-presidency. The announcement of liberal Hatfield at the earlier press conference had not helped. Thurmond told Nixon that if he chose a liberal, the South would no longer support him. There was the ultimate threat of Ronald Reagan against Richard Nixon. Nixon had foreseen it way back. Nixon tried to preserve all his options. Thurmond and Dent had their knives out. Even though they had told Nixon in Atlanta of their support, now they had Nixon just where they always had wanted him: squirming.

In the end, just as Thurmond and Dent and the Greenville Group had planned all along as they intermittently had pushed—or gently nudged—a theoretical Reagan candidacy, the threat of this real Reagan candidacy forced Nixon to cave and promise Thurmond that his choice for vice-president would be "acceptable to all sections of the party."[151] Thurmond at last had exacted his price for his support. Thurmond indeed would be the one who would coronate the King. Thurmond ended by warning Nixon that because of the Reagan threat, he had better tell the South "again what it wanted to hear."[152] That chance would be during the next morning, via a series of meetings that Nixon would have at the Hilton Plaza.[153] Nixon felt relieved that Thurmond had not abandoned him, for later he wrote that Thurmond, and Tower of Texas, were starting to shore up "the Southern dike against Reagan's rising waters."[154]

Back on the convention floor, New York City Mayor John Lindsay introduced the keynote speaker, Governor Dan Evans of Washington. As your author has reviewed elsewhere, in the spring, during Lindsay's campaigning in Oregon initially for Rockefeller as a surrogate and then when disappointed Rockefeller supporters had started the presidential boomlet for Lindsay, Lindsay had begun to take his own role more seriously. [155] In fact his biographer relates that although Lindsay mainly was seen as a potential vice-presidential running mate, his aides in April had been sent to Miami Beach to scout out campaign office space. They hoped to position Lindsay as a presidential alternative in case of a convention deadlock.[156] In July, the aides had set up a Lindsay headquarters at the Americana Hotel and set up a small communications network.[157] As discussed, Lindsay earlier had wrecked his own chances to be Reagan's vice-presidential choice, and both Nixon and Rockefeller were New Yorkers, which had precluded either from choosing Lindsay.

Evans, himself a possible vice-presidential choice as discussed earlier, remained a Rockefeller supporter. Yet in his speech, Evans, who had succeeded in physically distancing him from conservative Goldwater in 1964, suddenly borrowed conservative themes of Reagan, reminding his audience that the "increasing dominance of the federal government" had accomplished little. He pushed for private business to be used. As Reagan previously had said many times, Evans said that government "can't construct the solutions of the next three decades."[158] Evans certainly did not sound like someone who was supporting big-government Rockefeller, and indeed Evans' endorsement of Rockefeller was described by the press as "tepid."[159] Perhaps Evans had come full circle. From refusing to be photographed next to Goldwater in 1964, likely now Evans saw that he could with pride stand next to nominee Reagan. The exhausted delegates went back to their hotel rooms. After the big news of the Nixon choice of a liberal vice-president, coupled with the thrilling official announcement of the Reagan candidacy and the defections to conservative Reagan, what more excitement could be in store for Tuesday?

DAY 2, Tuesday, August 6

Apparently not all the Southern delegations got the word from Thurmond, or else not all believed what Nixon had promised. The 34 members of the Florida delegation declared that they would cast their 33 votes for Nixon, (Governor Kirk was for Rockefeller in hopes of becoming Rockefeller's choice for vice-president) *only* if they got a public pledge that Nixon only would choose a vice-president acceptable to the South—and that meant excluding Hatfield or Rockefeller or Lindsay.[160]

Nixon set about shoring up his defenses against the Reagan surge. But Nixon did not go to the Southern delegates; rather they came to him at his hotel. Thurmond and Dent had crafted the meeting ahead of time, but a member of the Florida delegation tape-recorded the whole thing and sent it to the *Miami Herald*. Through a long series of questions and answers, Nixon assured the delegates that he remained their man.[161] At one point, Thurmond told the assembled delegates, "I love Reagan, but Nixon's the one."[162] Dent saw "some delegates change right back from Reagan to Nixon" because of Thurmond's cajoling.[163]

Meanwhile Reagan continued his quest by holding meetings with delegates too. Nixon's team was fearful of more than just an isolated defection to Reagan here and there. One Nixon aide "was afraid that Reagan might get wholesale switches among the Southern delegates."[164] The aide noted that personally he had see how the Southern delegate's "heart beat for Reagan...Goldwater never had what Reagan's got."[165] Dent himself observed that unlike Rockefeller, Reagan's meetings with delegates indeed were being converted into "concrete votes," and the caucus setting was "perfectly attuned to his talents." Dent thought, "There is nothing more impressive than Ronnie Reagan behind closed doors."[166]

While Nixon was schmoozing the delegates, his operatives at the convention hall started using a new tactic to blunt the cascading movement to Reagan. The Nixon people got Barry Goldwater to start making the rounds to promote the candidacy of Reagan: *for vice-president*! Some delegates thought they were being told this by Goldwater because Reagan actually did want to become vice-president. Nixon forces were reminding delegates of the Time cover of the prior autumn, which, they reminded everyone, had shown Reagan in the second spot.[167] Nobody discussed that the article also could be interpreted as having Reagan on the top of the ticket. This would not be the first time Nixon would start such false rumors.

Reagan decided he had to meet with Thurmond again. After the prior meetings in Columbia in the fall of 1967 and in New Orleans the past May, now Reagan had to convince the same person to whom previously Reagan had denied interest in becoming a candidate.

So Reagan went to the Versailles Hotel, where Thurmond and the rest of the South Carolina delegation were staying. Thurmond reiterated that he was for Nixon. Not taking "No" for an answer, Reagan escorted Thurmond upstairs for a private 45-minute chat. Thurmond told Reagan how much he admired him, but it just was not his year.[168] After the meeting, Thurmond said he had told Reagan, "I would support him next time."[169] Thurmond would confide to White his true feelings after the convention, and indeed Thurmond would keep his word by voting for Reagan in 1976. Dent recalled that after the private meeting with Thurmond, Reagan "emerged with a long face....The Thurmond session had evidently drained and distressed him."[170] One historian termed the Reagan-Thurmond meeting as the "ultimate turning point."[171] But Reagan did not give up.

Reagan decided to bypass Thurmond and went directly to the South Carolina delegation meeting. He told them flat out that he would never accept the vice-presidential nod. Dent recalled that Reagan had answered all the delegate questions, but Thurmond's leadership, and Nixon having met them first, were just "too strong for Reagan to overcome."[172] One of the last Reagan holdouts in South Carolina's delegation, Bill Hunter, threw up the white flag and went for Nixon.[173]

Reagan would not quit. So Reagan bypassed both Thurmond and his South Carolina roadblock. After meeting with the Florida delegation, Reagan had lunch with the Mississippi delegation.[174] Mississippi's head was Clarke Reed, who never had forgotten the sleight Reagan had done to him in 1966 by not coming to his aid. Now Clarke Reed could take his revenge. Goldwater just had visited the Mississippi delegates on behalf of Nixon, and later Reed said that Goldwater had been of more help than Thurmond in keeping his delegation in line for Nixon.[175] Reagan also learned that the Mississippi delegates had been treated to a special boat trip by Thurmond—special because Thurmond steadied the boat for Nixon. Thurmond reviewed the veto power Nixon had given him over the choice of vice-president and all future Supreme Court nominees. Thurmond "persuaded them not to bolt for Reagan."[176]

With Reagan thus stymied when attempting to meet with the Mississippians, Reagan tried one last maneuver: calling their boss, Clarke Reed. He tried by asking Reed to keep an open mind and not commit to Nixon without hearing him out. Reagan asked, "I only want a chance. You've always said you wanted an open fight. OK, release your delegates." Now Reed had Reagan just where he wanted him and let him have it. He reminded Reagan of the time Reed had called Reagan asking a favor for help and Reagan had never called back. Reed told Reagan he would not release his delegates and advised Reagan, "You had better try where you have a few favors owing."[177]

Reagan still did not give up. He visited the Alabama and Louisiana delegations at the Di Lido Hotel, where they were housed. One Louisiana caucus leader told a delegate, "It breaks my heart that we can't get behind a fine man like Governor Reagan," but they were committed to Nixon on the first round.[178]

Mailer observed Reagan, as Reagan spoke briefly to the press when he left the Southern delegations. It was hard for Mailer to realize that Reagan was only 57, and was in fact two years older than Nixon, for Reagan "had a boy's face, no gray in his head."[179] Plus

Reagan, unlike Nixon, was "altogether at ease with the Press."[180] And unlike Nixon, Reagan had the confidence of the elected governor of a big state, had a public manner that was "so natural" and despite being 57, "had the presence of a man of thirty."[181]

Then one Reagan press aide held up his hand and asked for quiet. The aide whispered to Reagan the news of Eisenhower's latest medical setback of another heart attack. Reagan was somber with the news of the apparent rapid demise of his mentor and role model, but the unrelenting press hounded Reagan with repeated questions on how successful he had been at "prying delegates loose from Nixon."[182] Reagan responded saying he didn't know how successful he had been. "I can't tell you if we're gaining. I think we are, but I don't know."[183] Reagan faced the same conflicts that the delegates had: they wanted Reagan and told him so, yet they had to initially vote Nixon. So Reagan, as he left the meetings, had no true inkling if delegates were switching to him or not.[184] Reagan also had no inkling of what would happen to the general.

So where else could Reagan turn? Was Rockefeller gaining strength to thwart Nixon? At the time, Rockefeller's drive was reported as "completely bogged down" with "lassitude" and "failures of coordination."[185] Rockefeller himself, who had failed earlier in the day to appear on-time for an NBC broadcast and then found out later that his tardiness had caused the network to cancel the appearance altogether, smilingly told the press at 5:20 PM that Nixon would get no more than 550 first-ballot votes.[186]

But since Reagan's open announcement of his candidacy, as Reagan "worked his charm on a southern state delegation," Thurmond had been putting "out fires Reagan generated among conservatives and especially Southerners."[187] But Thurmond may have been firefighting against flames that would not die, because other observers saw clearly that Nixon's expected first ballot victory was "no longer secure."[188]

On ABC's *Evening News*, Rockefeller's camp claimed that Nixon's strength had dropped down to 515. Reporter Frank Reynolds noted that Reagan was stepping up his search for delegates although thus far no large blocs of delegates had changed.[189]

That evening for the full convention session, Everett Dirksen presented the report of the Platform Committee. Dirksen, despite previously proclaiming that Reagan, should he be the nominee, would be as fine as Lincoln in a future crisis, ended up supporting Nixon and worked closely with Nixon's floor manager to keep the Southern delegations in line.[190] Reagan's lack of conviction privately with Dirksen back in Eureka in 1967 had come full circle.

The evening edition of the *Miami Herald* hit the streets with the transcript of the tape, recorded earlier at the Nixon meeting with Southern delegates, but there had been no surprises in what Nixon had said. During this time, Goldwater, who earlier had failed in his mission to drum up delegate support for Reagan for vice-president, as a way to help Nixon, approached Reagan directly and brought up a Nixon-Reagan ticket, but Reagan "balked, insisting he wasn't interested."[191]

White prowled the corridors, while Reagan kept up his grueling pace of caucuses. But "the aroma of defeat" was in the air. One Reagan supporter muttered ruefully, "For months we sat around worrying among ourselves that too many appearances in the South would get people to talking about the Reagan Southern strategy. That's funny, because the guy with the real Southern strategy was Nixon—using Thurmond."[192]

The day did not end quietly for the Nixon forces, though, which suffered "more anxious moments…over the Reagan threat."[193] Reagan kept calling Florida delegates into his communications trailer for more cajoling. Dent noted that the women in the Florida delegation— by law half of the Florida delegates were women—would return from meeting Reagan "virtually swooning."[194] Because Reagan was particularly effective with women, there was more work for Thurmond and Dent to try to quelch the fires for Reagan. Florida Chairman Murfin, who previously had told White that he would vote for Reagan if White could get half of the Florida delegates to support Reagan, now changed his tune. Murfin "followed Thurmond's lead."[195] Murfin no longer showed any semblance of neutrality but became even more concerned whether he could "hold his delegation in line for Nixon."[196] He learned of a new Reagan attack on his delegation planned for the next day, and late at night Murfin got Dent on the phone.

THE LONG DAY 3-4: Wednesday August 7-Thursday August 8

As the nomination speeches approached, Nixon played the role of the "isolated, protected monarch."[197] The Nixon forces had expected that the last day of the convention would be calm and easy, but it would turn out to be the most hectic day of all.[198] In fact the day would become so cram-packed with political excitement that like Joshua, the day would last longer than 24 hours, and would not end until the wee hours of Thursday morning.

It began in a déjà vu fashion, like actor Bill Murray in *Ground Hog Day*. But on this day, it was no longer Monday with liberal Hatfield being the one Nixon was choosing. Now it was Wednesday. Yet it was as if the news of Monday—of Nixon screwing the South and allowing a new Reagan wave to crash on the Nixon hopes—was starting all over again. So Wednesday began with an Evans-Novak column which reported that now Nixon had requested, and had received, a report that there was no constitutional impediment to having another liberal as vice-president, this time Lindsay, a fellow New Yorker. Under the banner "Nixon Appears to be Reaching Toward the Left for Running Mate Despite Southern Hostility," Novak was fanning the flames of anti-Nixon feelings of betrayal in the South.[199] So Reagan's team made copies of Novak's article and started giving them out to Southern delegates. It was virtually a repeat of the *New York Times* article that had greeted delegates at the start of the convention. Being double-crossed by Nixon kept popping up within the Southern delegations. It would not be the last time that day that anti-Nixon fervor would be flamed by the distribution of newspapers.

During the day Nixon's aides were going over the nominating speech to be delivered by Agnew of Maryland and various seconding speeches, "especially one" by liberal Hatfield of Oregon, still also was being considered for the vice-presidency.[200] At the time, Hatfield reviewed his speech with Nixon's aides to agree to final wording on Vietnam.[201] Clearly, despite the vocal resentment from the Southern delegates, Nixon apparently had no qualms about choosing a liberal for his running mate. Having previously castigated the idea of a Rockefeller-Reagan ticket, what Eisenhower would say about a Nixon-Hatfield or Nixon-Lindsay ticket is anybody's guess.

At the same time Nixon was preparing Hatfield for the second spot, Nixon again counter-attacked the Reagan swell. This time, it was Thurmond—rather than Goldwater—who sent out rumors that Reagan had agreed to be Nixon's vice-president. This was the same tactic used by Goldwater earlier. Reagan again had to reply by telegram, this time sending out a nine-paragraph denial to every delegate. The telegram received by Senator Dirksen is shown.[202] The rumor persisted. Even two hours prior to the balloting, Reagan still was telling delegates from Nevada and Oklahoma that he would never accept the second spot.[203] Reagan's line amused his team, "Even if they tied and gagged me, I would find a way to signal 'No' by wiggling my ears."[204]

During the day, Reagan's two main efforts were to sway the Alabama and Florida delegations. The first state to declare its votes at the convention was seen as setting some of the general tone of what would occur later. Thus Alabama, the first state alphabetically, was important, yet it could yield its privilege to another state. The state chairman, Alfred Goldthwaite, remained the loyal Reagan supporter as seen, but his delegation was not yet a Reagan majority. By noon on Wednesday, Nixon's strength in Alabama was declining and hovered close to the critical number of thirteen of 26 delegates. White handed Rusher a floor pass and told him to relay the Nixon vice-presidential news to former Congressman James Martin of Alabama. White and Rusher hoped to "shake him loose" from his Nixon commitment.[205] Rusher later recalled that Martin sagged, saying in words that were politically quite incorrect to use, "Oh, Lord! If that's true, my delegation will make a lampshade out of me!" Martin went off to get assurances from Nixon.[206]

If Nixon's Alabama support fell below thirteen, there would be a flood to Reagan. That would make two states for Reagan. Nixon's representative in Alabama was being pressured to have Alabama yield to South Carolina in order for Strom Thurmond's name placed in nomination as favorite son; then Thurmond would withdraw in favor of Nixon. But Nixon's representative thought that such an arrangement would drive even more delegates to Reagan. Thus he came up with a compromise solution: Alabama would yield to California, so Reagan's name would be placed in nomination first as favorite son. In this way, the Alabama delegates hopefully would be placated and there would no further Nixon bleeding of support in Alabama.[207] Reagan had been pleased by the support from Alabama, but no new votes had been swayed.[208]

But the most serious situation was in Florida. Novak termed the situation in Florida a crisis which "almost changed the course of American history by flipping it to Reagan under the winner-take-all unit rule."[209] The 34-member Florida delegation that year, as discussed, was comprised of seventeen women, and one group of reporters described most of the latter as "crazy for Reagan."[210] These Floridians were not staying on the beach, but rather they were lodged inland at the Doral Country Club. Bill Murfin, state chairman, previously had gained this position with the help of a number of members of the delegation, who now in August were described as the "most fervent Reaganophiles."[211] Murfin also was a member of the Greenville Group, which had planned their big double-cross of Reagan. And Murfin had told Nixon long ago that in Florida, all was set for Nixon. At the same time, Governor Kirk, who earlier had declared for Rockefeller, hoping to join him in Washington, D.C. as vice-president, tried to wrestle control of his delegation away from Murfin. Kirk first proposed that he himself be nominated as favorite son, but this was defeated. Then he proposed that the whole group should vote for Reagan. An agreement emerged that a de facto unit rule would apply, such that whichever candidate got a majority, the rest of the delegates would switch to that preferred candidate.[212] Of course Clif White thought he had a private deal with Murfin that if Reagan got support from half the delegation, Murfin would vote for Reagan and with the unit-rule in place, Florida would be all for Reagan.

Late Tuesday evening, Murfin had learned that Reagan was sending out the big guns to Florida on Wednesday—Californians Senator William Knowland and Senate candidate Max Rafferty—to arm twist the Floridians. Sensing a make-or-break moment, Murfin urgently got Dent on the phone and reported that some of the women delegates were "almost hysterical" for Reagan. If Dent wanted to save the whole situation for Nixon, Dent had better "get Strom's ass over here before they turn up."[213]

Thurmond had been running around all day Wednesday shoring up "weak spots" for Nixon against the Reagan onslaught. When he got word of the major "slippage" in Florida and the imminent arrival of Reagan's forces, he rushed out to the hotel.[214]

So pro-Nixon Thurmond and Dent arrived just a few minutes before pro-Reagan Knowland and Rafferty. Dent proceeded to lay it on the line, and reportedly Thurmond at one point said that he had "veto power" over Nixon's choice for vice-president.[215] By the end of the morning, despite the cajoling of Knowland and Rafferty, nothing had changed. Thurmond had succeeded in keeping Florida as before: 14 for Reagan, 19 for Nixon, and one for Rockefeller.[216] But this apparent holding of the line by Thurmond and Dent for Nixon would be short-lived.

Reagan needed just three Florida delegates to switch, and if that happened then he would have 17 and Nixon 16, which because of the agreed-to unit rule would mean that the entire Florida delegation would swing to Reagan. And if Florida would successfully get out of its pre-convention commitment to Nixon, then likely the rest of the South, in addition to North Carolina and possibly Alabama by then, would hop on the Reagan bandwagon. Utah might switch back to Reagan too. It all depended upon getting just three delegates to change. Reagan ultimately actually may have convinced two to switch, because according to historian Jules Witcover, Clif White recalled later that actually it had come down to just one Florida delegate.[217]

So the American presidency hinged on one—possibly three—Florida delegate(s) switching and voting with his/her heart. And

Reagan would not give up. So he invited sixteen Florida delegates to his suite for lunch at the Deauville Hotel for another attempt at persuasion.

White by this time had the sixteen Florida votes that were needed for Murfin to be the seventeenth. But at that most critical time, Murfin did not honor his promise. Instead, Murfin threatened to resign as state chairman "if the delegation refused to hold for Nixon."[218]

At their final 2 PM state caucus, the pressure to switch to Reagan was enormous. Just before the group left for convention hall for the voting, Murfin insisted they honor the unit rule. White recalled, "It was really on that action that our chances were lost."[219] Some women delegates for Reagan wept. Rusher recalled that even Murfin's nerves "briefly gave way under the pressure and he wept a little" too.[220] Although four delegates abstained, Murfin's unit rule held for Nixon.[221]

After Nixon would be nominated, Rockefeller paid campaign staffer Melich later would write several letters which analyzed portions of the convention. She thanked Gingrich for his support and wished him well for his return to graduate school.[222] But in a more pointed letter, she reflected that she would never understand why the Reagan team did not poll the Florida delegation.[223] Historian Geoffrey Kabaservice noted that had the Reagan forces polled the Florida delegations directly, it could have "allowed its members to break free and vote for Reagan."[224]

Melich believed that if White had attempted to cause a disruption within the Florida delegation by having it polled on the floor, this action would signal that Nixon wasn't as strong as his operatives claimed. The majority of the Florida delegation would still be for Nixon. With Florida coming early in the nomination roll-call, Melich thought White's challenge would have been stopped by Nixon's people, yet it would have unsettled many delegations. The challenge could have stimulated others to change their vote on a second ballot. In the end, she believed Nixon would still prevail but his nomination would have taken longer and would have allowed the Reagan and Rockefeller operatives to negotiate for campaign policies and staff positions.[225] But as it turned out, Reagan did not give up.

So even though all seemed lost for Reagan with Florida and thus with the whole convention too, Reagan and Clif White continued the fight. During the convention proceedings, White and other Reagan delegate-hunters took a number of Florida delegates again to the Reagan trailer for additional last minute "personalized pleas" by Reagan.[226] They did indeed poll the Florida delegation as Melich later had reflected—up front and personal. But Nixon's men had monitored the situation and as soon as each delegate left the Reagan trailer, each was scooped up by a Nixon operative to start counter arguments.[227] Murfin "continued to sweat out the Reagan assault on his delegation."[228] Reporter Novak concluded, "The Reagan delegate hunters, led by F. Clifton White, were simply out-gunned in a majority of Southern states by Thurmond's massive authority."[229]

At 5:30 PM, just as the critical evening nominating session was about to begin, Tom Reed and Clif White did their final delegate count. They were disappointed that they had not achieved more. By their calculations, which closely matched those of CBS, Nixon would win on the first ballot with 682 votes, while Reagan would garner 180. Yet amongst the Nixon tally were some 40 delegates—mainly from Alabama, Florida and Mississippi—who still might switch. White laid it out for Reagan in the trailer. "We have one option left. We can fold the tent now. Or we can keep working and hope for a break." Reagan would not give up, answering, "Well, that's what we're here for, isn't it? Let's get back to work."[230]

Once again, Reagan did not want to give up. During the early evening as delegates prepared for the final session when voting would begin, Reagan concentrated on Alabama, Mississippi and Florida. Reagan calculated that all was not lost. If he could turn around Florida's unit rule, hold his own in Alabama, and steal a few more delegates from Mississippi, Nixon would be stopped without a first ballot victory.[231] So White told Reagan he would "spend the next few hours going after them."[232] White planned to corral these targeted delegates for a final attempt at changing minds.[233] Jim Martin, the Nixon leader in Alabama, remained constantly in doubt about Nixon, especially because back home, "most of their hearts belonged to Reagan."[234] At this point, Reagan needed some big break to stop Nixon. Nixon later recalled, "Nothing short of a miracle" could bring Reagan a victory.[235] White and Reed were hoping for one too.

Prior to the final session, Reagan continued to meet with individual delegates and small groups in the communications trailer, arguing that Nixon still could be stopped.[236] Nixon meanwhile needed a rest and left convention hall. Nixon boasted to two reporters about the fatal flaw of Reed's plan. Reagan "had blown" any chance of failing to take him on in at least one primary; any single defeat for Nixon could have "stuck him for good with his old loser image. Because (Reagan) didn't, he said, it was all over on the night of the Oregon primary."[237] *Ronald Reagan, Citizen Governor* had been a master stroke and Nixon had seen it as his major threat. But Reed's decision not to have

Reagan appear in person in Wisconsin, Nebraska, or Oregon, was indeed the fatal mistake. Rusher's last personal memory before the voting began was seeing Reagan in the communications trailer, still trying to corral, around a long table, more Mississippi delegates.[238]

Just before the main session, Reagan held a meeting with black leaders, including Reverend Ralph Abernathy of the Southern Christian Leadership Conference, to discuss his plans to combat poverty and reform welfare. Reagan favored welfare reform and cited a recent pilot program he had instituted in California to reform the system. He reiterated his compassion for the truly poor, those who could not provide for themselves, saying government and society had to help them. But those who could work needed to be trained to become self-sufficient.[239]

Reagan's regional directors and SFR and YAF allies kept bringing in delegates to the trailer.[240] Reagan would not give up. He needed to try every "conceivable chance."[241] Meanwhile, Ronald Reagan was about to be nominated to become president of the United States.

Endnotes

1. Chester et. al., p. 450
2. Quoted in Cannon, p. 268
3. Torrence, Elon, "New Ball Game, Says Bubb," *Dallas Times Herald*, 8/5/68
4. Chester et. al., p. 437
5. Novak, p. 167
6. Transcript, ABC News *Issues and Answers* telecast 1-2 PM, 8/4/1968, courtesy Dirksen Congressional Center, Pekin, IL
7. Novak, p. 168
8. Dent, p. 87
9. Dent, p. 87
10. White and Gill, p. 121
11. Reed, *Reagan Enigma*, p. 169
12. Chester et. al., p. 454-455
13. Skelton, George, "Though Wounded, California's GOP is Not Slain," *LA Times*, 7/31/2000
14. Thorburn, p. 168
15. Chester et. al., p. 449
16. Randolph, Gordon, "MGIC Chairman Heads Reagan Drive," *Milwaukee Journal*, 8/5/68, p. 10
17. Chester et. al., p. 457
18. Chester et. al., p. 457
19. Reston, James, "Delegates are asking Questions, but Are They asking the Ones that Matter?," *NYT*, 8/5/68, p. 19
20. Chester et. al., p. 458
21. Dent, p. 86
22. Dent, p. 87
23. Reed, *Reagan Enigma*, p. 169
24. Historian Lou Cannon relates that the Knowland proposed his idea first to Nofziger on August 7. Cannon, p. 268
25. Nolan, Pat, personal communication, 6/5/2013
26. Nolan, ibid
27. Dent, p. 91
28. Dent, p. 91
29. Mailer, p. 57
30. Chester et. al., p. 457

31. Dent, p. 85
32. Dent, p. 85
33. Dent, p. 85
34. Chester et. al., p. 441
35. Chester et. al., p. 449
36. Chester et. al., p. 449
37. Transcript, ABC News *Issues and Answers* telecast 1-2 PM, 8/4/1968, courtesy Dirksen Congressional Center, Pekin IL; Despite several attempts to discuss old recollections, Evans did not return phone calls to the author.
38. Mailer, p. 57
39. Novak, p. 167
40. *Face the Nation*, CBS Television, 8/4/1968
41. Novak, p. 167; Gibbs and Duffy, p. 216
42. Novak, p. 167
43. *Face the Nation*, CBS Television, 8/4/1968
44. Eisenhower, Dwight, Post-Presidential Diary 7/29/1968
45. Eisenhower, Dwight, Post-Presidential Diary 7/21/1968
46. Eisenhower, Dwight, Post-Presidential Diary 7/24/1968
47. Eisenhower, Dwight, Post-Presidential Diary 7/26/1968
48. Eisenhower, Dwight, Post-Presidential Diary, 7/30/1968
49. Eisenhower, Dwight, Post-Presidential Diary, 8/2/1968
50. Eisenhower, Dwight, Post-Presidential Diary 8/4/1968
51. Eisenhower, Dwight, "Communist Danger" Vital Speeches ital XXXIV #22, 9/1/68, p. 681
52. Eisenhower, David, p. 260
53. Sidey, Hugh, "The Smile and Sincerity In An Age of Contrivance," *Life*, 8/16/68, p. 4
54. *Newsweek*, 8/19/68, p. 24
55. Bass and Thompson, p. 225
56. Chester et. al., p. 457-458; Dent, p. 96
57. Bass and Thompson, p. 226
58. Witcover, p. 338
59. Witcover, p. 339
60. Hall, Gladwin, "Reagan Officially in race; Acts to Bar Nixon Sweep," *NYT*, 8/6/68, p. 1
61. Kramer, Joel, "Republican Convention in Miami is a 'Grotesque Number Game," *Harvard Crimson*, 8/6/68
62. *Newsweek*, 8/19/68, p. 24
63. Chester et. al., p. 457
64. White, p. 240
65. White, ibid
66. Chester et. al., p. 449
67. Reed, p. 27
68. *Newsweek*, 8/12/68, p. 9
69. Chester et. al., p. 450
70. Chester et. al., p. 450
71. Smith, William French, "Evolution of the Kitchen Cabinet" Oral History, Ronald Reagan Gubernatorial Series, Univ. California Bancroft Library, 1989, p. 41
72. *Newsweek*, 8/19/68, p. 24
73. Judis, p. 289
74. Dent, p. 92
75. Dent, p. 92
76. Dent, p. 92
77. Chester et. al., p. 449
78. Chester et. al., p. 449
79. Nofziger, p. 73
80. Hill, Gladwin, "Reagan Officially in Race; Acts to Bar Nixon Sweep," *NYT*, 8/6/68, p. 1
81. Kelley, p. 174
82. Reed, p. 27
83. Weinrod, pers int 5/21/2013
84. Chester et. al., p. 450
85. Hill, Gladwin, "Reagan Officially in Race; Acts to Bar Nixon Sweep," *NYT*, 8/6/68, p. 1
86. Weinrod, pers int 5/21/2013
87. Deaver, p. 22
88. Chester et. al., p. 450
89. RRL ,Tape 358 Part 1
90. Hill, op.cit.

91. Shapiro, Walter, "The Reagan Centennial: The Gipper Reconsidered," PoliticsDaily.com 1/30/2011
92. Reed, p. 27
93. Perlstein, p. 296
94. Gibbs and Duffy, p. 216
95. Kelley, p. 174
96. Quoted in Cannon, p. 268
97. "Reagan Move Is Too Late, Bubb Declares," *Evening Tribune*, 8/6/68, p. A6
98. "Henry Bubb Bubbles Over for Reagan," *Sacramento Union*, 8/6/68
99. Polczinski, Al, "Reagan Wins Top Honors in Bow at Kansas session for Undecided," *Wichita Eagle*, 8/6/68
100. Torrence Elon, "New Ball Game, Says Bubb," *Dallas Times Herald*, 8/5/68, p. 20A
101. Bass and Thompson, p. 226
102. Chester et. al., p. 437
103. Chester et. al., p. 437
104. Curtis Patrick, vol. I, p. 239
105. Hill, Gladwin, "Reagan Officially in Race; Acts to Bar Nixon Sweep," *NYT*, 8/6/68, p. 1
106. Perlstein, p. 298
107. Dent, p. 93
108. Bass and Thompson, p. 226
109. Bass and Thompson, p. 226
110. "Sock it to me" was a favored expression on the comedy show Laugh-In, in which Nixon would appear later
111. Bass and Thompson, p. 226
112. Bass and Thompson, p. 226
113. Perlstein, p. 298
114. Bass and Thompson, p. 226
115. Chester et. al., p. 437
116. Chester et. al., p. 456
117. Bass and Thompson, p. 225
118. Chester et. al., p. 456
119. Witcover, p. 339
120. Nixon, p. 309
121. Witcover, p. 340
122. Novak, p. 167
123. Chester et. al., p. 458
124. Chester et. al., p. 458
125. Chester et. al., p. 458
126. Dent, p. 90
127. Dent, p. 90
128. Dent, p. 90
129. http://tvnews.vanderbilt.edu/program.pl?ID=1530
130. http://tvnews.vanderbilt.edu/program.pl?ID=441722
131. William H. Thompson to Fred A Seaton, invitation for August 5, Fred A Seaton Collection, Dwight D Eisenhower Presidential Library
132. Dent, p. 95
133. Dent, p. 95
134. Dent, p. 95
135. Dent, p. 95
136. Dent, p. 95
137. Chester et. al., p. 458-459
138. Bass and Thompson, p. 226
139. Bass and Thompson, p. 226
140. Chester et. al., p. 436
141. Chester et. al., p. 437
142. Chester et. al., p. 437
143. *Newsweek*, 8/19/68, p. 25
144. Bass and Thompson, p. 227
145. Dent, p. 96
146. Dent, p. 96
147. Chester et. al., p. 459
148. Chester et. al., p. 459
149. Kopelson, Gene 2014A
150. Kopelson, Gene 2014D
151. Chester et. al., p. 460

152. Witcover, p. 342
153. Dent, p. 97
154. Nixon, p. 309
155. Kopelson 2014D
156. Cannato, p. 380
157. Cannato, p. 380
158. Evans, Daniel, "Keynote Address" Vital Speeches of the Day XXXIV No. 22, 9/1/68
159. *Newsweek*, 8/19/68, p. 25
160. Chester et. al., p. 460
161. Chester et. al., p. 461-465
162. Bass and Thompson, p. 229
163. *Newsweek*, 8/19/68, p. 27
164. Bass and Thompson, p. 229
165. Bass and Thompson, p. 229
166. Dent, p. 88
167. Dent, p. 89
168. Chester et. al., p. 465
169. Bass and Thompson, p. 230
170. Dent, p. 98
171. Evans, *The Education of Ronald Reagan*, p. 188
172. Dent, p. 98
173. Dent, p. 98
174. Reed, p. 28
175. Bass and Thurmond, p. 230
176. Pearson, Drew, "Washington Merry-go-Round," 8/19/68
177. Chester et. al., p. 465-466
178. Mailer, p. 72
179. Mailer, p. 71
180. Mailer, p. 71
181. Mailer, p. 71
182. Mailer, p. 72
183. Mailer, p. 72
184. Mailer, p. 73
185. Chester et. al., p. 466
186. Chester et. al., p. 466
187. Dent, p. 89
188. Mailer, p. 72
189. http://tvnews.vanderbilt.edu/program.pl?ID=1551
190. Chester et. al., p. 467
191. Witcover, p. 344
192. *Newsweek*, 8/19/68, p. 26
193. Dent, p. 98
194. Dent, p. 98
195. Evans, "The Educ of RR," p. 187
196. Dent, p. 99
197. Witcover, p. 345
198. Chester et. al., p. 467
199. Novak, p. 168
200. Witcover, p. 345
201. Witcover, p. 345-346
202. See Illustrations
203. *Newsweek*, 8/19/68, p. 26
204. White and Gill, p. 123
205. Rusher, p. 214
206. Rusher, ibid
207. Chester et. al., p. 469-470
208. Reed, p. 28
209. Novak, p. 168
210. Chester et. al., p. 467
211. Chester et. al., p. 468
212. Chester et. al., p. 468
213. Chester et. al., p. 468
214. Bass and Thompson, p. 230
215. Chester et. al., p. 468-469
216. Dent, p. 99

217. Witcover, p. 338
218. White and Gill, p. 123
219. White and Gill, p. 124
220. Rusher, p. 215
221. Chester et. al., p. 469
222. Tanya M. Melich to Newt Gingrich, letter 8/12/68, Tanya Melich Collection, Series II, Box 3, Folder 17, M.E. Grenander Dept. of Special Collections and Archives, University at Albany, State University of New York
223. Tanya M. Melich to The Honorable John J. Savage, letter 8/12/68, Tanya Melich Collection, Series II, Box 3, Folder 17, M.E. Grenander Dept. of Special Collections and Archives, University at Albany, State University of New York
224. Kabaservice, p. 242
225. Melich, personal interview 6/18/2014; Melich, personal communication 4/30/2015
226. Chester et. al.
227. Chester et. al., p. 469
228. Dent, p. 99
229. Novak, p. 168
230. White and Gill, p. 125
231. Dent, p. 99
232. Witcover, p. 346
233. Chester et. al., p. 472
234. Dent, p. 99-100
235. Nixon, p. 310
236. Witcover, p. 346
237. Witcover, p. 347
238. Rusher, p. 215
239. CBS Evening News, 8/7/1968
240. White and Gill, p. 125
241. White and Gill, ibid

CHAPTER 39: REAGAN IS NOMINATED

Reagan is the man "who has inspired a nation; a man who can restore the free world's faith in our beloved country. And yes, the man who can restore faith in ourselves, in our fellow man, in our country and in our God."

~ Ivy Baker Priest Stevens[1]

"The highlight of my political life."

~ Jim Gardner[2]

"No other Republican in our Nation can boast of a record like this. No other Republican promises so much in the way of victory. No other Republican can better challenge the might and money of our opposition." Americans "know he will do what he says he will do. They know he believes what he says he believes." Reagan will restore "the confidence of the world in America and our people's faith in themselves."

~ Bob Price[3]

"A man of common sense." Reagan had "real compassion for the underdog and the underprivileged" yet he demanded respect for "law and order and the rights of all citizens." Reagan was the man who could "restore greatness and grandeur and purpose" to America.

~ William Knowland[4]

The evening of Wednesday August 7 was the point when the years of hard work of Reagan's grass roots supporters finally were to be realized. But with White and Reed's final tally showing that Reagan and Rockefeller likely had not gathered enough strength to stop Nixon on the first ballot, only a big break—a miracle, as Mel Brooks might have written—could thrust Reagan into the nominee's spot. But the prayers of Reed and White, and by this point likely Reagan too, were about to be heard, as the long nominating process began at 5:30 PM. As planned, Alabama yielded to California, and thus Ronald Reagan's name, for the very first time in history, was placed in nomination for the presidency of the United States.

Ivy Baker Priest

It was quite fitting that the person who had the honors had a direct tie to Reagan's mentor. For Ivy Baker Priest Stevens had been former treasurer of the United States in the Eisenhower years and now was California's treasurer. Her future obituary, on June 23, 1975, would note that she had been the first woman to place a nomination for the presidency on behalf of Reagan that day. Of note, when she was treasurer of the country, she had appeared on the August 29, 1954 show of *What's My Line*, as contestants had to guess who she was and what her job was. Her 1958 autobiography, *Green Grows the Ivy*, of course does not discuss her role in 1968, and her personal papers, filed at the University of Utah, have no notes about her Reagan nomination speech.[5]

At a press conference on July 19 in Little Rock, a reporter had asked Reagan if he had decided who would place his name in nomination and he answered, "No; we've been talking about a few names" and added that the possibilities included "some of our own legislators, some of our own delegates, people from California."[6] Reagan had been proud that Priest, upon her return to California from the nation's capital, had joined his own administration in Sacramento. At his November 10, 1967 press conference in Seattle, Reagan had said he was "very fortunate" to have Ivy Baker Priest Stevens as his California state treasurer after having served as United States treasurer in the Eisenhower administration. Reagan cited her financial skills in that although she had $18Million less in funds to invest than her Democrat predecessor (due to Reagan cost-cutting), however she was able to achieve a greater total monetary return.[7] For her part, she often called Reagan "His Excellency."[8]

Mailer described her that evening as a "wretched speaker with parched, nasal, mean, stingy acid driving tones."[9] But this author, watching and listening to her on a DVD recording of her speech, found her voice pleasing and without any noticeable accent and having no acidic driving tones. Priest took the rostrum at 5:45 PM and was described as "white-haired and smiling in a blue lace dress."[10] She began by reminding her listeners that the Johnson administration was "confused and divided" and only offered solutions which were "the same disproven, antiquated answers which led to the failures of yesterday." But American now was "on the threshold of a new era," for which Republicans had the opportunity to "embark upon a recommitment to American ideals and excellence." Americans were crying out for "purpose, for direction, for leadership." California had faced such similar problems two years earlier, when they had been tired of a Democratic administration in Sacramento, which had provided "eight years of false promises and bankrupt programs." But California had come forward by choosing a "great new citizen leader." Citing Reagan's Ike-inspired campaign theme, she proclaimed that Reagan was a man "of integrity, compassion, and common sense; a man who could communicate, who could inspire and who could lead—a proven winner." After rounds of applause she continued. "What America needs today is a man with the courage to meet the problems, and to face with courage the issues and will not trade the demands of leadership for the comforts of expediency." Then she placed Reagan's name in nomination as the man "who has inspired a nation; a man who can restore the free world's faith in our beloved country. And yes, the man who can restore faith in ourselves, in our fellow man, in our country and in our God."[11]

Despite his earlier disparaging comments, Mailer did admit that Priest looked "confident, enthusiastic, round, sexy, warm, and gloriously vital."[12] Matt Lawson recalled fondly and with pride the pageantry of Ivy Baker Priest's speech.[13] Peter Murphy sat with the Oregon delegation, close to Governor McCall and Senator Hatfield. As Priest nominated Reagan, Murphy recalls, he was encouraged by Nixon supporters in the delegation to hold up his Reagan sign. He proudly joined the throngs in convention hall who all waved and cheered for Reagan.[14]

CBS anchor Walter Cronkite interrupted his live broadcast of Priest's speech to say that according to his network's count, Nixon had gone over the top. But the camera focused on California's delegates, whose members were wearing high sombrero hats. A few minutes later Cronkite interrupted again saying that Reagan was in the convention building, but was not in the hall yet, as he was still meeting with delegates privately to forestall a first ballot Nixon victory.

As Priest finished, pandemonium broke out. Delegates sang, "California here I Come" and "Dixie."[15] Others sang "Hey Look Me Over."[16] There was cheering, stomping, the waving of signs and placards, and general joy in the delegations. Delegates poured into the aisles with bands playing and state standards swaying above the crowds; some placards had slogans such as "I'm Gone on Ron."[17] CBS showed viewers many different Reagan signs. A CBS reporter interviewed Nancy Reagan during the demonstration and she said she was surprised by her husband's nomination and all the support he was getting. When asked if she or any of the other candidates' wives were involved in any discussions of strategy, she answered, "No."

Mailer saw five cages of balloons overhead, with Reagan catching one of them as it fell.[18] The demonstration for Reagan lasted twenty-two minutes, which one group of historians noted was the loudest compared to those later for Rockefeller or Nixon.[19] Bruce Schadler of SFR recalled looking all around, as he and so many others were standing and cheering for Reagan, and being very impressed by a "distinguished looking black man from California cheering for Reagan."[20] Matt Lawson, whose birthday was the next day, stood next to the wife of California National Committeeman Gardiner Johnson. Amidst all the cheering and wild yelling, their photograph later appeared in *Look*.[21]

Seconding Speeches

After the Priest Stevens nomination speech and the wild demonstrations, only ten minutes remained which were allocated for the seconding speeches.

Congressman Jim Gardner of North Carolina gave the first of the seconding speeches. Gardner reflected decades later that giving Reagan's seconding speech in 1968 had been the "highlight of my political life."[22] With the failure of Utah to stay in Reagan's camp and the decision by Ken Rogstad not to challenge the composition of the Washington State delegation, Gardner's North Carolina delegation remained the only one with a Reagan majority. Even though he had failed to persuade Thurmond to change his mind away from his support of Nixon, Gardner had held firm. As he seconded Reagan's nomination, Gardner made the delegates recall the dark days of 1964 with the "one bright spot that pierced the gloom" being Reagan's "The Speech." Gardner proclaimed that Republicans stood "on the threshold of its greatest hour," and he was indeed so pleased to second the nomination of Reagan.[23]

Next to the rostrum was Texas Congressman Bob Price, whose support and endorsement of Reagan during the spring had garnered him this honor. Price reminded the delegates that Republicans needed to nominate a proven winner and that Reagan had soundly defeated the California governor who had beaten Nixon. But the party also needed a man who not only was a winner, but needed someone who had coattails, for it might not be "much use" to have a Republican in the White House if Congress remained "overwhelmingly" Democrat. In 1966, Reagan had swept into office with him fully 26 new Republican legislators, four new statewide office holders, three new congressmen, and in three special elections since, had elected all 3. During 1967-1968, hundreds of thousands of people had turned out to see and hear Reagan and had donated "record amounts" to the party. Price declared emphatically, "No other Republican in our Nation can boast of a record like this. No other Republican promises so much in the way of victory. No other Republican can better challenge the might and money of our opposition." Now the age of television had dawned and Americans could sit in their homes and "look face to face with the candidates." Americans have seen Reagan and "know he will do what he says he will do. They know he believes what he says he believes." Reagan would restore America's greatness and restore "the confidence of the world in America and our people's faith in themselves."[24]

Last, California Senator William Knowland climbed up the stairs to speak. Knowland traced the history of open conventions within the Republican Party by citing 1860 and 1876, when Lincoln and Hayes, respectively, had not won on the first ballots but had been nominated on later ballots, and later for Garfield, it had taken a full 36 ballots. He urged each delegate to not be "mere rubber stamps," but to "fully assume his right and duty" by making a careful decision. Knowland saw in Reagan a man with leadership, principle, integrity, courage, and yes "a man of common sense." Reagan had a "real compassion for the underdog and the underprivileged" yet he demanded respect for "law and order and the rights of all citizens." Reagan was the man who could "restore greatness and grandeur and purpose" to America.[25] Knowland's biographers did not mention this speech in their book, *One Step from the White House*. Neither biographer has any files or notes about Knowland's speech, even though writer Paul Manolis did fly back to California with Reagan and Knowland after the convention.[26]

Mailer observed that once Reagan's name was placed in nomination and the seconding speeches and the demonstrations ended, "a monumental sense of tedium overtook the night."[27] There were nominating and seconding speeches for Rockefeller and Nixon and a few favorite sons, including Romney, all heading towards the final voting. At this point Mailer ascended to the top seating of the convention, where he sat alone at the end of the row until he looked up and saw a young man watching him.

Ron Docksai had stayed for two full weeks at the Fountainebleu and had been busy participating in many pro-Reagan rallies and demonstrations. He had seen several luminaries including Jackie Gleason, Clint Eastwood, and Congressman George H.W. Bush. But Docksai paid special attention to author Norman Mailer. Docksai had enjoyed watching Mailer being picked up each day in a fancy auto, while he and his fellow Reagan supporters had to take the free shuttle bus. Docksai recalled decades later that he enjoyed going to the top "nosebleed" section of the convention seating, occasionally to watch the proceedings from afar. Just after the three major candidates had been nominated that evening, Docksai noted a man who took a seat at the end of his bleacher. It was Mailer.

Mailer beckoned to Docksai and Docksai came and sat next to Mailer. After an uncomfortable long period of silence while Mailer was scribbling notes, Mailer asked Docksai where he was from and when Docksai answered New York City, Mailer's eyes lit up saying he himself was from Flushing. After Mailer then asked him what he was doing there, Docksai told Mailer all about Reagan, including Docksai having printed pro-Reagan posters and created special light bulbs that glowed in the dark with the words, "The Switch is On to Ron." Mailer scribbled notes but the two never saw each other again.[28]

The Last Minute Miracle for Reagan: Nixon-Hatfield

As delegates returned to convention hall for the evening session, they saw newsboys hawking a bulldog edition of the next morning's *Miami Herald* with the page-one banner headline that Oregon's liberal Mark Hatfield would indeed be Nixon's choice for running mate.[29] It was yet another—the third—newspaper report that sent shock waves through the delegations. Dent recalled that the story, plus the prior Evans-Novak column the morning before, had seemed most convincing and once again, he "suddenly got panicky."[30] Those two stories, added to the first one—as the convention opened—clearly made a "strong emotional impact on conservatives."[31]

Here was the hoped-for last-minute miracle for Tom Reed and Clif White and Ronald Reagan. The Reagan team sprang into action.[32] White ordered 2,000 copies of the newspaper.[33] At 8 PM, "squads of Reagan floor men" were seen moving quickly amongst the Southern delegations, giving out copies of the newspaper to every delegate and alternate they could find, "as if their political lives depended on it."[34] Actually they did. A great buzz began to spread like wildfire through the convention. Reed and White and Reagan's prayers for a last-minute break or miracle seemingly had been answered.

For an hour, White and Reed felt as if it were Monday night "all over again."[35] In fact, David Jones, the chairman of Students for Reagan, had gathered every SFR and YAF attendee he could find and they all joined the Reagan floor men with the newspaper copies that White had purchased.[36] They all enveloped the Southern delegates, telling as many as they could find, that Nixon was going to betray the South after all. Their votes must be changed to Reagan. Nixon would double-cross them after all, no matter what assurances Thurmond and Dent had given them. Jones' troops spread out across the floor and delivered the copies to every delegate and alternate they could find.[37]

Don Hodel of Oregon, still of course a Reagan supporter, was seated in front of the South Carolina delegation and recalled turning around to ask as many South Carolina delegates as he could what they thought of Reagan? He noted, "To a person (man and woman) they 'loved' him but they all said that 'Strom said that last time we voted our hearts. This time we vote for a winner.'"[38]

The Southern delegates began to waiver under the storm of Reagan youth handing out the hated news that Nixon would in fact double-cross them after all. Thurmond's assurances the day before were seemingly worthless.[39] Dent was watching the "pandemonium again" in the Southern delegations, knowing that if the story were true, that indeed "Tricky Dick" had in fact lied about waiting to make a decision on the choice of a running mate and had betrayed the South.

Rusher was handed a floor pass by Clif White and instructed to bring the news directly to Jim Martin in the Alabama delegation in the hope it would "shake him loose" from his commitment to Nixon.[40] Rusher's movements were reported to the Nixon team via walkie-talkie. Martin, in a phrase not intended to hurt any Jewish delegates nearby, for a second time exclaimed "Oh Lord! If that's true, my delegation will make a lampshade out of me! I'll go check it out."[41]

So the heads of the Mississippi and Alabama delegations, Clarke Reed and Martin, who had "the major panic" from the articles, ran to find Thurmond and Dent to explain what was happening. Then they told Thurmond that they would have to again canvas their delegates in light of Nixon's betrayal and the dramatic shift to Reagan. They felt that both delegations would need to skip the first ballot and see what other states were doing.[42]

Thurmond was described as "furious," telling the men they would have to get their delegations back solidly in line for Nixon.[43] Thurmond claimed that he knew the newspaper story could not possibly be true. Dent also "raced from delegation to delegation, insisting the story was not true."[44] Dent told delegates that Evans and Novak were Rockefeller supporters and thus their story was a plant to create panic.[45]

Then Clarke Reed of Mississippi pulled a trick from his bag. He challenged everyone from his delegation to a bet: he would wager $100 that the story was false. Despite raising his wager higher and higher, there were no takers. The head of the Georgia delegation did the same with a $1,000 wager.[46]

Dent did them one better. Dent found the writer of the story and corralled him in front of the Louisiana delegation. The delegates were frothing to vote for Reagan, but when Dent told the writer, "I'll have three hundred dollars with you; your story is wrong." The writer declined to take the wager, so triumphantly, Dent yelled what just had happened through a mega-phone to the delegates. The delegates calmed down and got back in line for Nixon.[47]

Hodel watched behind him as Thurmond then picked up his red phone with its direct line to Nixon. Thurmond confronted Nixon, who told Thurmond that the Hatfield rumor was false. But Hodel later recalled that the next morning, he would have breakfast with Hatfield's chief of staff, who would complain that Hatfield's chances to be vice-president had been destroyed by the newspaper-induced pandemonium, because in fact Nixon had promised the spot to Hatfield.[48] Fellow Oregonian, Governor Tom McCall, also recalled in his autobiography that he had been certain that Senator Hatfield and Nixon had a definite agreement. As soon as Nixon had won the Oregon primary back in May, Hatfield "threw himself" at Nixon; everything else seemed secondary. When Hatfield had defected from Rockefeller to Nixon, Rockefeller was disgusted.[49] Later it was learned that the source of the Hatfield story had been an "innocent" comment that had been made by Gerald Ford.[50]

So just before the rollcall began, Nixon workers were seen removing Nixon-Hatfield posters, which had been brought into the convention by several Oregon delegates.[51] Thurmond then grabbed his own megaphone in front of television cameras and announced that "the South loves Reagan, but it won't break."[52] It was time to vote.

Rusher walked back to the Reagan trailer command post and saw Reagan still talking earnestly around a long table to a final group of Mississippi delegates.[53] Reagan, White, Tom Reed and Rusher had hoped to pull a last rabbit out of their hats to stop Nixon on the first ballot. Finally, it was sinking in that they had lost. But one never knew what might occur during the actual roll call. Would a final miracle save the Reagan candidacy?

Endnotes

1. Priest Stevens, Ivy Baker, "Nomination Speech for Ronald Reagan" Official Report of the Proceedings of the Twenty-ninth Republican National Convention, Republican National Committee, 1968, p. 286-289
2. Gardner, pers int 3/27/2013
3. Price, Robert C., "Seconding Speech for Ronald Reagan" Official Report of the Proceedings of the Twenty-ninth Republican National Convention, Republican National Committee, 1968, p. 290-291
4. Knowland, William F., "Seconding Speech for Ronald Reagan" Official Report of the Proceedings of the twenty-ninth Republican National Committee, 1968, p. 292-293
5. Nepreis, Liz, personal communication 8/1/12
6. RRL, Tape 348
7. RR L, Tape 307
8. Vidal, Gore, "The Late Show," *The New York Review of Books*, 9/12/68
9. Mailer, p. 66
10. Wicker, Tom, "Nixon is Nominated on First Ballot," *NYT*, 8/9/68, p. 1
11. Priest Stevens, Ivy Baker "Nomination Speech for Ronald Reagan" Official Report of the Proceedings of the Twenty-ninth Republican National Convention, Republican National Committee, 1968, p. 286-289
12. Mailer, p. 67
13. Lawson, pers int 1/28/13
14. Peter Murphy, pers int 8/16/12
15. Mailer, p. 67
16. Wicker, Tom, "Nixon is Nominated on the First Ballot," *NYT*, 8/9/1968 p1
17. Wicker op.cit.
18. Mailer, p. 67
19. Chester et. al., p. 473
20. Schadler pers int 5/21/13
21. Lawson, personal communication, 3/31/2015
22. Gardner, pers int 3/27/2013
23. Gardner, James C., "Seconding Speech for Ronald Reagan" Official Report of the Proceedings of the Twenty-Ninth Republican National Convention" Republican National Committee, 1968, p. 290
24. Price, Robert C., "Seconding Speech for Ronald Reagan" Official Report of the Proceedings of the Twenty-ninth Republican National Convention, Republican National Committee, 1968, p. 290-291
25. Knowland, William F., "Seconding Speech for Ronald Reagan" Official Report of the Proceedings of the twenty-ninth Republican National Committee, 1968, p. 292-293
26. Manolis, Paul, personal interview 3/11/13; Johnson, Jim, personal communication 3/10/2013
27. Mailer, p. 67
28. Docksai, pers comm. 7/16/13
29. Bass and Thurmond p 230
30. Dent, p. 100
31. Dent, p. 100
32. White and Gill, p. 125-126
33. Evans, *The Education of Ronald Reagan*, p. 188
34. Chester et. al., p. 473
35. Chester et. al., p. 473
36. White and Gill, p. 125-126
37. White and Gill, p. 126
38. Hodel, pers comm. 10/7/2012
39. White and Gill, p. 126
40. Rusher, p. 214
41. Rusher, p. 214
42. Dent, p. 100
43. Chester et. al., p. 474
44. Bass and Thompson, p. 230
45. Dent, p. 100-101
46. Dent, p. 101

47. Chester et. al., p. 474; Bass and Thompson, p. 230
48. Hodel, pers comm. 10/7/2012
49. McCall, p. 106
50. Bass and Thompson, p. 231
51. McCall, p. 107
52. Chester et. al., p. 474
53. Rusher, p. 215

Chapter 40: Let's Make it Unanimous

"Adjourn! Adjourn!"

~ Pat Noland and Bruce Weinrod[1]

"Well, Ron, you're a young guy. You'll have another shot at this."

~ Richard Nixon[2]

At 1:19 AM on Thursday, August 8, the roll call voting began. Reagan was still in the trailer, "beseeching" Mississippi delegates to cast their 20 votes where their hearts lay.[3] Then Reagan went into the hall and sat together with Reed and the rest of the California delegation. Reed recalled Reagan's "piercing blue eyes" focus on the many delegates he had tried to persuade to join his quest to stop Nixon.[4]

For Reagan, the states at the beginning of the alphabet did not start out so badly. Alabama gave 12 for Reagan, and California added all 86. But in the end Florida's unit rule held and basically all votes went for Nixon. Mississippi held its unit rule too. But then a buzz began.

Pat Nolan recalled that as the voting hit the "L" and "M" states in their alphabetical order, there was a big effort to adjourn the proceedings. Nolan and his former Rockefeller Girls had stood outside the delegates' entrance and asked for extra credentials and tickets. There were three layers of security: barbed wire around the perimeter of the parking lots, doors at the entrance, and ticket inspections. A friend from California, wearing the official California Reagan delegation outfit—a black "Zorro" hat like the early California dons wore plus an orange V-shaped poncho with tassles—helped Nolan get in by distracting the security guard. Nolan ran across Dana Rohrabacher, back from Eastern Europe, and the two had managed to spirit in the two former Rockefeller Girls.[5]

Sitting in the bleachers, even as the voting tallies were announced, Nolan heard and saw that many delegates still were thinking of switching to Reagan, even into the wee hours of Thursday morning. They wanted to stop the proceedings to let the delegates take time to think about their votes and to nominate Reagan on Friday. They tried and tried to be recognized to place a motion of adjournment. The Reagan troops in the bleachers, Nolan and his friends, and Reagan activists on the floor, like Weinrod and many others, started to shout, "Adjourn! Adjourn!" Was the final miracle here at last? Would the convention be adjourned, and after a night to think of the consequences for the nation and the world, would the delegates return the next day and vote their hearts for Ronald Reagan?

Alas, the adjournment cries went unheeded. Convention Chairman Gerald Ford ruled them out of order and kept the proceedings going.[6] It would not be the last time Ford successfully would stop a late-inning Reagan drive to capture the nomination. As historian Craig Shirley has reviewed in detail, the next time would be in 1976. But it still was not yet over for Reagan's chances to be the nominee. After all, the goal was never to win on the first ballot. It was to stop Nixon and then win on the second or third ballot.

For at that point, it looked as if Reagan and Rockefeller had "actually halted Nixon short of the total he needed for nomination on the first ballot."[7] Then came "N" and New Jersey. When the news—that Reagan might still be catapulted to the nomination on the second ballot—was shared with the chairman of a county from New Jersey, the chairman—a Nixon supporter—quickly arranged that the Bergen County delegation split off from the state's slate. The slate, originally pledged to favorite son Clifford Case and not to Nixon, then went for Nixon.[8] That sealed Reagan's fate.

It was not until Wisconsin that Nixon finally got over the magic 667 votes. *RN* at last had survived the onslaught; he was the last *R* standing. Sitting in the California delegation, SFR member Matt Lawson looked at his watch. Mrs. Gardiner Johnson wished him a happy twenty-second birthday. But Matt was not happy.[9]

Neither was Reagan. Or was he alleviated that finally it was over? By then Reagan was back in the trailer, and he and White discussed a motion to make the vote unanimous. So Reagan headed back to the convention floor.[10]

Ultimately, Nixon would get only 25 votes more than the 667 required out of the 1,333 cast. At the very end, seeing the inevitable, Cliff White tipped off a few old friends that for Reagan it "was all over," and suggested they now vote for Nixon so as to go with the winner.[11] In the end, Nixon got 298 votes from 14 Southern and border states, although for most of these delegates, "Nixon was very much a second-choice candidate."[12] They really wanted Reagan and had hoped they could cast their true vote on the second ballot.

Reagan's ultimate tally was 182, including all 86 from California, 16 from the Reagan-majority state of North Carolina, 12 from Alabama, 15 from Texas, 6 from Washington and 5 from Idaho. Even after Reagan would call for a unanimous vote for Nixon, two delegates refused to budge and still voted for their hero.

Then magnanimous candidate Ronald Reagan ascended the platform. As he walked up, there was a "giant wave of applause."[13] Ford would not let Reagan come to the rostrum, citing convention rules. So while Reagan waited, and waited, Ford again thwarted Reagan by continuing to recognize delegations, one by one. Finally, Ford recognized a motion from Virginia to suspend the rules, and he let Reagan address the convention.[14] Was Reagan seething, standing there for many minutes awaiting Ford to permit him to address the convention?

At the podium in Miami Beach, observed Mailer, Reagan was smiling at the time and "looked curiously more happy than he had looked at any point in the convention." Reagan spoke with a mildness and a simplicity.[15] The delegates "cheered him wildly." He looked happy as if finally, "something had gone his way." Maybe Reagan's happiness was a sense of relief that it was Nixon's turn. Maybe it was too soon for him. His turn would come. Yet he wasn't getting any younger. But something important had gone his way. He had begun as a citizen candidate into a citizen governor concentrating on domestic issues. Now Ronald Reagan had transformed to become a world statesman who many across the nation thought should be president of the United States.

The color footage of Reagan showed him smiling against a crisp blue background atop the podium emblazoned with "Republican National Convention 1968." After the applause died down, the words in yellow "Nixon 1333" flashed across the screen. Reagan stated,

"We're gathered here with one common bond uniting us, and that is the knowledge that this great nation cannot stand or survive four more years of the policies that have been guiding us for too many of the recent years. Therefore because the only vehicle in the great two party system with the potential to replace the leadership now in Washington is the Republican Party, I hereby proudly move on behalf of my fellow Californians that this convention declare itself as unanimously and united behind the candidate Richard Nixon as the next President of the United States."[16]

Reagan's speech took 55 seconds. And then his 57-hour official candidacy was all over. But unofficially, so much had happened for so long, it all seemed a blur. In 1964, the Owosso group started it all. He first spoke out on Vietnam while in New Haven. At their first personal meeting, Ike certified him as presidential timbre during his gubernatorial campaign. In Seattle he spoke for the first time as a national political figure. Reagan made his first plans and multiple meetings with Reed and White to hunt for delegates and to campaign across the country. At his inauguration, Reagan saw the Reagan-for-President banner unfurled. Then came years of hard work, so many plane flights, hand shaking, breakfasts and dinners and lunches and barbecues, so many press conferences on land and in the air, so many speeches. The first campaign trip was to Eugene. The grand Vietnam debate triumph against Kennedy and calling for the Soviets to tear down the Berlin Wall. The cheering students in Omaha. Detente with Nixon in Bohemia Grove. Mentoring by Eisenhower via three more personal meetings and many phone calls and letters. Pressing about a surge in Vietnam. Threats to use nuclear weapons, threaten an amphibious invasion, threaten to mine Haiphong Harbor. The visits with Thurmond and Tower. The Milwaukee speech and starting his Wisconsin campaign with Don L. Taylor. The library dedication with Dirksen. The Landon Lecture. The Time cover. The governors cruise and many governors conferences. Riding horseback at the Oregon Veteran's Day parade and football game and his first speech devoted to world affairs. Visiting Lawrence-Livermore and learning about an anti-missile defense. Visiting veterans. His Chubb Fellowship at Yale. Honorary Seabee. Official trip to Mexicali. Proclamation on Croatia and the Latvian dancers. The Students for Reagan. His campaign swings to the West and South. Johnson's "unease" speech. Tet. The *U.S.S. Pueblo*. Johnson's withdrawal. His reinvigorated campaign after Kennedy's announcement. Bringing back Reed and White. Henry Bubb's Citizens for Reagan National Information Center. The King assassination. Writing the new White Paper speeches challenging Kennedy's candidacy. *Ronald Reagan, Citizen Governor*. The great first step in the Wisconsin primary. The huge next leap in Nebraska thanks to Dale Young. The trip to Idaho to meet his huge, enthusiastic Oregon campaign team and the disappointment that in Oregon he did not do even better. Speaking on Israel. The win in California with the tragedy of the Kennedy assassination. Antimissile defense. How to negotiate with communists. MacMillan and how not to negotiate with hostage takers. Searching for delegates. Giving his White Paper speeches with the most important having been in Cleveland and the final summation of his new role as world statesman in Amarillo: world affairs and military preparedness. The convention platform. His formal announcement. The final push for delegates. Can he stop

Nixon on the first ballot? Florida, his last hope, says No. At the very end, last-minute switches in New Jersey seal his fate.

Once Reagan finished his call for unity, Chairman Gerald Ford came to Reagan's left side as they exchanged a few words and shook hands before Reagan departed. As historian Craig Shirley has so vividly recreated, in eight short years, they would return to the convention once again to proclaim party unity in 1976 but with Ford as victor and Reagan once again not finishing in first place. Reagan left the podium and later was seen wearing a Nixon campaign button.

Rockefeller called Nixon to congratulate him, saying, "Ron didn't come through as good as he thought he would."[17] Before the delegates dispersed, Thurmond managed to get Reagan and Nixon together at the Fountainebleau. Nixon said, "Well, Ron, you're a young guy. You'll have another shot at this." Reagan countered, "Mr. Vice-President, you're three years older than I am."[18] Had Reagan thought his last, best shot for the presidency now was gone?

Reporters Evans and Novak saw clearly that it had been an "incredibly close affair."[19] Despite Reagan's lack of open campaigning and Nixon's unappealing personality, so "magnetic was Reagan's pull," that he almost pulled it off.[20] But there was one final issue for Reagan. Would Nixon now choose him as his running mate?

Endnotes

1.   Nolan, Pat, pers comm 6/5/2013; Bruce Weinrod pers int 1/30/2015
2.   Deaver, oral history, p. 8
3.   White, p. 247
4.   Reed, *The Reagan Enigma*, p. 172
5.   Nolan, Pat, pers comm., 6/5/2013
6.   Weinrod, pers int 1/30/2015
7.   Kabaservice, p. 243
8.   Kabaservice, p. 243
9.   Lawson, personal communication 3/31/2015
10. White and Gill, p. 127
11. Chester et. al., p. 435
12. Chester et. al., p. 435
13. Evans, "The Educ of RR," p. 188
14. Wicker, Tom, "Nixon is Nominated on the First Ballot," *NYT*, 8/8/1968, p. 1
15. Mailer, p. 70
16. Reagan, Ronald "Motion to Make the Nomination of the Honorable Richard M. Nixon Unanimous", Official report of the Proceedings of the Twenty-ninth Republican National Convention, Republican National Committee, 1968, p. 387
17. Witcover, p. 349
18. Deaver, oral history, p. 8
19. Evans and Novak, p. 40
20. ibid

PART FIVE

LOOKING AHEAD

CHAPTER 41: VICE PRESIDENT RONALD REAGAN

"I promised Ronald Reagan he will not be nominated tonight and we can't let him down."

~ Clif White[1]

"Even if they tied and gagged me, I would find a way to signal 'No' by wiggling my ears."

~ Ronald Reagan[2]

"Reagan's just an actor."

~ Richard Nixon[3]

Ronald Reagan had spent a good portion of his first campaign for president denying that he wanted to be vice-president. Speculation had begun in the summer of 1966, as some had thought Reagan might be offered the second spot if he threw his California delegates to Romney or Nixon. At Nixon's January 7, 1967, secret campaign strategy meeting, Reagan as vice- president had been rejected soundly. In September, 1967, Nofziger had been asked what would happen if party leaders knocked on Reagan's door with a vice-presidential nomination? Nofziger answered, "He won't answer the door!"[4] The rumors seemed to peak with the October, 1967 *Time* cover when he was paired with Rockefeller.

And Reagan wanted none of it. As discussed, Eisenhower had advised strongly against it and the two men had discussed the Sherman statement; we have seen how in many press conferences Reagan had reiterated Ike's and his own same thoughts on the subject. Some of the thickest files in the Oregon secretary of state's office had been letters advocating Reagan for vice-president.[5] When his name was placed on the Oregon ballot for vice-president in March, 1968, he had withdrawn promptly. Reagan had told the press he was not interested in the second spot on the ticket "in any way."[6] But then William Roberts of Spencer-Roberts had told the press the same month that if party leaders came to Reagan at the convention saying for the good of the country and the party, would he accept the second spot, Roberts said Reagan would not say, "No." A day later, Reagan, who like Ike had said he would not refuse his duty to country, had to refute Roberts.[7]

The same month, when Reagan had met with Eisenhower at Palm Springs, Reagan had confirmed to his mentor that he would not run as a candidate for vice-president. At the time, Eisenhower and Reagan had discussed a possible Nixon-Reagan ticket, which had been pushed by unnamed "less liberal" Eastern Republicans.[8]

In June, it had been reported that Nixon was considering a moderate as his running mate. At the time, Nixon told the press that he would choose his own running mate rather than let the convention decide. The reason was, "the convention would instantly choose Mr. Reagan."[9] Then by late June, Pearson reported that Nixon, needing California to win the nomination, reversed course and had offered Reagan the second spot.[10] In mid July, these feelings were confirmed: "most party leaders—and convention delegates—would choose conservative Ronald Reagan for Vice President."[11]

Just before the convention, the John Birch Society had made its threats over a Rockefeller-Reagan ticket. And his formal telegrams to delegates to counteract the Nixon rumors seemingly had put an end to the speculation. But now that Nixon was the nominee, could there still be a Vice-President Ronald Reagan in the future?

And at the convention, when the final set of rumors started by Thurmond and Nixon needed to be squelched and Reagan had been forced to send out telegrams, Reagan had proclaimed, "Even if they tied and gagged me, I would find a way to signal 'No' by wiggling my ears."[12]

Historians Gibbs and Duffy detail how Nixon's advisors, including Buchanan, Richard Whalen and Richard Allen, had been pressuring Nixon to choose Reagan. The more attractive the advisors made Reagan, the less Nixon would consider him. In the end, Nixon waved them off, saying, "Reagan's just an actor."[13] Nixon's private phrase for Reagan was "Glamor Boy."[14] Buchanan reviews his own efforts and those of Whalen to get Nixon to choose Reagan as his running mate.[15]

Nixon had won the nomination at 2:10 A.M. Thursday morning, and according to historians Chester et al, by 2:15 A.M., Nixon was in the solarium of his penthouse suite. At this first meeting to decide his running mate, Reagan's name was tossed out but no decision was made. So Nixon called a second meeting.[16] This new meeting included Dent, Thurmond, Finch, Knowland, Goldwater, Nunn, Dewey,

Murfin, Rhodes, Billy Graham, and Congressman Donald Rumsfeld. Eisenhower's Attorney General Herbert Brownell was present too. Dent recalled that "the sentiments for Reagan were strongest," although many doubted he would accept. Dent and Thurmond plugged for Reagan, with Reagan at the top of Thurmond's list.[17]

Surprisingly, Rhodes of Ohio, who had been Reagan's own choice for vice-president, gave Reagan "bad marks." Rhodes cited an unspecified poll, possibly the Rockefeller poll cited earlier, which supposedly showed Reagan would be a "bad drag" in industrial cities.[18] Rhodes said, "With Reagan on the ticket, we'd lose Ohio worse than 1964."[19]

Rumsfeld summarized the meeting and added that besides Dent and Thurmond, Murfin also made a pitch for Reagan. Governor Nunn's first choice was Reagan, as was Hawaii Senator Fong, who had been impressed by Reagan's first White Paper speech in Hawaii.[20]

Eventually, Nixon chose Spiro Agnew. Historian Peter Hannaford noted that political considerations aside, the two major reasons Nixon did not choose Reagan were rooted in jealousy: Reagan would upstage him and Reagan was taller.[21]

But if Nixon had changed his mind, and had chosen Reagan, it would have been Reagan to assume office after Nixon's subsequent resignation.

The possibility of Vice-President Ronald Reagan seemingly had died when Nixon selected Agnew as his running mate. But years later during the Nixon presidency, Agnew would resign amidst scandal. So Nixon once again would face the decision of choosing a vice-president. Would it be Reagan, by then retired from two successful terms as governor? In his memoirs, Nixon revealed that he met Democrat Mike Mansfield, who told Nixon that a Reagan nomination would meet "very strong opposition" in the Democratic Congress. But when Nixon asked 400 Republican leaders, Reagan's name, tied with Rockefeller's, was at the top of the list. Nixon thought the choice of either Reagan or Rockefeller would be too divisive, so he settled on Gerald Ford.[22]

As the convention ended, Nixon gave his acceptance speech. According to his biographer, William Safire, Nixon's call, "Let's win it for Ike" sounded too much like "Let's win it for the Gipper."[23] Nixon explained to Safire that the portion of his speech dealing with an "impossible dream," when Nixon had slightly modified his voice while he spoke, could not have been done by any other politician. But then Nixon frowned, thinking of Reagan. "Reagan's an actor, but I'd like to see him do that."[24] Nixon still could not see Reagan as more than an actor. But the American public had seen, for three years now, how one day Ronald Reagan would sit in the Oval Office.

Just before the convention ended, Reed was conferring with a Virginia delegate who wanted to place Reagan's name in nomination for vice-president. Reed was deciding whether to call the delegate to confirm plans. White knew that Reagan in no way wanted this to happen, so knowing a stampede to Reagan would occur, White told Reed, "Tom, if you pick up that phone, I'll shoot you. I promised Ronald Reagan he will not be nominated tonight and we can't let him down."[25] Meanwhile Ronald Reagan prepared to leave the Miami Beach convention.

Endnotes

1.   White and Gill, p. 128-129
2.   White and Gill, p. 123
3.   Gibbs and Duffy, p. 217-219
4.   "Reagan Urges escalation to Win the war 'Quickly,'" *NYT*, 9/13/1967, p. 5
5.   Davies, Lawrence E., "Reagan's Backers in Oregon Seek to Enlist Rockefeller's '64 Supporters," *NYT*, 12/24/1967, p. 33
6.   "Reagan is Staying in Race in Oregon," *NYT*, 3/20/1968, p. 33
7.   *US News and World Report*, 3/25/1968, p. 56; "Reagan Seen on Ticket," *Omaha World-Herald*, 3/27/1968
8.   "Reagan Bars Race for Vice President," *NYT*, 3/13/1968, p. 34
9.   Semple, Robert B., "Nixon Considering Moderate on Ticket," *NYT*, 6/30/1968, p. 1
10. Pearson, Drew, "Washington Merry-Go-Round," 6/24/1968
11. Newsweek, 7/15/1968, p. 15
12. White and Gill, p. 123
13. Gibbs and Duffy, p. 217-219
14. White, p. 251
15. Buchanan, p. 295-304
16. Chester et. al., p. 485-486
17. Chester et. al., p. 487
18. Dent, p. 102-103
19. Chester et. al., p. 487
20. Rumsfeld, Donald, Memo 8/8/1968, courtesy Dirksen Congressional Center, Pekin IL
21. Hannaford, p. 27-28
22. Nixon, p. 925-926
23. Safire, p. 55
24. Safire, p. 55
25. White and Gill, p. 128-129

CHAPTER 42: CONCLUSION—THERE'LL BE ANOTHER DAY

"I believe Reagan would have been nominated and would have been elected, by a bigger margin than Nixon. I also reject the Republican cliché that it was fortunate Reagan was not elected for another twelve years, by which time his ideological framework was better refined." Reagan's election in 1968 "would have averted Watergate and its dreadful consequences for the Republican Party, for conservatism, and for America."

~ Robert Novak[1]

"I hear you're having a wake...This is Ronald Reagan."

~ Ronald Reagan[2]

"He's finished. He's way too old to run for anything but reelection as governor."

~ Mike Wallace[3]

"You'll have another chance!"

~ Ronald Reagan[4]

"We'll fight another day!"

~ Ronald Reagan[5]

Counter-factual history is often the subject of essay examinations. Historian Arthur Schlesinger, Jr. delivered the Landon Lecture a few days after Nixon won the general election, and in his speech he discussed his initial thoughts on how RFK, had he lived, would have won instead. A year later in his classic biography of RFK, Schlesinger speculates in much more detail that if RFK had lived and become the Democratic nominee in 1968, he would have achieved party unity, won the fall election, and ushered in a golden age of liberal triumphs.[6] But historian and commentator Patrick Buchanan and historian Lewis Gould argued that none of this would have occurred. Buchanan felt the antipathy between RFK and Johnson was so intense, that not only would Democratic unity never have been achieved, but that likely

Johnson would have supported Nixon.[7] Similarly, Gould felt RFK was not a unifying factor and would have lost.[8]

As mentioned earlier, Buchanan also felt that even had Nixon been stopped on the first ballot, the convention would have returned to him later. But clearly with so many delegates chomping at the bit to vote for Reagan on the second ballot, what if Reagan had won the nomination? All three major Republican candidates sought party unity—even Rockefeller had made positive statements about Reagan, unlike what had happened in 1964. Very likely on the second or third ballot, Reagan would have emerged as nominee with the support of both Rockefeller and Nixon, especially if Reagan would have announced Nixon as secretary of state. Even Romney and Lindsay eventually would have had to support the Reagan-Rhodes ticket, given the political pressures to join their united party.

Could Reagan have won in 1968 if the apparatus for nomination were via primary elections, as now, rather than the combination of a few primaries, ascending chains of voting by party members at the local-county-state level, and favorite sons? Possibly, yes. As Henry A. Bubb had urged as the Miami Beach convention began, there had been no debates. In the second decade of the twenty-first century, many voters feel there are too many primary debates. What if 1968 Republican primary voters had seen one or more debates among Nixon, Reagan, Rockefeller and Romney? Would not Reagan, with his affability and charisma, wide experience of proven methods of down-sizing government in California, and his wide-reaching knowledge on world affairs, have won? Nixon would have been seen again as the two-time loser while Reagan was the winner. And with Nixon having lost the 1960 debate to John F. Kennedy and Reagan having won the May, 1967 debate against RFK, would not Republican voters cast their votes for a winner?

And what of the general election? Could conservative Reagan have defeated RFK (had he lived) or Humphrey? Given Reagan's profound debate triumph against RFK in 1967, in the fall of 1968 Reagan likely would have bested RFK or Humphrey in any further debates. At a point where the Great Society programs were falling apart amidst protests and riots, Reagan stood as the clear law and order candidate many had sought. And a 1968 nominee Reagan, who had been attacking Kennedy-Johnson domestic and foreign policies throughout 1966-1968, would have continued and expanded those themes. Reagan's success in downsizing California's state government would have been an inspiration for the nation to apply under a President Reagan in 1969. Reporter Robert Novak, whose multiple personal observations of the Reagan campaign were cited earlier, reflected later in his own autobiography that Reagan would have been elected by a wider margin than did Nixon.

The country at this point still wanted to win in Vietnam, and Reagan was the only candidate who offered the clear alternative of a path to victory, following what Eisenhower had accomplished in Korea and had recommended for Vietnam. There is a reasonably good chance that once the Great Communicator as a full-fledged nominee had laid out his vision for America to enter the 1970s, he would have won. Novak felt the same.

Reagan's 1966 success in attracting disillusioned Democrats, Independents, and Americans of Mexican descent had laid the groundwork for a massive electoral triumph in 1968. As discussed earlier, during the spring of 1968, Reagan had been the candidate whose signing of the Croatian Proclamation had the immediate consequence that large numbers of those minority communities, as seen by the waving banners in Cleveland, started switching to the Republican Party.

On the way home from the convention, recalled Pat Nolan, he visited some friends and relatives in Tennessee. He met them, a group of 37 Democrats, all eager to meet a boy from California who had attended the Republican convention. The 37 were split on whether to vote for Nixon or Humphrey. But to a person, each said that if Reagan had been the Republican nominee in 1968, all would have voted for Reagan. Even one particular man, appointed to his job by the Democratic governor, said he liked Reagan a lot.[9] The disillusioned Democrats—the Reagan Democrats, envisioned first by Ike—could have been out in force in the polling booths that fall had Reagan been the nominee.

What of the Wallace factor? Rusher speculated that had Reagan announced earlier that he was running as a bona fide candidate, and then won the nomination, there was no way Wallace would have achieved the votes of almost ten million voters that fall. With Reagan, rather than Nixon, as the Republican candidate, Humphrey would have lost by a wider margin.[10] Novak went even further, predicting that with Reagan as Republican nominee, Wallace might not even had run.

And what of a President Reagan in the White House in January, 1969? Rusher did some speculation of what a Reagan presidency would have meant.[11] Domestically, he would have begun downsizing the federal government along the lines of his successes in California. As Rusher reflected, the economic history of the 1970s would have been, in conservative terms, better.[12] And of course Watergate would have remained just a local destination in the nation's capital of which few had ever heard.

Of all the major authors cited earlier who previously have chronicled Reagan's efforts for 1968, none discussed Reagan's growth in the arena of world affairs. Only reporter Bill Boyarsky penned a discussion of Reagan's foreign policy declarations during this time, and Boyarsky's analysis was less than two pages. Calling Reagan's foreign policy views "controversial," Boyarsky only mentioned Reagan's views on Vietnam as "hawkish" and accused Reagan of not wanting to discuss specifics of Vietnam.[13] Clearly the latter was incorrect as indeed Reagan was the only candidate who made specific strategic and tactical military recommendations. Indeed politicians contemplating national office should take the lesson of Reagan in the 1960s seriously. Although Reagan initially ran for office for a domestic governor, initially he schooled himself on foreign affairs but then learned in detail from the master: Dwight Eisenhower. Reagan slowly and steadily spoke out, more and more, on world affairs, until in the spring of 1968 he gave five masterful White Paper addresses plus his summation speech on world affairs in Amarillo. He had become a world statesman.

As Reagan had said on the campaign trail so often, as a new occupant in the Oval Office, in January, 1969, he would have announced a complete reassessment of military strategy and tactics in Vietnam. He would have followed through on the threats he had learned from Eisenhower which both had wanted. Reagan would have asked Congress for a declaration of war and asked Americans to sacrifice, just as he had urged during the campaign. He would have staged naval drills off North Vietnam to threaten an amphibious invasion. He would have sought hot pursuit of Viet Cong and North Vietnamese into bases in neighboring countries. He would have mined and blockaded Haiphong Harbor. He would have increased the bombing of North Vietnam and likely bombed their dams. He would have ordered a massive troop surge. He would have threatened atomic annihilation. He would have not allowed any negotiations to drag on more than a few days. In short, he would have won the war.

But in world affairs, Reagan would not have been done. As Reagan had declared in Nebraska in June, 1967, Reagan wanted to change the structure of the United Nations, so as to prevent America from being overruled by smaller nations. The structure of the United Nations was not a known subject discussed between Eisenhower and Reagan. Yet just as Reagan, off the cuff, was quite knowledgeable about Theodore

Roosevelt and the Perdicaris Affair, it was this very same objection that Roosevelt had had about the idea of a League of Nations.[14] Thus likely Reagan truly was a student of Theodore Roosevelt as well. Reagan concluded that until the UN was reorganized, the United States could not "submit questions affecting our national interest to the U.N. and be confident of a fair hearing."[15]

As he had done for the first time during the RFK debate and several times after, Reagan would have called publicly, again, to tear down the Berlin Wall. He would have funded and begun his anti-ballistic missile shield along with more research into orbital defense. If he reached any agreements with the Soviets, he would insist on "trust but verify." Instead of just reacting to communist-inspired and funded problems, he would have been proactive by stirring up trouble, ordering huge counter insurgencies against communists in hotspots. The media and the Soviets had admitted that the communist economy could not keep up with the West; they could not provide both consumer goods and a strong military. Reagan would have entered into the same defense build-up, during the 1970s to counteract the damage of the Kennedy-Johnson years, as he would do in the 1980s to counteract the damage of the Carter years. Communism may have fallen, with freedom restored to Eastern Europe, a full decade earlier that what would occur. But one must admit, without the presence of the strong anti-communist partners in the 1980s like Margaret Thatcher and Pope John Paul II, and without a changed Soviet leader like Gorbachev, certainly a President Reagan in January, 1969, would have found it a much more formidable task. But such are the forlorn hopes of counter-factual essays.

In the end, had Nixon's nomination on the first ballot by those few votes all boiled down to Thurmond supporting Nixon to exact a political price? Clif White later told reporter Novak that Thurmond had confessed to him that in fact Thurmond would have preferred Reagan, but he did not want to be "marginalized in his new Party."[16] White later looked over lists of delegates and saw leaders from the 1964 conservative crusade. The problem was that conservative leaders, who would have formed the core of a Reagan candidacy, had been "preempted" by Nixon. And what was worse was that it had been conservative leaders who had gone for Nixon instead of Reagan.[17] Historian David Reinhard's review of modern era conservative Republicans agrees, feeling that the early Nixon endorsements from Buckley, Thurmond and Tower had "mortally wounded" Reagan's bid. Yet Reagan and his team had continued fighting until the end.

Rusher reflected that many delegates at Miami Beach had told him that they would have cast aside their commitments to Nixon on the first ballot had it made a difference. But if such votes would make no difference, why subject those delegates to further "politically crippling" ordeals?[18] Plus Rusher recalled, *Human Events* had supported Nixon while *National Review* and the American Conservative Union had hedged. Besides Reagan's grass roots activists, only the young—SFR and YAF—had supported Reagan openly, from the beginning, and again at the convention.[19]

Novak also confirmed some of the above essay thoughts, as he reflected that the future would have been brighter under a President Reagan in 1969. Had it not been for Thurmond, Novak felt, "I believe Reagan would have been nominated and would have been elected, by a bigger margin than Nixon. I also reject the Republican cliché that it was fortunate Reagan was not elected for another twelve years, by which time his ideological framework was better refined." Reagan's election in 1968 "would have averted Watergate and its dreadful consequences for the Republican Party, for conservatism, and for America."[20]

Or was the fault with campaign director Reed? To your author, Reed admitted that the fatal flaw in his campaign leadership for Reagan's first presidential campaign is that he did not want Reagan to visit any of the three opt-out states in 1968.[21] Reagan had campaigned in Oregon and Wisconsin under the guise of fundraising trips in 1967. Certainly Reagan could have returned to each of the three opt-out states in early 1968. During those critical times his visits and speeches could have at least turned Oregon into another vote tally triumph, rather than the flat unchanged tally compared to Nebraska that had derailed his effort. Likely he still would not have won Oregon, as Reed and Reagan had planned back in 1966. But a significant vote of more than forty percent might have made a huge difference to those other grass roots activists and delegates across the country who were hard at work for Reagan. Another lost potential opportunity was write-in Pennsylvania.

But clearly some of the fault lay with the candidate himself. Reagan had been through a successful primary and then general election in California. He had had major roles in 1962 for Nixon and in 1964 for Goldwater. Yet he put his faith almost entirely in his financial backers, in young Reed and in veteran White. In 1966, Reagan did not heed the advice of Spencer that more experienced experts were needed to run the campaign. Spencer also saw clearly that Reagan needed to tell voters that he wanted to be their president.

Up to the point of his finally becoming the dominant force at the top of his campaign in March, 1968, after his nemesis RFK entered the race, Reagan did not exert the forceful control that was needed.

Was Reagan's 1968 campaign worth it?

One recent Reagan biographer hardly mentions Reagan's first presidential campaign at all.[22] Most of the reflections of actual participants and interested historians were negative. Rusher's chapter title is "The Blunder of 1968," and he called Reagan's 1968 campaign "hesitant, belated, and almost half-hearted."[23] Shirley termed it, "ill-conceived, ill-timed, and too little, too late."[24] Historians Gibbs and Duffy termed it, "strange and muddled."[25] *Life* felt Reagan's campaign bid "was doomed by Reagan's own national irrelevancy."[26] Historian Bill Adler felt "the endeavor was nothing more than a forlorn hope. The Reagan camp made the fatal error of waiting until the opening of the convention to announce for Ronald Reagan."[27] Historian Andrew Johns felt Reagan, the dark-horse candidate, was "far too hawkish for the GOP, let alone the nation as a whole to be seriously considered as a candidate."[28] Yet as noted, the country still wanted to win the war at this time, and had just 25 votes gone the other way, the party likely would have nominated Reagan.

But what about all of his grass roots activists who had given their hearts to see Reagan elected president in 1968? After the convention, Sally and John Gram hosted a small gathering of friends and supporters in the Portland suburbs. She recalled clearly being "very disappointed" because "we worked really hard."[29] Suddenly the phone rang. Sally picked it up and a voice said, "I hear you're having a wake...This is Ronald Reagan." Sally recovered quickly, expressed her disappointment to the governor, and passed the phone around to others wishing to speak with Reagan including Mrs. Pearlman.[30] John recalled that Reagan was very kind and spoke to everyone at the gathering.[31] It was the second time Reagan had called the group of Oregon supporters after a defeat. But whereas in May his call was to express thanks for their hard work in the losing effort of his Oregon primary campaign, at that time there was still the convention to look forward to and the possibility of Reagan's nomination despite having lost in Oregon. But now this second thank you call in August, after the nomination of Nixon, seemed to the Oregon campaign staff to close the curtain on Ronald Reagan's bid for the presidency. In Wisconsin, Don L. Taylor commented that although many commentators judged Reagan's first presidential effort to have been a mistake,

Taylor believed, "It was a vital step in his career. He had energized thousands of loyal supporters and he won new converts that fall as he campaigned for Nixon in twenty-four states."[32] Walter Dilbeck remained very upset, feeling Reagan could have beaten Nixon if he had declared earlier. "He would have beaten Nixon."[33]

On the positive side, White's chapter termed the 1968 adventure a "Near Miss." Cannon reflected that 1968 prepared Reagan for sterner tests, as defeat in 1968 "laid the groundwork for victory."[34] Steven Hayward added that Reagan's campaign helped achieve party unity in 1968.[35]

Reed reviewed two important positive immediate direct effects: Reagan (not on the ballot) had achieved an actual major autumn 1968 general election triumph in California—winning direct control of the California Assembly and indirect control—via a tie brokered by Lt. Governor Finch—of the California Senate;[36] and Reagan being elected chairman of the Republican Governors in December.[37] Historian Lewis Gould observed that the only major contender "to emerge from the 1968 campaign with brighter prospects than when he began was Ronald Reagan."[38]

And what about running for the presidency again in the future? At the convention, as soon as Nixon had won the nomination, a number of Reagan backers changed their placards from "Reagan in '68" to "Reagan in '72."[39] Kathryn Forte of SFR had wondered during the convention why the delegates and students for Reagan were pushing so hard, when Nixon seemed to have it locked up. The answer she got was simple: "so Reagan will get the nomination the next time!"[40] Bruce Weinrod knew that Reagan had something special. Weinrod reflected that Reagan's 1968 loss was "a shame," as Weinrod thought it still had been winnable at the convention. Weinrod looked to the future: "We hoped he'd try again."[41] He sent out a thank you letter to all SFR members for their hard work in attempting to see Reagan nominated in 1968. Weinrod ended by urging his fellow SFR members to watch the progress of Reagan's governorship and, looking ahead to another Reagan candidacy in the future, to "spread word of its meaning and success."[42] Weinrod was laying the groundwork for the creation of a new SFR ahead.

Mailer noted that Reagan as an actor had played the good guy who didn't get the girl, but that was alright because he would get her the next time. At the convention, Reagan was "wildly popular with Republicans."[43] The conclusion was obvious: Reagan would get the prize—the nomination—the next time. Mailer's prescience about Reagan's future was vindicated not only by future events, but also by recent critics. Christopher Hitchens marveled at how Mailer had seen that Nixon was "the one" for 1968 but that very likely, Reagan "might well be the next one."[44] Frank Rich noted that Mailer had been "remarkably prescient," seeing Reagan as the one to ultimately ascend "from the ashes of Goldwaterism."[45]

Thus Reagan learned important lessons for the future: he learned the hard work it took to campaign, that his loyal public wanted to work for an active, avowed candidate, and that he had to take more direct control of the campaign apparatus and personnel. Cannon later added that 1968 was "vitally important" to Reagan's political career. By campaigning throughout the South and West and Midwest, Reagan realized he could become president, and those conservative grass roots Reagan activists would become the "core of his support in the decades ahead."[46] Reed added that Reagan learned a great deal about the nomination system and had recruited financial supporters from across the nation for the future.[47] Reed's summary was that 1968 was Reagan's "fiery furnace," the "crucible" that reshaped his perspectives and "hardened the steel in his spine."[48] It was his true— and needed—dress rehearsal.

Reagan also learned that although domestic issues were paramount in importance in most presidential elections, sometimes world affairs dominated. All the expertise Reagan had learned in foreign affairs would be stored away in his mind for future use. Most importantly, Ronald Reagan emerged from 1968 as a world statesman on the international stage.

Reagan Departs the Convention

Immediately after the vote, Pat Nolan recalled spotting Mike Wallace of CBS and asked if he thought Reagan had a chance to be elected president in the future. With the "certainty of declaring a three-day old corpse dead," Wallace's answer was immediate: "He's finished. He's way too old to run for anything but reelection as governor."[49]

Mike Thompson of SFR recalled that groups of YAF and SFR supporters left the convention hall, dejected, all carrying Reagan signs. Pat Noland and Ron Docksai were in the group. Nolan recalled their group was trying to figure their way back to the YAF headquarters at the Hotel Monte Carlo. Amidst a light drizzle, the paint on their hand painted Reagan-for-President signs was running.

Suddenly a limousine pulled up and started past them. They could see a hand reach out of the back seat and grab the driver. Then the car backed up and the back window came down. There was Ronald Reagan.

Reagan stuck out his head, smiled and thanked them for their support and countless hours of hard work on his behalf. Reagan quoted the words of William Wallace, "'They' can't take away your inner spirit or your will and readiness to regroup. We'll fight another day!" Looking directly with encouragement and conviction at Pat Nolan and Ron Docksai, Reagan gazed to the future, stating with hard, firm resolve, "You'll have another chance!"[50]

Rather than focusing on himself, but instead healing the wounds of his defeat, Reagan had reached out to his young supporters. Reagan wanted to make sure that Nolan and the rest were not discouraged. He offered them hope for the future. Nolan saw that from that very moment of defeat, Reagan had already "steeled himself for the task of running again for the presidency."[51]

So after all, all was not lost. There would be another fight in the future: another place, another time. Weinrod, Nolan, Schadler, Thompson, Docksai and countless other Students for Reagan, who had worked so long to see Ronald Reagan elected president in 1968, now knew there would be more conventions and future chances to battle for their hero, Ronald Reagan. [52][53][54][55] An area deserving of further research is Ronald Reagan's appeal to the young. Historian Craig Shirley has related how President Reagan's support among America's young voters was actually even higher than his high support among the general population, both during the elections of 1980 and 1984 and also when Reagan left office in 1989.[56] As summarized earlier by your author in the present work, Reagan's early involvement with YAF, his glowing rallies at the 1964 convention coupled with his clear dominance at the Young Republicans national convention in Omaha in 1967, and culminating with SFR in 1968, all demonstrate clearly that American youth's high esteem for Reagan began in the 1960s.

The Reagan limousine pulled away. Reagan would take a few days rest before flying West. His mentor, Ike, remained gravely ill at Walter Reed Army Hospital; who knew how much time he had left? His old nemesis, RFK, was gone too. Now as the general election would begin, he had to help Nixon. Then he had his own reelection campaign to run for 1970.

During his first campaign for the presidency, Reagan had seen a country drifting listlessly, whose citizens saw civil disobedience and violence at home and lack of strength abroad. Reagan had not approached the presidency as his next political step. Reagan had firm political convictions: smaller government and more individual freedom. He was not against government. He was against governmental programs that did not work. He wanted to bring common sense solutions to help the people. Reagan first had battled against a president who had complained of unease and despair in the land and who had been incapable of realizing that America had yearned for a new leader. Then Reagan had fought against Johnson's seeming replacement—his old nemesis, RFK. Reagan had provided the answer. He had forged his new role as world statesman.[57]

Indeed Reagan had learned a great deal from his presidential dress rehearsal. He had entered the campaign seeking the same small government goals he had when he had run for governor. He had succeeded quite well in accomplishing those tasks, and if he would become party nominee in the future, those same domestic goals—to apply now to lessen the massive federal bureaucracy—would always remain. Indeed as Reagan left the convention, Kennedy-Johnson's Great Society programs were still for the most part intact. As will be seen, in his heart, Reagan still knew he wanted to see them dismantled.

But what was new for Reagan during his first presidential campaign was his growth in foreign affairs. And due in no small part to his mentor Eisenhower, and Reagan's standing firm against the policies of RFK, at the close of his first presidential campaign, Reagan clearly had emerged as a world statesman. Reagan in 1968 now knew what he wanted to accomplish: get rid of the spirit of defeat— Johnson's "unease" and "despair" and "restlessness—and restore pride in a nation adrift, begin defeating communism via a booming economy, bring freedom to Eastern Europe, develop an antiballistic missile shield for the nation's defense, stand up to communism and indeed create trouble for communists abroad just as they had done in the Third World, negotiate from a position of strength with the communists, stand firm with Israel, and honor America's veterans from both Eisenhower's servicemen to those who had fought in Southeast Asia. Via the mentoring of Eisenhower, Reagan had turned his initial great dislike of communism into a firm set of principles, strategies and tactics.

If Nixon won and then would serve two terms, his own turn for the presidency could arrive in 1976. But thoughts of what might have been—President-Elect Ronald Reagan in 1968—would always remain. All in all, looking back with pride on what he had accomplished and then looking ahead to the future, it had been a great dress rehearsal.

Endnotes

1. Novak, p. 168
2. Sally Gram, pers comm. 9/22/12
3. Pat Nolan, pers comm. 6/5/2013
4. Nolan, p. 6
5. Docksai, Ron, pers comm. 7/16/13
6. Schlesinger
7. Buchanan
8. Gould, p. 85
9. Nolan, pers comm. 6/5/2013
10. Rusher, p. 217
11. Rusher, p. 216-217
12. ibid, p. 216
13. Boyarsky, p. 258
14. Thompson, p. 270, p. 291
15. Boyarsky, p. 258
16. Novak, p. 167
17. White and Gill, p. 111
18. Rusher, p. 216
19. Rusher, p. 216
20. Novak, p. 168
21. Reed, pers int, 10/2013
22. Brands
23. Rusher and Morrow, p. 206-209
24. Shirley, Reagan Revolution, p. 13
25. Gibbs and Duffy, p. 206
26. "Safe, Sane and Soporific," *Life*, 8/16/1968, p. 36
27. Adler, p. 147
28. Johns, p. 330
29. pers int 7/30/12
30. Sally Gram, pers comm. 9/22/12
31. John Gram, pers int 11/12/12
32. Taylor, p. 23-24
33. "Agnew Benefactor: High Roller, Mystery Man," *Washington Post*, 1/5/75, p. A4
34. Cannon, p. 270
35. Hayward, p. 211-212
36. Reed, The Reagan Enigma, p. 174
37. Reed, p. 34
38. Gould, p. 168
39. Hill, Gladwin, "Reagan cheerful Despite Setback," *NYT*, 8/9/1968, p. 18
40. Forte, Kathryn, pers comm. 4/28/13
41. Weinrod, pers int 5/21/2013
42. Weinrod letter to Students for Reagan, personal communication, 1/15/2015
43. Mailer, p. 70
44. Hitchens, Christopher, "Master of Conventions," *The Atlantic Monthly*, 8/19/2008
45. Rich, Frank, "How to Cover an Election," *The New York Review of Books*, 5/29/2008
46. Cannon, Lou, "Reagan Ran on Optimism," http://www.msbnc.com/id/27117516/ns/politics, 7/24/2012
47. Reed, *The Reagan Enigma*, p. 33-34
48. Reed, *The Reagan Enigma*, p 178
49. Pat Nolan, pers comm. 6/5/2013
50. Patrick Nolan Papers, LP429, California State Archives. Office of the Secretary of State, Sacramento, California, with permission of author; Docksai, pers comm. 7/16/2013
51. Nolan, pers comm. 6/5/2013
52. Docksai, pers comm. 7/16/13
53. Schadler, 5/21/13
54. Thorburn, p. 169
55. Pat Nolan, ibid
56. http://www.conservativebookclub.com/14012/author-interviews/what-is-ronald-reagans-legacy-author-interview-craig-shirley
57. President Reagan would receive the Legion d'Honneur for statesmanship in 1984 Brinkley. p. 2

CHAPTER 43: EPILOGUE—IKE AND DUTCH

"The good Lord knows what He is doing. This wasn't our turn."

~ Ronald Reagan[1]

"If South Carolina had withheld its votes, we might have made it."

~ Ronald Reagan[2]

Reagan was one of the very few "self-effacing men" who are "capable of inserting themselves into presidential politics."

~ William F. Buckley, Jr.[3]

"You have it exactly right, what I did, why I did it, what I expected."

~ Ronald Reagan[4]

Ronald Reagan was the "toughest debater he ever faced, and, obviously, he was right."[5]

~ Edward Kennedy[6]

A photo, "one of himself with Dwight Eisenhower that he had in every office since I've known him."

~ Michael Deaver[7]

"I Like Ike. I Love Ike!"

~ President Ronald Reagan[8]

"I never meant to go into politics. It wasn't my intention… But I ultimately went into politics because I wanted to protect something precious…Back in the 1960's when I began…the government was taking more of our money, more of our options, and more of our freedom. I went into politics in part to put up my hand and say 'Stop!' I was a citizen-politician. **Common sense** told us that when you put a big tax on something, the people will produce less of it. So we cut the people's tax rates and the people produced more than ever before…**Common sense** also told us that to preserve the peace, we'd have to become strong again after years of weakness and confusion. So we rebuilt our defenses." The superpowers had begun to "reduce their stockpiles of nuclear weapons."

~ President Ronald Reagan[9] (author's emphasis)

As soon as he got back to the hotel after having encouraged his SFR supporters, Reagan climbed a few stairs in his suite and gave a short speech thanking his close supporters. Then Reagan and White went to the adjacent suite. Nancy took off her husband's shoes and massaged his shoulders to "relieve the fatigue and tension" after the eighteen-hour day.[10] Outside the suite was White's fifteen year-old daughter, crying unconsolably. White didn't know what to do and went back inside to tell Reagan. The governor came out and put his arms around White's daughter: "The good Lord knows what He is doing. This wasn't our turn."[11] As Reagan had told everyone on the campaign trail from the beginning, if it were in God's plan and if the people had wanted him, then he, Reagan would accept the mantle. Obviously it wasn't—at least not yet. Nobody but Reagan, whose encouragement to the SFR members just had ended, was thinking that a President Reagan might still well be in the White House in the future. But now in 1968 it was Nixon's turn.

The next morning at 11 AM, Reagan called Nixon to offer congratulations. While Nixon was having his two meetings to choose a vice-president, the two former opponents chatted and planned for a meeting in California so Reagan could start campaigning for Nixon.[12] As Reagan left the hotel, there more were placards that had been altered to read, "Reagan in '72."[13]

Undoubtedly Reagan watched Nixon's acceptance speech. Whether Reagan agreed with writer William Safire (that Nixon's line, "Let's win it for Ike," sounded like a poor imitation of Reagan's famous Knute Rockne line, "Let's win one for the Gipper,") is not known.[14]

After the convention, the Secret Service protection that President Johnson had insisted upon for Reagan was withdrawn, and Ed Meese was left to determine new security measures for Reagan.[15] Meanwhile Ron and Nancy relaxed as they cruised the Florida Keys before flying back home.[16] On the way home, Reagan reflected, "How can you lose when you can go back to being governor of California? I'm not exactly unemployed."[17]

The morning after returning to Sacramento, Reagan told aide Tom Ellick, "It was a long shot!" "We gave it our best!"[18] Then Reagan wrote a letter of thanks to Henry A. Bubb, expressing his "deepest thanks" for the "many long hours" Bubb had given to the cause. Reagan thanked Bubb and his center and members for having "done their homework."[19] Clif White wrote a similar thank you letter to Bubb.[20] At his first post-convention press conference in Sacramento, when asked if the presidential bug was finally out of his system, Reagan answered, "There never was a presidential bug in my system."[21]

Reagan then read a column by William F. Buckley, Jr., which said in part that Reagan had been "expansively generous" and "considerate." Buckley felt that Reagan had followed the course of his grass roots activists, even though Reagan knew Nixon would win. Reagan was one of the very few "self-effacing men" who are "capable of inserting themselves into presidential politics."[22] Governor Reagan immediately telephoned Buckley. At the time, Buckley was on his yacht off the coast of Cozumel. When he was summoned by a bullhorn to return immediately to the Coast Guard station for an urgent message, and fearing the worst, that a family member had perished, Buckley got to a telephone. He was startled to hear the voice of Reagan. Reagan told Buckley, "You have it exactly right, what I did, why I did it, what I expected."[23]

Back in Washington, D.C., Bruce Weinrod wrote a letter of thanks, on behalf of the Students for Reagan Executive Committee, to those SFR members who had worked so hard during the winter, spring, and summer of 1968. To those members who had gone to the convention, Weinrod assured them that they had been "the key to the hastily, but amazingly well-organized effort" for Reagan.[24] Weinrod received a letter of thanks from William Rusher, in which Weinrod was thanked for his courage.[25] Shortly thereafter, Governor Reagan sent Weinrod a similar note of thanks.[26]

Then in a letter to Clif White, Reagan discussed his own personal feelings about the campaign. Reagan wrote that his campaign had prevented Nixon from moving to the left. Of course later events would prove Reagan's hopeful analysis of Nixon's future policies incorrect. Reagan added, "I have no regrets whatsoever, and no feeling that any of us fell short of what could be done."[27]

But soon thereafter, Reagan would deny there had been a campaign for the 1968 presidency. Historian Glen Moore reviews some of Reagan's post-convention recollections, or purported ignorance, of his 1968 campaign.[28]Similarly, Reed, in his recent memoir, remains mystified as to why both Ron and Nancy later had continued to deny that he had run for president first in 1968.[29] After all, Reed had met with Reagan at over one hundred meetings, in private or with others present—including Nancy as seen earlier—to plan and update the campaign. Reagan had flown almost every weekend for a year and a half to campaign, meet delegates, meet fellow Republicans, and set up local grass roots activist teams. In his later autobiography, Reagan would discuss 1968 in two pages and start his few campaign recollections in early 1968, as if everything from 1966 onwards had never happened.[30]

But the answer as to why Reagan denied it is basic human nature. Much of his campaign was hidden. And he had lost. Thus, reflected historian Lou Cannon, when Reagan had experienced his first political loss, he later denied its existence.[31] Reagan's hero Theodore Roosevelt, in his own autobiography as pointed out by historian David McCullough in his classic, *Mornings on Horseback*, shows how TR similarly failed to disclose his own first election loss: when he had failed, by running third, in his attempt to become the mayor of New York City (and also failed to mention one single word about his first wife, Alice Lee and their happy marriage until her tragic death giving birth to daughter Alice).[32] This is not to say that Reagan consciously was emulating TR by failing to disclose his first political failure. Rather it is human to forget, or at least in public not to bring attention to, life's failures.

In 1976, Reagan's second presidential campaign would be much more in the open, thus denying it would be impossible. In reality, Reagan was a fighter who did not like to lose. He lost in 1968 and his mind quickly relegated the memories to the far corners of his encyclopedic mind. Like TR, for sure Reagan knew quite well he had lost. But the past was over. After all, he next set his sights on helping Nixon win the presidency and then to seek his own reelection in 1970. But surely in the back of his mind was the promise he had made to the SFR students as they all had left the convention.

When Don Hodel would meet with President Reagan while being considered to become Reagan's secretary of energy, and later secretary of the interior, and after Hodel would mention he had been an alternate delegate sitting right in front of South Carolina and how close it had been for not nominating Nixon on the first ballot, Reagan would reflect, "If South Carolina had withheld its votes, we might have made it." With a "twinkling in his eyes," he would ask Hodel if he knew who the two most relieved people were when Reagan was not nominated in 1968? Hodel asked, "Who?" and Reagan answered, "Nancy and me!"[33] But the only time President Reagan publicly would reflect upon his 1968 campaign would be his moving tribute to his one-time nemesis.

Reconciliation with RFK and the Kennedys

On a warm spring day in early June 1981, exactly thirteen years after Senator Robert F. Kennedy had been assassinated, and just some two months and a week after an attempt had been made on his own life, President Ronald Reagan and surviving members of the Kennedy family, including Senator Edward M. Kennedy and Caroline and John F. Kennedy Jr., gathered in the Rose Garden of the White House.[34] Prior to the ceremony, the President had met with the Kennedy family in the Oval Office.[35] Nancy Reagan and Ethel Kennedy chatted "amiably".[36] Then Reagan presented a commemorative Congressional Gold Medal to Ethel Kennedy in honor of her husband, the slain senator. "As the President spoke, Ethel Kennedy nodded approval and leaned over to whisper something to Mrs. Reagan".[37] The 95th Congress had ordered that the medal be struck on November 1, 1978[38] but Jimmy Carter "never found time to do it,"[39] so it fell to Reagan, "Carter's more magnanimous successor,"[40] to make the presentation. Indeed President Reagan said to Ethel, "Mrs. Kennedy, this medal has been waiting patiently to be presented."[41] Reagan's diary entry for that evening read in part "Did however give a medal to Ethel Kennedy honoring Robt. K. It was voted by Cong. in 1978 and the former Pres. never presented it."[42]

How appropriate it was for President Reagan to have honored RFK in the Rose Garden. Historian Evan Thomas has reviewed how the idea of having a Medal of Honor ceremony at the White House, in which over 250 surviving Medal of Honor winners had gathered in the Rose Garden while JFK was president and while RFK had watched, had been RFK's idea.[43]

President Reagan spoke magnanimously of his former rival for the presidency in 1968 recalling, "His devotion for those less fortunate than himself are matters now for history…He roused the comfortable. He exposed the corrupt, remembered the forgotten, inspired his countrymen, and renewed and enriched the American conscience." Reagan said that on his own behalf, he "always appreciated his wit and his personal grace. And may I say I remember very vividly those last days of the California primary."[44]

Senator Ted Kennedy, the youngest and last remaining Kennedy son of that generation, who less than a year before in the Democratic Party had failed in his attempt to oust incumbent Carter, spoke next. After thanking the president, Kennedy reflected, "It is appropriate that he should receive it from you, for he understood so well that the common love of our country transcends all party identification….And you should know that after he debated you on international television in 1967, my brother Bob said that Ronald Reagan was the toughest debater he ever faced, and, obviously, he was right."[45]

Then Kennedy added to his prepared remarks saying, "Those of us who were with Robert Kennedy when he died in 1968 felt a special sense of relief this year, Mr. President, at your own recovery from the attack against you."[46]

After the ceremony, just prior to a meeting between Reagan and Charlton Heston, the Reagan's and the Kennedy's enjoyed iced tea and reminisced about "Bobby."[47] [48] The prior bitterness Reagan had felt against his nemesis, caused by all the hurts RFK had inflicted on Reagan in the 1960's, had long-since faded.

One historian, Michael Beran, found the 1981 occasion honoring RFK at the Reagan White House to be politically strange. Why "is" Ronald Reagan "paying elaborate-and apparently unfeigned—verbal homage" to Robert Kennedy? "It doesn't make sense."[49] In his 1981 remarks, Reagan had reminded his audience that during their shared 1968 presidential campaigns, RFK "was critical of bloated bureaucratic government.

The *New York Times* sneered: Reagan was playing politics with Bobby's reputation, turning him into an advocate of his (Reagan's) own vision of smaller government."[50] Historian Beran proceeded to discuss both the liberal and conservative sides of RFK. Liberal orthodoxy viewed RFK as purely of the political left wing, yet "Ronald Reagan…had the audacity to challenge this view of Bobby; few others have."[51] Beran continued, "Reagan was nearer the truth than he—or his listeners—knew".[52]

That day in June, 1981, President Reagan of course was recalling the time in the spring of 1968, when he had used RFK's apparent new conservative words at some campaign speeches—at the time attributed to RFK's trying to incorporate a law-and-order theme into his campaign to help attract votes—to create humorous opening jabs for his own speeches at the time. Three years later, President Reagan would have one additional opportunity to praise the Kennedys.

On June 24, 1985, President Reagan would speak at a fundraiser for the John F. Kennedy Library Foundation held at Senator Kennedy's

Virginia home. As reviewed not long ago by historian Jeffrey Lord and with a film version available, Senator Edward Kennedy and John F. Kennedy, Jr., would present Reagan with an American eagle statuette, which had been on President Kennedy's desk.[53] Senator Kennedy would tell the audience that he knew that his slain brother would have been pleased that the memento had been given to President Reagan. With Jacqueline Onassis and Ethel Kennedy applauding behind him, Reagan would thank Senator Kennedy and his nephew and then would call JFK a man who knew that America had had real adversaries and had tried to have America's defenses unsurpassed. Reagan did not elaborate on his reference, JFK's false 1960 campaign charges—the false "missile gap" charge—against Eisenhower and Nixon, but Reagan told the audience he had in fact campaigned and voted for the "other guy" (Nixon).[54]

Last, just as President Reagan in June, 1981 had been the one to give the Kennedy family the Congressional Gold Medal in honor of RFK, so too the medal would be awarded to Nancy and Ronald Reagan on May 16, 2002 (H.R. 3591)

President Reagan graciously had cast his comments about both RFK and JFK in positive yet also in conservative themes. In addition to reminiscing about RFK and JFK, Reagan would be the one who would reconcile America and its legacy in Korea and Vietnam.

Reconciling America and the Korean War

For more than a half-century after the fighting had ended, except for sporadic skirmishes, troops from North and South Korea still face each other across the Demilitarized Zone. Yet Ronald Reagan never forgot that Eisenhower had ended the fighting by his use of threats. The United States had suffered 100,000 wounded, 54,000 dead, and 8,000 missing in action. Many in America had long forgotten what the Korean War had been about. Ronald Reagan would make sure that Americans would understand and would honor the brave soldiers who had given so much.

In 1968, Ronald Reagan did not forget that North Korea was still our enemy. Only months after the GOP convention had ended, Reagan would find a new and very personal way to help the nation and its military. It was the still-unresolved incident that had tied together the Vietnam War with America's still-existing other "hot" military enemy, North Korea. Negotiations between the United States and North Korea finally would lead to the freeing of the crew of the *U.S.S. Pueblo*. Eleven months to the day from their capture, on

December 23, the crew would walk across the Bridge of No Return at Panmunjom.55 The crew and its captain, Lloyd Bucher, would arrive in San Diego to be reunited with loved ones on Christmas Eve, 1968. That same evening, the three Apollo 8 astronauts first would circle the moon and read from Genesis.

Bucher was described as "limping and appearing gaunt and gray." Governor Reagan—star in 1954 of *Prisoner of War*—was there now in real life to welcome home the brave captain, and former POW. Reagan would state for the nation, "I just want to say how proud all of us here are." Reagan then would express sympathy and joy to the families of the crew, "who knew the full measure of enemy brutality."56 In a scant twelve years, future President Reagan would welcome home another set of hostages, from Iran.

As soon as Reagan had become the Republican Party nominee for governor in June, 1966, within a week he had met with Eisenhower and their discussions of world affairs had begun. In February, 1981, within weeks of taking office, President Reagan would welcome President Chun Doo Hwan of the Republic of Korea as the first foreign leader to visit Reagan as the new leader of the Free World. As the two leaders met for the first time, it is difficult to imagine that Reagan did not think back to his mentor. The two presidents would issue a statement pledging to uphold the U.S.-Korea Mutual Defense Treaty, which had originated with President Eisenhower.

Two years later, President Reagan would make an official visit to South Korea. On November 12, 1983, President Reagan would address the National Assembly of the Republic of Korea in Seoul. In his remarks at the State Dinner, President Reagan's first words were about his mentor. President Reagan reflected on the visit of the president of South Korea to the White House shortly after the fighting in 1953 had ceased. Reagan cited Eisenhower's words, that the Free World owed a great debt of gratitude to the people of the Republic of Korea. Reagan would recall President Eisenhower's words, which had related the "courage, stamina, and self-sacrifice" of the Korean people. Reagan would relate that Ike had said at the time that the debt owed to the people of South Korea never could be repaid. President Reagan then would tell the assembly that the debt that Eisenhower had mentioned long since had been repaid. Ronald Reagan again would tie his own presidency directly back to the thread of ideals and policies begun a generation earlier by his mentor.

President Reagan would tell those assembled that America had shared their loss for the lives lost when the Soviet Union so recently had shot down a civilian aircraft, Korean Airlines Flight 007. Reagan would cite the year of 1983 as the thirtieth year of the mutual defense treaty between the Republic of Korea and America, signed under President Eisenhower. President Reagan would reiterate that the United States stood firm with South Korea: "In Korea, especially, we have learned the painful consequences of weakness...We stand with you to resist aggression from the North."[57] After his speech, President Reagan would tour the Demilitarized Zone.

On April 26, 1985, President Hwan would return to Washington, D.C. to revisit President Reagan. President Reagan would reflect upon his somber visit to the DMZ four years earlier. Then the two presidents would reaffirm their mutual defense treaty, begun with Eisenhower, and reaffirm the defense, economic and cultural ties, which would continue to bin together their two nations.[58]

During that same day, the theme of Korea would continue. President Reagan would honor his former acting colleague from their "shared" parts in the Korea War. Actor Harry Morgan, retired from his portrayal of Col. Potter in the long-running television hit show about the Korean War, *M*A*S*H*, received an honor at a Rose Garden ceremony. President Reagan would bestow a certificate of appreciation for Morgan having helped volunteers and veterans. Morgan would thank President Reagan and both former actors would reminisce about their joint 1954 Korean War film, *Prisoner of War*.[59]

Never forgetting the American soldiers of the Korean War, who had served under Eisenhower in the 1950s and still had served under his own leadership in the 1980s, in October 1986, President Reagan would sign a bill authorizing the establishment of a Korean War Memorial to be built in the nation's capital. Then President Reagan would appoint a Veterans Advisory Board to recommend the location of the site and its design. President Reagan also would turn his eyes to the major foreign conflict he had addressed in the 1960s, Vietnam.

Reagan Reconciles America and the Vietnam War

On May 9, 1970, Governor Reagan would be the keynote speaker at a Salute to the Armed Forces Ball, where bracelets were inscribed with the names of prisoners of war and those missing in action in Vietnam.[60] Decades later, the 2008 Republican presidential candidate and former POW in Vietnam, John McCain, would credit the agitation which Governor Reagan had created as a prime reason in his being moved to a cell with somewhat better conditions.

Also after 1968, Governor and Mrs. Reagan would continue their visits to wounded veterans. For example on October 15, 1970, a day which would have one of the largest demonstrations against the war, as she had with her husband in 1967 as discussed, Nancy again would visit wounded veterans at Letterman Army Hospital in San Francisco.[61]

In October 1971, Governor Reagan would visit South Vietnam as special representative of President Nixon and would meet President Thieu. In January, 1973, after the Paris Peace Accords would be signed, Reagan would host Thieu in Sacramento and would host dinners for returning prisoners of war.

Just after he would leave the governorship of California, Reagan would see the ignominious end of the war, as Saigon would fall in 1975 and American helicopters would try to help rescue as many loyal South Vietnamese as possible.

While running for the presidency for the third time in the summer of 1980, candidate Reagan would call Vietnam, "in truth, a noble cause. Those who died in that cause fought as well and as bravely as any Americans have ever fought in any war. They deserve our gratitude, our respect and our continuing concern."[62] That August, Reagan would speak to the Veterans of Foreign Wars and to the American Legion. He would use the same wording as he had in 1967-1968: that it was a just war, that America's soldiers should have been given the tools to win, and veterans should never be made to feel guilty that they had fought in Vietnam.[63] Once he was elected president, Reagan could do much more to re-educate the nation about the cause for which he had fought—so hard to win—from 1965 through 1968.

Historian H. Bruce Franklin discusses President Reagan's keen interest in a plan to find American POW/MIAs still in the jungles of Southeast Asia.[64] On January 28, 1983, President Reagan would address the National League of Families of American Prisoners and Missing in Southeast Asia. On May 1, 1983, President Reagan would visit the Vietnam Veterans Memorial Wall and lay a wreath of flowers. Meanwhile by June, a division of the Defense Intelligence Agency would be assigned the task of tracking down those missing.[65]

In April 1984, Reagan would tell the press, "We should have asked for a declaration of war and called it a war." When then asked if such a declaration might not have widened the Vietnam War, he would reflect back. In the early 1950s, Reagan had been in agreement with MacArthur and MacArthur's prophesy why not winning in Korea would make Vietnam the next communist target. This had been a major initial reason for supporting Eisenhower so long ago. In late

1967 when being interviewed by Harry Reasoner about the Citizens Committee report and being asked the same question about the war being widened, Eisenhower had answered an emphatic "No!"

So at the 1984 press conference, President Reagan would continue, "I know that there was great concern about the possibility of the war widening—just as there was in Korea, that prevented us from allowing General MacArthur to lead us to a victory in Korea. Everyone thought that you have to fight a war without winning it or you might find yourself in a bigger war. Well, maybe General MacArthur was right: there is no substitute for victory." Reagan and his mentor had remained steadfast in their desire to permit American servicemen to be given the tools to win.[66]

One month later, President Reagan again would have a chance to reflect upon Vietnam, when he would deliver a 1984 Memorial Day address honoring an unknown serviceman whose body had been returned from the land of the conflict. In front of a flag-draped coffin and at times with tears glistening, Reagan would tell the public that the lesson of Vietnam had been the "preciousness of human freedom." Reagan wanted Americans to rededicate themselves to securing answers to those still missing in action. To the families of those with still missing service men, sadly he noted, "Vietnam is not over for them." He would call on Hanoi to give "the fullest possible accounting" of the missing men and women. Reagan then would place the Congressional Medal of Honor, the same type as he had handed to RFK's family three years earlier, over the casket of the unknown soldier.[67]

That summer, President Reagan would declare the third Friday in July as National POW/MIA Recognition Day.[68]

Six months later at the dedication of the "Three Fighting Men" statue, which was to become an integral part of the nation's Vietnam Veterans Memorial, President Reagan again would help heal the wounds of Vietnam and help the nation move forward. Reagan would honor the families of those who had served or still were missing. Reagan would thank the gathered veterans for their courage and recognize that when they had returned home from Vietnam, "Little solace was given to you." Reagan would praise those who had served, as they "fought for freedom in a place where liberty was in danger. They put their lives in danger to help a people in a land far away from their own. Many sacrificed their lives in the name of duty, honor and country. All were patriots who lit the world with their fidelity and courage."[69]

On July 19, 1986, President Reagan would speak from the Oval Office on POW's and MIA's from Vietnam. His administration had been negotiating with Vietnam and Laos and as a result, more than any time since the war had ended, the remains of dead American soldiers had returned home . Reagan praised the dead American heroes: "These men died in battle for their country, and it's only right and fitting that they finally rest now in the Nation they loved so dearly and for which they so willingly sacrificed."[70]

Two years later in 1988, for his last Veterans Day speech, President Reagan again would reconcile those who had opposed and those who had favored the war. He would say, "Most of all, we remember the devotion and gallantry with which all of them ennobled their nation as they became champions of a noble cause." Citing the recent tragedies of the desperate fleeing boat people and the horrors of the killing fields in Cambodia, Reagan would explain, "Who can doubt that the cause for which our men fought was just?" Then coming full circle to the same Vietnam theme of his Veterans Day speech he had delivered during his first presidential campaign in Albany, Oregon, so long ago and for which he had been mentored by Eisenhower, Reagan would say, "We can all agree that we've learned one lesson: that young Americans must never again be sent to fight and die unless we are prepared to let them win." After praising Vietnam veterans and updating the country on his personal efforts to update crash sites to bring back the remains of missing servicemen, Reagan would end his speech by reciting the ancient Hebrew blessing from the *Torah*, or Old Testament: "The Lord will bless you and keep you, the Lord will make His face to shine upon you and give you peace, now and forever more."[71]

Repeatedly and whenever he could, including many visits to wounded veterans after 1968, Reagan both as governor and then as president would honor the veterans of World War II who had served under Eisenhower. Reagan honored the memories of America's soldiers who had fought in Korea and the veterans of Vietnam, whom both he and Eisenhower together had tried to help win the war. Reagan would bring closure to the conflict with which he had been associated for two decades.

Eisenhower's Protégé and Heir

At some point in their relationship, Eisenhower clearly started to view Reagan as more than just one of his political protégés or heirs. For besides the multiple meetings, letters, and phone conversations which seemingly were mainly about Eisenhower mentoring Reagan on domestic politics and then on foreign affairs, on at least one occasion the general had opened up to Reagan by confiding in Reagan his greatest failure as president. Reagan recalled years later, "Dwight Eisenhower once told me he believed that the biggest mistake he had made" was in appointing Earl Warren to the Supreme Court, because Warren had changed his judicial philosophy after the appointment.[72] This admission by Eisenhower to his protégé, made in private while Warren was still chief justice, is certainly yet another indication of the high esteem Eisenhower had placed in Reagan.

An area for future historians to explore is this exact and direct influence of Eisenhower's continuing into the Reagan presidency and the courts. Was candidate's Reagan antipathy, in the 1970s, to the Warren Court, a direct result of Eisenhower's admission? Was President Reagan's campaign promise in 1980, to appoint the first woman to the Supreme Court—and of course later fulfilled by his appointment of Sandra Day O'Connor—a direct link to Eisenhower's first advice to Reagan, to get women onto his staff?

Another area for exploration is the future roles that members of Reagan's 1968 campaign teams had on future Republican and national politics. As just one example, the Honorable Diarmuid O'Scannlain of the IXth Circuit Court of Appeals has traced his first having come to the attention of Reagan to the time period of his involvement in Reagan's 1968 Oregon primary campaign team.[73]

After Dwight Eisenhower would pass away in 1969, Governor and Mrs. Reagan, in Phoenix at the time, quickly would send a telegram of condolence to Mamie Eisenhower and their family at Walter Reed Army Hospital. It would read in part, "No words which we could express could possibly erase the sorrow and pain which you are experiencing on your loss nor is there anyway for us to express the deep sadness we feel in this hour…We loved Ike as our dear friend, we respected and admired as our leader, our general, our President."[74]

As soon as the Reagan's sent the telegram, Reagan's representative in the nation's capital, Edgar Gillenwaters, got an urgent call to prepare for Reagan to attend Eisenhower's funeral. Eisenhower's funeral was at National Cathedral and was attended by many heads of state. In the pew in front of the Reagan's and Gillenwaters was French President Charles De Gaulle. Gillenwaters observed De Gaulle's aide write down the name "Ronald Reagan" on a slip of paper for De Gaulle. De Gaulle then uncharacteristically turned around and looked eyeball to eyeball with Reagan for almost a full minute. As reviewed by historian Sebastian Reyn, De Gaulle at this time had been asked by Nixon to discuss with the North Vietnamese a future rebuilding program after an American withdrawal.[75] De Gaulle likely was aware of Reagan's conservative stances, for as the dignitaries left their pews, De Gaulle gave Reagan an extended handshake and did the same with Mrs. Reagan.[76] At a CSPAN event, historian Edmund Morris reiterated the meeting of Reagan and DeGaulle at Eisenhower's funeral.[77]

But the story of Eisenhower and Reagan, and the critical issues upon which Ike had mentored Reagan during the campaign, did not end with Eisenhower's death.

A year after Reagan's 1968 Amarillo speech and his concession to victor Nixon at the convention, Governor Reagan would speak in Rhode Island. Picking up on the theme he had espoused beginning in Albany, Oregon and which had continued in Cleveland and Amarillo, Reagan once again would tell his audience that America's greatest weapons had been "brought forward during the Eisenhower years." But Reagan now would have new information to add to his 1967-1968 campaign attacks on the neglects during the Kennedy-Johnson years. Reagan would cite a new study from the Strategic Studies Institute in London and would note, sadly, "The United States has now *lost* the ability to be the dominant power in the world." The Soviets now were overtaking America in missile capacity. Reagan would conclude, "Eight years of neglect have taken their toll."

Of more concern to Reagan was America's loss of desire to be the world's major superpower. Reagan cited the origin of the corrosion of America's will as due to protests against the Vietnam War, and he would proceed to cite activists' links to communist governments and the resultant alienation of many of America's young from society.[78]

In a 1975 radio address, Reagan would pay homage to Eisenhower, saying, "For many, his image as President is that of a genial golf player who didn't stir things up much and who in the main presided over a country that rode at anchor for 8 years."[79] Reagan then gave a fine tribute to his mentor by stating firmly, "Ike ended a war in Korea that had killed tens of thousands of our young men, and for the rest of his 8 years no young Americans were being shot at anywhere in the world. He also halted dead in its track the advance of communism. Big government didn't get any bigger and a citizen could go for an evening stroll in the park without getting bopped on the head...Never had a nation's wealth been so widely distributed and we were so strong that no one in the world ever thought about challenging us."[80]

In Reagan's speech delivered at the end of the 1976 Republican convention, historian Craig Shirley discusses how many of the delegates would bemoan that they had chosen the wrong candidate for the nomination. But what Reagan chose to say, an impromptu address without notes, indicates his continuing concern about nuclear weapons. Reagan reflected on what message he would leave in a time capsule to be opened in one hundred years. His message was that he hoped nuclear weapons had never been used and had been eliminated. It was again Eisenhower's "Atoms for Peace" speech theme, carried forth by Reagan from 1953 to 1976 to 2076.

When Reagan would run for president for the third time in the late 1970s, a major foreign policy controversy would surround President Carter's support for turning over the Panama Canal back to Panama. Candidate Reagan would be against the idea. But surprisingly, fellow conservative William F. Buckley, Jr., would be for it and the two conservatives would stage a televised debate. Just before the debate ended, Reagan would reveal that his thoughts and ideas on the canal had originated during one of his prior golf visits with Dwight Eisenhower.[81]Eisenhower, having been stationed in the Canal Zone in 1922 and under the mentorship of General Fox Conner, and having signed the Remon-Eisenhower treaty in 1955 with the follow-up negotiations in 1958 via his brother Milton's trip there, clearly foresaw that at some future point, his protégé Reagan might face new problems there.

As reviewed by historian Robert Ivies, during Reagan's 1980 presidential campaign, he frequently would sound the 1966 Eisenhower-inspired theme of "common sense." Reagan's optimism about America would be in stark contrast to Carter's attempt—via his "malaise" speech—to shift blame from himself to the American citizenry.[82] One now can see clearly that Reagan in 1980 would just be copying his own rhetorical style from 1966 and 1968. Reagan would transform his 1968 attacks against Johnson's "despair...restlessness" State of the Union address into attacks against Carter's malaise.

In the spring of 1980, in the midst of his third quest for the presidency, candidate Reagan would be interviewed and asked, "Who is your favorite president?" Reagan would answer that he could not choose only one, because there were obvious greats like Washington and Lincoln. Reiterating to the interviewer that he could not choose only one, Reagan suddenly switched the conversation and honed in on one person: Dwight Eisenhower. Reagan never disclosed that Ike had been his political mentor. It was during this time period, just prior to Professor Fred Greenstein's revolutionary reassessment of the Eisenhower years, that Eisenhower had not been placed highly by historians.

Reagan would tell the reporter that Eisenhower was "vastly underrated." Reagan would continue that Ike was a "darn good manager," because his brought to the presidency his expertise from the military when Ike had brought "all those diverse nations together." Eisenhower was the true team builder.

Reagan would end by reminding the reporter, "One thing that he did that's very little noticed. If you remember the furor over Quemoy and Matsu...He said, 'They'll have to climb over the Seventh Fleet.' Nobody tried to, and there was no war and Quemoy and Matsu remained free." Clearly, Ronald Reagan would take his exact campaign words praising Eisenhower from 1967 and 1968 and use them again in 1980.[83]

In his interview, candidate Reagan also would chastise incumbent Carter's use of empty threats against Iran. Reagan would cite President Carter's belated letter to Iran, which finally set an ultimatum to free the hostages, as being "five months late." Hearkening back to his own methods to deal, after the Pueblo crisis, with future hostages—agreed to by Harold MacMillan and likely via Eisenhower too—candidate Reagan would add, "The first 72 hours you explore the diplomatic channels." And then one uses military force.[84]

Reagan continued this theme, of his opponent's issuance of empty warnings to not cross a red line, by noting that Carter was "very careless with the credibility of this nation." Reagan cited Carter's speech, which had protested a Soviet brigade stationed in Cuba, and then nothing had happened. Then Carter sent a "very firm warning" that if the Soviet troops, massed on the border with Afghanistan, crossed the border, there would be "serious consequences." Reagan noted that the Soviets had crossed the border and there were, in fact, as of the time of the interview, no consequences.[85] Reagan knew from Eisenhower that threats were critically important, but if one made the threat, one had to be prepared to use the military options as necessary. In older terminology from his hero, Theodore Roosevelt, Carter had spoken loudly and carried no stick at all. In modern terminology (from President Obama's issuing an empty red line warning about Syria's use of chemical weapons), Carter had issued red line warnings and there were no consequences.

Candidate Reagan in 1980 would continue to be concerned about the treaties and alliances originally made by Eisenhower. As discussed by historian Lou Cannon, Reagan's running mate, George H.W. Bush would be sent to the Peoples Republic of China to mend fences. But Reagan would demonstrate he still was loyal to Taiwan, the Republic of China. Just as Bush would be departing, Reagan would announce the controversial policy that he favored establishment of an official liaison office in Taipei.[86]

Once Reagan would win election in 1980, just as Governor-elect Reagan had hired several prominent members of the Eisenhower administration to work for him in Sacramento, President Reagan similarly would hire one particular man who critically would help Reagan follow through on Eisenhower's mentoring to win the Cold War. Secretary of State George Shultz, who had been senior staff economist for President Eisenhower's Council of Economic Advisors, would meet Eisenhower for the last time after the 1968 convention. While the general remained at Walter Reed Hospital, Eisenhower would warn Shultz to take occasional time off from his soon-to-be hectic schedule as President-Elect Nixon's secretary of labor.[87] Mentioned earlier was President Reagan's appointment of Gil Robinson as special advisor to Secretary Shultz and later ambassador to the U.S. Information Agency, three decades after Robinson had been one of the youngest appointees of Eisenhower.[88]

Besides using it once again as a campaign theme in 1980, Reagan as president would continue to invoke the 1966 phrase "common sense" not infrequently. For example in 1981, when interviewed about his controversial interior secretary, Reagan would say that James Watt was trying to restore "common sense" to the office.[89] In his 1984 State of the Union Address, Reagan would reflect, "Preservation of our environment is not a liberal or a conservative challenge—it's common sense."[90]

Continuing Influence of Eisenhower on President Reagan's Domestic Policy

It is well beyond the scope of this book to examine the complete and detailed continuing influence of Eisenhower upon Reagan as president. That job awaits future historians. When analyzing presidential messages, statements, remarks, speeches, and addresses, it is clear that President Reagan invoked the memory of his mentor and predecessor whenever he could. Indeed it is correct to state that the president whom President Reagan quoted or cited most was President Eisenhower. President Reagan's direct quoting of Eisenhower's words, or praise for his programs, occurred at least 178 times, far out-stripping Reagan's references to any other of those specific of his predecessors whom prior historians have said were role models for Reagan, including either of the Roosevelt's, Lincoln or Coolidge.[91] What follows only highlights a portion of the many, many times President Reagan would invoke the memory of his mentor.

President Reagan would end his first Independence Day message stating, "As Dwight Eisenhower once said, 'There is nothing wrong with America that the faith, love of freedom, intelligence and energy of her citizens cannot cure.'"[92] At an October, 1981 swearing-in ceremony for members of his Export Council, President Reagan would cite President Eisenhower's 1957 message to Congress, when Eisenhower had said that international commerce led to a "just and lasting peace in the world."[93]Shortly after that address, in the only prior comment that your author could find on the direct relationship between the two men, one reporter would note that President Reagan had praised Ike "several times;" there was no further analysis of the relationship between the two men.[94]Later in 1981, the 25th anniversary year of Eisenhower's Interstate Highway System, President Reagan would call Eisenhower's program, "one of the most significant and far-reaching domestic programs in the history of the United States."[95]

In 1982, when signing the Intelligence Identities Protection Act, President Reagan would remind the audience that President Eisenhower had dedicated the cornerstone of the CIA's building: "'Heroes', he said, 'who are undecorated and unsung, whose only reward was the knowledge that their service to their country was unique and indispensible.'"[96] Ten days later for his second July 4th as president, President Reagan would speak of George Washington's courage at Valley Forge. Then President Reagan again would quote his mentor: "In the words of Dwight Eisenhower, 'Free men do not lose their patience, their courage, their faith because the obstacles are mountainous, the path uncharted.'"[97]

That autumn, President Reagan once again would deliver the Landon Lecture, as he had done fifteen years earlier on the campaign trail in the autumn of 1967, when he had been on the rostrum with Henry A. Bubb and had spoken about higher education. This time, President Reagan would speak about agriculture and Midwestern, conservative heartland values. Acknowledging Senator Dole in the audience, whom he had first met in June, 1968 at the Topeka barbecue where candidate Reagan had spoken from the hay podium, President Reagan then would cite fellow Kansan, his mentor Eisenhower: "I agree with your native son, Dwight Eisenhower, who said that without a prosperous agriculture there is no prosperity in America."[98]

In early 1983 when sending Congress his proposals for block grants to the states, President Reagan would address a theme that hearkened back to his joint recording with Eisenhower in 1962, *Mr. Lincoln's Party Today*. President Reagan reminded the nation, "In a 1957 speech to the National Governors Conference, President Eisenhower sounded the first words of caution about the trend towards increased central government control. He said: 'If present trends continue, the states are sure to degenerate into powerless satellites of the national government…The irony of the whole thing is accentuated as we recall that the national government was itself not the parent, but the creature of the states acting together. Yet today it is often made to appear that the creature, Frankenstein-like, is determined to destroy the creator.'"[99] Ike and Dutch's joint calls for smaller government hopefully would begin again under President Reagan's new policies.

Ike's conservative values again would be quoted by President Reagan at the dedication of an exhibit of cowboy art: "Another President from the West, Dwight Eisenhower of Abilene, Kansas, once said, 'Whatever America hopes to bring to pass in the world must first come to pass in the heart of America.'"[100]

During the summer of 1984, Hawaii would celebrate its 25th anniversary as a state. President Reagan would begin his proclamation by reminding the nation that it was President Eisenhower who had been the one who had proclaimed Hawaii as the nation's 500th state.[101]

What did President Reagan think of President Eisenhower's famed 1961 Farewell Address on the "military-industrial complex"? At the 1986 Conservative Political Action Conference, where in 1975 he had delivered another in his series of speeches using the phrase "pale pastels," which had morphed from "sickly pastels" back in 1967, President Reagan would remind his audience:

"And let me interject here two points that I think can be important this year. First, the question of defense spending. During the last few weeks, there've been a number of columns, editorials, or speeches calling for a slash in the military budget and quoting President Eisenhower as justification. President Eisenhower did warn about large concentrations of power like the military-industrial complex, but what's being left out is the context of that quote. In his farewell address to the American people, yes, he did warn us about the danger of an all-powerful military-industrial complex, but he also reminded us America must always be vigilant because, 'We face a hostile ideology—global in scope, atheistic in character, ruthless in purpose, and insidious in method.' The pundits haven't been quoting that part of his speech."[102]

The religious faiths of Presidents Reagan and Eisenhower have only been addressed by a few historians. On President Reagan's 75th birthday, February 6, 1986, he would attend the National Prayer Breakfast and would speak of Eisenhower's faith. Reagan would mention an incident from his mentor's 1952 presidential campaign.

Eisenhower had confided to a senator that just before D-Day, Reagan would relate, the general had a "startling and vivid spiritual experience—he had actually felt the hand of God guiding him, felt the presence of God." Reagan would continue that this, along with the support from colleagues and fiends, is what had gotten Ike through D-Day. Reagan would add, that only a short time after Ike's inauguration, President Eisenhower, in the White House, had confided to the same senator, "This is the loneliest house I've ever been in." It was at that point that Eisenhower was invited to, and attended, his first prayer breakfast.[103]

Continuing Influence of Eisenhower on President Reagan's Foreign Policy

Many historians have analyzed Reagan's foreign policy successes. For example, Henry Nau placed Reagan within the broad historical context of other activist presidents, such as Jefferson, Polk and Truman.[104] Another recent work assesses Regan's legacy in the world of the second decade of the twenty-first century.[105] Amongst President Reagan's fabled 4-by-6 inch cards he would use for delivering speeches would be one of his favorites which quoted Eisenhower: "The vital element in keeping the peace is our mil(itary) establishment. Our arms must be mighty, ready for instant action, so that no potential aggressor may be tempted to risk its own destruction."[106] Reagan loved Ike's "peace through strength."

Prior to President Reagan taking office, President Carter unilaterally would break the mutual defense treaty with Taiwan, which America had had with Taiwan ever since President Eisenhower had signed it decades earlier. Because Carter would break the treaty without Senate approval, Senator Barry Goldwater would sue President Carter (*Goldwater vs. Carter*). The Supreme Court would rule that Congress had not issued any formal opposition and the case was dismissed.

In 1972, President Nixon would make his historic opening to Red China. But Taiwan would be extremely worried. So Nixon would send Governor Reagan as his personal representative to assure Taiwan. Exactly a decade later, as reviewed by historian Harvey Feldman, the Reagan administration had difficult negotiations with the People's Republic of China. On August 17, 1982, President Reagan publicly would sign a communiqué in which America agreed to keep level, and then to reduce, its arm sales to Taiwan.

However, President Reagan would remain "disturbed by its possible effect on Taiwan and put little trust in Chinese promises to adhere to a peaceful solution." President Reagan had seen the successful treaty, which Eisenhower had established, unilaterally abrogated by President Carter. So Reagan would send his personal representative to meet the Taiwanese president to deliver orally six (later a total of eight) assurances to its long-standing ally. Reagan's action, in sending a personal representative to reassure Taiwan, is clearly the direct reflection of how Governor Reagan had helped Taiwan in 1972.[107]

As reviewed by historian Lou Cannon, when President Reagan would visit a communist country for the first time,[108] his speeches about Lincoln, freedom and free-market capitalism would be censored. When the communist leadership would press Reagan to cut back arm sales to Taiwan faster than planned, Reagan would refuse.[109]

Lebanon would be the tragic site of one of President Reagan's major foreign policy failures: the terrorist attack on the Marine barracks with the huge number of American deaths and the decision to withdraw. This would be in sharp contrast to President Eisenhower's 1958 success in Lebanon. But Reagan would not act in a vacuum: indeed Reagan would seek guidance from his long-deceased mentor. Historian Patrick Tyler has reviewed how, in the midst of the crisis, President Reagan would ask for an NSC review of exactly what Eisenhower had done in 1958. Circumstances on the ground clearly were different. And of course, his mentor was no longer alive. Yet Dutch would seek to know all the specifics of what his mentor, Ike, had done.[110] As noted, some have viewed Lebanon as Reagan's greatest foreign policy failure. When withdrawing American forces, Reagan may have recalled Eisenhower's warnings not to involve American soldiers in land wars in Asia. But President Reagan, like his mentor, knew that the major threat facing America remained the Soviet Union.

In February, 1981, during a State Dinner for British Prime Minister Margaret Thatcher, President Reagan would toast Churchill but also Eisenhower and MacMillan.[111] Two weeks later addressing Parliament in Canada, President Reagan would emphasize the many unities the two nations shared. President Reagan would reflect on President Eisenhower's 1953 address in the same spot and how Eisenhower had thanked Canada for its role in World War II. President Reagan would make special mention of the 1st Special Services, a combined American-Canadian force and how during the war, General Eisenhower had requested special reconnaissance from the force in Italy at Anzio and Rome.[112] Two weeks later, President Reagan would praise the Sister Cities International program: it was the 25th anniversary of the "great program" started by President Eisenhower. Reagan would reflect, "I'm sure he is looking down on us today and being very happy with what we have accomplished."[113]

On December 15, 1981 while meeting with Agostino Cardinal Casroli, Secretary of State to the Pope, and discussing communism, weapons and disarmament, Reagan would cite Eisenhower's 1953 United Nations speech: "President Eisenhower, at a time when the United States had a marked nuclear advantage over the Soviet Union, offered to turn over all nuclear weapons to an international authority. The world would be different today if the Soviets had not refused to join in this offer."[114]

At his 1982 State of the Union Address, President Reagan would remind Congress and the American nation that prior speakers had included Churchill and Douglas MacArthur. Then President Reagan would recall, "Dwight Eisenhower reminded us that peace was purchased only at the price of strength."[115]

Two months later, to mark the 25th anniversary of the Treaties of Rome, which had established the European Union, President Reagan would begin his talk by again citing his mentor: "In his State of the Union message in 1957, President Eisenhower welcomed the efforts of 'our European friends to develop an integrated community.' President Reagan would tell Europe that his administration would stay committed to Eisenhower's conclusion.[116]

On April 21, 1982 at a meeting of the National Security Council at which nuclear weapons negotiations with the Soviet Union were being discussed, Reagan again would invoke Eisenhower's name, reflecting, "Its too bad we cannot do…what Ike proposed on all nuclear weapons."[117]

On May 10, 1982 while answering the question of a student who would ask why we needed any weapons, Reagan again would speak glowingly about Eisenhower's "Atoms for Peace" proposal. After explaining to the student that the Soviets had rejected Eisenhower's 1953 proposal, Reagan would tell the student, **"So we're going to try again."**[118] (author's emphasis)

The next month, at the United Nations Special Session on Disarmament, President Reagan extensively would quote Eisenhower: "Our foreign policy, as President Eisenhower once said, 'is not difficult to state. We are for peace first, last, and always for very simple reasons…We know that only in a peaceful atmosphere, a peace with justice, one in which we can be confident, can America prosper as we have known prosperity in the past,' he said."

President Reagan would continue by reminding the world that President Eisenhower had pointed out that at the end of World War II, America was the only super power and had the only atomic weapons. But instead of garnering world domination, the United States had chosen a course of helping other nations recover from the ravages of war. They were the same words and phrases candidate Reagan and student Bill Bradley had uttered at the *Town Meeting of the World* debate so long ago.

President Reagan would conclude his U.N. address by recalling President Eisenhower's proposal for "Open Skies"—the early version of "Trust but Verify"—that the Soviets had, along with "Atoms for Peace"—rejected.[119]

According to historian Evan Thomas, President Eisenhower had looked to the future as his "ultimate, if distant, aim was disarmament—to rid the world of these 'terrible weapons.'"[120] He also felt that "Western nations had to keep the pressure on the Communist bloc until Marxism-Leninism collapsed from its own internal contradictions."[121] This was the essence of Eisenhower's private mentoring of Reagan and of Eisenhower's last speech, given to the 1968 convention, as discussed. Although Khrushchev did not join him in signing a test-ban treaty, which Eisenhower had hoped would have been the first step down the road towards peace, Eisenhower's goals clearly saw much of their fruition under the stewardship of his student, Ronald Reagan. As we have seen, it was Reagan in mid June 1968 who first warned that if the Soviets tried to equal America's military strength, then America stood ready to start a massive military build-up, which the Soviets could not match.

In the fall of 1983, President Reagan would recognize the silver anniversary of a joint defense research program. After congratulating Prime Minister Thatcher and the British people, President Reagan would remind both nations, "It was due to the foresight of President Eisenhower and Prime Minister MacMillan that the program was established and given the high-level government support required." President Reagan then would review Eisenhower and MacMillan's Declaration of Common Purpose, for both nations—later joined by Canada, Australia and New Zealand—to share defense technology.[122]

On December 8, 1983, the leader of the Soviet Union—Andropov—abruptly would cancel ongoing arms reduction talks and Reagan would have a few minutes to reflect and chat with reporters. Reagan would recall, "It was just thirty years ago today, on December

8th, 1953, that President Dwight Eisenhower made a speech on this very subject of nuclear weapons. And in that speech he said, 'To the making of these fateful decisions, the United States pledges before you…its determination to help solve the fearful atomic dilemma—to devote its entire heart and mind to find the way by which the miraculous inventiveness of man shall not be dedicated to his death, but consecrated to his life.' And **this administration endorses this view completely and this is what we are dedicated to.**"[123] [124] (author's emphasis) President Reagan thus had committed himself and his entire administration—as official policy—to completing the arms reduction proposals first made by his mentor so long ago.

And in one part of his 1984 State of the Union address, Reagan would address the people of the Soviet Union, asking why not do away with nuclear weapons. He would continue, "People of the Soviet, President Dwight Eisenhower, who fought by your side in World War II, said the essential struggle 'is not merely man against man or nation against nation. It is against war.'"[125]

President Reagan would have one unique military occasion, besides his Veterans Day and Vietnam memorial ceremonies cited earlier, with which to honor his beloved veterans. In what historians would describe as the first of Reagan's great speeches as president, Reagan would deliver a stirring speech on the beaches of Normandy to commemorate the fortieth anniversary of D-Day, which of course Eisenhower had led. Reagan would be the first president to visit Normandy. Historian Michael Beschloss reviewed that on the D-Day anniversary of June 4, 1954, President Eisenhower had stayed out of sight, quietly only releasing a written statement, which bespoke "volumes with its modesty and brevity." Ten years later, President Johnson had promised the nation that he would not leave its soil so soon after the Kennedy assassination. On the D-Day anniversary in 1974, President Nixon had been busy with Watergate and was preparing to leave for the Middle East.[126] Reagan would return to Omaha Beach for the 50th commemoration on June 6, 1994, shortly before his announcement that he had Alzheimer's Disease, but his visit in 1984 is the one best remembered.

Prior to the main commemorative speeches, Reagan would speak to reporter Walter Cronkite about Ike's troops and, according to historian Douglas Brinkley, about his own "idolatry of Eisenhower."[127] Then in front of teary-eyed American veterans, the first of President Reagan's two 1984 D-Day speeches, Reagan eloquently would praise the courage of Eisenhower's troops. Reagan's later second speech would commemorate those brave Americans who never made it home. Historians Douglas Brinkley and Paul Kengor have reviewed Reagan's 1984 D-Day commemoration speeches in *The Boys of Pointe Du Hoc* and in *American Spectator*, respectively.

IKE

As historian Douglas Brinkley has related, on the way home, President Reagan flew over and then personally spoke to the crew of the *USS Eisenhower*, which, along with its battle group, had been off shore during the ceremonies. As Reagan watched from above, the crew assembled into the formation spelling, "IKE." Reagan saluted and shouted to the radio, **"I like Ike. I Love Ike!"** (author's emphasis)[128] Reagan continued speaking to the crew, noting proudly that the D-Day landing was the "heroic operation that was planned and commanded by General Dwight D. Eisenhower. The memory of "Ike," our great allied leader, still inspires heroic efforts on both sides of the Atlantic."[129] Of course the crew had no idea of the private inspiration Ike had been to Reagan. Finally, Reagan had the chance to say to America and the world what Ike had meant to him.

President Reagan would view his mentor as heroic in many ways besides his military valor. After returning from the D-Day ceremonies, President Reagan quickly would get another chance to praise Eisenhower. On July 10, 1954, President Eisenhower had signed a bill establishing the Food for Peace program. Exactly thirty years later, President Reagan would reflect on these Eisenhower's accomplishments: that it was still the world's largest food aid program. Between 1954 and 1984, America had donated 653 billion pounds of food to over 100 countries and had helped some 1.8 billion people.

In 1967, candidate Reagan had said that Republicans gladly would support programs that actually helped people. His objection, then and throughout his political career, was that most Democratic programs had not worked. In 1984, President Reagan would praise his mentor's program that had been a triumphant success: "The record of progress is the result of what happened 30 years ago today, when Dwight D. Eisenhower picked up a pen and signed a piece of paper that quietly— and, with no great attention from the wise, he changed the world. I think Dwight D. Eisenhower would be very proud of what the Food for Peace program has accomplished."[130]

Inauguration Day for Eisenhower's second term had been on a Sunday in 1957, so he took the oath of office in a private White House ceremony with the formal inauguration in public the next Monday. It may have been just coincidence, but the pattern of January 20 falling on a Sunday occurs only every 28 years, and the next president to whom this would occur would be Reagan. Exactly 28 years later in 1985, Reagan would repeat Eisenhower's scenario.[131] And President Reagan, in his second Inaugural Address, again would carry forth Eisenhower's "Atoms for Peace" initiative: "We seek the total elimination one day of nuclear weapons from the face of the earth."[132]

In May, 1985, President Reagan would deliver an address at the Bergen-Belsen concentration camp. The controversial portion of the overall trip, to an SS cemetery and which would engender much domestic criticism and a rebuke from Elie Wiesel, is well beyond your author's present subject. Having used successfully the advice he had received so long ago in 1966 from Eisenhower to refute head-on the charges of anti-Semitism, Reagan would draw the lesson for his audience at Bergen-Belsen that the *Talmud* taught that the three gifts resulting from suffering—the *Torah*, the Land of Israel, and the World to Come—promised hope from the ashes of the six million slain by the Nazis.[133]

The year 1985 also would see the first true test for President Reagan of how to deal with hostages. In 1983, one significant aspect of the president's decision to invade Grenada would be that American medical students had been threatened and might become hostages, although certainly there were many other factors involved. His true test would be two years later.

For the *U.S.S. Pueblo* in the late 1960s and for the Iranian hostages in the late 1970s, Reagan had not been in power for either crisis to effect a quick, decisive reaction. Historian Jeffrey Lord recently compared how Presidents Johnson (the *U.S.S. Pueblo*) and Reagan each dealt with hostage crises. In 1985, the Italian cruise ship *Achille Lauro* would be hijacked by four terrorists from the Palestine Liberation Organization, who sought out American passengers and then proceeded to kill one, a wheelchair-bound elderly American Jew named Leon Klinghoffer, and threw his body overboard.

President Reagan would act quickly and decisively. Following his own dictums laid out in 1968 after the conversations and meetings with Eisenhower and Eisenhower's meeting with Harold MacMillan—after the *U.S.S. Pueblo* hijacking, the riots at Columbia University, the confirmation from MacMillan (that Reagan's declaration that action within the first 24 hours was critical in any future hostage crises was correct—Reagan in 1985 immediately would order jets launched from an American aircraft carrier to intercept an Egyptian plane which had been ferrying the hijackers to Italy. Reagan would order the terrorists' plane be escorted, forcibly, to a NATO base. When the Italian prime minister began sending his own jets to keep American jets and the terrorists away from Italy, Reagan called immediately and said he was going ahead with the forced landing regardless of what the Italian prime minister wanted. Unfortunately, the mastermind, Abu Abbas, would get away. Secretary of State Shultz would comment that Reagan's quick and forceful decisions and actions would clearly tell "terrorists and their sponsor states" that America would take decisive action from then on.[134]

In the summer of 1986, President Reagan would address the nation about his Strategic Defense Initiative. He would end his talk by citing and quoting Eisenhower: "The future will belong, no to the fainthearted, but to those who believe in it and prepare for it."[135]

In a final tribute to his advisor and mentor, President Reagan would appoint the members of the Dwight David Eisenhower Centennial Commission.[136] President Reagan would formally establish the commission on November 7, 1986.[137] As President Reagan's last year of office began, he would dedicate the renovated Army and Navy Club in the nation's capital. There, Reagan would tell the audience that he was pleased by the bust of Ike at the club and also noted that when he had passed by a photo of his old boss from World War II, General "Hap" Arnold, he could not resist snapping to attention. It certainly would please President Reagan to see reminders of his mentor and his first commanding officer when he had been in the First Motion Picture Unit so long ago.[138] And in final coincidence with his mentor, Ronald Reagan would pass away on June 5, 2004, the sixtieth anniversary of the day Eisenhower had made the most difficult decision of his own life and the day he had felt the presence of God: the orders to start D-Day.[139]

With President Reagan quoting and honoring the and memory of President Eisenhower so often, and with the calendar cycle of the Reagan years providing so many 25th and 30th policy and program anniversaries and commemorations of the Eisenhower years, one wonders whether President Reagan had made special requests of his staff and writers to provide the details of Eisenhower's words. But your author could find no such comments in any of a number of books by Reagan's close associates and staff. One also wonders how other presidents' citations of so many programs and quotes of one particular predecessor compares with how often President Reagan cited President Eisenhower. But the clear reason is the major theme of this work: Ike was Dutch's political mentor in the 1960s and Dutch clearly was not only an Ike protégé, in your author's opinion, Ronald Reagan was the most important protégé of Dwight Eisenhower.

The Eisenhower and Reagan Legacies

In retirement at Gettysburg and contemplating his legacy, Eisenhower still had reminders of his own major personal hero, Abraham Lincoln. As historian Evan Thomas relates, in Ike's small office where he took secure phone calls, "There was but one picture, a portrait of Lincoln."[140] And on top of his television was a small bust of the slain Lincoln.

Did Eisenhower ever wonder which future president might gaze upon Eisenhower in the future? Upon taking office in 1981, Ronald Reagan had Eisenhower's towering portrait hung in his Cabinet Room. And as historian Clark Judge has written, "A photograph of the former President also sat on the table behind Mr. Reagan's Oval Office desk; and in the President's private study next door, a bust of Eisenhower stood on a table near the President's favorite chair."[141]

Historian Judge speculated that President Reagan's apparent admiration for Eisenhower may have stemmed from Reagan's desire to reinvigorate a coalition to fight against the Soviet Union as Eisenhower had done against those same adversaries in the 1950's and against the Nazis in the 1940's. Judge added that another reason might have been that historian Fred Greenstein's *The Hidden-Hand Presidency* had just been published in 1982 and which had detailed, "How a President the intelligencia so disdained was smarter than critics imagined."[142]

But Ronald Reagan's admiration for, and homage to, Eisenhower clearly went much, much deeper than that. Eisenhower was Reagan's mentor and role model in the 1960s. Reagan sought to emulate Eisenhower as soon as he had joined Eisenhower in *Mr. Lincoln's Party Today* in 1962 and when that first Eisenhower letter of advice was handed to him by Freeman Gosden back in 1965. Reagan had declared that Eisenhower was his inspiration for the theme of the 1966 gubernatorial campaign. But Eisenhower was much more: he was the inspiration for Reagan's 1968 presidential campaign and that inspiration continued throughout the years of Reagan's presidency. As Ronald Reagan made his own set of difficult decisions during his eight years as president, from calling on Gorbachev to tear down the Berlin Wall to walking away from the Reykjavik summit because he refused to give up his Strategic Defense Initiative, he must have sought comfort by looking at the portrait, photograph, and bust of his old coach while recalling their shared roles in his 1966 and 1968 campaigns. As noted above in comments whose importance is only clear now that the present analysis has been completed, President

Reagan explained forcefully that some of his most important official policies were, in fact, continuations of Eisenhower's uncompleted policy goals brought to their fruition.

Commentator Jeffrey Lord brought Reagan's military policies to the public's attention in 2013, stating that President Obama, who was contemplating what action to take against Syria, might be wise to understand what Reagan had advised to his successors.[143] In late October, 1983, a day was planned for Reagan to play golf in Augusta, where Eisenhower had played so often that an "Eisenhower Cottage" had been built there. But he was awakened at four in the morning and met his secretary of state and his national security advisor in the Eisenhower Cottage living room to hear the news that America was asked to intervene militarily in Grenada. During the next day, a crazed gunman broke into the pro shop and held hostages. Knowing how to deal with hostages ever since Harold MacMillan had approved his ideas during the summer of 1968, quickly Reagan spoke to the man and he was captured successfully shortly thereafter. Exhausted, Reagan went to bed early, only to be awakened at 2:30 AM. In the Eisenhower Cottage living room again, Reagan met his advisors and was told that a suicide bomber had blown up the Marine barracks in Lebanon.

Was it fate that the two foreign crises during the Reagan administration in which Reagan had committed American troops were handled in part by the president from the Eisenhower Cottage? In Reagan's post-presidential autobiography, *An American Life*, he would create four principles for military action. These stated that American troops should not be committed unless the cause was vital to America's national interest; that if there were a commitment, then there must be clear intent and support to win; there must be support from the American people; and that combat was a last resort. Jeffrey Lord entitled his analysis that these were Reagan's rules. But they more appropriately should have been called Eisenhower's and Reagan's rules from Korea and Vietnam.

Eisenhower was out of office for seven years when historians began to reconsider his presidential accomplishments and the direct role he had played in those achievements. Starting with author Murray Kempton in 1967[144] to Princeton historian Fred Greenstein's seminal *The Hidden Hand Presidency* through historian Evan Thomas' *Ike's Bluff*, Eisenhower now is seen by many as a principled and activist president, whose style was "behind-the-scenes." Even a reassessment by Eisenhower biographer Stephen Ambrose confirmed the high marks historians continue to give to Ike as president.[145]

Yet Ronald Reagan, in the 1980 campaign interview cited above, hit the nail on the head in his positive assessment of Eisenhower. Greenstein was able to make his strong case only after Eisenhower era documents became available for study. Yet Greenstein in the late 1980s felt that Reagan's apparent administrative style could not measure up to that of Eisenhower. As Reagan was leaving office, Greenstein wrote that Reagan "was unusually passive in terms of engagement in subtler issues and seemed so insensitive to the workings of policy."[146] Greenstein made that judgment without access to critical Reagan administration documents, but he did leave the door open that he or others might change their minds once such documents might become available.[147] And just as Greenstein had foreseen, subsequently historians Martin and Annelise Anderson did have such access. As Greenstein had done for Eisenhower in 1982, they demonstrated clearly in *Reagan's Secret War* that like his mentor Eisenhower, Ronald Reagan had the same forceful decision-making prowess—with his style similarly appearing to be aloof—using the same hidden-hand techniques as his coach. Recently, Ed Meese, Reagan's Attorney General, and in agreement with this latter assessment, reflected that Eisenhower and Reagan each made extensive use of their cabinets and sub-cabinets to evaluate and set policies.[148]

Ike and Dutch

As mentioned briefly earlier, historian Doug Brinkley[149] and others[150] have felt that Reagan looked primarily to FDR as a role model, although the conclusion of the latter analysis is that Reagan emulated FDR's style but not his domestic policies. Eisenhower as a major Reagan role model has never been explored previously, except by the one sentence comment by a newspaper reporter in July, 1981, cited earlier.

The only academic works on Eisenhower and Reagan were brief analyses by historians Fred Greenstein, Paul Kengor, and Douglas Brinkley, and these works analyzed the governing styles and policies of the two presidents rather than discussing any direct link between the two men.[151][152][153] Indeed all three works are reminiscent of the December, 1967, magazine analysis by Julia Duscha, cited earlier, which had so disdainfully compared their two governing styles. Historian Stephen Ambrose briefly noted that Eisenhower and Reagan each had talked tough but maintained the peace, used covert CIA operations rather than overt military action in the Third World and had tremendous reserves of personal popularity.[154] Historian Douglas Brinkley noted that Reagan had inherited Ike's "infectious grin, gregarious demeanor, and 'hands off' style of leadership as his own."[155] Brinkley added that historians had overlooked "how much the Gipper stylistically modeled his presidency after Eisenhower's."[156] As noted earlier, Reagan's decision-making style, to reach a consensus in the cabinet, was very similar to that of Eisenhower. But it was not by chance. One can now see in the above analyses that President Reagan had again followed the path set by his mentor.

But as the present work has demonstrated for the first time, there was much more to Reagan's emulation of Ike than mere continuation of the style of governing. Reagan saw many of his domestic programs as continuations, or restorations, of Eisenhower's policies and initiatives. And in world affairs, in fact Reagan had continued Eisenhower's goal of defeating communism by seeing it to its final end via the use of the threat of military buildup. Eisenhower had mentored Reagan about military spending. And both had built their militaries. Analysts from the Heritage Foundation confirmed that Reagan and Eisenhower had achieved quite similar increases in military spending.[157] And Reagan had succeeded in throwing communism and its Berlin Wall onto the ash-heap of history without firing a shot. Ike would have been proud that his protégé Dutch had succeeded in completing his own goals.

There has been very little historical analysis of Eisenhower's post-presidential political involvement other than his eventual endorsing of Nixon and his televised speech to the 1968 Republican convention. And to your author's best knowledge, there has been almost no analysis of Ike's post-presidential diary until now. Various historians have discussed Eisenhower and his relationship to John F. Kennedy and his various foreign crises. Historian Andrew Johns, referenced earlier, chronicled Eisenhower's involvement with Kennedy and Johnson about Vietnam. Historian Kabaservice, cited earlier, provided some analysis of Eisenhower in the 1960s, especially the background about Eisenhower's Gettysburg conclave in 1962. None of these accounts discussed Eisenhower and Reagan. The most detailed account of Eisenhower in the decade of the 1960s, by his grandson David and his wife Julie, as referenced earlier, mentioned Eisenhower and Reagan only in a sentence. The present work is the first analysis to demonstrate clearly how involved Eisenhower remained in the world of Republican politics in the mid and late 1960s, and Eisenhower historian Fred Greenstein reflected to your author that such analysis has been needed to fill that historical void.[158]

Early analyses of Reagan's 1966 gubernatorial victory[159, 160] Cannon's classic work,[161] and several recent analyses by historians Mark Brilliant,[162] Kevin McKenna,[163] and Todd Holmes[164] all fail to discuss the direct Eisenhower-Reagan relationship. Gibbs and Duffy briefly mentioned the Eisenhower-Reagan relationship by calling it a "little-known" alliance and related that Eisenhower sent Reagan "advice and ideas directly and through intermediaries" plus "suggested ways Reagan could lay out a program, shorten his stump speech, and punch up his key phrases."[165] They speculated that Eisenhower's motive in helping Reagan was to help a fellow politician who had come to politics late in life. Historian Kabaservice's analysis, mentioned above, concluded that Eisenhower had no moderate Republican heirs.[166] A very recent Reagan biographer does not mention anything of the Eisenhower-Reagan relationship.[167] Of course the common perception is that Eisenhower and Reagan had virtually nothing in common, but the present analysis disproves this from the perspective of Eisenhower himself. In the mid 1960's, Eisenhower became Reagan's political mentor. Reagan followed Eisenhower's repeated advice virtually to the letter. And Eisenhower approved of Reagan, endorsed him, and certified him as presidential timbre.

Reed published his memoirs of his years with Reagan and admits that during that time, he had had no knowledge of the mentoring Eisenhower had been doing. It was not until your author's research brought it all to Reed's attention, and Reed acknowledges this in his book, which enabled him to see events in proper historical perspective.[168]

Did Eisenhower Advise Other Rising Republicans?

One may question whether Eisenhower's mentoring of Reagan was unique, or if indeed Eisenhower coached other rising Republicans in the mid 1960s and whether Reagan was just one of many Eisenhower political students. Eisenhower's private discussions and letters to Nixon in the mid 1960s are reviewed by historian Andrew Johns, but of course Nixon was not a political newcomer and needed no coaching per se from his old boss. The present author has been unable to document any letters, memos, or diary notes at the Eisenhower Presidential Library indicating that Eisenhower gave, other than to Reagan, any similar detailed and continuing political advice to any other rising Republicans at the time, including Hatfield, Percy, Romney, or Rockefeller.

Specifically, the Library has an interview transcript from 1965 wherein Eisenhower had felt that four men had been qualified to succeed him in 1960: Senator Henry Cabot Lodge, Vice-President

Nixon, General Alfred Gruenther, and Secretary of the Treasury Robert Anderson.[169] Eisenhower's comments had applied at the time specifically to 1960 and he was not asked about the 1968 election at the time of the 1965 interview.

During the time period Eisenhower initially coached Reagan, 1965-1966, Eisenhower's correspondence with Rockefeller consisted of one communication about the future of the party, and this single one was about Republican Party principles.[170] Eisenhower did wish Rockefeller good luck prior to the November, 1966 election.[171] But Eisenhower had no communication or diary entry about Rockefeller as a future presidential candidate, or any specific advice or suggestions Eisenhower had made in this regard. Similarly, there is no documentation about his advising George Romney or Mark Hatfield during the 1965-1968 timeframe either.

Reagan's Farewell Address

In a little-heralded diary entry of 1982, as he would begin tackling the multiple economic problems left by the Carter administration and the massive federal bureaucracy growing since the 1930s, President Reagan would reflect that the major emphasis of his domestic programs was not to undo FDR's New Deal but to undo Lyndon Johnson's Great Society: "I'm trying to undo the 'Great Society.' It was LBJ's war on poverty that led to our present mess."[172] Clearly Reagan's own 1966-1968 fighting against LBJ's policies during his first presidential campaign would never leave his mind. Indeed it would become the major domestic theme of his administration. As he would prepare to leave office, President Reagan would get the chance to assess how well he had done in dismantling these JFK-RFK-LBJ policies and in restoring the ideals and policies of Eisenhower.

President Ronald Reagan would deliver his own Farewell Address on January 11, 1989. His final speech shows a series of photographs on the desk behind him, and as historian Judge indicated, as the camera pans in, one cannot quite clearly discern Eisenhower's photograph. But what Reagan said spoke volumes of what he felt towards his mentor. Admittedly, Reagan did not mention Eisenhower by name. After all, Reagan stood high in his own light by accomplishing so much during his eight years. Reagan did not have to cite Eisenhower directly. Reagan's own words would lead directly back to the time Reagan first had entered politics and had sought the help of the general.

Reagan took pride that his two greatest accomplishments were "the economic recovery," and "the recovery of our morale. America is respected again in the world and looked to for leadership."173 He had righted the ship of state and returned it to the heading that President Eisenhower had established and which had been off-course for the 1960's and 1970's.

Reagan reflected back to his original observation of Eisenhower's perceived reluctance to run for the presidency and hearkened back to Eisenhower's first letter of advice, given to Reagan almost a quarter century earlier. That it was the people who should decide, both his and Eisenhower's philosophies at the beginning, returned to Reagan's thoughts when he said,

"I never meant to go into politics. It wasn't my intention…But I ultimately went into politics because I wanted to protect something precious…Back in the 1960's when I began…the government was taking more of our money, more of our options, and more of our freedom. I went into politics in part to put up my hand and say 'Stop!' I was a citizen-politician."174

Just as Eisenhower had seen himself as the Citizen-Solider, Reagan had continued on as the Citizen-Candidate to Citizen-Governor and had come full circle to being one of Eisenhower's major political heirs.

Although originally Reagan had begun speaking out about smaller government in his Hollywood days and as spokesman for *General Electric Theatre*, he got his 1966 campaign theme of common sense directly from Eisenhower. In his farewell, President Reagan reflected, "**Common sense** told us that when you put a big tax on something, the people will produce less of it. So we cut the people's tax rates and the people produced more than ever before."175 He continued, "**Common sense** also told us that to preserve the peace, we'd have to become strong again after years of weakness and confusion. So we rebuilt our defenses," and added that the superpowers had begun to "reduce their stockpiles of nuclear weapons."176 (author's emphasis) Was Eisenhower smiling behind him?

As noted earlier, Eisenhower famously had told Winston Churchill that Soviet leaders were all still "whores,"177 but in Reagan's Farewell Address, he told America that he thought Gorbachev was different. But "It's still trust but verify…It's still watch closely."178 Eisenhower, who had proposed Open Skies, couldn't have agreed more.

Reagan then urged Americans to teach their children about American history and American values lest they be forgotten. He spoke of the valor of Americans fighting in the Korean War, which

Eisenhower had ended. As he had for D-day in 1984, Reagan again spoke of the Omaha Beach landings during D-Day, which Eisenhower had directed. He spoke of the raid over Tokyo by Jimmy Doolittle, who later had become one of Eisenhower's advisors, Reagan's acquaintance in Oregon back on Veterans Day in 1967, and also the recipient of that fourth star pinned by President Reagan at the White House.

President Emeritus

Historian Craig Shirley recently has penned another critically important work, adding to his prior studies, now classics, of Reagan's 1976 and 1980 campaigns, this time analyzing Reagan's post-presidential years.[179] Given that your author's present work has emphasized events that were more than a full generation prior to Reagan's last decades of life, nevertheless, Shirley makes several important points about Reagan and Eisenhower. Shirley notes that Reagan was the last successful president since Eisenhower, and that both men were the only two presidents of the second half of the twentieth century to have left office more popular than when they were sworn in. Shirley also points out that Reagan had followed Ike's lead by telling the American public about medical issues, rather than the hidden concealment policies of other presidents.[180]

In June, 1989 in London, a quarter century after the death of the Greatest Briton, Reagan gave the Churchill Lecture at the English Speaking Union, where again he praised Churchill's love of freedom. Reagan visited Berlin at the former infamous Checkpoint Charlie and helped knock down a section of the Berlin Wall. It should never be forgotten that it was Ronald Reagan who first had called publicly to tear down the Berlin Wall on May 15, 1967 and the other stops on his first presidential quest elsewhere in 1967 and later in 1968 which have been reviewed by your author.

On June 27, 1990 at the Eisenhower Boyhood Home in Abilene, Reagan gave the commemorative address at the Centennial Celebration of Eisenhower's Birth. Reagan said nothing of their mentor-student relationship in the 1960s but noted that his old mentor had led the Allies, "not for territory but for justice, not for plunder but for righteousness." Stressing again the thread of freedom handed from Churchill to Eisenhower and then to Reagan, Reagan added, "He fought to extend to other people in other lands the freedom that every American knows." Reagan reminded his audience that Ike had "inspired Atoms for Peace and People-to-People." Reagan noted that

Eisenhower had not lived long enough to see the fulfillment of his yearnings for freedom for all mankind, but Ike knew it was only a matter of time. Reagan explained, "'Take courage', he said, "from the sure knowledge that the current of history flows toward freedom... In the long run, dictators and despotism must give way.'" Ronald Reagan, by his peaceful winning of the Cold War as envisioned by Eisenhower when they had met so long ago, had fulfilled the goals of freedom of Eisenhower and of Churchill.[181]

But even Reagan knew that his winning of the Cold War against the Soviet Union was not enough. In 1989 when the freedom-loving protestors at Tiananmen Square faced the tanks of the Red Chinese Army, Ronald Reagan spoke out and again called for freedom from communism.[182] One can only wonder how anguished Reagan might have been to see how his successor President Obama would not lift a finger to help the stirrings of freedom in Iran some two decades later or to award Communist Cuba with recognition without any freedom having been restored to its populace.

Ike and Dutch Together Again

Reagan's first public comments about a specific American anti-ballistic missile shield had been during the 1968 campaign, when as seen earlier, in Seattle in November, 1967, he had told the press he had been studying the subject and was in favor of increased spending in space weapons and later in July, 1968, he was not in favor of canceling the Sentinel program. But the idea did not entirely stay dormant until he would become president. On September 11, 1979, Reagan would reference his 1967-1968 insights about a missile shield by recalling, "There once was the beginning of a defense; an anti-ballistic missile system which we had invented and which the Soviets didn't have. We bargained that away actually for nothing."[183]

Long-time Reagan aide Michael Deaver recalled a long-treasured photograph of Reagan's: "one of himself with Eisenhower that he has had in every office since I've known him."[184] When President Reagan first would discuss his idea for a new strategic missile defense shield, the meeting would be held in the Cabinet Room. "To the President's right, hanging on the wall over the fireplace, was a three-foot high painting of Dwight D. Eisenhower, sternly gazing down on the generals in front of him. As the meeting began, you could almost feel that Eisenhower would have approved of what Reagan was about to do; after all, Reagan had selected this portrait to hang in the Cabinet Room."[185]

Perhaps President Reagan would reflect that his own new proposal for a strategic missile defense shield had its origin during the 1968 campaign, when, after his comments in Seattle, he had given his support to the Sentinel program after his visit to Dr. Teller at Lawrence-Livermore (preceded possibly by discussions with Strom Thurmond as discussed) and his opposition to the system's cancellation in mid 1968. Once the defensive shield was in place in the future, Reagan could fulfill the dream of eliminating nuclear weapons that had sprung directly from Eisenhower's 1953 proposal. Perhaps during their many private meetings discussing Reagan's primary and general election campaigns in 1966 and when they had discussed foreign affairs during Reagan's 1968 presidential campaign, the two men had discussed the issue of nuclear weapon elimination. But whereas Eisenhower had dealt with American nuclear superiority and a Soviet Union without massive of numbers of weapons, President Reagan would see that he needed the defensive shield technology first in order to make offensive weapons obsolete. Thus it was quite natural a location for President Reagan to be holding that critical meeting under General Eisenhower's watchful gaze.

Indeed on some football field above, coach Dwight Eisenhower was smiling down as a father figure, advisor and as a teacher on one of his major protégés and heirs, Ronald Reagan. For Eisenhower, who had despaired in 1960 that he might have no legacy to leave the American people, finally could see President Reagan had fulfilled the hopes for a better world that he did not live long enough to see.

And Ronald Reagan was looking up to the man who had been the inspiration for his own political life from governor in 1966 to candidate in 1968 to president in 1980. Historian Douglas Brinkley felt that with his 1984 D-Day address, President Reagan in effect had received the symbolic "D-Day baton" from Eisenhower. Reagan had told Walter Cronkite that day, "I will forever stand for Ike's D-Day veterans. They are my heroes, like they were his."[186]

But for both Ike and Reagan, their hearts belonged to football. And team players they were, in football and in politics. Although it had been decades since either of them had played the sport, they each had twice won the Political Super Bowl by winning the presidency and then by being re-elected with wider margins than the first time. Eisenhower had used his "hidden hand" techniques while he was president. But Ike had his other hand too. What Eisenhower really had done was to use his second hidden hand—with which he secretly had mentored Reagan in the 1960s—to pass the football of freedom and American excellence forward to Reagan.

Reagan then ran with it, past the 1960s, past the 1970s and even beyond the 1980s of his presidency. Well into the twenty-first century and beyond, whenever people yearn for freedom, democracy, and a strong America as leader of the Free World, and whenever people need inspiration and need leaders with moral clarity—who are not afraid to say what is right versus what is wrong—there can no finer role models than Ronald Reagan and Dwight Eisenhower. For Reagan, Ike's tutelage was critical. This political mentorship changed America's national priorities through the end of Reagan's presidency, whose effects still are very much with us today.

With the fall of communism in the 1980s and the massive reduction in nuclear weapons that was about to start, Reagan and Eisenhower could walk together proudly, originally as coach and student but now as full equals, into the Presidential Hall of Fame, sitting high up in the shining city upon the hill. Reagan had taken to heart the inspiring 1965 oration of Eisenhower, who had urged his fellow citizens to carry on the goals he had shared with Churchill: to free captive nations. And the Eisenhower and Reagan journey together had begun when coach Eisenhower first had mentored his new political student—all during Reagan's first campaign for the presidency. In the end, President Reagan would triumph by carrying forth the mantle of freedom that he had inherited from his heroes: Abraham Lincoln, Theodore Roosevelt, Calvin Coolidge, Winston Churchill and most of all, Dwight Eisenhower.

Endnotes

1. White and Gill, p. 128
2. Hodel, pers comm. 10/7/2012 and 7/10/2015
3. Buckley, William F., *The Reagan I Knew*, New York: Basic Books, 2008, p. 43-44
4. ibid, p. 43
5. Ayres, B Drummond Jr, "Reagan Joins a Kennedy Remembrance," *NYT*, 6/6/81, p. 1
6. Senator Edward Kennedy, describing how RFK's toughest opponent was Ronald Reagan, June, 1981
7. Deaver, p. 14
8. Brinkley, p. 214
9. Reagan, Ronald, "Farewell Address," 1/11/1989
10. White and Gill, p. 127
11. White and Gill, p. 128
12. Hill, Gladwin, "Reagan Cheerful Despite Setback," *NYT*, 8/9/1968, p. 18
13. ibid
14. Safire, p. 55
15. Patrick, Curtis, Vol. II, p. 224
16. Cannon, p. 270
17. Kelley, p. 175
18. Curtis Patrick I, p. 45
19. Ronald Reagan to Henry A. Bubb, letter 8/29/68, Henry A. Bubb Collection, University of Kansas Archives
20. White, Clif to Henry A. Bubb, letter 8/28/1968, Henry A. Bubb Collection, University of Kansas Archives

21. Cannon, Ronnie and Jesse, p. 275
22. Buckley, William F., "The Reagan I Knew," *New York: Basic Books*, 2008, p. 43-44
23. ibid, p. 43
24. Weinrod, Bruce letter to SFR members, undated, courtesy Bruce Weinrod
25. William A. Rusher to Bruce Weinrod, letter 8/28/68, courtesy Bruce Weinrod
26. Ronald Reagan to Bruce Weinrod, letter 9/30/1968, courtesy Bruce Weinrod
27. White and Gill, p. 131
28. Moore, p. 64
29. Reed, *The Reagan Enigma*, p. 178-179
30. Reagan, *An American Life*, p. 176-178
31. Lou Cannon, personal communication, 4/27/2015
32. McCullough, David. Both TR's mother and his wife died in less than a 24-hour span.
33. Hodel, pers comm. 10/7/2012 and 7/10/2015
34. Ayres, B Drummond Jr, "Reagan Joins a Kennedy Remembrance," *NYT*, 6/6/81, p. 1
35. "Remarks on Presenting the Robert F. Kennedy Medal to Mrs. Kennedy," Public Papers of President Ronald W. Reagan, June, 1981, The Ronald Reagan Presidential Library
36. Beran, p. xvi
37. Ayres, *NYT*, op.cit.
38. "Remarks" op. cit.
39. Beran, p. xv
40. Ibid
41. Ayres op.cit.
42. RRL, Diary entry 6/5/81; Reagan and Brinkley, p. 23
43. Thomas, Evan, "Prologue," *NYT Review of Books*, 9/10/2000
44. "Remarks" op.cit.
45. Ayres op.cit.
46. Ayres op.cit.
47. Ayres op.cit.
48. Most historians agree that RFK did not like to be called "Bobby" and preferred "Bob."
49. Beran, p. xvii
50. Beran, p. xviii
51. ibid
52. ibid
53. http://spectator.org/articles/56713/reagan%E2%80%99s-salute-jfk;   https://www.youtube.com/watch?v=jRhCC-6Wdp8
54. Reagan, Ronald, Remarks at a Fund-Raising Reception for the John F. Kennedy Library Foundation, 6/24/1985
55. Hahn, Cary, "Remembering the Christmas of 1968," *Marion Iowa Times*, 12/23/2008
56. "Pueblo Men, Loved Ones are Reunited" *Chicago Tribune*, 12/25/1968, sec. 1, p. 3
57. Reagan, Ronald, "Address Before the Korean National Assembly in Seoul," 11/12/1983
58. Reagan, Ronald, "Remarks Following Discussions with President Chun Doo Hwon of the Republic of Korea," 4/26/1985
59. Reagan, Ronald, "Remarks at a White House Ceremony Honoring Participants in the Retired Senior Volunteer Program," 4/26/1985
60. Cited in Franklin, H. Bruce, Missing in Action in the 21st Century, unpublished thesis, Rutgers University, 2013
61. Kelley
62. Quoted in Pendley, William Perry "How Ronald Reagan Saved the Vietnam Veterans Memorial," *Washington Times*, 11/10/2014
63. Cannon, p. 479
64. Franklin, op.cit.
65. Rosenthal, James, "The Myth of the Lost POWs," *New Republic*, 7/1/1985
66. "Reagan Gives Views on the Vietnam War," *NYT*, 4/5/1984
67. Reagan, Ronald, "Remarks at Memorial Day Ceremonies Honoring an Unknown Serviceman of the Vietnam Conflict," 5/28/1984
68. Rosenthal, op.cit.
69. Reagan, Ronald, "Remarks at Dedication Ceremonies for the Vietnam Veterans Memorial Statue," 11/11/1984
70. Reagan, Ronald, "Radio Address to the Nation on POW's and MIA's in Southeast Asia," 7/19/1986
71. Reagan, Ronald, "Remarks at the Veterans Day Ceremony at the Vietnam Veterans memorial," 11/11/1988
72. Reagan, *An American Life*, p. 279
73. http://howappealing.abovethelaw.com/20q/2003_03_01_20q-appellateblog_archive.html

74. Ronald and Nancy Reagan to Mamie Eisenhower, 3/28/69 telegram, 1969 File Series, Box 20, Eisenhower, Mamie Doud: Papers, 1894-1979, Dwight D. Eisenhower Presidential Library
75. Reyn, p. 343-345
76. Gillenwaters, p. 35-36
77. http://www.c-span.org/video/?107834-1/ronald-reagan-theodore-roosevelt
78. White and Gill, p. 137-138
79. Skinner, Reagan in his Own Hand, p. 253
80. Skinner, ibid, p. 254
81. https://www.youtube.com/watch?v=EWXMrnaZi-E; historian Adam Clymer reviews the politics of the pro- and anti-canal withdrawal forces in Drawing the Line at the Big Ditch. Lawrence: University of Kansas Press, 2008.
82. Ivies
83. "Reagan on Reagan," *Christian Science Monitor*, 4/4/1980
84. ibid
85. ibid
86. Cannon, p. 480-481
87. Van Natta, Don Jr., p. 77-78
88. Robinson, personal communication, 10/16/2015
89. Short, note 12, p. 149
90. Reagan, Ronald, "1984 State of the Union Address"
91. Appendix D; Reagan certainly did cite Washington and other Founding Father presidents often.
92. Reagan, Ronald, "Message on the Observance of Independence Day, 1981," 7/3/1981
93. Reagan, Ronald, "Remarks at the Swearing-In Ceremony for Members of the President's Export Council," 10/15/1981
94. Hart, Jeffrey, "Reagan and Ike," *Daily News*, 7/24/1981
95. Reagan, Ronald, "Proclamation 4879—Silver Anniversary Year of the National System of Interstate and Defense Highways," 10/29/1981
96. Reagan, Ronald, "Remarks on Signing the Intelligence Identities Protection Act of 1982," 6/23/1982
97. Reagan, Ronald, "Radio Address to the Nation on the Observance of Independence Day," 7/3/1982
98. Reagan, Ronald, "Remarks at Kansas State University at the Alfred M. Landon Lecture Series on Public Issues," 9/9/1982
99. Reagan, Ronald, "Message to Congress Transmitting Proposed Federal Legislation," 2/24/1983
100. Reagan, Ronald, "Remarks at the Opening of 'The American Cowboy' Exhibit at the Library of congress," 3/24/1983
101. Reagan, Ronald, "Proclamation 5230—Hawaii Statehood Silver Jubilee Day," 8/21/1984
102. Reagan, Ronald, "Remarks at the Annual Dinner of the Conservative Political Action Conference," 1/30/1986
103. Reagan, Ronald, "Remarks at the Annual National Prayer Breakfast," 2/6/1986
104. Nau
105. Chidester and Kengor
106. Anderson, Reagan's Secret War, p. 42
107. Feldman, Harvey, "President Reagan's Six Assurances to Taiwan and Their Meaning Today," *Heritage Foundation*, 10/2/2007
108. China in April 1984
109. Cannon, President Reagan, p. 420-423
110. Tyler, p. 288-289
111. Reagan, Ronald, "Toasts of the President and Prime Minister Margaret Thatcher of the United Kingdom at the State Dinner," 2/26/1981
112. Reagan, Ronald, "Address of the President and Prime Minister Elliott Trudeau of Canada Before a Joint Session of Parliament in Ottawa," 3/11/1981
113. Reagan, Ronald, "Remarks to Representatives of Sister Cities International," 3/27/1981
114. Anderson, p. 82
115. Reagan, Ronald, "State of the Union Address," 1/26/1982
116. Reagan, Ronald, "Statement on the 25th Anniversary of the European Community," 3/24/1982
117. Anderson, p. 106
118. Anderson, p. 107
119. Reagan, Ronald, "Remarks in New York, Before the United Nations General assembly Special Session Devoted to Disarmament," 6/17/1982
120. Thomas, Ike's Bluff, p. 109
121. Thomas, p. 144

122. Reagan, Ronald, "Statement on the 25th Anniversary of the Technical Cooperation Program," 10/13/1983
123. Anderson, p. 145
124. Reagan, Ronald, "Remarks and Question-and-Amswer Session with Reporters on Strategic Arms Reduction Talks," 12/8/1983
125. Anderson, p. 151
126. Beschloss, Michael, "Why Ike Wouldn't Celebrate the D-Day Anniversary," *NYT*, 5/19/2014
127. Brinkley, p. 214
128. Brinkley, p. 214
129. Reagan, Ronald, "Remarks by Telephone to the crew of the USS Eisenhower Following D-Day Ceremonies in Normandy," France, 6/6/1984
130. Reagan, Ronald, "Remarks on Signing the Food for Peace Day Proclamation" 7/10/1984
131. "1957 Presidential Inauguration" Dwight D. Eisenhower Presidential Library website
132. Reagan, Ronald. "Second Inaugural Address" 1/21/1985
133. Reagan, Ronald "Remarks at a Commemorative Ceremony at Bergen-Belsen Concentration Camp, 5/5/1985
134. Lord, Jeffrey, "Three Presidents and a Hijacking at Sea," *American Spectator*, 4/9/2009
135. Reagan, Ronald, "Radio Address to the Nation on the Strategic Defense Initiative," 7/12/1986
136. "Appointment of Four Members of the Dwight David Eisenhower Centennial Commission," 5/28/1987
137. Reagan, Ronald, "Statement on Signing the Bill Establishing the Dwight D. Eisenhower Centennial Commission," 11/7/1986
138. Reagan, Ronald, "Remarks at the Dedication Ceremony of the Army Navy Club," 1/12/1988
139. Brinkley, p. 218
140. Thomas, Ike's Bluff, p. 415
141. Judge, Clark, "Ronald Reagan at 100," *Claremont Review of Books*, XI, #1-2, winter/spring 2010-2011
142. Judge, ibid
143. Lord, Jeffrey, "Reagan's Rules for Military Action," *American Spectator*, 9/3/2013
144. Kempton, Murray "The Underestimation of Dwight D. Eisenhower," *Esquire*, 9/67, p. 108-109
145. Ambrose, Stephen, "The Age of Ike," *New Republic*, 5/9/1981
146. "What U.S. Scholars Think of the Reagan Presidency," *Christian Science Monitor*, 1/12/89, p. 3
147. Greenstein, p. 238
148. Meese, p. xviii
149. Brinkley, The Boys of Pointe du Hoc.
150. http://www.firstprinciplesjournal.com/articles.aspx?article=1082
151. Greenstein, Fred, "Ronald Reagan: Another Hidden-Hand Ike?" PS: Political Science and Politics 231, 1990, p. 7-13.
152. Kengor, Paul, "Comparing Presidents Reagan and Eisenhower," *Presidential Studies Quarterly* 282, 1998, p. 366
153. Brinkley, p. 214-215
154. Ambrose, Stephen, "How Great was Ronald Reagan?" online review by *The Heritage Foundation*, undated
155. Brinkley, p. 215
156. Brinkley, p. 215
157. Cited in Edwards, Lee, *The Essential Ronald Reagan*, New York: Roman and Littlefield, 2005, p. 103
158. Greenstein, Fred, personal interview, 1/4/2014
159. Boyarsky, Bill, *The Rise of Ronald Reagan*, New York: Random House, 1968.
160. Lewis, Joseph, *What Makes Reagan Run?*, New York: McGraw-Hill, 1968.
161. Cannon Lou, Governor Reagan, New York: Public Affairs, 2003.
162. Brilliant, Mark, *The Color of America Has Changed*, New York: Oxford University Press, 2010.
163. McKenna, Kevin, "The Total Campaign: How Ronald Reagan Overwhelmingly Won the California Gubernatorial Election of 1966," Undergraduate Thesis, Columbia University, 2010.
164. Holmes, Todd, "Economic Roots of Reaganism," *Western Historical Quarterly*, 411: Spring 2010, p. 59
165. Gibbs and Duffy op.cit., p. 202
166. Kabaservice, Geoffrey, *Rule and Ruin*, New York: Oxford University Press, 2013
167. Brands
168. Reed, Thomas, *The Reagan Enigma*, Los Angeles: Figueora Press, 2014, Acknowledgements

169. Post-Presidential Papers, 1965 Principal File, Box2 folder "AP-1 Morin, Pat", Dwight D. Eisenhower Presidential Library
170. Governor Nelson Rockefeller to Dwight Eisenhower, letter 12/22/1964, and Dwight Eisenhower to Governor Nelson Rockefeller, letter 1/4/1965, Post-Presidential Papers, 1965 Principal File, Box 44, folder "ROC", Dwight D. Eisenhower Presidential Library
171. Dwight Eisenhower to Governor Nelson Rockefeller, letter 11/7/1966, Post-Presidential Papers, 1966 Principal File, Box 11, folder "PL-4: Political Affairs, Funds" Dwight Eisenhower Presidential Library
172. http://www.firstprinciplesjournal.com/articles.aspx?article=1082
173. Reagan, Ronald, "Farewell Address", 1/11/89
174. ibid
175. ibid
176. ibid
177. Leaming, p. 243
178. ibid
179. Shirley, Last Act
180. Shirley, ibid, p. 9, p. 23, p. 127
181. *The Herington Times*, 8/9/1990
182. www.nbcuniversalarchives.com/nbcuni/clip/5112542724_007.do
183. Skinner, Reagan in His Own Hand, p. 120
184. Deaver, p. 14
185. Anderson, p. 116
186. Brinkley, p. 214-215

AFTERWORD

Shri Montek Singh Ahluwalia, who worked at the International Monetary Fund after Oxford, is the Deputy Chairman of the Planning Commission of the Republic of India.

Bill Bradley completed his studies at Oxford and became a basketball super-star in the NBA. In 1978 he ran for the U.S. Senate and faced Jeffrey Bell, a 1976 campaign planner for Reagan; Bradley won with 56% of the vote.[1] Bradley worked closely with President Reagan on budgetary matters (and actually agreed with Reagan's cuts to federal spending) and was the author of a bill which changed the tax code in 1986. Bradley said that Reagan never mentioned the 1967 *Town Meeting of the World* debate whenever the two men met. Bradley said that he himself did not mention the debate in either his own autobiography *Time Present, Time Past* nor was it mentioned in his biography *Senator* because he felt it was just a "moment in time." Senator Bradley remains close friends with his debate colleague Montek Singh. He kindly agreed to be interviewed by the author on September 14, 2012.

Dr. Francisco Bravo after 1968 became somewhat disenchanted with Governor Reagan.[2] Dr. Bravo died in 1990.

Henry A. Bubb stayed active in Republican Party politics in Kansas after 1968, but due to his age did not set up another Citizens for Reagan National Information Center in 1976 or 1980 or 1984. According to his son-in-law John C. Dicus, President Reagan chatted with Bubb many times, and Reagan sent a warm note of condolence to the Bubb and Dicus families upon Henry's death in 1989.

William F. Buckley, Jr. continued his feuding with Gore Vidal after the convention. Then Buckley began writing espionage novels in the 1970s. In 1990, he retired as editor of *National Review*. In 2008, Buckley was found dead at his desk, thought to be in the midst of writing a new book about Reagan.

Anderson Carter served in 1976 as national field director for the Reagan campaign, and in 1980 was deputy chairman for the Reagan for President Committee. In 1984 he served in a similar capacity as a consultant. During the Reagan administration, he served on a number of presidential committees. He died in 2000.

William P. Clark became Deputy Secretary of State, Secretary of the Interior, and National Security Advisor to President Reagan. Tom Reed reflected that Clark was "absolutely key" to Reagan's cold war policy that won the Cold War.[3] At the 1991 dedication of the Reagan Presidential Library, Clark was commended as the "longest serving Reagan appointee in successive years without interruption."[4] He was too ill to have been interviewed for this book and died in August, 2013.

Arthur H. Davis Jr. helped the Reagan campaigns in 1976 and 1980. He was appointed by President Reagan to be Ambassador to Paraguay and then to Panama. He died in 2000.

Dick Derham remained a Nixon supporter in 1968 and 1972. The enmity between the conservative and liberal wings of the Washington State Republican Party continued. Indeed at the 1970 state convention, the King County delegation was not seated, as the liberal forces sought to assure that there would be a majority in support of a convention platform plank approving the Evans-backed proposed constitutional amendment to permit a state income tax. Expelling a delegation that represented one-third of the state, which was deemed too risky in 1968, changed the philosophical complexion of the convention and allowed the Evans supporters to adopt the platform they wanted. After 1972 and looking toward 1976, the hard lessons learned from the 1968 efforts for Reagan included realizing they could not change the makeup of the credentials committee and its one vote per county structure. Therefore conservative Republicans made plans to ensure they had a majority of the members of the credentials committee by concentrating on building a truly statewide grassroots effort to increase conservative party members. Dick had met Frank Whetstone in March 1976 after his precinct caucus and Anderson Carter afterwards; they were the Reagan campaign officials in charge of western states then as in 1968. Dick became King County Chairman for Reagan in 1976 and 1980 and at the national convention was the Reagan floor leader on the Convention Rules Committee in 1976. In 1980 with a Reagan majority, he served as Chairman of the Convention Rules Committee. In 1983 Dick was appointed general counsel and then Assistant Administrator in the Agency for International Development. After returning home to Seattle in 1986 he resumed the practice of law but continued his activity in Republican grass roots activities. In 1991 he received 70% of the first ballot votes and was elected King County Chairman of the

Republican Party.[5] After retiring from law practice, Dick served as president of the Washington Policy Center—a state-level think tank focused on free market ideas. Clearly White and Rusher's analysis that one component of the growth of the conservative movement after the Goldwater era, national conservative think tanks such as the American Enterprise Institute[6] and the later-formed Heritage Foundation's State Policy Network formed in the 1990s, was now developing at the state level including the Pacific Northwest. These are all spin-offs of the first national Reagan campaign in 1968. By 2001 he served as one of the two Republicans on the state's four-member bipartisan Redistricting Commission. Today, he is no longer active in politics and met with your author in the summer of 2012 and again in 2014, along with Ned Lange.

Walter J. Dilbeck, Jr. pursued his Global League after 1968 but ultimately only four teams were secured. The Global League introduced the designated hitter and designated pinch runner and would have permitted unlimited substitutions like football. Opening Day was April 24, 1969 in Puerto Rico and after playing eleven games in Caracas, the league folded due to lack of monies, leaving players stranded.[7] Dilbeck claimed to have lost somewhere between $800,000 to $3 million on his Global League investments, and later after Vice-President Spiro Agnew resigned in disgrace, Dilbeck went into business with him.[8] Dilbeck died in 1991.

Ronald Docksai Sr., as National Chairman of YAF from 1970-1975, had the pleasure of introducing Ronald Reagan at the YAF 10th reunion in San Francisco. Docksai was also one of the founders of CPAC and introduced Reagan at several CPAC meetings. After serving as U.S. Health Policy Director for the U.S. House of Representatives from 1974-77, President Reagan nominated Docksai to serve as Assistant Secretary for Legislation, U.S. Dept. of Health and Human Services in February 1984. After Senate confirmation, he served until August, 1988. He was interviewed by your author in 2013.

Congressman Robert Dole, after the events in 1968, became Senator, Majority Leader, and Republican nominee for president in 1996. His accomplishments are too numerous to list here. But it should be noted that in 2016 he is charge of the Dwight Eisenhower Memorial.

Governor Dan Evans was instrumental in arranging for refugees from South Vietnam in 1975 to be welcomed in Seattle. He completed three terms and then became president of Evergreen College. When Senator Henry M. Jackson died in 1983, Evans completed his term, serving until 1989. Subsequently he served as Regent of the

University of Washington. He celebrated his 90th birthday in October, 2015. Evans was contacted by your author asking for his input, but the voicemail messages were never answered.

Diana Evans, along with Fred Van Natta, donated funds to keep Reagan's 1976 Oregon primary drive alive (see Fred Van Natta, below) and she was a delegate to the 1976 convention. Her roles in 1976 and 1980 were highlighted in *Time* magazine.[9] She attended the 1976 Kansas City convention and was heart-broken when Reagan lost to Ford. For all of her efforts in 1968 and 1976, she was made Oregon Campaign Chair for Reagan in 1980 and 1984 and attended those Republican conventions. In 1980 she was given the honor of giving one of the seconding speeches, which was never broadcast on national television, but was shown on a local Portland station. She met Reagan many times over those years but does not recall Reagan ever discussing the 1968 Oregon campaign. She and Peter Murphy made the front page of the *Oregonian* when they presented Reagan with a 50-lb. Chinook salmon on 9/27/80.[10] Diana was about to host a Republican Party picnic shortly after our personal interview ended in 2012. She was still active in 2014 in the Republican Party from her home in Salem but in 2015 is no longer active.

Kathryn Forte (now Mrs. Blackman) transferred to U.S.C. after the Miami Beach convention. She was head resident of the dormitory at where Patti Reagan also was a student. Today, she shuttles between homes in Los Angeles, Tucson, and the Kohala coast of Hawaii. She kindly sent the author her old files and papers on Students For Reagan, which she had kept for four decades.

James Gardner lost his race for governor of North Carolina in 1968 but did win election subsequently as lieutenant governor. When Reagan campaigned for him in late 1992, Gardner thanked Reagan for asking him to give the seconding speech in 1968 at Miami Beach. Reagan smiled.[11] Today, Gardner remains quite active in North Carolina Republican Party politics. In 2012 he served on the transition team for newly-elected Governor Pat McCrory and in 2013 was appointed chairman of the North Carolina Alcoholic Beverage Control Commission. He was interviewed by the author in his Rocky Mount business office in early 2013.

Newt Gingrich and his relationship with President Reagan was discussed recently.[12] Gingrich did not return any of the author's repeated requests for an interview.

Judge James C. Goode continued to serve as Linn County chair for Governor McCall. In 1969 he was selected as Linn County Veteran of the Year. He assumed the bench in 1981 and was elected for three terms.[13] He kindly consented to be interviewed by the author in the summer and fall of 2012. In 2015, Judge Goode retired.

General Andrew Goodpaster would receive the Presidential Medal of Freedom from President Reagan in 1984. He passed away in 2005.

Freeman Gosden continued playing golf and raising money for the Eisenhower Medical Center in Palm Desert. He died in 1982.

John Gram was promoted at Jantzen in 1980, so he could not help Reagan that year. But in 1984 he became Diana Evans' Oregon State Reagan co-chair and established a hundred local grass-roots Reagan offices throughout the state. He worked with the FBI and Secret Service prior to two of Reagan's visits to Portland that year. Today, he is no longer active in politics.

Sally Gram ran the advance office for President Reagan in 1984 when Diarmuid O'Scannlain was state chairman. Reagan campaigned in Oregon for a week, and Sally was in charge of hotel accommodations and used a fax machine for the first time. Reagan thanked her personally for her efforts. During that 1984 visit, Reagan's old swimming coach from Illinois had retired to Oregon and paid a visit to the president while Sally was there. Today, she is no longer active in politics but she and John hosted a reunion interview meeting of the 1968 Oregon campaign staff at their home when your author interviewed them in the summer of 2012.

Judge Paul Haerle returned to private law practice at the end of the first term of Governor Reagan in 1969 and never saw Reagan in person again. He was chairman of the California Republican Party and a member of the Republican National Committee from 1975-1977. He supported President Ford, a fellow graduate of Yale and the University of Michigan, in 1976 and did not participate in either the 1980 or 1984 Reagan campaigns. He kindly consented to be interviewed by the author in the fall of 2012.

Bob Hazen was asked to run for governor of Oregon in the 1970s but declined. During the Reagan administration he was asked to be Secretary of Energy but declined and suggested Don Hodel.[14] His son recalls that Hazen thought "Reagan was the best president ever made," and the family cherished a "stack of Christmas cards from the White House" to his dad.[15] In 1990 the U.S. government seized Benjamin Franklin Savings and Loan, yet in 1996 the Supreme Court found the federal governmental seizure had been unconstitutional. Bank shareholders sued the federal government for damages, and as of 2012, 22 years after the initial seizure, the case still was not settled.

Charlton Heston was asked by President Reagan to co-chair the National Endowments of the Arts and Humanities. He famously won a debate, about Reagan's anti-missile defense shield, against liberal actor Paul Newman. Heston then made a commercial advocating Reagan's "Star Wars" and was given special military clearance and narrated six training films on the U.S. nuclear program. Stuart Spencer tried to convince him to run for the Senate from California. When Heston died of Alzheimer's disease in 2008, Nancy Reagan praised him as one of her husband's closest friends and thanked him for his continued support of all for which Reagan had stood.[16]

Don Hodel was appointed administrator of the Bonneville Power Administration during the Nixon administration. Hodel relates that when he was reintroduced to President Reagan in 1981 and told the president that he had worked on his 1968 Oregon campaign, the President smiled and said, "I know." When discussing his loss in 1968, Reagan said that the "two most relieved people were Nancy and me." President Reagan appointed him Secretary of Energy from 1982-1985 and Secretary of the Interior from 1985-1989. After leaving Washington in 1989, he founded an energy consulting firm, and served for a time (1997-1999) as Ralph Reed's successor as president of Christian Coalition and later (2001-2003) as a board member and president of Focus on the Family, a media ministry. He was most kind in being interviewed several times in the summer and fall of 2012.

Jim Ince ran a Eureka College fundraiser featuring Reagan speaking at the Chicago Sheraton Hotel. Reagan's theme was helping small colleges survive financially and the event was a huge success. At the private reception that day, when Ince reminded Reagan that decades before he had brought those hot dogs to Reagan, who was announcing the football game in Des Moines, Reagan chuckled saying, "Jim, I really can't say I remember you, but I sure remember those hot dogs!" Ince did not campaign actively for Reagan in 1976, 1980 nor 1984. He kindly agreed to be interviewed by the author in January 2013.

David R. Jones became national vice-chairman of the Young Republican National Federation from 1969-1971 and was campaign director for James Buckley during his successful U.S. Senate election as a member of the Conservative Party. Afterwards he became executive director of the Tennessee Republican Party. President Reagan appointed Jones as chairman of the Commission on Student Financial Assistance. He died of lung cancer in April, 1998. The Fund for American Studies, for which he was a principal founder in 1967 and for which he served as president from 1974 until his death, in 1998 created the David R. Jones Center for Leadership in Philanthropy to honor his memory.

Senator Edward Kennedy died in 2009 and Nancy Reagan noted that Ted and Ron had been friends even though they were on opposite sides of the aisle.[17]

Henry Kissinger advised the Nixon transition team during the fall of 1968 and in his autobiography reviews how eventually the Nixon administration would adopt all of the dovish Vietnam policies of the 1968 Democratic platform.[18] Kissinger's candid opinion of Reagan was recorded on the Nixon White House tapes on November 17, 1971. Kissinger was asked by Nixon to evaluate Reagan, and Kissinger said at first, "He's a pretty decent guy." But when Nixon asked about his brains, Kissinger lashed into Reagan saying, "His brains are negligible...He's shallow...He's an actor." When looking far ahead and imagining if Reagan were elected to the White House, Kissinger thought the idea "inconceivable."[19] Yet Kissinger had no problem in 1980, four years out of power after Ford's defeat by Carter and as soon as Reagan became the nominee, to host a dinner party at his Manhattan apartment in honor of Nancy Reagan.[20] President Reagan's foreign policies against the Soviet Union, of trying to win the cold war, ran counter to Kissinger and Nixon's policy of détente. As noted below under Richard Nixon, Kissinger and Nixon attacked Reagan publicly over Reagan's planned negotiations with Gorbachev to eliminate ballistic missiles. Kissinger happily served on Reagan's Foreign Intelligence Advisory Board. In 2016, Kissinger is still an active diplomat of his country. His office did not return calls requesting an interview.

Matt Lawson traveled in 1976 and 1980 with Reagan during campaign stops as national deputy press secretary. Lawson recalled that he and Reagan never discussed the 1968 campaign. Today he is a venture capitalist in Orange County, California. He consented to a phone interview in January 2013.

Americus Liberator continued his quest for the presidency after the 1968 Nebraska Republican primary. He ran in the general election and wrote to President Johnson asking for Secret Service protection. He is the only man to have run against Ronald Reagan three separate times (1968, 1976, and 1980) and lost each time. He last ran for president in 1992 and later spoke about Reagan with fondness and great respect. He is buried next to his horse, Pard, in Valentine, Nebraska.[21]

John Lindsay would return home after Miami Beach and be astounded that a group of New York Teenage Republicans would mock him as they "idolized" Reagan.[22] Lindsay would lose the

Republican primary but win reelection as New York City mayor as an independent. He endorsed the Democrat when Rockefeller ran for reelection and then become a Democrat. He would run for president in 1972 but lose badly the Florida primary. He would pass away in 2000.

Maurice Harold Macmillan occasionally sparred with President Reagan's friend, British Prime Minister Margaret Thatcher. After Macmillan passed away in late 1986, President Reagan issued a memorial.

Tom McCall served two terms as governor. He was one of the first Republicans to call for Nixon's resignation after Watergate. He lost a third attempt at the governorship. He died in 1982.

Eugene McCarthy, after running against RFK in 1968, formally endorsed Reagan in 1980.[23]

Edwin Meese III became Governor Reagan's executive assistant and then chief of staff after 1968. In 1980 he was chief of staff of Reagan's campaign, headed the Transition Team, and became counselor to the president at the Cabinet level. From 1985-1988, he was attorney general of the United States. In 2006, Meese was part of the Iraq Study group and in 2008 was named the first Honorary Reagan Fellow of Eureka College. Since 1988, Meese today holds the Ronald Reagan Chair in Public Policy at the Heritage Center. Meese consented to be interviewed by this author in September 2012 and again in early 2013.

Tanya Melich wrote a book castigating the Republican Party, including the Reagan administration, for what she perceived to be the failings of its treatment of women. In 2015 she is no longer active in politics.

Peter Murphy was recruited by the Nixon campaign staff as soon as the Miami Beach convention was over and worked as a volunteer advance man. Once Gerald Ford became president, he worked for him for about seven months. But when Reagan ran against Ford, Peter immediately quit the Ford team to work for Reagan again. Peter recalled he was "ridiculed" by the Ford staff. In 1976 he became a delegate for Reagan and was chairman of one of four Reagan campaign districts in Oregon as well as state vice-chairman and finance chairman under Diana Evans. At the 1976 convention he recalled sitting about fifty feet away from a Reagan supporter who had a fist-fight with Nelson Rockefeller, which was an event captured by the national media. During the Reagan 1980 campaign, Reagan came to Eugene at the suggestion of Peter, who spoke to Ed Meese that he wanted Reagan to "take on the liberals." When large protests erupted on campus, Nancy Reagan told Peter, "You put my husband in a tough situation," but Reagan, the Great Communicator, overcame the difficulties. Peter and Diana Evans surprised the president by presenting him a 50 pound Chinook salmon, which Peter proudly recalled made the front page of the Oregonian.[24] That year Peter ran against Diarmuid O'Scannlain for Republican national committeeman and won. But they remained friends and later Peter wrote a letter to Ed Meese recommending Diarmuid for a federal judge appointment. When Ronald Reagan became president, Peter recalled meeting him about eight to ten times. Reagan did thank Peter for his long-time support. Although Reagan did not mention Peter's work in 1968 in Lane County as Reagan Chairman, Reagan did fondly mention the Albany parade and Corvallis football game. Certainly a personal highlight was when Peter was invited to travel with President Reagan in 1981 to go to Notre Dame. Peter also recalled that there were some preliminary discussions about an appointment as ambassador to Ireland but nothing came of them. As my summer 2012 interview with Peter Murphy ended, he was about to take his entire extended family to Ireland to attend a Notre Dame football game.[25] Your author and Peter met in the fall of 2015 when Notre Dame played Boston College at Fenway Park.

Richard Nixon had a decades-long intertwined relationship with Ronald Reagan after 1968. Three excellent sources that readers are encouraged to peruse are: Skinner, Anderson and Anderson for the Reagan-Nixon correspondence, Gibbs and Duffy's second Nixon-Reagan chapter on their relationship[26] in *The President's Club* and James Mann's *The Rebellion of Ronald Reagan*. These few tidbits are taken mainly from these three sources. During the Nixon administration, Nixon had Reagan make four overseas trips to visit eighteen heads of state, one of which Nixon benefitted from Reagan's own known anti-communist feelings: when Reagan reassured Chiang Kai-Shek after Nixon's China trip was announced. Reagan defended Nixon vigorously during Watergate until early August 1974 when he said he had changed his mind but did not think Nixon should resign. Two months after resigning, Nixon was hospitalized with phlebitis and Reagan called to cheer him up; but Reagan was distraught and cried.[27] Nixon had briefly considered naming Reagan vice-president after Agnew resigned. Once Reagan was the nominee in 1980, Nixon sent him campaign advice and urged specific Cabinet appointees for Reagan, including Al Haig but recommending not to hire George Schulz.[28] Nixon and President Reagan sparred over their differing views on the Cold War (Nixon and Kissinger for détente and Reagan for actually winning the Cold War) including a secret White House visit by Nixon to discuss Gorbachev and Reagan's proposal to eliminate ballistic missiles. Nixon felt that Reagan should not be permitted to negotiate with Gorbachev privately. After the Reykjavic summit, Nixon and Kissinger wrote a newspaper column publicly criticizing Reagan.[29] Reagan did appreciate Nixon's help in implementing welfare reforms. Reagan had called Nixon for advice from Camp David on how to proceed with negotiations with the Soviets and Nixon's advice was crucial when he recommended that Reagan list all those points that both sides had agreed on before proceeding to disagreements.[30] Nixon offered advice to Reagan on how to handle the Iran-Contra scandal.[31] Reagan returned the prior favor of overseas trips when he sent Nixon to Moscow to meet Gorbachev.[32] As the Reagan presidency was ending, Nixon offered advice on getting Reagan to campaign for nominee George H. W. Bush,[33] with the specific recommendation that Reagan make his last official campaign speech in San Diego on behalf of Bush.[34] Reagan attended the dedication of the Nixon Presidential Library in 1990 and Nixon returned the favor on November 4, 1991 when he attended the dedication of the Reagan Presidential Library. In reference to the struggles they had in 1968 over the film of Reagan that Tom Reed had created and used in the three major primaries, Nixon said, "By losing in 1962, I made it possible for Ronald Reagan to be elected governor in 1966." But in assessing the critical importance of the Reagan presidency for world history, Nixon recalled that at his famous kitchen debate with Khrushchev, the Soviet premiere had boasted, "Your grandchildren will live under communism." Nixon magnanimously then added, "Thanks in great part to the strong idealistic leadership of President Ronald Reagan, Khrushchev's grandchildren now live in freedom."

Lyn Nofziger helped form Citizens of the Republic in 1976 to help conservative candidates. He became President Reagan's first political director and helped persuade the president to stop the program of metrification of American measurement systems. He passed away in 2006.

Pat Nolan served in the California State Assembly in the 1970s and 1980s. He became Republican leader from 1984-1987 and minority floor leader from 1985-1986. He was recruited by Eureka College's fall 2012 course on the Reagan presidential campaigns where he spoke to historian Craig Shirley via skype-hookup about his 1968 experiences with Youth for Reagan and Students for Reagan.

Nolan kindly consented to be interviewed by the author in the spring of 2013. Today he is no longer active in politics.

The Honorable Diarmuid O'Scannlain received a thank you note from Governor Reagan after Miami Beach and then was invited to be Oregon chairman of the Youth for Nixon effort. In 1974 he ran for Congress in Oregon's first congressional district but lost. He attended the 1976, 1980 and 1984 Republican conventions. In 1976 he was a Ford delegate. He was elected Oregon Republican state chairman and was a national committeeman from Oregon as well. O'Scannlain was 1980 co-chairman of the Reagan campaign and recalled meeting Reagan at the Portland airport on May 18, 1980. It was the day Mt. Saint Helens exploded and there was concern as to whether Reagan's plane could land safely. O'Scannlain met and escorted Reagan to campaign events. He recalled that they may have discussed the 1968 campaign during that Reagan visit.[35] O'Scannlain became a consultant to the Office of the President-Elect from 1980-1981 and was team leader for the President's Private Sector Survey on Cost Control/Grace Commission from 1982-1983. He also chaired an advisory panel for the U.S. Secretary of Energy, Don Hodel, from 1983-1985. President Reagan nominated him to the United States Court of Appeals for the Ninth Circuit on August 8, 1986 and he was confirmed on September 25, 1986. O'Scannlain delivered a moving eulogy for William Rusher upon his death. The chambers of Judge O'Scannlain are in Portland where he graciously agreed to be interviewed by your author in the summer of 2012. On a wall of his office is displayed the certificate documentation of his appointment signed by President Reagan and Attorney General Edwin Meese. Today he remains busy on the Supreme Court IX Circuit Court of Appeals.

Donald Pearlman worked on his partner Diarmuid O'Scannlain's unsuccessful 1976 congressional campaign. At Hodel's invitation, he moved to Washington D.C. in 1982 to become executive assistant to secretary of energy, Don Hodel. He later served in the same role when Hodel became secretary of the interior. During the 1990s he became an expert on environmental matters and died at age 69 in 2005.

Congressman Robert Price lost his seat in 1974 as a general reaction to Watergate. Later he entered the Texas Senate. He had continued flying various Air Force fighters while serving in Congress including the SR-71 Blackbird. He passed away in 2004.

Nancy Reagan, being too ill during the research and writing of this book to be interviewed by your author, passed away in early March 2016.

Thomas C. Reed's experiences with Reagan are described in his recent memoir, *The Reagan Enigma*, for which your author supplied the research on the relationship of Reagan and Eisenhower and of Reagan and Robert Kennedy.

Nelson Rockefeller was later asked why he had failed in 1968 and answered, 'Have you ever been to a Republican convention?'[36] During a flight when interviewed by an Argentine journalist, he was asked why he had never been elected president. He answered, "I was in the wrong party."[37] Rockefeller stayed a Republican and became President Ford's vice-president once Nixon had resigned. At the 1976 convention, Rockefeller was not chosen, as he had asked Ford not to place his name in nomination previously. He died in 1979. In the 21st century, the Arkansas Republican Party hosts an annual Reagan-Rockefeller dinner in honor of the two Republicans; in 2012 the guest speaker was Governor Bobby Jindal of Louisiana.

Ken Rogstad remained chairman of the King Co. Republicans until 1970 and then focused his attention on his business. He did not have an active role in either the 1976 or 1980 Reagan committee and was not a delegate. However his wife's obituary (she died on June 26, 2012) related that both she and Ken did attend national Republican conventions from 1972 through 1984 but he was not an active delegate.[38] In the 1980's, he and his business H.W. Blackstock Co. were accused of bribing officials and consultants in Alaska to obtain $199 million in construction and supply contracts. The jury took only four hours to find them not guilty. After the verdict, a beaming Ken Rogstad said, "I'm scarred. I'm poor. But I'm happy." Rogstad's lawyer charged that the prosecutors were politically motivated and that Rogstad's firm was "run out of business."[39] He and his wife enjoyed boating on Puget Sound and the San Juan islands. Kenneth Rogstad died in the early years of the twenty-first century.

Congressman Dana Rohrabacher graduated college in 1969, and after obtaining his master's degree, he served Ronald Reagan as assistant press secretary during the 1976 and 1980 campaigns. From 1981-1988 he was one of President Reagan's senior speech writers. He helped formulate the Reagan Doctrine and the Reagan Economic Bill of Rights. Since 1988 he has served in Congress. Rohrabacher is quite proud of his many-decades-long friendship with Ronald Reagan, and his own office motto is "Fighting for Freedom and having fun." Rohrabacher's office is filled with personal photos of candidate and President Reagan. The congressman kindly consented to being interviewed in early 2013.

Former governor George Romney would be appointed by President Reagan to the President's Task Force for Private Sector Initiatives from 1981-1982. While exercising on a treadmill, George Romney died of a heart attack on July 26, 1995.

Francis Rothauge became an active Young Republican and newspaper editor. He and Van Natta are enthusiastic beekeepers. In 2014 he was interviewed by this author and today is no longer active in politics.

William A. Rusher's subsequent interactions with Reagan are highlighted in the two biographies cited in this work. He died in 2011.

Bob Schadler met Reagan in person at a 1972 meeting of the Inter-Collegiate Studies Institute. Schadler was in the U.S. Information Agency during the Reagan administration mainly as director of International Visitors and later as coordinator of Exchanges with Eastern Europe and the Soviet Union. He met the author for an interview in May, 2013.

O.J. Simpson had two subsequent interactions with Ronald Reagan and his family. According to Reagan biographer Lou Cannon, in *Ronnie and Jesse*, in 1969 after California Lt. Governor Bob Finch left to join the Nixon administration and Reagan was besieged with suggestions for a replacement, young son Ron suggested, "You ought to choose O.J. Simpson; he would definitely make the best lieutenant governor." Reagan's face "lit up with sheer pleasure and sincere delight" and agreed that OJ would be a good choice. Many years later while former President Reagan was deteriorating with Alzheimer's Disease, Nancy Reagan distracted herself "discussing the O.J. Simpson trial which she avidly watched on television."[40] At the time of this writing, Simpson remains in prison on gun charges.

Stuart Spencer ran Reagan's 1980 campaign as detailed in Craig Shirley's work. Spencer contributed some of his recollections in Reed's recent memoir. Despite several attempts, Spencer did not return phone messages left for him at his Palm Desert home in 2012 and 2013.

Shawn Steel is a practicing attorney. In 1995 he was elected treasurer of the California Republican Party. He was state party chairman from 2001-2003. In 2003 he co-founded the successful movement to recall Democrat Governor Gray Davis. From 2006 through the present he is Republican national committeeman from California. Steel's office is filled with political mementos, including a prize photograph with Barry Goldwater and several of Ronald Reagan. Steel did not meet Ronald Reagan after 1968 and never discussed the 1968 campaign with him. Steel consented to be interviewed in early 2013.

Arnold Steinberg became a political analyst in California. In 2015 he remains retired from politics and is writing his memoirs.

Ivy Baker Priest Stevens passed away in June, 1975, and her obituary notes that she was the first woman to place a nomination for president when she had for Reagan in August, 1968.

Don L. Taylor became a principal of Wisconsin Citizens for Reagan in 1976. In 1980, he was co-chairman for the Wisconsin Reagan effort and was floor leader for the Wisconsin delegation at the national convention. During the Reagan presidency, he met Reagan on many occasions in the White House. Don recalled that Reagan "always remembered his friends" with personal greetings, letters, and inclusion at White House meetings even occasionally with members of the Reagan Cabinet. Don and Reagan never again discussed the 1968 campaign in Wisconsin. For several decades, he was chairman of the Republican Party of Waukesha County. Upon his retirement, Governor Scott Walker proclaimed May 4, 2013 as "Don Taylor Day" throughout Wisconsin. He kindly consented to be interviewed by the author in the early winter of 2012-2013 and then again at a second interview in Wisconsin in June, 2013. In 2015 he remained active in the Walker for President campaign until Walker withdrew. Today he advises on conservative causes.

Randal C. Teague became the first student to receive scholarship assistance from the Fund for American Studies in 1969 and was editor of their publications in the 1970's. He was executive director of YAF from 1968-1971. Then he served as Economic Policy Analyst in the Nixon administration from 1971-1973 and then was chief of staff and legislative counsel to Rep. Jack Kemp from 1973-1979. He served on the Board and was treasurer of the American Conservative Union. Later he served at the Agency for International Development. In 1998 he became chairman of the Fund for American Studies. Today he remains a Washington D.C.-based attorney and lobbyist. He consented to be interviewed by the author in December, 2012.

Senator Strom Thurmond campaigned vigorously for Nixon in the fall of 1968 and was able to tell the South not to vote for George Wallace. Quietly, he voted for Reagan at the 1976 convention and campaigned actively for Reagan in 1980, even though initially he had supported John Connelly. During the Reagan administration, Thurmond was president pro tem of the Senate and as Judiciary Committee chairman, he guided Reagan's conservative nominees such as the first woman for the Supreme Court, Sandra Day O'Connor. In 1984, Reagan returned to South Carolina to campaign for Thurmond.

In 1997 he became the longest serving senator. Thurmond left the Senate in early 2003 and died a few months later.

Y.A. Tittle started a conservative blog in the 21st century and is retired from his and his son's insurance business. Your author attempted to speak with Mr. Tittle about his recollections of his May 1968 trip to Portland, but the calls were not returned. Sadly, Kennedy historian and sports author David Halberstam would perish in an automobile accident in 2007 while on the way to interview Tittle.

Kay Valory was appointed consumer advocate for the State of California by Governor Reagan and special assistant to the HUD regional administrator for Region Nine by President Reagan. She lived in northern California and consented to two phone interviews with the author in January 2013. She passed away in the fall of 2015.

Fred Van Natta recalled that after Miami Beach, Tom Reed hired him to manage the Republican Governor's Association meeting in Palm Springs November-December 1968 with special guest Bob Hope. Thirty-two Republican governors or governors-elect attended, as did Nixon and Agnew. During 1970-1976, he and Diana Evans "plotted" a Reagan comeback campaign. It was against President Ford that their mutual plans solidified in 1976. Fred recalled driving to Medford and Klamath Falls to meet southern Oregonians, asking for their support for Reagan the same day that he heard on the radio that Reagan turned his campaign around by winning the North Carolina primary. He and Diana were "greatly pleased." That year he and Diana Evans "personally put up the few thousand dollars that kept the fledgling Oregon campaign alive until then." Van Natta recalled in 1976 that "I remember how happy I was when he won a primary, because then we raised some money and got bailed out." He and Diana continued in 1980 and 1984 as the "Rabble-Rousing Reagan Rebels."[41] In precedent-setting case Van Natta v Keisling, in 1997 the Oregon Supreme Court ruled that citizens could contribute to political campaigns and groups without limitation as campaign contributions were to be considered a form of free speech. Van Natta had brought the suit because he feared unions could use their members for political purposes while individual citizens might be limited by proposed legislation. Fred still is active in the lobbying firm he founded, Van Natta Public Relations, has brought his daughter into the firm, and is an avid fisherman and beekeeper. He graciously arranged to meet the author along with several other 1968 Reagan Oregon campaigners in 2012. Van Natta was featured as a "rock star lobbyist" for the fall 2012 issue of *Willamette Lawyer*. Today he remains the longest living person in the Oregon capitol legislative process.

W. Bruce Weinrod continued to support Ronald Reagan and his approach to U.S. foreign policy in a variety of ways. held senior staff positions in the U.S. House and Senate including legislative director and counsel for Senator John Heinz. During the latter half of the Reagan administration, Weinrod was director of Foreign Policy and Defense Studies at the Heritage Foundation and met Reagan in person several times. President Reagan nominated him as board member of the U.S. Institute of Peace. Later under President George H.W. Bush, he became deputy assistant secretary of defense for European and NATO Policy and witnessed the removal of the infamous Checkpoint Charlie from Berlin. After Reagan left office, Senator Paul Laxalt, for whom Weinrod had worked years before, arranged for Weinrod to meet Reagan at his Century City, California office. As he was about to leave, Weinrod felt Reagan put his hand on his shoulder and asked if Weinrod had yet gone to the Reagan Library. When Weinrod told Reagan that he would soon, Reagan deadpanned, "You can use my name if it'll help!"[42] A few days later, Reagan told the nation he had Alzheimer's Disease. Weinrod was appointed by President George W. Bush as secretary of defense representative for Europe. Today he is managing director and general counsel for an international trade and technology firm and he kindly consented to be interviewed by the author in late 2012 and in 2013 and to supply the old documents of Students for Reagan.

Frank Whetstone initiated good will programs between his native Montana and Alberta, Canada. In 1980-1981, he served as senior adviser to the transition coordinator to the Reagan for President Committee. After chairing a committee to build better highways in the region, he was appointed by President Reagan to serve as Ccommissioner of the International Boundary Commission, United States and Canada.

F. Clifton White supported Ford in 1976. His biography cited here traced Reagan's rise to the presidency. President Reagan appointed him director of Radio Marti, which beamed free radio programming to communist Cuba. He died in 1993.

Dale L. Young attended the 1976 Republican convention in Kansas City as a Reagan supporter and an alternate delegate. His daughter was a *Reaganette*. He was Nebraska state campaign finance chair in 1980. He was elected as city council member in Lincoln and was appointed mayor to fill out the remainder of the term of his predecessor. He met President Reagan once in the 1980s but they did not discuss the 1968 campaign. Dale's son was a member of the White House press corps in the 1980s. Today Dale is retired from political activity but graciously agreed to be interviewed in 2012 and again in 2015.

Endnotes

1. Bell, now a member of the Board of Directors of the American Conservative Union and Senate candidate again in 2014, wrote "Indispensible Rusher" after Rusher's death: Bell, Jeffrey, "Indispensible Rusher" conservative.org, 179, 5/4/2011, p. 1-3
2. "Political Participation of Mexican Americans in California" Commission on Civil Rights, Washington D.C. 8/71, p. 16
3. Kengor and Doerner, p. 164
4. Kengor and Doerner, p. 336
5. "Derham Hopes to Revive Limping GOP-New Chairman in King County Wants Less Debt, More Volunteers," *Seattle Times*, 1/10/1991
6. White and Gill, p. 56
7. McKenna, Brian
8. Witcover, Jules "Agnew Benefactor: High Roller, Mystery Man," *Washington Post*, 1/5/75, p. A4
9. "The Long March," *Time*, 7/28/80, p. 30
10. "Candidate's Chinook," *The Oregonian*, 9/27/80, p. 1
11. Gardner, pers int 3/27/2013
12. Abrams, Elliott, "Gingrich and Reagan, " *National Review Online*, 1/25/2012
13. Judge James Goode, pers comm. 10/1/12
14. Syd Willett, pers comm. 6/15/12
15. Deck Hazen pers comm. 6/7/12
16. Ross, chapter 7
17. https://www.youtube.com/watch?v=wTIB96zDGpg
18. Kissinger, "The White House Years," p. 255-256
19. http://tapes.millercenter.virginia.edu/transcripts/index.php/Nixon/620-008
20. Mann, p. 25
21. Kopelson, Gene. 2014B
22. Cannato, p. 499-500
23. Deaver
24. "Candidate's Chinook," *The Oregonian*, 9/27/80, p. 1
25. Peter Murphy, pers int 8/16/12
26. "Reagan and Nixon: The Exile Returns," p. 353-371
27. Mann, p. 11-12
28. Mann, p. 13-14
29. Mann, p. 49-58, p. 232-235
30. Anderson, *Reagan's Secret War*, p. 220-221
31. Gibbs, p. 357
32. Gibbs, p. 359-362
33. Gibbs, p. 365-368
34. Gibbs, p. 368-371
35. O'Scann pers int 8/23/12
36. Persico, p. 80
37. Persico, p. 81
38. Dick Derham, pers comm
39. "Rogstad, Larkin Cleared in Alaska Bribery Trial," *Seattle Times*, 9/22/1980
40. Weinraub, Bernard, "The 40th President: The President's Widow," *NYT*, 6/7/04
41. Wong, Peter, "Reagan Leaves Varied Political Impact in Oregon," *Statesman Journal*, 6/12/2004, p. 3
42. Weinrod, Pers Int 5/21/13

APPENDICES

APPENDIX A
REAGAN FILES AT DWIGHT D. EISENHOWER
PRESIDENTIAL LIBRARY

Wedding Announcement   1
Recording Script   1
Telegrams   2*
Memo of Conversation   3
Letters:
     To DDE about RR   13
     From DDE about RR   14 (6 to Gosden and
                        transmitted to Reagan)

Direct Correspondence:
     RR to DDE   5
     DDE to RR   2

RR= Ronald Reagan; DDE=Dwight D. Eisenhower
Data does not include newspaper clippings

*1952 telegram (Reagan urging Ike to run for president) is not there.

APPENDIX B
REAGAN 1968 GRASS ROOTS PRESIDENTIAL CAMPAIGN ORGANIZATIONS

CO   Colorado Reagan for President Club
      Coloradans for Reagan

DC   Reagan for President
      Students for Reagan

ID   Idaho Friends of Reagan

IL   University of Illinois Draft Ronald Reagan for President Committee

KS   Kansas Citizens for Reagan
      Citizens for Reagan National Information Center

ME   Maine Students for Reagan
      Citizens for Reagan Committee

MI   Ronald Reagan for President in 1968 aka Republicans for Ronald Reagan

NE   Nebraskans for Reagan Committee

NH   Reagan for President Club
      New Hampshire Draft Reagan Committee
      Un-named (Jennet, MacDonald)

NY   Republicans for Ronald Reagan

OK   Oklahoma Republicans for Reagan

OR   Draft Reagan
      Citizens for Reagan
      Reagan for President
      Lane County Citizens for Reagan Committee
      Ronald Reagan for President Campaign Bus

TX   Citizens for Ronald Reagan
      Texans for Reagan

WI   Wisconsin Reagan for President Club

APPENDIX C
1968 REPUBLICAN PARTY CONVENTION
REAGAN TOTALS BY STATE (FIRST BALLOT)

AL 12	MO 3
CA 86	MT 3
CO 1	NM 5
FL 1	NC 16
GA 7	ND 1
ID 5	OK 7
IL 3	TX 15
IA 3	WA 6
LA 7	

APPENDIX D

President Reagan's Public References to his Republican Predecessors*

Eisenhower	178
Lincoln	101
Theodore Roosevelt	25
Coolidge	24
Nixon	15
Ford	13
Hoover	9
Taft	8
Harding	1

*It has been accepted by many historians, up to now, that Reagan viewed FDR, Coolidge, Taft, and Lincoln as his role models. As a comparison, President Reagan cited President Franklin Roosevelt (a Democrat) only 56 times. Compiled from Ronald Reagan Presidential Library (Speeches search engine)

APPENDIX E
REAGAN'S CAMPAIGN SPEECH DOMESTIC HIGHLIGHTS
(SEATTLE, NOVEMBER 10, 1967)

Reagan began his formal speech attacking government bureaucracy and inefficiency and got laughs when he said, "there's one sure way to make sure crime doesn't pay: let the government run it!" He then changed his focus to the Democrat Party and their recent expensive $1000 per plate fund-raising dinner by saying he could never figure out "how they can run these dinners at such a profit yet run the country at such a loss!" The contrast for the listeners, having just paid one-tenth that amount to hear Reagan, must have been striking.

He attacked Johnson's Great Society and the growth of the number of federal workers. He cited $425 million in government spending for promotion of government publicity by paraphrasing Winston Churchill, "never have so few spent so much to tell us so little" which was greeted with great applause.

Planting the seeds for comments he would use in later years, he cited the growth in the number of federal welfare programs by "a government program is the nearest thing we will see on this earth to eternal life." Specifically there were 100 new federal programs that had cost $3.5 billion per year in their first year but now cost $16.5 billion per year.

He attacked federal borrowing and Johnson's proposed 10% surtax. He disdained government waste by castigating a grant of $65 million to study coal mining in Middle Eastern countries "that don't produce any coal." He abhorred elite federal appointees who never had been elected and who were hired to solve problems supposedly "too complicated for the average citizen to understand."

He then softened his tone and focused on disaffected members of the Democratic Party by saying he was only attacking the democrat leadership and that he was sure there were many local Democrat citizens throughout the country who were disturbed about what was happening in the country.

Reagan then began to enumerate many examples of his successes in limiting government in just the first ten months since he took office. He cited a proposed federal program to be run in California in which chronically unemployed workers would be given work on open farmland. Although he normally would support this type of program, when he learned that the details of the program were that 17 workers were to be hired but that 7 government supervisors were to be hired also, he vetoed it. He was amused by a second proposal to fund a training course in picketing and demonstrating; he quickly vetoed that also.

Reagan decried that he had inherited a state system that had used no normal business practices. Learning that department heads were ordering new automobiles at retail prices, he put an immediate freeze on new car orders and instituted time-mileage-usage be documented. After three months, there was a surplus of state cars compared to their use and the use of gasoline dropped by 15%. He did not put a freeze on out-of-state travel but Reagan did insist that all such travel needed to be justified; afterwards such out-of-state travel dropped by 78%. By instituting common sense business practices of competitive bidding and consolidated buying, he saved millions of dollars for the cost of supplies. He took advantage of a free program from the phone company which then came in to analyze and recommend how to save money on telephone systems in state offices; Reagan announced he had just been told the state had thus saved $2 million.

Prior to his inauguration, the number of California state workers he said had been growing at a rate of 4-5.6% per year, although in other campaign speeches he cited 7% per year. Reagan put an immediate freeze on new hires and replacements. After just ten months, he had not only stopped the growth of the state workforce but he had created a 2.5% decline; this comment generated much applause. He also changed the physical location of the workforce. He consolidated state worker office space and design to conform to private business practices and was thus able to cancel the construction of a a previously-planned new state office building. Similarly he was able to fit an additional 1000 state workers into another building. In all, state workers went from occupying some 9 million square feet to just 7 million square feet. He was able to change the use of part-time workers. He found that state license expiration dates all occurred at the same time which required leasing of temporary office space and the hiring of temporary workers to handle the rush of work as licenses were about to expire. Reagan staggered the state license dates which ensured a constant workforce no longer needing year-end temporary workers nor any emergency additional office space rentals.

Reagan relished telling of a small matter that carried great personal satisfaction. His predecessor had apparently printed much excess stationery with his name imprinted at the top. Instead of throwing it out, Reagan instructed his secretary to use the paper for general office use but to X-out Governor Brown's name. When Reagan said he got "a certain amount of pleasure" in using it, there was much laughter in the audience.

Reagan then went back to comment on welfare as a "colossal and complete failure." But his biggest applause came when he commented that "It's time to stop being our brother's keeper and to start being our brother's brother. Maybe we will find that our brother can keep himself."

He closed on notes of unity of party and country. He declared, "We have it within our power to broaden the base of our party" and mentioned that many Democrats and former Democrats looked to Republicans for leadership because they could no longer follow Democrat leaders. "The leadership of that party has betrayed the members of that party."

Governor Reagan wanted Democrats to think about switching officially to join the Republicans when he again cited Winston Churchill: "Some men change principle for party and some men change party for principle." His appeal to future Reagan Democrats was in its infancy yet was clearly in his mind.

He ended by citing the new unity of the Republican Party after the 1966 election and felt the two-party system had been restored. He decried the labeling of liberal-Republican versus conservative-Republican. (RRL tape 307)

BIBLIOGRAPHY

Books

Adler, Bill. *Ronnie and Nancy*. New York: Crown Publishers, 1985.

Ambrose, Stephen. *Eisenhower: Soldier and President*. New York: Simon and Schuster, 1990.

Ambrose, Stephen. Nixon, *vol. 2: The Triumph of a Politician*, 1962-1972. Premier Digital Publishing, 1989.

Anderson, Martin and Anderson, Annelise. *Reagan's Secret War*. New York: Crown Publishers, 2009.

Andrew, John A. III. *The Other Side of the Sixties*. New Brunswick: Rutgers University Press, 1997.

Bass, Jack, and Thompson, Marilyn W. *Ol' Strom*. Marietta, Georgia: Longstreet Press, 1998.

Beran, Michael K. *The Last Patrician*. New York: St. Martins Press, 1998.

Black, Earl. Black, Merle. *The Rise of Southern Republicans*. Cambridge: Belknap Press, 2003.

Boyarsky, Bill. *The Rise of Ronald Reagan*. New York: Random House, 1968.

Bradley, Bill. *Time Present, Time Past*. New York: Village Books, 1966.

Brands, H. W. *Reagan*. New York: Doubleday, 2015.

Brilliant, Mark. *The Color of America Has Changed*. New York: Oxford University Press, 2010.

Brinkley, Douglas. *Cronkite*. New York: Harper Collins, 2012.

Brinkley, Douglas. *The Boys of Pointe du Hoc*. New York: Harper Collins, 2005. (All Brinkley citations are to this work unless otherwise specified)

Buchanan, Patrick. *The Greatest Comeback*. New York: Crown Forum, 2014.

Buckley, James Jr. *Bill Bradley, Basketball Hall of Famers Series, 2002*.

Buckley, William F. Jr. *The Reagan I Knew*. New York: Basic Books, 2008.

Burt, Kenneth. *The Search for a Civic Voice*. Claremont: Regina Books, 2007.

Cannato, William. *The Ungovernable City*. New York: Basic Books, 2001

Cannon, Lou. *Governor Reagan*. New York: Public Affairs, 2003. (all Cannon citations are to this work unless otherwise specified)

Cannon, Lou. *President Reagan: The Role of a Lifetime*. New York: Touchstone Books, 1991.

Cannon, Lou. *Ronnie and Jesse: A Political Odyssey*. Garden City, N.Y.: Doubleday, 1969.

Cheevers, Jack. *Act of War*. New York: Penguin Books, 2014.

Chester, Lewis, Hodgson, Godfrey, Page, Bruce. *An American Melodrama.* New York: The Viking Press, 1969.

Chidester, Jeffrey L. and Kengor, Paul (eds.) *Reagan's Legacy in a World Transformed.* Cambridge: Harvard University Press, 2015.

Clarke, Thurston. *The Last Campaign.* New York: Henry Holt and Co., 2008.

Colacello, Bob. *Ronnie and Nancy.* New York: Doubleday, 2004.

Cunningham, Sean. *Cowboy Conservatism.* Louisville: University of Kentucky Press, 2010.

Dallek, Matthew. *The Right Moment.* New York: Oxford University Press, 2000.

Deaver, Michael. *A Different Drummer.* New York: Harper Collins, 2000.

Dent, Harry S. *The Prodigal South Returns to Power.* New York: John Wiley and Sons, 1978.

Diamond, Edwin. *The Spot: The Rise of Political Advertising.* Cambridge: MIT Press, 1992.

Edwards, Anne. *Early Reagan.* London: Hodder and Stoughton Ltd., 1987.

Edwards, Lee. *Reagan: A Political Biography.* San Diego: Viewpoint Books, 1967.

Edwards, Lee. *The Essential Ronald Reagan.* New York: Roman and Littlefield, 2005.

Eisenhower, David, and Eisenhower, Julie. *Going Home to Glory.* New York: Simon and Schuster, 2010.

Eliot, Marc. *Reagan: The Hollywood Years.* New York: Harmony Books, 2008.

Evans, Thomas. *The Education of Ronald Reagan.* New York: Columbia University Press, 2008.

Evans, Rowland and Novak, Robert. *The Reagan Revolution.* New York: E.P. Dutton, 1981.

Frisk, David. *If Not Us, Who?* Wilmington, Delaware: ISI Books, 2012.

Gibbs, Nancy and Duffy, Michael. *The Presidents Club.* New York: Simon and Schuster, 2012.

Gilbert, Robert E. *The Tormented President: Calvin Coolidge.* Westport: Praeger Press, 2003.

Gould, Lewis L. *1968: The Election That Changed America.* Chicago: Ivan R. Dee, 1993.

Greenstein, Fred. *The Hidden-Hand Presidency.* New York: Basic Books, 1982.

Halberstam, David. *Unmitigated Odyssey.* New York: Random House, 1969.

Hanson, Victor Davis. *Carnage and Culture.* New York: Anchor Books, 2001.

Hanson, Victor Davis. *The Father of Us All.* New York: Bloomsbury Press, 2010.

Hayward, Steven F. *The Age of Reagan*. Roseville, California: Prima Publishing, 2001.

Hayward, Steven F. *Greatness*. New York: Random House, 2006.

Hoffman, Betty N. *Liberation*. Berkeley Heights, NJ: Enslow Publishers, 2012.

Isaacson, Walter. *Kissinger*. New York: Simon and Schuster, 2005.

Jacobs, Travis Beal. *Eisenhower at Columbia*. New Brunswick: Transaction Publishers, 2001.

Jenkinson, Clay. *Theodore Roosevelt in the Dakota Badlands*. Dickinson: Dickinson State University, 2006.

Johns, Andrew. *Vietnam's Second Front*. Lexington: University Press of Kentucky, 2010.

Judis, John B. *William F. Buckley Jr*. New York: Simon and Schuster, 1988.

Kabaservice, Geoffrey. *Rule and Ruin*. New York: Oxford University Press, 2013.

Kelley, Kitty. *Nancy Reagan*. New York: Simon and Schuster, 1991.

Kengor Paul. *The Crusader*. New York: HarperCollins, 2006.

Kengor, Paul and Doerner, Patricia. *The Judge: William P. Clarke*. San Francisco: Ignatius Press, 2007.

Kissinger, Henry. *White House Years*. Boston: Little, Brown and Co., 1979.

Kurlansky, Mark. *1968*. New York: Ballantine Books, 2004.

Larson, Arthur. *Eisenhower*. New York: Scribner, 1968.

Leaming, Barbara. *Churchill Defiant*. New York: Harper Collins, 2010.

Lewis, Joseph. *What Makes Reagan Run?* New York: McGraw-Hill, 1968.

Mailer, Norman. *Miami and the Siege of Chicago*. New York: The World Publishing Company, 1968.

McCall, Tom. *Maverick*. Portland, Oregon: Binford and Mort, 1977.

McCullough, David. *Mornings on Horseback*. New York: Simon and Schuster, 1982.

McGinnis, Joe. *The Selling of the President, 1968*. New York: Trident Press, 1969.

Meese, Edwin III, "Introduction," in Robinson, Gilbert. *Reagan Remembered*. New York: Beaufort Books, 2015.

Moldea, Dan. *Dark Victory*. New York: Viking Press, 1987.

Morrell, Margot. *Reagan's Journey*. New York: Threshold Editions, 2011.

Nasaw, David. *The Patriarch: The Remarkable Life and Turbulent Times of Joseph P. Kennedy*. 2014.

Nau, Henry. *Conservative Internationalism*. Princeton: Princeton University Press, 2013.

Newton, Jim. *Eisenhower: The White House Years*. New York: Random House, 2011.

Nixon, Richard. *RN*. New York: Grosset and Dunlop, 1978.

Nofziger, Lyn. *Nofziger*. Washington, D.C.: Regnery. 1992.

Novak, Robert D. *The Prince of Darkness*. New York: Random House, 2007.

Patrick, Curtis. *Reagan: What Was He Really Like? Vol. 1*. New York: Morgan James, 2011.

Patrick, Curtis. *Reagan: What Was He Really Like? Vol. 2*. New York: Morgan James, 2013.

Perlstein, Rick. *Nixonland*. New York: Scribner, 2008.

Persico, Joseph E. *The Imperial Rockefeller*. New York: Simon and Schuster, 1982.

Pipes, Kasey. *Ike's Final Battle*. Los Angeles: World Ahead Publishing, 2007.

Priest, Ivy Baker. *Green Grows the Ivy*. New York: McGraw Hill, 1958.

Pycior, Julie. *LBJ and Mexican-Americans*. Austin: University of Texas Press, 1997.

Reagan, Maureen. *First Father, First Daughter*. New York: Little Brown, 1989.

Reagan, Nancy. *My Turn*. New York: Random House, 1989.

Reagan, Ronald. *An American Life*. New York: Simon and Schuster, 1990.

Reagan, Ronald. *Where's the Rest of Me?* New York: Karz Publishers, 1981.

Reagan, Ronald and Brinkley, Douglas, ed. *The Reagan Diaries*. New York: Harper Perennial, 2007.

Reed, Thomas C. "Reagan for President in 1968!" chapter 8 in Reed, Thomas C. *An Insider's History of the Reagan Revolution 1958-1970*. unpublished manuscript. (all Reed citations are from this work unless specified as from *The Reagan Enigma*).

Reed, Thomas C. *The Reagan Enigma*. Los Angeles: University of Southern California Figueroa Press, 2014.

Reinhard, David. *The Republican Right Since 1945*. Louisville: University Press of Kentucky, 1983.

Reyn, Sebastian. *Atlantis Lost: The American Experience with De Gaulle 1958-1969*. Amsterdam: Amsterdam University Press, 2009.

Richardson, Darcy. *A Nation Divided: the 1968 Presidential Campaign*. Lincoln, NE: Writers Club Press, 2002.

Ritter, Kurt and Henry, David. *Ronald Reagan: The Great Communicator*. Westport: Greenwood Press, 1992.

Ross, Steven. *Hollywood Left and Right*. New York: Oxford University Press, 2011.

Rusher, William. *The Rise of the Right*. New York: William Morrow and Co., 1984.

Safire, William. *Before the Fall*. New York: Doubleday, 1975.

Schlesinger Jr., Arthur M. *Robert F. Kennedy and His Times*. New York: Ballantine Books, 1978.

Schweizer, Peter. *Reagan's War*. New York: Doubleday, 2002.

Shirley, Craig. *Last Act*. Nashville: Nelson Books, 2015.

Shirley, Craig. *Reagan's Revolution*. Nashville: Nelson Current, 2005.

Shirley, Craig. *Rendezvous With Destiny*. Wilmington: ISI Books, 2009.

Short, C. Brand. *Ronald Reagan and the Public Lands*. College Station: Texas A&M University Press, 1989.

Skinner, Kiron, Anderson, Annelise, Anderson, Martin. *Reagan in His Own Hand*. New York: Touchstone, 2001.

Skinner, Kiron, Anderson, Annelise, Anderson, Martin. *Reagan: A Life in Letters*. New York: Free Press, 2003.

Skinner, Kiron, Kudella, Serhiy, Bueno De Mesquita, Bruce, Rice, Condoleeza. *The Strategy of Campaigning*. Ann Arbor: University of Michigan Press, 2007.

Steffgen, Kent. *Here's the Rest of Him*. Reno: Forsight Books, 1968.

Tannenbaum, Nina. *The Nuclear Taboo*. New York: Cambridge University Press, 2007.

Taylor, Don L. *A Devotion to Liberty, Part III: 1966-1968, Early Efforts for Reagan*. Published privately.

Thomas, Evan. *Ike's Bluff*. New York: Little, Brown and Co., 2012.

Thomas, Evan. *Robert Kennedy: His Life*. New York: Simon and Schuster, 2000.

Thompson, J. Lee. *Never Call Retreat*. New York: Palgrave Macmillan, 2013.

Thorburn, Wayne. *A Generation Awakes*. Ottawa IL: Jameson Books, 2010.

Thurmond, Strom. *The Faith We Have Not Kept*. San Diego: Viewpoint Books, 1968.

Tyler, Patrick. *A World of Trouble: The White House and the Middle East*. New York: Farrar, Straus, and Giroux, 2009.

Van Natta, Don Jr. *First Off the Tee*. New York: Perseus Books, 2003.

Walth, Brent. *Fire At Eden's Gate*. Portland OR: Oregon Historical Society Press, 1994.

White, F. Clifton and Tuccille, Jerome. *Politics As a Noble Calling*. Ottawa IL: Jameson Books, 1994.

White, F. Clifton and Gill, William J. *Why Reagan Won.* Chicago: Regnery Gateway, 1981.

White, Theodore. *The Making of the President 1968.* New York: Atheneum Publishers, 1969.

Witcover, Jules. *The Resurrection of Richard Nixon.* New York: G.P. Putnam's Sons, 1970.

Scholarly and other articles

Allman, Joseph. "The 1968 Elections in Oregon." *Western Political Quarterly* 22(3), Sept. 1969, pp 517-525.

Clarke, Thurston. "The Last Good Campaign." *Vanity Fair.* 6/2008. (also published in book form)

Cox, Edward. "Grey Eminence: Fox Conner and the Art of Mentorship." *The Land Warfare Papers* 78W, Sept. 2010, pp 1-18.

Holmes, Todd. "The Economic Roots of Reaganism." *Western Historical Quarterly.* 41(1), Spring 2010, pp 55-80.

Holmes, Todd. "The Ever-Shrinking Middle Ground: Nelson Rockefeller in the Face of Reaganism." (research report, Rockefeller Archive Center, Sleepy Hollow, N.Y., 2011).

Ivie, Robert. "Speaking 'Common Sense' About the Soviet Threat: Reagan's Rhetorical Stance." *Western Journal of Speech Communication* 48 (Winter, 1984), pp 39-50.

Jonas, Frank H. and Harmer, John L. "The 1968 Election in California." *Western Political Quarterly.* 22(3), Sept. 1969, pp 468-474.

Kaufman, Robert W. "Ronald Reagan: A Republican Messiah?" *North American Review* 253(3) (May-June, 1968) pp 10-12.

Kopelson, Gene. 2014A. "The 1968 Nebraska Republican Primary." *Nebraska History*, Fall 2014, pp 162-172.

Kopelson, Gene. 2014B. "The Curious Candidacy of Americus Liberator." *Nebraska History*, Fall 2014, pp 174-175.

Kopelson, Gene. 2014C. "'Ya Basta?!': Ronald Reagan's 1966 Success with Mexican American Voters." *California History*, 2014, 94(4): 31-42.

Kopelson, Gene. 2014D. "The 1968 Oregon Republican Primary and the Decline of Liberal Republicanism." *Pacific Northwest Quarterly.* 2014, 105(2) (Spring), pp 73-84.

Kopelson, Gene. 2015. "Ike and Dutch: Mentor, Protégé, and Common Sense." Presented at the 125th Anniversary Commemoration of the Birth of Dwight D. Eisenhower, Dwight D. Eisenhower Presidential Library, Abilene KS, October 29, 2015; and at the Ronald W. Reagan Society, Eureka College, Eureka IL, 2016.

Kopelson, Gene. 2016. "A Skirmish in the Battle for Control of the Republican Party in Washington State." *Columbia*, Spring 2016, in press.

McKenna, Brian. "Global League." Society for Baseball Research, SABR Baseball Biography Project, 2008. (http:// sabr.org/bioproj/topic/global-league, accessed 3/11/2013)

McKenna, Kevin. "The Total Campaign: How Ronald Reagan Overwhelmingly Won the California Gubernatorial Election of 1966." Undergraduate Thesis, Columbia University, 2010.

Moore, Glen. "Ronald W. Reagan's Campaign for the Republican Party's 1968 Presidential Nomination." *Proceedings and Papers of the Georgia Association of Historians.* Vol. 13, 1992, pp 57-70.

Petrini, Maria. "An Exceptional Alliance: Johnson, Eisenhower, and the Vietnam War."http://millercenter.org/presidentialclassroom/exhibits/exceptional-alliance

Ritter, Kurt. "Ronald Reagan's 1960's Southern Rhetoric: Courting Conservatives for the GOP." *Southern Communication Journal.* 64(4), 1999, pp 333-345.

Scott-Smith, Giles. "Her Rather Ambitious Washington Program: Margaret Thatcher's International Visitor Program Visit to the United States in 1967." *British Contemporary History.* 17(4), winter 2003.

Vidal, Gore. "The Best Years of Our Lives." *New York Review of Books.* 9/29/1983 (also appeared in NYT 8/28/1983).

Special Collections

Reed, Thomas C. "Meetings and Telephone Exchanges Between Ronald Reagan and Thomas C. Reed, 1966-1968," herein abbreviated as Reagan-Reed with date and location, courtesy Thomas C. Reed.

Ronald Reagan Presidential Library Gubernatorial Audiotape Collection 1965-1974, Simi Valley, California, herein abbreviated as RRL with tape number.

Ronald Reagan Presidential Library Gubernatorial Videotape Collection includes *Town Meeting of the World* debate (5/15/1967), Eureka College Library Dedication (9/28/1967), *What About Ronald Reagan?* (12/12/1967), *Face the Nation* (8/4/1968) and Reagan Concession Speech at Miami Beach Convention (8/7/1968)

Post-Presidential Diaries of Dwight D. Eisenhower, Dwight D. Eisenhower Presidential Center, Abilene, Kansas, herein cited with diary date.

Shirley, Craig, "Reagan 101." Online course, Eureka College.

Personal Interviews

7/13/12 Dick Derham, in person
7/30/12 Fred Van Natta, John Gram, Sally Gram, Diana Evans, in person
8/3/12 Francine Pumphrey, phone
8/16/12, Peter Murphy, phone
8/16/12, Judge James Goode, phone
8/24/12 The Honorable Diarmuid O'Scannlain, in person
9/14/12 Peter Murphy, phone
9/14/12 Senator Bill Bradley, phone
9/17/12 John McCollister, phone
9/25/12 The Honorable Attorney General Edwin Meese III, phone
10/6/12 Dale L. Young, phone
10/17/12 Thomas C. Reed, in person

10/21/12 Don Hodel, phone
11/9/12 Austin Hoyt, phone
11/12/12 John Gram, phone
11/22/12 Judge Paul R. Haerle, phone
11/23/12 Don L. Taylor, phone
11/28/12 Congressman Toby Roth, phone
12/7/12 John C. Dicus, phone
12/27/12 Randy Teague, in person
12/27/12 R. Bruce Weinrod, in person
1/3/13 The Honorable Attorney General Edwin Meese III, phone
1/8/13 Congressman Dana Rohrabacher, phone
1/16/13 Shawn Steel, in person
1/17/13 Arnold Steinberg, phone
1/18/13 Kay Valory, phone
1/18/13 Jim Ince, phone
1/20/13 Kay Valory, phone
1/28/13 Matt Lawson, phone
3/11/13 Paul Manolis, phone
3/15/13 Ronald Docksai, phone
3/27/13 Congressman Jim Gardner, in person
5/18/13 Pat Nolan, phone
5/21/13 R. Bruce Weinrod and Bob Schadler, in person
6/2/13 Don L. Taylor, in person
6/8/13 Pat Nolan, phone
6/22/13 Curtis Patrick, phone
9/2/13 Thomas C. Reed, phone
10/2/13 Thomas C. Reed, phone
10/10/13: Damir Rados, phone
10/10/13: Zeljko Pavich: phone
10/20/13 Thomas C. Reed, in person
11/19/13: Damir Rados, phone
12/26/13: Andrew Polsky, phone
1/4/14: Fred Greenstein, phone
6/18/14: Tanya Melich, phone
8/8/14: Dick Derham and Edward Lange, in person
9/6/14: Thomas C. Reed, phone
11/14/14: Francis Rothauge, phone
1/30/15: Bruce Weinrod, phone
6/15/15: Dale L. Young, in person
7/14/15: Paul Pritchard, phone
8/17/15: Dan Rados, in person
11/19/15: Peter Murphy, in person
11/20/15: Morton Blackwell, phone
2/27/16: Doug Boyd, phone

Oral Histories

Davis, Arthur H., Jr., "Foreign Affairs Oral History Project," The Association for Diplomatic Studies and Training, 5/24/1991.

Miller Center of Public Affairs, Presidential Oral History Program. Ronald Reagan Oral History Project. Final Edited Transcript: Interview with Michael Deaver, Sept. 12, 2002.

Miller Center of Public Affairs, Presidential Oral History Program. Ronald Reagan Oral History Project. Final Edited Transcript: Interview with Stuart Spencer, Nov. 15-16, 2001.

Miller Center of Public Affairs, Presidential Oral History Program. Ronald Reagan Oral history Project. Final edited Transcript: Interview with Peter Hannaford, Jan. 10, 2003.

Gillenwaters, Edgar, "Washington Office Troubleshooter and Advocate for Commerce in California, 1967-1973" Ronald Reagan Gubernatorial Era Series, UC Berkeley Bancroft Library, 1985.

Haerle, Paul, "Ronald Reagan and Republican Party Politics in California 1965-1968" Ronald Reagan Gubernatorial Era series, UC Berkeley Bancroft Library, 1983.

Norm Skip Watts, "Observations of a Youthful Political Pro" Ronald Reagan Gubernatorial Era series, UC Berkeley Bancroft Library, 1983.

Smith, William French, "Evolution of the Kitchen Cabinet" Ronald Reagan Gubernatorial Era Series, UC Berkeley Bancroft Library, 1989.

INDEX

A

A Time for Choosing   21, 52, 58, 65-67, 70, 72-73, 78, 121, 150, 168, 170, 248, 353, 392, 397, 481
Abilene   11, 17, 31-32, 80, 107, 865, 881, 922-923
ABM Treaty, see Anti Ballistic Missile Shield   682, 683
Achille Lauro   496, 680, 872
Ahluwalia, Shri Montek Singh   213, 889
Ailes, Roger   234-235, 315
Alabama   275, 282, 284, 369, 528, 696-697, 699, 759, 782, 788, 791, 793, 799, 802-804, 806, 813, 819, 823, 825
Albany   301-302, 305, 307-308, 310, 312-313-314, 318, 338, 343, 442, 455, 461, 495, 546-548, 556, 566-567, 571, 643, 685, 718, 745, 858, 860, 897
Albany 1967 Veterans Day Parade   307-308, 310, 558, 718, 897
Albany Woodpeckers   307
Albuquerque   403, 481
All-Republican Conference   48
Alternatives   339
Altschuler, Sid   83
Amarillo   197, 350, 420, 480, 489, 589, 671, 678-680, 684-686, 745, 826, 838, 860
America the Beautiful, Reagan 1952 speech   73
American Conservative Union   75, 152, 840, 902, 905
Americans of Mexican descent   135, 429, 433, 436, 837
amphibious landings   192
An American Life   53-55, 132, 140, 271, 637, 640, 875, 885, 920
Annenberg, Walter   39
AntiBallistic Missile Shield, also see Strategic Defense Initiative   845
Anti-Semitism   103-104, 110, 625, 668, 872
Apollo 8   365, 854
Appling, Howard   590
Arizona   18, 275, 400, 448, 477, 481, 766
Arkansas   528, 686, 900
Asian-Americans   139
atomic weapons   34-36, 193-195, 351, 691, 869
Atoms for Peace   32, 34, 196, 861, 868-869, 872, 881
Aviophobia   279-280, 727

B

Babcock, Timothy   185, 228-229
Baltimore   475, 585, 688, 762
Barr, Charles   229
Barrett, William E.   510
Barshatky, David   640
Battaglia, Phil   136, 158
Bauer, Gary   400
Bay of Pigs   67, 74, 219, 540, 583
Bergen-Belsen concentration camp   104, 872, 887
Bergin, Thomas   326-332
Berlin Wall   13, 15, 24, 32, 73, 172, 211, 214-215, 312, 398, 523, 541, 602, 653, 660, 679, 691, 695, 826, 839, 874, 877, 881
Bilingual teachers   433
Birmingham   696-697, 701, 705
Bishop, Joey, see *The Joey Bishop Show*
Blacks   87, 198, 254, 291, 438-440, 476, 520, 522, 619, 629
Blackwell, Morton   285, 543
Bliss, Ray   133,145,387, 510,673, 754
Blocker, Dan   113
Boeing, William   417, 649
Bohemian Grove   243, 315, 826
Boise   403, 574, 582, 586-589, 603, 606
Bonanza   44, 55, 113, 243, 323
Boston   17-18, 62, 88, 91, 95, 100, 168, 331, 361, 394, 400, 441, 556, 670, 897, 919, 929
Boulder   403, 408, 484-485
Boyd, McDill   661
Bracero program   430
Bradley, Bill   207-213, 917
Bradley, Bruce   755
Bradley, Omar   103, 354
"Brainwashing" comment by Romney   927
Bravo, Dr. Francis   927
Brokaw, Tom   579, 594
Brooke, Edward   91
Brown, Edmund "Pat"   53
Bubb, Henry A., 17, 295, 319, 392, 400, 401, 406, 415, 420, 460, 471, 478, 551, 564, 638, 670, 671, 702, 703, 717, 729, 737, 754, 775, 779, 788, 790, 793, 836, 849, 864, 884, 889
Buchenwald concentration camp 927
Bucher, Capt. Lloyd   854
Buchwald, Art   542-543
Buckley, William F.   318, 321, 517, 884-885, 917
Budapest   695
Burghardt, William   438

YOUR AUTHOR

Gene Kopelson is president of the New England chapter, and on the Board of Trustees, of the Theodore Roosevelt Association; a Boston Churchillian; a holocaust educator; and a historian. He has written articles or lectured on TR's Great White Fleet, resistance to the Nazis, Reagan's 1966 Success with Hispanic Voters, and Republican Party politics.

He and his wife, Mindy, are avid cyclists and hikers. They maintain student-teacher book and video teaching trunks at the Holocaust Center for Humanity in Seattle and are active environmental stewards. Dr. Kopelson also is a cancer physician and internationally-recognized expert in radiation oncology.

Reagan's *1968 Dress Rehearsal: Ike, RFK, and Reagan's Emergence as a World Statesman* is his first book.

www.genekopelson.com